# TOWARDS THE E-SOCIETY:

## E-COMMERCE, E-BUSINESS, AND E-GOVERNMENT

## IFIP - The International Federation for Information Processing

IFIP was founded in 1960 under the auspices of UNESCO, following the First World Computer Congress held in Paris the previous year. An umbrella organization for societies working in information processing, IFIP's aim is two-fold: to support information processing within its member countries and to encourage technology transfer to developing nations. As its mission statement clearly states,

IFIP's mission is to be the leading, truly international, apolitical organization which encourages and assists in the development, exploitation and application of information technology for the benefit of all people.

IFIP is a non-profitmaking organization, run almost solely by 2500 volunteers. It operates through a number of technical committees, which organize events and publications. IFIP's events range from an international congress to local seminars, but the most important are:

- The IFIP World Computer Congress, held every second year;
- open conferences;
- working conferences.

The flagship event is the IFIP World Computer Congress, at which both invited and contributed papers are presented. Contributed papers are rigorously refereed and the rejection rate is high.

As with the Congress, participation in the open conferences is open to all and papers may be invited or submitted. Again, submitted papers are stringently refereed.

The working conferences are structured differently. They are usually run by a working group and attendance is small and by invitation only. Their purpose is to create an atmosphere conducive to innovation and development. Refereeing is less rigorous and papers are subjected to extensive group discussion.

Publications arising from IFIP events vary. The papers presented at the IFIP World Computer Congress and at open conferences are published as conference proceedings, while the results of the working conferences are often published as collections of selected and edited papers.

Any national society whose primary activity is in information may apply to become a full member of IFIP, although full membership is restricted to one society per country. Full members are entitled to vote at the annual General Assembly, National societies preferring a less committed involvement may apply for associate or corresponding membership. Associate members enjoy the same benefits as full members, but without voting rights. Corresponding members are not represented in IFIP bodies. Affiliated membership is open to non-national societies, and individual and honorary membership schemes are also offered.

# TOWARDS THE E-SOCIETY:

## E-Commerce, E-Business, and E-Government

***The First IFIP Conference on E-Commerce, E-Business, E-Government (I3E 2001) October 3-5, 2001, Zürich, Switzerland***

*Edited by*

**Beat Schmid**
*University of St. Gallen*
*Switzerland*

**Katarina Stanoevska-Slabeva**
*University of St. Gallen*
*Switzerland*

**Volker Tschammer**
*GMD FOKUS Berlin*
*Germany*

KLUWER ACADEMIC PUBLISHERS
BOSTON / DORDRECHT / LONDON

**Distributors for North, Central and South America:**
Kluwer Academic Publishers
101 Philip Drive
Assinippi Park
Norwell, Massachusetts 02061 USA
Telephone (781) 871-6600
Fax (781) 871-6528
E-Mail <kluwer@wkap.com>

**Distributors for all other countries:**
Kluwer Academic Publishers Group
Distribution Centre
Post Office Box 322
3300 AH Dordrecht, THE NETHERLANDS
Telephone 31 78 6392 392
Fax 31 78 6546 474
E-Mail <services@wkap.nl>

Electronic Services <http://www.wkap.nl>

**Library of Congress Cataloging-in-Publication Data**

IFIP Conference on E-Commerce, E-Business, E-Government (I3E 2001) (1st : 2001 : Zurich, Switzerland)
Towards the E-Society: E-commerce, E-business, and E-government / edited by Beat Schmid, Katarina Stanoevska-Slabeva, Volker Tschammer.
p. cm. — (International Federation for Information Processing; 74)
Includes bibliographical references.
ISBN 0-7923-7529-7
I. Schmid, Beat. II. Stanoevska-Slabeva, Katarina. III. Tschammer, Volker. IV. Title. V. International Federation for Information Processing (Series); 74.

2001038704



*Printed on acid-free paper.*

Printed in the United States of America.

# Contents

## Main Track - Part Four



## Main Track - Part Five

## Main Track - Part Six



## Minitrack One

# Conference Committees

## International Programme Committee

B. Schmid, Switzerland, (Chair)
V. Tschammer, Germany, (Co-chair)
D. Avison, France
M. Bichler, Austria
L. M. Camarinha-Matos, Portugal
W. Cellary, Poland
E. Clemons, USA
D. Deschoolmester, Belgium
J. Dietz, The Netherlands
F. Douglis, USA
J. H. P. Eloff, South Africa
S. Field, Switzerland
M. Funabashi, Japan
R. K. L. Gay, Singapore
B. C. Glasson, Australia
J. Griese, Switzerland
R. Grimm, Germany
D. Gritzalis, Greece
V. Hara, Finland
F. Kamoun, Tunisia
D. Khakhar, Sweden
K. Koen, South Africa
D. Konstantas, Switzerland
W. Lamersdorf, Germany
R. Lee, The Netherlands
C. Linnhof-Popien, Germany
T. Magedanz, Germany
M. Mendes, Brazil
M. Merz, Germany
Z. Milosevic, Australia
A. Molina, UK
P. Moody, Luxemburg
E. Neuhold, Germany
L. J. M. Nieuwenhuis, The Netherlands
V. Ouzounis, Germany
J. Palmer, USA
R. Posch, Austria
K. Rannenberg, UK
J. Skrbek, Czechia
K. Stanoevska-Slabeva, Switzerland
Ch. Steinfield, USA
M. Stolze, Switzerland
R. Suomi, Finland
P. Swatman, Germany
P. Timmers, Belgium
A. Tsalgatidou, Greece
M. Waidner, Switzerland
H. Weigand, The Netherlands
R. Wigand, USA
L. Yngstrom, Sweden
H.-D. Zimmermann, Switzerland

## Organizing Committee

K. Bauknecht, Switzerland,
(General Chair)
H. Haeuschen, Switzerland
L. Kuendig, Switzerland
L. G. Mason, Singapore
H. Rudin, Switzerland

## Steering Committee

B. Glasson, Australia
D. Khakhar, Sweden
J. Monteiro, Portugal
R. Posch, Austria
H. Rudin, Switzerland
V. Tschammer, Germany

# List of Reviewers

P. Aschmoneit
P.Balabko
A.Bartelt
U. Baumoel
R. Buehrer
M. Cole
C. Eikemeier
U. Geissler
J. Gerhard
M. Greunz
Th. Gordon
F. Habann
J. Haes
H. Haeuschen
S. Handschuh
D. Ingenhof
St. Klein
M, Klose
U. Lechner
S. Leist
M. Lenz
P. Mayr
V. Porak
Y. Pigneur
Ch. Reichmayr
R. Riedl
H. Rudin
A. Scharl
B. Schneider
B. Schopp
M. Schoop
P. Schubert
S. Seufert
Th. Stiffel
M. Ströbel
Y.-H. Tan
A.M. Tjoa
F. Ulrich

# Acknowledgements

The editors and the members of the Organizing Committee would like to thank the following sponsors of the conference:

- Credit Suisse, Zurich, Switzerland (www.credit-suisse.ch)
- SolCon GmbH, Zurich, Switzerland (www.solcon.ch)
- The Zurich Network, Zurich, Switzerland (www.zurichnetwork.ch)
- TKS – Teknosoft SA, Zurich, Switzerland (www.tks.ch)
- Winterthur Versicherungen, Winterthur, Switzerland (http://www.webinsurance.ch)

# Preface

I3E 2001 is the first in a series of conferences on e-commerce, e-business, and e-government organised by the three IFIP committees TC6, TC8, and TC11. It provides a forum, where users, engineers, and scientists from academia, industry, and government can present their latest findings in e-commerce, e-business, and e-government applications and the underlying technology to support those applications.

The conference comprises a main track and mini tracks dedicated to special topics. The papers presented in the main track were rigorously refereed and selected by the International Programme Committee of the conference. Thematically they were grouped in the following sessions:

- *Sessions on security and trust*, comprising nine papers referring to both trust and security in general as well as presenting specific concepts for enhancing trust in the digital society.
- *Session on inter-organisational transactions*, covering papers related to auditing of inter-organizational trade procedures, cross-organizational workflow and transactions in Business to Business platforms.
- *Session on virtual enterprises*, encompassing papers describing innovative approaches for creating virtual enterprises as well as describing examples of virtual enterprises in specific industries.
- *Session on online communities* containing three papers, which provide case studies of specific online communities and various concepts on how companies can build and harness the potential of online communities.
- *Sessions on strategies and business models* with papers describing specific business models as well as general overviews of specific approaches for E-Strategy formulation.
- *Session on customer relationships*, covering papers related to both mechanisms for evaluation of customer feedback and to various concepts for innovative customer services.
- *Session on online negotiations* with papers describing different approaches for online negotiations.

In addition to the main track, five mini tracks were organised by dedicated chairmen and programme committees. The mini-track chairs were responsible for the promotion of the mini track and the review process for papers submitted to the mini track. The mini tracks were selected by the International Program Committee of the conference from the submitted mini track proposals in reply to an open Call For Mini tracks. The following mini tracks were included in the conference programme:

- *Mini track on formal e-models*, chaired by Ulrike Lechner and Tiziana Margaria and comprising papers proposing various formal models for e-commerce and e-business;
- *Mini track on e-commerce-induced reengineering*, chaired by Majed Al-Mashari and containing papers describing the specifik aspects of e-commerce induced re-engineering.
- *Mini track on e-government*, chaired by Reinhard Riedl, Michael Gisler and Dieter Spaehni and encompassing nine papers describing case studies on specific e-government solutions in different countries and specific technical and business solutions enabling e-government.
- *Mini track on e-democracy*, chaired by Ake Gronlund and providing six papers with specific case studies and general reflection on e-democracy.
- *Mini-track on m-commerce*, chaired by Georgios I. Doukidis and Nikos Mylonopoulos and comprising papers on various aspects related to m-commerce as mobile payment solutions, adoption frameworks and functional models for m-commerce.

Many persons have contributed to make this conference a success. We would like to thank the members of the organising and programme committees, the authors and reviewers, the mini track chairs, the Universities of Zuerich and St. Gallen, GMD FOKUS Berlin, the IFIP Secretariat, and the sponsors of the conference.

*Beat Schmid Katarina Stanoevska-Slabeva Volker Tschammer*

*St. Gallen, Berlin, October 2001*

MAIN TRACK - PART ONE

# SECURITY AND TRUST

1

# Trust Based Contracting in Virtual Organizations:

## *A Concept Based on Contract Workflow Management Systems*

Lenz K.[*], Oberweis A.[*], Schneider S.[**]

[*] *Institute of Information Systems*
*University of Frankfurt/Main*

[**] *IBM Germany*
*Frankfurt/Main*

**Abstract**: For participants in virtual organizations it is necessary to work together on a temporary basis in order to solve specific problems. Both the search for adequate partners and the organizational set-up have to be very fast and efficient. The main difficulty of building a cooperation lies in finding the right balance between time-consuming, but safe ways based on traditional contracts, and less reliable, but faster ways based solely on traditional forms of trust. This paper introduces a contract/trust based solution and describes a computer-supported negotiation process to make the process of creating a virtual organization fast and safe at the same time. We propose an interorganizational workflow based on a combination of a minimal set of contractual documents supplemented by trust-based features. The workflow enables partners to establish a temporary cooperation agreement within a relatively short time. As workflow modelling language we have chosen so-called XML-nets, a novel variant of high level Petri nets which combines interorganizational workflow models with XML-document descriptions.

# 1. INTRODUCTION AND MOTIVATION

Virtual organizations consist of independent companies which use electronic networks, especially the internet, for a temporary cooperation [HaB97]. In the initial phase the companies interested in setting up a virtual organizations start looking for potential partners with complementary characteristics in their interaction with the client. The companies cooperate on a short-term basis to solve specific problems; once the problems are solved, the cooperation ends. In the era of the internet cooperation agreements must be established within an extremely short period of time in order to be able to successfully compete with rivals [SaV99]. Since the traditional ways of coming up with cooperation agreements are usually very time- and resource-consuming and since laws do not change as fast as technology does, a type of cooperation that is based on a trust model, might be an efficient alternative. This model (see for example [Lew99, MiF98]) does not rely on contracts but instead builds virtual organizations based only on trust-oriented partnerships. Even though trust-oriented relationships can be seen as relatively risky [Luh88] for all parties involved (especially because they might lead to opportunistic behaviour) they still provide clear competitive advantages and serve as a substitute for traditional hierarchical governance [KaJ99]. Yet, virtual organizations carry one important disadvantage: the conflict between the secure, but slow preparation mode of traditional cooperation agreements and the fast, but risky trust-based model of cooperation. This raises two basic questions which will be discussed in the following:

a) If a virtual organization needs a contract, how can the creation of this contract be speeded up?
b) If mutual trust helps to speed up the contracting process, how can potential/future members of virtual organizations develop and increase mutual trust?

"A contract is a promise or a set of promises for the breach of which the law gives a remedy, or the performance of which the law in some way recognizes as a duty." [Mac74, p.693]. We have already referred to the fact that virtual organizations present themselves as one single organizational unit when interacting with clients. For sales purposes, only one of the participants of a trust-based virtual organization directly interacts with the client. Since these relationships with the client are fixed in written contracts, the client interface of the virtual organization is the party that carries all business risks. All other relationships between the parties involved in the virtual organization are trust-based relationships and thus not contract-based. This means that the client interface is the only party who is liable for all delivered products and services towards the client, even for those delivered by other members of the virtual organization.

Contract management can be divided into several phases: planning and designing contracts, negotiation, conclusion and contract controlling [Ert99]. Because of their particular importance for virtual organizations, we focus on the negotiation and conclusion phases. Separating similar contracting problems, so called different levels of negotiation (Figure 1), will help to speed up and automate the process by bundling units of similar problems to find cooperation agreements.

In a first instance, intelligent software agents manage basic assumptions which are essential and the participants do not want further debates on. This kind of negotiation is relatively static but one of the fastest ways to find first agreements. For the discussion of more detailed questions during the next stage the partners have to use specific negotiation tools such as contract workflow management systems and other groupware tools like e-mail, video conferencing, etc.

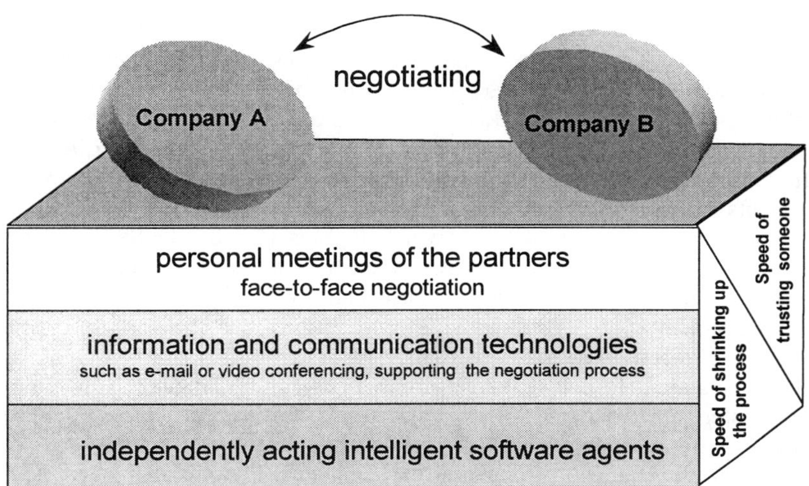


*Figure 1*: Negotiation Levels

One possible contract workflow will be described in the following sections of this paper. In a third instance, the partners have to discuss more complex topics in face-to-face meetings, which are more effective for building mutual trust, but at the same time are relatively expensive.

The model also uses software agents which are more efficient in matching basic assumptions, but are not able to cope with the process of establishing a trust-based relationship. In the following we concentrate on the issue of building mutual trust in virtual organizations, that is trust between the involved people. The three-step model presented in Figure 1 is meant to save time and to speed up the entire process by preventing time-consuming discussions. Furthermore, it allows for a more focused process since the partners have to be familiar with all the clearly structured steps towards agreement.

## 2. ELECTRONIC SUPPORT OF THE CONTRACTING PROCESS

"The term *contracting* is used to describe efforts by individuals to assign or to modify property rights. In this context, contracting includes bargaining among private claimants within groups..." [Lib89, p.4].

An overview of software agents to support contracting (in particular negotiating the first instance of the negotiation model) in electronic markets can be found in the WWW under URL http://www.agents.media.mit.edu/ groups/agents/publications/. In the following we focus on the second level, i.e. information and communication technologies to support the negotiation process, and especially on contract workflow management systems to support and speed up the process of writing up contractual agreements [HeW00] (compare also the COSMOS architecture under http://vsys-www.informatik.uni-hamburg.de and the project CrossFlow under http://www.crossflow.org). We analyze these contractual processes as a basis for developing contract workflow management systems. By using contract workflows different people in the companies involved can easily exchange documents.

Since so-called XML-nets [LeO01] allow the integration of electronic document exchange and interorganizational processes, they will be used to describe the process of finding agreements in a virtual organization. XML-nets support the exchange of documents which is represented by models of interorganizational business processes based on a novel variant of high-level Petri nets [Gen87, ObS96] and on XML (eXtensible Markup Language) [W3C00]. XML is a document declaration standard proposed by the World Wide Web Consortium (W3C, http://www.w3.org/). A so-called document type definition (DTD) describes the structure of valid XML documents of a certain type.

Petri nets are a formal graphical process description language which allows for the computer-supported analysis and validation of business processes [DeE00]. They consist of static components (the places, depicted by circles) and dynamic components (the transitions, depicted by rectangles) that are connected by directed arcs. Low-level Petri nets [Pet81] are well suited for the initial modeling of a complex workflow whereas high-level Petri nets like predicate/transition nets [Gen87] integrate behavior- and object-related aspects of workflows.

In XML-nets, the places are interpreted as containers for XML documents. The transitions and the corresponding descriptions of the document manipulation (i.e. the labels of the adjacent edges and the transition inscriptions) determine the flow of the documents. The Graphical XML Schema Definition Language (GXSL) ist used to model for each place in the net the structure of the respective valid XML documents. The GXSL based manipulation language XManiLa is used to model system dynamics [LeO01]. Due to the formal notation, well known analyzing methods and discrete simulation can be applied to XML-nets. Furthermore XML-nets can be directly interpreted by a respective workflow engine.

## 2.1 Process View: The Process of Contractual Agreements

As already mentioned, there are different phases in the process of setting up a cooperation between two organizations. The following scenario takes place after the potential partners have found each other and then have to negotiate their cooperation agreement (Figure 2). In this case, for example, company A creates an information document containing the issues of the project which the mutual software agents already agreed on and those which are still unclear.

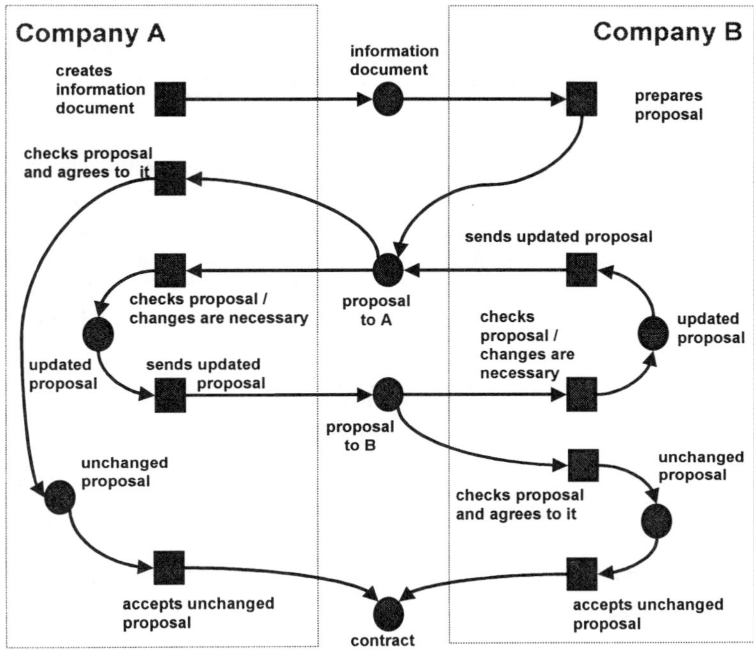


*Figure 2:* Complex Negotiation Process

If company B is able to deliver or produce the missing items it can fill in or change the relevant paragraphs and prepare a proposal document. This proposal document will be sent back to company A. In a simple case of contractual agreement company A will accept the proposal as it is; then a contract is closed. These issues are also discussed in the literature under the keyword *e-contracting* [GSS00]. Often the first proposal made by company B has to be changed, and company A then sends a new proposal to company B. The companies will iteratively exchange proposals until one proposal will be agreed upon in its entirety. This results in the following process: company A creates an information document describing the partnership in an organizational as well as a technical way. Company B prepares a proposal based on this information and sends it back to company A. Now company A has to check the proposal and either agrees to it and accepts it, which means that the contract is closed, or –which is more likely– that the companies have to re-negotiate their respective output of goods and services.

## 2.2 Document View: Document Structure of Contracts

The Petri net in Figure 2 describes the negotiation behavior of the two companies. Until now, the specification of the documents' structure is still missing. In order to describe the document flow of the negotiation process in detail we have to add information to the Petri net and thereby extend it to an XML-net. For each place of the Petri net, the respective type of documents has to be described by a graphical XML schema. XManiLA is then used for specifying the document manipulation by extended graphical XML schemas which label the edges in an XML-net[1] [LeO01].

In the given process three main documents are necessary: an information document, a proposal document, and a contract document. The information document (Figure 3) provides general information about the planned virtual organization *(planned_cooperation)* including the initiator, the background information and a description of the solution. Additionally, it contains the timeframe (*duration*) and the work which has to be done by the parties involved *(piece_of_work*). The *piece_of_work* element also describes the interfaces with all other related work products.

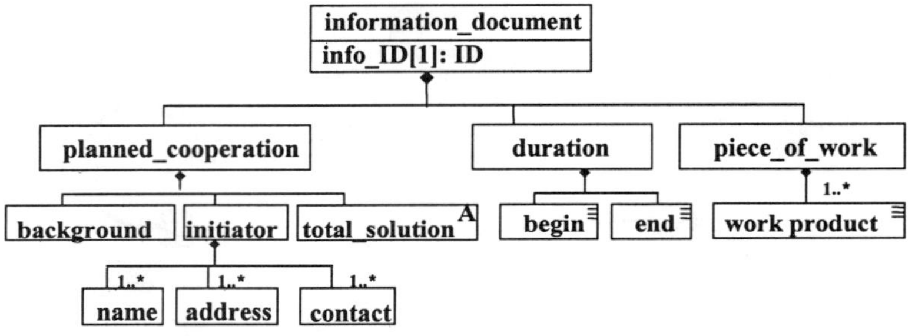


*Figure 3*: Graphical XML Schema for the Information Document

Once the information document has been received by company B, and if company B is interested in the suggested form of cooperation, the document will be transformed into a proposal. In addition to the information document, the proposal contains data about the partners, commercial business and legal terms, pieces of work which have to be achieved, and clearly defined hallmarks for the project planning process and arrangements about the cooperation.

The contract document (Figure 4) is similar to the proposal. In addition to the content of the proposal the sender expresses his intention to close the contract.

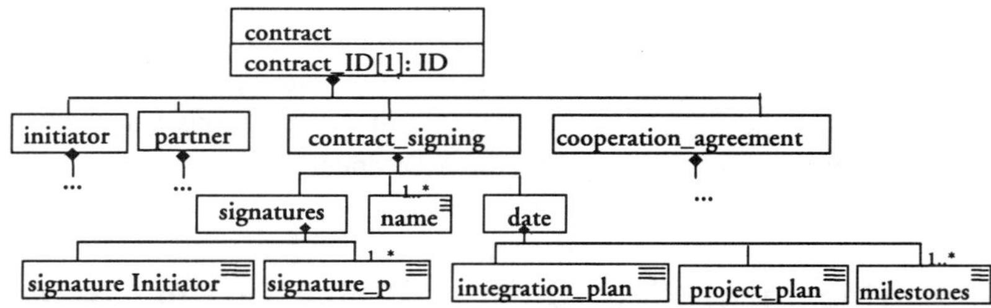


*Figure 4:* Graphical XML Schema for the Contract Document

1 Due to place limitations we cannot give a detailed introduction into XML-nets here. For further information concerning XML-Nets see, e.g., http://lwi2.wiwi.uni-frankfurt.de/projekte/xmlnet/default.htm.

The difference between a proposal and a contract is that both partners sign it, which proves their willingness to cooperate with each other (*contract_signing*). The cooperation contract describes the rights and duties of the partners. Enclosed are thus statements of contract partners (*contract_partner*), the commitments of the partners and legal aspects (*cooperation_agreement*).

We can now assign the schemas to the corresponding places of the Petri net in Figure 2, for example the GXS *in-formation_document* to the place 'document of information', the GXS *proposal* to the places 'proposal to A' and 'proposal to B' etc. Moreover the graphical XML schemas for the information document, the proposal and the contract serve as a basis for describing the manipulation of the documents during the negotiation process: From the GXS we can derive the extended GXSs, that describe insertion, deletion and manipulation operations on information documents, proposals, or contracts respectively. These operations are carried out whenever a transition occurs (i.e. whenever the event of operations on the documents takes place).The extended GXSs that we have assigned to the edges of the Petri net thereby exactly specify the documents that are manipulated by the occurring transition and the way these documents are manipulated. An excerpt of the resulting XML-net can be seen in Figure 5.

The graphical XML schemas *information_document* and *proposal* describe the documents contained in the places “information document” and “proposal to A”. The extended schemas serve as edge labels for specifying the operations on these documents for the transition “prepares proposal”. The black bar on the left side of the root element indicates that an information document is deleted and a new proposal document is created. Moreover, the usage of variables allows for ensuring equality of elements between the deleted and created document.

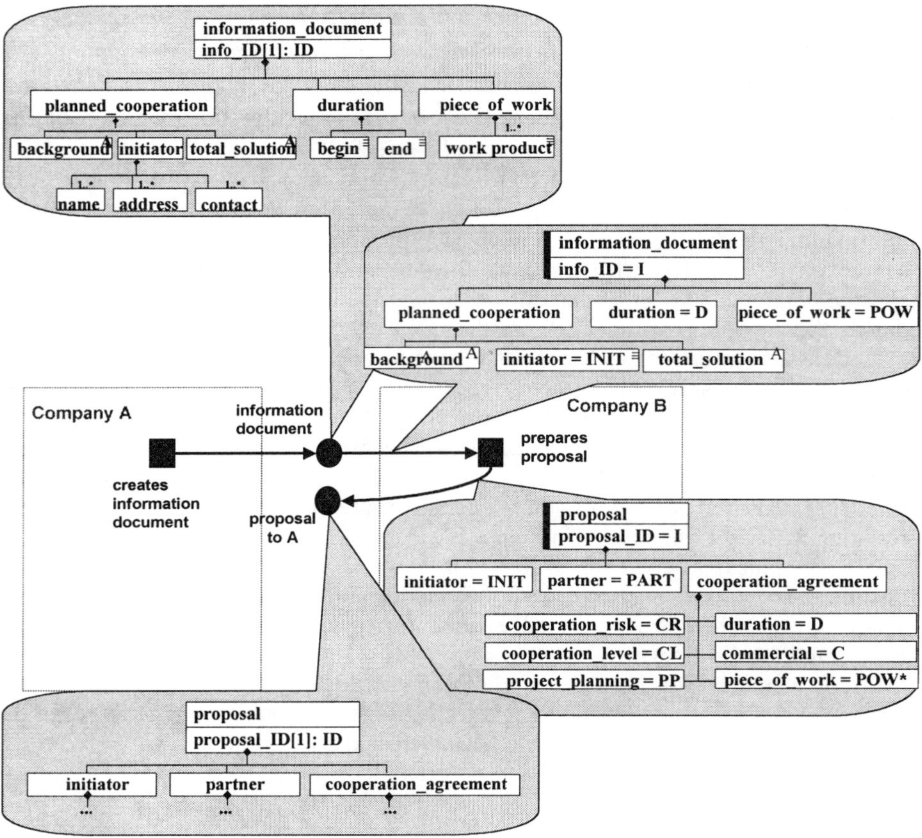


*Figure 5*: XML-net Excerpt of the Process

# 3. ACCELERATING THE PROCESS OF DEVELOPING TRUST

In virtual organizations trust needs to be managed [Zuc86]. This means that mechanisms for establishing and accelerating trust online and for preserving trust need to be introduced. Ishaya/Macaulay describe influencing mechanisms of the process of developing trust [IsM00] which leads to the following three patterns of mutual trust:

1. **Swift trust (trust by pressure[2]):** If there is only a short window of opportunity for a product or service and if the involved companies only have a very limited time frame available for working together and if there is only a minimal amount of shared objectives companies simply need to mutually assume their partners

2 See also www.ascusc.org/jcmc/vol3/issue4/jarvenpaa.html.

trustworthiness [MWK96]. In this case a self-fulfilling prophecy will lead to mutual trust. But this is a risky operation. We also call this phenomenon virtual trust, because in the initial phase the partners act as if they were actually trusting each other.

2. **Incremental trust:** In this case an actual exchange of purchased goods and services (trusted actions) leads to mutual trust. Both parties provide trusted actions and compare the results with their expectations based on their own preceding actions. The process of trust management is modeled by a place/transition net [Pet81] with infinite place capacity (Figure 6). The number of tokens in the place "mutual trust counter" increases with the number of trusted actions. Each company can set its own threshold for trusting the partner (e.g. company A five trust points).

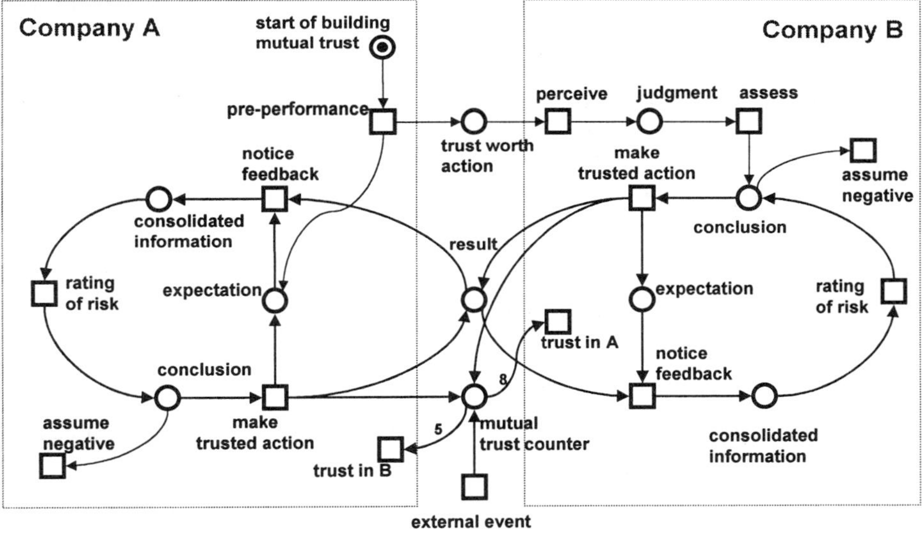


*Figure 6*: Petri Net for the Trust Management Process

Let us assume that company A executes a pre-performed trustworthy action and hands it over to company B. The evaluation carried out by company B leads to the conclusion that company B either decides to give the proposal a negative evaluation or to perform a trusted action as well. Company A receives the feedback, confirms the information, and uses it to compare the chances and risks of trusting company B.

Afterwards company A may either come to the conclusion that it is safe to perform another trusted action or it may seem more appropriate not to trust company B due to negative assumptions. If company A performs another trustworthy action company B will do the same. The more loops are made, the more trust there will be between the companies, and the faster the process of information exchange is, the faster mutual trust will increase. If there are more than two parties involved, there are further possibilities for building trust such as certificates issued by a (neutral) third party (see for example http://www.truste.com). Here we refer to social or relational trust, not to trust in the sense of technical mechanisms or certifications as for instance in the case of SSL. Trust can also be built up through reputation based on public opinion [SWZ99]. In this case computer systems collect, distribute and aggregate comments and collect past behavior of the participating organizations [Shn00]. Trust can also be measured with the help of a calculation system based on rewards and punishment. Therefore we integrate a mutual trust counter for gathering points of trustworthiness or the stage of reputation of the involved companies. Furthermore external events can influence these counters in case of increasing shares for example.

3. **Historical trust:** This form of building mutual trust by prediction requires partners who have personally known each other over a long period of time and have common shared values. This is a more familiar model and traditional way of emerging mutual trust which is obviously not suitable for virtual organizations.

Constructing trust in virtual organizations is difficult because of the anonymous character of the internet and the time pressure all participants are faced with. Thus a combination of incremental trust and swift trust can be used to speed up the process of contracting in virtual organizations and it can even become a part of or complement of the contract process to speed it up.

# 4. TRUST AS A PARTIAL SUBSTITUTE OF CONTRACTS

The concept described below is based on the idea that elements of trust can be used as a partial substitute for contracts to save negotiation time. In this case trust can replace parts of the negotiating process and of the negotiating documents. When you trust someone you don′t have to use all the paragraphs (suggested) of reducing risks only the one which are elementary based on the level you trust on. Trust is seen as an accepted instance of vulnerability to another party’s possible interference with one’s own sphere [FKH00], which makes purchases of goods and services a more risky venture and gives partners the possibility to opportunistic behavior. Building mutual trust in cyberspace depends on media richness [DLT87] and the social presence theory [SWC76]. This means that the more frequent the use of media during negotiation and the closer the resemblance of communications over the internet looks like a face-to-face conversation, the quicker mutual trust will increase. Thus the following requirements on contract workflow management systems are to be fulfilled:

1. It is necessary to work with different types of using common (internet) standards to accelerate the cycles of trust management. Using a variety of information and

communication technologies can help to speed up the process of building mutual trust (*trust view*).

2. It is also necessary to use supporting document and communication standards such as XML and TCP/IP to make it technically feasible for different organizations to be easily linked with each other (*technical view*).
3. It is necessary to use an interorganizational, well structured and well known process to make the agreements more transparent and comprehensible for the involved partners by using the negotiation model which helps to speed up these processes (*contractual view*).

In Figure 5 a combination of the contract and trust process is presented. For that purpose we combine the XML-net of the negotiation process (filled places and transitions) and the trust management process of Figure 7 (unfilled places and transitions) to a hybrid Petri net. The two nets are merged by overlapping transitions (merging transitions).

Let us assume that company A plans a virtual organization and starts by evaluating the risks that are associated with this project, e.g. the question of passing on important information to a third party. These evaluations are then used as the basis for preparing a document which contains the basic principles of the cooperation. These documents of principles also include the information document described before. When sending this document to company B, company A performs a trusted action. This trusted action can be seen as a progress on services, products or know how. The document that has been transmitted represents a contractual framework which provides a basic set of intentions and contains suggested general agreements about the cooperation, whereas in a traditional contract all agreements would have to be fixed in detail. For this framework the same document structure can be used; however, several paragraphs are intentionally left open. Company B evaluates the document, and after assessment it sends the framework back to company A which implies a trusted action. Until now a contract does not exist but instead only a document of understanding is available. While interacting the partners agree on basic assumptions and commitments which are the basis for a quick cooperation and – what is even more important – enables them to start working together right away.

In case of modifications, company B updates the framework and sends it back, together with a trusted action. Company A confirms the information and re-evaluates the risk of the cooperation. After that, company A either agrees on the framework (for that a certain numbers of trust points are a precondition for contracting and this may be different for both companies) or claims more updates on the framework. In this case the updates and trusted actions are sent to company B. Company B confirms the information and evaluates its own risks, too, before either agreeing or suggesting additional updates. If company A and B agree to the framework a minimal common ground exists which can then be complemented and put together with trusted actions into a cycle of trust-based relationship based on contracts. These cycles differ in the trust actions and negotiations involved. The benefit of this cycle-based proceeding is that it allows for the cooperation to start right away without a negotiated contract and without a partnership based only on trust. In the next cycle the partners agree on more detailed specific business needs as well as on shared values for the virtual organization.

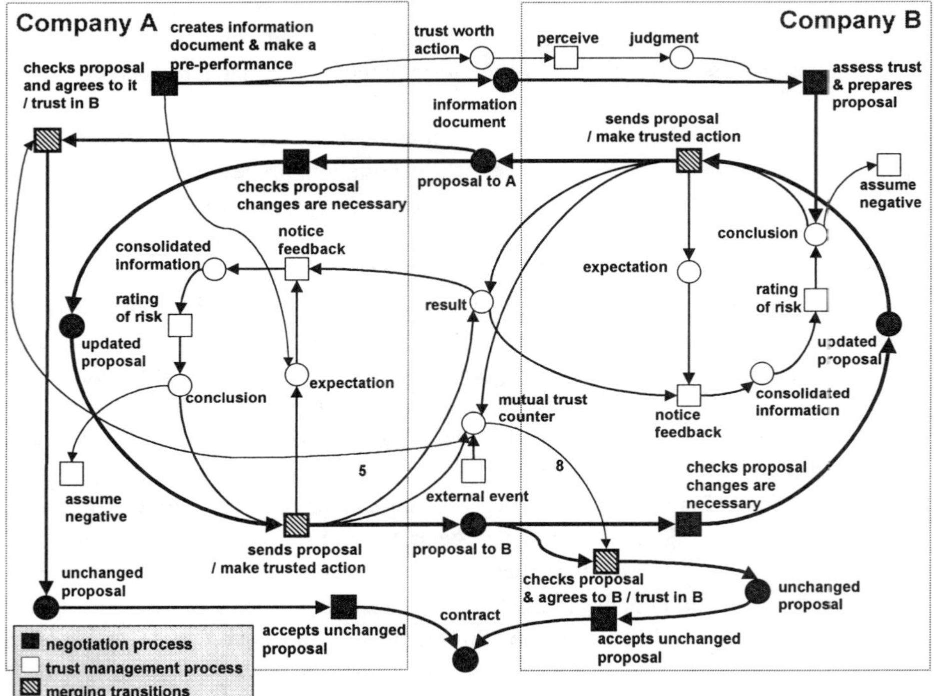


*Figure 7:* Petri Net of the Contract-Trust Process

Later the partners can manage cooperation with the help of trust rating models based on reputation, etc. There are models possible based on other hedging mechanisms which can be organized in an open form with no central instance (on the web), or they can be hosted by an independent third party. Whenever a virtual organization ends the partners evaluate each other according to negotiation habits, reliability, flexibility etc. Thus, companies accumulate so-called trust points, according to which they are classified into different risk classes. These classes correspond to categories of contractual paragraphs the companies use in the first phase of the contractual-trust-model. The number of trust points correlates with the number of necessary contractual agreements: the more trust points the higher the reputation and the lower the number of paragraphs and vice versa.

# 5. CONCLUSION

Building virtual organizations without contracts is a risky venture especially for the organization client interface. In this paper, we proposed a negotiation model that allows for accelerating the process of finding a cooperation agreement based on a contract. Building mutual trust is one of the main elements in this model. To make contract workflow management systems feasible, XML-nets are used which integrate the structure as well as the flow of the relevant documents. The main advantage for virtual organizations is that this model allows for an early start of the cooperation, even when the partners are still working on their agreements with the help of "documents of understanding" and "trusted actions", and finally leads to a negotiated contract.

XML-nets and additional trust rating models with the help of mutually treated trust counters are proposed for the specification on a contract workflow management system supporting virtual organizations. Further work of the project VirtO (http://lwi2.wiwi.uni-frankfurt.de/projekte/virto/ default.htm) at the University of Frankfurt aims at providing a detailed description and integration of trust building models (based on ratings, reputations, trusted actions, etc.) into the XML-nets. Currently we are developing a simple prototype simulator for XML-nets based on a native XML database system. We plan to use this simulator for the evaluation of our trust-contract process in addition to the application of analysis methods (like for example reachability analysis). We also plan to introduce integrity rules into XML-nets in order to specify requirements concerning the trust management process in a declarative way.

# 6. REFERENCES

[DeE00] Desel, J.; Erwin, T.: Modeling, Simulation and Analysis of Business Process; in: van der Aalst, W.; Desel, J.; Oberweis, A. (eds.), Business Process Management – Models, Techniques and Empirical Studies; LNCS 1806; 2000; pp. 129-141

[DLT87] Daft, R.L.; Lengel, R.H.; Trevino, L.K. (1987): Message Equivocality, Media Selection and Manager Performance - Implications for Information Systems; in: MIS Quarterly; December 1999; pp. 355-368

[Ert99] Ertel, D.: Turning Negotiating into a Corporate Capability; in: Harvard Business Revue; May-June 1999; p. 55- 70

[FKH00] Friedman, P.; Kahn, P.H.; Howe, D.C.: Trust Online; in: Communications of the ACM; December 2000; pp. 34-40

[Gen87] Genrich, H.J.: Predicate/transion nets; in: Brauer, W.; Reisig, W.; Rozenberg, G. (eds.); Petri Nets - Central Models and Their Properties; Advances in Petri Nets 1986; LNCS 254; 1987; pp. 207-247

[GSS00] Greunz, M.; Stanoevska-Slabeva, K.; Schopp, B.: Electronic Contracting with XML Containers; in: Jasper, H.; Küng, J.; Vossen, G. (eds.); Informationssysteme für E-Commerce, Linz; 2000; p. 11-27

[HaB97] Hardwick, M.; Bolton, R.: The Industrial Virtual Enterprise; in: Communications of the ACM; Vol. 40; 1997; pp. 59-60

[HeW00] Heuvel Van den, W.J.; Weigand, H.: Cross Organizational Workflow Integration Using Contracts; http://www.jeffsutherland.org/oopsla2000/vandenheuvel/vandenheuvel.htm; (2000-12-20)

[IsM00] Ishaya T.; Macaulasy, L.: The Role of Trust in Virtual Teams; in: Sieber, P.; Griese, J. (eds.): Organization Virtualness and Electronic Commerce; (www.virtual-organization.net); (2000-07-17)

[KaJ99] Karahannas, M.; Jones, M.; Interorganizational Systems and Trust in Strategic Alliances; in: Hansen, H.R.; Bichler, M.; Mahrer, H. (eds.); Proc. 8th European Conference in Information Systems, Austria , July 2000; pp. 346-357

[LeO01] Lenz, K.; Oberweis, A.: Modeling Interorganizational Workflows with XML nets; in Proc. Thirty-Fourth Hawaii International Conference on System Sciences (HICSS-34), Januar 2001

[Lew99] Lewis, J.D.: Trusted Partners – How Companies Build Mutual Trust and Win Together; New York; 1999

[Lib89] Libecap, G.D.: Contracting for Property Rights; Cambridge; 1989

[Luh88] Luhmann, N.: Familiarity, Confidence, Trust – Problems and Alternatives; in: Gambetta, D. (eds.); Trust – Making and Breaking Cooperative Relations; Oxford; 1988

[Mac74] Macneil, I.R.: The Many Futures of Contracts; in: Southern California Review; Vol. 47; 1974; pp. 691-816

[MiF98] Millmann, R.E.; Fugate, D.I.: Using Trust-Transference as a Persuasion Technique; an Empirical Field Investigation; in: Journal of Personal Selling and Sales Management; 08/1998; p. 56-57

[MWK96] Meyerson, M.; Weick, K.E.; Kramer, R..M.: Swift Trust and Temporary Groups; in Kramer, R..M; Tyler, T.R..: Trust in Organizations; London; 1996; pp. 166-195

[ObS96] Oberweis, A.; Sander, P.: Information System Behavior Specification by High-Level Petri Nets; in: ACM Transactions on Information Systems, 14(4); 1996; pp. 380-420

[Pet81] Peterson, J.L.: Petri Net Theory and the Modeling of Systems, Englewood Cliffs, 1981

[SaV99] Shapiro, C.; Varian, H.R.: Information Rules – a Strategic Guide to the Network Economy; Boston; 1999

[Shn00] Shneiderman, B.: Designing Trust into Online Experiences; in: Communications of the ACM; 12/2000; pp. 57-59

[SWC76] Short, J.W.; Williams, E; Christie, B.: The Social Psychology of Telecommunications; New York, 1976

[SWZ99] Sulin, B.; Whinston, A.; Zhang, H.: Building Trust in the Electronic Market Through an Economic Incentive Mechanism; in: Prabudda, D.; DeGross; (eds.); Proceedings of the 20th International Conference on Information Systems; December 1999; pp. 208-213

[W3C00] World Wide Web Consortium Recommendation: Extensible Markup Language (XML) 1.0; Technical Report; 6-October-2000; (http://www.w3/TR/2000/REC-xml-20000106)

[Zuc86] Zucker, L.G.: Production of Trust – Institutional Sources of Economic Structure; in: Research on Organizational Behavior; Vol. 8; 1986; pp. 53-111

# Trustbuilders and Trustbusters

*The Role of Trust Cues in Interfaces to e-Commerce Applications*

Jens Riegelsberger & M. Angela Sasse
*Hochschule der Künste Berlin & University College London*

**Abstract:** This paper investigates how interface design can help to overcome the proclaimed 'lack of trust' in e-commerce sites. Based on existing social science knowledge on trust, and our own exploratory study using Grounded Theory methods, we developed a model of consumer decision making in on-line shopping. Due to the separation in space and time when engaging in e-commerce, there is an *increased need for trust, rather than the oft-proclaimed lack of trust.* Based on this model we then review design guidelines through empirical tests. We focus on approaches that aim to increase trust by increasing the *social presence* of an interface. We identified cues in the user interface that help to build trust to some extent (*trustbuilders*), and some cues that have a great potential for destroying trust (*trustbusters*).

## 1. INTRODUCTION

Consider shopping in the real world: When a customer enters a shop for the first time, she sees the interior, goods and the sales staff. The customer may not conduct any risk evaluation at all, because shopping is a habit she does not perceive as risky. But the visual cues allow her to a evaluate the shop's professionalism, competence and trustworthiness via a comparison with other shops. The situation is different for shopping on the Internet: Most people do not shop habitually on the Internet and do not understand the underlying technology, and the risks are numerous. It is thus not surprising that one of the leading advertisers on the Internet is TRUSTe [15], an organisation that assigns seals to e-commerce enterprises that it considers 'trustworthy'. Consumers' *lack of trust* in e-commerce is often assumed to be one of the main reasons for the disappointing development of B2C e-commerce [21]. The aim of the research reported in this paper was to investigate whether – and which – elements of the user interface can contribute to building trust with customers.

## 2. RESEARCH APPROACH

Our research started with an exploratory approach: Firstly, we conducted a review of the sociology and social psychology literature on trust [study I]. This laid the conceptual basis for a series of in-depth interviews with 13 Internet users (8 e-shoppers, 5 non-shoppers). The interviews aimed to elicit their perception of risk, evaluation strategies for online-shops, and other intervening factors. The transcripts of the interviews were analysed using coding techniques from Grounded Theory [7, 28]. This process allowed us to construct a model of consumer decision-making in online-shopping [study II]. We analysed existing interface design guidelines for building 'trustworthy interfaces', and added the elements identified in the literature review [I] and our study [II]. This new set of guidelines was then subjected to an empirical test: Two semi-functional mock-ups of an online-shop (one incorporating the guidelines, the other not) were tested through an online experiment [study III]. 53 participants were randomly assigned to perform a trial shopping with one of the mock-ups. Their risk perceptions were elicited afterwards through an online questionnaire. The results of the interviews and answers to open-ended questions in the questionnaire indicated a high relevance of *personal interaction* for trust building. This insight formed the basis for another study, investigating how cues from human interaction can be applied to the interface to induce trust. Again, a literature review laid the foundation for further empirical research. Particular focus was given to the concept of *re-embedding* [6], and the related theories of *media richness* [20] and *social presence / telepresence* [12, 27]. We then performed an empirical test employing Walkthroughs [23, 25] with a mock-up and focussed interviews [14] with 15 participants [study IV].

## 3. TRUST

Consumer decision-making is a well-researched area. The prevailing cognitive model assumes that consumers search information on risks and benefits and weigh them against each other to reach a decision [5]. This model has, however, been criticised since it does not account for habitual decisions or affective reactions, nor the effect of trust in decision-making.

In complex situations (i.e. those which involve a large number of risks, or risks that are not well understood), individuals need to base their decisions on trust – or withdraw from the situation. Essentially, trust is a *device for reducing complexity* [13]. Various definitions of trust exist, and they agree that trust depends on: (1) an individual's ability to trust, (2) conventions; and (3) cues of trustworthiness [6, 13, 30]. Cues of trustworthiness - attributes of the entity to be trusted - are the focus of our research. They form a small empirical basis for the trusting person from which she may conclude on future behaviour of the entity in question. This has two implications: (1) to a certain extent, cues need to be seen as being given *unintentionally*, as a by-product of interaction; and (2) they need to be *congruent*: The perception of trustworthiness is easily undermined by a single cue to the contrary [13]. These results from the literature review [I] form the conceptual foundation of the model that is introduced in this paper.

# 4. RISKS IN E-COMMERCE

Table 1 gives an overview on the risks that have been mentioned by respondents, grouped according to the source of the risk [II]. It has, however, been shown that risk perception and trust towards an organisation and its technology are related [1].

*Table 1.* Risks in e-Commerce

| |
|---|
| 1. Risks that stem from the Internet include: |
| a) whether credit card data gets intercepted; |
| b) whether the data is transmitted correctly; |
| c) their own interaction with the system- i.e. whether they use it correctly |
| 2. Risks that are related to the physical absence of the online-retailer are: |
| a) whether the personal details they supply will be passed on to other parties; |
| b) whether the online-vendor will actually deliver the products or services. |

On-line shopping is thus a very complex situation in which people require more trust than in traditional shopping environments most would-be e-shoppers do not have sufficient experience - and hence expertise - to fully assess the underlying technology and its risks. The fact that e-commerce transactions are dis-associated in terms of time and geographical distance increases the complexity, and adds to the risk for the parties involved. The interviews [II] showed that risk perception depends on the knowledge and experience of potential e-shoppers.

## 4.1 Knowledge

Knowledgeable shoppers mainly consider risks related to individual online-vendors. Here the design of the interface has the highest impact. Very inexperienced Internet users see the greatest risk in the complexity of the system; some of them believe that even a trustworthy vendor is not capable of protecting them from the risks associated with the Internet. Furthermore, respondents who lack knowledge cannot judge the veracity and accuracy of media reports on Internet security. As a result of such reports, many would-be e-shoppers worry about risks that are non-existent or very small indeed [II, III].

## 4.2 Experience

Lack of experience can be seen as problem on an individual and collective level [I]. On an individual level, the prime risk that stems from a lack of experience is the danger of interacting incorrectly with the system - e.g. accidentally ordering an unwanted item. On a collective level, the lack of experience translates into absence of conventions. Many authors attribute the existing lack of trust to the relative novelty of the Internet [29, 30]. Once conventions have been established and individuals perform on-line shopping habitually, they argue, the trust problem will go away. People's trust is usually based on an *expectation of continuity* [13], and the basis for trusting is not usually re-evaluated for any specific decision. Our findings, however, suggest that the novelty of the medium - and thus the lack of habit and conventions - is only one of several factors increasing the demand for trust in on-line shopping [I, II].

The fact that customer and retailer in on-line shopping are separated in time and space is inherent in the medium, and will not be overcome with time - the 'trust problem' is therefore not likely to go away with increasing collective familiarity.

## 4.3 Separation in Space & Time

At the core of every economic transaction lies a situation known as *prisoner's dilemma* [11]: If both parties choose to maximise their own benefit (i.e. take the other party's exchange item, but keep their own), the transaction will not take place and both participants lose out. The risk of one party acting in this way can be minimised by co-presence of both parties: If I go to a shop and I do not receive the item after paying, I could exercise physical power on the shop assistant, or I could try to grab my money back. If the shop and I are embedded in the same legal system, I can trust the legal system to enforce the rules if necessary. If the transaction is separated in space, I may not have these options; thus, the transaction bears a higher risk and an increased demand for trust [I]. Furthermore, I cannot see the shop's interior nor the shop assistant, and thus I have few cues for my decision whether to trust this retailer or not [II].

Similarly, the separation in time (e.g. payment is made before goods are received) increases the risk of the transaction. If the goods are to be received within seconds after payment, the customer will realise quickly when she is being defrauded, and take remedial action. If a product ordered on-line is to be received after 2 weeks, it might be harder to track down the other party when it does not arrive [I, II].

This separation of transactions over space and time is called *dis-embedding* - a pervasive concept in modern societies, and by no means unique to on-line shopping. Catalogue shopping, for instance, faces the same problem. Due to the global nature of e-commerce, however, the degree of dis-embedding in e-commerce is higher.

Dis-embedded social systems and complex technology depend on an increased level of trust from all participants[6, 13]. We thus suggest that the oft-proclaimed 'lack of trust' in Internet shopping needs to be re-defined as an *increased need for trust*, based on the nature of the transaction - and currently - inexperience of the e-shoppers.

## 5. E-SHOPPER DECISION-MAKING

How then, we asked, do potential e-shoppers decide who to shop with in such a risky environment? The Grounded Theory analysis [II] identified three strategies that e-shoppers use, depending on their level of knowledge and experience with the Internet [Figure 1]. Ultimately, an e-shoppers' decision "*to buy, or not to buy*" is influenced by (1) the on-line retailer's performance when being evaluated by the potential e-shopper employing one of the identified strategies (e.g. whether the on-line retailer has a well-known brand), (2) the perceived benefit (e.g. how much they can save compared to other sources), and (3) their personal disposition (e.g. how high a risk they can bear)

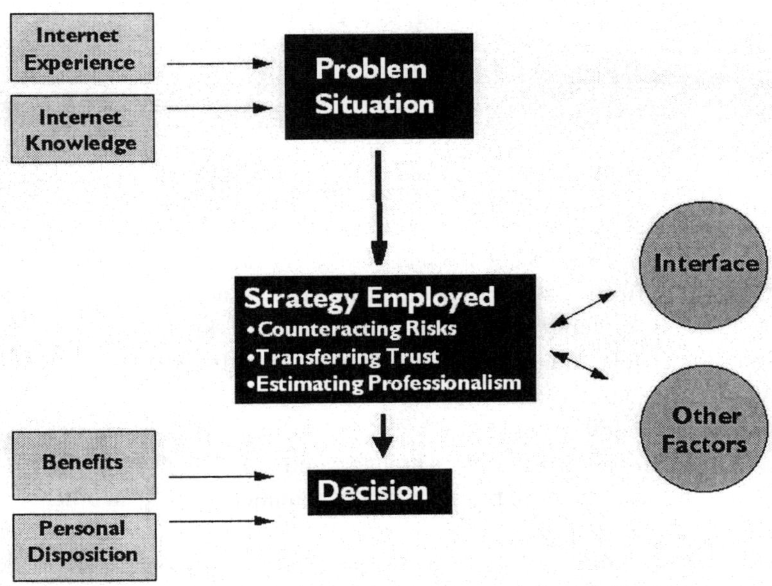


*Figure 1.* E-Shopper Decision Making

Inexperienced e-shoppers are likely to *transfer trust*: They will give on-line shopping a first try with retail organisations they are familiar with, or those that have been recommended to them. *Reputation* appears to be the biggest single influence when would-be e-shoppers decide to 'loose their virginity'. This importance of transferred trust gives established players who have a strong brand an advantage in e-commerce. At the same time, it exposes their traditional business to considerable risk, because trust transfer works in the other direction, too [1]. If I have a bad experience with the on-line shop, I may begin to doubt the competence of the organisation as a whole, and stop using the physical shop as well. Experienced e-shoppers build up a *repertoire* [19] of professional-looking e-commerce sites, similar to the one they have for traditional shops, and thus base their trust evaluation on interface factors - they estimate the on-line shop's professionalism. Very experienced and knowledgeable shoppers only consider specific risks (e.g. fulfilment), and try to counteract those directly (e.g. through checking for order tracking facilities). If they can identify a benefit by shopping on-line, they may even shop with an online-retailer that looks less professional. They have a strong sense of being in control when interacting via the Internet. We can expect *trust transfer* and *professionalism* to gain in importance as less knowledgeable e-shoppers enter the e-commerce arena.

# 6. CLOSING THE 'TRUST GAP'

## 6.1 Reducing Risk

The most obvious approach is to use technological solutions to directly address the risks involved in on-line shopping. This entails improved payment services, such as *Secure Electronic Transactions* (SET) or technological approaches to privacy like the *Platform for Privacy Preferences Project* (P3P). As mentioned before, these solutions will only be effective if the technological solutions are – at least in their basics – understood by e-shoppers. A further reduction of risks will be achieved when legal and regulatory frameworks – addressing the transaction itself, e-shoppers' privacy and statutory rights – have been established.

The risks that can be directly mitigated by interface design are *e-shoppers' own errors (1b)* and *faulty transmission (1c)*. Through good interaction design, the e-shopper can be assured that she does not accidentally commit herself to an order and that all data is received correctly. Examples include *status indicators, system feedback, displaying data already entered*, and *continuously displaying the products to be ordered* during the process.

*Fulfilment risks* (2b) can be reduced by giving alternative ways of contacting the online-vendor *(recourse)*, by *guaranteed response time*, or by the previously mentioned *order tracking*, which helps to minimise the impact of separation in time.

The experiment [III] with a mock online-shop showed that an interface with trust cues (including elements not specifically targeted at fulfilment risks) had the greatest effect on customers' apprehensions related to fulfilment.

## 6.2 Trust Transfer

There are several ways to address the inexperienced e-shopper's strategy of *trust transfer*. Here they have been grouped into *collective* and *individual* approaches. Collective approaches rely on the joint effort of several online-vendors; *trust/privacy seals* and *reputation mechanisms* are the most prevalent ones.

### 6.2.1 Collective Approaches

A seal is an icon assigned to an on-line retailer by an independent body, such as the previously mentioned TRUSTe. The success of such trust seal programs, however, is disputed. Results from Sapient / Studio Archetype & Cheskin [24] support the impact of trust seals, but Cranor et al. [3] and our research [II] suggest they are of limited use. E-shoppers respond to sites that proclaim their own trustworthiness with an irritated: "*well they would say that, wouldn't they.*" Rather, the site has to 'look and feel' trustworthy throughout the interaction.

Another way of transferring trust is a *reputation-sharing mechanism*, as currently used by on-line auctioneers such as eBay [11]. They aggregate individual e-shoppers' ratings of other participants' trustworthiness and, based on these, assign each participant a reputation rating. This approach could also be employed by trust seals: basing their approval on customer ratings - rather than solely on compliance with set guidelines - would increase their usefulness. Personalised reputation mechanisms that take account of how our friends rate an on-line retailer would model the real world more closely: We place the highest confidence in recommendations from friends who had prior experience with an on-line retailer [II]. This idea is incorporated in Amazon's *affiliate programme*: Providers of web sites are encouraged to link to products on Amazon.com. Thus, the trust would-be e-shoppers might have in individual sites is transferred to Amazon.com.

### 6.2.2 Individual Approaches

The role of an individual retailer's interface design in supporting the least experienced would-be shoppers' strategy of trust transfer is limited: Their focus is on inferring trustworthiness from personal recommendations or brand familiarity. An individual retailer's interface design here can only support trust through *endorsements* (e.g. from well-known experts), or through positive *customer comments*. The impact of these measures is, however, limited by two factors: Firstly, they themselves depend on a basic level of trust and credibility, as they could easily be forged. Secondly, interface elements with no function beyond emphasising trustworthiness were interpreted as signifiers of untrustworthiness by some respondents, because they are seen as an attempt at manipulation [IV]. A way out of this dilemma is to incorporate elements that communicate such information- e.g. *"we have a large customer base"* almost as a side-effect. An example are Amazon's *customer recommendations*. This element has functionality on its own right (customer response to books); at the same time, many customer recommendations suggest a large customer base without making this the central message [II].

While an individual online-retailer's interface design can only play a limited role in building trust with inexperienced Internet users, it can easily create mistrust through poor usability. Breakdown situations that stem from users' misguided interaction with the system are often attributed to the vendor's malfunctioning technology. Information that is overlooked by the user (e.g. terms & conditions) can create the impression that it has been wilfully withheld. Thus, trustworthy interface design is necessary but not sufficient for inexperienced would-be e-shoppers [II, III].

## 6.3 Estimating professionalism

For more experienced Internet users, the quality of the user interface is the most important factor when deciding whether to shop with an online-vendor or not. By complying with off-line business standards (e.g. *consistent graphic design, absence of technological failures, clear assignment of responsibilities, upfront disclosure of terms & conditions, shipping costs and availability*) and with web standards (e.g. *good URL* [17], *good usability, privacy policy, similarity in interaction design to well known sites*), an on-line retailer can signal professionalism and thus appear trustworthy. [4, 16, 26].

# 7. RE-EMBEDDING

We stated above that one of the consequences of separation in time and space (*dis-embedding*) is the lack of social cues available to the potential shopper (e.g. gesture or gaze). The importance of social cues as initial base for trust in human interaction has been stressed by both Luhmann and Goffmann [13, 8]. Cues that have been identified by social psychologists include non-verbal (e.g. gesture, gaze, proximity) and para-verbal ones (e.g. pitch, speed), but also content-based ones (e.g. competence, generosity) [10]. Thus, *re-embedding*, i.e. introducing face-to-face interaction in otherwise distant interaction, is a common approach to building trust: Business people and academics alike fly around the globe not only to negotiate or give presentations, but more importantly, to update their basis of trust in each others' work [6]. Experiments have shown that initial face-to-face contact in otherwise computer-mediated collaboration increases trust in workgroups. [22].

## 7.1 Virtual Re-embedding

The concept of re-embedding has high face validity. It is therefore not surprising that many authors champion the introduction of elements of face-to-face interaction (social cues) to the interface of online-retailers [16, 18, 26]. These recommendations are, however, rarely based on existing knowledge on the effects of mediated social cues.

These effects were first described by Short, Williams and Christie in their work on *social presence* [27] and later elaborated by Rice's work on *media richness* [20]. These concepts describe the effect of formal attributes of media on the social presence they afford (perceived similarity to face-to-face interaction). These concepts have been criticised for being to narrow because they focus on formal media attributes (e.g. fidelity of reproduction). A broader concept that also accounts for personal and situational intervening factors is that of *(tele-)presence*[12]. Based on these concepts, we assumed that an interface can transmit social cues (and thus communicate trustworthiness) when formal and content-based guidelines as stated by the above mentioned authors are adhered to. We call this approach *virtual re-embedding* [IV].

The capability of an online-vendor's interface to perform virtual re-embedding depends mainly on the modalities used (photographs, video, text, speech, etc.), and how they are implemented. A further result from research into the underlying concepts is that the effect of personal trust cues and social presence communicated through media strongly depends on personal and situational factors, of which only few have been identified (e.g. gender, media literacy, locus of control). There are two approaches to virtual re-embedding:

1. *Transparency*: Introducing staff on the online-vendor's site and providing means to communicate with them.
2. *Anthropomorphism*: Using agents that give cues of personal trustworthiness.

Anthropomorphism has been discussed in HCI for several years, however with a view to improving usability, rather than trust. The main point of criticism was that human-like agents generate expectations that which cannot be met by the system [31]. This disappointment is likely to decrease usability and trust (see above for the relation between trust and usability). Currently, there are systems being developed that allow conversation in a style similar to natural language while monitoring non- and para-verbal trust cues [2]. For Internet based e-tailing, however, they are not yet available.

## 7.2 Empirical test

Due to the above-mentioned problems associated with virtual re-embedding through anthropomorphism, the empirical part of study IV focused on the first approach (transparency). A mock-up incorporating various personal trust cues (photographs and names of customer service agents, chat & call-back opportunities, photographs of the company, photographs of a customer receiving an item) was subjected to walkthroughs.

The study revealed that (1) participants perceived cues of social interaction in the interface. The photographs and names received unprompted attention while the participants were completing their tasks. However, (2) participants varied strongly in their reaction towards these interface elements. The previously identified intervening variables (gender, usage experience, previous experience with vendor) explained variance only partially. A unexpected result was that (3) participants with a high level of distrust towards online-vendors rated the increased presence of online-retailers personnel (through e.g. chat facilities) as an additional risk, making them vulnerable to manipulation. The (4) reaction from very experienced and trusting Internet users were also negative: Virtual re-embedding added little benefit for them, while it 'cluttered' the interface. (5) Comparing the elements researched, those that offered a functionality (e.g. being introduced to a personal customer service agent) were received better than those without (e.g. photograph of a customer receiving an item).

The results endorse virtual re-embedding measures for medium-experienced shoppers. These measures should, however, also have functional benefits, Or they carry the risk of decreasing usability or being perceived as an intentional strategy for winning trust. The study thus confirmed the view from sociology [6, 13] that social cues are only perceived as trustworthy when they are seen as being given unintentionally. Relating this result to the concept of (tele-)presence allows to draw the conclusion that virtual re-embedding should be implemented by using 'rich' media (e.g. video) as they leave less room for controlling the cues given and thus are better signifiers of trustworthiness. This finding postpones virtual re-embedding to a time when very high bandwidth access is more widely available.

Finally, study IV confirmed the result from previous studies that (6) professional, consistent *graphic design* and *branding* are paramount. Social cues perceived as not conforming to the brand personality of the online-vendor resulted in extremely negative reactions. Thus, at present, virtual re-embedding measures should be carefully designed and integrated as part of the overall branding strategy.

## 8. CONCLUSIONS

The current 'lack of trust' in e-commerce needs be re-conceived as an *increased need for trust* due to the novelty and complexity of dis-embedded transactions on the Internet. Increased familiarity, technological and legal/regulatory solutions will help to reduce the current reluctance of customers, but cannot be expected to totally overcome it.

On an individual basis, online-vendors can decrease the risks perceived by potential shoppers by allowing them to make sure that they interact correctly with the system, and by allowing for recourse. Measures to be taken here include status bars and continuous visibility of the products ordered, as well as an order tracking facility after the order has been placed (including the possibility to cancel it).

The scope for building trust through the interface with inexperienced Internet users has been shown to be limited. They mainly rely on recommendations, brand familiarity and reputation, and are likely use trust in known retailers as a shortcut to avoid complex risk/benefit assessments. This means that established organisations will attract these e-shoppers by *trust transfer*, and they have to ensure that their online systems meet novice e-shoppers' expectations. Negative experiences will not only put individual e-shoppers off the online site, but generate the feeling that the company 'betrayed' their trust. They are likely to tell friends and relatives about the experience, thus damaging the organisation's *reputation*, which has been identified as key factor. *Endorsements* and *seals* depend on a basic level of trust and credibility. However, the negative impact of poor interface design and lack of usability on this group cannot be exaggerated.

In communicating trustworthiness to more experienced shoppers, the interface is of more help. These users have built a *repertoire* of sites and are able to evaluate an online-vendor against this repertoire. Hence, compliance with online and offline business standards is important. Important points are: upfront disclosure of availability, terms & conditions, shipping costs, breadth and depth of product offerings, absence of technological failures, speed, consistent graphic design, good usability, good URL, similarity to well known sites.

Interface elements that include elements of social interaction are also most likely to be successfully deployed in the group of medium-experienced e-shoppers. Here they have been discussed from the perspective of the sociological concept called re-embedding. However, care has to be taken not to intimidate inexperienced shoppers through higher presence, and not to disappoint experienced shoppers by elements without functionality other than giving cues of social interaction.

When discussing the problem of trust in e-commerce, it should be kept in mind that many individuals decide not to shop online simply because it does not offer enough benefits to them, and not because they distrust e-commerce. Thus, even well-crafted interfaces and virtual re-embedding elements are likely to build conversion (ration of shoppers to visitors) of one vendor relative to another – but not that of the whole market. This is likely to be reached through collective efforts (legal system, increased literacy, P3P) and through other individual efforts that are not necessarily part of the interface (brand building, unique functions offering new benefits).

Thus, most interface elements can be seen as *trust qualifiers*: They are unlikely to get non-shoppers over the 'trial-threshold'. If not taken care of, however, they have a great potential for destroying trust (***Trustbusters***) - not only trust in the e-shop, but also in the organisation's off-line counterparts. Using Herzberg's [9] term, they could be described as the *hygiene factors* of trust. ***Trustbuilders,*** on the other hand, are elements that either directly counteract the risks associated with e-commerce (risk-reducers) or have shown to build trust. The strongest trustbuilders, however, are factors outside the interface. Table 2 gives an overview.

*Table 2.* Trustbuilders & Trustbusters

| | Trustbuilders | Trustbusters |
|---|---|---|
| Interface Factors | – Status indicators<br>– Displaying data already entered<br>– Continuous visibility of products to be ordered<br>– Order Tracking<br>– Recourse<br>– Trial Runs<br>– Assignment of responsibilities<br>– Virtual Re-embedding coupled with functionality<br>– Communicating trust cues as by-products of functions. (e.g. user community, company history) | – Poor usability<br>– Inconsistent design<br>– Technological failures<br>– Long system response time<br>– Not complying to business & online standards<br>– Information on terms & conditions, shipping time, product availability positioned in a way they are easily overlooked by the user<br>– Intentional usage of personal trust cues without providing functionality<br>– Agents that generate expectations they cannot live up to |
| Other Factors | – Brand<br>– Reputation<br>– Reputation Sharing<br>– Affiliate Programmes | |

We have to keep in mind that this list will change over time, due to the previously mentioned dependence on what is perceived as 'standard'. Furthermore, it should not be seen as a basis for over-simplification: Trust perception depends strongly on personal and cultural factors. Thus, it might well be worth to provide separate interfaces for different customer segments.

## 9. REFERENCES

[1] Adams, A. & Sasse, M. A. (1999). Taming the Wolf in Sheep's Clothing: Privacy in multimedia communications. *Proceedings of ACM Multimedia '99*, 101-107.

[2] Cassell, J. & Bickmore, T. (2000). External Manifestations of Trustworthiness in the Interface. *Communications of the ACM*, 43(12), 50-56.

[3] Cranor, L. F.; Reagle, J.; Ackerman, M. S. (1999). Beyond Concern: Understanding Net Users Concerns about On-Line Privacy. http://www.research.att.com/resources/trs/TRs/99/99.4/99.4.3/report.htm

[4] Egger, F. N. (2000). Trust Me, I'm an Online Vendor: Towards a Model of Trust for E-Commerce System Design. In G. Szwillus & T. Turner (Eds.) (2000). *CHI2000 Extended Abstracts: Conference on Human Factors in Computing Systems*. The Hague, 101-102.

[5] Evans, M. J.; Moutinho, L.; Van Raaj, W. F. (1996). Applied Consumer Behaviour. Addison-Wesley: Harlow.

[6] Giddens, A. (1990). The Consequences of Modernity. Oxford: Polity Press.

[7] Glaser, B. G. & Strauss, A. (1967). The discovery of grounded theory: Strategies for qualitative research. Chicago: Aline Publications.

[8] Goffman, E. (1959). The Presentation of Self in Everyday Life. New York: Doubleday.

[9] Herzberg, F., Mausner, B. & Snyderman, B. B. (1959). The motivation to work. New York: Wiley.

[10] Klammer, M. (1989). Nonverbale Kommunikation beim Verkauf. Heidelberg: Physica.

[11] Kollock, P. (1999). The production of trust in online markets. *Advances in Group Processes*, 16.

[12] Lombard, M & Ditton, T. (1997). At the Heart of It All: The Concept of Presence. *Journal of Computer Mediated Communication*, 3(2).

[13] Luhmann, N. (1989). Vertrauen. Ein Mechanismus der Reduktion sozialer Komplexität. Stuttgart: Enke.

[14] Merton, R. K. & Kendall, P. L. (1946). The focussed interview. *American Journal of Sociology*, 51, 541-557.

[15] Nielsen Netrating Reporter (2001). http://www.nielsen-netratings.com/

[16] Nielsen, J. (07.03.1999). Trust or Bust: Communicating Trustworthiness in Web Design. http://www.useit.com/alertbox/990307.html

[17] Nielsen, J. (21.03.1999) URL as UI. Alertbox. http://www.useit.com/alertbox/990321.html

[18] Olson, J. S. & Olson, G. M. (2000). i2i Trust in E-Commerce. *Communications of the ACM*, 43(12). 41-44.

[19] Potter, M. & Wetherell, J. (1988). Discourse Analysis and the Identification of Interpretive Repertoires. In C. Antaki (Ed.). Analysing Everyday Explanation: A Casebook of Methods. London: Sage, 168-83.

[20] Rice, R. E. (1992). Task analyzability, use of new medium and effectiveness: A multi-site exploration of media richness. *Organization Science*, 3(4), 475-500.

[21] Reichheld, F. F. & Schefter, P. (2000). E-Loyalty: Your Secret Weapon on the Web. *Harvard Business Review*, 78(4), 105-113.

[22] Rocco, E. (1998). Trust breaks down in electronic contexts, but can be repaired by some initial face to face contact. *Proceedings of CHI 98*, 496-502.

[23] Rowley, D. E. & Rhoades, D. G. (1992). The cognitive jogthrough: a fast-paced user interface evaluation procedure. *Conference proceedings on Human factors in computing systems*, 389 – 395.

[24] Sapient / Studio Archetype & Cheskin Research (1999). eCommerce Trust Study. Studio Archetype / Cheskin. http://www.studioarchetype.com/cheskin

[25] Sasse, M. A. (1997). Eliciting and Describing Users' Models of Computer Systems. Doctoral Thesis. University of Birmingham.

[26] Shneiderman, B. (2000). Designing Trust into Online Experiences. *Communications of the ACM*, 43(12), 57-59.

[27] Short, J., Williams, E., Christie, B. (1976). The Social Psychology of Telecommunications. London: John Wiley & Sons.

[28] Strauss, A. & Corbin, J. (1998). Basics of Qualitative Research. Techniques and Procedures for Developing Grounded Theory. 2nd ed. Thousand Oaks: Sage.

[29] Swaminathan, V., Lepkowska-White, E., Bharat, P. R. (1999). Browsers or Buyers in Cyberspace? An Investigation of Factors Influencing Electronic Exchange. *Journal of Computer Mediated Communication*. 5(2).

[30] Winkel, O (1999). Die Förderung von Vertrauen, Glaubwürdigkeit und Verläßlichkeit in der digitalisierten Informationsgesellschaft. In Rössler, P. & Wirth, A. (1999). Glaubwürdigkeit im Internet. München: Fischer, 197-208.

[31] Winograd, T. & Flores, F. (1986). Understanding Computers & Cognition. Norwood, NJ: Ablex Corporation.

3

# A Taxonomy for Trusted Services

Jon Ølnes
*Norwegian Computing Centre (NR), P.O.Box 114 Blindern, N-0314 Oslo, Norway*[2]

**Abstract:** Electronic commerce must be trustworthy. This includes (technical) trust in the computerised systems and networks, and (organisational) trust in the honest intent of the counterparts. To establish trust, in general one has to rely upon infrastructures consisting of trusted services. In particular for organisational trust, a plethora of different services may be needed. This paper suggests a taxonomy to characterise trusted services in general. The virtues of a taxonomy are easier comparison and a common terminology, increased understanding, and facilitation of tasks like requirements specifications.

## 1. INTRODUCTION

In order to gain acceptance, electronic commerce must be trustworthy. Trust can be defined as "perceived lack of vulnerability". A trust decision implies a judgement about the vulnerability implied by a certain action, and thus a decision to carry out the action or not. The entity that decides upon this acceptance is ultimately always a human or a humanly controlled entity. As an example, the EU work on "qualified electronic signatures" and related certificates [2] is really about setting the requirements that digital signatures should fulfil in order to be trusted by the (humanly controlled) entities "EU" and "member state".

Trust decisions are not necessarily rational. Trust is a subjective decision, based on perceived, not real, vulnerability. Enough examples may be found where something (press coverage, lobbying organisations) blows minor vulnerabilities out of proportions, or alternatively attempts to turn severe vulnerabilities into trifles. Compiling available information, weighted by common sense and a sound scepticism towards the information, into rational trust decisions is a difficult task.

[2] Present affiliation: PKI Consulting Services AS, P.O.Box 1569 Vika, N-0118 Oslo, Norway. (Email: Jon.Olnes@pki.no ) Also part-time associate professor, University of Tromsø.

Trust may be established one-way (I trust my bank but my bank does not trust me) or mutually (we trust one another).

An electronic commerce arena may consist of large-scale systems (or rather large-scale connectivity between systems) and in principle arbitrary communication patterns. The actors may have no prior knowledge of one another, and thus no way to determine the trust to take in a counterpart. This calls for an infrastructure consisting of trusted services, commonly termed TTP-services (trusted third party). A plethora of different trusted services may exist for different purposes.

In this paper, the term TTP is used as a shorthand for any trusted service. The term is sometimes slightly misleading, as a trusted service need not always be provided by a neutral, *third* party. As one example, banks are usually trusted to take on several TTP roles for electronic commerce, even if the banks are highly involved in the financial transactions that result.

This paper focuses on a taxonomy to characterise trusted services and their roles, not that much on the topic of trust per se. There is ample literature on more or less formal trust metrics and reasoning about trust. This is discussed briefly in section 5 but in general the topic of formal trust reasoning is out of scope of this paper.

The virtues of a characterisation are an increased understanding of the roles of TTPs, better means to analyse the properties of the services, easier comparison between services, and facilitation of tasks like requirements specifications. The approach is more engineering-style than formal. The characteristics proposed are:

- service offered and type of trust mediated – technical or organisational (see 2);
- quality of service – as specified by the TTP's policy statements;
- proof handling – production, validation or storage of proofs;
- community of users;
- trust model – with respect to other TTP services;
- legal aspects, jurisdiction, responsibility and liability taken, need for agreements;
- communication pattern – on-line, off-line or in-line service, human user interface and programming (API) interfaces.

The characteristics are discussed in sections 2-7. Section 8 has a brief discussion on the role of licensing and certification. Section 9sums up the taxonomy in the form of a table. An example of an application of the taxonomy would have been beneficial, but a paper format unfortunately leaves no room for this.

## 2. TECHNICAL AND ORGANISATIONAL TRUST

Fundamentally, there are two different types of trust for electronic communication:

- *Technical trust*[3] in a computerised system and its components, i.e. that the system works as anticipated (reliability), is protected against attacks (security), and protects the interests of the user (safety).
- *Organisational trust* in the honest intent and willingness to co-operate of other actors / users of the system.

This is shown in *Figure* . Technical trust is in what Jøsang [5] calls "rational entities", computers and the like that behave according to programmed instructions. The most important property of rational entities is their security, i.e. that they have not been compromised. For the purposes of this paper the security term also includes reliability and safety. Organisational trust is in "passionate entities" in Jøsang's terms, i.e. entities that may behave according to will. This is related to questions like "will this person pay for the services" or "is this a serious dealer".

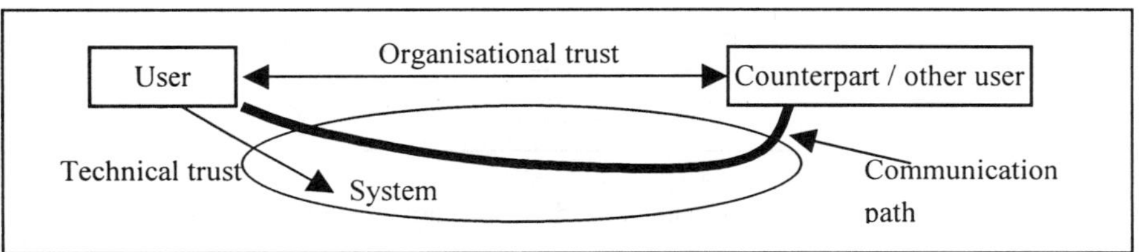


*Figure 1.* Technical and organisational trust.

Going back to the definition of trust as "perceived lack of vulnerability", it is clear that two different properties are important:

- The system / counterpart must be perceived as trustworthy; and
- The system / counterpart must really be sufficiently trustworthy.

These properties are to a certain degree independent. A rogue counterpart may have a very convincing appearance, while an honest one need not appear that way. It is perfectly possible to give the impression that an insecure system is secure, and a secure system does not necessarily give that impression. There may also be a conflict with respect to making security properties transparent and at the same time give an impression of security. The user interface and friendliness of a system clearly plays an important role in this context.

A limited number of actors can exchange information prior to communication, and can establish *direct* trust relationships by such ad hoc means. It is impossible to pre-establish such trust relationships for communication between a large number of (in principle arbitrary and unknown) actors. The general solution is to define some services as trusted, and derive trust between other actors from the trust in these services. In this, trust is regarded as a transitive property – we do not trust one another, but since both of us trust the TTP that vouches for the other party, we can still establish *indirect* trust. If we do not use the same TTP, we either have to obtain direct trust in more than one TTP, or the TTPs must apply a trust model that allows

3 The terminology technical / organisational trust is suggested by the author.

us to obtain indirect trust in the other party's TTP, resulting in a *chain of trust* between us. This is discussed further in 6.

The TTPs constitute an infrastructure. The two types of trust give rise to different kinds of TTP-services, as shown in *Figure* . TTPs for technical trust enable secure communication between possibly arbitrary actors. TTPs for organisational trust enable co-operation on presumably important matters between possibly arbitrary actors.

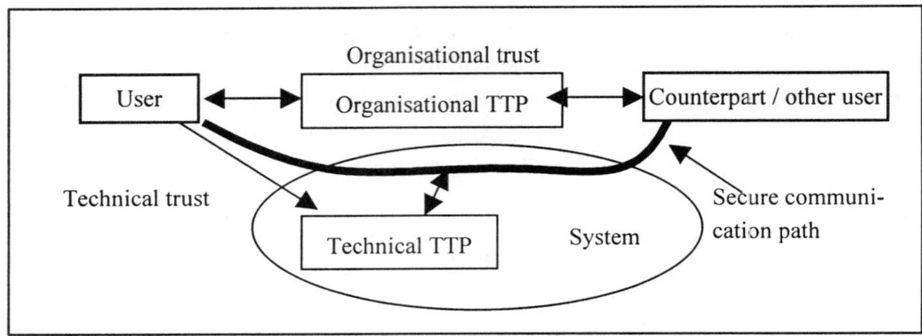


*Figure 2.* Technical and organisational TTPs.

## 2.1 Technical Trust and Security

No system is 100% secure. Determination of a "sufficient" level of security will vary from case to case dependent on the requirements. Too low *technical* trust means that a system cannot be used or that communication cannot take place. Technical TTP-services provide a certain guarantee that a sufficiently secure communication channel may be established. The most common example is a certificate authority that issues authentication certificates, which in turn may be used both for authentication and establishment of a secure communication channel.

Technical TTP-services, a certificate authority is a good example, may contribute to organisational trust by providing knowledge for the user's trust decision. However, it is a frequent mistake to assume that authentication implies trust. Knowing your counterpart does not necessarily make you trust him.

## 2.2 Organisational Trust and Accountability

Reflections about what one wants to communicate *about* (or co-operate on) with a counterpart that one communicates *with*, are commonplace in daily life. The answers are given by the level of trust taken in the counterpart. A low level of *organisational* trust implies that co-operation cannot take place, or alternatively that strong accountability measures must be in place in order to prove and prosecute malicious behaviour. For accountability event logging may often be sufficient.

Stronger accountability services, i.e. non-repudiation, can only be achieved by use of digital signatures and / or TTPs for storing of proofs.

For electronic commerce, visual impression should not imply trust. A backstreet store in a large city gives an impression of the risk of buying something there. For its electronic commerce service, the same store may have a totally different appearance.

Organisational TTPs are commonplace in everyday (physical) life, although one does not normally reflect on the necessity of such actors. The textbook example of a commerce TTP actor is a broker that mediates trade between parties. Electronic broking is an active research area.

Organisational TTPs are not needed in an infrastructure for secure *communication.* But the TTP services are needed – or at least desired – to obtain trustworthy electronic *commerce* (given a broad interpretation of this term). In this aspect, the organisational TTPs are parts of value chains for electronic commerce. Organisational trust and organisational TTP roles are generally not well defined nor understood in today's electronic commerce. As of today, a reasonable assumption seems to be that where a TTP role exists in "traditional" commerce, its electronic counterpart may also be needed, with approximately the same purpose. Only experience will show if this picture is correct, or if roles will appear, disappear or get new content if eventually electronic commerce will develop to something entirely different from traditional commerce.

## 3. PROOF HANDLING – THE PURPOSE OF A TTP

A TTP plays a role with respect to the knowledge upon which an actor decides a level of trust. The TTP *produces*, *validates*, or *stores* proofs of statements. Examples of statements are: "I am NN", "I have the right to charge bank account xxxxx", "I have sent message M at time T", "I intend to pay for the goods that I just ordered", or "I run a trustworthy business". It follows that "proof" may be a bit strong word in some cases – a better term might be "plausibility". A TTP may be delegated the responsibility for producing certain information, e.g. cryptographic keys. An important characteristic of a TTP is its role in proof handling, e.g.:

- A certificate authority *produces* electronic IDs, i.e. proofs of identity[4];
- A notary service *stores* proofs related to certain documents or actions;
- An OCSP (On-line Certificate Status Protocol) [10] service *validates* certificates and returns their status (valid, suspended, revoked, etc.).

[4] The electronic ID is only part of the proof. It is only valid when accompanying some piece of information that proves that the originator is in possession of the correct private key.

Proofs can be suitable for human evaluation, or they may be meant for automatic processing by programs and services. This may pose entirely different requirements with respect to representation of the proofs.

# 4. COMMUNICATING WITH A TTP

A TTP will one way or another be involved in the communication between the actors. Depending on its role in the communication protocol a TTP is denoted as:

- Off-line – does not participate in the communication, but the actors rely on the TTP having produced the necessary proofs in advance;
- On-line – the actors communicate directly, but at least one of them must communicate with the TTP during the communication session, at the time of session establishment or later;
- In-line – all communication between the actors passes through the TTP.

This is shown in Figure 3. The most common example of an off-line TTP is a certificate authority for authentication certificates. An example of an on-line TTP is an OCSP [10] service for validation of certificates. An example of an in-line TTP is a service that provides anonymity. A broker may also operate an in-line service. Even an off-line TTP may offer on-line services, but these services are not necessarily trusted. One example is an on-line certificate directory, which may or may not be a trusted service.

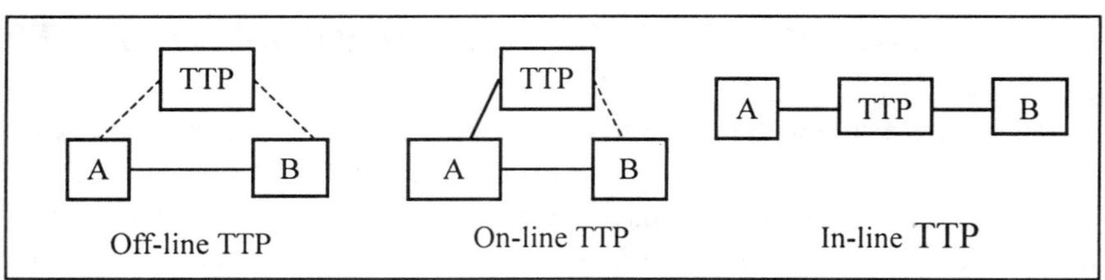


*Figure 3.* Communicating with a TTP.

A TTP must offer interfaces towards its users. This may be interfaces intended for human users, protocol interfaces that can act as the server side for defined communication protocols, or application program interfaces (API) related to use of component based systems and middleware. An interface may be message based, i.e. well-defined messages are exchanged between the user and the TTP, or call-based, usually by means of remote procedure calls. For on-line and in-line TTPs, the need for interfaces is obvious. An off-line TTP needs to offer interfaces in order to handle requests for production of proofs, like certificates, and for adjunct on-line services, like a directory, if offered.

# 5. QUALITY OF SERVICE AND QUALITY OF TRUST

An actor's subjective trust evaluation decides whether or not a certain action may be performed, perhaps under certain additional requirements like accountability. When a TTP is involved, the first decision is to what degree the TTP is trusted, and secondly to what degree actors that the TTP vouches for can be trusted. A decision to trust a TTP implies access to all actors / services for which trust is mediated by this TTP. It does not necessarily imply trust in all such actors, but distrust in the TTP implies distrust in the actors.

There is ample literature on approaches to metrics, based on various formal logics, for analysis of trust properties, see for example [1], [6], [7], [8]. Reiter and Stubblebine [8] provide a comparison of some approaches and suggest design principles for metrics. Most papers are particularly targeted at authentication and certificate chains, but the approaches can in most cases be generalised to other trusted services and trust models. Formal reasoning is valuable for a thorough analysis, probably mainly from a system engineering viewpoint. The benefit with respect to trust decisions taken by ordinary users is marginal. Since this paper is about characteristics of trusted services, and not trust per se, a further discussion on formal approaches to trust modelling and metrics is out of scope.

In the context of this paper, an important question is how, in a practical sense, an actor can establish a level of trust in a TTP. The trust is based on knowledge and assumptions (which will always carry an element of uncertainty). In practice, the most important parts of the knowledge are probably the actor that is responsible for the TTP, the name ("brand") of the service, and references to (recommendations from) other actors that trust the service.

Following these characteristics, the quality of the service comes next in importance. To enable determination of the quality of service, a TTP needs to have the following basic properties:

- Available policy statements that give a clear indication of the quality level and other aspects of the service like liabilities – a certificate policy is one example;
- An implementation that fulfils the level given by e.g. the certificate policy – conformance may be backed by third-party evaluation (see 8);
- Frequently objectivity with respect to the actors it serves.

The last property is not always necessary. As one example, a bank may take trusted roles for electronic commerce even if the bank is highly involved in the financial transactions that take place. In such cases, the term Trusted *Third* Party is slightly misleading, but we will nevertheless keep the term TTP for any trusted service, even provided by one of the communicating actors.

Figuring out the quality of a particular TTP service by simply reading its policy will usually not be practical. A policy (most certificate policies may serve as excellent examples) may be a complex and rather impenetrable document, even to people with reasonable competence in the problem area. Policies may even be written in a language unknown to the reader, and may refer to laws and regulations that belong to an unknown jurisdiction.

For practical purposes, quality of service should refer to a limited number of discrete values. An example may be different classes of authentication certificates, like Verisign[5] certificates of classes 1-3 (increasing quality). Here, the level is simply claimed by the service provider. Instead, more objective criteria may be established, where a provider may either give a self-assessment about compliance with a certain level, or some kind of certification or licensing may be given (see 7). "Qualified certificate" [2] is one such objective level indicator.

Getting hold of the quality indicator is the next problem. The EU Directive mandates a "qualified" indicator in the certificates themselves, but in most cases certificates will only have a reference to the policy, that is still impenetrable.

This may be solved by trusted validation services, which can be queried for information about other TTP services. One example may be a service that receives certificates issues by "any" certificate authority, and returns an authoritative answer about the validity of the certificate in question along with information about its quality level. This is discussed a bit further in 6.3.

Another approach is taken by the US Federal PKI specifications[6], which include a bridge certificate authority that will (voluntary agreement) cross-certify with the certificate authorities that serve the Federal administration. The bridge defines a number of discrete quality levels, and indicates, in a cross-certificate, the correct policy mapping (see 6.2) towards the policy of the service in question.

The quality of a service does not automatically indicate the trust level, but the quality level is an important characteristic for the taxonomy. The quality level is one more piece of information upon which quality of trust can be based. An actor may trust services of documented equal quality to different degrees, e.g. decide to trust only certain issuers of qualified certificates.

# 6. TRUST MODELS, RELATIONSHIPS BETWEEN TTPS

## 6.1 Trust Models and Scaling

Users will select certain TTPs that they decide to trust. Of course, other users may select other TTPs offering the same services. Requirements for communication between users of different TTP services are evident. This calls for trust models involving several TTPs. Three trust models can be seen:

[5] http://www.verisign.com

[6] See http://csrc.nist.gov/pki

- Monolithic, or trust list, i.e. only completely separate services – a user must establish trust separately in each of the TTPs;
- Hierarchies, where a TTP is approved (e.g. has a certificate issued by) a TTP at a higher level, and so on through possibly several levels back to a trusted root;
- Web of trust, where pairs of TTPs mutually (one-way is possible, but not common) recognise one another – e.g. through cross-certification,

A monolithic structure does not scale. Similarly, a web of trust structure involving a large number of TTPs will be unmanageable. Hierarchies have well-known scaling properties, but in this context even a hierarchical structuring has its problems. It is fairly clear that one will not end up with a situation where all TTP services of a particular kind are members of one common hierarchy. One is always left with an element of a monolithic trust model, in the form of direct trust in several trust structures.

Trust structures are nevertheless useful. As one example, Norwegian banks develop specifications for a common electronic ID service called BankID. This is a considerable simplification with respect to the situation where each bank has its own solution.

A hybrid structure is formed by combining a hierarchical structure with a web of trust structure. Whether this is allowed or not, and in case at which level in the hierarchy, is decided by the policies in force. Mutual recognition at the root level will effectively chain complete hierarchies, while mutual recognition at lower levels will chain sub-trees or single services. Finding a trust path between actors in a hybrid model (or even in a large-scale web of trust) is very difficult in practice.

## 6.2 Trust Models and Quality Level

Neither a web of trust model nor hierarchies necessarily mean a consistent quality level of the TTPs involved. The approval represented by e.g. cross-certification may be related only to an assurance that the other TTP runs according to its specified policy, whatever its quality. Such models enable recognition of other TTP services, and processing (e.g. certificate processing) related to the service, but users still have to determine separately the quality of all TTPs.

Rather, a user wants an indication that a given TTP has at a well-known quality, even if the TTP is only indirectly trusted. For web of trust this is achieved by "policy mapping", which implies a mutual recognition that the services are compatible. Within a hierarchy, a consistent policy level is obtained by posing requirements on the policies. A TTP that is not a leaf node of the hierarchy will postulate policy requirements that a TTP at lower levels must adhere to in order to become a member of the hierarchy.

As stated in 5, an actor may not necessarily take an equal trust in all services of a given quality level. Furthermore, the length of the trust chain becomes a new parameter in the trust determination. But more often than not, a user will accept a service at a well-known quality level if it is a member of a trust structure that the user recognises.

Deep hierarchies, as originally suggested by the PEM specifications [9], are discouraged because of the length of the trust chains and the time-consuming processing. The trust model is one of the main reasons for PEM's failure.

The present direction is towards "shallow hierarchies". Below a root, that typically determines (the level of) the policies in the hierarchy, there is one level of TTPs that in turn service the users. Thus long chains are avoided, and finding a path is easy. The Norwegian BankID project is one example of such a structure, with one CA per bank under a common root. Identrus[7], an initiative taken by some of the world's largest banks, potentially adds one more layer. The Identrus root-CA issues certificates only for the large banks (level 1), while smaller banks must obtain certificates from level 1 CAs, which additionally serve customers directly.

## 6.3 Meta–TTPs

Even given trust structures, a user is faced with a large number of TTPs that the user must decide to trust or not for a given purpose. An approach to solving this is meta-TTPs that answer requests about the quality and other aspects of other TTPs.

An example is an on-line certificate validation service. When receiving a certificate, a user will, without any processing of his own, ship the certificate off to the validation service. This service returns the status of the certificate (valid, revoked, suspended, expired) and possibly extra information derived from the certificate, like the values of certain fields or attributes. It may also return a quality level indicator. (As discussed in 5, the quality of TTP services should preferably be categorised into a limited number of discrete levels.) Based on the response, the user will decide to trust or not in order: the issuer, the certificate, and the actor for which the certificate has been issued. A particular validation service may not know everything, but as with all other TTP services, it may be part of a larger trust structure.

Conceptually, this may be regarded a two-level trust hierarchy, with the meta-TTP as the root, and the services it answers for at the second level. A meta-TTP must rely on a registry of services with given characteristics, compiled by the meta-TTP itself, or by other sources. According to the EU Directive [2] issuers of qualified certificates must be registered. The same goes for various TTP-roles that require a license in order to operate.

The interesting feature is that users may request information related to TTP services that they know nothing of, without referring to any kind of trust structure. A user may send any certificate to a validation service, regardless of who the issuer of the certificate is, and get back the information the user needs for his trust decision.

[7] http://www.identrus.com

The ultimate situation is that this may make all other trust structures void, since trust in TTPs may either be direct, or indirect through a meta-TTP.

## 7. LEGAL ASPECTS, LIABILITY, AGREEMENTS, USERS, PAYMENT

Part of the quality of a TTP is the degree of certainty of the information supplied or handled by the service. If a user suffers damage because of a mistake or failure by a TTP, severe legal implications may result. Any TTP needs to take precautions, and the legal conditions for use of the service should be clearly stated in the policy. The first step here is identification of jurisdiction and applicable law. Additionally, the TTP will impose limitations on the liability taken in case of failures, usually in the form of statements like not accepting liability if the service is used for a transaction above a certain value, or if the user's actions imply carelessness or violate the TTP's policy.

Relevant laws and regulations may to some extent dictate the liabilities that the TTP must take, and other aspects of its operation. Other issues here are the need for a license in order to be allowed to operate the service, and compliance with laws in areas such as privacy.

While statements like "use of the service implies that one has accepted the conditions stated in the policy" are commonplace, explicit formal agreements between a TTP and other actors are usually also needed. As one example, a certificate authority may require a signature on a written agreement before issuing a certificate to a person, even if the contents of the agreement are covered by the certificate policy. Agreements are also needed towards other TTPs in common trust structures[8], and with actors that somehow assist in the provision of the service. Examples here are registration authorities assisting certificate authorities and outsourcing of parts of services.

A common problem for TTPs is that no agreement need to exist with a party that relies on the TTP's proofs. As one example, an actor that receives a certificate issued by a given certificate authority will in general not have an agreement with the certificate authority. Liabilities towards such relying parties with respect to mistakes by the TTP should be covered by the TTP's policy, but this is nevertheless a difficult legal area.

The legal environment is one important parameter for identification of the customers of the service, and may be especially important if an international market is targeted. However, commercial issues will usually be more important – which market segments will the TTP aim at in order to make a profit out of the operation?

[8] Experience shows that the complexity of the legal aspects of cross-certification may make the process almost prohibitive.

Is the service open to anyone, or is it accessible only to a restricted community? The latter points directly at another important question: how is payment settled for use of the service? Several models are possible here, from subscription fee via per use fee (with a variety of payment methods) to free use. A discussion of payment models is outside the scope here.

# 8. LICENSING, EVALUATION, CERTIFICATION

Certain organisational roles require a license to operate. Examples are lawyer, medical practitioner, bank, real estate broker, and numerous others. Frequently such roles will be of a TTP type. What we see is really a trust hierarchy. TTPs at higher level certify the rights and credibility of TTPs at the leaf level by issuing a license for a certain role. Electronic license certificates, e.g. to licensed lawyers, should be issued for easy accessibility to other actors.

A license may require an evaluation and certification procedure. The roles, and the trust structure, of such a system are shown in *Figure* . A license granting body[9] is in charge of licensing of the actors that may perform evaluations according to certain criteria, and actors that are entitled to issue certificates of compliance with the criteria. Evaluator and certificate issuer will often be the same actor, but the roles are conceptually different. This is a confidence-building, and thus trust-building, system, making properties like quality and security visible.

There are several standards and systems for certification, with the ISO9000 series for quality as the most well known. The ISO14000 series provides certification with respect to environmental requirements. In security, ISO17799 [4] will be used. Certification may be requested by an actor at its own discretion, e.g. because this will lead to a market advantage, or it may be required by a license granting body in order to obtain a license for a certain role.

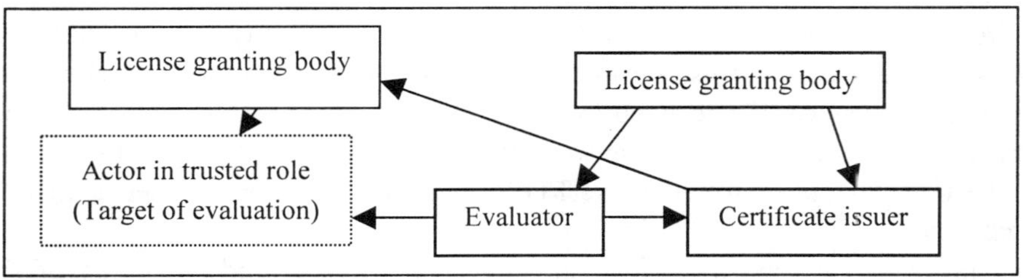


*Figure 4.* Evaluation, certification, and licensing.

[9] The term "accreditation" is usual for this role, but this is just a special case of licensing.

Similarly, security evaluation of (part of) a technical system may be done, e.g. according to the ISO15408 criteria [3]. This provides a guarantee that the system fulfils certain security criteria, given a certain class of environment. Technical system evaluation and certification may be a prerequisite for certain roles, e.g. with respect to systems used to store or process certain kinds of information.

# 9. THE TAXONOMY – TABLE FORMAT

Based on the discussions in the previous sections, the following table sums up the suggested taxonomy:

| **Characteristic** | **Parameters** | **Description** |
|---|---|---|
| Service type | Name of service | E.g. certificate authority, lawyer, broker, notary service |
| | Type of trust mediated | Technical/organisational – technical may contribute to both |
| | Trusted functions | E.g. authentication, payment transfer, key management, safe electronic commerce |
| | Adjunct services | E.g. directory service for a cert. authority |
| Quality of service | Policy reference | Policy defines most aspects of the service |
| | Service level | Derived from policy – preferably one of a discrete number of alternatives |
| | Owner | Who is behind the service? |
| | Brand name and references | Brand name for the service. Reference to actors that accept the TTP |
| Proof handling | Produce/validate/store | Part of protocols between actors |
| User community | Leaf-TTP or not | Wrt. trust models: Serves users directly or role wrt. other TTPs (e.g. root of cert. hierarchy, or license granting authority) |
| | Identification of customers | Restricted group or not |
| | Restrictions / requirements | Only certain application areas or open – depends on legal environment |
| | Payment model | Who pays, and billing method |
| Trust model | Trust structures and/or named counterparts | Trust structures or named TTPs that the service relates to, including trust model (hierarchy, web-of-trust etc.) |
| Legal aspects | Jurisdiction and law | Must be named in policy |
| | Licenses needed | In order to operate service |
| | Certifications needed | ISO17799, ISO15408 etc. |
| | Agreements needed | With users, authorities and other parties |
| | Liabilities taken | Important for most TTPs and for users |
| Comm. pattern | Off-line/on-line/in-line | Wrt. to protocols between actors |
| | Human/user interface | If access directly from human users |
| | API characteristics | Syncronous or asyncronous, message based or call based, standards and other interface specifications (message formats, protocols, APIs, middleware etc.) |

## 10. CONCLUSION

This paper suggests a taxonomy for TTP services. Such a characterisation may help understanding of the area, may provide guidance when comparing services and may help e.g. in writing of requirements specifications. The services are characterised according to type of service offered including type of trust mediated (in the security of the technical systems or in the trustworthiness of the counterparts that one wants to co-operate with), community of users, trust model (hierarchy, monolithic, web of trust) with respect to other TTPs, quality of service, proof handling (production, storage, validation), and communication pattern (off-line, on-line, in-line TTP).

**Acknowledgement.** The work on this paper has been carried out as a part of the (Harmonization for the Security of Web Technologies) HARP project, partly funded by the EU under the IST research programme.

## 11. REFERENCES

[1] T.Beth, M.Borcherding and B.Klein, Valuation of Trust in Open Systems, Proceedings of the 1994 European Symposium on Research in Computer Security (ESORICS '94), 1994.

[2] EU, Community Framework for Electronic Signatures, Directive 1999/93/EC of the European Parliament and of the Council, December 1999.

[3] ISO15408, Evaluation Criteria for IT Security, Parts 1-3, 1999.

[4] ISO/IEC 17799, Information Security Management – Code of Practice for Information Security Management, 2000.

[5] A.Jøsang, The Right Type of Trust for Distributed Systems, Proceedings of the 1996 New Security Paradigms Workshop, 1996.

[6] A.Jøsang and S.J.Knapskog, A Metric for Trusted Systems, Proceedings of the 21st National Security Conference, 1998.

[7] U.Maurer, Modelling a Public-Key Infrastructure, Proceedings of the 1996 European Symposium on Research in Computer Security (ESORICS '96), 1996.

[8] M.K.Reiter and S.G.Stubblebine, Authentication Metric Analysis and Design, ACM Transactions on Information and System Security, Vol. 2, No. 2, pp 138-158, May 1999.

[9] RFC1421-1424, Privacy Enhancement for Internet Electronic mail (PEM), 1993.

[10] RFC2560, Internet X.509 Public Key Infrastructure Online Certificate Status Protocol, June 1999.

4

# System Models, e-Risks and e-Trust

*Towards bridging the gap?*

Theo Dimitrakos

*Central Laboratory of the Research Councils, Rutherford Appleton Laboratory, Oxon, UK*

**Abstract:** Motivated by an industrial application, we introduce a working model of trust in e-commerce, and offer a classification of trust in e-services. Emphasis is also placed on the combination of risk analysis and role-based modelling to support trust management solutions.

## 1. INTRODUCTION

The issue of trust in e-commerce is central for businesses as electronic services based on ubiquitous media (e.g. Internet, WWW, mobile phones) proliferate. The UK is the largest e-commerce market in Europe [1], and although smaller than the US, it has been closing the gap relative to the size of the economy. The e-service market is predicted to rise to between 4% and 7% of GDP by 2003 for the countries shown in *Figure 1*. However, there is still major concern about user confidence in e-services. Year 2000 started with high hopes and many promising e-commerce start-ups but the bubble soon burst with many of them going out of business by the fourth quarter. In addition to well-thought business plans, if e-business ventures are to prosper, there is a prominent need to improve consumer confidence in e-services.

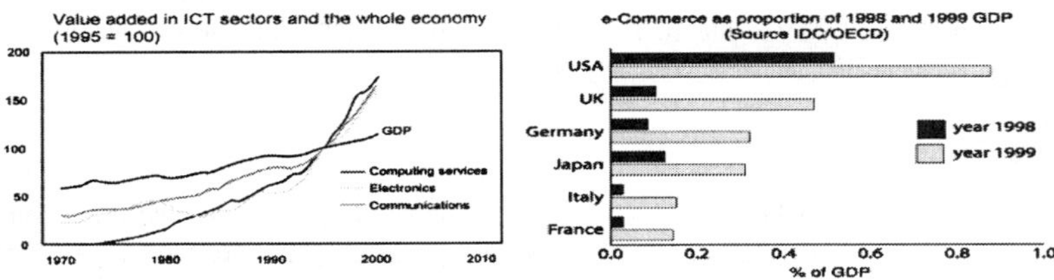


*Figure 1*. Sources: IDC/OECD (left) and "Success in 2005", UK ESRC (right)

Differing trust relationships can be found among the parties involved in a contract, and the emerging virtual communities require richer models of trust, in order to distinguish between them, and accommodate them in the context of a specific service. To build consumer confidence, e-commerce platform providers need to improve the existing technology in order to capture, measure and manage the trusting relationships that underlie such services. If e-commerce is to achieve the same levels of acceptance as traditional commerce, trust management has to become an intrinsic part of it.

Current solutions fail to incorporate in their decision making evidence or opinions collected by an agent through the agent's own experience, or via communication with other agents who cohabit the system. This makes the evolution of e-commerce systems harder and impedes their ability to adapt to changes in trust and to set up new relationships. In order to be able to handle trust dynamics, future solutions will have to incorporate methods to simulate learning, reasoning and analysing transactional and environmental risks with respect to the agents' view of the system they inhabit.

Motivated by an industrial application (section 2), this paper introduces a working model of trust in e-commerce (section 3) and a trust management scheme (section 4) including a classification of the basic types of trust underlying e-services. We suggest that the needs for flexibility and scalability are better addressed by separating the trust management framework from the purpose of the application, and we emphasise that risk management and role-based modelling can be combined to support trust management solutions. More specifically, we find roles to be well suited for modelling service-specific aspects of trust and particularly helpful for identifying and analysing cases where trust may be transferable. We also anticipate that risk management can guide an agent through transforming a mere *inclination* to trust into a carefully considered *intention* to trust, and through endorsing dependable *behaviour* as a realisation of the agent's dependable *intentions* to trust.

## 2. MOTIVATING EXAMPLE

As a motivating example, we summarise the Home Shopping Tool (HST) component of the ACTIVE platform[10], which will be used as one of the test-beds in the CORAS project[11].

[10] Developed in the ESPRIT EP 27046 project which aimed to introduce an e-commerce platform for integrated retail services, providing an intelligent interface upon which the trading parties (retailers, suppliers and consumers) establish a tied and trusted relationship.

[11] CORAS (IST-2000-25031) is an industry lead European project developing a framework for precise, unambiguous, and efficient risk analysis of security critical systems. The framework will be evaluated in major user trials in e-commerce and e-medicine.

HST delivers a personalised, targeted marketing experience through the realisation of a variety of services including personalised shopping, catalogue information, product search and recommendations, sales negotiation, e-payment, and user management facilities. Specific consumer information is gathered for the purpose of behaviour analysis and can be made available to the platform operator.

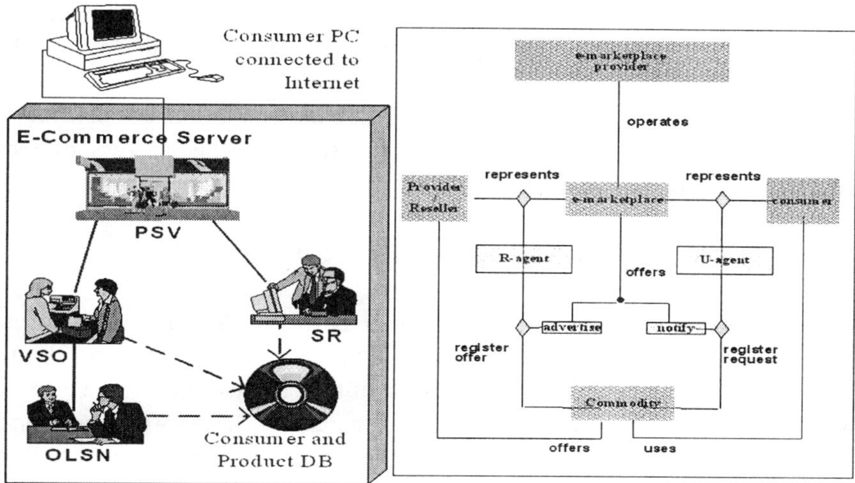


*Figure 2.* HSP components and basic business entities & relationships underlying OSLN

Notably, consumers and suppliers are provided with an agent-based automated bargaining mechanism that allows customers to find and negotiate products with various suppliers, and suppliers to promote their products and attract consumers. The agents get involved in a negotiation process and try to reach a mutual agreement according to the mandates given by their creators.

These services are offered to the users with the help of the following software modules depicted in *Figure 2*: The Virtual Shopping Operator (VSO), the Shopping Recommender (SR), the On-line Sales Negotiator (OLSN) and the Personalised Store Visualiser (PSV).

In the course of the CORAS project, this platform will be modelled in order to perform security risk analysis. We will further analyse these models (in parallel to CORAS) and use them as indicative examples to relate basic security and fairness properties to trust. During this analysis we will assess the effectiveness of, and further develop, the model of trust outlined in this paper. The results of the security risk analysis being conducted in CORAS will be used as input to our working model of trust management.

# 3. TRUST IN E-COMMERCE

In the physical world, we derive much of our notions of trust from the tangible nature of the entities in our environment. Our trust relies on personal contact, the tangibility of the objects and services, the difficulty of fraudulence and a clearly defined legal framework. Personal contact in virtual communities is limited, the legal framework is vague and the objects and services under negotiation are less tangible. The traditional notions of trust need to be rethought, and suitable models of trust in e-commerce have to be developed.

In this section we provide a rigorous definition of trust in e-commerce and analyse some general properties of trust proposed following surveys of recent attempts to formalise this concept [2],[3].

## 3.1 A working definition of Trust in e-Commerce

Although the importance of trust has been recognised, there is no consensus in the literature on what trust is. On the other hand, as it is elaborated in [3], many researchers assume an (unprovided) definition of trust and use the term in a specific way related to access control or to paying for purchases. In [2] we survey various attempts to provide some definition of trust that is suitable for e-commerce. Some aspects of these definitions are common, other are complementary. For example, [8] emphasises that trust is a belief in the competence of an entity within a specified context, while [3] lay stress on that the entity that manifests trust (the "trustor") is the human - not the system. They also emphasise that trust is in part subjective. A somewhat similar view is expressed in [4] where entities are distinguished into *passionate*, who have free will, and *rational,* who don't. According to [3],[4] trustors are *passionate* entities. The definition in [6] focuses on another aspect of trust: in commerce, *trust is relative to a business relationship*. One entity may trust another entity for one specific business and not in general. This diversity of the purpose of trust is also mentioned in [4] but not incorporated into a definition. Finally, none of the above emphasises that trust is not only inherently measurable but also it exists and evolves in time. We define trust as follows.

**Definition 1:** *Trust of a party A in a party B for a service X is the measurable belief of A in that B will behave dependably for a specified period within a specified context.*

**Remarks:**

- A party can be an individual entity, a collective of humans or processes, or a system; (obviously, the trustor must be an entity that can form a belief).
- The term service is used in a deliberately broad sense to include transactions, recommendations, issuing certificates, underwriting, etc.

- The above mentioned period may be in the past, the duration of the service, future (a scheduled or forecasted critical time slot), or always.
- Dependability is used broadly to include *security, safety, reliability, timeliness, and maintainability* (following [7]).
- The term context refers to the relevant service agreements, service history, technology infrastructure, legislative and regulatory frameworks that may apply.
- Trust may combine objective information with subjective opinion formed on the basis of factual evidence and recommendation by a mediating authority.
- Trust allows one agent to reasonably rely for a critical period on behaviour or on information communicated by another agent. Its value relates to the subjective probability that an agent will perform a particular action (which the trustor may not be able to monitor) within a context that affects the trustor's own actions.

Notably, our definition differs from [4],[5] with respect to the trusting subjects. Intelligent agents who negotiate can be either humans or programs and in both cases they need to manifest trust intentions and establish trusting relationships. Intelligent software agents are adaptive autonomous programs featuring the ability to acquire knowledge and to alter their behaviour through learning and exercise. Their decision making can be enhanced so that they form trust intentions and make decisions relying on trust. Our definition differs from [3],[6],[10] with respect to the inherent measurability and the subjective nature of trust. It also differs from [3],[4],[7],[8] in that trust differentiates between services and it is active for critical periods of time.

We also note that distrust, accounting to what extent we can ignore one's claims about her own or a third party's trustworthiness and their proclaimed actions or commitments, is modelled as a measurable belief in that a party will behave *non-dependably* for a critical period within a specified context. Distrust is useful in order to revoke previously agreed trust, obstruct the propagation of trust, ignore recommendations, and communicate that a party is "blacklisted" for a class of potential business transactions.

## 3.2 Properties of Trust and Distrust

The particular characteristics of trust may differ from business to business. Nevertheless, there are some common delimiters that indicate the existence of general principles governing trust in e-commerce.

**Proposition 2:** The following are general properties of trust and distrust.

P1. *Trust is relativised to some business transaction.* A may trust B to drive her car but not to baby-sit.

P2. *Trust is a measurable belief.* A may trust B more than A trusts C for the same business.

P3. *Trust is directed.* A may trust B to be a profitable customer but B may distrust A to be a retailer worth buying from.

P4. *Trust exists in time.* The fact that A trusted B in the past does not in itself guarantee that A will trust B in the future. B's performance and other relevant information may lead A to re-evaluate her trust in B.

P5. *Trust evolves in time, even within the same transaction.* During a business transaction, the more A realises she can depend on B the more A trusts B. On the other hand, A's trust in B may decrease if B proves to be less dependable than A anticipated.

P6. *Trust between collectives does not necessarily distribute to trust between their members.* On the assumption that A trusts a group of contractors to deliver (as a group) in a collaborative project, one cannot conclude that A trusts each member of the team to deliver independently.

P7. *Trust is reflexive, yet trust in oneself is measurable.* A may trust her lawyer to win a case in court more than she trusts herself to do it. Self-assessment underlies the ability of an agent to delegate or offer a task to another agent in order to improve efficiency or reduce risk.

### 3.2.1 Propagation of trust

As we elaborate in the sequel, at least unintentional transferability of trust within a locus may be acceptable in specific contexts. *Note that "transferability" in our case corresponds to influencing the level of trust rather than relational transitivity.* We distinguish three special *roles* that entities mediating in a trust relationship can play. These roles are *guarantors, intermediaries*, and *advisors*. Note that an entity may play more than one mediating role in a business relationship.

***Guarantor*** is a party taking the responsibility that the obligations of the parties she guarantees for are fulfilled at an agreed standard. Guarantors assist the establishment or facilitate the increase of trust for a specific transaction by underwriting (a part of) the risk associated with the transaction. A typical example is a credit card company.

***Intermediary*** is a party that intervenes between other parties in a business transaction and mediates so that they establish a business relationship with or without their knowledge. We distinguish the following types of intermediary:

– *Transparent:* an intermediary that identifies the parties she is mediating between to each other. An example is `Lloydstsb.com`, a bank, who offer to their on-line customers a comprehensive car rental and flight booking service powered by `Expedia.co.uk`, an on-line travel agency. A trivial example is an entity that simply redirects to another entity.

– *Translucent*: an intermediary that identifies the existence of the parties she mediates between but not their identity. An example is a retailer advertising product delivery by courier without identifying which delivery company is responsible for this.

- *Overcast:* an intermediary that hides the existence of the parties she is mediating between from each other. Examples include virtual enterprises, and ventures selectively outsourcing tasks to unidentified strategic allies.
- *Proxy:* an intermediary who is authorised to act as a substitute of another entity.

***Advisor*** is a party that offers recommendations about the dependability of another party. Advisors include the authorities maintaining blacklists for a community. Examples include, credit scoring authorities and reputation systems.

**Proposition 3:** Trust and distrust propagate according to the following rules:

P8. *(Dis)trust is not transferred along an overcast intermediary.* Assume that A (dis)trusts an overcast intermediary T for a service X provided by B. Since A is not aware that B provides the service, her (dis)trust is placed in T.

P9. *Trust is transferred along transparent intermediaries – distrust is not.* Assume that, for a service X, A trusts a transparent intermediary T mediating for B. By agreeing to the service, A expresses trust in B for X instigated by T's mediation.

P10. *(Dis)trust in a subcontractor of a transparent intermediary is transferred to (dis)trust in the intermediary.* If a party A (dis)trusts a subcontractor of a transparent intermediary T for a service X, then A is inclined to (dis)trust T for this particular service.

P11. *Trust is transferred anonymously along translucent intermediaries – distrust is not.* Assume that A trusts a translucent intermediary T for X and T trusts B to subserve for X. By agreeing to the service, A effectively expresses trust in a third party to subserve for X without necessarily knowing identity of that party.

P12. *Trust in an advisor is transferred to the recommended party - distrust is not.* The more A trusts T the more she relies on her recommendation.

P13. *Distrust in a recommended party is transferred to the advisor – trust is not.* A's distrust in a party B recommended by T for a service X prompts A to question T's competence as an advisor for X.

P14. *Advisors distinguish between recommendations based on "first hand" and "second hand" evidence. In the latter case they ought to identify their sources.* If $T_1$ and $T_2$ both pass to A advise by T as their own observations then T gains an unfair advantage in influencing A. See section 4.2 of [9] for further analysis.

P15. *Distrust propagates through trust and it obstructs the propagation of trust.* If A distrusts an intermediary T for a service X then A will ignore T's mediation to the extent of the distrust.

Note that P9, P10 and P12, P13 allow for trust and distrust to be transferred in opposite directions. This does not necessarily result in a conflict. The opposite initial values will affect each other and the final decision will depend on the resulting balance between trust and distrust in each party, and the tendencies of the trustor. This would not have been possible, had trust been viewed as a binary operator, because transitivity of trust would have lead to inconsistency.

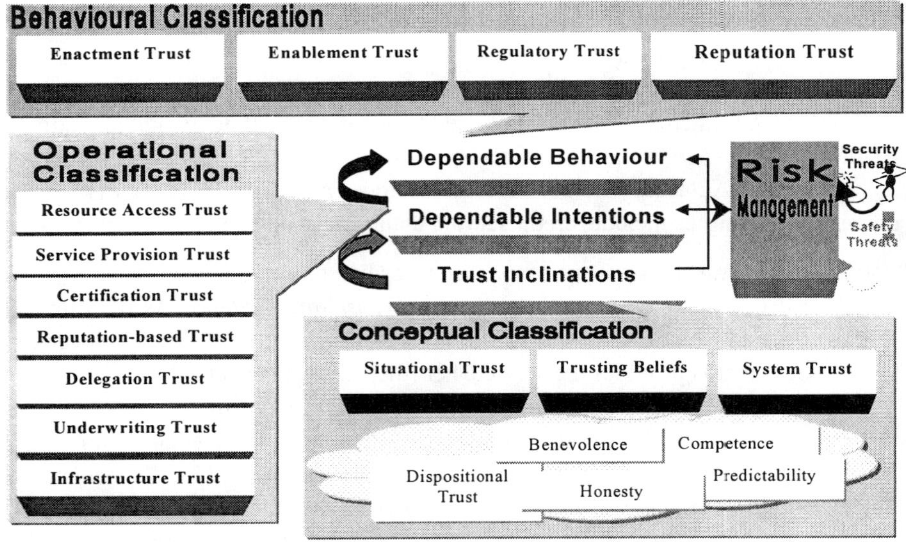


*Figure 3.* A pictorial overview of the proposed trust-management scheme

# 4. TRUST MANAGEMENT

The term *trust management* was introduced in [10] addressing the problem of developing a *"coherent intellectual framework...for the study of security policies, security credentials and trust relationships"*. It was the first time that issues such as *providing a unified mechanism*, *locality of control,* and most importantly, *separating mechanism from policy* were paid enough attention. Indeed, solutions to the shortcomings of existing trust management systems can be better addressed by separating the trust management framework from the purpose of the application. To achieve this, we need to systematise the development of control mechanisms and trust-based policies across all aspects of dependability, including security.

Trust management aims to provide a coherent framework for determining the conditions under which a party A takes the risk to depend on a party B with respect to a service X for a specific period within a specific context, and even though negative consequences are possible. Increasing the levels of trust facilitates processes to become more efficient but also increases the risk of allowing for the exploitation of vulnerabilities. One would consequently aim, in principle, to *maximise trust while minimising risk*. Hence, trust management subsumes and relies on risk management:

1. One may employ tailored risk analysis in order to analyse environmental risks and assess the most tangible aspects of trust (e.g. the dependability of the information technology infrastructure).

2. Risk management allows us to weight transaction risk against trust, evaluate the impact of a failure in trust and help device countermeasures.

Note that the above two analyse different types of risk (cf. section 4.1.4).

## 4.1 Classifications of trust

Trust management becomes more tractable in the presence of a conceptual classification of the different aspects of trust and the different ways they influence behaviour. For this purpose, we have adapted the conceptual framework proposed in [7]. Our adaptation extends the approach proposed in [11] and includes the following concepts summarised in *Figure 3.*

### 4.1.1 Trust inclinations

Trust inclinations is an intentionally broad term referring to the tendencies of an agent. These are typically influenced by the agent's own view of the environment it inhabits, by the extent it is willing to depend on another potentially unknown agent in a given circumstance, and by the extent it perceives the known institutions and infrastructure to be dependable.

The following classification focuses on trust inclinations inherent in an agent or acquired through the agent's exposure to an environment. (See also *Figure 3.*)

**Situational trust** measures the extent to which a party is willing to depend on an unspecified party in a specific role and a given circumstance.

**Beliefs** describe an agent's schema about the environment it inhabits. Four categories of primitives contribute to belief formation [7]:

- *benevolence*, i.e. the belief that one cares about the others welfare;
- *honesty*, i.e. that one makes an agreement in good faith;
- *competence*, i.e. that one is able to perform a specific task;
- *predictability*, i.e. that one's behaviour is predictable in a given situation.

**Dispositional trust** is a fifth primitive referring to an agent's persistent tendency to trust oneself and others across a wide spectrum of situations.

**System trust** measures the extent to which an agent believes that it can depend on the known institutional structures such as legislative, regulatory, reputation systems and the underlying technology infrastructure.

### 4.1.2 Dependable intentions

Dependable Intentions describe the extent to which a party is willing to depend on other parties (including oneself) for a specified period, within a specified context and in relation to a specific service. Dependable intentions can be modelled within policies, where a **policy** is viewed as *"a rule that can be used to change the behaviour of a system"* (following [12]). In decentralised open distributed systems, policies apply *within a locus*, i.e., a subsystem. As perception and knowledge evolve, an agent may find herself in a position where, according to one policy, pursuing a business relationship with another agent is to her interest, but according to another policy, the same business relationship with the same agent has to be avoided. **Meta-policies** (i.e., policies *"about which policies can coexist in the system or what are permitted attribute values for a valid policy"* [12]) are particularly useful for resolving such conflicts [13].

An operational classification of trust relates to this viewpoint (*Figure 3*), focusing on how the intention to trust is controlled and exercised.

- **Resource Access Trust:** for the purposes of a service X, A trusts B to access resources that A controls. This type of trust forms the basis for authorisation policies that specify actions the trusted party can perform on the resources, and constraints that apply such as time periods for when the access is permitted.
- **Provision of Service Trust:** A trusts B to for a service X that does not involve access to A's resources. Application service providers (ASPs) are typical examples of entities that would require service provision trust to be established.
- **Certification-based Trust:** A trusts a B for a service X on the basis of criteria relating to the set of certificates presented to A by B and provided by a third party C. Certificates are commonly used to authenticate identity or membership of a group.
- **Reputation-based Trust:** A trusts B for a service X on the basis of criteria relating to the opinions of other parties who have considered interacting with B in the past for similar services. Examples include reputation systems in e-auctions such as `eBay.com`. This type of trust is often complementary to certification-based trust.
- **Delegation Trust:** For a service X, A trusts B to make decisions on A's behalf about resources that A owns or controls. Examples include the delegation of decisions regarding investment to one's financial advisor.
- **Underwriting Trust:** A trusts B for a service X based on criteria related to the reduction of risk caused by the intervention of a third party C underwriting X. Examples include insurance companies underwriting loss or damage, and credit-card companies guaranteeing payment for a purchase.
- **Infrastructure Trust:** For the purposes of a service X, party A trusts the base infrastructure (subsystem B) upon which the provision of a service will take place.

### 4.1.3 Dependable behaviour

Dependable behaviour describes the extent to which a party behaves dependably. It implies acceptance of risks (potential of negative consequences) and their effect. At this level, the agent's inclinations and intentions have been analysed and endorsed resulting in patterns of behaviour.

The following classes of trust relate to this viewpoint (*Figure 3*), focusing on the roles of the stakeholders as they engage in a business relationship.

- **Enactment trust** is the trust between parties that engage in a business relationship through e-services, including customers and retailers.
- **Enablement trust** is the trust in those who enable or mediate in the provision of e-services including the technology and platform providers.
- **Regulatory trust** is the trust in the legislative, regulatory, standardisation and advisory bodies for e-business at a local or a global level.
- **Reputation trust** is the trust in reputation systems or the recommendation of arbitrary agents.

#### 4.1.4 Risk management

Risk management is the *"total process of identifying, controlling and minimising the impact of uncertain events"* [14]. Risk management often involves a form of risk analysis. The latter is *"the process of identifying risks, determining their magnitude, and identifying areas needing safeguards"* [14]. Risk analysis is critical for achieving the right means of abstracting information from reality into a formal model. Its importance has been recognised in the process industry and finance – business areas where elegant methods for risk management have been developed. As is depicted in *Figure 3*, we see risk management supporting the analysis of trust inclinations leading to the formation of trust intentions, and the analysis of trust intentions leading to the endorsement of dependable behaviour. We anticipate different kinds of risks to be analysed in these two phases. The focus in the former case is on analysing the effect that an agent's persistent tendencies and risks from the environment have on the formation of this agent's trust for a specific service. The focus in the latter case is on balancing intentions to trust against interaction risks in order to endorse an informed and dependable behaviour.

Ideally, risk management should be applied across all aspects of dependability. However, the increasing complexity of today's systems urges the improvement of existing methods of analysing systems and their specification in order to increase the likelihood that all possible threats are taken into consideration. There is therefore a need for combining different risk analysis methodologies with respect to the system architecture. For example, qualitative methodologies for analysing risk lack the ability to account for the dependencies between events, but are effective in identifying potential hazards and failures in trust within the system, whereas tree-based techniques take into consideration the dependencies between each event. We are not aware of an already developed integrated approach to system modelling and risk analysis, where the architecture of the information system model is used to guide the combined application of risk analysis techniques. This need is being addressed in CORAS [15],[16] for the area of security risk analysis. We aim to build on the work of CORAS extending the integrated risk analysis and system-modelling framework to support analysing trust in e-services.

## 5. CONCLUSION

The pliability of the emerging communication media, the complexity of plausible interactions in virtual communities and the frequency of critical interactions among people who are relative strangers lead to problems that may not arise in traditional social settings. Yet, the same pliability abides an unprecedented degree of engineering and allows for solutions to many of these problems. However, effective solutions require interdisciplinary approaches requiring the integration of tools from cognitive sciences and economics in addition to telecommunications and computing.

In this paper, we introduced a rigorous model of trust in e-commerce and presented general properties of trust that underlie e-services, highlighting a role-based approach to the analysis of (unintentional) transfer of trust. We proceeded by proposing a trust management scheme, which included *(i).* an hierarchical decomposition of trust into inclinations, intentions and behaviour; *(ii).* a classification of the basic types of trust in each viewpoint. We suggested that risk analysis and role-based modelling can be combined to support the formation of trust intentions and the endorsement of dependable behaviour based on trust.

Concluding, we provided evidence of emerging methods, formalisms and conceptual frameworks which, if appropriately integrated, can bridge the gap between systems modelling, trust and risk management in e-commerce. However, there is still a long way to go. Further work and foreseen research challenges include:

- *To formalise and evaluate the proposed role-based model of trust in e-commerce.* (Preliminary results have been reported in [17] and [18]).
- *To extend on-going work* [15] *on integrating systems modelling and security risk analysis by correlating risks with trust.* This also involves understanding how to combine suitable risk analysis methods across different areas of dependability.
- *To develop risk management techniques supporting the transition between trust inclinations, intentions and dependable behaviour.* An output is to produce practical guidelines for the attention of regulators and technology providers on how to maximise trust and minimise risk in different e-service scenarios.
- *To embody trust-based decision making in the policy-based management of decentralised open distributed systems.* This involves enhancing the management of decentralised distributed systems with methods to simulate learning, reasoning and analysing transactional and environmental risks, and enabling the *dynamic evaluation* of the trust associated with each transaction.

- *To embody trust elements in contract negotiation, execution monitoring, re-negotiation and arbitration.* This involves modelling legal issues concerning the status of electronic agents as participants in the process of contract formation.
- *To experiment with developing a virtual marketplace from scratch, taking trust issues into account throughout the development lifecycle.*

## 6. ACKNOWLEDGEMENT

Motivating and fruitful discussions with the CORAS partners and the participants of the CLRC/CORAS workshop on *"Semi-formal Modelling, e-Risk and e-Trust"*[12] contributed to the improvement of this paper.

## 7. REFERENCES

[1] UK-online Annual Report, year 2000, http://wwww.ukonline.gov.uk
[2] T. Dimitrakos. System-models, e-Risks and e-Trust. CLRC working paper. http://www.itd.clrc.ac.uk/PublicationAbstract/1331
[3] T. Grandison and M. Sloman. *A Survey of Trust in Internet Applications* IEEE Communications Surveys and Tutorials, Fourth Quarter 2000.
[4] A. Kini and J. Choobineh, *Trust in Electronic Commerce: Definition and Theoretical Consideration.* Proc. 31st International Conference on System Sciences, IEEE, 1998.
[5] A. Jøsang, *The right type of trust for distributed systems.* Proc. of the New Security Paradigms Workshop, ACM, 1996.
[6] S. Jones, TRUST-EC: requirements for Trust and Confidence in E-Commerce, European Commission, Joint Research Centre, 1999.
[7] J.C. Laprie, *Dependability: Basic Concepts and Terminology,* Springer-Verlag, 1992. D.H. McKnight and N.L. Chervany. *The Meanings of Trust.* Technical Report MISRC Working Paper Series 96-04, University of Minnesota, 1996. See also [19]
[8] A. Jøsang and N. Tran. *Trust Management for E-Commerce.* Virtual Banking 2000.
[9] A. Jøsang. *An Algebra for Assessing Trust in Certification Chains.* In Proc. Network and Distributed Systems Security Symposium. The Internet Society, 1999.
[10] M. Blaze, J. Feigenbaum and J. Lacy, *Decentralized Trust Management.* Proc. IEEE Conference on Security and Privacy, Oakland, CA. May 1996
[11] D. Povey, *Developing Electronic Trust Policies Using a Risk Management Model.* In LNCS, Vol. 1740, Springer-Verlag, 1999.
[12] N. Damianou, N. Dulay, E Lupu and M. Sloman. *The Ponder Policy Specification Language* Proc. Policy 2001: Workshop on Policies for Distributed Systems and Networks, Bristol, UK, 29-31 Jan. 2001, Springer-Verlag LNCS 1995, pp. 18-39
[13] E.C. Lupu and M. Sloman, *Conflicts in Policy-Based Distributed Systems Management.* IEEE Trans. on Software Engineering, 25(6): 852-869 Nov.1999.

[12] Workshop hosted at Rutherford Appleton Laboratory in conjunction to the 2nd CORAS meeting. See http://www.itd.clrc.ac.uk/Activity/CORAS+1087 for contributed talks.

[14] *Information technology-Security techniques-Guidelines for the management of IT Security (GMITS)Part1: Concepts and models for IT Security.* ISO/IEC TR13335-1:1996

[15] K. Stølen. CORAS: A Platform for Risk Analysis of Security Critical Systems. Proc. The International Conference on Dependable Systems and Networks, 2001 (To appear)

[16] *CORAS Web* http://www.nr.no/coras See also http://www.itd.clrc.ac.uk/Activity/CORAS

[17] T. Dimitrakos, *Modelling Trust in e-Commerce.* Proc. AI 2001 workshop: Novel E-Commerce Applications of Agents. Ottawa, Canada, NRC-44883, June 2001.

[18] T. Dimitrakos and J.C. Bicarregui. *Towards modelling e-trust.* Proc. 3rd Panhellenic Symposium on Logic, Anogia academic village, Crete, Greece, July 2001.

[19] D.H. McKnight and N.L. Chervany. *What is Trust? A Conceptual Analysis and an Interdisciplinary Model.* Proc. The 2000 Americas Conference on Information Systems (AMCIS2000). AIS, Long Beach, CA, August 2000

5

# Digital Evidence

*Designing a Trusted Third Party Service for Securing E-vidence*

Nicklas Lundblad
*Swedish Research Institute for Information Technology*

**Abstract**: The evolution of an information society is accompanied by the growth of digital materials and transactions. It is in some cases necessary to use these digital materials and transactions as evidence in legal processes. The value of digital evidence is, however, hard to determine. In this paper some basic requirements and suggestions for a trusted third party model that can be used to secure digital evidence is given. A first sketch of a general typology of digital evidence is offered and discussed.

## 1. INTRODUCTION

### 1.1 The nature and growth of digital evidence

There is no single definition of what constitutes digital evidence, and it might be problematic to try to define, crisply, what is and what isn't digital evidence. If an e-mail has been printed out, for example, it might be considered to be a kind of digital evidence, since it originated from a digital original.

There are, however, some attempts at defining digital evidence. One such definition (SWGDE 1999) is interesting and might prove valuable: "*Digital Evidence:* Information of probative value stored or transmitted in digital form". It is far to early to say what different new technologies might change the evidentiary landscape.

It suffices to say that digital evidence is something that is used as evidence in a court of law and that is avaliable primarily in digital format. By enumerating different kinds of digital evidence the definition will be made clearer later on.

There are several reasons to examine digital evidence from a legal standpoint. Some of the most important are:

- Digital evidence is easy to manipulate. The integrity of the material being used as evidence is open to different forms of attack. Files, screen dumps, documents and other digital materials are easy to fabricate or modify.
- Digital evidence is more anonymous than regular evidence. An e-mail, or a web page, is less attached to a person than is a physical letter or a statement in some other kind. The change of medium, from paper to computer, increases the number of possible senders or originators.
- Digital evidence is highly technological. The form and content are interwoven and must be considered as a whole in deciding the evidentiary value of the material in question. Consider the fact that digital evidence often will be encrypted or hidden. (Denning and Baugh 2000)
- Digital evidence is hard to submit to court. The actual processes of submitting the digital evidence is extremely open to attack, and the general level of knowledge in court when it comes to these kinds of evidence is low.

The legal system is not used to handling this kind of evidence. There are, however, good reasons to assume that digital evidence will become a more and more frequent means of proving facts in cases pertaining to electronic commerce. This implies that we have to learn more about digital evidence and find ways of securing digital evidence in satisfactory ways.

## 1.2 Digital evidence –some introductory remarks

There exists – today – commercial firms that work with *existing* digital evidence and offer services in the area. One such firm, Digital Evidence, offers pre-trial assistance and evidence acquisition (Digital Evidence 2001):

> At Digital Evidence Inc., we are experts in a wide variety of computer investigation techniques. We can assist you by examining a large assortment of computer platforms and media to locate information which is important to your case.

The services offered by Digital Evidence are services tailored to help the police, lawyers or other actors after the fact. In contrast to this we could discuss how to pre-emptively design systems so that they capture evidence during the transaction. The perspectives differ slighly from each other. In the first case the aim is to evaluate and restore digital material that can be used in court. In the second case the objective is to create processes and systems such that evidence or material of evidentiary value (potential evidentiary value) are created when using the system. The TTP-services drawn up in this paper are pre-emptive in the sense that they try to capture evidence in new and safe ways. This suggests two different categories of digital evidence: constructed and recovered.

Digital evidence is going to become more complex. Most of what we consider today is static evidence – pictures, email et cetera – but it is far from unlikely that we will need to secure processes or sessions in the future. This new kind of dynamic evidence will require much more from the securing party. This also suggests two different categories: time stamp evidence (which would be evidence gathered at a certain point in time) and session evidence (which would be evidence that is arranged into sequences and timelines).

The field can be divided into an empirical perspective and a constructive perspective. The first perspective studies how we can handle what we find today as digital evidence, and deals with complicated issues on how to decrypt data that has been encrypted to hide evidence, how to intercept email, filter data et cetera. (Eoghan 2000) The second deals with designing systems that generate essentially new kinds or stronger kinds of digital evidence. This paper mainly deals with the second perspective.

This paper works with what is a distinctly Swedish legal perspective. In Sweden evidence law is not designed to be statutory, i.e. formal in any way. Anything might be entered as evidence and the court then has to decide what the value of the evidence presented is. We will thus speak about evidentiary value as an analogue variable. In some systems the opposite will hold true; evidence laws will be designed to admit only certain kinds of pre-defined categories of evidence. Practice will look different in those legal systems.

## 2. TYPES OF DIGITAL EVIDENCE

### 2.1 Introduction

The process of securing digital evidence can almost always be referred to as a form of *printing*, where the document is put through a process where it is time stamped and secured/signed in it's present form. Secure printing is a main theme of the service this paper describes. We often will refer to signing and encrypting documents without considering the method of doing so. This does not mean that the form of signing and encryption is, in itself, unimportant – quite the contrary – but it falls besides the main theme of the paper. The TTP-service/services described in this paper will presumably coexist with an advanced public key infrastructure.

Generally, however, there are some qualities that all systems that collect or construct digital evidence must share. These systems must be trusted, in the sense that their technical architecture and design must comply with accepted security standards. Pfleeger (1997) and Camp (2000) discuss in greater detail what this means for systems handling any kind of material that needs to be trusted. It should be noted that these requirements also apply to systems securing digital evidence.

## 2.2 Web pages

Regular web pages are, of course, the subjects of legal examination quite often. The reasons are many: copied text, unlawful links, illegal pictures, or content that in any other way violates a law, contract or other legal enforceable rules might necessitate an exmination. If the examiner decides that the material is in any way unlawful it might be necessary to submit web pages as evidence.

Web pages are, by themselves, hardly secure. It is easy to alter the content of a web page and any judge that is given a web page should reasonably ask him or herself what the value of that piece of digital evidence is. If the submitting party can then not show that the evidence was produced in a secure and trusted way the evidentiary value assigned to the web page should be close to zero.

How can web pages then be secured? One possible way would be to develop a browser plugin that stores the web page and encrypts it with a timestamp. Such a program might also save the page in multiple places and media, at once, ensuring redundancy. It would work as a sort of camera, taking 'pictures' of the web and then storing them in a way as to ensure their security. The material stored could, among other media, be printed out in a relatively safe format such as the portable document format (pdf), to ensure that it is not tampered with.

The repository can easily be distributed and the browser can be one or more – depending on the level of security desired. The page is then signed with a collection of data pertaining to the page, it's IP-number, time viewed, author metadata et cetera.

There will have to be a certain, safe storage solution behind the entire concept. This goes for all the following types of digital evidence and is, in itself, a problem of some magnitude. It is important to note that if the material, once secured, is not kept safe, the evidentiary value will be heavily reduced.

## 2.3 Digital documents

In the growing number of cases where digital documents are the only documents that exist in a certain case it is necessary to submit them as evidence. Here we can deal with everything from carefully formatted XML-documents to Microsoft Word documents, or even simple ASCII text messages (S2ML 2001).

Again the process of printing these (in the form of screen dumps or any other form) to a safe format, like pdf, with some amendments, time-stamps and other additions might serve the purpose of generating medium-safe evidence.

## 2.4 E-mail

That e-mail can be used as evidence in court is something that everyone familiar with the Microsoft Trial is aware of. A company's email is in fact often a liability.

The evidential value of e-mail, however, should really be considered small to non-existent if the company itself submits it. There are however models that remedy this.

The methods available to secure email are many. Three seem especially important:

- The BCC-plugin model (BCC here stands for Blind Carbon Copy, and is a mode of sending e-mail).
- The Dual SMTP model
- The Dual POP/IMAP model

The first two secures mail that has been sent. The third secures mail that arrives to a certain address.

The BCC-plug in model is a simple add-on program that allows the user to send a copy of all outgoing mail to a secure storage solution. In this way a record of all sent mail is drawn up, and questions concerning what was and was not said can authoratively be laid to rest.

This plug-in might easily be configured to allow the user to choose what mail is copied, or it can be locked, so that all e-mail is copied. The configuration will of course affect the value of the evidence.

The Dual SMTP solution works in much the same way, but it does not utilise the secure link between TTP and Sender that is assumed to exist in the BCC Plug In case. The Dual POP/IMAP solution is likewise merely a device that copies all incoming mail to a locked account for future reference. This, also, can be accomplished at both server and client level. The choice will of course affect the security achieved.

## 2.5 Log files

Another important form of evidence is a log file. These files might very well be used to prove unlawful computer break-ins or hacking crimes. Log Ffiles can be used to construct evidence in several different ways. The deposition of log files is one way, and then the log file basically works as any kind of digital document. A stronger form of evidence is generated if the log file is outsourced to a TTP, and the logs actually handled by the TTP.

## 2.6 Digital payments and receipts

In a world where the number of digital payments and receipts grow rapidly there is a need for a way to create evidential value for these new forms of payment. Everything from e-cash to electronic invoices require careful thinking when it comes to how we strengthen their evidentiary values.

The existing secure standards in this field are interesting subjects of study in this field.(Westland and Clark 2000).

## 2.7 Procurement processes

Aside from the pure static digital phenomena described above – where they all have in common that they are *files* – we might also see the need for a new kind of evidence: evidence of a recorded process, such as a procurement process. The reasons may be varying: we might want to ensure that a public procurement has been performed according to legal protocol, or we might be anxious to see that all bids were opened at the same time, or, indeed, opened at all. We might not settle for data about single files here, but instead require recordings of processes. It is interesting to note that these recordings will then be log files and subsequently handled as such. Public procurement is one especially interesting area here, and the issue is undergoing study in Sweden.

# 3. A SKETCH OF A DIGITAL EVIDENCE STANDARD

## 3.1 Standard architecture in general

This first sketch of a standard architecture is made up of three layers: legal, organisational and technological. The thought behind this division is quite simple. It is necessary to understand that none of these levels alone is enough to ensure good evidence. Legal formalities might be useless against sloppy technology or an unsecured organisation, and vice versa. A service designed to secure evidence must consist of careful design on all three levels.

### 3.1.1 Legal Layer

The legal layer consists of rules of evidence, the structure of evidence and the lawful capture of evidence. There are several different factors that have to be taken into account here:

- What counts as evidence? Are there formal requirements or does the system allow for a free test of evidence?
- What, usually, is interesting in the evidence? That is, what does the evidence consist of? How are these parts digitally rendered?
- Are there formal requirements on the collection of evidence? What if it has been collected unlawfully?

These, and many other questions forces the service provider to establish a legal checklist that he must use in all cases where he collects evidence. Such a checklist is a necessary tool in a service that aims to deliver high value digital evidence. The checklist should also be anchored in courts and responsible authorities, and be made public, preferrably by displaying it on the web site. The issue of public display is important in that it gurantees that flaws in the checklist are illuminated by the public eye.

### 3.1.2 Organisational

Firstly it should be mentioned that the organisational layer differs heavily in the two cases where the TTP is a private actor, and where the TTP is a public actor. Here we will primarily deal with the first case. Should public TTPs be established it is to be expected that they will be provided with due instructions from the constituting actors.

The organisational level is more complicated than the legal. What is needed is the equivalence of what is called Certification Practice Statements in regard to the issuing of digital certificates. An *Evidence Securing Statement* (ESS) is required. This should describe, amongst other things:

- How a request for the securing of evidence is received and acted upon
- How evidence is secured, by whom and by what means
- How evidence is stored and redundancy in storage ensured
- What aspects of evidence are ensured and in what order
- Liability limits
- Education and selection of evidence securing staff

The ESS should also be made public and used to create a widespread trust in the service. It is furthermore important to open these processes for review, certainly by allowing lawyers to request review into log files and technology solutions under a set of given circumstances.

The organisational layer also encompasses the different forms of evidence a securing party is ready to offer, which in essence determine the service structure. There are many different forms of evidence, and it should be obvious that the business model of the trusted third party should be constructed to offer the highest possible degree of flexibility. Several variations are possible:

- **Time.** It should be possible to secure evidence for a limited time, for, say two weeks, and then have it erased. It should also be possible to secure evidence a number of times (i.e. every week at different hours) in a sequence, to show that certain content on a web site was posted for a certain time.
- **Security level.** It should be possible to secure evidence with different levels of security. The processes and methods used can vary, for example, and the number of samplings can vary as well. The evidence can be collected in real time with legal counsel present.
- **Redundancy.** This is in part also a matter of security, but if the service secures screen dumps from a hundred different servers or simply from one, this matters. The level of redundancy in the system is also something that effects the strength of the evidence collected.

- **Media.** It is of course also possible to print the material on paper, burn CDs and or save the material in digital format only.

These issues, the construction of the business model of the service, should also be openly published, since they affect the evidentiary value.

### 3.1.3 Technological

The technological layer requires a careful design of an *Evidence Securing Infrastructure* (ESI) – an infrastructure that technologically allows for the safest and most efficient securing of evidence possible.

Elements in this infrastructure and process should be:

- **A sound amount of redundancy in collecting evidence.** It should not be possible to fool the system by showing a certain page for a certain IP-number, for example. The system should use distributed securing servers, so that the securing process is untraceable as such. This is an important requirement. The securing of evidence should normally not be discernable from regular use.
- **Timestamp technologies that are tamper proof.** Software needs to be developed that signs screen dumps or e-mail immediately in a way that no one should be able to change.
- **Safe storage utilities.** The storage and saving of material should be a) distributed and b) time resistant. Safe server parks and other means might be necessary to use in certain cases.
- **Encryption technologies.** To ensure that someone who does not have access rights does not access evidence, all collected evidence should be stored in encrypted form.
- **Sampling technology.** Technology that can vary collection point in the network (i.e. from what IP-number the evidence is collected, or what server) and that is capable of securing evidence at random times.

These technologies offer a good beginning of the technological layer's construction, but this needs to be tested and prototyped.

## 3.2 Two Cases

The best way to illustrate what a evidence-securing TTP service would do is to offer to sample cases. The cases offered below are intentionally chosen to show normal and non-spectacular problem situations where digital evidence might be useful.

### 3.2.1 Intellectual property issues

The owner of digitalpets.com notices that his competitor, analoguepets.com seems to have copied digitalpets.com web site layout and a few useful search functions that digitalpets.com has developed. He seeks legal advice and the lawyer submits a request for the securing of three kinds of digital evidence: a screen dump, a saved web page and a session in the search functions for both sites.

The submission reaches the Trusted Third Party that immediately registers it in it's log file. Then two certified evidence clerks starts to work. The screen dump is secured by the use of *Secure Screen Dump* – a software that timestamps the screen dump by pinging a number of atomic clocks on the Internet, and then encrypts the file and a signature made of the file for storage in the Trusted Third Party's secure server park. A web page is saved the same way, through another tool, and then a session is recorded in the search tool, and safely stored.

The evidence receipt is sent to the legal counsel, who then puts together a letter to the would-be offender and states that digital evidence has been secured by a trusted third party, and that they would like to see him immediately desist in using the layout and search tools used by digitalpets.com.

If the matter goes to court the evidence is collected from the third party, and then submitted in accordance with due process.

### 3.2.2 Digital contracts

The earlier example was quite simple, and the evidence easily collected. In this case we will describe a more complex situation, where a contract is negotiated and signed, and subsequently deposited with the Trusted Third Party. Company A starts negotiations with Company B on a large contract. To ensure that all evidence is secured they sign an initial agreement in which they specify that all negotiations will take place on a trusted third party platform and that they will not consider themselves legal obligated until a contract has been deposited with aforementioned trusted third party.

The negotiations consist of carefully phrased email that is sent via a special mail server that copies, and timestamps all communications via the trusted third party. The material is then gathered and saved. When the draft of a contract becomes finalised both parties electronically sign it and deposit it with the trusted third party. The contract's evidentiary value is thus strengthened immensely compared to if it only had been accessible to the parties involved. The TTP then also signs the contracts and submits it to safe storage. It might be necessary to make this storage blind – to ensure that the companies suffer no extra security exposure in storing the information with the TTP.

# 4. POTENTIAL PROBLEMS

## 4.1 Legal

In the legal layer we find many of the hardest problems we need to solve. In this subsection we will discuss issues of intellectual property rights and privacy.

### 4.1.1 Intellectual property rights

Consider the first case offered above. What if the party being sued replies with a counter claim stating that the screen dump a web page copying indeed constitutes illegal copying and an infringement of his/her intellectual property rights? How should such a claim be met?

It could be argued that evidence never is subject to counter claims like this, but if the trusted third party is a private actor or organisation the problem suddenly becomes more complex. We then have to take into account the various IPR laws and try to see if there are exceptions under which securing evidence might be subsumed.

This is a real problem, even if it seems simple enough, and with IPR-laws being revised we need to think about instances like the sampling of digital evidence where a form of fair use exemption would be in order.

### 4.1.2 Privacy

One particularly interesting problem – in the European Union at least – is how the collection and securing of evidence is viewed under the European Data Protection Directive.[13] The provisions of this directive put heavy demands on the collection of evidence that contains personal data. The articles and rules state quite clearly that several prerequisites must be fulfilled. Not only must such a collection comply with the basic requirements in article 6 of the directive, he or she must also fulfill the consentoriented criteria offered in article 7. Both articles are too long to quote here.

Consider both cases above: the negotiation material, as well as the screen dumps might contain personal data (names, telephone numbers, e-mail addresses et cetera). How should then a claim to the effect that the collection of such evidence is illegal under the data protection directive be handled?

There is a provision in the directive that might be applicable here, in article 7 p f). The balancing of legitimate interests of the individual and the third party. It might be argued here that the interest of securing evidence supersedes the interest of the

[13] Directive 95/46/EC of the European Parliament and of the Council of 24 October 1995 on the protection of individuals with regard to the processing of personal data and on the free movement of such data. Hereinafter: the data protection directive.

individual. The problem, however, is not a trivial one. Indeed: if the directive would be interpreted literally many of the services described would not be possible. Many of the provisions in both article 6 and 7 put severe limitations on the collection of evidence that contains personal data.

### 4.1.3 Liability

The chief problem for an actor deciding to act as a trusted third party is, of course, liability. Given that all other issues resolves well, this one is still enough to dissuade a private organisation from taking the role of trusted third party, and to secure evidence.

We see a growing number of phenomena today where liability might very well slow the development of much needed services. This goes for the traditional certificate authority role as well as the more differentiated trusted third party role. This must be solved. In part the problem can be solved with insurance solutions, but it is also important to look at disclaimers and contractual limitations of liability.

Today, however, the problem remains largely unsolved.

### 4.1.4 Company secrets

When acting as a trusted third party an organisation will run the risk of storing and accessing what must be regarded as company secrets. It is therefore necessary to develop blind systems, where the TTP can store and secure evidence without having access to it, or without knowing what the evidence consists of. Such blind solutions might take some time to develop, but the technology is available today (see Brands, 2000).

## 4.2 Organisational

There are also organisational problems that need to be solved. These often deal with business issues that remain unsolved, since the TTP-market in all essentials is new.[14]

### 4.2.1 Bankruptcy

If the TTP is a private organisation or an actor, he or she will risk bankruptcy. The issue will then arise of what to do with the data/evidence collected. This issue must be resolved by creating a back-up plan for these kinds of actors in case of bankruptcy, but they can also be solved by choosing suitable actors – actors with

[14] Even if it is possible to argue that it bears a strong resemblance to earlier services in the field of trust that we have seen such as *Notarius Publicus*.

staying power and well-established trust services, such as the Chambers of Commerce or certain bank federations.

### 4.2.2 Sales of data

Another issue that needs to be resolved is the ownership of the evidence collected. This is a relatively small issue, but it deserves to be mentioned. The matter could probably be solved by contractual provisions.

## 4.3 Technological

Among the technological problems that must be solved we find the usual important issues of security, integrity, non-repudiation, redundancy et cetera. It is worth mentioning however that the technological problems are the least pressing in the design of an evidence-securing service.

### 4.3.1 System weaknesses

One issue that however deserves mentioning is the possible existence of system weaknesses. If it turns out that the evidence provided by the TTP is vulnerable to a certain attack, all previous evidence must and can be called into question. This is a nightmare eventuality for the designers of services like this, but it must be taken into consideration.

# 5. FUTURE DEVELOPMENTS

A service of the kind described here is quite simple and still also quite useful. It is interesting to reflect on the evolution of this kind of service, and how the evidence situation at large might develop. In this section three different scenarios will be considered.

## 5.1 Secure zones

One likely and interesting scenario features what we might call secure zones. Instead of securing single pieces of evidence, we might visualise systems that record and monitor all activity in certain well-defined logical subnets. These subnets – secure zones – might then be regarded as evidence safe, i.e. that all that happens can be introduced as evidence in court.

The development of business webs and secure extranets offer us prototypes of how this might look in the future. There is no question: we need secure sub nets. The question is how secure they can become.

## 5.2 Evidence markup languages and automatic dispute resolution

Another interesting scenario is one where XML and other mark-up languages might be used to generate evidence templates that can be used to standardise on-line evidence. These templates might then be used in highly automatic dispute resolution systems, where claims and counter claims can be automatically evaluated. Such a dispute resolution might be binding or merely used to indicate where a true process would end, but it would still be interesting to use and see.

# 6. REFERENCES

Brands, Stefan A Rethinking Public Key Infrastructures and Digital Certificates: Building in Privacy (MIT Press 2000)

Camp, L Jean Trust and Risk in Internet Commerce (MIT Press 2000)

Denning, Dorothy E and Baugh, William E "Hiding Crimes in Cyberspace" in Cybercrime: Law Enforcement, Security and Surveillance in the Information Age (Routledge: New York 2000)

Digital Evidence web site http://www.digital-evidence.com [2001-02-13]

Digital Evidence: Standards and Principles Scientific Working Group on Digital Evidence (SWGDE) International Organization on Digital Evidence (IOCE) October 1999 in Forensic Science Communications April 2000 vol 2 number 2, http://zeraw.nbase.com/programs/lab/fsc/backissu/april2000/swgde.htm [2001-02-13]

Eoghan, Casey Digital Evidence and Computer Crime: Forensic Science, Computers, and the Internet (Academic Press, 2000)

Pfleeger, Carles P. Security in Computing 2$^{nd}$ ed (Prentice Hall 1997)

Security Services Markup Language http://www.s2ml.org/index.cfm [2001-02-13]

Stephenson, Peter Investigating Computer-Related Crime (CRC Press 1999)

Westland, J. Christopher and Clark, Theodore H.K. Global Electronic Commerce: Theory and Case Studies (MIT Press 2000)

# 6

# Security Requirements of E-Business Processes

Konstantin Knorr[1] and Susanne Röhrig[2]
[1]*Department of Information Technology, University of Zurich, Winterthurerstrasse 190, CH – 8057 Zurich, knorr@ifi.unizh.ch*
[2]*SWISSiT Informationstechnik AG, Hauptbahnhofstrasse 12, CH – 4501 Solothurn roehrig@swiss-it.ch*

**Abstract:** This paper presents an open framework for the analysis of security requirements of business processes in electronic commerce. The most important dimensions of the framework are security objectives (confidentiality, integrity, availability, accountability), the phases of and the places/parties involved in the process. The approach is of open nature so that it can be adapted to the heterogeneous needs of different application scenarios. The discussion of business processes within a virtual shopping mall illustrates the capacity and potential of the framework

## 1. INTRODUCTION

Over the last years enterprises and individuals have started to conduct business over computer networks, especially the Internet. This development is commonly summarized as electronic business (e-business). Zwass [22] defines e-business as business connections, which make use of electronic media. One of the major characteristics is that partners do not necessarily have to know each other prior to their business interaction [15].

Despite its wide use and opportunities, e-business has not grown to its full potential – one of its most important obstacles being the lack of adequate security measures as well as difficulties to specify adequate security requirements. An abundance of research about security in e-business can be found in literature. As a start reference, we suggest the final report of the SEMPER (Secure Electronic Market Place for Europe) project [11].

The framework for security requirements of e-business processes (EBPs) proposed in this article can be seen as the continuation of the research done in [10],

[16] and [17], where a two-dimensional model to quantify security is established. The dimensions are the security objectives and the places of an e-business transaction. This article adds other dimensions (the phase of an EBP). Wang and Wulf [21] use an approach similar to our framework. They propose a general framework for security measurement in computer systems. Compared to the framework presented here, they neglect the process dimension.

Herrmann and Pernul [6][7] argue that security requirements vary with the perspective taken. They identify different perspectives (informational, functional, dynamic, and organizational) which are closely related to the different elements of a workflow specification. In comparison with our approach, the authors focus on legal issues such as intellectual property, legal bindings, and privacy.

This article introduces a framework to structure security requirements of an EBP. Since information security is a very broad topic, we concentrate on security objectives, which have a precise definition and meaning. Security is often associated only with confidentiality of data, especially by non-security experts. How fatal this mis-interpretation can be, has been proven by the large mail virus epidemics in the last two years. Our framework takes into account all relevant security objectives such as the availability of data and systems, which is very important because of the distributed nature of e-business.

Since there is a high diversity concerning structure and nature of EBPs, we work on a high level of abstraction and identify four phases, which all EBPs have in common. The division used in this article originated with Schmid [18]. A further discussion will follow in Section 2.3.

We will show that security requirements of EBPs are dependent of three different factors, also referred to as dimensions:

- security objectives,
- place and party of the EBP and
- the different phases of the process

Figure 1 illustrates the idea of dimensions for the analysis of security requirements, additional dimensions will be identified and contrasted later on. The framework allows for a structured analysis of security in EBPs since a matrix can be used to illustrate the different dimensions. Security measures can be arranged in this matrix according to the security requirements.

The remainder of this paper has the following structure: Section 2 discusses the dimensions of our framework. Section 3 applies the framework to a sample business scenario of a virtual shopping mall. A discussion of the results, open questions and related work follows in Section 4, before future research areas conclude this paper.

# 2. DIMENSIONS OF THE FRAMEWORK

Our framework analyzes security using several dimensions such as security objectives, parties/places and phases of the EBP under consideration. Each of these dimensions consists of so-called *elements*, e.g. the dimension *phases* comprises four elements, one of these elements is the *negotiation phase*. The purpose of this section is to describe the major dimensions of our framework and identify the elements relevant for every dimension.

Please note that the framework is designed to be open, i.e. it can be adjusted through adding or removing dimensions and/or elements. In our opinion the dimensions discussed in Sections 2.1, 2.2 and 2.3 are the most important and influential ones in an e-business setting. Section 2.4 discusses further dimensions, which could be used to extend our framework.

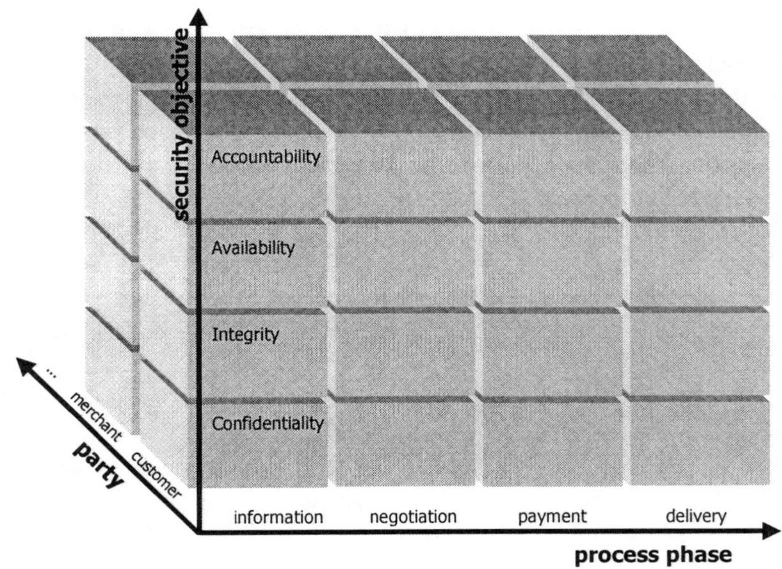


*Figure 1.* Dimensions of the framework organized in a matrix

## 2.1 Security Objectives

A security objective is the contribution to security that a system or a product is intended to achieve [1]. The term *security objective* must not be confused with security services that are defined in [20] as "a processing or communication service that is provided by a system to give a specific kind of protection to system resources" or — with more emphasis on communication in [8] — as "a service, provided by a layer of communicating open systems, which ensures adequate security of the system or of data transfer". Therefore, security objectives are the goals that are to be achieved, while security services are means to achieve these goals.

Traditionally, when talking about data security, three security objectives are addressed: confidentiality, integrity, and availability [4]. To better suit the needs of e-business with all its legal aspects, more security objectives have been identified recently, the most important one being accountability.

- **Confidentiality** describes the state in which data is protected from unauthorized disclosure, e.g. a loss of confidentiality occurs when the content of a communication or a file is disclosed.
- **Integrity** means that the data has not been altered or destroyed, which can be done accidentally (e.g. transmission errors) or with malicious intent (e.g. sabotage).
- **Availability** refers to the fact that authorized persons can access data and systems within an appropriate period of time. Reasons for loss of availability may be attacks or instabilities of the system.
- **Accountability**: If the accountability of a system is guaranteed, the participants of a communication activity can be sure that their communication partner is the one he or she claims to be. Thus, the communication partners can be held accountable for their actions.

Note that the four objectives are of different nature. While confidentiality and integrity are mainly about data – e.g. single bits, data packets in a protocol environment, data base entries, or documents of word processing program – availability is primarily associated with computer systems and secondarily with the data of the system. Accountability is used in connection with subjects and data.

Besides the four objectives stated above, others have been identified – like **unobservability** and **authenticity** to name only a few. Nonetheless, our selection is not a random one, since all security objectives can be described in terms of the classical three. Unobservability, e.g., can be regarded as confidentiality concerning the circumstances of a communication, whereas accountability may be expressed as integrity of data defining the sender or recipient of a communication. Because of its high importance for e-business, accountability was included in our list of security objective. A reason to restrict the framework to four objectives was to keep its granularity on a manageable level.

In this paper, we define *security mechanisms* (or *security measures*) as software, hardware, organizational procedures, protocols, or algorithms, which are used to increase the level of one or more security objectives. Digital signatures, for example, are used for accountability and integrity, whereas a backup server room is a measure to increase availability. *Security requirements* of an EBP express the importance of the different security objectives, e.g. the need for confidentiality may be high in one setting while availability will be rated high in another.

## 2.2 Parties

Electronic commerce (e-commerce) is a subset of electronic business (e-business). While e-business focuses on the support of business between two or more partners through information technology (IT) with the overall objective to increase the efficiency of the underlying business processes, e-commerce is only about trade relationships using IT support [2]. Concerning the parties involved, Gaugler [5] differentiates four categories of e-business:

- Business-to-Business (B2B), if two companies establish a trade relation,
- Business-to-Consumer (B2C), if a company and a consumer establish a trade relation,
- Business-to-Public (B2P), if a company and a public administration do business, and
- Public-to-Consumer (B2P), if a public administration and a consumer do business.

Under certain circumstances, more than two parties can be involved in an e-business setting. Examples of parties not mentioned above are:

- **Certification Authorities** for the establishment and maintenance of public key infrastructures needed for digital signatures
- **Trusted Third Parties** (such as notary services, lawyers or courts) in case of legal disputes between the trading partners.
- **Banks** or **credit card companies** if special electronic payment systems (e.g. electronic cash or SET [19]) are implemented.

Each of the parties involved in e-commerce may have a different conception of security in an EBP. In the extreme these requirements may even contradict each other. Example: On the one hand a customer of an online trader wants his personal data such as address, shopping preferences, and credit card number to be kept confidential and deleted after the transaction is completely settled. On the other hand the online trader might be tempted to use these data for marketing purposes or even sell the personal data of its customers to a web marketing company to increase his revenue.

The above considerations clearly show the need to include the dimension *parties* in our security framework. In a sample scenario that will follow in Section 3 we will restrict ourselves to a B2C example with two parties: customer and merchant.

## 2.3 Phases of an EBP

An important concept for this paper is that of a process, to be more precise that of a business process. A business process has a clearly defined start and end condition and consists of several tasks. A typical example is the handling of an insurance claim, where the start condition could be a car accident and the end condition the arrival of a specific amount of money at a bank account. Examples of tasks are the creation of a claim form, the approval of the claim (both by an insurance employee) or the assessment of the car by an external assessor. We define an e-business process (EBP) as a business process in the context of e-business. Popular examples are the ordering and payment of books, CDs or flights over the Internet.

Next to security objectives and parties we will include different phases of an EBP in our framework. It is intuitively clear that the security aspects change during the execution of an EBP. E.g. the integrity of prices for products on a web page is important in an early stage, while accountability is an integral component of payment.

Since EBPs are heterogeneous, we have to find a process model that is suitable for most processes in e-business. To be manageable, this model will be on a high level of abstraction. Such a general model has been introduced by Schmid [18] who identifies three phases:

1. During the **information phase** the parties try to find partners, compare them, clarify their trade relation, and specify the products to be exchanged. These actions are not legally binding.
2. In the **contracting phase** the parties decide on their partners according to their decision criteria and work out and sign a contract about their trade relation.
3. Finally, in the **delivery phase** payment and delivery is done and eventually a new transaction is prepared.

The three phases are supposed to be executed in chronological order. In cases of irregularities or exceptions a reverse step might be necessary or the process might even be started over again. Unfortunately, the delivery phase proves to be too coarse for the analysis of security requirements, since the delivery phase combines payment and delivery, which clearly have different security requirements. Therefore, we extend the model of Schmid to the following four phases:

- information
- contracting
- payment
- delivery

Please note that the chronological order of the last two phases depends on the type of EBP. Next to a sequential order – such as prepaid payment systems using coupons or electronic cash and pay-after systems using credit cards – a parallel execution is possible, which is also know as pay-now systems.

As mentioned above and as will be shown in the sample scenario in Section 3, security requirements and mechanisms vary according to the phases. Figure 2 gives an (incomplete) overview of security mechanisms that may be used in the four different phases. Since typically in an EBP the information and telecommunication systems on the company's side are more complex and numerous, research has focused on this area. Damm *et al.* [3] give an overview.

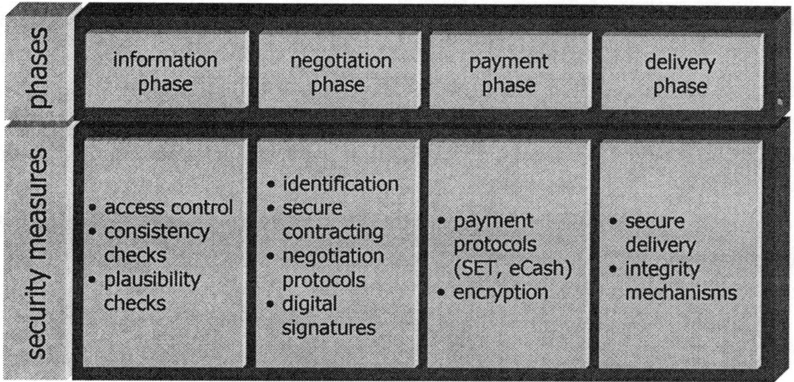


*Figure 2.* Security mechanisms and measures in the different phases of an EBP

## 2.4 Additional Dimensions

Next to the dimensions discussed above, there are other ones, which have an effect on security in an EBP. Manchala [13] identifies the **monetary height** of the transaction and the **shopping history** of the consumer as factors relevant for trust in e-commerce. Clearly, these factors are possible dimensions for our framework, too. A company might activate additional security mechanisms for a customer if this customer has had problems with paying goods in the past or if the customer orders goods of an exceptionally high value. Alternatively, if the shopping history of a customer has shown his trustworthiness the security mechanisms may be lowered. Also, customers might be concerned about paying a company if there are rumors about bankruptcy.

Additionally, the different **sites** of an EBP can be used as another dimension. The following three sites are typical for a simple EBP because of its distributed nature:

- merchant's site,
- customer's site, and
- transmission way (the Internet).

This distinction has been used and analyzed in [10] and [16]. The security requirements on the transmission way may vary, e.g. the delivery of an electronic document is less demanding concerning the availability of the Internet than the broadcast/streaming of a movie or concert. Nevertheless, a customer or merchant will typically not have the means to change the structure of security mechanisms outside their domains – especially since many other parties such as network providers, telecommunication companies, hardware and software companies, etc. may be involved in between.

The **physical location** (such as address and country) of customer and merchant might be of interest, too. On the one hand an Internet user might have objections ordering goods from specific countries. On the other hand, an online dealer might not be allowed to deliver goods to certain countries because of trade regulations.

The **type of process** has great impact on security requirements. The process of filling out an online questionnaire to obtain a free homepage raises less security questions than an online banking transaction such as a money transfer or the purchase of shares. Our framework is capable of structuring such differences.

Clearly, the **type of product** changes the security requirements. As we will show in the sample process, a book and online-video require different security mechanisms during the delivery phase.

To be precise, another dimension – the **data ownership** dimension – should be included in our framework. When talking about security objectives (e.g. confidentiality) at a specific party (e.g. merchant) it is not a priori clear whose data are under consideration. It could be the merchant's as well as the customer's data. Nevertheless, usually the customer will give sensitive information such as credit card number and address to the merchant.

In the remainder of this paper – especially in the sample scenario – we will restrict ourselves to the discussion of the three major dimensions *security objective*, *party*, and *phase* in order to keep the granularity of the framework on a manageable level. Other dimensions, which have been topic of this section, will be mentioned but not discussed in depth.

# 3. SAMPLE SCENARIO

This section shows how to apply our framework to a sample scenario. Röhrig, Knorr, and Noser [16] analyzed the security of M3L: the Mall of the Multimedia Labs (MML) at the Department of Information Technology, University of Zurich. M3L offers products and services of the department such as online courses, research papers, PhD theses, "musical objects", and services in the area of automatic, additive fabrication (stereolithography). Müller [14] gives a detailed technical description of M3L.

In what follows the security requirements within shopping processes in the M3L will be analyzed. We concentrate on two parties (customer, merchant). The evaluation will include three values: *low*, *medium*, and *high*. Here, *low* means that the party concerned has no particular interest in this security objective; *medium* denotes that the party wants this security objective to be protected, while *high* indicates that this security objective is considered essential.

In the information phase a customer browses the content of M3L. Since the products offered are not customizable and the terms of business are pre-defined, the negotiation phase consists of putting the desired goods into the virtual "shopping cart" and ordering them by clicking the respective buttons of M3L's user interface. During the payment phase either credit card transactions or the SET (Secure

Electronic Transactions, cf. [19]) payment system may be used. The delivery of goods can be done online, because most of M3L's products (e.g. music or online courses) are digital and can be sent over the Internet.

The security requirements for both parties of the business process (customer and merchant) during the four phases will be explored in the next paragraphs.

During the **information phase** the customer wants to find out whether the goods offered by M3L meet his demands and to compare them with the products of other shops. The data under consideration for the confidentiality and integrity therefore is the information contained in the M3L web pages. The customer will have low demands concerning the confidentiality of this data. Nonetheless, the data he collects is the basis for his decision to buy certain goods. Therefore, he wants them to be correct, i.e. of a certain integrity. If he cannot access the web site of M3L, he will visit other merchants; the availability of the M3L server is quite unimportant to him. In case the customer wants to make use of the merchant's offer, he expects that the terms presented on the web site are the ones that apply when he purchases the goods; accountability is therefore important for him.

The merchant, however, wants to present his offers to potential customers in a correct and easy-to-use manner. If the chance arises to find out more about the prospective buyers, he will do so. This might contradict the customer's aim to reveal as few personal data as possible. To allow for the customer to access a correct image of the merchant's offer, integrity is an important aim of the merchant. The same applies for the availability the M3L service, since the customer could easily use the offers of a competitor. Of course, this problem applies much more to Internet shops selling consumer goods (like books) that are also offered by competitors.

The security requirements of customer and merchant during the information phase are summarized in Table 1.

*Table 1:* Security requirements during the information phase

| | **Confidentiality** | **Integrity** | **Availability** | **Accountability** |
|---|---|---|---|---|
| **Customer** | low | high | low | High |
| **Merchant** | low | medium | high | Medium |

During the **negotiation phase**, a contract between the parties is made. This means, that the customer will have to reveal more personal information, which will make him more sensitive about confidentiality. Furthermore integrity and accountability of data concerning the contract are important for him, because it is his basis for agreeing to this contract. The availability of the M3L server, however, will be of low importance for him, since he still has the opportunity to change his supplier.

For the merchant the confidentiality of the customer's data will be only as important as demanded by legal regulations (e.g. privacy laws). Integrity and accountability for him are at least as important as for his customer. Because he is aware that the customer can still change to a competitor's offer, the availability of his systems is a major concern.

The security requirements of both parties during the negotiation phase are shown in Table 2.

*Table 2.* Security requirements during the negotiation phase

| | Confidentiality | Integrity | Availability | Accountability |
|---|---|---|---|---|
| **Customer** | high | high | low | High |
| **Merchant** | medium | high | high | High |

During the **payment phase** the data necessary to pay the goods are transmitted to the merchant. If credit card payment is used, this means that the credit card number of the customer is sent over the Internet. For this reason the customer will have high requirements concerning the confidentiality of his data, whereas the integrity of the data is less relevant for him; in the worst case he would be obliged to send the data a second time. The same applies for availability; if a customer cannot send his payment information, it is only a nuisance since he will have to try another time. Accountability is ranked *high* as the customer wants to be able to prove that he has paid the goods he ordered.

For the merchant it is more important that the credit card number is transmitted in a correct than in a secret manner. Confidentiality will therefore be only his aim as it is used to gain this customer's trust, whereas the integrity will be of high importance for him. This is also the case for availability. If a customer cannot send his payment information, this means that the merchant will be paid to a later time, which results in loss of interest, or in the worst case that the customer wants to break off the whole deal. Moreover, accountability during the payment phase is extremely important for him, since this helps him to prove that a payment was issued or not.

For both customer and merchant the security requirements during the payment phase are presented in Table 3.

*Table 3:* Security requirements during the payment phase

| | Confidentiality | Integrity | Availability | Accountability |
|---|---|---|---|---|
| **Customer** | high | medium | medium | High |
| **Merchant** | medium | high | high | High |

During the **delivery phase** the security requirements vary as to the kind of product that is delivered. In the M3L scenario these goods are either stream data (music or video) or files (research papers or PhD theses). In both cases the customer's requirements on confidentiality will be medium or low, since the data transmitted has already been published and does not reveal personal information. Of course, if somebody tracks the customer's online orders over a longer time, he gets a fairly good idea of the consumer's preferences. The customer's demands on integrity and availability will be quite high, since he wants to get exactly and without delay the product he ordered and paid for. The accountability will not be of high concern for him, because he is less interested in the originator of the good than the good itself.

During the delivery phase the merchant will have high demands on confidentiality. Since he earns money by selling the product, it is important for him that only the buyer can read it. For him the integrity of the data will be only as important as necessary for not annoying his customer. If the goods he is about to deliver consist of streaming data, the availability of the network and IT infrastructure will be very important for the merchant, since a failure might effect his future sales. In case research information is transmitted, availability is less important than in case of streaming video. As to accountability, it is important for the merchant, that the customer cannot deny that he received the goods. A summary of security requirements during the delivery phase is shown in Table 4.

*Table 4:* Security requirements during the delivery phase

| | **Confidentiality** | **Integrity** | **Availability** | **Accountability** |
|---|---|---|---|---|
| **Customer** | medium | high | high | Medium |
| **Merchant** | high | medium | high (video)<br>medium (paper) | High |

# 4. DISCUSSION AND FUTURE WORK

## 4.1 Discussion

This paper introduced an open framework for security of EBPs and applied this framework to a sample scenario. *Security objectives*, *parties*, and *phases* have been identified as the most important dimensions of the framework. Additionally, other dimensions have been discussed such as the shopping history and physical location of merchant and customer, type and the monetary height of the product. We have shown in a sample scenario that security requirements are quite different concerning parties and phases and may even contradict each other.

Our framework is of open nature, i.e. dimensions and/or elements of dimensions can be added or removed according to the characteristics of the EBP under consideration. Thus, the security matrix can be adapted to the individual needs of the EBP. An EBP with a strong need for anonymity could include anonymity as an additional security objective. If the monetary height of the product is of interest this could lead to the integration of the additional dimension *product value*.

We identify the following application areas of our framework:

- The multi-dimensional security matrix resulting from the framework (cf. Fig. 1) can be used to analyze security requirements and contrast them to security mechanisms which is an important aid for application developers designing new or rebuilding existing process-oriented e-business applications (e.g. workflow systems). This approach guarantees that during design or redesign of an e-business application no security objective is forgotten or neglected.
- Since security mechanisms are expensive, our approach can be used by companies to distribute a limited security budget to the different security objectives.
- Because an analysis as discussed above shows clearly the different intents of the partners of an e-business transaction, it may be used as a foundation for the merchant's security as well as his policy on the use of customer data.
- If the granularity of an analysis based on the framework is increased by using a complete process specification and identifying security objectives for each element of it (i.e. for each participant, each artefact, and each action) such a model can be used further to implement a security policy. First, contradictions within the security policy itself can be pointed out and eliminated. Such an elimination is necessary, as contradicting security requirements might increase and sharpen the comsumers' awareness for security in e-business. Secondly, by using a matrix that assigns security services to security objectives, the model can be used to derive those services that have to be implemented in order to reach the defined security objectives. An example of this procedure is given in [12], a software prototype that facilitates and automates those tasks is in preparation.
- Furthermore, the framework can be used as a basis for a quantification of security [10][16] and risk analysis in EBPs.

We stressed the open nature of our framework by giving a list of potential additional dimensions in Section 2.4. This list is by no means complete. In order to generalize our approach, a systematic classification of all major dimensions has to be established.

The focus of this paper has been on e-commerce environments. Other non-commercial areas have specific security requirements, which could be analyzed with our framework:

- One important area of public life is administration and government. The use of information technology and the streamlining of processes in this setting have become known as electronic government. We plan to apply the framework to processes in this area and hope to find and characterize differences to EBPs.
- Another security-sensitive area is health care where process automation plays an important role in cost reduction [9]. Security is of paramount importance in this environment since – in the worst case – human life may be threatened if appropriate security mechanisms are not in place. Therefore, we think that the

analysis of security requirements in health care processes is an important future research direction.

## 5. ACKNOWLEDGEMENTS

Konstantin Knorr's work was funded by the Canton of Zurich. Both authors would like to thank Helmut Kneer for his support concerning the final layout of the paper. Susanne Röhrig would like to thank her collegues at SWISSiT Informationstechnik AG for their help and patience.

## 6. REFERENCES

[1] Abrams, M.D., Jajodia, S., Podell, H.J. (eds.). *Information Security: An Integrated Collection of Essays*. IEEE Computer Society Press, 1995.

[2] Bauknecht, Kurt. *Electronic Business — Potentiale, Rahmenbedingungen & Anwendungsfelder*. Unterlagen zum Fortbildungsseminar in Informatik, Institut für Informatik der Universität Zürich, 22.-23. September 1999.

[3] Damm, D.; Kirsch, P.; Schlienger, T.; Teufel, S.; Weidner, H.; Zurfluh, U. *Rapid Secure Development — Ein Verfahren zur Definition eines Internet-Sicherheitskonzeptes*. Institutsbericht Nr. 99.01, Institut für Informatik der Universität Zürich, Februar 1999.

[4] Department of Commerce, National Bureau of Standards. *Guidelines for Security of Computer Application*. Federal Information Processing Standards Publication 73, June 1980.

[5] Gaugler, Thomas. *Interorganisatorische Informationssysteme (IOS): Ein Gestaltungsrahmen für das Informationsmanagement*. Dissertation, Institut für Informatik, Universität Zürich, 2000.

[6] Herrmann, Gaby; Pernul, Günter. „*Viewing Security from Different Perspectives*. In: Proceedings of the 11$^{th}$ International Bled Electronic Commerce Conference, Slovenia, 1998, pp. 89-103.

[7] Herrmann, Gaby; Pernul, Günter. *Zur Bedeutung von Sicherheit in interorganisationellen Workflows*. WIRTSCHAFTSINFORMATIK, 39 (1997) 3: 217-224.

[8] ISO/IEC 7498-2. *Information Processing Systems – Open System Interconnection – Basic Reference Model – Part 2: Security Architecture*. 1989.

[9] Knorr, Konstantin; Calzo, Pino; Röhrig, Susanne; Teufel, Stephanie. *Prozessmodellierung im Krankenhaus*. In: Tagungsband der 4. Internationalen Tagung Wirtschaftsinformatik, Saarbrücken, März 1999, S. 587-604.

[10] Knorr, Konstantin; Röhrig, Susanne. *Security of Electronic Business Applications – Structure and Quantification*. In: Proceedings of the 1st International Conference on Electronic Commerce and Web Technologies EC-Web 2000, Greenwich, UK, Sep. 2000, pp. 25-37.

[11] Lacoste, G.; Pfitzmann, B.; Steiner, M.; Waidner, M. (Hrsg.). *SEMPER — Secure Electronic Marketplace for Europe*. LNCS 1854, Springer, 2000.

[12] Meier, Arion; Röhrig, Susanne. *Sicherheitsanforderungen für elektronische Verträge: Ein prozessbasierter Ansatz*. Arbeitskonferenz Elektronische Geschäftsprozesse (eBusiness Processes), Klagenfurt, Austria, September 2001.

[13] Manchala, Daniel W. *E-Commerce Trust Metrics and Models*. IEEE Internet Computing, March/April 2000, pp. 36-44.

[14] Müller, Roger. *3D eShopping-Mall*. Diplomarbeit am Institut für Informatik, Universität Zürich, Dezember 2000.

[15] Nabil, Adam R.; Yesha, Yelena (Eds.). *Electronic Commerce: Current Research Issues and Applications*. LNCS 1028, Springer, Heidelberg, 1996.

[16] Röhrig, Susanne; Knorr, Konstantin; Noser, Hansrudi. *Sicherheit von E-Business Anwendungen: Struktur und Quantifizierung*. WIRTSCHAFTSINFORMATIK, 42(2000) 6: 499-507.

[17] Röhrig, Susanne; Knorr, Konstantin. *Towards a Secure Web-Based Healthcare Application*. In: Proceedings of the 8th European Conference on Information Systems, Vienna, July 2000, Vol. 2, pp 1323-1330.

[18] Schmid, B.: „*Elektronische Märkte*. Wirtschaftsinformatik 35(1993)5: 465-480.

[19] SET Secure Electronic Transaction Specification. Book 1: Business Description, Version 1.0, http://www.setco.org, 1997.

[20] Shirey, R.: *Internet Security Glossary*. Request for Comments 2828, May 2000.

[21] Wang, Chenxi; Wulf, William. *Towards a Framework for Security Measurement*. In: Proceedings of the 9th annual IFIP WG 11.3 Working Conference on Database Security, pp. 3-7, Lake Tahoe, CA, August 1995.

[22] Zwass, Vladimir. *Electronic Commerce: Structures and Issues*. International Journal of Electronic Commerce, 1(1):3-23, 1996.

7

# Performance Analysis of Smart Card-Based Fingerprint Recognition For Secure User Authentication


Youn-Hee Gil[1], Yongwha Chung[1], Dosung Ahn[2], Jihyun Moon[2] and Hakil Kim[2]

*1 Biometrics Technology Research Team, Electronics and Telecommunications Research Institute, 161 Kajong-dong, Yusong-gu, Daejon, 305-350, Korea {yhgil,ywchung}@etri.re.kr*

*2 Department of Automation Engineering, Inha University, Yonghyun-dong 253, Nam-gu, Incheon, 402-751, Korea, dosung@email.com, jieney@innocent.com, hikim@inha.ac.kr*



**Abstract:** In the modern electronic world, authentication of a person is an important task in many areas of day-to-day life. Using a biometrics to authenticate a person's identity has several advantages over the present practices of Personal Identification Number stored in smart cards. However, there is an open issue of integrating biometrics into the smart cards. Typical authenticating algorithms by using biometrics may not be executed in real-time on the resource-constrained smart cards. In this paper, we analyse first the performance requirement of the biometric authentication on the smart cards. Then, to satisfy the requirement, we have developed a light-weighted finger recognition algorithm. Finally, we investigate the possibility of integration of the algorithm into the smart card. Based on our simulation results, a smart card can be designed such that the card can encapsulate all the critical information including the biometrics data, and perform all the comparison securely inside the smart card without any data leaking out.


## 1. INTRODUCTION

Smart card, chip card, or IC card[1-3], which is a credit card sized plastic card, embedded with a special type of hardwired logic or a microprocessor to hold critical information securely, is a good choice of light-weighted hardware assisted cryptographic devices for protection at the client side when conducting some kinds of online activities, such as E-commerce, E-business, and E-government. Especially, the smart card is used as a PKI storage device because chips are tamper-resistant.

Computations on the chips involved in authentication of digital signature and key exchange are more secure as they are isolated from other parts of an operating system. The smart card also enables credentials and other private information to be portable between computers at work, home, or on the road.

In recent years, there is an increasing trend of using biometrics, which refers the personal biological characteristics used for authentication or identification. It relies on "something that you are", therefore can inherently differentiate between an authorized person and a fraudulent imposter. Compared with using the four-digit Personal Identification Number(PIN), it can be more secure to use the biometric information of size 500B for protection of the critical data. Furthermore, biometric information has no concern to be forgotten. Smart cards play an important role in biometrics[4-6]. In general identification system, the biometric templates are often stored in a central database. With the central storage of a biometric data, there is an open issue of misuse of the biometric information for the purpose the owner may not be aware of. We can decentralize the database storage part into millions of smart cards and give it to the owners after authorization of it.

However, most of these systems have a common characteristic that the biometrics authentication process is solely accomplished out of the smart card processor[3]. For example, in fingerprint-based smart card system, the critical fingerprint master template information needs to be insecurely released into the external fingerprint reader from the card to be compared with the input fingerprint template. To heighten security level, the comparison of the master template with the fingerprint sample needs to be performed by the in-card processor, i.e., match-on-card[6], not the external reader.

In this paper, we examine whether the in-card processor can execute the entire authentication and verification steps. If so, all of the critical information including the biometrics data can be encapsulated in the card, and all the computation can be performed securely inside the card without any data leaking out. Although it's not possible, at least, the in-card processor should be capable of the matching and verification process. That is, the smart card does not only perform the ordinary PIN verification and certification storage, but also involve the biometrics authentication. However, the processing power of the in-card processor is very limited. Thus, performance requirements of the biometric authentication steps on the in-card processor should be analyzed first. Then, to satisfy the requirement, we have developed a light-weighted finger recognition algorithm. To investigate this feasibility of the in-card processor, we conducted performance analysis of our fingerprint matching algorithm with an instruction set simulator. The simulation results showed that the card could encapsulate the biometrics data and perform the comparison securely inside the card without any data leaking out.

The organization of the paper is as follows. Overview of the smart card system considered in this paper is given in Section 2. In Section 3, the selected biometrics authentication system is explained. Performance analysis results are shown in Section 4, and concluding remarks are made in Section 5.

## 2. SMART CARD SYSTEM

A smart card resembles a credit card in terms of physical look and size with one or more semiconductor devices attached to a module embedded in the card. More specifically, the smart card is a portable, very secure, low cost, and intelligent device capable of manipulating and storing data. This intelligence is due to an in-card processor that is suitable for use in a wide range of applications[1-3].

Figure. 1 shows the smart card system we are developing[7], and its characteristics are summarized as follows:

***Hardware.*** The in-card processor is a 32-bit ARM7TDMI[8] to manipulate and interpret data. The memory in the smart card consists of three different types. The ROM is used for the smart Card Operating System(COS) and is usually embedded during manufacture. The RAM is used by the COS as temporary storage area. The user available data segments are allocated in the EEPROM. The size of each memory type is 64KB, 1KB, 40KB for ROM, RAM, EEPROM, respectively. The first two types of memory are not available for user access. Several levels of access security are supported in the EEPROM. The methods of assigning access security can be controlled through use of a PIN or a biometric template or using cryptography. The smart card also include the Crypto-Coprocessor and the Random Number Generator(RNG) to perform cryptographic algorithms in real-time. Finally, for the contact interface, the external interface module is included.

***Software.*** From the time of smart card manufacture to the end of loading application and usage by consumers, different kinds of software are used to handle smart cards. The Card OS(COS) is a vendor dependent component of the software, and supports a file system on the EEPROM storage, command interpretation, and security options for the data stored on the smart card. During initialization and personalization, application specific data structures are loaded. During the usage of the smart card, the card interacts with the application through the Application Programming Interface(API). The smart card also includes the Java Virtual Machine to support multiple applications. The details of the targeted smart card can be found in [7].

Note that, because of the area restriction of the smart card chip, we select ATM7TDMI. However, the maximum performance of the in-card processor is 60 Million Instructions Per Second(MIPS) and the maximum clock rate of it is 66 MHz. This processing power is very limited compared with the typical PCs having 800 MHz Pentium III. Thus, very careful performance analysis is required to integrate the biometrics into the resource-constrained smart card system.

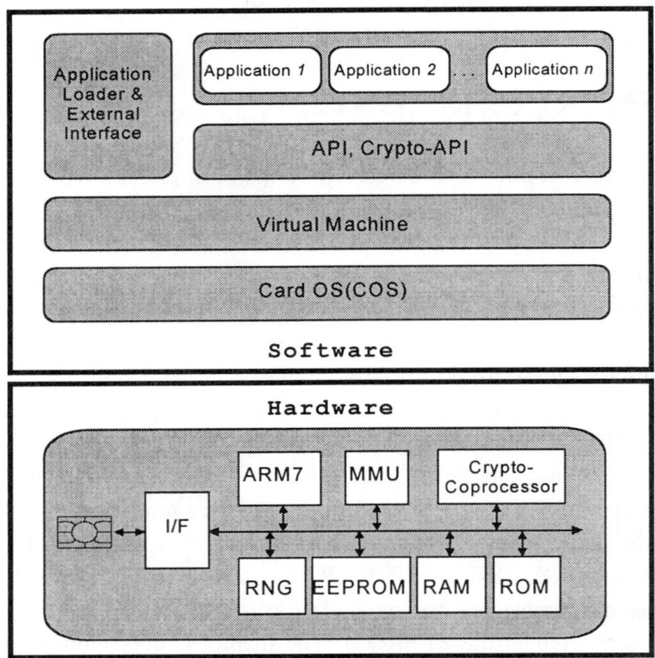


*Figure 1.* Target Smart Card System [7]

# 3. SELECTED BIOMETRICS AUTHENTICATION

In this paper, fingerprint is chosen as the biometrics for authentication as it is more mature in terms of the algorithm availability and feasibility, while the other kinds of biometrics, such as the iris and face, may not be well suited to an ordinary smart card processor with respect to its limited processing power. Note that the problem of resolving the identity of a person can be categorized into two distinct types of problems. Authentication or verification refers to the problem of confirming or denying a person's claimed identity, whereas identification or recognition refers to the problem of establishing a subject's identity. That is, the authentication system matches a person's claimed identity to his/her previously enrolled pattern(i.e., "one-to-one" comparison). However, the identification system identifies a person from the entire enrolled population by searching a database for a match(i.e., "one-to-many" comparison). In this paper, we only focus on the authentication system by using smart cards with biometrics.

Fingerprint is especially suitable as a method to authenticate users to use smart cards. This can be elaborated by considering the time complexity of the algorithm.

Whether the in-card processor is capable to execute the entire fingerprint matching algorithm in real-time depends on the time complexity. In the following, we briefly describe the fingerprint matching system used in our research.

The technique for fingerprint matching has been developed in the field of image processing. Generally, when we want to compare two fingerprint images, it is needless and wasteful to accomplish this by repeating pixel-by-pixel checkup. On the contrary, it is better to pre-process the images so that the unique features of the fingerprint images are extracted first, and then simply compare these features instead. Here, such kinds of domain specific features for fingerprint matching are called minutiae[4]. Minutiae refer to the ridge ends and ridge bifurcations of a fingerprint.

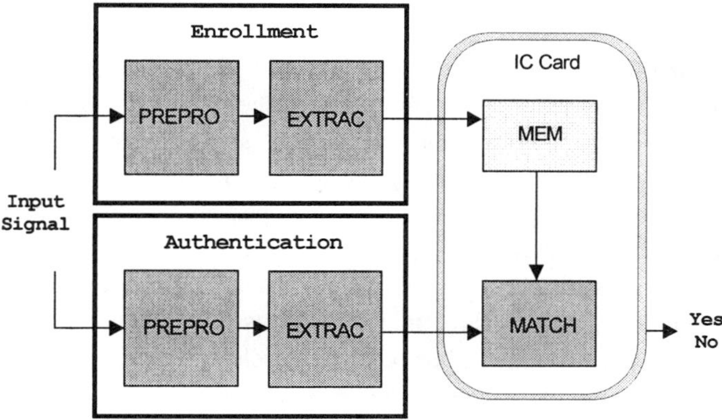


*Figure 2.* Fingerprint Matching System using Smart Card

Figure. 2 shows the general steps in the fingerprint matching system using smart cards. The system operates in two phases. In the off-line enrollment phase, minutiae are extracted and stored in the smart card. In the on-line authentication phase, the stored minutiae and the minutiae from live fingerprint are presented to the system, and then the similarity between them is examined. This authentication phase consists of the following three steps:

***Image Pre-Processing.*** This refers to the refinement of the original fingerprint image against image distortion obtained from the fingerprint sensor. It consists of three stages. Binary conversion stage applies low-pass filter to smooth the high frequency regions of the print and threshold to each sub-segment of the image. Thinning stage generates one-pixel-width skeleton image by considering each pixel with its neighbors. In positioning stage, the skeleton obtained is transformed and/or rotated such that valid minutiae information can be extracted.

***Minutiae Extraction.*** This refers to the extraction of feature in the fingerprint image. After this step, some of the minutiae are selected and stored into a template file, which includes the position, orientation, and type(ridge ending or bifurcation) of minutiae. However, false minutiae can be extracted due to the noise during the image acquisition step and/or information loss in the pre-processing step. The false minutiae deteriorate overall accuracy significantly in the succeeding matching step. Therefore, we have developed a method to remove such false minutiae using ridge distance information and various types of noises. Another advantage of this removing method is to reduce the execution time by eliminating unnecessary computation due to false minutiae. The details of our false-minutiae removing algorithm can be found in [9].

***Minutiae Matching.*** When user's fingerprint image is obtained, we use image processing techniques before turning the image into a skeleton image as explained above. After getting thinned image, we find out minutiae points in it. Note that the correction for scaling, translation, and rotation of the image are needed before starting the matching step.

Based on the minutiae, we compare the input fingerprint image with the template file. Actually, minutiae matching is composed of the alignment stage and matching stage. Alignment is the most time consuming step in the whole fingerprint recognition, thus success of optimizing the alignment stage is the key to achieve real-time performance. Therefore, we have developed an alignment algorithm using specific data structure called as "clique", which can optimize the search space. "Clique" is the data structure consisted of information derived from the triangle-shaped three minutiae, such as three minutiae points and orientation, and the radius of circumcircle. Especially, the radius of circumcircle can be used as the search key because there exists only one in one triangle-shaped form.

In order to get the clique data structure, we select three minutiae by picking up the first and second nearest minutiae point from one minutia using Euclidean distance measurement. Figure 3 represents these three minutiae and the circumcircle formed using them. After getting the center of the circumcircle and three inter angles between three minutiae points, the three minutiae can be arranged according to the angles. The right side point of the largest inter angle ($\alpha$) is the first, and the second and third point are chosen as clockwise direction from it.

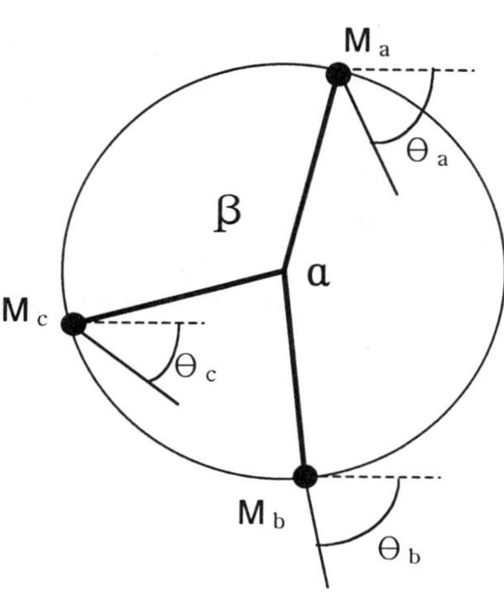


*Figure 3.* Geometry of 3 minutiae clique

The structure of clique is consist of the radius of circumcircle $(r)$, two inter angle $(\alpha,\beta)$, three orientations $(\theta_a,\theta_b,\theta_c)$, and three types $(\zeta_a,\zeta_b,\zeta)$ as below:

$Ci = \{r,\alpha,\beta,\theta_a,\theta_b,\theta_c,\zeta_a,\zeta_b,\zeta_c\}$, *where* $i = 1,2,\ldots,N$, and $N$ is the number of clique.

Given a fingerprint image, we extract all of the possible triple minutiae sets to be get ready for construction clique. Here, the number of clique is defined as $n \times {}_kC_2$, $2 \le k \le n-1$ when n is the number of feature points. Selecting meaningful k is important and affects to the performance. The complexity of blind search between two fingerprint images, each of which has $n_t$, $n_s$ minutiae points, is between the range $\{\Theta(n_t n_s),\ \Theta(n_t^3 n_s^3)\}$. By using the radius of circumcircle as the search key, search space can be reduced compared with the exhaustive search. After using our minutiae matching algorithm, the number of points that matches can be obtained. Then, the match score could be measured by normalizing with the number of input minutiae. This score is in the range {0,1}, where 1 corresponds to a perfect pattern match. The details of the clique algorithm can be found in [10].

# 4. PERFORMANCE REQUIREMENT ANALYSIS

Our light-weighted minutiae matching algorithm developed to satisfy the resource constraint is applicable to the smart card environment perfectly because of its real-time performance.

To establish an objective assessment of our system, sample image pairs of size 832 ×768 selected from the NIST Special Database 14[11] have been used to estimate the performance numbers. The simulator we used is the Simple Scalar[12] which models the behavior of a microprocessor in software on a host system.

To characterize the computational requirement of each step in the fingerprint matching system, we break down the instructions into six components as shown in Table 1. The low-level step(Pre-Processing) needs a lot of integer computations. However, the high-level step(Minutiae Matching) involves less ALU operations and more load/store operations.

Table 1. Distribution of Instructions Executed

| Step | Load | Store | Uncond Branch | Cond Branch | Int Comp | FP Comp |
|---|---|---|---|---|---|---|
| Pre-Processing | 67,937,581 (18%) | 11,720,360 (3%) | 3,075,362 (1%) | 56,968,411 (15%) | 227,089,206 (62%) | 92,242 (1%) |
| Minutiae Extraction | 19,004,017 (23%) | 2,873,822 (3%) | 817,493 (1%) | 11,010,208 (13%) | 50,034,953 (59%) | 1,115,595 (1%) |
| Minutiae Matching | 3,640,392 (18%) | 2,600,846 (13%) | 219,109 (1%) | 1,933,178 (10%) | 8,738,570 (43%) | 2,992,937 (15%) |

To show the performance requirement of the in-card processor, the number of instructions and the estimated execution time on the 8-bit Intel-8051 and 32-bit ARM7-based smart cards are summarized in Table 2.

In Table 2, we present estimated result per each step.

Table 2. Summary of Simulation Results

| Step | Total No of Instructions | Estimated time on 8051 | Estimated Time on ARM7 |
|---|---|---|---|
| Pre-Processing | 366,883,251 | 158.6 sec | 6.1 sec |
| Minutiae Extraction | 84,856,108 | 36.4 sec | 1.4 sec |
| Minutiae Matching | 20,125,037 | 7.8 sec | 0.3 sec |

According to the Table 2, it is impossible to assign minutiae extraction or matching step as well as pre-processing to the 8051 chip. This is because computation using biometric information requires much memory and time. However, ARM7 shows improved result. Using this can make match-on-card to be realized. Currently, 32-bit smart card is somewhat expensive to be applied for ordinary system. Nevertheless, it can be good solution for the system that should be guaranteed very high-level security such as E-Commerce, E-Business, and E-Government.

With respect to the limited processing power of the in-card processor, all of the three steps above can't be assigned to the in-card processor. Instead, we consider assigning only the third step to the in-card processor, which is the minutiae matching. This is because the first two steps involve rigid image processing computation, which is too exhaustive to be executed in the in-card processor. These computation steps can be easily carried out in real-time by a fingerprint capture device or a smart card terminal equipped with at least a 500 MIPS processor. Therefore, the whole computational steps can be performed in real-time, and the smart card can encapsulate the biometrics data and perform the comparison securely inside the card without any data leaking out.

## 5. CONCLUDING REMARKS

Smart card is a model of very secure storage, and biometrics is the ultimate technology for authentication. The two can be combined in many applications to enhance both the security and authentication. However, a careful analysis is required to integrate the biometrics into the smart cards because the smart cards have very limited resources.

Our performance analysis shows that the use of a 32-bit smart card processor is feasible in order to conduct the fingerprint authentication actively with respect to the advanced techniques in fingerprint image comparison. In contrast to the traditional PIN verification currently being used, this further enhances the security issues in adopting the smart card into many emerging applications such as:

- making legally binding digital signatures for E-commerce, on-line documentation signing, contracts, taxation, legal applications
- access to the system that should be guaranteed very high level security in government especially such as Department of Defense
- user authentication used in internet banking or electronic commerce
- gaining access to secure websites.

## 6. REFERENCES

[ 1 ] Dreifus, H. and Monk, T.: Smart Cards. John Wiley & Sons (1997)
[ 2 ] CardTech/SecureTech.: Proc. of the CardTech/SecureTech 2000 Conference (2000)
[ 3 ] Mearns, C. and Jones, D.: The Smart Card. SJB Research (1999)

[ 4 ] Jain, A., Bole, R., and Panakanti, S.: Biometrics – Personal Identification in Networked Society. Kluwer Academic Publishers (1999)
[ 5 ] Pankanti, S., Bolle, R., and Jain, A.: Biometrics: The Future of Identification. IEEE Com-puter, Vol. 33, No. 2 (2000) 46-49
[ 6 ] Biometric Consortium.: Proc. of the Biometric Consortium 2000 Conference (2000)
[ 7 ] Kim, H. et al.: Specification for the Next-Generation IC Card System(Korean). Technical Report, ETRI (2000)
[ 8 ] Furber, S.: ARM System-on-Chip Architecture. Addison-Wesley (2000)
[ 9 ] Kim, H. and Kim, H.: Rotation-Scale-Translation-Intensity Invariant Algorithm for Finger-print Identification(Korean). Journal of The Institute of Electronics Engineers of Korea, Vol. 35, No. 6 (1998) 838-850
[ 10 ] Ahn, D. and Kim, H.: Fingerprint Recognition Algorithm using Clique(Korean). Technical Report, Inha University (2000)
[ 11 ] http://www.itl.nist.gov /iaui/vip/fing/fing.html
[ 12 ] Burger, D. and Austin, T.: The SimpleScalar Tool Set, Version 2.0. Technical Report, University of Wisconsin (1997)

8

# Fingerprint Authentication System For Smart Cards

Nikkou Kaku, Takahiko Murayama and Shuichiro Yamamoto
*NTT Information Sharing Platform Laboratories, NTT Corporation*

**Abstract**: Among the several methods that enable fingerprint authentication of card holders, the one that executes the matching process on the smart card chip is the most important. The Pattern matching method, such as [1], is of no use for smart cards, because it takes too much time to adjust the position between the input image and template image. So we have developed an algorithm (FTA: Free Turning Algorithm) using minutiae that does not need the position correcting process. In this paper, we describe the basic effectiveness of this algorithm and a prototype system that implements it on a smart card.

## 1. INTRODUCTION

Smart cards have attracted a great deal of public attention because of their high security and the variety of services they enable, and they have been introduced in various fields. Although the personal identification number (PIN) is widely used as a method of authenticating card holders (for example, for magnetic-stripe ATM cards), biometrics (fingerprints and irises etc.) are expected to replace it because biometrics overcome the problems of users forgetting their PINs or having them stolen[2]. Fingerprint-based methods are especially practicable, because the error rate is comparatively low and the hardware is cheap. The three models shown in Table 1 are considered typical models that can be used for a fingerprint authentication system. They are the Server Authentication Model (SAM), Fingerprint Scanner Authentication Model (FSAM), and Smart Card Authentication Model (SCAM).

*Table 1.* Typical Models of a Fingerprint Authentication System for Smart Cards

| Model | Recognition engine location |
|---|---|
| SAM | Host server |
| FSAM | Fingerprint scanner |
| SCAM | Smart card chip |

Comparing them, SCAM has several advantages.

1. It is user-friendly in that card holders can manage their fingerprints with their smart cards by themselves.
2. It can reduce the cost of administering and maintaining the database of template fingerprints.

However, it is not practical for implementing a pattern-matching algorithm such as [1] in smart cards, because the algorithm requires too much time to adjust the input and template image positions. Therefore, we have developed an algorithm (FTA: Free Turning Algorithm) that does not need positional correction between the input and template images. FTA can omit this step because it uses a feature vector (the Relative Vector) composed of components describing the relationship between two minutiae (e.g., distance). Consequently, a card holder can be authenticated by touching the fingerprint scanner at any angle. If chip-sized fingerprint scanners are embedded in contactless smart cards in the future, the features of FTA will be particularly effective because card holders are likely to present their cards at various angles.

Section 2 explains the problems of implementing the algorithm [1] in smart cards. Section 3 describes our algorithm, FTA, which is evaluated in Section 4. Section 5 describes a prototype system implementing our algorithm in smart cards. Section 6 concludes this paper.

## 2. THE PROBLEM WITH THE THINNED IMAGE PATTERN-MATCHING ALGORITHM

The pattern-matching algorithm [1] adjusts the positions of a binarized input image and a thinned template image by moving them relative to each other in the vertical and horizontal directions and rotating them. The two images are then compared by matching the corresponding pixels at each position. Consequently, the computational complexity of the pattern-matching algorithm [1] is high (Fig.1). We found that executing the algorithm for matching the binarized input image and the thinned template image (size: 256×256 pixels), without correcting the position, took 8 seconds on a smart card with a 5-MHz processing speed, a 4-kbit ROM, and a 512-kbit Flash memory. Therefore, the algorithm would need about 53 minutes to match those two images by the usual procedure including positional correction on the smart card[15].

[15] The algorithm [1] adjusts the relative positions by 10 pixels vertically, 10 pixels horizontally, and 4 degrees of rotation.

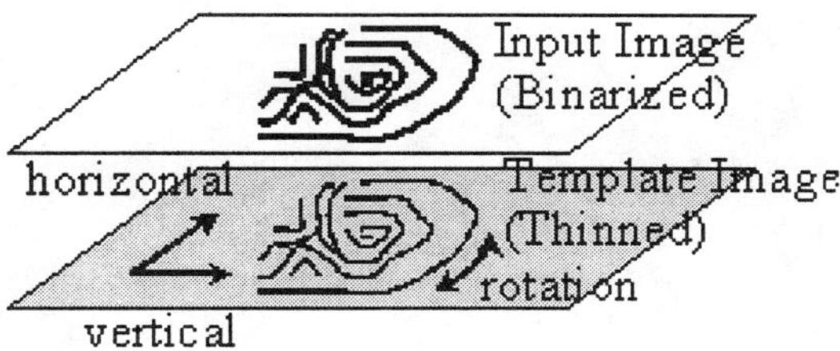


*Figure 1.* Thinned Image Pattern Matching Algorithm

## 3. FREE TURNING ALGORITHM (FTA)

### 3.1 Relative Vector

We define the following vector which forms the basis for the Relative Vector. We call the vector Extension, because it can be regarded as an extension of the ordinary feature vector $P(x,y,\theta)$.

**Definition 1:** Extension

We define a coordinate system $C$ whose origin is at the center point of the fingerprint image [16]. We define the extraction region ER as the region enclosed by a circle of radius $r$ centered on the origin. And we number the minutiae counterclockwise in order of increasing distance from the origin (Fig.2).

[16] For example, if the image size is 256×256, then the origin of $C$ is at (128,128).

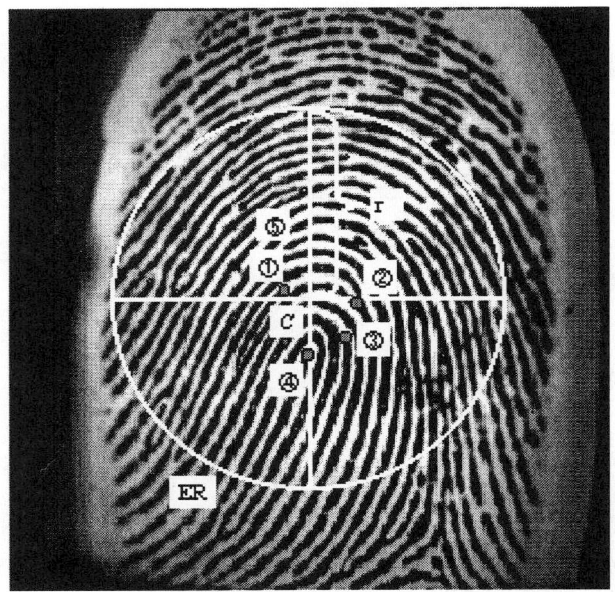


*Figure 2.* Extraction Region

Now we define the Extension $m_i$ (Fig.3 [17]).

$$m_i = ( x_i, y_i, \theta_{(i,trace(1))}, \ldots, \theta_{(i,trace(N))}, kind_i, i )$$

Here□

a) $x_i$, $y_i$ are coordinates of $C$.
b) $trace(n)( n = 1, \ldots, N ) \in \{ 1, 2, \ldots \}$ and $trace(1) < trace(2) < \ldots < trace(N)$. The $trace(n)$ is the number of pixels when tracing the ridge. And $n$ is the ID number of a tracing point [18].
c) $\theta_{(i,trace(n))}$ $(0 \leq \theta_{(i,trace(n))} < 2\pi)$ is the angle of the vector starting at the location of $m_i$ and ending at the location found by tracing the ridge $trace(n)$ pixels, to $C$. If $m_i$ is a ridge bifurcation, we trace the ridge that has obtuse angles on both sides.
d) $kind_i$ indicates the kind of minutiae. If $m_i$ is a ridge bifurcation, then $kind_i = 0$. If $m_i$ is a ridge ending, then $kind_i = 1$.
e) $i$ is the ID number of $m_i$.

[17] Figure 3 shows an example of the Relative Vector of the ridge bifurcation described in Fig.2 No.□. For ease of explanation, we move the origin of $C$ to the location of the ridge bifurcation.

[18] A tracing point is a point that can be found by tracing the ridge.

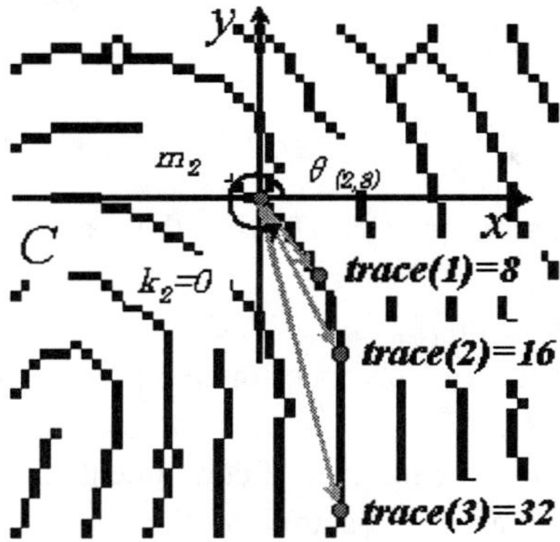


*Figure 3.* Extension

**Definition 2:** Relative Vector

Using Extension $m_i$, $m_j$, we define the Relative Vector $m_{ij}$ (Fig.4).

$$m_{ij} = ( len_{ij}, d\theta_{(ij,trace(1))}, \ldots, d\theta_{(ij,trace(N))}, kind_{ij}, i, j )$$

Here,

a) $len_{ij} = ( (x_i - x_j)^2 + (y_i - y_j)^2 )^{1/2}$
b) $d\theta_{(ij,trace(n))} = | \theta_{(i,trace(n))} - \theta_{(j,trace(n))} |$
c) if $\pi < d\theta_{(ij,trace(n))} < 2\pi$ then
d) $d\theta_{(ij,trace(n))} = 2\pi - |\theta_{(i,trace(n))} - \theta_{(j,trace(n))}|$
e) $kind_{ij} = 0$ ( if $kind_i = kind_j = 0$ )
f) $= 1$( if $kind_i = kind_j = 1$ )
g) $= 2$( if $kind_i = 0$, $kind_j = 1$ or $kind_i = 1$, $kind_j = 0$ )
h) This indicates a kind of Relative Vector.
i) $i$ is the ID number of $m_i$ and $j$ is the ID number of $m_j$.

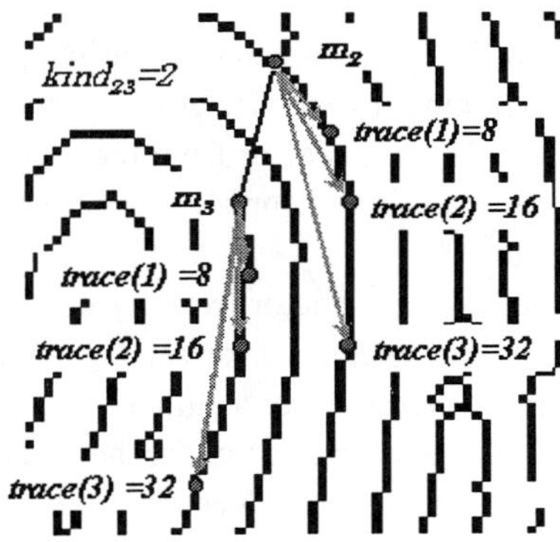


*Figure 4.* Relative Vector

## 3.2 FTA Overview

We present the complete FTA algorithm in Appendix. Here, we give an overview of it.

First, let us define some notation. Define the set of Relative Vectors of the template image as $R = \{ m^r_{ij} \}$,

$$m^r_{ij} = ( len^r_{ij}, d\theta^r_{(ij,trace(1))}, \ldots, d\theta^r_{(ij,trace(N))}, kind^r_{ij}, i^r, j^r )$$

and define the set of Relative Vectors of the input image as $S = \{ m^s_{ij} \}$.

$$m^s_{ij} = ( len^s_{ij}, d\theta^s_{(ij,trace(1))}, \ldots, d\theta^s_{(ij,trace(N))}, kind^s_{ij}, i^s, j^s )$$

The notation |A| describes the number of components of the set $A$. The basic idea of FTA is matching the Relative Vectors of the input image with the Relative Vectors of the template image (Fig.5).

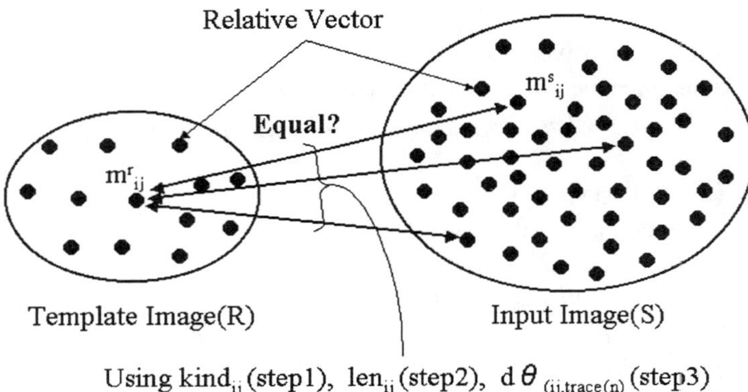


*Figure 5.* FTA Overview

The steps of the algorithm are as follows.

**[step 0]** Using $len_{ij}$, sort the Relative Vectors of the template image in ascending order and assign a number to each Relative Vector.

**[step 1]** Using $kind_{ij}$, find the Relative Vector from the input image that corresponds to the Relative Vector of the template image. Make set $A_1$ composed by such Relative Vectors.

**[step 2]** Using $len_{ij}$, find the Relative Vector from $A_1$ corresponding to the Relative Vector of the template image. Make set $A_2$ composed by such Relative Vectors. Here, the difference in length of the Relative Vectors of the template and input images has to be under the threshold ( *THR_LEN* ).

**[step 3]** Using *d_ang*[*n*], sort the Relative Vectors of $A_2$. This sort is executed $N$ times. If $m^s_{ij}$, which have a minimum *d_ang*[*n*] in each sorting process are identical to each other and all minimum *d_ang*[*n*] in each sorting process are under the corresponding threshold *THR_ANG*[*n*], then add one to the *count*. Otherwise, go back to **step 1**.

**[step 4]** If *RATE* (*count* /|*R*|), which is the matching rate of the Relative Vectors of the input and template images is over the threshold( *THR* ), then the input image is identical to the template image. Otherwise, the input image is not identical to the template image.

## 4. EXPERIMENT

We conducted three experiments to evaluate the False Acceptance Rate (FAR), False Rejection Rate (FRR), and Equal Error Rate (EER) of FTA. We used a fingerprint database openly available on the Worldwide Web[19], which contains scanned fingerprint images from twenty-one subjects, who each provided eight fingerprint images from the same finger. The database is composed of 168 (21×8) fingerprint images and the resolution of each image is about 350 dpi. We conducted 147 (=(8-1)×21) matching tests between the same subjects, and 3360 (=8×20×21) matching tests between different subjects. An example of the database is shown in Figs. 6 and 7 [20]. We applied three types of preprocessing: smoothing, binarizing, and thinning.

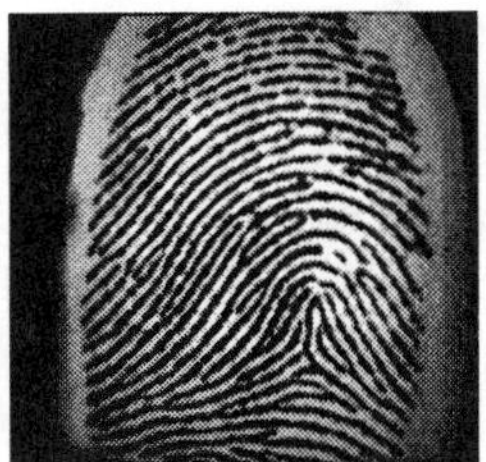

*Figure 6.* fp1-4

*Figure 7.* fp17-5

[19] http://bias.csr.unibo.it/research/biolab/bio_tree.html

[20] Here, fp1-4 denotes the fourth fingerprint image of subject no. 1 and fp17-5 the fifth fingerprint image of subject no. 17.

Table 2 shows the parameters of the three experiments.

*Table 2.* Parameters

| | \|R\| | \|S\| | N | trace(1) | Trace(2) | trace(3) |
|---|---|---|---|---|---|---|
| Experiment 1 | 45 | 190 | 2 | 5 | 10 | - |
| Experiment 2 | 45 | 190 | 2 | 18 | 20 | - |
| Experiment 3 | 45 | 190 | 3 | 5 | 10 | 15 |

Here, $|R|$ and $|S|$ are the numbers of Relative Vectors of the template and input images, respectively. $N$ is the number of tracing points. And *trace*(1), *trace*(2), and *trace*(3) are the numbers of pixels of the first, second, and third tracing points, respectively. In these experiments, we defined the maximum of *trace*(n) as 20 pixels, because few minutiae were detected when it was over 20.

## 4.1 Preliminary experiment

We decided the template image of each subject and the FTA threshold by the following methods.

### 4.1.1 Deciding the template image

Using eight fingerprint images of the same subject, we conducted a round-robin matching on the condition that the threshold of the length difference (*THR_LEN*) and the threshold of the angle difference (*THR_ANG*[*n*]) were maximum[21]. We then take the template image to be the image having the maximum average matching score ( *count* /$|R|$).

Table 3 [22] shows the template image of each experiment decided by this method.

[21] The difference in length, i.e., $|len^s_{ij} - len^s_{ij}|$, did not exceed 160 (pixels), because we defined the radius of the Extraction Region as 80 (pixels). And the difference in angle, i.e., $|d\theta^s_{(ij,trace(n)} - d\theta_{(ij,trace(n)}|$ $(n = 1, \ldots, N)$, did not exceed $\pi$. Therefore, we defined *THR_ LEN* and *THR_ANG*[*n*] as 160 (pixels) and 4 (radians), respectively.

[22] We abbreviate fp in Table 3. And because of a lack of Relative Vectors, we could not define a template image for some conditions.

*Table 3.* Template Images

| Subject | Experiment 1 | Experiment 2 | Experiment 3 |
|---|---|---|---|
| 1 | 1-1 | 1-3 | 1-3 |
| 2 | 2-8 | 2-5 | 2-1 |
| 3 | 3-3 | 3-1 | 3-3 |
| 4 | 4-2 | 4-1 | 4-2 |
| 5 | 5-7 or 5-8 | 5-4 | 5-4 |
| 6 | 6-4 | 6-6 | 6-4 |
| 7 | 7-5 | 7-1 | 7-1 |
| 8 | 8-3 | 8-3 | 8-8 |
| 9 | 9-5 | 9-5 | 9-5 or 9-6 |
| 10 | 10-4 | 10-1 | 10-4 |
| 11 | - | - | 11-5 |
| 12 | 12-5 | 12-8 | 12-1 |
| 13 | 13-6 | 13-7 | 13-6 |
| 14 | 14-4 | 14-8 | 14-4 |
| 15 | 15-3 | 15-4 | 15-4 |
| 16 | 16-7 | 16-6 | 16-2 or 16-5 |
| 17 | 17-2 | 17-6 | 17-2 |
| 18 | 18-3 | 18-3 | 18-6 |
| 19 | - | - | - |
| 20 | 20-3 | 20-4 | 20-8 |
| 21 | - | - | - |

### 4.1.2 Deciding the threshold

Using the template images shown in Table 3, we conducted matching tests for the same subjects and among different subjects on condition that *THR_LEN* and *THR_ANG*[*n*] were both maximum. Then we plotted their cumulative frequency distributions of $|len^s_{ij} - len^s_{ij}|$, which were calculated in the matching tests for the same and among different subjects, respectively. We define the interval maximizing the difference of these cumulative frequencies as the threshold *THR_LEN*.

Similarly, we plotted the cumulative frequency distributions of $|d\theta^s_{(ij,trace(n)} - d\theta^r_{(ij,trace(n)}|$, which were calculated in the matching tests for the same subject and among different subjects, respectively. We define the interval maximizing the difference of these cumulative frequencies as the threshold *THR_ANG*[*n*].

Table 4 shows the threshold for each experiment decided by these procedures.

*Table 4.* Thresholds

| | *THR_LEN* | *THR_ANG*[0] | *THR_ANG*[1] | *THR_ANG*[2] |
|---|---|---|---|---|
| Experiment 1 | 1.6 | 0.2 | 0.216 | - |
| Experiment 2 | 2.1 | 0.162 | 0.222 | - |
| Experiment 3 | 2.1 | 0.221 | 0.206 | 0.242 |

## 4.2 Experimental Results and Evaluation

Figures 8, 9 and 10 show the FAR-FRRs of experiments 1, 2, and 3, respectively.

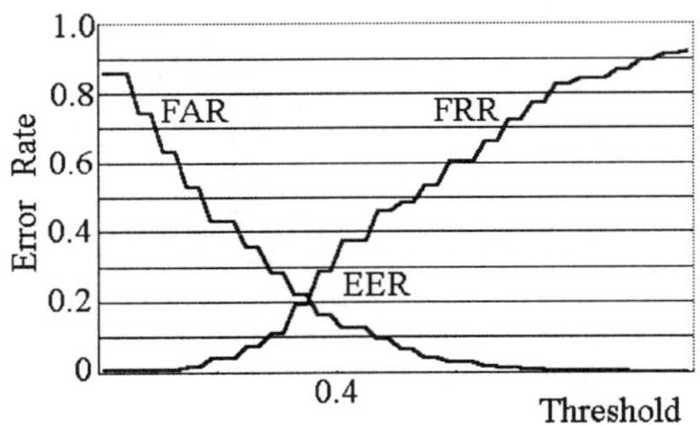


*Figure 8.* FAR-FRR of Experiment 1

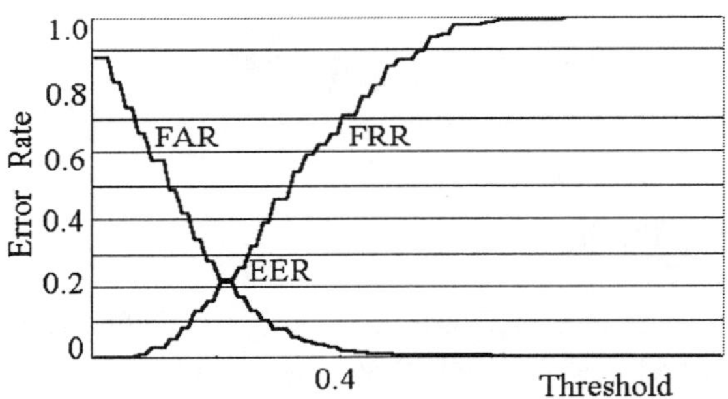


*Figure 9.* FAR-FRR of Experiment 2

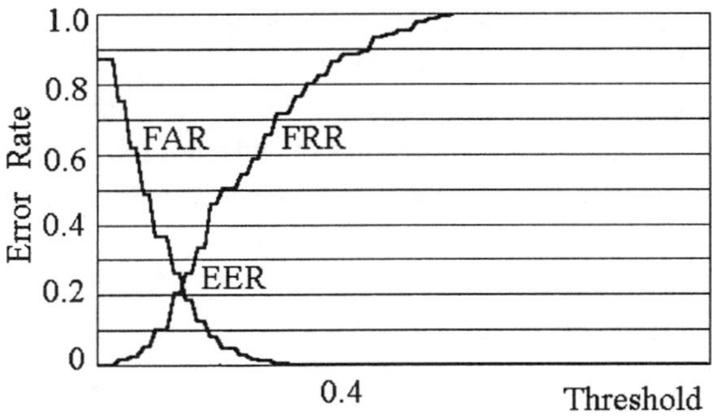


*Figure 10.* FAR-FRR of Experiment 3

Comparing Figs. 8 and 9, we can see that the EER does not change with the number of pixels of the tracing point. Similarly, comparing Figs. 8 and 10, we can see that it does not change with the number of tracing points, either. Therefore, we can conclude that the EER of FTA is approximately 0.2.

Next we consider the possibility of improving the EER of FTA by analyzing the results of experiment 1. Figure 11 shows that the individual EERs of the subjects varied widely in experiment 1. To determine the cause of this variation, we examined every thinned image of each subject. We found many false minutiae caused by interrupted ridge lines in the thinned images of subjects who had a high EER, but few false minutiae in the thinned images of subjects who had a low EER [23].

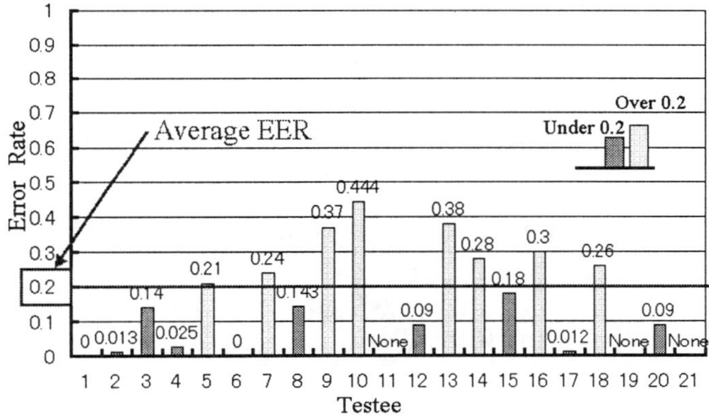


*Figure 11.* EER for each Subject in Experiment 1

Table 5 shows the rate of false minutiae occurring in the thinned images of typical subjects. Figures 12 and 13 show the thinned images of fp1-1 and fp10-4, respectively. In Figs. 12 and 13, the symbol ■ represents false minutiae and • represents true minutiae.

*Table 5.* Average Rate of False Minutiae and EER

| Subject | Average Rate of False Minutiae | EER |
|---|---|---|
| 1 | 0.2 | 0 |
| 3 | 0.6 | 0.14 |
| 5 | 0.825 | 0.21 |
| 10 | 0.85 | 0.444 |

[23] We examined the minutiae detected by the FTA manually.

*Figure 12.* Thinned Image (fp1-1)

*Figure 13.* Thinned Image (fp10-4)

From the above discussion, we conclude that the authentication accuracy of FTA can be improved by reducing the occurrence of false minutiae caused by interrupted ridge lines. We have demonstrated the basic effectiveness of FTA.

## 5. PROTOTYPE SYSTEM

In this section we describe the prototype system used to implement our algorithm on a smart card. Figure 14 shows the processing procedure of the prototype system, and Figure 15 shows the prototype itself.

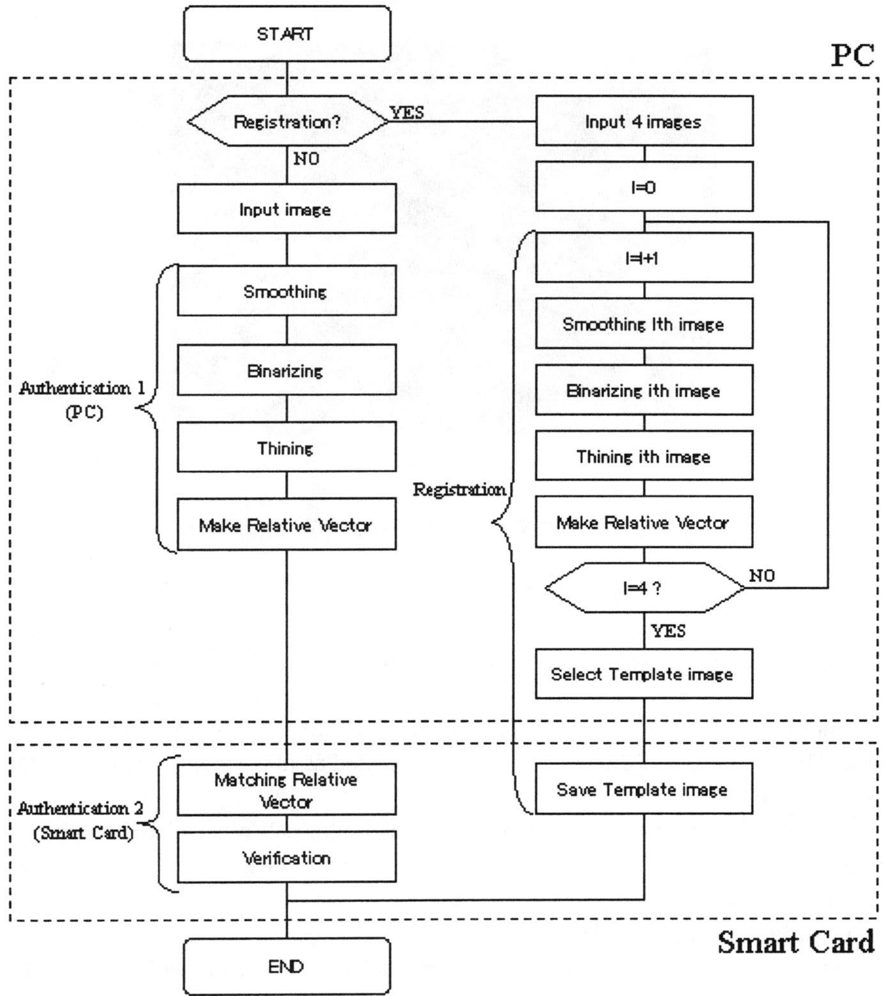


*Figure 14.* Prototype System Procedure

*Figure 15.* Prototype System

## 5.1 Overview of each process

Here, we briefly explain each process of the prototype system (Fig.14).

**Smoothing.** The 256×256 pixel gray-scale image was smoothed with a 3×3 mask. The brightness of the center point was defined as the average brightness of the eight neighbors.

**Binarizing.** We refer to a 4×4 pixel area as a block. We calculated the average brightness for every block, and the average brightness for a 3×3 block area. Using the latter, we binarized the 3×3 block area.

**Thinning.** We used the Hilditch algorithm[3].

**Make Relative Vector.** After detecting the minutiae, we made the Relative Vector as explained in Section 3.1.

**Choose template image.** We conducted round-robin matching for four input images. We used the image with the highest average matching score as the template image.

**Matching.** The Relative Vector of the input image was matched to the Relative Vector of the template image.

## 5.2 Evaluation of prototype system

We evaluated the processing speed of our prototype system under the conditions shown in Table 6. Table 7 shows the evaluation results.

*Table 6.* Evaluation Conditions

| PC | 266MHz |
|---|---|
| Smart Card | CPU:5MHz,ROM:4kbits,RAM:512kbits |
| Image | 256×256,gray-scale image |

*Table 7.* Results(See Fig.14)

| Procedure | Time |
|---|---|
| Registration | 8s |
| Authentication 1(PC) | 2s |
| Authentication 2(Smart Card) | 6s |

# 6. CONCLUSION

We have developed an algorithm, FTA, that has low computational complexity and does not need position correction between input and template images in order to execute fingerprint authentication on a smart card chip. We have demonstrated the basic effectiveness of FTA and made a prototype system.

With the FTA implemented on the smart card, the FTA matching process takes six seconds. Our goal is to reduce the FTA matching time to within one second through an optimum implementation.

**References**

[1]Tetsuji KOBAYASHI,"A Fingerprint Verification Method Using Thinned Image Pattern Matching," IEICE TRANSA-CTIONS,Vol.J79-D-□,No.3,pp.330-340,March 1996.

[2]Youichi SETO," Personal authentication technology using biometrics ", SICE Vol.37,No.6, pp.395-401,1998.

[3]J. Hilditch,"Linear skeletons from square cupboards", Machine Intelligence 6, Edinburgh Univ. Press, pp. 404-420, 1969.

**Appendix**

Define the set of Relative Vectors of a template image as $R = \{ m^r_{ij} \}$,

$m^r_{ij} = ( len^r_{ij}, d\theta^r_{(ij,trace(1))}, \ldots, d\theta^r_{(ij,trace(N))}, kind^r_{ij}, i^r, j^r )$

and define the set of Relative Vectors of an input image as $S = \{ m^s_{ij} \}$,

$m^s_{ij} = ( len^s_{ij}, d\theta^s_{(ij,trace(1))}, \ldots, d\theta^s_{(ij,trace(N))}, kind^s_{ij}, i^s, j^s )$

and,$N \geq 2$.

**main( ){**

( *step 0* )

Using $len^r_{ij}$, sort the set $R$ in ascending order ;

Give a number to each Relative Vector in that order

$m^r_{ij\text{-}order} = ( len^r_{ij\text{-}order}, d\theta^r_{(ij\text{-}order,trace(1))}, \ldots, d\theta^r_{(ij\text{-}order,trace(N))}, kind^r_{ij\text{-}order}, i^r, j^r )$ ;

count=0 ;

**for(** $order = 1$; $order \leq |R|$; $order{+}{+}$ **){**

( *step 1* )

Make set $A_1 = \{ m^s_{ij} \mid kind^s_{ij} = kind^s_{ij\text{-}order} \}$ ;

( *step 2* )

Make set $A_{1.5} = \{ m^s_{ij} \mid m^s_{ij} \in A_1 , \quad | len^s_{ij} - len^r_{ij\text{-}order} | \leq THR\_LEN \}$
**for(** $x = 0; x < 3; x{+}{+}$ **){**
Search $m^s_{ij}$ from the set $A_{1.5}$
which has minimum $|len^s_{ij} - len^r_{ij\text{-}order}|$ ;
Add $m^s_{ij}$ to set $A_2$ ;
Delete $m^s_{ij}$ from set $A_{1.5}$ ;
**}**
( *step 3* )
**for(** $n{=}1;\ n \leq N;\ n{+}{+}$ **){**
Search for $m^s_{ij}$ from set $A_2$ which has
minimum $|d\theta^s_{(ij\text{-}order, trace(n))} - d\theta^r_{(ij\text{-}order, trace(n))}|$ ;
Substitute $d\_ang[n]$ for such
$|d\theta^s_{(ij\text{-}order, trace(n))} - d\theta^r_{(ij\text{-}order, trace(n))}|$ ;
Substitute $i^x, j^x$ for $i^s, j^s$, respectively,
where $i^s, j^s$ are ID numbers of such $m^s_{ij}$ ;
**if(** $d\_ang[n] \leq THR\_ANG[n]$ **){** $i^s[n] = i^x ; j^s[n] = j^x$ ;
**if(** $i^s[1] = \ldots = i^s[n]$ && $j^s[1] = \ldots = j^s[n]$ && $n = N$ **){**
/* Final Loop */
count++ ;
}
**} else {**
break ;
}
}
}
( *step 4* )
**if(** $count / |R| \geq THR$ **){**
Matching OK ;
**} else {**
Matching NG ;
}
}

9

# Tamper-Resistance Network:

## *an Inforastructure for moving electronic tokens*

Kimio Kuramitsu and Ken Sakamura

*Interfaculty Initiative in Information Studies, University of Tokyo, 7-3-1 Hongo Bunkyo-ku, Tokyo 113-0033. Japan, Phone: (+81) 3 5841 2484 / Facsimile: (+81) 3 5841 8459, {kuramitsu, sakamura} @iii.u-tokyo.ac.jp*

**Abstract:** Moving electronic tokens or tickets over networks makes business processes more effective. At the same time, such a movement will sometimes produce disturbed results, such as illegal copies, unauthorized disclosures, and accidental destructions. Tamper Resistance Network (TRN) is a secure distribution infrastructure networked among smartcards and other tamper-proof devices. Over TRN, we can move tokens electronically, preventing from being duplicated or lost. In order to enhance the security of online token trading, the control of atomicity and the trace of the movement are discussed. In addition, we will present an initial experimentation, where electronic tickets are sold, exchanged, and examined over the prototyped TRN implementation.

## 1. INTRODUCTION

A token, or a ticket, is information with *value*. Information technology today opens up great possibilities for digitalizing tokens and its applications. In particular, a tamper-proof personal device such as a smartcard can protect data from illegal copies and unauthorized modification. Using such a device, we can secure the value of electronic tokens.

Furthermore, a token is essentially a moving object; many kinds of tickets allow a buyer to transfer a ticket to others. Even a nonnegotiable token such as an airline ticket could be distributed through an intermediary, like a travel agency. Accordingly, the *transferability* is very important for implementing electronic token applications. The objective of this study is to secure the transfer of tokens among tamper-proof devices.

The starting point of our approach is, say, a virtual private network among tamper-proof devices. An encrypted session directly opened between two devices can extend tamper-resistance to a token moving over the network. Furthermore, we will discuss two characteristics that make the encrypted network more reliable and more secure.

1. **Atomicity.** The transfer of electronic token is an all-or-nothing processing between two devices. The token should neither be doubled nor lost, even if the communication is interrupted with malicious intents.
2. **Traceability.** The movement of token should be traceable. While ticketing companies are forced to take good care of users' privacy, they must also prevent, say, "bad money drives out good."

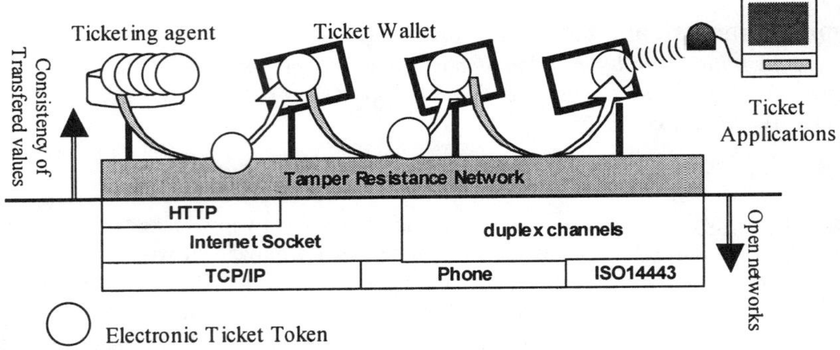


*Figure1.* The Layered Architecture of Tamper Resistance Network

Tamper Resistance Network (TRN), we will propose here, is a networked environment that enables to ensure the consistency of tokens, distributed among all of the personal devices. The number of tokens distributed over TRN is controlled, and illegally duplicated tokens are detectable. Furthermore, we design TRN as an infrastructure for multiple ticketing vendors; that is, the TRN provides every company with the common secure channel, on which each can setup ticketing applications originally.

This paper presents the design of the TRN infrastructure and its initial implementation. The remainder of the paper is organized as follows. Section 2 overviews the concept of TRN and summarizes its requirements. Section 3 designs the TRN scheme. Section 4 discusses the atomicity of TRN and the security enhancement of the traceability. Section 5 describes a prototyped implementation in the experimental project. Section 6 concludes the paper.

# 2. ELECTRONIC TRANSFERABLE TOKEN

## 2.1 Motivation

First of all, let us imagine a hard ticket to a popular event, such as the World Cup soccer and an Olympic game. Vacant seats are not desirable for both the organizer and people who want to attend the game. We consider that electronic transferable tickets will reduce unused tickets and vacant seats; for example, a person who suddenly cancels the game can send his or her ticket to a remote buyer. Also, a secondary marketplace that an authorized broker organizes will inject liquidity of tokens over the Internet.

The movement of tokens, however, results in heightened risks of destroying value, for example, illegal copies, unauthorized disclosures and accidental destructions. Thus, many ticketing systems restrict online transfer. The smartcard-based ticket is regarded as a semi-digitalized solution, where a ticket is exchanged physically although stored electronically. More recently, NTT's Digital Ticket system extends the trading of tickets on smartcard through trusted third parties. [12] However, the transfer through a mediator seems to be inefficient, too complex and less scalable. In addition, some people dislikes even trusted parties in terms of trading privacy.

Our fundamental approach to Tamper Resistance Network is based on two-party communication. A ticket wallet (depicted in the next section) directly sends an electronic token to another wallet. In this context, the TRN could be said to be a virtual private network, tunneling over open networks, authenticating with each other, and encrypting traffic. Indeed, there are not a few standards proposed for secure communication between smartcards. (The typical example is Modex's Value Transfer Protocol [13]) The uniqueness is that the security of TRN is designed to ensure the consistency of tokens distributed among the set of personal wallets. The atomicity control makes the basis of transfer more reliable. The traceability of the transfer, furthermore, enables the recovery of lost tokens and the detection of illegal tokens distributed on the public.

## 2.2 Ticket Wallet

The user must store an electronic token on a personal *ticket wallet* device. The tamper proof hardware is essential for protecting stored objects from unauthorized disclosure and modification. Its core is a secure integrated circuit computer, consists of multiple components – CPU, a cryptographic coprocessor, dynamic RAM and nonvolatile storage such as E2PROM and FeRAM and communication peripherals – combined with a single chip. The software that controls the transfer of token is installable on the chip.

Smartcard is one of the typical tamper resistance hardware, which embeds a secure chip in a plastic case [5]. However, the smartcard is not necessary suitable to store transferable tokens, because the plastic case gives no help to know the changing content of the card. The user will need some user interfaces to browse the content of token or send a token to another. We have therefore envisioned a smart phone-based ticket wallet. Using user interface and communication capability that the smart-phone supports, the user can easily exchange tokens. Figure 2 illustrates a portable phone, on which a secure chip is installed.

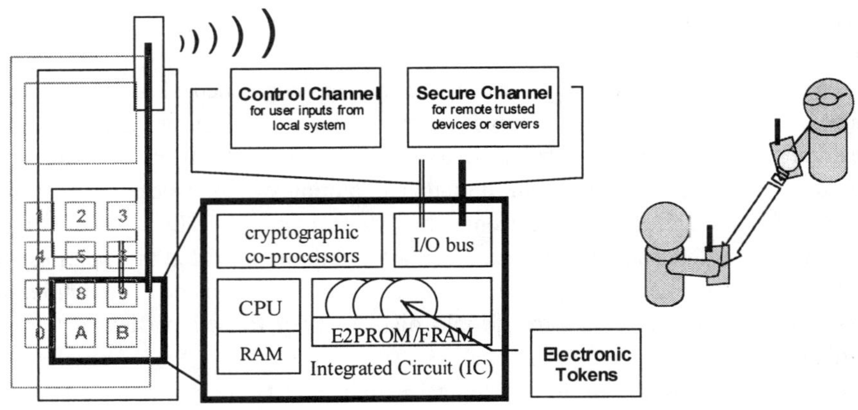


*Figure 2.* The Phone-based Ticket Wallet

Note that the TRN infrastructure should be designed as device-independent. In particular, inexpensive smartcards are useful for disposal ticket wallet devices. Accordingly, important is the compatibility with the smartcard technology that is limited in memory and processing resources. For example, the state of the art contact-less smartcard only supports an 8~16bit CPU, a 16~32K ROM for program module, 512bytes of RAM and 4~16K EEPROM for data storage. Although higher performance chips are under development, we should pay attention to its compactness.

## 2.3 Scope and Requirements

Tamper Resistance Network is a secure distribution environment, where a token can move from one wallet to another. In each wallet, a TRN driver will be installed, which authenticates a communicating entity, opens an encrypted session, and control the transfer of tokens. We premise that the TRN driver is certificated and protected from illegal disclosures and modifications, as well as a token object.

For the authentication and encryption, many techniques are now available on smartcard. [5] In the section 3.2, we will present one of the authentication schemes that satisfy the TRN session. Over them, we will add two features: *transaction control* and *movement trace*. Here we define the "ACID" properties that the TRN driver should ensure.

- **Atomicity**. The transfer of token is an all-or-nothing processing between two devices. The interruption must restart to complete the transferred or untransferred status (without any external coordinators).
- **Consistency**. The restart timing of the interrupted transfer is unpredictable, because the token is moved in suspicious circumstances. The token should neither be doubled nor eliminated from start to end transaction.
- **Isolation**. A token owner must have the ability to retransfer the received token to another wallet as a new transaction.
- **Durability**. The wallet must record logging information to restart and synchronize the interrupted transaction.

Ideally, the control of atomicity enables us to ensure the consistency of distributed tokens over the TRN environment. However, unexpected accidents and troubles might occur. The record of movements also helps detect such accidents and recover (or at least minimize) system troubles. We therefore need to trace moving tokens over the TRN.

Note that the TRN infrastructure proposed in this paper only discusses the scheme of transferring and tracing a data object. We will not specify any format of token, or the semantics of each token. Many applications today encode a ticket object using ASN.1 BER TLV's (type-length-value) record. [5] In addition, ISO7816-4 defines Application Protocol Data Unit to interact commands to access the record stored on smartcard. The TRN is defined only with the management of token movement, independent of a specific format and access method.

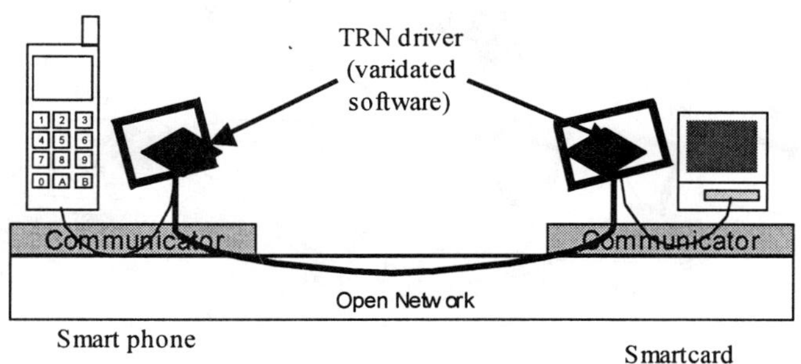


*Figure 3.* The TRN Driver is Installed in the Secure Chip

# 3. TAMPER REGISTANCE NETWORK

Tamper Resistance Network is a networked environment, where we can move electronic tokens from one tamper-proof device to another. To secure the movements on the TRN, we design the two protocol schemes, *token atomicity* and *transfer traceabilitiy,* over an *authenticated* session. Note that we premise that the TRN scheme designed in this section will work on a half duplex channel.

## 3.1 Overview

The TRN environment is comprised of several kinds of entities: a certification authority, ticketing agents, token objects and token devices. To start, we first define a small amount of preliminary notations. Let **C** be a finite set of ticketing agent $C_i$, **D** be a finite set of the devices $D_i$, and **O** be a finite set of token object $O_i$. Throughout the paper, we use the notation shown in Table 1.

| | |
|---|---|
| A→B: m | Entity A send a message to another entity |
| m1, m2 | The concatenation of messages m1 and m2 |
| k(m) | Message m encrypted using a cryptographic key k |
| $pk_A, sk_A$ | A pair of public and private keys of entity A. |
| $[m]_A$ | A digital certificate (signature) for message m by entity A |
| h(m) | A cryptographic digest of message m |

*Table 1.* Notation used for Protocol and Cryptographic Operation

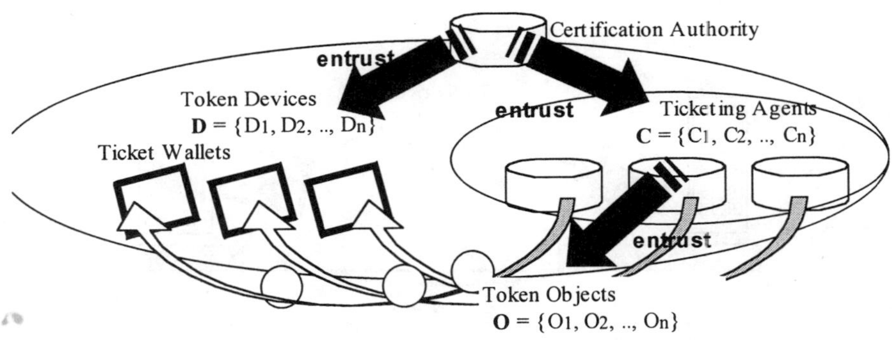


*Figure 4.* The Certification Relationship Between Entities in TRN

**Definiton1.** A *certification authority* is a primary trusted entity that controls the whole authenticity of the remainder of all entities (represented as $\mathbf{C} \times \mathbf{D} \times \mathbf{O}$) on

TRN. The authority has a pair of *root asymmetric key* {$pk_{CA}$, $sk_{CA}$}, and can issue digital certificate $[m]_{CA}$ for any messages.

**Definition2.** A *ticketing agent* $C_i$ is a creator of ticket objects. To issue a certificate for the token object, $C_i$ has a pair of asymmetric key {$pk_{Ci}$, $sk_{Ci}$}. The certification authority registers the certificate $[pk_{Ci}]_{CA}$ for the public-key $pk_{Ci}$.

**Definition3.** A *token device* $D_i$ is a communicating entity, including service servers by the certification authority and each ticketing agent as well as personal ticket wallets. It has a tuple of [$id_i$, $pk_{Di}$, $sk_{Di}$, $[idi, pk_{Di}]_{CA}$, $pk_{CA}$], where $id_i$ is a unique identifier of $D_i$, and a set of {$pk_{Di}$, $sk_{Di}$} is an asymmetric key to authenticate an encrypted session. The certificate $[id_i, pk_{Di}]_{CA}$ ensures the authenticity of device $D_i$ under the trust of the authority, and $pk_{CA}$ is used to verify the certificate.

**Definition4.** A *token object* $O_i$ is a tuple of [$oid_i$, $[oid_i]_{Cj}$, $body_i$], where $oid_i$ is a unique object identifier of $O_i$ and $[oid_i]_{Cj}$ is a certificate for $O_i$ by $C_j$, that is, the creator of $O_i$ is a ticketing agent $C_j$. The $body_i$ is the body of the object, including a variety of token's properties.

Figure 4 shows the confidential relationship of these entities over the TRN environment. The certification authority gives one's trust to all ticketing agents and token devices. Each entrusted ticketing agent creates token objects over *certificate hierarchy*. The token objects can be moved between entrusted devices.

## 3.2 Authenticated Session

To start, we will define the TRN session, where two devices communicate together through an authenticated and encrypted stream. Generally, we can generally use a challenge-response authentication or a shared secret key to authenticate trust of smartcard. Also, these techniques are regarded as enough secure over smartcards. [5] However, the important thing to trace moving tokens is to authenticate the identification of communicating entity, as well as trust of them. Accordingly, we introduce a PKI-based authentication [1] that can identify each device. Following shows that the device $D_A$ starts to authenticate $D_B$.

**Step1.** The device $D_A$ initializes a session, and then sends the device identifier and its certificate to another device.

$$D_A \rightarrow D_B: id_A, pk_A, [id_A, pk_A]_{CA}$$

The device $D_B$, after receiving $[id_A, pk_A]_{CA}$, verifies the certificate using the public-key $pk_{CA}$. If verified, $D_B$ can trust $id_A$ and $pk_A$ on the basis of the confidence of the certification authority. Note that since the certificate $[id_A, pk_A]_{CA}$ is public information, $D_B$ should not at this step believe in a device at the other end of the line.

**Step2.** The device $D_B$ generates a random number $rnd_B$ and then encrypts it using the received public-key $pk_A$. In addition, the encrypted number is signed with the secret-key $sk_B$ for avoiding *man-in-the-middle- attack.* $D_B$ sends those of data, following the identification information of $D_B$.

$$D_B \rightarrow D_A: id_B, pk_B\ [id_B, pk_B]_{CA}\ ,\ pk_A(rnd_B),\ [pk_A(rnd_B)]_B$$

**Step3**. $D_A$ decrypts the number $pk_A(rnd_B)$ using $sk_A$, and at the same time verifies the signature $[pk_A(rnd_B)]_B$ using $pk_B$. If verified, $D_A$ also generates a random number and sends it to $D_B$ as well.

$$D_A \rightarrow D_B: pk_B(\underline{rnd_A}), [pk_B(\underline{rnd_A})]_A$$

Ultimately, both of $D_A$ and $D_B$ finish initializing a new session by exchanging random numbers through the encryptions by one another's public keys. Therefore, $D_A$ and $D_B$ can create a common symmetric key $\underline{k_{AB}}$ at each end.

$$h(rnd_{A}, rnd_{B}) \rightarrow k_{AB}; \textit{ a session key}$$

Note that $D_A$ and $D_B$ may need to send a greeting message to each other for testing the session key (for example, $D_A \rightarrow D_B$: $k_{AB}$("hello") )

**Definition5.** A *TRN session* is denoted as a relation *s* of $[id_i, id_j, k_{ij}]$, where $id_i$ and $id_j$ is a pair of authenticated identifiers of communicating entities $D_i$ and $D_j$, and $k_{ij}$ is a session key dynamically generated at the current session. (Notice that we must implement the session that can detect *reply attack*[24] )

## 3.3 Token Atomicity

If an electronic product were transferred as a simple monolithic object, the sender and the receiver will repeat ACK for ACK endlessly. Our approach begins with the extension of an object $O_i$ to an electronic transferable token.

### 3.3.1 Status of Moving token

The movement of token could be thought of a status transition between two devices. To represent the status of a moving token, we define the following two parameters, which adds to $O_i$.

1. **value** parameter is a flag that determines whether the corresponding token is available, and whether the token is trustable.
2. **from-to** parameter is a record that represents where the corresponding token came from, or where the token will go to.

**Definition 6**. A *transferable token* or a status of moving $O_i$ is denoted as a relation *t* of [$oid_i$ $value_i$, from-$to_i$], where $oid_i$ is an identifier of $O_i$, The $value_i$, is an element of {enabled, disabled, trustless, trustless_disabled}, and from-$to_i$ is an element of the union set of {any, no} and **D**. Table 2 summarizes the semantics of *t* used in this paper.

[24] Some malicious users may attempt to defraud the TRN system reusing encryption messages. A unique identifier for each packet helps detect the replay of duplicated messages in the same session.

| **Status** | **Semantics** |
|---|---|
| $t[oid_i$ enabled, any] | Complete token |
| $t[oid_i$ disabled, $id_B]$ | Disabled token, except for moving to the device $id_B$. |
| $t[oid_i$ trustless_disabled, $id_A]$ | Trustless and disabled token, moved from the device $id_A$ |
| $t[oid_i$ trustless, $id_A]$ | Trustless token, moved from the device $id_A$ |
| $t$[null] | Deleted ticket |

*Table2:* The Semantics of Moving Ticket *t*

### 3.3.2 Applied 2PC protocol

A two-phase commit (2PC) protocol is a basic scheme that synchronizes the status of transactions among multiple distributed systems. [3] We apply 2PC scheme to the status transition of *t* between two entities. Let $M_{2PC}$ = {"copy", "copied", "commit", "committed", "true", "false"} be a set of protocol messages. Over a session s[$id_A$, $id_B$, $k_{AB}$], the ticket $O_i$ is transferred from $D_A$ to $D_B$ as follows.

**Step1.** $D_A$ first disables $O_i$ (complete ticket) and sets the destination $id_B$ at the from-to field (that is, $t$[oid$_i$ enabled, any] ➔$t$[oid$_i$ disabled, $id_B$]), and then starts to copy $O_i$ onto $D_B$.

$D_A$➔$D_B$: $k_{AB}$("copy", $O_i$)

**Step2.** $D_B$ stores the received O*i* as $t$[oid$_i$ trustless_disabled, $id_A$], and then returns an ACK message.

$D_B$➔$D_A$: $k_{AB}$("copied", true)

**Step3.** $D_A$ deletes $O_i$ from the storage, and then commits the transfer of oid$_i$

$D_A$➔$D_B$: $k_{AB}$("commit", oid$_i$)

**Step4.** $D_B$ switches the value parameter from trustless_disable to trustless, (that is, $t$[oid$_i$ trustless_disabled, $id_A$] ➔$t$[oid$_i$ trustless, $id_A$]), and then returns an ACK for the commitment.

$D_B$➔$D_A$: $k_{AB}$("committed", true)

Finally, $D_A$ deletes the ticket status $t$[oid$_i$ disabled, $id_A$] and finally closes the transaction

Sometimes, the receiver entity ($D_B$ above) cannot store $O_i$, because of owner's rejection or out of memory. In such cases, $D_B$ must respond the $k_{AB}$("copied", false) message at Step2. Then, $D_A$ aborts the transaction, roll-backing the status from $t[oid_i$ disabled, $id_B]$ to $t[oid_i$ enabled, any]. Figure 5 illustrates full sequence diagrams at the committed and aborted transfer.

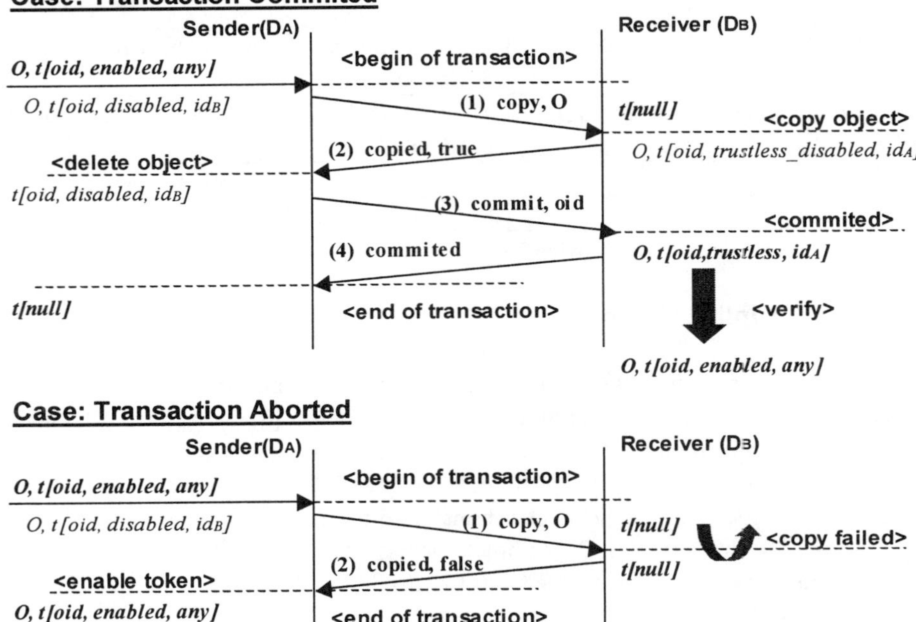


*Figure 5.* Protocol Sequence in the Transfer Transaction

Note that we already reported an atomic 2PC transfer scheme for an untraceable token [7]. This section extends the 2PC scheme to a traceable token. In short, it is possible to control whether we should trace the transfer or not, at Step4. If an untraceable token is committed, $D_B$ only have to set the complete ticket as $t$[oid$_i$ enabled, any]. For furthermore information, we will refer to our earlier work [7].

## 3.4 Traceability

A relative problem with the transferability is the *credibility* of received tokens. Under environment where multiple venders can issue tickets, can you really trust an electronic ticket just entitled "Olympic Baseball Game"? Thus, the token $O_i$ just after received should be restricted as trustless. In order to use the trustless token (or move to another devices), the owner first has to check the authenticity represented by $[oid_i]_{Cj}$. In this case, the verification of $[oid_i]_{Cj}$ requires the public-key of the creator $C_j$, but a resource limited device cannot store public-keys of all agents on **C**. Thus, the ticket wallet has to retrieve the public-key for $[oid_i]_{Cj}$ from the certification authority. Let $M_{Auth}$ = {"seekfor", "seeked"} be a set of protocol messages. Following shows the authentication of O*i* over a new session $s[id_B, id_{CA}, k_{BCA}]$.

**Step1.** $D_B$ seeks for the public key of the creator of $O_i$. At this time, the status of $O_i$ is represented as $t$[oid$_i$ trustless, $id_A$], where $id_A$ represents the identifier of the sender.

$$D_B \rightarrow D_{CA}: k_{BCA}(\text{“seekfor”}, oid_i, id_A)$$

**Step2.** The certification authority records the movement as a tuple of [oid$_i$, $id_A$, $id_B$] (note that, $id_B$ stems from the present session), and then returns the public key of the creator of $O_i$.

$$D_{CA} \rightarrow D_B: k_{BCA}(\text{“seeked”}, pk_{Cj})$$

$D_B$ verifies the certificate $[oid_i]_{Cj}$, and, if verified, switches the status from $t$[oid$_i$ trustless, $id_A$] to $t$[oid$_i$ enabled, any].

Due to resource constraints, we cannot record a chain of all movements on each token or device. However, this scheme can notify the certification authority of each movement of $O_i$, before the token owner uses or moves the token. The authority on the other hand can combine the notifications and complete the chain of all movements among devices.

**Definition** 7. A *token movement* is recorded as a tuple of [oid$_i$ id$_l$, id$_k$], which means that the object $O_i$ was moved from id$_l$ to id$_k$.

# 4. DISCUSSION

## 4.1 ACID properties

In the transfer of a token object between particular two devices, the status of $t$ is finite. Let the trustless status $t$[oid, trustless, id$_A$] on $D_B$ be regarded as the same as the complete ticket $t$[oid, trustless, id$_A$], because the process of ticket verification in Section 3.4 is independent of that of the transfer. Table 3 addresses all pairs of the statuses (I) ~ (IV), transferred between $D_A$ and $D_B$. Figure 6 illustrates the status transition diagram in the transfer of $O_i$. Here we will show a brief proof of the ACID properties in TRN.

- **Consistency**. Whenever the transfer is interrupted, the status of $t$ is determined as one of (II) ~ (V). At each status of (II) ~ (V), the value of $t$ on $D_A$ and $D_B$ is not simultaneously enabled. At the any status, the object $O_i$ remains upon at least one device. Therefore, TRN never doubles the value nor lost the object completely.
- **Atomicity**. In TRN, the sender plays a role in a transaction coordinator that resumes interrupted transactions. From viewpoints of $D_A$, the discriminable interrupted status is limited; $D_A$ can only differ (II) and (III) from (IV) and (V), in terms of the presence of $O_i$. Thus, $D_A$ restarts the transaction as follows. If the transfer is interrupted at (II) or (III), $D_A$ resends the message $k_{AB}$(copy, $O_i$). On the other hand, at (IV) or (V), $D_A$ resends the message $k_{AB}$ (commit, oid$_i$).

- **Durability.** Both of the restarting messages (copy $O_i$ and commit $oid_i$) are generatable from the status of token respectively. Furthermore, the recipient ($id_B$) in the ongoing transfer is recorded in the from-to field.
- **Isolation.** At (V), the owner of $D_B$ can move $O_i$ to other device, because the message committed is generatable from *t*[*null*].

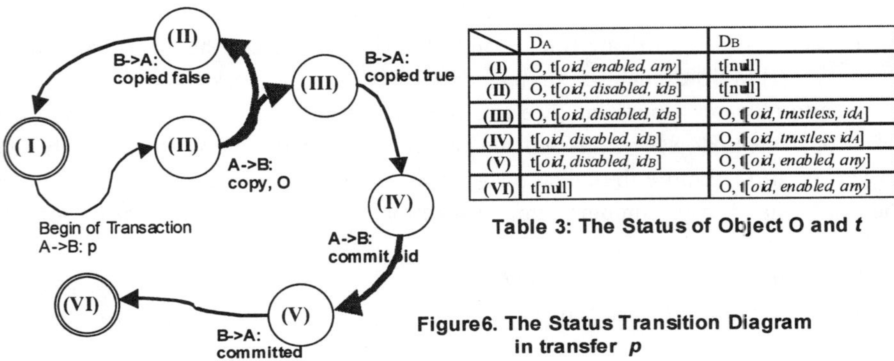


| | DA | DB |
|---|---|---|
| (I) | O, t[*oid, enabled, any*] | t[null] |
| (II) | O, t[*oid, disabled, idB*] | t[null] |
| (III) | O, t[*oid, disabled, idB*] | O, t[*oid, trustless, idA*] |
| (IV) | t[*oid, disabled, idB*] | O, t[*oid, trustless idA*] |
| (V) | t[*oid, disabled, idB*] | O, t[*oid, enabled, any*] |
| (VI) | t[null] | O, t[*oid, enabled, any*] |

**Table 3: The Status of Object O and *t***

**Figure6. The Status Transition Diagram in transfer *p***

## 4.2 Traceability, Security, and Privacy

Here we will discuss how the traceability affects security, reliability, and privacy in the TRN infrastructure.

- **Detection.** A remarkable advantage with the traceability is that it enables the certification authority to detect device disclosures. The certification authority always analyzes the flow of tokens, and if finding the branch that means that the illegally duplicated tokens are distributed, the authority can stop the flow and block suspicious devices. That is, the TRN infrastructure has the ability to keep the consistency (and the number) of distributed tokens on its running.
- **Recovery.** An electronic token stored on the device might be broken by hardware longevity or natural disturbance such as radial ray and electromagnetic wave. (In order to enhance tamper resistance against a physical analysis, such breakdowns are also desirable) The tracing of the movement help detect the device, where a token will be lost for the last time. A ticketing agent will (if possible) reissue a lost token for the right owner.
- **Privacy.** A unique identifier is assigned to each personal device, but it doesn't associate with a particular personal identification. If there is no map from device to person, privacy could be preserved. But this is ideally a hope. To bring it all down to earth, someone will make the mapping. In order for the users to control privacy matter, the TRN infrastructure should permit the use of disposable (or recyclable) devices, as the need arises.

# 5. PROTOTYPED IMPLEMENTATION

In the JIPDEC[25] project, we experimented the transferability of electronic tickets over TRN. This section presents our initial implemented prototypes in the experimental project.

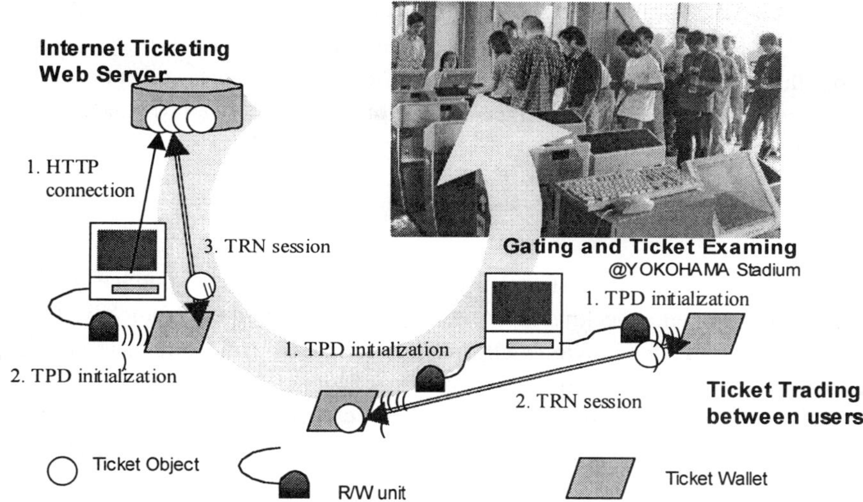


*Figure 7*. The Overview of Experimental Environment for Digital Ticketing.

## 5.1 Experimental Environments

The JIPDEC project assumes three ticket applications; (1) a user buying tickets online can receive electronic tickets directly from an Internet ticketing server to his or her personal ticket wallet; (2) the users also can freely exchange the tickets between ticket wallets; (3) ultimately, ticket examiners can check a ticket correctly at gating systems. Figure 7 shows the overview of experimental environment.

- **Ticketing Server.** We implemented the Internet ticketing service on a Servlet-based web server. Here we regard the server as one of the token devices on **D.** Our implemented servlet can switch a HTTP/1.1 session to a TRN session with Switching-Protocol ("Protocol-Upgrade: TRN").
- **Ticket Wallet.** Initially, we developed a personal ticket wallet on the small Java device, named PFU BossaNova™ [9]. Although BossaNova has no proper tamper resistances for its memory, it supports GUI-based touch panel and IrDA communication. After the initial implementation, we developed more secure

[25] JIPDEC (Japan Information Processing DEvelopment Center) is an EC promotion institute sponsored by Japanese government. Available at http://www.jipdec.or.jp/.

wallet using a tamper proof security box that supports elliptic curve cryptographic engine and ISO14443 based communication capability. (This security box is originally developed as an emulation test-bed of contact-less smartcard.) Both types of wallet can connect to a PC through a R/W unit.

- **Ticket browser.** The token devices are by nature passive. To browse and operate a personal wallet device, we used a PC as a user interface. For example, when you want to buy a ticket, you first connect the server with a HTTP request, and then turn to the TRN mode. At the same time, you start polling your wallet on the end of R/W unit. After that, the PC exchange authentication and succeeding encrypted tokens over TRN. From viewpoints of TRN, the server and the wallet never trust mediated PC.

## 5.2 Summary

More than 100 persons tested to use our prototype system for purchasing tickets, exchanging them, and checking their entrance to the stadium electronically. The size of messages to transfer $n$ byte-length token is estimated as follows: sent size (copy and commit) is about $n + 40$ bytes; received size (copied and committed) is 48 bytes. Moreover, the required size of logging field in each transfer is *value* (1 byte) and *from-to* (4 bytes) with a token object itself. The logging size is small enough to implement the TRN broker on the limited recourses.

# 6. CONCLUSION

The electronic transferability of tokens is a double-edged sword for organizations that conduct electronic business on the Internet. The main contribution of Tamper Resistance Network (TRN) is to provide us with a secure distribution environment that allows us to move tokens electronically without risk of duplicating or destroying them. The control of atomicity and the trace of movement are provided to enhance the security of trading between smartcards or other tamper-proof device.

This paper addressed the experimental prototype for the distribution of electronic tickets on TRN. The finding of the experimentation is that the TRN framework is useful to setup online business selling electronic tickets through the Web. Future directions we will investigate include additional security evaluation, fair-exchange, and PKI design based on business models.

# 7. REFERENCE


1. C. Adams and S. Lloyd. Understanding the Public-Key Infrastructure, Macmillan Technology Series, 1999.
2. S. Araki. The Memory Stick. IEEE Micro, pages40-46, July-August 2000.
3. P. Bernstein and E. Newcomer. Principles of Transac-tion Processing. Morgan Kaufmann Publishers, 1997.
4. W. Diffie and M Hellman. New Direction in Cryptog-raphy, IEEE Trans. on Information Theory, pages 644-654, IT-22, 6, 1976.
5. U. Hansmann, M. S. Nicklous, T. Schack. F. Seliger. Smart Card Application Development Using Java. Springer, 2000.
6. S. Kent and R. Atkinson. Security Architecture for the Internet Protocol. IETF RFC 2401, Nov. 1998. Avail-able at http://www.rfc-editor.org/rfc/rfc2401.txt
7. K. Kuramitsu et al. TTP: Secure ACID Transfer Protocol for Electronic Ticket between Personal Tamper-Proof Devices. In *Proceedings of the 24th Annual International Computer Software & Applications Conference (IEEE COMPSAC2000)*, Oct. 2000.
8. K. Kuramitsu and K. Sakamura. PCO: EC Content Description Language Supporting Distributed Schema across the Internet. Journal of IPSJ, pages 110-122. Vol. 41 No.1, Jan.2000.
9. PFU BossaNova Homepage, available at http://www.pfu.co.jp/BossaNova/.
10. W. Townsley et al., Layer Two Tunneling Protocol (L2TP), IETF RFC 2661, Aug. 1999. available at http://www.rfc-editor.org/rfc/rfc2661.txt
11. J.D. Tygar. Atomicity in Electronic Commerce. In Proceeding of the 5th Annual ACM Symposium on Principles of Distributed Computing. May 1996.
12. Matsuyama and K. Fujimura. Distributed Digital-Ticket Management for Rights Trading System, In Proceedings of the ACM EC'99, November 1999.
13. Mondex Electronic Cash. Available at http://www.mondex.com/

MAIN TRACK - PART TWO

# INTER-ORGANISATIONAL TRANSACTIONS

10

# Pattern-directed Auditing of Inter-organisational Trade Procedures

Ronald M. Lee[1], Roger W.H. Bons[2], René W. Wagenaar[3]
*[1]Erasmus University Research Institute for Decision and Information Systems (EURIDIS), The Netherlands;*

*[2]Philips International BV - Corporate IT, eBusiness Support Strategy and Planning, Eindhoven, The Netherlands;*

*[3]Rotterdam School of Management, Dept. Decision and Information Systems, Erasmus University Rotterdam*

**Abstract:** In open business-to-business electronic commerce, when trading with parties where no prior trade relationships or trust exist, the parties need to rely on inter-organizational trade procedures that control trading risks. These trade procedures have to be audited to identify potential control weaknesses and the resulting fraud potential, including the risks associated with the communication medium used to support the execution of these procedures.

This article is an initial step towards establishing a theory on the auditing of inter-organizational (trade) procedures. A set of generic principles is proposed for inter-organizational trade procedures, which includes the analysis of potential control weaknesses associated with the technical communication infrastructure. We show how this theory can be supported using automated techniques, and illustrate using the example of a documentary credit procedure.

## 1. THE NEED FOR INTER-ORGANISATIONAL PROCEDURES

Following the wave of business to consumer (B2C) electronic commerce, the focus is now shifting to business to business applications. In this article the object of analysis are the procedures used to exchange the information that is needed for the execution of a business transaction.

More and more, these procedures are becoming automated, in the form of electronic trade procedures, that are generic and re-usable among different sets of parties. Reaching agreement on how to use electronic trade procedures not only involves the design of an acceptable procedure to be used, but also involves detailed legal and technical arrangements. Since in most countries an electronic message (business document) is not by default acceptable in a court of law, a specific contract[26] has to be made to deal with any legal problem that might arise from replacing traditional paper documents with electronic messages. The process of reaching these agreements can become quite costly and introduces a highly relationship-specific cost in the establishment of an electronic link between trading partners.

These high relationship-specific costs associated with electronic messaging have resulted in a situation in which it has been applied mainly for long-term, stable trading relationships among trusting partners. The procedures used in these relationships focus on reducing the co-ordination costs the parties have to incur for exchanging their products or services. For instance, logistical concepts such as Just In Time delivery are highly supported by the electronic exchange of (operational) data. If something goes wrong during the transaction, the parties will jointly try to find a solution that does not endanger the continuation of their long-lasting relationship.

However, increasingly dynamic competition and globalization are pushing for a more open form of business-to-business electronic messaging -- that is applicable in shorter term relationships involving a small number of transactions and without a pre-existing trust among the parties. As in the past, such new forms of messaging will continue to require detailed specification of the procedures to be used to exchange the messages. However, the negotiation costs to agree upon these procedures should be minimized in order to lower the entry barriers.

An example of an approach that could contribute to the lowering of these negotiation costs is the notion of electronic trade procedures, as being developed by the Business Process Analysis Group (BPAWG), of the UNITED NATIONS CENTER FOR TRADE FACILITATION AND ELECTRONIC BUSINESS (UN/CEFACT). A related concept is that of "Open-edi" as defined by the International Standards Organization (ISO) working group (IEC JTC1/SC30/SC32). This initiative strives towards the construction of tools for the standardization of inter-organizational procedures, using formal specifications of these procedures (called "Open-edi Scenarios", [ISO, 1996]).

However, in these more open kinds of circumstances, where the trading partners do not know or fully trust each other, they will require more 'control information' about each other's behavior during the execution of a transaction. Parties may be subject to opportunistic behavior of their counter-party, yielding a clear and present danger of loosing money. Thus, if parties cannot trust each other, they have to be able to rely on the procedures they use to interact.

In international trade, this has lead to well-established (paper-based) procedures controlling with these risks and the introduction of parties such as inspection agencies and banks to serve as trusted intermediaries. An example of such a procedure is the Documentary Credit procedure [ICC, 1994], which is discussed in more detail below. Other examples include the Incoterms, which standardize the

[26] These contracts are referred to as 'Interchange Agreements'.

delivery terms in a sales contract [ICC, 1990] and (inter)national customs procedures.

In order to support the formal specification of inter-organizational procedures, our previous research has resulted in the Documentary Petri Net (DPN) formalism. This formalism builds upon classical Petri Nets [Petri, 1962; Peterson, 1981], with some extensions to enable the modeling of electronic trade procedures. Each of the roles is modeled as a separate DPN model. The transitions of the Petri Net represent the activities to be performed within the role. In addition to the classical Petri Net, two additional types of places are introduced: document places and goods places. They are introduced to make a clear graphical distinction between control places and places that represent the transfer of information or goods. The interested reader is referred to [Lee, 1999; 2000] for a more extensive discussion on the DPN formalism.

These DPN models are built using the CASE tool InterProcs[27], a modeling tool developed by Lee [1992, 1999, 2000]. InterProcs offers a graphical user interface with which Documentary Petri Nets can be drawn. Furthermore, since InterProcs embeds a Prolog engine, rule-bases can be added to a Documentary Petri Net model, allowing automatic reasoning about modeled trade procedures. The pattern recognition approach presented below is an example of this.

Summarizing this first section, we have identified the need for the specification of inter-organizational procedures. Such procedures have existed for centuries in the paper-based world, but their importance increases now the world has entered the era of electronic commerce. Especially when non-trusting trading partners are doing business with each other, they have to have a clear understanding of the procedures they are going to use to govern their transactions. This will lead toward a further rationalization and formalization of inter-organizational trade procedures. To support this process, our previous research resulted in the Documentary Petri Net formalism and the InterProcs tool. In this article, we introduce a theory for auditing inter-organizational procedures to assess their trustworthiness.

## 2. THE AUDITING OF INTER-ORGANISATIONAL PROCEDURES.

With the emergence of electronic commerce companies may quickly encounter new ways of doing business. Not only will they be able to do business with companies from different (trading) cultures, but also the type of business may differ. An example of the latter is the purchase of multi-media data (music, books etc.), in which not only the purchasing, but also the actual delivery process is conducted through an electronic network. Trading parties must be able to rely on the ability of the procedures governing their transactions to control the risks associated with doing business at arms' length.

[27] InterProcs was originally developed in Prolog, but has since been re-implemented in Java, providing for operational models both as executable applets and for standalone design. The current version of InterProcs is available at the Web site: http://abduction.euridis.fbk.eur.nl/projects/InterProcs.html.

In addition to this, the character of the controls could change as well. Using modern technology, the traditional paper-based controls could be replaced by more efficient and/or effective electronic controls. In the Port of Rotterdam, several pilot studies have shown that huge benefits can be achieved, both with respect to cost savings in the execution of the controls and cost savings related to a better management of the risks (less damage).

It is clear from the previous discussion that the assessment of the trustworthiness of inter-organizational procedures becomes a crucial factor in the successful adoption of these procedures. Developments in (open) electronic commerce not only require the porting of existing, paper-based, procedures into an electronic setting, but also trigger the development of totally new procedures. Our research offers the first steps towards the establishment of a theory on inter-organizational auditing.

Participants in business transactions will strive to reduce the risk of non-performance by implementing inter-organizational controls. An obvious way to do this is to conduct business only with those parties one trusts. However, in the open trading relationships this trust is typically not present and the risks have to be reduced by exchanging additional control information. Parties fully depend on the reliability of the messages received when deciding whether or not they have to perform some activity. If the underlying message was wrong or manipulated, this can lead to a substantial loss for that party.

In the linguistic philosophy literature, this control functionality of information has been referred to as 'Speech Acts' [Austin, 1962; Searle, 1969]. This theory deals with 'performative documents', which change the 'societal state' of the parties exchanging them. For instance, a party making an offer towards another party has created a conditional obligation by sending such a message. With respect to the performative function of EDI messages, several authors have proposed a taxonomy of different classes of messages (see for instance [Lee, 1992; Moore, 1996]).

Based on parallels with internal accountancy theory, we have constructed an initial set of 'general principles' for the construction of safe trade procedures, based on principles in the internal auditing literature. These modifications solely consist of the replacement of the internal auditing terms 'operational task', 'control task', 'document', 'agent' and 'position' with 'primary activity', 'control activity', 'information parcel', 'organization' and 'role' respectively. We do not claim the completeness of this list; its sole function is to provide a starting point for further research. For instance, existing rules on collusion between agents in internal auditing literature can be easily translated into rules for collusion between companies, resulting in fraud schemes.

1. If a primary activity is performed by one role, another role should testify the completion thereof using some information parcel. The primary activity should precede the control activity. The role responsible for the control activity should be different from the role executing the primary activity. Furthermore, the organizations playing the roles should not be connected.
2. If a role executes a primary activity and some information parcel is issued by another role to testify this, this information parcel should be received by the

executing role as well. This principle constitutes the detective controls as mentioned in the previous sections

3. If a role A executes a primary activity, the result of which triggers the execution of another primary activity in a role B, an information parcel must be issued by another role C to testify this if role B cannot witness the execution of role A's activity. This document must be received and checked by role B.
4. If a certain item (goods/funds) is physically transferred from on role to another, the receiving role must identify itself using some document. This transfer should occur after the identification took place.
5. If a certain item is physically transferred from one role to another, the receiving role should certify the status of the item as it is received using some document. The transfer of this document and the exchange of the item should occur simultaneously.
6. If an intermediary organization is used for the (physical) transfer of an item, a report should be received by the principal from both the intermediary agent and the receiver of the item.

# 3. COMPUTER AIDED SUPPORT FOR THE AUDITING OF INTER-ORGANISATIONAL PROCEDURES

## 3.1 A Pattern Recognition Approach For Internal Auditing

In this section we will introduce the computational technique of "audit daemons" (Lee, 1991), which was applied to internal auditing in the dissertation work of Chen (1992). The purpose of Chen's work was to "develop a theoretical foundation for building a knowledge-based system, which can accept a model of an internal accounting control system as input and produce the identification of fraud potentials as output". Chen based his theory on a schema-based reasoning approach, integrating the schema theory of knowledge representation from cognitive psychology and pattern recognition in the field of Artificial Intelligence. The internal accounting control system is modeled using the Documentary Petri Net (DPN) formalism.

The knowledge base containing the general principles for internal auditing is constructed as follows. Chen starts by identifying control patterns of accounting procedures. Control patterns are "stereotypical relationships between agents, tasks, and information repositories". They serve as "screening criteria for auditors to identify control weaknesses". The control patterns are based on the control objectives to be achieved over the operating tasks and are represented using a logic-based language.

These control patterns serve as the starting point for the auditing process as they specify the way it ought to be. Deviations of such control patterns (control weaknesses) are called "audit patterns". If a pattern of a control weakness is recognized in a given internal accountancy control system, a warning has to be raised. Since the control patterns are specified using a logic-based language, the audit patterns can be easily inferred from the control patterns using a logical negation. This process is followed on all the control patterns specified, resulting in a set of audit patterns.

The audit patterns in their turn are used to identify the illegal actions that could be taken by an agent in charge of an operating task. For this purpose Chen introduces audit rules, which take the audit patterns as their antecedent and contain explicit warnings as their consequent, which have to be pronounced by the system in case they are matched.

The automated evaluation process takes these audit rules and a Petri Net model of an internal accounting control system as input. For this purpose Chen identified "control primitives", which are in fact the conditions in the audit rules. He distinguishes "procedural control primitives" and "organizational control primitives". The organizational control primitives are checked using the organizational structure of the control system. The procedural control primitives have to be checked by analyzing the Petri Net model of the internal accounting control system. Pattern recognition is used to map the Petri Net model to the control primitives as they are found in the rules. These control primitives are represented as 'audit daemons'. Figure 1 shows the audit daemons for the control primitives **task(X:A)** and the **follows(X:A, Y:B)** primitives as they were used by Chen.

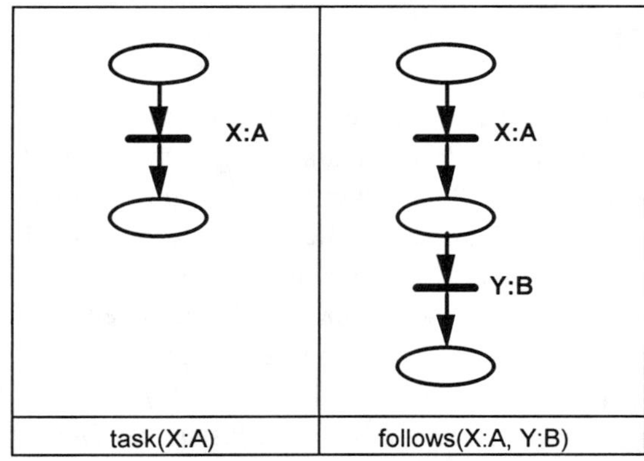


*Figure 1.* Two examples of audit daemons

This concludes our review of Chen's analysis approach. In the next section the application of this approach in the domain of inter-organizational trade procedures is addressed.

## 3.2 The Pattern Recognition Approach Applied To Inter-Organizational Procedures

In this section the analysis method of Chen is applied to the inter-organizational context. First some of Chen's definitions are adapted for the inter-organizational context. The set of conditions that have to be evaluated for the audit rules in this example consists of the following predicates:

## 3.3 The Pattern Recognition Approach Applied To Inter-Organizational Procedures

In this section the analysis method of Chen is applied to the inter-organizational context. First some of Chen's definitions are adapted for the inter-organizational context. The set of conditions that have to be evaluated for the audit rules in this example consists of the following predicates:

**activity(Role1: PA)**
**testify(Role2, Role1:PA, Doc)**
**follow(Role1: PA1, Role2: PA2)**
**Role1 <> Role2**
**occupy(Role1, Company1)**
**socially_detached(Company1, Company2)**

These conditions have to be evaluated based on the DPN model of the procedure under investigation. The conditions 'activity', 'testify' and 'follow' are procedural control primitives, whereas 'occupy', 'principal', '<>' and 'socially_detached' are organizational control primitives. The procedural control primitives are checked using audit daemons (see Figure 1), the organizational control primitives are checked based on the underlying logic-based language representation. It should be noted that for the control conditions referring to a performative action (in this case 'testify') a more detailed description may be used, in terms of a procedural audit daemon. For instance, in case of the certification of goods, the Communication Chain for transferring a certificate of origin from the inspection agency to the consignee satisfies the predicate

**testify(inspection_agency, shipper: produce_goods, certificate_of_origin)**.

# 4. EXAMPLE: THE DOCUMENTARY CREDIT PROCEDURE.

In order to illustrate how the analysis process can be supported by an automated tool, this section contains a small example of the documentary credit procedure. This is a procedure that facilitates the exchange of goods against money between a buyer and seller who do not trust each other completely. It is fully governed by the exchange of (performative!) documents that control the behaviour of the seller on behalf of the buyer.

The seller has to obtain these documents and present them to his bank. All parties have an underlying contract (the Letter of Credit), which specifies exactly which documents are requested, based on the underlying sales contract. Upon presentation of a correct set of documents, the 'corresponding bank' will pay the seller. In its turn, the corresponding bank will be able to retrieve its money from the issuing bank by forwarding the documents.

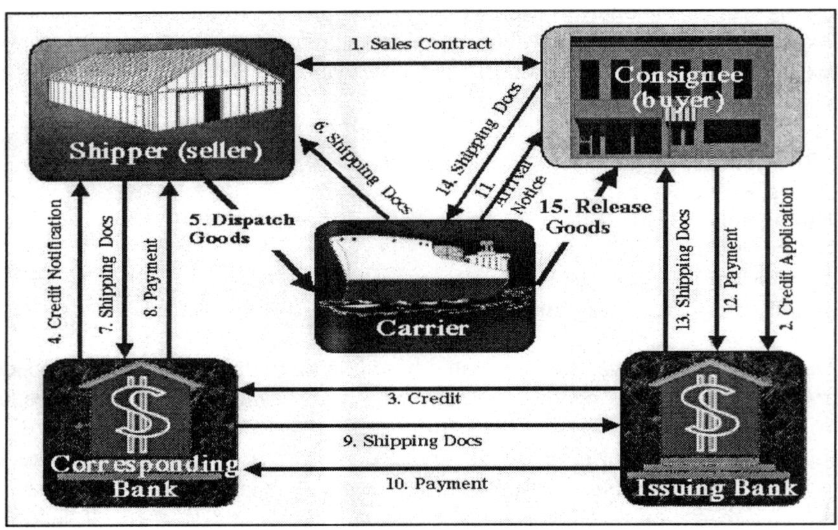


*Figure 2.* A Simplified Documentary Credit Procedure

Finally, the issuing bank will forward the documents to the buyer in exchange for the price. Note that the buyer needs these documents to be able to claim the goods once they arrive at the port (especially the 'bill of lading' is used for this purpose). The procedure is still fully based on paper, and is usually only used for large transactions.

Instead of the informal specification in Figure 2, the formal analysis requires the specification of an trade procedure in terms of roles and information parcels. In Figure 3, the DPN role model for the seller (called 'shipper') is shown as an example. Similar models are constructed for the other roles as well. The individual role models are 'glued' together at their document/goods places, representing the inter-organizational exchanges of information.

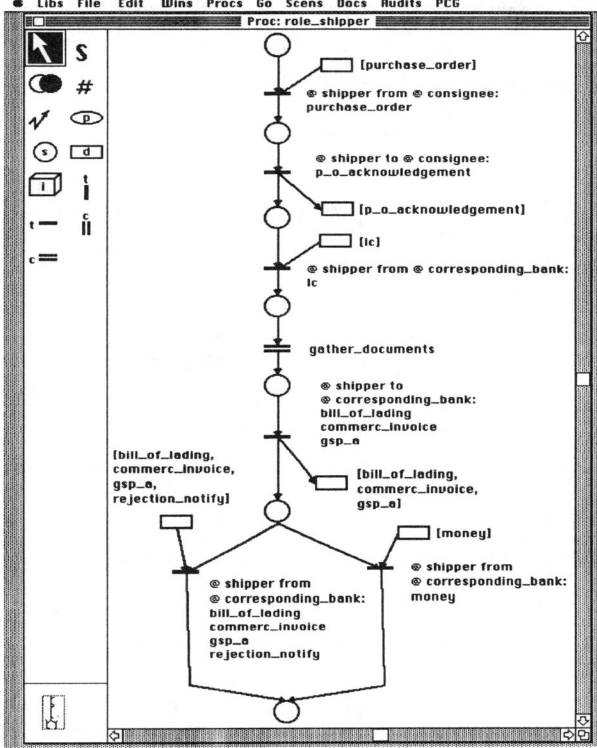


*Figure 3.* The DPN model of the shipper role

As a next step, the general principles presented above are instantiated in order to be usable in this domain. This is done using the Table 1, which is the result of a literature review in this area (especially the Incoterms [ICC, 1990]). It lists the primary activities governed by the documentary credit procedure, specifies the documents needed to control them and identifies the roles responsible for performing these controls.

| PRIMARY ACTIVITY | CONTROL DOCUMENT | CONTROLLI NG PARTY |
|---|---|---|
| producing the goods | certificate of origin | inspection agency |
| packaging the goods | certificate, packing list, b/l | inspection agency, carrier |
| arranging transportation | b/l, CMR, airwaybill, CTA | carrier |
| paying the transportation | b/l, CMR, airwaybill, CTA | carrier |
| arranging insurance | insurance contract | insurance company |
| delivering the goods to carrier | b/l, CMR, airwaybill, CTA | carrier |
| transferring the property | b/l, CMR, airwaybill, CTA | carrier |

*Table 1:* Relationship between primary activities and control documents used to control them.

The generic rules presented earlier can now be instantiated with parameters that refer to specific roles and documents as listed in Table 1[28]. This yields a huge set of rules that have to be satisfied in a proper documentary credit procedure. Note that the rules specified in Table 1 only consider the relationship between buyer and seller and have to be extended to deal with the relationships between these parties and the banks involved.

In this article we use two example cases to illustrate the results of the analysis process. In the first case, the wrong type of document was used to evidence the transfer of the property. The shipper issued a 'delivery order' himself, which did evidence that he gave the assignment to the carrier to transport the goods, but did not provide the buyer with sufficient documentation to claim the goods. In fact, some other party did in fact claim the goods from the carrier instead. The analysis of the DPN model of this situation warns against this possibility since it will not find a proper document to evidence the transfer of the property.

In the second case, an insecure medium was used to transfer the information, which allowed the shipper to forge both the bill of lading and the certificate of origin. A fax message was used to transfer both of these documents. Normally, the receiving party should have rejected this document for exactly this reason. Although this example seems to be irrelevant for the analysis of trade procedures, it does show what can happen if not the proper security measures have been taken. The analysis of the DPN model of this case warns that the technical security requirements (non-repudiation etc.) have not been fulfilled, since it can not find the proper controlling

[28] The rules for the analysis of the technical infrastructure have been instantiated already since they are not domain specific.

activities in the specification of the Message Transporting Service used for the transfer of the documents.

# 5. CONCLUSIONS AND FUTURE RESEARCH DIRECTIONS.

The main contribution of this paper was the introduction of a new theory on the auditing of inter-organizational procedures. This entails the analysis of inter-organizational trade procedures on how trustworthy they are. Based on the similarities between the analysis of inter-organizational control systems and internal accounting control systems an initial set of generic principles for inter-organizational trade procedures has been presented. In addition to this, control weaknesses caused by the use of a communication medium have been addressed in a similar fashion as well.

In order to support this theory, we have extended the InterProcs tool, that uses a pattern recognition approach for the auditing of internal accounting control systems. Since the problem domains are very similar, the same technique could be applied in the inter-organizational context as well. Some minor additions were needed to deal with the complexity of recursive control rules in the area of the technical communication infrastructure. The working of the tool has been briefly illustrated using examples from the documentary credit domain.

Future research has to improve this initial theory based on more empirical knowledge, covering multiple application domains. The list of general principles should be completed and national differences, but also differences per industry, should be reflected in these rules. The communication technologies have not been examined in sufficient detail to claim completeness of the auditing rules on this area either. Several projects are on their way to construct such rules, especially with respect the use of encryption and trusted third parties in electronic commerce.

# 6. REFERENCES

Austin, J.L., *How to DO things with words*, Harvard University Press, Cambridge, MA, 1962.

Bons, R.W.H., Lee, R.M., Wagenaar, R.W., Wrigley, C.D., *Modelling Inter-organizational Trade Procedures Using Documentary Petri Nets*, Proceedings Hawaii International Conference on System Sciences (HICSS) 28, Hawaii, USA, pp. III/189-198, January, 1995.

Bons, R.W.H., Lee, R.M., and Wagenaar, R.W. "Computer-Aided Auditing of Inter-organizational Trade Procedures", *Intelligent Systems in Accounting, Finance and Management*, Special Issue on Electronic Commerce, ed. Jae Kyu Lee, 1999

Bons, R.W.H, Dignum, F., Lee, R.M and Tan, Y-H. "A Formal Specification of Automated Auditing of Trustworthy Trade procedures for Open Electronic Commerce", *Proceedings of the Hawaii International Conference on System Sciences*, January, 1999.

Chen, Kuo-Tay. *Schematic Evaluation of Internal Accounting Control Systems*, University of Texas at Austin, USA, PhD Dissertation, 1992.

Dewitz, S. K., Lee, R. M., *Legal Procedures as Formal Conversations: Contracting on a Performative Network*, Proceedings of International Conference on Information Systems, Boston, U.S.A., pp. 53-65, December, 1989.

Elsas, P., *Computational Auditing*, PhD thesis Free University Amsterdam, Netherlands, September, 1996.

Frielink, A.B., De Heer, H.J. (eds.), *Leerboek Accountantscontrole* , Stenfert Kroese, Volumes I, IIa and IIb, Leiden, Antwerpen, (in Dutch), 1985 (I), 1987 (IIa), 1989(IIb).

Garfunkel, S. , *PGP: Pretty Good Privacy*, O'Reilly & Associates, Inc., U.S.A., 1995.

ICC, *Incoterms 1990*, International Chamber of Commerce publication number 461, 1990.

ICC, *The Uniform Customs and Practices for Documentary Credit Procedures*, International Chamber of Commerce publication number 500, Paris, France, January, 1994.

ISO, *The Open-edi Conceptual Model*, ISO/IEC JTC1/SWG-EDI, Document N222, 1991.

ISO, *The Open-edi Reference Model*, IS 14662, ISO/IEC JTC1/SC30, 1996.

Lee, R.M., "Auditing as Pattern Recognition: Automated Analysis of Documentary Procedures", Working Paper, Department of Management Sciences and Information Systems, University of Texas at Austin, August 1991.

Lee, R.M., *Dynamic Modeling of Documentary Procedures: A CASE for EDI*, Proceedings of Third International Working Conference on Dynamic Modeling of Information Systems, Noordwijkerhout, Netherlands, June, 1992.

Lee, R.M. "Distributed Electronic Trade Scenarios: Representation, Design, Prototyping", *International Journal on Electronic Commerce :* Special Issue on Formal Aspects of Digital Commerce, eds. S. O. Kimbough and R.M. Lee, Vol 3, No 1, 1999, pp. 23-26.

Lee, R.M. "Documentary Petri Nets: A Modeling Represention for Electronic Trade Procedures" *Business Process Management: Models, Techniques, and Empirical Studies*, eds. W. Aalst, J. Desel, A. Oberweis, Springer, 2000, pp. 359-375.

Lee, R.M., Bons, R.W.H., Wrigley, C.D., Wagenaar, R.W., *Automated Design of Electronic Trade Procedures Using Documentary Petri Nets*, Proceedings Fourth International Conference on Dynamic Modeling and Information Systems, Noordwijkerhout, Netherlands, pp. 137-150, September, 1994.

Lee, R.M., Bons, R.W.H., *Soft-Coded Trade Procedures for Open-EDI*, International Journal of Electronic Commerce, pp. 27-50, Volume 1 Number 1, 1996.

Moore, S.A., *Testing Speech Act Theory and its applicability to EDI & other computer-processable messages*, Proceedings of the 29th Hawaii Intenational Conference on System Sciences, Hawaii, U.S.A., pp.30-38, January, 1996.

Peterson, J. L., *Petri Net Theory and the Modeling of Systems*, Prentice-Hall, 1981.

Petri, C.A., *Kommunikation mit Automaten*, PhD thesis University of Bonn,, Germany, 1962.

Searle, J., *Speech Acts: An Essay in the Philosophy of Language*, Cambridge University Press, London, UK, 1969.

Starreveld, R.W., De Mare, H.B., Joëls, E.J., *Bestuurlijke Informatieverzorging*, Samsom Bedrijfsinformatie, Part I & II, Alphen a/d Rijn, Netherlands, (in Dutch), 1995.

Van Tulder, R., Wagenaar, R.W. (eds.), *Omgaan met Dilemma's: Zeven Cases in Strategie en Informatie Technologie in Mainport Rotterdam*, Kluwer Bedrijfswetenschappen, Deventer, Netherlands, (in Dutch), 1995.

Wagenaar, R. W., *Business network redesign - Lessons from the Port of Rotterdam Simulation game*, Proceedings Conference on interorganizational systems in the global environment, Bled, Slovenia, September, 1992.

Wrigley, C.D., *EDI transaction protocols in international trade*, Proceedings Conference on interorganizational systems in the global environment, Bled, Slovenia, September, 1992.

11

# Cross-organizational Workflow Management

*General approaches and their suitability for engineering processes*

Ottokar Kulendik[1], Kurt Rothermel[1], Reiner Siebert[2]
*[1] University of Stuttgart, Institute of Parallel and Distributed High-Performance Systems, Stuttgart, Germany*
*2 DaimlerChrysler Research & Technology, Lab. IT für Engineering, Ulm, Germany*

**Abstract:** Cross-organizational workflow management deals with the need for transparent and controlled process automation across organizational boundaries. Cooperation between manufacturers and suppliers in the field of engineering requires coupling of parallel workflows of autonomous organization units. So far, several approaches with different architectures exist but they address this field of application differently. This paper presents some requirements of cross-organizational workflow management in the engineering domain by using an application scenario. Existing research approaches are classified distinguishing used specification schemata and expressiveness concerning cross-workflow dependencies. We describe a new approach in a class that matches the presented requirements.

## 1. INTRODUCTION

The situation on today's markets forces companies to reposition themselves, to rethink their core competencies, and to cooperate with each other. Increasing availability of e-business in the economic landscape is basis for automation of business processes. For established cooperation relations, permanent cost pressure increases the need for a stronger integration and even standardization of business processes, e.g. between manufacturers and suppliers. Common base for the cooperation support can be the coupling of business processes realized as workflows. This problem arises specifically where manufacturers and suppliers cooperatively develop vehicles. To achieve control over and changeability of cross-organizational development processes, they can be supported using workflow management. Important goals for the support of these engineering processes are the following ones.

**Support for activity-specific participation and divided development responsibility.** On the one hand, suppliers in the engineering domain may participate in specific activities of manufacturers' processes. On the other hand, as we will show below with the help of a scenario, in general suppliers may have own workflows that run parallel to manufacturers' ones. There may be multiple dependencies in between such workflows. In such cases, suppliers, like manufacturers, participate in an enormous part of a development process and perform iterations of constructive change and digital and physical validation of CAD models. They coordinate the development and are accountable for developed parts and modules in that they fulfil the requirements. Of course, due to complex dependencies between construction and validation departments in today's simultaneous engineering processes, this case is also relevant for in-house processes in large companies where individual development departments have their own processes and may even be geographically distributed. Cross-organizational workflow management should support divided development responsibility.

**Integration of existing workflows and workflow management systems.** Manufacturers and suppliers have their own information systems and business processes. So, instead of centralized processing and prescription of systems and processes, their integration should be achieved to maintain the autonomy of different organizations concerning information and business process management. Because of this, existing workflows and heterogeneous workflow management systems have to be integrated into cross-organizational workflows. It cannot be assumed that one workflow system prevails against others due to the increasing diversity of these systems (cf.[1]). Workflow systems in operation are more and more integrated into special purpose and application systems like e.g. enterprise resource planning, engineering data management, or enterprise application integration. A definition of new workflows should not be enforced where possible to reduce set-up effort.

**Support for engineering processes.** While parts of development processes are well-structured and can be planned and defined a priori, as we will see in the scenario below, process support for collaborative engineering processes has to support unstructured parts of work by allowing dynamic decisions concerning activity sequence and refinement, long-running activities and unstructured process parts as well as a coarse-grained specification[2]. These requirements are reflected differently by specific systems developed in research[2,3] or systems in operation like PDM systems with limited workflow support.

How should an approach for cross-organizational workflow management in this environment look like? To date, several research approaches for cross-organizational workflow management have been developed. Using a scenario from the engineering domain, we explore some requirements for an approach in this field of application. We describe a reference model and use it to classify existing approaches along the identified requirements. We then describe our own approach chosen in a class which matches the requirements best. After discussing related work, we conclude and give an outlook on future work.

# 2. REQUIREMENTS

The following scenario is a simplified illustration of a part of a development process for a vehicle's body. Background is a cooperation project with an engineering supplier that bears responsibility for a module like the side door. Figure 1 shows an early phase of the entire development process where only construction and simulation departments are involved on both sides. Depicted is a high-level view on activities visible to both manufacturer and supplier that are realized by detailed internal workflows.

## 2.1 Scenario

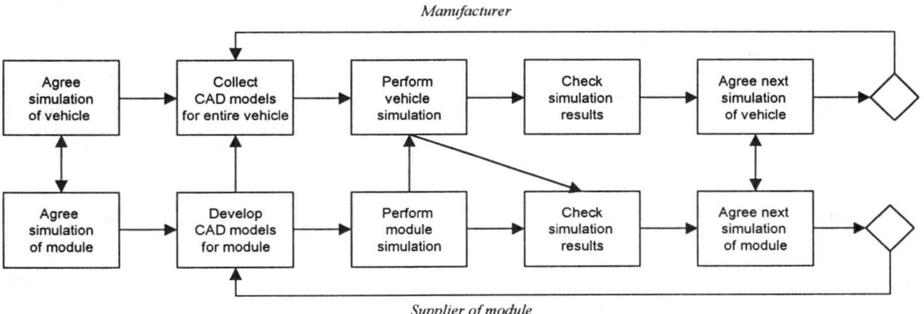


*Figure 1.* Scenario

The workflow is triggered at the beginning of a new development phase where some changes resulting from feedback of preceding phases have to be elaborated and the digital vehicle should fulfil some safety and quality requirement specifications that are digitally verified. At first, project leaders of development of both manufacturer and supplier come to an agreement concerning deadlines for the minor development phases up to a milestone at the end of the major development phase. In the scenario shown, these are deadlines for preparing a new version of CAD models of the module and for getting back simulation results. The supplier develops the CAD models agreed upon and transfers them to the manufacturer. Then, the supplier performs a module simulation, e.g. a dent simulation. The manufacturer receives the results and starts a simulation of the entire vehicle using the same CAD models, e.g. for a crash simulation. After simulation, results are transferred to the supplier. Meanwhile, the project leaders of development of both supplier and manufacturer evaluate results of the simulation. If a problem in one or both simulation occurs, optimisations and another iteration before the end of this development phase are necessary and are again agreed by both project leaders of development.

## 2.2 Requirements

Bearing this scenario in mind, we explore some requirements for cross-organizational workflow management.

**Coupling of parallel workflows with multiple cross-organizational workflow dependencies.** As shown in the scenario, the supplier has an own workflow that runs parallel to the manufacturer's one. In contrast to a call of a remote subworkflow with dependencies only during calling and getting back results, there are multiple control and data flow dependencies in between the workflows. This situation is typical for scenarios with divided responsibility for development because of the need for coordination and tight cooperation along aggregation or neighbourhood relationships of parts, modules and entire body of the vehicle.

**Common view on cross-organizational workflows for participating organizations.** Especially when responsibility for product development is divided, manufacturers need a view on suppliers' planned or running workflows, organizational structure, and data; and so do suppliers. Specifically, concerning aspects of function, information, and behaviour, specification information with respect to planned course of activities and data is important; as well as monitoring information like state of the process, etc. Regarding organizational aspects, contact persons or performers of planned, running, or past activities are important, for instance to cope with information demand concerning simulation results. This process transparency is needed due to a high degree of dependency between involved processes. It increases level of knowledge of managing as well as of operative process participants. It also achieves a better identification with the entire process and thereby finally enhances process quality. To cope with the obvious need of privacy and abstraction when integrating internal workflows, a specific view onto internal workflows is desirable to make them visible externally for specifying how workflows should be coupled and for monitoring by other organizations.

**Adaptations of cross-organizational and internal workflows.** After the configuration of cross-organizational workflows those workflows as well as workflows of manufacturers or suppliers have to be adapted to new project scopes and responsibilities, or to actual demands concerning safety, quality or innovation. This can result in the need for additional activities, e.g. added checks or quality assurance examinations. To keep change effort low, changes of cross-organizational workflows should not result in changes of internal workflows of organizations, and vice versa.

**Complex cross-organizational control and data flow dependencies.** As with intra-organizational workflows, control and data flow dependencies should be able to be restricted to certain conditions. For example, it is aspired that several control flows can be synchronized, e.g. using an AND-join or an OR-join[4], if the manufacturer has to wait for the completion of another module's CAD models by another supplier. To support overlapping activities like e.g. the agreement shown in the scenario, more complex inter-activity dependencies than just successor-relationships are desired. Furthermore, in the engineering domain, specification of dependencies between workflows with unstructured parts should be supported. For instance, if two developers of neighboured parts should level out their models, a sequence of their activities may not be defined a priori, but the existence of predefined intermediate states of workflow data.

# 3. GENERAL APPROACHES

In order to be able to differentiate between approaches we describe a reference model in the following that helps to derive a classification system for approaches. The model which we derive reflects the need for providing an external representation of internal workflows which was mentioned in the second requirement above. We then use the model to distinguish two criteria of existing approaches: in what kind of schema dependencies between the workflows are specified (direct/indirect coupling), and the expressiveness of the model for specifying dependencies between workflows (subworkflow/multiple dependencies).

## 3.1 Reference architecture

To describe and to compare different approaches for cross-organizational workflow management, we look at how these workflows are specified. Following the terminology of [5], in the following workflow schema model denotes an abstract idea of a workflow. An approach for cross-organizational workflow management may choose to specify a workflow schema model using a workflow schema, that means a workflow of its own. A schema is a specification in a formal textual or graphical language. It may be structured into different sub-schemata regarding the different workflow aspects of function (activities performed), information (use and flow of workflow data), behaviour (sequence of activities), organization (roles that perform activities), and operation (tools for performing activities). The reference architecture consists of the three entities: high-level workflow schema model, external workflow schema model, and internal workflow schema model (cf. figure 2). After describing these entities, we can distinguish between approach classes regarding how the high-level workflow schema model is specified, and how dependencies between workflows are expressed. We compare the resulting classes of approaches concerning the requirements.

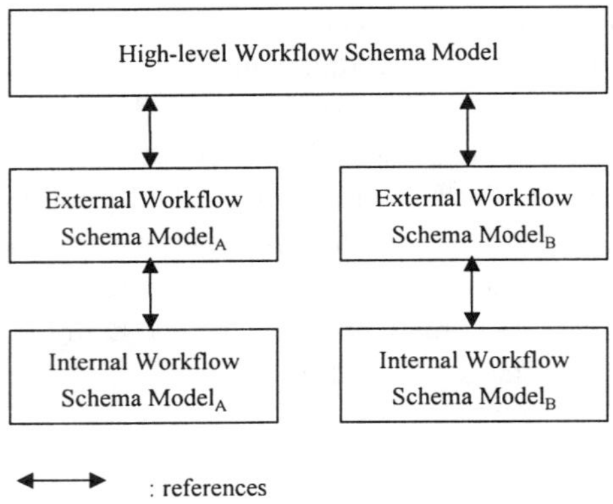


*Figure 2.* Reference model

*The high-level workflow schema model* comprises those parts of a cross-organizational workflow in which several organizations take part. Specifically, it describes which organizations take part in which workflows. Therefore, it references corresponding external workflow schema models of each organization.

*The external workflow schema model* describes a workflow part of a high-level workflow which belongs to an organization. It contains externally visible aspects of a workflow and so it supports encapsulation for privacy and abstraction purpose. This schema model is independent of any concrete participation in a cross-organizational workflow.

*The internal workflow schema model* describes an internal workflow of an organization. It consists of the full workflow specification needed for execution, e.g. aspects of function, information, behaviour, organization, and operation. Because it contains confidential details of the organization, e.g. the workflow structure and data, and unnecessary details, the internal model is just visible to the own organization. The internal workflow schema model is specified by an internal workflow schema that is managed by an internal workflow management system. The internal workflow management systems of different organizations may be heterogeneous.

In contrast to the internal workflow schema model, existing approaches do not always specify the other both schema models by workflow schemata. However, an external workflow schema model is at least conceptually separated from an internal schema model. This schema can be used to mask heterogeneous workflows and workflow systems to the high-level workflow, therefore some approaches specify further schemata in order to map between external and internal schemata or to integrate external into high-level schemata. A detailed discussion of these schemata and distributed implementation of logical components lies beyond the scope of this paper.

In the following, we first use the specification of the high-level workflow schema model as characteristic criterion for an approach's architecture. We mainly distinguish between two general approach classes, direct and indirect coupling, and some specific variants. Independent of this difference, we examine as a further criterion how dependencies between workflows of different organizations are specified.

## 3.2 Direct coupling vs. indirect coupling

With respect to how a high-level workflow schema model is specified externally or inside internal workflow schemata, we can distinguish between direct and indirect coupling.

*Direct coupling* integrates existing workflow management systems without using an additional schema for the high-level schema model (cf. figure 3). Using this approach, an organization extends its internal workflow schema by importing an external workflow schema of another organization. So, dependencies between workflow parts of different organizations are specified inside internal workflow schemata, and a high-level workflow schema model is specified by these internal and external workflow schemata. During execution time, internal workflow management systems instantiate internal workflow schemata and manage the workflow instances. In case of control or data flow dependencies with another workflow they interact with other internal workflow management systems by using an integration layer. The topology of the interaction is according to the dependencies between the corresponding external and internal workflow schemata. Examples are ACEFlow[6], CrossFlow[7], Mokassin[8], and WAGS[9].

*Direct coupling with high-level workflow schema* is a hybrid form of direct and indirect coupling concerning specification schemata and execution architecture: during specification time, a high-level workflow schema is specified, during execution time the architecture corresponds to direct coupling. After specification, the high-level schema is divided into organization specific external and internal schemata. Each organization may implement generated external schemata respectively extend or refine generated internal schemata that are then executed by their internal workflow management systems. To allow for that, high-level workflow schemata are often structured by using special concepts that support an easy division of the high-level schema. Interworkflow[10] supports this approach. It provides additional support for top-down modelling of cross-organizational workflows. In the following, we consider direct coupling with high-level workflow schema as a special case of direct coupling because both classes of approaches have basically the same schemata during execution time.

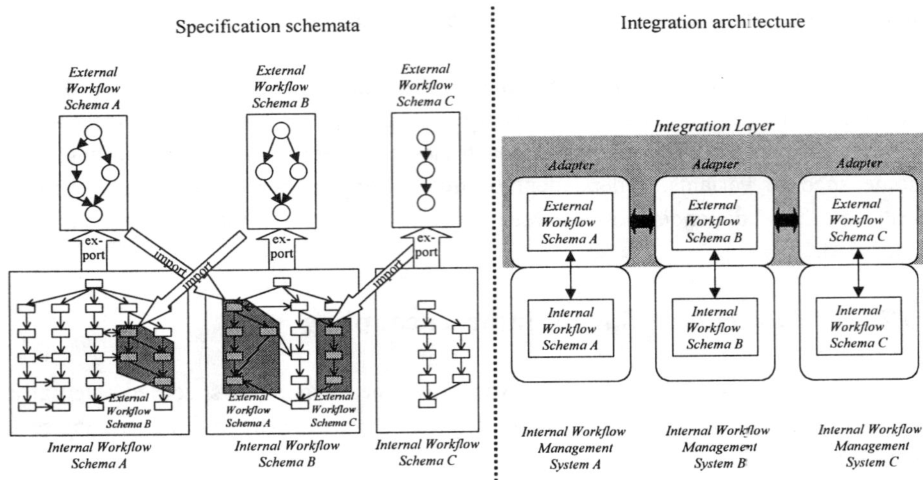


*Figure 3.* Direct coupling

*Indirect coupling* uses an additional high-level workflow schema for specifying a cross-organizational workflow. Depending on whether a high-level workflow schema is managed by a centralized or a decentralized system, we can distinguish between two variants of indirect coupling.

*Centralized indirect coupling* aims to support a centrally coordinated cooperation, where a high-level workflow schema model is specified and executed in an additional central workflow system. WISE[11], CMI[12], and eFlow[13] belong to this class. In this kind of approach a high-level workflow schema model is specified in a high-level workflow schema. The high-level workflow schema is managed by a high-level workflow management system, and instances of it are executed there. This system is a special workflow management system for managing cross-organizational workflows.

For specification purpose the high-level workflow management system may offer specific concepts. So, a high-level workflow schema contains references to external workflow schemata that are involved in the cross-organizational process and specifies control and data flow dependencies between them. Since it is a workflow management system on its own, it can contain own activities that are performed by members of the organization unit that operates it. The schema may further contain coupling-specific control flow constructs as multiple calls of one subworkflow, dynamic binding and some more; or it may use other shared components like an organization service covering all organizations involved.

During execution the high-level workflow management system centrally manages high-level workflow instances. It interacts with internal workflow management systems to ensure dependencies between high-level workflow parts. The interaction is hierarchical, i.e. systems of the participants just interact with the high-level system and not directly with each other. The existing internal workflow management systems are integrated with the high-level system using adapters located in the high-level system or in the internal system. The interaction is realized using one or several middleware systems.

*Decentralized indirect coupling* manages high-level workflow schemata by using a decentralized system that consists of high-level components which belong to each participating organization (cf. figure 4). Control and data flow dependencies are specified in a specific high-level dependency schema between external workflow schemata. So, in contrast to centralized indirect coupling, the high-level workflow schema may not contain own activities that are not defined inside one of the external workflow schemata of participating organizations. During runtime, dependencies are realized by interactions between high-level components that together form one logical high-level workflow management system, while high-level workflow state inquiries result in polling of high-level components. Adapters integrate existing internal workflow management systems with high-level components. Examples are Process Fractals[14], referential Petri-nets[15], MariFlow[16], and VEC[17].

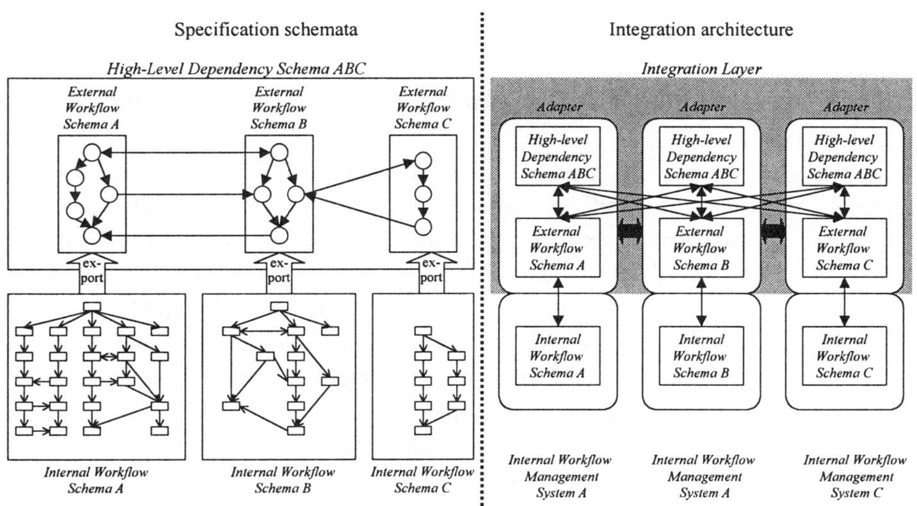


*Figure 4.* Decentralized indirect coupling

**Comparison to relevant requirements.** Indirect coupling can realize a common view using its additional high-level schemata. Direct coupling fails to support this common view well because high-level workflow schemata are specified by internal workflow schemata and are managed by internal workflow management systems that are private to organizations and should not be accessible by other organizations. In addition, a common view of a high-level workflow only using external workflow schemata as available in indirect coupling can be used simultaneously by all participating organizations because no internal workflow schema is involved.

Since indirect coupling uses an own schema to specify dependencies between external workflow schemata, it is much better in supporting adaptations of high-level workflows and internal workflows. In contrast to that, direct coupling requires a change of an internal workflow schema if a different external workflow schema has to be used, e.g. when a different organization participates.

For similar reason, indirect coupling allows specification of complex dependencies more easily than direct coupling. Because dependencies can be specified in own schemata that can be designed independent from underlying internal workflow management systems' concepts, specific dependency concepts for cross-organizational workflow management can be added more easily in these approaches as functionality can be added outside of existing systems. Though, concrete extensions may require extensions of internal systems as well and therefore their integration into specific systems have to be considered in detail. Note that despite of these issues, direct coupling has the advantage of allowing reuse of tools for monitoring of a high-level workflow easier than indirect coupling. However, this is a characteristic we do not require.

## 3.3 Subworkflow dependencies vs. multiple dependencies

Approaches of direct as well as of indirect coupling differ concerning how dependencies between workflows can be specified. Several approaches support *subworkflow dependencies* between two workflows [6,11,16,17]. This corresponds to outsourcing of an activity. If workflow WA has a subworkflow dependency to workflow WB, WA transfers control and data on start of WB, WB is performed, and WA gets back control and result data after completion of WB. An external workflow schema then just specifies a signature of WB for coupling. Interface 4 defined by the WfMC[18] that describes an interoperability interface for workflow management systems is usable for realizing subworkflow dependencies.

Other approaches [7-10,12-15] use more complex external workflow schemata to allow for *multiple dependencies between workflows*. These approaches describe not just input and output parameters but intermediate states and data of workflows as well. Control flow dependencies can be made conditional on these intermediate states. Input data can be communicated to a workflow which already started, output data like intermediate results can be obtained before ending. Intermediary states and their association with needed input data or output data are often specified by using events that signal state changes.

**Comparison to relevant requirements.** As we explained in the section on requirements, we need to support multiple dependencies between workflows of autonomous organizations. While it is in principle possible to divide workflow dependencies into several subworkflow dependencies, this would not be sufficient to cope with these requirements because it would lead to several subworkflows controlled by a calling workflow. This would not allow a called organization unit to define a workflow continuously and autonomously. Furthermore, "call-back" subworkflows and complex call sequences would be needed to return intermediate results to a calling workflow.

## 4. A SPECIFIC APPROACH

Our comparison between classification criteria and identified requirements suggests that an approach of indirect coupling with multiple dependencies suits our application domain best. The evaluation considered the potential of each detected class of approaches rather than characteristics of concrete instances of approaches. Especially in order to realize the requirements of providing a common view and supporting complex cross-organizational dependencies, we use expressive external workflow schemata that specify the information needed for coupling as well as for monitoring, and different types of dependency specifications.

Following the general approach of decentralized indirect coupling, we propose the following architectural model (see figure 5). From bottom to top: the internal workflow layer contains internally defined and managed workflow schemata. The external workflow layer contains external workflow schemata used for coupling and for monitoring. The layer also can specify a mapping between internal and external workflow schema, which is not further described in the scope of this paper. The linkage specification describes how workflow dependencies are bound to the external workflow schema. The workflow dependency layer specifies with a configuration schema control and data flow dependencies of the workflows that together form a high-level workflow. In addition to the mentioned schemata, the layers contain the corresponding instances as well.

*The external workflow schema* describes externally visible aspects of function, information, behaviour, and organization. An operational aspect is not described. The functional aspect describes activities performed by the workflow and input and output relations to data objects of the informational aspect. The informational aspect describes workflow-relevant data, i.e. control data objects and production data objects. Workflow data objects are described by name, type, and location. Analogously, the organizational aspect is realized by reference to a (potentially external) organization service. In addition to roles and persons that perform activities, contact persons for an activity are referenced. For all aspects, schema as well as instance information is available, e.g. the organizational aspects allow us to retrieve which person performed a certain activity, and so on.

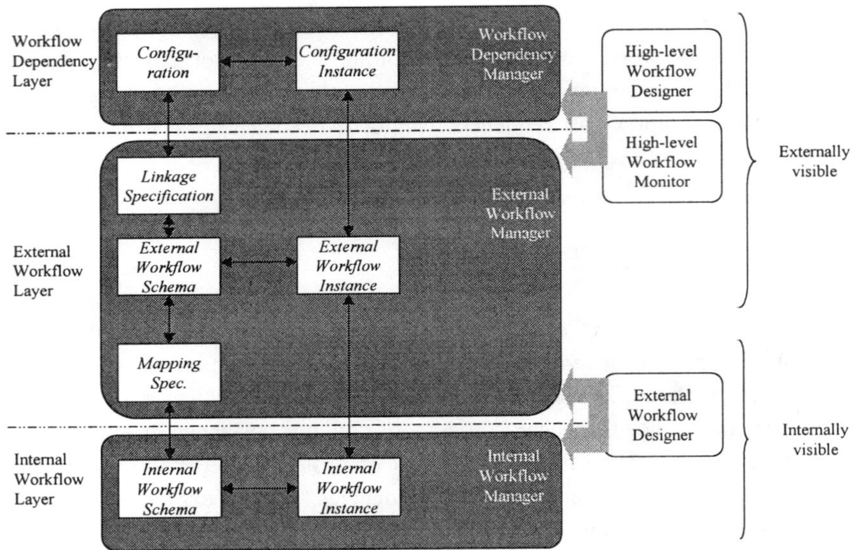


*Figure 4.* Proposed solution approach

The dependencies between the participating organizations are defined using a common configuration schema that specifies the dependencies, dependency endpoints that are assigned inside the external workflow schema, and the linkage specification between those schemata. In the *linkage specificatio*n, dependencies are bound to dependency endpoints. For example, a simple data flow dependency is bound to a data flow exit of a sending organization's workflow and a data flow entry of a receiving organization's workflow. This allows for a decentralized and autonomous specification: an organization can specify on its own which activities consume the output of an agreed data flow dependency, and it can change this specification, e.g. if a newly inserted activity should get the output data instead.

*Dependencies* are multiple relations that can be bound to dependency endpoints, i.e. entries and exits. Control flow dependencies describe constraints concerning execution behaviour of workflows, activities, or control constructs. A control flow dependency is connected to one or more control exits and one entry, and may contain a condition. A condition specifies in terms of the exits' states in which case the entry is activated, e.g. to model a control flow join using a logical AND. Data flow dependencies model the transfer of data between different workflows. A data flow dependency connects a data exit to a data entry. It is evaluated in case of a data state change of an exit. Data flow dependencies specify one or more assignments between data content items of data exits and data content items of data entries. Dependencies may further be associated with conditions which describe in what case data is transferred.

*Dependency endpoints* are part of the external workflow schema. They specify endpoints of the workflow, i.e. entries and exits of control and data flow. Sources for control and data dependency points specified in the external workflow schema may be control construct execution states or workflow data states, or application-specific events. Control flow entries and exits can be assigned to specific activity and control construct execution states, e.g. started or finished, with the semantics that the activity or control construct state can be triggered respectively delayed by a control flow dependency. Data flow entries are associated with activity input data or workflow input data states, data flow exits can be associated to activity output data or states of workflow output data. If a structure of an external workflow schema is not fully specified due to an unstructured or previously unforeseen course of activities, changes of workflow data may be used as control flow exits. In addition, application-specific input and output events may be used as control or data flow entries and exits. They can be assigned to parts of an external workflow schema later. Together, this allows us to model dependencies even where a course of activities is not known during dependency modelling time, but needed data input or produced output or some intermediate events are known in advance.

## 5. DISCUSSION OF RELATED WORK

As described in the section on classification, several approaches focus on subworkflow dependencies between cross-organizational workflows. Some workflow approaches focus on distribution, availability, and heterogeneity of workflows. Work dealing with similar issues as this paper engages in is Process Fractals, Mokassin, CMI, and referential Petri-nets.

Process Fractals[14] follow decentralized indirect coupling. In that approach, the external workflow schema is divided into an event-based interface used for coupling and a specific representation used for monitoring. Cross-organizational control flow is modelled by using binding input events of one interface to output events of another and vice versa. Complex cross-workflow dependencies as e.g. AND-joins are not supported. Data flow is bound to these control flow transitions and is realized by moving or copying documents that have a commonly known type. The organizational aspect concentrates on large-scale aspects like dependencies between organizations; monitoring of small-scale organizational information is not aimed at.

Mokassin[8] supports direct coupling with multiple dependencies using a decentralized agent-based infrastructure. Here, specification does not focus on separating internal and external representation but on separating interface and implementation of a workflow. With this, the approach does not aim on supporting organizational information for monitoring purpose or a separated external view on an internal workflow. An interface representation may contain a state graph specifying events that an implementation generates. Complex control and data flow dependencies are supported and can be added by a modeller.

CMI[12] supports centralized indirect coupling using a high-level workflow schema in which workflows of different organizations are imported as specific activities. The external workflow schema contains a state chart where possible interactions with the service are specified by methods that can either be called on such external workflows. Specific concepts of the high-level workflow management system are e.g. activities that can perform multiple calls on external workflows.

Referential Petri-nets[15] focus on Petri-net based modelling of cross-organizational workflows. Inheritance concepts between external and internal workflow schemata are developed, to support for controlled compatible extensions.

# 6. SUMMARY AND OUTLOOK

Cross-organizational workflow management for cooperation in the field of engineering has to support situations characterized by activity-specific participation and divided responsibility of development, integration of existing workflows and their management systems, and unstructured process parts. As we explained by using the scenario, for the support of cross-organizational engineering process we require: 1) Coupling of parallel workflows with multiple dependencies, 2) Common view on cross-organizational workflows for participating organizations, 3) Adaptations of cross-organizational and internal workflows, and 4) Complex control and data flow dependency specifications.

To examine existing approaches, we classified them along used specification schemata, complexity of the cross-organizational dependencies, and execution architectures. Some approaches are not that suitable to support adaptations of cross-organizational and internal workflows because they require change of internal workflows when cross-organizational workflows change; or participating organizations do not have a common view on cross-organizational workflows. Other approaches have just a simple subworkflow-based dependency model that makes it difficult to couple parallel workflows.

The favoured architectural class couples existing workflow management systems directly but specifies cross-organizational workflow dependencies in a specific specification and execution layer. The approach we have proposed showed how the selected architectural class can fulfil the identified requirements by using an expressive external workflow representation. Furthermore, it supported complex control and data flow dependencies across organizations. To avoid changes of the dependency schema, these dependencies can be linked to the workflows decentralized and autonomously by each participating organization.

Right now, we are detailing the model and will refine the architectural specification. To assure integration with existing systems, we are going to examine those systems to derive at a generic workflow meta schema and architecture. This provides the base for developing a detailed integration approach. In addition, issues like the support for change of schema and compatibility, and specific security requirements will further be evaluated.

# 7. REFERENCES

[1] Bussler C. Enterprise-wide workflow management. IEEE Concurrency 1999; 3:32-43.

[2] Reinert J., Ritter N. Applying ECA-Rules in DB-based Design Environments. Proceedings of the GI-Fachtagung CAD'98; 1998 Mar 5 - 6; Darmstadt. Informatik Xpress 9. Bonn: Gesellschaft für Informatik [u.a.], 1998.

[3] Beuter T., Schneider P., Dadam P., The WEP Model: Adaptive Workflow-Management for Engineering Processes. Proceedings of the European Concurrent Engineering Conference (ECEC'98); Erlangen-Nürnberg, 1998 Apr 26 – 29. Society for Computer Simulation; 1998.

[4] Workflow Management Coalition. Terminology & Glossary. WFMC-TC-1011, 3.0, 1999. http://www.wfmc.org/.

[5] Jablonski S., Böhm M., Schulze W. (edts.) Workflow-Management: Entwicklung von Anwendungen und Systemen. Heidelberg: dpunkt-Verlag, 1997.

[6] Stricker C., Riboni S., Kradolfer M., Taylor J. Market-based Workflow Management for Supply Chains of Services. Proceedings of the 33rd Hawaii International Conference on System Sciences (HICSS-33); Maui, Hawaii; 2000 Jan 4 – 7. IEEE Computer Society Press, 2000.

[7] Hoffner Y., Ludwig H., Gülcü C., Grefen P. Architecture for Cross-Organisational Business Processes. Proceedings of the Second International Workshop on Advanced Issues of E-Commerce and Web-Based Information Systems (WECWIS2000); 2000 Jun 8 - 9; Milpitas. IEEE Computer Society, 2000.

[8] Gronemann B., Joeris G., Scheil S., Steinfort M., Wache H. Supporting Cross-Organizational Engineering Processes by Distributed Collaborative Workflow Management - The MOKASSIN Approach. Proceedings of the 2nd Symposium on Concurrent Multidisciplinary Engineering (CME'99) / 3rd International Conference on Global Engineering Networking (GEN'99); 1999 Sep 14 - 15; Bremen. Bremen: Hochschule Bremen, Institut of Aerospace-Technology - Reports, 1999.

[9] Riempp G., Nastansky L. From islands to flexible business process networks – enabling the interaction of distributed workflow management systems. Proceedings of the 5th European Conference on Information Systems, Vol. 1; 1997 Jun 19 - 21; University College Cork, Cork, Ireland. Cork: Cork Publ. Ltd, 1997.

[10] Hiramatsu K., Okada K.-I., Matsushita Y., Hayami H. Interworkflow System: Coordination of Each Workflow System among Multiple Organizations. Proceedings of the 3rd IFCIS International Conference on Cooperative Information Systems (CoopIS'98); 1998 August 20 - 22; New York City. IEEE Computer Society Press, 1998.

[11] Lazcano A., Alonso G., Schuldt H., Schuler C. The WISE approach to Electronic Commerce. International Journal of Computer Systems Science & Engineering, 2000; 5:343-355.

[12] Schuster H., Baker D., Cichocki A., Georgakopoulos D., Rusinkiewicz M. The Collaboration Management Infrastructure. Proceedings of the 16th International

Conference on Data Engineering (ICDE'2000); San Diego, USA, 2000 February 29 - March 3. IEEE Computer Society Press, 2000.

[13] Casati, F., Ilnicki, S., Jin, L., Shan, M.-C. An Open, Flexible, and Configurable System for E-Service Composition. Tech. report, HP Laboratories Palo Alto, HPL-2000-41, 2000.

[14] Lindert F. Modelling inter-organizational processes with process model fragments. Proceedings of the GI-Workshop Enterprise-wide and Cross-enterprise Workflow Management: Concepts, Systems, Applications, Informatik'99; 1999 October 5 - 9, Paderborn. Ulm: Universität Ulm, Ulmer Informatik-Berichte, 1999.

[15] Van der Aalst W.M.P, Moldt D., Wienberg F. Enacting Interorganizational Workflows using Nets in Nets. Proceedings of the 1999 Workflow Management Conference; 1999, November, 9; Münster: University of Münster, 1999.

[16] Dogac A., Beeri C., Tumer A., Ezbiderli M., Tatbul N., Icdem C., Erus G., Cetinkaya O., Hamali N. MariFlow: A Workflow Management System for Maritime Industry. In: Guedes Soares, C., Brodda, J. (edts.): Application of Information Technologies to the Maritime Industries, Edicoes Salamandra, Lisbon, 1999.

[17] Ludwig H., Whittingham K. Virtual Enterprise Coordinator – Agreement-Driven Gateways for Cross-Organisational Workflow Management. Proceedings of the International Joint Conference on Work Activities Coordination and Collaboration (WACC '99); 1999 February 22 - 25; San Francisco. ACM Software Eng. Notes, Volume 24, Number 2, 1999.

[18] Workflow Management Coalition. Interoperability Abstract Specification. WFMC-TC-1012, 1.0, Oct. 1996. http://www.wfmc.org/.

12

# Modelling a Business To Business Intermediation Platform

A. K. Kaltabani, M. A. Lambrou, G. T. Karetsos, M. E. Anagnostou
*National Technical University of Athens, Department of Electrical Engineering and Computer Science, 9, Heroon Polytechneiou Str. 15780 Zografou Athens, Greece, e-mail:{akalt, marial,karetsos,miltos}@telecom.ntua.gr, Tel: +30-1-7721512, Fax:+30-1-22534*

**Abstract:** Our proposition concerns an architectural model of a broker assisted, business to business e-commerce system. The presented brokerage platform is designed against business and technical requirements, within the transformational B2B landscape, which might push forward either centralised or proliferate, symbiotic brokerage models or even render them all invalid. In our paper, we merely elaborate on the design of a modular, scalable and extensible component-based brokerage system for complex, B2B services transactions. To this end, firstly, a particular conceptualization of a complex services transactions lifecycle is presented. Secondly, the functionality of the components comprising the designed brokerage platform is provided. Thirdly, the interactions among the identified components are given for indicative service procedures. The derived architectural model is proposed as applicable to various business domains in the aid of efficient business to business processes alignment.

## 1. INTRODUCTION

In this paper, we present a particular brokerage platform, compliant to business to business models and respective systems implementation requirements, that is considered applicable across a number of diverse business domains. The main proposition of our work is a generic, modular, scalable and reusable architectural model of the envisaged business to business brokerage system, enabled by an informed and comprehensive examination of the requirements and determinants shaping the electronic intermediation and business to business arena, nowadays and in the near future. Examining and questioning dominant trends and propositions concerning brokerage and B2B models and systems, enable the presented results.

Moreover, the specific architectural approach is derived by correspondingly exercising the concepts, methodologies and practices of the service engineering domain.

Our paper is structured as follows: In section 2, we overview the evolution of the electronic intermediation phenomenon and as related in particular with emerging business to business models, services and systems. In section 3, a description of the brokerage functionality is given, whereas, in section 4 the detailed architectural aspects and tasks are addressed, for presenting the static and dynamic view of the brokerage platform. Finally, in section 5, conclusions and discussion on the future work are given.

## 2. THE EVOLUTION OF ELECTRONIC INTERMEDIATION AND BUSINESS TO BUSINESS TRANSACTIONS SYSTEMS

In e-commerce literature, the overall electronic intermediation theme, as well as its relevance and relationship with particular business to business issues, have attracted considerable attention and generated quite comprehensive analyses. Equally important experimentations and commercial exploitation of respective software systems [1, 2] have been, in parallel, achieved.

A number of [3,4,5,6,7] authors report that business transactions, over communication networks and in particular over Web, typically involve all types of intermediaries, not just the traditional wholesalers and retailers, but specialised content providers, search engines, affiliate sites and networks, Internet service providers, the backbone providers, software makers, the advertising networks, and many other entities and players to be generated.

Obviously electronic commerce practices and system capabilities can simultaneously allow suppliers to suppress one or several intermediaries in a distributed network (because of a public shared infrastructure and a direct contact), but it can also provide the opportunity to create new intermediaries in some domains by the provision of added-value in classifying, integrating or managing information and services, among others. Bakos [4,8] hypothesizes that large scale globally distributed intermediaries, formed by industry participants in collaboration with IT companies, will emerge in marketplace. Either by capturing dominant market share in a single industry or by becoming electronic market makers across a number of industries such intermediaries will be capable of sustaining a competitive advantage by securing economies of scale and scope.

First generation electronic brokerage systems, applicable both to business to business and business to customer markets, exploited the value propositions stemming from three formative roles [1,4 ,9]:

1. *aggregation* of buyer demand and seller offers (products, services), thus enabling economies of scale and scope and normalizing the negotiation power of the involved players, within a market.
2. provision of an enhanced market institution and platform of *trust* for the overall services transaction.
3. *facilitation* to the market and involved players by streamlining the information exchange and the coordination of the respective processes. Consequently, perform an efficient *matching* of the complex specifications of the demand and supply side characteristics.

Organisations and e-commerce systems that employed successfully, most often in an integrated manner, the aforementioned aspects and as conditioned by the specificities of the markets (consumer, industrial) within which those organisations operate, represent the early phase of the e-brokerage models. It is that brokerage model that also critically shaped the evolution of the business to business landscape, in particular. This brokerage model is often quoted and interpreted as the "exchange-like model", gaining insight, in specific, from the financial markets evolution [5, 10]. Currently, we already observe clear trends towards a fragmentation of the offered brokerage services, beyond the above described model, as provided by distinct, complementary or symbiotic second-generation brokerage, business to business models. Such business models, and following up the analysis of Wise et al [**Fehler! Textmarke nicht definiert.**], can be viewed as including:

a) *mega-brokers* that may act as central hubs or intermediation platforms for the execution of most transactions and for buyer – supplier communication and coordination, resembling the classical e-broker.
b) *specialist originators* that automate, in particular, the buyer decision making process, which is especially vital for complex products and services, and subsequently channel the transactions to the brokerage platform for execution.
*c)* *solution providers* can operate separately from open hubs by embedding the product sale into a suite of valuable and thus indispensable services.
*d)* *sell side asset brokers* that operate in a rough compliance with a peer to peer paradigm, in which suppliers can trade among themselves, some times after initial transactions with buyers are made on the central hubs or mega brokers.

It is in this very same context, however, that the notion of "napsterization of business to business transactions" appears to considerably challenge the current evolution path, as above described. Following the McAfee argument [9], if companies can complete complex transactions among themselves through peer-to-peer networks and interoperable complex business processes software, the need for centralized brokerage systems decreases dramatically.

Against this background, we subsequently present a particular business to business brokerage platform, and we argue that, although it encapsulates the *centralized-broker* or *mega broker* design principles, it is extensible to a number of the evolutionary, proliferate brokerage models such as the *solution provider* or the *sell side asset broker* paradigms. Its potential accommodation to a dominant peer to peer, business to business transaction landscape will be subject to further study.

## 3. DESCRIPTION OF THE BROKER ASSISTED E-COMMERCE TRANSACTIONS SYSTEM

In this section we present an outline of the proposed brokerage platform, driven by the specific requirements of the involved actors determining its conception, use and operation. This is primarily achieved by envisioning the construction of a generic, reusable and scalable business-to-business (B2B) brokerage framework, and by a conceptualization of the complex service transaction lifecycle and its particular functional decomposition.

In the proposed complex services transactions model we consider three basic domains that is the User Domain, the Service Provider Domain and the Broker Domain, which actually represents the specific brokerage platform domain. The particular interactions that take place among these three domains mirror our understanding and approach to a complex e-commerce service transactions lifecycle and its refined phases. In more detail we design the following phases:

- The request formulation and solutions pre-processing
- The solutions identification and bilateral negotiation
- The solutions evaluation
- The transaction execution and payment

Apart from the functionality necessary for executing the above phases' processes, in the broker domain, the complex knowledge representation is handled by means of Ontology technology [11] to efficiently represent and manipulate the static and dynamic aspects of complex services semantics in different business applications. The presented overall design approach caters for a tripartite and synergistic solution building and negotiation protocol, as is illustrated in the following Figure .

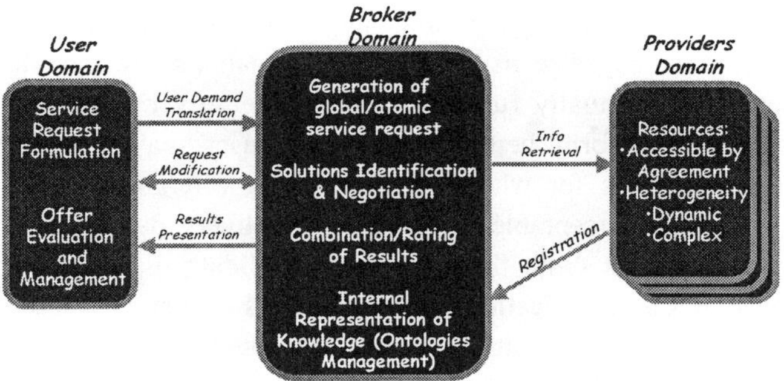


Figure 1: The Brokerage system design approach

The proposed system [12] will be able to handle complex services composed by a set of simple services. A simple or atomic service is defined as to be provided as a whole by an external, affiliated provider, so the system handles to a certain extent the internal complexity (if any) of that service, thus, allowing for a strong provider perspective. The notion of a complex service is also introduced so as to ensure that the specific brokerage platform can manipulate a wide range of bundled services, and thus, at the same time, complying with a customer-centric approach. In the sequel, the functionality of the complex services transaction e-commerce system is described.

After a customer has successfully accessed the system, he/she may construct requests by browsing a hierarchical menu of provided services, in specific business domain(s). The menu presented to a given user is built dynamically and is personalized based on the knowledge of the user's profile and the history of his previous requests. The platform interactively guides the user in the definition of the desired complex service. The knowledge required to dynamically formulate a complex service request that is compliant with the system is provided by means of the Ontology technology capabilities supported by the platform. Upon the user request validation by the system and the confirmation by the user, the system will invoke its internal brokering functionality in order to find an acceptable solution. In the case that several offers are found, the system proceeds with their evaluation, based on the customer preferences indicated in his profile, or other criteria.

When the solution identification phase is completed, the system will present a solution to the customer. The solution may be presented in several ways depending on the customer preferences. The platform is designed so as to support the co-operation with and servicing to three generic classes of providers that are currently met and even anticipated to operate in the e-commerce arena, in the near future. In specific, a brokerage system capabilities as the one described in this paper, can be exploited by service providers that allow for an extensive and online access to the brokered resources (affiliate service providers), and to the ones that allow for a limited access and consequently limited automation in service delivery (on-line service providers). It may also be used, in a minimalist sense though, by services providers that do not actually run any e-commerce server. The customer of the described brokerage platform, hereafter denoted as user, may redefine the attribute values of simple services for which no satisfactory offers have been found, e.g. increase the maximum acceptable price, modify delivery dates, or other terms of service provision. In this case, the system will validate the updated request and perform a new solution identification process, until a satisfactory solution is found.

Once the proposed solution has been accepted, a corresponding service reservation takes place and the system proceeds with the subsequent phase that is the transaction execution and payment phase. In this later phase, the platform performs the necessary interactions with the service provider domains in order to actually proceed with e-commerce services provision and delivery, which were during the previous phases successfully brokered and reserved. The interactions taking place in this later phase comply with the all-or-nothingness principle that is the complete service reservation will be delivered by the appropriate provider.

## 3.1 Federation aspects of a brokerage system

One aspect that needs to be addressed when designing a brokerage system is its capability to federate with other such systems specialized in similar, complementary, or ancillary business domains. This is important for the system's scalability whenever a requirement for expansion either in geographical or in business terms emerges. Scalability is also critical when we come to the system's robustness and business value, since users can take advantage of Service Providers (SPs) not directly attached to their home broker and thus the probability to satisfy their demands is increased.

The establishment of a federation among brokers poses a number of technical requirements. First and foremost, a federation agreement should exist between any pair of brokers that are willing to cooperate and seamlessly support their attached users. This is achieved through a mutual registration procedure and knowledge exchange. Second, a query redirection and result handling mechanism should exist that takes care of the information exchanges between the home broker and the remote ones. Third, each broker should update its information regarding its federated brokers either after a predefined interval or whenever a major change has occurred in one of each federated brokers.

The system we describe can relatively easily support federation with enhancements in the Ontology Manager's database to care for the federated brokers and the corresponding remote SPs. However, a detailed analysis of the exact federation mechanisms falls out of the scope of this paper, being an issue of our future work in the area of the design of brokerage services.

Finally, it is essential to note that the introduced federation metaphor and its corresponding technical mechanisms are seen as particularly meaningful in the current transformational phase concerning the operation of robust and advantageous brokerage, business to business models, as discussed in section 2. Such a federation policy might apply to the presented system, in its capacity either as a mega broker cooperating with a broker of a similar scope, in the same or a complementary business domain, or as a proliferate brokerage model in synergy with its complementary ones.

# 4. ARCHITECTURAL MODEL OF THE BUSINESS TO BUSINESS BROKERAGE SYSTEM

In the following, we present the design of the proposed brokerage system architecture, as being enabled by the exploitation of the service engineering framework [13,14,15,16,17] concepts, methodologies and practices. More precisely, in the sequel, we elaborate on the tasks and results of the identification of the system architecture components, and the definition of the component interfaces and the component interactions, falling within the service analysis and service design phases of the above framework [13]. To this end, we adopt a two-fold approach. First, in sub-section 4.1, we illustrate the brokerage architecture components, that is a static view of our system, while in sub-section 4.2, we elaborate on these component intercommunications, providing a dynamic view of the system.

## 4.1 Component based system model

In this section, we focus on the description of the functionality of the main components' that our brokerage system comprises [18]. Each one of these components is further analysed in the next paragraphs. As illustrated in Figure , the components that have been identified are the following:

- The *User Manager* component that is the first access point for the user to the brokerage system. It carries out all the managing user oriented activities and collaborates with the Ontology Manager for formulating the service requests.
- The *Provider Manager* component that participates in the solution building and actually keeps information for the service providers themselves and the services they offer.
- The *Solution Builder* component that is responsible for formulating a service solution corresponding to the service request by collaborating with the User Manager, the Provider Manager and the Ontology Manager.

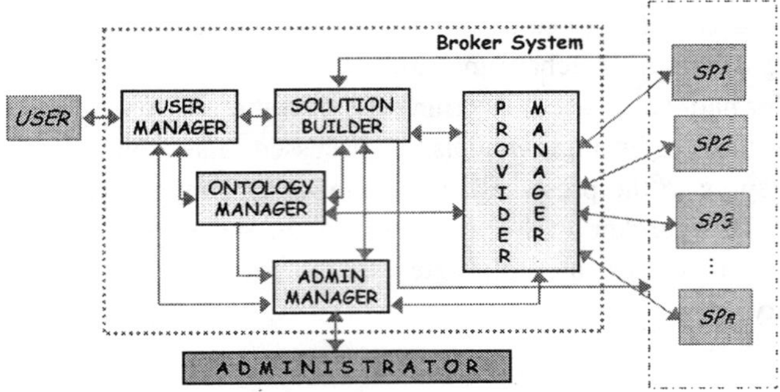


Figure 2: Main view of the system architecture

- The *Ontology Manager* component that handles the interactions of the brokerage system components with the ontologies that model the knowledge of the complex services.
- Finally, the *Administrator Manager* component that is responsible for the control of the overall brokerage system.

Focusing on the User Manager we identify the components that are illustrated in Figure . First of all, an interface abstraction layer that comprises the *User Interface Handler* and the *Graphical Manager* enables the connection of the user to the system and is responsible for handling the information exchanges between the customer and the rest of the components of the system.

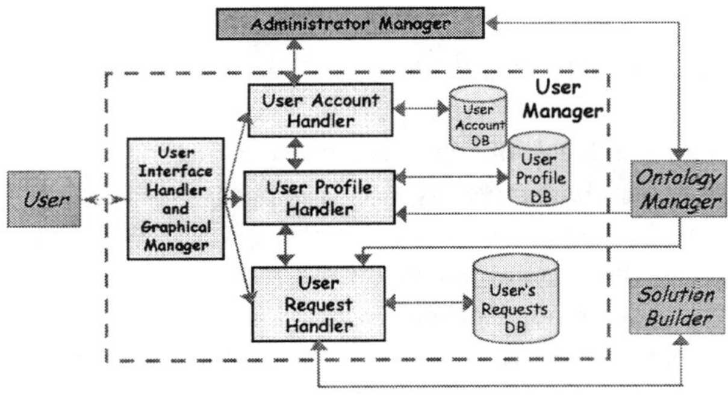


Figure 3: User Manager

The user is able to perform both managing and transaction-related activities through our brokerage system. Regarding the *managing activities*, the customer is able to create, modify or delete his account that consists of a username and a password through the *User Account Handler*. This refers to the users who have a full subscription to the system and take full advantage of it. Other types of users, having various levels of access and use rights to the system, are also foreseen. Moreover, the user profile that keeps not only personal information about the user but also his own preferences and constraints related to the complex services is managed through the *User Profile Handler*. As it is defined in [**Fehler! Textmarke nicht definiert.**], the complex services are described in terms of ontologies, and the User Profile Handler retrieves from them the necessary elements for service provision handling.

On the other hand, the *transaction-related* activities take place when the customer expresses the need for a complex service by means of a suitable request. The aim of the *User Request Handler* is to manage all interactions with the user during and all along the procurement of a complex service. That means to help the user expressing his request as dialoguing with the *Solution Builder* and the *Ontology Manager* as well as modifying the request when no satisfactory solutions are found.

Symmetrically to the User Manager, within the Provider Manager the following components are defined (see Figure). Firstly, as in case of the user side, there is a need for a *Provider Interface Handler* and a *Graphical Manager* that allows each service provider to be connected to the system.

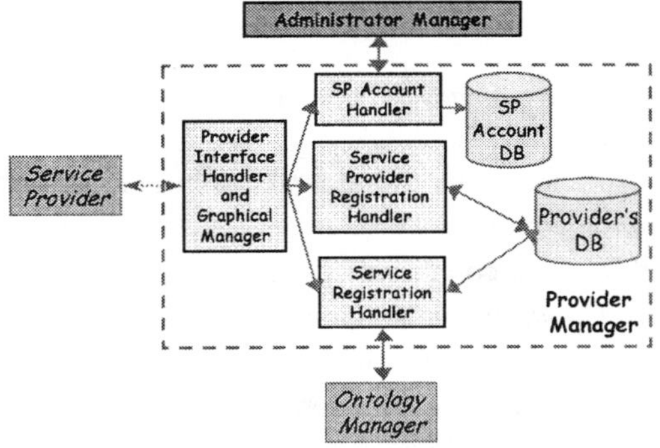


*Figure 4:* Provider Manager

The *SPAccount Handler* is responsible for creating and handling (e.g., modifying, deleting) the service provider account while all the related elements are kept in the proper database. Moreover, all the mandatory parameters related to SP registration data and required by the system (e.g., company data, business sector, type of services the SP can provide) are managed by the *Service Provider Registration Handler.* Finally, the detailed service content registration is handled by the *Service Registration Handler*. In specific, there is a co-operation between the *Ontology Manager* and the *Service Registration Handler* whenever an alternation to the provider offers' takes place. The main concern is the description of the provider offers in a way coherent with the rest of brokerage platform, i.e. relate the service provider's offer to the right element of the ontology.

The Solution Builder represents the core functionality of the overall system. The components that are identified are depicted in Figure . As already mentioned, the complex service consists of atomic services that may be provided by more than one service providers. In this sense, the *Solutions Pre-Processor* component is responsible for the identification of the candidate service providers that may offer solutions according to the user service request. This is achieved with the participation of the Provider Manager form where complete information about the SPs' offers is obtained.

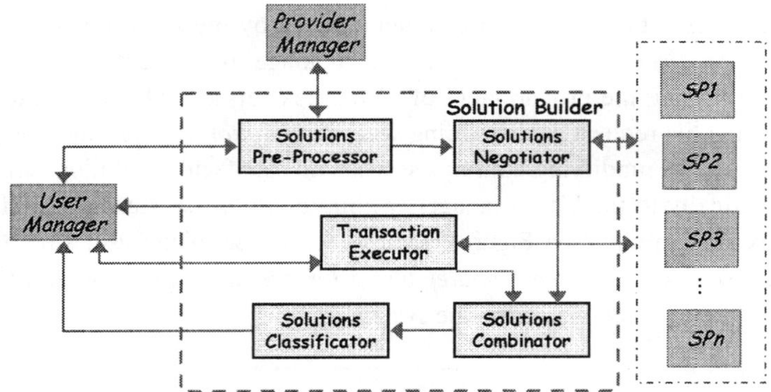


*Figure 5*: Solution Builder

Based on the constraints set by the user, the solution negotiation takes place by the *Solutions Negotiator* component that is designed in order to identify the actual service solutions with a close collaboration with the specific service providers. The role of the *Solution Combinator* component is to group the various solutions according to the system's business criteria. Moreover, the *Solution Classificator* component is responsible for the evaluation of the service offers according to the user defined criteria (e.g., price, delivery date etc). The customer himself is the one that takes the final decision either to accept or to reject the proposed solutions. The user has also the ability to modify his request if the solutions that are presented to him are not still satisfactory. Then, a new negotiation phase takes place. If the user accepts the offer of his complex request, the transaction execution begins which is handled by the *Transaction Executor* component that encapsulates the logic necessary for the transaction confirmation and payment. Specifically, the user reserves the offer and then, the service providers are contacted in order to confirm that the offers are still valid. If one of the reservations fails, the whole transaction is aborted. In the normal case, where all the reservations are kept for the specific user, the payment procedure takes place and when it is successfully completed, the system informs the user that he will be offered, provided the requested service.

## 4.2 Brokerage system component interactions

Following, the dynamic model of the proposed brokerage system is provided by highlighting the main procedures that take place during the complex service transactions lifecycle. We emphasize on the solution building that is described in terms of message sequence charts (MSCs) while the rest of the procedures are described in less detail. Firstly, the User and the Service Provider Registration procedures are explained.

In the first one, the User Domain, the User Manager and the Administrator are involved. A user registration request is completed by means of two main processes: *(a)* The *User Account Management* in which the definition and management of user access rights and system use for all types of users (i.e., registered, identified and anonymous) is carried out and, *(b)* the *User Profile Management* process, in which the definition and management of general properties, personal data and transaction preferences for all types of users is carried out.

Secondly, in the Service Provider Registration procedure the Service Providers domain, the Provider Manager as well as the Administrator domain are involved. Apart from the *Provider Account Management,* which is designed in a symmetrical and reusable form with respect to the user respective part, there is also the *Provider Registration Management* process. Specifically, this process deals with the definition of the terms of the access agreement with the brokerage system for the affiliate providers, as well as the definition and management of the offered service attributes for all types of providers. The affiliate providers provide all the information (i.e., complete service attributes and values offer) to the system, while the online and offline providers give only a subset of this information in the system's catalogue form.

In the following Figure , the dynamic model of the Service Request Handling, the Solution Negotiation and Evaluation is highlighted. Specifically, after being authenticated into the system, the user is able to formulate an informed complex service request as based on previous existing demands which can either reuse or modify or build a new request from scratch. In the first case, the complex service request being reused is validated with the collaboration of the User Manager, the Ontology Manager and the Solution Builder. In the case of a request modification, the detailed atomic services, subsequently formulated, are validated (updated) with the collaboration of the User Manager, the Ontology Manager and the Solution Builder. In the later case of building a new request from scratch, the user formulates his request based on the current complex service template that the Ontology Manager forwards to the user side. The next step is the retrieval of the candidate service providers identities that offer solutions corresponding to each atomic service request. This is achieved by means of interaction between the Solution Builder and the Provider Manager.

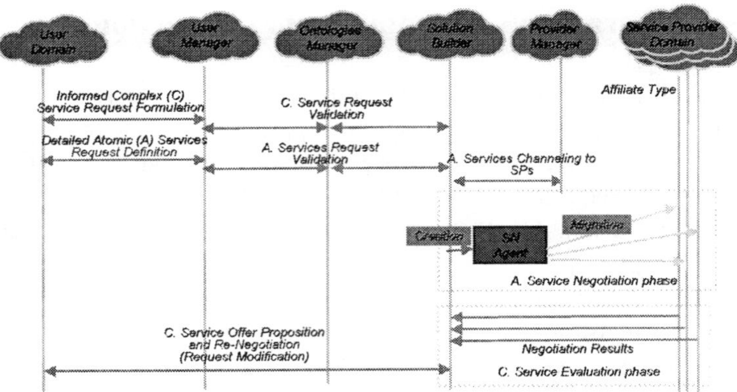


*Figure 6:* Complex Service Request Handling Procedure

Focusing on the processes that comprise the solution building, we provide the message sequence charts in Figure  and Figure , in which the detailed interactions among the identified service components are shown. In this respect, we start with the solution negotiation that begins when the *Service Request Validator* (SRV) which is a part of the Solution Pre-Processor component sends the corresponding message to the *Negotiator Controller* (NC) (*NegotiateServiceRequest()*) who in turn creates and instantiates a *Single Negotiator* (SN) for each atomic service. The SN is created as an agent that migrates to the identified Service Providers $SP_{ik}$ machines (where the $SP_k$ provider offers the *i* type of atomic service, i=1,..n and k=1,..m), in order to get the exact service offers for each atomic service. The *GetServiceOffer()* method is invoked and for the affiliate providers a full offer containing the requested static and dynamic elements may be found. Regarding the online or offline providers there is also the need to be contacted offline by the user.

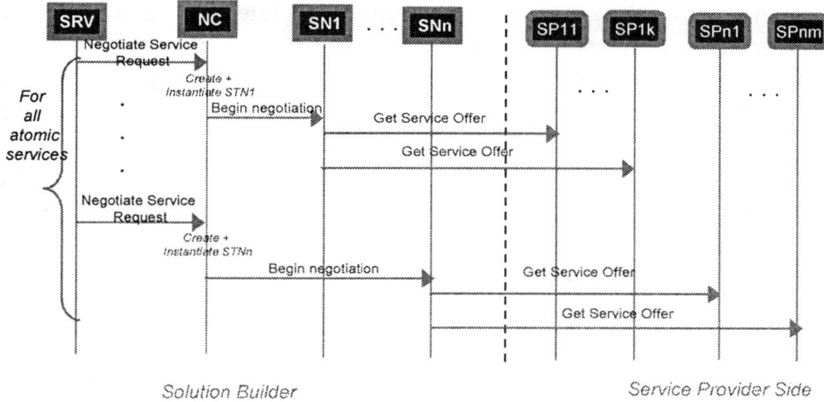


Figure 7: Solution Negotiation Procedure

The reply is returned by the service providers and is forwarding to the user via the NC and URH. In case the user is not satisfied from the offers or he wants to modify his request, then the *ModifyServiceRequest()* method (Figure ) of the URH is invoked and a new search and negotiation between the user and the providers takes place until both sides are fully satisfied.

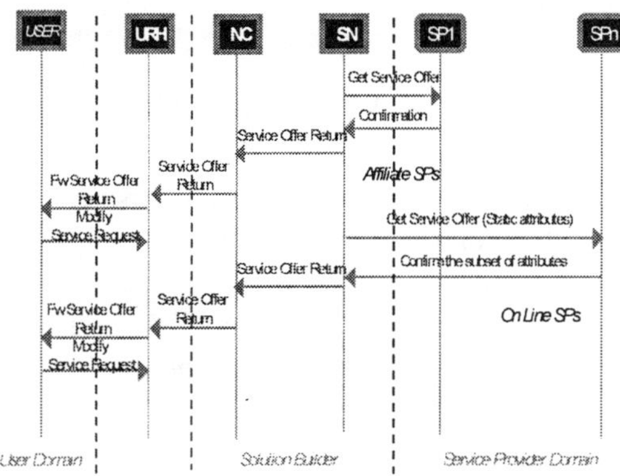


Figure 8: Single Provider Negotiation Procedure

The negotiation results are collected in the Solution Builder and the complex service evaluation phase follows. This process consists of a two level filtering according to the brokerage system and user defined criteria. This is achieved by means of detailed interaction between refined components of the Solution Builder. Specifically, when the atomic service offer is created and returned to the NC there is the possibility the user has had specified in his profile that he prefers to see the offers in the form of the complex solution. Moreover, he has the right to request more than one solutions. In the event of such a user preference the NC forwards the offer (*FwAtomicServiceOffer()*) to the *Solution Combinator Component* (SCC) which in turn creates the complex solution based on the brokerage system business criteria. The offer is forwarded (*FwGlobalSolution()*) to the *Solution Classificator Component* (SRC), where the solution rating takes place based on weighted, user defined criteria. Finally, the complex offer is displayed to the user through the URH (*ShowGlobalOffer()*).In turn, the user is able to either accept one of the proposed solutions (*ChooseOneOffer()*), meaning that the negotiation phase is over, or to re-negotiate the solutions, which is essentially the modification of his service request (*ModifyServiceRequest()*).

Within the complex services transactions execution, a concluding phase is distinguished that comprises transaction confirmation, resources reservation and payment functionality. This will take place after the user has accepted and chosen the offered complex services. The *Transaction Controller* (TC) requests the corresponding *Single Transaction Negotiator* (STN) to make the reservation of the atomic services. Then, the STN contacts the related service provider in order to reserve its offer and makes the last checks. The confirmation is returned to the URH via the TC who in turn invokes to make the payment the *Payment Manager* (PM). The Payment Manager abstracts the functionality necessary to complete the payment process and the result is made known to the URH. The completion of the payment indicates the transaction completion as well.

## 5. CONCLUSIONS AND DISCUSSION

In this paper, we present a particular business to business brokerage architectural model. Such as model, aims at, primarily, meeting the requirements for comprehensive, reusable and scalable component-based frameworks, in the aid of complex e-commerce transactions services provision. The designed brokerage platform has been constructed upon a refined requirements analysis exercise and an iterative service design process, that have explicitly taken into account the needs and constrains of specific business domains. These domains represent the B2B publishing and the B2B retail sectors, against the conjuctural and structural forces shaping their transformation into the Internet economy. In devising the proposed brokerage platform, we undertake the tasks to identify refined software components and test their intercommunications for certain service scenarios and procedures, which tasks are, in detail, presented in this paper. Moreover, while challenging the proposed brokerage system capabilities and robustness, we anticipate and enforce its relevance and usefulness into the rapidly changing B2B landscape, by discussing a brokerage federation policy, to be considered in detail in our future design work.

# 6. ACKNOWLEDGEMENTS

This work was supported by the Commission of the European Communities within the IST Programme Smart-EC (IST-1999-10130). The authors would like to warmly thank their Smart-EC colleagues.

# 7. REFERENCES

[1] Martin Bichler, Arie Segev, "A Brokerage Framework for Internet Commerce", Distributed and Parallel Databases, Vol.7, Number 2, pp.133-148, April 1999 http://haas.berkeley.edu/citm/wp-1031.pdf

[2] M.Lambrou, G.Karetsos, E.Protonotarios, "A Service Analysis and Service Design Framework for the Implementation of a generic Brokerage Service", Advances in Information Technologies: The Business Challenge, pp. 226-233, IOS press,1998.

[3] Garr N., "Hypermediation: Commerce as Clickstreams", *Harvard Business Review*, January-February 2000.

[4] Bailey, J. P., Bakos J. Y., "An exploratory study of the emerging role of the electronic intermediaries", *International Journal of Electronic Commerce*, Spring 1997.

[5] Wise R. et al., "Beyond the Exchange: The Future of B2B", *Harvard Business Review*, November-December 2000.

[6] Chircu A., Kauffman R., "Reintermediation strategies in business-to-business electronic commerce", *International Journal of Electronic Commerce*, Fall 2000.

[7] M.B. Sarkar, B. Butler, and C. Steinfield, Intermediaries and cybermediaries: a continuing role for mediating players in the electronic marketplace, Journal of Computer-Mediated Communication **1**(3) (1996), http://jcmc.huji.ac.il/vol1/issue3/sarkar.html.

[8] Bakos J.Y.," The emerging role of electronic marketplaces on the Internet", Communications of the ACM, August 1998.

[9] McAfee A., "The Napsterization of B2B", *Harvard Business Review*, January-February 2000.

[10] Ming Fan, Jan Stallaert, Andrew B. Whinston, "The Internet and the Future of Financial Markets", *Communications of the ACM,* November 2000/Vol. 43, No. 11

[11] M. Fernandez Lopez, "Overview of methodologies for building ontologies", Proceedings of the IJCAI-99 workshop on Ontologies and Problem-Solving Methods (KRR5) (http://sunsite.informatik.rwth-aachen.de/Publications/CEUR-WS/Vol-18)

[12] Smart-EC: Support for Mediation And bRokering for Electronic Commerce, IST-1999-10130, RTD Project, Deliverable 3.1, "Service Specifications".

[13] E. Tzifa, P. Demestichas, M. Lambrou, A. Kaltabani, S. Kotrotsos, M.Anagnostou, "Advanced service creation environment: Practices implementation and application", *Technologies for the Information Society: Development and Opportunities*, pp. 466-473, IOS press, 1998.

[14] P.P.Demestichas, N.P.Polydorou, A.K.Kaltabani, N.I.Liossis, S.A.Kotrotsos, E.C.Tzifa, M.E.Anagnostou, "Issues in Service Creation for Future Open Distributed Processing Environments", ICC'99

[15] J. Rumbaugh, M. Blaha, W. Premerlani, F. Eddy, W. Leversen, Object-oriented modeling and design, Prentice Hall, Englewood Cliffs, NJ, 1991.

[16] TINA-C Deliverable, Definition of service architecture, Version 5.0, 1997

[17] TINA-C, TINA business model and reference points 4.0, Baseline Document, 1997

[18] Smart-EC: Support for Mediation And bRokering for Electronic Commerce, IST-1999-10130 RTD Project, Deliverable 4.1, "Smart-EC Architecture V1".

MAIN TRACK - PART THREE

# VIRTUAL ENTERPRISES

# 13

# Towards Dynamic Virtual Enterprises

Vaggelis Ouzounis, Volker Tschammer
*ECCO – Electronic Commerce Center of Competence, GMD-Fokus, Kaiserin-Augusta-Allee 31, D-10589, Berlin,Germany, Email: (ouzounis, tschammer)@fokus.gmd.de*

**Abstract**: Virtual Enterprises (VEs) enable the deployment of distributed business processes among different partners in order to shorten development and manufacturing cycles, reduce time to market and operational costs, increase customer satisfaction, and operate on global scale and reach. Dynamic virtual enterprises are an emerging category of VEs, where the different partners are being selected dynamically during business process execution based on market-driven criteria and negotiation. In this paper, we discuss concepts and technologies that are considered to satisfy key requirements of dynamic virtual enterprises, and propose DIVE, a framework for the specification, execution and management of shared business processes in dynamic virtual enterprises.

## 1. INTRODUCTION

In the digital economy, companies are continuously seeking for new ways of business in order to cope with the increasing competitive pressure generated by the global market place. The need for global scale and reach, short development and manufacturing cycles, reduced time-to-market and operational costs, increased customer satisfaction, and rapid adaptation to new market changes has led companies to intensify automation, collaboration, and distribution (Applegate 96, Malone 91, Ouzounis 98a). The Internet is increasingly becoming the general basis for such purposes together with its advanced services, including electronic market places and the World Wide Web. New organisational forms develop, like collaborative commerce and virtual enterprises. In such virtual, collaborative organisations, partners, particularly small and medium enterprises (SMEs), can concentrate on their own core-competence and exploit partners' resources and capacities.

In this paper, we discuss concepts and technologies that satisfy key requirements of dynamic virtual enterprises, and propose DIVE, a framework for the specification, execution, and management of shared business processes.

## 2. DYNAMIC VIRTUAL ENTERPRISES

Distribution of tasks and co-operation has been a central aspect of trade and business since centuries. Manifold relationships between enterprises and parts of enterprises, often invisible for the customer, have contributed to the goal of satisfying the customer's needs for timely and high quality services. In the digital economy, where many of those relationships are realised via the Internet, new forms of business must develop which support communication and co-operation between distributed and automated business processes. Such Internet-based, collaborative organisations are usually called virtual organisations or virtual enterprises.

Virtual enterprises are characterised by the following properties (Ouzounis 98b, Ouzounis 99):

- the processes which take share in the business are distributed via distant partner organisations,
- the partners are autonomous, i.e. there need not be other co-operation or dependency outside their engagement in the virtual enterprise,
- the partners engaged in the virtual enterprise are organised internally in a way that they can delegate some or all of their business processes and resources totally or partially to the virtual organisation,
- the partners have made agreements about common goals, negotiated how to reach these goals, assigned roles and distributed responsibilities, defined how the processes and resources have to be introduced, shared, used, and administered, developed procedures of problem handling, and made agreements about how to share profits and losses,
- the partners use common information and communication infrastructures in order to support collaboration and co-ordination during the life-cycle of the virtual enterprise.

Virtual enterprises are not a new concept in management studies (Malone 91, Ouzounis 99, Camarinha-Matos 99). Some of the big manufacturing companies have already business relationships with their suppliers and customers based on electronic procedures and protocols, such as EDI (Filos 00). These "virtual" business relationships enable the sharing of business processes and resources via electronic information and communication services. However, the level of integration and the usage characteristics of information and communication technologies vary and are often not optimal. Most of the activities are still performed manually and the cost of implementing and integrating electronic solutions as well as the time required to deploy virtual enterprise concepts are high (Lin 96).

Based on the criteria described above, two categories of virtual enterprises can be defined, namely static virtual enterprises and dynamic virtual enterprises (DVEs). In the case of static virtual enterprises the business partners are linked statically, i.e. the relationships between partners are fixed and the shared business processes have pre-defined interfaces, are tightly coupled, and are customised according to the partners' environments and requirements. Changes during the execution of business processes are not foreseen, except for critical situations, like failures or loss of partners.

In dynamic virtual enterprises the business partners are found and linked dynamically, on-demand, and according to the requirements of the customers with the help of the services provided by a virtual market place (Nwana 99). The business relationships in a dynamic virtual enterprise can change continuously based on market-driven criteria. The virtual market place provides services for the registration of business process offerings based on generic, well-known process templates. Business domains that want to engage in virtual enterprise relationships can register offers at the market place in relation to the process templates. Whenever a business domain wants to use a particular process, it is visiting the virtual market place and locates all the potential partners that can provide the required process. As soon as the market place search has resulted in a list of candidate partners, the partner selection process starts. Included in the process are negotiations about the capacities and services required and contracting about the roles and tasks of each partner. The negotiation process can be performed manually, or automatically. The result of it is usually a contract, which regulates the business relationships established. With the support of the virtual market place, the number and role of partners can easily be adapted to the requirements of customers and the currently available capacities and abilities of the partners. This is a significant evolutionary step, which lets virtual enterprises take advantage of the demand and supply regulated by an open, Internet-based market (Schuldt 99).

Consequently, from a business point of view, dynamic virtual enterprises appear to be the most promising approach. However, from the technical point of view, the required solutions and systems are more complex and more sophisticated. Therefore, evaluating and integrating actual information and communication technologies is an important step towards an efficient, flexible, and easy-to-use support environment for dynamic virtual enterprises.

# 3. TECHNOLOGIES FOR DYNAMIC VIRTUAL ENTERPRISES

In the following, we describe technologies of particular interest to dynamic virtual enterprises, including those which support the exchange of information in loosely coupled inter-organisational environments, the co-operation of automated business components, the control of work processes across organisational boundaries, and the dynamic mediation of business process providers and users.

## 3.1 Information Exchange Between Loosely Coupled Systems

Systems supporting the information exchange between the loosely coupled systems of dynamic virtual enterprises must enable asynchronous transactions across organisational boundaries, flexibly support application domain-specific types and formats of information, and allow for autonomous behaviour of the communicating and co-operating business processes.

**EDI.** EDI (Electronic Data Interchange) is a standard format for exchanging business data. An EDI message contains a string of data elements, each of which represents a singular fact, such as a price, or a product model number. One or more of such strings form a transaction set, which is the EDI equivalent to a message. A transaction set often consists of what would usually be contained in a typical business document or form.

EDI transactions are typically performed asynchronously to the execution of business processes. This satisfies one requirement of loosely coupled environments and cross-organisational information exchange in virtual enterprises. The current format of EDI messages is static and cannot be extended easily. The scope and context of EDI documents is limited and rather impossible to change, and thus, it is difficult to use EDI as the basis for general-purpose inter-domain business process execution and management. EDI transactions, as currently defined, only support electronic commerce interactions. The business document definitions provided have been considered inadequate for many other application scenarios. To address this issue, the EDI standards organisations, like EDIFACT and ANSI X.12, have developed sets of documents for various industries and business sectors. Using these document definitions, the customisation required per business relationship can be reduced, though in general, per-relationship integration and customisation work is still required.

Under these circumstances, EDI is best suited for long-term and stable business relationships between organisations, which are powerful enough to make significant investments into electronic relationships. Business processes that are not related to electronic commerce, such as supply chain optimisation or product design, are best performed outside the EDI context. In general, each new EDI relationship requires new customisation and integration work. These relationships are not easily established and return on EDI investment is gained only over long periods of time, not over short-term transactions.

**DCBS.** Distributed component based systems (DCBSs) are widely used for distributed computing and information processing due to the simplicity, ease of integration and deployment, high degree of distribution, standard underlying distributed protocols, like CORBA-IIOP and RMI, and middleware services. Back-end systems and clients integrate with the distributed framework using the application programming interfaces (APIs) and object models exposed by the underlying levels of the architecture. While clients are insulated from the APIs of the back-end systems, they are tightly bound to the APIs provided by the framework (Orfali 96).

This design choice has two implications. First, by using object binding as the interaction technique, DCBS applications must be adopted all at once by all participants in the cross-organisation relationship. Upgrades to back-end systems, the component framework, and the business application must be co-ordinated across all participants. Second, because of the tight binding, the same object model must be adopted for communication and co-operation across different business domains. This poses a significant barrier to interworking in cross-organisational environments. Additionally, the DCBS frameworks do not provide a complete solution, but instead serve as the starting point for developers to build applications. By building on the framework, developers can more quickly complete applications and leverage the code in the framework that takes care of many of the mechanical details needed for a successful distributed application. Finally, these choices make the DCBS frameworks most appropriate for deployment inside a single company that needs to link multiple distributed divisions or sites. In general, DCBSs are considered inadequate for use in a dynamic virtual enterprise environments because of their tight coupling model (Tombros 00).

**Messaging Systems.** Messaging systems, in contrast to DCBSs, are not based on a static and tightly coupled component model and do not require compatible middleware services (Filos 00). Messaging systems separate the interface of services from the corresponding modules, which provide these services and, thus, hide the complexities of the server components and systems from the client. In this way, they support asynchronous and loosely coupled relationships among different business domains.

However, there are some drawbacks with messaging systems, too. One of the key problems is that there exist different proposals for a message specification language, i.e. for specifying the envelope and the content of the message. The protocols currently used actually specify their message envelope in XML and follow their own description approach for the included content. Another problem is the lack of generic messaging standards. This results in incompatibilities among different system implementations and makes the integration of business processes across different domains more difficult. The biggest problem, finally, is the specification of an adequate ontology, i.e. a set of concepts describing entities and interactions, such as things, events, and relations, for an agreed-upon vocabulary for each of the different business sectors (Georgakopoulos 98). Standard ontologies would enable the rapid integration and deployment of messaging systems in different application areas. In general, messaging systems have certain benefits over existing DCBS in dynamic virtual enterprises due to the asynchronous and loosely coupled approach, the independence among the interfaces of components and the component bodies, and – if available - the well-defined ontologies.

## 3.2 Co-operation of Automated Business Components

**Intelligent mobile agents**. Intelligent mobile agents combine many of the benefits offered by messaging systems and DCBSs. Agent systems are loosely coupled and communicate asynchronously (Breugst 98). Messages exchanged are well defined through the FIPA agent communication language standard (FIPA 98). Agents realise the concept of ontologies, which makes them more flexible and autonomous and, agent systems are deployed within a distributed object-oriented framework, like CORBA or Java, and thus can access any type of standard business component.

Through these combined benefits, agent systems support autonomy and flexibility, scalability, and adaptability. Flexibility is supported by the distinct communication and co-operation models which have been developed for agent-based systems, scalability comes from the migration capabilities of agents, and adaptability relies on their inherent intelligence. Furthermore, due to the object-oriented concepts used to implement agent platforms and agents the integration with existing technologies is facilitated (Choy 99).

Intelligent mobile agents can be used in different ways to solve virtual enterprise problems. One way is to use an agent based business process management system which controls and co-ordinates the execution of virtual enterprise business processes in a distributed, autonomous, and flexible way. Another way is to use agents for the dynamic selection of partners and the negotiation phase among different virtual enterprise partners (Bellifernine 99). Agents can also be used to manage and co-ordinate the provision of virtual marketplace services.

Although agent technology is a good candidate for the support of virtual enterprises, there are some problems as well. One of the key issues currently is the requirement for a mobile agent platform for the provision of agent life cycle and migration management services (Martesson 98). Several agent platforms have been developed so far, which, however, are mostly incompatible between each other. Agents sitting on different platforms have difficulties in communication and co-operation. Migration between different platforms is nearly impossible and – if actually achieved – relies on dedicated solutions. Current standardisation activities, like OMG-MASIF and FIPA, deal with these problems.

## 3.3 Control of Work Processes Across Organisational Boundaries

**Workflow Management Systems.** Workflow management systems are used to specify, execute, manage, and streamline business processes. Workflow management systems in general provide several functions, which can be used for business process execution and control across the organisational boundaries, existing within a virtual enterprise (Grefen 99). Workflow management systems can monitor and control the execution of hierarchical systems of processes and sub-processes, defined by dedicated business modelling tools and business process specification languages.

However, conventional workflow management systems have certain drawbacks in relation to the virtual enterprise concept. One of the main problems is their limited autonomy and flexibility (Miller 98). So far there are no extensions to the existing business process specification languages towards the support of cross-organisational business processes (Bolcer 99). Furthermore, invocation of remote business processes should be preceded by access control, authorisation, and contract checks. Current workflow systems do not provide such mechanisms. Finally, in current workflow systems, shared business processes are structured inflexibly with respect to sub-processes that have to be executed remotely, i.e. the virtual enterprise partners which are to provide those processes are specified statically. Consequently, this approach is suitable for static virtual enterprises only and not for dynamic ones, where the partners, which are to provide parts of the shared business process are not known in advance, and where the remote domains can be selected dynamically, after negotiation and during the business process execution (Tombros 00).

In dynamic virtual enterprises a workflow management system must deal with the fact that for the same business process specification different instances can exist. For every instance a set of different partners may be selected according to the needs and requirements of the process. Standards, currently proposed, are not directly dealing with market-based cross-organisational business process execution and management (Bolcer 99). Critical open issues, like inter-domain workflow execution and management, business process specification languages for inter-domain business processes, and dynamic selection of workflow providers during process execution are not effectively discussed. A message-based approach with corresponding XML message requests and responses is currently considered as a solution to support the required degree of autonomy and flexibility in dynamic virtual enterprises (Ouzounis 98b).

Agent-based workflow management systems are to solve several of these problems. Control of business processes shared between multiple business domains can be assigned to agents which are either deployed directly in each of the domains involved or can migrate from domain to domain as required by the processes structure. Agents arriving at a domain invoke the required sub-process and after successful termination of their task either return back to their home agency or migrate to another domain in order to invoke another sub-process. The remote domains can authenticate and authorise the requesting agents based on electronic contracts that have been established during the negotiation phase. However, most of the issues related to such agent-based workflow management systems, cross-organisational business process execution, and dynamic selection of partners are still under investigation and stable, well-defined solutions and concepts are missing.

## 3.4 Dynamic Mediation of Business Process Providers and Users

**Virtual Market Places.** Virtual market places are central parts of dynamic virtual enterprises. They increase flexibility and scalability through their search and mediation functions and support the selection of business partners during the establishment and reconfiguration of dynamic virtual enterprises. A market place can administer offerings for business processes made by potential providers and can perform searches for partners satisfying required quality attributes. The search and matchmaking services can be further complemented by advanced services, like electronic negotiation and contracting. With respect to negotiations mechanisms applied to the dynamic and automated selection of business processes, the bidding model and the bargaining model are favoured compared to the auction models.

Intelligent mobile agents can be a profitable technical implementation of such functionality due to their inherent autonomy, adaptability, and learning characteristics (Magedanz 99). However, most current implementations of agent-based virtual market places do not consider emerging FIPA agent standards. Furthermore, most of the negotiation approaches, techniques, and models have basically concentrated on B2C and C2C electronic commerce and are not addressing the needs of business-to-business market places and dynamic virtual enterprises. Although some of the above techniques can be extended for the dynamic selection of partners in virtual enterprises based on service templates, this area is considered new and further research is needed. Certain key issues like agent communication language, ontology, negotiation protocol, and negotiation strategy need to be clarified and extended for application in dynamic virtual enterprises.

Despite these problems, intelligent mobile agents can provide the basis for the new generation of open, flexible, autonomous, and distributed systems for the management and execution of business processes in dynamic virtual enterprises.

# 4. DIVE – AGENT-BASED LIFE CYCLE MANAGEMENT FOR DYNAMIC VIRTUAL ENTERPRISES

In the following, we introduce DIVE, a life cycle management approach for dynamic virtual enterprises. It is to realise dynamic virtual enterprise concepts based on agent technology and virtual market places.

In our case, the virtual enterprise life-cycle model consists of two key phases. These phases are the Business Process Specification and Registration Phase and the Business Process Execution and Management Phase.

## 4.1 Business Process Specification and Registration

During the Business Process Specification Phase a virtual enterprise candidate partner specifies its offer for a business processes. Such a process is a hierarchical structure consisting of the root process and a tree of sub-processes. Sub-processes that cannot be further sub-divided are called tasks. Tasks are the actually activities performed by a resource business object, such as a software component, a device, or a robot. A business process offer can be utilised during the execution and management phase either as a self-contained process or as a sub-process of a defined higher-level process. The specification of business processes is done using the DIVE business process definition language. For every business process, the input parameters, the output parameters, the sub-processes, the tasks, and the conditions among the sub-processes and tasks are specified. Additionally, every sub-process and task is specified as a local or remote entity. Local entities are those, which can be entirely performed by the offering domain, while remote entities are those which must be provided by remote domains. Furthermore, for every specified task the associated business objects are specified.

Within DIVE, each business object is encapsulated and represented by a specific agent, called Resource Provider Agent (RPA). In this way, autonomous agents handle legacy services provided by existing distributed objects that are physically located at different network locations. The result of a business process specification in DIVE is an XML-encoded document, which can be interpreted for execution during the business process execution and management phase. During the process registration phase a business domain which wants to participate in dynamic virtual enterprise relationships registers its processes at the virtual market place. The market place administers the type of the process offer together with the attributes to be taken into account during the process execution and management phase.

## 4.2 Business Process Execution and Management

After successful registration, the offering business domain becomes a virtual enterprise candidate and the business process can be executed upon request from a customer or from a higher-level business process. When a request arrives, it is directed to a virtual enterprise representative, which creates an instance of the process. First the process description is retrieved from the business process repository. Then it is interpreted and the execution of the process is started. The virtual enterprise representative is realised in DIVE by a Personal User Agent (PUA). Each request is administered by a dedicated PUA. The PUA forwards the request to the DIVE agent-based business process management system, which instantiates, interprets, and executes the business process by means of a set of co-operating agents, called Workflow Provider Agents (WPAs).

Communication and co-operation between the WPA and RPA agents, if they all belong to the same domain, are based upon an intra-domain ontology, which comprises the set of messages defined within the domain for the exchange between WPA and RPA agents.

If a sub-process has been specified as remote, then the corresponding WPA creates a specialised negotiation agent, called Requestor Negotiation Agent (RNA), and sends it to the virtual market place in order to locate potential virtual enterprise candidate partners for the required remote sub-process. Upon request, the virtual market place informs the RNA about all the potential virtual enterprise candidate partners. After that, the RNA starts the negotiation process by contacting the negotiation agents located in each candidate partner. These agents are called Provider Negotiation Agents (PNA). The negotiation process is performed among the RNA and PNAs by using a negotiation protocol and a negotiation ontology. The negotiation protocol used is the FIPA Contract Net protocol, a modified version of the original Contract Net protocol. The result of this negotiation process is the selection and contracting of the best virtual enterprise candidate domain according to the constraint given by both sides and the compromise negotiated.

As soon as a virtual enterprise partner for a particular remote process has been selected and contracted, the PNA returns back to his original location and informs the corresponding WPA agent about the selected partner. Then, the WPA contacts that partner domain and requests the execution of the business process by referring to the contract id that has been fixed during the negotiation process. The virtual enterprise partner domain checks the list of existing contracts and starts the execution of the requested process if a legitimate contract is found. The agent responsible for the access control and authorisation is called Domain Representative (DR) agent.

A customer that has requested the execution of a business process can influence and manage the process during execution time. The main operations that can be performed are suspension, resumption, and termination of the process execution.

Every request of the customer is served initially by the virtual enterprise representative domain. All the WPA and RPA agents, related to the execution of the business process instance, are suspended, resumed, or terminated according to the customer's request. In addition to the activities within the representative domain, all the remote sub-processes and tasks, which have been started in the context of the business process, are suspended, resumed, or terminated, too. Therefore, similar requests are issued and sent from the virtual enterprise representative to the corresponding virtual enterprise partners. Whenever the DR agent of a virtual enterprise partner gets a request to suspend, resume, or terminate an existing local business process, it checks the contract id, and if correct orders the related internal WPA and RPA agents to resume, suspend, or terminate. In that way, unauthorised requests for process suspension, resumption, or termination are not served. The communication and co-ordination between the different agents responsible for remote business processes are regulated by an inter-domain ontology. The inter-domain ontology is actually the set of messages that the agents are allowed to exchange during the execution and management of remote business processes. In addition to the execution control actions provided, the customer can request information about the current status of the business process. Similar to the information flow for execution control, the virtual enterprise representative requests from all agents associated with this process, local or remote, to declare their current status. When a process finally completes its operation, the DR agent of the virtual enterprise representative partner is informed. Then, the DR agent informs the customer by posting to it the output results of the process and other status information, like the time of completion. If a fatal problem occurs during the execution of a process, the WPA agent responsible for the process instance informs the DR agent that the execution of this process cannot be continued and consequently, the WPA agent aborts itself. The DR agent informs either the customer or the associated virtual enterprise partner, about this event and stops the execution of the business process.

## 4.3 The DIVE Virtual Marketplace

The virtual market place plays the role of a third party administrative domain within the virtual enterprise. It provides matchmaking services to the virtual enterprise partners. The virtual market place administers a set of so-called service types, which represent the business process types defined and describe in a consistent way the interface of business processes The market place enables virtual enterprise candidate partners to register and administer offers in relation to defined service types and virtual enterprise representatives to search for potential partners that can provide particular business processes associated with existing service types. For every service type, the name of the type and a set of named properties are specified. The name of the service type is the name of the business process, while the input and output parameters of the process are named properties of the service type. Additionally, extra properties, related with the negotiation phase, are included in the service type. Service types are managed by the virtual market place administrator. The service type management includes creation, deletion, modification, and retrieval of service types.

Virtual enterprise candidate partners that want to register their process offerings at the market place must match each offer with an existing service type or must initiate the creation of a new type. For a common understanding between the partners making an offer and the domains looking for matching offers, it is necessary that every service offer is an instance of a given service type. Each offer assigns values to the properties defined by the type. Each candidate domain is responsible for its service offers. Actions, which a candidate domain can perform on its offers, include the registration of an offer, the withdrawal, the listing of offers and the modification of an offer.

Virtual enterprise representatives that want to find suitable partners, which can provide a particular process, retrieve from the market place all the registered offers that satisfy given constraints. The search and matchmaking functions required, are provided by the market place. Therefore, the basic functions, which the market place must provide, include service type management, service offer management, and service offer retrieval management.

## 5. CONCLUSIONS

Based on the development, testing, and validation of the DIVE framework, the following conclusions can be drawn according to the selection of technologies and the design decisions during implementation:

Openness has been achieved due to flexible, XML-based ontologies for the management of shared business processes and the negotiation process. The use of open, interoperable standard technologies like XML, FIPA, FIPA-ACL, and Java also increases the openness of the system.

Dynamicity, flexibility and evolution are due to the dynamic selection of virtual enterprise partners and the automated negotiation during business process execution and management.

Asynchronous and loosely coupled communication has been achieved through communication mechanisms supported by a FIPA platform. In general, the intelligent agents communicate asynchronously and loosely coupled by message exchanges through the FIPA agent communication channel (ACC).

Distribution and scalability are due to the autonomous and distributed execution and management of shared business processes by means of intelligent, autonomous agents located in different administrative domains.

Autonomy has been achieved due to the asynchronous and loosely coupled communication of agents during the execution and management of business processes.

Intelligence is due to the deployment of artificial intelligence techniques during the business process execution and management. For that reason, special mechanisms have been developed and tested for the integration of rule engines like the JESS rule engine for the assertion of conditions related to the control flow in business processes.

Apart from those benefits, a key drawback has been identified. This drawback is the lack of performance. Performance limitations mostly originate from the extra time required for parsing the messages, the asynchronous message transportation imposed by the FIPA ACC, the migration of agents, and the performance characteristics of the underlying agent platform.

Although the presented work intended to provide a coherent solution for the management of dynamic intelligent virtual enterprises, certain issues are still subject to further improvement and research. These are the negotiation strategy algorithms for automated negotiation and partner selection, fault tolerance and exception handling during the execution of shared business processes, and secure inter-domain communication during inter-domain process execution. These and other open issues are addressed by two international projects, recently initiated, namely COVE (Cove 01) and THINKcreative.

## 6. REFERENCES

Applegate, L. M., C.W. Holsapple, R. Kalakota, F. J. Radermacher, and A. B. Whinston (1996). "Electronic Commerce: Building Blocks of New Business Opportunity". Journal of Organizational Computing and Electronic Commerce, vol. 6, no. 1, Addision Wesley 1994, ISBN 0-201-42289-1.

Bellifernine, F., G. Rimassa, and A. Poggi (1999). "JADE: A FIPA Compliant Agent Framework". 4th International Conference and Exhibition on the Practical Applications of Intelligent Agents and Multi-Agent Systems (PAAM 99), London.

Bolcer, G. A. and G. Kaiser (1999). "SWAP: Leveraging the Web to Manage Workflow". IEEE Internet Computing, Jan/Feb 1999.

Breugst, M., L. Hagen, and T. Magedanz (1998a). "Impacts of Mobile Agent Technology on Mobile Communication System Evolution". IEEE Personal Communications Magazine, vol. 5, no. 4.

Camarinha-Matos, L. M. and H. Afsarmanesh (eds) (1999). "Infrastructures for Virtual Enterrises. Networking Industrial Enterprises". IFIP TC5 WG5.3 / PRODNET Working Conference for Virtual Enterprises (PRO-VE '99), Porto, Portugal, October 1999, Kluwer Academic Publishers.

Choy, S., M. Breugst, and T. Magedanz (1999). "Beyond Mobile Agents with CORBA - Towards Mobile CORBA Objects", 6th ACTS Conference on Intelligence in Services and Networks (IS&N), H. Zuidweg et a. (Eds.), IS&N 99, ISBN: 3-540-65895-5, Springer-Verlag, 1999.

COVE Project, http://www.uninova.pt/~cove/coveproject.htm

Filos, E. and V. Ouzounis (2000). "Virtual Organisations: Technologies, Trends, Standards and the Contribution of the European RTD Programmes". International Journal of Computer Applications in Technology, Special Issue: "Applications in Industry of Product and Process Modeling Using Standards", Virtual-organisation.net, "Newsletter", Vol. 1, No. 3-4, 1997.

FIPA (1998) http://www.fipa.org/spec/FIPA98.html.

Georgakopoulos, D. (1998). "Collaboration Management Infrastructure for Comprehensive Process and Service Management". International Symposium on Advanced Database Support for Workflow Management, Enschede, The Netherlands, May, 1998.

Gibon, P., J.-F. Clavier, S. Loison (1999). "Support for Electronic Data Interchange in Infrastructures for Virtual Enterprises". Networking Industrial Enterprises. IFIP TC5 WG5.3 / PRODNET Working Conference for Virtual Enterprises (PRO-VE '99), Porto, Portugal, October 1999, Kluwer Academic Publishers.

Grefen, J., B. Pernini, and G. Sanchez (Eds, 1999). "Database Support for Workflow Management: The WIDE Project". Kluwer Academic Publishers, ISB7923-8414-8.

Lin, F. (1996). "Reengineering the Order Fulfillment Process in Supply Chain Networks: A Multiagent Information Systems Approach" Ph.D. Thesis, University of Illinois at Urbana-Champaign.

Magedanz, T. (Ed.) (1999). Special Issue on "Mobile Agents in Intelligent Networks and Mobile Communication Systems" in Computer Networks Journal, ELSEVIER Publisher, Netherlands, vol. 31, no. 10, July 1999.

Malone, T. W. and J. F. Rockart (1991). Computers, Networks, and the Corporation. Scientific American vol. 265, no. 3. pp. 128-136. R. Gestner, "Using Objects for Workflow Enabling of Standard Application Software", http://laser.cs.umass.edu/workflow/gestner.html , 1996.

Martesson, N., R. Mackay, and S. Björgvinsson (eds) (1998). "Changing the Ways We Work. Shaping the ICT-Solutions for the Next Century". Conference on Integration in Manufacturing, Göteborg, Sweden, October 1998.

Miller J, A. Sheth, K. Kochut, and D. Palaniswami (1998). "The Future of Web-Based Workflows". International Workshop on Research Directions in Process Technology, Nancy, France.

Nwana H, D. Ndumu, L. Lee, and J. Collis (1999). "ZEUS: A Toolkit for Building Distributed Multi-Agent Systems". In: Applied Artifical Intelligence Journal, vol 13, no. 1, 1999. http://www.labs.bt.com/projects/agents/index.htm.

Ouzounis, V. (1998a). "Electronic Commerce Commercial Scenarios, Business Models and Technologies for SME's", European Multimedia, Microprocessor Systems and Electronic Commerce Conference and Exposition (EMMSEC 98), Bordeaux, France September 1998.

Ouzounis, V. (1998b). "Electronic Commerce and New Ways of Work – An R&D RoadMap", European Commission –Directoral General III, 1998.

Ouzounis, V. and V. Tschammer (1999). "A Framework for Virtual Enterprise Support Services". 32nd International Conference on System Sciences (HICSS-32), Maoui, Hawaii, January 1999.

Orfali, R. (1996). "The Essential Distributed Objects Survival Guide ", John Wiley and Sons, ISBN 0-471-12993-3, 1996.

Schuldt, H., H. J. Schek, and G. Alonso (1999). "Transactional Coordination Agents for Composite Systems." International Database Engineering and Applications Symposium (IDEAS'99). Montreal, Canada, August 1999.

Stricker, C., S. Riboni, M. Kradolfer, and J. Taylor (2000). "Market-based Workflow Management for Supply Chains of Services". 33rd International Conference on System Sciences (HICSS-33), Maui, Hawaii, January 2000.

Tombros, D. and A. Geppert (2000). "Building Extensible Workflow Systems Using an Event-Based Infrastructure". 12th Conference on Advanced Information Systems Engineering, Stockholm, Sweden, June 2000.

14

# A Semi-Automated Brokerage for a Virtual Organization of Mould and Die Industries in Brazil

Ricardo J. Rabelo [1]; Rolando V. Vallejos [2]

[1] *Federal University of Santa Catarina, Department of Automation and Systems, Brazil (rabelo@das.ufsc.br).*

[2] *University of Caxias do Sul, Department of Mechanical Engineering, Brazil (rvvallej@ucs.tche.br).*

**Abstract:** This paper addresses a semi-automated process of brokerage for a virtual organization of mould and die industries located in the south of Brazil called VIRFEBRAS. This process is represented by a multi-agent-based decision support system that helps a human-broker in the selection of the group of enterprises within VIRFEBRAS which better fits a given business opportunity. This decision is not automated, but rather made via an agreement among the human-broker and all the members. Each enterprise will have a Production and Planning Control system that in turn feeds the whole system with updated data about its current / planned capabilities, enabling global optimizations and trust. Some implementation results are presented and next directions are pointed.

## 1. INTRODUCTION

The need to augment the competitiveness has been pushing most of the enterprises over the world to invest in new methods of organization and work, and in advanced manufacturing and information technologies. VIRFEBRAS – *Virtual Organization of Mould and Die Industries of Brazil* – is a Virtual Organization made up of nine mould and die SMEs in the city of Caxias do Sul, located in the south of Brazil. Caxias do Sul is nationally seen as a mould and die *cluster*. A *cluster* is seen as a group of enterprises that have the potential and the will to cooperate and therefore may become the partners in a Virtual Enterprise (VE) (Camarinha et al.,

99a). It was created as a strategic answer to face the current market needs, in the sense that the business potentialities and competitiveness of the enterprises could be increased in the global market if they behaved as a stronger coalition, gathering the sum of their individual capacities.

In the VIRFEBRAS[29] context, the importance of brokerage emerges in the creation phase of a virtual enterprise, when it is necessary to decide on the appropriate set of skills and resources to respond to a given business opportunity. In fact, the broker concept is wider, with its use also in the VE operation phase, when it is necessary to change a partner. Brokerage is an activity – normally coordinated by a human assistant called *broker* – that aims at searching for business opportunities over the world and to bring them into the cluster of enterprises he/she represents (Camarinha et al., 99b).

This paper presents a multi-agent-based decision support system that assists a human-broker in the selection of the team of enterprises within VIRFEBRAS that better fits a given business. This development is one of the actions of a regional industrial qualification program for the mould and die industry, lead by the Mechanical Department of the University of Caxias do Sul, regarding the problems and peculiarities of this sector.

This work represents an improvement of the first system version presented in (Rabelo et al., 2000a), developed in the scope of the INCO-DC MASSYVE project (MASSYVE, 2000). The paper is organized as follows: Chapter 2 gives a general overview of the current Brazilian scenario in the mould and die sector and the VIRFEBRAS context. Chapter 3 stresses the brokerage approach. Chapter 4 describes the brokerage scenario within VIRFEBRAS. Chapter 5 introduces the system architecture. Chapter 6 shows some results of the developed system, and Chapter 7 discusses the results and points the next steps of this work.

## 2. MOULD AND DIE INDUSTRY SCENARIO

In Brazil, the mould and die industry is going through a crucial moment, presenting some particularities. The mould and die sector requires specialized labor; most of the mold and die projects and manufacturing processes are based on previous experiences, sometimes without technological innovations. The customer usually decides to purchase a mould or die considering three main factors: *quality*, *cost* and *delivery time* (Santos, 97). However, another factor is emerging in importance: the *agility* in the business negotiation process.

[29] VIRFEBRAS companies: Indústria de Matrizes Bisol Ltda., Coprima Metalúrgica Ltda., JR Oliveira Indústria Metalúrgica Ltda., CJN Indústria de Matrizes Ltda., Elite Indústria de Matrizes Ltda., Gama Indústria de Matrizes Ltda., Tokyo Indústrias de Matrizes Ltda., Sildre Indústria de Matrizes Ltda., and Matrizes Sadel Ltda.

To be competitive a Brazilian mold and die industry must accomplish the delivery time previously agreed with the customer, with appropriate costs and the requested quality. It has been clearly seen that the biggest problem a mold and die industry has to improve its level of competitiveness is related to the quality of the Production Planning and Control systems (PPC). In this type of industry, the PPCs should be very sensible and efficient to deal with constant modifications in the schedules as the mould project uses to receive many alterations along its manufacturing. This situation also makes the process planning and scheduling very difficult considering the available resources in a certain period of time. The finite nature of the manufacture resources creates delivery priority conflicts, that become more problematic with unforeseen events, such as machine damage, employee absenteeism, delay in the delivery of materials and components, etc. (Santos, 97).

In the VIRFEBRAS scenario, one possibility to make business is when customer orders arrive via the broker. Two major problems usually occur. The first one is related to the complexity to provide a reliable answer to the customer. There can be so many possibilities of teams of members to fit a given business that it makes the broker's job extremely hard and complex, when he/she should focus on gathering new business opportunities. In this context, the importance of a brokerage, as the one being proposed here, ascends in significance as it is almost impossible for a human being to generate all possibilities of teams (i.e. possible VEs within VIRFEBRAS) and to evaluate every schedule. Thus, a non-assisted generation may imply a less profitable coalition in terms of final cost and delivery time and, in the worst case, the loss of the business opportunity. The second problem is related to the agility to provide the client with a fast but consistent answer. Regarding the complexity mentioned above, the broker should have some supporting system that helps him/her to speed up the whole process of announcing the opportunity, generating the possibilities, analyzing them, selecting one and finally giving a final answer. In this sense, a good brokerage system can offer the required agility that nowadays is a must in terms of competitiveness.

The nine mold and die industries that constitute VIRFEBRAS are on different organization and automation levels, each one having its own culture, methodologies and characteristics, some of them desirable to be kept. In spite of this, VIRFEBRAS is going to have its own / common "quality stamp" to differentiate it from other enterprises or similar clusters. Several actions have been pursued in order to have a certain degree of homogeneity in the enterprises so that, for instance, their "chances" can be equivalent and hence the trust building among the members can be reinforced. One of these actions is to provide every enterprise with a reliable – and the same – PPC & Scheduler (PPCS) system. In other words, it can be said that information technology serves to homogenize / encapsulate the differences among the enterprises from the broker's point of view.

The current implantation of the PPCS systems is extremely important to obtain in an efficient way the large volume of information that the operators and the production manager should periodically provide. Part of the qualification methodology being applied tries to guarantee that an enterprise has the PPCS systems implanted after a process of internal reorganization. Actually, the PPCS system is viewed as crucial. The answers (bids) to be sent to the broker are based on the information the system suggests and it should reflect as much as possible the effective and planned shop-floor occupation, especially considering that a mould usually has its project modified many times along the process. Keeping the delivery time is one of the most important competitive keys in the tool and die industries.

The information about the enterprises' capacities are shared among all the members, allowing for global, cooperative and constant optimizations in the enterprises' schedules. Therefore, and using the same PPCS software, a reliable information gathering is essential to reinforce – again – the trust building, one critic aspect in the success of a virtual organization.

# 3. THE BROKERAGE APPROACH

An alternative to analyze business opportunities for the VIRFEBRAS is the figure of a *broker*. The broker is a human specialist who represents VIRFEBRAS and who has two main roles: to look for new business opportunities / to manage their reception, and to coordinate the process of selecting the most suitable consortium of enterprises for every opportunity.

In order to improve the agility in business management, a supporting software module is suggested. By means of a *broker agent* an acquired *business opportunity – a set of moulds* – is transformed into a distributed business process (DBP) that is split into business processes (BP), where each BP corresponds to an individual mould or die. The individual mould/die tenders are then distributed among the VIRFEBRAS enterprises. Depending on the business requirements and the available capacities and skills, it may happen that various alternatives of teams of enterprises ("internal" VEs) that can accomplish the various BPs may be found, and further the most adequate coalition should be then elected. Figure 1 illustrates the idea of having several possible VEs within the cluster to attend a given DBP, where three VEs capable to accomplish it are formed (only VE1 has BPs explicitly assigned to the enterprises). Notice that a given enterprise "E" can get more than one BP (mould) and that it can be involved in several VEs or opportunities simultaneously.

The VE life cycle involves a number of phases, basically VE creation and configuration, VE operation, VE evolution, and VE dissolution (Spinosa et al., 98), comprising the phases of business opportunity identification, and partners search and selection. This work is currently focused on the VE creation phase. It presents a multi-agent-based decision support system – the *MASSYVE Mould Broker (MMB) System* – (i) to assist the VIRFEBRAS' human broker in the decision-making process of evaluating and suggesting the most adequate consortium of enterprises for a given package of moulds, and (ii) to support some basis to optimize the package's schedules regarding the information come from the PPCS systems. As the cluster members are potential competitors, the final decision is made by a management board and not by the broker. However, the decision is based on the broker's analysis, represented by the set of alternative consortia generated (and evaluated) by the system.

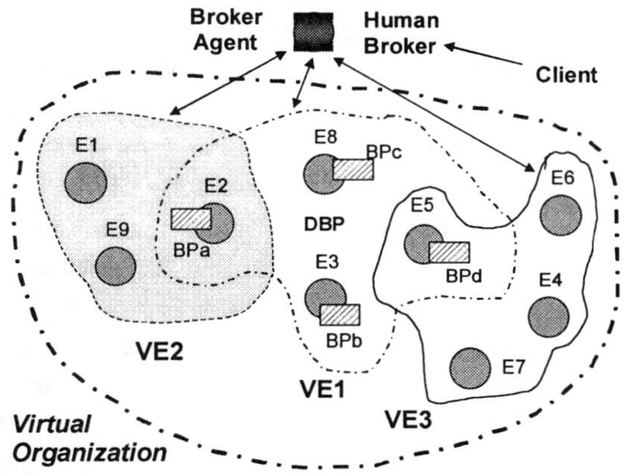


*Figure 1.* A VE scenario within VIRFEBRAS

# 4. THE BROKERAGE SCENARIO

In the current VIRFEBRAS scenario, the enterprises receive client orders both directly (i.e. in the traditional way) and via the broker. A client order can involve an individual or a set of moulds and/or dies. The client may also indicate if the mould maker can or cannot subcontract other mould makers for each mould. A client order can arrive at the broker with a detailed specification or as a draft. In the latter case, a number of interactions among the client and the involved enterprises are required until the final proposal is agreed.

Regarding the MMB prototype being developed, the system validation and testing have been made gradually, comprising the following (partial but real) scenario for the client orders arriving at the VIRFEBRAS' broker:

1. a client order arrives as a set, i.e. as a group of individual moulds;
2. considering quality control and trust aspects required by the client, in any case an interested enterprise cannot subcontract another enterprise, even if it belongs to the cluster;
3. a client order has all information completely and precisely specified when it arrives at the broker.

A client order specifies the mould size (in *tons*), its type (*mould* or *die*), the part material (*aluminum* or *plastic*, or *die*), and the due date (for each mould or for the entire package). The mould drawing is usually sent as well, but it is not dealt with for brokerage purposes. For the broker, the technical competence of each VIRFEBRAS member is represented in terms of its *capacities*, namely the *mould size* and *type* that each one can manufacture.

Four basic steps are carried out in the VIRFEBRAS brokerage system life cycle:

1. for each business opportunity, the broker analyzes the package (DBP) and identifies who are the potential candidate enterprises for each mould or die (BP), invites them to bid, and finally distributes the client order among the enterprises whose competence fits the tender;
2. the involved enterprises should receive, analyze and bid in the case they are interested and capable to satisfy the BP's requirements. A bid requires the direct intervention of the enterprise's manager so that the price can be provided and eventually the proposed delivery date from the PPCS can be refined. Once the bid is sent to the broker, the enterprise books its agenda for that business until it receives the final decision if the BP has been assigned to it or not;
3. having positive bids, alternatives of VE for a given DBP are formed;
4. after the evaluation of every alternative and the election of the suitable VE, the VE is created and the involved enterprises are noticed about the final result, corresponding to the final commitment to the given business.

# 5. A MULTI-AGENT ARCHITECTURE

Multi-agent Systems (MAS) represents a suitable approach for modeling the enterprises that can participate in a VE, since they can exhibit some relevant capabilities like autonomy, interaction with other agents, decentralized and distributed decision-making, scalability, flexibility in the creation of coalitions, among many other (Rabelo et al., 98). Therefore, the MAS approach is quite suitable to support the VIRFEBRAS requirements. Applying a MAS approach to this brokerage activity implies that agents have to exchange information with each other so that a set of consortia of enterprises capable to perform a given package can be identified. Once these consortia are generated, the selection criteria are based on the *lowest global cost* and the *shortest delivery date*, in this priority order.

## 5.1 The MMB System Architecture

In order to cope with the VIRFEBRAS scenario requirements, four hierarchical and heterogeneous *classes* of agents have been designed:

– Mould-Broker (MB): it is the global system supervisor, acting as the more direct interface between the system and the human broker.

- Facilitator (F): it represents the logical set of enterprises that have a given technical competence. Therefore, the mould-broker agent first sends a call for tenders to the facilitators whose competence area fits the client's order *type*. This speeds up the contract process as well as avoids the unnecessary message exchange among agents that are not potential bidders.
- Enterprise-Agent (EA): it represents every enterprise of the cluster into the multi-agent community.
- Consortium (C): it is a temporary agent created to manage the process of generating VE alternatives for a certain package based on the bids received from the enterprise-agents. Once the broker and VIRFEBRAS board decide for the best schedule and awards it to the involved enterprise-agents, the respective consortium agent dismantles itself.

## 5.2 Control Information Flow

Figure 2 illustrates the essential control information flow among the MMB agents' *classes*. One important aspect to be highlighted in the MMB system is the direct involvement of the enterprises' representative in the negotiation process. In the mould and die sector, the *quotation* and the specification of the *delivery date* are two pieces of "lethal" information to be sent to the broker. Even small mistakes can imply a huge loss. Hence it is fundamental for the manager – at least at this stage of the system – to have these information "under his/her control". Therefore, when the enterprise-agents receive a tender and make their computation, the manager is asked to manually feed it with those information. It means that, although agents are used to give more agility in the brokerage process, humans make the decisions. It corresponds to a *hybrid* or *semi-automated* approach as the managers acts directly both in the interaction with the agents, and in the final election of the best composition of enterprises for a given package.

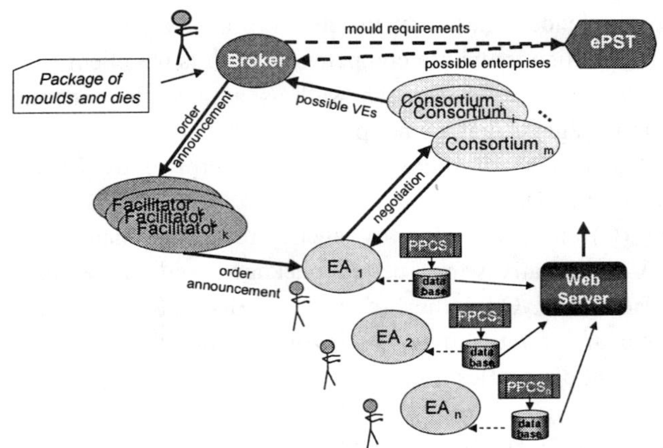


*Figure 2.* The Control Information Flow in the MMB System

## 5.3 Other approaches for information integration

In the figure 2 two next developments are included. The first one is the integration of the MMB system with the VIRFEBRAS Web Server. Such server can be seen as a very simple *extranet*, allowing each member to see the planned/current capacity of the other members. This information is produced by each PPCS and made available in the respective members' databases, and the enterprise manager takes it into account when he/she needs to feed the agent with the delivery date. Equivalent information integration could be done in the case of enterprises that have some supporting system for quotation, hence also helping the manager to feed the agent with the price. The second development step foreseen is the integration with a complementary partners search and selection tool (ePST tool), like the one developed in (Camarinha et al., 99b), to find the missing partners outside in case not enough resources or skills are found inside the cluster.

Related to the integration of the VIRFEBRAS Web Server, PPCSs and databases (the "internal modules") with the MMB system, some aspects should be pointed out. As mentioned above, there is no direct integration among these two entities so far (dashed line between the enterprise-agents and the other systems). One can note the simplicity or triviality of the general architecture to integrate the internal modules themselves. However, it is an approach that is very simple to be implanted at the enterprises, it does not require very specialized people in informatics, it is cheap and very easy to be understood and used by the manager and by other enterprise people. All these advantages themselves justify the approach in spite of some limitations. At this stage of maturation of VIRFEBRAS and the people involved, the most important aspect is that the system works and attends the basic requirement, which is to provide a way to share information about the members' capacities. At this moment, very sophisticated solutions could hazard the tough work of convincing the entrepreneurs about the advantages of the whole philosophy, and trust building.

On the other hand, some more advanced directions are going to be evaluated. It will not be the case of addressing other possible frameworks for the web-based implementation solution specifically, as this would be just a matter of software engineering to some extent. But the approaches to support more efficient interoperation among agents and those internal modules as a whole deserve some comments. In this context, the problem is how an enterprise-agent can get the information about the capacities (or other information, simple or complex) of the other in an integrated way, directed communicating with the internal modules. In general, this problem can be viewed as an *agentification* process.

*Agentification* means to develop a wrapper around the required/involved subsystems so that their particularities and heterogeneities can be encapsulated and a transparent front-end can be established (Rabelo et al., 94). In (Rabelo et al., 2000b), for instance, an agentification was developed to support a transparent communication with a web-server, where the multi-agent system protocol encapsulated HTTP commands. In a more sophisticated approach (Rabelo et al., 2000c), the concepts of federated and distributed databases are applied in order to support agents/enterprises autonomy and privacy, and better information management and integration, where the agents can have access to the required information within the VIRFEBRAS borders no matter how and where it is stored. In the case of the integration with the PPCS, it would require some re-engineering in it in terms of developing an integration layer (an API, as open and standard as possible) to support its interoperation with the agent, like the one described in (Camarinha et al, 99b). Other different not web-based approaches are going to be investigated as well, namely workflow-based ones, which offer a more tight control and advanced coordination capabilities among the applications/agents that act as information providers and information consumers (Rabelo et al., 2000b). Summarizing, the importance of investigating more advanced approaches and effective integration mechanisms is related to the preparation of the enterprises to run in a B2B environment, a must nowadays in this era of electronic commerce.

## 5.4 The Brokerage Flow in the VIRFEBRAS

The interactions among agents must be coordinated in a way that the desired multi-agent system can behave properly according to the VIRFEBRAS control rules. The Contract-net protocol (Davis, 80) is used to coordinate information exchange among the agents in order to form VE alternatives. After a package is split into individual moulds (or dies), a tender of every mould is spread out over the VIRFEBRAS enterprise-agents. Once received (via Facilitators), the agents evaluate the tenders and based on their agenda and capabilities, send a positive or negative answer to the Consortium agent (specially created to collect the bids related to the given package). After receiving the bids from all the interested enterprises, several possible coalitions of agent-enterprises are created. Each coalition represents a VE with a schedule, which can be evaluated through some objective performance metrics. The human-broker, with the results of the several Consortium-agents usually presented in the system, evaluates the most suitable coalitions for each package together with the managers of the enterprises in a board meeting.

# 6. IMPLEMENTATION EXAMPLE

An analogy with the VE life scenario could be made to better explain the phases necessary to run the MMB system being developed for the VIRFEBRAS cluster. Firstly the VE should be created and configured, i.e. the MMB agents should be identified and launched. Once a VE is created it can operate, i.e. once the MMB agents are launched they can execute the roles for which they have been created (see section 5.1). This section starts with the procedures to create and launch the MMB system, and after this an example is given of each of the four steps (see chapter 4).

## 6.1 "Derivation" of the MASSYVE Mould Broker System

The developed system corresponds to a set of instances of every MMBS agent classes, "derived" according to the VIRFEBRAS characteristics. The instantiation of the MMBS agents for VIRFEBRAS is composed of:

- *1 Mould-Broker;*
- *3 Facilitators (plastic mould, aluminum mould, and die competence areas);*
- *9 Enterprise-Agents (one per enterprise).*

The first action the system user should do is to launch the system itself. Once the system is logically defined and all the agents are identified including the specification of on which PC (host, IP address and port), each agent will be executed. The links among agents represent the necessary (and configurable) communication possibilities. Since the consortium agents are dynamically created when a package arrives, they are not initially modeled. Furthermore, each agent has its particular graphical interface when launched, through which the respective enterprise manager can interact with. After the launching of the system, the MMB system gets ready to receive client orders from the market. In the current implementation, as the MMB system is being tested by the VIRFEBRAS broker, all the agents have been launched in the same PC, which means that the broker is the person who feeds the agents on behalf of their representatives.

## 6.2 Package announcement and bidding

When the broker receives a client order, it should be sent to the enterprise-agents for evaluation and further bidding. Figure 4 shows the interface of one agent and the details of the tender received. Some of the agent interfaces are "hidden" in the figure in order to allow a better visualization. Figure 5 shows the interface though which the enterprise manager is called to indicate the delivery date and price.

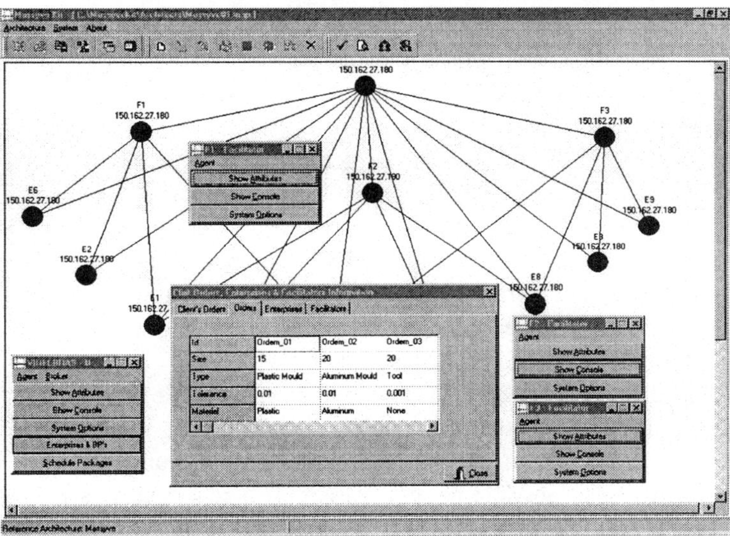


*Figure 4.* A package of moulds is received

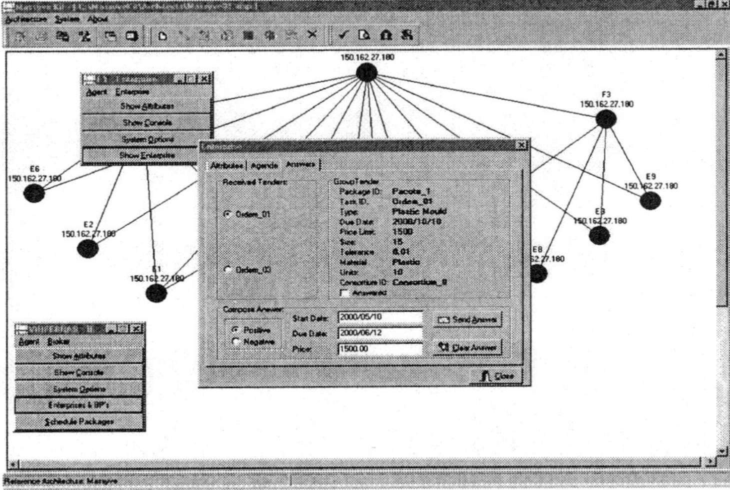


*Figure 5.* Bidding, with human intervention

## 6.3 VE Evaluation and Selection

After the contract-net processing according to the MMBS control information flow, a set of possible VEs are created. Depending on the package characteristics and on the enterprise availability, one enterprise can get more than one mould. The set of alternatives are evaluated by the human broker who consults, following the VIRFEBRAS rules, all of its members for taking the final decision about the suitable VE for the package. The evaluation considers the global lowest cost and shortest delivery date, using the information sent by the agents in their biding.

Figure 6 shows an interface where several VEs (with their respective schedules) were formed for a given package. In this case, only four VEs appear. However, depending on the number of alternatives generated, it is possible to see them in groups of four VEs. It is possible to zoom on each alternative and evaluate each one individually too. The performance indicators, which are the base for the decision, are provided at two levels: intra-organizational (i.e. the impact inside each enterprise) as showed in figure 6, and intra-organizational (i.e. considering the vision upon the whole VE). The broker makes a pre-evaluation on the VEs generated and takes the final decision with the VIRFEBRAS representatives.

Regarding the usual / relatively large number of possible VEs generated for a given package, the system offers to the broker the option to see / to "bring" the *n* best schedules firstly, ordering them according to the selection criteria price and/or delivery date. It is also possible to store these best n schedules in a historical file, organized by several "access keys".

The MMBS system prototype has been developed in C++ / UML on a PC / Windows-NT platform, and it has used the supporting software MASSYVE KIT Tool (MASSYVE, 2000) to generate the infrastructure of the multi-agent system. Once launched, each agent takes about 2-3 MB of memory. The agents use a particular high-level protocol and TCP/IP to communicate with each other.

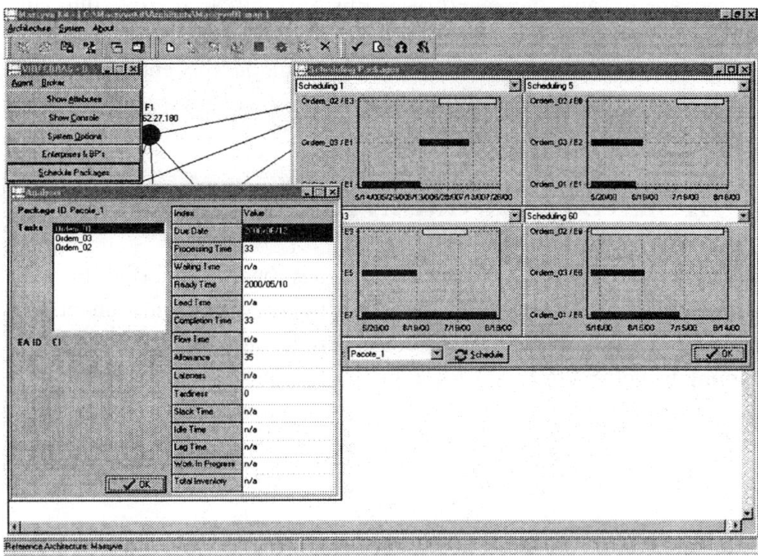


*Figure 6.* Evaluating possible VEs

# 6. CONCLUSIONS AND NEXT STEPS

This paper described a work being done at the VIRFEBRAS virtual organization, which is focused on the mould and die sector. A semi-automated brokerage system is proposed to assist the human broker in the selection of the most suitable team within VIRFEBRAS to accomplish a given business opportunity. The selection criteria are the lowest price and shortest delivery date. The system prototype developed – the MASSYVE Mould Broker System – is a decision-support system based on the multi-agent technology.

Initially it is intended to qualify the nine mould and die industries which currently composes VIRFEBRAS, enabling them to co-operate in the context of *Virtual Enterprises* by making them more competitive in the global market. Upon satisfactory results the intention is to transfer this work methodology to other mold and die industries of the Caxias do Sul cluster and possibly nationally. In fact, this work aims to prepare the VIRFEBRAS enterprises properly to run in a B2B scenario through the Internet.

This work is part of an ongoing initiative towards a wider and more generic brokerage tool, which is being installed for testing in the VIRFEBRAS. In this sense, and although already useful for this organization as it is now, next developments are being planned. It involves the implementation of procedures to support subcontracting as well as to refine the information models used while the enterprises gain more awareness and trust in the system. Besides that, the integration between the agents and the enterprises PPCS is foreseen, regarding the natural evolution of the VIRFEBRAS computational environment. In the medium-term it is intended to improve the negotiation protocol among the enterprises/agents, also including some supervision capabilities during the VE operation phase.

## 7. ACKNOWLEDGMENTS

The development of the MMB system has been supported by CNPq (The Brazilian Council for Research and Scientific Development) under the project DAMASCOS. Thanks to Mr. Maurício Andrade and Mr. Carlos Gesser for the programming tasks, and to Mrs. Flávia Saretta for the suggestions in the final text.

## 8. REFERENCES

[1] Camarinha-Matos, L. M.; Afsarmanesh, H. (1999a), The Virtual Enterprise Concept, in *Infrastructures for Virtual Enterprises – Networking Industrial Enterprises*, Eds. L. M. Camarinha-Matos and H. Afsarmanesh, Kluwer Academic Publishers, pp.3-14.

[2] Camarinha-Matos, L. M.; Cardoso, T. (1999b), Selection of Partners for a Virtual Enterprise, in *Infrastructures for Virtual Enterprises – Networking Industrial Enterprises*, Eds. L. M. Camarinha-Matos and H. Afsarmanesh, Kluwer Academic Publishers, pp.259-278.

[3] Camarinha-Matos, L. M.; Santos Silva, V.; Rabelo, R. J. (1999c), Production Planning and Control in a Virtual Enterprise, *in Infrastructures for Virtual Enterprises*, Eds. L. M. Camarinha-Matos and H. Afsarmanesh, Kluwer Academic Publishers, pp.219-232.

[4] Davis, R. (1980), The Contract Net Protocol: High-Level Communication and Control in a Distributed Problem Solver, *IEEE Trans. on Systems, Man, and Cybernetics*, 29, pp.1104-1113.

[5] MASSYVE (2000), http://centaurus.dee.fct.unl.pt/~massyve.

[6] Rabelo, R. J.; Camarinha-Matos, L.M. (1994), Negotiation in Multiagent Based Dynamic Scheduling, in *International Journal on Robotics and Computer Integrated Manufacturing*, Vol 11 N 4, pp.303-310, Pergamon.

[7]Rabelo R. J.; Camarinha-Matos, L. M.; Afsarmanesh, H. (1998), Multiagent-based Agile Scheduling, *International Journal of Robotics and Autonomous Systems, Special Issue on Multi-Agent Systems Applications*, N 27 pp. 15-28, North-Holland, ISSN 0921-8890.

[8]Rabelo, R. J.; Camarinha-Matos, L.M.; Vallejos, R. V. (2000a), Agent-based Brokerage for Virtual Enterprise Creation in the Moulds Industry, in *E-Business and Virtual Enterprises*, Eds. L. M. Camarinha-Matos, H. Afsarmanesh and R. J. Rabelo. Kluwer Academic Publishers, pp.281-290.

[9]Rabelo, R. J.; Klen, A. P.; Ferreira, A. C. (2000b), For a Smart Coordination of Distributed Business Processes, in *Advances in Networked Enterprises*, Eds. L. M. Camarinha-Matos, H. Afsarmanesh, Heinz-H Erbe, Kluwer Academic Publishers, ISBN 0-7923-7958-6, pp.81-90.

[10]Rabelo, R. J.; Afsarmanesh, H.; Camarinha-Matos, L. M. (2000c), Federated Multi-Agent Schduling in Virtual Enterprises, in *E-Business and Virtual Enterprises*, Eds. L. M.

Camarinha-Matos, H. Afsarmanesh, and Ricardo Rabelo, Kluwer Acad., ISBN 0-7923-7205-0, pp. 270-281.

[11]Santos, S. M. (1997) *O conceito de planejamento fino e controle da produção aplicado a ambientes de ferramentarias.* [in Portuguese], Master Thesis, Federal University of Santa Catarina.

[12]Spinosa, L. M.; Rabelo, R. J.; Klen, A. P. (1998), High-Level Coordination of Business Processes in a Virtual Enterprise, in Global. of Manufact. Digital Communic. Era of the 21st Century, Eds. Jacucci, G., Olling, G. J., Preiss, K. and Wozny, M., Kluwer Academic Publishers, pp. 725-736.

15

# An Engineering Approach to Develop Business Networks

Rainer Alt, Christian Reichmayr, Thomas Puschmann, Florian Leser and Hubert Oesterle
Institute of Information Management, University of St. Gallen
Mueller-Friedberg-Strasse 8, CH-9000 St. Gallen, Switzerland
Phone: (+41) 71 224 2420 / Facsimile: (+41) 71 224 2777
{Firstname.Lastname}@unisg.ch

**Abstract:** In order to attain Business Networking goals, such as the simple and fast exchange of transactions, increased customer care or reduced inventories, business partners have to be convinced about new ideas, new business processes among them and new (information) systems. For implementation to be successful, a variety of decisions will have to be taken concerning strategy, process and systems. Business Networking projects require a methodical approach completely different from that of traditional ERP implementations. The proposed method therefore guides managers in designing and implementing cooperation-intensive business networks. It covers aspects from strategy to implementation and follows the principles of method engineering. The 'Woodbridge'-Cases illustrates the method in practice.

## 1. CHALLENGES OF IMPLEMENTING BUSINESS NETWORKS

### 1.1 Questions in Implementing Business Networks

Following Kalakota/Robinson [1] companies are implementing eBusiness strategies in three areas: electronic commerce (sales and procurement), supply chain management (logistics) and customer relationship management (marketing and after sales). In order to characterise the development of these strategies for the B2B sector, the concept of Business Networking has been proposed [2]. Business Networking focuses in the first place on projects between business partners with a high co-operation intensity. Short-term, spot transactions are neglected in the following since they do not prevail in the B2B sector.

Thus, the implementation of business networks will focus on co-operative structures, which have been described as hybrids between markets and hierarchies in the organisational literature [3], [4]. Generally, we refer to long-term relationships between at least two key suppliers and/or customers who conduct transactions with medium frequency and information breadth[30]. Our experience in several projects which aimed at shaping interaction among business partners, an area we refer to as Business Networking proposed [2], yielded that a variety of critical questions have to be answered:

– What are the potentials of co-operation and in which area will Business Networking yield the most benefits? What are possible co-operation scenarios, how can they be specified and evaluated?
– In order to reach Business Networking goals, such as improved customer care or reduced inventories, how can business partners get convinced, business processes among the partners agreed upon, and the strategic and process scenario translated into enabling IT applications?
– How to evaluate applications that can be integrated into existing system landscapes? What are the implications of the networking solution for the overall application and service architecture?
– What is a proven sequence for proceeding in a Business Networking project? What are the major steps and what are suitable techniques for ensuring quick and successful implementation?

## 1.2 Existing Approaches and Requirements

Methods are proven to helpful address these issues systematically, to take advantage of the experience gained in other projects, and to ensure the proper documentation of project activities. In the first place, a method for Business Networking has to take into account the specifics of inter-business relationships. The main areas are all aspects associated with co-operation, the extended supply chain and new (electronic) services. Existing methods emerged primarily from the three areas shown in Table 1: co-operation management, process (re-)design, and implementation of Business Networking systems.

However, these methods show shortcomings in three respects:

– *They focus on a specific level of the Business Engineering model, i.e. they emphasise either the strategy, process or system level.* They do not provide guidance from the co-operation strategy through to the implementation of a Business Networking system. For example, the methods for co-operation management offer valuable insights into setting up and managing co-operations,

[30] The breadth of information describes the variety of exchanged information, e.g. not only transaction information, such as price, volume, article description, but also planning data and the like.

but do not address the selection, configuration, and implementation of systems supporting these relationships.

- *They frequently have only a low level of formalisation.* Systematic methods require a meta model, a procedure model, techniques, a role model, as well as result documents. Many methods, especially in strategy development and co-operation management, include only a procedure model and some techniques. Structured documentation of the result is often lacking, despite the fact that these documents form an important input for system implementation.
- *They do not provide support for networking processes.* The networking processes consist of electronic commerce (EC), supply chain management (SCM), customer relationship management (CRM) and the like. Existing methods are either generalised (e.g. BPR methods) or focus on designing particular networking processes (e.g. supply chain methods)

The goal is to present an initial outline of a method for Business Networking. The following requirements can be noted:

- The method should provide support for co-operation-intensive projects in the design, measurement, and implementation of collaboration processes.
- It should include new business models, potentials of electronic processes (e.g. EC, SCM), as well as the implications of using new Information Systems (IS).
- The method should take 'eService-provider' into account - a new form of organisation that (1) support co-operation between companies and/or consumers, (2) are largely electronic, i.e. with no manual intervention, (3) are accessible via computers or smart appliances, (4) can be used individually or as a package, (5) are highly standardized, and (6) are charged according to use [5].
- It should include standardisation efforts – the concept of the 'Business Bus'. It describes the totality of technical, applications and business standards on which software solutions, electronic services, etc. are based. These include EDIFACT, cXML, RosettaNet, OAGIS (Open Application Group Integration Specification) and OAMAS (Open Applications Group Middleware API), de facto standards for business objects such as those in the SAP environment (incl. the BAPIs as methods) or those of Microsoft's BizTalk, process standards like CPFR, and finally "laws" for Business Networking, e.g. generally valid rules for dealing with delays in delivery as now agreed in some cases between the participants in a supply chain [2], [6].
- It should include knowledge of existing methods and follow the design principles of method engineering [7].

| Strengths | Weaknesses | Examples |
|---|---|---|
| **Methods for Co-operation Management** | | |
| - Propose examples of models for establishing and managing co-operations<br>- Often include political and social aspects | - Lack advice on specific types of co-operations and the role of IT<br>- Inadequate specificity concerning business processes | [8], [9], [10], [11], [12] |
| **Methods for Business Process (Re-)Design** | | |
| - Generalised and applicable to a variety of industries<br><br>- Methods for supply chain management (SCM) include specific supply chain knowledge | - Inadequate extended supply chain focus and know-ledge of co-operations<br>- SCM methods neglect other processes, e.g. customer relationship processes | [13], see overview in [14]<br>[15], [16] |
| ***Methods for IS Implementation*** | | |
| - Include vital specifics for imple-menting Business Networking Systems (e.g. SCM-, EC-systems) | - Methods are vendor and/or tool-specific and are weak at the strategy and process levels | [17], [18], [19], [20] |

*Table1.* Overview of Existing Methods in Business Networking

## 1.3 Benefits of an Engineering Approach

Method engineering is an approach developed by Gutzwiller/Heym [7], [21] to ensure the systematic development of methods. It has been used in the definition of various methods which are being used successfully in practice. Methods based on method engineering principles consist of five building blocks (see Figure 1):

- The *procedure model* contains the recommended sequence of all top-level activities. For example, a method for business process redesign may start with a preliminary analysis, continue with macro-design and finish with micro-design [22].
- *Techniques* describe how one or more results can be achieved. For example, a technique to measure supply chain performance includes the steps that have to be undertaken as well as various metrics, and provides hints on how to complete result documents. Tools, such as the ARIS Toolset [23], may support the application of techniques.
- *Result documents* are produced for the documentation of results and represent an important input for the specification of IT requirements. A result document for analysing as-is processes, for example, would be a process architecture.

- *Roles* describe who is participating in a project at a certain stage. These are determined by the decisions which have to be taken and the knowledge required to complete the result documents.
- The *meta model* contains the main objects of design and the relationships between these objects. For example, a method for business process redesign would specify that processes produce outputs and consist of activities.

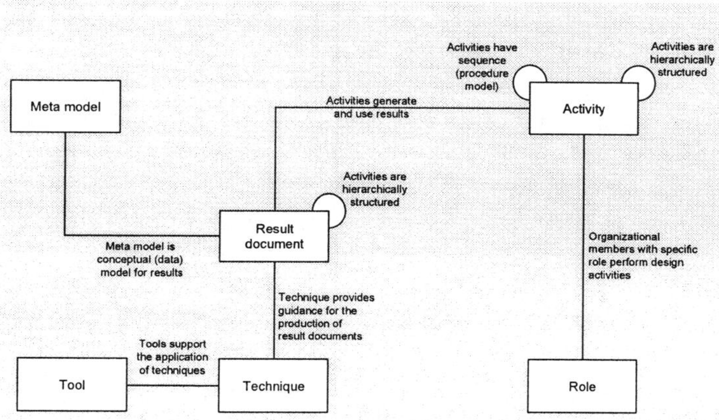


*Figure 1.* Elements of Method Engineering [7]

Besides helping to structure a project, methods are used to facilitate training and (self-)learning. In providing a common language they improve communication between people with heterogeneous backgrounds. Another advantage is that formalisation enables knowledge transfer, i.e. example result documents elaborated in one project can be used in another similar project. Experience has shown that these benefits are apt to lead to improvements in terms of hard (time, cost, quality) and soft (flexibility and knowledge) factors.

## 2. TOWARDS A METHOD FOR BUSINESS NETWORKING

In the following chapter, the structure of a method will be described which provides techniques that are applicable to all Business Networking strategies. The key features of the method are:

- the consistent usage of aspects relevant to co-operation at the strategy, process and IS level,
- the usage of method engineering which comprises a meta model, a role model, a procedure model and techniques plus various result documents, and

- the representation of project experiences gained out of eBusiness and SCM-projects from 8 partner companies – Bayer AG, Robert Bosch GmbH, Deutsche Telekom AG, ETA SA (The Swatch Group), Hiserv GmbH, Hoffman-La Roche, Riverwood Int., and SAP AG.

## 2.1 Design Areas of a Method for Business Networking

The advantage of the Business Networking method is that it can start from existing and established approaches in business engineering. As shown in the left columns of Figure 2, business engineering "structures the organisation, data and function dimensions at the business strategy, process and information systems levels." [24]. The method for Business Networking proposes three co-operation-specific enhancements:

- *Metrics.* Besides well-known process metrics, peculiarities of quality, time, cost, and flexibility, the method also includes measurements for collaboration processes. These include the efficiency of setting up relationships with a new Organisation Unit (OU), the implementation of an EDI link to a new OU, and the like.
- *Co-operation management.* Although Business Networking is IT-enabled, Business Networking projects are not primarily technical projects and require substantial co-operation management skills. This includes selecting and convincing business partners, generating trust, defining win-win situations and co-operation contracts, conflict management, initiating pilot projects, setting up project teams, co-operation controlling procedures etc.
- *Networking.* Business Networking builds on a new business model. On the strategy level this includes new co-operation models, on the process level new forms of electronic co-ordination (e.g. multi-vendor product catalogues, supply chain scenarios), and on the systems level the use of eServices-providers and the design of the business bus.

The method's systematic approach involves successively elaborating and refining the content of the three dimensions. In the case of co-operation management, for example, the structure of the initial co-operation concept is retained when drawing up the co-operation contract - additional details are merely added. The co-operation contract in turn serves as the basis for co-operation controlling. In the same way, initial assessments of networkability are successively refined into concrete and quantitative indicators.

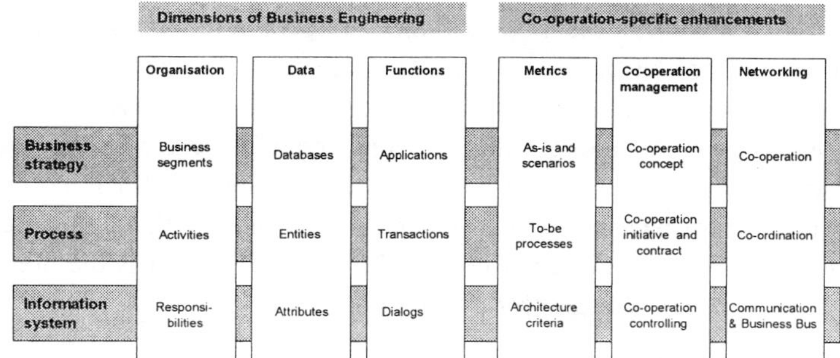


*Figure2.* Dimensions of Business Engineering and Co-operation-specific Enhancements

## 2.2 Meta Model

According to Brenner [25], a meta model is the conceptual data model of the results of a method and represents the constituent parts of the major design results of a method. Its purpose is to ensure consistency, providing a rapid overview of description and design areas and the terminology employed. The terms and their interrelationships are explained for each level (strategy, process, IS). Figure 3 shows the meta model at the strategy level with its entities and relationships. The gray scaled entities reflect the relationships to the process layer below.

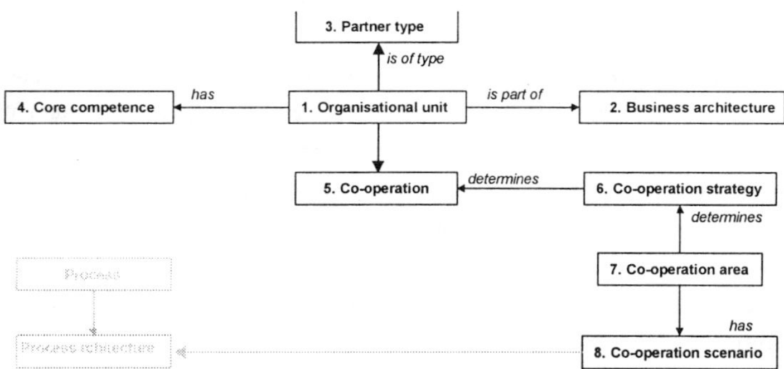


*Figure3.* Meta Model at Strategy Level

## 2.3 Role Model

The assignment of activities to ultimate units of responsibility is referred to as the role model. Roles are assumed by a business unit or individual employees, and involve tasks, competencies and responsibilities. The role model starts off by distinguishing the familiar roles of the people concerned: moderator, decision-maker, responsible and supporter.

In addition to inwardly oriented BPR methods, co-operation projects require a role model which includes the roles of the co-operation partners. The method assumes that an initiator has a co-operation idea and successively concretises it. The first step takes place in the initiator's own company with an assessment of the co-operation idea (or vision), along with its scope, benefits and consequences. The decision whether to go ahead with a concrete co-operation project in co-operation with one or more pilot partners is then made on the basis of this assessment. The experience systematically collected from the pilot partner project is the prerequisite for winning several partners and/or for a roll-out.

## 2.4 Procedure Model

The Business Networking method assumes that co-operations not only have common characteristics but are also similar in their implementation. This procedure model was obtained in several partner projects and distinguishes the four top-level activities 'analyse, design, plan/implement' (see Figure 4):

- *Analysis of co-operation potentials.* First, an analysis is undertaken to determine the area(s) with the highest returns for Business Networking. Often, a quick preliminary study of 2-3 weeks is conducted for this purpose. The result of this phase is a co-operation concept which is presented to top management.
- *Design and evaluation of scenarios.* Based on a co-operation concept, the specific design alternatives are developed and evaluated. This phase is performed jointly with the co-operation partner and leads to a co-operation contract.
- *Planning and implementation of pilot projects.* Based on the co-operation contract, individual projects are carried out, e.g. process reengineering, EC or Advanced Planning System (APS) implementation. This phase links with the implementation methods of system vendors (e.g. SAP's ASAP).
- *Continuation.* Depending on the success of the pilot projects (and other criteria) it will be decided how the pilot solution is to be continued. Possible decisions are (1) roll out the solution to other OUs, (2) discontinue the pilot, and/or (3) pursue other co-operation projects.

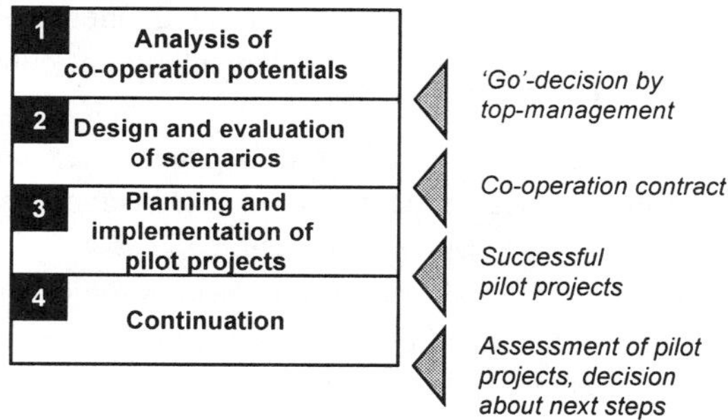


*Figure4.* Procedure Model of the Business Networking Method

## 2.5 Techniques

Procedure models define the temporal, logical sequence of steps in a problem-solving process [26]. The goals and results of each of the four phases of the Business Networking method are achieved by means of techniques which consist of a detailed procedure and result documents. The 11 techniques in total (see Figure 5) are explained below.

| method CCiBN | |
|---|---|
| Phase 1<br>Analysis of co-operation potentials | 1.1 Selection of co-operation area and project scope |
| | 1.2 As-is process and application architecture |
| | 1.3 Co-operation scenarios and metrics |
| | 1.4 Co-operation concept |
| Phase 2<br>Design and evaluation of scenarios | 2.1 Selection pilot partners |
| | 2.2 Process analysis |
| | 2.3 Design of application architecture |
| | 2.4 Co-operation initiative |
| Phase 3<br>Planning and implementation of pilot projects | 3.1 Management of project portfolio |
| | (internal project) |
| Phase 4<br>Continuation | 4.1 Operational co-operation management |
| | 4.2 Continuation |

*Figure5.* Phases and Techniques of the Business Networking Method

**Phase 1: Analysis of co-operation potentials**

*1.1 Selection of co-operation area and project scope.* The areas in which co-operation is to take place are specified. The starting points are the co-operation goals and the co-operation road map which shows possible areas of co-operation. A performance analysis is carried out for assessment purposes, and the project initiator determines the relevant dimensions of the project and the composition of the project team.

*1.2 As-is process and application architecture.* The as-is business, process and application network is modelled, taking into account the defined project scope. As-is analysis is the prerequisite for the design and implementation of optimised structures and processes.

*1.3 Goals, potentials and architecture of the to-be process network.* Collaboration scenarios, consisting of the business, process and IS architecture, are developed and evaluated according to the extent to which they meet the goals.

*1.4 Co-operation concept.* The main result document is the co-operation concept which is presented to the potential pilot partners at the beginning of the second phase (technique 2.1) and corresponds to a letter of intent. In order to achieve this result, the project initiator defines partner profiles, draws up a rough assessment of benefit categories (win-win situation) and selects the preferred type of partner.

**Phase 2: Design and evaluation of scenarios**

*2.1 Pilot partner selection.* The initiator selects the partners for the pilot project. The objective is to identify partners who have an interest in a quick win. The technique also includes team-building activities.

*2.2 Process analysis.* The focus is on defining the to-be process architecture. This involves selecting the strategic alignment and the basic processes. The objective is to develop the best suited process scenarios for which a standard software application already exists; i.e. the idea is not to develop a 'best case scenario' but one which can best be depicted in applications.

*2.3 Design of IS architecture.* The definitive choice of applications and eServices is made for the best suited application / eService scenario. The scenario is analysed to identify any shortcomings with regard to the processes modelled. This is followed by an analysis to determine how these gaps can be filled in terms of IS.

*2.4 Co-operation initiative.* This technique completes the co-operation contract in respect of common goals, obligations and resource deployment. The objective is to bring together the results obtained prior to implementation and, in particular, to review cost and benefit elements.

**Phase 3: Planning and implementation of pilot projects**

*1.1 Management of the project portfolio.* The inter-organisational activities required to achieve goals in respect of deadlines, costs and target fulfilment levels have to be co-ordinated. The methodological support for project realisation is not part of the Business Networking method; this is where the specific approaches of the project initiator, the pilot partners and the software manufacturer (e.g. ASAP for APO) come in.

*(Execution of internal partner projects).* Executes defined projects and monitors the delivery of results. It is not an integral element of the Business Networking method.

**Phase 4: Continuation**

*4.1 Establish operational co-operation management.* The objective is to ensure that the co-operation runs smoothly and that the co-operation goals are actually fulfilled.

*4.2 Continuation decision.* A final review of the pilot project is performed and the success of the project communicated to the decision-makers. In addition, a 'business case' is drawn up to gain (roll out) partners and the success of the co-operation is marketed at the inter-organisational level. Finally, a decision is made on how to proceed, i.e. roll-out to other partners or follow on with a new co-operation project.

Although the method proposes an ideal sequence of activities, we are aware that certain projects require modifications. For this reason, each technique contains a clear description of the required inputs. This permits lower starting points, parallel activities, cycles and the like. In order to provide some insight into the individual phases and techniques a reference case will be described.

# 3. REFERENCE CASE WOODBRIDGE, INT.

The Woodbridge case that focuses on SCM-issues is fictitious and was developed in order to provide a general and neutral example to explain the use of the Business Networking method.

Woodbridge, Int. located in Seattle, Washington, is a long-established, international manufacturer of cardboard, aluminium and plastic packaging materials. The main customer in the USA is Walters Best in Richmond, Kentucky. Walters Best produces different types of pasta that are packaged with plastics from Woodbridge. Walters Best sells the pasta to its end-customers, i.e. supermarkets, wholesalers, etc. Woodbridge has its own car pool to deliver the materials to Walters Best distribution center.

## 3.1 Phase 1: Analysis of Co-operation Potentials

Over the last two years Woodbridge ran into financial difficulties for the first time. The reasons for this, as shown by internal analyses, were a new competitive situation, rising costs and quality demands. Management's first reaction was to perform various analyses, i.e. potentials and risks, stakeholder, as-is customer, market and portfolio analyses, etc. It was then decided to define new co-operation concepts, open up new markets in South America and increase the level of customer service.

### 3.1.1 Selection of Co-operation Area and Project Scope

In order to improve external relationships it was decided to improve forecasting capabilities. In the past, it was not possible to exchange future demand figures electronically with business partners and no advanced planning system was in place to calculate different production plans. Customer demand was exchanged by telephone on a monthly basis only. Problems arising from this were:

- poor production capacity utilisation,
- high inventory stock levels at Woodbridge and Walters Best,
- no flexible reaction to changing demands, i.e. special offers, postponements, etc.

The results of all analyses revealed weaknesses in logistics and warehousing.

### 3.1.2 As-is Process and IS Architecture

The as-is situations of the following three result documents were established: business architecture, process architecture and IS architecture. The as-is business architecture shows a geographic overview of all linked business units, i.e. warehouses, plants, distribution centers, wholesalers, and, of course, end-customers (see Figure 6).

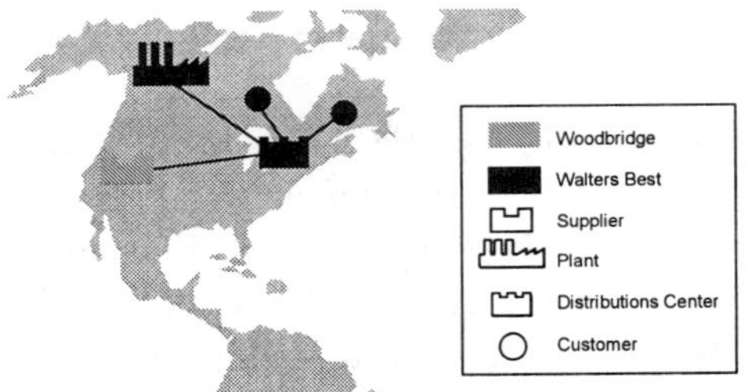


*Figure6.* As-Is Business Architecture

The process architecture consists of a macro and a micro level similar to established BPR methods [24]. The as-is process architecture describes all flows of information, goods and funds that are exchanged between business units (see Figure 7). The as-is process architecture at a more detailed (micro) level describes the main processes of the business units and their inputs and outputs within an activity chain diagram (see Figure 8).

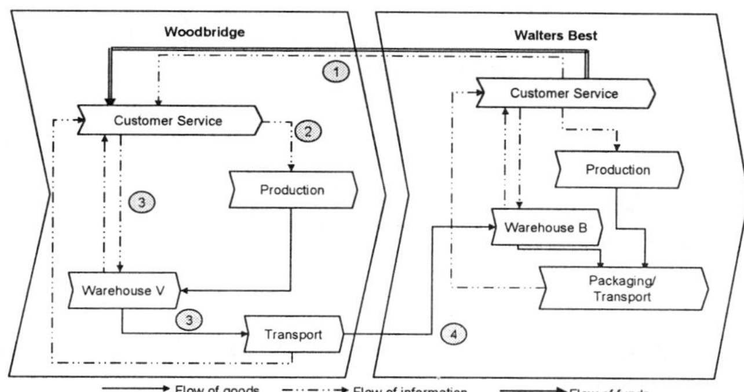


*Figure 7.* As-Is Process Architecture – Macro

At the beginning of the project the customer service from Walters Best ordered plastic materials from the Woodbridge customer service by telephone (1). Woodbridge produced an account of these orders along with past trends (2), and delivered plastics from warehouse V to warehouse B (3 & 4).

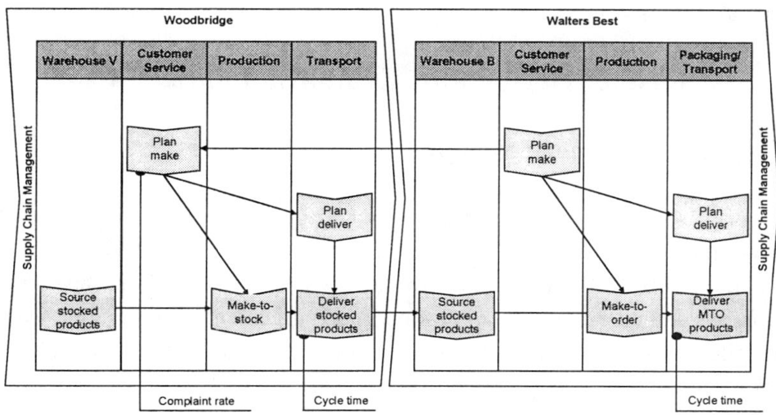


*Figure 8.* As-Is Process Architecture - Micro

As indicated in Figure 7 and Figure 8, there was neither an integrated planning function for the complete supply chain and future demands, nor an EC-solution to facilitate data exchange. Both enterprises only used ERP systems to plan their internal production (plan make), delivery (plan deliver), etc. (see Figure 9).

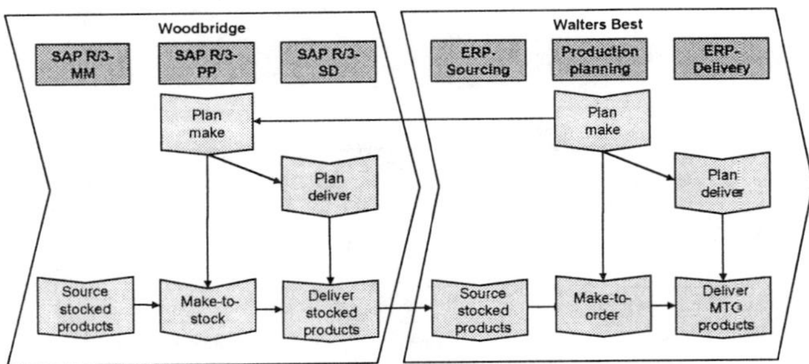


*Figure 9.* As-Is IS Architecture

### 3.1.3 Goals, Potentials and Architecture of the to-be Process Network

For the purpose of developing efficient collaboration scenarios, Woodbridge decided to consider benchmarking databases and best practices in the sector, such as Riverwood International. As a result, a Vendor Managed Inventory (VMI)[31] scenario was established to solve the problems in production and warehousing. An eService scenario was developed to solve the problems in shipment. The VMI scenario was to help decrease the costs of warehousing by about 40%, and the eService scenario was to help simplify the shipment process and decrease costs by about 20%.

## 3.2 Phase 2: Design and Evaluation of Scenarios

### 3.2.1 Pilot Partner Selection

Woodbridge analysed the market in South America and selected three corporations with which they considered co-operation to be a viable proposition: Wheat Ind., Brewers Finest and Delta Choc.[32] Walters Best and these new corporations signed a preliminary co-operation agreement. Walters Best was defined as the pilot partner and the others as partners for the continuation phase of the project when the pilot was rolled out.

### 3.2.2 Process Analysis

Woodbridge and its partners held various workshops in order to obtain a clear picture of how the benefits could be shared within the collaboration scenario, i.e. the

[31] VMI is a supply chain strategy that helps a company to collaborate with its customers to gather individual demand forecasts and synchronizes forecasts with local production plans to achieve greater flexibility in the planning and manufacturing process.

[32] Wheat, Ind. produces cereal products, Brewers Finest is a large brewery and Delta Choc. produces various sweets.

win-win situation. The overall co-operation principles, performance and co-operation goals were also defined. This included, for example, how to deal with conflicts, trust building and management, behavior in relation to competitors and collaboration processes. Finally, the main performance indicators for the scenario were fixed (see Table 2).

| **Scenario** | **Process** | **Metric** | **As-is Value** |
|---|---|---|---|
| VMI | Make-to-Stock | Capacity utilisation | 40% |
| VMI | Make-to-Stock | Unit cost | US$ 1m |
| eService | Deliver Stocked Products | Order fulfilment cycle time | 5 days |
| eService | Plan Deliver | Order management cost per ton of plastic | US$ 15,000 |

*Table2:* Metrics of Scenarios at Start of Project

The to-be business architecture shows the pilot project and the continuation partners, all warehouses, distribution centers, plants, etc. (see Figure 10).

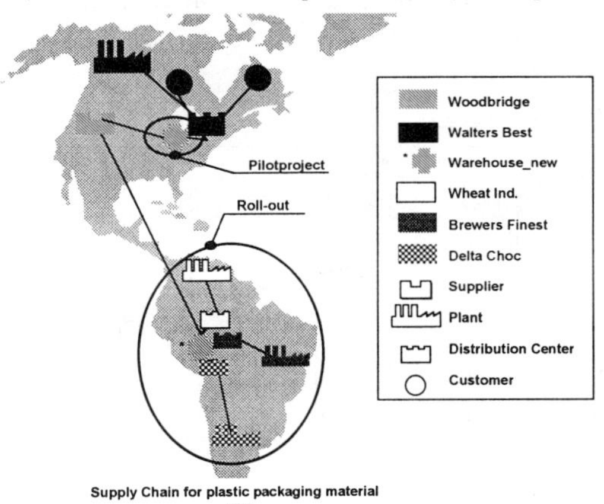


*Figure10.* To-Be Business Architecture

While the responsibilities of the various customer services remained unchanged, Warehouse V and the new Warehouse B are now managed by Woodbridge. It is responsible for product availabilities and stock level optimisation. Transport has been completely outsourced to a new partner, eLogistics (see Figure 11).

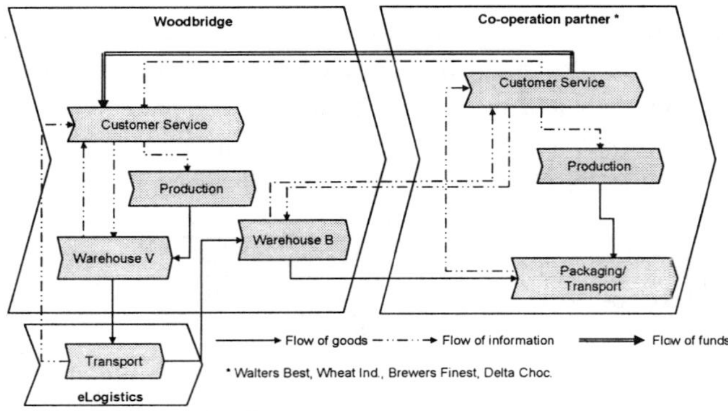


*Figure11.* The To-Be Process Architecture – Macro

These facts are again depicted in Figure 12 'Source stocked products' now belongs to Woodbridge and 'Plan deliver' and 'Deliver stocked products' to eLogistics. For the interaction with eLogistics an EC solution was established to facilitate requests for required capacities, availabilities and status information by developing two new processes: 'Inform MTO service' and 'Contract MTO service'.

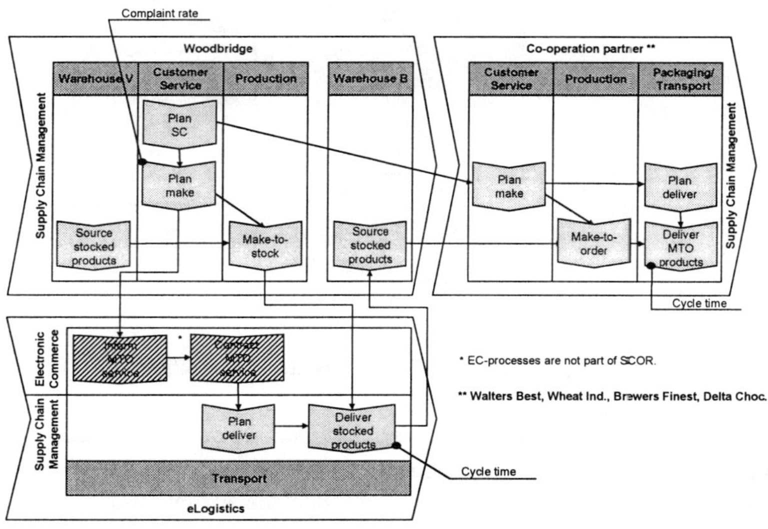


*Figure12.* To-Be Process Architecture - Micro

### 3.2.3 Design of IS Architecture

To manage the new warehouses and continuous forecasting, Woodbridge implemented an APS that has various interfaces to the core ERP systems of Woodbridge and partners. On the other hand, Woodbridge uses an electronic catalogue system from eLogistics that shows availabilities and conditions of transporters (see Figure 13) as well as the status of parcels to be delivered to partners and to Woodbridge itself via the Internet.

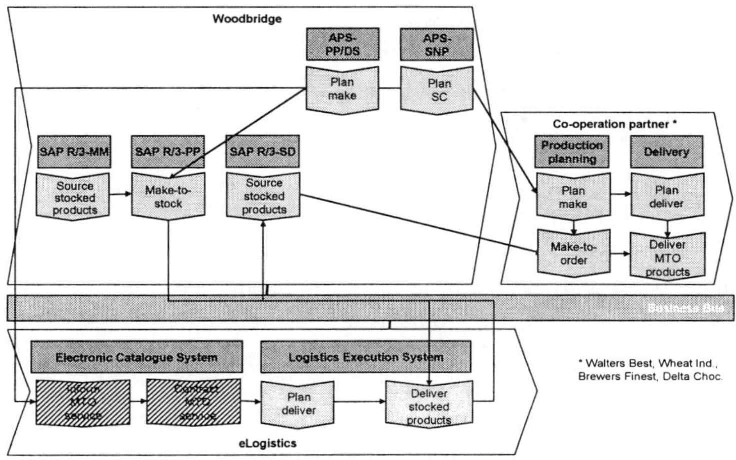


*Figure13.* To-Be IS Architecture

## 3.3 Phase 4: Continuation

At the end of the project a final evaluation of the main goals was conducted. Table 3 shows one result document out of technique '4.1 Establish Operational Co-operation Management'. Final, the project led to significant reductions in all core metrics.

| Scenario | Process | Metric | To-be Value |
|---|---|---|---|
| VMI | Make-to-Stock | Capacity utilisation | 85% |
| VMI | Make-to-Stock | Unit cost | US$ 560,000 |
| eService | Deliver Stocked Products | Order fulfilment cycle time | 1.5 days |
| eService | Plan Deliver | Order management cost per ton of plastic | US$ 8.500 |

*Table3:* Metrics of Scenarios at End of Project

# 4. CONCLUSION

Due to their specific characteristics, Business Networking or co-operation projects require additional steps and competencies in project work and procedure. Although a variety of methods are available, these methods present significant shortcomings since they either focus only on strategic aspects, do not include knowledge of networking processes, or else provide only a low level of formalisation.

The advantages of a method for Business Networking are that it:

- provides an integrative framework that includes all activities relevant to analysing, designing, planning/implementing and continuing Business Networking projects. It offers a structured path from (strategic) analysis and conceptualisation to implementation. Strengths of existing methods can be integrated.
- facilitates inter-organisational project management by providing a common procedure model, using understandable techniques and result documents as well as role descriptions. This helps to structure a shared project plan, to determine which tasks have to be performed and to decide who should be involved at which stage of the project. Problems arising from different corporate cultures, languages and systems can be avoided.
- addresses critical success factors relevant to Business Networking. The success of Business Networking projects is often determined by non-technical, i.e. organisational and political factors. Examples are creating win-win situations, homogenisation of master data and the like.
- supports knowledge management by transferring knowledge relating to prior and ongoing projects. It includes success factors and best practices as well as critical configuration and implementation know-how. Besides helping to provide direct benefits for project management, the method improves employee training. In doing so, it increases the flexibility and responsiveness of an organisation to cope with future networking challenges.

The information age presents a variety of challenges to management. The implications and opportunities are dynamic and the method for Business Networking represents a solid foundation for tackling these challenges in a systematic way. We see two areas in which the method can be extended:

- *Interaction with knowledge management.* The increasing volume of electronic transactions handled via Business Networking systems presents an important source for extracting information about customers. The integration of transaction-oriented and relationship-oriented Business Networking systems will provide new perspectives for creating tailored and efficient customer service.
- *Development of eServices.* Electronic services will be an important part of Business Networking in the future. How eServices can be developed or how they can be integrated at business, process and IS level are questions to be addressed in further development of the method.
- *Electronic marketplaces.* In comparison with long-term supply chain projects, co-operation with business partners by means of electronic marketplaces is frequently of a short-term nature. Extending the method to include techniques which also cover systems of this kind represents another direction in which the method might be developed.

# 5. REFERENCE


14. Kalakota, R., and Robinson, M. e-Business: Roadmap for Success. Reading (MA) etc.: Addison Wesley Longman, 1999.
15. Österle, H. "Enterprise in the Information Age." In Business Networking: Shaping Enterprise Relationships on the Internet, ed. Hubert Österle, Elgar Fleisch, and Rainer Alt, 2. ed., 17-54. Berlin etc.: Springer, 2001.
16. Fleisch, E. Das Netzwerkunternehmen - Strategien und Prozesse zur Steigerung der Wettbewerbsfähigkeit in der "Networked Economy". Heidelberg: Springer, 2001.
17. Wigand, R. T., Picot, A., and Reichwald, R. Information, Organization and Management. Chichester: Wiley & Sons, 1997.
18. Alt, R., Puschmann, T., and Reichmayr, C. "Strategien zum Business Networking." HMD - Praxis der Wirtschaftsinformatik, Volume 38, Number 217, 2001, pp. 43-55.
19. Puschmann, T., and Alt, R. "Enterprise Application: The Case of the Robert Bosch Group." A paper delivered at the Thirty-Fourth Annual Hawaii International Conference on System Sciences, Hawaii, 2001.
20. Gutzwiller, T. A. Das CC RIM-Referenzmodell für den Entwurf von betrieblichen, transaktionsorientierten Informationssystemen. Heidelberg: Physica, 1994.
21. Doz, Y. L., and Hamel, G. Alliance Advantage: The Art of Creating Value through Partnering. Boston: Harvard Business School Press, 1998.
22. Gomez-Casseres, B. The Alliance Revolution - The New Shape of Business Rivalry. Cambridge: Harvard University Press, 1996.
23. Håkansson, H., and Snehota, I. Developing Relationships in Business Networks. London etc.: Routledge, 1995.
24. Chisholm, R. F. Developing Network Organizations: Learning from Practice and Theory. Bonn etc.: Addison Wesley Longman, 1998.
25. Sydow, J. Strategische Netzwerke: Evolution und Organisation. Wiesbaden: Gabler, 1992.
26. Davenport, T. H. Process Innovation: Reengineering Work Through Information Technology. Boston: Harvard Business School Press, 1993.
27. Hess, T., and Brecht, L. State of the Art des Business Process Redesign. Wiesbaden: Gabler, 1995.
28. Bowersox, D. J., and Closs, D. J. Logistical Management: The Integrated Supply Chain Process. New York etc.: McGraw-Hill, 1996.
29. Christopher, M. Logistics and Supply Chain Management: Strategies for Reducing Costs and Improving Services. 2 ed. London: Financial Times/Pitman Publishing, 1998.
30. SAP. "Global ASAP, Version 1.0, CD-ROM." , Juni 1999. 1999.
31. IMG, A. PROMET SSW: Method for the Implementation of Standard Application Software Packages, Release 3.0. St. Gallen: IMG AG, 1998b.
32. i2. Rhythm - An Overview. Irving: i2 Technologies, 1997a.
33. Syncra. QuickWin: Guide to Trading Partner Collaboration. : Syncra Software, Inc., 1998.
34. Heym, M., and Österle, H. "Computer-aided Methodology Engineering." Information and Software Technology, Volume 35, Number 6, 1993, pp. 345-354.
35. IMG. PROMET BPR, Methodenhandbuch für den Entwurf von Geschäftsprozessen, Version 2.0. St. Gallen: Information Management Group/Institut für Wirtschaftsinformatik Universität St. Gallen, 1997b.
36. Scheer, A.-W. ARIS - Business Process Frameworks. Berlin etc.: Springer, 1995.

37. Österle, H. Business in the Information Age: Heading for New Processes. Berlin etc.: Springer, 1995.
38. Brenner, C. Techniken und Metamodell des Business Engineering. St. Gallen: Institute for Information Management, University of St. Gallen, 1995. Doctoral Thesis.
39. Heinen, E. Industriebetriebslehre: Entscheidungen im Industriebetrieb. 9 ed. Wiesbaden: Gabler, 1991.

MAIN TRACK - PART FOUR

# ONLINE COMMUNITIES

16

# The Community Model of Content Management

Johannes Hummel and Ulrike Lechner
*mcm*institute *for Media and Communications Management, University of St.Gallen*
Johannes.Hummel@unisg.ch and Ulrike.Lechner@unisg.ch

**Abstract:** Peer-to-peer architectures for sharing pieces of music illustrate how quickly consumers adopt novel structures - as long as they provide clear incentives. The services MP3.com, Napster, and gnutella are alternatives to the classical architecture of the value chain in which the music industry had a prominent role. We present a community model for content management and analyze system architectures, value chains, the relation between content and community management, and the trend towards peer-to-peer architectures. We argue that the traditional content is being increasingly embedded in a social, economic and organizational context and that therefore content management can hardly be separated from community management. We explain this comparing traditional and novel peer-to-peer content and community management of the music industry.

## 1. MOTIVATION AND INTRODUCTION

Information and communication technology does not only provide new kinds of content, but also new designs for the production, packaging, multiplying and distribution of it. As a consequence, novel business models occur where new actors are involved in various processes along the value chain.

This paper contributes to the discussion of the impact of technology on business models for content management. Our example is the music industry. This industry with the traditional offline industry and the novel services such as MP3.com, Napster.com, and gnutella is a prominent example of the role of technology in the change of the creation of economic value through new business models for content management. We focus on one particular business model, *virtual communities,* and argue that community and content management are inseparable in the novel services for content management. We present the community model for content management, discuss it and illustrate it with the novel structures in the music industry.

This paper is organized as follows. First, we analyse the characteristics of content on the Internet as a digital product (Sect. 2). Second, we look at the role of communities regarding the management of content (Sect. 3). In this chapter, we describe types and functions of communities as business models and focus on the technology as a prerequisite for content management. In the fourth section (Sect. 4), we illustrate our description using the example of services and communities in the music industry. We close this paper with a short discussion of the findings (Sect. 5).

## 2. CONTENT ON THE INTERNET

The notion of content is closely related to the kind of medium that transfers it. In traditional one-way mass media content is typically a product of the media industry. Newspaper articles, television spots, sport coverage etc. are being produced, packed, multiplied, and distributed by the media industry. A piece of content, i.e., a television show or a newspaper article is in itself a sensible unit. The traditional communication channels assemble pieces of content according to their format and multiply and distribute the (packaged) content.

This is being changed through technology. Due to Internet and its digital technology content has a much broader meaning in the sense of an information good (Allen 1990). The *characteristics of content on the Internet* and its differences to content in the traditional media industry are shown briefly on four aspects:

1. Content is digital. Most contents are digital or have a digital counterpart. E.g., the mp3 format is a digital counterpart to analogous as well as other digital formats such as, e.g., CD-formate or disks and cassettes. There is both conventional and digital broadcasting and television. Digital contents can be distributed and processed with the means of information technology. As the digital technology becomes a commodity everybody can easily create, package or modify content. Moreover, digital contents are accessible to machines of all kind for processing - this increases the availability of contents and makes the contents more valuable than conventional counterparts (Shapiro and Varian, 1999).
2. Content is linked. As the Internet can be seen as an electronic network, the content is embedded in and part of this network. Compare the isolated web pages to pages as part of a Web site or of an information system or online application. An isolated site or a single web-page is practically valueless - it will hardly be visited. Only if a page is linked, it is accessed through customers and becomes valuable. In many cases, the value of the content results from a direct link of information to transactions, e.g., through hyperlinks or from links between pure information on products and transaction services to buy those products (cf. (Shapiro and Varian, 1999)). Still, this content and its link structures need to be structured and organized (Stanoevska-Slabeva and Schmid, 2000).

3. Content is interactive. As every participant is recipient and sender at the same time, the Internet allows interactivity in a much broader way than traditional media. There is traditional passive content, as e.g., the one on books, television, or broadcasting. Particular to the new media are interactive contents with some interaction between user and application or among users. Interactive contents may solve problems presented to them and adapt to users' needs. Therefore, the producer of content is not only the media industry, but also every participant in the Internet (Schmid 2000). This leads to the consequence that it changes over time with the media and the community interacting with the content.
4. Content is embedded in a social, economic and organizational environment. Individual content is sometimes very valuable for other participants. As the Internet does not only have the cultural function of information as traditional media, but also the economic function of commerce and the social function of community, this content spills over to these functions (cf. Sect. 3.2). E.g., in the Internet everybody can provide information about products. The experiences that consumers share are considered to be more trustworthy and valuable than information provided by producers. (Schubert, 1999; Schubert and Ginsburg, 2000; Hagel III and Armstrong, 1997)

The characteristics of content as shown above have several consequences on the whole value chain of the media industry. Not only the sources of content are much broader, as every participant is a potential creator and sender of content. But also as the Internet does not only allow one-to-many communication as the traditional media, but also many-to-one or many-to-many kind of communication, all steps of the value chain can be implemented following a new design. This leads to increasing competition on every stage of the value chain, as new business models occur for every part of the value chain, allowing new actors to participate and to manage the processes. As a consequence, the management of content is getting one of the most important functions to keep or get revenues from. The pure content, as produced typically by the media industry, is adorned with other contributions by the community. Here, content and the social environment of the community become inseparable. Moreover, with the novel peer-to-peer architectures, a transaction infrastructure for peers has emerged in the music sector. This article describes one of the most fascinating examples of this which has a deep impact on the business model for the media industry - the phenomenon of virtual communities and their peer-to-peer services as a possibility to manage and distribute music files through the consumers.

# 3. COMMUNITIES AS A MODEL FOR CONTENT MANAGEMENT ON THE INTERNET

In this chapter, we describe virtual communities, their functions, and their role as a business model for community management. First, we take a closer look at the prerequisite for the development of these communities, the development of multi-directional communication, and peer-to-peer architectures as a consequence of the interactive technology of the Internet. On this basis, we describe virtual communities, their functions, and the business model "virtual community" in more detail.

## 3.1 System architectures - infrastructures for communities

The information and communication technology of the Internet provides platforms to create content as described above. On these platforms, interaction is part of the creation of content and of economic value. Three basic architectures for interaction can be differentiated (depicted in *Figure. 1*). In mass communication, the traditional model of the media industry, communication is unidirectional. Contents are being produced and distributed to the consumers through channels which allow hardly any feedback or consumer contribution. The possibility of easier and less costly interaction through the medium Internet changed the transactional model profoundly. In mass customization, communication channels are interactive - content can be exchanged between consumer and producer/intermediary rather than transmitted from producers to consumers. A little feedback from the consumer enables the producer/intermediary to tailor the communication to the individual consumer. However, there is an information and communication asymmetry; typically, the producer has more information.

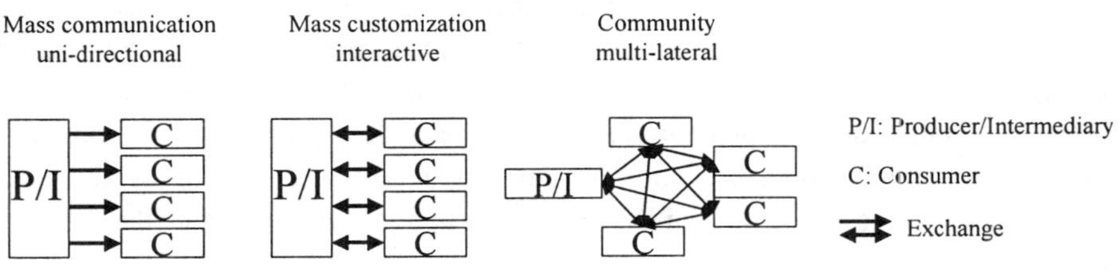


*Figure. 1* Interaction models

This asymmetry decreases in the community model as all interaction partners are able to communicate with each other. Computer science refers to this architecture as peer-to-peer. All members of the community are able to participate in communication on an equal basis, i.e., as peers. Internet has a peer-to-peer architecture in the sense that every participant may initiate communication to anybody connected to this network. The service WWW allows everybody to publish and retrieve information from the Internet. Only recently, the interest in peer-to-peer architectures surged. Currently, the predominant transaction is the sharing of files (e.g., gnutella), and of storage or processing capacity (e.g., seti@home).

Uni-directional, interactive and multi-lateral communication channels induce new architectures for the distribution of information. Characteristic of unidirectional communication is a client-server architecture with a powerful server that manages information, its flow, and weak clients. The position of the server is weakened and the position of the clients is strengthened in the interactive communication channel. The community model of computing induces an organization where all participants interact on an equal basis with respect to communication and computation.

Information and communication technology provides novel means to gather, process, distribute, and communicate information and content. Depending on their abilities for information processing and communication this technology allows in particular the consumers to become peers in the creation, sharing and management of common content. In business, such a communication design is often referred to as a "community". But what is a community all about?

## 3.2 Communities and the role of content

The term "virtual community" has established itself for communities in which communication is facilitated by electronic media, in particular, for communities where interaction takes place on the Internet. (Rheingold, 1993). Online community is a synonym for "virtual community". Over time various aspects of virtual or online communities have been discussed in literature: social, political, and economic aspects and the perception of virtual communities has changed over time from a social phenomenon to a valid business model (Hummel and Lechner, 2000).

The creation of economic value in this business model results especially from the content and knowledge, the participants bring into the community (Timmers, 1998). The members of a community may contribute to the creation of economic value with various kinds of contributions: information, product reviews, recommendations, pieces of music, files to be shared. The community contributes pieces of content similar to the contents produced by the media industry. Virtual communities, however, provide the social and economic environment that meets human needs and the contents that communities produce can hardly be separated from this context.

There are sociological, economic, and technological views on virtual communities. The first sociological definitions came from Taylor and Licklider who saw the community potential of electronic networks in 1968. They described their vision of a virtual community "...in most fields they will consist of geographically separated members, sometimes grouped in small clusters and sometimes working individually. They will be communities not of common location but of common interest..." (Licklider and Taylor, 1968).

Probably best known is the definition of Howard Rheingold (Rheingold, 1993). He defines virtual communities first as purely related to the Internet. From his point of view virtual communities are "...social aggregations that emerge from the Net when enough people carry on those public discussions long enough, with sufficient human feeling, to form webs of personal relationships in cyberspace" (Rheingold, 1993). Later, he also emphasizes the importance of the connection between real and virtual communities. Due to his experience with the virtual community "The well" (well.com), he sees communities as "....a group of people who may or may not meet one another face to face, and who exchange words and ideas through the mediation of computer bulletin boards and networks" (Rheingold, 1994).

In a similar way, somehow seeming a little transfigured, argue Godwin and Jones. Godwin is of the opinion "...but in cyberspace, increasingly, the dream is not just „owning a house" – it's living in the right neighborhood (Godwin, 1994)". Jones even speaks of "virtual settlement (Jones, 1997)". Figallo is later stressing the meaning of common values writing "...according to that definition, members of a community feel a part of it. They form relationships and bonds of trust with other members and with you, the community host. Those relationships lead to exchanges and interactions that bring value to members" (Figallo, 1998).

From the view of computer-mediated-communication the most important elements of a virtual community are shared resources, common values, and reciprocal behavior. Whittaker et al. write in their definition "...members have a shared goal, interest, need,...engage in repeated, active participation,...have access to shared resources, reciprocity of information,...shared context of social conventions..." (Whittaker et al. 1997). Preece extends this view on the necessity of common rules „...an online community consists of: People, who want to interact socially... policies ...that guide people's interactions (and) computer systems, to support and mediate social interaction..." (Preece, 2000).

Hagel and Armstrong were the first who broke with the view of virtual communities as sociological phenomenon (Hagel III and Armstrong, 1997). They see in virtual communities a business model which uses communication on the Internet to create electronic market places and to increase customer loyalty. Referring to Rheingold they define virtual communities "...but virtual communities are more than just a sociological phenomenon. What starts off as a group drawn together by common interests ends up as group with a critical mass of purchasing power, partly thanks to the fact that communities allow members to exchange information on such things as a product's price and quality"(Hagel III and Armstrong, 1997). Following (Timmers, 1998), we consider "Virtual Community" to be a business model in electronic markets distinguished by "The ultimate value of virtual communities is coming from the members (customers or partners) who add their information ... ".

Virtual communities are socio-economic business models. Regarding *economic* functions, commercially-oriented virtual communities can contain, in general, all economic functions that are part of other Internet-intermediates.

Today, the business model of virtual communities is well differentiated. *Figure 2* depicts the five kinds of commercially relevant communities and their content.

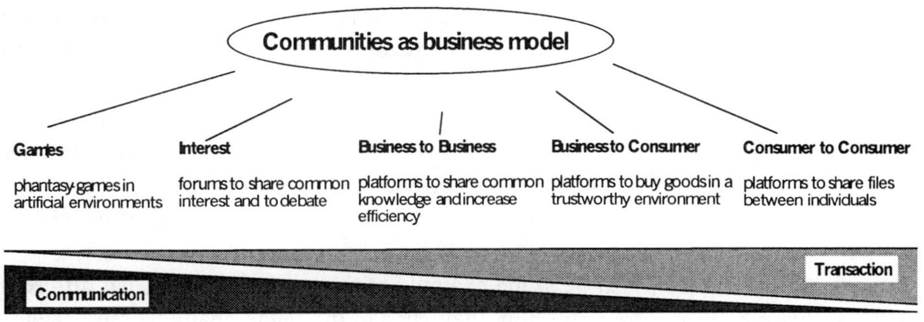


*Figure 2.* Communities, their platforms and content

The purpose of game communities is playing interactive in artificial environments with other members. Communities of interest are forums to meet people and to debate with them about a common interest. In Business-to-Business communities people of the same profession meet each other, debate about business related issues, and make transactions regarding their business. Business-to-Consumer communities create a trustworthy environment where consumers are more willing to buy from the shop(s), offering this community. Finally, in Consumer-to-Consumer communities, individuals trade goods between each other without a commercial intermediary.

In all of these kinds of communities (depicted in Figure 2), content plays a mutual role. In game communities, participants create content in the way of "real" goods, as they explore resources, deal with each other or build their houses etc. In communities of interest, the participants use the forum to exchange thoughts or news. They bring in their own content and contribute to the existing content others brought in. In all transaction oriented communities from business-to-business over business-to-consumer to consumer-to-consumer we find two kinds of content. The first one is information which is shared or exchanged between all participants. In this way, content has the economic characteristics of an information good. The other ones are recommendations, reviews, and ratings of buyers and sellers and participants of chats etc. They help to create a social and economic environment to facilitate transactions through the building of trust, reducing complexity and transaction costs. Communities create extra value through combining both kinds of content.

Content has therefore different meanings in these business models. And it can be managed by all different participants of the community as well as by the technology itself (cf. for the services (Stanoevska-Slabeva and Schmid, 2000)). All participants can create or exchange content within the community. But also technology is playing a more and more important role regarding the creation of content. Think of the recommendation services of many online shops. The medium observes the transactions of participants, detects the social structure in terms of profiles and interests, and communicates the respective recommendations on which goods to buy. The exchange of information relevant for a customer segment is fully automated. Most likely such a communication does not meet the need for social relations and maybe this interaction does not foster trust. Similar to consumer contributed reviews the recommendation provides information about relevant and good products - based on the assumption that those eventually are being bought by more consumers.

In the following we illustrate at the example of the music industry what different kinds of this model occurred and how they change the value chain. These changes result in new possibilities to manage the most important content of this industry – music files. It is accompanied by a switching of power from the traditional media industry to third party services and consumers.

# 4. CONTENT MANAGEMENT IN THE MUSIC SECTOR

In the past years a variety of new models for content management in the music industry have been implemented. MP3.com, Napster.com, and gnutella are examples for services for Online content management. In this section, we discuss their architectures for the creation of economic value through content management and explore the trend toward a community model for content management. We consider first the system architecture (Sect. 4.1.1) and then discuss the value chain with actors, roles, and the interaction on these architectures (Sect. 4.1.2). This first part is dedicated to the interaction infrastructure for community management with processes and interaction in content management. Then, we discuss the impact of content management to the social systems and the individual participating in the social system (Sect. 4.2).

## 4.1 Four models of content management

Subsequently, we present four models and their system architectures (1) The traditional business models of the music industry (2) mp3.com as a client-server architecture (3) napster.com as a combination of client-server and peer-to-peer architecture and (4) gnutella as an example for a pure peer-to-peer architecture.

### 4.1.1 System architectures

The system architecture with components and interaction channels distinguish the technology of content management. The four architectures are depicted in *Figure* . We observe that the classic architecture of the traditional music industry with unidirectional communication channels is being succeeded by a client-server with bidirectional communication channels. The consumers and artists communicate with the service. MP3.com is an example for an implementation of this architecture. Napster.com exemplifies a combined client-server with peer-to-peer architecture. Further on, there are pure peer-to-peer architectures as, e.g., gnutella.

Within this development, a hierarchical model, where the music industry used to have a strong position is being accompanied by novel architectures that follow the community paradigm, i.e., with self-organization and symmetric positions of all actors. These architectures reflect the actors and their infrastructure for content management. They allow the actors to manage content in various ways throughout the whole value chain. Subsequently, we analyze the value chain and the processes of content management more in detail and compare again the various models.

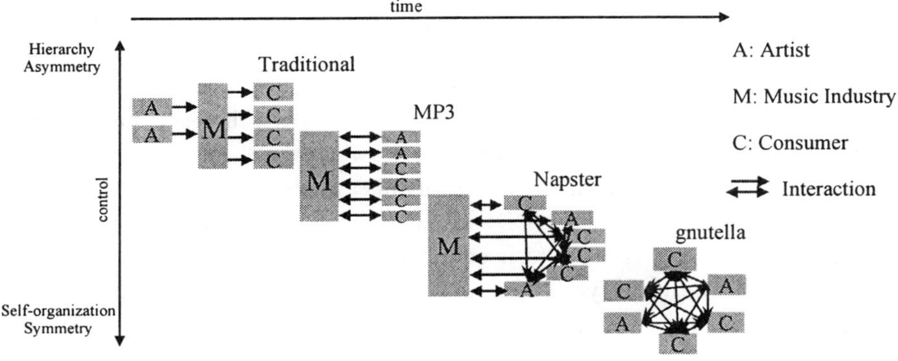


*Figure 3.* System architectures for content management in the music industry

### 4.1.2 Value Chain and Communication Design

In terms of value creation we suggest to distinguish seven steps in the value chain and the respective communication model. In the *traditional uni-directional value chain of the music industry* as depicted in Figure (Music Ind.), the artist is responsible for the creative part, the idea. The contents are being established. Here, artists and music industry work together. Then, the product is packaged, marketed, multiplied, and distributed. The music industry occupies these stages in the creation of economic value. The role of the consumer consists just in buying the product.

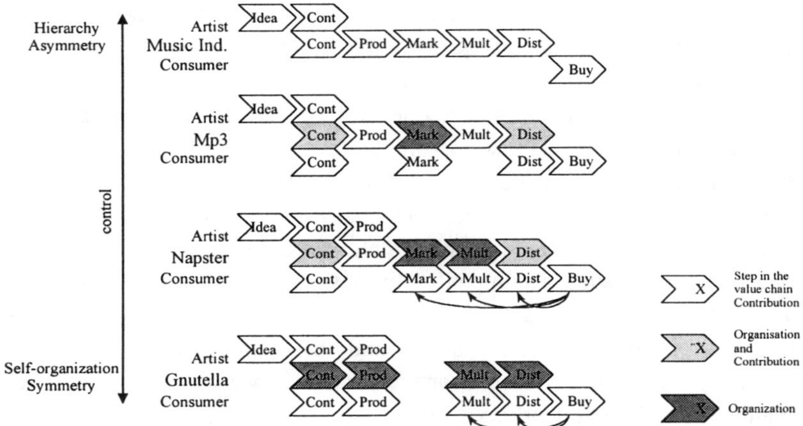


*Figure 4.* Value chains in the music industry

The novel services for content management - MP3, Napster and gnutella - implement these steps in the value chain in a different ways. Each service is briefly introduced. Then, its value chain, as depicted in Figure is analyzed.

*MP3.com* considers itself to be an online repository of the users music files to facilitate access to those pieces of music everywhere on the Internet (mp3.com). Users upload pieces of music - or identify themselves in the so-called beamer services as owners of a carrier (CD) for some piece of music. Each user has its account to access the pieces of music online. Access to music is granted via Internet technology. MP3 provides (yet unknown) artists to publish a CD online and offers to produce, ship, and offer CDs on demand.

MP3 offers a recommendation service that points out artists and music and various services of community interaction. The server has files, registry and, because of the interaction services, all information about the consumers and the artists.

In terms of the value chain the consumers, service, and artists contribute mp3 files. The service of MP3 contributes the storage space for content and some means to structure and organize the access to content, e.g., in search engines and directories. The consumers take over the marketing through reviews and within a recommendation service for peer groups. MP3.com just structures and organizes those contributions. They play an essential role for the distribution part of the value chain. MP3.com again just organizes this.

Thus, MP3 implements three steps in the value chain different from the music industry: the production of contents, the marketing, and the distribution. In all three cases, the consumers take over some role in contribution of contents - Mp3.com provides the means for structuring and organizing and allows for some interrelation between community and contents. However, only the step marketing follows a community architecture; the consumers interact following a community model.

*Napster.com* considers itself as "the world leading file sharing community" (napster.com). The server Napster.com offers a directory of lists of files to be shared and software to participate in the community. Each Napster client offers mp3 files of a dedicated folder on the hard-disk of the client to be shared to the community and allows to register all those files in the central directory, i.e. each client is client and server for sharing files. To search a file, the Napster client accesses the server. Swapping of files takes place following a peer-to-peer architecture. Napster.com has all the information necessary for community management. Every community member contributes content, storage facilities for files and digitized profiles.

In terms of the value chain depicted in Figure the service itself is involved in the marketing, multiplying, and distribution of the titles. The decision of a consumer to download (buy) a mp3 file influences the marketing implemented in a recommendation service. This dependency is represented as backwards arrows. Note that consumers themselves provide the resources for multiplication and distribution and trigger multiplication and distribution. This is also depicted as backwards arrows. Compared to the traditional model Napster implements four steps of the value chain in a novel way: production of contents, marketing, distribution, and multiplication. More steps of the value chain follow a community model - it is the community which contributes as peers to marketing, multiplication, distribution, and contents following in each step a community architecture. Moreover, Napster has features such as, e.g., buddy lists and allows for blocking certain users - such that the social aspects of a community and the content management within this community are more interrelated. Thus, Napster's architecture of the value chain is more peer-to-peer and the social function of community spills over to content management.

*Gnutella* is a file-sharing application without any central structure. It is widely used to swap any kind of files. Gnutella clients form a self-organizing net of peers. Searching for files and swapping of files are exercised in a peer-to-peer architecture. A gnutella client is client and server for files. It offers all files in a dedicated directory to be shared on the net, swaps files, searches for files, routes messages and requests files. There is *no* central service.

Gnutella clients do not offer any community building services, as communication or recommendation services; there is no marketing in gnutella's value chain. The value chain of gnutella shows that - apart from marketing - all steps are taken over by the consumers. They contribute the content, do multiplication and distribution (by their decisions to upload and download music). The service just facilitates all these interactions of the consumers.

In the development of the value chains, we see that various steps are implemented in a peer-to-peer architecture and that the pure content management of the traditional music industry gets interrelated with the community and its function. The contents in the community systems such as, e.g., Napster or gnutella is inseparable from the community: it is the community that contributes contents, marketing, multiplication, and distribution - the server only facilitates and structures the interaction.

Note however, that those value chains can hardly be considered isolated. The marketing done by the music industry plays an important role in all value chains - in all online services users need to know which titles they are interested in. This knowledge and the interest profiles are the basis for the recommendation services.

The developments in this sector are technology driven, but the consumer has an important role: the clear incentives motivate consumers to adopt these novel technologies and services. Since content and community and content management and community management are becoming increasingly inseparable one may ask how a community evolves using such a service and how individual strategy and community welfare relate to one another. This is discussed in the following section.

## 4.2 Member and community management

As shown above, all these communities rely on a variety of communication technology that enables various ways of interaction. Common to all these technologies is the fact that they are network technologies. Therefore one can expect that these business models are driven by network effects which are due to system feedbacks. Positive feedback describes the effect that the strong get stronger and the weak get weaker. Conversely, negative feedback describes that the strong get weaker and the weak get stronger. When the value of a good or service to one user depends on how many other users there are economists say that this product exhibits network externalities or network effects (Shapiro and Varian, 1999). Network effects are often the result of positive feedback effects.

As information and communications technology is changing from a technology for information processing to a communication technology these network effects play a more and more important role. Hagel and Armstrong refer to positive network effects as a major driver for the development of communities (Hagel III and Armstrong, 1997). On the first glance, all the four models described above seem to be the same regarding network effects. The more users such a service has, the more contents it is going to have and the more attractive it becomes. A more detailed view on the different technologies and on particular aspects shows however that some of the these technologies do also have specific negative feedbacks. Subsequently, we discuss the relation between a single user's contribution to the network and the effect that this has for its benefit from the network. One would expect that the architectures that resemble communication networks most closely, i.e. the architectures most closely to peer-to-peer architectures, are more likely to exhibit positive feedback effects. We argue that in fact these architectures display negative feedback. In this section, we explore the network effects and consumer benefit for the stages of the value chain of Sect. 4.1.2 contents, marketing, multiplication and distribution.

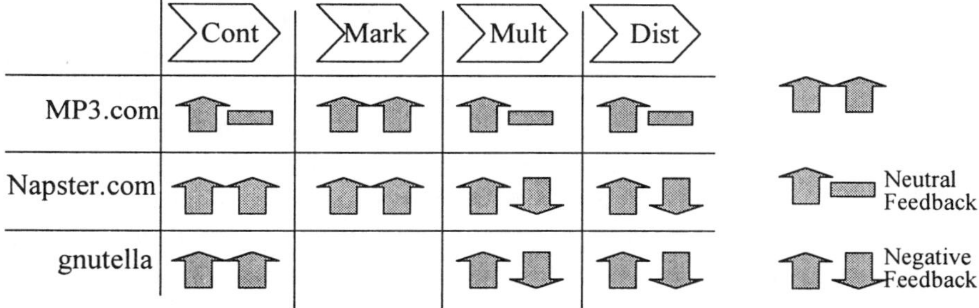


*Figure 5.* Feedback effects

Let us consider *content* and the correlation between the files a user contributes and the benefit a user has from contributing. The consumer has at MP3.com a neutral and at Napster.com and Gnutella positive feedback through an increase of the number of contributed files. All contents a user contributes are stored and available online such that the single user benefits from the storage capacity and the reliability of the network. This is some (relatively small) benefit that exceeds the mere increase of available files by increasing the number of files contributed. At MP3 the user basically has exactly those files at his disposal that she stores online - the increase in contribution equals the benefit, i.e. there is neutral feedback. Concerning *marketing* the important features are recommendation services. Those services improve with the number of transactions a single user and the whole community perform. This means a positive feedback at MP3 and Napster. Another relevant feature at Napster.com is the service that allows a user to govern who may download files from her computer. Many users are willing to share files only with those who also contribute and the service allows to block unwanted users from download. Both MP3 and Napster have here a positive feedback - the more information and files a user contributes - the better. In gnutella there is no such benefit, since there is no marketing.

In *multiplication* and *distribution* the feedback is either neutral or negative. On Napster and gnutella users do not only share files but also storage capacity and bandwidth. The one who contributes files shares his bandwidth with the users that download files from his computer. The consequence is a negative feedback for the individual user. The more and more popular files an individual offers, the more of his bandwidth is consumed by the ones downloading the files. Thus, at Napster and gnutella there is a negative feedback at this step of the value chain. Empirical studies show the asymmetry in contribution and the effect that people lie in terms of their speed of connection to the Internet such that they are not the ones who are selected as servers for a download (Adar and Huberman, 2000). At MP3, all users share the connection to the server, but not the "last mile". At this service the contributions do not inflict multiplication and distribution - we regard them to be neutral.

To sum up this analysis. Network effects do not apply to all three file sharing services. Moreover it is contribution of content that makes the least difference - the users have little positive or neutral feedback there. We assume that users of the services weigh the benefit that they have from the service as a storage device much lower than the negative feedback from distribution and multiplication. The disadvantage of sharing bandwidth with other users is clear for the one who contributes files. Thus, negative feedback in multiplication and distribution applying at Napster and gnutella outweights the positive or neutral feedback in contribution. The growth rate at Napster is high - a clear indicator for positive feedback and network effects. This again is then most likely due to the positive feedback of Napster in marketing. Moreover, Napster provides means for the management of the negative feedback effect in multiplication/distribution - a user can block users (typically the ones who do not contribute themselves) from downloading. Thus, marketing with the recommendation services display positive feedback - blocking users helps to manage the negative feedback. Marketing and this management of relations establish the connection between the contents and the social environment. It is the social environment and its the relation to content that differentiates the services and feedback effects.

This case illustrates that the management of those contents that used to be the product of the media industry does not distinguish the different services for content management. It is the linkage between ``pure" content and user contributed content and between content and the social environment that distinguishes the services. Hereby, content management and management of the community are inseparably interrelated and pieces of music alone do not make up the value of a network. The pure content is embedded in the social structure of the community with profiles, recommendations reviews, and personal relations. It is this social structure and the management of the community that distinguishes the services - not the mp3 files.

# 5. COMMUNITIES AS TOOL FOR CONSUMER CONTROL

The new characteristics of content in the Internet has at least two consequences for the economic situation along the value chain. First, the management of content gets more and more important for the creation of value. Second, the new business models allow various new and different ways of managing this content which undermine obviously the power of the traditional players in the markets. Communities and peer-to-peer architectures lead to more similarity in terms of contribution and power and between the different actors along the value chain. As the example of the music industry shows, there is a rapid development of various business models in this field which give more influence on the management of content to the consumers. The fact that content is digital allows more people to contribute. The fact that content needs to be linked allows for different kinds of contents to be joined and new organizational forms of the contents. The fact that it is interactive allows for new ways of interaction among all actors in the value creation. Most important, however, is that content becomes inseparable from the social, political, and organizational environment. The community attaches its structure to the content, e.g., in reviews, recommendations or personal relations and the content management influences the social, economic, and organizational structure of any community. Particular to the novel systems is that the community with authors, actors and consumers that structure and organize the transactions takes over the power in those systems.

These developments are driven by technology and the consumers. None of this models is older than two years, but they have already become very popular. But the novel architectures support more than "communication and information" - they are the basis for transaction and organize the community to take over a number of functions the media industry or intermediaries used to occupy. The socio-economic business model "community" gains a novel relevance in various application fields. The music sector and in particular the alliance of Napster and Bertelsmann and all the legal approaches to stop the developments illustrate that novel, originally technology driven designs may change a value chain and a whole industrial sector.

**Acknowledgements.** We are indebted to the anonymous referees for valuable comments. We are also indebted to B. Buchet for proofreading. The work of Ulrike Lechner is sponsored by the Swiss National Funds in an endowed professorship.

# 6. REFERENCE LIST


Adar, E. and Huberman, B. (2000) Freeriding on Gnutella. *Firstmonday* **5**,

Figallo, C. (1998) *Hosting Web Communities: Building Relationships, Increasing Customer Loyality, and Maintaining a Competitive Edge*, Wiley Computer Publishing.

Godwin, M. (1994) Nine Principles for Making Virtual Communities. *Wired*

Haertsch, P. (2000) *Wettbewerbsstrategien für Electronic Commerce*, Josef Eul Verlag .

Hagel III, J. and Armstrong, A. (1997) *Net Gain: Expanding markets through virtual communities*,

Hummel, J. and Lechner, U. (2001) Communities - The role of technology. In: European Conference on Information Systems (ECIS 2001). To appear. 2001.

Jones, Q. (1997) Virtual Communities, Virtual Settlement & Cyber-Archaelogy: A Theoretical Outline. *JCMC* **3**,

Levine, R., Locke, C., Searls, D. and Weinberger, D. (1999) *The cluetrain manifesto. The end of business as usual*, Perseus Books.

Licklider, J.C.R. and Taylor, W. (1968) The computer as a Communication Device. *Science and Technology* 21-40.

Preece, J. (2000) *Online Communities*, 1 edn. New York:

Rheingold, H. (1994) A Slice of Life in my virtual community. In: Haramsin, L.M., (Ed.)

Rheingold, H. (1993) *The virtual community: homesteading on the electronic frontier*, Addison-Wesley.

Schmid, B.F. (2000) Was is new in the digital economy? *EM-The Int. Journal of Electronic Markets and Business Media*, 11(1).

Schubert, P. (1999) *Virtuelle Transaktionsgemeinschaften im Electronic Commerce: Management, Marketing und Soziale Umwelt.*, Josef Eul Verlag.

Schubert, P. and Ginsburg, M. (2000) Virtual Communities of Transaction: The Role of Personalization in Electronic Commerce. *EM - Electronic Markets.The International Journal of Electronic Markets and Business Media,* 10(4).

Shapiro, C. and Varian, H. (1999) *Information Rules: A Strategic Guide to the Network Economy*, Harvard Business School.

Stanoevska-Slabeva, K. and Schmid, B.F. (2000) Community Supporting Platforms. *EM-The Int. Journal of Electronic Markets and Business Media*, 10(4).

Timmers, P. (1998) Business Models for Electronic Markets. *EM - Electronic Markets.The International Journal of Electronic Markets and Business Media* 8(3).

Whittaker, Issacs and O'Day (1997) Widening the web. Workshop report on the theory and practice of physical and Network communities. Report from ACM CHI.

17

# Learning About the Online Customer:

## *an interpretive case study of building digital customer relations in online entertainment*

Annakarin Nyberg & Ola Henfridsson

*Center for Digital Business and Department of Informati!cs, Umesaring; University, Sweden*

**Abstract**: This paper explores the challenges and opportunities involved in building digital customer relations in online entertainment. In doing this, the paper presents an interpretive case study of the release of the Swedish computer game developer Daydream's new on-line game Clusterball. In releasing this game, Daydream intended to bypass three stages – publicists, distributors and retailers – in the computer gaming value chain. With little prior experience of consumers, this bypass required that the company established a platform for learning about and from its entertainment consumers. Our particular interest in this paper is with digital customer relations and how a computer game and its related virtual community can provide opportunities to build such relations for learning about the online customer.

## 1. INTRODUCTION

Mediating customer relations over the Internet is becoming more widespread. This tendency can be observed among both e-commerce companies and more traditional retailers and producers. Inspired by visions about blending richness and reach [Evans and Wurster 1999, 2000] and one-to-one marketing [Peppers and Rogers, 1997; Pine 1993], many organizations explore what this digitalisation offers for streamlining as well as improving customer relations.

Even though digital customer relations are increasing in number and scope, the area can be considered relatively unexplored in terms of documented research. Apart from promising research on the general level [see e.g., Orlikowski, 1999], we need more research about the specific nature of the "customer in the machine" [Hughes et al, 1999]. How can we understand digital customer relations? How can we learn about and from the online customer? What are the organizational consequences of online customer relations? These questions are at the centre of attention in this paper.

Empirically, the paper builds on an interpretive case study [Klein and Myers, 1999; Walsham, 1995] of the process by which the Swedish computer game developer Daydream Software handled their customer relations digitally. In releasing the online game Clusterball, the company intended to bypass three stages – publicists, distributors and retailers – in the computer gaming value chain. With little prior experience of consumers, the bypass attempts required that Daydream established a platform for learning about the customer. In terms of technology, there are two technologies at the centre of attention – the game itself and the Clusterball community. In exploring the role of these technologies in Daydream's attempts to understand and learn about its Clusterball customers, this paper intends to create a better understanding of the nature of digital customer relations and, furthermore, how a computer game and its related virtual community can provide opportunities to build such relations for learning about the customer.

There are several reasons why this is important. Firstly, in view of the discrepancy between the expectations and actual outcomes of many B2C-efforts, one might say that we need to know more about business processes mediated over the Internet. Noting that many B2C-customers are disappointed about the service level offered [Hoffman and Novak, 2000; Nyberg and Lindh, 2000; Reichheld and Schefter, 2000], customer relations seems an extra relevant domain where more knowledge is needed. Secondly, despite initial visions about one-to-one marketing, it seems that many CRM-efforts result in automating the customer relation. In contrast with these discouraging results, our interest is in how "learning about the online customer" can be a two-sided process of the "informating" (Zuboff 1988) kind. More knowledge about how to establish such relations online can be useful for improving the functioning of internetworked organizations (Orlikowski 1999).

This paper is structured as follows. Section two explores the related literature, while section three outlines the research strategy. Section four presents the background to Daydream and their new on-line computer game Clusterball. Section five interprets the case, while section six concludes this paper.

## 2. DIGITAL ORGANIZATIONS: RELATED LITERATURE

There is little doubt that the role of information technology (IT) in current organizations is slowly changing. While its traditional role was a supportive one, many researchers have observed how this technology becomes more and more embedded in the core business processes of modern organizations [see e.g., Ciborra et al, 2000, Zuboff, 1988]. Rather than only being used for streamlining already existing processes, new technologies such as CRM-systems and KM-systems are intended to result in new ways of doing business. In understanding the nature of digital customer relations, therefore, we believe that there are good reasons to look a bit closer at the body of literature exploring the increasingly intertwined nature of information technology and organizations. This literature provides some guidance in our efforts to understand what happens when the role of information technology increasingly lies at core business processes such as sales and customer relations.

As early as in the beginning of the nineties, Orlikowski and Robey (1991) observed how information technology enables and restricts organizational structuring; Ciborra and Lanzara (1994) noted how the design and use of IT is enabled as well as restricted by so-called formative contexts; and Orlikowski and Gash (1994) outlined how key actors' assumptions were important for understanding information systems in organizations. This body of research was important in that it documented and explored the increasingly embedded nature of IT and organizations. Later on, in refining the research within this area, the IS community has adopted new approaches such as actor-network theory [see e.g., Hanseth and Monteiro, 1997; Walsham, 1996; Walsham and Sahay, 1999]. This refinement could be seen as an adaptation to the increasingly complex character of the intertwining between non-human actors such as standards, software, and hardware and human actors.

In view of the emerging number of digital organizations, i.e., organizations that mediate most of their business processes over the Internet, various researchers have searched for good labels for these organizations. Research and exploration around the concept virtual organizations have been around for some years now [Davidow and Malone, 1992; Hedberg et al, 1997], while inter-networked organizations [Orlikowski, 1999] and cybermediaries [Jin and Robey, 1999] are recent terms used to describe and explore this kind of organizations. Despite labels used, Orlikowski's (1999) exploration of how internetworked technologies such as email, web publishing tools, intra-nets, extranets, and hypertext systems in general influence organizations in ways not easily understood and predicted gives a good view of the complexity involved in digital organizations. So, "why are organizations investing in internetworking", Orlikowski (1999, p. 5) asks, suggesting that the core questions concern how open organizations should be with their stakeholders. Needless to say, internetworking implies openness, a notion that most organizations adhere to. However, implementing this openness in terms of making workers, work processes, and so on, public knowledge is another issue.

The two sections following the research strategy section present a case study where a certain degree of openness was intended in the customer-company relation for learning about and from the customer. The case study will show how digital customer relations are characterized by transparency and time and place independency, and, furthermore, it shows how these characteristics can lead to both organizational opportunities and consequences. These observations can be useful for any company in digitalizing its customer relations for improving their ability to learn from and about the customer.

# 3. RESEARCH STRATEGY

This study can be broadly described as an interpretive case study [Klein and Myers, 1999; Walsham, 1995]. Interpretive case studies are valuable for tracing assumptions, interpretations and problems of involved actors. The involved actors are important here, because the IS researcher's understanding of the studied phenomenon is created through the meanings that these actors associate with it [Orlikowski and Baroudi, 1991]. In seeking such understanding, however, the IS researcher needs to be involved in the daily activities taking place at the researched site.

Between January 2000 and October 2000, in-depth studies of the planning, design, and release of the technologies associated with Daydream's on-line computer game Clusterball have been conducted by a team of three researchers (of which two are the authors). The ten-month study can be divided into three phases. Between January and March, we took part in meetings and discussions and we also spent time to learn about the employees, their assignments and working routines. As a result, we got a notion of the every day work at Daydream that was useful in going from observing the company into a more active participation. In March 2000, we started to take more active part in the process. Two complete working places were set up for two of the members of the research team and, starting in April, half time was spent at Daydream Software for participant observation. From April to September 2000, we conducted 600 hours of participant observation. During this phase, we were, to some extent, intervening in the studied process. For instance, we took responsibility for things such as evaluating the company's web sites and creating customer scenarios intended to support the initial utilization of the CRM-database. October was spent verifying and complementing the data collected.

Two things guided the choice of research site. Firstly, Daydream represents leading practice in that they almost exclusively use information technologies such as CRM-technologies and virtual communities to handle their customer relations. To fruitfully explore, assess and predict the nature of digital customer relations, it can be considered important to study the organizational or social contexts in which new technologies for doing that are tried out. Secondly, we had very good access to this company, which is an important factor when conducting interpretive studies. We gained this access through Daydream's CEO, who introduced us to special problems associated with customers in the computer gaming industry.

## 3.1 Data sources

The data sources were of different kinds: participant observation, interventions, website data, meeting protocols, e-mail correspondence, press releases, and field notes. We kept diaries of 600 hours of participant observation at the company. Everything that happened during a working day was written down and commented.

These notes have been important tools in the data analysis. In particular, they have been useful for reconstruct the process in terms of events and dates. Website data was an important source of data. For instance, at one of the web sites – shareholders' corner – shareholders could express their thoughts about the company and discuss the commercial potential of its products with other shareholders. Another example is the public forum, a community in which the Clusterball players could discuss the game. These kinds of information were important to understand what challenges the company was facing in terms of customer relations. Being a company quotated on the stock market, Daydream also issued press releases covering their present status to shareholders, the media and other interested parties. Another way of communicating these messages were through two types of e-mails, the "scoreboard" and the "devarea". The e-mails were sent to people registered in Daydream's CRM-database. The scoreboard and the devarea contain information about the current and future products and the daily work related to those.

# 4. BACKGROUND AND CONTEXT TO THE CLUSTERBALL CASE

## 4.1 Daydream – the company

Daydream Software is a Swedish computer game developer that has attracted a lot of attention over the years. In 1996, the company was introduced at the Swedish stock market and the expectations on the small company were high. Daydream employs about 65 persons (November 2000) and constitutes one of the global actors on the computer gaming market, which is renowned for fierce competition, emerging trends, and shifting customer behaviour. Over the years, the computer gaming industry has experienced rapid growth and innovation. Datamonitor (1999) expects, for instance, the US and European market to grow around 15% annually between 1998 and 2003. Because of rapid diffusion of personal computers in combination with increasing capacity of game consoles such as the Playstation™, the industry has been able to continuously deliver more advanced graphics and technical features. In view of this development, it is not surprising that the computer gaming market is considered a very competitive one, where small misjudgements about its future direction can erode market leadership. In times when virtual commerce and entertainment tend to converge, there are many possible future scenarios of the computer gaming market. Among these scenarios, the on-line game distributed, played and paid for over the Internet is one model that many believe in.

## 4.2 Clusterball – the game

Out of the three released computer games, Daydream's third game Clusterball was made available on the Clusterball community website in July 2000. Clusterball is an on-line computer game that allows an infinite number of geographically dispersed players to play against each other. As part of Daydream's non-violence strategy, the game is marketed as a sports game, in which the player flies a ship with which he or she can pick balls from designated places diffused in a 3D-landscape. Besides being rated as a good computer game in the press, the game also creates new opportunities to learn about the customers. The downloading process, for instance, enables learning about the customers through the gathering of customer information. As the first venue of the game is downloaded, Daydream does not gather any information about its customers, nor do they charge anything. The venue is for free. The second venue is received after the gamer has filled out a form of registration. This procedure can be considered as a non-monetary payment. The registration form includes two types of questions; optional questions, like what hardware or software the gamer use, and compulsory questions, like the gamers nationality, age, sex and e-mail address. If a gamer admits to the gathering of personal related data, it will get access to the Clusterball community, which non-registered gamers do not. The registration process is the first step in the direction of getting to know the gamers, and eventually, of creating relations. If the gamer finds the game appealing and wants more than two venues, these venues have to be bought.

All data that is gathered via the registration, the game, or other game related events, is registered in a customer relationship management database (CRM-database). In combination with database management tools, the database is used to analyse the data and to segment gamers into suitable groups. The groups are formed due to what messages that is communicated. The CRM-database and the database management tools, makes it possible to manage and to analyse large amounts of data in ways that would not have been possible otherwise.

## 4.3 Clusterball – the community

As a step in the endeavour to affiliate the Clusterball gamers to the game and the company, Daydream has developed a virtual community (Hagel and Armstrong 1997). The community is built upon a set of common interests – computer gaming in general, and Clusterball in particular. The shared interests are also a basic condition for the very existence of the community. The community is available at the Clusterball web site (www.clusterball.com) to which everybody gets access. However, it is only registered gamers who have access to the virtual community.

The community can be considered as a potential source of knowledge about the customers. Within the community, gamers are exchanging ideas and are able to comment on, for example, the game, its participants, or the company. Every now and then, for reasons like aggressive or flaming de-bates, or for congratulating successful Clusterball gamers, Daydream employees take part in the discussions. The community also renders the possibility to help each other; it creates an affinity to the other customers and to Daydream as well. The discussions are a valuable source through which Daydream can get hold of ideas or positive and negative critique regarding the company or the game. The community, in combination with the CRM-database, creates good opportunities to track the gamers in what way they are using the offered online services. Based upon this, Daydream can learn about the gamers and get an understanding of how needs best will be satisfied.

# 5. THE CLUSTERBALL CASE: ORGANIZATIONAL CHALLENGES IN LEARNING ABOUT THE ONLINE CUSTOMER

This section outlines the challenge that Daydream was confronted in their attempts to bypass three stages of the computer gaming value chain, and how this required the company to learn about the online customer. The section shows how visions about CRM-database management, virtual communities, and online gaming were put into practice in the context of the on-line computer game Clusterball.

## 5.1 Daydream's challenge

Because Clusterball is distributed, played and paid for over the Internet, the game enables Daydream to bypass three stages – publicists, distributors and retailers – in the value chain. This bypass was a considerable challenge to Daydream as they had little prior experience of selling directly to consumers. The value chain of Daydream's two CD-based games, Safecracker and Traitors gate, included publicists, distributors and retailers and, consequently, these intermediaries also gathered most of the customer-related data. In other words, Daydream needed to build a social and technological platform for learning about their customers.

Needing a more developed understanding of game consumers, Daydream had to deal with the situation and decide how and to what extent they would be able to learn about their customers. As we will see in the following subsections this dealing was far from trivial.

## 5.2 The pre-release phase (December 1999 - July 2000)

In December 1999, Daydream announced that they were looking for test gamers for Clusterball at the Clusterball website. One criterion for becoming a test gamer was to fill in a registration form about personal related data. The gamers signed up via the Clusterball website and, as a result of this registration, Daydream found the CRM-database slowly growing in number of players.

In the short run, these players were valuable for finding bugs as well as testing game idea itself. In the longer perspective, they constituted the first customer base on which Daydream could establish an initial understanding about Clusterball. In April 2000, the research team was assigned the responsibility to do initial data analysis the database. As the number of test gamers increased, the need for the database management tools became more obvious. During the 29th of May 2000, a Daydream representative and the researchers attended a course on Power Play. This course was intended to provide a better understanding of the potential of using customer data in marketing and diffusion of the game.

One important issue in learning about the Clusterball customer was to decide what and how much information that would be collected when releasing the game. During a marketing department meeting on May 5, 2000, the issue of how much information the company would be able to collect about the gamers without making them find such gathering too integrity violating was discussed. In view of the fact that the new Clusterball website would be released in the later part of June 2000, this was an important question in need of an answer. At this stage, the problem was not lack of ideas about ways of collecting data, but rather whether one critical market segment, the "hard-core" gamers, would allow any registration. There were some controversies over this issue between the marketing department and the game developers; while the marketers wanted to collect as much information as possible, the game developers were more reluctant to such collecting. Without a decision, however, the web designer would not be able to the place from which the potential Clusterball gamers would get hold of the form of registering,

Shortly before releasing Clusterball, Daydream became aware of the need of organizational changes. The removal of publicists, distributors and retailers was not straightforward; it implied new and changed work practices as Daydream had to build an organization that could handle end customer relations. The release date was set, and changed, quite some times. At this stage, many stakeholders – stockholders, eager gamers, as well as mass media – put Daydream under pressure and the company had to take decisions with little analysis of their consequences. Consequently, it was not unusual for Daydream to reconsider their short-term priorities. Ideas generated at brainstorming sessions on the use of collected customer data, for instance, had to be put on hold despite obvious advantages in using them. Another but related example is the work with the CRM-database and the management tools. Despite that Daydream had both available customer data and educated staff in May; it was not until September 2000 the CRM-database was used for analysing purposes. Up-coming circumstances tended to arise and they made the everyday work unforeseeable and difficult to plan. One additional factor that contributed to the difficulties was that Daydream was dealing with technologies in new and yet unexplored ways – they had no first movers to copy. Daydream had to learn by trial and error.

## 5.3 The post-release phase (July 2000-October 2000)

On the 17th of July 2000, Clusterball was released at www. clusterball.com. The game was well received by critics and as the number of Clusterball gamers increased, the Clusterball community began to be more frequently utilized. Realizing that the community was one key source of knowledge Daydream became aware of the need for someone responsible for the forum – a community manager. The "community manager's" main task would be to keep the community going and to communicate and collaborate with the gamers. The involvement and the supervision of the community opened up for new possibilities. The community was valuable since its member's possessed knowledge about the game and about computer gaming in general. By following the discussions in the forum, and to encourage and comment on ideas from gamers, Daydream could trace needs and wishes of their customers. Such needs and wishes were also explicitly asked for:

"...we at Daydream are listening to what the community wants." ["Lobo" from Daydream in the on-line forum, 2000-09-04.]

Daydream made use of this potential a number of times. There are several examples of how ideas, expressed and discussed in the forum, became realized in the game. One such example is the pre-chat for gamers who have joined a game. While waiting for the remaining gamers to join, the gamers can communicate with each other. Implemented as a new patch of the game, the pre-chat was released in October 2000, only three months after releasing the game. Another example is the request for individualizing the appearance of the Clusterball ship. This request became an appreciated reality as a ship tutorial was available at the Clusterball community on November 5, 2000.

Not surprisingly, the forum was not only used for exchanging and discussing ideas in a constructive and creative way. Because it provides the opportunity for all registered gamers to act without any particular restrictions, the emergence of undesired discussions cannot be avoided. There are examples of how Daydream's "community manager" has had to intervene and rebuke inappropriate behaviour at times when discussions have became to overheated or aggressive. This type of intervention is a delicate matter, as it is often important to take immediate action without downplay the open and productive atmosphere.

# 6. ORGANIZATIONAL ISSUES OF DIGITAL CUSTOMER RELATIONS

On the basis of the case study of Clusterball and the involved technologies for mediating customer relations, we have identified two properties of digital customer relations: time and place independency and transparency. This section of the paper describes these properties and explores their organizational opportunities and consequences (see Table 1).

*Table 1*. Overview of digital customer relations in the Clusterball case

| Properties | Organizational opportunities and consequences | Illustrative examples |
|---|---|---|
| Time- and place independency | Co-design | • New patches released based on customer suggestions (e.g., individualized skins and the pre chat opportunity |
| Transparency | Fast sense-and-respond | • Daydream's appointment of a community member |

Firstly, time and place independency can be considered an important property of digital customer relations. As mediating technologies, the game and the community could be utilized independent of time and place, which created good opportunities for gamers to get together and exchange ideas about the game. Time and place independency enabled Daydream to get access to the Clusterball players' collected knowledge and, in the Clusterball case, we can see how Daydream used this knowledge for enabling a sort of co-design of the game. In this regard, there are several examples of how customers were part of the development of Clusterball. As mentioned in section five, the pre chat and the ability to individualize the appearance of the Clusterball ship are illustrative examples. In this way the customer's opinions, interpretations, beliefs, and desires can be part of creating a better game. This co-design suggests changes in the traditional roles of game developers and players, where the border between the customers and the developers are becoming more and more diffuse. The customers are no longer customers in a traditional sense; in line with the "open source" movement, [see e.g., Ljungberg, 2000; Raymond, 1999], they have turned into co-designers of the game.

Secondly, digital customer relations are also characterized by transparency. All members of the Clusterball community can follow and interact within the forum. As a result, Daydream had to be alert to uncomfortable opinions and requests. Animated activity and members who were eager to discuss distinguished the community. As a result, the possibility to intervene in real-time imposes demands on Daydream to act, or at least, comment topics that arise in the community. Daydream was not only expected to intervene, the company was also expected to act fast. Every now and then, the discussions become heated and, as a consequence, Daydream employees were, more or less, forced to step in and sometimes also to rebuke the actors. Whether the topics were of positive or negative nature, the transparency property requires action to be taken. In the line with Orlikowski's [1999] discussion of internetworked organizations, this openness is something that stretches beyond Daydream's control.

The transparency property imposes demands on fast sense-and-respond to customer behaviour. In view of the transparency of changed attitudes and desires, new ideas and thinking can be turned into practice quickly. As Bradley and Nolan [1998] outline, value in the "network era" requires that sense-and-respond business strategies replace make-and-sell strategies. In the short run, this property cuts both ways. It enables organizations to keep informed to be able to re-configure, but it also undermines some of the stability needed for streamlining business processes.

## 7. CONCLUSION

This paper explores the nature of digital customer relations in the context of online entertainment. In particular, the paper takes a closer look at how the Swedish game developer Daydream had to learn about their online customers in the context of releasing its new online game Clusterball. In this specific case, two technologies – the game itself and the Clusterball community website – were involved in the mediation of customer relations. In fact, most of what Daydream knew about their customers was mediated through these technologies; this fact makes this case a useful illustration of what characterizes digital customer relations.

In our efforts to understand the nature of digital customer relations, two properties were identified in the collected data: time and place independency and transparency. We suggest that these properties are important themes in the design, assessment, and improvement of digital organizations.

## 8. REFERENCES

Bradley, S. P., & Nolan, R. L. (Eds.). (1998). Sense and Respond - Capturing Value in the Net-work Era. Boston, MA: Harvard Business School Press.

Ciborra, U. C., & Lanzara, G. F. (1994). Formative Contexts and Information Technology: Under-standing the Dynamics of Innovation in Organizations. Accounting, Management & In-formation Technologies, 4(2), 61-86.

Ciborra, C., Braa, K., Cordella, A., Dahlbom, B., Failla, A., Hanseth, O., Hepsö, V., Ljungberg, J., Monteiro, E., & Simon, K. A. (Eds.). (2000). From Control to Drift - The Dynamics of Corporate Information Infrastructures. Oxford: Oxford University Press.

Evans, P. and T. S. Wurster (1999). Getting Real About Virtual Commerce. Harvard Business Review (November-December): 85-94.

Evans, P., & Wurster, T. S. (2000). Blown to Bits - How the New Economics of Information Transforms Strategy. Boston, MA: Harvard Business School.

Datamonitor (1999). "Electronic games: booming prospects for the new millennium." Datamonitor.

Davidow, W. H., & Malone, M. S. (1992). The Virtual Corporation. New York: Harper Collins.

Hagel, J. and A. Armstrong (1997). Net Gain - expanding markets through virtual communities. Boston, MA, Harvard Business School Press.

Hanseth, O., & Monteiro, E. (1997). Inscribing Behaviour in Information Infrastructure Standards. Accting., Mgmt. & Info. Tech., 7(4), 183-211.

Hedberg, B., Dahlgren, G., Hansson, J., & Olve, N.-G. (1997). Virtual Organizations and Beyond. Chichester: Wiley.

Hoffman, D. L., & Novak, T. P. (2000). How to acquire customers on the Web. Harvard Business Review, 78(3), 179-183.

Jin, L., & Robey, D. (1999). Explaining Cybermediation: An Organizational Analysis of Electronic Retailing. International Journal of Electronic Commerce, 3(4), 47-65.

Klein, H. K., & Myers, M. D. (1999). A Set of Principles for Conducting and Evaluating Interpretive Field Studies in Information Systems. MIS Quartely, 23(1), 67-93.

Ljungberg, J. (2000). Open Source Movements as a Model for Organizing, Proceedings of ECIS2000 .

Nyberg, A., & Lindh, H. (2000). Online Customer Relationships - an Empirical Study of ten Swedish online retailers. Proceedings of IRIS23, 951-967.

Orlikowski. (1999). The Truth is Not Out There: An Enacted View of the "Digital Economy". Presented at the "Understanding the Digital Economy: Data, Tools, and Research," on May 25 & 26, 1999 at the Department of Commerce in Washington, DC.

Orlikowski, W. J., & Baroudi, J. J. (1991). Studying information technology in organizations: Research approaches and assumptions. Information Systems Research, 2(1), 1-28.

Orlikowski, W. J., & Robey, D. (1991). Information technology and structuring of organisations. Information Systems Research, 2(1), 1-28.

Peppers, D. and M. Rogers (1997). Enterprise One-to-One: Tools for Building Unbreakable Customer Relationships in the Interactive Age, Piatkus.

Pine, B. J. (1993). Mass Customization - The New Frontier in Business Competition. Boston, MA, Harvard Business School.

Raymond, E. S. (1999). The Cathedral & the Bazaar - Musings on Linux and open source by an accidental revolutionary. Beijing: O'Reilly.

Reichheld, F. F., & Schefter, P. (2000). E-loyalty: Your secret weapon on the Web. Harvard Business Review, 78(4), 105-11

Walsham, G. (1995). Interpretive case studies in IS research: nature and method. Eur. J. Inf. Systs., 4, 74-81.

Walsham, G. (1996). Actor-Network Theory and IS Research: Current Status and Future Prospects. In W. Orlikowski, G. Walsham, M. R. Jones, & J. I. DeGross (Eds.), Information technology and changes in organisational work. (pp. 466-480): Chapman & Hall.

Walsham, G., & Sahay, S. (1999). GIS for District-Level Administration in India: Problems and Opportunities. MIS Quarterly, 23(1).

Zuboff, S. (1988). In the age of the smart machine: The future of work and power. New York: Basic Books.

# 18

# Information Dissemination in Virtual Communities as Challenge to Real World Companies

Christopher Lueg
*Department of Information Systems, University of Technology Sydney (UTS)*

**Abstract:** The event of the Internet and its web-related services in particular has enabled business-related online communities (also referred to as communities of commerce) that are centered around companies and their web sites. Creating and nurturing such online communities is expected to be a key element in gaining and sustaining customer loyalty in the age of 'empowered fruit flies'. However, apart from such explicitly business-friendly communities, the Internet has also enabled a variety of business-independent online communities which may disseminate at the speed of light information about companies, their products, their bright sides, and their dark spots. The effectiveness of information sharing observed in a particular online community indicates that the Internet has enabled a variety of novel ways to affect companies, their reputations, and their businesses. A look at the relevant literature suggests that traditional security management is not yet prepared to cope with these new challenges.

## 1. INTRODUCTION

The importance of the Internet as communication medium has increased significantly over the past few years and so has commercial interest in online communities. The Internet and its web-related services in particular have enabled so-called communities of commerce (Bressler and Grantham, 2000) which are communities that are centered around companies and their web sites. Creating and nurturing such business-related online communities is expected to be a key element in gaining and sustaining customer loyalty in the age of 'empowered fruit flies' which denotes that ``low-attention-span creatures with big wallets [...] move swiftly from one sweet fruit to the next in search of the best pricing, highest convenience, and quickest satisfaction" (Colony, 2000). Typical examples of communities of commerce are the social interactions that occur in the context of Amazon.com's virtual bookstore and eBay's virtual market place.

Apart from enabling such business-related online communities, the Internet has enabled a huge variety of online communities that are not related to businesses and that may pursue interests that are quite different from corporate interests. Such communities may be beneficial to a company they like by conveying a positive image but they may also be detrimental to a company's reputation and business by spreading information that contributes to a negative (or more realistic) image. Business-independent communities are difficult to address for companies and ways to influence or even control such communities are limited. It is tempting to underestimate the power of online communities-and online communication in general-as online communities may be relatively small in terms of members. Nevertheless, such communities may strongly effect a company. The lever is the virtually unlimited dissemination of information.

In this paper, we describe an online community that has formed to share experiences with fast food products and we outline that this community is an environment where effective information sharing is happening. Considering the growing importance of online communities and online communication in general, we argue that the Internet has enabled a variety of novel ways to affect companies, their reputations, and their businesses. A look at the relevant literature suggests that information management and security management are not yet prepared to cope with these new challenges. Companies in particular have to understand that the forces of the Internet can hardly be controlled; the challenge is to understand how to react to them (Bressler and Grantham, 2000).

## 2. MOTIVATION: INFORMATION DISSEMINATION IN A COMMUNITY

According to Williams and Cothrel (2000), online communities are groups of people who engage in many-to-many interactions online and form wherever people with common interests are able to interact. In this sense, the term "community" is used in a more general sense than in sociological research (e.g., Wellman and Gulia, 1999) where sharing beliefs or a feeling of belonging to the same community is considered essential for viewing a social groups as community.

In this paper, we focus on particular newsgroup which is situated in the global conferencing system Usenet news. Usenet being founded in the early Eighties is one of the oldest and probably the largest conferencing systems of its kind. Usenet is purely text-based and it is used by thousands of users who contribute more than a million messages per day, generating a daily network traffic of more than a hundred gigabytes. Collecting precise usage data is rather difficult as the largest part of user interaction with Usenet is invisible; messages only reflect active contributions to

Usenet whereas the much more frequent activity of reading messages remains invisible (Lueg, 2000).

Research has found Usenet newsgroups be capable of forming and hosting communities (e.g., Roberts, 1998). Interest in Usenet is increasing (again) as newsgroups have been identified as places where is effective community building and information dissemination can be observed.

## 2.1 The Online Community dafff

In this paper, we focus on the Usenet newsgroup *dafff*. The name of the newsgroup is an abbreviation of the newsgroup's location within a particular internationally distributed newsgroup hierarchy. *dafff* qualifies as a community in the sense of Williams and Cothrel (2000) as its members are engaging in many-to-many interactions and the motivation for the engagement is the shared interest in certain products. In addition, *dafff* members share certain attitudes, such as expecting posters to behave according to the Usenet netiquette and its rules of good conduct. Also, they maintain shared artefacts, such as a list of answers to frequently asked questions (FAQ) and a web site that is used as a central repository for information, such as the FAQ, that are relevant to the newsgroup and their interests. The newsgroup's participants are well connected in terms of electronic communication so that information can be distributed rapidly. The shared interest in a particular topic is the basis for the newsgroup which suggests to view the newsgroup as a community of interest (Carotenuto et al., 1999).

The *dafff* newsgroup has formed to discuss "fast food" which is a generic name for food as offered by companies such as McDonald's, Burger King, KFC, Pizza Hut, Taco Bell, Hungry Jack's, Wendy's, and Subway. Fast food could be characterized as food that is prepared and consumed within minutes. Typical fast food products are hamburgers, French fries, pizzas, and sandwiches, which are usually served in combination with soft drinks, such as Coca Cola and Pepsi Cola.

## 2.2 Information Sharing in the *dafff* Community

Experiences with fast food and the respective restaurants are shared and discussed in the *dafff* newsgroup. Information being contributed by newsgroup members range from the quality of food and service (e.g., food temperature and consistency; speed of service; friendliness of employees; responsiveness to questions and critiques) in particular restaurants to regional differences in what restaurants offer. In one particular case, a newsgroup member reported that he or she observed the (in Germany strictly forbidden) re-use of food products that were returned by an unsatisfied customer.

Of particular interest are hamburger restaurants. In the case of one particular hamburger giant, information range from knowing which restaurants are operated by the giant itself and which are operated by franchise partners to details of internal quality control systems that are intended to ensure product quality. These quality control systems are a frequent topic as they directly influence the food experience in fast food restaurants. Fast food companies seem to face the problem that their freshly made products should be consumed within short periods of time to ensure product quality (depending on the actual product, products may be stored in the warmer for a few minutes). According to internal quality standards, products not served after this time should be discarded.

One of the two most popular hamburger companies marks its freshly made products according to the time left until the products should be discarded. Its main competitor uses a number-based flag system to indicate until when products may be kept. In both cases, details of the quality control systems and the meaning of the indicators used are not communicated to customers. As a consequence, customers ultimately have to trust the companies that only freshly made food is served and that overdue food is indeed discarded.

Some members of the newsgroup community, however, knew about the quality control systems used and contributed these information to discussions in the newsgroup. Almost all members of the newsgroup are now able to assess how fresh products really are when they are served. Observations reported by newsgroup members indicate that it happens that overdue food products are not discarded as demanded by internal company policies. In the case of the company using the flag-based system, it seems to happen that sometimes quality control indicators are manipulated to pretend a later production time. As a result, food served may not be as fresh as demanded by company policies. In the case of some restaurants of that particular company, newsgroup members reported they could observe that the flag system was not used at all so that it were impossible even for employees to assess freshness of products they were serving to customers.

Information about the quality control system system, how it is intended to be used and how it may be abused, has become part of the community's "organizational memory" and is described in the newsgroup's FAQ. In this sense, it is not only information sharing but knowledge sharing that can be observed in the community as statements indicate that members effectively learned how to apply the information when visiting fast food restaurants.

## 2.3 The Scope of the *dafff* Community

The newsgroup's FAQ is available on the web site that is maintained by some of the newsgroup members. New participants in the newsgroup are pointed towards to web site when information related to topics covered by the FAQ are being requested. Discussions as well as the FAQ can easily be found when using a regular search engine, such as Google (http://www.google.com). In addition, it is reasonable to assume that members share their knowledge with real world friends and colleagues when physically visiting fast food restaurants. *dafff* members are physically located Germany and a few other countries which means that they are able to collect information from a rather large physical area.

Put in a nutshell, the scope of the community exceeds the particular newsgroup by far; the community and the corresponding web site have the potential to become a widely recognized fast food information resource on the Internet. Given the growing recognition of the Internet's importance to companies (e.g., Kalish, 1997; Reuters, 1997), it is not unlikely that some of the fast food companies discussed in the newsgroup are already monitoring the ongoing discussions. In fact, some members are known to be current employees of fast food companies discussed in the newsgroup.

Community members may also use other online communication channels, such as email, mailing lists, chats, instant messenger, and other newsgroups, to disseminate information they received in a community. Furthermore, members of online communities are real persons in the end who meet family members at home, friends at the movies, and colleagues at their workplaces which means that rumors can be expected to be disseminated in the real world as well.

Related to the problem of virtually unlimited information dissemination is that that communication is no longer limited to their specific social contexts. Search engines, such as Alta Vista and Google, preserve information for years and have empowered casual users to find information that was published almost anywhere on the Internet. Online archives, such as Deja.com (now Google.com) allow users to search billions of web pages and articles that were published in the global conferencing system Usenet news. This means that even casual users have access to a vast amount of information (positive and negative; true and false) that has been said about particular companies and their products. A further implication is that communication is removed from its original context. As Grudin (2001) puts it: "[...] capturing context digitally alters it fundamentally. The context that is captured is removed from its context, namely the context that is not captured". This de-situating is especially relevant when considering the community example discussed in this paper. A quick glance at the discussions in this community could suggest that ``fast food bashing" occurs but in fact the community is a ``fan" community mostly consisting of members that love fast food.

## 2.4 Communities as Chance for Corporations

From a business perspective, the *dafff* community is especially interesting as most community members share a positive attitude towards fast food despite some negative experiences. This means that the community and its web site are different from increasingly popular ``revenge" web sites, such as McSpotlight (http://www.mcspotlight.org) or Living Wages (http://www.nikewages.com), providing information about the fast food giant McDonald's and the sports equipment giant Nike, respectively.

Empirical evidence exists that members of the *dafff* community are interested in increasing the quality of the products they like and the service they enjoy. Apart from revealing and discussing dark spots, newsgroup members also report on good experiences in particular restaurants and how they liked certain products (especially in the case of new and limited "special offers"). However, implications of the "quality problem" discussed above should not be underestimated. Discussion statements indicate that several newsgroup members understand the quality problem in such a way that they question the company's attitude towards its own quality standards *in general* which means that they question other standards of the company as well.

In the case of online communities with a rather positive attitude towards companies and their products, companies may have the chance to establish communication with online communities in order to prevent damage and to actually improve their services. For example, the observations concerning disregard of the internal quality control system could be used to investigate incidents.

## 2.5 Supporting Communication With Online Communities

The members of the *dafff* community are mainly located in Germany. A review of the German web sites of the two most popular fast food companies in the newsgroup suggests that additional communication channels would be required to establish communication between companies and online communities As reported in Lueg (2001a), the current web sites typically lack ways to provide feedback online or to communicate with each other. Instead, online customers are referred to sending faxes or providing feedback in restaurants. According to experiences discussed in the newsgroup, the latter can be at least frustrating if customers address disregard of the internal quality control systems. Reviews of the companies' web sites in countries all over the world showed similar results in most cases. Interestingly, Japan with its specific culture is treated differently.

A range of ways to support communication with business-friendly online communities has been outlined in Lueg (2001a). In a nutshell, the communication strategy should be based on interaction and feedback; the communication goal should be to prevent deterioration of reputation through isolated events and to improve reputation through transparency. The message should be that despite bad experiences the company still is a trustworthy company offering quality products, that the company does not intend to hide grievances, and that the company investigates and resolves incidents as soon as possible after they have been reported.

Certainly, providing additional communication channels involves certain risks. Appropriate communication requires considerable expertise (domain knowledge, legal knowledge, PR knowledge, etc.) and still communication may fail if the company's reaction to incidents does not meet what is expected.

# 3. ONLINE COMMUNICATION AS CHALLENGE TO COMPANIES

Providing new communication channels always introduces additional risks as communication channels may be abused for information-level Denial-of-Service (DoS) attacks (see below for a definition). In a more general sense, the speed with which information can be disseminated within online communities and among user of the Internet in general indicates that information dissemination in the age of the Internet should be considered a serious challenge for companies.

It is widely acknowledged that computer security is an important topic and the state-of-the-art in computer security provides some protection against threats ranging from hackers trying to break into corporate computer systems to DoS attacks. Companies should be able to reduce vulnerabilities as well as the potential impact of still successful attacks.

However, information sharing in Usenet newsgroups suggests that potentially threatening activities that are based on the virtually unrestricted dissemination of information are becoming more and more important. Examples for information that may be disseminated are rumors, gossip, urban legends, and last but not least purposely false information. Computer viruses, such as the Melissa virus or the more recent Love Letter virus, infecting computers all over the world within a few hours, have demonstrated the speed of information dissemination in the age of the Internet.

A famous example for the threat potential of information dissemination in Usenet newsgroups and on the Internet in general is the urban legend that the American designer Tommy Hilfiger appeared on the Oprah Winfrey Show (an extremely popular show in the US) and made racist comments about several groups, after which he was tossed off the set by Winfrey. In fact, Hilfiger has never appeared on or taped an episode of Winfrey's show but the legend spread so rapidly and generated so much controversy among customers and potential customers that the company was forced to respond on the net (Ulfelder, 1997). See Lueg (2001b) for a discussion of how online communication may affect real world companies.

It is necessary to distinguish such information-based attacks from network-based attacks, such as regular DoS attacks, as network-based attacks are easier to address due to their technical nature. Lueg (2001b) defines information-level attacks as attacks that are based on the dissemination of information in such a way that companies, their operations, and their reputations may be affected. Dissemination may be active as in the case of sending email or passive as in the case of setting up web sites.

The primary lever of an information-level attack is the content of a message rather than its form. Sending faked inquiries to service accounts (e.g., feedback channels for online communities) to eat up resources would qualify as information-based attack as it is the content of the messages that would provide the lever for the attack. Examples for information-based threats are the setting up of so-called revenge web sites and the disseminating of false or biased information as in the case of the false Hilfiger accusation. Dissemination of information that is likely to trigger specific counter reactions as in the case of ``joe jobs" also qualifies as information-based threat. A joe job denotes abusing an opponent's identity for spamming. The intended effect of a joe job is that the apparent sender is blamed for spamming (i.e., damaged reputation) with the ultimate goal that the opponent is being dropped by his Internet service provider.

The computer security related literature does not provide much information on how to address information-level threats. A look at the relevant literature suggests that the focus is on making corporate computer systems and networks secure in order to protect them against direct undesirable activities. Topics discussed at specialized computer security conferences, such as the Australasian Conference on Information Security and Privacy (ACISP), range from authentication and encryption to access control and intrusion detection. Threatening activities that are based on the dissemination of information, however, are happening outside secure environments. (Lueg, 2001b).

Companies, such as CyberAlert (http://www.cyberalert.com), IntelliSeek (http://www.intelliseek.com), and eWatch (http://www.ewatch.com), have recognized the threat potential and offer specific tools that allow to search the web and other information sources to find out "what is `being said about [a] company and its products', and that provides `a way to identify potentially damaging rumors' " (Manktelow, 2001). However, the strengths and weaknesses of these tools are largely unknown and information on how to incorporate information-level threats into security management are hard to find. See Lueg (2001b) for a discussion of the current situation. Ebbinghouse (2001) provides an overview of several ways to address problems with online information.

# 4. CONCLUSIONS AND FUTURE RESEARCH DIRECTIONS

In this paper, we have outlined that not only the creation of new business-related online communities (so-called communities of commerce) but also the appropriate consideration of existing online communities is increasingly important in the age of the Internet. As a matter of fact, companies cannot control information dissemination in online communities but they can (and they will have to) react to the fact that more and more of their real world customers are members in online communities as well. Moreover, the virtually unrestricted information dissemination on the Internet should be considered a serious challenge to companies.

The focus of this paper was on one particular community and its potential impact on real world companies. We are extending our investigation to cover communities in a variety of online environments as we consider the community under investigation as a representative for a new breed of online communities that can either support or harm companies.

Another strand of work focuses on the development of a framework for assessing information-level activities and the incorporation of information-level security management into existing security management frameworks.

## 5. ACKNOWLEDGEMENTS

The author would like to thank Ingrid Slembek and the anonymous reviewers for their comments on drafts of this paper, Robert James Steele for pointing to the Manktelow article, and Paul Verhoeven for insights about Bug Planet.

## 6. REFERENCES

Bressler, S. and Grantham, C. E. (2000). Communities of Commerce: Building Internet Business Communities to Accelerate Growth, Minimize Risk, and Increase Customer Loyalty. McGraw-Hill.

Carotenuto, L., Etienne, W., Fontaine, M., Friedman, J., Newberg, H., Muller, M., Simpson, M., Slusher, J., and Stevenson, K. (1999). CommunitySpace: Toward flexible support for voluntary knowledge communities. In Proceedings of the Workshop "Changing Places", London, UK.

Colony, G.F. (2000). My View: Empowered Fruit Flies. Forrester Research, June, p2.

Grudin, J. (2001). Desituating action: Digital representation of context. Human-Computer Interaction, 16(2-3).

Ebbinghouse, C. (2001). You have been misinformed-now what?: Attacking dangerous data. Searcher, 9(4).

Kalish, J. (1997). P.R. firms surf the net. Reuters. Available online at http://www.mcspotlight.org/media/press/reuters_14feb97.html.

Lueg, C. (2000). Supporting social navigation in Usenet newsgroups. In Proceedings of the Workshop "Social Navigation-A Design Approach?" at the Annual ACM SIGCHI Conference on Computer-Human Interaction (CHI 2000), The Hague, The Netherlands.

Lueg, C. (2001a). Virtual Communities as Challenges to Real Companies. In Proceedings of the Pacific Asia Conference on Information Systems (PACIS 2001), Seoul, Korea

Lueg, C. (2001b). The Role of Information Systems in Information-Level Security Management. Submitted to ACIS 2001.

Manktelow, N. (2001). Net chatter is a data goldmine. IT News from The Age and the Sydney Morning Herald http://www.it.fairfax.com.au/e-commerce/20010227/A25453-2001Feb27.html.

Reuters (1997). P.R. Firms Seek Image Control on the Internet. http://www.infowar.com/class_1/class1_zn.html-ssi.

Roberts, T. L. (1998). Are newsgroups virtual communities? In Proceedings of the Annual ACM SIGCHI Conference on Human Factors in Computing Systems (CHI'98), pages 360-367, New York, NY. ACM Press.

Ulfelder, S. (1997). Lies, damn lies and the Internet. Computerworld. http://www.computerworld.com/cwi/story/0,1199,NAV47STO6800,00.htm.

Wellman, B. and Gulia, M. (1999). Virtual communities as communities. In Smith, M. A. and Kollock, P., editors, Communities in Cyberspace, pages 167-194. Routledge, London, UK.

Williams, R. L. and Cothrel, J. (2000). Four smart ways to run online communities. Sloan Management Review, 41(4):81-91.

MAIN TRACK - PART FIVE

# STRATEGIES AND BUSINESS MODELS

19

# Insights into IST and E-business Strategy Development

David H. Brown and Paul J. Robinson
*The Management School, Lancaster University*

**Abstract:** As organisations move further into the e-business era they face new opportunities and challenges in developing their business to accommodate this evolving environment. Of considerable importance is the development of IST and e-business strategies. Instead of just focusing on the phenomenon of the virtual world this research takes a wider perspective of strategy development by exploring the themes from both a business and IST strategy perspective, whilst incorporating key areas of the e-business domain. The experiences discussed in the paper illustrate the need for direction and flexibility; the importance of formal planning and an evolving relationship between information technology and business.

## 1. INTRODUCTION

The setting for this paper is a now familiar one – the continuing extraordinary commitment by organisations to e-business despite the recent failures of many internet companies. In 1999 business-to-business (B2B) and business-to-consumer (B2C) transactions were estimated to be £2.8 billion and these are expected to grow tenfold by 2002. Globally this figure is likely to exceed £650 billion (Financial Times, 2000). For these organisations the decision to engage in e-business was invariably a strategic level commitment and would lead to major implications for suppliers and customer relationships, internal organisational processes and information systems and technology (IST). The latter is crucial since without appropriate IST provision there can be no effective e-business. So how do these organisations come to commit the resources needed to become e-enabled? To what extent were these initiatives business or technology led, or neither?

These questions sit at the core of this paper which presents the results of a pilot multiple case-study research project to explore the IST strategy development processes in organisations that have developed e-business initiatives. The area of IST strategy formulation has long proved a difficult one for organisations (for example, see Earl, 1989 and Ward, 1996). As information technology (IT) becomes increasingly integrated into organisational processes then the evaluation of how IT dependent initiatives – such as e-business – needs to reflect the organisational and process implications. No longer can the problem be delineated and treated as a technical one subservient to the business case. The problem is further exacerbated by the fact that IT, and the means by which it can be made available to organisations, are both subject to rapid change. This change may or may not prove to be significant to any given organisation but they cannot be ignored and need to be evaluated. In an interconnected world (locally and globally) externalities may require an organisation to change its technology, or processes, or both.

Within such a context, unravelling and comprehending the processes that lead to strategic commitments is difficult but necessary if future decisions are to be better informed. Even if organisations have an audit trail in the form of policy documents, business proposals and meeting minutes the passage of time, and the politicisation in the decision process, make the final interpretation of events problematic. The advent of e-business initiatives, however, offers an empirical opportunity which this ongoing research seeks to exploit. By definition e-business initiatives are recent and in the companies considered all occurred in the last two years. The possibility existed therefore, to explore the organisational processes leading to the strategic IT based commitments through recent documentation and the testimony of the actors in the situation. The organisations chosen for the research are those that have traditionally traded in the 'physical' world and are now transitioning into the 'virtual' world. This meant a realistic view of IST and e-business strategy development was taken without the risk of distortion from the dot.com start-ups, which, in the main, have had quite different strategic justifications.

The structure of the paper is as follows. To place the research in context the paper commences with an overview of the impacts of e-business and provides an insight into e-business strategy development. Following this the main concepts of business and IST strategy literature are discussed which lead into a brief discussion of the research approach undertaken. The main discussion focuses upon the empirical results obtained from the three case organisations and relates them to the main strategy concepts previously highlighted. Bringing together the main points discussed and highlighting areas of further research concludes the paper.

## 2. IMPACTS OF E-BUSINESS

In the e-business era, organisations are able to utilise modern technologies to conduct business in new and innovative ways over the World Wide Web. For the purpose of this research a generic definition of e-business will be used, as follows:

> "...the seamless application of information and communication technologies from its point of origin to its endpoint along the entire value chain of business processes conducted electronically and designed to enable the accomplishment of a business goal..."
>
> Wigand (1997, p 5)

This includes B2B, B2C, e-service, e-trading and e-commerce. Since the potential of e-business was realised there has been a plethora of articles and books describing how this new paradigm can affect business, markets and industry. This paper does not attempt to cover all the available literature but will merely highlight some of the major impacts and forces summarised from various authors and researchers. The potential impacts of e-business are seen to be:

- **Increased acceleration of change** – Technology driven growth and change is accelerating (Ticoll et al, 1998). The internet could lead to product life cycles being reduced with more frequent introduction of products (Sawy et al, 1999). Customer's needs could change more rapidly, making them difficult to predict (Barabba, 1998).
- **Cost Reduction** – Utilising internet technologies can reduce the costs of communication between suppliers and customers, allowing for cost effective customer service and market research (Bickerton, 1998). Transaction costs can be dramatically affected during the purchase of products (Wigand, 1997).
- **Value Chain Changes** – Electronic business could lead to the disintermediation and reintermediation of intermediaries in the value chain, along with increased empowerment for customers (Bakos, 1998). This would lead to major changes in the value chain.
- **Blurring of industry and organisational boundaries** – Boundaries of industry and organisations could be blurred due to the convergence of technology. Technology could essentially redefine the nature of competition (Barabba, 1998).
- **Market Impacts** – Bakos (1998), summarises a number of key points on how markets could be affected by e-business. These impacts include: changes in product offerings, impact of information goods, lowering of search costs, facilitation of information sharing and new types of price discoveries.
- **New Interorganisation business forms** – As a direct result of the internet new cost effective interorganisational systems have led to the development of new

internet based communities. Current examples include Portals, Virtual Trade Communities and Guaranteed Electronic Markets (Ticoll et al, 1999; Lockett and Brown, 2000)

The above impacts and forces illustrate that organisations are facing not only potential opportunities but also major challenges as the e-business era develops. As argued by Chen (2000) the validity of being a purely web-based business is now being questioned. As the economy is calming down from the initial dot.com furore, traditional organisations are under increased pressure to move into the virtual world alongside their physical world. Bickerton (1998), notes that many organisations in the UK (and possibly around the world) are assessing how best to use internet technologies to improve business. As argued by Hitt (1998), Earl (2000) and Venkatraman (2000), organisations now face more complexity and uncertainty. Even though there have been major developments in the area of e-business there are still great challenges ahead for organisations. Venkatraman (2000, p 16) summarises this succinctly:

> "... the business landscape is fuzzy and fast changing – we are navigating unchartered waters...".

Downes and Mui (2000), argue that strategy development in the e-business era needs to be approached from a creative angle. Many authors believe that traditional approaches to strategy development are no longer suited to the modern turbulent environment. The model advocated by Downes is one that proposes organisations can shape the environment in which it exists. The three phases of strategy development include reshaping the landscape, building new connections and redefining the interior. This model attempts to create the building blocks to allow lucky foresight to occur, instead of creating a deliberate strategy.

Venkatraman (2000), argues for the need to develop strategies that simultaneously builds on current business models and creates new business models. Both Venkatraman and Downes emphasise the need for experimentation during the strategy development process to allow for flexibility and the testing of ideas. As a contrast, Timmers (2000), shows in his e-business research that formal planning still has a major role to play in strategy development. However, organisations are struggling to integrate legacy and new strategies. In terms of IT usage Wigand (1997) and Earl (2000), both argue that a key element is the organisational processes. IT fulfils a two-way role in organisations that enables value to be delivered. Not only does the business strategy and organisational processes define IT but IT is also an enabler for new business processes and strategies.

# 3. ASPECTS OF BUSINESS AND IST STRATEGY DEVELOPMENT

The term IST strategy is used to emphasise both the Information Systems (IS) and IT aspects of the organisation. Checkland conceptualised the role of IS in organisations in terms of a 'serving' and 'served' system. The 'served' system is the actual business, which is served by IS within the organisation, the 'serving' system. This concept is illustrated through the work of Earl (1989, developed in Galliers, 1991 and extended in Galliers, 1999). This work denotes that business needs are essentially the 'why' and the IST strategy comprises the 'what', 'how', 'when' and the 'who' of the organisation. IST strategy is therefore concerned with ensuring the business strategy can be implemented successfully.

The need to align both IT and business has been discussed for many years by many authors (for example, see Scott Morton, 1991; Ward, 1996 etc). As noted by Earl (1999) 90% of IST strategy literature discusses this area which underlines its relevance to effective IST strategy development. Put simply, without alignment the 'why' of the organisation cannot be fulfilled.

De Wit & Meyer (1995), have provided a useful three dimensional framework for the debate on strategic development:

- Strategy Process – 'How' strategies come about
- Strategy Content – The output of the strategic process, the 'What'
- Strategy Context – The set of circumstances which both Process and Content were determined, the 'Where', 'When', 'Who' and 'Why'

Ideally all three dimensions will feature in the strategy development process. This paper makes use of the Dewit & Meyer framework to structure the discussion. Having determined the context in the previous section, the following discussion focuses upon the process and content aspects of strategy development. The aim of this section is to highlight the key debates in order to determine their role in the IST and e-business strategy development process. The forces of e-business mean that as organisations experience both continuous (steady and evolutionary) and discontinuous (radical and intermediate) change the impacts on their strategy development will vary. During times of continuous change the impacts may not be too fierce and may mean a slight reorientation of the strategy. However, now and then this relative stability is punctuated by a major event within the environment (e-business) and suddenly evolution turns into revolution, as organisations need to take a 'quantum leap' to adapt to the changes occurring (Mintzberg, 1987).

As noted by Nutt (1998), the activation for change can develop from both the internal and external environments. More specifically, Trompenaars (1996), argues that organisations interact with transactional, socio-political and contextual environments. Within these environments there are various forces impacting on the organisation that affect strategy development, including internal forces (information constraints, politics and history) and external forces (legal, fiscal and legitimacy constraints). When coupled with the forces created by e-business the pressures facing organisations are great, as noted by Hamel (1997, p. 1):

> *"...the economic sea change now under way will drive an extraordinary amount of wealth creation over the next few decades... wealth will also get destroyed, as new business models drive out the old. That much is obvious..."*

Hamel points out that strategy is a key element for an organisation to be able to take advantage of business opportunities. The process of development can take many forms and as noted by Chase (1998), organisations are unique, therefore no two strategies will be the same. This is also supported by Ansoff (1994), who argues that organisations can take different strategic approaches depending upon the varying environmental challenges that they experience. Traditional approaches to strategy development have emphasised the importance of strategic planning. Quinn (1994), argues that planning is important as it creates discipline to look towards the future, expresses goals, allocates resources and helps to instil a long-term perspective in the organisation. However, planning approaches have been criticised for being to rational and deliberate. Mintzberg (1985), argues that it is actually difficult to follow a purely deliberate approach to strategy development as precise intentions would need to exist, be common and be realised as exactly as intended within the organisation. He notes that planning is important but is not the whole process because an element of flexibility is needed to allow for changes in the environment (continuous and discontinuous). Mintzberg believes that strategies need to incorporate both deliberate and emergent aspects to allow for control *and* flexibility, as intended strategies are not always realised as planned (Mintzberg, 1987).

Heracleous (1998) argues that it is important to incorporate strategic thinking in the strategy process. He notes that strategic thinking questions the strategic parameters currently in place. The planning aspect implements the direction chosen (derived from the strategic thinking) and helps to configure the organisation. Fowler and Lord (1998) also accept the role of strategic thinking in strategy development. They note that executives tend to use intuition to develop strategies and do not necessarily rely on sophisticated formal techniques.

With regards to strategy content, the main concern in the literature tends to focus upon whether an outside-in or inside-out approach is taken. The outside-in perspective is based around the concept of positioning. This determines whether an organisation's profitability is above or below industry average (Porter, 1985). Porter (1979), argues that the essence of strategy is coping with competition by matching the organisations strengths and weaknesses to the environment. The approach attempts to position the organisation to take advantage of opportunities in the environment so that a competitive advantage can be developed through various strategies. Porter (as discussed in Clarke, 1994), argues that organisations can develop competitive advantages by assessing the five forces within their industry and taking their strategic stance. The competitive advantage is delivered through how activities are arranged and performed in the value chain of the organisation relative to its industry in which the organisation exists.

IST strategy development has been heavily influenced by the work of Porter (Clarke, 1994). Using Porters work as a basis, IT was believed to be a key enabler of competitive advantages for organisations. As noted by Lambert and Peppard (1993) and Clarke (ibid), the traditional view of IT is one that emphasises IT being aligned with business needs. The Business Strategy essentially drives the IST strategy. However, IT has developed and matured considerably over the years.

In more recent years the inside-out perspective has developed. Hamel (1993), believes too much focus has been placed on environmental fit and not enough on resource leverage. Itami (1987), argues that various internal assets are in fact a source of competitive advantage. The key to the inside-out approach is based on leveraging resources, capabilities and competencies that are used to create a sustainable competitive advantage. Schoemaker (1992,) illustrates that the outside-in and inside-out approaches can in fact be integrated, as they are complimentary approaches. The model he proposes revolves around four key processes, which are: generating scenarios; conducting competitive analysis; analysing the organisations and competitor's competencies; and developing a vision by identifying strategic options. This approach utilises key aspects of both outside-in and inside-out perspectives. Earl (1999), proposes that strategists need to view IT from an 'opportunity' perspective. In this view, IT should be used to open up new ways of doing business (inside-out). This view is even more important in the e-business era as IT could have more influence over business because of the reliance of IT in order to implement an e-business approach. This now brings into play the investment aspects of IST strategy. With IT becoming more critical to organisations the investments in this technology can be classified as 'strategic' in that it will affect and contribute to the organisations future growth (Easterby-Smith, 1996). An investment so critical would need to be reflected in the strategy development process and would have major influence on the direction taken. However, due to the uncertainty surrounding e-business benefits and technology, it could be difficult for organisations to justify and make these strategic investments.

## 4. RESEARCH APROACH

The empirical research was conducted using a multiple case-study approach. Guidelines for adopting this approach are those provided by Yin (1994). Three case organisations were selected from a range of possibilities. Table 1 shows a high-level comparison of the case organisations used for this research project. The organisations are all placed in different industries and differ in terms of size and turnover.

*Table 1:* Comparison of Case Organisations

| | FoodCo | RetailCo | PrintCo |
|---|---|---|---|
| Industry | Retail – Food | Retail – General | Printing, |
| Location | UK | UK – Northwest | Multi-national |
| Turnover | £1,917.7 million | £787 million | Europe = $5.3 billion |
| No. of employees | 20,000 | 10,500 | UK – 4000 (Global = 94000) |
| E-business Initiative | Product purchasing and delivery | Product purchasing and delivery | Product purchasing and delivery |
| Structure | Centralised | Divisional | Centralised |

The actual data was collected from a number of sources including, websites, annual reports, company documents and primarily performing semi-structured interviews within the three organisations. These organisations have been chosen for a number of reasons:

- They are all established organisations (Bricks and Mortar)
- They have developed e-business initiatives within the last 2 years
- They are drawn from a cross section of organisations and industries

Within these organisations key personnel were selected to conduct interviews with. The choice of sample was directed by their involvement in one or more of the following areas:

- General business strategy development
- IST strategy development
- E-business initiative

The use of semi-structured interviews was chosen for their qualitative fit in the research approach. Wherever possible multiple interviews were conducted which allowed the different perspectives and key issues to emerge. These were complimented with document analysis. They allowed the research to gain greater depth and help to discover the views, the experiences and how the interviewees made sense of the situation.

# 5. RESEARCH RESULTS AND DISCUSSION

A number of themes have emerged from the research, which deals with the trigger for change, mechanisms for implementing the decision, and the perspective and integration of IT into the business strategy. Each of these themes will be discussed separately in this section. Table 2 illustrates the main findings from the three case organisations.

*Table 2.* Main Research Findings

| | FoodCo | RetailCo | PrintCo |
|---|---|---|---|
| Trigger of Change | CEO intuition | CEO intuition | Operational needs |
| View of IT | Opportunistic and support | Opportunistic and support | Opportunistic and support |
| Relationship between IT and Business | IT and business influence each other | IT and business influence each other | IT and business influence each other |
| Focus of IST | IT and processes to deliver advantage | IT and processes to deliver advantage | IT and processes to deliver advantage |
| Strategy process directed by | Business and IT Directors | Senior Planning Manager | Use of strategic intent |
| Role of Planning | Control and communication | Control and communication | Control and direction |
| Flexibility of planning | Quarterly reviews | Decisions made outside the process | Decisions made outside the process |
| Strategy Focus | Outside-in and inside-out | Outside-in and inside-out | Outside-in and inside-out |
| Investment Focus | Investment not that severe | Difficult to justify - uncertainty | Operational |

## 5.1 Trigger for change

All case organisations experienced the 'punctuation' phenomenon caused by e-business. Having traded through a period of relative stability, the organisations strategic direction was impacted on in a major way by the need to develop an e-business approach. The significance of this move is apparent because developing e-business facilities within these cases was not just concerned with simply implementing a web site to communicate to the outside world. As noted earlier, the opportunities and challenges created by e-business are great, not only as another sales channel but also in terms of the impacts this approach can have on the whole organisation.

The trigger for change differed between organisations. The literature emphasises the need for formal analysis of the organisational environments to determine the future direction of the business. In all cases the trigger of change was not the result of formal analysis. For Retailco and Foodco the trigger for change came from the CEO of the organisation. He had 'decided' that e-business facilities were needed within the business. The decisions by the CEO's were believed to have been influenced by the strategic moves of competitors and also through informal discussions within their social network. In this sense the move to e-business was seen to be a competitive move and not just for operational needs. Printco's move to e-business was triggered in a slightly different way. This was not the result of a decision from the CEO but was influenced by the operational needs of the organisation. Prior to moving into e-business, Printco found themselves under increasing pressure from suppliers and customers to develop an e-business approach. The main reason for this pressure was to reduce operational costs. All three examples illustrate the impact e-business can have on organisations. Not only is there pressure from competitors who are developing new and innovative approaches to conduct business. There is also pressure from within the value system to ensure e-business facilities exist so that operating costs can be reduced across the whole system.

## 5.2 Mechanism for implementing the decision

Following the 'official' decision to adopt an e-business approach the case organisations illustrated distinct approaches during the initial stages of strategy development. Foodco tended to tackle the situation from an operational angle. Basically, they would incorporate the operational requirements of the initiative within their current business model. As the initiative developed the role and direction would be slowly integrated in the strategy development process. Retailco attacked their initiative from a more radical stance. To allow for flexibility of the development they completely relaxed the traditional internal business controls to allow the experimentation of ideas. Once Printco had realised the requirement of e-business it was immediately integrated within the strategy development process.

Although each organisation expressed that the initiative did impact on them, the level of impact varied between organisations. For Foodco, the impact was less severe then that felt by Retailco and Printco. Prior to the e-business initiative launched by Foodco they had spent a number of years developing various approaches to customer delivery facilities. This meant that e-business was more of a technical issue for them to develop, as the logistical infrastructure was already in place. A major concern for Foodco was therefore integrating the new technology into their traditional business. Within Printco and Retailco, the punctuation caused by e-business was viewed as major event in terms of organisational impacts. Retailco felt the issue was so important that a new business division was initiated to develop this new approach. They believed it was important to allow for the testing of new ideas without impacting on other areas of the business.

For all case organisations formal planning played a major role in the development of IST and e-business strategies. Planning in these organisations was not the whole strategy process but created the capability to allocate resources, communicate ideas and provide control (as noted by Quinn, 1994). The creative thinking of the strategists drove the strategy development process. Foodco and Retailco both emphasised the need for creative thinking. The strategists were questioning the strategic parameters currently being followed in their organisations. Planning was used as a tool to configure the organisation and implement the direction that had been decided.

Although concern is expressed about the rigidity of planning in strategy development, it seems in reality that planning does not necessarily have to restrict the flexibility of the strategy process. The planning processes in all cases were annually based. FoodCo's flexibility in its planning process was evident by performing a quarterly review of the strategy plan; essentially a smaller version of the annual planning process was completed every three months. Both PrintCo and RetailCo also had flexibility in their process to make decisions outside the planning process. Any major decisions made would then be fed back into the strategy process as and when required. This degree of flexibility also supports the earlier discussions on strategies being both deliberate and emergent. The planning process was seen as a key element but all cases acknowledged the importance of a certain amount of flexibility to respond to the changing business needs. This allowed all cases to respond to both continuous and discontinuous change in the environments they interact with.

In terms of strategy focus, all organisations showed signs of incorporating both an inside-out and an outside-in approach. The general focus in all cases was one that reflects the model proposed by Schoemaker (1992). Scenario planning was used (in various forms) to generate potential futures. Detailed analysis of competitive moves, internal and competitor's capabilities and technological trend was conducted. This was not a linear process but was iterative as the strategy process was unravelled. Competitive and IT analysis was used to determine the strategic use of IT within the organisation. However, the high-level role of IT was an implicit given, as the e-business initiative would not be possible without some level of IT. The main focus was on the business capabilities that IT could deliver and ultimately the potential advantages to be gained from using this technology.

Although all organisations adopted a combination of inside-out and outside-in approaches only Foodco emphasised the potential advantages that could be gained from focusing on the inside-out approach. The majority of their effort was focused towards a combination of both approaches. However, at various times the focus would shift towards purely an inside-out approach as they attempted to influence the market. The evidence of this is illustrated in the success of their e-business initiative in their industry sector as they have led the market in e-business with many competitors adopting their business model.

## 5.3 Perspective and integration of IT into the business strategy

With the advent of the e-business initiatives within the case organisations there seemed to be a slowly changing perception of the role of IT in these organisations. All cases, especially FoodCo illustrated a view of IT that places it firmly in what Earl (1999), calls the 'opportunity' approach. Here IT is not simply viewed as a supporting role (which was also evident) but in fact IT is the driver of new opportunities and business models. This perspective illustrates an evolving role of IT within the case organisations. IT was no longer viewed as being submissive towards business needs, as in the traditional view discussed by Lambert and Peppard (1993). With the advent of e-business this relationship changed from being simply a one-way influence were the business strategy drove the IST strategy. The role of IT in the cases organisations is one were IT would actually drive some business capabilities. Alignment of the two domains is therefore essential. Without it the capabilities offered by e-business could not be fulfilled. The key leverage that brings together the two areas of IST and business is essentially the processes that need to be fulfilled in the organisations. This supports the model proposed by Wigand (1997) in that process is the central linkage of business and IST capabilities. The strategic process undertaken within the cases was an iterative one that allowed them to develop the capabilities required.

Even though this view was evident, there was also concern expressed towards the uncertainty surrounding the capabilities of e-business technologies. To overcome this problem great emphasis was placed upon the assessment of the external and internal IT environments. This was to ensure the technological capabilities existed and also that the case organisations had the resources and capabilities to implement such technologies. The uncertainty aspect was also reflected in the approach taken to making 'strategic' investments. For Retailco the relaxing of internal controls meant that it was difficult to justify the investment made. Because of the impact of e-business the organisation followed a 'wait and see' approach to investment. Foodco's investment approach was less severe due to the logistical infrastructure already in place. Finally, Printco felt they could justify the investment, as the e-business facilities were needed for operational requirements.

The above discussion highlights some key high-level aspects of IST and e-business Strategy development. This research illustrates that some of the traditional aspects such as formal planning and competitive advantage are being integrated with more creative and IT driven approaches to strategy development. As the business environment becomes more complex and turbulent, the strategy development process requires creativity and flexibility but also direction, control and focus offered by the more 'traditional' strategy aspects. It seems as though the focus of many recent publications believing that 'traditional' approaches to strategy are no longer useful maybe too generalised as the case organisations illustrated a combination of a number of strategy development aspects.

# 6. CONCLUSION

This paper has discussed how a number of organisations have developed IST and e-business strategies over the last few years. Using a number of core literature domains the research highlighted how strategy development could occur within the business world. The concepts and theories were then tested within three case organisations that have developed e-business initiatives over the last 24 months. The results of this research make interesting reading and can be summarised as follows.

First, it is evident that the role of IT is evolving within the organisations, no longer is the business strategy leading the IST strategy. The two domains are starting to influence each other as the dependence on IT becomes greater due to e-business requirements. Second, there is great uncertainty regarding the technological capabilities currently available. This is reminiscent of the early days of IT when IT graduated out of the 'back office' onto the desks of users. In time, as technologies develop the confidence in the new technologies may also develop. Third, to cope with this uncertainty, internal controls were relaxed to allow for flexibility. Forth, formal planning during IST strategy development still plays an important role for organisations. However, it is important that a degree of flexibility exists in order to cope with both continuous and discontinuous change occurring in the environment is which the organisations interact. Fifth, strategic investment perspectives can vary depending on the uncertainty of the initiative. Finally, there exists a view that strategy development (e-business and IST) incorporates both elements of the outside-in and inside-out schools.

This research is part of a three-year program investigating strategy development in the e-business era. This paper has highlighted a number of questions to be addressed in further research. Initial questions include ones concerned with the strategic learning and decision implementation within organisations. Examples of these questions are: Following a major strategic re-orientation, such as e-business, has the organisations learnt from the experience for future changes? What implications restrict the translation of the initial strategic idea into reality? How are strategic ideas justified to the organisational members who decide on its feasibility? The next stage of the research is to conduct action research within a global organisation that is moving into the e-business domain. The research conducted in this paper will therefore help to focus future research being undertaken.

# 7. ACKNOWLEDGEMENTS

The authors would like to acknowledge the involvement of the three case organisations that wish to remain anonymous that participated in the research. Also, for The Lancaster University Management School for the support and resources required to complete this research.

# 8. REFERENCES


Ansoff, I., 1994, A Response to Henry Minztberg's Rethinking Strategic Planning,, *Long Range Planning*, June, pp 31-32

Bakos, Y., 1998, The emerging role of electronic market places on the internet, *Communications of the ACM,* August, pp 35-42

Barabba, V., 1998, Revisiting Platos Cave in Tapscott, D.; Lowy, A. and Ticoll et al, D., 1998, *Blueprint to the Digital Economy*, Mcgraw Hill, New York

Bickerton, P., 1998, *Delivering Business Benefit through Internet technologies,* Business Information Review, March, pp 40-49

Chase, R., 1998, *Creating a Knowledge Management Business Strategy,* Management Trends Int., London

Chen, S., and Leteney, F., 2000, Get Real! Managing the next stage of internet retail, *European Management Journal*, Vol 18 No 5, pp 519-528

Clarke, R., 1994, *The Path of Development of Strategic Information Systems Theory*, Xamax Consultancy US

De Wit, B. and Meyer, R., 1994, *Strategy Process, Content, Context. An International Perspective,* West Publishing, USA

Downes, L. and Mui, C., 2000, *Unleashing the Killer Application: Digital Strategies for Market Dominance*, Harvard Business School, Boston

Earl, M., 1989, *Management Strategies for Information Technology,* Prentice Hall, England

Earl, M., 1999, Strategy Making in the Information Age., In Currie, W and Galliers, B *Rethinking Management Information Systems,* Oxford Univeristy Press, England

Earl, M., 2000, Evolving the E-Business, *Business Strategy Review*, Vol 11 Iss 2, pp 33-38

Easterby-Smith, M. and Junshan, G., 1996, Vision, Mechansim and Logic in Brown, D and Porter, R, 1996, *Management Issues in China,: Volume 1*, Routledge, London.

Financial Times, 2000, The battle for Internet customers, 19th Jan, ITI

Fowler, S. and Lord, M., 1998, Decision Processes and uncertainty: Corporate strategy in China, in Hitt, M; Ricart I Costa, J and Nixon, R 1998 *Managing Strategically in an Interconnected World*, John Wiley and Sons, Chichester

Galliers, R., 1991, Strategic Information Systems Planning: myths, reality and guidelines for successful implementation, *European Journal of Information Systems,* pp 55-64 1(1)

Galliers, R., 1999, Towards the integration of e-business, knowledge management and policy considerations within an information systems strategy framework, *Journal of Strategic Information Systems*, pp 229-234, No 8

Hamel, G., 1997, *The Search for Strategy,* Strategos

Hamel, G. and Prahalad, C., 1993, Strategy as Stretch and Leverage, *Harvard Business Review*, March/April, pp 75-85

Heracleous, L., 1998, Strategic Thinking or Strategic Planning?, *Long Range Planning,* June, pp 481-488

Hitt, M.; Ricart I. Costa, J. and Nixon, R., 1998, *Managing Strategically in an Interconnected World*, John Wiley and Sons, Chichester

Itami, H., 1987, *Mobilising Invisible Assets,* Harvard University Press, USA

Lambert, R. and Peppard, J., 1993, Information Technology and New Organisational Forms: Destination and no road map, *Journal of Strategic Information Systems,* Sept, pp 180-205

Locket, N and Brown, D, 2000, eclusters: The potential for the emergence of digital enterprise communities enabled by one or more intermediaries in SMEs, *Knowledge and Process Management*, Vol 7 No 3, pp 196-200

Mintzberg, H. and Waters, J., 1985, Of Strategies, Deliberate and Emergent in De Wit, B. and Meyer, R., 1994, *Strategy Process, Content, Context. An International Perspective,* West Publishing, USA

Mintzberg, H., 1987, Crafting Strategy, Harvard Business Review, July-Aug

Nutt, P., 1998, Framing Strategic Decisions, *Organisation Science*, Vol 9 No 2, March

Porter, M., 1979, How Competitive Forces Shape Strategy, *Harvard Business Review,* Mar-Apr, pp 137-145

Porter, M, 1985, *Competitive Advantage: Creating and Sustaining Superior Performance*, Macmillan, USA

Sawy, E. et al, 1999, Value Innovation in the Electronic Commence, *MIS Quarterly,* Sept, pp 305-336

Schoemaker, P., 1992, How to Link Vision to Core Capabilities, *Sloan Management Review* Fall, pp 67-83

Scott-Morton, M., 1991, The corporation of the 1990's: Information Technology and Organisational Transformation, Oxford University Press, New York

Ticoll, D. et al, 1998, Joined at the Bit, in Tapscott, D.; Lowy, A. and Ticoll, D., 1998, Blueprint to the Digital Economy, Mcgraw Hill, New York

Timmers, P., 2000, Electronic Commerce - Strategies and models for Business to Business Trading, John Wiley and Sons, England

Trompenaars, T., 1996, Resolving international conflict: Culture and Business Strategy, Business Strategy Review, Vol 7 No 3, pp 51-68

Venktramen, N., 2000, Five steps to a Dot-Com strategy: How to find your footing on the web, Sloan Management Review, pp 15-28, Spring

Ward, J. and Griffiths, P., 1996, 2nd Edition, Strategic Planning for Information Systems, John Wiley and Sons, London

Wigand, R., 1997, Electronic Commerce: Definition, theory and context, The Information Society, pp 1-16 13

Yin, R., 1994, 2nd Edition, Case Study Research - Design and Methods, Sage, London

20

# E-commerce strategy formulation

Les Labuschagne and Jan Eloff
*RAU Standard Bank Academy of Information Technology, Rand Afrikaans University, South Africa, LL@ na.rau.ac.za*

**Abstract:** Many large organisations find it difficult to develop an e-commerce strategy. Senior management should first develop a comprehensive understanding of what it means to become e-commerce enabled before deciding whether or not to pursue that route. With e-commerce comes major changes that must be carefully planned and coordinated to avoid chaos and confusion. The aim of this paper is to provide an approach to develop an e-commerce strategy for large organisations. An e-commerce strategy, in its most simplistic form, consists of three steps, namely: determining where the organisation is; where it wants to go; and the best way of moving from the one to the other.

## 1. INTRODUCTION

The growth in electronic commerce (e-commerce) as a discipline has been unprecedented in the field of information technology. Both industry and academia have realised its importance, resulting in much research being done into its various facets. There are a number of success stories but, unfortunately, even more failures. The popular media has generated a lot of "hype" around e-commerce, especially business-to-consumer (B2C) e-commerce, and many "horror-stories" abound. Numerous surveys have been conducted which highlight the drawbacks or problems with e-commerce, and most of these point to security as an overriding problem [ERNS96][ERNS99]. In reality, however, many different technologies exist that address most security concerns [GREE00][LABa00]. The main problem with many failed e-commerce initiatives is the seeming lack of senior management support as well as a general lack of understanding – amongst senior managers – of the fundamental issues that constitute a successful e-commerce environment [ERNS96][LABb00]. This paper suggests a practical, top-down approach for transforming a traditional organisation into one that is e-commerce enabled. The suggested approach is based on well-known and proven management techniques to facilitate a wider acceptance by senior management.

## 2. THE BUSINESS ENVIRONMENT

For the small, start-up organisation, engaging in e-commerce is relatively easy and inexpensive, as is evident from the number of "dot.coms" that have sprung up over the past two years. Large corporates and multi-nationals are, however, experiencing difficulty realising the full potential of e-commerce. For such an organisation, it is not just a matter of selling products over the Internet, but rather changing its business philosophy as well as the industry in which it operates.

Organisations are attempting to adapt their imperfect business processes and systems to become e-commerce enabled. Many failed e-commerce initiatives can be attributed to the GIGO (garbage-in, garbage-out) principle. A struggling organisation with poor processes and systems will not become successful just because it has become e-commerce enabled. In such examples, e-commerce did not fail, but it was a case of the organisation being doomed from the start.

Before embarking on any e-commerce initiatives, it is essential that there is a proper understanding of what is required from the organisation [LABb00]. There are seven factors that govern an e-commerce enabled organisation [ROSS00][ROSS01]:

1. Convergence – In e-commerce, the convergence of business and technology drives the organisation. Technology has become a business enabler and creates new business opportunities. The traditional roles of CEO and CIO are becoming integrated and, in future, will become the responsibility of just one person.
2. Streamlining – All business processes, both internal and external, must constantly be analysed to seek ways to make improvements. Streamlining also involves the creation of new business process which, in turn, might lead to a need for new or additional infrastructure. Organisations can no longer function in isolation of customers, partners and suppliers.
3. Technology awareness – The e-commerce enabled organisation must keep abreast of technological developments as such developments create new opportunities. CEOs of the future will need a solid understanding of both the business and technological aspects affecting their organisations and industry.
4. Flat-and-flexible organisational structure – The e-commerce industry is a fast-paced one with little time for bureaucracy. The organisational structure needs to be adapted to become mobile and flexible in response to change. Employees must be empowered to make decisions and utilise opportunities. This means that the functional organisational structure of the past is inadequate and that new structures, such as project and matrix organisation structures, are required [SCHW00].

5. Information-centricity – E-commerce differentiates itself from traditional commerce in the sense that information, rather than a physical product, is the primary asset. Therefore, a more aggressive approach to information gathering, storing and retrieval needs to be followed. Many organisations have mountains of data, some information, but very little knowledge.
6. Customer-centricity – The focus of e-commerce is on the individual customer, rather than on the anonymous masses. This is sometimes referred to as mass-customisation where products and services intended for the masses are packaged for the individual. Customers want to be treated as individuals which means that organisations must get to know their customers as individuals.
7. Web assurance – E-commerce removes the need for physical presence but at the same time creates a lack of trust due to its face-less and place-less nature. Traditional organisations use a physical presence to establish initial trust with customers. With e-commerce, this is not always possible and, therefore, requires a different approach. One method of achieving initial trust is to have the organisation verified by a trusted party [ARTH01].

Once an organisation understands and accepts the above factors, it can start to develop an e-commerce strategy to change from its existing form into an e-commerce enabled entity. The main success factor for transforming an organisation is an excellent strategy [KALA97]. The development and implementation of a strategy is referred to as the strategic planning cycle and consists of four phases [TURB00]. These phases are illustrated graphically in figure 1 below:

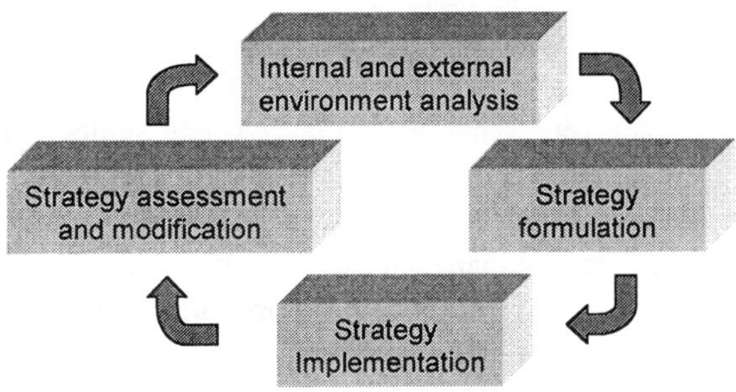


*Figure 1.* Strategic planning cycle

The following paragraph addresses the first two steps, namely internal and external environment analysis and strategy formulation.

# 3. E-COMMERCE STRATEGY

Strategy is defined as "the long-range plans to effectively manage environmental opportunities and threats in light of corporate strengths and weaknesses" [TURB00]. Intuitively, strategy can also be defined as the process of determining:

- where the organisation is;
- where it wants to be; and
- the way to get there.

Many proven techniques and tools exist that can be used for this purpose. By using familiar and proven techniques, top management is put at ease, as there is already enough unfamiliar territory within e-commerce. A SWOT (strengths-weaknesses-opportunities-threats) analysis can be used to determine where the organisation is. The Robson's five forces model [YEAT96] (an adaptation of Porter's five forces model), can be used to determine where the organisations wants to be. With the information gathered in the previous two steps, a plan can be developed to move from the one to the other.

## 3.1 Where the organisation is

The first step, to determine where the organisation is, can be achieved by using a SWOT analysis. The four components of SWOT need to be analysed to determine both internal and external organisational factors.

When looking at the internal factors, one approach is to view the organisation as consisting of three layers, with each layer broken down into more detail. The three layers are [ROSS01]:

1. Business direction – represents the top layer where strategic decisions are made by top-management.
2. Business architecture – represents the business units responsible for the core business processes that are managed by functional management.
3. Business infrastructure – represents the supporting services needed for the core business processes that are managed by operational managers.

These three layers are depicted graphically in figure 2 below:

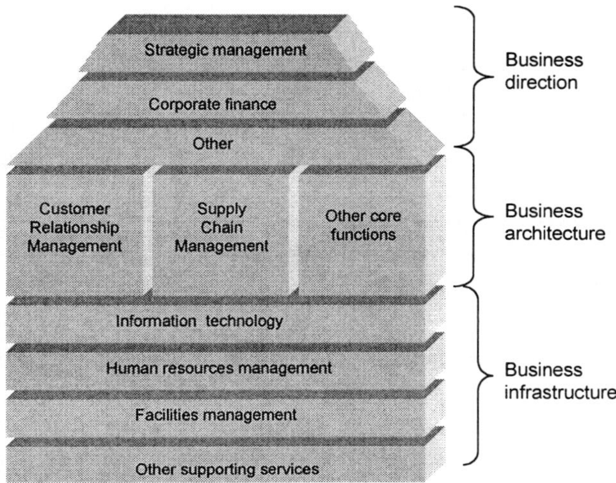


*Figure 2* – Three-layer organisational view

Following is a discussion regarding each layer.

### 3.1.1 Business direction layer

On the business direction layer, the existing strategy must be analysed to see if it can be adapted to include e-commerce. If not, a strategic decision needs to be made as to the future direction of the organisation. Top-management must be in agreement regarding the change in strategy, as this decision needs to be filtered down to everyone in the organisation. If some top managers do not support the initiative, there is a very good chance that it will fail [SCHW00]. E-commerce strategies will, in most cases, require innovative business models and/or business process re-engineering. It is seldom that a physical organisation will be converted into one that is an e-commerce enabled without using either of these.

Once the strategic direction has been decided, the e-commerce initiative must be funded. This is where corporate finance plays a very important role. Few organisations will have the financial resources available to fund a complete transformation. In most cases, a phased approach to implementing e-commerce is recommended. Each phase can then be financed separately. It is also possible to start planning for the allocation of funds over a certain time period. Corporate finance is also responsible for determining the financial viability of investing in an e-commerce initiative.

### 3.1.2 Business architecture layer

Once the strategic direction has been set and financial resources have been allocated, the business architecture can be analysed to determine the core business functions and the relationship between the systems in these functions. As a minimum, most organisations should have some form of customer relationship management (CRM) and supply chain management (SCM), even if it is in its most basic form. Depending on the type of organisation, other functions need to be analysed as well.

### 3.1.3 Business infrastructure layer

Lastly, the business infrastructure needs to be analysed to see what is already available. As a minimum, most organisations will have some form of information technology infrastructure, human resources management and facilities management. In many cases the organisation might already have some e-commerce components in place, for example a Web presence, an intranet and e-mail facilities. These can be used as the foundation for the e-commerce initiative.

At this point an organisation should have a good idea of its own strengths and weaknesses. An analysis of the market and the industry the organisation operates within should give insight into the opportunities and threats. This is sometimes referred to as Industry and Competitive Analysis. The next step is to determine where the organisation wants to be.

## 3.2 Where the organisation wants to be

To determine where it is that the organisation would like to be, a number of questions need to be asked. Wendy Robson took Porter's five forces model and adapted it to what is now known as Robson's five forces model for information systems opportunities [YEAT96]. The application of Robson's model to e-commerce is shown in figure 3 below.

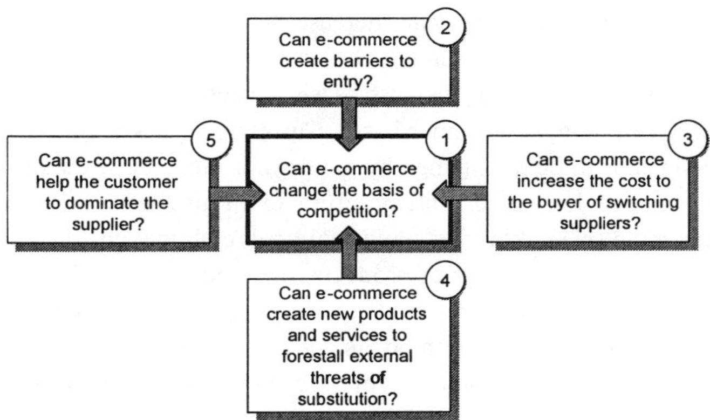


*Figure 3.* Robson's five forces model applied to e-commerce

After referring to figure 3 above, the first question to ask is whether e-commerce can change the basis of competition. There is no point embarking on e-commerce if no benefit is to be derived from it. The answer to this question can be [TURB00]:

– the organisation achieves competitive advantage (offensive approach)
– the organisation is able to level the playing fields and compete with much bigger competitors (offensive approach)
– the organisation needs to go this route for business survival reasons (defensive approach)

The ideal situation for any organisation is to create a new market by providing a new product or service. Whoever is first in this new market is usually perceived as the market leader. The market leader is now in a position to make up the rules for this new marketplace by which any future competitors need to abide. A typical example is Amazon.com — the first Internet-based bookseller. Any other organisation wanting to enter this market will be measured against Amazon.com.

The next question to answer is whether e-commerce can create barriers to entry. In a free market, any venture that is profitable is bound to attract new competitors. The ideal is to provide a product or service that discourages anyone else from entering the market and thereby maintaining a monopoly. Despite the fact that e-commerce can level the playing fields, many small organisations are unable to compete with the resources available in bigger corporates to develop large and sophisticated back-end systems. This is especially the case when it comes to using technologies such as data warehousing, data mining and knowledge management. The investment made thus far by Amazon.com in information technology runs into millions of dollars. Any competitor planning to enter this market will need to make a substantial investment to compete with such a strong and well-established entity. Another problem is that Amazon.com has been able to collect valuable information on its customers for a number of years. A new entrant will not have this information, nor will it be able to purchase it.

The third question is whether e-commerce can increase the cost to the buyer of switching suppliers. Ideally, an organisation wants to build up a loyal customer base as repeat business costs much less than new business. Using incentives and getting to know the customer can create a loyal customer base. Customers quickly get into a convenience-habit, which needs to be maintained by the organisation. An example is where Amazon.com, despite its low-price strategy, offers extra discounts to loyal customers. Part of the incentive scheme involves a virtual book club that customers can belong to, and, after purchasing a number of products, they receive free gifts or additional discounts. This is sometimes referred to as a virtual community. Customers are also given specific information on books and other products based on their preferences and past purchases. Customers, therefore, build up a relationship with the organisation. The effort involved for a customer to move from a familiar environment to an unfamiliar one where a relationship must still be established — and where there are no immediate benefits — will discourage most customers from making such a move. In e-commerce, trust also plays a very important role, as trust is developed over time, and few customers are prepared to move from a trusted environment to one where trust must still be established.

The fourth question is whether e-commerce can generate new products or services to forestall external threats of substitutions. Most products and services evolve over time and the organisation itself needs to be able to evolve accordingly. New products and services are, in many cases, the result of developments in technology. Organisations must either prevent the acceptance by customers of these new products and services, or be geared to accommodate any such substitutions. Going back to the example of online bookstores, one new development in the book market is electronic books or e-books. Books are published on disk and a special viewing device is used to read the book. Should physical books be substituted with electronic books in the future, Amazon.com will be geared for this. Amazon.com has already started distribution of electronic books, thereby preparing the business to accommodate this possible substitution of products.

The fifth question is whether e-commerce can help the customer to dominate the supplier. In most cases the individual customer has very little bargaining power. By consolidating the bargaining power of individuals, organisations can act as intermediaries and take full advantage of bulk purchases. Amazon.com is able to sell books at very competitive prices, lower than traditional bookstores, due to bulk purchases from book wholesalers. These savings can then be passed on to the customer. Amazon.com also passes demand-information through to the book wholesalers to ensure a supply that matches demand.

At this point the organisation knows where it is and where it wants to go. The next step is developing a plan to get from one to the other.

## 3.3 The way to get there

By mapping the information obtained from step two, where the organisation wants to be, onto step one, where the organisation is, different areas will be identified that must be adapted or created to enable e-commerce. The information obtained from questions one and two in step two is used to change the existing strategic direction of the organisation, as illustrated in figure 2. The information obtained from question three is used in CRM in determining what has to be done to become e-commerce enabled. The information obtained from question four is used in SCM to determine how substitute products or services can be accommodated. The information obtained from question five is used by both CRM and SCM to determine better ways of serving the customer. The relationship between where the organisation wants to be, to where it is, is shown in figure 4 below.

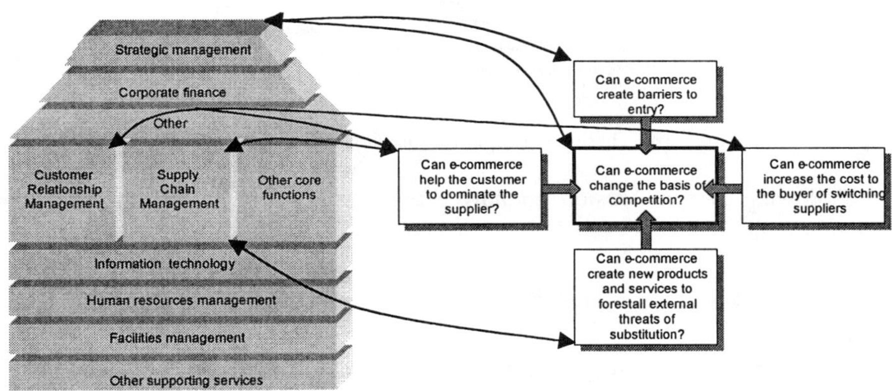


*Figure 4* – Relating where the organisation wants to be to where it is

During this process an organisation may realise that there are some new areas that have to be established within the organisation. The new e-commerce enabled organisation, based on its e-commerce strategy, might therefore resemble figure 5 below [ROSS01]:

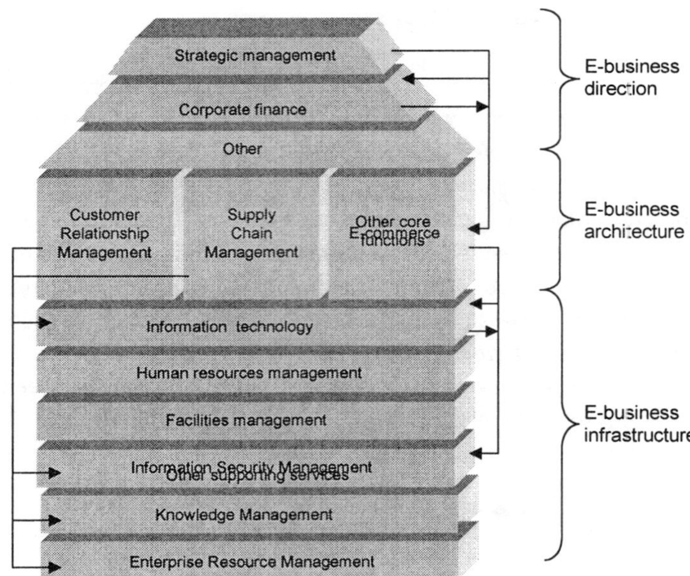


*Figure 5* – Three-layer organisation view incorporating e-commerce

Following is a discussion on how e-commerce would change the traditional organisation:

### 3.3.1 E-business direction

Top-management is responsible for setting and executing the new e-commerce strategy. Part of e-commerce strategy formulation must include investigating issues such as taxation, foreign exchange, legislation, multilateral contracts and role and policy of government [SCHN00].

### 3.3.2 E-business architecture

On the e-business architecture layer, e-commerce might be seen as a core function of the organisation and should therefore be a business unit on its own. For the purpose of this paper, e-commerce is defines as the exchange of goods and/or services for money using Internet technology as a supporting infrastructure. This unit must address several issues that include:

- **Electronic contracting.** Contracts are used in the physical world to bind two parties to an agreement and to protect them from one another. The use of contracts is considered good business practice by most large organisations. In the e-commerce environment, it is sometimes impossible for two parties to have the physical contact necessary for signing contracts before engaging in business.

This does not mean that contracts must now be abolished. Digital signatures can be used to sign electronic contracts [TURB00].

Contracts are still required for e-commerce, for the same purpose as for the physical world and is a prerequisite for procurement, negotiations, bidding and auctioning [SCHN00].

- **Electronic payment.** In cases where transactions are performed and money must be transferred, a secure electronic payment system must be implemented. For regular, large-sum transactions, using e-cash, credit cards or e-cheques becomes inadequate. The wide variety of electronic payment systems available presents an organisation with a choice. Electronic payment systems have to be integrated into the financial institution's systems. It goes without saying that security is very important if fraudulent transactions are to be prevented [GREE00].
- **Web assurance.** An organisation wants its customers and business partners to trust its processes and systems. One way to establish trust is to have processes and systems audited by, for example, an audit firm that will provide certification that the organisation complies with baseline controls [ARTH01]. Web assurance generally means looking at security, privacy, and consumer protection. Web assurance is similar to quality standards in concept, where in the future only organisations that have been certified will engage in e-commerce with one another. Organisations that provide such services include TRUSTe [TRUS01], Better Business Bureau (BBB) and Online Privacy Alliance [TURB00].

The CRM unit is responsible for both pre-sales and post-sales activities such as ordering, settlement, delivery, payment and customer care [ROSS01]. This unit, therefore, must work closely with the e-commerce, information technology and information security management units when it comes to electronic payment systems.

The CRM unit is responsible for analysing and managing the supply chains by using tools such as work flow management. This unit must work closely with the CRM unit to be able to exploit JIT (just-in-time) delivery of goods and services [TURB00].

The abovementioned issues are just some of the important ones and are by no means an exhaustive list.

### 3.3.3 E-business infrastructure

Based on the additional needs of the e-business architecture layer, the Information technology unit must expand its capabilities and develop additional expertise in areas such as smart cards, biometrics, digital certificates and encryption. More e-commerce enabling knowledge is required for, as an example, new information and communication platforms and mobile agents [SCHN00][TURB00].

The Human resources unit might not experience any drastic changes but could give valuable input to the CRM unit.

Facilities management traditionally looked at the management of, for example, physical security, air conditioning and telephony. Many of these services now makes use of computer technology in the related products. There is a definite overlap between the facilities management, information security management and the information technology units.

Based on the needs of the e-commerce unit, the establishment of a separate information security management unit might be required. This unit must work closely with the e-commerce and information technology units to implement the security infrastructure needed for secure transactions [GREE00]. The information security management unit is responsible for the non-technical aspects of security, while the information technology unit is responsible for the technical aspects. This unit must address several issues that include:

- **Certification and accreditation.** Security is a key issue for most organisations in conducting transactions over the Internet. An organisation might want to be certified as complying with some Information Security Standard, for example the BS7799, to provide potential customers and business partners with the peace of mind that it is proactively addressing security. Certification is only one component of web assurance, as discussed earlier.
- **Public key infrastructure.** Should an organisation decide to use public key encryption as its backbone for secure transactions, a public key infrastructure must be implemented. Once implemented, it needs to be managed and maintained, which requires dedicated resources and commitment. The use of a public key infrastructure does not automatically guarantee trust. A concerted effort is required to get the buy-in from all interested parties.

To enable CRM and SCM to effectively perform their functions, a knowledge management and an enterprise resource management division might have to be established. The enterprise resources management division is responsible for ensuring that all systems within the organisation are integrated to eliminate inconsistent information and data redundancy brought on by having large amounts of data. Data warehouses can be used for this purpose, as well as to improve on efficiency. The knowledge management unit uses techniques such as data mining to find patterns and trends in the data warehouses. This knowledge is, in turn, used by the organisation to improve its CRM and SCM functions [TURB00].

The above mentioned issues are just some of the important ones and are by no means an exhaustive list.

The next step, as shown in figure 1, is to implement the strategy and to regularly assess its performance [SCHN00]. Based on the results of the assessment the strategy might have to be modified or changed. It is very important that the strategy sets out to achieve a quantifiable goal, as many e-commerce failures are a result of unrealistic expectations. Strategy formulation is part science, part art.

# 4. CONCLUSION

For many organisations, e-commerce seems like an unrealistic dream. The reason for this is that large corporates and multi-nationals are like big ships that turn slowly. It is impossible to expect these organisations to change overnight to become e-commerce enabled. As with any other major organisational change, it is important to have strategy that will give direction to all involved. Many e-commerce initiatives have failed in the past because organisations focus on components of e-commerce rather than taking a holistic approach.

The top-down approach suggested in this article will assist senior executives by providing a starting point for taking an organisation down the e-commerce road — without getting lost in the detail.

# 5. REFERENCES

[ARTH01] Arthur Andersen, http://www.arthurandersen.com/, 2001

[ERNS96] Executive guide to e-commerce, Ernst & Young International, Release 1 – September 1996

[ERNS99] E-Commerce — 1999 Special Report Technology in Financial Services, Ernst & Young International, SCORE Retrieval File No. J00226, 1999

[GREE00] Electronic commerce — Security, Risk Management and Control, M. Greenstein & T.M. Feinman, McGraw-Hill Higher Education, ISBN 0-07-229289-X, 2000

[KALA97] Electronic Commerce: A Manager's Approach, R. Kalakota, A.B. Whinston, ISBN 0-201-88067-9, Addison Wesley Inc, 1997

[LABa00] A framework for electronic commerce security, L. Labuschagne, Information Security for Global Information Structures, p. 441 – 450, Kluwer Academic Press, ISBN 0-7923-7914-4, 2000

[LABb00] Electronic commerce: The information security challenge, L. Labuschagne & J.H.P. Eloff, Information Management & Computer Security, p. 154 – 157, ISSN 0968-5227, Volume 8 Number 3, 2000

[ROSS00] The Enterprise-wide Electronic Business (EWEB) Model — An Electronic-business (EB) Solution, A. Rossudowska, L. Labuschagne, SH. von. Solms, Proceedings of 16th World Computer Congress, ISBN 7-900049-66-5/TP.66, IFIP, 2000

[ROSS01] The EWEB Framework – A guideline to an enterprise-wide electronic business, A. Rossudowska, Rand Afrikaans University, Masters thesis, Rand Afrikaans University Library, South Africa, 2001

[SCHN00] Electronic Commerce, G.P. Schneider, J.T. Perry, ISBN 0-7600-1179-6, Course Technology – Thomson Learning, 2000

[SCHW00] Information Technology Project Management, K. Schwalbe, Course technologies – Thomson Learning, ISBN 0-7600-1180-X, 2000

[TRUS01] TRUSTe, http://www.truste.com, 2001

[TURB00] Electronic Commerce: A Managerial Perspective, E. Turban et al, ISBN 0-13-975285-4, Prentice Hall Inc., 2000

[YEAT96] Project Management for Information Systems, D. Yeates, J. Cadle, ISBN 0 273 62019 3, Pitman Publishing, 1996

21

# Business Models for Information Goods Electronic Commerce

*Conceptual Framework and Analysis of Examples*

Fons Wijnhoven

*University of Twente; P.O. Box 217, 7500 AE Enschede, Netherlands; email: a.b.j.m.wijnhoven@sms.utwente.nl*

**Abstract**: Electronic commerce studies have created important models for the trade of physical goods via Internet. These models are not easily suitable for the trade of information goods. Lowly codified information goods are hard to represent unambiguously among trading partners, their property rights are hard to secure, and the determination of volume and price is difficult. Highly codified information goods are easier traded by markets but have different levels of abstraction, which leads to specific requirements for their business models. The article analyses several information goods trade models that are derived from the framework presented.

## 1. THE NATURE OF INFORMATION GOODS

In markets, the good traded must be comparable to a commodity, this means highly codified and non asset specific (of potential value for many buyers). The transactions are governed through classical contract law: sharp in by clear agreement; sharp out by clear performance- in which the identity of the parties is irrelevant (Williamson, 1991: 271). Information goods though often are less codified and thus require intense communications to be understood. Additionally, the information good may be more asset specific, implying that it is of use for only a limited group. These exchange and product uncertainties require more elastic contracting mechanisms. If the contracting parties maintain autonomy but are bilaterally dependent to a nontrivial degree, the contracts will not be complete, and "(1) contemplate unanticipated disturbance for which adaptation is needed, (2) provide a tolerance zone within which misalignment will be absorbed, (3) requires information disclosure and substantiation if adaptation is proposed, and (4) provides for arbitration in the event voluntary agreement fails" (Williamson, 1991: 272). This is what Williamson calls hybrid transaction governance, and some other authors call clans (cf. Ciborra, 1987) or networks (cf Liebeskind et al, 1996). High asset specific goods are infeasible to supply by hybrids, because their ownership conditions are such strict that the unspecificity of ownership common to hybrids have to be avoided even if the asset is highly codified. This thus requires the information exchange to be governed by hierarchy. Hierarchy has preference over markets and hybrids when many contract disturbances happen, ande the principal is allowed to make the decision himself. Following Furubotn & Pejovich (1974) three types of property rights exist (1) the right of use, (2) the right of changing forms and structure of the transferred good, and (3) the right to reap the profits of the good. Picot, Bortenlanger, & Rohrl (1997) add a fourth property right essential for markets: (4) the right to sell the good. Because information exchanges implicate the transfer of information from a supplier to a buyer, the exchange partners arrange some kind of payment. This payment may result from the work of the invisible hand (the market), mutual understanding and networking (the handshaking in hybrids), and fiat in hierarchies. Because prices are hard to define in hybrids (Liebeskind et al, 1996), the payment for use mostly consists of invitations for collaboration on further development, and sharing profits when the information good can be sold or exploited. In the hierarchy, the most important ownership is the right to reap the profits exclusively.

Following Boisot (1998: 14) information (goods) may be classified along the dimensions of their level of codification and abstractness. Codification helps to give form to a knowledge asset, for instance by representing it in a language or mass-produced artefact. High codification implies that the representation is unambiguous for different receivers of the tokens. Abstraction refers to the level that information and knowledge can be applied more generally and is less restricted in scope.

Information goods are representations of events, objects, and ideas, which are codified such that they may be exchanged. Though the abstraction level may determine the level of control over processes (Bohn, 1994; Wijnhoven, 1999) and as such is basic for the business value of information goods, the codification level determines the efficiency of possible exchanges (Boisot, 1998). Low codification levels obstruct the market exchange of information goods, because it may be unclear for the buyer what actually will be sold. As such low codification goods are more effectively exchanged in networks, where reputation determines much of the expected value, and higher risks of poor value deliveries are acceptable. High codification, in return, enables to tag a price to the commodity and also enables others to deliver comparable products that create market competition. Consequently, markets only enable highly codified information products to be exchanged, though if they are highly asset specific, they will have to be exchanged via hierarchies for the sake of maximum exploitation of the property rights. Low codified information goods require a conversion process to make them suitable for market exchanges, if they are not asset specific. Given the different levels of abstraction and codification, several information goods may be identified (see table 1).

*Table.1* A classification and examples of information goods

| Exchange governance | Market | Hybrid | | Hierarchy | |
|---|---|---|---|---|---|
| **Codification** | **High** | **Low** | **High** | **Low** | **High** |
| Abstraction low | Data delivery services; News, journals; Infotainment | Qualitative observations & reports; Gossip | Data sets | Gossip; Business intelligence reports | Databases |
| Abstraction moderate | Magazines | Research in progress results; Ideas & notions | Shared resources for academic group | Organisational routines & norms; Undocumented policies | Management reports; Documented business policies |
| Abstraction high | Professional services; Courseware; Scientific publishing; Patents; Insurances. | Theory ideas Paradigms | Scientific software; Models; Sponsored scientific books & CD-ROMs | Business and management consulting; Skills | Knowledge-based systems; ERP; Business models; R&D. |

This article focuses on the information markets and the related information goods. Section two analyses the problems of information goods trade by electronic commerce systems, and section three proposes a generic way of designing business models that cope with these problems. Sections four, five and six analyse business models that cope with low, moderate and high abstract information goods. Finally, section seven analyses and discusses the differences and generics of these models.

## 2. PROBLEMS OF INFORMATION GOODS TRADE VIA E-COMMERCE

Electronic commerce aims at "...the seamless application of information and communication technology from its point of origin to its endpoint along the entire value chain..." (Wigand, 1997: 5). Electronic commerce may reduce transaction and co-ordination costs, because (1) it allows more information to be communicated in the same unit of time, (2) it enables a tighter linkage between buyers and sellers, (3) it may create an electronic marketplace where buyers and sellers trade, and (4) it enables the strategic deployment of linkages and networks among co-operating firms. Electronic commerce systems enable the replacement of inefficient intermediaries (Wigand, 1997: 4). The extent to which intermediaries can be replaced by electronic means is dependent on the level to which (lowly codified) pre-execution expertise is required. Picot et al (1997:114-115) therefore split consulting-driven from execution-driven transactions. An example of an execution-driven transaction is the booking of a flight, when the travel agency books the flight and provides no extra services. Consultant-driven transactions cannot be disintermediated because they rely on tacit knowledge. An example is the underwriting of a life insurance policy.

Kambil & Van Heck (1998) distinguish several trade processes and trade context processes. The trade processes involve the search and valuation of offers from suppliers and buyers, the logistics for transporting the goods, the payment and settlements, the verification of the quality and features of the product offered, the authentication of the trading partners, and the monitoring of conformance to the contract or agreement among the parties. The trade context processes may exist of communication and computer support, product representation, legitimisation for the validation of exchange agreements, influence structures and processes to enforce obligations or penalties to reduce opportunism risks, and a legal or institutional structure to resolve disputes.

All these trade activities have opportunities and specific problems when they want to trade information goods. These are listed below.

1. Search. Search engines, portals, and electronic agents may reduce the search costs for potential buyers. Sometimes the number of potential offers may be an overabundance, requiring evaluation methods like reputation indicators and certifying intermediaries (also see 2 and 5 below).
2. Valuation. A variety of new price discovery means (electronic auctions, bidding processes and negotiation via electronic agents) exist that differentially attribute costs to buyers, sellers and intermediaries. These may be applied to information goods as well, though the role of certification and reputation management may be more dominant.
3. Logistics. The logistic problems for the delivery of tangible goods via e-commerce may be huge. In contrast, information goods offer excellent opportunities for transaction costs reductions via Internet delivery. Divisibility of many information goods realises mass-customisation. Security problems (property rights theft) though are large.
4. Payment & settlements. Third parties may provide the infrastructures to reduce for exchange risks, consisting of banking and legal services. The divisibility of information goods enables to stop delivery when payment is not done (subscription principle), and thus the payment risk in information goods is probably easier controlled than in physical goods trade.
5. Authentication. The authenticity of the trading parties in electronic commerce is required. Third parties may monitor conformance to the contract or agreement among parties, so that dispute resolution can be based on agreed data. A special

problem for information goods is the ease of producing illegal copies, though this may be easily recognised.

6. Communications & computing. Improved processing, storage, input-output, and software technologies, transform the co-ordination capabilities of stakeholders in each process. This is especially true for information goods, where a strong merge of production, logistics and distribution may happen. Consequently, mass customisation is rather easily realised.
7. Product representation. Product representation determines how the product attributes are specified to the buyer or third parties. Too much representation, though, removes the trade value of information goods, but too less is insufficient for making buying decisions.
8. Legitimisation of transaction. Trade and exchange agreement can be validated on-line, by connections with credit card firms (which guarantee payment), checking the authority for transactions by PIN codes and membership numbers. This is most useful for information goods.
9. Influence structures & processes. Explicit mentioning of the terms and conditions of the trade may reduce dispute problems, but only when existing relevant legal and transaction data is available, reliable, and is easily transferred to enforcement actors.
10. Dispute resolution. Probably legal institutes must be adjusted to settle legal problems in electronic commerce, but the law will need innovations and not much experience (jurisprudence) may exist yet. This problem may be larger with information goods, because the property rights of information goods are more difficult to describe and secure.

Several principles of trade mentioned by Kambill & Van Heck are hard to apply in the context of information goods because of the codification (representation), property rights, and pricing problems involved.

# 3. CONCEPTS FOR THE ANALYSIS OF INFORMATION GOODS TRADE PROCESSES

Because information goods are easily and cheaply produced and distributed to clients, the actual process of information goods creation for many information goods can be done in close interaction with the end consumers. This means that information goods creation processes should be included in the information goods business models. The information goods creation management process helps to make the good to a commodity that can be easily sold to generate the highest revenues. Some of the most important subprocesses of this activity are to help clients find the product (search), to realise the authenticity of the product (through e.g. copyrights), and to make attractive product representations that help clients to make buying decisions. Also after-sales services may be developed to increase the client's expected future product value. The actual production of the information good is an important part of the business model, because it will enable more or less mass-customisation. As stated before, information goods may theoretically have nearly unlimited opportunities of mass-customisation, and the production facility is thus an important part of the model, which requires specific communication and computing facilities, influence structures and processes. Finally, information goods require a retail and distribution facility, which is able to value the product, logistically deliver, settles payments, legitimise the transactions and efficiently treat disputes. This results in the classification of activities and processes for information goods trade as listed below (Clemons et al, 2001).

- Information goods creation process, by e.g. artist, writer, reporter, researcher, photographer.
- Information goods creation management: selection of content, promotion, contract writers and creators, edit, generate sponsorship, certify correctness, accuracy, timeliness and suitability
- Information goods production: bundle data to packs, combine it for cross-selling (e.g. advertisements), print, distribute to subscribers and retailers
- Information goods retail and distribution: by subscription services, news agencies, news stands, convenience stores and other outlets

We describe some of the market trade examples of table 1 following the processes and activities listed here. The resulting models are analysed in section seven with respect to their similarities and differences among the three levels of abstraction of information goods.

# 4. BUSINESS MODELS FOR LOW ABSTRACT INFORMATION GOODS

Table 1 mentioned the following low abstraction information goods: data delivery services, news services, and infotainment (popular music and books). Because news service is a specific example of data delivery services, only the data delivery services and the infotainment examples will be discussed in this section.

## 4.1 Data delivery service

The information supplier delivers elementary data to the acquisition activity of the service, and helps to fill the structure and content of the product platform. Next these data may be analysed, integrated, synthesised, added and standardised, and consequently stored and made easily available to clients to facilitate customised client needs. These acquisition, refinement, and storage and retrieval facilitations are the information goods creation process. The distribution process is similar to the retail process and thus also includes the contracting and product presentation. The buyer receives information packages, and submits information needs specifications to the access tools and information product family resource. These data delivery services thus deliver customised information packs and access to large data resources. These services are also called information refineries (Meyer & Zack, 1996). See figure 1 for a model of the data delivery service.

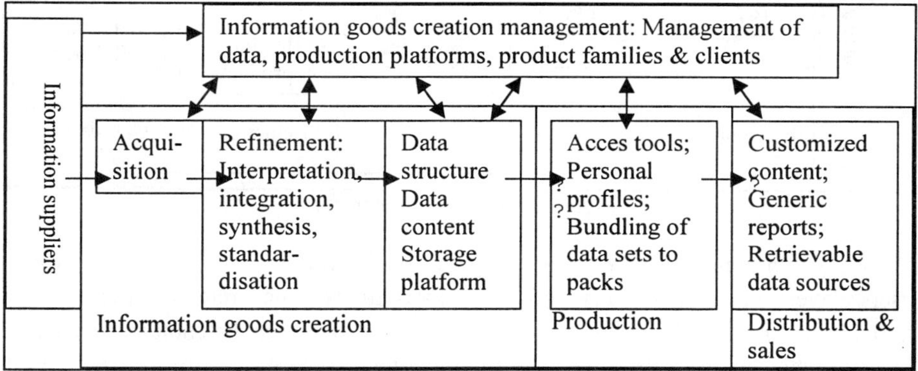


*Figure 1.* Data delivery services trade model

Modern new services can be organised as data delivery services, while improving the customisation and topicality (real time news), and reducing the production and delivery costs. As addition though, they need a certification process to manage the quality if the supplied data and maintain the reputation of the service.

## 4.2 Infotainment service

Infotainment is a broad term for software for fun. Basically an artist or group of artists produce a piece of art, like a movie, a piece of music, or a game. The artist(s) first create a composition, arrangement, script or initial game design and tries to convince a recording company to arrange the facilities to produce the idea, and sell and distribute it. There is a tendency for music groups and game developers to create the products on their own, which means that the artist (group) and the product creation management firm are the same people, but often the investments and the commercial expertises needed are insufficient for this unity (cf. Clemons & Lang, 2000). The information goods creation manager also facilitates the bundling of pieces of the art product to optimally suit specific market groups and so to make the product more attractive. Information goods of this kind can be delivered in hardcopy and digital form. The digital form, though more sensitive for violations of copyrights, enable more flexibility in the delivery and customisation of the good. Also the distribution and production cost are less. See figure 2 for a model of the Infotainment trade.

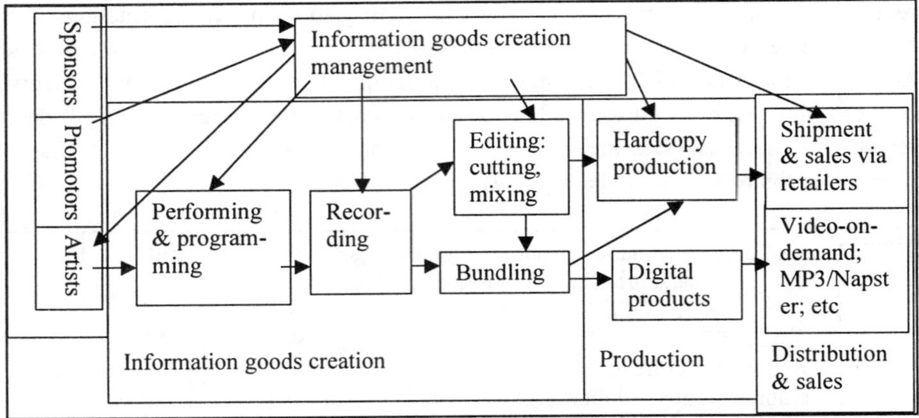


*Figure 2.* Model of infotainment

Many infotainment services require a continuous development, while users/players and designers discover new opportunities or generate new ideas related to the basic product. After some time the many new ideas may be combined to a new release, which may be supplied via shops as CD-Roms or via the Internet-based product supply site. Consequently, the management of the exchanges of users and designers is a most important part of product management, and the information goods creation management.

# 5. BUSINESS MODEL FOR MODERATE ABSTRACT INFORMATION GOODS: MAGAZINES

Magazines publish articles with a higher level of abstraction than news services. This implies that more content expertise has to be added. Consequently, the information goods creation process is more intense and takes more time. Additionally, magazines have to hire external expertise to check the quality of the product or to add to it when the editors have insufficient depth of knowledge. Some information goods buyers may be expected to be more knowledgeable and can add sometimes by delivering their comments. The readers may want more resources and may be interested to reuse articles, though they do not know which and when. The most important additions to the news services thus are (1) the research process, (2) acquiring external expertise for additions and review, and (3) resources for readers. See figure 3 for a model of a magazine.

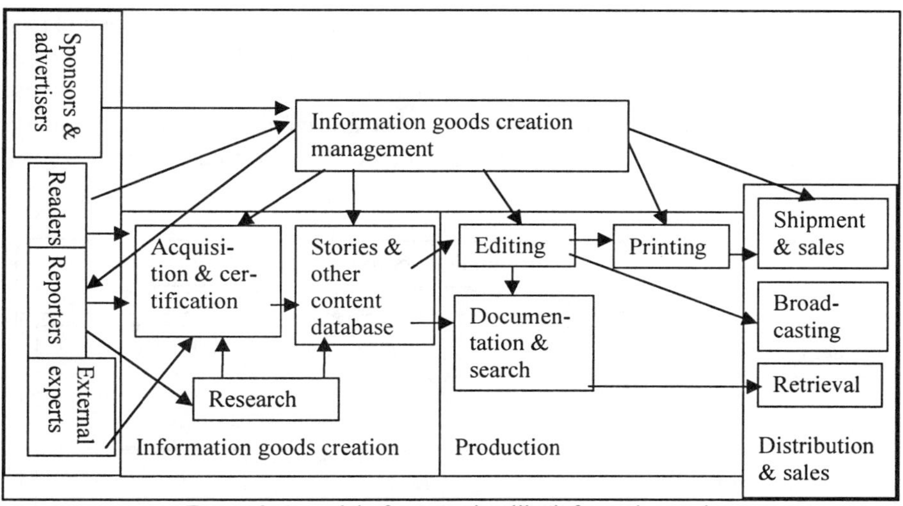


*Figure 3.* A model of a magazine-like information trade

# 6. BUSINESS MODELS FOR HIGHLY ABSTRACT INFORMATION GOODS

Table 1 mentioned five examples of high abstract information goods: professional services, courseware, scientific publications, patents, and insurances. Lack of space reduces this discussion to professional services and patent trade here.

## 6.1 Professional services marketing

Professional services have a high level of abstraction and consequently it may be difficult to codify them fully. As far as they are not fully codifiable, other trade mechanisms than markets are more useful (Liebeskind et al, 1996; Williamson, 1991). Most hospitals, organisation consultants and educational institutes have web-sites, which help clients to make an initial diagnosis, an initial analysis, or give information concerning research results and courses. Many of these sites are free of charge, because they help to develop a need among prospects for more profitable services, which are difficult to codify. To understand the typicalities of such professional services marketing, lets analyse the case of CapGeminiErnst&Young's Dutch operational benchmark service. CGEY clients can fill in a form consisting of benchmark items. The data submitted are compared to data from other firms, and some diagnosis and advice is given. Via the system, clients receive a well-grounded advice, combining theoretic insights, expertise and data. They pay a small fee for the service. Sometimes they will be able to solve the detected problems themselves, but they may also hire the professionals from CGEY or another organisation consultancy firms. At least two different types of products may be delivered: (1) the electronic advice via the website, and (2) professional skills. The information goods production thus has two production lanes, and these lanes built on data, expertise (case experiences), and theoretical insights, that are modified to the consultancy systems and the consultancy method. See figure 4 for a model of professional service trade.

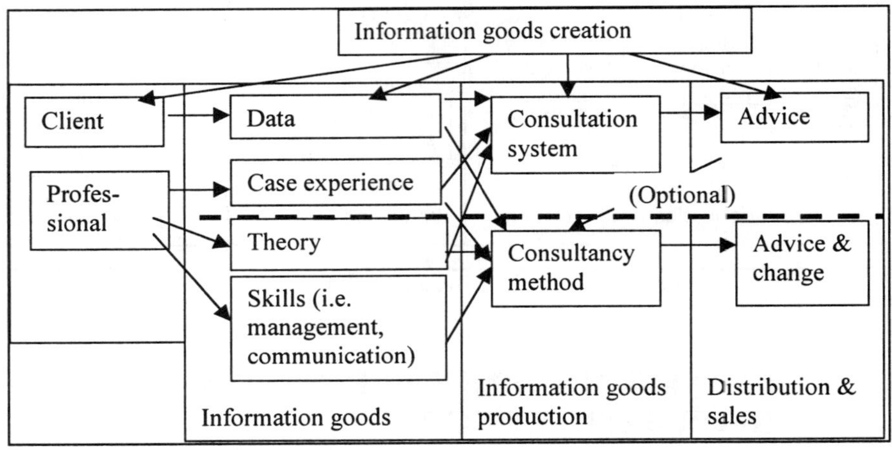


*Figure 4.* Professional service marketing-like information goods trade

Typical for this information trade process is that some of the information goods are hard to codify, and thus are difficult to trade via markets (this is represented as everything below the dashed line in the figure 4), and are certainly not to be traded by electronic commerce. These low codification goods though are important complements to the codified goods.

## 6.2 Patent trade

Though patents are representations of highly abstract knowledge, they are suitable for codification. This means that they are described such that other people can use them in a profitable way when they pay for its use. This makes patents as information goods, particularly suitable for market trade.

Because using a patent is only possible through coming to an agreement with a patent owner, the actual production requires the public publication of the patent, a valuation of the patent and the negotiation and contracting. These production processes are combined within the Yet2.com site. Yet2.com wants to be a global patent marketplace, by giving clients (searchers and potential buyers of patent licenses) access to owners of advanced technologies. Several leading technological firms are sponsors of Yet2.com, and they share their patents via Yet2.com with the market. The Yet2.com site gives information for valuation and pricing of patents, via its "done deals database", assists in structuring a deal by providing past deals as a frame of reference, and helps to learn about royalty rates in similar transactions. Yet2.com also gives assistance in legal services like patent prosecution, trainee programs, setting up legal protection. The site gives multiple references to other firms that can help by providing their professional services, and as such is a professional services marketing site as well. The information good is created via the review of a patent submitted for publication and the actual delivery of it as an information good via publication (hardcopy or on-line). This review (the job of patent and trademark offices and authorities) focuses on removing ambiguity in the patent description, and checking the novelty of the invention. The results of these reviews are processed by specialised publishers like Derwent via hardcopy prints and on-line databases. See figure 5 for a model of patent trade.

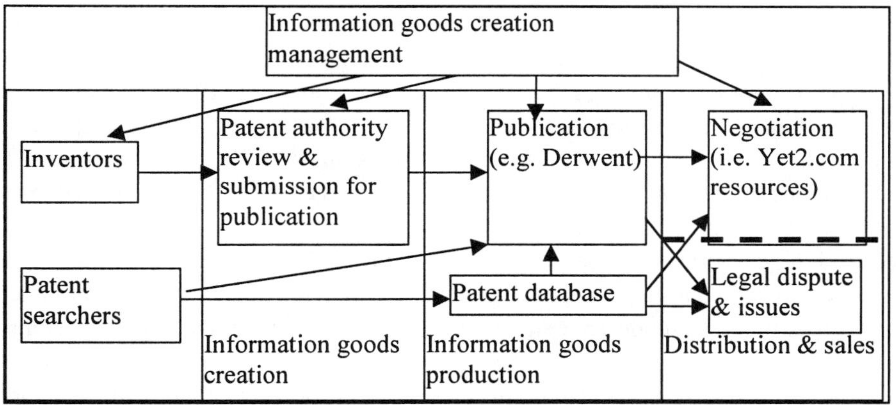


*Figure 5.* A model of patent trade

The elements below the dashed line have low levels of codification and are hard to trade via electronic commerce systems.

## 7. CONCLUSIONS AND DISCUSSION

Although this study does not pretend to be complete on all possible information good trade models -the cases have been selected as examples within a framework- several conclusions for theory and practice can be drawn. These conclusions result from a comparison of the models among different information goods abstraction levels, and within similar abstraction levels.

Trade models for moderate abstract goods require the addition of more expertise than for the low abstract good trade process. This expertise often has to be insourced, and requires review and commenting activities of (external) experts. High abstract goods can hardly be traded completely by electronic means, and requires supplementary human commercial interactions to deliver the information goods completely. Electronic commerce systems for high abstract goods thus need a human expertise supplement in its production and delivery processes for clients who want more.

Within the low abstract information goods group, the models differ on:

The level of human interaction needed. With some goods an execution-driven process may satisfy, whereas with other goods clients need access tools to create their own end product.

The level of bundling and customisation of the information good. For instance books are completely bundled information goods, whereas data delivery services may supply unbundled data.

The virtual or physical nature of the supplied good. Most low abstraction information goods models enable virtual as well as physical deliveries.

Within the moderately abstract group the most important difference may be the level of user/reader/consumer interaction in the information goods creation process. Electronic reader platforms may facilitate discussions and facilitate further critical explorations by the reader. This may be extended to reader involvement in magazine production activities.

With high abstract information goods the major differences are:

The level of completeness of the product codification. High abstract information goods mostly have a codifiable and noncodifiable part. The noncodifiable part also requires a consultant-driven trade process.

The leading actor in the market. In some cases the product creator owns the trade system (i.e. insurance firms), whereas in other cases the product creator and buyer community may own the trade system (e.g. some scientific communities).

The inter-organisational nature of the trade system. Some information goods require the collaboration of several specialised information good creators (i.e. the patent trade market of Yet2.com).

Sections 2 and 3 mentioned that information goods trade has specific complications because of its goods representation, property rights, and pricing problems. But at the same time, information goods can profit more from electronic media for reducing transaction costs, and improving producer-buyer interactions. Electronic media also enable more integration in the value chain and opportunities of exploiting this. All the information goods trade models have high opportunities of customisation and intense user/client involvement in product creation and production. The access tools, though important for customisation, make information good trade systems very sensitive for property rights violations.

Information goods business models at a meta-level share actor roles, information goods creation activities, information goods production activities, distribution and sales activities, and the co-ordinating tasks of information goods creation management. Further analysis and design of the models architectures require considering several organisational and information technological decisions. Though some significant insights are accomplished on concepts and models of information goods trade, this article is just a start to further systematic exploration of information goods electronic commerce. Much more practice has to be documented and analysed, resulting in the development of management instruments.

# 8. REFERENCES

Bohn, R.E., Measuring and managing technological knowledge. Sloan Management Review, 1994; Fall: 61-73

Boisot, M. H., *Knowledge Assets: Securing Competitive Advantage in the Information Economy*. Oxford [etc.]: Oxford University Press, 1998.

Ciborra, C. U., Research agenda for a transaction costs approach to information systems. In: *Critical Issues in Information Systems Research,* R.J. Boland, R.A. Hirschheim (eds.), Chichester: Wiley: 253-274, 1987.

Clemons, E.K., Lang, K.R., *Newly Vulnerable Markets in an Age of Pure Information Products: An Analysis of Online Music and Online News*. Not published working paper, University of Science & Technology, Hong Kong, 2000.

Furubotn, E., Pejovich, S., *The Economics of Property Rights*. Cambridge, MA: Ballinger, 1974.

Kambil, A., Van Heck, E., Reengineering the dutch flower auctions: A framework for analyzing exchange organizations. Information Systems Research, 1998; 9: March: 1-19.

Liebeskind, J.L., Oliver, A.L., Zucker, L., Brewer, M., Social networks, learning, and flexibility: Sourcing scientific knowledge in new biotechnology firms. *Organization Science*, 1996; 7 (4): 428-443.

Meyer, M. H., Zack, M.H., The design and development of information products. *Sloan Management Review*, 1996; 37 (3): 43-59.

Picot, A, Bortenlanger, C., Rohrl, H., Organization of electronic markets: Contributions from the new institutional economics. The Information Society, 1997; 13: 107-123.

Wigand, R.T., Electronic Commerce: Definition, Theory, and Context. The Information Society, 1997; 13 (1): 1-16.

Wijnhoven, F., Development scenarios for organizational memory information systems. Journal of MIS, 1999; 16 (1): 121-146.

Williamson, O. E., Comparative economic organization: The analysis of discrete structural alternatives. Administrative Science Quarterly, 1991; 36: 269-196.

22

# Implications of e-Commerce for Banking and Finance

Michael S. H. Heng
*University of South Australia*

**Abstract:** The aim of the paper is to show that e-commerce holds the potential to transform banking and financial systems. First, banks and financial firms can use the technology and business practice of e-commerce to market their products to the customers. Second, e-commerce provides a business opportunity for banks to offer new products and services to serve the needs of e-commerce. Third, the new business environment associated with e-commerce provides opportunity for institutional innovations in banking and finance, which can help to lay a sounder foundation for the international financial system. The paper focuses on the second and third aspects.

## 1. INTRODUCTION

Before e-commerce captured public imagination and business participation, the Internet was seen by the conservative and established banks as at best just another distribution channel. The advent of e-commerce has changed such perception.[33] Now almost every financial firm, from the most prestigious Wall Street investment bank to the provider of micro credit to the very poor, has found that it has no choice but to invest in an Internet strategy. "And having invested in it, it will need to persuade its customers to use it. (Long 2000)" Bank customers who enjoy the convenience of on-line purchase from Amazon.com may expect their banks to improve the services. However, banks and financial firms need to be more than becoming Internet savvy and embracing the practices of e-commerce. They need to see themselves as worthy contributors of e-business and to play their roles in a positive way in institutional innovators. The aim of the paper is to show that e-commerce holds the potential to transform banking and financial systems in a radical way.

[33] It must be noted here that innovative financial firms, e.g. e-trade and Schwab,. can claim some credit for their contribution to e-commerce.

There are three aspects in which e-commerce can affect banking and finance. First, banks and financial firms can use the technology and business practice of e-commerce to market their products to the customers. Second, e-commerce provides a business opportunity for banks to offer new products and services to serve the needs of e-commerce. Third, the new business environment associated with e-commerce holds potential for institutional innovations in banking and finance, which can help to lay a sounder foundation for the international financial system. The paper focuses on the second and third aspects. For the sake of completeness, the first aspect will be discussed here in the Introduction. Separate sections below will be devoted to dealing with the second and third aspects in greater detail.

Now, let us consider the first aspect. As customers we are witnessing these changes before our nose as banks adopt the Internet infrastructure and business practices of e-commerce. Many of us would have direct experience with electronic banking, for example Internet bank and e-brokerage, and have seen the disappearance of some brick-and-mortar branches of our familiar banks. The beauty of Internet banking lies in its low cost, convenience and availability. It enables banks and financial companies to offer services with the following qualities: 24-hour, seven-days-a-week availability, convenience, fast delivery, customer focus and personal service. Banks can reduce the time taken to approve mortgage application from weeks to hours. Many of the back office activities like data entry are now performed by the customers, reducing costs and improving services. The commercial use of the 128-bit encryption opens the way for secure on-line financial transaction. The Internet as a technological platform is to financial transaction what money as a common medium of exchange is to the economy. Just consider the convenience and flexibility provided by money in economic activity. Much more important than these is the need for bans and financial firms to operate in a *radically new* way. For example, act as an open shop for customers to buy services from you and your competitors. It is founded on the on-line world principle of getting the customers coming back to you, and has been adopted by Fidelity and Schwab selling competitors' mutual funds on their websites (Keen 2001).

Second, e-commerce represents a business opportunity for banks to offer new products and services to serve the needs of e-commerce. E-commerce has created a demand for low cost facility for micro payments (Choi et al 1997). Some other areas wherein banks can develop services are: protection for e-commerce participants against fraud, electronic billing and assistance for small businesses (Wenninger 2000), acting as information intermediary to safeguard the privacy of on-line customers, and acting as a rating agency for e-commerce.

Third, the new business environment associated with e-commerce represents an opportunity for re-structuring the banking and financial systems. As the capital market is assuming more and more the role of financing business ventures, banks have become less crucial as intermediary between savers and investors. Together with the dangers associated with moral hazard, this forms a good reason for governments to withdraw the safety net from banks and set up an independent agency to operate on a totally secure basis the payment and transaction systems. Another potential impact is that central banks may find it more difficult to set interest rates, thereby giving up their important function in monetary policy.

There is a strong historical precedent to the second and third aspects I just outlined in the two passages above. Many of the standard business practices of banks today evolved in response to the needs of modern commerce[34]. Modern commerce also shaped the business environment, which in turn introduced some major institutional innovations. A significant one was the commodity exchange which evolved to become the stock exchange, and futures market.

The rest of the paper is organized as follows. The next section will give a brief review of the development of banks in modern Europe, showing how banking emerged as an established business activity in response to the needs of commerce. Subsequently, section 3 describes some areas where banks are offering or can offer new services to support e-commerce. Section 4 discusses two main areas where e-commerce and the Internet can provide the opportunity to restructure the banking and financial systems, and the possible effects on financing of public projects. I close the paper with a conclusion in section 5.

## 2. LEARNING FROM ECONOMIC HISTORY

The early history of banking in the West can be read as a story of the evolution of banks in the process of meeting the needs of modern commerce. Banks in Europe began as moneychangers who specialized in assaying and valuing the coins used in the market centres (De Roover 1948; Lane and Muller 1985; Summer 1971). In the early 13th century, cities like Venice, Florence and Genoa bloomed and grew to become economic and cultural engines. These cities drove and expressed new aspirations and ways of thinking directed to material purposes, in the process creating new social behaviours. Venice was a great commercial centre, and it was here that banking for the first time separated itself from the changing of money (Roberts 1996). They evolved to become deposit banks, acting as custodians of their clients' money. This proved to be very useful to traders who gradually learned to trust the banks. With traders coming to accept book entry transfers as payment for their merchandise, banks acquired the role as payment intermediary between buyers and sellers. As long as the depositors could trust the banks, most of their money was laying idle there. This was soon discovered by the bankers. They realized that they could hold some reserves against deposits, and could lend out the rest against some

[34] Commerce had existed as early as the division of labour ushered in by the agricultural revolution. But commerce then had not stimulated the emergence of banks in the form that we know it. The task was left to modern commerce, i.e. commerce in modern history.

collateral or invest in promising business ventures. "Banks began when men saw from experience that there was not sufficient money in specie for great commerce and great enterprise." (Summer 1971, p.200.) With this new business activity, they carried out an additional role as financial intermediary between savers and investors/borrowers or become investors themselves. The second role allowed banks to provide liquidity in the economy. This has far-reaching economic consequences, both in the form of economic benefits and risks.

The intellectual life in Italy at that time was fermenting and vigorous. Florence was the focus of the most intense and influential cultural activity in the whole of Europe. From 1350 to 1450, more scholars, artists, scientists, architects, and poets lived and worked in Italy than anywhere else in the western world. Many of them came from other countries to participate and contribute to that great unplanned historical phenomenon known later as the Renaissance. "Europe went, as it were, to school there." (Roberts 1996: p.193.) Against this background of intellectual vitality, flourishing commerce brought with it a chain of institutional innovations. The Bill of Exchange appeared in the 13$^{th}$ century along with the first bankers. Limited liability was known in Florence in 1408, and marine insurance was available before that (Roberts 1996). Double entry bookkeeping evolved to meet the needs of merchants (Bodie and Merton 1998). By 1500, Italians had invented new credit instruments for the financing of international commerce. The Amsterdam stock exchange was established in early 17$^{th}$ century (Braudel 1968). The 19$^{th}$ century saw the regular market being replaced by continuous trading, purchase by sample, the rise of shop keeping, and replacement of fairs by produce exchanges or bourses.

The contribution of traders to the establishment of banks is well documented (Summer 1971; Clough and Cole 1968). In Europe, banks were established in centres of great foreign commerce such as Venice, Amsterdam, Hamburg and Nuremberg. It was "merchant capital which created markets, financed manufactures, floated the American colonial economies and launched banking and insurance." (Grassby 1970: p.106.) Even today, we still see the role of traders as modest providers of credit to peasants and farmers in developing countries. In emerging economies the activities of traders promote not only the more efficient deployment of available resources, but also the growth of resources (Bauer 1991).

Traders were risk-takers who under the right conditions underwent a metamorphosis to become financial and industrial capitalists. The instruments of capitalism were invented in the course of turning the wheels of commerce. For this paper, the most significant one is the principle and practice of limited liability. The practice of limiting the liability of passive partners made it easier for companies to attract investors to participate in new business ventures. It provided an efficient means for entrepreneurs to pool together public financial resources by selling them shares on the stock exchange. It is an instrument for sharing risks and profits that proved crucial in the growth of capitalism.

# 3. NEW PRODUCTS AND SERVICES TO SERVE E-COMMERCE

Commerce in our age inevitably involves monetary transaction. It would thus come as no surprise that e-commerce could affect banking in a very fundamental way, and would be affected by the ways banks respond to the new demands. For example, e-commerce will further undermine the power of bank branches (Lawrence et al 1998). It is also a business opportunity for banks to offer new products and services to serve the needs of e-commerce. In the following sub-sections below, we look at five areas where banks can offer their services to electronic commerce - payment services, information intermediary, rating services, fraud protection, and providing technological support for small businesses to enter e-commerce.

## 3.1 Payment and Billing Services

Credit card is one of the few remarkable innovations introduced successfully by banks in the last five decades (Drucker 1999), and it is currently being used extensively in B2C electronic commerce. But it is an expensive means of payment for e-commerce and many on-line shoppers will prefer other forms of paying their purchase (Long 2000). So will many on-line retailers who have to cough up set up and transaction costs and 2-3% of every payment. Moreover credit cards are not suitable for person-to-person trade on the Internet. Such inadequacy shows up in on-line auction. The American government has expressed misgivings about the reliance on credit cards for e-commerce. In short, e-commerce has created a demand for low cost facility for micro payments and flexible payment (Choi et al 1997; Long 2000).

New ways of on-line payments are appearing in the market, such as deduction from a pre-paid account, electronic billing services, direct transfer out of bank accounts. An interesting one is provided by X.com and PayPal which allows account holders to email money to each other (Long 2000).

## 3.2 As Information Intermediary

A recent issue of *The Economist* (Dec 9th 2000) reports the possibility for credit card companies and banks to act as information intermediaries. In such a construction, a bank customer downloads software from the bank that he knows and can trust. With the help of the software he can browse without the target websites knowing his identity at all. When he decides to buy an article on-line, the software generates a new identity for him, with a fictitious name and e-mail address, a coded postal address, and a one-off credit card number. The new identity is sent, via the online merchant, back to the bank. The bank would then check the details of the transaction and approves the transaction. The post office receives a decoded address label and the coded name.

## 3.3 Rating Services

Trading in cyberspace has its risk. This is the sense of uncertainty associated with lack of relevant information that matters (Bodie and Merton 1998). It is similar to the risk faced by buyers in nascent industrial societies when they began buying goods produced by strangers. Before the Industrial Revolution, they bought shoes from the shoemaker whom they knew directly or whom they knew from friends in the community. In the new business environment brought on by the Industrial Revolution, they had no such direct knowledge, and brand emerged as an innovation to serve customers' need for identification when buying products made by "strangers".

There are interesting parallels in the new trading environment in cyberspace. For example, there is a demand for rating agencies whose main function is to monitor and grade, on a regular basis, the quality of goods and services, as well as to rate the ability of buyers and sellers to meet their commitment. The electronic market supports an efficient use of information dispersed among economic agents. It provides a concrete example of a rational economic order, as described by Hayek (1945). He argues that the economic problem of society is a problem of the utilization of knowledge not given to anyone in its totality. "The peculiar character of the problem of a *rational economic order* is determined precisely by the fact that the knowledge of the circumstances of which we must make use never exists in concentrated or integrated form, but solely as the dispersed bits of incomplete and contradictory knowledge which all the separate individuals possess. (emphasis added, ibid, p.519)".

## 3.4 Fraud Protection

Besides the issues about quality, there is the related concern of fraud which is often expressed by on-line customers. From the seller's point of view, there is a new need for him to be guaranteed that the buyers would pay. Banks can enter the picture by being a supportive party in on-line transaction. A buyer of a car (say) offered for sales on-line would get the quality guarantee from a rating agency. After striking the deal with the seller, he would deposit the money with the bank associated with the electronic market. As soon as the buyer is given the keys of the car, the seller can collect the money from the bank. A business opportunity is thus created for banks with global spread, to offer a service that has some parallels to letter of credit.

There is a related business in the area of verifying identities (Wenninger 2000). Banks can offer a product that would protect e-commerce participants against fraud arising from false identities. With the help of encryption technique, a bank would certify the identities of its own account holders and act on behalf of its account holders to verify the identities of account holders at other banks. Such intermediary role increases the security of the on-line business.

## 3.5 Other Support to Business Clients in E-Commerce

E-commerce provides a new avenue for a few of the biggest commercial banks with technological capabilities to offer other business firms the technology to conduct business-to-business e-commerce (Wenninger 2000). These big players are assuming the role of automating the entire information flow associated with the procurement and distribution of goods and services among B2B partners[35]. Being information based and related to financial transactions, these services are seen by banks as an extension of the cash management services they have been providing to large corporations.

Banks with technological know-how can offer their expertise to assist businesses to participate in e-commerce. In concrete terms, they can help smaller firms set up the infrastructure and payment capabilities to engage in e-commerce. A few banks are offering small businesses in coping with the negotiation of volume discounts from vendors and electronic procurement services (Dalton 1999; Wilder 1999).

# 4. INSTITUTIONAL INNOVATION OF BANKING AND FINANCE

The new business environment associated with e-commerce represents an occasion for the banking system to re-structure as part of the bigger project of setting up a new financial architecture. The more profound consequences are in the broader area of financial systems where the Internet serves as the technological platform for all kinds of financial transactions, the so-called e-finance. Here I touch on two potential impacts. The first is the function of central banks in the area of monetary policy; the second is the stability of international financial systems and the modus operandi of national politics. It has been argued that Internet related technologies could increase the speed of financial operations, raising the question of how interest rates should be set and whether the short end of interest setting needs to become shorter *i.e.* time units smaller than a day (Friedman 1999b). Some economists have even envisaged a world where technological developments emasculate altogether the monetary controls of central banks (King 1999). This could occur if new technologies (and regulators) permitted real time pricing and exchange of goods across the Internet without the intercession of an independent

[35] Fore more information, please refer to corporate and institutional e-commerce services available at www.chase.com and www.citibank.com/singapore/gct/english (Wenninger 2000).

monetary system administered by a central bank. In such an environment the government earns no seignorage and would no longer be able to provide liquidity support by printing money.

The second potential impact is in international financial systems and national politics. Currently, banks are being squeezed from both the deposit and payment system side and the lending side (Claessens et al 2000). On the deposit and payment system side, many deposits substitutes are emerging and many non-banks such as mutual funds are offering transaction accounts. With Internet banking, consumers no longer have to pay high prices to transfer money from one country to another. On the lending side, the technology and deregulation allow non-deposit-taking financial institutions and capital markets to serve many more segments of borrowers including small and medium size borrowers. Transaction costs are lower, information is better and more widely available. I concur with Claessens et al (2000) in arguing that current developments in technology and deregulation are eroding the special nature of banks. An opportunity now presents itself for governments to re-evaluate the overall need for a public safety net.

This position is echoed by Heng and Peters (2001) who work out the idea in greater detail. In an unpublished paper, they explain that conditions are ripe for the re-invention of a core component of the banking system by having an autonomous institution to house the deposit accounts of individuals and companies. This institution would own and operate the payment and settlement systems. It is not profit-orientated, and will be managed by experienced bankers reputed for their competence, prudence and integrity. The new structure does not provide deposit guarantee for commercial banks, thereby removing a key factor of moral hazard. One manifestation of moral hazard was the reckless lending practices of banks in rich countries to East Asian companies. This was a crucial factor in the Asian economic crisis (Friedman 1999a). By encouraging banks to be more prudent in their lending habits, the new set-up would contribute to a sounder financial system in emerging economies and a sounder international financial architecture. The proposed set-up would constitute an important building block in a new international financial architecture. Banks could continue to thrive but they would need to innovate and earn their revenue by providing value-added services to their customers.

If accepted and implemented, Heng and Peters' (2001) proposal has two very interesting consequences. First, it removes one key factor in moral hazard which is diagnosed to be a cause in financial crises (Eichengreen 1999). So while the modern information technology infrastructure has made the financial market more volatile, it also provides an opportunity for designing a sounder and more stable international financial architecture. Second, the new setup would remove from politicians the powerful lever of supplying loans to their pet projects or supporters. The public would have a bigger say in the allocation of the public money. Politicians are then required to persuade the public of the merits of financing projects on the basis of, say, strategic long-term value for the economy, defense, or cultural life. The long-term consequences of this for the countries concerned will certainly be very interesting to watch.

# 5. CONCLUSION

Electronic commerce is associated with IT as an enabler, facilitator, and even inhibitor of business activities both within and among all types of organizations (Applegate et al 1996). It is thus creating enormous interest in the world of IT as well as many other industries (Pan et al 2000). There is little doubt that growth in this area will continue as more organizations join in the festivities, establishing and cultivating business relationships, performing business transactions, distributing knowledge, and implementing competitive strategy. Corporate life, particularly in America, is being transformed by the Internet (Micklethwait and Wooldridge 2000). Banks and financial firms are currently operating in such a new business environment, and they are responding to the changes in myriad ways.

The new environment provides an opportunity for banks and financial firms to develop new products and services. They can even to enter the traditional turf of technological firms. However, business players from other fields are planning to engage or are already moving into the traditional hunting grounds of banks and financial companies. Microsoft and computer network companies are known to be gearing up to offer financial services to the public. Of late, telephone companies are planning to allow customers to use their mobile phones to pay for goods and services. The charge will be added onto the monthly telephone bill of the customers. With the advent of Wireless Application Protocol (WAP) technology, mobile phones can provide customers with direct access to the Internet. This would enable mobile online shoppers to use their WAP phones to make purchases without having a credit card. And as pointed by one reviewer, in Finland people already pay through mobile phones through calling, not even througn WAP

Another source of competitive pressure comes from the relatively business activity known as navigation (Evans and Wurster 1999; Wenninger 2000). Navigators or intelligent search agents are information aggregators which search the web for similar products across a large number of companies, compare them for attributes such as prices, terms of delivery and goodies, and report their findings to the on-line customers. Banks and financial firms will have to compete with a bigger number of players, and face serious threats from nimble and innovative newcomers like Charles Schwab.

Banks and financial firms are sailing into new water that holds both promises and dangers. On one hand they have the know-how specific to banking and financial, and for the large players, they enjoy the trust of their customers. But they are burdened with legacy systems consisting of their management structures, reward systems and computer systems. They would certainly have to prepare themselves properly for the cut and thrust of life in the brave new world.

One of the most important challenges facing organizations in the age of electronic commerce has become the development of new business strategies and models. New business models are challenging the logic and assumptions of traditional models. Referring to the chapter 1 or first phase of electronic commerce, Keen (2001) recalls that the focus was on the technology as the driver. "Now companies are recognizing that this is about commerce: business models, process/technology integration, service, and relationships (Keen 2001, p.164)." This is a manifestation of the fact that the new environment presents opportunities for some and threats for others. Bill Gates knows that competition today is not among products, but among business models; irrelevance is a bigger risk than inefficiency (Turban et al 2000, p.xxvii). Indeed, inability to outgrow the dominant, outdated business design and thinking is often what leads to business failure (Kalakota and Robinson 1999). The pressure is now on companies to function in a state of more or less constant transformation. Senior management has to live with the challenges of earning revenues from well-tested practices while being prepared to experiment with new ideas which may undo these old practices.

As a way to study the impact of e-commerce, I turn to the early history banking and its relation to modern commerce, for history is indispensable in shaping our understanding. If history can be a guide to us, then we may see e-commerce exerting radical changes in banking and finance. Some of these changes have happened while others are emergent. Of these, the changes with the most far-reaching consequences are likely to be those in the area of institutional innovation. If carried out successfully, they would help to strengthen the international financial system.

**Acknowledgement**: The author would like to thank the three anonymous reviewers for their thoughtful comments.

# 6. REFERENCES

Applegate, L. M. et al 1996. Electronic commerce: building blocks of new business opportunity. Journal of Organizational Computing and Electronic Commerce, vol.6, no.1, p.1-10

Bauer, P. 1991. The development frontier: essays in applied economics. Cambridge, MA: Harvard University Press

Bodie, Z. and Merton, R. C. 1998. Finance London: Prentice-Hall

Braudel, F. 1985. Civilization and capitalism volume 2 – the wheels of commerce. London: Fontana Press

Choi, S. Y. et al 1997. The economics of electronic commerce. Indianapolis: Macmillan

Classens, S., Glaessner, T. and Klingebiel, D. 2000. Electronic finance: reshaping the financial landscape around the world. Presented at the joint conference of the World Bank, the IMF and *International Finance* 11 July 2000 Washington DC, available at www.worldbank.org/research/interest/conf/upcoming/papersjuly11/papjuly11.htm

Clough, S. B. and Cole, C. W. 1968, Economic history of Europe, 3rd edition. Boston: D C Heath and Company

Dalton, G. 1999. Wells Fargo turns to web hosting. Information Week Sept 20

De Roover, R. 1948. Money, banking and credit in mediaeval Bruges. Cambridge, MA: The Mediaeval Academy of America

Drucker, P. 1999. Innovate or die. The Economist, 25 Sept.

Eichengreen, B. 1999. Toward a new international financial architecture: a practical post-Asia agenda. Washington, DC: Institute of International Economics

Evans, P. and Wurster, T. S. 1999. Getting real about virtual commerce. Harvard Business Review Nov-Dec, p.85-94

Friedman, T. 1999a. The Lexus and the olive tree. London: HarperCollins

Friedman, B. 1999b. The future of monetary policy. *International Finance* Vol.2, no.3 p.321-338

Grassby, R. 1970. English merchant capitalism in the late seventeenth century. Past & Present, vol. 46, p.87-107

Hayek F.A. 1945. "The use of knowledge in society," *American Economic Review*, vol. 35, no. 4, (Sept), 1945 p.519-530.

Heng, S. H. and Peters, S. C. A . 2001. The Internet and an Opportunity to Re-invent the Banking System. Unpublished research paper, Vrije Universiteit Amsterdam

Kalakota R. and Robinson, M. 1999. e-Business: Roadmap for success. Reading, MA: Addison Wesley

Keen, P. G. W. 2001. Relationships: the electronic commerce imperative. In G .W. Dickson and G. DeSanctis (eds.) Information Technology and the Future Enterprise. Upper Saddle River, NJ:Prentice Hall, p.163-185

King, M. 1999. Challenges for monetary policy: new and old. Paper prepared for the Symposium on New Challenges for Monetary `Policy. Jackson Hole, Wyoming.

Lane, F. and Mueller, R. 1985. Money and banking in medieval and Renaissance Venice, Baltimore: John Hopkins University Press

Lawrence, E. et al 1998. Internet commerce. New York: Wiley.

Long, S. 2000. Survey of on-line finance. The Economist, 20 May 2000

Micklethwait, J. and Wooldridge, A. 2000. A future perfect. London: Heinemann.

Pan, S. L., Hsieh, M. H. and Chen, H. 2000. Managing knowledge in electronic commerce era: a case study of online learning centre. Proc. Of 4th Pacific Asia Conference on Information Systems 1-3 June Hong Kong

Roberts, J. M. 1996. A history o f Europe. Oxford: Helicon

Summer, William G. (ed.) 1971. A history of banking in all the leading nations volume 1.New York: Kelley Publishers

Turban, E., Lee, J., King, D. & Chung, H.M. 2000. Electronic Commerce: a managerial perspective. Prentice Hall, New Jersey

Wenninger, J. 2000. The emerging role of banks in e-commerce. Current Issues in Economics and Finance, vol.6, no.3, p.1-6

Wilder, C. 1999. Wells Fargo provides procurement - banks to offer web buying for business customers. Information Week Aug 10

23

# Electronic Commerce Use in Small and Medium-Sized Enterprises:
## *Some Evidence from Northeastern United States*

Fahri Karakaya and Omar Khalil
*University of Massachusetts Dartmouth*

**Abstract**: The Internet and Electronic Commerce (EC) related practices were surveyed in ninety-four small and mid-sized enterprises (SMEs) from a region of the Northeastern United States. Only 6.3 percent of the firms' sales was found to be attributable to e-commerce business. The results suggest some relationships of a firm's sales and profitability on one hand and the firm's Internet use on the other hand. Firms that rated their profitability and sales levels to be higher seem to have higher use of the Internet to gather distributor and vendor information, to conduct online purchasing, and to promote their products online. The majority of the firms surveyed tend to use e-mail to a great extent for communications internally among employees and externally with customers, vendors and distributors. Higher levels of e-mail usage for internal and external communications tend to associate with higher levels of reported sales and profitability. However, the findings suggest that most of the SMEs do not employ the Internet to its full capacity. In order for SMEs to advance their EC activities they need to develop their own EC strategies and to secure the managerial, human, financial, and technological resources to effectively implement them.

# 1. INTRODUCTION

The ever growing Internet use and EC activities are evident in the experts' and researchers' statistics and estimates. For example, the number of Internet users in 1997 was 170 million worldwide, and this number is expected to grow to approximately 350 million by 2005 (O'Shea, 1999). Currently there are 148.7 million Internet users in North America, 86.6 million users in Western Europe, 57.6 million users in Asia Pacific, 10.8 million users in South/Central America, 9.5 million users in Eastern Europe, and 7.5 million users in Middle East/Africa.

Similarly, the number of publicly accessible Web pages is expected to grow from 800 million today to 8 billion by 2002 (Moeller 1999).

Further, EC is growing exponentially. Back in 1997, the global EC was estimated at $10 billion, exceeded $13 billion in 1998, but is predicted to rise to $200-300 billion by 2002 (Morphett , 1999), and to increase to $3 trillion by 2003 (Aaron, Maurizio, and Skillen, 1999; O'Shea, 1999). In the U.S., 40 percent of U.S. households are now online and 40 million consumers have shopped online in the year 2000. It is also expected that by the year 2003, there will be over 60 million shoppers online. (Cyberdialogue, 2000). Forrester Research Inc. forecasts that by 2002, Internet commerce among U.S. businesses alone (U.S. business-to-business Internet commerce) will be $327 billion up from year 2000's estimate of $17 billion. The business-to-business portion of EC is estimated to be 78 percent of the total dollar value of electronic transactions, and it's estimated that the consumer e-commerce will grow to $108 billion in 2003 (Hof 1999).

Therefore, EC has been accepted as a bona fide business practice in the commercial world (Davis & Garcia-Sierra, 1999). Industry Week (1999) quotes the head of Motorola's electronic commerce department as saying; "Anyone not making the change to Web-based commerce within the next year would probably be locked out of their business for good." While many businesses, small and med-sized enterprises (SMEs) in particular, have web sites and claim to practice EC, little is known on how much they use the Internet to conduct business online, how extensively they employ the many E-Commerce tools that are available, whether the businesses that employ E-Commerce tools are more successful than the ones that do not, and whether firm size influences the extent of employing of e-commerce tools. With this in mind, this study was designed to explore the extent of EC use by SMEs located in a region of the Northeastern United States.

## 2. BACKGROUND

The Web is poised to become the medium by which companies buy, trade, make contacts, exchange data and information, discuss designs, and locate companies. Although EC can be defined from different perspectives (e.g., communication, business process, service and online), perhaps a useful way to view it is to link it to trading. EC is trading by means of new communication technology. It includes all aspects of trading such as commercial market making, making, ordering, supply chain management and the transfer of money (Garnett and Skevington, 1999).

EC fosters building better relationships among customers, producers, and suppliers. Its implementation harnesses networked resources to further the exchange of business transactions in a more efficient and cost effective manner (Aaron, Maurizio, and Skillen, 1999). It contributes to economic efficiency in such ways as shrinking distances and timescale, lowering distribution and transaction costs, speeding product development, disseminating more information to buyers and sellers, and enlarging customer choice and supplier reach (Levis, 1996).

As a consequence of EC growth, small and medium-sized enterprises (SMEs) face pressures from supply chain reorganization that exclude them or reduce their role to sub-contracting, and from the closure of independent retailers (Rhodes & Carter, 1998). Because online competitors are forcing customized responses to customers' demands, SMEs must provide services that eclipse products as the source customer value, match production to real-time customer demand, and float prices with current market conditions. Designed for efficiency in an environment of slow change, SMEs' business practices must be dismantled and rebuilt to support mass customization, open finance, and business process outsourcing (McCarthy, 1999).

Fortunately, the Internet is a potential force in democratization of capitalism, and offers SMEs and consumers dramatic new possibilities in the global marketplace (Quelch & Klein, 1996). Potential EC benefits for SMEs include increased research capabilities, more efficient sourcing and purchasing, reduced administration time and expense, more effective data exchanges, increased visibility and sales, and use as a customer service tool (Davis & Garcia-Sierra, 1999).

SMEs are expected to recognize and seek strategic benefits with EC, and to invest heavily in web technologies and in web-based systems. However, the development of Internet-based strategies by SMEs to meet the challenge of large firms depends on the internal firm dynamics, including willingness-or resistance-to undertake major changes in practice and the external contexts, particularly the financial, technological, political and regulatory environments (Rhodes & Carter, 1998). Future plans and policies that aim at advancing SMEs adoption and practice of EC must depend on accumulated empirical evidence on the current EC practices, problems, and potentials. This investigation is designed to profile EC practice of a number of SMEs located in a region of the Northeastern United States.

# 3. METHOD

In order to profile EC practice among SMEs, a survey was designed in cooperation with the five area business executives and pretested. After minor modifications, the survey along with a personalized letter and a return envelope were mailed to 490 firms located in a region of the Northeastern United States in May 2000.

The firms were selected using a stratified sampling procedure that employed the area zip codes. The cover letters were directed at the contact persons listed in the database asking them to route the survey to the individual(s) responsible for e-commerce activities. Ninety-four companies responded to the survey (19%).

## 3.1 Demographics of the Responding Firms:

Fifty-four percent of the responding firms were manufacturers, 20% service firms, 10% distributors, 8% retailers, and 8% others. The responding companies indicate that on average only 6.3 percent of their sales was attributable to e-commerce business. It is important to note that 58 percent of the businesses (50 organizations) indicates that zero percent of their sales was attributable to e-commerce. Only five companies attribute 25 percent or more of their sales to e-commerce. On average, the responding firms have engaged on e-commerce for approximately 17 months (ranging from zero to five years). The responding firms also report that their sales and profits have been in the range of very good and good (mean ratings of 3.6 and 3.46 respectively, measured as 3=good and 4=very good). The average size of the responding businesses was 127 employees ranging from a minimum of 0 employee to maximum of 1954 employees.

# 4. RESULTS

The analysis of the 94 area companies indicates that many businesses have access to the Internet and many are already doing business online. However, most businesses use the Internet on a limited scale and need assistance in a variety of technical and non-technical areas. Ninety two percent of the firms has access to the Internet and 73 percent has web sites. However, on average, only one out of four companies (25%) utilize the Internet regularly in conducting business, including, online promotion, online sales and purchase, online customer service, and gathering online marketing, vendor, and distributor data. Overall, most of the businesses surveyed have Internet presence in order to provide information about their products and services.

## 4.1 Internet Use and Company profitability and Sales

The Internet usage varies among the responding companies. While some are heavy Internet users others use the Internet on a limited basis. Table 1 shows the types of Internet use and the rating of company profits by the respondents. As one may note, despite the fact that the majority of the firms have web sites, only a small percent of them utilize the advanced Internet tools. Most of the activities listed in Table1are "only occasional usage."

Analysis of variance (ANOVA) was performed to examine whether the Internet usage varies by company profitability and company sales levels. The respondents rated their profitability and sales levels on a five-point scale, ranging from very poor to excellent. Similarly, the respondents rated their various types of Internet usage, ranging from always to never use. In performing the ANOVA, the Internet usage variables were employed as multi dichotomous while company profitability and sales were treated as dependent variables. The means in Table 1 Indicate the Internet usage activities and one could assess the extent of these activities from the means.

Two of the seven variables shown in Table 1 show statistically significant relationship between company profitability levels and Internet usage. The companies that always gather distributor information through the Internet rated their profitability levels higher than the respondents who do the same occasionally, never, and almost always (mean=5.0 vs. 3.33, 3.52, and 3.67 respectively). Companies that always conduct online purchase transactions rated themselves more profitable than the companies that perform online purchases almost always, occasionally, and never (mean=4.5 vs. 3.11, 3.41 and 3.44 respectively).

In addition, post hoc tests (Duncan's Multiple Range Test) indicate that there are other differences among the firms with different profitability levels. Those firms that always use the Internet to gather vendor information are more profitable than the firms who use the Internet occasionally doing the same activity (mean=4.40 vs. 3.34 respectively). Similarly, firms using the Internet to promote their products always rated themselves as more profitable than the firms never using the Internet for promotion purposes (mean=4.09 vs. 3.21 respectively).

| Internet Use | Mean | F-Value | P-Value | Post Hoc Test |
|---|---|---|---|---|
| Gather Marketing Research Data | 1.18 | 1.14 | .34 | ------- |
| Gather Vendor Information | 1.24 | 1.87 | .14 | 1&3 |
| Gather Distributor Information | 1.00 | 2.94 | .03 | 0,1,2 & 3* |
| Promotion through Internet | 1.26 | 2.00 | .12 | 0&3 |
| Conduct Online Sales transactions | 0.78 | 0.98 | .41 | --------- |
| Conduct Online Purchases | 0.85 | 2.64 | .05 | 0, 1,2&3 |
| Conduct Online Customer Surveys | 0.44 | 1.13 | .34 | --------- |

Scale: Internet use activities were measured as: Never =0; occasionally=1; almost always=2, and always=3. Profitability variable was measured on a five-point scale as Excellent, Very Good, Good, poor, Very Poor.

*Should be read as there is a difference in company profits between firms always gathering distributor information and companies gathering distributor information almost always, occasionally, and never.

*Table 1.* Types of Internet Use by RespondingFirms and Relationship with Company Profits

Table 2 shows the ANOVA and post hoc test results for company sales as rated by the responding firms. As it was the case with company profitability, the firms that use the Internet extensively (always) to gather distributor information rate their sales higher than the companies that never or occasionally gather distributor information through Internet (mean=5 vs. 3.31, 3.60 respectively). The Duncan's Multiple Range Test also showed that there is a statistically significant difference in the sales levels of companies that utilize the Internet in conducting customer surveys occasionally (mean=4.06) and never (mean=3.41).

While the ANOVA results were statistically insignificant, promotion through Internet and conducting online purchases were found to be related to company sales levels in the post hoc tests performed. Firms that consider themselves as using the Internet always (mean=4.30) for promotion rate their sales levels higher than the firms that utilize the Internet occasionally (mean=3.53) or never (mean=3.38) for promotion. Similarly, The firms that always use the Internet for online purchasing rate themselves as having higher sales levels than firms conducting online purchases occasionally and never (mean=4.5 vs. 3.60, 3.51 respectively).

| Internet Use | Mean | F-Value | P-Value | Post Hoc Test |
|---|---|---|---|---|
| Gather Marketing Research Data | 1.18 | 0.74 | .53 | ------------- |
| Gather Vendor Information | 1.24 | 1.32 | .27 | ------------ |
| Gather Distributor Information | 1.00 | 3.27 | .03 | 0,1 & 3* |
| Promotion through Internet | 1.26 | 2.08 | .10 | 0,1& 3 |
| Conduct Online Sales transactions | 0.78 | 1.24 | .30 | ----------- |
| Conduct Online Purchases | 0.85 | 1.89 | .13 | 0,2 & 3 |
| Conduct Online Customer Surveys | 0.44 | 2.75 | .05 | 0&1 |

Scale: Internet use activities were measured as never=0; occasionally=1; almost always=2, and always=3. Sales variable was measured on a five-point scale as Excellent, Very Good, Good, poor, Very Poor.

*Should be read as: there is a difference between firms gathering distributor information through Internet always and occasionally and never.

*Table 2.* Types of Internet Use by RespondingFirms and Relationship with Company Sales

## 4.2 E-Mail Usage and Company Profitability and Sales:

The vast majority of the responding firms use e-mail for one reason or another. More specifically:

- 72 percent use e-mail to communicate within their organizations,
- 78 percent use e-mail to communicate with vendors,
- 75 percent use e-mail to communicate with distributors, and
- 85 percent use e-mail to communicate with customers.

Indeed, e-mail usage appears to be the most Internet activity utilized by companies. One respondent commented "The first thing I do when I start work in the morning is to check my e-mail." To examine the relationship between the type of e-mail usage and company profitability and sales, ANOVA and post hoc tests (Duncan's Multiple Range Tests) were performed. The results indicate there are statistically significant relationships (see Table 3). Companies that use e-mail to communicate internally always, almost always, and occasionally rate themselves as more profitable than the firms that never use e-mail (mean=4.0; 3.56; 3.71 vs. 3.03). In other words, those firms that utilize e-mail more frequently to communicate with their employees rate themselves as more profitable compared to the ones that never use e-mail to communicate internally. Firms using e-mail to communicate with distributors always rate themselves as more profitable compared to the firms communicating with distributors through e-mail occasionally or never (mean=4.60 vs. 3.31, 3.35 respectively). Similarly, companies that use e-mail always, almost always, and occasionally to communicate with customers rate their profitability levels higher than the ones that never use e-mail to communicate with distributors (mean=4.00; 3.54; 3.50 vs. 2.72 respectively).

| Internet Use | Mean | F-Value | P-Value | Post Hoc Tests |
|---|---|---|---|---|
| Use E-mail to communicate within organization | 1.31 | 4.26 | .00 | 0&1,2,3* |
| Use E-mail to communicate with vendors | 1.22 | 1.28 | .29 | ------- |
| Use E-mail to communicate with distributors | 1.10 | 3.03 | .03 | 3&0,1 |
| Use E-mail to communicate customers | 1.32 | 3.15 | .03 | 3&0,1,2 |

Usage of E-mail was measured as on a four point scale as: Never =0; occasionally=1; almost always=2, and always=3

*Should be read as there is a statistically significant difference in company profits between firms never using e-mail to communicate within their organization and using e-mail occasionally, almost always, always to communicate within the organization.

*Table 3.* Types of E-Mail Use by Responding Firms and Relationship with Company Profits

The examination of company sales levels as related to type of e-mail use shows that all five types of e-mail use are related to company sales (see Table 4). Firms that always use e-mail to communicate within the organization have higher sales levels than those that never use e-mail in communicating within the organization (mean=4.20 vs. 3.27 respectively). Similarly, companies using e-mail almost always to communicate with vendors rate their sales higher than the ones who don't (mean=4.00 vs. 3.16 respectively). Firms that use e-mail always to communicate with distributors rate their sales higher than the ones who use e-mail occasionally or

never to do the same (4.60 vs. 3.50, 3.30 respectively). Firms that utilize e-mail almost always to communicate with distributors also rate their sales higher than the firms who don't (mean=4.00 vs. 3.30). In examining the relationship between sales and the level of communication with customers, the ANOVA showed only a weak relationship exists (p=.059). The post hoc tests indicate that firms using e-mail always to communicate with customers
have higher sales levels than the ones that use e-mail occasionally or never (mean=4.22 vs. 3.43, 3.27).

| Internet Use | Mean | F-Value | P-Value | Post Hoc Tests |
|---|---|---|---|---|
| Use E-mail to communicate within organization | 1.31 | 3.57 | .02 | 0&3* |
| Use E-mail to communicate with vendors | 1.22 | 3.01 | .04 | 0&2 |
| Use E-mail to communicate with distributors | 1.10 | 3.94 | .01 | 3&0,1 and 2&0 |
| Use E-mail to communicate customers | 1.32 | 2.58 | .06 | 3&0,1 |

*Table 4 continued.*

E-mail usage was measured as on a four point scale as: Never =0; occasionally=1; almost always=2, and always=3

*Should be read as there is a statistically significant difference in company sales between firms never using e-mail to communicate within their organization and the firms using e-mail always to communicate within the organization.

*Table 4.* Types of E-mail Use by Responding Firms and Relationship with Company Sales

## 4.3 Internet Use and Company profitability and Sales

To examine the relationship between company size and web site contents, one would expect that larger firms would have more elaborate or comprehensive web sites. Most of the companies reported to have web-sites sites include company and product information (over 90%). However, Only 17 percent of the firms have stock/inventory status of their products and 35 percent of the firms have online sales transaction capabilities on their web sites. While these two web functions are important in business operations, they require technical know how and are costly to integrate into web sites. Therefore, one would expect that larger companies to have these and other costly tools such as interactive customer service software. Table 5 shows the means of the companies in terms of the number of employees and whether they differ or not. Three of the tested nine web site content variables through t-tests differ between the relatively large and relatively small size firms. The average size of the firms with online catalogs on their web sites is 160 employees. This compares to companies with average employee size of 128 employees having no online catalogs. Similarly, relatively larger companies disclose company financial data on their web sites (average size of employees 483 vs. 135). However, one should interpret this with caution since only seven percent of the companies have this information available on their web sites. The third variable that was statistically significant was "links to other company web sites (e.g., suppliers, distributors or customers). Compared to the relatively smaller size firms, the web sites of the relatively larger firms contain more links to other sites.

| | Presence of Content | Company Size (Mean Number of Employees) | | T-Stats. | Ssignificance Level |
|---|---|---|---|---|---|
| Web Page Content | % | Yes | No | t-value | p-value |
| Company Information | 93 | 167* | 17 | 1.0 | .29 |
| Product Information | 91 | 164 | 65 | 0.75 | .46 |
| Hyperlinks to other Sites | 44 | 237 | 89 | 2.03 | .05 |
| Online sales transactions | 35 | 120 | 173 | 0.78 | .43 |
| Stock/Inventory Status | 17 | 171 | 153 | 0.20 | .84 |
| Online Catalogue | 53 | 160 | 128 | 2.03 | .05 |
| Customer Service Area | 54 | 155 | 157 | 0.97 | .74 |
| Other company Advertisements | 29 | 129 | 168 | 0.59 | .56 |
| Company Financial Data | 7 | 483 | 135 | 2.31 | .02 |

Reflects company size average in terms of employees.

*Table 5.* Relationships between Company Size and Web-site Contents

## 5. DISCUSSION AND CONCLUSIONS

Ninety-four SMEs from a region in the Northeastern United States were surveyed in order to profile their Internet and EC practices. The majority of the responding firms have started recently to use the Internet for one reason or another. Most of the businesses surveyed use the Internet to provide information about their products and services. However, on average, approximately 6 percent of the surveyed firms' sales are attributed to EC. Further, only one from every four firms utilize the Internet regularly in conducting business (e.g., promotion, sales, purchases, customer service, and gathering online marketing, vendor and distributor data).

The results suggest some relationships of a firm's sales and profitability on one hand and the firm's Internet use on the other hand. Firms that rated their profitability and sales levels to be higher seem to have higher use of the Internet to gather distributor and vendor information, to conduct online purchasing, and to promote their products online. The majority of the firms surveyed tend to use e-mail to a great extent for communications internally among employees and externally with customers, vendors and distributors. In addition, higher levels of e-mail usage for internal and external communications tend to associate with higher levels of reported sales and profitability. Finally, larger firms tend to have online financial data, online catalog, and their we-sites tend to have more links to other sites.

A more advanced use of the Internet requires more managerial and technical resources. Since larger firms are expected to be more resourceful, compared to the smaller ones, a firm's size may influence the breadth and depth of its Internet use. Fore example, the findings of this investigation suggest that that most of the surveyed SMEs do not employ the Internet to its full capacity. Many still think EC is just having a web page. But EC is much more than that. A firm engaging in EC must create a business infrastructure to go with it. Also, EC requires substantial infrastructure planning with the intention of avoiding putting together an EC site in a few weeks on underpowered hardware equipped with narrow pipes, ill considered software and no data management strategy.

SMEs are hindered by the inadequate investment in skills and technologies, compared to large companies. Other issues include security, cost, and resistance (Davis & Garcia-Sierra, 1999). Successful application requires positive attitudes towards information technology and the ability to identify and solve the problems that possibly accompany EC. SMEs need to understand the development of web presence sites is becoming a competitive necessity, particularly the need to establish online storefront.

Finally, SMEs also need to know the barriers to entry; the difficulty in establishing a market leadership position, and the cost of entry will increase in direct proportion to the delay in investing in web technology and EC applications (O'Shea, 1999). To get to this point, SMEs need to keep in mind the need for developing their own EC strategies. They need to focus on EC infrastructure, strong partnerships and the core products and structure in order to ensure that online business will be effectively conducted in the digital economy era.

# 6. REFERENCES

Aaron, R., Decina, M., and Skillen, R. (1999), Electronic commerce: Enablers and implications, IEEE Communications Magazine, September, pp. 4752.

Davies, A.J. and Garcia-Sierra, A.J., (1999), Implementing electronic commerce in SMEs—three case studies, BT Technology Journal, Vol 17, No. 3, pp. 97-111.

Garrett, S.G.E., Skevington, P.J., (1999), An introduction to eCommerce, BT Technology Journal, Vol. 17, No. 3, pp. 11-16.

Hof, Robert (1999), "Is that E-Commerce Roadkill I see?"*Business Week*, (September 27), EB 96.

Levis, K., (1996), Electronic Commerce, *British Telecommunications Engineering*, Vol. 14, No. 4, pp. 281-285.

McCarthy, J.C., 91999), The social impact of electronic commerce, IEEE Communications Magazine, September, pp. 53-57.

Moeller, Michael (1999), "A Hidden Goldmine Called Inktomi," *Business Week*, (September 27), EB 72-73.

Morphett, I., 1999, Foreword, *BT Technology Journal*, Vol. 17, No. 3.

O'Shea, E., (1999), IEEE Communications Magazine, September, pp. 83-86.

Quelch, J.A., and Klein, L.R., (1996), The Internet and international marketing, Sloan Management Review, Spring, pp. 60-75.

Rhodes, R., and Carter, R., (1998), Electronic commerce technologies and changing product distribution, Int. J. Technology Management, Vol. 15, Nos 1-2, pp. 31-48.

24

# The Development of E-Commerce in Malaysia

Ainin Sulaiman, Rohana Jani, Shamshul Bahri
*Faculty of Business and Accountancy, University of Malaya, 50603 Kuala Lumpur*

**Abstract**: E-Commerce has become an important tool in handling different types of business activities emerging from the convergence of several information technologies and business practices. Although E-Commerce has been seen to be an effective and efficient way of doing business, the degree/extend of adoption is still not as extensive and with some reservations amongst both users and non-users. The paper focuses on the analysis of primary data collected via questionnaire on adoption of E-Commerce applications and its constraints. As expected, the results showed that e-mail was the most widely adopted E-Commerce application mainly due to a minimal cost involved in the implementation. The results also revealed that about 27% of the respondents did not adopt any kind of E-Commerce applications and nearly 75% of them can be considered as low users (i.e. utilizing less than five applications). Security has been indicated by many to be the top main reason for not adopting E-Commerce.

## 1. INTRODUCTION

E-Commerce is now emerging from the convergence of several information technologies and business practices. Among the principal technologies directly enabling modern E-Commerce are computer networking and telecommunications, client/servers computing, multimedia, information retrieval systems and electronic data interchange. E-Commerce is of considerable value whereby it acts as a platform for the formulation of new customer management strategies. This is mainly because E-Commerce directly connects buyers and sellers, support fully digital information exchanges between them and suppress the limit of time and place. In addition, E-Commerce support interactivity and therefore can dynamically adapt to customer behavior and can be updated in real time, therefore it is always up to date.

The importance of E-Commerce can be seen from the increase in size of Internet users and growth of electronic commerce worldwide (Strauss and Frost, 1999). In

Malaysia, a report in The Star IN-TECH April, 18 2000, indicated that in 1995 there were only 7,000 Internet users and in 1999, the size increased by hundred percent (700,000). In addition, The E-Commerce spending in 1997 was RM 12.54 million and this figure is expected to increase to RM 2.46 billion by the year 2002.

The increase in Internet usage and E-Commerce spending in Malaysia is spearheaded by the Malaysian Government, via the creation of the Multimedia Super Corridor (MSC). The MSC provides low telecommunication tariffs, no censorship on the Internet, plus a well developed IT infrastructure of fibre optic cabling. This complements the rise and growth of the Internet and E-Commerce activities (www.mdc.com.my).

Although E-Commerce is in its early stage of usage in Malaysia, it is expected to change the way organisations carry out their daily transactions. By using E-Commerce, organisations will have an added value, whereby it can improve, transform, and redefine their organisations (Bloch et al, 1996).

E-Commerce comprise of a wide range of activities. It is not only exchange of products, services and information electronically (Kalakota and Whinston, 1997) but it also includes new advancement to advertising, market research, customer support service, order and delivery and financial transactions (payment) (Turban et al, 2000).

This study focuses on E-Commerce applications pertaining to these areas. It explores the extent of usage of these E-Commerce applications in Malaysia, namely amongst the Manufacturing, Services and Agriculture/Construction sector.

The paper begins by describing the various ways in which organisations can conduct E-Commerce. It continues with a description of the research methodology, a discussion of the findings, in particular the applications that are most and least widely used. It then proceeds with an analysis of the level of E-Commerce applications by the various organisations. Finally, the paper reveals factors which hinder E-Commerce adoption among the selected organisations.

## 2. COMMERCE ON THE INTERNET

According to The World Trade Organisation (WTO) E-Commerce can be illustrated by reviewing the usage of Internet. The Internet can be used for a mulitude of exchanges and transactions, including e-mails, leisure reading and searching for information (browsing or surfing), advertising and promoting personal or business causes, linking people, selling, purchasing or providing services. It can be concluded that the Internet provides a powerful platform for organisations to conduct E-Commerce.

Advertising includes providing information about the company and its product and services. This can be carried out by displaying the information on the organisation web sites, using a third party website or by means of electronic catalogues. A survey of the World Wide Web shows that more and more organisations are putting their catalogues online.

In carrying out market research online organisations can keep in touch with the market environment i.e.: what their competitors is 'up to' and the changing trends of consumers' taste and preferences (Fletcher, 1990). In addition, organisations can also use Internet to monitor their competitors and utilize the Internet for suppliers' evaluation. This would add value to the organisations' procurement decisions as the Internet provides another source of suppliers evaluation (Haynes et al., 1998).

Order and delivery applications include online application/registration, processing sales order and coordinating procurement with suppliers. Some companies provide an online shopping facilities whereby potential customers can shop online. They then uses courier agents to deliver the products. These courier agents on the other hand provides potential customers with services that helps them keep track and trace the movements of their products.

The most important process in any business transactions is making payments or receiving money for the products and services provided. There are companies which allow their customers to pay their online purchases using credit cards. Lately, multimedia technologies have brought about the existence of the smart cards and prepaid cards. Smart cards have been introduced in Malaysia through one of the seven Malaysia Multimedia Super corridor's flagship application (Ainin & Lee S.L, 1997).

The most common customer support services are the e-mail and FAQ (Frequently Asked Questions) (Kiani, 1998). In addition, customers can lodge complaints or make enquiries by filling online forms. More and more organisations with websites are using these applications extensively.

According to surveys carried out on the use of E-Commerce (Cockburn and Wilson, 1996; Hoffman et al., 1996; Jones and Vijayasarathy, 1998; Haynes et.al, 1998) most organisations use Internet as a vehicle for publicity and advertising, such as providing information about their products. Few companies allow potential customers to order and pay through the Internet.

The results of a survey (Soh et al, 1997) conducted in Singapore illustrated that most of the organisations surveyed used E-Commerce for markerting and advertising, customer support, information gathering and to a lesser degree, electronic transactions such as order and delivery and payment.

Similar study conducted in Greece, indicated that organisations used E-Commerce to ensure on-time delivery of their products and services and provide customers information about products. The studied also showed that the less active usage was online payment and placing orders online.

# 3. RESEARCH METHODOLOGY

## 3.1 Sources of Data

The study utilized both secondary and primary data. The secondary data was based on literature pertaining to the area of interest. Besides hard copy of the literature, soft copy of articles obtained through the Internet was also considered as references. This is to review and understand concepts related to the area of research. Questionnaires were used to collect primary data.

The questionnaire consists of two main sections. The first section comprises of questions on E-Commerce applications and the level/status of adoption of each application, that is, whether or not it is in use, intention to use within the next 2 and 3 years or no intention to use at all. The respondents were asked mainly questions on the type of electronic applications (i.e. Electronic Marketing, Electronic Advertising, Customer Support Service, Order and Delivery and Payment) used by their organization as well as the levels of the usage of each application. This section is designed to capture the trends of the E-Commerce applications adoption among the respondents (organizations).

The second section of the questionnaire required the respondents to rate the level of perceptions regarding factors that hindered them from using more E-Commerce applications. The response was based upon a 5 interval Likert Scale, where 1= 'strongly disagree' and 5 = 'strongly agree'.

The questionnaires were then mailed to the selected organizations. The target respondent was the Chief Executive Officer of the organization or their Information System/Technology (IS/T) Directors or equivalent. A mailing list was then compiled (from the Federation of Malaysian Manufacturer (FMM) Directory, Malaysian Industry Development Authorities (MIDA), and National Productivity Corporation) and the questionnaires were distributed accordingly.

The mailing list (Table 1) consisted of 6468 organizations representing the various sectors of the economy, namely Services (47%), Manufacturing (46%) and Agricultural/Construction (7%).

*Table 1 :* Distribution of Questionnaires by Sector

| Industry | No. of Questionnaires | Percentages (%) |
|---|---|---|
| Manufacturing | 3001 | 46 |
| Agriculture/Construction | 425 | 7 |
| Services | 3042 | 47 |
| **Total** | **N = 6468** | **100** |

A total of 590 responds were received (a response rate of 9%), out of which , 45.4% were from the Manufacturing sector, nearly 45% from Services and 7% from Construction/Agriculture sector. Although this sample may not be a total representation of the population (N = 6468). the data gathered provide us with useful empirical and important background information on E-Commerce usage in Malaysia, particularly in the selected sectors mentioned above.

## 3.2 Methods for Data Analysis

The data analysis method mainly involved descriptive summary through cross-tabulation and frequency distribution of variables of interest. These display provide the overall distribution of the data and highlights any significant features of the variables in the study. A Chi-square test is applied to look at association between factors.

# 4. ADOPTION OF E-COMMERCE APPLICATIONS

## 4.1 Types of E-Commerce Applications Used

Table 2 illustrates the trends of E-Commerce applications adoption in Malaysia. The figures clearly reveal that the top three currently most utilized applications are e-mail (59.7%) followed by homepage/own business website (33%) and displaying company information and the product services offered at 32.5%. Although e-mail was widely used, there were still a fairly large percentage (about 21%) of the organisations that did not intend to use it at all. This was probably because they did not plan to have Internet access.

***Table 2*** Adoption of Applications

| Applications | In Use | | Use within 2 year | | Use within 3 year | | Do not Intend to use at all | |
|---|---|---|---|---|---|---|---|---|
| | Freq. | % | Freq | % | Freq | % | Freq | % |
| Communication e-mai | 352 | 59.7 | 87 | 14.7 | 26 | 4.4 | 125 | 21.2 |
| Home page/ Own websi | 194 | 32.9 | 193 | 32.7 | 55 | 9.3 | 148 | 25.1 |
| Displaying company information and the product/services offered | 192 | 32.5 | 184 | 31.2 | 46 | 7.8 | 168 | 28.5 |
| Handling customers feedback/queries on-line | 98 | 16.6 | 200 | 33.9 | 69 | 11.7 | 223 | 37.8 |
| Credit cards | 97 | 16.4 | 97 | 16.4 | 55 | 9.3 | 341 | 57.8 |
| Research on competitors | 92 | 15.6 | 166 | 28.1 | 86 | 14.6 | 246 | 41.7 |
| On-line application/ registration | 82 | 13.9 | 171 | 29 | 64 | 10.8 | 273 | 46.3 |
| Third party website | 79 | 13.4 | 101 | 17.1 | 40 | 6.8 | 370 | 62.7 |
| On-line help – product updates | 76 | 12.9 | 207 | 35.1 | 61 | 10.3 | 246 | 41.7 |
| Processing sales order from customers on-line | 74 | 12.5 | 197 | 33.4 | 93 | 15.8 | 226 | 38.3 |
| Research and evaluation of new suppliers | 73 | 12.4 | 177 | 30 | 84 | 14.2 | 256 | 43.4 |
| Research on consumer preference | 71 | 12 | 164 | 27 | 82 | 13 | 273 | 46.3 |
| On-line help – Frequently asked question (FAQ) | 70 | 11.9 | 193 | 32.7 | 58 | 9.8 | 269 | 45.6 |
| Tracking incoming and outgoing good delivery | 53 | 9 | 169 | 28.6 | 91 | 15.4 | 277 | 46.9 |
| Electronic catalogues | 51 | 8.6 | 172 | 29.2 | 70 | 11.9 | 296 | 50.2 |
| Co-ordinating procurement with suppliers on-line | 38 | 6.4 | 201 | 34.1 | 99 | 16.8 | 252 | 42.7 |
| Prepaid cards | 24 | 4.1 | 84 | 14.2 | 52 | 8.8 | 430 | 72.9 |
| Smart cards | 22 | 3.7 | 100 | 16.9 | 70 | 11.9 | 398 | 67.5 |

Among the eighteen E-Commerce applications studied, e-mail was probably the cheapest to implement. In fact the organizations did not have to invest a lot of money to communicate via e-mail as no software or extra hardware were needed. This may be and indications that many organizations were still not ready enough to invest a large sum of money to adopt E-Commerce. Assuming that the organizations were already using computers (equipped with modems), all they needed to do were to register with a service provider to gain access to the Internet for a minimal fee. This implied that it is readily available. In addition, a survey of the World Wide Web showed that there are several companies or search engines that provide free web-based email service. Thus, the expenses incurred will be only for the adoption of the Internet time, whereby charges are based on the local telephone call rates.

On the other hand, applications such as coordinating procurement, monitoring trading and tracking incoming and outgoing goods were not widely used. This is so since these applications require a substantial amount of investment, thus only a few can actually afford to implement them within their organizations. This further substantiated the reason why e-mail is most widely used.

Looking at the mode of payments, 16.4% of the organisations were currently using credit cards for payments while 57.8% showed no interest of doing so. This implied that the organisations were concerned about the authentication of the payment system The number of organisations using smart cards and prepaid cards were also very low (less than 5% each) and the increase in adoption within the next three years was expected to be minimal. Furthermore, the number of organisations that did not intend to use either smart cards or prepaid cards was very high (more than 55%). This once again indicated that majority of the organisations were not ready to use these mode of payment as the technology is still new and there are not many success stories on its adoption. Nevertheless, with the implementation of the smart card flagship application by the government within the next few years the adoption of smart card is expected to increase.

These findings support the studies conducted by Bloch et. al.(1996), Cockburn and Wilson, (1996), Soh et al (1997) and Kardaras and Papathanassiou (2000). In addition, we would expect similar findings, if similar research is to be conducted in any country which is just embarking on E-Commerce such as Malaysia's neighboring countries like Thailand, Indonesia and Brunei.

## 4.2 Level of E-Commerce Adoption

Table 3 presents the distribution of total number of E-Commerce applications adoption by the organizations.The number of adoption range between "no usage" to "a maximum of 15" applications used. A total of 18 applications was listed and none of the organizations used all the 18 applications studied. From this table we can observe that nearly 27% of the respondents did not use any kind E-Commerce applications whereas only 1.5 % used more than 10 E-Commerce applications.

About 39.5% used between 1 to 3 types of applications. Next we look at the degree of adoption. Data was grouped into low and high adoption based on the overall percentage distribution. Low user refers to range of adoption between 0 to 4 applications whereas high user is from 5 to 15 applications. It can be then concluded that the level of adoption is very low with nearly 75% of the respondents were low users and 25 % as high users. These figures reflect that Malaysian organisation is still slow in adopting E-Commerce.

*Table 3 :* Total Number of E-Commerce Applications Adopted by Organisations

| Total | Frequency | Percentage (%) |
|---|---|---|
| 0 | 158 | 26.8 |
| 1 | 89 | 15.1 |
| 2 | 68 | 11.5 |
| 3 | 76 | 12.9 |
| 4 | 54 | 9.2 |
| 5 | 33 | 5.6 |
| 6 | 35 | 5.9 |
| 7 | 21 | 3.6 |
| 8 | 15 | 2.5 |
| 9 | 17 | 2.9 |
| 10 | 11 | 1.9 |
| 11 | 4 | .7 |
| 12 | 3 | .5 |
| 13 | 3 | .5 |
| 15 | 3 | .5 |
| Total | 590 | 100.0 |

Detailed analysis by sectors (manufacturing, construction/agriculture and services) and number of applications used shows a significant relationship between the two variables, as reflected in Table 4. This implies that rate of E-Commerce adoption to some extend depends on the type of organizations or business involved. This is clearly reflected by the percentage distribution shown in Table 4. However, it was found that there is no significant relationship between size of organization (small medium versus large) and rate of adoption (Table 5). Small medium organizations in this case refer to those with less than 150 employees while large organizations are those with more than 150 employees.

***Table 4:*** Distribution of Adoption by Sectors

| Adoptions | SECTORS | | | | | | | |
|---|---|---|---|---|---|---|---|---|
| | Manufacturing | | Construction /Agriculture | | Services | | Total | |
| | Freq | % | Freq | % | Freq | % | Freq | % |
| Low users | 213 | 47.9 | 48 | 10.8 | 184 | 41.3 | 445 | 100 |
| High users | 55 | 37.9 | 11 | 7.6 | 79 | 54.5 | 145 | 100 |
| Total | 268 | 45.4 | 59 | 10 | 263 | 44.6 | 590 | 100 |
| Chi-square test | $\chi^2 = 7.729$ (p-value = 0.021) , low users = 0 – 4 applications : high users = 5 – 15 applications | | | | | | | |

***Table 5:*** Distribution of Adoption by Size of Organisations

| Adoptions | SIZE | | | | | |
|---|---|---|---|---|---|---|
| | Small/Medium | | Large | | Total | |
| | Freq | % | Freq | % | Freq | % |
| Low users | 239 | 53.7 | 206 | 46.3 | 445 | 100 |
| High users | 70 | 48.3 | 75 | 51.7 | 145 | 100 |
| Total | 309 | 52.4 | 281 | 47.6 | 590 | 100 |
| Chi-square test | $\chi^2 = 1.294$ (p-value = 0.255); small < 150 employees ; large > 150 employees low users = 0 – 4 applications : high users = 5 – 15 applications | | | | | |

Table 5 reveals that 51.7% of large organizations are high users of E-Commerce applications while 48.3% of the small medium organizations are high users. This finding is consistent with earlier findings in an Indian E-Commerce survey (Rao, 2000).

# 5. FACTORS HINDERING ADOPTION

Besides studying the trends of E-Commerce applications in Malaysia, it is useful and interesting to explore why these organizations are not fully utilizing the applications. It was found that the top four reasons given by the respondents were as follows:

- Insufficient security to prevent hacking and viruses (27.8%)
- Sales and marketing requires high human interaction (25.8%)
- Insufficient security for on-line credit payment transaction (23.7%)
- Cost of setting up of E-Commerce is high (23.6%)

The findings indicated that security issues seemed to be the main barrier to the implementation of E-Commerce. The organizations were reluctant to use E-Commerce as they felt that the transactions conducted electronically were open to hackers and viruses, which are beyond their control. They were also skeptical about the security measures that were implemented to safeguard on-line payment transactions.

These are similar to the findings of the research conducted on the Small Medium Enterprises (SME) in Australia (Lawrence et.al, 1998), the survey conducted by United Kingdom based Industrial Research Bureau (Computimes, Feb. 2000) and Indian E-Commerce survey (Rao, 2000) whereby all the studies illustrated that electronic security is the single major barrier to E-Commerce.

Besides security, the study indicated that financial concerns were also a barrier to E-Commerce implementation. The organizations perceived that the cost of setting up E-Commerce infrastructure is high, therefore they do not intend to use E-Commerce applications in their organizations. Although this was indicated by 24% of the organizations, review of the literature had indicated that application such as E-mail is very cheap to use. Creation of website also does not incur much cost (cost varies according to design) if designed and maintained by vendors. Electronic advertising using banner on a third party website costs as little as RM400. Hence, we can conclude here that the reason given by the organizations was what they perceived and not based on actual know-how.

# 6. CONCLUSION AND IMPLICATIONS

This study is part of a larger study carried out by the authors in collaboration with the Malaysian National Productivity Corporation. The study was aimed at identifying the level of E-Commerce adoption among Malaysian business organisations. Although more than 6000 questionnaires were distributed, less than ten percent responded.

A total of eighteen applications categorized as electronic marketing, electronic advertising, customer support service, order and delivery and payment were studied.

The study has indicated that the level of E-Commerce adoption among Malaysian organisations are still relatively low. 26.8% were not adopting any E-Commerce applications at all while 75% of the organisations were adopting less than five applications.

The study showed that the most widely used application was communication via the e-mail. It was also found that less than five percent of the organisations actually used the smart card and prepaid card applications. Hence, although Malaysian business organisations do use E-Commerce applications, the adoption was still minimal. This also implied that the use of E-Commerce in Malaysia as a mode of payments, is still lagging. In addition, the results also indicated that Malaysian organisations were still not ready to invest heavily in E-Commerce despite both e-mail and creation of websites are among the cheapest applications to implement and use.

Detailed analysis by sectors (manufacturing, construction/agriculture and services) and number of applications adopted showed a significant relationship between the two variables. This implied that rate of E-Commerce adoption to some extend depends on the type of organizations or business involved. However, it was found that there was no significant association between size of organization (small medium versus large) and rate of adoption

There are various reasons as to why organizations do not use E-Commerce extensively. The findings of this research seem to be similar to those of other studies that aim to elucidate factors that hinder organizations in adopting E-Commerce in either developed or developing countries such as India and Indonesia. Therefore, the cornerstone of Malaysia's move into E-Commerce lies in the transformation of its legal and regulatory environment to support companies undertaking E-commerce. This includes the drafting of the Multimedia Convergence Act, which creates an up-to-date communications framework. The Act will be implemented along with the following five high-impact cyber laws: The Digital Signature Cyber Law, The Multimedia Intellectual Property Cyber Law, The computer Crime Cyber law, The Telemedicine Development Cyber law and The Electronic Government Cyber law. Nevertheless the formulation of laws is not sufficient therefore the Government has to play a bigger and more aggressive role in enforcing the laws especially those related to the privacy and security issues if we want to see the increase in E-Commerce adoption among Malaysian organizations

Although Malaysia's E-Commerce activities are increasing, the developed countries such as USA and Europe are seen to be in a more advantageous position as they have the latest technology, knowledge and highly skilled and talented human resource. In addition, they are also in a better position in terms of infrastructure, education and suppliers of products and services. Most importantly they have a bigger market share and better access to market. MSC is suppose to be the Malaysian catalyst for E-Commerce infrastructure and human resource development. However, since E-Commerce in Malaysia is still at the infancy stage,it is still early to make any conclusive statements as to whether the MSC has successfully encouraged the growth of E-Commerce in Malaysia.

## 7. REFERENCES


Ainin S.and Lee S.L, (1998), Smart cards: Towards Management Excellence, *Proceedings of the Association of Asian Management*, Malaysia.

Bloch M, Yves and Segev A., *The Road of Electronic Commerce - a Business Value Framework. Gaining Competitive Advantage and Some Research Issues*," March 1996.

Clarke R. (1993), *The Strategic Intent of On-Line Trading Systems : A Case Study in National Livestock Marketing*, Xamax Consultancy Pty Ltd.

Clarke. R (1993), *EDI Is But One Element of Electronic Commerce*, Xamax Consultancy Ptd Ltd.

Cook, David and Sellers. D (1995), *Launching a business on the Web,* Que Corporation.

Cockburn C and Wilson T (1996), Business use of the WWW, *International Journal of Information Management*, vol 16:2.

Fletcher (1990), *Marketing Management and Information Technology,* Prentice Hall.

Foo, Fran (1998), "Becoming a role model for e-commerce," *The Star: In-Tech,* September 22 1998, pp. 33-34.

Gummesson. E (1997), "*Relationship Marketing (RM) and the Imaginary Organization Proceedings of the European Marketing Academy Conference,"* ESSEC, Paris. In Miers, Derek and Hutton, Graham (1988), "The Strategic Challenges of Electronic Commerce," England.

Haynes. P, Becherer. R, Helms. M (1998), " Small and mid-sized businesses and Internet use: unrealised potential?," *Internet Research: Electronic Networking Application and Policy*, Volume 8, number 3, pp.229-235.

Hoffman. D, Novak. T, Chatterje. P (1996), Commercial Scenarios for the Web: Opportunities and Challenges", Project 2000: Research Program on Marketing in Computer-Mediated Environments, Own Graduate School of management, Vanderbilt University.

Kalakota. R, Whinston. A (1997), *Electronic Commerce : A Manager's Guide*, Addison Wesley.

Kardaras D and Papathanassiou E., (2000), The development of B2C e-commerce in Greece, *Internet Research*, vol 10:4, pp 1066-2243.

Kosiur. D (1997), *Understanding Electronic Commerce*, Microsoft Press.

Kiani, Riza.G (1998), " Marketing Opportunities in the digital world," *Internet research: Electronic Networking Applications and policy,* Volume 8, number 2, pp. 185-194.

Lawrence. E, Corbitt. B, Tidwell. A, Fisher. J, Lawrence. J (1998), *Internet Commerce : Digital Models For Business*, John Wiley & Sons Australia, Ltd.

Rao S., (2000), E-Commerce:The medium is the mart, *New Library World*, vol 101:1154-2000, pp53-59.

Soh. C, Quee.M, Fong. G, Chew. D, Reid. E (1997), " The use of the Internet for business: the experience of early adopters in Singapore," *Internet Research: Electronic Network Application and Policy,* Volume 7, number 3, pp. 217-228.

Straus J. and Frost R. (1999), *Marketing on the Internet*, Prentice Hall, Upper Saddle River, NJ.

Timmers P.(1999), Electronic *Commerce:Strategies and Models for Business to Business Trading*, John Wiley & Sons, Chichester.

Tull D and Hawkins D., (1987), *Markerting Research*, Macmillian Publishing Company, New York,

Turban E., Lee J., King D., Chung H.M (2000), *Electronic Commerce: A Managerial Perspective* (1st. Edition), Prentice-Hall, Inc.,

Zwass V.(1998), "*Structure and Macro-Level Impacts of Electronic Commerce : From Technological Infrastructure to Electronic Market Places*" in Emerging Information Technologies ed. Kenneth E. Kendall, Thousand Oaks, CA: Saga Publications.

25

# Employing the Balanced Scorecard for the Online Media Business

*A Conceptual Framework*

Markus Anding and Thomas Hess
*University of Goettingen, Germany*

**Abstract:** The new performance measurement system Balanced Scorecard tries to overcome drawbacks of traditional financial measurement systems by focusing on a company's individual strategies. These strategies derive from critical success factors. In the media sector, general critical success factors can be analysed, building a basis for deriving specific company strategies and measures. By analysing market forces and company resources, the factors Critical Mass, Customer Relations, Cooperations, Innovation, Leading Technologies, Competent Employees and Optimised Processes are found and – based on these factors – reasonable measures are elaborated. In combination with financial measures these build a generic model for individual Balanced Scorecards in the online media sector, helping companies to streamline the process of a Balanced Scorecard implementation.

## 1. INTRODUCTION

The media sector is one of the industries evolving most quickly at present and especially online companies develop wide varieties of business models and e-commerce strategies. Yet many companies neglect the elaborate implementation of these strategies as they focus on operational activities and omit the measurement of factors which are most critical for their success – possibly because they don't even know them. The paper on hand presents general critical success factors of online media companies as a basis for the implementation of a Balanced Scorecard – a management system which helps to implement strategies and measure business performance by analysing a company from different perspectives and not only focussing on financials. This paper develops a generic model for the design of individual Balanced Scorecards for online media companies. So far, a company has to extensively analyse its strategies and success factors prior to the implementation of a Balanced Scorecard. Using a generic model as a guideline, this process can be streamlined.

The underlying methodology is based on the theoretical analysis of market forces and internal resources of online companies. These are combined to a set of critical success factors, relevant to this specific type of companies. Further on, typical measures for these success factors build a framework which a company can adapt. The background of this analysis was a cooperation project with three online media companies which have developed individual Balanced Scorecards based on this model.

# 2. BASIC CONSIDERATIONS

## 2.1 The Balanced Scorecard

Apparent drawbacks of traditional performance measurement systems built the starting point for a research project, carried out in the early nineties by Robert S. Kaplan and David P. Norton with twelve US-companies (Kaplan/Norton, 1997). It was targeted on overcoming the disadvantages of measurement systems based solely on financial figures and ex post information, e.g. the DuPont-System (Horvath, 1991). Due to their concentration on financial "hard facts" these systems neglect factors with ample influence on business performance – so called "soft facts" – like customer satisfaction or employee fluctuation. Though they can hardly be expressed mathematically exact, soft facts carry a big stake in analysing the condition of a company. So it was found by Ernst & Young, that an investor's decisions are based to 35% on non-financial figures (Low/Siesfield, 2000).

The basic outcome of the research project was the Balanced Scorecard – a system which completes existing financial measurement schemes with non-financial indicators of a company's past and future performance. Altogether the system combines monetary and non-monetary, internal and external as well as short- and long term indicators what makes it "balanced".

The Balanced Scorecard approach pursues two main purposes. First, the implementation of strategies – from the management level through the hierarchy as far as the conversion into operational action – is supported by a continuous process of formulating, communicating, implementing and adapting strategies. Second, the acquisition and presentation of information, thus the effectiveness and quality of decision making, is enhanced by the design of the Balanced Scorecard – as a balanced key figure system. So the Balanced Scorecard consists of a Management- as well as a Measurement System(Weber/Schäffer, 1998) and can be seen in the aspects of strategy implementation and performance measurement.

The authors of the Balanced Scorecard have split the measurement system into several perspectives representing the main stakeholders of a company, especially shareholders (financial perspective), customers (customer perspective) and employees (learning and growth perspective) (Kaplan/Norton, 1997). A perspective of internal processes was added to represent most important business processes. Figure 1 depicts this generic system.

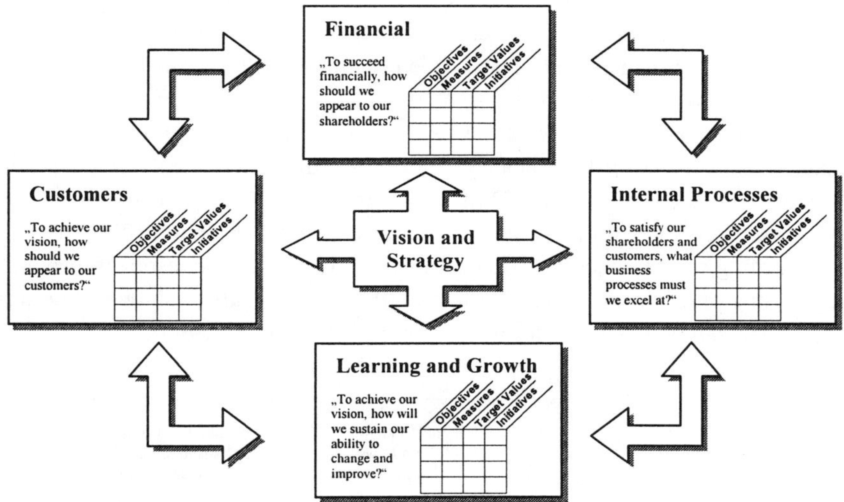


*Figure 1.* The generic Balanced Scorecard System (Kaplan/Norton, 1997).

Each perspective comprises a number of critical success factors expressed by business objectives for which measures are defined. Target values are assigned to each measure and initiatives are specified which are planned to be taken in order to reach the objectives. Additionally an objective can be associated with a specific person who bears the corresponding responsibility. In companies with considerable hierarchies, the measurement system can be distributed top-down through these hierarchies, reproducing the system on each level in the company and fractionising targets relevant to each success factor. This ensures the implementation of the company's strategies on each hierarchical level.

It is to be highlighted, that the Balanced Scorecard perspectives are not independent from one another – they show cause-and-effect relationships (Kaplan/Norton, 1997), which means that a changing measure in one perspective affects or can affect other measures in other perspectives. For instance the financial yield of a company can be affected by a change in customer satisfaction.

## 2.2 Business models of the online media sector

In order to derive particularities of the Balanced Scorecard in online companies, general characteristics of the media sector will be discussed in the following and an overview of relevant business models will be given.

Media products can be classified according to the technology primarily used for distributing content. Killius/Mueller-Oerlinghausen (1999) define print-, broadcasting- and online media whereas Hacker (1999) classifies the fields of print-, electronic-, broadcasting- and pre-recorded media in more detail. Further on these fields can be broken down into sub-sectors – e.g. newspapers, journals and books in the field of print media – whereas the field of electronic media splits into offline and online. In the following this paper will focus on the latter one – on online media which distinguishes itself from offline media by having a permanent connection to a service provider, such as online streaming music in comparison to offline CD music.

According to the generic value chain, which consists of investment, production, sales, billing and consumption (Zerdick et al., 2000), figure 2 shows value adding levels which can be identified for media companies (Hacker, 1999):

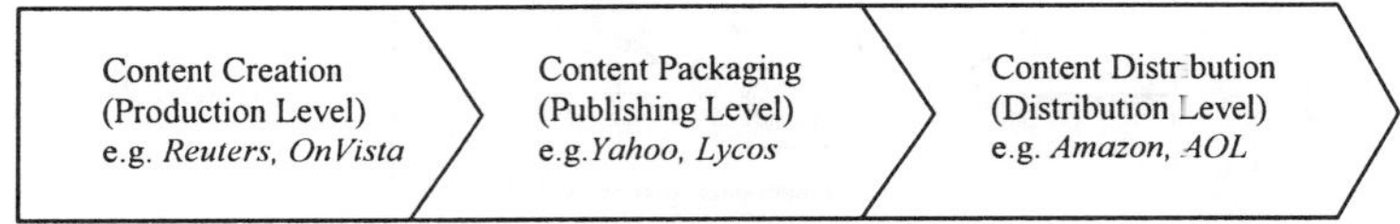


*Figure 2.* Media value chain

Besides continuous changes in these value chain elements of typical media production, even traditional value chain elements of the trading sector are affected by developments in the media branch. Especially in the field of distribution a desintermediation and virtualisation of wholesale- and retail levels takes place, transferring these levels partly or completely into the online-sector.

The performance measurement of a company depends largely on its business objectives which in the media branch can be of economic as well as of arty and publicity nature. In the following – for building the basis for a Balanced Scorecard framework – only companies with focus on economic objectives will be taken into consideration[36].

A business model describes the characteristics of a company and comprises the questions *"What is being sold to whom?"*, *"Which input is being acquired from whom"* and *"How is the production process to be designed?"*. The main focus for

[36] Which does not mean that the Balanced Scorecard is not suitable for arty-focused companies, but sticking to the generic model, a Balanced Scorecard has an economic focus.

online business models lies in the underlying revenue model, which is – in comparison to traditional media business models – often the real innovation.

Media business models in general can be categorised according to the level of the value chain they are operating in. Thus there exist companies which create, package or distribute content. Schumann/Hess (2000) classify online business models into *Content Provider*, *Broker* and *Service Provider.*

Content Providers produce genuine content or product supplements, brokers are portals or aggregators who categorise and structure offers of content- and service providers. The latter model in the form of virtual communities is described by Hagel/Armstrong (1997)as the central element of the online business landscape of the future. Finally, service providers deliver the infrastructure, the physical and logical components which enable online business.

The revenue model of online companies often covers a combination of different revenue sources. These are defined by Zerdick et al. (2000) as *advertising, subsidisation via state, subscription/fees* as well as *transaction charges.*

## 3. IMPLICATIONS FOR A BALANCED SCORECARD IN ONLINE COMPANIES

The methodology of deriving a Balanced Scorecard for the online business can comprise two basic steps – according to the generic procedure described by Kaplan/Norton (1997). First, specific critical success factors of the online business shall be derived by analysing general market forces as well as primary company resources in the online sector and the illustrated business models. Based on these factors, typical perspectives, indicators and key figures will be compiled as shown in Figure 3.

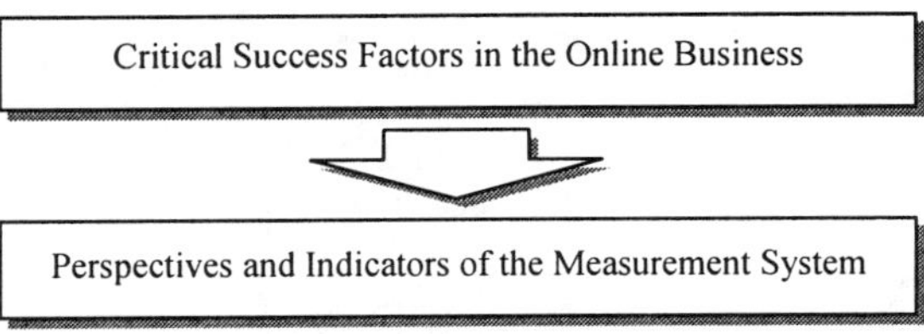


*Figure 3.* Basic steps for deriving Balanced Scorecards

This procedure reflects the main steps in the general implementation process of a Balanced Scorecard.

## 3.1 Critical success factors of the online business as a starting point

A company's critical success factors can be derived by analysing the company from market-based (external) and resource-based (internal) aspects (For the resource based view see (Wernerfelt, 1984), for the aspects mentioned see (Schumann/Hess, 2000), also (Böhning-Spohr/Hess, 2000)). On one hand, the environment of a company – i.e. the market – comprises a number of factors which the company has to align its strategies with – in a specific way according to the company's branch. On the other hand, a company owns internal resources it can use to gain competitive advantage. These two aspects will now be discussed referring to online companies.

### 3.1.1 The market based view

The market-based aspect consolidates in Porter's five market-forces, which are *Industry competitors*, *New market entrants*, *Buyers*, *Suppliers* and *Substitute products*, shown in Figure 4 – with examples for the online business and arrows depicting the specific strength of these forces.

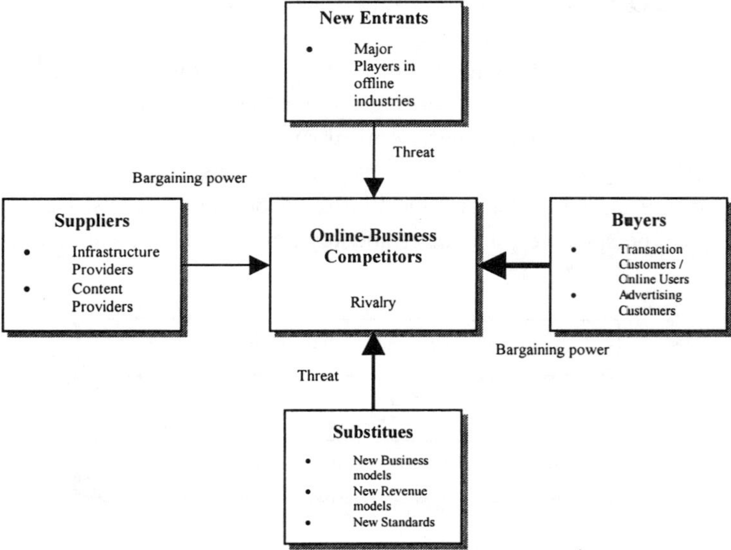


*Figure 4.* Porter's Five Forces in the online business (Porter, 1980)

**Rivalry in the online business.** Rivalry of incumbents in the online business is slightly different in the business models of Content Providers, Brokers and Service Providers. Where the first mainly face competition in the advertising market, the latter one primarily concentrates on consumers looking for internet access and online transactions. In the advertising market, size and quality of a company's user basis is crucial for success. Therefore it is important to bind a big part of the online-time of most of the users, i.e. to win a "Share of mind" and collect information about them, which is valuable for advertising customers. For that reason, establishing a strong brand is of central significance (Manning, 2000), often ending in heavy brand competition among a few big players (Hagel/Amstrong, 1997). Thus, quality, success and costs of marketing are of major importance for Content Providers and Brokers.

In contrast, the transaction- and access-market, characterised by homogeneous services[37], is focused on satisfying and locking in customers by means of outstanding service as well as optimisation of processes and – as a consequence thereof – the reduction of costs, since rivalry in the homogeneous access-market embodies in price battles. Additionally, sheer size in respect of economies of scale matters in this market too.

**New entrants.** Due to high marketing expenses and long cash-to-cash cycles[38], new entrants need huge cash backing to become real competitors for established players. Therefore the rivalry strategies mentioned above serve as entry barriers too. On the other hand, technological barriers are rather small, because hardware is getting cheaper and online-businesses can be put up within shortest time. Incumbents can face this danger with own innovations and investment, trying to stay ahead in technological advance. Beyond that, the business models of online companies and its components can be copied very easily. Entry barriers in this field can be built by patents (Laidlaw, 2000).

**Substitutes**. Since new products are developed at high speed in the online business, the threat of substitutes is relatively high (Laidlaw, 2000). Content Providers and Brokers mainly face intangible "products" like new business- or revenue models, whereas Service Providers confront material products like network components or software programs. New developments and new standards – emerging quickly due to the high transparency in the online market – cannot be inhibited. So established companies have to recognise and follow new trends in order to use them for themselves[39]. Here, a company's ability to innovate and its financial strength are crucial – especially because the speed of developing and offering new products is essential.

**Suppliers.** Infrastructure- and content providers are the major groups of suppliers in the online business. Their bargaining power is highly correlated to the individuality of their products. Therefore, standardisation is a way to limit the power

37 So are the services of call by call internet providers and online retailers not highly differentiated among competitors.

38 The cash-to-cash cycle measures the time from the initial cash outflow to the time when cash is received from customers. As for the term, see Kaplan/Norton (1997), pp. 56.

39 An example is given by the music industry, when music labels were mistaken trying to prevent the usage of MP3 files for the distribution of music.

of suppliers, although too much standardisation can have the adverse effect of reducing own individuality in respect of the customers.

**Buyers.** The online market shows high transparency and low switching costs for customers. In addition to standard offerings they require surplus value and services tailored to their specific needs instead of mass products. The need to offer additional value forces companies to cooperate with others, especially if this additional value cannot be created using the company's core competencies. So called "Lock In" strategies try to prevent customers from switching. A customer is locked in when the effort of switching is higher than the possible profit. Thus, companies raise this effort by customising services ("mass customisation") and differentiating their offers, so that customers – once used to the specific offerings of a company and having defined their user profile – are less likely to switch to rivals.

Summarising the factors discussed so far, four general market based critical success factors, significant for all the three online business models, can be outlined: the achievement of a *critical mass*, entering into *cooperations*, developing *innovations* and strengthening *customer relations*.

### 3.1.2 The resource based view

According to PORTER, the origins of competitive advantage are the competencies that firms possess (Porter, 1991), which are embodied in a firms resources. Prahald/Hamel (1990) state that core competencies provide potential access to a wide variety of markets, they make a significant contribution to the perceived customer benefits of the products and they are difficult for competitors to imitate.

Two crucial resources for online companies – which can hardly be substituted or imitated – are employees and information systems (Schuhmann/Haess, 2000).

Creative employees provide the intellectual capital of a company (Brinker, 2000), thus lay the basis for its success. They create content for content providers, package content for brokers and take care of information systems for service providers. Employees are to be acquired and retained[40] – two requirements for human resource management which have to be taken into consideration when designing the employee perspective of a Balanced Scorecard.

Information systems for two reasons (Hasan/Tibbits, 2000) have a special relation to the Balanced Scorecard. First, information systems are widely used for implementing this performance measurement system. Second, technology mostly is so important for online companies, that it has to have special emphasis in the Balanced Scorecard system.[41]. If online companies neglect IT strategies, they won't

[40] This is particularly important on the IT labour market, where specialists are rare. See Boyd (2000).

[41] For that reason even dedicated IT Scorecards have been developed. See Van Grembergen/Van Bruggen (2000).

have a chance in competing with rivals in the long term. Reasonable alternatives are: leading the market with own innovations and products, or following the market by adopting a leading rival's technology (see Götze/Mikus, 1999).

Besides that, internal business processes can be seen as critical success factors too, although they strongly depend on the ability of work force and information systems. Business processes are assessed by analysing their quality (i.e. error rate) an speed (in online business models expressed by the period between starting and finishing a transaction) as well as the costs they bring about.

The resource based success factors of online companies can be subsumed to *competent employees*, *leading technologies* and *optimised processes*.

Figure 5 shows a synopsis of the seven general success factors defined.

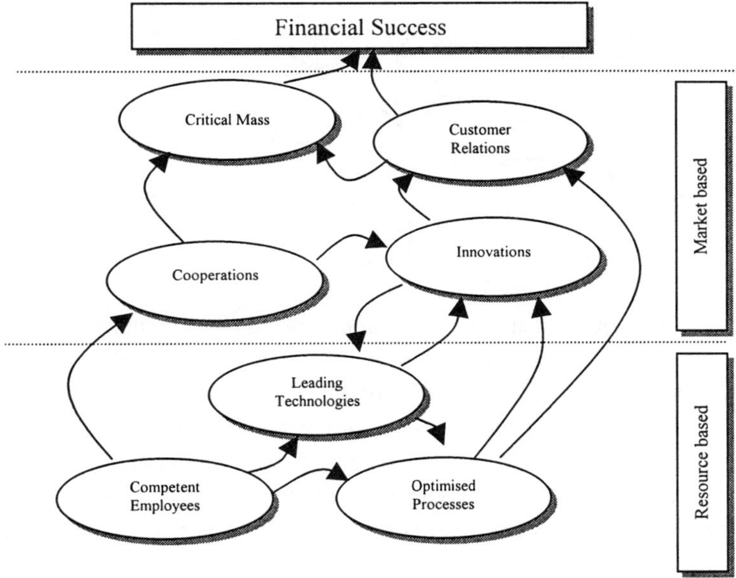


*Figure 5.* Critical success factors of online business models and their relations

As Figure 6 illustrates, critical success factors are not independent from one another, but show cause-and-effect relationships which are hardly to be quantified and which in this paper will not be analysed in detail. Generally they are an important subject of discussion when a Balanced Scorecard is developed. On top of this cause-and-effect chain the financial success depicts the topmost performance indicator.

## 3.2 Deduction of indicators and perspectives of the Balanced Scorecard

After having defined general critical success factors, a selection of indicators for these factors will be compiled and reasonable assignments of these indicators to perspectives will be discussed as shown in Figure 6.

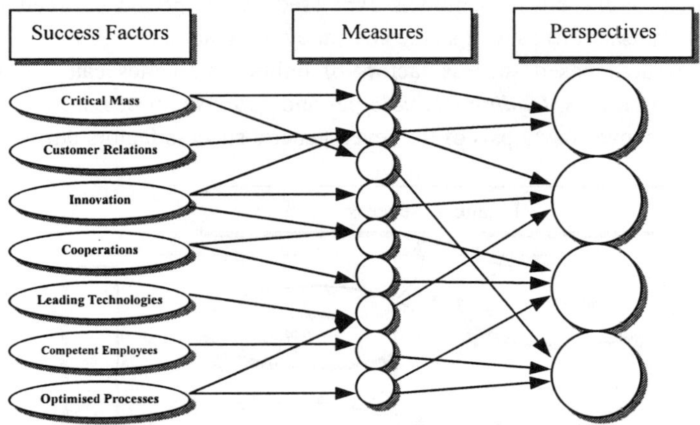


*Figure 6.* Assignment of measures to success factors and aggregation to perspectives

**Critical Mass.** The critical mass is the number of users/ consumers or the turnover/ market share of an online company which is necessary for the company to survive and grow out of own means. Intuitive growth indicators are the *number of customers/ consumers*, the *turnover* and *market share* as well as the growth rates of these. Marketing – necessary for reaching the critical mass – can be analysed by a broad range of measures in the fields of customer acquisition and -retention; like *conversion rate*, *turnover with new customers* or *number of return buyers*; as well as measures for website activity.

**Customer Relations.** Individualisation, already common for customers of B2B-business models, is coming up in B2C too. The intensity of customer relations is growing in both models and the need of measuring them differently is vanishing. *Customer satisfaction* is a core measure. It is created by services tailored to customer needs, presuming an extensive *knowledge* about their characteristics. Other measures for customer satisfaction are the *rate of returning customers*, *customer turnover* and *number of complaints*. A *customer satisfaction index* can be built of these factors. Customer *lock in* and *profitability* indicate a customer's value for the company and, especially in B2B-models, the *number of individual services delivered* and the *number of customer contacts* in a period indicate the commitment between customer and company. Individualisation in B2C-models can be measured by the number of *individual data fields* in the customer database.

**Cooperations.**Cooperations can significantly support reaching the critical mass. The success of cooperations can be measured by the *additional value or turnover* or by *synergies* they generate. The *speed* of entering into new markets and developing new products as well as the market share can rise through cooperations and can be a measure for their success. To reduce complexity, a company could build a *cooperation index*, weighing the effects mentioned according to their importance for the company.

**Innovation.** Innovation splits into two processes of identifying customer needs and creating new products. It can be measured concentrating on the process itself as well as on the quality of its result. Measures for the innovation process can be *time to market (Friedag/Schmidt, 2000)* of new products, *break even time (Kaplan/Norton, 1997)*, the *period between two product generations* or the *rate of new innovations which eventually become new products*. The *R&D budget* additionally is an ex ante value driver for the innovation process. The innovation result can be analysed by the *time advantage over rivals*, the number of *customer needs identified* or the *share of turnover of new products*.

**Leading Technologies.** Technologies and information systems can be described by the parameters *availability* and *performance*, further on by *costs*, *complexity* and *level of standardisation*. Availability is measured by *uptime*, i.e. the share of time in which a system can be accessed. The extent to which a company is technology leader can be measured by its *ability to innovate* and a *comparison to competitors*. Value drivers for these are the *R&D-budget* and the *competence of the work force*. Technology measures are especially important for service providers whereas content providers and brokers focus rather on human capital.

**Competent Employees.** The performance of employees is defined by their *satisfaction*, their *loyalty* and *productivity* (Kaplan/Norton, 1997). A way of determining satisfaction and loyalty is to build an *index* of elements of a questionnaire as well as analysing employee *fluctuation*. *Employee turnover*, their *level of proficiency* and *error rates* are productivity measures. These ex-post indicators can be replenished by Performance drivers like *scheduled days for further education* or the *extent of variable payment*. Having a particularly high importance for online companies, the employee factor in the Balanced Scorecard tends to be described by a wider variety of measures in comparison to other branches such as the producing industry.

**Optimised Processes.** Due to a tendency of shortening temporal distances, basically production processes[42] are subject of optimisation strategies, targeting the *speed of transactions*, the *speed of solving problems*, the *performance of systems* and *process costs*. Particularly content providers focus on *quality* and *actuality of*

[42] Production processes exist besides innovation- and customer service processes. In the online business they principally cover the operation of systems and business transactions.

*content created*, whereas service providers and partly brokers concentrate on *efficiency* and *costs* of logistics and project management.

After having defined a set of key measures for online companies, suitable perspectives for an online-Balanced Scorecard are to be chosen.

In comparison to other branches, a Balanced Scorecard in the online sector has to be focused especially on information technology – which here has not only a supporting function – and in more a holistic way on a company's market than on customers themselves. Therefore perspectives for IT-potential and Market/Customers are essential. Internal processes are primarily relevant for service providers whereas employees play more a significant role for content providers and brokers. Depending on a company's estimation of their importance, employee- and IT-potentials as well as processes can be combined to single perspectives. This may be a "future readiness perspective" as defined by Hasan/Tibbits (2000), which concentrates on upcoming opportunities and challenges. Eventually a financial perspective is to be mentioned, which is compulsory for companies of any kind which have financial profit objectives. Here the measure *customer lifetime value* plays a key role in the field of B2C e-business as it depicts the present value of a single customer, including present- and future revenues, variable costs and marketing expenses.

Table 1 summarises the discussed measures and recommends an allocation to perspectives, which up to now have been used in three business cases, as mentioned chapter 1.

***Table 1: Critical success factors, key measures and perspectives.***

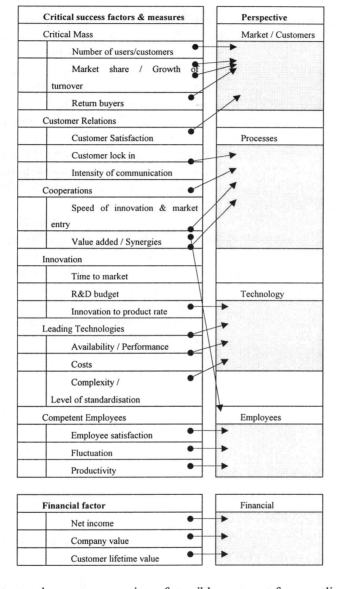

| Critical success factors & measures | | Perspective |
|---|---|---|
| Critical Mass | | Market / Customers |
| | Number of users/customers | |
| | Market share / Growth of turnover | |
| | Return buyers | |
| Customer Relations | | |
| | Customer Satisfaction | Processes |
| | Customer lock in | |
| | Intensity of communication | |
| Cooperations | | |
| | Speed of innovation & market entry | |
| | Value added / Synergies | |
| Innovation | | |
| | Time to market | |
| | R&D budget | Technology |
| | Innovation to product rate | |
| Leading Technologies | | |
| | Availability / Performance | |
| | Costs | |
| | Complexity / Level of standardisation | |
| Competent Employees | | Employees |
| | Employee satisfaction | |
| | Fluctuation | |
| | Productivity | |

| Financial factor | | Financial |
|---|---|---|
| | Net income | |
| | Company value | |
| | Customer lifetime value | |

This paper only gave an overview of possible measures for an online Balanced Scorecard. Therefore a more elaborate set of measures can be found at a dedicated website on the internet (see www.wi2.wiso.uni-goettingen.de/forschung/dm/bsc/bsc.htm).

# 4. CONCLUSION AND OUTLOOK

The paper on hand has tried to sketch the characteristics of a Balanced Scorecard in the online media sector. The result – a generic model of success factors, perspectives and reasonable measures – can be used as a framework for online companies which want to build their own Balanced Scorecard. So far, a company that wants to implement a Balanced Scorecard has to start analysing it's critical success factors, discuss strategies and develop measures. The model on hand can streamline this process by indicating a direction. It is a first step towards a partly standardised concept for developing Balanced Scorecards in the media sector and solves the problem of finding a direction for a Balanced Scorecard implementation. Although different kinds of media companies (Content providers, brokers, service providers) are surely not to be managed and measured identically, the discussed model can be a starting point for either of them.

From another perspective, the standardised development of a Balanced Scorecard can be seen critical, since a constituting element of the system is the analysis and communication of the company's strategy within an elaborate implementation process – skipping that by using a framework could end up in a less company specific Balanced Scorecard. Thus the presented generic model is not aimed at omitting important implementation steps, it should be a guideline.

The mentioned cause-and-effect relationships and the inherent Balanced Scorecard management cycle were only discussed marginally in this paper and can be subjects of further analysis. The dynamics of the media sector and the lack of time for analytical activities – especially in growth companies – can cause difficulties for these intentions.

Due to missing long term studies on the Balanced Scorecard in media companies an empirical validation and verification of the findings in this paper is not available yet.

# 5. REFERENCES

*Ansoff, I.* (1965): Corporate Strategy, New York.

*Böhning-Spohr, P./Hess, T.* (2000): Geschäftsmodelle inhalteorientierter Online-Angebote, Arbeitspapiere der Abt. Wirtschaftsinformatik II, University of Goettingen, Nr.1/2000, Goettingen, 2000.

*Brinker, B.* (1999): Intellectual Capital: Tomorrow's Assets, Today's Challange, CPA Working Paper, http://www.cpavision.org/vision, Download on 2000-08-25.

*Götze, U./Mikus, B.* (1999): Strategisches Management, Chemnitz, 1999.

*Hacker, T.* (1999): Vernetzung und Modularisierung – (Re)Organisation von Medienunternehmen, in: Schumann, M./Hess, T. (1999, Editors): Medienunternehmen im digitalen Zeitalter, Wiesbaden.

*Hagel III, J./Armstrong, Arthur G.* (1997): net gain – expanding marktes through virtual communities, Harvard Business School Press, Boston/Massachusetts, 1997.

*Hasan, H./Tibbits, H.R.* (2000): Strategic Management of Electronic Commerce: an adaption of the Balanced Scorecard, http://www.uow.edu.au/~ hasan/aica/hasan-tibbits.htm, Download on 2000-08-11.

*Horváth, P.* (1991): Controlling, 4. Ed., Vahlen.

*Kaplan, R.S./Norton, D.P.* (1997): Balanced Scorecard, German translation by Péter Horváth, Stuttgart, 1997.

*Killius, N./Mueller-Oerlinghausen, J.* (1999): Innovative Geschäftsmodelle in digitalen Medien, in: Schumann, M., Hess, T. (1999, Hrsg.): Medienunternehmen im digitalen Zeitalter, Wiesbaden, p. 139-153.

*Laidlaw F.J.* (2000): Acceleration of Technology Development – The Experience of 28 Projects Funded in 1991, http://www.atp.nist.gov/eao/ir-6047.htm, Download on 2000-11-07.

*Manning, R.* (2000): Internet Branding and the User Experience, http://www.clickz.com/cgi-bin/gt/print.html?article=1516, 2000-03-31, Download on 2000-10-29.

*Porter, M.E.* (1980), Competitive strategy: Techniques for analysing industries and competitors. New York: The Free Press

*Porter, M.E.* (1991): Towards a Dynamic Theory of Strategy, in: Strategic Management Journal, Nr. 12, p. 95-117.

*Prahalad, C.K, Hamel, G.* (1990): The core competence of the corporation, in: Harvard Business Review, Nr. 68, p. 79-91.

*Schumann, M./Hess, T.* (2000): Grundfragen der Medienwirtschaft, Berlin/Heidelberg.

*Van Grembergen, W./Van Bruggen, R.* (2000): Measuring and improving corporate information technology through the balanced scorecard, http://is.twi.tudelft.nl.ejise/vol1/issue1/paper3/paper.html, Download on 2000-08-20.

*Weber, J./Schäffer, U.* (1998): Balanced Scorecard, Advanced Controlling Reihe: Neue Aufgabenfelder und Instrumente, Band 8, Vallendar, 1998.

*Wernerfelt, B.* (1984): The resource-based view of the firm, in: Strategic Management Journal, Nr. 5, p. 171-180.

*Zerdick, A./Picot, A./Schrape, K./Artopé A./Goldhammer, K./Lange, U.T./Vierkannt, E./López-Escobar, E./Silverstone, R.* (2000): E-Conomics – Strategies for the Digital Marketplace, Berlin/Heidelberg.

26

# A Model for Value-added Internet Service Provisioning

Helmut Kneer, Urs Zurfluh, Burkhard Stiller[2]
*Department of Information Technology IFI, University of Zurich, Switzerland*
*[2]Computer Engineering and Networks Laboratory TIK, ETH Zürich, Switzerland*

**Abstract:** Today's Internet represents a multi-provider environment as a basis for global service delivery with a set of services, business roles, and strategies. The integration of data and telecommunication, especially for multimedia services, requires Quality-of-Service (QoS) for the transport of data. Furthermore, it demands a value-added Internet with communication and network services as well as charging functions between entities and services. This paper defines business roles and their responsibilities as well as business strategies, communication policies, and interacting roles and services. A fully defined business process as part of a business model and independent from technology is used to illustrate value-added Internet service provisioning.

## 1. INTRODUCTION

Due to the fast growing Internet and the global extent of Internet access even for regular home users, existing business models have changed and new ones arisen. New E-Commerce applications and services offer a wide spectrum of possibilities to do business electronically. Due to available bandwidth and powerful hardware, recently the idea arose to use the Internet infrastructure for an integration of data and telecommunication to entertain customers with multimedia data and services like video streams or teleconferencing.

A crucial point for the transfer of high-quality data is the fact that traffic congestion occurs in the Internet, which makes reliable transmission of delay-sensitive data difficult or even impossible. High-quality Internet applications or services are very susceptible to delayed delivery of data packets, since their quality strongly depends on reliable network parameters like data throughput, bandwidth, and latency. Unfortunately, packet forwarding in today's Internet works on a best-effort base, which results in poor quality for multiplexed audio or video streams, especially when network congestion occurs. One solution to overcome this problem is the introduction of a multi-service-level Internet, which offers different service levels and the desired Quality-of-Service (QoS) for certain high-quality data transfer. This necessitates the reservation of network resources based on pricing models 0. Within the CATI project (Charging and Accounting Technologies for the Internet) enabling technologies were designed to implement charging and accounting of Internet services based on the reservation of network resources 0.

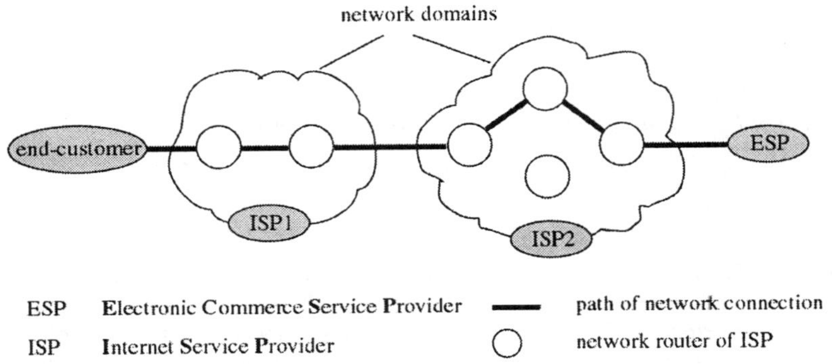


*Figure 1.* Multi-provider business scenario

Economic incentives for providing high-quality end-to-end communication imply the development and usage of E-Commerce services that contribute an added value to the service provisioning over IP infrastructure. Interacting and cooperating business roles are required to perform service delivery based on pre-defined policies.

Figure 1 shows a business scenario with an end-customer electronically connected to an E-Commerce Service Provider (ESP) that represents a merchant offering information (in form of both physical and non-tangible goods) and services over the Internet. The clouds in between symbolize the network domain with the underlying network infrastructure of the network providers. These network providers carry different roles and provide several value-added services while transferring data from sender to receiver. Thus, they are called Internet Service Provider (ISP). There may be one or several ISPs involved in the scenario, depending on the network fragmentation of the ISPs and the geographical distances between end-customer and ESP.

If the end-customer (or one of her communication agents that is responsible for communication-related tasks) decides to make use of one of the ESP's offered goods or services, different steps need to be performed before. Service parameters and policies need to be negotiated among business entities before the connection to the ESP can be established and maintained. Possible applications of such a scenario include IP telephony, teleconferencing, data backups, the transmission of financial feeds, and the transfer of video or audio on demand (VoD, AoD).

This paper is organized as follows. Based on the multi-provider scenario, Section 2 defines business roles and relationships. It defines a set of differentiated services and discusses controlling business policies and their use to the Internet services market. Section 3 describes the overall charging process between different roles for the delivered services. Section 4 contains a fully defined business process showing the temporal coherence between business roles and services. Finally, Section 5 summarizes the paper, draws conclusions, and outlooks on future work.

# 2. ROLES, SERVICES, AND POLICIES

The growing deployment of E-Commerce applications and the convergence of data and telecommunication make the introduction of proper business models and well-defined business processes indispensable. Applying business models in the technical area of telecommunication require a set of mechanisms being available for performing charging and billing functionality, especially for QoS-based end-to-end communication. This section includes a description of business roles and defines the corresponding services they provide but also their underlying strategies and policies.

## 2.1 Roles

A role in a role model is characterized by a certain functionality and scope of duties. Roles in business and technical environments have the advantage to logically separate the business model and define what tasks and resources are used by them and what responsibilities the different roles take. L.G. Lawrence 0 defines a role as "... mainly a definition of a job at the lowest level of granularity used in the organization. According to the business concerned it may be in a position description, establishment position statement or other term which addresses what must be done by the occupant of that job regardless of who that person is". A role can inherit purely technical as well as administrative functions. Furthermore, the concept of roles is advantageous for the security, quality, and resource management. Securing data and managing resources can be based on role-access relationships where certain business entities are assigned to roles with restricted functionality.

We want to focus on the roles of ESP, ISP, end-customer, and Customer Premises Network (CPN) knowing that there are more than just these few and that these roles are not limited to the interface but to the quality of the service they provide 0. An instance of a role will interact and communicate with another instance of a role in order to provide a service. Additionally, one business entity can fulfil the tasks of several roles and thus adopt these roles. One example is Akamai 0 that takes the role of both ISP and ESP by providing access networks and content.

The role of an **E-Commerce Service Provider (ESP)** symbolizes a merchant within the business relationship with an end-customer. The ESP offers products, contents, and services online via the World Wide Web (WWW) to every Internet user in the world and represents the seller of goods. Within the following, "goods" are considered a general term for any kind of product, content, of service that is offered or sold electronically on the Internet.

The role of an **end-customer** symbolizes a customer at the end point of a communication connection with the ESP. The end-customer can get online information about the offered goods within the ESP's catalogue and may choose electronically by clicking on certain items. The end-customer can even compare prices of different sellers and thus find the optimal product or service concerning quality and price. It is also possible that end-customers are affiliated to a **Customer Premises Network (CPN)**, e.g., a LAN of an enterprise or a university that groups end-customers and establishes the connection to the Access ISP. A CPN represents a group of users in terms of a common policy and conceals individual end-customers from the Access ISP.

The role of an Internet Service Provider (ISP) is divided into the roles of Access ISP and Core ISP according to their scope of network provider duties and the range of hardware and software equipment. Access ISPs support local access to internal or external networks and provide Internet connection between end-customers, be it directly or through a CPN. Many Core ISPs increase the reach of Access ISPs to a global extent and form the backbone of the Internet. They handle the data transport interconnecting multiple Access ISPs. There might be none or more than one instance of a Core ISP involved in a communication connection between end-customer and ESP. It depends on the connectivity of the ISPs and the geographical distance of end-customer and ESP. In case there is only one instance of an ISP involved between end-customer and ESP, it takes the role of both Access ISP and Core ISP. Thus, the role of Access ISP and Core ISP may be physically inherent in one business entity.

## 2.2 Service Model

Figure 2a shows a service model with the previously defined roles of the end-customer, ESP, and ISP in form of ovals. The model abstracts from the technical solution where the end-customer is connected to an ESP via the IP infrastructure of an Access ISP. Instead, the service model is based on the business relationship between end-customer and ESP including different services that are provided on top of the IP infrastructure of the ISP. The end-customer uses the E-Commerce Service, offered by the ESP, as an interface for further value-added service provisioning. This E-commerce service comprises the offer of products, content, and services that are offered online by the ESP (e.g., furniture, CDs, online books or magazines, audio-on-demand, video-on-demand, Internet games).

Figure 2a also implies the possibility for the end-customer to directly use the IP infrastructure offered by the ISP in order to communicate over the TCP/IP-based infrastructure. This might be useful to up or download data onto or from a file server with no extra services and without any time restrictions for the communication. Ordering an E-Commerce service from the ESP gives the end-customer a wide range of accompanying value-added services that can be recombined and added to increase the value of the E-Commerce service.

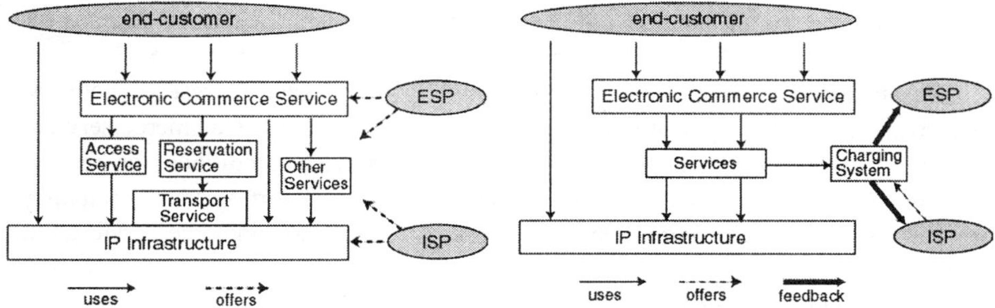


*Figure 2a.* Service model including roles and services

*Figure 2b.* Service model extended by the feedback mechanism of the charging system

The module **Other Services** combines services such as security service, synchronization service, charging service, etc. **Access Service** is offered to end-customers to connect to the Internet via ISP platform. Service functionality comprises among others access control, charging and billing, logging in and out. An Access ISP holds the position of the closest ISP to end-customer and ESP, which is a special role since access conditions are individually and contractually fixed. Access conditions determine the kind of connection such as its bandwidth, availability, or security measures, but also pricing models for the Internet access. Since these conditions are fixed on a contractual base in form of Service Level Agreements (SLA) 0, they have to be kept otherwise reimbursements have to be settled to compensate the failure. Internet access implies global connectivity with a local connection to the Access ISP, and thus, the price of a local phone call.

**Transport Service** provided by the role of the ISPs is of fundamental importance for the quality of the delivered communication services. Data needs to be carried reliably from one end point to another. Packet forwarding on today's Internet works on a best-effort basis, which means that single packets are transmitted independently from each other from sender to receiver as fast as possible. However, transmitting video or audio frames with good quality requires a type of network connection with a certain guaranteed bandwidth or maximum delay. A video or audio stream is delay-sensitive which requires timeliness of packet delivery and only allows small variations in the transfer rate due to buffering mechanisms. The service quality of the stream depends on the delay between every transmitted frame where the frame size varies depending on the amount of changes in the picture. Thus, the transfer rate varies from frame to frame. A video conference on the other hand is rate-sensitive and needs to constantly transmit frames of the same size. Providing a high-quality video conference stream requires a guaranteed bandwidth with a certain constant data transport rate 0. One solution for ISPs to provide reliable transport services according to the required QoS of the E-Commerce service is to firstly classify traffic into different service classes and, secondly, to treat data packets differently depending on the service class and the according price 0. Consequently, the quality of an E-Commerce service depends on many factors, but mainly on the quality of the underlying transport service.

**Reservation Service** can be provided by ISPs in order to reserve network resources for data transport but also by the ESP to reserve an E-Commerce service. The reservation service negotiates and stipulates service conditions for the E-Commerce service and network parameters for the transport service (including Internet access). Depending on the requirements for the E-Commerce service, the end-customer chooses the desired QoS for the transport service by selecting the appropriate QoS parameters (e.g., bandwidth, latency, loss rates), which in turn affect the price. Three different kinds of service reservation can be distinguished:

1. An immediate short-term reservation where the end-customer reserves a service immediately for one period no longer than the default (e.g. 30 seconds).
2. An immediate long-term reservation where the end-customer reserves a service immediately for a period longer than the default (e.g. several minutes).
3. A reservation in advance where the end-customer reserves a service that will be delivered in the future.

## 2.1 Strategies and Policies

As described implicitly by the previous two sections, strategies and policies inherently form a major constituent for roles to enable a structured interaction. Note that strategy at this point defines the set of business rules for establishing, controlling, and operating service provisioning. This terminology applied here is addressed to the higher layer, termed business layer. The technical management of communication networks, in particular with respect to policies, determines all details in a given communications layer to allow for the automated decision on, e.g., access rights, security levels, performance issues, or service quality. Therefore, a policy based on economic incentives within the communications layers is a means for business management strategies and business cases.

Interaction between different ISPs is based on a federal approach, where entities are widely self-dependent and responsible for their service delivery, but where the Access ISP has a special role as the point of contact for the end-customer in order to technically set up an E-Commerce service. To be able to implement such an approach in the Internet, a set of communication means is essential, basically driven by the Internet and its protocols as well as existing management means. SLAs form such crucial technical means to implement a business process depending on an ISP strategy. They are applied between business entities in general, ISPs as well as end-customers, to negotiate business conditions on a contractual basis. They define a.o. a service control policy that regulates objectives and responsibilities for the service delivery under a given business process.

Considering the economic dimensions of strategies and policies, the approach to charge for communication services is an essential constituent for a business process. Therefore, the charging of services (as described in Section 3) needs to be supported by appropriate technology 0, 0. In addition, the performance in economic terms of the service delivery between service providers shall be based on a "win-win" strategy, which implies service delivery and financial compensation until the service has finished or failed. This implies fair business relationships among providers, since no financial losses result from service failures. The effects of such a strategy, backed by SLAs, policies, and network management functionality will be illustrated by a particular business process (cf. Section 4). The process is applied specifically onto three different Internet technologies to argue that the strategy as well as instances of policy sets are independent from the underlying technology.

# 3. CHARGING COMMUNICATIONS

A commercialized Internet requires a variety of communication services (as illustrated in Section 2.2) which encompass technical ones as well as economic ones. While the functionality of technical services includes IP packet delivery, reliability and error control, or security features, economic services focus on feedback information from service usage to optimize the revenue of E-Commerce services.

Based on the scenario of Figure 1, a charging approach within a business process requires a system interface for a commercial information transfer between ESPs and ISPs in order to optimize business strategies. Optimizing service provisioning requires accounting of services on a timely basis. Traditionally, this accounting has been performed on longer time-scales, nowadays a short-term is envisioned. This leads to the necessity to map these technically accounted information onto a financial dimension in a similar time-scale. Therefore, a charge calculation function will become the major tool for optimizing business strategies and revenues, since soft real-time charging provides important feedback for service providers. This may allow ESPs to select an optimal provider for IP services at a given time. Potentially, an in-operation communication could be switched dynamically, however, technical restrictions have to be considered closely before practical solutions will be available. A similar concept is applicable to all service provider roles as defined above, where cash flow and further economic factors are to be optimized.

As depicted in Figure 2b, the charging system represents that component in the described service model of Figure 2a, which performs mapping tasks from technically accounted parameters of an IP infrastructure and its usage by end-customers onto financial values required to provide feedback signals to both ESPs and ISPs. However, technical parameters need to be completed by QoS information directed to the ESP in case a content sensitive data transport service has failed, e.g., a file backup. However, QoS information directed to the ESP is required to cancel the E-Commerce service and its charges if content sensitive data has been damaged.

A charging system and its communications facilities 0 requires a clear differentiation of tasks and functions to be implemented for the network. Within the Internet, an initial step to organize those tasks has been performed 0 and they offer the necessary functionality to perform economically- as well as technically-driven control and optimization functions. The charging tasks with the customer billing (termed billing) and the subsequent payment (termed payment) can be embraced and modeled in a clearing phase (cf. Section 4), which basically compensates effort and expenses[43].

## 3.1 Billing

Billing can be considered a service itself, which could be outsourced from the service providers' core business. Billing implies the process of collecting all relevant information from a charge calculation function and accumulating it onto the customer's bill. The bill summarizes all charges to a final amount that the customer needs to pay either per service or on a regular base (e.g. monthly, weekly).

The ESP bills the end-customer for the ordered product, the delivered service (including reservation), or the provided digital content. Access and Core ISPs bill a.o. for Internet Access[44], transport, and reservation services, and especially the charge for the transport service depends on the applied pricing model, including QoS value specifications. The price for these provided services may consist fully or partially of the following three basic components: (1) an access charge for the network access, (2) a one-time connection charge for the connection setup, and (3) a usage charge based on time, volume, or QoS for the provided service. Accordingly, the charge covers used network resources and the maintenance of the network infrastructure. Usage-based pricing schemes are applied to charge the customer for the actual amount of used network resources 0. It could even be possible that the

[43] As denoted in Section 3.2, clearing can also be done in advance, especially if the service customer is unknown to the service provider.

[44] In case of a direct dial-in connection between the ESP and the end-customer, no Internet Access service is required and the transport service is charged as a direct phone call from the end-customer to the ESP.

transport charge is shared proportionately between the ESP and the end-customer, e.g., collect calls where the callee pays.

Final prices for E-Commerce, Internet access, and transport service sometimes include an optional charge for their reservation. Figure 3 illustrates the coherence between the different services and the billing for their delivery. Horizontally listed, there is the E-Commerce service on top of the Internet access service and the underlying transport service. Reservations for all these services can be made independently from each other. Billing can be performed separately for the horizontally listed services with or without charges for the reservation service.

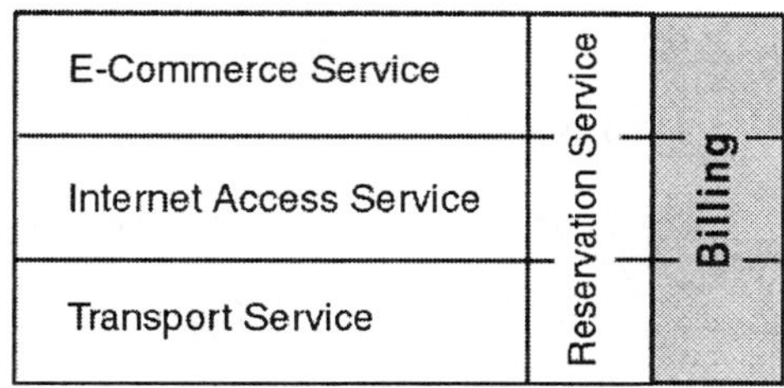


*Figure 3.* Coherence of different services with billing

With classical billing, customers receive a monthly bill with a list of charges for the claimed goods. The scheme can be applied in a single-provider environment with a classic business relationship between the merchant and the customer. Different billing schemes have to be applied in a multi-provider environment (cf. Figure 1) where the service performance depends on the cooperation of multiple entities.

Edge billing is a scheme applicable for billing transport and reservation services along a path of ISPs. Charges from every ISP are added to one final bill. The end-customer or the ESP (or both) pays the total amount to the Access ISP, which deducts its share and passes the rest on to the next ISP along the path. The next ISP also deducts only its share and forwards the rest. This process continues along the paths until the end of network connection. Certainly, bilateral agreements between neighboring ISPs would perform better in terms of effort, but asymmetrical traffic flows and quite drastically changing traffic volumes over time require a flexible solution to short-term service setups. A centralized billing model consists of several bills that are passed directly from the ISPs to the end-customer, which results in a complex situation for the end-customer. A hybrid model is a combination of both edge billing and centralized billing. Other billing schemes comprise clearing centers to perform the clearing between involved entities 0.

## 3.2 Payment

The payment process is a well-defined scheme, which stipulates how money is exchanged between customer and service provider. In case an end-customer wants to remain anonymously (e.g. using a public phone), payments are made in advance (pre-paid). E-Commerce services where the end-customer is known to at least one service provider (e.g. calling from a stationary phone) the payment process is executed afterwards (post-paid). Figure 4 shows our developed model for classifying payment mechanisms according to anonymous or registered end-customers.

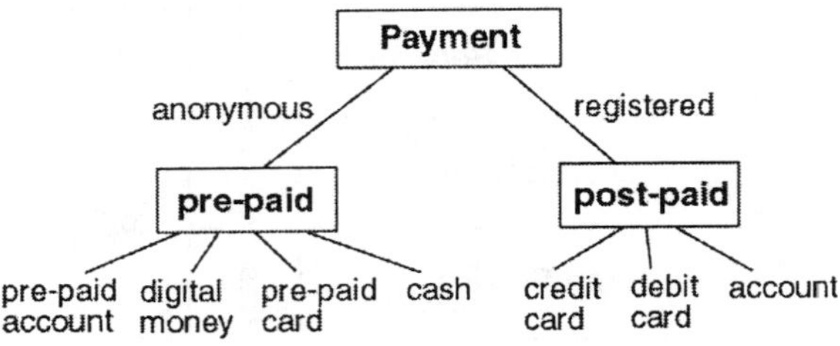


*Figure 4.* Classification of payment mechanisms

The tree structure shows peculiarities for both anonymous pre-paid and registered post-paid payments. Credit and debit cards as well as regular accounts are used for conventional payments where the customer has a registered bank account. Cash and pre-paid cards (e.g., telephone cards) are anonymous means of payment – well known today. Digital money is just a logical representation of monetary units and is also used anonymously, whereas pre-paid accounts are used with a pseudonym where the service availability depends on the current account balance.

# 4. BUSINESS PROCESS

This section describes the business process derived from the E-Commerce scenario of Figure 1 where an end-customer requests an E-Commerce service from an ESP. This includes the demand for any of the previously mentioned additional services. The flow of this business process is restricted to only the operative sequence of steps and phases without specifying any strategies for negotiating service parameters or taking market situations into consideration. The business process is part of a business model 0 and it shows the different coherent phases and their correlation with the previously identified roles and services 0. Furthermore, these phases are mapped onto Internet protocol architectures such as best-effort Internet, IntServ, and DiffServ resulting in approaches to solve tasks of these phases (cf. Figure 6). The business process contains four different but coherent phases: (1) contracting phase, (2) reservation phase, (3) service phase, and (4) clearing phase.

The initial **contracting phase** is run through only once to introduce the business partners to each other on a contractual base for further cooperation and service provisioning. Initially, the end-customer logs in with a service provider - be it an ESP or ISP - to request a service. If the end-customer is already known to the service provider, meaning a contract exists already, the contracting phase is skipped.

Figure 5 shows the business process in form of a flow chart, where the clouds show sub-phases of the four coherent phases and the rhombuses symbolize "forks in the road" that decide which way the process leads. Attached to the clouds are the roles in the gray boxes that represent the involved actors of that sub-phase. After the contracting phase is run through, the business process leads into the **reservation phase** where different services and their parameters are negotiated. The end-customer logs in with the service provider again to actually reserve a service.

In an optional specific information phase the end-customer gets customer specific information about the short-term market situation, e.g., price tender, network traffic, or com-parison with other service providers. If no service has been previously reserved the service parameters have to be negotiated among the business entities within the negotiation phase. As mentioned in Section 2.2, services can be reserved immediately for a short term, immediately for a longer term, or in advance. It is important to note that the negotiation phase for the Integrated Services Internet (IntServ) runs differently from the one for the Differentiated Services Internet (DiffServ). IntServ sup-ports the negotiation of service parameters based on single end-to-end flows whereas DiffServ traffic is based on the notion of aggregated flows with fixed numbers of service levels which requires longer termed service negotiation on a per IP packet-basis.

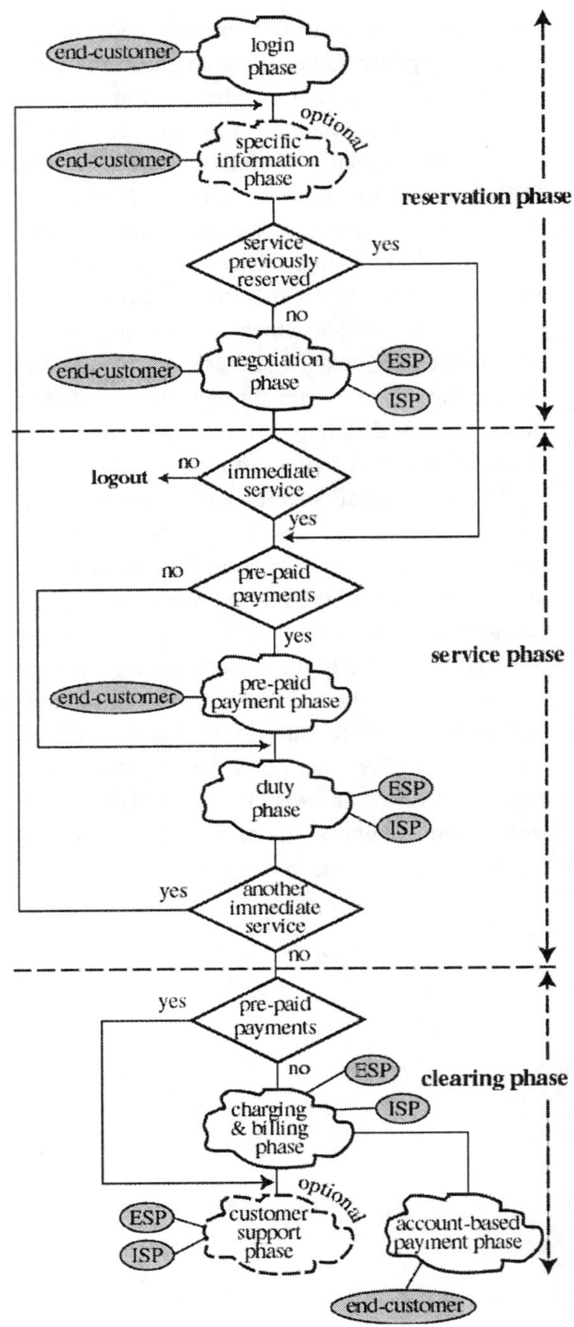


*Figure 5.* Entire business process including reservation, service, and clearing phase

In the subsequent **service phase**, the performance of the requested services takes place. If no immediate service is desired the end-customer logs out. Of course, the end-customer can log out at any point during the whole business process. If an immediate service is desired by a registered end-customer the actual service is performed within the duty phase. However, if the end-customer decided to remain anonymous, pre-paid payments have to be made within the pre-paid payment phase before the service is performed. If another immediate service is desired the business process loops back into the specific information phase to rerun the reservation phase. Again, this loop is very short termed (e.g., 30 seconds) and flow based in case of IntServ and longer termed (e.g., whole service duration) in case of DiffServ.

| | | best effort | IntServ | DiffServ |
|---|---|---|---|---|
| reservation phase | service previously reserved | not possible | check for existing or reserved flow | check DSCP usage of microflows at border router |
| | negotiation phase | no negotiation | RSVP messages btw. ESP & end-customer | res. requests btw. bandwidth brokers |
| service phase | pre-paid payment phase | no payment since no resources are reserved | pre-paid payments within IP packets for a certain period of time (e.g., 10 minutes) | |
| | duty phase | IP packet routing with no priorities | IP packets with flow labeling | IP packets with DSCP marked for PHB |
| | another immediate service | possible anytime with no guarantee | new RSVP message (default 30 seconds) | similar DSCP marking scheme for packets of a microflow |
| clearing phase | charging and billing phase | no charges | charges for single flows with same flow label | charges for counted IP packets per DSCP |
| | account-based payment phase | no payment | adding identified charges to a customer bill | |

*Figure 6.* Phases of the business process mapped onto different architectures

The final **clearing phase** includes charging, billing, and payment for the delivered service with account-based post-paid payments if the end-customer is registered. The charging and billing phase comprises the accumulation of user specific information to calculate the final price for the service and also the subsequent sending of the bill. Post-paid payments are made within the account-based payment phase for example with credit card, debit card, or regular money transfer. A final, optional customer support phase concludes the business process where the service provider has the chance to get any feedback from the end-customer concerning the performance of the service.

Figure 6 compares a best-effort Internet with the IntServ and DiffServ framework and how they could technically support tasks within some exemplary sub-phases and decision points. It illustrates how best-effort does not foresee any resource reservation or service differentiation. IntServ approaches with RSVP as a signaling protocol are based on single flows, whereas DiffServ handles aggregated flows with guaranteed per-hop behaviors (PHB) for packets with similar DiffServ

Code Point (DSCP). The negotiation within DiffServ is handled by Bandwidth Brokers (BB) of different DiffServ domains 0. A micro-flow is a single instance of an application-to-application flow of packets identified by source and destination address, protocol id, and source port.

# 1. CONCLUSIONS AND FUTURE WORK

Business entities and their roles and responsibilities determine basic components of a business process, which is developed for a future value-added Internet. A clear separation of these players, a concise definition of the services they offer, and a characterization of their interactions and mechanisms allow the definition of open business processes. This openness is essential for tomorrow's markets in the Internet, covering charging and accounting for products, contents, and services using network resources. On a network level it is the transport service that implements reliable QoS-based end-to-end communication with different service levels. The usage of the Internet as a platform for electronic business requires a higher level of abstraction with well-defined business processes and business models including special cooperating roles and services based on appropriate policies.

Within the previously shown multi-provider scenario, it is especially the clearing process with clearing, billing, and payment for delivered services that is crucial for the economic success of an E-Commerce application. It must remain open, whether the pure transport-related charging and its corresponding billing will be valid for every single service in the Internet. Regularly changing Internet technologies and a broad variety of service providers and customers with different single demands and expectations complicate development and use of generic business processes and require an exact differentiation of E-Commerce scenarios. However, the business process as demonstrated in Figure 5 made a step towards an integration of E-Commerce and service delivery through the introduction of contractual agreements, charging mechanisms, billing, and payment. Also, the potential of having business processes handy, of having efficient technology in place, and of having simulation experiences available for charging and accounting issues in the Internet provides the basis for experimentation as well as long-term collection of experiences. Although the INDEX project collected first results 0, various questions need further investigations: the applicability of various pricing models 0, its dependencies on business models, and applicability of fine-grained and scalable accounting tools.

The business process clearly distinguished pre-paid payments from account-based payments for the settlement of services. Clearing is part of the economic policy that regulates financial compensation of services. The policy considers registered as well as anonymous end-customers, but prefers account-based payments in case of service failures, when pre-paid payments have been made already.

Account-based payments are advantageous, since clearing is performed on a pay-per-use base where only the actual received service is paid after service delivery.

Furthermore, future work needs to be done in embedding the technological know-how into economic models and business. Figure 6 shows basic approaches how to map the phases of the business process onto technological Internet architectures but more work is required to further develop these ideas. Reservation of network resources could be performed by using intelligent agents as bandwidth brokers. Dynamic usage-based pricing models are designed and need to be operated. Payment methods are still lacking trust for many electronic business applications. The handling of anonymous service customers should be the focus of investigations for QoS-based end-to-end service provisioning in a value-added Internet. The growing number of mobile Internet users and new mobile Internet technology is a clear indication for changing expectations of today's service markets.

## 2. ACKNOWLEDGEMENTS

This work has been performed in the framework of the projects Charging and Accounting Technology for the Internet – CATI (CAPIV No. 5003-054559/1 and MEDeB No. 5003-054560/1) and ANAISOFT (No. 5003-057753/1) which have been funded by the Swiss National Science Foundation, SNF, Bern, Switzerland. The authors like to acknowledge many discussions with their project colleagues.

## 3. REFERENCES

[1] Akamai: Delivering a Better Internet; URL: http://www.akamai.com, January 2001.

[2] J. Altmann, B. Rupp, P. Varaiya: Effects of Pricing on Internet User Behavior; Netnomics, Vol. 3, No. 1, pp 67-84, June 2001.

[3 ] K. Downes, M. Ford, H.K. Lew, S. Spanier, T. Stevenson: Internetworking Technologies Handbook; 2nd Edition, Macmillan Technical Publishing, Indianapolis, U.S.A., 1998.

[4] N. Foukia, D. Billard, P. Reichl, B. Stiller: User Behavior for a Pricing Scheme in a Multi-provider Scenario; Workshop on Internet Service Quality Economics, Cambridge, Massachusetts, U.S.A., MIT, Session 5, December 2-3, 1999.

[5] U. Kaiser: Sicherheits- und Kostenaspekte in elektronischen Zahlungssystemen für RSVP; Institut für Technische Informatik und Kommunikationsnetze, TIK, ETH Zürich, Student's Thesis, August 1998.

[6] I. Khalil, T. Braun: Implementation of a Bandwidth Broker for Dynamic End-to-End Resource Reservation in Outsourced Virtual Private Networks; The Conference on Leading Edge and Practical Computer Networking (LCN 2000), November 9-10, 2000, Tampa, Florida.

[7] H. Kneer, U. Zurfluh, B. Stiller: Modeling the Provisioning of Value-added Internet Services and Reservations in a Multi-provider Environment; TIK Report No. 110, ETH Zürich, Computer Engineering and Networkds Laboratory TIK, Switzerland, May 2001.

[8] H. Kneer, U. Zurfluh, G. Dermler, and B. Stiller: A Business Model for Charging and Accounting of Internet Services; International Conference on Electronic Commerce and Web Technologies (EC-Web 2000), pp. 429-441, Greenwich, U.K., September 4-6, 2000.
[9] L.G. Lawrence: The Role of Roles; Computers & Security, Vol. 12, pp. 15-21, 1993.
[10] P. Reichl, S. Leinen, B. Stiller: A Practical Review of Pricing and Cost Recovery for Internet Services; 2nd Berlin Internet Economics Workshop (IEW'99), Berlin, Germany, May 28–29, 1999. Session "Survey I".
[11] B. Stiller, T. Braun, M. Günter, B. Plattner: The CATI Project – Charging and Accounting Technology for the Internet; Springer Verlag, Berlin, Germany, Lecture Notes in Computer Science, Vol. 1629, 5th European Conference on Multimedia Applications, Services, and Techniques (ECMAST'99), pp 281–296, Madrid, Spain, May 26–28, 1999.
[12] B. Stiller, J. Gerke, P. Reichl, P. Flury: Management of Differentiated Services Usage by the Cumulus Pricing Scheme and a Generic Internet Charging System; IEEE/IFIP Symposium on Integrated Network Management (IM'2001), pp 93-106, Seattle, Washington, U.S.A., May 14-17, 2001.
[13] UUNET: Service Level Agreements; URL: http://www2.uu.net/customer/sla, 2001.

MAIN TRACK - PART SIX

# CUSTOMER RELATIONSHIPS

27

# A Mechanism for Evaluating Feedback of E-Commerce Sites

Karen Renaud, Paula Kotzé, and Tobias van Dyk
*Department of Computer Science and Information Systems, University of South Africa*

**Abstract:** The developers of e-commerce applications have a problem in gauging the knowledge and expertise of end-users. The developer must therefore design the interface to the system so that the use thereof is sufficiently intuitive to require the minimum of background knowledge. Developers need to enhance the usability of their web sites so that incidental users will find the site rewarding and enticing, and encourage them to explore further. This paper will explore the role of feedback as a valuable tool in enhancing the interpretability of e-commerce applications. We discuss firstly how applications may be designed to make use of an enriched model of application feedback, and secondly how developers may evaluate their sites so as to gauge the efficacy of the currently provided feedback. We propose a novel method for analysing the purchasing phase of the e-commerce experience. We then introduce an evaluation method for determining whether a particular site provides adequate feedback or not. Three sites were evaluated using the proposed model, and the results of this evaluation are analysed.

## 1. INTRODUCTION

Organisations can hardly afford to ignore the E-Commerce (EC) alternative to traditional marketing [1]. EC users will seldom complain about badly-designed sites and the first inkling of a problem may come only from analysis of usage patterns which will very possibly come too late to enable corrective action to be taken, or damage to be prevented. Such patterns, as derived from logs, are very difficult to interpret [13], as is demonstrated by Rosenstein in his study of server logs [20]. According to Rohn [19], there are two important things an EC site should do in order to be successful:

- attract additional customers, and
- reduce workload for the sales force.

Keeping current customers might be even more important [9]. EC purveyors can never become complacent because EC frees users from restraints which previously forced them to use sub-standard retail stores [8, 13]. Many researchers rate ease of use as being of critical importance to the EC process [11]. Bad usability is often blamed for causing the failure of sites [9, 19].

In this paper we have chosen to discuss one particular aspect of web-site usability, namely that of feedback. We will advocate the extensive use of feedback to increase the interpretability of systems, thus enhancing the ease of use of these systems. Section 2 will explore the nature of feedback in EC

applications. It is necessary, however, to convert this discussion about the merits of feedback to a methodology for evaluating proposed EC web site pages. Before such a methodology can be provided it is necessary to understand the nature of the EC shopping experience, and this will be discussed in Section 3. Section 4 proposes a feedback evaluation methodology for EC systems. Section 5 discusses the results of an evaluation which was conducted on three large EC sites. Section 6 concludes.

## 2. FEEDBACK

Feedback serves a behavioural purpose in the interaction between users and computers, with the computer fulfilling the same role as a conversational participant [16]. Only by means of feedback can participants in a conversation detect faults in the understanding of what is said [5]. The success of the human-computer 'conversation' will depend on the user being able to gauge the 'knowledge' of the application. Feedback must make the 'knowledge' of the application, based on previous inputs, tangible and accessible in order to fulfil its role adequately in the face of an untutored and unreliable user population.

The conversational model of user interaction, with respect to the current computer usage paradigm of recognition rather than recall [4], leads us to consider users as reacting according to the way they interpret the state of the system. The quality of the feedback provided by the system can assist in enabling an understanding of the state of the system and becomes very important when the system is prone to long response times, a common occurrence in e-commerce systems.

### 2.1 Use of Feedback

It is necessary to consider the purpose of any feedback, and the way a user can be expected to make use of such feedback as is provided. The Oxford English Dictionary (OED) defines feedback as: *signifying a response*, *modifying the behaviour of the user* and *promoting understanding*. The traditional role of feedback in human-computer interaction is often seen exclusively as pertaining to the first use.

The extension of the feedback concept to include all the features will enable EC sites to give better and adequate feedback to users.

It has been noted by various researchers that a discourse typically has an incremental quality about it [3]. Dix [4] argues that it is difficult for users to manage and visualise this "sense of history" in their interaction with the computer. Often the application's only concession to a user's need for this is the provision of an undo facility. This provides a type of historical function but the user often needs to reverse the state of the system in order to see what happened before.

It is therefore appropriate to consider the need for the portrayal of previous system states so that the user can refer to it in order to understand the present state of the system. Historical functions are routinely provided by web browsers, such as a history of sites visited and bookmarks, but we feel that this history should be more finely grained than that. The user needs to have a history of their interaction *within* particular web sites. We postulate that good feedback should involve giving the user both immediate *and* archival feedback. There are several difficulties in providing such feedback, such as the difference in technical expertise between the developers and the users of e-commerce sites, the naïvety and unknown nature of e-commerce end-users, and the distributed nature of e-commerce systems, which makes them prone to outages and unpredictable behaviour.

## 2.2 Recommendations

Developers need to have guidelines to ensure that adequate feedback is provided. This section draws the conclusion that developers need to provide the following:

- **immediate feedback:** signal a response to each user action, explain unusual occurrences such as delays, display relevant system state clearly.
- **archival feedback:** provide a historical function which allows users to check on previous actions without changing the state of the system. Always provide the facility for users to check on their progress through any process which has specific stages.

This feedback satisfies the OED definition of the purpose of feedback. Having defined feedback, we now develop a model of the EC shopping process. This will enable us to arrive at an EC-specific set of guidelines for determining feedback quality. The next section provides such a model, and Section 4 uses this model and the findings of this section to derive the required guidelines.

# 3. ANALYSIS OF THE E-COMMERCE PURCHASING EXPERIENCE

Guttman *et al.* [7] identify six stages of customer purchasing behaviour: need identification, product brokering, merchant brokering, negotiation, purchase and delivery, and service and evaluation. O'Keefe and McEachern [14] propose a model with only five processes: need recognition, information search, evaluation, purchase, and after- purchase evaluation. Singh *et al.* [21] break up the EC process into three activities: identifying and finding a vendor, purchasing and tracking. We will examine only one of Singh's processes - namely the one that everyone refers to as the *purchase* task. This task can be split up into two distinct stages, as shown in Figure 1.

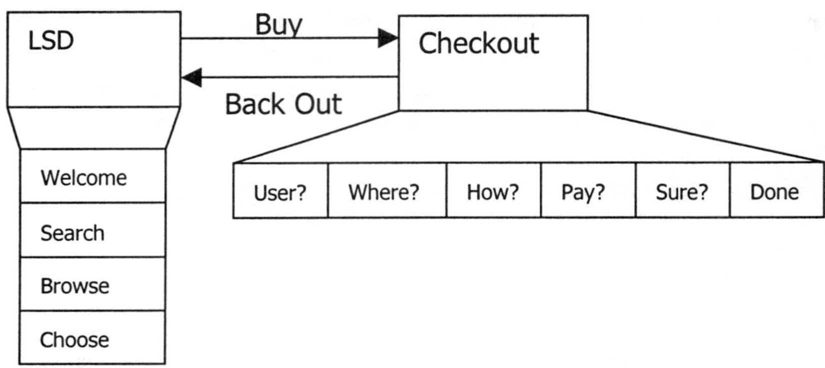


*Figure 1.* The Two Phases and Ten Stages of the Purchase Task.

1. *Look, See and Decide (LSD):* This stage will typically be used to look at available products, compare them, and to make a decision about whether or not to purchase products. This may be done one or more times until the consumer has found products which satisfy his or her needs. This phase is intensely user-driven because the user is looking at and assimilating information continuously. It has the following substages which can be traversed iteratively and in varying sequences: Welcome; Search; Browse; and Choose.

2. *Checkout:* When the users trigger this stage they have made their choice of offered products and decided to make a purchase. They now have to provide certain details, such as their address and credit card details. This stage is system-driven and changes the paradigm of the interaction process from user initiative to system initiative. Feedback is of critical importance during this stage - users who feel that they have lost control can simply leave the site without any embarrassment — unlike a user who is standing at a checkout till in a supermarket. This stage is typically

composed of at least the following steps, which should be navigated in a serial fashion: User? Where? How? Payment? Sure? and Done. Only one of the previous steps has elicited much research interest ie. Payment [10].

# 4. METHOD

The feedback and information requirements of a user during the LSD stage are very different from those required by the checkout stage. The differences in operation between these phases make it beneficial to develop two different strategies for evaluating web pages since some sites will support one stage far better than the other and one single evaluation process is unlikely to suit both stages.

In deriving an evaluation method it was necessary to combine the findings of various researchers. Ravden and Johnson [17] propose a checklist-based evaluation mechanism which rates interfaces from various perspectives such as visual clarity, consistency, compatibility, explicitness, appropriate functionality, informative feedback, control, error handling and finally, user guidance and support.

We have selected elements from the most relevant of Ravden and Johnson's categories in order to set up one complete feedback evaluation mechanism, for each stage, which will ensure that an EC page provides adequate and complete feedback. The evaluation metrics for the LSD phase are shown in Table 1.

The metrics for the checkout phase are somewhat different, because of the linear and structured nature of the process. The metrics are given in Table 2. The following section will describe how these metrics were applied to three EC sites, and comment about the efficacy of the proposed evaluation mechanism. In order to evaluate EC web pages, a score is given for each of the above questions as follows:

- Never (0) - the feature is never available.
- Sometimes (1) - the feature is seldom there.
- Mostly (2) - the feature is usually there.
- Always (3) - the feature is universally available.

The scores are then determined per stage, and per site, in the form of a percentage where 100% indicates a site giving a user perfect feedback and sites scoring 0% might as well give up and close shop. The scores per feature in each stage were calculated by adding up the score for each page making up the stage and awarding a total for each particular feature. The scores for each feature were then totalled to arrive at a percentage per site per purchasing stage.

# 5. EVALUATION

We chose three sites to apply the metrics to. Booksellers like Amazon (www.amazon.ac.uk) are the pioneers in this field and we felt that their site would be a good one to evaluate. We therefore chose two other bookseller's sites to compare it to - namely Books Online (www.uk.bol.com) and Kalahari (www.kalahari.net). We purchased various products from each EC site, and evaluated the process. Our final scores for each site, arrived at after discussion and consensus of all the authors, are given in Tables 1 and 2.

| **Evaluation of System Feedback Quality: LSD Stage** | | Amazon Max 9 | Kalahari Max 9 | BOL Max 9 |
|---|---|---|---|---|
| 1 | Is it clear what a user must do to search for a product? [9, 13] | 6 | 6 | 7 |
| 2 | Does the search engine offer alternatives if a search fails? [10] | 9 | 3 | 0 |
| 3 | Does the system inform the user of the reasons for delays? [12] | 5 | 3 | 3 |
| 4 | Are different types of information clearly separated? [2] | 7 | 5 | 9 |
| 5 | Was information readily available? [9, 15] | 6 | 6 | 6 |
| 6 | Is it clear what needs to be done to select a product? | 9 | 6 | 6 |
| 7 | Can the user undo a product selection? [12] | 9 | 6 | 8 |
| 8 | Is it clear what must be done to make the transition to Checkout? | 6 | 6 | 9 |
| 9 | Does the system allow users to check on previous searches? [18] | 0 | 0 | 0 |
| 10 | Is jargon user-centric? [12] | 6 | 6 | 6 |
| 11 | Is there a help facility? [22, 15] | 9 | 9 | 9 |
| | Percentage | 73% | 57% | 64% |

*Table 1:* Evaluation Metrics for the LSD Stage

## 5.1 Discussion

One notices from Tables 1 and 2 that some metrics scored markedly well or badly. A low score should wave a red flag at the developer and can be used to indicate a problem area. A high score shows that the developer has one a good job in providing adequate feedback for that particular feature of the site. This section will discuss the low and high scoring feedback features of the three sites.

| **Evaluation of System Feedback Quality: Checkout Stage** | | Amazon Max 18 | Kalahari Max 9 | BOL Max 15 |
|---|---|---|---|---|
| 1 | Are instructions and messages concise and positive? [13] | 12 | 6 | 9 |
| 2 | Are instructions clear and prompts unambiguous? [13] | 12 | 6 | 12 |
| 3 | Are possible actions clear? | 11 | 5 | 11 |
| 4 | Is it clear what a user must do to take an action? [9, 13] | 13 | 5 | 13 |
| 5 | Is the required format of user inputs clearly indicated? [15] | 15 | 7 | 10 |
| 6 | Are user actions linked to changes in the interface? | 13 | 6 | 12 |
| 7 | Is there always an appropriate response to user actions? | 12 | 6 | 13 |
| 8 | Does the system inform the user of the success or failure of their actions? | 14 | 6 | 11 |
| 9 | Does he system inform users of the reasons for delays? [11] | 11 | 3 | 5 |
| | Do error messages indicate: | | | |
| 10.1 | What errors are? | 12 | 6 | 13 |
| 10.2 | Where errors are? | 6 | 3 | 10 |
| 10.3 | Why they have occurred? | 6 | 1 | 13 |
| 10.4 | How the user should recover? | 10 | 6 | 8 |
| 11 | Is it clear what the user has to do to complete the task? | 11 | 5 | 14 |
| 12 | Does the system indicate the current stage? [22] | 17 | 3 | 15 |
| 13 | Was information always readily available? [9, 15] | 9 | 6 | 12 |
| 14 | Can the user easily back out of the process? [12] | 10 | 2 | 3 |
| 15 | Is final purchase is confirmed by the user? | 18 | 9 | 15 |
| 16 | Can users check on inputs provided during the process? [18] | 9 | 6 | 3 |
| 17 | Is jargon and terminology user-centric? | 12 | 6 | 9 |
| 18 | Is there a help facility? [22, 15] | 16 | 9 | 15 |
| | Percentage | 66% | 59% | 72% |

*Table 2:* Evaluation Metrics for the Checkout Phase

### 5.1.1 Low Scores

Two criteria stand out particularly: the lack of a historical facility and inadequate reasons for long or unexpected delays. None of the evaluated sites allow users to remind themselves of previous search criteria. A user searching for a specific type of book may type in many different search parameters and may easily forget which parameters have been tried before, especially after a period of time has elapsed. It would be helpful to have a drop-down menu which can be activated by the user in order to see previous search criteria.

In the same vein, there is also a need for the user to be reminded, as they progress through the checkout stage, of their previous inputs. Some sites do provide this but it is often not done consistently.

The other controversial score is the one allocated to the question: *Does the system inform the user of the reasons for delays?* Most browsers give observable feedback on page-fetch delays and anticipated completion times. However, many sites, including the ones evaluated, seem to rely completely on this facility rather than providing the user with some sort of site-specific indicator of site access (hit-rate). A user who is given access to such an indicator will perhaps be more patient when sites take a long time to respond.

A feature which we had considered to be essential and basic to good practice, namely that of indicating the substage throughout the checkout stage, was almost absent in the Kalahari site. The user becomes disoriented because the checkout stage encompasses various substages and they have no way of knowing where they are in the process.

### 5.1.2 High Scores

Some positive features should also be mentioned. The e-mail confirmation sent out by all three sites is a very good feature. The scores allocated to help facilities were high for all the sites — and this is particularly good with respect to site usability. What is good for an EC user is automatically good for the site too.

Another universal feedback feature is the requirement that the user positively confirm their transaction. This eliminates possible errors later when users find that they have made a mistake and not picked it up in time. All evaluated sites offer a final page which displays all choices made for the transaction, allows the user to check these choices, and waits for the user to confirm before processing the order. All sites also send the user an e-mail confirming the order so that the user can still exercise a form of recovery, via e-mail, if he or she wishes to cancel the order.

Amazon always attempts to offer alternatives when a search does not produce any results. Another feature provided by both Amazon and BOL is their usage of a customer-driven rating system. Although this is not feedback in the traditional EC sense it is undeniably valuable to potential customers.

## 6. CONCLUSION

Feedback can be used to assist the user in understanding the functionality and requirements of an EC application and can be effectively harnessed to ensure that users do not simply give up on sites. We have identified two distinct and dissimilar phases during the shopping cycle and have applied stage-specific evaluation metrics to them. This provides an evaluation mechanism which can be used by developers to flag problem feedback areas.

# 7. REFERENCES

[1] K. Bennet and J. Slonim. The electronic commerce position paper. ACM Computing Surveys, 28(4es):112, 1996.

[2] J. A. Borges, I. Morales, and N. J. Rodriguez. Page Design Guidelines Developed Through Usability Testing. In [8], chapter 11, pages 137 - 152. 1998.

[3] G. Carenini and J. D. Moore. Generating Explanations in Context. In Proceedings of the 1993 International Workshop on Intelligent User Interfaces, Session 6: User Support, pages 175-182, 1993.

[4] A. J. Dix. Closing the loop: modelling action, perception and information. In M. F. C. T. Catarci, S. Levialdi, and G. Santucci, editors, AVI'96 - Advanced Visual Interfaces, pages 20-28. ACM Press, 1991.

[5] F. L. Engel and R. Haakma. Expectations and Feedback in User-System Communication. International Journal of Man-Machine Studies, 39(3):427-452, 1993.

[6] C. Forsythe, E. Grose, and J. Ratner, editors. Human Factors and Web Development. Lawrence Erlbaum, Mahwah, New Jersey, 1998.

[7] R. H. Guttman and A. G. M. ans P Maes. Agent-mediated electronic commerce: a survey. Knowledge Engineering Review, 13:147-159, 1998.

[8] G. Huaubl and V. Trifts. Cosumer decision Making in Online Shopping Environments: The Effects of Interactive Decision Aids. Marketing Science, 19(1):4-21, Winter 2000.

[9] M. G. Helander and H. M. Khalid. Modeling the customer in electronic commerce. Applied Ergonomics, 31:609-619, 2000.

[10] J. Jahng, H. Jain, and K. Ramamurthy. Effective Design of Electronic Commerce Environments: A Proposed Theory of Congruence and an Illustration. IEEE Transactions on Systems, Man and Cybernetics - Part A: Systems,and Humans., 30(4):456-471, July 2000.

[11] G. E. Miles and A. Howes. Framework for understanding human factors in web-based electronic commerce. International Journal of Human Computer Studies, 52(1):131-163, 2000.

[12] J. Nielsen. useit.com: Jakob nielsen's website. useit.com: usable information technology. http://www.useit.com.

[13] J. Nielsen and D. Norman. Usability on the Web Isn't A Luxury. Information Week, January 14 2000. http://www.informationweek.com/773/web.htm.

[14] R. M. O'Keefe and T. McEachern. Web-based customer decision support systems. Communications of the ACM, 41:71-78, 1998.

[15] P. Paper. Making Online Information Usable.http://www.world.std.com/uieweb/online.htm.

[16] M. A. Perez-Quinones and J. L. Sibert. Negotiating User-Initiated Cancellation and Interruption Requests. In Proceedings of ACM CHI 96 Conference on Human Factors in Computing Systems, volume 2 of SHORT PAPERS: Models, pages 267-268, 1996.

[17] S. J. Ravden and G. I. Johnson. Evaluating Usability of Human-Computer Interfaces: A Practical Method. John Wiley and Sons, 1989.

[18] K. Renaud and R. Cooper. Feedback in Human-Computer Interaction - Characteristics and Recommendations. South African Computing Journal, (26), 2000.

[19] J. A. Rohn. Creating usable E-commerce sites. STDVIEW: Standard View, the ACM Journal on Standardization, 6, 1998.

[20] M. Rosenstein. What is actually taking place on web sites: e-commerce lessons from web server logs. In Proceedings of the 2nd ACM conference on Electronic commerce, pages 38-43, Minneapolis, MN USA, October 17 - 20, 2000.

[21] M. Singh, A. K. Jain, and M. P. Singh. E-Commerce over communicators: Challenges and solutions for user interfaces. In Proceedings of the ACM Conference on Electronic Commerce (EC-99), pages 177-186, N.Y., Nov. 3-5 1999. ACM Press.

[22] R. Tilson, J. Dong, S. Martin, and E. Kieke. A Comparison of Two Current E-Commerce Sites. In ACM 16th International Conference on Systems Documentation, Web Navigation, pages 87-92, 1998.

28

# Feature-oriented vs. Needs-oriented Product Access for Non-Expert Online Shoppers

Daniel Felix[1], Christoph Niederberger[1], Patrick Steiger[2] & Markus Stolze[3]
[1] *ETH Zurich, Technoparkstrasse 1, CH-8005 Zurich, Switzerland*
[2] *PricewaterhouseCoopers, Affolternstrasse 52, CH-8050 Zurich, Switzerland*
[3] *IBM Research, Zurich Research Laboratory, Säumerstrasse 4, 8803 Rüschlikon, Switzerland*
*felix@iha.bepr.ethz.ch, patrick.steiger@ch.pwcglobal.com, mrs@zurich.ibm.com*[*]

**Abstract:** Most online shops today organise their product catalogue in a feature-oriented way. This can cause problems for shoppers who have only limited knowledge of product features. An alternative is to organizing product information in a needs-oriented way. Here possible ways of using the product build the focus of attention. In this study we compared reported preference of catalogue access of non-expert shoppers when confronted with either feature-oriented or needs-oriented access to a catalogue of digital cameras.

## 1. INTRODUCTION

An important success factor for online shops is the way in which they help shoppers identify appropriate purchases (Hagen et al, 2000). Currently we can identify three main ways in which online shops help visitors find the products they desire:

- Hierarchically organised catalogues,
- Feature-oriented catalogues (search & browse based on product features),
- Needs-oriented catalogues (search & browse based on shopper needs).

The traditional way of supporting a product search in an online shop is to present the products in a *hierarchically organised online-catalogue*. The challenge for hierarchically organised online-catalogues is to match category labels to shopper expectations and interests. A shopper looking for a video camera might wonder whether TV or Photo is the correct section to search. Similarly, a shopper looking

* This work was supported by the affiliated organizations of the authors and by the Swiss Priority Program ICS grant "Management of Customer Relationship".

for a computer with at least 50 GB of hard-disk space and at least 900 MHz CPU might not be well served by having to make a premature commitment about whether he prefers a desktop or a laptop computer (Stolze 1999).

This latter issue is addressed by *feature-oriented online-catalogues* (Steiger and Stolze, 1997). Here shoppers are presented with a form for specifying their requirements and preferences with respect to the desired features of a product. Once completed, the form is used to compile a query that is run against the database of all available products. The matching products are then returned in a list for inspection by the shopper. Feature-oriented search of products in the online catalogue can be problematic if shoppers are not experts in the product domain. For example it can be difficult for a non-expert in the domain of digital cameras to specify the mega-pixel resolution the camera should support, or how many photos the camera should be able to store.

This problem is addressed by *needs-oriented online-catalogues*. Instead of asking shoppers about desired features of a product, these catalogues elicit shoppers' needs and the way shoppers intend to use the desired product. Thus, a needs-oriented catalogue would try to determine what kind of photos the shopper intends to take and whether he or she plans to take the camera on extended trips.

To our knowledge only few online shops support shoppers in their search for products in a needs-oriented way. One of the exceptions is the IBM online store (http://commerce.www.ibm.com) that uses the metaphor of a sales assistant to guide users through an interview in order to determine their needs and ultimately presenting them with a personalised selection of products. Recently some of the feature-oriented catalogues (e.g. the CNet desktop decision maker: http://computers.cnet.com) have added support to help potential shoppers identify their feature-oriented requirements profile based on a fixed set of questions about the intended use of the product.

## 2. GOAL

The starting point of our investigation was the hypothesis that communicating with a non-expert shopper in a needs-oriented way would be more appropriate than approaching him or her in a feature-oriented way. We expected that due to the lacking knowledge of the domain, especially product novices (cf. Figure 1) would be better served when presented with a needs-oriented organization of the online-catalogue. To investigate this hypothesis we performed an experimental study. Below we first describe the experimental setup, then present the results and discuss our conclusions.

| | Domain Knowledge | Familiarity with Product |
|---|---|---|
| **Expert** | *Profound*<br>knows all terms<br>knows relevance of product features | *Partial*<br>specific expectations about range of products offered by a shop |
| **Advanced User** | *Limited*<br>basic understanding of concepts<br>knows most terms and many product features | *Limited*<br>rough expectations about range of products offered by a shop |
| **Novice** | *None*<br>limited knowledge of terms in that domain<br>not able to map individual needs to product feature preferences | *None*<br>no expectations about the range of products offered by a shop |

*Figure 1.* Three categories of online shoppers.

## 3. TEST SETUP

The test consisted of two test series. Each series consisted of a sequence of two system-guided question-and-answer sessions, one in which needs-oriented questions were asked, and the other, in which feature-oriented questions were asked. In order to investigate the influence of the sequence of these sessions, the test subjects were split into two groups, one group (Series A) began the test with the needs-oriented, the other (Series B) with the feature-oriented questions. After each session the data sheets of the three top-ranked cameras were presented to the users. Depending on the type of session, the information on these sheets was presented in a different order. If the questions were needs-oriented, then information on how well the given camera supported different uses was presented first. Otherwise the information about camera features was presented first.

### 3.1 Test Subjects

Twenty volunteers (aged 20 to 60) where tested. All subjects owned a traditional photo camera, but none of them owned a digital camera. All subjects were non-experts with respect to the domain of digital cameras.

### 3.2 Test Procedure

The tests were structured as follows. In the first step, test persons were asked to answer a set of questions regarding their expertise in the area of digital cameras. Only non-experts were admitted to the actual test.

Then, the first advice session was conducted: The test persons had to use the sales assistance system described below. The system asked ten questions concerning the person's needs or the features of the desired digital camera, depending on which of the two groups the subject belonged to. Based on the answers given, the 25 available digital cameras were ranked. The subjects then received the data sheets of the three top-ranked digital cameras, from which they were asked to select the camera they found the most appealing. The subjects were then asked to answer a questionnaire to assess the quality of the sales consultation for that session.

For the second session, the procedure was repeated with the other type of sales consultation (needs-oriented or feature-oriented). After completing both sessions, a questionnaire for final evaluation was presented. This allowed the subjects to compare the two modes of advice and to indicate their preference. At the end of the test the subjects received a small compensation for their time invested.

## 3.3 Sales Assistance System

In our tests we used the same system to ask ten needs-oriented and ten feature-oriented questions. The question screens were simple HTML pages that contained only a title, the question texts and the set of potential answers as active hyperlinks. The HTML pages were generated by a Java Server Page (JSP) that called a custom inference engine that identified the next best question to be presented to the user. Single clicking on an answer led to the display of the next question, i.e. only a single answer could be given to each question. Most questions included a "don't care" response.

The inference engine stored user answers and computed the current "best" question among the remaining unanswered questions. For this it used the stored "ability profiles" of the cameras. The profiles list the answers that affect the suitability of a camera in a positive or negative way. For the needs-oriented dialogs the profiles referenced to the needs-oriented questions and for the feature-oriented dialogs the profile referred to the feature-oriented questions. Figure 2 shows a sample (needs-oriented) profile of a camera. In the test we used an elimination strategy to determine the next best question. According to this strategy the best question is that with the highest potential for collecting negative evidence about the siutability of all the cameras under consideration.

```
<product id="23">
  <name>"Camera 23"</name>
  <url>camera23.html</url>
  <relevanceRules>
    <rule>
      <questionId Idref="Q_usage"/>
      <answerId Idref="A_usage_private"/>
      <relevance> + </relevance>
    </rule>
    <rule>
      <questionId Idref="Q_weight"/>
      <answerId Idref=" A_weight_light"/>
      <relevance> - - </ relevance>
    </rule>
    ...
  </relevanceRule>
</product>
```

*Figure 2.* Example of a camera description that contains needs-oriented rules of how answers given by a user affect the relevancy of the camera for that user.

# 4. RESULTS

In tables 1 and 2, the results of the two test series are listed. These results are discussed in the subsequent section.

| Subject No | Satisfaction with (first) session **N** | Satisfaction with (second) session **F** | Which session was more pleasant to use? | Which type of advice is better suited for novices? | Which session yielded better results? |
|---|---|---|---|---|---|
| 1 | 2 | 2 | F | N | F |
| 2 | 1 | 1 | F | F | F |
| 3 | -1 | 1 | F | N | F |
| 4 | 1 | 2 | F | N | F |
| 5 | 1 | 1 | F | F | F |
| 6 | 0 | 1 | F | N | F |
| 7 | 2 | 2 | N | N | N |
| 8 | 1 | 1 | F | N | N |
| 9 | 1 | 1 | N | N | N |
| 10 | 1 | 1 | F | N | F |
| Average | **0,9** | **1,3** | **8F/2N** | **2F/8N** | **7F/3N** |

*Table 1.* Results of test series A, where in the first session needs-oriented (N) and in the second session feature-oriented (F) questions were asked. Satisfaction is rated from very high (2) to very low (-2).

| Subject No | Satisfaction with (first) session **F** | Satisfaction with (second) session **N** | Which session was more pleasant to use? | Which type of advice is better suited for novices? | Which session yielded better results? |
|---|---|---|---|---|---|
| 11 | 1 | 2 | N | N | Both |
| 12 | 1 | 1 | N | N | Both |
| 13 | 1 | 1 | N | N | F |
| 14 | 1 | 0 | F | N | F |
| 15 | -1 | 0 | N | N | F |
| 16 | 1 | 1 | N | N | N |
| 17 | 1 | 0 | N | N | F |
| 18 | 1 | 0 | F | N | F |
| 19 | -1 | 1 | N | N | N |
| 20 | 0 | 1 | N | N | N |
| Average | **0,5** | **0,7** | **2F/8N** | **10N** | **5F/3N** |

*Table 2.* Results of test series B, where first feature-oriented (F) and then needs-oriented (N) questions were asked. Satisfaction is rated from very high (2) to very low (-2).

# 5. DISCUSSION

Given the relatively low number of test subjects a quantitative interpretation of the data must be approached with caution. Initially, when designing the experiment, we had hoped to confirm the almost 'trivial' hypothesis, i.e. that novices prefer a needs-oriented style of dialog vs. a feature-oriented. In fact we expected this result to be so strong that even a small number of test subjects would be sufficient to prove the point. After analysing the test data, however, we were surprised to find that the situation was not as clear-cut as we had initially assumed. Nevertheless, 18 out of the 20 non-experts we tested recommended the needs-oriented interviewing style for novices.

If we focus on the first session in each series–which reflects the situation of a client starting to use a Web site–our test data is still consistent with the hypothesis that non-expert users prefer the needs-oriented style of advice (average satisfaction level N 0.9 vs. F 0.5). However, with a difference of 0.4 on a scale from -2 to 2, the observed effect is quite small. Given the number of test subjects, the difference is not significant and could be coincidental.

The situation even reverses if we examine the average satisfaction levels after the second session. Here the feature-oriented dialog style received a higher average score (1.3) than the needs-oriented style (0.7).

Interestingly, eight users (six in series A, two in series B, whom we categorised as novices in the domain of digital cameras) did not seem to consider themselves novices, because at the end of the test they all personally preferred F but recommended N for novices. We believe that this is because these eight subjects are advanced users (cf. Fig. 1) who feel they understand the feature-space of digital cameras. After they underwent both kinds of advisory processes, they preferred to specify products directly in terms of features.

At least in some cases, however, the self-reported preference did not match the observations of the experimenter. In a number of cases persons were observed to have difficulty answering the feature-oriented questions, but still reported an overall preference for the feature-oriented dialog style. Part of the reason for this might be that advertising for digital cameras currently focuses on product features. This might precondition people into believing that these products should be selected in a feature-oriented way. We found evidence in support of this when one of our test persons mentioned (even before starting the test) that he just seen an advertisement for "3-Mega Pixel Cameras" and thus was predisposed to look for this feature.

## 5.1 Learning Effect

A proposed explanation for the phenomenon that users perceived themselves as advanced users after having completed the test might be that during the two sessions the subjects experienced a learning process. This interpretation is supported by the fact that in both series the second session received higher satisfaction scores than the first one. Closer inspection reveals that answering the needs-oriented before the feature-oriented questions, as in series A, enhanced the acceptance of the feature-oriented approach more (from N 0.9 to F 1.3) than if users started with the feature-oriented questions (test series B: from F 0.5 to N 0.7). However, this effect is not strong enough to be statistically significant given our sample size. Thus, while data suggests that non-expert users gain more domain knowledge from first answering needs-oriented questions, a larger sample size would be needed to prove this point.

We believe that the learning effect between sessions is partially caused by the fact that test persons after the first session had the opportunity to review the resulting set of cameras that were best suited to their stated needs. Thereby they were able to perform contextualised learning. This means that they could derive the relationship of needs and features from the three camera fact sheets presented: it was possible for them to see how the selected needs (series A) referred to the presented features and vice versa (series B).

## 5.2 Design Implications

From this test, we can derive the tentative recommendation can that non-expert shoppers should start with a needs-oriented style of advice. However, they should not be locked in the 'beginner mode' but should be given the option of switching between feature-oriented and needs-oriented ways of specifying their product requirements.

Related to the flexibility of switching modes is the insight–confirming a well-known postulation in the field of Human Computer Interaction–that visitors to a commercial Web site selling complex products should be given the option of (implicitly or explicitly) classifying their level of experience. The Web site then should provide an adapted user interface including targeted product selection advice in a needs- or feature-oriented way.

In addition to this more static adaptation it might also make sense to explore methods that opportunistically combine needs-oriented and feature-oriented ways of addressing shoppers.

### 5.3 Further Research

This study is a first step towards understanding how information about expected product-use can be exploited in online-catalogues to guide shoppers more effectively to desired products. Further research is needed in other domains and in other countries to gain additional insight into the relationship between the needs-oriented and the feature-oriented approaches of helping users select appropriate products. It should also be interesting to extend the focus of the investigation and explore whether other dialog styles and the presentation of other types of product information would show a greater effect. Given our current results, it seems promising to regard the navigation of non-expert shoppers as a learning process that needs to be supported.

## 6. REFERENCES

Hagen, P. R., Manning, H., and Paul, Y. Must Search Stink? Forrester Report, 2000.

Steiger, P., and Stolze, M. Effective Product Selection in Electronic Catalogs. Proceedings of CHI '97 (Atlanta GA, April 1997), ACM Press, 291-292.

Stolze, M. Comparative Study of Analytical Product Selection Support Mechanisms. Proceedings of INTERACT 99, (Edinburgh UK, August 1999), IFIP/IOS Press, 45-53.

URLs (checked February 20, 2001):
http://commerce.www.ibm.com
http://computers.cnet.com

29

# An Architecture For Web-Based Post-Sales Service In A Flexible Manufacturing Environment

Weidong Zhang[1], Frans Coenen[2] and Paul Leng[2]
[1]*School of Computer Science, University of Windsor, Canada N9B 3P4*
[2]*Department of Computer Science, University of Liverpool, UK L69 7ZF*

**Abstract**: Providing effective and efficient post-sales services is a significant issue facing industries operating in a flexible environment. The main problem is that the great diversity of the potential product range may make it impracticable to provide conventional support documentation for all versions offered. In this paper we explore some approaches of web-based information systems to support post-sales services in a customised manufacturing context. The major objective is to integrate various new technologies of Internet, Database and Expert Systems, such as JavaServer Page and Servlet Technology, JDBC, and Model-Based Methods, to supply on-line maintenance and diagnostic support to field service engineers.

## 1. INTRODUCTION

One aspect of commerce for which the Internet may be especially relevant is in the provision of post-sales services. It is becoming increasingly common for manufacturing industries to tailor their operation to be more in line with their customer requirements than (say) 10 years ago. That is to say that instead of offering a range of (say) 6 versions of a product, starting with a "deluxe" model at the top and working down to an "economy" model at the bottom; individual customisation is offered for the entire product range. This serves to increase the desirability of the product and (it is hoped) will encourage a corresponding increase in sales. There are, however, a number of difficulties associated with this approach, especially in respect of post-sales service.

For example, when perhaps 10,000 versions of a product are on offer, the storage of data concerning each version becomes problematic. More seriously the quantity of maintenance data required for an appropriate level of after sales service becomes increasingly difficult to 1) provide (in an effective manner) and 2) update. This is exacerbated when, as is often the case, the manufacturer is operating in a global market place. Thus although after sales services (i.e. maintenance) are seen as an important issue with respect to customer loyalty, there are issues concerning the provision of appropriate maintenance data that need to be addressed.

The issue of the provision and updating of maintenance information for manufacturers of the form described above is the principal concern of this paper. The aim of the paper is thus to provide a mechanism whereby maintenance information can be provided in a globally effective manner in such a way that it is both current and correct. In the delivery of field service information, the service agent in the field will hope to obtain information on demand, with minimal delay, after quoting only a brief product reference, ideally a unique identification found on the product. This information will be delivered by the product manufacturer and/or the parts suppliers. The obvious medium for the provision of the desired data is the Internet. However there are a number of issues to be considered. For instance the nature of the desired maintenance information, the presentation of the data, and the generation of the required information.

The rest of the paper is arranged as follows: 2. System Scenario, which identifies the basic entities and information involved in the proposed system; 3. Related Work, which reviews the previous research and development in related fields; 4. System Architecture, which specifies the system processes, system components and their relationships; 5. System Implementation, which describes the implementation architecture and the underlying techniques; and 6. Discussion and Conclusion, which discusses related issues and summaries the main findings and future work.

## 2. SYSTEM SCENARIO

In the delivery of field service information, three key entities are involved (see Figure 1). First, the service agent in the field will hope to obtain information on demand, with minimal delay, after quoting only a brief product reference, ideally a unique identification found on the product. This information will be delivered by the product manufacturer and/or the parts suppliers. In a conventional environment, it would be possible for the relevant data to be extracted from the product catalogue directly. In the flexible context we are considering, however, it will be necessary to create the information required by reference to the product design data and, thence, to data relating to the components of the product. The kinds of information delivered could be very diverse; we will briefly consider some of the more important categories.

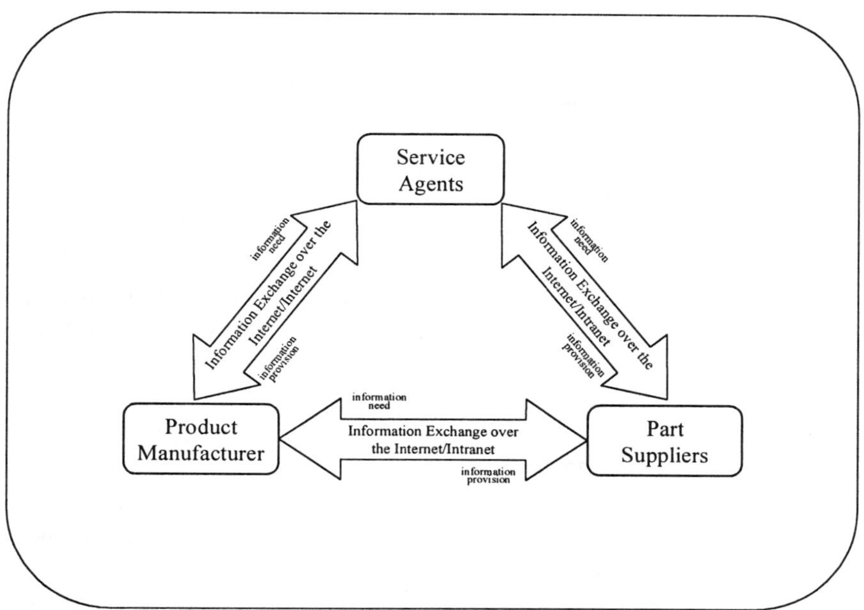


*Figure 1.* System scenario

## 2.1 Textual and other descriptive data

Usually, simple text descriptions will be a central feature of the information provided. In an online context, the presentation of text can be augmented and structured using hypermedia techniques [5], and the information incorporated may then include other non-textual data, including photographs, video clips, and animations. In an engineering context, detailed product information in the form of plans, engineering drawings, and design data will also be essential, possibly including access to a product database.

## 2.2 Product modelling

Even when dynamically generated and augmented by non-textual information, product documentation is essentially an organisation of data into a convenient and manageable form. Product modelling goes beyond this, in presenting information on the appearance and behaviour of the product in a form which allows the user (in this case, the service agent) to interact with the description: for example, to configure the model with locally-applicable data, to conduct experiments, and to focus on specific features. Virtual Reality (VR) languages, for example VRML [4] and Java3D [14], allow product models to be built which incorporate 3D graphics and enable "fly through" simulation to illustrate behaviour.

## 2.3 Expert knowledge

Much of the information used by service engineers, as with other skilled professionals, may take the form not just of factual data but also of accumulated expertise. As in other domains such as medicine in which diagnosis is central, Knowledge-Based Systems may be expected to have a role here. Production rule systems [3] have been favoured by the Expert System community for many years, particularly for diagnostic systems which may often be represented readily in terms of "if-then-else" rules, and there continues to be active research into rule-based diagnosis in many contexts [12].

## 2.4 Case-based data

Another important basis for fault diagnosis in the field is the use of case data describing possible faults, symptoms, verification procedures, and repairs. Case-Based reasoning (CBR) systems [15] typically store case histories in some form of data organisation, fronted by a reasoning system. New cases are investigated by presenting relevant case data to the system which then attempts to match this with recorded histories in order to identify similar cases which may provide relevant information.

# 3. RELATED WORK

Each of the information categories mentioned above has been widely used in systems for diagnosis and/or explanation generation in a variety of domains. A distinction can be made between systems that are essentially descriptive, i.e. producing documentation for the target domain, and those that provide a model of aspects of the domain that can be used for experiment and/or to reason about the domain. When dealing with complex structures, however, even systems which do not attempt to simulate behaviour will require to model the target domain in some detail.

A useful review of current work in model-based and qualitative reasoning is provided by Hunt, Lee and Price [9]. Different types of model include, in particular, structural models, which attempt to capture important physical or logical relationships of components of the target system, and functional models, which derive the operation of the system from information about the functional behaviour of its components. An example of an essentially structural model is that described by

Xue, Yadav and Norrie [17] for use in building product design. This system also incorporates a knowledge-based system to generate building product descriptions automatically.

For our purposes, structural information is important: because the modelled product may be entirely new to the service agent, it will be essential to produce a model that he/she can readily relate to the real product, identifying components and their physical relationships. However, it will also be necessary, to describe operational procedures and for fault diagnosis, to build into the model representations of functional behaviour. Compositional modelling [7] derives a behavioural model from a knowledge base of the behaviour of components and their environment. Iwasaki et al [10] describe a web-based compositional modelling system, CDME, which formulates behaviour models of physical systems from domain knowledge. In CDME this knowledge is principally represented at two levels: an ontological level, which defines the vocabulary of the system, and a physical level, which describes aspects of behaviour in terms of this vocabulary.

The INT-OP project [1], concerned with the generation of operating procedures for chemical process plants, also incorporates elements of both descriptive and operational modelling. The system, CEP (Chemical Engineering Planner) produces plans which define sequences of actions to bring about specified changes in the plant. The basis of the system is a detailed model of the domain. Although the target domain of this project is more complex than the one we are considering, and the output more specialised, a number of elements of the work are relevant to our discussion. The plant model used defines a hierarchy of components and the connections between them, and a conclusion of the project was that the effort required to create this was substantial, and that tools to assist in domain development are vital. A further element of the model is a set of "pairs", defining associations between components. The significance of this in our context is that, for example, a fault identified in one component of the system may in fact be caused by a problem arising in a different component, with no close physical connection to the one under consideration.

A number of key issues emerge from the research described in the literature. The first is the need to integrate model-based aspects of the system with other elements. Hunt et al [9] observe that even in model-based diagnosis, much of the information that is necessary is not model-based, and includes data such as failure likelihoods for different components, and heuristics for fault localisation. Secondly, the need to derive information about a target product from data relating to its components calls for the use of intelligence in this integration. Finally, both these issues point to the central role carried by the organisational structure of data in the system. This needs to incorporate not only a detailed structural model of the target domain, but also behavioural information and representations of all the different kinds of information which may be called upon by the service agent. In the following section we outline the architecture of a system to meet these requirements.

# 4. SYSTEM ARCHITECTURE

Figure 2 illustrates a top-level processing procedure of the proposed system.

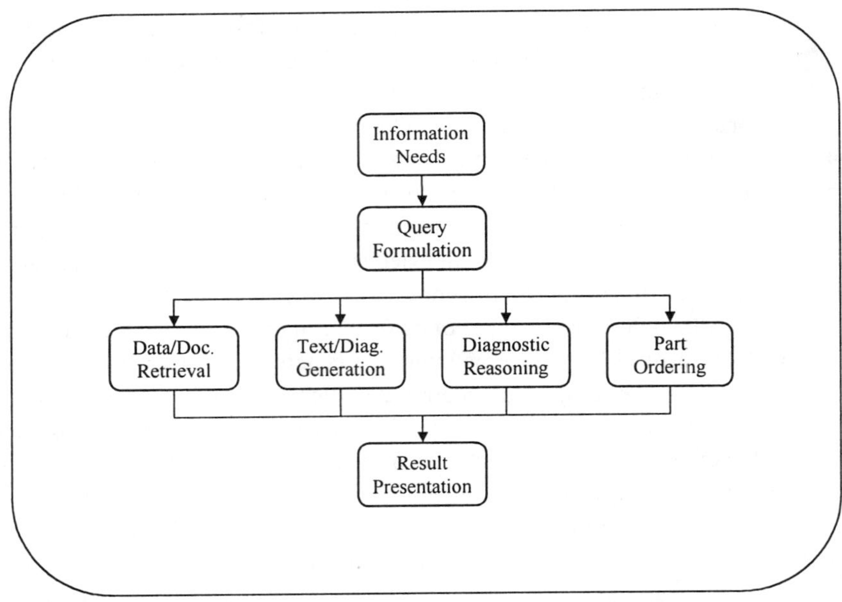


*Figure 2.* Processing procedure

Field engineers or other users raise Information Needs from their practical work. From these are formulated formal queries that the system can understand. According to the queries, one or more of the following could happen: Data/Document Retrieval, Text/Diagram Generation, Diagnostic Reasoning, or Part Ordering. Data/Document retrieval means finding some pre-stored data/documents which could satisfy the users needs; these could be of different media, such as text, image, audio, etc. Text/diagram generation uses text or diagrams for components of the product to create composite representations, for instance, 3D diagrams of products. Diagnostic reasoning addresses the other central aim of the system, to assist the engineer in fault diagnosis and repair. It may make use of techniques including case-based and rule-based systems to support this function. Finally, Part Ordering is provided to enable the engineer to obtain replacement parts when necessary. The result presentation takes the outcomes from the above processes for display to the user. Figure 3 shows a preliminary architecture for a system to support these processes.

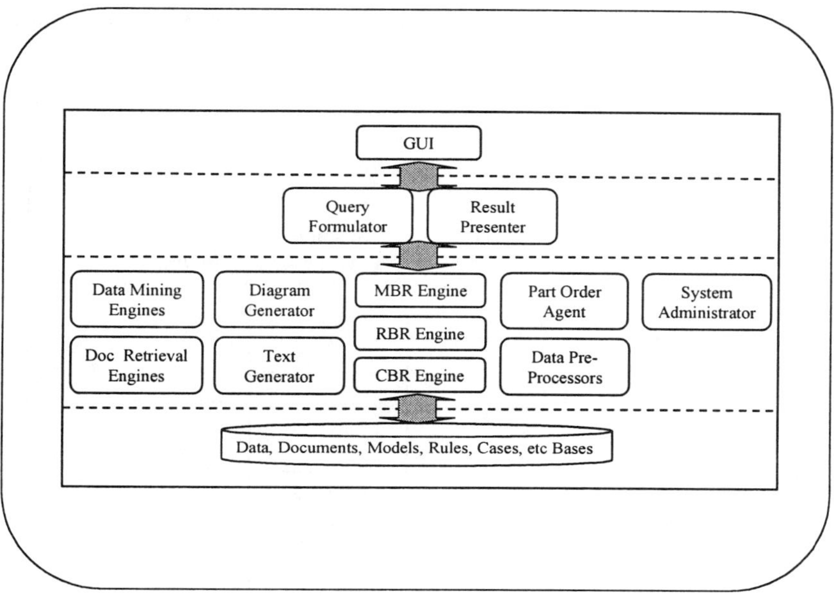


*Figure 3.* Integrated system framework

The system components included in this framework can be divided into four groups: User Interface (Graphic User Interface, User Requirement Formulator, Result Presenter); Processing Agents (Data/Document Retrieval Engines, Text/Diagram Generators, Diagnostic Reasoning Engines, Part Order Agent, etc); Administrative Agents (Data Pre-processors and System administrator); and Databases (data bases, document bases, model bases, rule bases, and case bases). Most of these components have a direct correspondence to the processes of Figure 3. The implementation envisaged represents system components in the form of servers or agents operating over the Internet; this could be refined with different kinds of architecture techniques, for example, Multi-Tier Client-Server and Multi-Agent Architectures. [6, 16].

## 5. SYSTEM IMPLEMENTATION

Figure 4 illustrates the architecture of the system implementation. This can be classified into four levels. From the left, the first is the client-side presentation, which includes pure HTML, Java Applets, and combinations of the two. This kind of presentation provides choices for graphical user interfaces across a company's Intranet or on the World Wide Web. Support for simple HTML means quicker prototypes, and support for a broader range of clients. Additionally, the Java plugin can be automatically downloaded to provide added applet support when necessary.

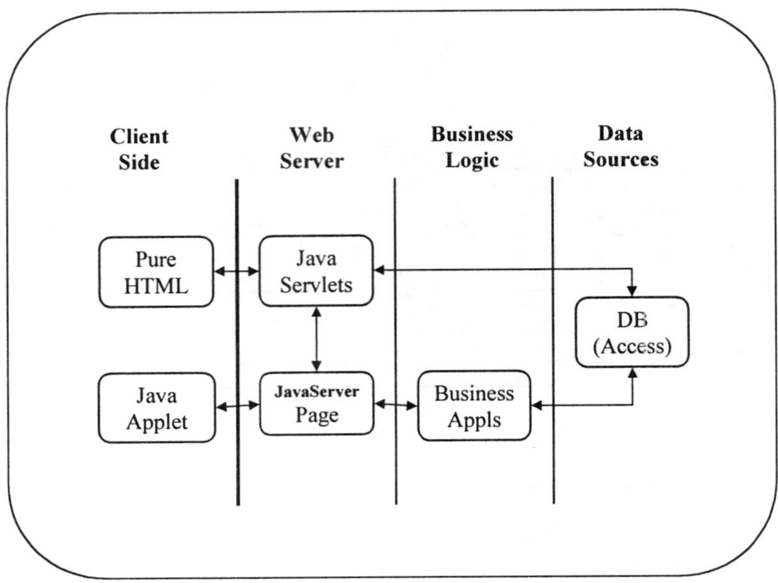


*Figure 4.* System Implementation architecture

At the second level is the Server-Side presentation, including Java Servlets and JavaServer Pages, and at the third level, Server-side business logic. The main technology here is JavaBeans. Enterprise JavaBeans (EJB) technology gives developers the ability to model objects by defining two distinct types of components: Session Beans and Entity Beans. Session Beans represent behaviours associated with client sessions – for example, a user purchase transaction – while Entity Beans represent collections of data, such as rows in a relational database, and encapsulate operations on the data they represent. Entity Beans are persistent, surviving as long as the data they are associated with remains viable. In this case, they provide a path to the final level, the database.

## 6. DISCUSSION AND CONCLUSION

The key issue identified in the architecture we have outlined is *integration*, which has two aspects: firstly, the integration of information relating to components of the product to create a composite picture, and secondly, the integration of the different forms of representation and modelling used. The first is the role of the diagram generator and text generator system components. The use of static "canned" information, however well-organised and presented, does not fully meet the demands of a flexible production process. The problem is, essentially, that the description of the product as a whole is more than a simple concatenation of the descriptions of its components. Dynamic explanation generation [13] can be used to reduce repetition of information and to produce a more coherent overall product description. This technique, however, applies only to text. A greater challenge is created by the need to pull together all the elements of the documentation of components, textual and other, into a single, integrated product description. This process may be seen as an aspect of product design, and appropriate design techniques, such as the use of CAD software, may have a role here.

The second major function of the system is to assist in the diagnosis of faults in service, and this is the principal purpose of the Model-Based, Rule-Based and Case-Based Reasoning components of the system. Operational simulation via a product model is particularly significant in this respect. Added intelligence may be provided by model-based reasoning [8], in which the model is manipulated by appropriate reasoning routines. A common approach is to use a "perfect" product model to generate a simulation of the correct behaviour of the system, and then to introduce faults to the model in an attempt to replicate the observed behaviour of the (faulty) real product. Model-based systems have in recent years found favour with industry, for example in the Tiger project [6]. Used in isolation, however, they suffer from the drawback that little or no explanation may be provided to supplement the observed model behaviour, so again, integration with the representational elements of the system is called for. Another goal is to integrate Knowledge-Based Systems with modelling techniques, including model-based reasoning and VR interfaces. Intelligent VR agents (IVRA) [2] adds intelligence to virtual reality to produce autonomous agents that model physical behaviour, using intelligence to guide the use of VR.

The Case-Based Reasoning element is also primarily to support fault diagnosis. CBR systems need not incorporate large databases; very often, a case base of some 100 previous histories will be sufficient to give useful pointers. In the present context, there are issues to be resolved concerning the matching of case data. Because the product under consideration may, in the extreme case, be unique, there may be no case histories relating to this particular model. Hence, it will be necessary for the CBR system to look for matches not just with the circumstances of the present case but also with the product model, in order to find, for example, cases in which a similar but not identical product has been involved.

# 7. REFERENCES

1 Aylett, R., Petley, P., Chung, P.W.H., Soutter., J. and Rushton, A. Generating Operating Procedures for Chemical Process Plants. Integrated Manufacturing Systems: The International Journal of Manufacturing Technology Management. 1999; 6:328-42

2 Ballin, D. and Aylett, R. *Intelligent Virtual Environment and Virtual Agents. Tutorial Material.* 19th SGES, 1999.

3 Buchanan, B.G. and Shortliffe, E.H. *Rule Based Expert Systems - The MYCIN Experiments of the Stanford Heuristic Programming Project.* Addison-Wesley, 1984.

4 Carey, R., Bell, G. and Marrin, C. *The Virtual Reality Modeling Language (VRML97). ISO/IEC 14772-1.* The VRML Consortium Inc, 1997.

5 Crowder, R.M., Wills, G., Heath I. and Hall, W. The Application of Hypermedia in the Factory Information Environment. Proc "FACTORY 2000" Conference; Cambridge: IEE Conference Publication 435, 1997.

6 Edwards, J. *3-Tier Client/Server at Work.* Wiley, 1998.

7 Falkenhainer, B. and Forbus, K. Compositional Modeling: Finding the Right Model for the Job. Artificial Intelligence, 1991; 51:1-3

8 Hunt, J.E, Lee, M.H. and Price, C.J. Progress in applying model based and qualitative reasoning to industrial applications. The MONET Newsletter, 1998; 1.

9 Hunt, J.E. Model Based and Qualitative Reasoning: Industrial Application. Proc 1st Int Workshop on Model-Based and Qualitative Reasoning - Perspectives for Industrial Applications; ECAI'96; Budapest; 1996.

10 Iwasaki, Y., Farquar, A., Fikes, R. and Rice, J. A Web-Based Compositional Modelling System for Sharing of Physical Knowledge. Proc 15th Int Joint Conf on AI; AAAI Press, 1997.

11 Milne, R., Nicol, C., Trave-Massuyes, L., Quevedo, J., Ghallab, M., Bousson, K., Dousson, C., Aguilar, J. and Guasch, A. TIGER: Real Time Situation Assessment of Dynamic Systems. Intelligent Systems Engineering Journal, 1994; 3.

12 Moulton, M. A Rule-Based Incident Tracking System. In *Applications and Innovations in Expert Systems V,* Macintosh, A. and Milne, R., eds. London: SGES Publications, 1997.

13 Rubinoff, R. Adapting Mumble: Experiences with Natural Language Generation. Proc AAAI-86; 1986.

14. Sowiztal, H., Rushworth, K. and Deening, M. *The Java 3D API Specification.* Addison-Wesley, 1998.

15 Watson, I. *Applying Case-Based Reasoning: Techniques for Enterprise Systems.* London: Morgan Kaufman, 1997.

16 M. Wooldridge, N. R. Jennings, and D. Kinny. A Methodology for Agent-Oriented Analysis and Design. In *Agents'99: Proceedings of the Third International Conference on Autonomous Agents,* O. Etzioni, J. P. Muller, and J. Bradshaw, eds, Seattle, WA, May 1998.

17 Xue, D., Yadav, S. and Norrie, D.H. Development of an Intelligent System for Building Product Design and Manufacturing - Part1: Product Modelling and Design. 1999

30

# Efficient Winner Determination Techniques for Internet Multi-Unit Auctions

Achal Bassamboo[1], Manish Gupta[2], and Sandeep Juneja[3]
*Stanford University[1]: IBM India Research Lab., Delhi[2]: Indian Institute of Technology, Delhi[3]*

**Abstract**: In this paper we develop algorithms for efficiently processing bids in a single item, $N$ unit ($N \geq 1$) open cry auction for a large class of winner determination rules. Existing techniques consider all previously submitted bids along with the new arrivals to update the current set of winners. We propose that at most $N$ "potential winner bids" amongst the previously submitted bids need to be used for such updates, thus significantly reducing the computation time and memory requirements. This is crucial when a large number of auctions are being conducted simultaneously. For a commonly used greedy auction rule we show that the expected number of potential winner bids may be much less than $N$ under reasonable probabilistic assumptions.

## 1. INTRODUCTION

The phenomenon of a website attracting millions of users in a short duration is becoming increasingly frequent. On July 14, 1998, the Guinness Book of World Records recognized the 1998 Olympic Games Web Site for two world records (see Iyenger et. al. 1998). The first was for receiving 634.7 million requests over the 16 days of the Olympic games. The second was set when 110,414 hits were received in a single minute around the time of the Women's Figure Skating. We have come a long way since then. The use of Internet to facilitate commerce, and in particular auctions, has also been growing at a rapid rate. It is not unreasonable to expect that an auction sale of a superstar's memorabilia in a sports event may attract thousands of bidders. Such a large number of participants in an auction can put immense load at a web server.

We refer the reader to McAfee and McMillan (1987) and Milgrom (1989) for a comprehensive survey on auctions theory. Varian (1995) provides an overview of the design of economic mechanisms for auctions. Wurman et. al. (2000) present an extensive breakdown of the auction space that captures the essential similarities and differences of many auction mechanisms in a format more descriptive and useful than simple taxonomies. Sandholm (1999) presents a scalable search algorithm for optimal winner determination in a combinatorial auction. Internet commerce technologies for different kinds of auctions: open-cry, sealed bid, and Dutch auction (see Kumar and Feldman 1998a, 1998b) have been developed for Websphere Commerce Suite (WCS 4.1), IBM's commerce server. While Kumar and Feldman (1998a), (1998b) describe how these auctions may be conducted on the Internet, they do not discuss issues related to improving performance and scalability of these auctions.

In this paper our focus is on quickly determining winner bids in an open-cry auction for $N$ units ($N \geq 1$) of a single item. For such auctions, an obvious allocation strategy is to assign the units to the bidders in a descending order of the price/unit offered by them. However, this may not be feasible all the time. For example, a bid desiring multiple units that wants "all or nothing" may be rejected if the quantity demanded is not available. Also, the same bid may be accepted at a later time (and a previously accepted bid rejected) if a newly arriving bid makes it attractive and feasible to include it along with the rejected bid in the list of "current winners". Due to such complications, the existing packages such as WCS 4.1, at any time during an ongoing auction, combine the newly arrived bids with all the ones that had arrived earlier to determine the current set of winners based on the auction rules. In such cases, if the number of bids is large, the processing delays may be large and the server may even breakdown. Our main contribution is that we show that under a large class of auction rules (including those that are practically implemented) significant computational improvement over naive methods is possible in determining current set of winners. In particular, we introduce the notion of maintaining a small subset of well chosen "potential winner bids" amongst all the bids that have arrived at any time during an ongoing auction. The remaining bids may be rejected as "loser bids", i.e., they have no chance to qualify as winner bids in the future. We develop two such potential winner sets. The first one is simple to identify and update and is referred to as the "Coarse Filter Structure" (**CFS**). We show that the number of bids in CFS at any time is $O(N\log N)$[45]. The second one is more intricate and is referred to as the "Refined Filter Structure" (**RFS**). We show that RFS may contain at most $N$ bids at any time. These structures considerably reduce the response times to the bidders and the computer storage requirements since this reduced list of potential winner bids can be maintained as a set of persistent objects in the main memory for quick access and modification. An

[45] A function f(N) is said to be O(g(N)) if there exists a constant K>0 so that $f(N) \leq K\,g(N)$ for all N sufficiently large. It is said to be $\Theta(g(N))$ if there exist constants $0<K_1<K_2$ so that $K_1\,g(N) < f(N) \leq K_2\,g(N)$ for all N sufficiently large.

additional benefit of this is that the loser bids get an opportunity to quickly revise their bids.

We focus on two commonly used rules for selecting winners: namely, the greedy rule and the knapsack rule (explained in Section 2). The greedy rule is the most popular rule due to the simplicity both in explaining it to a lay person and in its implementation. We develop algorithms that quickly update RFS (O(log $N$) per bid) when the greedy rules are used. We also show that under greedy rules and under some reasonable assumptions on the probability distribution of the bid size, if the average bid size is $\Theta(N^{\alpha})$ ($0 < \alpha < 1$), then the expected number of bids in RFS is $\Theta(N^{1-\alpha})$.

There exists some literature related to the online knapsack problem (see Leuker 1998, Marchetti-Spaccamela 1995). Their focus is somewhat different from ours as they consider auctions where the final decision on whether a bid is a winner or a loser is made as soon as an arriving bid is analyzed. This benefit of speedier decision-making is at a cost that the solutions obtained may be sub-optimal. We, on the other hand, decide whether a bid is a potential winner bid or a loser bid at the time of its arrival. Our solution is always optimal.

In this paper, we theoretically demonstrate that the proposed algorithms offer significant improvement over the current naive implementations. To keep the exposition short, simulation experiments are not reported. The interested reader is referred to Bassamboo et. al. (2000) to view the orders of magnitude of the computational gains confirmed by the simulation experiments.

In Section 2 the commonly used winner determination auction rules for open cry auctions are reviewed. In particular, we review the existing implementation of WCS 4.1. In Section 3, assumptions on the auction rules considered are stated. In particular, CFS is identified and a theorem identifying the RFS is stated and proved. The updating techniques for RFS under the greedy rule are discussed in Section 4. This section also states a theorem describing the order of magnitude of the expected number of bids in RFS for large values of $N$. Finally in Section 5, we briefly discuss issues such as the bidder utility functions supported by the bid structure that we consider and the problems related to processing *order bids*, (i.e., a software agent that bids on behalf of a human bidder).

## 2. OPEN-CRY AUCTION: AN OVERVIEW

In an open-cry auction (also popularly known as “English” auction) of a single item with multiple units, the seller may specify the minimum starting bid. She may also specify a minimum bid increment that a new bid needs to have over the current best price (based on bids of current winners) to be eligible[46]. All currently eligible bids are displayed to the users. The set of current winning bids (based on pre-specified auction rules) is also identified. At the time of bidding, the bidder specifies the number of units desired. A bidder may also specify whether she would accept *partial* quantity or not. Once the bidding phase is over, the bidders with the high bids get the items being auctioned, but the price they pay could be different from what they bid. In a discriminative auction, also known as a Yankee auction, the winners pay the amount that they bid. In a non-discriminative auction the winning bidders pay the price paid by the winning bidder with the lowest bid. This is currently the trend on the Internet; sites like www.ebay.com use this methodology for auctioning off multiple items.

## 2.1 Greedy Rules for Winner Determination

Some notation is needed before we describe the greedy rules for winner determination. Recall that *N* denotes the number of units on a single item multi-unit open-cry auction. For any bid *b* let val(*b*) denote the price per unit offered. Let Q(*b*) denote the quantity requested in the bid and let T(*b*) denote the time of arrival of the bid. Note that if a bid *b* is willing to accept partial assignment of the quantity bid, then from winner determination viewpoint we may treat *b* as comprising Q(*b*) identical bids, each bidding for a single unit. This allows us to assume, without loss of generality that all bids in the auction do not accept partial assignments, i.e., **they want all or nothing**. Let R denote a set of rules of an open cry auction. For example, we set R=``greedy", when the greedy method of winner determination (see Section 2.2) is used and set it to ``knapsack" when the knapsack rules (see Section 2.3) are used. Let W(R, Z, *N*) denote the winner bids amongst bids Z in an auction for *N* units of a single item, where winners are selected using rules R.

Given a set of bids Z, *an example* of greedy rules for winner determination would typically sort all the bids so that given any two bids $b_i$ and $b_j$, the sorting places $b_i$ above $b_j$ iff:

- $val(b_i) > val(b_j)$ or,
- $val(b_i) = val(b_j)$ and $Q(b_i) > Q(b_j)$, or,
- $val(b_i) = val(b_j)$, $Q(b_i) = Q(b_j)$ and $T(b_i) < T(b_j)$.

We use the convention $b_i > b_j$ (resp., $b_i < b_j$) to mean that bid $b_i$ is placed above (resp., below) bid $b_j$ in the sorted list. In case $b_i = b_j$ one may break the tie arbitrarily by assuming small perturbations in the time of bid arrival. We refer to this method of sorting as *gsort*.

[46] A bid is considered eligible if at the time of submission it passes all the checks such as check on bidder's creditworthiness, minimum bid criteria, etc.

## 2.2 Winner determination algorithm

In this section we outline the algorithm, **A1**, that considers a set of bids Z sorted according to gsort and determines W(greedy, Z, *N*). The algorithm **A1** proceeds in a straightforward recursive manner. At any step it tries to satisfy the demand of the top-most bid in the sorted list with the available quantity (initially, this equals *N*). If the demand cannot be satisfied, the corresponding bid is rejected. Otherwise the demand is met and the available quantity is reduced by that demand, and the next bid in the sorted list is considered. The algorithm terminates when either all the bids have been considered or when the available quantity reduces to zero, whichever occurs first. Some notation is needed to facilitate the listing of the pseudocode for **A1**. Let $(b_1, b_2, \ldots, b_n)$ denote the list of bids in Z sorted in descending order using gsort. Let $X_i$ denote the available quantity when the bid $b_i$ is considered for allocation. The pseudocode is as follows:

```
Ψ = ∅, X_1 = N,  j = 1;
while (Z ≠ ∅ and X_j ≠ 0) {
   if    (Q(b_j) > X_j) X_{j+1}= X_j;
   else  Ψ = Ψ ∪ { b_j }, X_{j+1}= X_j - Q(b_j);          . . . . . . . . . . . . . (1)
   Z = Z - {b_j}, j = j + 1;
}
```

The set $\Psi$ returned from this algorithm denotes the set W(greedy, Z, *N*). Later we shall see that the RFS under greedy rules can be obtained by a slight modification of the above algorithm.

In practice, some variants of greedy rules may sort in a slightly different manner from gsort (e.g., if the two bids quote the same value per unit, then one may be selected over the other at random). To keep things simple we focus on the greedy rule that sorts using gsort and selects winners as described by **A1**. As will become apparent to the reader, *the key ideas of this paper can be adjusted to suit variants of the greedy rule through simple modifications.*

## 2.3 Knapsack rules for Winner Determination

A seller's revenue is maximized when winners are computed by solving an integer knapsack problem (see, e.g., Horowitz and Sahni 1990). To see this precisely, consider again the set $Z = (b_1, b_2, \ldots, b_n)$. Let $(\boldsymbol{I}_i: i=1, \ldots, n)$ be a solution to the integer program:

maximize $\sum_{i=1}^{n} I_i * val(b_i) * Q(b_i)$ such that

$\sum_{i=1}^{n} I_i * Q(b_i) \leq N$, and $(I_i : i = 1,\ldots, n)$ equals 1 or 0. Then W(knapsack, Z, $N$) consists of each bid $b_i$ for which $\boldsymbol{I_i} = 1$. Since the winner bids obtained using the greedy rule form a feasible solution to this problem, the seller's revenue under greedy rule is less than or equal to his revenue under knapsack rule. However, it is easily seen that if all the bids either request a single item or are partial bids, i.e., bidders are ready to accept any quantity less than what is requested in their bids, then the greedy solution is equivalent to the knapsack solution.

## 2.4 Implementation of Winner Determination in WCS 4.1

Assume that the auction starts at time t=0 and continues till time $t=T_{end}$. For $0 \leq t_1 \leq t_2 \leq T_{end}$, let $S(t_1, t_2)$ denote the set of bids that arrive after time $t_1$ and before or at time $t_2$. Let S(t) denote S(0,t). The winner determination algorithm in WCS 4.1 works as follows: All arriving bids are stored in a database. A process that computes winner bids runs periodically every $\tau$ seconds (currently $\tau$ is kept at 90 seconds). During run $k \geq 1$ of this process (at time $k\tau$), all the bids in the database are considered, i.e., the set of bids $S((k-1)\tau)$ that were present at the time of the last run, as well as the set of bids $S((k-1)\tau, k\tau)$ that arrived after the last run. The greedy rules (i.e., algorithm **A1**) are used to determine the new set of winners from the resulting set $S(k\tau) = S((k-1)\tau) \cup S((k-1)\tau, k\tau)$.

To get an approximate idea of the computational effort involved, let m denote the cardinality of the set $S((k-1)\tau, k\tau)$ and l denote the cardinality of the set $S((k-1)\tau)$. Clearly, in the above algorithm, the computational effort for sorting the newly arrived m bids along with the existing (already sorted) l bids is O(m log(m+l)) (see, e.g., Cormen et. al. 1990). In addition, in the worst case **A1** may require considering each bid from the sorted list to determine the current set of winners (for large m, this will happen if most bids do not get the quantity they desire). Therefore, the additional computational effort in finding the current winners is in the worst case O(m+l). During peak load, m may be quite large (much larger than $N$) and thus large amount of computational effort may be required. In the next section we present algorithms that drastically reduce this effort.

# 3. IDENTIFYING THE SET OF POTENTIAL WINNERS

We first motivate the need to identify a set of potential winners through an example. Denote each bid by a pair of numbers; the first denotes the price/unit and the second denotes the quantity required (assume that all bids ask for all or nothing). Assume that the greedy rules are used to determine the winners. Now suppose that $N = 5$ and the following 6 bids have arrived in an ongoing auction: (25, 5), (23, 3), (20, 4), (18, 4), (17, 2) and (10, 1). Clearly the first bid is the only one in the current winners set. We address the problem of determining which amongst the loser bids may in future become a winner bid and which amongst them can never in future become a winner bid and hence need not be considered in future winner determination. Note that if the only bid that arrives next is (30, 4) then along with it bid (10, 1) becomes a winner. Similarly, if (30, 3) is the only other bid to arrive, then along with it bid (17, 2) becomes a winner. Similarly, arrival of an appropriate bid could make (23, 3) a winner bid. It is easy to see that the bids (20, 4) and (18, 4) can never be winners, since the bid (23, 3) always supersedes both of them. Thus, the potential winner set includes (25, 5), (23, 3), (17,2) and (10,1).

In this section we make a set of assumptions that impose minimal restrictions and cover a large class of practically implemented rules for open-cry auctions. We also identify CFS and RFS and show that under these assumptions, at any time t, CFS (resp., RFS) retains at most $O(N \log N)$ (resp., $N$) bids from the set S(t) to determine winners of the auction at any time in future. Some notation is needed for this purpose.

Let $S^*(t)$ denote the bids $S(t, T_{end})$. Let $S_q(t) \subseteq S(t)$ denote the set of all bids in S(t) asking for quantity q for $q \leq N$. For notational simplicity we suppress the reference to t and let S, $S^*$, $S_q$ denote S(t), $S^*(t)$, $S_q(t)$ whenever this does not cause confusion. It is worth keeping in mind that the results shown below involving S and $S^*$ hold for *any* two disjoint sets S and $S^*$.

**Assumption 1** *Under the set of rules R, there exists a sorting criteria* **C** *for the bids in* $S_q$ ($q \leq N$) *such that any bid in the list sorted using* **C** *belongs to the winner set W(R, S, N) only if all the bids above it in the list belong to W(R, S, N).*

Note that this assumption is satisfied by the greedy and the knapsack rules when the sorting amongst bids asking for the same quantity is based on the bid value, e.g., under gsort (for example, (20, 4) is preferred over (18, 4) both under greedy as well as knapsack rules).

For any set Z, let |Z| denote its cardinality. For any number x, let $\lfloor x \rfloor$ denote the greatest integer less than or equal to x. When Assumption 1 holds, and if $|S_q| \geq \lfloor N/q \rfloor$, then let $T_q(S_q)$ denote the set of top $\lfloor N/q \rfloor$ bids of the set $S_q$ under **C**. Otherwise, if $|S_q| < \lfloor N/q \rfloor$ then let $T_q(S_q) = S_q$. Let $T(S) = \bigcup_{q=1}^{N} T_q(S_q)$. The following proposition easily follows from Assumption 1:

**Proposition 1** *Under Assumption 1,* $W(R, S \cup S^*, N) = W(R, T(S) \cup S^*, N)$.

This result implies that in any ongoing auction, if Assumption 1 holds, then all potential winner bids from set S lie in the subset T(S). In particular, the bids in the set S - T(S) clearly are the loser bids and can be rejected. We refer to T(S) as the Coarse Filter Structure (**CFS**).

**Lemma 1** *The following relation holds:* $|T(S)| \leq N(1+\log N)$.

**Proof:** Note that $|T(S)| = \sum_{q=1}^{N} |T(S_q)| \leq \sum_{q=1}^{N} N/q = N(1+\sum_{q=2}^{N} 1/q)$. The result follows by noting that $1/q \leq \int_{q-1}^{q} 1/x \, dx$. □

Thus, under Assumption 1, $O(N \log N)$ bids need to be kept at any time and the rest can be discarded. We now show that the number of potential winners can be further reduced under the following two assumptions:

**Assumption 2** *Under the set of rules R, for all N, if* $b \in Z$ *and* $b \notin W(R, Z, N)$*, then* $W(R, Z, N) = W(R, Z - \{b\}, N)$.

Thus, under this assumption, the removal of any loser bid from the set of bids Z does not alter the set of winner bids.

**Assumption 3** *Under the set of rules R, for all N, if* $b \in W(R, Z, N)$ *then:* $W(R, Z - \{b\}, N - Q(b)) = W(R, Z, N) - \{b\}$

.

Thus, if one winner bid b is assigned Q(b) units of the item, the remaining winners (call them B) are not assigned any unit and the remaining $N$-Q(b) units are re-auctioned to the Z - {b} bids, then the winners of the re-auction are the unassigned winners of the previous auction, i.e., the set B. Many practically conceivable rules for the open-cry auction satisfy Assumptions 2 and 3. In particular, it is easily seen that the greedy and the knapsack rules do satisfy these assumptions.

For notational brevity let G(R, S, N) denote the set $\bigcup_{q=1}^{N} W(R, S, q)$, let $Z_1$ denote the set $W(R, S \cup S^*, N) \cap S$ and let $Z_2$ denote the set $W(R, S \cup S^*, N) \cap S^*$. Thus $Z_1$ denotes the final auction winners that have already arrived (i.e., belong to the set S) and $Z_2$ denotes the final auction winners that are yet to arrive (i.e., belong to the set $S^*$). Note that if the bids in $Z_2$ require q units then the bids in $Z_1$ require $N$ - q units (assuming that all $N$ units are allocated). Intuitively one then expects that $Z_1 = W(R, S, N - q)$, since this is the best way to allocate $N$ - q units to bids in S. Since, q can take any value from 0 to $N$, it is reasonable to expect that $Z_1 \subseteq G(R, S, N)$. This is proved in the following theorem (its proof is given in the Appendix). We also show that the number of bids in G(R, S, $N$) (and hence $Z_1$) is upper bounded by $N$.

**Theorem 1** *If R satisfies Assumptions 2 and 3, then*

$$Z_1 \subseteq G(R, S, N). \quad \ldots \ldots \ldots \ldots \ldots (2)$$

*In addition, for all* $j \geq 1$,

$$|G(R, S, j)| \leq |G(R, S, j - 1)| + 1 \leq j. \quad \ldots \ldots \ldots (3)$$

Thus, the above theorem states that if Assumptions 2 and 3 hold then at any time t, at most $N$ bids amongst S are potential winners. In particular, the bids in S - G(R, S, $N$) are the loser bids that can be rejected. We shall henceforth refer to G(R, S, $N$) as the Refined Filter Structure (**RFS**). Note that it is easy to construct an $S^*$ so that $Z_2$ requires any quantity from 0 to N. Therefore any set (W(R, S, q): $1 \leq q \leq N$) can be a subset of a winner set for an appropriate $S^*$. In particular, for any bid $b \in$ G(R, S, $N$), there exists an $S^*$ so that b is a final winner bid. It follows that RFS cannot be further trimmed. Suppose that, in an auction, we wish to compute the current set of winners at discrete time intervals ($t_1$, $t_2$, ..., $t_k$). Then the above theorem suggests that, at any time $t_i$, we retain only the bids in G(R, S($t_i$), $N$) and use them to compute W(R, S($t_i$), $N$).

## 3.1 Updating CFS

Note that CFS is easy to update as the new bids arrive. If the newly arrived bid requires q units then it may be inserted in $T_q(S_q)$ in O(log ($N$)) time (using binary sort techniques). Furthermore, if, after announcing the current set of winners, an auction receives a large number of bids (much larger than $N$), then there is a significant chance that an arrived bid will not change CFS. It may then be desirable to first compare the newly arrived bid requiring q units with the last bid in the set $T_q(S_q)$, and reject the lower of the two (only if $|T_q(S_q)| = \lfloor N/q \rfloor$).

# 4. UPDATING RFS UNDER GREEDY RULES

It is noteworthy that when knapsack winner determination rules are used, updating RFS may be computationally expensive and hence CFS may be preferred over RFS. We refer the reader to Bassamboo et. al. (2000) for a discussion on how RFS may be updated using standard dynamic programming techniques under knapsack rules. Fortunately, greedy rules have a nice recursive structure that may be exploited to efficiently compute RFS. Lemma 2 states the key recursive relationship that proves useful in efficiently determining RFS under greedy rules. To aid in its statement let r(x, y) denote max(x - y, y - 1), let n denote the cardinality of the set of bids Z and let ($b_1$, $b_2$, ..., $b_n$) denote the list of these bids sorted in descending order using gsort.

**Lemma 2** *For $j \geq Q(b_1)$,*

$$G(greedy, Z, j) = \{b_1\} \cup G(greedy, Z - \{b_1\}, r(j, Q(b_1)). \quad (4)$$

*For $j < Q(b_1)$,*

$$G(greedy, Z, j) = G(greedy, Z - \{b_1\}, j). \quad (5)$$

Proof of Lemma 2 is given in the appendix. In view of this lemma, the algorithm for determining G(greedy, Z, *N*) is a simple modification of **A1**. This algorithm, call it **A2**, is identical to **A1** except that in (1), the step $X_{j+1} = X_j - Q(b_j)$ is replaced by $X_{j+1} = r(X_j, Q(b_j))$.

Note that the output $\Psi$ is the set G(greedy, Z, *N*) and that the elements in $\Psi$ may easily be maintained as a sorted list (based on gsort). Also, analogous to **A1**, for all j, after bids $\{b_1, b_2, \ldots, b_{j-1}\}$ have been examined, **A2** proceeds recursively to solve the smaller problem of determining G(greedy, $Z^j$, $X_j$), where $Z^j = \{b_j, \ldots, b_n\}$. The computational effort required in the above algorithm is O(n log n) for sorting Z, and O(n) for finding G(greedy, Z, *N*). For large set Z the effort required in sorting it can be high. We refer the reader to Bassamboo et. al. (2000) for updating procedures that do not require the sorted Z. In particular, it discusses RFS updating techniques that require O(log N) updating computational effort per bid.

## 4.1 Expected number of potential winner bids

Although, we have an upper bound of *N* on G(greedy, Z, *N*) and it is easy to create cases where this bound is achieved (e.g., when all the top bids request a single item), simulation experiments show that number of bids in G(greedy, Z, *N*) is typically much smaller (see Bassamboo et. al. 2000). We now conduct an order of magnitude analysis of the expected number of bids in G(greedy, Z, *N*) under some reasonable assumptions on the probability distribution of bid sizes. Our conclusion is that for large *N*, this expectation typically is much smaller than *N*. Let $\tau$ denote the number of bids in the set G(greedy, Z, *N*).

Assumption 4 explains the class of probability distributions on the sizes of bids that we consider. This assumption is somewhat restrictive to avoid undue mathematical technicalities. It however covers many cases of practical relevance (as discussed later) and provides insight explaining the order of magnitude of the expected number of bids in G(greedy, Z, *N*).

**Assumption 4** *There exist positive numbers $\overline{Q}$, $\beta$, $\gamma$ and $0 \leq \alpha \leq 1$ such that $\overline{Q} = \Theta(N^{\alpha})$, and $\beta/N^{\alpha} \leq P(Q(b_i) = q) \leq \gamma/N^{\alpha}$ for $q \leq \overline{Q}$ for all $i \leq n$ and $P(Q(b_i) = q)=0$ otherwise for all $i \leq n$.*

For example, the case where each $Q(b_i)$ takes values from 1 to $N$ with equal probability is modeled by taking $\alpha = 1, \overline{Q} = N$ and $\beta = \gamma = 1$. To capture the setting where the bids are predominantly small in size, we may consider a smaller $\overline{Q}$, for example, $\overline{Q} = \Theta(\sqrt{N})$ or $\overline{Q} = \Theta(1)$. We now state the main theorem of this section. Its proof involves lengthy technicalities and is given in Bassamboo et. al. (2000).

**Theorem 2** *Under Assumption 4,* $E(\tau) = \Theta(N^{1-\alpha}) + O(\log N)$.

# 5. DISCUSSION OF SOME PRACTICAL ISSUES

## 5.1 Bidders with Decreasing Marginal Utility Functions[47]

Economic theory postulates that most bidders have decreasing marginal utility functions. It is noteworthy that the bids permitted in our discussion can support such bidders. Thus, suppose that the bidder is willing to bid $v_1$ for the first unit, $v_2$ for the second unit, ..., $v_k$ for k-th unit, where $v_1 > v_2 > \cdots > v_k > 0$. Then she may maximize her utility function by sending k bids each of size 1 and price $v_1, v_2, \ldots, v_k$, respectively. Clearly, a bid with price $v_i$ wins only if bids with price $v_j$ win for all $j < i$ (both under greedy and knapsack rules). However, when $v_i$'s are not monotonically non-increasing (e.g., first unit is worth \$0, second is worth \$5 and the third is worth \$4), further research is needed to determine efficient computation techniques.

## 5.2 Order Bids

At most of the Internet sites conducting open-cry auctions, the bidders are given the option of placing a regular bid (i.e., bid where a unique bid value is specified) or placing an *order bid* (also called *proxy bid*), i.e., a software agent that bids on behalf of a human bidder. An order bid differs from the regular bid in the sense that it specifies the bidder's *maximum bidding limit* instead of a unique bid value. The following simple assumption (satisfied by both greedy and knapsack rules) on the auction rules makes winner determination straightforward, even when order bids are involved:

**Assumption 5** *Under auction rules R, if* $b \in W(R, S, N)$ *for a given val(b), then, keeping all else fixed,* $b \in W(R, S, N)$ *even if val(b) is increased.*

[47] We thank Terence Kelly (Univ. of Michigan) for pointing this out and for related discussions.

Thus, to determine the winners in an auction that allows regular bids and order bids, each order bid may be treated as a regular bid with the maximum bidding limit treated as its bid value. Thus an order bid may only send a single bid. The issue of the amount the order bid needs to pay is a complex one, that will be addressed by the authors elsewhere.

# 6. CONCLUSION AND FURTHER RESEARCH AREAS

In this paper we introduced the concept that for a large class of winner determination rules, at any time in an ongoing auction, amongst all the arrived bids, it is possible to identify a small subset that contains all potential winner bids. We focussed on multiple N unit single item auction. For this auction we identified the minimal subset of potential winner bids and showed that it contains at most N bids. We further showed that on an average this number may be much less than N if the bids arriving require large quantities. We demonstrated that this approach may provide computational benefits as well as improved response times to customers.

The following are some issues arising from this work that need further attention: In our analysis we assumed that the bidder may not retract or modify her bid. Theory needs to be developed to address this. Research is also needed to see how these ideas extend to combinatorial auctions where more than one item is auctioned. In this paper we focussed on bids that demanded all or nothing. We discussed that if a bidder has a marginally decreasing utility function then her bids can be easily incorporated in our framework. Further research is needed to efficiently identify winner bids and potential winner bids when the bidder utility function is more general.

# 7. APPENDIX

**PROOF of Theorem 1:** Assumption 2 implies that $Z_1 \cup Z_2 = W(R, S \cup Z_2, N)$. Assumption 3 further implies that $Z_1 = W(R, S, N - \Sigma_{\beta \in Z2} Q(b))$ from which (2) follows. We prove (3) using induction on the number of identical items on auction. Note that $|G(R, S, 1)|$ equals 0 or 1, depending on whether W(R, S, 1) is empty or not. Assume that (3) holds for all $j \leq m$. We now show that it holds for m+1 by assuming the contrary and showing a contradiction. Thus, suppose that there exist bids $b_1, b_2 \in G(R, S, m+1)$ and $b_1, b_2 \notin G(R, S, m)$. This implies that $b_1, b_2 \in W(R, S, m+1)$. From Assumption 3, we have that $W(R, S - \{b_1\}, m+1 - Q(b_1)) = W(R, S, m+1) - \{b_1\}$. Since $W(R, S - \{b_1\}, m+1 - Q(b_1)) \subseteq G(R, S, m)$, it follows that $b_2 \in G(R, S, m)$ giving us the desired contradiction. □

**PROOF of Lemma 2:** Note that (5) straightforward since $b_1$ is too big to belong to any W(R, S, i) for ($i \leq j$). Now we prove (4). Again for $i < Q(b_1)$, it is obvious that:

$$W(\text{greedy}, Z, i) = W(\text{greedy}, Z - \{b_1\}, i). \quad \ldots\ldots\ldots\ldots\ldots\ldots (6)$$

From greedy rules it is clear that for ($i = Q(b_1), \ldots, j$), $b_1$ will belong to the set W(R, S, i) and the remaining quantity $i - Q(b_1)$ will be satisfied from amongst the bids $Z - \{b_1\}$, i.e.,

$$W(\text{greedy}, Z, i) = b_1 \cup W(\text{greedy}, Z - \{b_1\}, i - Q(b_1)). \quad \ldots\ldots\ldots (7)$$

Hence, from (6) and (7), taking the union of W(greedy, Z, i) for $i \leq j$, it follows that

$$G(\text{greedy}, Z, j) = (\cup_{i=1}^{Q(b_1)-1} W(\text{greedy}, Z - \{b_1\}, i)) \cup \{b_1\} \cup (\cup_{k=1}^{j-Q(b_1)} W(\text{greedy}, Z - \{b_1\}, k))$$

and (4) follows.

## 8. REFERENCES


BASSAMBOO, A., M. GUPTA AND S. JUNEJA. 2000. Efficient Winner Determination Techniques for Internet Single Item Multi-Unit Open-Cry Auctions. IBM Research Report RI 0027.

CORMEN, T. H., C. E. LEISERSON AND R. L. RIVEST. 1990. *Introduction to Algorithms.* The MIT Press.

HOROWITZ, E. AND S. SAHNI. 1990. *Fundamentals of Computer Algorithms*. Computer Science Press.

IYENGER, A., J. CHALLENGER, D. DIAS AND P. DANZIG. 1998. Techniques for Designing High-Performance Web Sites. IBM Research Report RC21324.

KUMAR, M. AND S. I. FELDMAN. 1998. *Internet Auctions.* http://www.ibm.com/iac/papers/auction_fp.pdf.

KUMAR, M. AND S. I. FELDMAN. 1998. Business Negotiations on the Internet. *Inet'98.* Geneva, Switzerland.

LEUKER, G. 1998. Average-Case Analysis of Off-line and On-line Knapsack Problems. *Mathematical Programming* **29** (2): 277-305.

MARCHETTI-SPACCAMELA, A. AND C. VERCELLIS. 1995. On-line Knapsack Problems. *Mathematical Programming* **68** (1): 73-104.

MCAFEE, R. P. AND J. MCMILLAN. 1987. Auctions and Bidding. *Journal of Economic Literature* **25**: 699-738.

MILGROM, P. 1989. Auctions and Bidding: a primer. *Journal of Economic Perspective* **3** (3):3-22.

SANDHOLM, T. 1999. An Algorithm for Optimal Winner Determination in Combinatorial Auctions. *International Joint Conference on Artificial Intelligence (IJCAI)*. Stockholm, Sweden: 542-547.

VARIAN, H. R. 1995. Economic Mechanism Design for Computerized Agents. *Usenix Workshop on Electronic Commerce*. New York.

WURMAN, P., M. WELLMAN AND W. WALSH. 2000. A Parametrization of the Auction Design Space, *Games and Economic Behavior*.

31

# "Figaro should be in Sydney by the 2nd of July" - Contracting in many-to-many e-services

Olivera Marjanovic[*)] and Zoran Milosevic[#)]
*[*)]School of Information Systems, Technology and Management, University of New South Wales, Sydney, Australia, o.marjanovic@unsw.edu.au*

*[#)]Distributed Systems Technology Centre (DSTC), Brisbane, Australia, zoran@dstc.edu.au*

**Abstract:** Dynamic e-business is the latest development in e-commerce that is based on a concept of many-to-many e-services where applications (services) can be wrapped and presented as independent e-services or composed to create new e-services. This paper investigates a problem of contract preparation in many-to-many e-services by combining temporal and deontic logic. Contract composition is illustrated by an example called "eBigMove".

## 1. INTRODUCTION

Dynamic e-business is the latest development in e-commerce that involves rapid teaming of companies with both familiar and new business partners in pursuit of specific business objectives. It is based on a concept of many-to-many e-services where applications (services), possibly offered by different companies, can be wrapped and presented as independent e-services that, in turn, could be further composed to create new e-services (Durante et al., 2000). Furthermore, to provide added value, it should be possible to customize and deploy composite e-services in a very flexible and efficient way. Thus, it is not hard to imagine that composition of e-services poses a unique set of technical challenges such as coordination, security, data integrity, dynamic modification etc.

Currently, there are many companies that already offer or are in the process of developing technical platforms and solutions to support dynamic composition of e-services. For example, HP's E-speak platform (Kuno, 2000), Microsoft's Windows DNA (including BizTalk), IBM's San Francisco Framework etc. For more details these technical infrastructures see (Kuno, 2000). As technical components are becoming available, the IT community is shifting its interest from technical platform issues toward modeling of business interactions in composite e-services.

In order to ensure legality and protect interests of all parties involved in e-services, business interactions are regulated by contracts. Consequently, many-to-many e-services poses some interesting challenges in the area of e-contracting.

The main objective of this paper is to investigate a problem of contract preparation in many-to-many e-services. The proposed model is based on a combination of temporal and deontic logic used to express obligations, permissions and prohibitions as well as various temporal constraints and estimates. To illustrate contract composition including verification of its temporal and deontic consistency, we use a simple example of many-to-many e-services called "eBigMove".

## 2. MOTIVATING EXAMPLE

At the time of writing, one of the authors of this paper is about to move interstate. As all people who have ever moved their house know, the "big move" requires contacting a number of agents and service providers in order to move people, pets, furniture and cars and get them at their destination on time. Thus, it is necessary to arrange furniture shipment, transport of cars, reserve and buy plain tickets, organise a move for Figaro the cat etc.

The big move is, in fact, a scheduling problem constrained by a number of temporal constraints imposed both by service providers and customers. For example, different furniture removalists have different schedules and take different time to provide a service (e.g. one provides a service 4 times per week and on average takes 2-3 days to deliver furniture). Figaro the cat, should fly on the same flight as its owners and if that is not possible, it should not arrive before its owners. Cars should be delivered after the owners arrive, otherwise the price for this service will increase to include daily parking fee at the airport depot. Customers (and preferably their furniture and pets) should be in Sydney by 2$^{nd}$ of July.

All service providers are independent i.e. they are not interested (expected) to coordinate their activities in any way. Thus coordination involves a lot of phone calls and paper work as customers have to negotiate individual contracts with each service provider, manually "compose" (i.e. schedule) their own "big move" and coordinate individual services.

Now imagine being able to find a service provider that is able to arrange a composite many-to-many e-service called "eBigMove". So, the customers wouldn't need to communicate with all individual service providers and manually coordinate their services. The provider of "eBigMove" would not only compose and coordinate individual services but also monitor their execution and, if necessary, replace one service with another one on the fly (e.g. in a very unlike case of airline strike).

Having in mind that different customers may have different requirements in terms of their temporal constraints, preferred service providers or priorities, this relatively simple problem of composition of individual services, can turn out to be very complex. More examples of complex many-to-many services can be found in construction industry (where a general constructor subcontracts a number of service providers from various specialty areas), film industry, telecommunication, software engineering etc. Note that, in general, companies forming coalition to pursue market opportunities are not a new concept. However, "the manual and tedious process required to form these coalitions limits the number of market opportunities that can be pursued" (Nayak et al. 2001, pg.2) as coalitions cannot be formed quickly enough to meet market demands. In the following sections of this paper we will concentrate on the problem of contract composition and illustrate how responsibilities and actions of individual service providers can be scheduled and coordinated.

# 3. E-CONTRACT BUILDING BLOCKS

## 3.1 The Reference Model of Open Distributed Processing

The reference model of open distributed processing (RM-ODP) (ISO/IEC, 1998) is increasingly being used for modeling of complex, open distributed systems. Its part called *the enterprise viewpoint* has been used as a practical framework for modeling of virtual enterprises, in particular e-contracts in B2B services (see for example Herring and Milosevic, 2001). In this section, we provide a brief overview of the basic concepts applicable to e-contracting.

A contract is an agreement governing part of the collective behaviour expressed in terms of roles and their responsibilities (obligations, permissions and prohibitions). An obligation is a prescription that a particular behaviour is required. An obligation is fulfilled by the occurrence of the prescribed behaviour. A permission is a prescription that a particular behaviour is allowed to occur. A permission is equivalent to there being no obligation for the behaviour not to occur. A prohibition is a prescription that a particular behaviour must not occur. A prohibition is equivalent to there being an obligation for the behaviour not to occur. To formally model obligations, permissions and prohibitions we use a formal logic called deontic logic. This logic was introduced by von Wright (1968) and later widely applied to modeling of organizational knowledge: see for example: Lee (1988), ISO/IEC WD 15414 (1998), Cole et al. (2001) etc.

## 3.2 Modeling of Time

The ODP-RM Enterprise view is yet to address the temporal nature of obligations, permissions and prohibitions (Cole et al, 2001). However, proper modeling of temporal constraints is critical for many-to-many e-services especially for their selection, scheduling, monitoring and coordination. Modeling of time and temporal reasoning have been investigated for many years in many disciplines including artificial intelligence (see for example: (Allen, 1981), (McDermot, 1982), Dehter et. al, 1991), temporal databases (see for example: (Jajodia et al. 1998), software engineering (Manna & Pneuli, 1979) etc. However, in this section we will limit our discussion to the basic temporal concepts used in e-contracting.

- **Absolute time**

An absolute time value (also called time point) is commonly specified in terms of UTC (Universal Coordinated Time). A pair absolute of time values *(t1, t2)* such that *t1* precedes *t2* ($t1 \leq t2$) is called a time interval.

- **Relative time**

A concept of relative time is used to model time duration that is independent from any time point e.g. 2 days, 5 hours.

- **Repetitive (periodic) time**

A repetitive time is a set of ordered time points such that the distance between two consecutive time points is constant and corresponds to some relative time value d. Thus, a repetitive time value can be represented as:

$$r = (tb, te, d)$$

where tb and te correspond to the beginning and end of a time interval that represents the domain of the repetitive time while *d* is a relative time value.

- **Temporal constraints**

Temporal constraints are different rules that regulate the order, timing and duration of individual actions. *Hard* temporal constraints usually result in some consequences if the corresponding action is not performed as required (e.g. late grant applications are not accepted). Soft temporal constraints imply that the original temporal constraints could be relaxed under certain circumstances.

- **Notation**

The following notation is used for formal definitions of various constraints:

- *action-id* is a unique action identifier
- *temporal-operator* ∈ {"<", "≤", "=" ">", " ≥ "} is used for comparison of either two relative time values or two absolute time values
- *d-limit* is a relative time value that corresponds to the prescribed time limit
- *type* ∈ {h,s} determines the type of temporal constraint i.e. *h* corresponds to *hard* and *s* to *soft* temporal constraint.
- *temporal-reference*∈{'b','e'} is used to denote beginning 'b' or end 'e' of an action.
- *deadline* is an absolute time value e.g. *Date1*, *Date2* etc.

- *time-period* is a relative time value that determines the period of repetition of an action
- *b-time-point* and *e-time-point* two absolute time points that determine a domain of repetitive time
- *otime* denotes an absolute time value when an action is estimated to occur

The above notation should be used when interpreting the following definitions of temporal constraints.

- **Formal definition of temporal constraints**

*A duration constraint* limits *duration* of individual actions as follows:

*Duration (action-id, temporal-operator, d-limit, type)*

For example:

*Duration (ai, ≤, d, h)*

prescribes that action *ai must* take no more than *d* time.

*Duration (ai, ≥, d, s)*

prescribes that action *ai should* take no less than *d* time to complete.

*An absolute deadline constraint* limits in terms of absolute time, when an action must/should finish (e.g. the deadline for grant applications is 15.March, 2001, 5pm).

*A_Deadline (action-id, temporal-reference, temporal-operator, deadline, type)*

For example:

*A_Deadline(ai, e, ≤, Date1, h)*

prescribes that action *ai must* be completed no later than *Date1*.

*A_Deadline(ai, b, ≤, Date1, s)*

prescribes that action *ai should* start no later than *Date1*.

A *relative deadline constraint* limits when an action *must/should begin/end* relative to the *beginning/end* of another action. The distance between two reference points is expressed in terms of relative time. Formally:

*R_Deadline(action1-id, temporal-reference, temporal-operator, action2-id, temporal reference, distance, type)*

For example,

*R_Deadline (aj, b, ≤, ai, e, d, h)*

prescribes that action *aj* must start no later than *d* time after action *ai* is completed.

Note that relative deadline constraints can be also used to prescribe order of individual actions. For example,

*R_Deadline (aj, b, =, ai, b, -, s)*

prescribes that actions *ai* and *aj* should start at the same time.

Periodic deadlines are temporal constraints used to prescribe the occurrence of an action in terms of repetitive time. Formally,

*P_Deadline (action-id, temporal reference, time-period, b-time-point, e-time-point, type)*

For example:

*P_Deadline (ai, e, d, Date1, Date2, h)*

prescribes that action *ai must* be completed every *d* time starting from *Date1* until *Date2* is reached.

A set of temporal constraints is *mutually consistent*, if and only if it is possible to find any assignment of temporal attributes (beginning, end and duration) for all actions such that all temporal constraints can be satisfied.

- **Temporal estimates**

*Temporal estimates* describe estimated duration and order of individual actions. They are usually based on the accumulated experience and are important for scheduling of individual actions and resource planning.

Formally,

*EDuration (action-id, temporal-operator, d-limit)*

For example:

*EDuration (ai, =, d)*

is interpreted that action *ai* could take (usually takes) *d* time to complete.

*Estimated occurrence* is used to express the fact that an action could occur after/before some absolute time or periodically every d time.

*EOccurence (action-id, temporal-reference, temporal-operator, otime)*

For example:

*EOccurence (ai, b, <, Date1)*

indicates that *ai* could start before *Date1*.

*Estimated order* is used to express how an action could start/end relative to the beginning/end of another action.

*EOrder(action1-id, temporal-reference, temporal-operator, action2-id, temporal-reference)*

For example:

*EOrder(ai, b, <, aj, b)*

is interpreted that action *ai* could start before action *aj* starts.

## 3.3 Deontic constraints

In role-based models (such as for example e-contracting), roles and their responsibilities have to be specified explicitly to prevent any possible misunderstanding or ambiguity. In terms of temporal attributes, a contract specification includes two temporal attributes: an absolute time indicating when the contract was signed and a time interval that specify the period of contract's validity. Formally, a contract can be specified as follows (note that for simplicity all other attributes are omitted):

*C (contract-id, ..., date-signed, c-begin, c-end)*

where c-begin and c-end determine the period of contract validity.

Now suppose that contract ci is signed on Date1 and has a period of validity is (cb, ce).

*C (ci, ..., Date1, cb, ce)*

As already stated, a contract is formally defined as a set of deontic constraints assigned to various roles. Our representation of deontic constraints is based on deontic logic that is extended to include the concept of time.

- **Obligations**

An obligation can be formally represented as:

*O(role, action-id, temporal-reference, temporal-operator, deadline, tdistance, ob, oe)*

where *role* is obliged to perform *action-id* either by the *Deadline* or every *tdistance* starting from *ob* until *oe* is reached. Note that *(ob, oe)* is the period of validity of this deontic constraint. This deontic constraint is properly defined if the following conditions are satisfied:

- Time interval (ob, oe) has to be contained within (cb, ce) i.e.

$$cb \leq ob \leq oe \leq ce$$

- Absolute time value deadline has to be within the period of validity of this deontic constraint i.e.

$$ob \leq deadline \leq oe$$

- In the case of repetitive time, Role must be able to perform *action* at least once i.

$$ob + tdistance \leq oe$$

The following are some examples of obligations:

*O(r1, ai, e, ≤, Date1, -, t1, t2)*

it prescribes that role *r1* is obliged to finish action *a1* no later than *Date1*. This obligation is valid from time *t1* to *t2*. Observe that *tdistance* attribute is not applicable to this type of deontic constraint. This deontic constraint will generate two temporal constraints as follows:

If Date1 = t2 then the deadline could not be extended and both generated temporal constraints will be hard:

*A-Deadline (a1, e, ≤, Date1, h)*

*A-Deadline (a1, b, >, t1, h)*

However, if Date1< t2 then the first temporal constraint will become soft:

*A-Deadline (a1, e, ≤, Date1, s)*

- **Permissions**

A permission can be formally represented as:

*P(role, action-id, temporal-reference, temporal-operator, deadline, tdistance, pb, pe)*

indicates that *role* is permitted to perform *action-id* either by the *deadline* or every *tdistance* starting from *pb* until *pe* is reached.

Similarly to obligations, a permission has to be valid during the period of contract's validity; absolute time value deadline has to be within the period of validity of this permission; and in a case of repetitive time, a role should be able to perform action-id at least once. For example:

*P(r1, ai, b, >, Date1, -, t1, t2)*

states that role *r1* is permitted to start action *ai* after *Date1* and it is valid from time *t1* to *t2*.

Permissions do not result in temporal constraints as they don't prescribe that action *ai* must occur. Rather, two temporal estimates will be generated as follows:

$$EOccurence\ (ai,\ b,\ >,\ Date1)$$

$$EOccurence\ (ai,\ e,\ \leq,\ t2)$$

meaning that action *ai* could be expected to start after Date1 and finish by t2.

The following is an example of periodic permission:

$$P(r2,\ ai,\ b,\ =,\ -,\ d,\ pb,\ pe)$$

that can be interpreted as role *r2* is permitted to perform action ai every d time starting from *pb* until *pe* is reached. This will generate a number of temporal estimates:

$$EOccurence\ (ai,\ b,\ =,\ pb+d)$$
$$EOccurence\ (ai,\ b,\ =,\ pb+2d)$$

The number of temporal estimates is equal to the maximum number n such that:

$$pb + nd \leq pe$$

- **Prohibitions**

As already stated prohibitions are used to express that an action is forbidden to happen. Formally,

*F(role, action-id, temporal-reference, temporal-operator, atime, fb, fe)*

states that role is forbidden to perform action-id during a certain period of time - that is determined by absolute time value *atime* and the period of validity of this deontic constraint: *fb* and *fe*. Note that prohibitions are defined for a period of time rather than repetitively. Similarly to permissions and obligations, this deontic constraint is properly defined if its period of validity is within the period of contract's validity and *atime* is within *(fb,fe)*.

# 4. COMPOSITION OF AN E-CONTRACT IN MANY TO MANY E-SERVICES

In a simple contract, it is possible to start from deontic constraints and then schedule corresponding actions based on generated temporal constraints. However, in complex many-to-many services, the same process cannot be easily applied because it is very difficult to specify deontic constraints (in particular their temporal attributes) without prior scheduling of individual actions. Furthermore, complex e-contracts may involve a large number of service providers (each with different temporal constraints and estimates). Thus scheduling of individual services (i.e. their beginning and end times, their order and estimated durations) can be very challenging and can involve several iterations.

To start the scheduling process, we propose to use a time visualisation method called a time map (as depicted by Figure1). Nodes of this map are absolute time points that correspond to beginning/end time of individual actions. Arcs are relative time values that correspond to distance between time points (e.g. duration of an action). All arcs are labelled by temporal operators ( e.g. "<") and some by relative time values indicating time limits ("<d1") – meaning that the distance between two time points should be less than d1. An absolute time value attached a node correspond to a deadline or estimated occurrence. To indicate repetitive time, a set of absolute time values is attached to a node. To distinguish temporal constraints from estimates, a darker font/colour is used.

Note that a time map constructed in this way may not contain all actions. The challenge of a proper scheduling is to find out how these additional actions can be linked with the rest of the time map in order to specify their order, duration and expected beginning/end times. As a solution to this problem we propose to modify and apply the Floyd-Warshal all pair shortest algorithm (Dechter et. al. 1991) that is used in artificial intelligence for temporal constraint networks. The algorithm has to be modified to take into account time estimates and repetitive time. The actual specification of this algorithm is out of the scope of this paper.

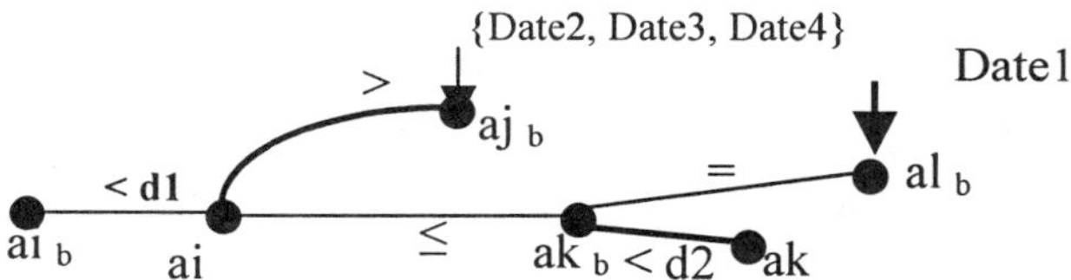


*Figure 1.* An example of a time map

Once when a possible schedule is found (as a result of this algorithm), it will be used for specification of deontic constraints for all service providers. The next step is to verify mutual consistency of the resulting deontic constraints. For example, deontic inconsistency will arise when the same role is both obliged and forbidden, or both permitted and forbidden to do the same action at the same time. In other words, if a role is obliged to perform an action during a particular period of time, it has to be permitted to do it at the same time. Only when all deontic constraints are specified and verified, it is possible to formulate individual contracts for all service providers.

## 5. WILL FIGARO BE IN SYDNEY BY THE 2ND OF JULY?

To illustrate the introduced procedure of contract composition, let us go back to the example introduced in Section 2. So how to get Figaro the cat, its owners and preferably their furniture and cars to Sydney by the 2nd of July. The provider of eBigMove service will start from the required actions and temporal constraints specified by customers:

- Transport people by the 2nd of July (assume that this corresponds to action *a1*)
- Transport Figaro at the same time or after its owners by no later than the 2nd of July (action *a2*)
- Transport cars so that arrive in Sydney after its owners etc. (action *a3*)

Then the provider has to take into account various time estimates:

- A flight takes 1h.
- Car transport takes between 1 and 2 days and it is organised every 3 days etc.

These temporal constraints and estimates can be represented as:

*A_Deadline( a1, e, ≤, "2/7/2001: 19:00:00 +10", h)*
*R_Deadline(a2, b, =, a1, b, 0, h)*
*R_Deadline (a2, e, =, a1, e, 0, h)*
*E_Order (a3, e, >, a1, e)*
*EDuration(a3, ≤, 2days)*
*EDuration(a1, =, 1h)*
*EOccurence (a3, b, "27/6/2001: 8:00:00 +10")*
*EOccurence (a3, b, "30/6/2001: 8:00:00 +10")*
*EOccurence(a3, b, "3/7/2001: 8:00:00 + 10")*

Then, the eBigMove provider will compose an initial time map (Figure 2).

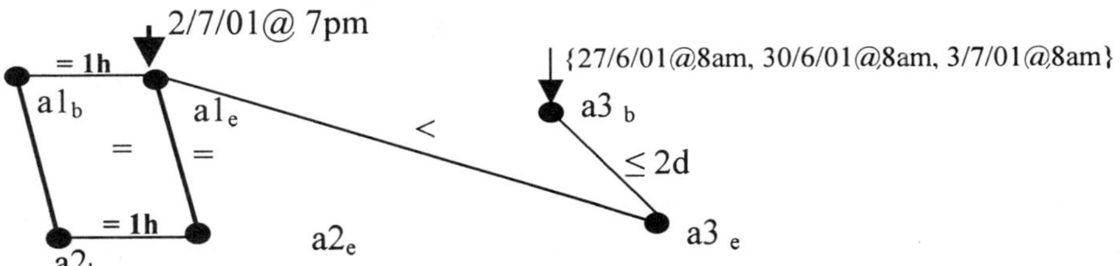


*Figure 2:* An initial time map for "eBigMove" composite e-service

Then, every time when a new service provider is selected, a set of new temporal constraints and estimates will be added to the existing time map. For example: A furniture removalist provides a service 4 times per week and usually takes 2-3 days to deliver it (Suppose that this action called "furniture delivery" is identified as *a4*). Furthermore, they require the customers to be present when furniture is packed for the transport (e.g. for insurance purposes), etc. This will result in an additional temporal constraint:

*R_Deadline( a1, b, ≥, a4, b)*

As a result, the two new nodes that correspond to $a4_b$ and $a4_e$ will be added to the map as well as a relative deadline constraint between $a1_b$ and $a4_b$.

Hence, scheduling of individual actions (services) is an interactive process where temporal constraints and estimates of potential service providers are removed, added and modified until a time schedule is found such that all temporal constraints are satisfied. Note that, the same schedule has to satisfy other constraints specified by the customer such as cost, quality etc. that are removed from this consideration for simplicity. In a case that a schedule cannot be found, then the customer is contacted and some of the initial temporal constraints are removed/modified and the whole process is repeated again.

When a schedule is found, the time map is then used to derive deontic constraints for all service providers. For example, the following obligation will be derived:

*O(Furniture-removalist, a4, e, ≤, "3/7/2001: 8:00:00 + 10", "30/6/2001: 9:00:00 + 10", "4/7/2001: 16:00:00 + 10")*

It indicates that a furniture removalist is obliged to deliver furniture preferably by 3rd of July at 8 a.m. but no later than the 4th of July 4pm and the contract was signed on the 30th of June at 8am.

When all deontic constraints are determined in this way and verified to prevent any possible inconsistency, the individual contracts can be signed. Note that the customer signs the contract only with eBigMove and they then sign a number of contracts with individual service providers. Thus, all these contracts are interrelated.

When all contracts are signed, the next step would be to monitor their execution and if necessary use the time map again to refine temporal constraints and fine tune execution of individual actions as well as coordinate the run-time replacement of one service provider with another. So will Figaro get to Sydney by the 2nd of July? Only if corresponding deontic constraints are satisfied!

After the same service is provided a number of times, the accumulated experience can be used to create new time estimates as well as to select the service providers that will satisfy customer requirements in the best possible way. However, monitoring of contract execution and analysis of the accumulated experience are out of the scope of this paper.

Although the previous example is relatively simple, it illustrates the complexity of contract composition and execution. Note that the introduced model can be further extended to deal with temporal constraints that are the function of different parameters e.g. price. In that case the scheduling algorithm has to be modified as well. This area is one of our future challenges.

# 6. RELATED WORK

A B2B Enterprise Model introduced by (Milosevic & Bond, 1995) is used as a basis of an enterprise model for many-to-many e-services. This model is currently being implemented using BizTalk technology and XML messaging (for more details see Herring & Milosevic, 2001). In order to support many-to-many e-contracting, we propose to extend the original model with a component called *contract verificator*. This decision support component needs to provide tools for construction and analysis of time maps, automatic scheduling of individual services (based on the

Floyd-Warshal all pair shortest algorithm) as well as tools for user-friendly specification of deontic constraints and automatic verification of their consistency.

Other related work in the area of e-contracting includes EU-funded COSMOS project (see Griffel et al., 1998 ) that provides the set of services that facilitate the use of e-contracts. Much of the system deals with lower-level communication and representation issues rather than more contract-specific issues.

In the area many-to-many e-services, one of the leading research and development groups is certainly the HP group (see Durante et. al., 2000; Kuno, 2000). Their projects include development of technical architecture e-services as well as modeling and composition of e-services. However, they do not consider e-contracting aspects.

## 7. CONCLUSIONS

The main objective of this paper was to investigate a problem of contract preparation in many-to-many e-services. The process of contract composition and preparation is based on a combination of temporal and deontic logic. This paper argues that proper support during contract preparation is crucial for the process of forming short or long-term coalitions (i.e. virtual enterprises) to pursue market opportunities. This is especially important for small business as they are not required to have very sophisticated technical platforms to be able to participate in service provisioning.

Our future work in this area will also include monitoring of complex e-service execution, dynamic composition of services during run-time and analysis of the accumulated experience on service execution. We envisage that the work presented in this paper, sets a good foundation for all of these future research challenges.

## 8. ACKNOWLEDGMENT

The work reported in this paper has been funded in part by the Cooperative Research Centres Program through the Department of the Prime Minister and Cabinet of the Commonwealth Government of Australia.

## 9. REFERENCES:

Allen, J.F. (1981), "An interval based representation of temporal knowledge", in *Proc. 7th Int. Joint Conf. On Artificial Intelligence*, 221 – 226.

Cole, J. et al. (2001), "Author Obliged to Submit Paper before 4 July: Policies in an Enterprise Specification", *Policy2001 workshop*, Bristol, UK, January.

Dechter, R., Meiri, I., Pearl, J. (1991), "Temporal constraint networks", *Artificial Intelligence*, 49, 61-95.

Durante, A. et al. (2000), "A Model for the E-Service Marketplace", *Hewlett-Packard Company.*

Griffel, F. et al. (1998), "Electronic Contracting with COSMOS – How to Establish, Negotiate and Execute Electronic Contracts on the Internet", *EDOC'98 Workshop*, La Jolla, California, USA.

Herring, C. and Milosevic, Z. (2001), "Implementing B2B Contracts Using BizTalk", *Proc. of HICSS-34 Conference*, Hawaii, Honolulu.

ISO/IEC WD 15414. (1998), *Open Distributed Processing – Reference Model – Enterprise Viewpoint*, January.

Jajodia, E.S. and Sripada, S. (Eds.) (1998), *Temporal Databases – Research and Practice, Lecture Notes in Computer Science*, 1399.

Kuno, H. (2000), "Surveying the E-Services Technical Landscape", *Hewlett-Packard Company.*

Lee, R.M. (1998), "A logic model for electronic contracting", *Decision Support Systems*, 4, 27-44.

Mana, Z. and Pnueli, A. (1979) "The modal logic of programs', *Lecture Notes in Computer Science*, Vol.71, Springer Verlag, 385 – 411.

McDermott (1982), "A temporal logic for reasoning about actions and plans", *Cognitive Science* 6, 101 - 155.

Milosevic, Z. and Bond, a. (1995), "Electronic commerce on the Internet: What is still missing?", *Proc. of the 5th Conference of the Internet Society*, pg. 245-254, Honolulu.

Nayak, N. et. al. (2001), "Virtual Enterprises – Building Blocks for Dynamic e-Business", *Workshop on Information Technology for Virtual Enterprises* (ITVE), Gold Coast.

von Wright, C.G. (1968), "an Essay in Deontic Logic and the General Theory of Action", *Acta Philosophica Fennica*, 21, North-Holland.

32

# Trading among Untrusted Partners via Voucher Trading System

Ko Fujimura and Masayuki Terada
*NTT Information Sharing Platform Laboratories*

**Abstract**: To provide highly usable electronic commerce systems at lower cost, it is important to utilize and co-ordinate the function-specific application service providers (ASPs) that are distributed throughout the Internet such as those providing matching, payment, and delivery services. In order to coordinate independent services that have not yet established trust among each other, this paper proposes to use electronic "vouchers" to link untrusted trading partners. A voucher is a digital representation of rights to claim goods or services and can be securely transferred between trading partners using the Voucher Trading System (VTS). This paper clarifies the basic functionalities that VTS should provide for coordinating untrusted trading partners.

## 1. INTRODUCTION

Electronic commerce (e-commerce) is generally conducted in three phases: (1) the marketing/matching phase in which consumers search for merchandise they want to purchase and negotiate with vendors, (2) the contract/payment phase in which the desired merchandise are ordered and purchased, and (3) the delivery/service phase in which the purchased merchandise are delivered or services are rendered.

Many e-commerce systems now provide all of the three phases mentioned above, but their level of usability is limited because of their excessive development costs. A recent trend is the establishment of highly usable and low-priced Application Service Providers (ASPs) that provide services restricted to a specific phase. Recently, product manufacturers and service providers have started constructing marketing channels to consumers by coordinating component ASPs (Figure 1). The reason for this is that this type of direct channel can reduce the costs of the value chain, and each of the three phases can be flexibly combined to satisfy the consumers' diverse requirements. On the other hand, in this form, the delay of each phase becomes significant as described below. Technology that co-ordinates these dispersed independent services is a key goal for realizing the next generation of e-commerce.

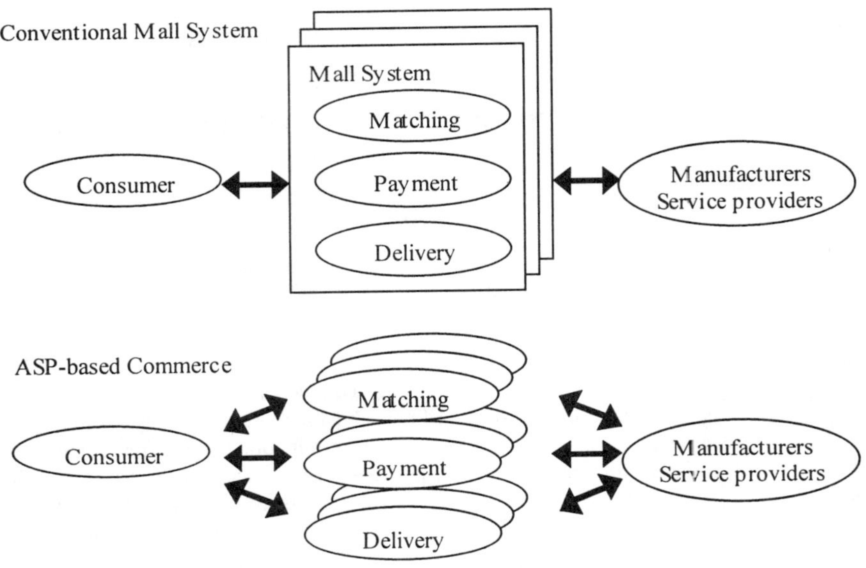


*Figure 1.* Transition in e-commerce

**Specialization.** When the three phases are provided by different, autonomous organizations, completion of service provision demands that the physically separated organizations must be able to co-operate with each other. In general, though the term is e-commerce, not all the phases are electronic. Searching for merchandise and negotiating in the matching phase are performed on the Internet, but the payment for and the delivery of merchandise will often be conducted at convenience stores or convention halls in the real world.

**Time dispersion.** There is no delay between the payment and delivery phases when the merchandise is exchanged for money. However, in the transportation or entertainment industry, payments are generally made for future services. For example, a passenger purchases a ticket before riding on a train. By collecting the money from the consumers beforehand, the number of cancellations can be reduced and important resources such as seats on a train or in a theater can be better utilized. In these cases, the time between payment and delivery can range from several minutes to several months.

Throughout history, physical "slips of paper" called tickets or coupons have been used for coordinating these spatially and temporally dispersed processes. The tickets or coupons are considered to be a physical representation of rights to claim goods and services. In other words, as the result of the payment transaction, the generic value represented by "money" is exchanged for specific rights represented by "slips of paper" and these slips of paper are used to confirm prior payment at the time the goods or services are delivered. These slips of paper representing rights do not just fill the gap between payment and delivery, they also represent a medium that fills the gap between the matching and payment phases. A discount coupon that represents the right to purchase items at certain price, or a queuing ticket that represents the right to purchase certain goods are examples of such use.

We believe that the trend towards dispersed e-commerce demands the creation of a new digital medium that can take the place of slips of paper. We call such a digital medium *voucher* in this paper. Unlike electronic money, vouchers exhibit a wide diversity in terms of the types of rights involved and issuers. Vouchers may be issued by individuals or companies, and the contents will vary widely. For this reason, if each specific voucher required a dedicated system, the implementation costs would be excessive. We, therefore, believe that a generic Voucher Trading System (VTS) capable of trading a wide variety of vouchers in which a large number of issuers can participate and share costs is essential.

This paper proposes a generic VTS model that can be implemented in several ways. We use application examples in discussing how independent dispersed trading partners who have not yet established trust amongst each other can be coordinated through VTS intermediation.

The rest of the paper is organized as follows. Section 2 provides a survey of related works. Section 3 describes the model of the proposed VTS. Section 4 describes a synopsis and the characteristics of typical implementation models. Section 5 presents application examples and discusses the benefits of the VTS. Section 6 discusses standardization issues and proposes a wallet architecture that achieves interoperability without sacrificing implementation flexibility. In this section, the trust model assumed in the architecture is also presented. Section 7 concludes the paper.

## 2. RELATED WORK

There are several previous studies that provide technologies useful for VTS implementation. Since the 1980s, hundreds of schemes have been proposed for implementing "electronic cash" [17]. Some of them can also be applied for implementing VTS, especially for preventing double-spending. This paper thus does not intend to propose a new/particular method for preventing double spending. Instead, this paper clarifies the basic functionalities that VTS should provide for coordinating untrusted trading partners.

TEDIS, EDIBOL [14], and Mandate [12] address the technical, business, and legal issues of circulating financial instruments, e.g., electronic checks and Bill of Lading. They also made many suggestions collected through their experience with pilot systems. The main focus of these works is large scale B2B transactions in which PKI or trustworthy identifiers of trading partners can be assumed. To the contrary, this paper focus on B2C or C2C transactions in which cost sharing is essential, and PKI cannot be assumed.

SEMPER [11] provides a generic payment service framework that allows users to handle several payment schemes in a flexible way. Its approach is comparable to ours, but our goal is to provide a more simple solution by assuming the VTS model.

Ricardo System [8] and SOX [10] provide a payment platform that enables a wide-range of financial instruments to be traded. Their system introduces a value description system called Ricardian Contract, which specifies two separate issuer entities, i.e., legal issuer and technical issuer. The legal issuer is responsible for backing the value of the instruments and the technical issuer is responsible for managing the instruments. This separation is also a key concept of this paper and we present a formal model.

We have also developed an implementation of VTS called FlexTicket and presented some techniques in previous papers. [6][7] are early studies that address the language needed to define diverse types of rights. In [13][15], we presented protocols that assured the "genuineness" of vouchers that were circulated. However, none of the previous papers focused on the business aspects of VTS.

This paper is based on a discussion within the IETF trade WG[48] and presents details of background and implementation models, in addition to the requirements, terminologies, and standardization interfaces presented in [4][5].

# 3. RIGHTS TRADING MODEL

## 3.1 Vouchers

A voucher[49] is a digital representation of the right to claim goods or services. A voucher is generated by an issuer when the issuer (e.g., manufacturer or service provider) makes a certain promise to a holder (e.g., consumer). This paper thus defines a voucher as follows:

**Definition.** Let $I$ be a voucher issuer, $H$ be a holder, $P$ be the issuer's promise to the holder. A *voucher* is defined as the 3-tuple of $<I, P, H>$.

Vouchers differ from electronic cash since $I$ and $P$ can represent a wide variety of issuers and contents, respectively. Contents can cover a wide range: one voucher may state that it can be exchanged for a hamburger, another may state that it can be

[48] The IETF trade WG mainly addresses B2C payment protocols and has developed IOTP [1] which encapsulates and supports diverse types of payment systems.

[49] The previous studies often call this concept "ticket," "right," or "bearer instrument [9]."

exchanged for one night's lodging, while a third may state that it can be exchanged for 2 dollars worth of train travel. The contents of a voucher can even represent some monetary value; the voucher may indicate that it can be exchanged for 100 dollars worth of merchandise. (Note: *P* does not need to be described in terms of a natural language provide the contents of the vouchers are specified. For example, the contents can be defined by XML to facilitate machine processing, and the identifier or hash value of the XML document can be used to specify *P*.)

## 3.2 Participants

In this paper, the VTS consists of four participants: the issuer, the holder (or user), collector, and VTS provider. The roles of each participant are as follows:

**Issuer:** Creates and issues a voucher. Guarantees the contents of the voucher.

**Holder (or user):** Owns the voucher. Transfers and redeems the voucher to other users or collector.

**Collector (or examiner):** Collects the voucher: generally accompanied by the transfer of goods or the rendering of services. Note that the roles of collector and issuer can be done by the same entity.

**VTS provider:** Provides the VTS and guarantees that there are no duplicate assignments or multiple use of vouchers.

The issuer generates the voucher, *<I, P, H>*, and the vouchers are circulated among users in the VTS until finally they are collected. The VTS provider provides the trading system to the issuer, user, and collector, and is assumed to be trusted by the other participants (Figure 2).

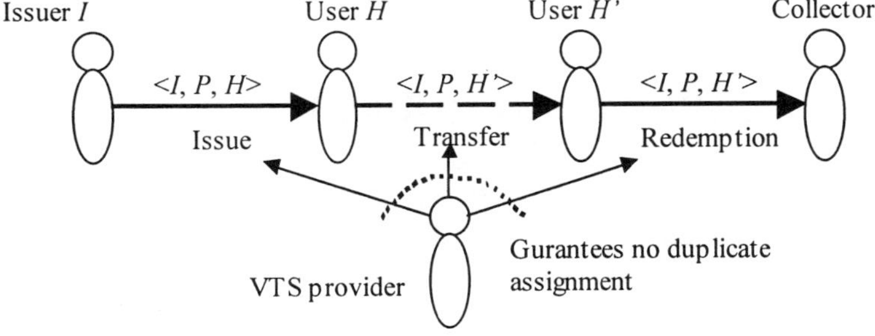


*Figure 2.* Participants and roles

## 3.3 Voucher Trading System

The purpose of the VTS is to provide a means of circulating issuer-generated vouchers among the users. The system must satisfy the three requirements described below:

**Prevention of forgery**: It must be impossible to counterfeit vouchers. Only the issuer generates vouchers.

**Prevention of alteration**: It must be impossible to alter vouchers during circulation.

**Prevention of reproduction**: It must be impossible to reproduce or copy vouchers during circulation. Multiple transfers or duplicate redemptions are to be prohibited.

A formal definition of a system that satisfies these requirements is given below.

**Definition.** A *Voucher Trading System* is a system that logically manages a set of valid vouchers $R \subset \{<I, P, H> \mid I \in \mathrm{I}, P \in \mathrm{P}, H \in \mathrm{H}>\}$ where I is the set of issuers, P is the set of promises, and H is the set of holders; VTS prevents the vouchers from being modified or reproduced except as part of the three transactions of issue, transfer, and redemption. The initial state of R is an empty set.

**Issue:** An *issue transaction* is the action that creates the tuple <*I, P, H*> and adds it to R to reflect the issuer's intention.

**Transfer:** A *transfer transaction* is the action that rewrites the tuple of <*I, P, H*>($\in$R) as <*I, P, H'*>($H \neq H'$) to reflect the original holder *H*'s intention.

**Redemption:** There are two redemption transactions: presentation and consumption. A *presentation transaction* is the action that shows the tuple of <*I, P, H*>($\in$R) to reflect the holder's, *H*, intention. In this case, the ownership of the voucher is retained when the voucher is redeemed, e.g., redemption of licenses or passports. A *consumption transaction* is the action that deletes the tuple of <*I, P, H*>($\in$R) to reflect *H*'s intention. In this case, the ownership of the voucher may be voided or the number of times it is valid reduced when the voucher is redeemed, e.g., redemption of event tickets or telephone cards.

# 4. IMPLEMENTATION MODELS

The Voucher set, R, described in Section 3, is logical, and management can be centralized on a network server or it can be dispersed across portable devices (e.g., smart cards) maintained by the users. This section gives a synopsis and the characteristics of these implementation styles.

**(1) Server storage type**

In this model, the VTS provider manages a centralized server in which sets of 3-tuple <*I, P, H*> entries is stored. The issuing of a voucher in this model is done by authenticating *I* and storing a new entry, <*I, P, H*>, in the server. The transfer of a voucher is done by authenticating user *H* and rewriting the entry contained in the server with <*I, P, H'*>, where *H'* is the new holder of the voucher. The consumption of a voucher is done by authenticating user *H* and deleting the entry contained in the server (see [13] for an example).

A key feature of this model is that the center's cost for development and operation can be shared among the many participating issuers.

**(2) Portable storage type**

In this model, the VTS provider supplies each user *H* with portable devices (e.g., smart cards) that store sets of 2-tuple <*I*, *P*> entries. A voucher is issued in this model by authenticating *I* and storing a new entry, <*I*, *P*>, in the tamper-resistant storage of a portable device managed by user *H*. The transfer of a voucher is conducted by generating the digital signature that proves entry <*I*, *P*> was erased from the tamper-resistant storage of *H*'s portable device (this authenticates the sender's portable device) and sending it to the recipient's portable device. The receiving portable device then verifies the digital signature and stores entry <*I*, *P*> in its tamper-resistant storage. The consumption of a voucher is done by generating the digital signature that proves entry <*I*, *P*> was erased from the tamper-resistant storage of *H*'s portable device and sending it to the collector (see [15] for an example).

This model is similar to (1) above in the sense that the smart cards issued by the VTS provider can be shared by multiple issuers resulting in a decrease in the costs of card issuance and program development. Furthermore, since the redemption of vouchers can be done offline, this model is superior to the server storage type model in terms of communication cost and availability. However, since a smart card reader/writer is required at the user terminal, this model is not so popular at this moment.

The above two models are typical implementation examples of the VTS proposed in this paper. In many existing types of digital ticket systems, the issuer himself manages the issued tickets or vouchers. These types are also supported by VTS; the roles of issuer and VTS provider are merged. Typical implementation examples of such existing systems are given below and comparisons of these types are made.

**(3) Issuer-managed server storage type**

In this model, a set of 2-tuple <*P*, *H*> entries is stored on a server managed by the issuer. Vouchers are issued, transferred, or consumed in this model by authenticating *H* and adding, rewriting, or deleting the entries on the server database, respectively. One difference of this model from (1) above is that authentication of the issuer is unnecessary since the issuer is also the debtor. Moreover, on the user side, user authentication can be easily established by using a credit card or ID card. For these reasons, many instances have been developed such as the ticket-less service of airlines and a concert ticket system.

**(4) Issuer-managed portable storage type**

In this model, each issuer of vouchers supplies users with portable devices (e.g., smart cards) that store sets of promise *P* entries. The assumption is that a user must have one smart card from each issuer. Vouchers are issued, transferred, or consumed in this model by authenticating *H* (the validity of the card is authenticated) and adding, rewriting, or deleting the entries in the tamper-resistant storage of the portable device, respectively. Since this method is easy to implement and enables high-speed processing, it has spread throughout the transportation industry in the form of the smart-card-based passenger ticket. Most current systems, however, do not have transfer functionality nor do they allow transfer over the Internet.

In the models where the issuer is the manager of the voucher ((3) and (4) above), the system is not fair from the user's point of view since the issuer can illegally erase the voucher from memory or repudiate the existence of the voucher. Therefore, as an application requirement, the user must trust the issuer as in the case with transportation companies. Additionally, as described in Section 1, each user in this model must develop a system capable of issuance, examination, etc., even though it is difficult for a small business to create an operation center or to issue smart cards independently. For these reasons, we believe that the model in which the tasks of voucher administration are delegated to the VTS provider is superior. One high priority goal is to minimize the trading cost of inexpensive tickets and coupons such as meal and prepaid tickets. For these applications, the portable storage type seems to be most suitable. Table 1 shows the relationships among the features of the different models.

| Type | Characteristics | Non-Repudiation | Cost sharing (Card issuance, Center operation) | Offline capability (Low communication cost) |
|---|---|---|---|---|
| Third party management | Server | Yes | Yes | No |
| | Portable device | Yes | Yes | Yes |
| Issuer management | Server | No | No | No |
| | Potable device | No | No | Yes |

*Table 1.* Characteristics of voucher management methods

## 5. APPLICATION EXAMPLES

This section describes, using a typical e-commerce example involving matching, payment, and delivery, how vouchers are traded using the proposed VTS, and why VTS is effective for coordinating untrusted trading partners.

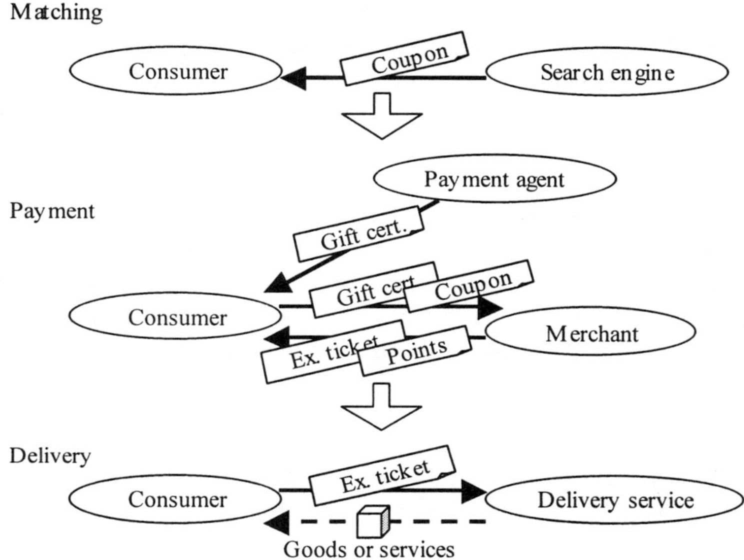


*Figure 3.* Typical transaction example of using vouchers

Figure 3 shows a typical e-commerce example of a consumer searching for merchandise and making a purchase:

**Matching**: A consumer uses a search engine to locate the desired merchandise and acquires a coupon that represents rights to purchase that merchandise at a discounted price.

**Payment**: The consumer purchases gift certificates from a payment agent site since "real" cash is not suitable for transferring credit. When cash is used to pay for gift certificates at a publicly accessible terminal such as an ATM terminal, the gift certificates are stored on a smart card in exchange for the cash. After getting the gift certificates, the consumer redeems the coupon and gift certificates at the merchant site; in exchange he/she acquires an exchange ticket for the merchandise and loyalty points.

**Delivery**: The consumer transfers the exchange ticket to the delivery service site and specifies the address to which the merchandise is to be sent.

In this example, the coupon coordinates the matching and payment phases while the exchange ticket coordinates payment and delivery phases. In particular, note that the exchange ticket ensures the cooperation of the mutually independent entities of consumer, merchant, and delivery service. In other words, there is no need to exchange contracts among the consumer, delivery service, and the merchant beforehand. The merchant exchanges the merchandise for the exchange ticket from the delivery service and the delivery service exchanges the merchandise for the exchange ticket from the consumer (Figure 4). This is possible even though the participants involved in the transactions may not directly trust each other; all trust the vouchers themselves. For example, even if the delivery service does not trust the consumer, the merchant that issued the exchange ticket is trusted, and if the VTS guarantees that there is no duplication of the exchange ticket, there is no problem in exchanging the exchange ticket for the merchandise. In the same way, even if the merchant does not trust the delivery service, the issuance of the exchange ticket can be verified, and if the VTS guarantees that there is no duplication of the exchange ticket, there is no problem in exchanging the exchange ticket for the merchandise. In other words, if there is trust in the issuer and the VTS, the trust of the user is not an absolute necessity. In general, it is difficult to manage the trust of individuals, so this characteristic of the VTS is especially effective in B2C or C2C transactions.

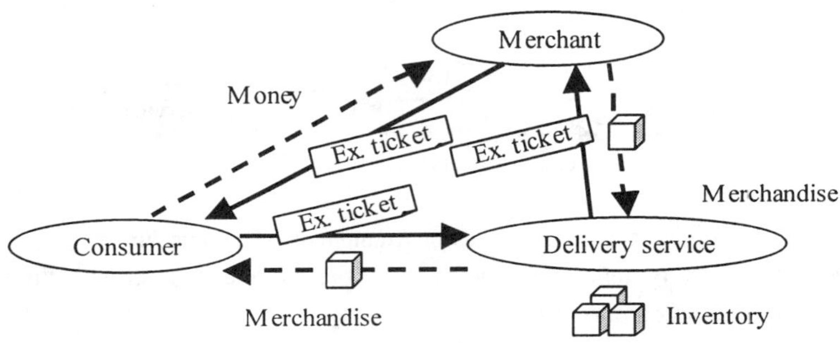


*Figure 4.* Trading with untrusted trading partners

Moreover, the transactions that involve vouchers have other desirable features such as privacy protection. For example in the above exchange ticket scenario, the consumer can contact the delivery service by himself, the merchant does not even need to know any personal information such as the delivery address. Furthermore, by designating a publicly accessible site such as a convenience store as the receiving point, the delivery service is prevented from learning the address of the consumer.

# 6. WALLET ARCHITECTURE

## 6.1 Processing Model

In order to realize the full benefits of VTS described in the above sections, a common VTS should be shared among a large number of consumers and services. A single VTS provider, however, is also impractical, because security level and performance requirements differ with the application. For discount coupons or event tickets, for example, the portable storage type VTS is often preferred, whereas for bonds or securities, the server storage type VTS is preferred. Moreover, each issuer must have the right to specify the trusted VTS providers delegated to circulate the vouchers, because if the VTS provider illegally copies the vouchers, the issuer would incur a loss due to the illegal copying.

Multiple VTS, however, will rise the issue of interoperability and may force consumers to install a "digital wallet" for each VTS. For these reasons, we believe some standard specifications should be developed to achieve interoperability. As shown in Section 4, however, there are several ways of implementing the VTS and technologies are continuously changing. It is impractical to define standard protocols for issuing, transferring, or redeeming voucher at this moment.

To provide implementation flexibility, we propose a modular wallet architecture that allows additional VTSs to be added as modules. In this architecture, instead of specifying a standard voucher transfer protocol, two specifications, i.e., Voucher Component and VTS API specifications, are standardized (Figure 5) [4] [5].

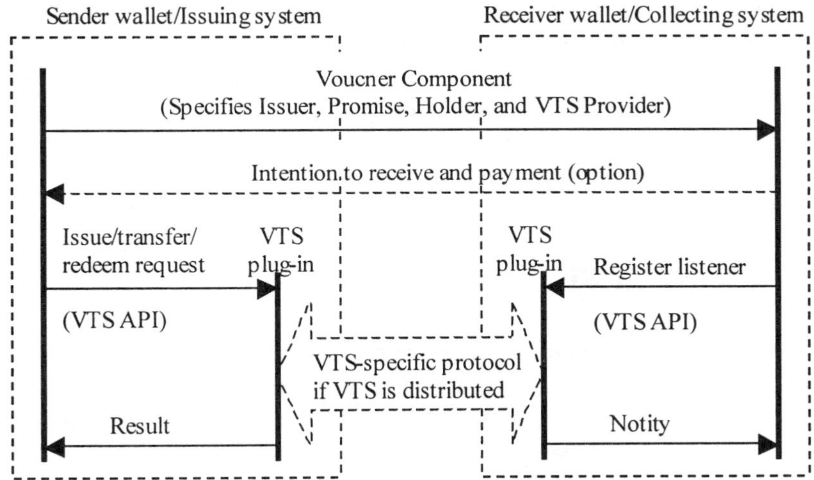


*Figure 5.* Wallet architecture with VTS plug-ins

The Voucher Component is an XML component that contains branding information for letting the receiver know which VTS plug-in can be used for receiving the voucher. The component also contains standard properties needed to display the entities in the wallet, e.g., name of the issuer and the title of the voucher.

After sender and receiver agree on what vouchers are to be traded and which VTS is to be used, the issuing system or wallet system requests the corresponding VTS plug-in to permit the issue, transfer, or redeem transactions to be performed via the standard VTS API. The VTS then rewrites the ownership of the voucher using a VTS-specific protocol. Finally, a completion result/notify is sent to the wallet systems or issuing/collecting systems.

## 6.2 Trust Model

A voucher is trusted if the Issuer and VTS Provider are trusted, since the Issuer is responsible for the contents of the voucher and the VTS Provider is responsible for preventing ownership from being assigned to multiple users. The trust level required for Issuer and VTS Provider depends on the type (or Promise) of the voucher. To provide the information needed for verification, we propose to specify the conditions of Issuer and VTS Provider in the Voucher Component and given as input to the verifier, which is provided as a function of the wallet system. The trust in a voucher is thus verified through the Voucher Component. This model enables trading partners to verify their trust in the voucher regardless of the trust in the partners.

In this model, the Voucher Component is the root of trust and must be delivered securely, since a forged voucher could be verified as valid if a malicious user could alter the Voucher Component. Delivery of the Voucher Component exceeds the scope of this paper, since existing technologies, such as XML digital signature [2] SSL [3], or IPSEC [16], can be used. Note that the Voucher Component does not have to be sent from the sender of the voucher. It can be directly delivered from the issuer or trusted third party using SSL. Note also that a set of trusted Voucher Components can be pre-downloaded before conducting a transaction.

# 7. CONCLUSION

E-commerce systems on the Internet are becoming increasingly complicated and diverse. Against this backdrop, technologies that coordinate multiple e-commerce services are becoming more important. This paper proposed a Voucher Trading System (VTS) for coordinating transactions conducted among untrusted trading partners, such as consumers, and matching, payment, and delivery services. This approach enables companies or individuals to trade goods or services via the Internet without demanding trust in the identity of trading partners. All that is needed is trust in the vouchers themselves, just like the paper-securities-based transactions of the real world.

This paper proposed a VTS model and showed that it can be realized in several ways. This paper also discussed the importance of standardization and proposed an architecture that achieves interoperability without sacrificing implementation flexibility. We are currently developing Voucher Component and VTS API specifications in the IETF trade WG to establish voucher trading as the infrastructure of e-commerce.

# 8. ACKNOWLEDGEMENT

This work is based on discussions within the IETF trade WG. I would like to thank all active members of the WG, especially Donald E. Eastlake 3rd, Ian Grigg, and Renato Iannella for providing encouragement and helpful comments.

# 9. REFERENCES

[1] D. Burdett, "Internet Open Trading Protocol – IOTP Version 1.0," RFC 2801, IETF, 2000.

[2] D. Eastlake, J. Reagle, D. Sole, et al., "XML-Signature Syntax and Processing," W3C Candidate Recommendation, W3C, <http://www.w3.org/TR/xmldsig-core/>, 2000.

[3] A. Freier, P. Karlton, and P. Kocher, "The SSL Protocol Version 3.0," IETF Internet Draft, <http://home.netscape.com/eng/ssl3/draft302.txt>, 1996.

[4] K. Fujimura, "Requirements for Generic Voucher Trading," IETF Internet Draft, draft-ietf-trade-drt-requirements-02.txt, 2001.

[5] K. Fujimura and M. Terada, "XML Voucher: Generic Voucher Language," IETF Internet Draft, draft-ietf-trade-voucher-lang-01.txt, 2001.

[6] K. Fujimura and Y. Nakajima, "General-purpose Digital Ticket Framework," *3rd USENIX Workshop on Electronic Commerce*, pp. 177-186, 1998.

[7] K. Fujimura, H. Kuno, M. Terada, K. Matsuyama, Y. Mizuno, and J. Sekine, "Digital-Ticket-Controlled Digital Ticket Circulation," *8th USENIX Security Symposium*, pp. 229-238, 1999.

[8] I. Grigg, "Financial Cryptography in 7 Layers," *Pre-proceedings of the Fourth Annual Conference of Financial Cryptography*, 2000.

[9] R. A. Hettinga, "A Market Model for Digital Bearer Instrument Underwriting," <http://www.philodox.com/modelpaper.html>, 1998.

[10] G. Howland, "Development of an Open and Flexible Payment System," Systemics Ltd., <http://www.systemics.com/docs/sox/overview.html>

[11] G. Lacoste, B. Pfitzmann, M. Steiner, and M. Waidner (Eds.), "SEMPER - Secure Electronic Marketplace for Europe," LNCS 1854, Springer-Verlag, 2000.

[12] MANDATE II Consortium, "MANDATE final report," Draft version 2.0, 1998.

[13] K. Matsuyama and K. Fujimura, "Distributed Digital-Ticket Management for Rights Trading System," *1st ACM Conferences on Electronic Commerce*, pp. 110-118, 1999.

[14] A. Schmidt, "TEDIS II - EDICON final report," 1997.

[15] M. Terada, H. Kuno, M. Hanadate, and K. Fujimura, "Copy Prevention Scheme for Right Trading Infrastructure," *4th Smart Card Research and Advanced Application Conference (CARDIS)*, IFIP 52, Kluwer Academic Publishers, 2000.

[16] R. Thayer, N. Doraswamy, and R. Glenn, "IP Security Document Roadmap," RFC2411, IETF, 1998.

[17] P. Wayner, "Digital Cash," Academic Press Ltd., 1997.

MINITRACK ONE

# FORMAL E-MODELS

**Minitrack chairs:**

Ulrike Lechner, University of St. Gallen, Switzerland,
Ulrike.Lechner@unisg.ch

Tiziana Margaria
University of Dortmund and MetaFrame, Germany
Tiziana.Margaria@metaframe.com

33

# The Influence of Market Uncertainties on Business Models for Online Music

Willms Buhse
*Dept. of General and Industrial Management, Technical University of Munich, Germany, and Bertelsmann Digital World Services, New York*

**Abstract** This paper will examine and categorize potential business model scenarios for online music. The virtualization of music leads to market uncertainties. On the supply side, the offering party might not be able to sufficiently privatize online music. On the demand side, with a changing cost structure for digital goods, consumers might not be willing to pay directly for digital goods so that revenues would have to be collected indirectly by public or private entities. As a result, business models for online music can be categorized into four scenarios. In the first scenario, online music is used to promote the traditional offline business while in the second scenario, consumers are willing to pay for additional services to access online music. The third scenario is significantly different from the first two scenarios as music providers are expected to be able to protect their content by using digital rights management technology. In the fourth scenario peer-to-peer technologies allow consumers to use a mechanism called super distribution with which they can share and recommend songs. The paper concludes with a recommendation to music companies to position themselves in all four scenarios.

## 1. INTRODUCTION

This paper will examine and categorize potential business model scenarios for online music. In this article, online music is defined as commercially available digital music that is distributed over networks like the Internet. Thereby music has become the ideal case study for digital commerce with its unique availability in digital form on billions of CDs. From the beginning online distribution became an underground phenomenon (Pettauer, 2000). The music industry, though small in its market size, has become a prominent case study for new technology concepts, introduced by companies like Napster for peer-to-peer file sharing, RealNetworks for streaming media, InterTrust for digital rights management and others. Forecasts from analysts regarding the market size for online-music, vary significantly between 7.8b US $ (Forrester), 2.6b US $ (Jupiter) and 1.9b US $ (Market Tracking International) (Becker and Ziegler, 2000).

Though much literature can be found prognosticating a significant change in the competitive environment of the music industry, little research exists on the combination of revenue models and property rights in the field of online music (Zerdick et al., 1999). The starting point for this analysis is the assumption that the basic principle of the electronic market as an efficient allocation mechanism works. But uncertainties on both the supply and demand side of the electronic market are leading to insufficiencies. In the following, two significant consequences regarding the business models caused by the virtualization of music are analyzed: first the cost structure for the delivery is structured differently and thereby revenues might be affected. Second the protection of copyrights has become more difficult in today's networks. Combining these two uncertainties into a scenario matrix, case studies will be given for each of the resulting four categories. Concluding remarks are made about possible positioning of companies in the music industry.

## 2. DEMAND-SIDE: COST STRUCTURE AND REVENUE MODELS

According to Forsa, the majority of the Internet users (69 percent) in Germany are not willing to pay for information or entertainment on the net.[50] One reason that may limit the willingness to pay for online-music may lie in the loss of a physical representation of the artist's work, which has become a collectible good with comprehensive artwork associated with it.[51]

Information goods are characterized by having high fixed costs, or first-copy costs, but very low incremental costs (Skiera, 1999). In the case of the music industry, the production of the master-copy accumulates a high amount of costs, while the production of additional copies can be estimated as marginal costs (Kelly, 1998). A study conducted in England, Germany, Italy and France by Doglio/Richeri found that in the music industry, the first-copy cost amounts to an average of 21.1 percent, followed by manufacturing costs of 8.5 percent. The highest per-unit cost is attributable to marketing and sales with 49.9 percent, with the remaining 20.5 percent allocated to label costs and margin (Doglio and Richeri, 1996). Cost elements, which might be affected are not only limited to manufacturing costs, but retail obsolesce, returns, physical distribution and transport. On the other hand, costs

[50] Forsa-Study conducted from October, 26th – 29th, 2000 with 1005 internet users in Germany

[51] In fact, a trend similar to the times of the LP, when printing costs for booklets increased in contrast to the production cost of the CD itself

for technology, bandwidth and customer service have to be factored in. Consequently, the benefits of digital distribution do not significantly change the per-unit cost at current volumes. It does however offer the possibility to distribute in much larger quantities than in the physical world.

As a result, the Internet seems to have a significant impact on the music industry's revenue model and thereby on the competitive environment. In the literature, revenues are divided into two main categories: *direct revenues* which result from the consumer, and *indirect revenues* which are refinanced through associated products via public or private entities (Zerdick et al., 1999). While in the literature a separation between different revenue streams seems possible, in the business environment, a wide spectrum of combinations can be found just like a newspaper might have revenue streams from advertising, subscription and single transactions. Additionally, in the television market, which closely resembles the music industry, the revenues tend to grow towards direct revenues. Ten years ago, direct and indirect revenues were split equal, while today, direct revenues mainly from subscriptions increased to 58 percent, compared to 42 percent for advertising based indirect revenues (Veronis Suhler & Associate 1998). The possible reason for this is consumer preferences regarding the allocation of their limited time (Berman et al. 2000).

# 3. SUPPLY-SIDE: PUBLIC AND PRIVATE GOODS

The theory of public goods holds that goods have different characteristics whether or not there is rivalry or non-rivalry in using them. *Public goods* are *non-excludable* and *non-rivalrous* in consumption while private goods are sold to those who can afford to pay the market price.

In the music market, broadcasting as a public good is used to promote songs while CDs function as a container for music sold as private goods (Tschmuck, 2000). *Copyrights* are a means of establishing the boundaries between who is allowed to use a particular good and under which conditions, and who is not allowed to use it. Developments in technology seem to take away the grounds for these boundaries. Burke has shown how technological developments in the past gave rise to changes in copyright (Burke, 1996). At the same time, piracy has always had a significant share in the music market. In 1999, according to IFPI about 1.9b units of illegal copies were found with a value of 4,1b US $ leading to a hypothetical market share of 36 percent (IFPI, 2000). On the Internet, piracy has become an even larger mass phenomenon due to the availability of perfect digital copies. With non-excludable online-music, end consumers become *free riders*, which are not willing to pay the market price for music as long as others might be accessing the music for free (Heinrich, 1994).

Traditionally, the distribution of music is dominated by an oligopoly of five major labels. For these music labels, the economic value lies in their artist contracts and in the exclusive distribution for recordings, which enables promotional distribution channels like free TV or radio (Thurow, 1994). Statistically, infrequent consumption of music albums as private goods accounts for about one hour, with revenues of 68 US $ per music listener per year. On the other hand, public broadcast amounts to frequent but superficial consumption of 3 hours a day. This results in 58 US $ in advertising revenues for the broadcast stations per year, from which music labels receive a much smaller percentage than from the album sales.[52] As a result, the music industry shows high interest in privatizing the music in order to generate higher revenues not only from traditional products but also from the online market. Increasing online piracy challenges the privatization of online music, therefore the music industry has started a number of legal, marketing, educational, and technology initiatives.

Law suits from the RIAA against MP3.com, Scour and Napster and others in the U.S. demonstrate the music industry's efforts to minimize copyright infringement. Though the industry might reach successes in certain countries, concepts like "Offshore-Web-Hosting" from companies like HavenCo.Com or Offshore.com.ai and de-central file sharing systems like Gnutella and FreeNet might well continue to operate despite law suits and even drive consumers to "underground" systems (Schreirer, 2000).

From a technology point of view, the music industry started the Secure Digital Music Initiative (SDMI) to develop specifications jointly with technology companies like Microsoft, IBM and many others. Many doubt that the music industry can successfully introduce security mechanisms that are either unbreakable or at least can raise the barrier for piracy without creating unproportional high costs (Albers et al., 1999). Many examples in other media industries like currently the DVD-protection scheme have shown failures of secure protection mechanisms (DeCSS). Additionally, on the Internet only a single copy (even by re-digitizing from analog versions) made available is sufficient to be globally distributed in a short period of time leading to a total loss of control by the owner. But it is quite possible that the biggest challenge the music industry is facing is not hackers but instead infrastructure. Today's infrastructure with 200m multimedia PCs, 1b CD-audio-devices and 17b unprotected audio CDs with 150.000 different titles will be very difficult to replace (Gurley, 2000).

[52] Bertelsmann internal research

# 4. FOUR BUSINESS MODEL SCENARIOS

The goal of using scenarios is to categorize various business models according to several case studies involving new distribution mechanisms like file sharing, digital rights management and super distribution. As in the previous chapters described, the virtualization of music has two significant consequences regarding the business models: first the cost structure for the delivery is structured differently and thereby revenues might be affected. Second the protection of copyrights has become more difficult in today's networks.

*Table 3.* Scenario matrix for online music

| | **Public Good** | **Private Good** |
|---|---|---|
| **Indirect Revenues** | Open-Source-Filesharing | Subscription Systems |
| **Direct Revenues** | Music Service Provider | Superdistribution |

Four scenarios can be deduced by combining these two uncertainties into a matrix, which represents both, supply and demand. In this article, for each of the scenarios, one case study is described and possible revenue models are given.

## Assumptions

These four business model scenarios are subject to the following assumptions:

- in the mid- to long-term, no business models will be viable which infringe on copyright laws. However, there might be systems without commercial interest that face no legal consequences for enabling illegal copies. Open-source-file sharing systems belong to this category.
- revenue models are based on rational entrepreneurial decisions, excluding artistic, voluntary or otherwise motivated scenarios.
- Most importantly, these scenarios anticipate a slow migration towards online technologies. Meaning, traditional media companies maintain distribution control over physical storage media like CD and DVD. The hypothesis from Zerdick et al. states that electronic markets do not lead to an immediate substitution of the existent value chain. Nevertheless it is leading to a constant erosion of traditional value chains and the orientation towards the demand side (Zerdick et al., 1999).

## 4.1 First Scenario: Open Source File Sharing Systems

Within less than two years, Napster became the largest music library ever with about 1b titles, without economic incentive, marketing activities, and even more important without involvement of the music industry (Becker and Ziegler, 2000). At a very high level, file sharing systems or peer-to-peer-networks (P2P) aggregate and distribute information. With either central or de-central listings, files be can searched for, transferred and stored locally. The main challenge for content owners is its mass phenomena. Since its launch, Napster attracted almost 70 Million users who knowingly violate copyright laws.

While Napster through its partnership with Bertelsmann plans membership fees and the compensation of content owners, other open-source-file-sharing systems are developed without any commercial purpose. Their purpose is to freely distribute information beyond any control. Examples are Gnutella developed by Gene Kan and FreeNet designed by Ian Clarke. Both are designed to run de-centralized, which makes it almost impossible to control or shut down their operations. As a result, besides music files, other illegal content like children pornography and terrorist instructions can be found. The main challenge of these systems is that they only can scale with resources like content, bandwidth and storage from their users. As their content can be viewed as public goods, these systems attract *free riders* not willing to give any contribution in return. During a study of the Gnutella Network, it was found, that 70 percent of the users don't give any contribution to the system, and that half of the searches were answered by just one percent of the participants (Adar and Huberman, 2000). Apart from significant loss of system performance with longer search and download times, it adds vulnerability to the system as it might collapse with the shut down of few peers. On the other hand, there are concepts like seti@home with users voluntarily contributing resources in exchange for prestige and reputation. As a result, file-sharing systems seem to be able to overcome today's challenges and will play an important role in the distribution of online music.

How can the music industry embrace such systems to generate revenues? Revenues can be generated indirectly from online music in return for the value of consumers' attention (Seidel, 1993). This can be used to promote either the physical album or the artist in order to reach more popularity and thereby earn higher merchandising and advertising revenue. As a result, with online music being a public good, the combination of online and offline business by integrating online-music and traditional marketing and distribution seems a profitable business model (Tomczak et al., 2000), (Zerdick et al., 1999). Despite legal battles from RIAA arguing that illegal copies cannibalize album sales, market studies are inconclusive at this point. Jupiter identified Napster usage as one of the most important factors for increased music purchases (Sinnreich et al., 2000). On the other hand, VNU found album sales decreasing in record stores close to universities, where file sharing supposingly reaches high usage among students (VNU Entertainment Marketing Solutions, 2000). Creed offered their hit song in 1999 from 100 web sites for free downloads, and in the process stimulated their album sales. Coincidentally their album "Human Clay" reached the top of the billboard charts.[53] A recent example is the partnership between the online retailer CDNow and Napster, where the file sharing system receives a commission of about 15 percent for every album sale.

Nevertheless, substitution of traditional media like CDs and DVD-Audio might increase as soon as a comparable infrastructure for online music exists. Physical goods have always served as "containers" for services. For example, a CD has no intrinsic value, only the value of delivering music. In the age of downloadable music, though, the CD loses its value as a container for music (Rifkin, 2000).

## 4.2 Second Scenario: Music Service Provider

Provided online music is a public good, collecting direct payments seems almost impossible unless, the value lies primarily in the functionality and services, rather than in the content itself (Deutsche Bank, 2000). In this scenario, instead of copy protection, service-oriented new business models are developed that prevent the motive to copy. Besides content, these services offer convenience, reliability and fast access to music almost anywhere and at anytime and are referred to as the *celestial jukebox*. This services sector is expected to grow from 2.5m today to 12.3m in 2003 in the U.S (Black, 2000). Ultimately, those companies would have to combine content, community, application services, context and search functionality. Personalization plays a crucial role in attracting consumers and providing lock-in (Heinrich, 1999). In the networked economy, these versions and even individual products and services are achievable due to smaller transaction and production/service costs (Piller, 1998). Using a feedback loop mechanism for online-music, personal playlists can be generated, recommended, updated and shared among other users. Online music, with about three min title length can generate comprehensive sets of data over time, provided 4 hours of daily music consumption, 80 songs might be rated on a daily basis almost automatically. Large description data bases like Moodlogic or Gigabeat can analyze relationships among titles and artists according to rhythm, instruments, contextual information and even mood.

It might be easy to maintain a piracy site with some illegal copies, but to provide access, payment mechanisms and customer service to many thousand people simultaneously is a more complex task. Which companies might position themselves in the role of music service providers? First, relationships, such as those established by radio or television stations, emphasize repeat visits. They have already proven their ability for selection and aggregation of music (Hull et al., 2000). Second, those with existing billing and services relationships like ISPs and TelCos, e.g. AOL TW. Third, there are companies with a link to end devices, like hardware-, OS-software-,

[53] Committee on Intellectual Property Rights and the Emerging Information Infrastructure (2000), p. 80f

and CE-device-manufacturers, though they might as well bet on copy protection technologies as they are able to choose and set standards. Nevertheless, under current copyright law, most companies might have to negotiate licenses either directly with the music labels, their syndication partners or through royalty collecting entities, in order to be able to offer these services.

## 4.3 Third Scenario: Subscription Models

Protection technologies play an important role in determining whether a media product is a public or a private good. In scenarios three and four, online music is considered a private good, as content owners are able to restrict access to the content and thereby introduce the possibility to exclude free riders and charge for their online music. To securely protect online music, all major labels incorporate *digital rights management* technologies, which basically fall into four categories: first the *access* is controlled with authentication and/or encryption mechanisms. Second, the *usage* is controlled according to rules that are set by the distributor of the music. This determines how the user can interface with the information, e.g., listen-only rights, where the user is unable to save or distribute the music. Third a *tracking* mechanism allows the information provider to track subsequent use with watermarking and digital footprints. Fourth and last, *payment* systems enable the information provider to generate revenue for the rights granted to the user. As a result of inefficient micro payment systems, subscription models are viewed as a method to overcome high transaction costs (Picot et al., 2001).

For subscription models watermarking can provide important contributions to the field of intellectual property protection within a more extensive security framework for identification and proof of ownership, which is comparable to IRSC-Codes used by the GEMA for recognition of CD-Audios (Goldhammer and Zerdick, 1999). By embedding a watermark into the compressed audio signal during delivery, the customers are aware that a watermark may identify them (Tang, 1998). Hence, they can be made responsible if the signal is found outside the legal domain by a trigger technology, even in a decompressed and analog representation.[54] In contrast to encryption technologies, watermarks could be used with today's infrastructure for CD-Audio as well as MP3-devices. Subscriptions bundle a large number of information goods for a fixed price. In a variety of circumstances, a multi-product monopolist can extract substantially higher profits by offering one or more bundles of information goods than by offering the same goods separately (Bakos and Brynjolffson, 1999). At the same time, bundling can be used to introduce new artists

[54] Specifications for such an infrastructure is currently designed by the Secure Digital Music Initiative. www.sdmi.org SDMI, Document Nr. pdwg99070802, „SDMI Portable Device Specification Part 1, Version 1.0“, p. 21

and titles as a strategy to overcome the information paradox, which states that the value of an information can't be determined a *priori* of consumption.

In this scenario, for the first time in their history, music labels have the opportunity to create a continuous relationship with the end consumer. This relationship offers a foundation on which music labels can generate revenues. The subscription model may represent a mix between indirect and direct revenues with the option of consumption combined with transparent pricing (Zerdick et al., 1999), (Sinnreich, 2000). Forrester expects additional revenues from subscriptions of 3.3b US $ (Schreirer, 2000). A premium membership might offer a flatrate, eventually combined with services from the second scenario, while an advertising-based membership might limit access in quantity, time or actuality.

## 4.4 Fourth Scenario: Super-Distribution

In 1990, a visionary architecture was developed for the distribution of digital goods. The Japanese Ryoichi Mori coined the term *Superdistribution* for this new concept of licensing information (Mori, 1990); (Cox, 1996); (Morin, 1999). The fundamental idea is to allow free distribution of digital content, while controlling access to usage and changes with the content owner defining the terms. According to his prototype, called Software Service System (SSS), which was implemented as a peer-to-peer-architecture, the following components must be available (Morin, 1999):

- a persistent *cryptographic wrapper* must stay in place when the digital property is used, copied, redistributed, etc.
- a *digital rights management system* with a trusted tool that tracks the deals and the usage associated with the access to the digital property
- *payment information* have to be exchanges securely among the parties

After securely encrypting the music with a key, the package can be digitally delivered to the consumers end device (Tang, 1998). There, the locally installed trusted tool gains access to the digital content with an unlock key which leaves the file locally encrypted and streams the digital content into the memory for "on the fly" decryption. The user, who has agreed to the terms and conditions of use, has now the license to access the content. His usage is recorded and the transaction is reported to a clearinghouse to initiate payments and backup system information. Using the superdistribution concept, consumers can recommend and share files among each other via email, FTP, physical media and even file sharing networks. Still the copyright is being protected and the content owner maintains control and determines payment collection.

Under the third scenario, bundling was mentioned as being attractive for content companies to extract higher profits. In the music industry, this has always been the case with album sales, where only one or two hits from an entire album initiate the purchase. Digital products possess optimal de-bundling capability, which in return can be re-bundled again for custom-mixes (Albers et al., 1998), (Kulle, 1998). With digital downloads and superdistribution, consumers might start "cherry picking" their hits and thereby endanger the traditional revenue model of album sales. In this scenario, using digital rights management and superdistribution, major labels maintain control over the distribution of music and might even be able to enforce their copyrights more than in the traditional world.

## 5. CONCLUSION

In this paper scenarios for online business models that depend on uncertainties on the supply and demand side of the music industry were examined. It was argued that on the one hand, online music could either be a public or a private good, due to insufficiencies in absolute content protection. On the other hand, the willingness for consumers to pay for digital goods might determine the nature for direct or indirect revenue streams. As a result, consistent business models in all four scenarios were developed. The scenarios have shown that there is a spectrum of potential revenue streams for online music both as public and private goods. Therefore, the main distinction between the scenarios depends on the supply side, where copyright for online music can either be protected by technical means or not.

Although online music distribution has been in place for some time, it is too early to determine which scenarios will evolve. Nevertheless, it is quite possible for all these scenarios to exist in parallel under certain market conditions. In this case, it is assumed that all four scenarios can come into affect during the life cycle of an online music release. Starting with the secure superdistribution concept (scenario 4) at the time of release, followed by a time lag for subscription based accessibility (scenario 3). Over (short or long) time, the value might decrease and with hackers distributing illegal copies, the release might become widely accessible as a public good. Then services might be offered (scenario 2) and at the same time additional value from the user's attention for promotion and advertising might be extracted (scenario 1). Therefore, the music labels should prepare themselves to claim strategic positions in all four scenarios, otherwise their traditionally dominant role in the music market, and the barrier-to-entry that currently prevents external competition will diminish. I would like to conclude with Shapiro & Varian that content owners should maximize the value of their digital goods and should not secure them for the sake of protection (Shapiro and Varian 1998). Therefore, the optimal strategy is not only to reduce the motives for copy infringement, but at the same time to increase the accessibility for consumers to digital products and services.

# 6. REFERENCES

Adar E., Huberman B. (2000) Free Riding on Gnutella, http://www.firstmonday.org/issues/issue5_10/adar/index.html, viewed at December 10th, 2000

Albers S., Clement M., Peters K. (1998) Marketing mit Interaktiven Medien. Strategien zum Markterfolg, Frankfurt am Main

Albers S., Clement M., Skiera B. (1999) Wie sollen die Produkte vertrieben werden? – Distributionspolitik. In: Albers S., Clement M. et al. E-Commerce – Einstieg, Strategie und Umsetzung im Unternehmen. Frankfurt, pp. 79-94

Bakos Y., Brynjolffson E. (1999) Bundling information Goods: Pricing, profits and Efficiency, Working Paper

Becker, A.; Ziegler, M. (2000) Wanted: A survival plan for the music industry – Napster and the consequences, Diebold Study

Benjamin, Robert; Wigand, Rolf (1995) Electronic Markets and Virtual Value Chains on the Information Superhighway. In: Sloan Management Review, winter, pp. 62 - 72.

Berman, S., McCelellan, B. et al. (2000) The Future of the Entertainment and Media Industries: 2005, PriceWaterhouseCoopers, New York

Black, L. (2000) Understanding Consumer Demand to create business models that work, Webnoize research, SGAE, Madrid, 25. 10. 2000

Burke, A.E (1996) How Effective Are International Copyright Conventions in the Music Industry? Journal of Cultural Economics, volume 20, number 1, pp. 51-66

Choi, S.Y., D.O. Stahl, and A.B. Whinston (1997) The Economics of Electronic Commerce. Macmillan Technical Publishing

Committee on Intellectual Property Rights and the Emerging Information Infrastructure (2000) The Digital Dilemma – Intellectual Property in the Information Age. National Academy Press, Washington

Cox, Brad (1996) Superdistribution: Objects as Property on the Electronic Frontier, Addison-Wiley

Deutsch Bank (2000) New Media Mechanics - Value of Content Online

Doglio, D.; Richeri, G. (1996) The Economics of Publishing: Prospects for Online Distribution, Centro Studi Salvador, Telecom Italia, Venice

Evans, P.; Wurster T. (1999) Blown to Bits - How the new economics of information transforms strategy. Harvard Business School Press, Boston, Massachusetts

Forsa-Study (2000) viewed at http://www.berlinonline.de/wissen/computer/internet/.html/200011/net01105.html

Goldhammer, K.; Zerdick, A. (1999) Rundfunk Online – Entwicklung und Perspektiven des Internets für Hörfunk- und Fernsehanbieter, Berlin

Gurley, W. (2000) Digital music: The real law is Moore's law, Fortune; New York; Oct 2, 2000;; Volume: 142, Issue: 7 pp. 268f.

Heinrich, J. (1994) Medienökonomie, Vol. 1 Opladen Westdt. Verlag

Heinrich, J. (1999) Medienökonomie, Vol. 2 Opladen Westdt. Verlag

Hull, G.P.; Greco, A.P.; Martin, S. (2000): The Structure of the Radio Industry, in: Greco, A. (2000): The Media and Entertainment Industries. Readings in Mass Communications, Boston, pp. 122-156

IFPI (2000) Piracy Report 2000, June 2000

Kelly, K. (1998) New Rules for the New Economy. 10 Radical Strategies for a Connected World. Viking Press, New York

Kulle, Jürgen (1998) Ökonomie der Musikindustrie: Eine Analyse der körperlichen und unkörperlichen Verwertung von Musik mit Hilfe von Tonträgern und Netzen, Frankfurt a. M.

Morin, Jean-Henry (1999) Commercial Electronic Publishing over Open Networks: A Global Approach Based on Mobile objects (Agents). Dissertation University of Geneva

Mori, R. (1990) Superdistribution: The Concept and the Architecture. The Transactions of the IEICE E73, No 7.

Pettauer, Richard (2000) Die Blitzkarriere von MP3. Micafocus 1: Reales Musikschaffen Für Einen Virtuellen Markt, March 18th 2000, http://www.mica.at/mf_pettau_p.html, viewed at 10.10.2000

Picot, A.; Reichwald, R.; Wigand, R. (2001) Die grenzenlose Unternehmung, 4. Ed., Wiesbaden

Piller, F. T. (1998) Kundenindividuelle Massenproduktion. Die Wettbewerbsstrategie der Zukunft, München.

Rifkin, J (2000) The Future of Digital Music: Is There an Upside to Downloading? Hearing Statements U.S. Senate Committee on the Judiciary, viewed at http://www.senate.gov/~judiciary/7112000_jg.htm

Schreirer, E.(2000) Content out of Control, The Forrester Report, Cambridge, MA

SDMI (2000) SDMI Portable Device Specification Part 1, Version 1.0, Document Nr. pdwg99070802, p. 21

Seidel, N. (1993) Rundfunkökonomie: Organisation, Finanzierung und Management von Rundfunkunternehmen, Wiesbaden

Shapiro, C.; Varian, H.R. (1998) Information Rules. A Strategic Guide to the Network Economy, Boston

Sinnreich, A. (2000) Digital Music Subscriptions: Post-Napster Product Formats, Jupiter Studie,

Skiera, B. (1999) Wie teuer sollen die Produkte sein? – Preispolitik. In: Albers, S.; Clement, M. et al. (Hrsg.) E-Commerce – Einstieg, Strategie und Umsetzung im Unternehmen. Frankfurt, pp. 94-108

Tang, Puay (1998) How Electronic Publishers are Protecting against Privacy: Doubts about Technical Systems of Protection The Information Society Vol. 14, n. 1, pp. 19-31

Thurow, N. (1994) Die digitale Verwertung von Musik aus der Sicht von Schallplattenproduzenten und ausübenden Künstlern, in: Becker, Jürgen / Dreier, Thomas, Urheberrecht und digitale Technologien, Vortragssammlung der Sitzung des Instituts für Urheber- und Medienrecht, UFITA-Schriftenreihe, Baden-Baden, p. 77

Tomczak, T. et al. (2000) Online-Distribution als innovativer Absatzkanal. In:

Tschmuck, P. (2000) Internetökonomie und Musikwirtschaft. During: Micafocus 1: Reales Musikschaffen Für Einen Virtuellen Markt, March 18th, 2000, http://www.mica.at/mf_tschmuck_p.html, viewed at 10.10.2000

Veronis Suhler & Associate (1998), Communications Forecast

VNU Entertainment Marketing Solutions (2000) Measuring the Influence of Music File Sharing, New York

Zerdick, A. et al.. (1999) Die Internet-Ökonomie – Strategien für die digitale Wirtschaft. Springer, Berlin, Heidelberg (u.a.)

34

# An Approach to Knowledge Management Support in E-Business Processes

Ingrid Slembek

*Faculty of Information Technology, University of Technology, Sydney (UTS) and the CRC for Enterprise Distributed Systems Technology, Australia*

**Abstract:** Knowledge is increasingly being identified as the key resource of the enterprise [4]. One approach to managing this key resource is to focus on the support of organisational knowledge creation in business processes. We propose the use of a framework for business process management as the vehicle to deliver this support. Employing the theory of organisational knowledge creation developed by Nonaka [9], we identify the presence of enabling conditions required to promote knowledge creation by making comparisons with a target established for the process. Tailored knowledge management services are proposed to strengthen these enabling conditions, and we show how the framework can assist the process in their integration. Our approach is particularly suitable for delivering support to e-business processes implemented with information technology. An illustration is provided using threat identification, a knowledge intensive activity of the risk management process.

## 1. INTRODUCTION

The strong increase in global business competition since the early 90's [8] and advances in information technology have accounted for the rapid spread of e-business practices in many industries. These practices [7, 14] have resulted in a shift towards a higher degree of complexity in business processes, permitting vendors to be linked with their geographically distributed customers and suppliers to form a single virtual organisation [1].

Within the set of e-business processes we can identify those that are knowledge intensive, in which existing individual and organisational knowledge is used to create new knowledge for the competitive benefit of the organisation. In such processes, organisational knowledge is created through the dynamics of the interaction of people working together to solve problems [9]. We call them knowledge intensive business processes, simply referring to them in this paper as processes for short.

Our goal is to support processes with an emphasis on organisational knowledge creation, in line with the increasing emphasis on knowledge as a vital organisational resource [6]. We accomplish this by applying a framework, based on Continuous Process Improvement (CPI) techniques, developed for business process management in our earlier research [12]. CPI, an approach that stems from the area of Business Process Management (BPM), is continuous and iterative in nature [5] and thus suitable for use with dynamic, emerging processes. The framework has been designed with the aim of making process stakeholders aware of and facilitating the treatment of weaknesses detected in the processes. This proactive approach to support provides feedback on current process performance as compared with an organisational target. It is designed to be applied in an iterative manner, periodically cycling through the steps of data collection, analysis, evaluation, and the provision of feedback and remediation assistance to the process under examination. The architecture of the BPM framework has been designed to obtain process data seamlessly from the application software used to support the process, making it well-suited to use with e-business processes.

In this paper we refine the BPM framework to provide specific knowledge management support in processes, using Nonaka's widely-referenced [3, 5, 6] theory of organisational knowledge creation [9] as the basis for these refinements. We illustrate its application with a knowledge intensive e-business process from the area of risk management, with a focus on identifying knowledge management services to support organisational knowledge creation in the process. This focus emphasises the importance of knowledge as an organisational resource and its contribution to the successful outcome of the process.

The next section of this paper briefly introduces the essential elements of Nonaka's spiral of knowledge creation and the BPM framework. In section 3, we demonstrate the framework's capability to identify knowledge management services to address weaknesses in the process under study. This paper finishes with a summary that includes a discussion on future research directions.

## 2. ORGANISATIONAL KNOWLEDGE CREATION AND THE BPM FRAMEWORK

We briefly describe Nonaka's theory [9] of the dynamics of organisational knowledge creation, and how it has been functionally translated in our BPM framework [12], in order to provide the reader with the background required to follow the illustration of the framework's operation in the next section.

Nonaka's theory is based on his study of Japanese companies involved in product innovation. Knowledge comes in two basic forms, tacit, or experiential, knowledge and explicit, or codified, knowledge. An important concept of the theory is that by cycling through the four modes of knowledge conversion (tacit to tacit, tacit to explicit, explicit to explicit and explicit to tacit) in a spiral manner, knowledge is created. Through the shared experiences and interaction between individuals engaged in this spiral of knowledge creation, it is possible to create organisational knowledge that would otherwise not have been arrived at by individuals working on their own.

The model of organisational knowledge creation contains five phases: the sharing of tacit knowledge between team members; creating concepts based on successive rounds of tacit knowledge sharing; the justification or testing of created concepts; the building of a model or prototype based on the justified concepts; and cross-levelling – the distribution of new knowledge throughout the organisation [10]. These five phases repeat as many times as are necessary until concepts are refined and crystallised into a new product or service.

There are five enabling conditions which Nonaka identifies as essential to the successful promotion of the knowledge spiral: intention, autonomy, creative chaos, redundancy and requisite variety [10]. Intention indicates that the organisational goals for the process are clearly known to participants. Autonomy indicates that the process team has the independence to organise itself and take decisions. Creative chaos means that the team is faced with challenges in the process which they must work together to address. Redundancy is a condition that applies to the intentional overlapping of information available to the process team, providing it with more than the minimum required to perform its work. The final enabling condition, requisite variety, ensures that team members have information available to them in various forms through quick and flexible channels [10]. These enabling conditions are present in varying degrees in each phase of organisational knowledge creation.

The BPM framework was designed to provide three major functions, which have been tailored here to detect and address weaknesses in the enabling conditions. The first function, the business process object (Interface), is responsible for communications with the process, collecting data from and providing feedback to it. The second function provides business process data analysis (Analyser), taking the raw data collected from the process by the Interface and analysing it to identify the five organisational knowledge creation phases and the five enabling conditions which have been characterised for the process in each phase. The last function, the business process assessor (Assessor), evaluates the enabling conditions for each organisational knowledge creation phase against a pre-defined target, making recommendations for the adjustment of knowledge management services in the process to address any weaknesses detected. The Interface may facilitate their addition or removal if requested by the process, concluding a cycle of the BPM framework's operation. A more detailed explanation of the generic operation of the framework is presented in [12].

# 3. KNOWLEDGE MANAGEMENT SERVICES FOR AN E-BUSINESS PROCESS

In this section, the risk management process is described at a high level, followed by a walk through of the framework's application to an activity within the process. Emphasis is placed on the assessment of enabling conditions and the need for knowledge management services in a process to support organisational knowledge creation.

Risk management, as defined in the Australian and New Zealand standard, AS/NZS 4360 [13], consists of a series of activities which assist in identifying, prioritising and helping stakeholders actively make decisions about the risks they face. This standard defines the classic sequential activities involved in risk management as: establishment of context; identification of threats; assessment of risk; and treatment of risk. Monitoring and review occurs in parallel with the other activities, and if an issue is identified, a new cycle of the process is initiated from that point in the sequence of activities. The risk management process was chosen for this illustration because it is highly knowledge intensive and relies on the strong presence of enabling conditions for a successful outcome.

For our illustration, we have selected an organisation that has decided to consolidate and relocate its data centre resources in a new building, hence triggering a full cycle of the risk management process. We focus on the threat identification activity because it displays typical characteristics of an organisational knowledge creation process, including a multifunctional team of people who engage in data gathering, sorting and analysis [9].

## 3.1 Analysis of the Organisational Knowledge Creation Phases

Figure 1 shows a model of the activity for our threat identification example. The rich picture notation employed in the model is borrowed from the soft systems methodology developed by Checkland and Scholes [2]. The many roles participating in the threat identification activity are shown on the left, linked through the cloud-shaped activity to the artefacts that they use or create in the course of fulfilling their duties. Many of the team members are located at different sites, and rely on email, file servers and other information technology to support their collaboration. The artefacts shown here are all used as input information in identifying threats, with the exception of the threat ID list, which is created by the process. Some roles are filled by more than one person, such as with the Business Operations Area Stakeholder, which is taken by one or more participant(s) from each area, resulting in a relatively large team.

We now demonstrate how the BPM framework identifies weaknesses in the threat identification activity's knowledge resourcing. Process data is collected by the Interface as specified by the Analyser. The Analyser goes on to distinguish the threat identification activity in terms of the phases of organisational knowledge creation.

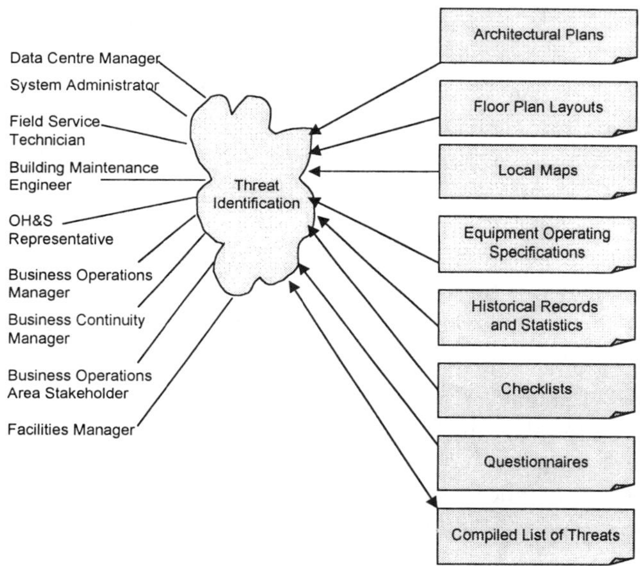


*Figure 1.* Rich picture of the threat identification activity

In phase 1, sharing of tacit knowledge, the organisation puts together a multifunctional team whose members represent particular business stakeholders with an interest in the continuous operation of the enterprise's data centre. An objective of this team is to assess the risk to business service continuity of the data centre's computing resources. Team members visit the new data centre location, touring its building and the surrounding streets. An opportunity for sharing tacit knowledge between team members occurs on this visit. Once an understanding of the scope and nature of the threat identification exercise is gained by the team members, phase 2, concept creation, is entered. Each team member contributes possible threats to business service continuity by drawing on their experience and on information at their disposal. This information may take the form of architectural plans, floor plan layouts and area maps; equipment operating specifications; historical records and insurance statistics; expert opinion, such as might be expressed in community of practice discussion forums or newsgroups; and any other information which might prove relevant based on the nature of the threatened business service(s). The identification of threats may be facilitated through the use of checklists, questionnaires or other tools. Preliminary lists of threats are drawn up and refined in small group meetings held by threat type, including natural and man-made disasters and organisational threats. During phase 3, concept justification, with the initial list of threats compiled, the business continuity manager meets with team members representing different business operations areas to flush out further threats that may have been overlooked. Techniques employed may include scenario, fault tree, systems or other similar analysis; brainstorming and other techniques to systematically identify further threats in the areas exposed in the previous phase. The business continuity manager presents a list of identified threats to the represented business areas in order to gain agreement on and cover off any remaining threats before an overall rollup occurs at the organisational level in phase 4, building of an archetype. The business continuity manager compiles the threats by business operations area and distributes the list to the entire team. A workshop involving all team members is held, during which the representatives from each business operations area present the identified threats to the team for discussion and feedback. Following the workshop and the resolution of any resulting action items, a comprehensive list of threats is issued to the team by the business continuity manager for consideration in the next stage of risk management. In phase 5, cross-levelling of knowledge, lists of identified threats compiled during the threat identification activity are archived with other records about the risk management process. These lists reflect the organisational knowledge gained during the current activity and may provide useful input knowledge during a future iteration of the activity.

## 3.2 Assessment of Enabling Conditions

Once the Analyser has completed identification of the organisational knowledge creation phases in the process, the Assessor compares the actual enabling conditions detected against a target previously established for the process. A comparison of these is shown in Table 1, in which the letter T represents the target and the letter A the actual. Enabling conditions are listed in the leftmost column and the organisational knowledge creation phases appear in the header row.

*Table 4.* Assessment of the threat identification activity's enabling conditions

| | Phase 1 | Phase 2 | Phase 3 | Phase 4 | Phase 5 |
|---|---|---|---|---|---|
| Intention | T, A | T, A | T, A | T, A | T, A |
| Autonomy | T, A | T, A | T, A | T, A | T, A |
| Creative Chaos | - | T, A | - | - | - |
| Redundancy | T, A | T, A (weak) | T, A | T, A | - |
| Requisite Variety | T, A | T, A (weak) | T, A | - | - |

Intention is clearly present at the process level through the use of the AS/NZS standard and through quality procedures in use in the organisation. This condition is expected and present in all of the organisational knowledge creation phases. Autonomy is evident through the presence of the self-organising team, whose members represent a broad range of functional areas in the organisation. This condition is expected and present in all of the organisational knowledge creation phases. Creative chaos does not factor significantly in the threat identification activity, except in phase 2, when the initial lists of threats are being compiled. In the example, the desired chaos is supplied by the challenge posed by relocation of the data centre. The nature of threat identification relies on a rich redundancy of experience and information, which is reflected in the target. Some of the team members have previously worked in departments currently represented by other members, and have held similar positions in the past. Redundancy of information should be strongly present in threat identification. Available information is drawn from the business operation and functional areas represented, but few overlapping sources were detected. This yields a weak match with the target. The final enabling condition, requisite variety, is important in threat identification since a sufficiently comprehensive list of threats will be produced only by looking at the problem from many different angles. Access to a wider variety of information sources would provide more sources for potential threats. The actual state of this enabling condition yields a weak match with the target.

## 3.3 Identification of Knowledge Management Services

After evaluation of the actual status of the enabling conditions against the target established for the process, specialised knowledge management services are recommended for inclusion in the process in a bid to bolster support for the organisational knowledge creation phases. We look at the services that are proposed to address the weaknesses identified in the information redundancy and requisite variety enabling conditions.

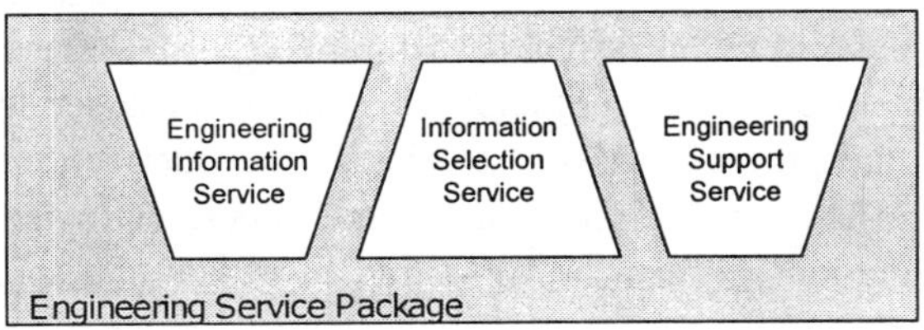


*Figure 2.* Knowledge management service package

As determined in the previous section, there is insufficient overlap, as well as lack of variety, in the information available to team members to aid in threat identification. Knowledge management services are identified through consultation with the process stakeholder and packaged by the Assessor to address these shortcomings. These services may be pre-existing in a service library or may need to be custom built. The information sources currently used by the team are evaluated and other sources applicable to the task are identified for inclusion in an information service. To support the project team members representing the building and maintenance department, an engineering information service for building-related matters supplies access to maps, drawings, architectural plans, product information and specifications for the construction materials used in the building; manufacturer and independent product fault reports; general civil engineering publications; reports by insurance bodies; and so on. For additional sources and variety of information, a support service is added that provides access to external professional discussions sponsored by civil engineering professional associations and online hotline support facilities from a consortium of international reinsurance companies. Included with the support service are internal discussion forums to which all employees in the building and maintenance department can contribute to aid in problem solving. An information selection service provides intelligent search tools for quickly locating relevant information in the support and information services. It includes filters that improve the usability of the statistical data often used with risk management by presenting it in various, including graphical, formats. Similar packages of information and support services are proposed to support the other functional areas represented by the project team.

When the threat identification activity has been completed, the search service can be used to extract important issues from the discussions for archival purposes. Thus, when modifications are made to the data centre infrastructure and the threat identification activity is revisited, a history of previous issues and decisions are available to assist the project team in putting the changes into context.

## 3.4 Provision of Feedback to the Process

With assessment complete, the Assessor provides its evaluation to the Interface, which formats and communicates it to the process. If the evaluation contains recommendations for the addition of knowledge management services, as is the case in our example, the process can elect to engage the Interface to assist with their implementation. The degree to which automated support is provided will depend on the level of integration between the BPM framework and the application software underlying the process. In the case of the engineering service package, the Interface might be asked to install one or more of the recommended services in the process and establish access to them for the building maintenance engineer and facilities manager on the project team, as well as for all employees in the building and maintenance department. Authorised process stakeholders can manually add or remove the knowledge management services as required.

The CPI nature of the BPM framework facilitates a review of the process on a regular basis, either automatically initiated by the Interface or manually by an authorised process stakeholder. Each time a review is performed, the results of the evaluation are recorded and made available to process stakeholders. Upon completion of the process, the process log is preserved in the organisational memory along with other process data of organisational interest. Records of the knowledge management services used for a specific risk management process can be used as a basis for recommending services for subsequent instances of the same process.

# 4. CONCLUSIONS AND FUTURE DIRECTIONS

In this paper, we have approached the problem of providing support for e-business processes by offering knowledge management services to strengthen their organisational knowledge creation conditions. This was accomplished through the application of a CPI-based framework for business process management. The framework was adapted to identify the phases of Nonaka's spiral of organisational knowledge creation [10], and then to evaluate the presence of its enabling conditions against an established target for the process. Knowledge management services were selected to address identified deficiencies in the enabling conditions, and selectively integrated into the sample process. We demonstrated the operation of the framework's assessment function with an activity from the risk management process.

We recognise that additional work needs to be done to further develop our approach to the support of organisational knowledge creation in processes. The analysis of organisational knowledge creation enabling patterns in processes is required to develop targets for use during assessment. Matching criteria need to be established to aid in the automatic selection of knowledge management services to support identified areas of weakness in enabling conditions. The sourcing of services is also an issue. Each organisation can build its own library of services, but a more effective approach may be to seamlessly source services from vendors connected via the Internet and to negotiate for their use.

Future directions for our research include the characterisation of knowledge intensive processes in terms of knowledge management services, the refinement of an assessment approach for the identification of enabling conditions within organisational knowledge creation phases, and a business component design of the BPM framework to provide knowledge management services. We plan to interview participants in various knowledge intensive processes to define knowledge management services that are characteristic of these processes, and test our findings through the construction of a prototype. Progress made towards the definition of processes in terms of knowledge management services will help to refine the requirements for successful e-business collaboration. Designing the business process management framework as a set of business components will deliver the flexibility and rapid response to changing business needs required to keep e-business processes competitive [11]. It also provides a structure within which knowledge management services can be easily added and adapted to meet business needs.

**Acknowledgements:** The work reported in this paper has been funded in part by the Co-operative Research Centre Programme through the Australian Government's Department of the Industry, Science and Resources.

The author would like to thank Luke Cole, Valérie Gay, Dennis Hagarty, Christopher Lueg and the reviewers for their comments on drafts of this paper.

# 5. REFERENCES

1. Bultje, R. and van Wijk, J. Taxonomy of Virtual Organisations, Based on Definitions, Characteristics and Typology. *VoNet: The Newsletter @http://www.virtual-organization.net, 2* (3). 7-20.
2. Checkland, P. and Scholes, J. *Soft Systems Methodology in Action*. Wiley, Chichester, West Sussex, England, 1990.
3. Davenport, T.H. and Prusak, L. *Working Knowledge: How Organizations Manage What They Know*. Harvard Business School Press, Boston, Mass, 1998.
4. Drucker, P.F. *Post-Capitalist Society*. HarperBusiness, New York, NY, 1993.
5. Hammer, M. and Champy, J. *Reengineering the Corporation: A Manifesto for Business Revolution*. Allen & Unwin, St Leonards, NSW, 1996.
6. Johannessen, J.-A., Olaisen, J. and Olsen, B. Mismanagement of tacit knowledge: the importance of tacit knowledge, the danger of information technology, and what to do about it. *International Journal of Information Management, 21*. 3-20.
7. Kalakota, R. and Robinson, M. *E-Business : Roadmap for Success*. Addison-Wesley, Reading, Mass, 1999.
8. Kock, N. Benefits for Virtual Organizations from Distributed Groups. *Communications of the ACM, 43* (11). 107-112.
9. Nonaka, I. A dynamic theory of organizational knowledge creation. *Organization Science, 5* (1). 14-37.
10. Nonaka, I. and Takeuchi, H. *The Knowledge-Creating Company : How Japanese Companies Create the Dynamics of Innovation*. Oxford University Press, New York, 1995.
11. Riggins, F.J. and Rhee, H.-K., Developing the Learning Network Using Extranets. in *Proceedings of the Thirty-First Hawaiian Conference on Systems Sciences*, (Hawaii, 1998).
12. Slembek, I. and Gay, V., An Architecture for the Support of Knowledge-Intensive e-Business Processes. in *Proceedings of the 6th International Conference on Object Oriented Information Systems*, (London, 2000), Springer Verlag, 113-120.
13. Standards_Australia *AS/NZS 4360: Risk Management*. Standards Association of Australia, Strathfield, NSW, 1999.
14. Yang, J. and Papazoglou, M.P. Interoperation Support for Electronic Business. *Communications of the ACM, 43* (6). 39-47.

35

# Electronic Reverse Auctions - Success Metrics & Dynamics

Ido Millet, Diane H. Parente, John L. Fizel, Ray R. Venkataraman
*Penn State Erie, School of Business, Erie, PA 16563-1400*

**Abstract**: This paper describes an on-going study analyzing thousands of electronic procurement auctions conducted by a large multinational firm. We describe the challenges of developing metrics for auction success and auction dynamics and how these metrics improve our ability to model, understand, and manage this domain. Since we are in the initial stages of our study and since many of our findings are confidential, this paper is limited to describing the metrics and the relationships investigated between supplier experience, supplier participation levels, late bidding behavior, and electronic reverse auction success. By the time of the presentation, we expect to obtain permission to reveal more details about our findings.

## 1. INTRODUCTION

Online auctions are rapidly increasing in popularity and importance (Gaudin, 2000; Lucking-Reiley, 2000; Rupley, 2000; Shaw, 1999). While the business-to-consumer (B2C) has been the most popular category of online auctions, business-to-business (B2B) online auctions are emerging as a prominent business model (Rupley, 2000). In 1999 alone, B2B online auctions totaled $109 billion worth of transactions, and that number is expected to grow to $1.3 trillion by 2003 (Gaudin, 2000).

Within the category of B2B online auctions there has been rapid development of reverse auctions (Turban et al., 2000) and many companies are achieving substantial savings through such online procurement auctions (Brunelli, 2000; Schwartz and Mendel, 1999). In reverse auctions the buying company hosts the online auction and extends invitations to potential suppliers to bid on announced request-for-quotations (RFQs). The supplier with the lowest price wins the contract.

While B2B procurement auctions are clearly a significant phenomenon, there is a dearth of empirical research on the performance and dynamics of these auctions. In order to support such empirical research, metrics for online auction success and related factors must be established. This paper describes the type of metrics and analysis used in studying thousands of electronic procurement auctions conducted by a large multinational firm.

Since we are in the initial stages of our study and since many of our findings are confidential, we limit our discussion to a description of the metrics and the relationships investigated between supplier experience, supplier participation levels, late bidding behavior, and electronic reverse auction success. We begin by describing auction success metrics. We then turn to supplier participation metrics, supplier experience metrics, and late bidding behavior metrics. The paper concludes with examples of how these metrics can help us research, understand, and manage electronic procurement auctions. By the time of the presentation, we expect to obtain permission to reveal more details about our findings.

## 2. AUCTION SUCCESS METRICS

As one of the reviewers of this paper pointed out, measuring auction success is an important yet elusive task. The reviewer observed that success should be measured as the auction effectiveness at finding the optimal market price. Since optimal market price is typically an unknown, we must rely upon surrogate measures.

A typical approach is to measure reverse auction success in terms of price reduction for the product or products included in the procurement process. This metric, as one of the paper reviewers pointed out, is far from ideal, since further auction cycles for the same product would probably fail to generate similar price reductions. However, since we are currently in the early stages of applying online procurement auctions and since reporting of price reduction holds an obvious appeal to management, it is the metric of choice in current literature.

For example, the Navy officials in NAVSUP estimate a 28.9% savings off the purchase price for their components through reverse auctions (Anonymous, 2000). Similarly, Quaker Oats reports millions of dollars in savings by purchasing via reverse online auctions (Brunelli, 2000). However, it is not clear how these savings should be measured.

In many cases, the purchased item has no prior price or no prior price at the same purchase volume. Furthermore, prior purchase prices may fail to reflect existing market and production conditions. For example, the cost of raw materials or components can change dramatically over a short period. In our case study, the corporate buyer sets a starting bid for the auction, a price that may be below the prior contract price and is expected to reflect current market conditions. However, we have to assurance that the starting bid price set by the corporate buyer is a realistic and unbiased estimate.

In short, while measuring auction success can be accomplished by comparing the winning lowest bid price to a reference starting price, we must select from a number of alternatives for identifying the reference starting price. In our case study, we have identified three main alternatives for a starting price reference point: a) the staring bid price set by the corporate buyer, b) the actual price paid by the corporation in the last purchase of that product or service, and c) the first or highest bid price submitted during the auction.

As discussed above, the first two alternatives can result in missing or biased reference points and hence we elected to use the difference between the maximum and minimum bids as the main measure of auction success. It should be noted however that we found very high correlations between the three alternative measures of auction success.

Once a measure of auction success is established, we found a large number of interesting correlations between auction success and various factors. The rest of the paper will discuss three of these factors.

## 3. SUPPLIER PARTICIPATION METRICS

Theoretical and empirical analysis of traditional auctions has clearly established that more bidders will improve the winning bid (see, for example,Brannman et al., 1987). However, our analysis of B2B procurement auctions suggests that bidder participation is a multi-stage process and that each stage is critical to developing effective auction participation rates. We developed a set of metrics to measure the level of participation response at each of these stages. These metrics include measures such as: a) number of suppliers invited, b) number and percent of suppliers who accepted the invitation, c) number and percent of suppliers who actually logged in to the online reverse auction site, d) number and percent of suppliers who actually submitted bids, and e) number of actual bids.

Statistical analysis shows that all of these metrics are significant factors in explaining auction success. We then discovered various factors that can explain and even influence supplier participation levels. For example, by inviting an optimal number of suppliers to an optimally sized auction, conducted over an optimal time window, auction success may be improved.

It was during that phase of the investigation that we asked ourselves if supplier experience in online auctions could be a useful predictor of participation levels and auction success.

# 4. SUPPLIER EXPERIENCE METRICS

Bidder experience has been recognized by prior research as an important factor in investigating auction dynamics (Andreoni and Miller, 1995; Kagel, 1998; Phillips et al., 1991; Wilcox, 2000). Since we had no access to information about supplier experience in B2B procurement auctions in general, we considered metrics that measure participation experience as reflected by the data set of the corporation itself. This was facilitated by the fact that the data set included the participation and bidding history for thousands of online auction events.

Using our data set, supplier participation experience could be measured in a variety of ways: a) number of times a supplier accepted an invitation to participate, b) number of times a supplier logged in to previous auctions, c) number of bids submitted by the supplier in previous auctions, and d) number of previous auctions where the supplier submitted the winning bids. The number of auctions previously won by a bidder has been used by Wilcox in a recent empirical investigation of eBay auctions (2000). However, this measure seems overly restrictive and was probably used due to lack of alternative data. We have no conclusions yet about which of these alternative metrics is the most significant, but we have several initial findings.

Our preliminary investigation focused on the experience metric of number of times a supplier has logged-in to previous auctions. We found a significant correlation between average level of supplier experience in each auction and the success of that auction. We also found that different levels of supplier experience resulted in different auction dynamics, such as late bidding behavior.

The significance of these findings is that corporate buyers can influence the level of experience in the bidder pool since they invite specific suppliers to each auction event. By providing the buyers with guidelines about optimal average experience level for each auction type and experience level profiles for each supplier, the buyer can manage the invitation process to produce a supplier pool that is closer to prescribed levels of experience. For example, if the invited pool of suppliers is too inexperienced, an exception report can alert the buyer to that fact.

# 5. SUPPLIER SUITABILITY METRICS

One of the reviewers of this paper correctly observed that supplier suitability to provide the requested product or service is a major factor in determining auction success. Due to lack of data on supplier suitability, this factor was outside the scope of our initial investigation. However, we hope to address this issue by suggesting to our case firm that suitability metrics be subjectively assigned by the buyers as they invite each supplier to participate in the auction.

# 6. LATE BIDDING BEHAVIOR

Late bidding behavior occurs in reverse auctions when suppliers submit bids towards the end of the auction time window. Theory and empirical research indicate that in auctions where the buyer is uncertain about the value of the purchased item, late bidding behavior arises (Milgrom and Weber, 1982; Wilcox, 2000). One reason for this phenomenon is that by delaying their bids, participants can use pricing information in other bids as a mechanism for gathering information about the common value attributed to the auctioned item by others.

In the case of reverse auctions, we can apply symmetrical reasoning and expect more pronounced late bidding behavior when suppliers are uncertain about the cost or risks involved in producing the requested item. Our initial findings indicate that indeed late bidding behavior is a significant phenomenon in B2B reverse auctions. It is correlated with auction success and is influenced by a variety of factors, including supplier participation levels, supplier experience, and product type.

Simple metrics of late bidding behavior include number and percent of bids submitted in the last period of the auction time window. These metrics show significant correlations with the factors above. However, more sophisticated metrics of late bidding behavior show even greater promise in clarifying auction dynamics.

# 7. CONCLUSIONS

While we are only in the initial phases of our research, work is already in progress within the corporation to apply the metrics and initial findings to the management and control of online procurement auctions. The objective is to carefully adjust factors that are under management or buyer control in order to increase auction success.

Future research is needed to test the applicability of our findings to other organizational and auction type settings. For example, will auction participation dynamics and their relationships to auction success change significantly once much of the profit margin has been squeezed out due to repeated auction cycles? Price savings in initial auctions may capture reductions in both transaction and production costs. However, price savings in subsequent auctions must be generated almost exclusively from continued efficiencies in production, and from the inclusion of newer, lower-cost suppliers.

Future research is also needed to expand the number of success factors modeled and investigated. Factors such as trust, security, auction web site content, design and features were outside the scope of our initial investigation.

Online auctions provide a unique opportunity to apply theory, data mining techniques, and information technology to the development of better models and understanding of auction dynamics. We hope that this paper contributes to our ability to address this research agenda.

# 8. REFERENCES

Andreoni, J. and J. Miller, "Auctions with Artificial Adaptive Agents," Games and Economic Behavior, 10: 1 (1995), 39-64.

Anonymous, "Revisiting reverse auctions," Agency Sales, 30: 9 (2000), 31-33.

Brannman, L., J.D. Klein, and L.W. Weiss, "The price effects of increased competition in auction markets," The Review of Economics and Statistics, 69: 1 (1987), 24-32.

Brunelli, M., "Online auctions save millions for Quaker Oats and SmithKline Beecham," in Purchasing 128 (2000).

Gaudin, S., "Auction action," in Network World 17 (2000).

Kagel, J.H., "Cross-game Learning: Experimental Evidence from First-price and English Common Value Auctions," Economics Letters, 49 (1998), 163-70.

Lucking-Reiley, D., "Auctions on the Internet: What's being auctioned, and how?," Journal of Industrial Economics, 48: 3 (2000), 227-52.

Milgrom, P. and R.J. Weber, "ATheory of Auctions and Competitive Bidding," Econometrica, 50 (1982), 1089-122.

Phillips, O.R., R.C. Battalio, and K. C.A., "Sunk and Opportunity Costs in Valuation and Bidding," Southern Economic Journal, 58: 1 (1991), 112-28.

Rupley, S., "Biz-to-Biz auctions," in PC Magazine (2000).

Schwartz, E. and B. Mendel, "Auctions preserve pricing: New business model helps suppliers retain price integrity," InfoWorld, 21: 42 (1999), 12.

Shaw, M.J., "Electronic commerce: Review of critical research issues," Information Systems Frontiers, 1: 1 (1999), 95-106.

Turban, E., J. Lee, D. King, and M.H. Chung, Electronic commerce: A managerial perspective. Prentice Hall: New Jersey (2000).

Wilcox, R.T., "Experts and Amateurs: The Role of Experience in Internet Auctions," Marketing Letters, 11: 4 (2000), 363-74.

36

# Security Modelling for Electronic Commerce: The Common Electronic Purse Specifications*

Jan Jürjens[1] and Guido Wimmel[2]

[1]*Computing Laboratory, University of Oxford, email: jan@comlab.ox.ac.uk*

[2]*Dept. of Computer Science, Munich University of Technology, email: wimmel@in.tum.de*

**Abstract:** Designing security-critical systems correctly is very difficult. We present work on software engineering of security critical systems, supported by the CASE tool AUTOFOCUS.

Security critical systems are specified with extended structure diagrams, message sequence charts for the protocols and statecharts for the attacker, translated into an AUTOFOCUS system model and examined for security weaknesses using model checking. Additionally, the specifications could be simulated or tested - which is a first step towards integration of cryptographic primitives, intuitive graphical modelling, simulation and model checking.

We explain our method at the example of a part of the Common Electronic Purse Specifications (CEPS), and comment on potential of vulnerability and consequences for the design.

## 1. INTRODUCTION

Security aspects have become an increasingly important issue in developing distributed systems, especially in the electronic business sector. Because failures of security mechanisms may cause very high potential damage (e.g., loss of money through fraud), the correctness of such systems is crucial.

Designing security critical systems correctly is difficult. Also, it is easy to misunderstand assumptions on the environment in which e.g. protocols are to be used and what their secure functioning may rely on. Security violations often occur

* This work was partially supported by the Studienstiftung des deutschen Volkes, and by the German Ministry of Economics within the FairPay project

at the boundaries between security mechanisms and the general system (Gollmann, 1999; Anderson, 2001).

Therefore, the consideration of security aspects has to be integrated into general systems development (Anderson, 1994). Common modelling techniques used in industry, such as collaboration diagrams, state charts and message sequence charts have to be tailored for that purpose. For instance, (Jürjens, 2001c) presents first work towards that goal by extending the UML (Unified Modelling Language).

On the other hand, to ensure the correctness of the systems, the models have to be sufficiently precise, to be able to state security properties in an unambiguous way and to formally verify their truth or find possible weaknesses, using mathematical reasoning or automated verification with model checkers.

In this work, we show how to model and reason about a security-critical protocol (the purchase transaction) of the Common Electronic Purse Specifications CEPS (CEPSCO, 2000), supported by the CASE tool AUTOFOCUS (Huber et al., 1998a; Huber et al., 1998b). CEPS is a candidate for a globally interoperable electronic purse standard supported by organisations (including Visa International) representing 90 percent of the world's electronic purse cards and likely to become an accepted standard (Asokan et al., 2000). This makes its security an important goal.

We specify cryptographic protocols using message sequence charts (MSCs), in a way similar to the usual informal notation of security protocols. These specifications can be translated mechanically into an AUTOFOCUS system model consisting of state transition diagrams (STDs) (Krüger, 2000). Together with the modelled adversary, this system is checked for security weaknesses automatically using the model checker SMV connected to AUTOFOCUS to verify the desired security properties of the protocol.

Our approach has the benefits of combining intuitive graphical modelling, simulation and model checking, and allows to represent counterexamples as MSCs. Since the AUTOFOCUS tool is closely related to the formal development method Focus (Broy et al., 1992), our approach also supports formal proofs in this framework, allowing to build on results such as (Lotz, 1997). The intruder model used is rather flexible, the adversary can switch between acting as one or another party, intercept only certain messages or learn certain keys etc.

In the following subsection we present some background information and refer to related work. In Section 2, we give an overview over the Common Electronic Purse Specifications, specify the part under consideration and explain the security threat model. In Section 3, we introduce the notation of AUTOFOCUS and use it to investigate the above specification. We end with a conclusion and indicate further planned work.

## 1.1 Security-Assurance Using Formal Tools

There has been extensive research in using formal methods to verify security protocols, following an abstract way to describe protocols in (Dolev and Yao, 1983). A few examples are (Burrows et al., 1989; Lowe 1996; Paulson 1998; Pfitzmann and Waidner 2001); an overview is in (Gritzalis et al., 1999; Ryan et al., 2001). Smart card protocols have been investigated using formal logic in (Abadi et al., 1993). (Gollmann, 2000) points out the need to consider the underlying physical layer in formal security investigations.

While many case-studies consider protocols from the academic literature (usually presented in a much more tractable form), notable examples of verifications of smart-card payment system used in practice can be found in (Anderson, 1999; Stepney et al., 2000).

As an example for the treatment of security in the context of general systems engineering, (Jürjens, 2001c) presents work towards using the UML notation in security engineering which is applied to the CEPS load transaction in (Jürjens, 2001a).

AUTOFOCUS has been used for security in (Wimmel and Wißpeintner, 2001), the underlying Focus model in (Lotz, 1997).

# 2. CEPS

We give an overview over the Common Electronic Purse Specifications and specify the (simplified) purchase transaction to be investigated.

Stored value smart cards ("electronic purses") have been proposed to allow cash-free point-of-sale (POS) transactions offering more fraud protection than credit cards: Their built-in chip can perform cryptographic operations which allows transaction-bound authentication[55] (whereas credit card numbers are valid until the card is stopped, enabling misuse). The card contains an account balance that is adjusted when loading the card or purchasing goods.

Here we consider the central part of CEPS, the purchase transaction, which allows the cardholder to use the electronic value on a card to pay for goods. The participants involved in the transaction protocol are the customer's card and the merchant's POS device. The POS device contains a Purchase Security Application Module (PSAM) (a smart-card) that is used to store and process data and assumed to be tamper-resistant. During the transaction, the account balance in the card is decremented, and the balance in the PSAM is incremented by the corresponding amount. The card issuer later receives transaction logs.

[55]For a discussion of authentication cf. (Gollmann, 1996).

In addition to transactions using public terminals it is intended to use CEPS-cards for transactions over the Internet (CEPSCO, 2000, Bus. Req.).

## 2.1 Specification of CEPS Purchase Transaction

Apart from incremental transactions not considered here, security functionality is provided only by the PSAM (and not the rest of the POS device). Thus our protocol participants are the CEP card $C$ and the PSAM $M$ (with public and private keys $K_C$ and $K_C^{-1}$ resp. $K_M$ and $K_M^{-1}$, where the public keys are exchanged before the transaction). The protocol consists of the following steps (see Fig. 3 for a formal specification by AUTOFOCUS MSCs):

1. PSAM → Card: $\mathrm{Init}(\{\{SK_{PS}\}_{K_M^{-1}}\}_{K_C})$
2. Card → PSAM: $\mathrm{Resp}(\{S\}_{SK_{PS}})$
3. PSAM → Card: OK

The PSAM initiates the transaction after the CEP card is inserted into the POS device, by sending a message containing a freshly created session key $SK_{PS}$ signed by $M$ and encrypted with $C$'s public key. Whenever the card receives a message after being inserted into the POS device, it tries to decrypt it with its private key and checks its signature with $M$'s public key. If this is successful, $C$ responds with a message containing $S$ encrypted under the received session key (otherwise it waits for the next message). $S$ contains identification data to authenticate the card and transaction data for logging purposes (and validation by the card issuer later). We assume that only $C$ can produce $S$ and that $M$ can verify if a received message is such an $S$ produced by $C$ (in practice, this is achieved by having $C$ sign the message) and therefore model $S$ simply as a secret value (to simplify mechanical verification). Finally, after $M$ receives a message encrypted under $SK_{PS}$ it stores the contents and ends with a message OK. We leave out some message parts that are only relevant for logging.

## 2.2 Security Threat Model

The CEP specifications require the smart card and the PSAM (but not the POS device (CEPSCO, 2000, Bus Req. p. 13, Funct. req. p. 20) to be tamper-proof. The purchase transaction is supposed to provide mutual authentication between the terminal and the card using a chain of certificates of which the first is issued by a Certification Authority and the last contains the card's or PSAM's public key.

The smart card is inserted into a POS device and can thus communicate with the PSAM. Since there is no direct communication between the cardholder and her card, the information displayed by the POS device regarding the transaction has to be trusted at the point of transaction. Security for the customer against fraud by the merchant is supposed to be provided through logging the (signed) transaction details and a posteriori settlement involving the card issuer. Similarly, security for the merchant against the customer is supposed to be provided by exchanging the purchased good only for a signed message from the card containing the transaction details, for which the merchant will receive the corresponding monetary amount from the issuer afterwards. The idea is that risk of fraud is kept small since fraud should be detected in the settlement later and certificates of cards or PSAMs actively involved in fraud can be revoked.

In our formal investigation, we consider the following two threat scenarios to see if they allow an attack: A sufficiently motivated adversary makes a POS device publicly available (for ATMs, such cases are reported in (Anderson, 1994)) which only communicates with the card (to receive transaction information) and returns the card with an error message, without actually having completed a transaction.

In the first scenario, the attacker then uses a smart card including the information obtained from the earlier interaction and tries to attack a merchant's POS device by buying goods with transaction messages signed by the earlier attacked card. If the attack succeeds, the attacker terminal or card do not show up in the audit trail at all, so the attacker cannot be made responsible. This scenario corresponds to an attempted attack (also called "man-in-the-middle" attack) where the attacker first communicates with the attacked card (in the role of a PSAM) and then with the attacked PSAM (in the role of a card).

In the second, more sophisticated scenario the attacker could try to attack an inserted card as above, and in parallel a PSAM in a POS device set up by a merchant in an unsupervised place by tampering with the POS device (not assumed to be tamper-proof) in order to directly communicate with the PSAM. Via a radio connection the attacker could thus communicate both with the attacked card and the attacked PSAM (if he succeeds in synchronising the two events). Thus he could buy goods with transaction messages signed by the card attacked at the same time. Again the attacker terminal or card do not show up in the audit trail. In this scenario the attacker communicates with the attacked card and the attacked PSAM in parallel.

This scenario is more realistic when using CEPS for transactions over the Internet, as intended (CEPSCO, 2000, Bus. Req.). Then, the mentioned synchronisation is much easier to realise, since the attacker needs to initiate his purchase over the Internet only when the attacked card is inserted into the modified terminal and can pay directly with the attacked card. Of course, the purchase should be anonymous (e.g. access to multimedia content).

# 3. INVESTIGATING CEPS WITH AUTOFOCUS

In this chapter, we show how to specify security critical systems using the CASE tool AUTOFOCUS/Quest (Huber et al., 1998a; Slotosch, 1998; Phillips and Slotosch, 1999) recently developed at Munich University of Technology with the goal to combine user-friendly graphical system design using common description techniques such as collaboration diagrams, state charts and message sequence charts, and support of simulation, code generation and formal verification of correctness.

(Jürjens, 2001b) gives a specification language to represent cryptographic primitives in Focus (Broy et al., 1992), the formal foundation of AUTOFOCUS. On the basis of this and an earlier case study — an AUTOFOCUS model of the Needham-Schroeder public key protocol — we present a framework for AUTOFOCUS specifications of such systems. The Focus specification language in (Jürjens, 2001b) and the AUTOFOCUS model are closely related and can easily be translated into each other, so simulation, verification, code generation and model checking in AUTOFOCUS are supported as well as formal proofs using the Focus method.

System specifications in AUTOFOCUS make use of the following views:

- **System Structure Diagrams (SSDs)** are similar to data flow resp. collaboration diagrams and describe the structure and the interface of a system. In the SSD view, a system consists of a number of communicating components, which have input and output ports to allow for sending and receiving messages of a particular data type. The ports can be connected via channels, making it possible for the components to exchange data. SSDs can be hierarchical, i.e. a component belonging to an SSD can have a substructure that is defined by an SSD itself. Besides, the components in an SSD can be associated with local variables.
- **Data Type Definitions (DTDs)** define the data types used in the model, with the functional language Quest (Phillips and Slotosch, 1999). In addition to basic types as integer, user-defined hierarchic data types are offered that are similar to those in functional programming languages.
- **State Transition Diagrams (STDs)** represent extended finite automata and are used to describe the behaviour of a component in an SSD. The automata consist of a set States of states, and a set $Tr \subseteq \text{States} \times \text{States} \times \text{PRE\_EXP} \times \text{INP\_EXP} \times \text{OUT\_EXP} \times \text{POST\_EXP}$ of transitions, where
  - PRE_EXP are boolean terms on local variables and variables bound in INP_EXP representing a **precondition** for transition firing.
  - INP_EXP denotes **input patterns** of the form $inp_1?x;inp_2?y;...$ (i.e., reading values from input channels). The $x,y$ can also be pattern matching expressions (which will be explained later).
  - OUT_EXP denotes **output expressions** of the form $out_1!term_1;out_2!term_2;...$ (output values of expressions to ports)
  - POST_EXP are **postconditions** of the form $lvar_1{:=}term_1;lvar_2{:=}term_2;...$ (sets local variables to the values of $term_i$, which can include local variables and variables bound in INP_EXP).
- In AUTOFOCUS, a transition $(s,t,p,i,o,q)$ from $s$ to $t$ is annotated with $p{:}i{:}o{:}q$. Leaving out components is interpreted as **true** for pre-conditions, and as the empty list in the other cases. A transition is executable if the input patterns

match the values at the input channels and the precondition is true. At each clock tick, one executable transition in each component fires, outputs the values specified by the output patterns and sets the local variables according to the postcondition. The values at the output ports can be read by the connected components in the next clock cycle.

- **Extended Event Traces (EETs)** finally make it possible to describe exemplary system runs, similar to MSCs (ITU, 1996).
- The Quest extensions (Slotosch, 1998) to AUTOFOCUS offer various connections to programming languages and formal verification tools, such as Java code generation, model checking using SMV, and bounded model checking and test case generation (Wimmel et al., 2000).

# 4. SPECIFICATION OF SECURITY CRITICAL SYSTEMS IN AUTOFOCUS

### 4.1.1 Abstract System Model

Figure 1 shows an abstract system model (high-level design) of the CEPS purchase transaction. The system consists of two components `Card` and `PSAM`, which are connected via channels. In addition to conventional system structure diagrams, one can use security tags (Wimmel and Wißpeintner, 2001) to specify properties relevant for security evaluations. In this case, the channels are labelled with "public", which means that they can be accessed by an intruder. Moreover, the protocol between the two parties is specified.

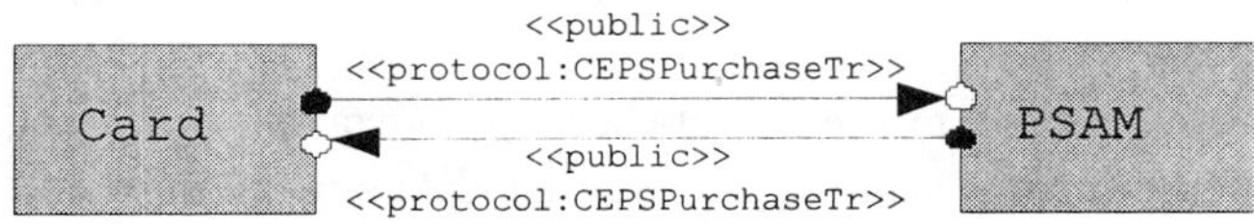


*Figure 1.* Abstract System Model for CEPS

The abstract system model must then be refined into system structure, behaviour and data type views to allow for concrete security analyses.

### 4.1.2 System Structure Diagram

Figure 2 shows the system structure diagram of the system. It corresponds to the system model shown in Fig. 1. However, there is now an additional component `Intruder`. As the channel between `PSAM` and `Card` in Fig. 1 was marked "public", all messages between `PSAM` and `Card` have to pass this component, which thus can access and manipulate the messages. The additional channels `rndi` into the intruder are explained later.

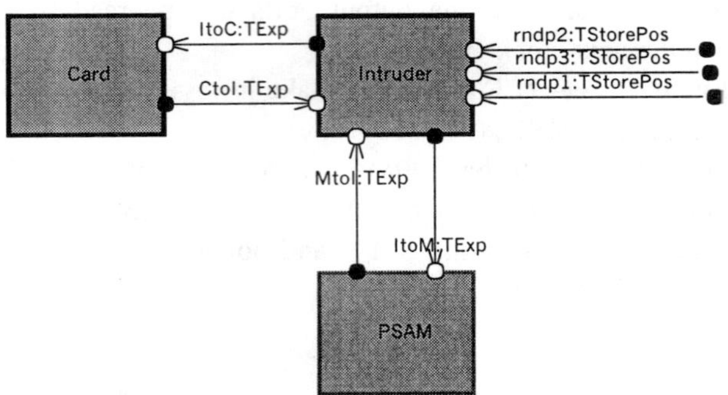


*Figure 2.* System Structure Diagram for CEPS System

### 4.1.3 Data Type Definition

The messages that can be sent through the channels are cryptographic expressions. A cryptographic expressions can be a basic element such as an empty message, a key or a name, or an encrypted expression (under a certain key), or a concatenation of two expressions. This is represented by the following AUTOFOCUS data type definition:

```
data TKey = KM_ | KM | KC_ | KC | SKPS | SKI | S;
data TExp = Empty | Key(TKey) | Encr(TKey,TExp)
  | Concat(TExp,TExp);
```

The keys given in the definition of `TKey` correspond to the keys used in the specification shown in Section 2.1. `KC_` denotes $K_C^{-1}$, and an additional secret key `SKI` was added for the intruder.

However, to be able to use model-checking to examine vulnerabilities, the data types need to be finite. Therefore the recursive data type `TExp` must be replaced by a non-recursive one. This is straightforward to accomplish if we note that in our system we only have two possible types of valid messages: a message of the form $\{x\}_{K1}$ and a message $\{\{x\}_{K1}\}_{K2}$. We thus represent these by the new data types `TEncr1` and `TEncr2`. `TExp` can now either be `Empty` or consist of one of these data types:

```
data TExp = Empty | Exp1(exp1:TEncr1) |
Exp2(exp2:TEncr2);
data TEncr1 = Encr1(keyenc1:TKey, expenc1:TKey);
data TEncr2 = Encr2(keyenc2:TKey, expenc2:TEncr1);
```

Expressions can now be represented by constructor terms. For example, `Exp1(Encr1(SKPS,S))` corresponds to $\{S\}_{SK_{PS}}$, and

`Exp2(Encr2(KM,Encr1(KC_,SKPS)))` corresponds to $\{\{SK_{PS}\}_{K_C^{-1}}\}_{K_M}$. From the first message (say it is stored in a variable `x`), the key can be extracted using selectors: `keyenc1(exp1(x))` gives `SKPS`.

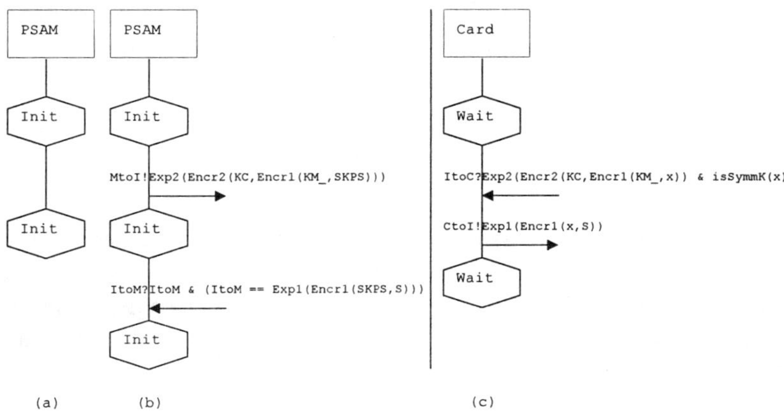


*Figure 3.* AutoFocus MSCs for CEPS System

### 4.1.4 Behaviour of the PSAM

The PSAM and the card execute the protocol *CEPSPurchaseTr*, which is specified using message sequence charts (MSCs). Figure 3(a),(b) show the AUTOFOCUS MSCs specifying the behaviour of the PSAM (conf. Fig. 1 – the message `OK` was left out because it has no security related meaning). In this figure, diamond shaped elements denote states. Thus, the PSAM can either wait in the `Init` state, or execute the protocol. Figure 4 shows the state transition diagram generated from this representation. MSCs are particularly suitable for specifying cryptograpic protocols as they represent sequential executions and correspond to the usual informal notation.

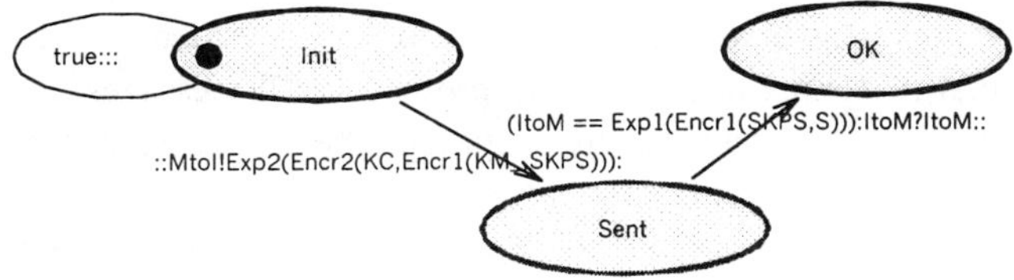


Figure 4. State Transition Diagram for the PSAM

#### 4.1.5 Behaviour of the Card

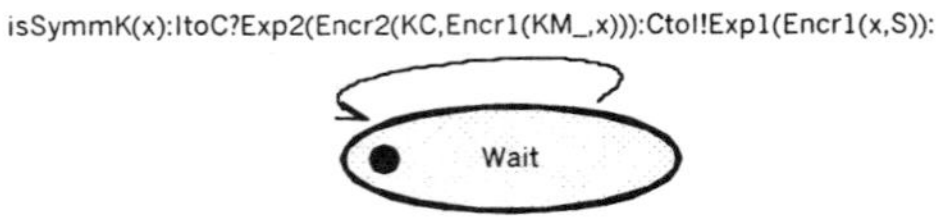


*Figure 5.* State Transition Diagram for the Card

Figure 5 shows the state transition diagram for the Card, generated from the specification in Fig. 3(c). This also demonstrates how *input patterns* can be used in AUTOFOCUS to make transition annotations more readable. The pattern `ItoC?Exp2(Encr2(KC,Encr1(KM_,x)))` is an abbreviation for `ItoC?ItoC` and the precondition

```
is_Exp2(ItoC)∧is_Encr2(exp2(ItoC))    ∧
keyenc2(exp2(ItoC))==KC
        ∧ ...
```

and binding of the variable *x* to `expenc1(expenc2(exp2(ItoC)))`.

In addition, the card makes sure that the key sent to it is a symmetric one. This is done by checking *`isSymmK(x)`*, which is given as a *function definition*, with obvious meaning:

```
fun isSymmK(SKPS) = True
  | isSymmK(SKI) = True
  | isSymmK(x) = False;
```

#### 4.1.6 The Intruder Model

The above model specifies the data types, system structure and behaviour of the involved parties for the CEPS purchase transaction. This system could now be simulated and tested using AUTOFOCUS.

To be able to investigate vulnerabilities, we use an intruder model commonly employed in formal reasoning about security protocols. All messages in the system are sent via the intruder, who can thus intercept them, learn secrets in the messages, and generate own messages or replay messages.

As the intruder model is highly nondeterministic and allows many different executions, it is best specified by an STD (see Figure 6). For readability, some transitions are annotated with a text label instead of the full annotation (which is shown by the CASE tool on a mouse click).

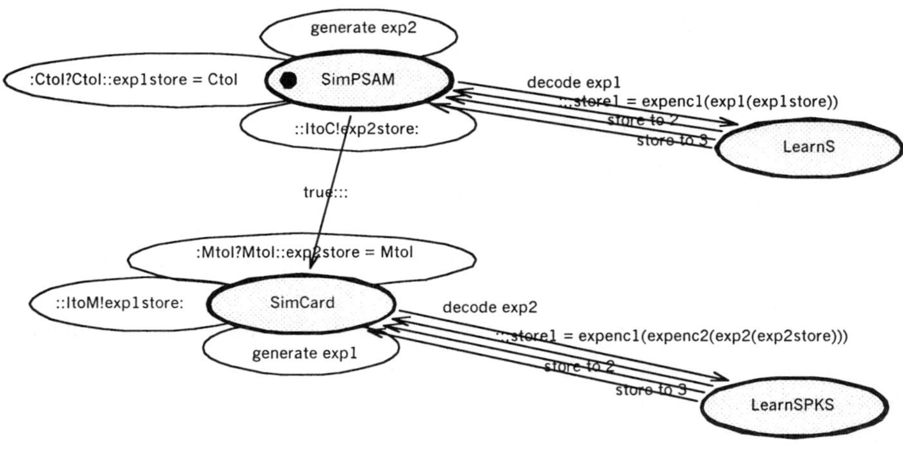


*Figure 6.* State Transition Diagram for the Intruder

The intruder can store two messages (local variables `exp1store` and `exp2store`), one of each type (`Exp1` and `Exp2`), and three keys (local variables `store1,2,3`). It has four states: `SimPSAM`, `SimCard`, `LearnS`, and `LearnSKPS`. In state `SimPSAM` it acts as the PSAM, reading messages from channel `CtoI` and storing them. The transition to `LearnS` labelled `decode exp1` can be executed if the intruder can decrypt the message in the store (which is of the form `Exp1(Encr(k,x)))` and learn the secret `x` contained in it. This is the case if the intruder has the key `k` somewhere in his key store. To model the searching of the store, the input channels `rndi` nondeterministically provide the intruder with a store position he can choose a key from, to compare it with the key used for encryption. Altogether, the `decode exp1` transition is given as

```
(is_Exp1(exp1store) && (keyenc1(exp1(exp1store)) ==
retrkey(store1,store2,store3,p1))):rndp1?p1::
```

where `retrkey` is a function choosing one of `store1`, `store2` ,`store3` depending on `p1`. In the transitions back to `SimPSAM`, the content of the message is stored in one of the three possible places.

In a similar way, the transition `generate exp2` chooses keys from the store to build up a message of the type `TExp2` to be sent to the card. Finally, the remaining transition just replays an expression stored in `exp2store`.

The intruder can also nondeterministically move to state `SimCard` where he simulates the card, in an analogous way to state `SimPSAM`.

Note that in this model, the intruder can only first act as the PSAM, and then as the Card. This restriction can be removed by adding a transition from `SimCard` to

SimPSAM. The model can also be tailored, e.g. not to allow the intruder to act as the PSAM at all, or not to learn certain keys or intercept particular messages etc.

## 4.2 Model Checking

The system specification described above specifies the behaviour of the CEPS purchase transaction protocol in presence of a hostile intruder. This specification can now be simulated or tested. In this paper we concentrate on model checking to examine the protocol with respect to possible vulnerabilities.

We consider a vulnerability a behaviour which leads to the PSAM reaching the OK state without prior having received the transaction information $S$ created by its *immediate* communication partner. Note that this is different from the situation of Internet protocols where communication is usually passed on by third parties (and possibly the adversary) due to the physical situation. Here, the holder of the card directly communicating with the PSAM receives the purchased goods without further authentication, which motivates the above definition. Since in our model the PSAM communicates directly only with the adversary, it is sufficient to check if it ever reaches the OK state.

The intruder first acts as the PSAM, only communicating with the card (state SimPSAM), and later as as the card (SimCard, only communicating with the PSAM). When there is an execution such that the PSAM reaches the state OK, the intruder managed to trick the PSAM into authenticating him.

For this purpose, we use the AUTOFOCUS connection to the model checker SMV. The property we check is AG¬(PSAM.State=*OK*), meaning in all reachable states (AG) the PSAM does not reach the stats OK in presence of the intruder.

If the property is violated, this indicates a vulnerability, and the model checker outputs a corresponding trace. Such a trace can then be automatically converted into an MSC and visualized in AUTOFOCUS.

Whether or not this situation arises depends on which keys the attacker possesses initially and how freely he can move between the states SimCard and SimPSAM. Below, we explain some scenarios we examined. Model checking took approximately 5 minutes on a SUN UltraSparc 2 (200 MHz, 1GB RAM).

- If the intruder only possesses the public keys KC, KM and his private key SKI, the model checker does not find an attack. Thus, we can conclude that with respect to the chosen attacker model, the CEPS purchase transaction has been shown to be correct. Due to the restrictions of the model, this is no full proof of course — further evaluation of the protocol can be carried out later by more thorough methods as theorem proving (automatically or by hand).[56]
- Assuming the private keys KC_ and KM_ leaked somehow, so the intruder could get hold of them. Then of course he can authenticate himself to the PSAM. The

[56]However, the restrictions could be justified with arguments similar as given in (Lowe, 1996)

model-checker correctly indicates this and outputs a corresponding MSC, which graphically visualizes the behaviour of the system in this case for the developer. Such *execution traces* can be generated by the model checker for many different kinds of specifications of possible runs (whether security related or not) and make it possible to test the implementation of the system or find and correct mistakes in the specification.

- Both private keys have to leak at the same time - if only one key leaks, the model checker does not find an attack. Thus, in the first threat scenario described in Section 2.2, no attack is possible without leaking keys.
- If one allows the intruder to move freely between the states `SimCard` and `SimPSAM` — as in the second threat scenario from Section 2.2 where the intruder communicates with the attacked card and the attacked PSAM in parallel — we find that the PSAM can actually reach the state `OK`. This is possible even if the intruder does not possess any keys. The corresponding execution trace is displayed in Figure 7 and shows the attacker acting as a relay, i.e. waiting for a message from the PSAM (in the `SimCard` mode), forwarding it to the card, waiting for the reply (in the `SimPSAM` mode) and forwarding it to the PSAM. The dashed lines represent time ticks (each tick corresponds to the execution of a transition in the automata). We can see that the intruder takes a number of ticks to record the messages before he can produce an answer. If the PSAM and the card wait for messages, this does not restrict the model. In addition, there is a spurious fake message from the intruder, which is ignored by the card (this message was generated by the model checker as part of the counterexample — in our model the intruder can sent any fake messages at any time).
- If we rule out this kind of behaviour (e.g., by not allowing the intruder to replay both messages), again no attack can be found.

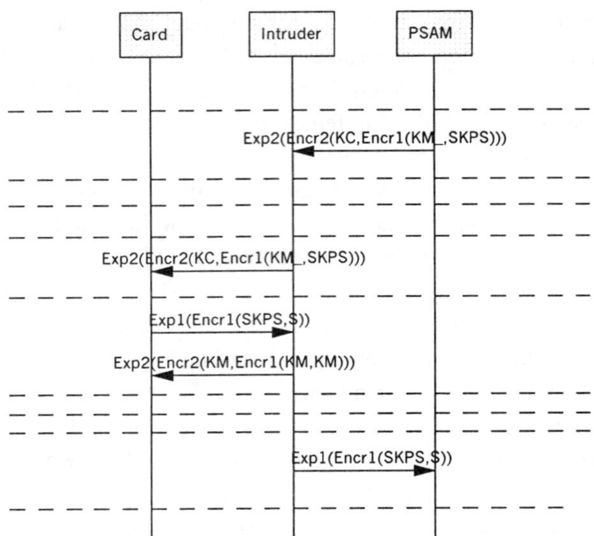


*Figure 7.* MSC for potential vulnerability in CEPS System

## 4.3 Interpretation of results

Our model showed that the CEPS purchase transaction is resistant to attacks of an intruder trying to have itself illegimately authenticated by the PSAM — except for the second, more sophisticated, threat scenario. As explained, this is no full proof of the correctness of the protocol.

The indicated potential vulnerability is present since firstly the card cannot communicate directly with the cardholder during the transaction and secondly CEPS does not include the entire POS device in the security perimeter. An intruder being able to attack a card and a PSAM in a remote place at the same time could therefore carry out purchase transactions with the attacked PSAM on the account of the attacked card. Given the card specifications (no own display) to avoid the first cause one would have to employ a challenge and response between card and user via the terminal, as suggested in (Abadi et al., 1993), which may however not always be practical. So the right conclusion may be to increase security by securing the Card Acceptance Devices (CAD) of (unattended) POS devices so that communication with the PSAM is only possible with proper smart cards without contact to the outside of the POS device, and not possible by bypassing the CAD.

Note that the scenario given in Figure 7 would not at all be considered a vulnerability in the context of Internet protocols, where it is assumed that an attacker may act as a relay. This again shows the importance of considering the underlying physical situation when investigating security of systems (Gollmann, 2000). Note also that even though the scenario pointed out above does not require any cryptographic operations on the side of the adversary, our model does of course perform these (under the usual restrictions regarding key knowledge) in the general case. Of course, the message exchange in Figure 7 does not require use of model checking techniques to be found, however, a benefit of formal methods is that they require the investigator to be very explicit about the assumptions (on the underlying physical security), which may be why the scenario has gone unnoticed so far.

Future work includes a more formal justification showing that an infinite-state adversary is no more powerful than the used finite-state one by computing the transitive closure of the possible actions.

# 5. CONCLUSION AND FUTURE WORK

We investigated the security of the currently developed Common Electronic Purse Specifications (CEPS) using the CASE tool AUTOFOCUS. Benefits of our approach include the possibility to specify and verify cryptographic protocols in the framework of a CASE tool, which enables a treatment in the context of system development. Since security violations often occur at the boundaries between security mechanisms (such as protocols) and the general system (Anderson, 2001), being able to treat protocols in the context of the system allows a more adequate security assessment. Besides these methodological benefits, we deliver concrete results on the security of the payment systems to be developed and fielded according to the CEPS. Our investigation showed a potential weakness arising from the fact that according to CEPS, the POS device is not part of the security perimeter and especially from the intended future use over the Internet. Due to space constraints we could only consider one part of the CEPS. Other parts are left for further work.

Note that the protocol considered is relatively simple. Our motivation was not to push the frontier of model checking technology but to indicate how to incorporate formal techniques for security engineering into general system development.

This work is only a first step towards "computer-aided security engineering". We intend to go further beyond the scope of formal methods as it is previously mostly applied in computer security by considering vulnerabilities arising from the way security mechanisms are employed in the system context and by employing tools beyond model-checking and theorem-proving (such as specification-based testing which we recently applied to firewall design (Jürjens and Wimmel, 2001)).

# REFERENCES

M. Abadi, M.Burrows, C.Kaufman, and B.Lampson. Authentication and delegation with smart-cards. *Science of Computer Programming*, 21(2):93–113, 1993.

R.Anderson. Why cryptosystems fail. *Communications of the ACM*, 37(11):32–40, November 1994.

R.Anderson. The formal verification of a payment system. In Mike Hinchey and Jonathan Bowen, editors, *Industrial-Strength Formal Methods in Practice*. Springer, 1999.

R.Anderson. *Security Engineering: A Guide to Building Dependable Distributed Systems*. Wiley, 2001.

N.Asokan, P.Janson, M.Steiner, and M.Waidner. The state of the art in electronic payment systems. *Advances in Computers*, 53, 2000.

M.Burrows, M.Abadi, and R.Needham. A logic of authentication. *Proceedings of the Royal Society of London A*, 426:233–271, 1989.

M.Broy, F.Dederich, C.Dendorfer, M.Fuchs, T.Gritzner, and R.Weber. The design of distributed systems - an introduction to FOCUS. Technical Report TUM-I9202, Technische Universität München, 1992.

CEPSCO. Common Electronic Purse Specifications, 2000. Business Requirements vers. 7.0, Functional Requirements vers. 6.3, Technical Specification vers.2.2, available from http://www.cepsco.com.

D.Dolev and A.Yao. On the security of public key protocols. *IEEE Transactions on Information Theory*, 29(2):198–208, 1983.

D.Gollmann. What do we mean by entity authentication ? In *IEEE Symposium on Security and Privacy*, 1996.

D.Gollmann. *Computer Security*. J. Wiley, 1999.

D. Gollmann. On the verification of cryptographic protocols - a tale of two committees. In *Workshop on Security Architectures and Information Flow*, volume 32 of *Electronical Notes in Theoretical Computer Science*, 2000.

Stefanos Gritzalis, Diomidis Spinellis, and Panagiotis Georgiadis. Security protocols over open networks and distributed systems: Formal methods for their analysis, design, and verification. *Computer Communications*, 22(8):695–707, 1999.

F.Huber, S.Molterer, A.Rausch, B.Schätz, M.Sihling, and O.Slotosch. Tool supported Specification and Simulation of Distributed Systems. In *International Symposium on Software Engineering for Parallel and Distributed Systems*, pages 155–164, 1998.

F.Huber, S.Molterer, B.Schätz, O.Slotosch, and A.Vilbig. Traffic Lights – An AUTOFOCUS Case Study. In *1998 International Conference on Application of Concurrency to System Design*, pages 282–294. IEEE Computer Society, 1998.

ITU. ITU-TS Recommendation Z.120: Message Sequence Chart (MSC). ITU-TS, Geneva, 1996.

Jan Jürjens. Object-oriented modelling of audit security for smart-card payment schemes. In P. Paradinas, editor, *IFIP/SEC 2001 – 16th International Conference on Information Security*. Kluwer, 2001a.

Jan Jürjens. Secrecy-preserving refinement. In *Formal Methods Europe*, LNCS. Springer, 2001b.

Jan Jürjens. Towards development of secure systems using UML. In H. Hußmann, editor, *Fundamental Approaches to Software Engineering (FASE/ETAPS, International Conference)*, LNCS. Springer, 2001c.

J.Jürjens and G.Wimmel. Specification-based Testing of Firewalls. In *Andrei Ershov 4th International Conference "Perspectives of System Informatics" (PSI'01)*. Springer, 2001. To appear.

I.Krüger. *Distributed System Design with Message Sequence Charts*. PhD thesis, Technische Universität München, 2000.

V.Lotz. Threat scenarios as a means to formally develop secure systems. *Journal of Computer Security 5*, pages 31–67, 1997.

G.Lowe. Breaking and fixing the Needham-Schroeder Public-Key Protocol using FDR. In Margaria and Steffen, editors, *TACAS*, volume 1055 of *LNCS*. Springer, 1996.

Lawrence C. Paulson. The inductive approach to verifying cryptographic protocols. *Journal of Computer Security*, 6(1–2):85–128, 1998.

J.Philipps and O.Slotosch. The Quest for Correct Systems: Model Checking of Diagramms and Datatypes. In *Asia Pacific Software Engineering Conference 1999*, 1999.

Birgit Pfitzmann and Michael Waidner. A model for asynchronous reactive systems and its applications to secure message transmissions. In *IEEE Symposium on Security and Privacy*, 2001.

P.Ryan, S.Schneider, M.Goldsmith, G. Lowe, and B. Roscoe. *Analysis and Design of Security Protocols*. Addison Wesley, 2001.

S.Stepney, D.Cooper, and J.Woodcock. *An Electronic Purse: Specification, Refinement, and Proof.* Oxford University Computing Laboratory, 2000. Technical Monograph PRG-126.

O.Slotosch. Quest: Overview over the Project. In D.Hutter, W.Stephan, PTraverso, and M.Ullmann, editors, *Applied Formal Methods - FM-Trends 98*, pages 346–350. Springer LNCS 1641, 1998.

G.Wimmel, H.Lötzbeyer, A.Pretschner, and O.Slotosch. Specification Based Test Sequence Generation with Propositional Logic. *Journal on Software Testing Verification and Reliability*, 10, 2000.

G.Wimmel and A.Wißpeitner. Extended description techniques for security engineering. In P.Paradinas, editor, *IFIP/SEC 2001 – 16th International Conference on Information Security*. Kluwer, 2001.

37

# A Three-Phase Model of Electronic Marketplaces for Software Components in Chemical Engineering

Mareike Schoop, Jörg Köller, Thomas List, Christoph Quix
*Informatik V (Information Systems), RWTH Aachen, 52056 Aachen, Germany*
*{schoop,koeller,list,quix}@informatik.rwth-aachen.de*

**Abstract**: Electronic marketplaces in the business-to-business operate in different branches. Abstracting from these realisations of the concept of an electronic marketplace, we can derive a general model of a business transaction with the following three phases. Starting with a search for new business partners, successful negotiations lead to a contract which then needs to be fulfilled. In this paper, these three phases will be discussed in detail, emphasising the problems with current practices in electronic marketplaces. An extended model that overcomes these problems will be presented and applied to the context of trading of software components for chemical engineering.

## 1. INTRODUCTION

Electronic marketplaces in the business-to-business area have been the subject of research for a number of years. These types of marketplaces provide a forum for bringing together buyers and sellers with the aim of enabling and supporting trade. In recent years we have seen different implementations of the concept of an e-marketplace. For example, some approaches (such as [www.baunetz.de]) concentrate on providing facilities for finding new partners. Interactions leading to a business deal and fulfilling the related contract are not supported and thus need to take place outside the marketplace. Other approaches (such as [www.chemunity.com]) automate the interactions. No search is possible but a request is directly sent to approved suppliers in an auction-like manner.

In general, we can abstract from the different implementations onto a general model of a business transaction. Starting with a search for new business partners, successful negotiations lead to a contract which needs to be fulfilled. Such a three-phase model (search, negotiate, fulfil) has been used in many facets [SS01] and sometimes integrated with other views on business processes [SL98].

In this paper we will present the model in detail and discuss the current practices for each of the three phases. Problems will be pointed out and extensions to the current practices will be proposed to overcome the problems. Thus a new comprehensive model will be presented (section 2). The application context of trading software components for chemical engineering, that requires a sophisticated electronic marketplace will be introduced (sections 3 and 4). Our model will then be applied to the context, showing the specific requirements of such a marketplace (section 5). This paper concludes with a discussion of our approach.

## 2. A MODEL FOR A B2B E-COMMERCE PROCESS

During a commerce process, the involved participants usually go through three phases. Firstly, a party looks for potential business partners. A buyer wants to find relevant suppliers of the product (s)he is looking for; a seller might want to find potential customers for the products (s)he can supply. After locating potential (new) partners, the second step is to come to an agreement that is acceptable to all partners. Partners might bargain about the price, might find a compromise about the delivery dates, might negotiate about quality aspects of the products. The aim is to finalise a contract that specifies the business deal. Therefore, this second phase concerns negotiation about details of the agreement. If the negotiation is successful then a business deal is struck and the outcome is a contract which will then have to be processed by the partners in the third phase, e.g. concerning logistics, payment etc. The general model that can be extracted from the above observations is one of three phases.

The search phase is about finding business partners; the negotiation phase is about finding agreements leading to a contract; the fulfilment phase concerns the execution of the contract. The three-phase model is independent of any technological means, i.e. it is valid for traditional commerce processes as well as for electronic commerce interactions (see its application in the MEMO – Mediating and Monitoring Electronic Commerce – Project[57]). For example, a buyer might look for potential suppliers in the yellow pages, in the catalogues of chambers of commerce or on the internet.

In this paper we will concentrate on *electronic marketplaces for business-to-business electronic commerce.* The current practices in such marketplaces can best be discussed using an example of an existing business-to-business marketplace of the chemical industry called *chemUnity*[58]. A buyer's request containing information about the product (s)he wants to purchase, its type and concentration, the delivery address and time is transferred via the marketplace to all potential suppliers as specified by the buyer. Suppliers have a fixed amount of time (usually 25 hours) to react. Those who choose to send an offer will be taken into account. The best offer is determined by the marketplace based on the buyer's selection criteria. If the best

[57] http://www.abnamro.com/ memo/
[58] http://www.chemunity.com

offer is within the price range indicated by the buyer, then the transaction is completed and the following obligations exist: The seller must supply the product(s) indicated in the original request whereas the buyer must provide the payment according to the offer received.

Abstracting from the example, we can state general observations concerning the three phases in electronic marketplaces as follows.

The search phase consists of (extended) keyword search based on some classification, e.g. a product catalogue, a list of companies in a certain branch etc. Using these kinds of search mechanisms presupposes good knowledge of the search items by the search party and an appropriately structured search domain. For example, if a company would like to find new business contacts or would like to find suppliers of certain products that have different names in different companies, then keyword-based search is clearly insufficient.

The protocols of electronic negotiations that are usually supported in electronic marketplaces are auctions or electronic catalogues. In the latter case, the option is one of "take it or leave it" – either to order at the price specified in the catalogue or not to enter into the business transaction at all. Auctions can be useful for settings as described above. However, even in the example of *chemUnity* certain problems are obvious. Complex negotiations cannot be supported by such a model. For example, the cheapest supplier might not be the one offering the best quality, the cheapest supplier might not be trustworthy, the third cheapest supplier might be able to deliver much quicker than the cheapest one etc. Furthermore, if negotiations concern frame contracts, then a different negotiation protocol is required. Highly interactive exchanges that occur in traditional commerce can be transferred to electronic commerce where, on the one hand, the potential of information technology can be exploited to offer new functionalities and to support effective interactions and, on the other hand, information technology cannot (and indeed should not) replace the human negotiator by an automated software agent but rather support human negotiators in their tasks [SQ01].

The fulfilment phase is the one that is usually covered best in any electronic marketplace. Payment models are supported (usually payment by credit card) and an integration with the companies' logistic systems is achieved. If all goes well after the contract has been finalised then such a model is sufficient. However, if disagreements occur between the parties as to which obligations need to be fulfilled, whether certain duties have been carried out according to the agreements made during the negotiation etc., there is hardly any support to help solving such problems. No history behind an agreement is usually provided that could help the parties themselves or an independent third party to understand why certain agreements have been reached and where the specific problem lies.

To summarise, there are potential problems with respect to current practises for all three phases. Nowadays there exist a number of electronic marketplaces for different branches. Therefore, a (new) marketplace requires additional functionalities for all phases to make it attractive to participants and to distinguish it from its competitors. For example, to capture different relations between concepts, semantic search mechanisms need to be provided so that similar and related information can be found; a new negotiation protocol is required that is interaction-based and supports the communication-intensive exchanges in complex negotiations; different payment models should be provided to capture the different needs of various application contexts. Furthermore, a monitoring component could help to observe the interactions and trace them back in case of conflicts.

The three-phase model will be used throughout the present paper. Section 3 and 4 will present the area of trading software components for the chemical industry as one example application area of our work. The three phases will be reconsidered in section 5 in relation to the application area. In particular, we will discuss the realisation of some of the additional functionalities discussed above for the specific context.

# 3. CONTEXT: SOFTWARE COMPONENTS FOR THE CHEMICAL INDUSTRY

This section presents an application domain, namely the usage and trading of software components in computer aided process engineering (CAPE).

## 3.1 Software components

Modern software systems, especially large enterprise systems, tend to grow more and more complex but require at the same time increased flexibility. This flexibility facilitates easy integration of new subsystems or the extraction of functionality of parts of the system to be used elsewhere. Additionally, managing interdependencies between different subsystems in a complex enterprise environment has become a challenging task for software engineers. Therefore, the component-based approach for design and implementation has become popular and has been proven to be useful [Ho00].

Software components can be considered as the next step beyond objects. Based on existing definitions the term "software component" is used in this paper as follows: "A software component is an executable, stand-alone piece of software with a clearly defined interface and behaviour." The component's interface allows other pieces of software (e.g. other components) to access its functionality. There are different middleware approaches facilitating the implementation and deployment of software components by providing low level communication infrastructure, component lifecycle management, transaction services, and similar services such as (D)COM and COM+, CORBA, and Enterprise Java. In addition, several proprietary middleware systems exist.

The fact that software components are stand-alone pieces of software which can be delivered and deployed in a given environment makes them a good candidate for being traded on the web in a component marketplace. Several concepts and technical architectures for web-based component marketplaces have been developed [JGR99, Be98, BKR96, WRMT95]. However, all of these marketplaces follow a horizontal approach, i.e. the type of components that can be sold is not limited to specific domains. The horizontal approach can become a problem for various reasons (see sections 3.3 and 4)

## 3.2 CAPE-OPEN components

The challenges for software engineering concerning integration and flexibility of complex software systems depicted above are also relevant to the CAPE domain, especially to process simulation. Process simulators are tools designed to create mathematical models of manufacturing facilities for processing and/or transforming materials. Chemical manufacturing through continuous or batch processing, polymer processing, and oil refining are examples of such processes. Process simulators are central for designing new processes; they are also used extensively to predict behaviour of existing or proposed processes. Designing and simulating such processes is a very complex task which typically involves many different tools with strong interrelations. Most of these tools are highly specialised, expensive, and require much expertise to be run and maintained. Therefore, process simulation can be seen as a perfect candidate for applying component techniques for mutual integration and data exchange.

However, two years ago no component-based architectures were used because most existing systems had a FORTRAN core which is not even object-oriented. The tools used for process simulation were closed, monolithic applications which made it almost impossible to include new components from other vendors or to combine these tools [CO96]. However, such integration and combination is desirable, as the manual exchange of data between those application is tedious and error prone. Additionally, these tools were (and still are) highly heterogeneous because they may run on simple PCs using Windows or mainframes using Unix. To combine these tools each of them must be divided up into standardised components with defined interfaces.

This problem was addressed by the European CAPE-OPEN initiative in which the chemical industries and major vendors of process simulation software have accomplished a standard of open interfaces for process simulation software [BJ99a,BJ99b]. The overall outcome of CAPE-OPEN was the definition of a conceptual design and interface specifications for simulators which consist of an assembly of relatively large software components. Standard components of a process simulator have been identified [CO98] and the semantics of these components and their interdependencies have been clearly defined in terms of UML diagrams, COM and CORBA interface definitions, and textual descriptions [http://www.global-cape-open.org].

## 3.3 Requirements for a CAPE-OPEN marketplace

In the previous section we have discussed that software components are good candidates for being sold in a web-based marketplace. We have also pointed out that for making a marketplace attractive, additional services should be offered which can be effectively designed for a vertical, i.e. domain-specific, marketplace only. We will now present a set of services for trading CAPE-OPEN components via the web. In contrast to a horizontal component marketplace the CAPE-OPEN components have the following properties.

In the CAPE domain, there are only a few component types with approximately 15 different interfaces. The behaviour of a component, i.e. the way it can be integrated and used, is precisely defined. This allows us to integrate an automated standard-compliance test in the marketplace assuring a certain level of quality of the components offered. This means that if a user owns a CAPE-OPEN simulator executive and buys a CAPE-OPEN unit (s)he can be sure that it will work. Although the components' behaviour is standardised they differ widely in their internal functionality. In case of units this means that there are components for various purposes (e.g. reactors, distillation columns, etc.) which may differ only in very subtle details that can be crucial for the success of a simulation. These differences can be described exactly only because there is a underlying common terminology. Therefore, we can include a powerful semantic product search in the marketplace which would be difficult to implement in the horizontal case. Since the behaviour of the components is highly standardised, the interrelations of components available in the marketplace can be made explicit. Similar to the semantic specification of the component itself it can also be described which other components are necessary to perform a calculation. For example, it can be specified that a specific reactor unit implementation needs a thermodynamics package supporting certain properties and calculation methods. This can be used for linking components in the marketplace that will interoperate smoothly. All CAPE-OPEN interfaces are designed to run in a distributed environment. Therefore, the marketplace can support not only classical licensing models such as buying or renting components. Rather it is also possible to take licence models into account which are based on application service provider (ASP) approaches (see [KLJ01]). Additionally, due to the domain focus of the marketplace, specific user support can be offered in terms of FAQ's discussion groups, or expert forums.

Defining and offering the above services for unspecified software products is difficult as will be discussed in the next section. Another problem is that describing the exact functionality of a component (not only in terms of their interface definition) is a non trivial task. In our case this problem is solved by offering only a very limited range of components with a functionality that is clearly defined by the software standard.

# 4. APPLYING THE MODEL TO THE CONTEXT

In section 2, we have presented a model for a business-to-business electronic commerce transaction. It consists of three phases: search for products and business partners, negotiation about the contract, and fulfilment of the contract. Based on the requirements for a marketplace for software components, we will now apply the three-phase model to our application context.

The marketplace provides support for the three main phases search, negotiation and fulfilment, based on extended services which are required for this context. These services are certification and classification of components and management of licenses for components as described in the previous section. The architecture of the marketplace itself is component-based so that new services and functionalities can easily be integrated. In the following, each of the three main phases and the extended services will be presented in more detail.

## 4.1 The Search Phase

In our context of software components for the chemical industry, we will use a combination of different searching technologies. This idea has also been used in the MEMO Project [Le00, Je00]. The user can start to explore the information on the marketplace by browsing through an ontology of concepts. While browsing, the user can compose a query for a normal keyword-based search engine. The basic data model for the ontology consists of concepts which might be related to several other concepts and might have a number of attributes or properties (see upper part of figure 1).

As mentioned in section 4, finding the right component for a specific context of a chemical simulation can be difficult because of the complex requirements which have to be fulfilled. The static properties of a component (given through its interface) are well defined by the CAPE-OPEN standard. The standard describes basically three relevant interface types; the components implementing these interfaces will then be used in a CAPE-OPEN compliant process simulator. The three interfaces describe material (thermodynamics) properties, (chemical engineering) units and numerical solvers. To simulate a specific plant, a user has to choose a unit for each apparatus of the plant, specify a numerical solver for the units and the materials for the feed of the plant.

The realisation of the search engine for components faced two main problems. On the one hand there is a large variety of components for each interface type. The hierarchical structure of the ontology is used so that the engineer can easily navigate through the units. This structure is based on the model CliP [BSM01] which itself is based on pdXi, an application protocol of the STEP initiative [ISO 10303]. The extended data model for the ontology is shown in figure 3 (only the first hierarchy level is displayed).

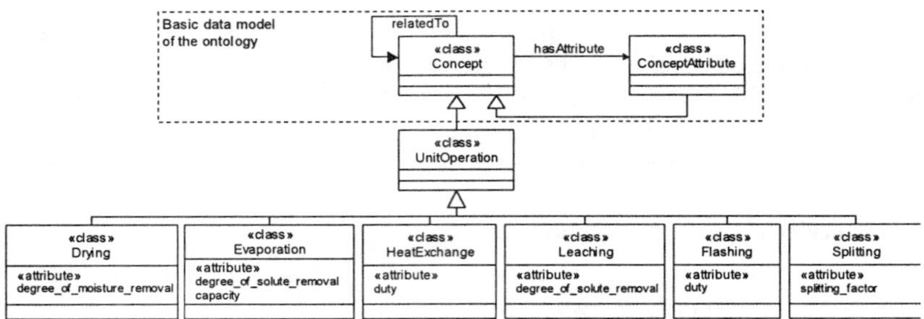


*Figure 1.* Data model of the ontology including the CliP hierarchy

The ontology now enables the engineer to find the apparatus (s)he wants to simulate. Units on the other hand only specify a mathematical model for an apparatus. There are many different mathematical models (and therefore many different units) that can be used to simulate one and the same apparatus. To find the right one, the chemical engineer has to take into account many constraints. For example, not every unit can be used with every numerical solver, certain numerical solvers cannot be combined in the same plant, and different mathematical models (that are coded into the units) might be better in certain situations which depend on the pressure used in the plant, the temperature and other properties. Some of these conditions, such as "which combinations of solvers can be used together", are known and can be modelled into our ontology, see figure 2 which contains the extensions to the data model of the ontology that is used to formulate relations between units and solvers. Some of these conditions have the form of a simple rule (such as "the pressure that is used in a reactor has to be supported by the solver"). These conditions are expressed using the terms of the data model of the ontology and can be used to narrow a search explicitly through specifying the properties used by the conditions. Other conditions are based on relations between certain solvers and units (such as "solver A is known to work well with unit B"). These conditions are formulated by explicitly instantiating attributes of the data model on the instance level of the ontology. To formulate a relationship between two units that is not contained in the data model, the general `relatedTo`-Attribute can be instantiated. These relationships cannot be used to formulate a search query on the ontology, but can be used to navigate through the products. For example there can be a link between the units A and B that states that unit B can be used for free if unit A is bought.

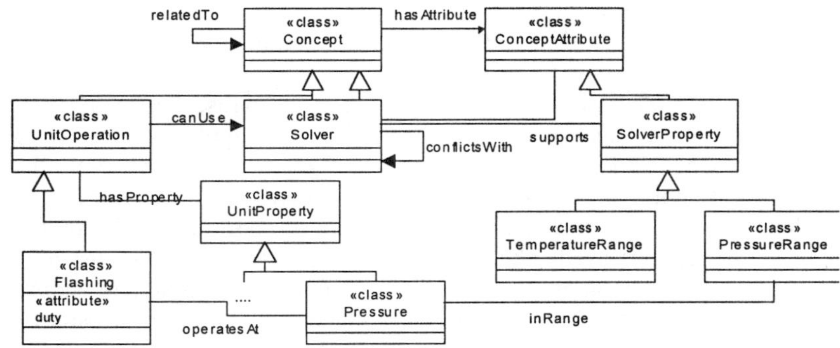


*Figure 2.* Relationship between units and solvers

In addition to the product-oriented ontology, our ontology contains first approaches to describe services related to the components. We describe vendors that offer components and consulting services related to these components. During a search an engineer can switch between the product view and the corresponding vendor view or navigate a "consulting" link to find vendors that offer consulting services for a specific component. In the future this basic system will be extended to enable the specification of properties of a potential component to find vendors that can develop a very specialised component.

To summarise, the main advantage of our approach for searching is based on a semantically rich ontology which provides a clear understanding of the domain. Based on this information, the user is able to specify precise search criteria that go far beyond the possibilities of normal keyword-based search. This is especially useful in an application context where the products differ only in a few properties. The ontology is (indirectly) based on a domain standard so that an engineer can use the search without special knowledge.

## 4.2 The Negotiation Phase

The result of the search phase is a list of components the developer is interested in and the suppliers of these components. Alternatively, the search phase can end with a list of companies the developer wants to negotiate with about a more complex product (e.g. a component which is not yet completely specified or consulting and technical support that has to be included). In addition, the user can negotiate with a company about a frame contract which applies especially to the case of a company offering several components that a developer is interested in. By doing so, the developer does not have to negotiate about every small component (s)he is going to purchase in the future.

One of the key problems in the negotiation phase is that there is no negotiation model which is appropriate for all kinds of transactions. As mentioned before, this phase can range from a simple catalogue-like ordering process to complex peer-to-peer negotiations about individual (frame) contracts. These more complicated contracts are not only about the licensing of a software component, but might also include information about consulting or technical support, the requirements for the component etc. Therefore, we envision a flexible negotiation module which supports multiple negotiation models.

In the simplest negotiation model, the products are presented with their properties and prices in an electronic catalogue. This model applies especially to "off-the-shelf" components, i.e. components that are ready to deploy with the CAPE-OPEN process simulator. The off-the-shelf components can be bought just as they are – the different variants, license models and support models with the corresponding prices are displayed. The buyer of the software component can only choose between these fixed components. For example, an engineer is able to choose the models which fits his needs best. There is no bargaining between the customer and the supplier about the price or the functionality of the component.

Another popular negotiation model in electronic commerce are auctions. Although in our opinion auctions are in general less applicable in this context, auctions should be supported by the marketplace. For example, a company might be looking for a component that fulfils certain requirements. Instead of searching for a supplier, the company can publish a request for quotations and start a reverse auction. As price is certainly not the only criterion for a customer, multi-attribute auctions should also be taken into account.

To support the more difficult case of complex negotiations that can, for example, occur when complex components, consulting services, or technical support are concerned a novel negotiation protocol is offered. This protocol emphasises the exchange of communication acts involved in negotiations and is interaction-based. We will present a brief introduction of our model; the interested reader is referred to [Sch99, SQ01] for more detailed discussions.

The approach is based on speech act elements [Ha81, Se69] and formal logics [DW95, Sch98] and supports structured electronic message exchange. Each message has a certain type (e.g. offer, request, counter-offer, discussion, quotation) that specifies how the message content is meant. The negotiation steps follow a characteristic pattern. For example, a supplier's offer can only be answered by a customer's counter-offer, acceptance, rejection, or discussion request and not by another offer of the supplier. The content of messages is represented in a semi-formal way, linked to the ontology. Taken together, the structured approach helps to prevent most misunderstandings about what exactly is meant in this type of written communication, thereby making the obligations of each partner during a negotiation explicit. The formalisation of our approach enables reasoning about the obligations. The content of negotiations can be accessed in various ways, e.g. by content (all messages concerning numerical solvers), type (all offers by company A), obligations (all open obligations, all unfulfilled obligations of company B), people involved (all messages sent by X), time (all request sent between 5/5/00 and 8/2/01) and various combinations (all offers by company X sent in 2000 that have been accepted and not yet fulfilled).

Since the message exchange is done in a structured way and the exchanges are stored, they can be used later in case of conflicts to find out what was agreed and which obligations were accepted during a negotiation.

A similar model can be used for the negotiation of frame contracts. A frame contract is a "parameterised" contract which specifies the general conditions of business relations. In the context of software components, a frame contract might specify consulting and technical support, pricing and licensing, etc. Frame contracts are necessary because chemical engineering companies are often major companies that usually need more than one component of a supplier. Both parties, customers and suppliers, may be interested in long-term business relationships. The marketplace allows negotiations about frame contracts. The conditions of these contracts are taken into account when prices are calculated. If a frame contract exists between the two companies, the customer can later order components easily by referring to the frame contract. Some conditions do not have to be discussed again as they are specified in the frame contract.

To summarise, the marketplace offers several negotiation models. Depending on the situation, the customer or the supplier can choose a model for a transaction. Independent of the negotiation model, all negotiation data can be recorded by the marketplace (if both parties agree). This enables the traceability of the negotiation. The trace of the negotiation can be used in legal conflicts. Making the obligations of the business partners explicit enables the monitoring of the execution of the contract during the fulfilment phase.

## 4.3 The Fulfilment Phase

Support during the fulfilment phase is given in many different ways. First, the component has to be "delivered" to the customer. Therefore, a secure download mechanism has to established that allows only authorised users access to the software. We do not plan to develop a new mechanism, rather we will rely on existing technologies.

After the component has been transferred to the customer's site, it has to be ensured that the software is not used more often as allowed in the contract. Therefore, license servers are required to control the use of the component. Different types of licenses or payment models can be handled by the marketplace. In this context, a trusted third party (TTP) can be involved to handle payment and to monitor the contract execution. The TTP controls whether both parties act according to the contract.

The payment model for off-the-shelf components can be based on a license server system. A license server has to be installed at the local network of the engineering company, called the local license server. Depending on the license model in use for a specific component, the local license server needs an online connection to the central license server of the marketplace or the TTP. The implementation supports local user control to ensure that only qualified and authorised users have access to the components. A "pay-per-use" model can also be supported by a license server.

The way a simulation component is actually bought depends on how the customer is registered at the marketplace and whether the customer has a frame contract with the supplier. Ideally, the engineer can select the component, download it and plug it into the simulator. The local license server is notified about the new license situation via the Internet, billing is done according to the agreements in the frame contract. The TTP can be involved to collect the billing information.

If no frame contract is applicable, the user can still choose to "buy" the simulation component according to the conditions given in the contract. License models that do not work on a pre-paid basis are not available. The user can download the component, license information will only be sent to the user when the payment is verified. The business transaction here is done via the marketplace, the TTP acts as a monitor and keeps logs of each transaction.

As the marketplace or the TTP can provide a license server, the license server has to provide several functionalities. The billing information for the use of components is recorded and the licenses issued by the software vendors are managed. On the one hand, a library or an interface with functions to retrieve license information from the server or to update license information on the server will be provided. These functions can be built into the components by the component developer. On the other hand, the software company must be able to maintain the licenses, e.g. issue new licenses, upgrade licenses, remove licenses. These functions will be provided by a special interface for software companies to the license server of the marketplace or the TTP.

Finally, consulting and support activities can be included in a contract about software components. Especially for consulting activities (be it for chemical engineering simulations or for general business or IT aspects) it is problematic to formulate a contract that covers all detailed specifications that were discussed in the negotiation. In the case of a misunderstanding between customer and consultant about the extent of consulting, the contract and its links to the negotiation trace can be used to resolve a potential conflict.

## 4.4 Data Management

Data management is one of the core services of the marketplace. Although the user has no direct interface to the data management module of the marketplace, the quality of this module may have an impact on the other modules. We will briefly discuss the functionalities which have to be delivered by the data management component. A more detailed discussion about the requirements for a business data management component can be found in [QS00].

Firstly, all the data of the marketplace has to be managed in an integrated way. As many different modules form the marketplace software, many different data models will be in use. Since data needs to be exchanged between the modules, the data management module has to manage the data in a common model. Different views on this data model will be provided as a mapping from the common data model to the specific data model of the module. Furthermore, data has to be integrated from external sources such as product catalogues, company profiles or ontologies.

A common data model of component data is especially important for searching as the information about software components should be comparable. On the other hand, a supplier wants to present his/her product in a unique look-and-feel to be distinct from other components. Therefore, data presentation can be customised based on the needs of the users of the marketplace.

The ontologies (cf. sec. 5.1) are also managed by the data management module. If a new component is registered at the marketplace, it has to be classified into the ontology. The search module is then able to access this information. Facilities for ontology maintenance will also be provided as the ontology for software components will certainly evolve over time. The data model for ontologies is currently being implemented in an extensible way, so that new classes and relationships can be added later on.

Finally, access rights and user profiles have to be managed. Not every user of the marketplace is allowed to see everything. In particular, data of negotiations and contracts should only be accessible by the parties involved in the negotiation. A company may provide additional information to its customers via the marketplace.

## 4.5 Implementation Issues

The proposed extension for the different phases of the electronic commerce process as described above are embedded in an overall architecture of the marketplace. Each functionality is encapsulated in one or more modules. Furthermore modules capture the transaction data. Our approach is to have a middle layer between the data modules and the ones implementing functionality to achieve the possibility to adapt the functions to different marketplace structures. It is not our goal to implement a general framework for electronic marketplaces but to offer functionality that can be combined with existing software solutions. The modules are implemented as Enterprise Java Beans (EJBs) according to the Java 2 Enterprise Edition. We use the Inprise Application Server as EJB container. We have implemented the data layer using entity beans. These beans can be replaced by an existing software solution for electronic marketplaces. The middle layer between functionality and data is realised as a set of session beans that implement a well-defined set of interfaces. The modules implementing the advanced functionality rely on these interfaces. To replace the data layer with another existing marketplace solution the session beans have to be rewritten according to the interfaces.

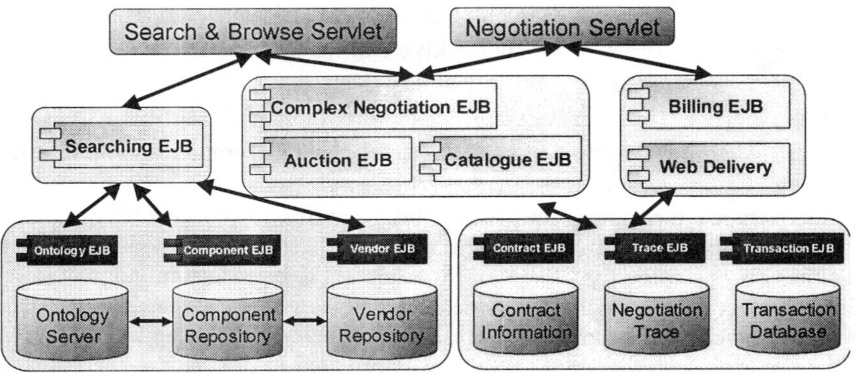


*Figure 3.* Overall architecture

The overall architecture is depictured in figure 3. There are several (logical) separate databases for the ontology, the components and vendor information and databases for contract information, a store for the business transactions and a trace database for the negotiation and fulfilment trace. Some databases have strong interrelations (for example ontology and component database). The coordination of the databases is realised by the data management module using a meta database (not depicted in figure 3). The middle layer consists of entity beans that encapsulate the database access and have to be tailored according to the underlying system. The search and negotiation modules are implemented as session beans that access the databases through the middle layer entity beans. The user interface is currently realised by web-based servlets. In the case of the negotiation we have three different modules in use, each representing a different business model: Auctions, complex negotiations and catalogue-based buying. These modules have to use the transaction and trace beans to create new data (business transactions and negotiation logs). Billing and delivery is then done using the related beans.

The overall architecture allows a flexible integration of services such as the ontology-based search engine or the negotiation modules with a marketplace. New alternative or additional services can be added easily. The data abstraction based on the entity bean-middle layer and the data management enables the use of the services on different marketplaces.

# 5. CONCLUSION

Electronic marketplaces exist in many facets. However, in order to be acceptable to users, the three phases of an electronic commerce process, namely search, negotiate, fulfil, need to be supported efficiently. We have discussed the problems with the current practices for all of the phases. For example, keyword-based search mechanisms presuppose a good knowledge of the search item and a search space that is constructed accordingly. A number of horizontal and vertical marketplaces are in operation. In order to be competitive and distinct, a marketplace nowadays thus needs to offer additional functionalities. The useful additions depend on the branch the marketplace is designed for. Therefore, most of the functionalities make only sense when developing vertical marketplaces. For example, we discussed the idea of ontology-based semantic search mechanisms.

Our extended three-phase model has been applied to the context of software components for the chemical industry. In order to show its generalisability, the model has also been used in other contexts such as the construction industry (cf. the MEMO project [www.abnamro.com/memo]). The approach presented in this paper can be combined with other frameworks. For example, the marketplace *chemUnity* could be extended by the functionalities we presented in this paper. Therefore, our model is not an implementation model but a conceptual basis for an implementation.

To summarise, we have presented a sophisticated model for a holistic support of the three phases extended by innovative services that provides an efficient framework for electronic marketplaces in the context of software components for chemical engineering. The model enables efficient support of business transactions ranging from a search module consisting of sophisticated semantic search and keyword-based search, over a negotiation module offering simple electronic catalogues, auction models, and support of complex highly interactive negotiations, to different payment models and licence models in the fulfilment phase.

# 6. REFERENCES

[Be98] A. Behle, An Internet-based Information System for Cooperative Software Reuse, In *Proc. of 5th IEEE International Conference on Software Reuse*, pp 236-245, 1998.

[BJ99a] B. Braunschweig , M. Jarke, A. Becks, J. Köller and C. Tresp: Designing Standards for Open Simulation Environments in the Chemical Industries: A Computer-Supported Use-Case Approach. In *Proc. of the 9th Annual Int. Symposium of the Int. Council on Systems Engineering*, Brighton, England, June, 1999.

[BJ99b] B. Braunschweig, M. Jarke, J. Köller, W. Marquardt and L .v. Wedel: CAPE-OPEN - experiences from a standardization effort in chemical industries. In *Proc. Intl. Conf. Standardization and Innovation in Information Technology (SIIT99)*, Aachen 1999.

[BKR96] P. Buxmann, W. König and F. Rose: The Java Repository – An Electronic Intermediary for Java Resources, In *Proc. of the 7th Int'l Conference of the International Information Management Assoc.*, 1996.

[BSM01] B. Bayer, R. Schneider and W. Marquardt: Integration of Data Models for Process Design - First Steps and Experiences. In *Computers & Chemical Engineering* **24** (2000), 599-605.

[CO96] CAPE-OPEN, Project Programme, Annex I, Brite/EuRam Be 3512, 1996.

[CO98] CAPE-OPEN, Conceptual Design Document 2. http://www. global-cape-open.org/CAPE-OPEN_standard.html, 1998.

[CO00] Global CAPE-OPEN Master Plan for CAPE-OPEN Laboratories Network, Global CAPE-OPEN project deliverable, 2000.

[DW95] F. Dignum and H. Weigand: Communication and Deontic Logic. In R.J. Wieringa and R. Feenstra (eds), Information *Systems, Correctness and Reusability, Proc. of ISCORE-94 Workshop*, Singapore, pp. 242-260, 1995.

[Ha81] J. Habermas: Theorie des kommunikativen Handelns, volume 1: Handlungsrationalität und gesellschaftliche Rationalisierung. Suhrkamp, Frankfurt am Main, 1981.

[Ho00] J. Hopkins: Component Primer, Comm. ACM, 43(10), October 2000.

[ISO 10303] ISO 10303: Part 231, Process Engineering Data: Process Design and Process Specifications of Major Equipment. ISO TC 184/SC4/WG3 N740 (1998).

[Je00] M.A. Jeusfeld: Business data structures for B2B commerce. In Proc. Conf. EMISA – Methods for Developing Information Systems and their Application, Information Systems for E-Commerce (EMISA-2000), Linz, Austria, 2000.

[JGR99] H.-A. Jacobsen, O. Günther and G. Riessen: Component Leasing on the World Wide Web, In *Proc. of the $1^{st}$ ACM Conf. Electronic Commerce*, ACM Press, 1999.

[KLJ01] J. Köller, T. List and M. Jarke: Designing a Component Store for Chemical Engineering Software Solutions, In *Proc. $34^{th}$ Hawaiian Intl. Conf. On System Sciences (HICSS-34)*, Maui, 2001.

[Le00] C.J. Leune: Final document on searching, querying and discovering mechanisms. *MEMO Deliverable 1.4*, July 2000 (http://www.abnamro.com/memo/).

[QS00] C. Quix and M. Schoop: Facilitating Business-to-Business Electronic Commerce for Small and Medium-Sized Enterprises. In *Proc. of the First Intl. Conf. on Electronic*

*Commerce and Web Technologies (EC-Web 2000),* Greenwich, UK, Springer-Verlag, pp. 442-451, September 2000.

[Sch98] M. Schoop: *Towards Effective Multidisciplinary Communication: A Language-Action Approach to* Cooperative Documentation Systems. PhD Thesis, The University of Manchester, UK, 1998.

[Sch99] M. Schoop: A Theoretical Framework for Speech Act Based Negotiation in Electronic Commerce. In S. Klein, B. Schneider (eds), *Negotiations and Interactions in Electronic Markets, Proc. 6th Research Symposium on Emerging Electronic Markets (RSEEM),* Münster, Germany, pp. 79-89, 1999.

[Se69] J. Searle: Speech Acts: An Essay in the Philosophy of Language. Cambridge University Press, Cambridge, 1969.

[SL98] B. Schmid and M. Lindemann: Elements of a Reference Model Electronic Markets. *Proc. 31st Hawaiian Intl. Conf. On System Sciences (HICSS-31),* Hawaii, 1998.

[SQ01] M. Schoop and C. Quix: DOC.COM: Combining document and communication management for negotiation support in business-to-business electronic commerce. In *Proc. 34th Hawaiian Intl. Conf. On System Sciences (HICSS-34),* Maui, 2001.

[SS01] S. Schmitt and B. Schneider: Einsatzpotentiale der KI im Electronic Commerce. *Künstliche Intelligenz*, 1/01:5-11, 2001.

[WRMT95] E. Whitehead, J. Robbins, N. Medvidovic and N. Taylor: Software Architecture: Foundation of a Software Component Marketplace, In *Proc. 1st International Workshop on Architectures for Software Systems*, Seattle WA, April 24-25, 1995, 276-282.

38

# The communicative logic of negotiation in B2B e-commerce

Hans Weigand
*Tilburg University*

**Abstract**: Negotiation is an important challenge for B2B e-commerce that is hardly supported by current systems. In this paper, we present a short overview of different perspectives on negotiation and describe the ESPRIT project MeMo (Mediating and Monitoring Electronic Commerce) which aims at supporting B2B negotiation. A prototype has been built and tested in the Dutch construction industry. Our aim in this paper is a formal logical analysis of negotiation protocols. Dynamic Deontic Logic is used as a starting point for our model, but, as we argue, some extensions of this framework are necessary. A formal analysis of so-called norm-based negotiation is presented. Some alternative negotiation protocols are discussed as well.

## 1. INTRODUCTION

Negotiation is a key component in e-commerce. In automated negotiation, computational agents find and prepare contracts on behalf of the real-world parties they represent. The automation saves human negotiation time and computational agents are sometimes better at finding deals in combinatorally and strategically complex settings. An example of a system supporting such agent negotiation is the eMediator system built at Washington University (Sandholm, 1999). However, it is only in relatively well-structured areas that the use of automated negotiation pays off. In most business settings, negotiation will remain to be performed by humans. In such a case, negotiation support systems can be of help. An example of a negotiation support system is the INSPIRE systems built by Gregory Kersten at Carleton University (Kersten & Noronha, 1997).

In Electronic Commerce, market transactions are supposed to consist of a couple of phases (e.g. Lindemann & Schmid, 1999). In the information phase, customer and supplier find each other. When an offer is made, the agreement phase starts. The result of the agreement phase is a legally binding contract. In the settlement or fulfilment phase, the agreed-upon terms of the contract are fulfilled by delivery of products and payment. Sometimes, an after-sales phase is distinguished. In such a model, negotiation is located in the agreement phase.

In this paper, we first provide a brief overview of the MeMo project. In section 3, we present an overview of different perspectives on negotiation. In section 4, we introduce the Dynamic Deontic Logic that we take as starting point for our formal model, and section 5 provides a formal analysis of so-called norm-based negotiation using the Dynamic Deontic Logic. In section 6, some alternative negotiation protocols are discussed.

# 2. MEDIATING & MONITORING ELECTRONIC COMMERCE

Electronic Commerce is doing business via electronic networks such as for example Internet and World Wide Web (WWW). Electronic commerce can be seen as the successor of Electronic Data Interchange (EDI), but it goes far beyond EDI in that it aims at supporting the complete external business processes. Information about potential business partners can be obtained, through specialised databases, chambers of commerce, and lately also through the WWW. Also the fulfilment of the transaction is well supported.

However, there is practically no support for the connecting stage of contract negotiation. This stage has to be done manually. This is a major obstacle for the uptake of electronic commerce by Small and Medium Size Enterprises (SME's). Big companies can usually afford to undertake the time and money consuming enterprise of negotiating interchange agreements, because they can establish long-term relations with their suppliers (or customers) and they have the expertise in house. The MeMo system is one of the first solutions aimed at SME's.

## 2.1 Negotiation and Contracting Mechanism

The Negotiation Module of MeMo supports business-to-business negotiation and contract building. The precondition for business relations is a relation of trust between all business partners. This relation of trust depends on personal contact on the one hand and on contracts and legislation on the other. The MeMo negotiation module does not replace human informal communication, but enables human agents to structure their communication using a Formal Language for Business Communication. Since the results of the negotiation are typically laid down in a contract, it also offers a repository of standard contracts and a shared workspace in which a standard document can be adapted by the partners to their particular need. It facilitates different scenarios and provides SMEs with safe "negotiation rooms".

Since language is often a big barrier for international trade, especially for small companies in Europe, the Negotiation Module also contains a multilingual thesaurus in which key terms of international trade are given in multiple languages. In this way, it is possible for the human agents to personalise their MeMo interface to their particular language. By all these means, MeMo is one of the first systems that really facilitate business negotiation via the Internet.

## 2.2 User Evaluation

In order to involve a group of SMEs in the project, MeMo has formed a SMEs Round Table in Spain, in Germany and in the Netherlands. These user group round tables provide the ideal environment to continually discuss the incremental developments and test the EC-Brokering Service (ECBS) with SME user companies. The most extensive evaluation of the system has taken place in the Dutch constructing industry.

One of the results of this evaluation was that traditional non-automated negotiation causes the agreements to contain many errors, resulting in high failure costs in the fulfilment stage. An integrated system like MeMo can help to reduce data errors. Another result was that negotiation means quite different things for different roles in the value chain, and that a system like MeMo must be tuned to a particular role before it can be used effectively. For example, a wholesaler negotiates with manufacturers about frame-contracts on a yearly basis. He negotiates with contractors on a project-basis. During and after these negotiations, he forwards specific orders (electronically) to the manufacturers within the boundaries of the frame contract. Negotiation and fulfilment are not strictly separated, since contracts are modified and updated many times before the final delivery. Contractors negotiate with wholesalers on a project-basis, and do this typically by asking quotes from several parties and then using this information in bargaining. The bargaining is seldom about the price only, but more often about delivery schemes and extra services.

# 3. PERSPECTIVES ON NEGOTIATION

A classical model of negotiation was introduced by Gulliver (1979). This process model consists of eight phases:

1. search for arena
2. agenda definition
3. exploring the field (emphasis on differences)

4. narrowing differences
5. preliminaries to final bargaining
6. final bargaining
7. post-negotiation phase
8. ritualization of outcome (signing of contract)

According to Kersten, negotiations involve two or more participants engaged in two types of complex activities: communication and decision making. The communication can be modelled using for example Speech Act Theory (e.g. Chang & Woo, 1994). The decision making occurs at two levels: individual and interdividual. The contract is typically based on an exchange of goods or services. Hence neither of the parties can decide on the contract on its own: they are interdependent. In that sense, the decision to come to an agreement is a group decision. On the other hand, each participant has his own objectives that he tries to fulfill. The decision whether a certain bid is acceptable or not, is an individual decision of one actor.

In this paper, the perspective is communicational (Habermas, 1981; Schoop & Quix, 2001). Negotiation moves are analyzed as communicative actions that have a certain effect in the social world (the world of norms and commitments), the subject world (the world of values and beliefs) and, at the end of the day, also in the object world (the world of accomplishments). We will not go into the decision problems. The social and cognitive perspectives are taken into account as far as they are relevant to the communication process.

If negotiation is about arriving at an agreement, a typology of negotiations can be based on the basis for the other party to accept the agreement. *Why does the other party agree to sign the contract?* One reason can be that he is obliged to do this. In other words, the party is supposed to be motivated by norms (at least partly). This leads to a type of negotiation that we call norm-based, and which corresponds with the classical quotation process. Another reason for signing is that he wants to do it. In other words, the party is supposed to be motivated by goals (at least partly). This leads to a type of negotiation that we call goal-based. In this type of negotiation, the parties try to fix common or mutually accepted goals. In addition to these two types, we identify what we call document-based negotiation. In this type of negotiation, the contract is built up in small steps. This type of negotiation does not look at the motivation of the parties, but tries to achieve the goal of a signed contract by getting agreement on the various parts first. In section 5, we will focus on norm-based negotiation as it turns out to be the most common in the application domain of the MeMo system. A few remarks on the other types will be made in section 6.

# 4. DYNAMIC DEONTIC LOGIC

In (Verharen, 1998) and in various articles (e.g. Weigand et al, 1997), a formal logic has been described for modelling communication. It is based on Dynamic Deontic Logic and extended to include speech acts. Instead of repeating all the formal definitions here, we limit ourselves to a vocabulary and some examples of its application in business process modelling.

| | |
|---|---|
| $O(\alpha)$ | action $\alpha$ is obliged (possibly with indices i and j to indicate the agent and principal) |
| $[\alpha]\phi$ | (Dynamic Logic) after action $\alpha$, formula $\phi$ holds |
| Auth($\alpha$) | action $\alpha$ is authorized (where the action is a speech act) |
| DIR | directive (based on charity (c) or authorization (a) – the latter meaning that the request claims to be authorized by a previous agreement or norm) |

*Examples*:

$[DIR_c(i,j,give\text{-}quotation(j,i,g,p))]\ O_{ji}(give\text{-}quotation(j,i,g,p)\ OR\ refuse(j))$

*After a request for a quotation (i.e. a directive based on charity) the company is obliged to give the quotation or send a refusal. This follows from the generic business rule that a request for a service offered is always answered.*

$$[give\text{-}quotation(j,i,g,p)]\ auth(i,DIR_a(i,j,deliver(j,i,g,p)))$$

*If a company gives a quotation for a certain price (p) the client is authorized to order the product (g) for that price. (i.e. a meaning definition for give-quotation).*

$$auth(i,DIR_a(i,j,deliver(j,i,g,p))) \Rightarrow [DIR_a(i,j,deliver(j,i,g,p))]$$
$$(O_{ji}(deliver(j,i,g,p))\ AND\ [deliver(j,i,g,p)]\ auth(j,DIR_a(j,i,pay(i,j,p))))$$

*If a customer is authorized to order a product for a certain price (i.e. a quotation has been given for that price) then the company is obliged to deliver the product after the customer has ordered it. After delivery of the product, the company is authorized to order the customer to pay for it.*

The logic can also be used to reason about violations:

$$O_{ij}(i,j,ship(i,j,goods)) \Rightarrow [\tilde{\ }ship(i,j,goods)]\ (O_{ij}(i,j,pay(100))$$
$$AND\ auth(i,j,DIR_a(i,j,ship(i,j,other\_goods))))$$

*if i is obliged to ship the goods and he does not do it, he is obliged to pay a fine and the other party j is authorized to request (other) goods*

Besides O and auth, we include one more primitive operator in the deontic specification language. This is acc, for accomplishment. acc( $\alpha$) means that action $\alpha$ has been executed. As with O and auth, it takes typically two messages, one of both parties, to establish such a fact.

The DDL model recognizes that communicative acts are joint efforts, and that requests do not automatically create an obligation. However, the fact that business negotiation is really an interaction in which two objectives have to be synchronized, is not sufficiently accounted for. (Weigand & vd Heuvel, 1998) have developed 5 levels of "meta-patterns" starting with the speech act level. Of particular importance here is what they call the level of transaction. A transaction is defined as the minimal sequence of speech acts that has a deontic effect. The typical case is a REQUEST followed by an ACCEPT. Although it can be agreed upon by the parties that a simple REQUEST already creates an obligation, we prefer to assign deontic effects to transactions only, even if in some case the transaction consists of only one speech act.

## 5. NORM-BASED NEGOTIATION

Let us consider an order message. As we have seen, this is analyzed logically as a request (illocution) for the delivery of a product (propositional content). A request contains an implicit validity claim: why should the other party honor the request? In (Weigand et al, 1997) three possible validity motivations have been distinguished: charity, authorization and power. Power is not applicable normally in a market environment. Charity means that the other party is not obliged in any way to honor the request, but he may decide to do so himself, and then, after his commit, an obligation is created. This is a real possibility, but there are certain disadvantages. If the buyer mentions a price, he runs the risk that the price is too high or too low. If it is too high, the seller will accept the order, but the buyer could have made a better deal. If it is too low, the seller will not accept the order and the negotiation may terminate immediately. Another disadvantage of a charity-based order from the perspective of the buyer is that he cannot compare different sellers, since the discussion is about the order, and so when the two parties arrive at an agreement, the order is placed and the buyer cannot withdraw anymore. And finally, since the order is charity-based, he does not know whether the seller will respond, or will respond timely. This uncertainty is often unacceptable in a business environment. We conclude that an authorized request is to be preferred over a charity-based one.

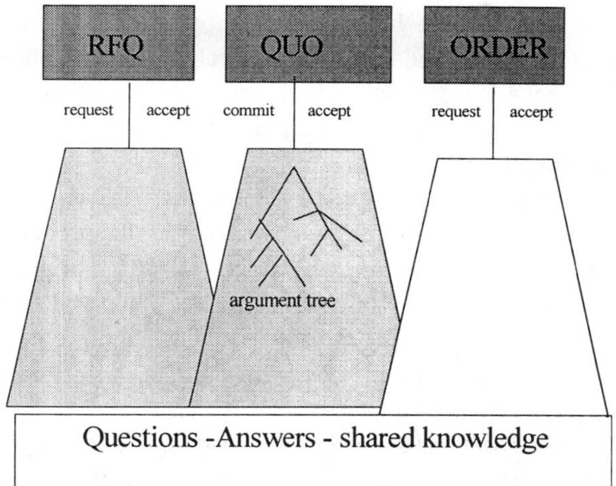


*Figure1.* Main phases of the negotiation, with discussion layer and discourse layer below

When the order is authorized, the question is where this authorization stems from. In B2C relationships, shops are identified as such and prices are listed. These *listed prices* authorize the consumer to order (or request) a product for that price. In B2B relationships, it is less common to use listed prices. This implies that the authorization must be granted first. Of course, this is exactly what a *quotation* message does. In speech-act theory this is analyzed as an authorization message, a message that creates an authorization (namely, to order). The quotation itself is an action on behalf of the supplier that must be triggered somehow and possibly also authorized. For that reason, there is usually a message before, the *request for quotation (RFQ)*, by means of which the buyer request for a quotation message. This request is usually based on charity; the other party commits to this request voluntarily. The RFQ authorizes the seller to send a quotation.

## 5.1 The main phases of norm-based negotiation

This logical reconstruction of the pre-ordering communication leads to a distinction in at least two phases: the RFQ phase and the QUO phase. In the simple case, these messages (and their uptake by the other party) are sufficient. But if something is unclear or not satisfactory to one of the parties, a discussion can start (Fig.1). In terms of the Language/Action Perspective, a *break-down* occurs. A break-down means that a discussion starts and only after having finished this discussion, the phase can be closed (Reijswoud, 1996).

In the MeMo view, the discussion in the RFQ phase centers around the identification of the goals of the transaction. This includes the identification of the participants themselves ("who are you?") as well as the precise identification of the product ("what do you want?"). In terms of Winograd (1988), the discussion is a *conversation for clarification* and the typical speech-acts in this phase are questions and answers. The discussion ends when both parties have sufficient confidence that the intended transaction is properly identified (to both) and the seller commits himself to make a quotation.

In the QUO phase, the seller fulfils his obligation to send a quotation. This quotation contains an authorization for the buyer to order the product. It may contain alternatives (different products, or different prices for different product quantities). A discussion can start on this proposal that in terms of Winograd takes the form of a *conversation for possibilities* and the typical speech acts are proposals and counter-proposals. The discussion ends when both parties accept one or more proposals and the buyer accepts the (modified) quotation.

It should be noted that often the quotation message *also* contains a (conditional) request to the buyer to pay the quoted price. Accepting a quotation implies accepting this request. Again, a discussion may arise in the case of a break-down. This discussion typically takes the form of a *bidding process* and the typical speech acts are bids and counter-bids. The discussion ends when both parties agree on a certain price. The bidding process can be structured by using a monotonic concession protocol (Zlotkin & Rosenschein, 1996) which means that a next bid is always stronger than a previous one (in plain words, the buyer only goes up with his bid and the seller only goes down). Note that this bidding process can run in parallel to the conversation for possibilities, although the parties can also decide to finish this conversation first. The advantage of doing the bidding at the end, is that price gets less attention during the exploration of the possibilities, which will probably result in more alternatives to be considered and worked out. However, if the goods or service are not very specific and easy to describe, the price may be the most important decision factor, and hence is better taken into account immediately. Our research in the Dutch construction industry showed the following picture: first, a quotation process is performed in which price is the most important attribute. Then one or two suppliers are selected and negotiations start with them in which all kinds of possibilities are explored. In terms of the formal model used here, this means that within the QUO phase, there is a bidding process first, followed by a conversation for possibilities.

After the quotation is accepted by the buyer, there is no contract yet. The buyer can negotiate several quotations from different suppliers and then choose the one that fits him best. At this point, different scenarios can be followed. One is that the buyer fills in a purchase order or some other formal contract. After having being signed by both parties, this contract is binding and contains not just authorizations, but obligations of both parties to perform their part. It is also possible that a frame contract is set up and afterwards, a delivery order is sent in accordance with the frame contract. The most simple case is that the buyer sends an order to the seller and the seller accepts this (note that normally, the seller is obliged to accept the order since it is authorized by the quotation).

Also in the ordering phase, a discussion can arise. From the negotiation perspective, we are only interested in discussions about the contract, so we ignore discussion about a delivery order after a contract has been signed. In the MeMo system, this discussion is not done by means of speech acts, but by collaborative writing (document-based negotiation). Both parties have access to a shared workspace in which the draft contract is stored as a document. Parties can update this document into a newer version. The "discussion" ends when both parties agree on a certain version.

## 5.2 Logical semantics of the quotation phases

Summarizing, from a logical view on negotiation we distinguish four phases and their postconditions:

[identification] *social world*: O(y,quote(y,x,p)).
*subject world*: ident(x, i),ident(y,j), Des(x,p)

In words: the parties mutually know the identity of x, the identity of y, and that x desires product p. This is a change in the subject world. The change in the social world is that y has an obligation to send a quote. p is a product description.

[proposal] *social world*: auth(x,order(x,y,p))
*object world*: DONE(y,quote(y,x,p))

In words: x is authorized to order product p from y, and the obligation of y to send a quote has been fulfilled. Note that the price still needs to be determined.

[bidding] *social world:* auth(y,invoice(y,x,f))

In words, y is authorized to invoice x for the amount f - where invoice means: request to pay.

([quotation] = [proposal] + [bidding])

[contracting] *social world*: O(y,deliver(y,x,p)), O(x,pay(x,y,f)).

In words: y has an obligation to deliver and x has an obligation to pay. There may be additional clauses, for example, requiring the seller to deliver *before* sending the invoice. In the case of a frame order, both obligations are conditional (the condition can be the delivery order message, or a stock status change).

All these phases are essential in the sense that they have a specific effect on the social world, but each phase may be passed in one step, or may contain an extensive discussion. The second and third phase (proposal/ bidding) are often done in the same message exchange. The advantage of having four phases is that the discussions in each phase can focus on one issue at the time.

## 5.3 Tender-based negotiation

In the above, we assumed one seller and one buyer. However, it is also possible to negotiate with several parties at the same time. Instead of a request-for-quotation, the buyer can send a tender to a set of sellers. After receiving the bids, the buyer typically selects the cheapest one (or best one, given multiple criteria), and puts his order. The phases are the same as in quotation-based negotiation; the bidders are typically *obliged* to perform the transaction when they are selected, so it also a kind of norm-based negotiation.

Roughly, two subtypes of tender-based negotiation can be distinguished. In one type, the tender procedure is pre-defined, and all parties involved are informed about the rules of the game. The buyer is usually *obliged* to select the cheapest (or best) bid. There is no room for discussion. The bids may or may not be revealed to the other bidders. In the other type, the tender-based negotiation is nothing but the performance of a number of quotation-based negotiations in parallel. The buyer can use information that he receives in one negotiation to press the party in another negotiation. There are no rules defined for all parties, and in each negotiation there is the possibility of discussion.

The advantages of a formally defined tender protocol are (a) the efficiency of the process, (b) and built-in guarantees for a fair competition. A disadvantage is that, since discussion is excluded, the subject of the tender must be clearly defined in advance. Also the evaluation criteria are determined in advance (most often, this is the price), which leaves little room for suppliers to distinguish themselves with special services.

The MeMo system does not only support quotation-based negotiation, but also tender-based ones. The shared workspace can be used to publish the details of the tender and tender procedure.

## 6. GOAL-BASED AND DOCUMENT-BASED NEGOTIATION

Besides norm-based negotiation we distinguish goal-based negotiation and document-based negotiation.

*Goal-based negotiation* does not aim at an authorization, but assumes that the parties (whether human or software agents) are motivated by goals. Hence, if a deal can be defined that meets the goal of the other party, this will motivate him to agree.

A goal-based negotiation protocol may consist of four main phases: (1) the introduction, in which the parties greet each other and introduce themselves, (2) goal identification – in which the parties express some of their goals, typically only after being asked, (3) exploration – in which the parties suggest opportunities, alternative ways of achieving the mutual goals, and (4) agreement in which one of the alternatives is agreed upon by both partners, perhaps with some small modifications. The exploration phase may be diverging first and converging in the end. The speech acts in the first introductory phase are greetings and self-introductions, the speech acts in the second goal identification phase are mainly questions and answers in the form of expressives, the speech acts in the third phase are suggestions and expressions of agreement/disagreement. Finally, the agreement phase consists mainly of proposals. Not only in the second phase, but in all phases, questions are very important, to make the parties express their goals and their proposals. This is in sharp contrast with the typical norm-based negotiation, where requests are predominant.

Negotiation styles are influenced by cultural backgrounds (Ulijn & Strother, 1995), and it may be the case that the goal-based negotiation is closer to the Oriental cyclic style. It is important to note that whereas norm-based negotiation is grounded in what Habermas calls the social world, the goal-based negotiation is grounded in what Habermas calls the subject world. It may be argued that goal-based negotiation lends itself less well to computer-mediated forms. It is not supported yet in the MeMo prototype.

*Document-based negotiation* is a negotiation process in which some document – typically the contract – plays a pivotal role. It can work very well if a document template is available, such as the contract templates issued by the International Chamber of Commerce. The process proceeds in steps determined by the contents of the contract. The clauses of the contract are grouped, and in each step, one set of clauses is discussed. After some agreement is reached, the next group of clauses is considered. Finally, when a preliminary agreement (soft commitment) is reached on all parts, the parties discuss the whole. A document-based negotiation is especially interesting in complicated situations, such as in international sales. In such cases, it is better to first see if an agreement is possible at all, and the legal safeguards are sufficient, before bargaining about the price, or other one-dimensional parameters such as delivery time, makes any sense. Document-based negotiation is currently supported in the MeMo prototype in the form of a contract base with a number of template documents and a negotiation protocol around this contract.

# 7. CONCLUSION

In this paper, we have described the MeMo system and the negotiation support it currently offers. We have described the formal semantics of norm-based negotiation using Dynamic Deontic Logic. In addition, we have sketched two other negotiation types. The MeMo system aims at flexible negotiation support; instead of imposing one protocol on each negotiation session, the parties can choose a preferable protocol themselves. So in the case of a sales contract, the quotation-based protocol can be used, while for the negotiation about an agency contract, a document-based protocol is more appropriate. Combinations are possible as well.

# 8. ACKNOWLEDGEMENTS

The research is partly supported by the European ESPRIT project "MeMo: Mediating and Monitoring Electronic Commerce", No 26895 (1999-2001) (http://www.abnammro.com/memo/). Participants are ABN-AMRO bank (NL), RWTH Aachen (D), Center-AR Tilburg (NL), IMK Checkmark (NL), EKD (E), Sarenet (E) and Atos/Origin (E).

# 9. REFERENCES

Chang, M. & C.Woo, 1994 A speech-act based negotiation protocol: design, implementation and test use *ACM Trans. on Information Systems 12(*4), pp360-382.

Habermas, J., 1981. *Theorie des kommunikativen Handelns*. Suhrkamp (2 volumes).

Gulliver, P., 1979. *Disputes and Negotiations*. Academic Press.

Kersten, G., & S.Noronha, 1997. Negotiations and the Internet: user expectations and acceptance. Interneg Research.

Lindemann, M.& B. Schmid, 1999. Framework for Specifying, Building and Operating Electronic Markets. *Int. Journal on Electronic Commerce (3), 2*, pp.7-21.

Reijswoud,V.E. van, 1996. *The structure of business communication: theory, model and application.* Ph.D. Thesis, Delft University of Technology.

Sandholm, T., 1999. Automated Negotiation. *Comm. of the ACM* 42(3).

Schoop, M., Ch. Quix, 2001. DOC.COM: Combining document and communication management for negotiation support in business-to-business electronic commerce. *Proc. HICSS '01*, IEEE Press.

Ulijn, J. & J.B. Strother, 1995. *Communicating in Business and Technology: From psycholinguistic theory to international practice*. Peter Lang GmbH, Frankfurt.

Verharen, E., 1998. *A Language-Action Perspective on the design of cooperative information agents*. Ph.D. Thesis, Tilburg University.

Weigand. H., F. Dignum, E.Verharen, 1997. Integrated Semantics for Information and Communication Systems. In: R. Meersman, L. Mark (eds), *Database Application Semantics*. Chapman & Hall

Weigand, H. & vd Heuvel, W.J., 1998. Meta-patterns for Electronic Commerce Transactions based on FLBC. *Proc. HICSS'98*. IEEE Press.

Winograd, T., 1988. A Language/Action Perspective on the design of cooperative work. In: I.Greif (ed), *Computer Supported Cooperative Work: A book of readings*. Morgan Kaufmann, San Mateo.

Zlotkin, G., J.S. Rosenschein, 1994. Rules of encounter - Designing conventions for automated negotiations among computers. MIT Press.

39

# Hierarchical Knowledge and Meta-Observations

Reinhard Riedl
*Department of Information Technology, University of Zurich*

**Abstract:** We present a model machinery for the generation of aggregating views of knowledge, the coupling of localized knowledge, and for carrying out meta-observations, which record the dynamics of a knowledge generating system. The machinery is based on the only assumption, that we can monitor events in a system. Thus it applies to all e-business applications with client/server computing.

## 1. THE COGNITIVE PERSPECTIVE

E-business often requires the exchange of textual information between partners in differing situations and with a different social, educational, or cultural background. Information is exchanged then as text data, whose interpretation depends on the problem context of the producer, and of the receiver, respectively, as well as on their respective ontologies. Thus, if context and/or ontology differ, the exchange of information is likely to fail. This fudamental problem, is often described as the problem of meaning and relevance. Seen from the perspective of cognitive science, one may understand meaning as a pointer, which affiliates an affordance in an ecological niche with an icon, which is usually a data object, e.g. a word in a text. On the one hand, pointers may be interally valued by a numerical inference value, which desribes the relevance with respect to affordances. On the other hand, pointers as a whole may be externally valued by relevance number which describes the relevance of the icon (embedded in a larger information object) for the receiver of information.

Inference network models with two layers may be used to subsumize and model these pointers, and affinity matrices can be used to represent the relationship between affordances and icons. Inference network models have been used before in information retrieval and information filtering [1], while affinity matrices have been used for data-affinity based load balancing in high performance distributed computing. In both cases, we have formal representations at hand, which can be generalized to similar structures. A survey of these formal modeling approaches can be found in [11].

The relevance of icons can equivalently be modeled with inference networks consisting of two layers, or with affinity matrices, respectively. The canonical composition of inference network models, and the canonical matrix multiplication, respectively, may thus be used to jointly model meaning and relevance. Thus any larger textual information object can be modeled straightforwardly, as long as its components do not interfere with each other. The latter is for example true for digitalized personal documents in inter-organisational e-government [12]. We shall elaborate on these representations below.

In our picture, knowledge implies the ability to identify the pointers and to learn from experience how to improve that identification. The identification is a process rather than a single activity, which may be performed in a moment or in a series of steps. Knowledge management technology can facilitate faster or more accurate identification by

- supporting the human identification process
- automating the process and providing computed results to the human user or
- collecting and presenting experience, which can be used to construct or update automatic identification algorithms or human knowledge on how to perform the identifications.

In this paper, we shall primarily focus on the third task, and we shall explain how monitoring in client/server computing can be exploited to come up with formal knowledge representations.

## 2. THE ENGINEERING PERSPECTIVE

Recently, there has been started considerable work on higher order knowledge mining, compare for example the approach in [13] based on clausal form logic [6]. While most of these approaches are founded in database engineering, our approach stems from distributed systems engineering.

Distributed systems[59] are message-oriented and adhere to the service paradigm. This is both true for high performance computing and for information sharing systems, and it even applies in parts and to some extent for distributed mainframe environments. There are two basic communication paradigms implemented, namely request/reply interaction and messaging based on some queueing service. The Middle-ware is responsible for the execution of communication and in doing this, it usually supplies additional support for distributed computing, such as security services, transaction semantics, and computing context (e.g. virtual synchrony).

[59] equivalently, we may speak of client/server systems

Events and event models play an essential role in Middle-ware managed systems. For example, next to the naming service, the event service is a primary service in CORBA or CORBA-like systems. Among others, Middle-ware provides us event tracing mechanisms, and with basic functionality to evaluate these recordings and to apply them, e.g. for non-repudiation services. While most of this add-on functionality primarily generates order relations, it is also possible to put services on top of it, which supply us with inference relations, e.g. for data-affinity based load balancing in distributed computing environments.

As these capabilities are creating demand, considerable work is being done on the extraction of knowledge from these event tracings. The reasons for doing that are quite diverse, ranging from meta-benchmarking approaches over performance tuning and information system re-engineering to actual knowledge mining. The natural next step of this work is to develop tools for engineering of the knowledge extracted and for the monitoring of the observation extraction process itself.

Part of this monitoring is the creation of meta-observation on the internal structure of knowledge bases and knowledge representations, which constitutes some particular form of higher-order knowledge. In this paper, we present a modeling machinery, which merges and generalizes some of the knowledge models applied for actual engineering tasks in distributed systems.

## 3. THE MODEL BASELINE

First, we present the basic framework for our approach to knowledge modeling. The standing thesis in behind is, that knowledge can be generated from the clustering of observations of well identified and classified events. Thus knowledge grounding is performed by event classification. This defines clear restrictions on the scope of applicability of our theoretic framework, or rather, it identifies the place of our `tool-box' in the chain of knowledge generation.

The input to our model are the observations of classified events, i.e. events[60] with well defined, observable a priori conditions, and well defined a posteriori conditions. The output of our model, or, more precisely, the output of a machine implementing (part of) the machinery defined by the model, are views of the knowledge represented by the classified observations, couplings of different, localized knowledge representations, and meta-observation reports.

Both views and meta-observation reports represent higher-order knowledge to a different extent: Views plainly describe aggregated knowledge, while meta-observation reports inform us about the internal structure of observations, e.g. their dynamics. Moreover, our model framework also supports the coupling of localized knowledge, represented by views. This includes the coupling of automatically

[60] The term event does not imply that it has no extension in time.

generated knowledge[61], i.e. grounding categorization, with human expert knowledge.

We shall proceed as follows: We first define the basic model and we introduce two representations of it, one in terms of hierarchical graphs and the other in terms of numerical matrices. The representation with hierarchical graphs enables us to define skew views of the knowledge, where part of the knowledge is aggregated and another part is not.

The representation with matrices enables us to give numerical pictures of these graphs as well as of their aggregated views. Finally, we explain how local knowledge may be combined technically with other knowledge. Combinations are worked out on the the level of representations only, in order to avoid a mixing up of the physical observations and their homomorphic (virtual) images in our model.

## 3.1 Events, a priori observables, a posteriori observables, and profiles

In our approach, knowledge is a localized model of the correlation between a priori observables and posteriori observables, which is formally represented by inference matrices, as they appear in inference network models ([5]), where they are also sometimes called link matrices. This model is drawn from the observation of events and the structuring of these events. Each event is associated the same a priori observables and the same a posteriori observables. In the following, the event set will be denoted by E. The set of a priori observations is denoted by O- and the set a priori observable states is denoted by S-. The set of a posteriori observations is denoted by O+ and the set a posteriori observable states is denoted by S+. Formally, observables are mappings between the event set and the set of states. We omit a detailed formal introduction and we refer to [11]. For the two sets of states, we introduce the concept of profiles. Profiles are sets of states. We requite that the set of a priori profiles, and the set of a posteriori profiles are atomic lattices (whose order structure is defined by set inclusion). As usual, a subset of disjunct profiles is called a partitioning (with respect to a given lattice of profiles). Partitionings define new observables, when the original observables are composed with a mapping representing the set inclusion of the original states into the new states. In the following, we shall assume that the lattices of profiles consists of a (finite) sequence of refined partitionings.

**Definition 1:** We define knowledge as the quintuple (**E**, O-, O+, T, P), where E denotes the set of classified observations or observed, classified events, O- and O+ denote the observables, and T and P denote lattices of profiles.

[61] where automatic generation is based on available classification

## 3.2 Graph representations

Knowledge as defined above can be represented as a VH-graph ([7]). We shall not bother the reader with explicit definitions, but rather we shall explain the concept to be applied. We may represent states as nodes in a bipartite base-graph, and we may represent events as edges. VH-graphs have in addtion a hierachical, i.e. tree-like, structure, where the nodes of the base-graph are embedded into the hierachy. Cuts are non-comparable sets of elements of the hierachy, and views corresponding to a cut collapse all structure of the base-graph "below" the cut. Thus, parts of the base-graph may be aggregated, while other parts may be shown in full detail. That is, we may zoom into the system at critical parts and still work with a moderately complex view, when we aggregate other parts.

Due to our assumptions above, the union of the both lattices of profiles provides us with an appropriate hierachy, and thus we can create hierachical views of the knowledge quintuple defined above. Please note that if we allow various edges between the same pair of nodes, the VH-graphs are in one-to-one correspondence with the knowledge qintuples. Further, we can merge two knowledge quintuples represented as bipartite graphs, by applying the construction principle for the composition of relations. This results in a representation for the composed knowledge as a new bipartite graph, whose nodes consist of the a priori states of the first quintuple and of the a posteriori states of the second quintuple, while for each pair of edges ((u,v), (x,y)), v=x, (u,v) an event in the first quintuple, and (x,y) and event in the second qintuple,there is an edge (u, y) in the new bipartite graph.

The graph representation reveals that our approach to formal knowledge representations is in the spirit of rule-based systems. This defines some constraints on its applicability, but on the other hand it links event monitoring directly with an autmated generation of rule sets, which reflects what is actually happening in a client/server system. The main advantage of graph representations is that they allow a visualisation of rules, where hierachical views provide an opportunity to focus attention on selected parts of the system and to aggregate others.

We conclude with

**Definition 2:** Given a knowledge quintuple (**E**, O-, O+, T, P), the affiliated hierachical knowledge is the union of all knowledge quintuples, which can be constructed from it by applying the technique of generating views.

By abuse of terminology, hierachical knoewledge is a set homomorphic images of the original knowledge, whose size is determined by the profile latices.

## 3.3 Matrix representations

Assume again that we have given a knowledge quintuple (**E**, O-, O+, T, P) as above. We now introduce the footprint matrix representation and the reference matrix representation of knowledge according to the following scheme

- lines correspond to states of a priori observables
- columns correspond to states of a posteriori observables
- entries correspond to events, where integer counting leads to reference matrices and Boolean counting leads to footprint matrices
- there is no semantic meaning in the enumeration of lines and columns
- states may be replaced by sets of states, namely profiles

Again we omit details. The scheme sketched enables us to provide matrix representation for knowledge quintuples, as well as for the affiliated hierachical knowledge. Note that forming a homomorphic image is done by addition of lines and/or columns, and that the combination of knowledge corresponds to matrix multiplication.

If we reverse the order of relations and if we normalize entries such that we get a probabbility matrix, then we obtain the inference values for an inference network model consisting of two layers. Again, combination is done by matrix multiplication.

### 3.4 Some Remarks

In many application scenarios, one type of view is exactly what one is interested in. However, if we are interested in the internal structure of a set of observations it is exactly the diversity of view, which enables us to `measure' this structure [9].

There is some duality between a priori observables and a posteriori observables. They are essentially a view position. Exchanging them changes corresponds to a matrix transposition. Ignoring normalization issues, the change of view corresponds to the change between reference matrices and inference matrices.

Our framework essentially stems from the modeling of decision problems with decision tasks, a priori observables, and a posteriori observables. Decisions are made upon the observation of a priori observables and the quality of the decisions is a function of the a posteriori observables. Therefore, it is critical for good solutions to understand the correlation of a priori and a posteriori observables. (Cf. [10]). There are various different interpretations possible. Our basic understanding is, that any matrix entry specifies something like a rule linking the a priori state and the posteriori state. This rule may be understood as an inference rule, or some conditional probability.

## 4. IMPLEMENTATION TECHNIQUE

Next, we discuss basic formal techniques for the implementation of knowledge generators relying on our model framework.

## 4.1 Generation of hierarchies

Hierarchies of a priori profiles arise from the clustering of natural partitionings. Above we have defined a machinery to represent knowledge with respect to such hierarchies. However, which hierarchies are we to choose?

This depends on the problem context, of course. The general strategy will be to find satisfactory solutions for the following problem: Find a hierarchy of profiles such that each a priori profile is as homogeneous as possible with respect to the posteriori observables of their class members (because otherwise the inference rule associated had little relevance), that any two a priori profiles are as distinct as possible with respect to their a posteriori observables (because otherwise the associated inference rules would have little meaning), and that all profiles are neither too small (as then they would lack statistical relevance) nor too large (because we are interested knowledge as fine-grained as possible). Note that analogously, we can also ask for a posteriori profiles fulfilling the same requirements for a priori observables.

There are various different possibilities to formalize these requirements, and there are various methods to obtain the desired hierarchies: classical clustering algorithms based on a distance function on the set of a posteriori observables (in case of a priori profiles) or on the set of a priori observables (in case of a posteriori profiles), neural network clustering, algorithms choosing a configuration whose matrix representation is as close as possible to a block diagonal matrix, or which optimizes some independent reference model (cf [2]), and some further more. A discussion of these issues is beyond the scope of this paper.

## 4.2 Meta-observations

Meta-observations concern the event system as a whole. We use them to judge on the relevance of observations. There are various possibilities for analyzing observations

- the intrinsic algebraic structure as it is addressed by the optimization problems indicated above
- the intrinsic algebraic structure as it is represented by semigroup role structure (cf [9])
- the comparison with natural languages measuring the Heaps and the Zipf exponent (cp [11]).
- One example of the last is the footprint growth function, which stems from Heap's law:

**Definition 3:** The relevance of the observations are described by the growth of the footprint of the (ordered) events with respect to the a priori and a posteriori observables.

Heaps observed that in natural language texts this functions grows like a polynomial with exponent one half, i.e. similar as the supremum function of one-dimensional Brownian motion.

## 4.3 Architecture

Finally we depict the architecture for knowledge mining, where the model machinery discussed is situated in.

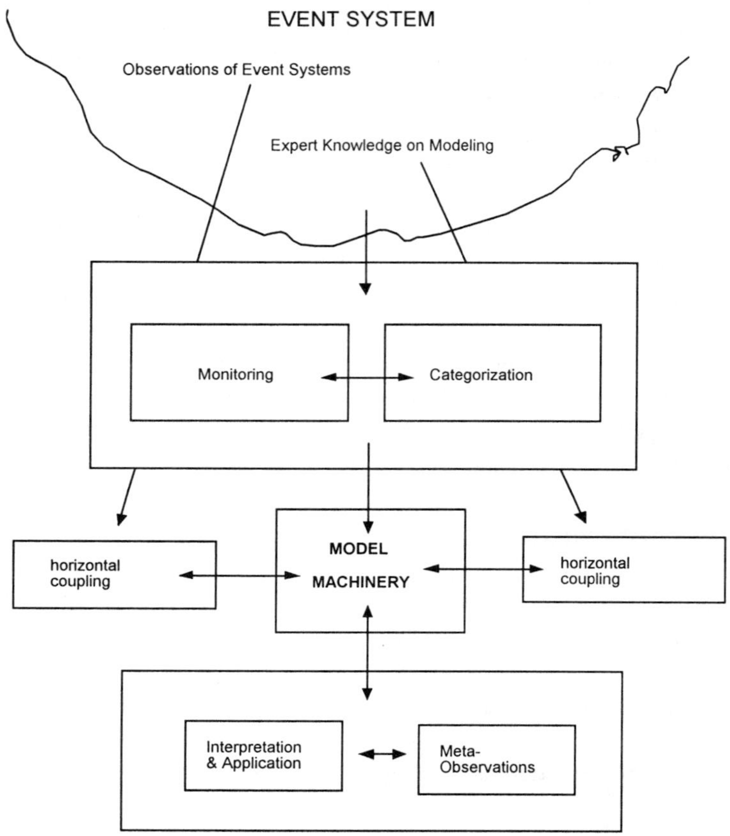


The architecture consists of four levels: the system, where measures are taken (called event system above), the layer with monitoring and primary categorization tools feeding our model framework with data, the implementation of our model framework, which makes use of automatic and expert categorization, and the layer with tools for interpretation and application of the hierarchical views and the couplings of different knowledge representations. There, the meta-observation tools are situated as well, since they are needed for the relevance ranking of knowledge representations.

## 4.4 Applications

There is a wide range of applications for our machinery in e-business:

- customer profiling in market research
- psychological analyses of user behaviour in virtual venues or communities
- design of information agents supporting users of large Intranets, design of e-brokers for customer-supplier matching in virtual markets, or personalied guidance of users through administration processes in e-government
- optimization of native code generators in Bytecode compilation
- optimization of load distribution in high performance transaction processing
- sociological analyses of information societies

In all these cases, we can monitor natural events, such as client requests, data object accesses, etc. and hierachical knowledge representation plays an important role for the design and the implementation of applications. Typically, a priori profiles describe the identity of an active person or object, while a posteriori profiles desribe what is really done, or which ressources are really requested. Indeed, applications im e-business with monitoring of client requests range from psychology and sociology to performance management.

We have performed meta-observations for various different scenarios, such as DB/DC transaction processing, accesses to web-pages in web-sites, and requests for search-engines. This revealed that Heaps and Zipf's Law are more or less valid in all scenarios, but the coefficients depend on the actual scenario. In some scenarios they clearly reflect the dynamics of the system, while in other scenarios they may also represent static patterns of access distributions.

# 5. CONCLUSIONS

We have presented a formal machinery for knowledge engineering. Due to its genericity it applies to a wide range of knowledge mining scenarios in distributed computing and distributed information systems. Part of this machinery has been implemented in joint research projects with industry. While the workflow for knowledge extraction is well understood in parts, so far little is understood of the internal structure of event systems.

# 6. REFERENCES

[1] Belkin, N.J., and Croft, W.C., Information Filtering and Information Retrieval: Two sides of the Same Coin, Comm. of the ACM, Vol 35, No 2, 1992;

[2] E. Born, T. Delica, W. Ehrl, L. Richter, R. Riedl, Characterization of Workloads for Distributed DB/DC-Processing, J. on Information Science, 1997;

[3] J. Heaps, Information Retrieval - Computational and Theoretical Aspects, Academic Press 1978

[4] C Lueg and R. Riedl, How Information Technology Could Benefit from Modern Approaches to Knowledge Management, Proceedings of the 3rd Conference on Practical Applications of Knowledge Management - PAKM 2000, Basel 2000

[5] J. Pearl, Probabilistic Reasoning in Intelligent Systems: Networks of Plausible Inference, Morgan Kaufmann, 1998

[6] T. Richards: Clausal Form Logic: An Introduction to the Logic of Computer Reasoning, Addison Wesley, 1989

[7] M. W. Richter, VH-Graphs - A New Approach to Hierarchical Graphs and their Application to Object-oriented Programming, Thesis, Univ. of Zurich, 1998

[8] R. Riedl: Agents for Customer Support in Electronic Commerce: Agents as Performing Actors, ACM SIGUCCS Conference 1999, Denver, Colorado 1999;

[9] R. Riedl: Usage of Trace Data for the Deduction of Role Structures and the Comparison of Knowledge Societies, 3rd Int. Conf. on Cognition Technology, San Francisco 1999

[10] R. Riedl: The Impact of Workload on Simulation Results for Distributed Transaction Processing, Proc. HPCN Europe '99, Amsterdam 1999;

[11] R. Riedl: Need for Database Trace Benchmarks, in R. Eigenmann, Performance Evaluation with Realistic applications, MIT-Press, 2001

[12| R. Riedl, Document-based Interorganisational Information Exchange , accepted for Proceedings of SIGDOC 2001, Santa Fe 2001

[13] H. Spiliopoulou, J. F. Roddick: Higher Order Mining: Modelling and Mining the Results of Knowledge Discovery. In Proc. Second International Conference on Data Mining Methods and Databases, Cambridge, UK, WIT Press, 2000

MINITRACK TWO

# E-COMMERCE-INDUCED REENGINEERING

**Minitrack Chair:**

Majed Al-Mashari
King Saud University, Saudi Arabia, malmashari@yahoo.com

40

# ERP Implementation: An Integrative Methodology

Abdullah Al-Mudimigh[1], Mohamed Zairi[1] and Majed Al-Mashari[2]
[1]*European Centre for TQM, University of Bradford, UK*
[2]*College of Computer and Information Science, King Saud University, Saudi Arabia*

**Abstract:** Though ERP systems are being widely implemented in many organisations, there is a lack of unified implementation methodologies that reflect the essential critical factors of success. Research developing such methodologies has been scarce. This paper fills this gap by proposing an integrative methodology based on an extensive review of the essential critical factors of success. Following the generic proposed methodology and framework, it is argued that success can be yielded in implementing ERP systems.

## 1. INTRODUCTION

Many companies are radically changing their information technology strategies to maintain a competitive advantage, become more responsive to change markets, and deliver better service at lower cost by purchasing off-the-shelf integrated ERP software instead of developing IT systems in-house (Davenport, 2000; Holland and Light, 1999).

Overall, ERP is a relatively new phenomenon, and the research related to it is not extensive (Al-Mashari, 2000; Nah et al., 2001; Parr, et al., 1999), and its implementation methodologies are still developing. Several approaches and methodologies have been introduced by a number of authors and practitioners (e.g. Al-Mashari, 2000; Gibson, et al., 1999; Bancroft, et al., 1998; Computer Technology Research, 1999; Welti, 1999, Holland and Light, 1999; Bingi, et at., 1999; Markus, et at. 2000; Al-Mashari and Zairi, 2000). However, and generally speaking, there has not yet been a common comprehensive or holistic approach to ERP implementation.

This paper proposes a holistic framework for ERP implementation based on an extensive review of the factors and the essential elements that contribute to success in the context of ERP implementation. The following sections provide an overview of the proposed framework and a detailed discussion of its elements.

# 2. INTEGRATIVE FRAMEWORK FOR ERP IMPLEMENTATION

In essence, there are critical issues that must be carefully considered to ensure successful implementation of an ERP system project. Based on the vast literature review conducted on ERP system implementation, this research has derived a framework of ERP system implementation depicted on Figure 1.

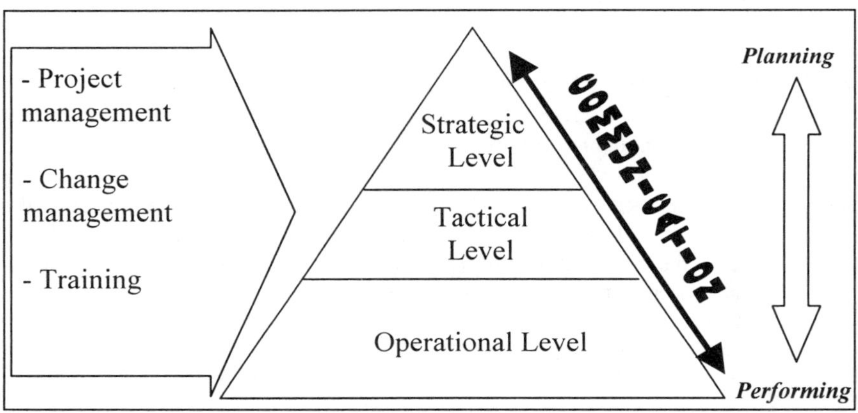


*Figure 1.* Holistic ERP System Implementation Project framework

As the figure shows, there are critical factors hypothesised to play a more overriding role in the project of ERP implementation. On the other hand, they should be ongoing throughout all implementation's levels. These factors are project management, change management, training, and communication.

The figure also shows that the implementation ERP system has been subdivided into three levels: strategic, tactical, and operational. Each level contains a number of critical factors. The factors of strategic level are current legacy system evaluation, project vision and objective, ERP implementation strategy, top management support and commitment, business case, and benchmarking. The factors of tactical (managerial) level are client consultation, hiring consultants, business process reengineering (BPR), ERP software and vendor selection, and implementation approach. Operational level contains business process modelling, configuring system, final preparation, and go live.

These levels of implementation, however, are not independent of each other and each level should be used to drive to the next level, for example, strategic level should be used to drive to the tactical level, and each level has to be well managed. Moreover, there is a direct relationship between the implementation's levels at which a decision is taken and characteristics of the information required to support decision making (Bocij, et al. 1999).

The following sections will discuss all the levels of successful ERP implementation and its factors. Moreover, the discussion will be based on a comprehensive review of the literature.

# 3. FRAMEWORK ELEMENTS

## 3.1 Project Management

ERP implementation is challenging, costly, and risky. Consequently, to achieve the desired benefits, the ERP system implementation must be carefully managed and monitored. It is in this respect that project management becomes important, if not crucial for success. Hoffer et al. (1998) argue that the project management activities span the life of the project from initiating the project to closing it.

Project management deals with various aspects of the project, such as planning, organisation, information system acquisition, personnel selection, and management and monitoring of software implementation (Peak, 2000). The project management is a practised system necessary to govern a project and to deliver quality products.

Initially, the project manager, in conjunction with the steering committee, will select the project team. Due to the wide ranging impact of ERP software, The members of the project team should ideally be from management or supervisory positions (Bancroft, et al., 1998), and have the authority to make decision regarding how a process will be completed (Computer Technology research Corporation, 1999).

The project manager must have skills to govern the project successfully (Welti, 1999; Bancroft, et al., 1998) including being a coach, cheerleader, flexible, confidante, mentor, stress resistance, communicative, and visionary.

### 3.1.1 Project Schedule and Plans

Slevin and Pinto (1987) define project schedule and plans as the detailed specification of the individual action steps required accomplishing the project's goals. If the project has failed, the fact that not every detail of the plan was pursued be typically used as the rationale for the project's failure.

### 3.1.2 Monitoring and Feedback

Slevin and Pinto (1987) define the monitoring and feedback factor as the timely provision of comprehensive control information at each stage in the implementation process. This is one of the project manager's fundamental tasks (Welti, 1999).

### 3.1.3 Risk Management

Risk management can decrease the number of unexpected crises and deviation from budget and schedule, providing advance warning as problems begin to develop (Peak, 2000). It is the competence to handle unexpected crises and deviations from the plan (Slevin and Pinto, 1987). Any deviation from the implementation project budget, schedule, and defined project goals must be identified and tracked carefully, with appropriate corrective action taken.

## 3.2 Change Management

Cooke and Peterson (1998) identify change management, in terms of adopting an ERP system, as activities, processes, and methodologies that support employee understanding and organisational shifts during the implementation of ERP systems and reengineering initiatives. Many ERP implementation failures have been caused by the lack of focus on 'the soft issues', i.e. the business process and change management (Sumner, 1999).

An ERP systems package has a major impact on organisations, especially on their staff (Welti, 1999). Thus, change management is essential for preparing a company to the introduction of an ERP system, and its successful implementation. ALVEO (Welti, 1999) prepared its employees for the coming change through management support, information, communication, and training.

Overall, top management commitment, education and training, communication are critical success factors of any change management (Norris et al., 2000).

## 3.3 Training

ERP systems are extremely complex systems and demand rigorous training. Installing an ERP software package without adequate end-user preparation could yield to drastic consequences. Inadequate or lack of training has been one of the most significant reasons of many ERP systems failure (Kelley, et al., 1999).

ERP training should address all aspects of the system, be continuous and based on knowledge transfer principles wherever consultants are involved (Davenport, 1998b). Welti (1999) cites that every level in the orgainsation class and the various users require different training.

## 3.4 Communication

Communication is one of the most challenging and difficult tasks in any ERP implementation project (Welti, 1999). Slevin and Pinto (1987) define communication as the provision of an appropriate network and necessary data to all key factors in the project implementation. Communication has to cover the scope, objectives, and tasks of an ERP implementation project (Sumner, 1999).

## 3.5 Strategic Level

The decisions made at this level significantly change the manner in which business is being done (Bocij, et al. 1999) and these decisions are the responsibility of top management (Turban, et al., 1999).

The following sections will discuss these factors based on the literature reviewed.

### 3.5.1 Current Legacy System Evaluation

Adolph (1996) points out that the legacy system contains the existing information technology (hardware and software), business processes, organisation structure, and culture.

In a sense, Holland and Light (1999) argue that the nature and scale of problem that are likely to be encountered could be defined by evaluating the existing legacy system. If organisation's legacy systems are extremely complex, with multiple technology platforms and a variety of procedures to manage common business processes, then the amount of technical and organisational change required is high. Otherwise, if the organisation has already got common business processes and a simple technical architecture, change requirements are low.

ERP systems depend on sophisticated IT infrastructure. It is clear that ERP implementation involves a complex transition from legacy information systems and business processes to an integrated IT infrastructure and common business process throughout the organisation (Gibson, et al. 1999).

### 3.5.2 Project Vision and Objective

Slevin and Pinto (1987) define project vision as the initial clarity of goals and general direction, while Bocij, et al. (1999) define it as an image of a future direction that everyone can remember and follow.

A global survey showed that an understanding of business objectives and clear vision are key success factors (Cooke and Peterson, 1998). However, at this stage in the ERP project, the vision should provide a direction and general objective, and no details are required. Welti, (1999) suggests that the project definition should not contain specific goals or strategy and should determine the purpose of the project. The next step would be to determine the ERP objectives.

### 3.5.3 ERP Implementation Strategy

The ERP implementation strategy will be reviewed to determine the impact of ERP system implementation on the enterprise, while the strategy of ERP system implementation will be overviewed, with details, within the tactical level.

The company has to have a clear understanding of the business implications to avoid a potential peril of failures. Building an implementation strategy for an ERP system project needs to be strongly based on both the business case developed and the results of the series benchmarking test. It should also ensure a full alignment with overall business strategy (Al-Mashari and Zairi, 2000).

### 3.5.4 Top Management Support/Commitment

Top management support was consistently identified as the most important and crucial success factor in ERP system implementation projects (Welti, 1999; Davenport, 1998a; Sumner, 1999; Bingi, et al., 1999; Bancroft, et al., 1998).

Welti (1999) suggests that active top management is important to provide enough resources, fast decisions, and support the acceptance of the project throughout the company. The top management support and commitment does not end with initiation and facilitation, but must extend to the full implementation of an ERP system. They should continually monitor the progress of the project and provide direction to the implementation teams (Bingi, et al, 1999).

### 3.5.5 Business Case

A strong business case can control a project's scope (Industry Week, 1998). It considers project objective, needs, and benefits. Moreover, a business case can help to convince people of the need for change, and therefore, their commitment to it (Industry Week, 1998).

Cooke and Peterson (1998) point out that to ensure a business-specific result, the business case needs to be translated down to those who are deploying the actual systems. Moreover, they mention that, based on a global survey, the development of a strong business case was one of the key success factors.

### 3.5.6 Benchmarking

Benchmarking is a technique for learning from other people. Bocij et al. (1999) suggest that the result of a series of benchmarking exercises could be compared against similar items in order to make the best selection.

Al-Mashari and Zairi (2000) argue that the benchmarking can play a significant role in shaping the strategic direction to be taken for change introduction using ERP package.

## 3.6 Tactical Level

At the tactical level, also termed managerial level, the medium-term planning of ERP specific organisational issues are largely concerned, where the decisions are made by middle managers (Turban, et al., 1999).

The following sections will discuss a comprehensive list of factors at this level, tactical, based on the literature reviewed.

### 3.6.1 Client Consultation

Slevin and Pinto (1987) define client consultation as the communication and consultation with, and active listening to, all affected parties, manly the client. They argued that the consultation with clients should occur early in the process, otherwise the chance of subsequent client acceptance will be lowered.

It is essential for an organisation to keep their clients aware for their future project to avoid miss-convince.

### 3.6.2 Hiring Consultants

Due to the complexities of implementing an ERP system, most companies choose to hire consultants to help them select, configure, and implement the system. Welti (1999) argues that the success of a project depends on the capabilities of the consultants because they have in-depth knowledge of the software.

However, with new technology, it is often critical to acquire external expertise, including vendor support, to facilitate successful implementation (Sumner, 1999). IT research firm Gartner Group (Computer Technology Research Corporation, 1999) argues that the ratio of consulting costs to software costs could reach up to 3:1. Clearly, it is a critical success factor, and has to be managed and monitored very carefully.

### 3.6.3 Business Process Reengineering (BPR)

As mentioned before, there are two main options to implement ERP systems: modify an ERP system package to suit the organisation's requirements or the implementation of an ERP system package with minimum deviation from the standard settings (Holland and Light, 1999). However, ERP systems are built on best practices that are followed in the industry, and to successfully install ERP, all the processes in a company should conform to the ERP model (Davenport, 1998a; Sumner, 1999). Therefore, to take a full advantage of an ERP software, business process redesign is seen as a prerequisite.

Davenport (1998a), Bingi, et al. (1999), Al-Mashari and Zairi (2000), Holland and Light (1999), Gibson, et al. (1999), O'Leary (2000), and Davenport (2000) all agree that the enterprise consensus is required to reengineer a company's core business processes to align them with the model implicit within the ERP package to take advantage of the ERP system. Companies that do not follow this philosophy are likely to face major difficulties (Bancroft, et al., 1998; Gibson, et al., 1999).

The persisting question at this point is when should a company do business process reengineering? before, during, or after ERP package implementation. In fact, some companies have implemented ERP system package prior to BPR project (e.g. ALVEO (Welti, 1999)) to avoid the trouble of a BPR project. If the corporate structure and processes fit well with ERP system package, this approach is possible (Bancroft, et al., 1998). While, some companies started with BPR prior to ERP package (e.g. Digital Equipment (Bancroft, et al., 1998)). Thus answering this question will depend highly on the company's specific situation and as status quo.

In general, the decision as to when BPR should take place in ERP system package implementation, (before, during, or after) remains dependent on the business situation (Bancroft, et al., 1998).

### 3.6.4 ERP Software/Vendor Selection

Selecting new ERP system software is a difficult task and one of the most risky decisions that most companies face. Moreover, ERP package is not like other off-the-shelf package such as word-processing, spreadsheet, or database software, but rather sophisticated and complex software for the areas of enterprise processes.

An enterprise should choose an expert and a clear method to help select the software system. The complexity of selecting ERP package software can add a lot of time to the ERP system project (Computer Technology Research Corporation, 1999).

### 3.6.5 Implementation Approach

The company has to take a fundamental decision regarding the implementation approach and clearly select a focused path. There are aspects, such as organisational structure, resources, attitude toward change, or distance between the various production facilities, that influence the company's decision to select ERP system implementation approach. There are three main implementation approaches: step-by-step, big bang, and roll-out. The roll-out approach, which may be implemented as a step-by-step or big bang, creates a model implementation at one site, which is then rolled out to other (Welti, 1999).

However, small and medium size enterprise (SME) cannot afford to spend years on a software project like large enterprise. Therefore, vendors and consultants of ERP system have responded with methods and tactics specifically designed to keep ERP system projects moving. Most enterprises now use a rapid implementation approach, e.g. AcceleratedSAP, or ASAP, (Computer Technology Research

Corporation, 1999). In this regards, companies should consult with ERP software package vendors and implementation partners to understand more regarding specific details of rapid methodology.

## 3.7 Operational Level

Although installing an ERP software package is not as difficult as getting the enterprise soft elements in line with all the change imperatives, its critical role in yielding optimum outcomes from implementation cannot be over-emphasised (Al-Mashari and Zairi, 2000). In essence, there is no development requirement, rather, it is business processes (Bancroft, et al., 1998).

For this phase, there are numerous tools used during an ERP package system implementation supported by several ERP package vendors.

The following sections will discuss the steps at this level based on the literature review conducted.

### 3.7.1 Business process Modelling

In this step, the project team determines how the system will work, not in the technical sense but in terms of the processes the company uses to accomplish different tasks, and how the business will operate after the ERP system package is in use. SAP calls this task "business process blueprint".

The business process modelling is the complete description of how an enterprise will implement the ERP system package to support its business activities (Buck-Emden, 2000).

### 3.7.2 Configuring System

Configuring an ERP system package is largely a matter of making compromises and of balancing the way the enterprise wants to work with the way the ERP package system lets it works (Davenport, 1998a).

Configuration does not mean the modification of the ERP package, but rather the set-up and configuration of all usage options that are possible in an ERP software package (Buck-Emden, 2000).

The process of configuration differs fundamentally from programming. Configuration involves adapting the generic functionality of the software package to the needs of a particular company, while programming involves creating new functionality of application (Markus and Tanis, 2000).

### 3.7.3 Final Preparation

Before going live on an ERP system, all necessary adjustments, in order to prepare the system and business for production start-up, have to be made. The system must be tested to make sure that it works technically and the business process configurations are practical (Computer Technology Research Corporation, 1999).

It is important in this step to assess the end-user well training (Welti, 1999). In general, all testing must be completely prepared and seriously carried out whether for integration or for migration.

Testing helps companies avoid potential problems that might negatively impact customers (Bancroft, et al., 1998). The project teams should test the user-acceptance to gather the more intangible feedback about ERP system package materials (Computer Technology Research Corporation, 1999).

### 3.7.4 Go Live

This is the final step of the ERP package implementation; it is also referred to as "going into production". It has two major steps: activating the system and transitioning from the old system to the new system (Computer Technology Research Corporation, 1999).

Going live usually goes off-hours (e.g. weekend, holiday, etc.), to allow project teams to monitor how the system performs (Computer Technology Research Corporation, 1999).

By the end of this step, the project management prepares for the acceptance of the productive environment by the steering committee (Appelrath and Ritter, 2000).

## 4. CONCLUSION

This paper has made a unique contribution by proposing a holistic framework for ERP implementation. Since the field of IT support systems has moved away from stand alone, dedicated solutions with localised impact to more integrated flexible enterprise wide systems, a fresh approach was needed. In essence, this is the unique contribution that ERP systems bring with them. Not only do they address organisational systems from a Business Process Change perspective, but furthermore, the software configuration is geared towards creating seamlessness and an integrated 'value chain'.

In essence, the paper recognises a series of critical issues that must be carefully considered to ensure successful implementation of an ERP system project. These factors culminate in the proposed model depicted in Figure 1. The proposed model makes a worthwhile contribution since it has clearly identified factors that are beyond the issues of project management that other authors have been referring to in the literature. Furthermore by adhering to the various levels of application of ERP systems, will ensure that organisations can derive maximum benefits from ERP systems and that the decision making process and the flow of information happens in a seamless, corporate-wide perspective. One additional feature of the proposed model which is very worthwhile pointing is that there is a dual process of planning and performing which synchronises the various activities of organisational systems and ensures that there is goal congruence and performance effective delivery outcomes.

# 5. REFERENCES

Adolph, W. (1996) "Cash Cow in the Tar Pit: Reengineering a Legacy System", IEEE Software, May, pp. 41-47.

Al-Mashari, M. (2000) "Constructs of Process Change Management in ERP Context: A Focus on SAP R/3." Proceedings of the Americans Conference on Information Systems (AMICS).

Al-Mashari, M. and Zairi, M. (2000) "The effective application of SAP R/3: a proposed model of best practice." Logistics Information Management, 13(3), pp. 156-166.

Apperlrath, H. and Ritter, J. (2000) "SAP R/3 Implementation: Method and Tools." Springer, Germany.

Bancroft, N.; Seip, H. and Sprengel, A. (1998) "Implementing SAP R/3: How to introduce a large system into a large organization." Manning Publication Co., USA.

Bingi, P.; Sharma, M. and Godla, J. (1999) "Critical Issues Affecting an ERP Implementation." Information management, summer, pp.7-14.

Bocij, P.; Chaffey, D.; Greasley, A. and Hickie, S. (1999) "Business Information Systems: Technology, Development and Management." Financial Times Management, London.

Buck-Emden, R. (2000) "The SAP R/3 System: An introduction to ERP and business software technology." ADDISON-WESLEY, USA.

Computer technology Research Corporation (1999) "Enterprise Resource Planning: Integrating Applications and Business Process Across the Enterprise." Computer Technology Research Corporation, USA.

Cooke, D. and Peterson, W. (1998) "SAP Implementation: Strategies and results." Research report 1217-98-RR, The Conference Board, New York.

Davenport, T. (1998a) "Putting the Enterprise into the Enterprise System." Harvard Business Review, July-August, pp. 121-131.

Davenport, T. (1998b) "Think Tank: Making the most of an information-rich environment." CIO Magazine, December 1.

Davenport, T. (2000) "Mission Critical: Realizing the Promise of Enterprise Systems." Harvard Business School Press, USA.

Gibson, N.; Holland, C. and Light, B. (1999) "A Case Study of a Fast Track SAP R/3 Implementation at Guilbert." Electronic Markets, June, pp.190-193.

Hoffer, J.; George, J. and Valacich, J. (1998) "Modern Systems Analysis and Design." (2nd Ed.), Addison-Wesley, Reading, MA.

Holland, C. and Light, B. (1999) "A Critical Success Factors Model for ERP Implementation." IEEE Software, May/June, pp. 30-35.

Industry Week, (1998) "Just in case", Industry Week, 246(15), p. 28.

Markus, M, Tanis, C., Fenema, P. (2000) "Multisite ERP Implementation." Communication of the ACM, 43(4), pp. 42-46.

Markus, M. and Tanis, C. (2000) "The Enterprise System Experience - From Adoption to Success." In Framing the Domains of IT Management Research: Projecting the Future Through the Past, Pinnaflex Educational Resources, Inc., (Zmud, R., ed.).

Nah, F., Lau, L. and Kuang, J. (2001) "Critical factors for successful implementation of enterprise systems." Business Process Management Journal, 7(3), pp.285-296.

Norris, G.; Hurley, J.; Hartley, K.; Dunleavy, J. and Balls, J. (2000) "E-Business and ERP: Transforming the Enterprise." John Wiley & Sons, Inc., New York, USA.

O'Leary, D. (2000) "Enterprise Resource Planning Systems: Systems, Life Cycle, Electronic Commerce, and Risk." Cambridge University Press, USA.

Parr, A.; Shanks, G. and Drake, P. (1999) "The Identification of Necessary Factors for Successful Implementation of ERP System." Proceedings of IFIP Conference on New Information Technology in Organizational Processes: Field Studies and Theoretical Reflections on the Future of Work, St Louis, Missouri, USA, August.

Peak, D. (2000) "Project Management." In INTERNATIONAL ENCYCLOPEDIA OF BUSINESS & MANAGEMENT (IEBM), THE HANDBOOK OF INFORMATION TECHNOLOGY IN BUSINESS, (Zeleny, M., ed.), London.

Slevin, D. and Pinto, J. (1987) "Balancing Strategy and Tactics in Project Implementation." Sloan Management Review, Fall, pp. 33-44.

Sumner, M. (1999) " Critical Success Factors in Enterprise Wide Information Management Systems Projects." Proceedings of the Americans Conference on Information Systems (AMICS).

Turban, E.; McLean, E. and Wetherbe, J. (1999) "Information Technology for Management: Making Connections for Strategic Advantage." John Wiley & Sons, USA.

Welti, N. (1999) "Successful SAP R/3 Implementation: Practical Management of ERP projects." Addison Wesley Longaman Limited, USA

# 41

# Web-driven Management Thinking: A Look at Business Process Redesign in the Age of the Web

Ned Kock
*Temple University, 1810 N. 13th Street, Speakman Hall 210C, Philadelphia, PA 19122, USA*

**Abstract:** Traditionally, management thinking has preceded and quite possibly driven the adoption and use of information technologies (IT) in organizations. That is, management schools (of thought) that emphasize certain types of work structures usually appear earlier than IT geared at supporting those work structures. This situation has undoubtedly changed recently, arguably around the mid-1990s, with the explosion in the commercial use of the Internet and particularly the Web. A first step towards a new management framework to help organizations benefit from modern Web-based IT is proposed and discussed in this paper. Our goal is to provide some basic elements that can be used by managers and researchers as a starting point for a broader management model. As such, we focus on a particular set of activities associated with team coordination and communication in production and service delivery business processes. Our framework is based on our experiences in 30 business process redesign projects conducted in partnership with 15 US organizations from 1997 to 2000.

## 1. INTRODUCTION

Traditionally, management thinking has preceded and quite possibly driven the adoption and use of information technologies (IT) in organizations. That is, management schools (of thought) that emphasize certain types of work structures usually appear earlier than IT geared at supporting those work structures. This situation has undoubtedly changed recently, arguably around the mid-1990s, with the explosion in the commercial use of the Internet and particularly the Web. The emergence of e-commerce, e-trade, e-business, and other *e-'s* has clearly led to creation of new organizational forms, management challenges, and related management ideas. For example, the Web has led to the development or expansion of the following types of organizations (Ashkenas et al., 1995; Christensen, 1998; Davidow and Malone, 1992; Grudin, 1994).

- "Internet startups", whose market value vastly exceeds what traditional price/earnings standards for company market valuation stipulate, placing these companies in an advantageous competitive position right at their inception due to the initial amount of capital that is available to them.
- "Internet portals", whose market value depends much more heavily on the number of visitors (first time or repeat) they can draw than on their revenues, profitability or other traditional market value measures.
- "Virtual organizations", which operate with no or few physical assets and distribution channels.
- "Boundaryless organizations", in which geographical barriers to teamwork and market reach are virtually eliminated.

The examples above only scratch the surface as far as the potential that this "disruptive technology" which is the Internet can have on organizational structure and, in consequence, management thinking. The adoption of management ideas that are aligned with the collaboration potential afforded by the Internet and the Web can place companies at tremendously advantageous positions in their industries, at least at a certain point in their evolution as organizational entities, as illustrated by Dell Computer, Federal Express, E-Trade and Amazon.com. The reasons for this are many, and range from the capacity to benefit from lower barriers to new entrants, to the ability to attract large infusions of capital at the beginning of their life cycle, to the development and continuous use of highly streamlined distribution and workflow management processes.

This paper proposes and discusses a first step towards a new management framework to help organizations benefit from modern Web-based IT. Our framework is developed based on a broad review of 30 business process redesign projects conducted by us in 15 organizations from 1997 to 2000.

## 2. NEW ORGANIZATIONAL MODELS SUPPORTED BY THE WEB AND KEY MANAGEMENT SCHOOLS OF THE 1900S

At the time of writing, the type of management thinking discussed in the previous section was not well defined and shaped in the form of a single management school. Nevertheless, is has been easy to find organizations trying to adapt ideas from old and existing management schools to the new environment of Web-based IT. Table 1 summarizes key management schools that emerged in the late 1900s, before the use of the Web became widespread.

*Table 1:* Key management schools of the 1900s

| Management school | Main figure(s) | Period | Main thesis |
|---|---|---|---|
| Total quality management | Deming, Juran | Began in the 1950s, first in Japan, reaching the US in the 1980s | Organizational improvement should focus on processes, not problems, and related quality issues. Productivity improvement cannot be realized without quality improvement. Line employees and customers, not only managers, should be deeply involved in quality improvement initiatives (Deming, 1986; Juran, 1989). |
| Organizational learning | Revans, Argyris, Senge | Began in the 1960s | Workers as well as managers can continuously improve the organization in which they work by freely sharing and questioning their knowledge and personal beliefs in a trusting organizational environment (Argyris, 1992; Revans, 1991; Senge, 1990). |
| Excellence | Peters, Kanter | Began in the 1980s | Excellent organizations change continuously in order to satisfy their customers. This change is both top-down and bottom-up, i.e., it is driven by managers as well as line workers (Peters and Waterman, 1982; Kanter, 1995). |
| Reengineering | Hammer, Davenport | Began in the 1990s | Organizations should radically redesign their processes from time to time in order to remain competitive. This redesign should be top-down, i.e., primarily led by top managers (Davenport, 1993; Hammer and Champy, 1993). |

Trying to adapt ideas from old and existing management schools (such as those in Table 1) to the new environment of Web-based IT has its advantages, but is difficult to accomplish in practice. There are two key reasons for this. The first is that some of the new Web-based IT have emerged to support new organizational forms that are often incompatible with one single management school. This makes it difficult to match a single management school with Web-based IT. The second reason is that existing management schools usually propose ideas that are, at some level, contradictory with each other, often because they were developed on the premise that other management schools proposed ideas that did not work in practice (e.g., reengineering vs. total quality management). Moreover, given the tendency of business writers to focus on one or a few business ideas and propose them as a panacea, it is difficult to find a good match between single existing management schools and emerging Web-based IT. What appears to be needed is a generic framework that ties together relevant management ideas that help organizations strategically and operationally align themselves with new Web-based IT.

It is beyond the scope of this article to propose a new management school. Even "describing" in the detail a new management school would increase the length of this paper beyond the space available. Given this, a first step towards a new management framework to help organizations benefit from modern Web-based IT is proposed and discussed in the next section. Our goal is to provide some basic elements that can be used by managers and researchers as a starting point for a broader management model. As such, we focus on a particular set of activities associated with team coordination and communication in production and service delivery business processes.

## 3. A SIMPLE FRAMEWORK FOR SUPPORTING PROCESSES WITH WEB-BASED IT

A great deal of our work at the Process Design and IT Group at Temple University's E-Business Institute revolves around the use of IT to support various team-based business processes. Since 1997, we have been working with a number of companies in the Philadelphia Metropolitan Area, the US Department of Defense, and a few defense contractors, in the analysis and redesign of their business processes, leveraging the resources provided by the Web to support new intra-organizational processes through "intranets", and new inter-organizational processes through "extranets". Some of the companies we have worked with toward this end were Prudential Insurance, Metro One Telecommunications, Sheraton Hotels, Day & Zimmermann, Delaware Investments, Penn Mutual and Andersen Consulting. The defense contractors we have worked with were Lockheed Martin and Computer Sciences Corporation.

After several projects, each involving different managers, consultants and key employees, some patterns started to emerge that seemed relatively independent of characteristics of the organization, processes, or people involved. While the organizations and processes targeted had their own peculiarities, we seemed to invariably arrive at a similar final result. This final result was, in all projects, a new process (we analyzed and redesigned over 30 processes from more than 15 organizations from 1997 to 2000). Processes analyzed included marketing, sales, inventory control, production, distribution, service delivery, and procurement. Production, service delivery and procurement processes were among the most frequent types of processes redesigned. In these, some generic features were particularly similar across redesigned processes in different companies. These are illustrated in Figure 1 and can be summarized as follows:

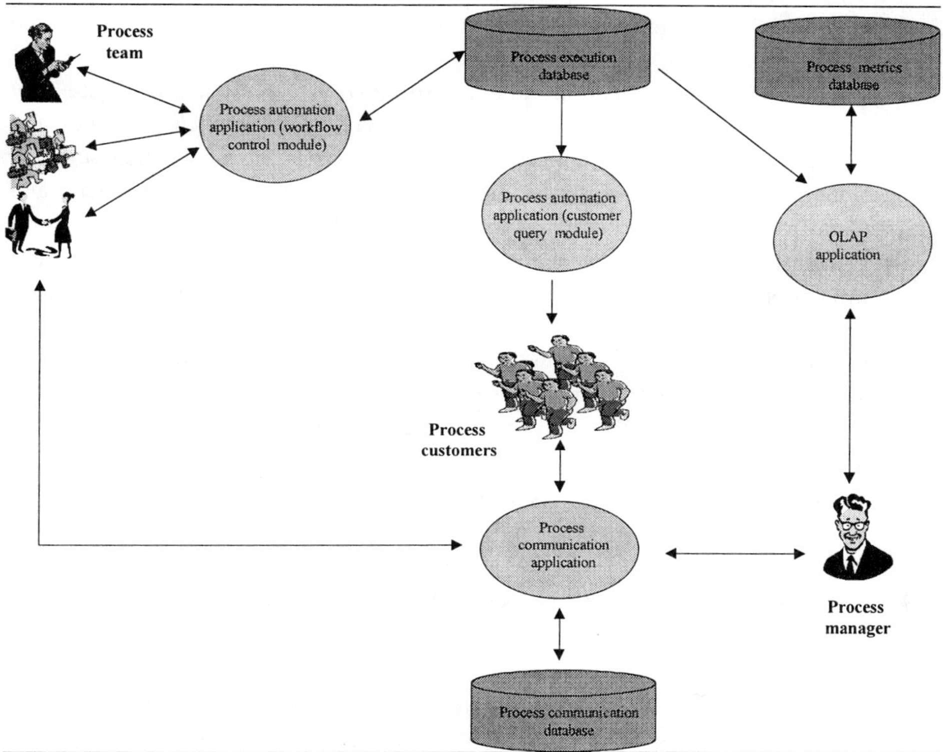


*Figure 1.* A generic model to implement processes enabled by Web-based IT

**A Web-based workflow control module**, represented in Figure 1 by the oval described as "Process automation application (workflow control module)". This is a computer application module that automates the execution of a process, from beginning to end, reminding process team members of tasks under their responsibility and allowing them to update the execution status of those tasks. This module populates a **process execution database** that stores data about process execution, represented in the figure by the drum symbol described as "Process execution database".

**A Web-based customer query module**, represented in Figure 1 by the oval described as "Process automation application (customer query module)", whose main function is to give customer access to process execution status data. For customers requesting an external telephone line repair, for example, this module would provide information about repair status.

**A Web-based OLAP (Online Analytical Processing) application**, represented in Figure 1 by the oval described as "OLAP application", whose main function is to allow the process manager to generate (and customize the generation of) process metrics periodically. Process metrics provide a simplified view of the productivity and quality of a process and can be used for continuous improvement of the processes.

**A Web-based process communication application**, represented in Figure 1 by the oval described as "Process communication application", which populates and provides access to a **process communication database**. This application supports continuous communication between the process manager, process customers, and process team and may incorporate the following Web-based components:

- **A repository of summarized process metrics and process improvement initiatives** aimed at improving the outcomes of the metrics. Usually the process manager maintains this repository.
- **A discussion forum** that allows process customers to communicate with each other as well as with process team members and the process manager.
- **A knowledge base** with key data needed by process team members to execute their respective activities in the process, and process customers, so they can use outputs of the process more efficiently and effectively.

# 4. A PRACTICAL EXAMPLE: A WEB-BASED "HELD DESK"

One of the most common processes of IT organizations that provide technology support to parent companies is the "help desk" process, which is used here to illustrate the generic process framework outlined in the previous section. It is through the help desk process that internal users are enabled to do their work using IT. Help desk activities include new accounts (e.g., email, proxy, dial-up, selected applications) creation, office applications training, general hardware and software support, network cabling set up, and database hosting, among others. The help desk process is a key process for both IT organization and parent company. The IT organization's budget is often defined by the quality and volume of help desk-related services provided to internal IT users.

A practical implementation of a help desk process using the Web-based IT model discussed in the previous section is shown in Figure 2. The relative position and shape of the main process elements is the same as in Figure 1 so that the reader can easily relate generic elements (shown in Figure 1) with their more specific counterparts in the implementation example shown in Figure 2.

In this practical implementation, the user interface is a Web browser (e.g., Netscape Navigator, Internet Explorer etc.) and, as such, is common to all users. All applications are Web-enabled and run on Web servers (or clusters of Web servers).

The communication medium between Web servers and browsers is the Internet (although it could have been an intranet or local area network supporting Web communication protocols). This configuration allows any of the process "actors" (i.e., process manager, process team members and process customers) to use the system anywhere-anytime. Specific implementation elements are discussed below.

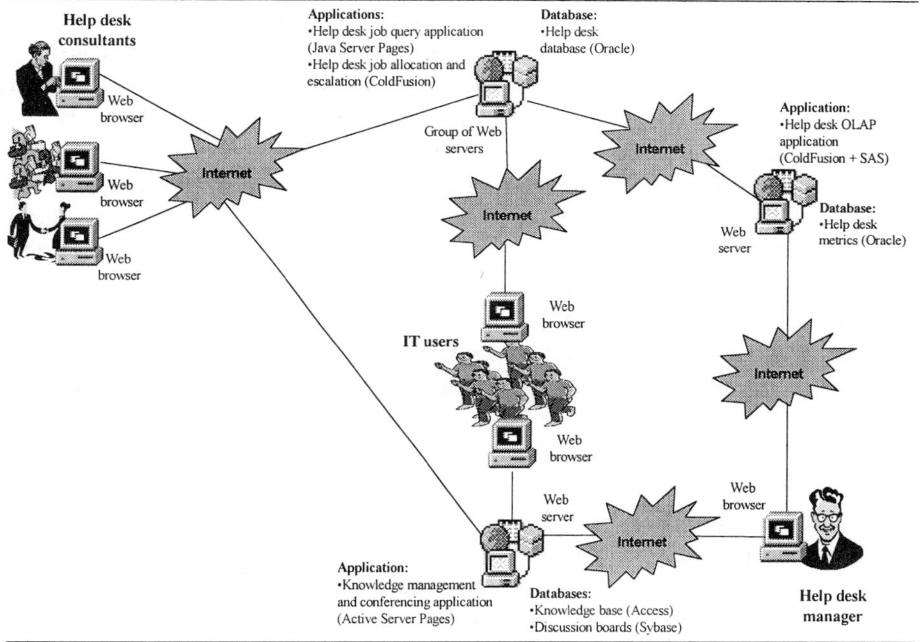


*Figure 2.* A Web-based "help desk" implementation of the generic Web-based IT model

**A Web-based workflow control module**, is implemented as a help desk job allocation and escalation application, developed using ColdFusion (a Web development platform commercialized by Allaire Corporation) by a third-party software developer (and modeled after the popular Remedy Help Desk system). This application populates an Oracle **help desk database** that stores data about help desk "jobs" (e.g., requests for support and follow-up activities).

**A Web-based customer query module**, is implemented as a help desk job query application, developed with Java Server Pages (or Servlets, which are standard pieces of Java code that run on the Web server), which allows IT users to monitor the status of their help desk jobs. This application runs on the same group of Web servers (which could be seen as one large Web server) as the help desk job allocation and escalation application and performs queries against the same help desk database populated by that application (although without modifying the database).

**A Web-based OLAP (Online Analytical Processing) application**, is implemented as a help desk OLAP application, developed using ColdFusion and SAS (an OLAP application development platform), that allows the help desk manager to generate (and customize the generation of) help desk quality and productivity metrics periodically. The application populates an Oracle help desk metrics database. Examples of metrics are number of help desk jobs of a certain category (e.g., network troubleshooting) solved within 2 hours of the request for help, number of complaints by IT users, number of help desk jobs handled by a particular individual or group of individuals, percentage of recurring problems etc.

**A Web-based process communication application**, is implemented as a knowledge management and conferencing application, developed with Active Server Pages (standard pieces of VBScript code – itself similar to Microsoft's Visual Basic language code – that run on the Web server), which populates and provides access to two databases: **an Access knowledge base and a Sybase discussion board database**. The application also allows the help desk manager to post process metrics periodically, which are converted by the application into standard HTML and shown as a series of static Web pages. This application supports continuous communication between the help desk manager, IT users, and the help desk team. It incorporates the following Web-based components:

- **A discussion forum** that allows IT users to communicate with each other as well as with help desk consultants and the help desk manager in a more personal and less structured way than through help desk jobs. This discussion forum also works as a continuous two-way information exchange forum between local IT "gurus" (e.g., a salesperson who knows a lot about a sales IT application and who helps his colleagues in the Sales Department) and help desk consultants.
- **A knowledge base** with key knowledge needed by help desk consultants to execute their respective activities in the process. This knowledge base is also used by selected IT users (e.g., the local IT "gurus" mentioned above) for self-help.

# 5. LINKS WITH DIFFERENT MANAGEMENT SCHOOLS AND RELATED IDEAS

It is important to stress that the process redesign initiatives that led to variations of the generic model discussed here were guided by a common methodology called MetaProi, which stands for <u>Meta</u>-process for <u>Pro</u>cess <u>I</u>mprovement (see Kock, 1999). In spite of this, the fact that the model shown on Figure 1 emerged from process redesign efforts involving different people in different companies is still remarkable. After all, senior management and consultants were involved, and they agreed that the new processes were either optimal or close to optimal. This convergence is also an indication of the existence of underlying management ideas that are likely to surface if awareness about current Web-based IT potential exists. Further inspection also suggests that even though these management ideas, which surfaced in process redesign discussions, are not tied to a single management school, they are obviously aligned with several schools (as shown on Table 2).

*Table 2:* Management ideas, related schools and process features

| Management idea | Management schools | Process feature(s) |
|---|---|---|
| Direct management control on teams should be reduced to a minimum. Process-level control should be automated as much as possible. | Excellence, Reengineering. | Workflow control automation. |
| Customers should have instant access to process execution status. | Total quality management, reengineering. | Automated customer query support. |
| Process metrics should be periodically analyzed and used to incrementally improve processes. | Total quality management. | OLAP-based process metrics generation. |
| Customers should be allowed access to process performance data and related process improvement initiatives, and asked for their advice on how to improve processes. | Excellence, total quality management, organizational learning. | Process metrics and improvement initiatives repository, discussion forum. |
| Customers should be given full and decentralized access to process-related data so they can solve some process-related problems themselves. | Reengineering, organizational learning. | Process knowledge base. |

The "Process feature(s)" column on Table 2 describes features of the generic process model that are highly dependent on IT, particularly in the last two rows (repository, discussion forum, and knowledge base). Those features would not have been present if senior management was not willing to implement the management ideas described in the first column of Table 2, which in turn became more popular with the emergence of four contemporary management schools: total quality management, organizational learning, excellence, and reengineering. Still, one cannot convincingly argue that management thinking is driving the use of the technology. Not only do these four management schools differ significantly from each other, but they also have a different following (e.g., organizational learning proponents often suggest their management school as a "softer" and more "people-oriented" alternative to reengineering). It is more likely that modern Web-based IT force the adoption of management ideas that do not have a single and coherent source.

The idea that information technology should drive organizational design has been proposed by many business thinkers, including reengineering co-inventor Tom Davenport (1993) – in fact, this was one of the early areas of disagreement between him and other proponents of reengineering led by Hammer and Champy (1993). Yet, letting information technology define how processes are structured shifts a great deal of the responsibility on how to manage organizations to software developers and systems integrators, who arguably do not know the processes of the organizations they serve as well as their (internal or external) customers do. Moreover, software developers and system integrators need to sell their products and services to many organizations in order to maximize their profits, which is bound to decrease potential competitive advantages for their corporate customers. After all, if you have the same processes and enabling technologies as your competition, how can you possibly get ahead of them?

## 6. CONCLUSION

From a practical perspective, the generic process model discussed above can be seen as an "archetype process", which can be used as a "template" for the design of optimal business processes. After all, it is based on a number of process redesign efforts that led to the same high-level result. Using it may save organizations precious time and resources that would otherwise be wasted "reinventing the wheel".

From a more philosophical perspective, the process model can be seen as a first step in the direction of a new management school. This new school's principles should guide the selection and implementation of Web-based IT to enable optimal processes, rather than the other way around. One of the key concepts underlying this new management school is that of "virtual communities" of process team members, users and managers, brought together in creative ways through the use of Web-based IT. Such virtual communities should, among other things, promote collaboration between customers and suppliers, by allowing them to communicate and share information and knowledge independently of traditional time and distance constraints.

## 7. REFERENCES

Argyris, C. (1992), *On Organizational Learning*, Blackwell, Cambridge, MA.

Ashkenas, R., Ulrich, D., Jick, T. and Kerr, S. (1995), *The Boundaryless Organization*, Jossey-Bass, San Francisco, CA.

Christensen, C.M. (1998), *The Innovator's Dilemma: When New Technologies Cause Great Firms to Fail*, Harvard Business School Press, Cambridge, MA.

Davenport, T.H. (1993), *Process Innovation*, Harvard Business Press, Boston, MA.

Davidow, W.H. and Malone, M.S. (1992), *The Virtual Corporation*, HarperCollins, New York, NY.

Deming, W.E. (1986), *Out of The Crisis*, Center for Advanced Engineering Study, Massachusetts Institute of Technology,Cambridge, MA.

Grudin, J. (1994), CSCW: History and Focus, *IEEE Computer*, V.27, No.5, pp. 19-26.

Hammer, M. and Champy, J. (1993), *Reengineering the Corporation*, Harper Business, New York, NY.

Juran, J. (1989), *Juran on Leadership for Quality*, The Free Press, New York, NY.

Kanter, R.M. (1995), Mastering Change, *Learning Organizations: Developing Cultures for Tomorrow's Workplace*, Chawla, S. and Renesch, J. (Eds), Productivity Press, Portland, OR, pp. 71-83.

Kock, N. (1999), *Process Improvement and Organizational Learning: The Role of Collaboration Technologies*, Idea Group Publishing, Hershey, PA.

Peters, T.J. and Waterman, R.H., Jr. (1982), *In Search of Excellence*, Harper & Row, New York, NY.

Revans, R. (1991), Getting Mixed up With Others?, *Proceedings of The First World Congress on Action Research*, V. 2, Collins, C. & Chippendale, P. (Eds), Acorn, Sunnybank Hills, Queensland, Australia, pp. 157-194.

Senge, P.M. (1990), *The Fifth Discipline*, Doubleday, New York, NY.

42

# e-Engineering through e-Business Change Management

Colin G. Ash and Janice M. Burn
*Edith Cowan University*

**Abstract**: This paper reports on a longitudinal study of e-business change management in ERP enabled organisations. Twenty organisations agreed to participate in the study and data was collected through ongoing e-dialogue and face to face interviews over a two year period. An analysis of the findings led to the adoption of a model proposing various antecedents to successful e-business change management in ERP environments. Multiple case studies with varying dimensions of e-business scope are described in context of this model and a detailed case study of an organisation with a highly innovative project is used to illustrate the facilitators that lead to e-business project success.

## 1. INTRODUCTION

Numerous papers have been written about e-business and how this concept will change the way companies do business, characterised by rapid exchange of information within a virtual network of customers and suppliers working together to create value-added processes (Ticoll et al, 1998; El Sawy et al, 1999; Wigand and Benjamin, 1998; Jansen et al, 1999; Burn and Barnett, 2000). However, little information is available on how to successfully integrate e-Business projects with ongoing ERP implementations or already productive ERP systems (Hesterbrink, 1999; Holland and Light, 1999).). As more and more established organisations realise that they need to form alliances with their customers, partners and suppliers over the Internet, e-business integration with ERP systems becomes a critical issue (Gable, 1998; Markus and Tanis, 2000).

This combination of technologies offers established companies the opportunity to build interactive relationships with their partners and suppliers, improve efficiency and extend their reach, all at a very low cost. For example, GE estimates to save $500 million to $700 million of its purchasing costs over three years and cut purchasing cycles by as much as 50% (Hesterbrink, 1999: p3). The Norwegian company Statoil, processes more than 350,000 invoices annually, and awards over 40,000 contracts through web enabled ERP commerce. The company expects a considerable improvement in the ratio of invoices to orders as well as a tangible contribution to revenue (SAP, 1999; Venkatraman et al, 1999). Eventually, both companies expect to buy the majority of their purchases through Web-based bidding systems. Faced with such e-business innovations companies are looking for effective solutions to marry the two technologies for strategic advantage. Inevitably this will have a major impact on their employee workforce, the processes they have to perform and their skill requirements. The workforce has had to embrace a new culture as a knowledge based community with far more flexible work roles. Increasingly, we are seeing the large traditional organisation breaking up and the emergence of new, networked organisational forms in which work is conducted by temporary teams that cross organisation lines. (Markus, Manville and Agres, 2000).

In this new climate, organisations have to learn new approaches to managing a workforce of knowledge workers, yet little information is available on how to implement this successfully and how to ensure more effective personnel performance as a result. Drucker (1998) suggests that the traditional role of managers telling workers what to do is no longer viable and instead managers must direct people as if they were unpaid volunteers, tied to the organisation by commitment to its aims and purposes and often expecting to participate in its governance.

This paper reports on the findings from multiple case studies of e-business projects in ERP enabled organisations. The key findings from each case study are captured into a theoretical framework for e-business change management. A detailed analysis of one major project using this framework illustrates the suitability of using this as a model for evaluating success factors. The case presents a recently implemented e-business project in personnel management within the energy services division of *Engineer.com*, at one of its overseas locations. The company uses SAP R/3 as its global ERP solution. Rather than emphasising technological issues the focus is now clearly on cultural change and organisational performance issues (Pereira, 1999) and the factors that empower employees to support large-scale change. In particular it looks at the motivational factors influencing employees to initiate change in the face of these new realities and the implications for management in the learning organisation.

## 2. E-BUSINESS AND ERP

Venkatraman and Henderson, (1998) have defined an e-business model for the learning organisation that promotes harmony over three vectors – customer/market interaction, asset sourcing and knowledge leverage supported by a strong information technology platform. They see this as the virtual organising model for the 21st Century and as such a management strategy in itself.

Figure 1 gives a view of an organisation using an Enterprise Resource Planning (ERP) system such as SAP, as an integrated system to enable knowledge management across the three vectors of the organisation.

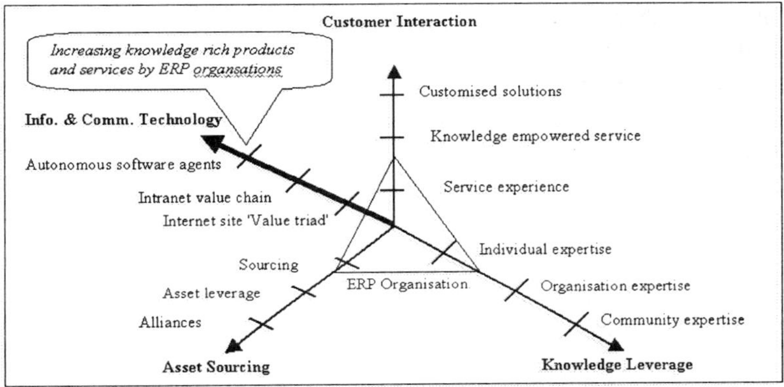


*Figure 1.* e-Business and ERP

(i) Customer interaction (B2C) refers to the extent to which an organisation virtually interacts with the market defined at three levels of greater virtual progression. (ii) Asset sourcing (B2B) refers to competency leveraging from varying complexity. (iii) Knowledge leverage (B2E) refers to access to expertise beyond the organisation.

This model acted as the initial basis for investigating how far along the three vectors organisations had implemented integrated e-business through ERP systems.

Kalakota, (1999) states "*the creation and implementation of an e-business project is inextricably linked to the management of change*" (Kalakota et al, 1999; p 60).

This requires systematic attention to learning processes, organisational culture, technology infrastructure, people and systems thinking. Hesterbrink (1999) further emphasises the importance of alignment of those dimensions with respect to ERP and e-Business implementations. e-Business change is defined here as an organisational initiative to design an e-business project.

> "to achieve significant (breakthrough) improvements in performance (eg quality, responsiveness, cost, flexibility, satisfaction, shareholder value, and other critical e-business measures) through changes in relationships between management, information, technology, organisational structure, and people" (Guha, et al, 1997: p 121).

Planning and managing such systems requires an integrated multi-dimensional approach across the e-business and the development of new business process models (Kumar and Crook, 1999; Scheer and Habermann, 2000).

Therefore, in any examination of outcomes, consideration should be given to (a) the environmental conditions for change and (b) the ability of the organisation to manage change in those conditions. Outcomes of e-business change can be measured at various levels of the broad complex phenomenon of any e-ERP project. Previous studies by Guha et al (1997) indicate successful e-business projects should tend to have facilitators over many dimensions but also failure is most likely to occur where too little consideration has been given to key factors such as cultural readiness or change management.

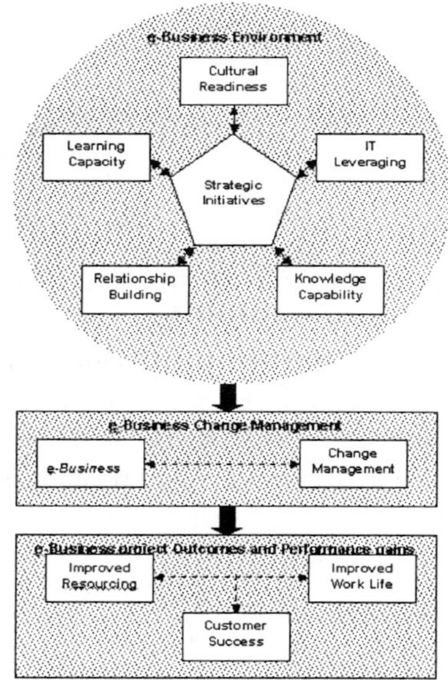


*Figure 2:* Theoretical Framework of e-Business Change Management (Adapted from Guha et al, 1997)

*"Any significant business process change requires a strategic initiative where top managers act as leaders in defining and communicating a vision of change. The organisational environment, with ready culture, a willingness to share knowledge, balanced network relationships, and a capacity to learn, should facilitate the* ***implementation*** *of prescribed e-business management and change management.*

*Both of these are requisite for customer success and ultimately in achieving measurable and sustainable competitive performance" (p 121).*

Increasingly, organisations are realising that importance must be given to improving quality of work-life issues. If effectively managed, employees should ultimately be more productive in their work tasks and better able to serve customers, suppliers, and business partners. The key constructs that can be probed here are: gaps between effectiveness expectations (goals) and actual performance improvements, eg employee work satisfaction, efficient resourcing, and customer interaction (Venkatraman and Henderson, 1998).

The model in Figure 2 was used in this study to identify facilitators and inhibitors of successful e-business change. The relationships presented in the framework are based on relevant work in organisational change, strategic management innovation, and information systems. The general thesis of the framework is adapted from Guha's et al, (1997) work on "business process change management"

# 3. BACKGROUND TO STUDY

## 3.1 Case Selection

"Embedded" multiple case-study analysis was chosen to investigate the research questions concerning the complex phenomenon of e-business change projects. Embedded approaches enlist the use of multiple units of analysis; (1) the company (strategy), (2) the project team, (3) the project. This triangulation attempts to validate primary data. The case-studies selection criterion required a major e-business project, which had organisational implications. Also, as the focus was on studying antecedents to organisational performance, a homogeneous set of projects (having similar initiatives) with variance across cases but with the same outcome measures - cost, responsiveness, flexibility, satisfaction, shareholder value, and other e-business metrics – was required

To identify the sites, a search using secondary literature, web sites, and SAP related industry consultants were contacted to identify major e-ERP projects (Ash, 2000). There were three stages to the investigation: the initial stage focused on ten local (West Australian) organisations and the subsequent development of mini-case studies; stage two was expanded to include a further ten overseas organisations (with a more restricted selection criteria) and the development of an additional seven mini-cases; stage three was a return visit to eight of the organisations to develop full case histories. In each case a senior IT/SAP project manager was contacted for interviews.

## 3.2 Investigations of Overseas SAP Sites

In November 1999, initial interviews in ten sites, were conducted in person by visiting each organisation at their headquarters. Senior e-business project managers were questioned about "the benefits and barriers arising from extending their R/3 business processes onto the Internet" (Ash, 2000). Sites were selected using a set of *e-Business activity* selection criteria:

– It should involve a major e-Business project with organisational implications.
– The project should have been completed.
– At some point the project should have an expected breakthrough performance.
– The project should focus on cross-functional business activities.
– Initial assessment of outcomes should be unambiguous (Guha et al, 1997).

A repeat visit to each of eight sites was performed in June/July 2000 to collect the detailed information for this study, using the following protocol. In each case the focal point of contact was the most senior level IT/SAP project manager. Multiple archival documents, as well as many conversations via e-mail. A qualitative structured interview questionnaire was used during the second visits to collect primary data for the study from eight (8) SAP worldwide sites (Table 1).

*Table 1: All Case Organisations Interviewed*

| Criterion of Project | Bank | Biotech | Charity | Comp-uter | Employ-ment | Engin-eering | Scitech | Society |
|---|---|---|---|---|---|---|---|---|
| *1. Major e-business project* | B2E | B2B | B2C | B2B | B2E/B | B2E | B2B/C | B2C |
| *2. Project completed* | Locally | Yes | Sept | Yes | Yes | Locally | Yes | Yes |
| *3. Expected breakthrough* | Yes | Yes | Yes | Yes | Yes | Yes | Yes | Yes |
| *4. Cross functional focus* | Yes | Yes | Yes | Yes | Yes | Yes | Yes | Yes |
| *5. Unambiguous outcomes* | Yes | Yes | Yes | Yes | No | Yes | Yes | No |
| **Size of Organisation** | Large | Medium | Small | Large | Large | Large | Large | Small |
| **Significance of Project** | Medium | High | High | High | High | Innova-tive | High | High |

*Eg Case 1. - Bank [Large] Business-to-Employee (B2E) "Employee Intranet"*
*Case 2. - Biotech [Medium] Business-to-Business (B2B) "e-Procurement"*
*Case 3. - Society [Small] Business-to-Customer (B2C) "Online Ordering"*

In Table 1, Engineer.com stands out from the other cases as highly innovative because of its global potential and project content. For **Engineer.com,** employee resourcing for offshore oil and gas projects is expensive, complex, and dynamic (Baark, 1999). Managers need to make informed decisions when skilled worker schedules change. To optimise worker overtime requires access to employment records in real-time, at remote locations, under critical circumstances, and knowledge of all local employment. There are significant penalties in Norway for employing foreign workers over an agreed time quota.

# 4. EVALUATING AN E-ERP SUCCESS (CASE 4)

**Engineer.com – "Management Reporting and Personnel System"**

This in-house Intranet using R/3 personnel data, is an incremental HR Internet initiative for project management of offshore skilled agency workers. Its application has proven to be a major tool for supporting decision making for minimising labour costs. It has been expanded to include a computer hardware tracking system. With the aid of computer graphics this Intranet systems provides a simple "walk-up" user interface for casual users, for example project managers who have little or no training on the R/3 HR sub-system. Further, the use of mobile phone technology has enabled access to the intranet by the project managers whilst offshore.

Data was collected using a structured questionnaire that extracted three levels of detail (Table 2). By analysing the data and comments captured from the interviews, a summary of comments was first constructed. These comments helped focus on the individual contributions of the components of the research or business framework. Each component of the framework was rated as having a positive (+ve) or negative (-ve) contribution towards the Intranet project. In some cases, both positive and negative contributions were found from one component variable.

*Table 2: Summary of Findings for each component of the e-Business Framework*

| **Business Framework** *Components* | Rating +ve / -ve | Summary of Comments |
|---|---|---|
| **Environment** | | |
| *Strategic Initiatives* | +ve & -ve | A pro-active, incremental HR Internet initiative to manage offshore agency skilled workers - cost minimisation. Some initial resistance to use of m-commerce. |
| *Cultural Readiness* | +ve & -ve | The introduction was reasonably well accepted by the users within the local division. Some resistance was evidenced from the users of the local sister division. |
| *IT Leveragability* | +ve | This HR manager web-enabled reporting system was implemented to leverage R/3 integration strength. It made superior use of graphics in reporting. |
| *Knowledge Capability* | +ve | Made good use of insights into the Norwegian employment regulations, helped in the sharing of knowledge. |
| *Relationship building* | +ve | *Knowledge capability* enabled an improved activity in the HR workplace and improved inter-organisational linkages. |
| *Learning Capacity* | +ve | Instructor led training at upper levels of key users. Also Intranet documents for users to reference and to support learning by. |
| **Management** | | |
| *Change Mgt Practice* | +ve | Participative change tactic resulted in an evolutionary change. |
| *e-Bus Mgt Practice* | +ve | Some technical improvements from feedback on the use of reporting tools. |
| **Performance Gains** | | |
| *Expectations & actual performance* | *small gap* | No significant gap between effectiveness expectations and actual performance |
| *Working life* | Highly +ve (for a small project) | Improved user satisfaction – a current study by HQ has recommended this in-house intranet using R/3 personnel tables, be adopted globally. Also, it has been expanded to include two more HR reporting tools. |
| *For agency workers* | | cost savings (+ ve), reliability (+ve) |
| *Business resourcing* | N/A | Not applicable |
| *Customer interaction* | N/A | In the future... |

Key: +ve = facilitator, -ve = inhibitor; + & - = facilitator & inhibitor

The results given in Table 2 show that a high overall level of success was achieved. The column of ratings draws attention to the importance of having positive contribution from all the components (synergy) for the project to be successful (Guha et al,1997). However, two components were rated as having both a positive and negative influences. To understand these summarised findings, a more in depth discussion follows for each of the three main dimensions of e-business change - the **change environment**, the **management of change**, and the **outcomes and performance gains**.

## 4.1 Change Environment

**Strategic Initiatives** This IT innovation sprang from the insights of one of the company's local HR professional staff members. This is in spite of autocratic decision making from the central administration. It was observed that poor project management of the number days worked for each agency employee could cause excessive labour cost. The local government regulations for offshore labour have very strict penalties.

**Cultural Readiness** In the project, the HR staff project team showed a desire to initiate change. The change agent was the practical leadership of the HR staff.. *"We are very proud of this Intranet solution."*

According to Mintzberg and Westley, (1992), a visionary leader is a single leader who influences change. For Engineer.com the leadership showed inspiration for the development of a practical solution that overcame management obstacles. As senior management remarked after the implementation. *"This Internet enabled ERP environment will serve to facilitate global collaboration throughout the company".*

There remained, however, the partner organisation professional rivalry. A culture of resistance to accept change was introduced from a key partner.

**Network Relationships** For Engineer.com, the project demonstrated positive cooperation with the local agency government and the beginnings of cross-functional cooperation. As IT management stated " Our Web-base solution assists the most casual user with global, personalised, and secure access to our corporate information on demand".

**Learning Capacity** In the project, learning by doing and learning from others helped improve the professional end-user IT skills. This enabled project managers to adapt to a quality decision making scenario.

**IT Leveragability and Knowledge Capability** For Engineer.com, the project demonstrated positive local leadership, superior IT design for improved learning, and business-to-employee communication, but with some collaborative resistance. To overcome resistance to change, each must be aligned (along with the enabling technology) to the strategic initiatives to overcome resistance to change (Hesterbrink, 1999).

## 4.2 e-Business Change Management

**Change Management** In the e-business management practice, the pattern of change was reported to be a participative change tactic resulting in an evolutionary change. This was viewed as a "waterfall" progression of change, starting with an alleviation of dissatisfaction by HR professionals and eventually arriving at a well managed process:

alleviation of dissatisfaction,
↳ vision for change,
↳ evolutionary change tactics,
↳ well-managed process for change

**e-Business Management** The team based structure involving HR and IT personnel was felt to be critical to the success of the project and allowed for the growth and transfer of knowledge among the team members. The use of graphics in combination with the web tools and techniques also had positive influence on the use by casual professional users.

## 4.3 Outcomes and Performance gains

**Outcomes** It was reported that from the outset the project showed an improvement in one of the outcome constructs - the quality of work life (QWL). However, within the area of **performance gains,** improved business resourcing was seen as most significant (positive). As a measure of its success and/or acceptance, the Intranet solution was expanded to include the IT department's computer hardware tracking system.

**Performance Gains** The performance gains were achieved from two sources; labour cost savings in hiring agency contract employees, and access to reliable (real-time) employee data via mobile technology. The project enabled efficiency gains from minimising of offshore labour costs, and effectiveness gains from optimising opportunity labour costs. For example, when the offshore work was delayed or ahead of schedule, the on site project managers had mobile phone access to online real-time data for deciding on the optimal allocation of agency workers. This type of cost savings through operational efficiencies of labour resourcing, can be compared to those cost savings (efficiencies) in the e-procurement case studies.

## 4.4 Case Summary

This case study shows how one small group within a large global organisation succeeded in making the HR business processes of their ERP systems available over the Internet. The human resources (HR) staff at one location were motivated to initiate an e-business project and to form a team with IT staff and user project managers to develop a suitable system. A "personnel management intranet" was developed and by leveraging the power of graphics and Internet technology extended the reach of the ERP (HR) business processes, for casual users. The knowledge contribution from all members of the team enabled them to implement this project leading to significant improvement in organisational performance. The primary beneficiaries were the offshore project managers, who needed access to the HR employee tables for personnel management and gained this through the innovative use of mobile technology. The result was one of considerable costs saving and greatly improved staff resourcing through improved decision making by the project managers when working off shore.

The intrinsic motivation and self-management of autonomous knowledge within the development team played an important role in the successful implementation. The emphasis was very much more on collective performance rather than individual but at the same time development and maintenance of personal and professional reputations was a significant driver.

Interestingly, while the project was rated highly successful there was strong opposition from their partner operations to implement the same system and this came from the counterpart HR staff who had not been exposed to the participative development process. Further, the organisational management were lukewarm in their support initially, viewing the proposed system as a threat to a strongly centralised control culture. Once the results broke down their initial resistance, management "assumed" responsibility for the success and leadership for global implementation.

*"We are beginning to recognise the potential benefits of leveraging our SAP R/3 business processes through the new Web-based environment"*

# 5. CONCLUSIONS

An established research framework of e-Business change is used to identify the factors for success of this e-business project within an ERP environment. The results confirm that a successful project was found to have facilitators in all components of the business framework, including the change environment and project management. Further there is the implication that; the least successful e-business projects will have inhibitors in both dimensions, especially in the area of cultural readiness and change management. In this case study conflict arose between local project management initiatives versus a centralised autocratic global ERP deployment. This highlights the need to encourage the balancing of conflicting organisational knowledge, when contemplating the adoption of e-business solutions.

The case presented was used to test the suitability of an established research framework for gathering evidence to identify the factors for success of an e-business project. In order to avoid an original IT-centric position, we emphasise the importance of managing the change of e-business projects. This research framework was chosen as a methodology for its ability to examine complex phenomena. It is seen as evolutionary in nature, and was content driven. It is primarily a diagnostic tool for identifying factors contributing to success of new business models. It is not seen as a prognostic tool. It specifically explores the areas related to the successful learning organisation where the key issues remain as people oriented business issues.

In the future as e-business activities become common place, corporate portals for empowering employees will be considered as a competitive necessity. The next wave of economic advantage lies in revenue generation from new business opportunities in other business-to-business models, such as business-to-consumer for customer satisfaction. These are complex problems that can never be solved with technology alone. They require leadership, appropriate problem solving skills, lots of hard work and executive commitment and a culture that embraces the ideals of the learning organisation (a team and community oriented work process). The organisational design, learning environment, and human-to-human communication and collaboration must be aligned to the enabling technology. "One should always keep in mind the balance between people, business processes, and technology" (Carlson, 1995). In a labour force of cross-functional virtual teams management will be more about motivation and governance may be largely a question of self-regulation rather than traditional managerial control. IT professionals may well be better equipped for this change given the large "community of practice" with a strong, shared culture of technical professionalism and their extended use of technology for communication and decision making.

# 6. REFERENCES

Ash, C.G. (2000) An e-Commerce Model for Extending ERP Systems onto the Internet: An Australian Perspective, In Proceedings of the International Conference of Enterprise Information Systems, ICEIS'2000, Stafford, UK 4-7 July.

Baark, E, (1999) Engineering Consultancy: An Assessment of IT-enabled International delivery of services, Technology Analysis & Strategic Management, March, Vol 11, No 1 pp 55-74

Boey, P. Grasso, M. Sabatino, G. Sayeed, I. (1999) Architecting eBusiness Solutions, Vol II No. 7 [http://www.cutter.com/consortium/freestuff/dcar9907.html]

Burn, J. M. and Barnett, M. L. (2000) Emerging Virtual Models for Global e-commerce - world wide retailing in the e-grocery business. Special Millennium Issue of Journal of Global Information Technology Management, Vol 3, No. 1, pp 18-32.

Carlson, DA (1995) Harnessing the Flow of Knowledge, [http://www.dimensional.com/~dcarlson/papers/KnowFlow.htm]

Drucker, P. F. (1998) *Management's New Paradigms*, Forbes, Oct. 5, pp 152-177.

EL Sawy, O. A., Malhotra, A., Gosain, S. AND Young, K. M. (1999) IT-Intensive Value Innovation in the Electronic Economy: Insights from Marshall Industries. MIS Quarterly, Vol 23, No 3, pp 305-335.

Gable, G. G. (1998). Large Packaged Software: a neglected technology? Editorial, Journal of Global Information Management 6(3), pp3-4.

Guha, S. Grover, V. Kettinger, W.J. Eng, J.T.C. (1997) Business Process Change and Organisational Performance: Exploring an Antecedent Model, Journal of Management Information Systems, Vol. 14, No1, pp. 119-154.

Hesterbrink, C. (1999) e-Business and ERP: Bringing two Paradigms together, PriceWaterhouse Coopers, Sept.

Holland, C. P. and Light, B. (1999). Generic Information Systems Design Strategies. Americas Conference on Information Systems, Milwaukee, August.

Jansen, W., Steenbakkers, W. AND Jagers, H. Electronic Commerce and Virtual Organisations. Special Issue of eJov (Vol. 1, No. 1) pp 54-68.

Kalakota, R. Robinson, M. (1999), *e-Business: Roadmap for Success*, Addison-Wesley Longman, MA, USA

Kumar, R. L. and Crook, C. W. A. (1999) Multi-Disciplinary Framework for the Management of Interorganisational Systems, The Data Base for Advances in Information Systems, Vol. 30 (1).

Markus, M. L., Manville, B. and Agres, C. E. (2000). What makes a virtual organisation work? Sloan Management Review, Vol. 42 (1), pp 13-26.

Markus, M. L. C., and Tanis, C (2000). Multisite ERP Implementations. Communications of the ACM 43(40, pp 42-46.

Mintzberg, H. Westley, F. (1992) Cycles of Organisational Change, Strategic Mangement Journal, 13, pp. 39-59

Pereira, R.E. (1999) Resource View Theory Analysis of SAP as a Source of Competitive Advantage for Firms, The Database for Advances in Information Systems, Winter 1999, Vol. 30, No. 1; 38-46

SAP (1999) SAP B2B Procurement at Statoil (1999) No 64, p.18 [http://www.sap.com/sapinfo.net/industries/]

Scheer, A. W. and Habermann, F. (2000) Making ERP a Success. Communications of the ACM 43(4), pp 57-61.

Ticoll, D., Lowry, A. and Kalakota, R. (1998) Joined at the Bit, in *Blueprint to the Digital Economy creating wealth in the era of e-business* Don Tapscott, Alex Lowy and David Ticoll, McGraw-Hill

Venkatraman, N. Henderson, J.C. (1998), Real strategies for Virtual Organising, Sloan Management Review, Fall '98, 33-48.

Venkatraman, N, Tanriverdi, H, Stokke, P (1999). It it working? Working from home at Statoil, Norway. Europen Management Journal, 17 (5), pp 513-531.

Wigand, R.T., and Benjamin, R.I. (1995). Electronic Commerce: Effects on electronic markets, Journal of Computer-Mediated Communication [On-line], 1 (3), http://www.ascusc.org/jcmc/vol1/issue3/wigand.html

MINITRACK THREE

# M-COMMERCE

**Minitrack Chairs:**
Georgios I. Doukidis
Athens University of Economics and Business, Greece,
gjd@aueb.gr

Nikos Mylonopoulos
Athens Laboratory of Business Administration, Greece,
nmylonop@alba.edu.gr

43

# A Conditional E-Coupon Service For Location-Aware Mobile Commerce

Hui Luo, N. K. Shankaranarayanan
*AT&T Labs – Research, Middletown, NJ 07748, USA*

**Abstract:** This paper presents the concept and theory of a conditional electronic coupon (CEC) service as an optimal wireless targeted advertising scheme to promote location-aware mobile commerce. The key idea of CEC service is to advertise stores conditionally, i.e., distributing e-coupons for a store to mobile customers only if the number of mobile customers requesting such e-coupons exceeds a threshold. Using the CEC service, mobile customers stand a good chance to obtain e-coupons from some local stores shortly before they go shopping there, and participating stores are guaranteed to make maximum extra profits in a statistical sense by issuing e-coupons.

## 1. BACKGROUND

As more and more wireless devices are connected to the Internet, many have predicted that mobile commerce will take off soon, just like e-commerce booming in recent years. However, mobile commerce may not necessarily be an e-commerce copy over wireless connections, because location information of wireless service subscribers could play a significant role in mobile commerce scenarios.

Location-based wireless applications have been under intensive investigation since FCC required that wireless service providers must be able to identify the locations of cellular phone users making 911 calls after Oct. 1, 2001 [1]. Various commercial uses derived from this requirement have been proposed. For example, a mobile visitor can use his WAP phone to ask a server for information like "where is the closest restaurant?" [2]. For another example, a store may send e-coupons to mobile customers passing by the store and thus hopefully brings in more traffic [3]. The first example describes a location-assisted information retrieval service, which requires mobile customer's location information to be submitted to the server along with the query message. The second example describes a location-aware wireless targeted advertising scheme, which mandates the locations of nearby mobile customers to be monitored closely by some system on behalf of the store.

Since advertising is a huge business, location-aware wireless targeted advertising, as a brand new advertising scheme potentially, has caught tremendous attention. Although it is favored by wireless service providers who are eager to open new revenue source, at present it is not clear whether this idea will become a serious business, because there are many important issues unsolved.

One major issue raised by mobile consumer group is privacy. Although some preliminary market study shows that about 60 percent of participating mobile consumers think wireless targeted advertisements are valuable and 27 percent of them say they like to switch to wireless service providers carrying the wireless targeted advertising service [4], the privacy concern has been weighing in mobile consumer's mind and it might threaten the wireless targeted advertising business from taking off [5]. The argument herein is that mobile consumers have to worry about the fact that their 24/7 locations are purposely monitored, which might fall into mishandling hands.

Another major issue is a technical problem for wireless service providers. In order to send a targeted advertisement for a participating store to some mobile customers at right time in right place, the locations of these mobile customers must be monitored closely. To do so, all mobile devices must frequently send location data to the network, and thus cause significant uplink signaling traffic that may eventually overflow the network. The situation could get worse if location identification methods are network-based or network-assisted because they need consume significant computing resources from the network [6].

Probably the most important issue is a business question that will be asked by stores before they are willing to pay for the wireless targeted advertising service --- is wireless targeted advertising effective and cost-efficient compared with other advertising methods? The answer largely remains unknown, although it can be argued that wireless targeted advertising may be more effective because the potential customers (the targeted mobile customers) are physically close to the advertised stores when they receive the targeted advertisements, and that wireless targeted advertising should be of low cost because the advertisements are only broadcast in local areas of participating stores.

Bearing the privacy concern, technical problem, and business question in mind, we invented a new wireless targeted advertising scheme, called a CEC service, to promote location-aware mobile commerce. The rest of this paper will present details of the CEC service concept and demonstrate quantitatively that the CEC service is an optimal wireless targeted advertising scheme, which can benefit mobile customers, participating stores, and wireless service providers.

# 2. CONCEPT

## 2.1 Overview

The CEC service concept consists of three key ideas: (1) mobile customers send requests to a CEC server and indicate they wish to receive e-coupons from some local stores shortly before they go shopping; (2) in turn, the CEC server will distribute e-coupons for a store to these mobile customers and, optionally, all nearby mobile customers if the number of mobile customers requesting such e-coupons equals or exceeds a threshold; and (3) the store pays an advertising fee every time after its e-coupons are distributed. The CEC service provider (which could be a wireless service provider) never unconditionally pushes advertisements to mobile customers, as done by conventional advertising methods.

With these key ideas, the CEC service can significantly improve advertising effectiveness and cost-efficiency, because (1) e-coupons are distributed to mobile customers who explicitly request such e-coupons, hence they may probably shop the store after receiving desired e-coupons; and (2) e-coupons are distributed to a number of mobile customers, which equals or exceeds a threshold that assures, in a statistical sense, the store can make profit after paying the advertising fee to the CEC service provider. In addition, the CEC service gets rid of the technical problem for wireless targeted advertising because its operation is based on requests made by mobile customers. The accurate location information of mobile customers are conveniently embedded in these requests, and therefore mobile devices do not need to send periodical location update messages to wireless networks. The CEC service also eliminates the privacy concern, because it does not track the locations of mobile customers. A mobile user's location is exposed to the CEC service provider only at the moment when the user is making the request, and the user is willing to do so.

## 2.2 System Architecture

The exemplary system architecture given below is a high-level description with some data structures highlighted, which is presented to clarify the concept and theory of the proposed CEC service. It does not include all details for a real implementation.

In order to provide the CEC service, a CEC service provider needs to run a CEC server on the Internet, which is a combination of a CEC controller, a Web server, and a database. The Web server provides Web interfaces for mobile customers to browse local stores, to request e-coupons from some specific stores using store names or from a group of stores offering similar goods or services using keywords, to confirm redeem of e-coupons, and to request e-coupon quotas. The Web server also provides Web interfaces for participating stores to edit their mobile commerce profiles and to predefine e-coupons.

Every participating store has a mobile commerce profile in the CEC database, and the CEC service provider does not charge the store for maintaining its profile. The store profile data structure is given below in C syntax.

```
struct store_profile {
    char[32] store_id;
    char[64] store_name;
    char[64] store_address;
    char[64] billing_information;
    char[64] instant_contact_address;
    char[64] business_type;
    int number_of_coupons;
    struct e_coupon * first_e_coupon_pointer;
    int number_of_pending_requests;
    struct store_pending_request * first_pending_request_pointer;
    float estimated_number_of_redeems;
    int number_of_pending_redeems;
  struct pending_redeem * first_pending_redeem_pointer;

}
```

Where, instant_contact_address could be a phone number, an instant messaging address, or an email address, by which the CEC service provider can notify the store as soon as it distributed e-coupons for the store; business_type is described by a set of keywords, which can be used to determine whether the store is a candidate store in case that mobile customers use keywords instead of store names in their requests.

In the profile, the store also needs to define one or more e-coupons. Every e-coupon is associated with some conditions, including time (when e-coupons can be distributed), range (where e-coupons should be distributed), and a profit margin (how much profit the store can make from a mobile customer using this e-coupon). The data structure of e-coupon is given below.

```
struct e_coupon {
    struct timing time_condition;
    strcut range range_condition;
    float profit_margin;
    char[128] coupon_text;
    struct e_coupon * next_e_coupon_pointer;
}
```

Where, profit_margin is the most important parameter, from which the CEC controller can calculate a threshold for the store and therefore can determine whether the store's e-coupon should be distributed.

Every mobile customer who signs on the CEC service has a mobile commerce profile in the CEC database. Its data structure is given below.

```
struct customer_profile {
```

```
    char[32] customer_id;
    char[64] instant_contact_address;
    int coupon_quota;
    int number_of_pending_requests;
    struct customer_pending_request * first_pending_request_pointer;
    int number_of_pending_coupons;
  struct pending_coupons * first_pending_redeem_pointer;
}
```

Where, instant_contact_address could be a cellular phone number, an SMS address, or a mobile email address belonging to a cellular phone or other mobile device capable of supplying location information. Whenever a mobile customer uses his mobile device to contact the CEC Web server, his location information and his instant contacting address are included as header parameters in the HTTP request message and submitted to the CEC Web server.

All fields in customer_profile are under control of the CEC service provider. The mobile customer can only read some fields, such as instant_contact_address, coupon_quota, and number_of_pending_requests. Among these fields, the most important parameter is coupon_quota. At the first time when a mobile customer uses the CEC service or at the beginning of a long cycle (such a week or a month), a small value is assigned to coupon_quota in the customer profile. After the mobile customer requests an e-coupon, coupon_quota decreases by one. If he cannot get the desired e-coupon, or if he gets the e-coupon and redeems it at the store, coupon_quota increases by one. If coupon_quota is equal to zero, the mobile customer cannot request any e-coupons until the beginning of next cycle. The reason why the coupon_quota parameter is introduced in mobile customer's profile is to prevent an irresponsible mobile customer from abusing the CEC service, because a fundamental assumption for the CEC service is that a mobile customer will redeem at least one of e-coupons received upon his request at a very high probability. Using e-coupon quota is a good compromise between giving mobile customers maximum freedom and protecting store's interest. With a positive coupon_quota, a mobile customer can have a few chances not to redeem any received e-coupons if none of them is attractive. In order to encourage mobile customers to be co-operative, the CEC service provider shall issue some bonus e-coupon quota to a mobile customer after he redeems a certain number of received e-coupons.

## 2.3 How It Works

Before a mobile customer goes shopping, he uses his mobile device to contact the CEC Web server. He can request e-coupons from specific stores by specifying store names or from a group of stores by specifying keywords that describe the business type of stores.

After receiving the e-coupon request, the CEC Web server sends an HTTP response message back to the mobile customer, which tells the mobile customer remained quota and expected time to receive e-coupons (it is possible that the mobile customer cannot receive any e-coupon). The CEC Web server then passes the request message (along with location information and instant contact address of the mobile customer) to the CEC controller.

After receiving the request message, the CEC controller does not immediately decide whether e-coupons should be distributed to the mobile customer. Instead, the CEC controller makes such decision at the end of a processing cycle, which is about 5 to 10 minutes. Before a processing cycle ends, the CEC controller simply logs such request in the mobile customer's profile and all candidate store profiles. Where, a store is considered a candidate store if the time and range conditions for the store to issue e-coupons are satisfied and if the business type or store name is specified in the request message. To log a request made by the mobile customer, the CEC controller needs to complete the following jobs.

1. Creating a customer_pending_request record in the mobile customer's profile, which contains the request time and the IDs of all candidate stores.
2. Decreasing coupon_quota by one in the mobile customer's profile.
3. Creating a store_pending_request record in every candidate store's profile, which contains the request time and the mobile customer's ID.
4. Increasing estimated_number_of_redeems by a proper value for every candidate store, where the increment can be chosen to equal one divided by the number of candidate stores (this is why we need the assumption that a mobile customer will probably redeem at least one of e-coupons received upon his request; there could be better estimates for this increment).

The data structure of customer_pending_request is given below.

```
struct customer_pending_request {
  struct time request_time;
  int number_of_candidate_stores;
  struct candidate_store * first_candidate_store_pointer;
  struct customer_pending_request * next_pending_request_pointer;
}
```

Where, request_time serves as an identifier of the pending request made by the mobile customer; number_of_candidate_stores is the number of stores where the mobile customer's request is pending; first_candidate_store_pointer points to the first candidate store that starts a chain of all candidate stores, which has the following data structure,

```
struct candidate_store {
  char[32] store_id;
```

```
    struct candidate_store * next_candidate_store_pointer;
}
```

The data structure of store_pending_request is given below.

```
struct store_pending_request {
    struct time request_time;
    char[32] customer_id;
    struct store_pending_request * next_pending_request_pointer;
}
```

When a processing cycle is finished, the CEC controller performs the following operations with every participating store in a random order (the store whose profile is processed later has more advantage, so the processing order must be randomly chosen if all participating stores pay the same advertising fee to the CEC service provider).

1. The CEC controller finds the effective e-coupon at current time in the store profile, and calculates the best threshold for the store, which is equal to the advertising fee divided by the product of estimated_number_of_redeems times profit_margin.
2. If number_of_pending_request is less than the threshold, the CEC controller does not distribute e-coupons for this store. Instead, the CEC controller increases estimated_number_of_redeems accordingly in profiles of other candidate stores that have not been processed (this is why the store whose profile is processed later has more advantage).
3. Otherwise, the CEC controller needs to distribute the store's e-coupon to mobile customers who requested it in this processing cycle. In this case, the CEC controller needs to complete the following jobs: (1) creating a pending_coupon record in the store profile, which includes a serial number, a redeem confirmation number, the e-coupon text, the issuing time, the expiring time, the number of mobile customers who will receive this e-coupon, and an estimated number of mobile customers who will redeem the e-coupon at the store; (2) sending the pending_coupon record to the store via its instant contact address; (3) creating a pending_redeem record in profiles of mobile customers who will receive this e-coupon, which includes a serial number, the request time, the issuing time, the ID of the issuing store, the e-coupon text, and the expiring time; and (4) the CEC controller sends the pending_redeem record to all mobile customers who requested the e-coupon in this processing cycle.
4. The CEC controller removes all store_pending_request records from the store profile and resets estimated_number_of_redeems to zero in the store profile.

In addition to processing store profiles, the CEC also performs the following operations with every mobile customer profile.

1. The CEC controller checks whether a pending_redeem record has the same request_time value as that of some customer_pending_request record.

2. If this is not the case, coupon_quota increases by one in the mobile customer's profile.
3. The CEC controller removes all customer_pending_request records from the mobile customer profile.

The data structure of pending_coupon is given below.

```
struct pending_coupon {
  char[32] serial_number;
  char[32] redeem_confirmation_number;
  struct time issuing_time;
  struct time expiring_time;
  char[128] coupon_text;
  int number_of_recipents;
  int estimated_number_of_redeems;
  int number_of_redeems;
}
```

Where, serial_number is used for mobile customers to claim the e-coupon at the issuing store; redeem_confirmation_number is a secret number known only by the store, which may be used for mobile customers to confirm with the CEC service provider that they have redeemed their e-coupons; number_of_recipients, estimated_number_of_redeems, and number_of_redeems can be used for the issuing store to estimate the effectiveness of its e-coupon.

The data structure of pending_redeem is given below.

```
struct pending_redeem {
  char[32] serial_number;
  char[32] store_id;
  struct time request_time;
  struct time issuing_time;
  struct time expiring_time;
  char[128] coupon_text;
}
```

Where, the value of request_time is equal to that of request_time in the corresponding customer_pending_request record.

After receiving desired e-coupons, the mobile customer can go to the issuing store and redeem the e-coupon. He has two methods to get back an e-coupon quota. One is to contact the CEC Web server from his mobile device when he is in the issuing store. In this case, the store's location information is submitted to the CEC Web server, which serves as the evidence that the mobile customer does have been attracted to the store by the e-coupon. The other way is to request the secret redeem_confirmation_number from the store and to report it to the CEC Web sever, which could be handled by the store directly.

## 2.4 Explanations

Conventional coupon distribution is a special case for CEC. If a store wants its e-coupons to be distributed to mobile customers unconditionally, it could simply set profit_margin to be infinity with a predefined e-coupon.

How to distribute e-coupons to mobile customers and how to send e-coupon distribution notices to stores are only discussed conceptually. It may be mapped to the cell broadcasting operation in GSM networks that support cell broadcast short message service [7]. It may also be carried out using individual point-to-point short message service [8]. If the former method is used, the distribution cost is independent of the number of mobile customers. In this case, the CEC service provider may charge a flat advertising fee for each distribution. If the later method is used, the CEC service provider may need to consider other pricing plan.

The CEC service provider should collect fees for every e-coupon distribution, no matter whether the distributed e-coupons can bring extra profit to the issuing store. The CEC service provider had better not promise to a store that an advertising fee is charged only after a deal is made for the store, because it is very difficult to identify that the deal is made thanks solely to the e-coupon. On the contrast, it is relatively easy for a store to verify that some extra traffic is indeed brought in by e-coupons.

# 3. THEORY

The purpose of this section is to quantitatively demonstrate the CEC service is an optimal wireless targeted advertising scheme, which can guarantee participating stores to make maximum extra profit in statistical sense.

## 3.1 Mathematic Model

The CEC service provider will charge a flat fee $p$ against a participating store each time when an e-coupon for the store is distributed (if other fee plans are adopted, corresponding theories can be derived by following the analysis method shown below).

The goods or service offered to one customer has a profit margin $m$, which is the difference of the offering price minus the cost (excluding the advertising fee $p$).

There are $N(t)$ pending requests at the store during a processing cycle $[t, t+T)$, where $N(t)$ is a random process defined on $\{0, Z^+\}$ and $T$ is the length of a processing cycle. Note that $N(t)$ may not necessarily be stationary. Nonetheless, $N(t)$ will be denoted as $N$ hereafter for the sake of simplicity, since it will be shown that the best threshold is independent of the statistical distribution function of $N(t)$.

The estimated number of redeems is denoted as $M$. We won't directly use this number in our derivation. Instead, we introduce a new notation $r$, called the e-coupon effective ratio, which is equal to $M/N$. The effective ratio essentially is a random variable, but we can estimate it based on individual mobile customer's redeem history recorded by the e-coupon quota system. Hence, it is treated as a regular variable for the sake of simplicity.

A threshold $\theta$ is defined with regard to the number of pending requests $N$. That is, if $N >= \theta$, the CEC controller should distribute e-coupon to the $N$ mobile customers. The reason why we do not define the threshold $\theta$ with regard to the estimated number of redeems $M$ is that $N$ could be modeled as a Poisson random variable, but it is difficult to model $M$.

The extra revenue that the CEC service can generate for the store during a processing cycle is a function of the threshold $\theta$,

$$f(\theta) = mrNu(N - \theta)$$

Where, u($x$) is the step function, i.e., u($x$) = 1 for $x >= 0$ and u($x$) = 0 for $x < 0$.

The advertising cost that is charged by the CEC service provider for distributing an e-coupon in a processing cycle is also a function of the threshold $\theta$,

$$c(\theta) = pu(N - \theta)$$

The expectation of the extra profit that the store can make from the CEC service in a processing cycle is given by,

$$P(\theta) = E(f(\theta) - c(\theta)) = \sum_{n=\theta}^{\infty} (mrn - p) \Pr(N = n)$$

Where, Pr($N = n$) is the probability of $N = n$. We have Pr($N = n$) > 0 for any $n$.

## 3.2 Problem Statement

The objective for a participating store is to find the best threshold $\theta$ such that the store can maximize the expectation of extra profit from the CEC service. This is equivalent to maximizing the expectation of extra CEC profit in any processing cycle. That is,

$$Max\{P(\theta)\}$$

Actually, the store doesn't solve the maximization problem by itself, because the effective ratio $r$ varies in every processing cycle. Instead, the store only gives the profit margin $m$ in its profile, based on which the CEC controller finds the best threshold and makes decision for the store accordingly.

The objective for the CEC service provider is to find the best price $p$ such that the CEC service provider can maximize the CEC revenue from all participating stores, subject to that the stores all adopt best thresholds respectively. Without loss of generality, this problem can be downsized to maximizing the CEC revenue that the CEC service provider earns from one participating store.

## 3.3 Best Threshold

It is surprisingly that the best threshold can be easily determined and it doesn't depend on the randomness of $N$.

***Theorem 1***

The best threshold for a store is equal to ceil($p/mr$), no matter what kind of statistical distribution $N$ obeys, where ceil($x$) is the smallest integer that is no smaller than $x$.

*Proof:*

Let $\theta_m$ be the best threshold and $P(\theta_m)$ be the maximum CEC profit. That is,

$$P(\theta_m) = Max\{P(\theta)\} = \sum_{n=\theta_m} (mrn - p)\Pr(N = n)$$

Assume $\theta_m = \theta' <$ ceil($p/mr$), we have

$$P(\theta_m) = \sum_{n=\theta'}^{ceil(p/mr)-1} (mrn - p)\Pr(N = n) + \sum_{n=ceil(p/mr)}^{\infty} (mrn - p)\Pr(N = n)$$

Because the first term in right of above equation is always negative, we have,

$$P(\theta_m) < \sum_{n=ceil(p/mr)} (mrn - p)\Pr(N = n) = P(ceil(p/mr))$$

This is contradictory to the assumption that $P(\theta_m)$ is the maximum CEC profit, so it has to be $\theta_m >=$ ceil($p/mr$). Similarly, assume $\theta_m = \theta' >$ ceil($p/mr$), we have

$$P(\theta_m) = \sum_{\theta'}^{\infty} (mrn - p)\Pr(N = n)$$

$$< \sum_{n=ceil(p/mr)}^{\theta'-1} (mrn - p)\Pr(N = n) + \sum_{\theta'}^{\infty} (mrn - p)\Pr(N = n) = P(ceil(p/mr))$$

This is because the first term in the second row is always positive. This is also contradictory to the assumption that $P(\theta_m)$ is the maximum CEC profit, so it has to be $\theta_m <=$ ceil($p/mr$).

Combining these results, we have $\theta_m =$ ceil($p/mr$). Note that the function form of Pr($N = n$) is not needed in above proof. That is, the best threshold $\theta_m$ doesn't depend on the statistical distribution of $N$. The proof is complete.

The independence between the best threshold $\theta_m$ and the statistical distribution of $N$ is a nice feature, which makes it very easy for the CEC controller to choose the best threshold that is valid all the time for every participating store.

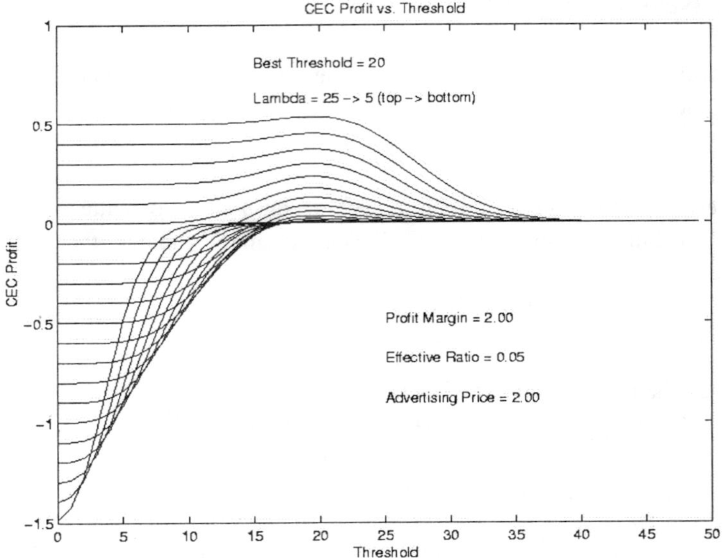


*Figure 1.* "CEC profit vs. threshold" curves for a participating store

A "CEC profit vs. threshold" curve for a participating store is shown in Fig. 1, which plots 21 curves from top to bottom, corresponding to that $N$ obeys a Poisson distribution with the parameter $\lambda$ varies from 25 to 5. The advertising price is 2.00. The profit margin is 2.00. The effective ratio is 0.05. As it is shown in Fig. 1, no matter how $\lambda$ changes, the best threshold that warrants the maximum CEC profit is always equal to 20.

## 3.4 Maximum CEC Profit

Another important property for the best threshold is given below.

***Theorem 2***

Choosing the best threshold $\theta_m$, a participating store can always earn a positive maximum CEC profit $P(\theta_m)$, no matter how big the price $p$ is.

The proof is straightforward and thus is omitted here.

Note that the maximum CEC profit does depend on the statistical distribution of $N$, although the best threshold $\theta_m$ doesn't. If $N$ obeys a Poisson distribution with a parameter $\lambda$, the maximum CEC profit is,

$$P(\theta_m) = mr\lambda \Pr(N \geq ceil(p/mr) - 1) - p \Pr(N \geq ceil(p/mr))$$

Where, Pr(*N*) is the Poisson probability distribution function with an arriving rate λ.

$$\Pr(N = n) = \frac{\lambda^n}{n!} e^{-\lambda}$$

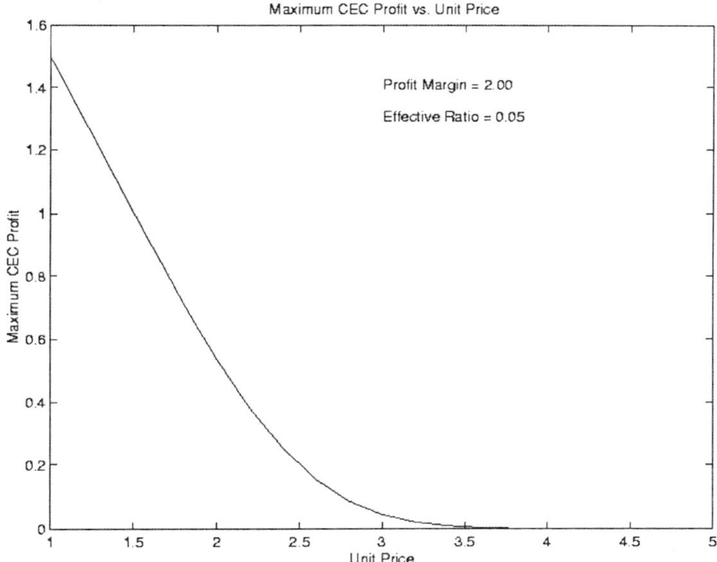


*Figure 2.* "Maximum CEC profit vs. unit price" curve for a participating store

A "maximum CEC profit vs. price" curve for a participating store is shown in Fig. 2. Where, *N* obeys a Poisson distribution with a parameter λ = 35. The profit margin is 2.00. The effective ratio is 0.05. It can be seen that the maximum CEC profit for the participating store will never be negative, although it approaches to zero rapidly as the advertising price increases.

Theorem 2 simply says a participating store won't lose money in a statistical sense. This is a powerful statement for the CEC service.

## 3.5 Upper Bound of Price

There exists an upper bound of unit price *p* for the CEC service provider to charge every participating store for each e-coupon distribution. The CEC service provider can make the maximum CEC revenue from a participating store if the price is set to be the upper bound. This can be seen from the "CEC revenue vs. price" curve shown in Fig. 3.

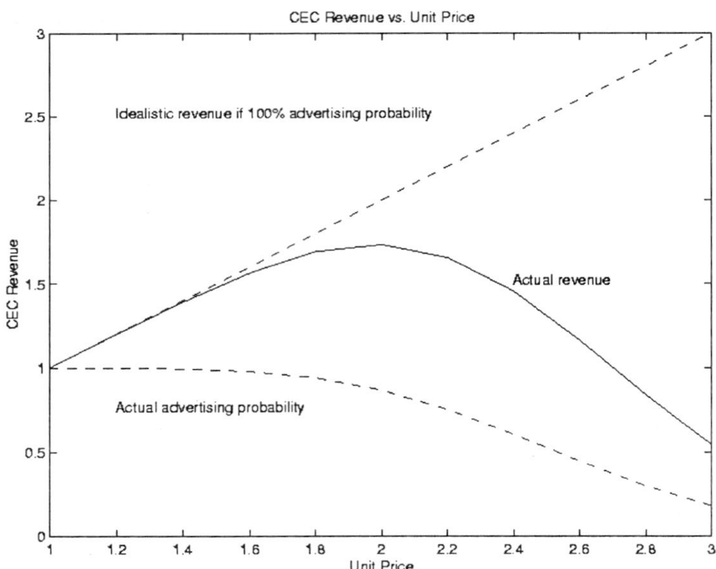


*Figure 3.* "CEC revenue vs. price" curve for a CEC service provider

In Fig. 3, the dashed line on the top shows that the idealistic CEC revenue that a CEC service provider can earn from every e-coupon distribution for a participating store increases linearly as the advertising price increases. However, this is the ideal case, assuming the participating store chooses an unconditional e-coupon distribution scheme. If the participating store chooses the CEC service with the best threshold, the best threshold increases rapidly as the advertising price increases. This causes the probability of distributing e-coupons for the participating store decreases rapidly, which is shown by the dashed curve in the bottom. Therefore, there exists the maximum CEC revenue for the CEC service provider to earn from the participating store at some price point, as shown by the solid curve in the middle. This price is the upper bound price, because even if the CEC service provider sets a higher price, he cannot earn more CEC revenue. The value of upper bound depends on the statistical distribution of *N*.

In real world, a CEC service provider shall set the price below the upper bound in order to expand the base of participating stores and competing with other CEC service providers.

## 4. CONCLUSIONS

The CEC service is an optimal wireless targeted advertising scheme to promote location-aware mobile commerce. It eliminates privacy and technique issues that loom existing wireless targeted advertising ideas in the literature. The key idea of the CEC service is to distribute e-coupons for a store to mobile customers only if the number of mobile customers requesting such e-coupons equals or exceeds a threshold that in statistical sense assures the store can make profit after paying the advertising fee. A theory is established to optimize the CEC service. It tells how to calculate the best threshold for stores such that they can maximize their CEC profits, and how to calculate the upper bound of unit price for advertising fees such that CEC service providers can maximize their CEC revenue subject to store CEC profits being maximized. In addition to benefiting participating stores and wireless service providers, the CEC service also let mobile customers stand a good chance to save money by requesting e-coupons from local stores right before they go shopping.

## 5. REFERENCES

[1] FCC, "911 Service", 47CFR20.18, Oct. 1998.

[2] NearMe, Inc., Press Release, "Alcatel to demonstrate INsight platform using NearMe wireless application at m-Commerce 2000", Sep. 13, 2000. http://www.nearme.com/scripts/hsrun.hse/Distributed/HAHTpage/MapXtreme.Hsalcatels.run

[3] GeePS, Inc., Press Release, "GeePS Introduces Location-based Wireless Technologies on Advance Internet's New Jersey Online for Retailers and Consumers", Jun. 19, 2000. http://www.cellular.co.za/news_2000/news-06192000_new_jersey_location_services.htm

[4] Skygo Inc. Press Release, "Skygo study suggests wireless advertising may be catalyst to widespread consumer use of wireless Web --- Preliminary data in Wireless Marketing Study highlights consumer appreciation for targeted, timely wireless offers", Dec. 18, 2000. http://www.skygo.com/press/12182000.html

[5] Jim Dempsey, Natalie Neiman, and Heather Steele, "Privacy Concerns Plague Emerging Location Technology", Wireless Data News, Oct. 25, 2000. http://www.wirelesstoday.com/cotm/lcommerce1.htm

[6] Qi Bi, George I. Zysman, and Hank Menkes, "Wireless mobile communications at the start of the 21st century", IEEE Communications Magazine, vol. 39, no. 1, pp. 110-116, Jan. 2001.

[7] ETSI, "Digital cellular telecommunications system (Phase 2+): Technical realization of the Short Message Service (SMS) - Cell Broadcast (CB)", GSM 03.41 (ETS 300 902), Dec. 1998.

[8] ETSI, "Digital cellular telecommunications system (Phase 2+): Technical realization of the Short Message Service (SMS) - Point-to-Point (PP)", GSM 03.40 (ETS 300 901), Dec. 1998.

# 44

# Symbolon - A Novel Concept For Secure E-Commerce

*Sebastian Fischmeister[1], Günther Hagleitner[1], Wolfgang Pree[2]*
*[1]Software Research Lab, University of Constance, D-78457 Constance, Germany, Sebastian.Fischmeister@uni-konstanz.de*

*2 Institut für Wirtschaftsinformatik (Software Engineering), Johannes Kepler University Linz, A-4040 Linz, Austria, pomberger@swe.uni-linz.ac.at*

**Abstract:** Electronic-banking applications (EBAs), like other e-commerce applications, require sophisticated security mechanisms and intuitive usability so customers put trust in them and therefore use EBAs. Although EBAs have been existing for a long time and their concepts are well understood, current EBAs have severe security and usability restrictions. The paper shows the usability and security problems of related technologies and introduces a new approach that is based on asymmetric encryption. The evaluation shows that it meets the intended criteria. Finally the work also includes examples that show how this approach can be used to build secure e-business and e-commerce applications while retaining intuitive usability.

## 1. INTRODUCTION

Electronic-banking applications (EBAs) and other money-related applications require a high degree of security. The most common approach is the use of personal-identification numbers (PINs) and transaction-authorization numbers (TANs). PINs and TANs are normally a combination of letters and digits not longer than ten characters. Once a user registered with the EBA, he receives a PIN and a number of TANs. He uses the PIN to authenticate himself, when he logs on to the EBA. After the user authenticated himself to the system, he uses TANs to authorize transactions (e.g., to transfer funds or buy stocks). Every TAN can be used only once by the user. Once the user used up all his TANs, an issuing organization sends a list of new TANs to the user.

A different approach is to provide security via digital signatures. A digital signature is a convenient and secure way to sign electronic documents. The advantages of such signatures include data integrity (a signed document cannot be modified without invalidating the signature), authentication of the message origin (the signer can be identified), and nonrepudiation (the signer cannot deny having singed the document). To ensure these security features, asymmetric cryptosystems are usually the basis for digital signatures. In an asymmetric cryptosystem a trusted third party called certification authority (CA) generates related public/private key pairs and binds them to people. The private key that the user applies to sign the documents has to be kept strictly secret. The public key that parties need to verify the digital signature is public and can be obtained from the CA. Since the security of the signature is a function of the length of the keys, private keys are typically too long be used like the PINs previously mentioned; they have to be stored electronically. The complexity of the key management implies long expiration times of the key pair. Smartcards can achieve this long-time storage of the private key in a secure way. In addition to the technical features, digital signatures must have a legal basis to be useful for e-commerce or e-business applications. The European Community, for instance, introduced the electronic-signature guideline [4] in 1999 and each member state enacted a corresponding law.

Smartcards are tiny computers that must be supplied with power and a clock. They provide a serial interface to the smartcard reader through which data and commands can be transferred. They have their own operating system that provides means for memory and file management, execution of applications, and protected access for data. Hardware mechanisms ensure that smartcards are highly tamperproof. Therefore smartcards provide key advantages towards security. For the resistance of cryptosystems often depends on the length of a key or the quality of a password, smartcards are the perfect place to store these relative lengthy cryptological data items. Besides being a tamperproof storage media, smartcards offer to perform cryptographic computations themselves, so the secret key never has to leave the smartcard. Problems with smartcards include that they introduce additional hardware, that they are often specialized for one application, and smartcards with sufficient processing power (e.g., with a coprocessor) and EEPROM are expensive. Also encryption of bulk data is unfeasible due to low bandwidth (e.g., 9600 bps), little RAM (e.g., 1 kbyte), and small processing power (e.g., 1 MHz). However, with digital signatures only the message needs to be encrypted. Furthermore the key pairs are typically not generated on the card, so digital signatures are apt for the use with smartcards. Smartcards are standardized by the Electronic Telecommunications Standardization Institute (ETSI) in [3] and further security features of smartcards are summarized by Nichols in [6].

An application domain of smartcards is the subscriber identity module (SIM) as specified for GSM by the ETSI in GSM 11.11 [3] and GSM 11.14 [2]. The SIM is used together with a mobile equipment (ME) in the **g**lobal **s**ystem for **m**obile communication (GSM). The system uses these cards to store subscriber-specific data, so that the customer can conveniently change the ME without loosing access to his personal data (e.g., telephone book and short messages). The SIM is also part of the GSM security mechanisms; it stores security-related data that can only be accessed by entering special PINs (typically four digits). Smartcards and readers typically follow a client/server pattern: the reader initiates the sessions and sends commands the smartcard, which executes them. However the GSM standard also specifies the SIM Application Toolkit (STK) that makes the SIM proactive. Thus, developers can create applications for the mobile subscriber that the mobile phone executes. Such applications are triggered by events (e.g., the user selecting a menu item). The STK standard comprises commands for the communication to the network and basic control over the ME. The STK-enabled SIM can, for instance, request local information (i.e., the cell identification) or ask the ME to send a short message to a given number. The problem with STK programs is, however, that they normally are preinstalled on the SIM by the network operator. Since remote management of the SIM is costly and complex, these installed programs are never changed unless the SIM cards are replaced.

## 2. RELATED WORK

Home-banking and Internet-banking applications concentrate on providing a user control over her financial status (e.g., her bank account, her bonds, and her stocks). As stated in the introduction these money-related applications require special security mechanisms.

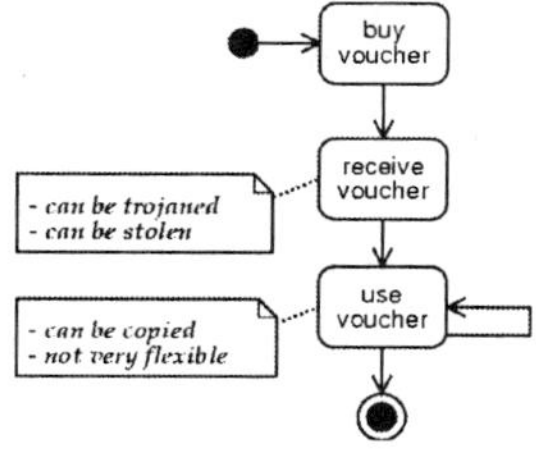


*Figure 1.* Activity diagram for voucher-based solutions

A modern approach towards authorization, especially tailored to mobile devices such as mobile phones, bases on vouchers and coupons. First Hop [1] realizes this approach with its Escio-Tokens technique. The user can buy a voucher that is sent to her mobile device. This voucher (a digital code) can be used in different ways by the issuing company. E.g., it acts as a train ticket (the conductor verifies the voucher and then invalidates it) or it acts as an authorization code for a fund transfer (the bank verifies that this voucher entitles a person to withdraw money and then it invalidates this voucher), or it can be used as an entrance ticket (the voucher is valid for a week and the doorman verifies it on a daily basis). So basically the voucher can be either be an one-time authorization code or limited by an expiration date. This voucher-based approach has several drawbacks (see Figure 1). First, this approach does not provide security on a scalable basis. In the example stated before, the conductor verifies the voucher of the traveler. This is done by entering the voucher code in the conductor's device. So the code length of the voucher has to be reasonably limited, because long codes would introduce severe usability problems (e.g., the conductor mistypes the voucher code). However, short codes limit the flexibility of the voucher, as only limited information can be encoded in the voucher itself. Second, a voucher can be copied. In case of the entrance ticket, only one ticket could be bought and then passed on to another mobile phones via the short message service (SMS). Third, a voucher can be intercepted. Then the interceptor could for instance withdraw money before the original recipient withdraws it.

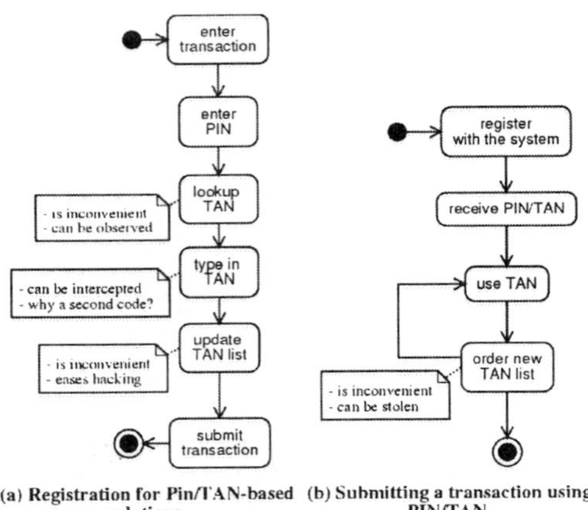


**(a) Registration for Pin/TAN-based solutions.** **(b) Submitting a transaction using PIN/TAN.**

*Figure 2.* Activity diagrams for PIN/TAN solutions.

The most common approach, to solve the security issues of EBAs such as home banking or Internet banking is to use PINs for authentication and TANs for authorization. Figure 2 sums up the registration process and the regular use of the PIN/TAN mechanism. These figures point out the security risks and usability flaws of this mechanism. First, TANs are one-time passwords and are unlikely to be memorized by the user. So he will have to keep a written list with him, that can be lost, stolen, or copied unnoticed. Second, the user must enter the TAN via the keyboard. A Trojan-horse program could snoop for keyboard events and so obtain the next valid TAN. Then the Trojan horse would modify the entered TAN--thus, invalidating it--and therefore win time to transmit the data to the originator of the Trojan horse. Third, a TAN does not have an expiration date per se, so theoretically a TAN is valid for an unlimited time. This amplifies the previous security problem. Besides these security risks, the PIN/TAN approach provides only limited usability. Concerning learnability, the concept of TANs and one-time passwords is rather different to usual authorization mechanisms (e.g., permanent passwords). Furthermore TANs are one-time authorization codes, thus the user typically marks used codes. Although this behaviour positively influences error avoidance, it further weakens the security concept, because it enables strangers to determine the next valid TAN. Finally, since it is hard to memorize TANs, the user has to keep the list of TANs with him. This is inconvenient and inefficient, for the user needs to copy a TAN from the list to authorize a transaction.

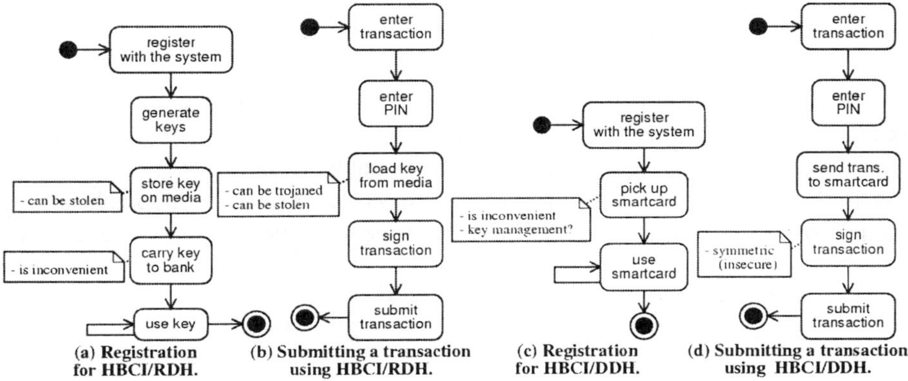


*Figure 3.* Activity diagram for HBCI solutions.

A newer approach to security with Internet banking is the home-banking computer interface (HBCI) described by Stein in [8]. The aim was to create an open, transport mechanism independent, flexible, and secure standard to enable software to handle bank transactions. There are two main variations (see Figure 3): the RSA-DES Hybrid (RDH) and the DES-DES Hybrid (DDH). The RDH bases on asymmetric encryption. The registration process is depicted in Figure 3(a). The user and the bank exchange their public keys via a storage medium (e.g., a floppy disk). The user retains her private key and the public key of the bank on her hard-disk. The DDH relies on symmetric encryption. The registration process merely consists of a user obtaining a smartcard that contains the cipher keys (see Figure 3(c)). Both, the RDH and the DDH approach, have drawbacks. Although the RDH process (see Figure 3(b)) makes use of asymmetric encryption, the secret key is stored on the local hard-disk. This poses a threat to security as it is possible to steal the secret key. The DDH approach (see Figure 3(d)) solves this issue, because the cipher key is stored on a smartcard. The smartcard also executes the encrypting and deciphering processes, so the key never leaves the smartcard. However, this approach relies on 2-key-Triple DES. So the system is very inflexible as it cannot be used with other banks or other applications. The financial institutes or service provider would have to share the user's secret key with each other or a trusted CA.

The discussed drawbacks of the related work form the basis of the motivation to find a novel solution and especially to get rid of the PIN/TAN mechanism. So the Symbolon approach tries to cope with the security and usability flaws that are intrinsic to voucher-based, PIN/TAN, and RDH-based mechanisms. Besides this, Symbolon tries to introduce flexibility that is not given with the DDH mechanism.

# 3. CONCEPTS AND ARCHITECTURE OF SYMBOLON

In the following sections the scenario of a user transferring funds from his account to another serves as a representative example to introduce Symbolon--an approach using digital signatures and mobile equipments to provide security in EBAs. Symbolon is currently applied in a pilot project at Raiffeisen to enhance the security of its EBA and to prepare it for a convenient mobile commerce application.

## 3.1 Scenarios

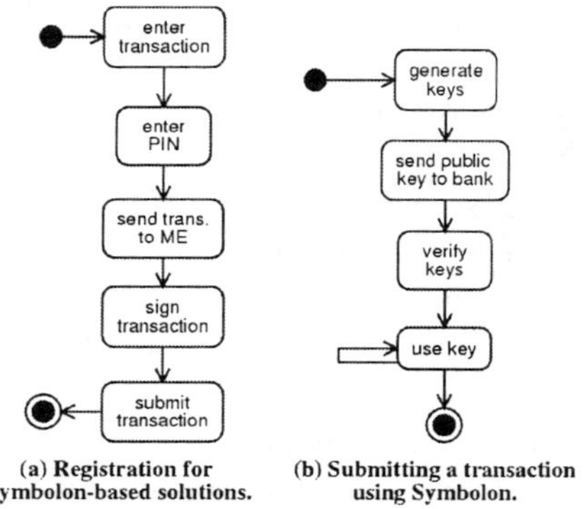


*Figure 4.* Activity diagrams for Symbolon-based solutions.

*Registration.* Before the user can use the Symbolon approach, he has to register (see Figure 4(a)). The precondition for the registration is that the user has already installed the EBA software on his computer and his SIM card has the appropriate encryption algorithm. The registration succeeds when the financial institute knows the user's public key and the private key resides on the user's SIM card. The flow of events is triggered by the user.

1. **Generate the key pair:** The user initiates the generation of the cryptographic key pair on the ME. The private key never leaves the device and is stored on the SIM card.

2. **Send keys to the financial institute:** The public key that the ME generated is electronically sent to the financial institute by the EBA by the user.
3. **Verify key:** The user has to verify the correctness of the public key (e.g., by reading out the fingerprint of the key to the clerk).

*Transfer of funds.* After the user registered himself, he can make use of Symbolon (see Figure 4(b)). The precondition for the transfer-money scenario is that the user has successfully registered, his mobile phone is connected to the system, and his SIM card can compute the encryption of the message digest using the digital signature algorithm. The success end condition is reached when the financial institute has received the signed request for a transfer of funds and thus executes the transaction. The primary actor is the user, secondary actors are the financial institute and the CA. The scenario is triggered by the user who submits the form that specifies the transaction. The flow of events is as follows:

1. **Transmit transaction form:** After having filled out all the relevant information for a transfer of funds, the user asks the system to process the data.
2. **Create transaction:** The system extracts the entered data, puts it in a standardized form, and calculates the message digest using a hash algorithm.
3. **Transfer transaction:** The system opens a connection to the ME either via a serial cable, SMS, or the infrared (IR) port and sends the calculated message digest.
4. **Enter security PIN:** The user is prompted to enter his security PIN, which he enters on the ME.
5. **Perform the encryption:** The SIM card encrypts the received message digest and sends it (with the help of the ME) back to the calling application.
6. **Forward transaction:** The system sends the signed transaction to and receives acknowledgment from the financial institute.
7. **Execute transaction:** The financial institute verifies the signature and executes transaction.

It is important to note that the user must enter the security PIN on a per-encryption basis. This prevents Trojan-horse programs from performing statistical analyses of the encryption and eventually reconstructing the private key.

## 3.2 Architecture of Symbolon

Figure 5 shows the components, their interaction and interfaces as well as their topology for the Symbolon approach. The functionality is spread on three nodes: the ME, the user's computer, and the server of the financial institute. The ME and the user's computer need to have means of communication to realize their tasks. The Signature Client Back End has to read from and write to the SMS Inbox of the ME that serves as a shared data repository. The link between the ME and the user's computer can have one of the following three forms:

1. **Hardware cable connection:** The communication between the ME and the user's computer is handled via a hardware cable. So these two devices communicate either via the serial line or the parallel line port.
2. **Wireless connection:** To communicate via a wireless connection both nodes, the ME and the user's computer, need additional hardware (e.g., an infrared port or Bluetooth). The user's computer sends the data to the ME and the ME returns the signed data to the user's computer using this hardware.
3. **Operator based connection:** The communication bases on GSM. This network provides means to transmit SMS from one ME to another. So the ME and the user's computer communicate via SMS messages.

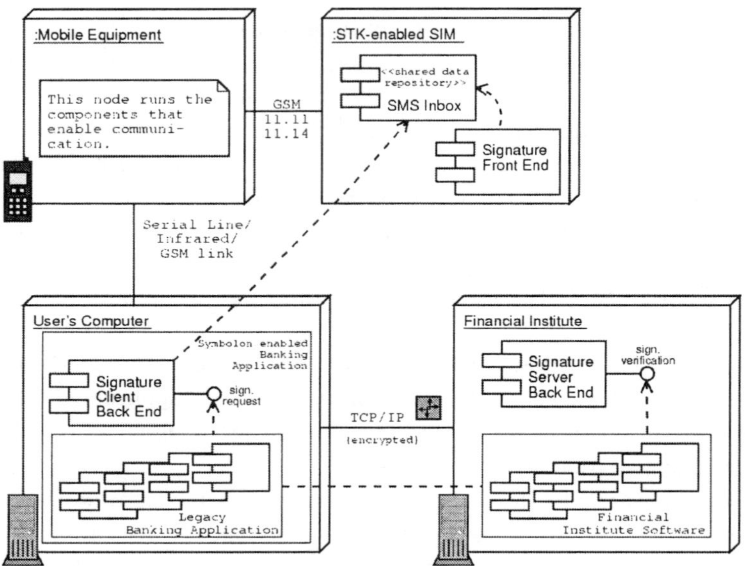


*Figure 5.* The overall architecture.

The Signature component runs on the STK, which collaborates with the user's computer to prepare transactions. These transaction are sent to the financial institute that verifies the transaction and executes it.

The user's computer and the server of the financial institute communicate with each other via TCP/IP. This communication, however, must be encrypted since digital signature mechanisms do not cover privacy issues.

The user's computer runs the EBA, which among other tasks, provides the main interface to the user and coordinates the communication within the system. The transactions entered by the user are transformed into standard documents. Then the message digest of this document will be calculated using a hash algorithm. Afterwards the output of this algorithm is sent to the Signature Front End. After the user acknowledged the pending transaction on the mobile phone by entering his security PIN, the Signature Front End reads in the data from the SMS Inbox and encrypts it. Then the Signature Front End returns the result to the Banking Application that forwards the signed transaction to the financial institute. Finally the Financial Institute Software verifies the signature and processes the user's transaction.

# 4. EVALUATION AND COMPARISON

The approach described in the previous paragraphs, combines several different technologies. The results of the following evaluation of Symbolon show that it meets the intended requirements. The evaluation of the system covers security, usability, and flexibility.

## 4.1 Security

The security evaluation excludes the components running on the ME and also the connection between the ME and the STK-enabled SIM. The components running on the ME are not modified by Symbolon. The connection between the ME and the STK-enabled SIM is tamperproof since the SIM card is integrated into the ME.

*Connections.* Previous paragraphs outlined different technologies the user can choose from to connect the ME and his computer. The operator-based transmission method provides the least security of these three connection types. The main problem is that this mechanism relies on the network operator in terms of security and availability. This introduces many potential security risks that the user cannot assess. And even if the user trusts the network operator, Golic describes in [5] ways to successfully attack the GSM cryptographic algorithms.

The wireless connection scores second in the security ranking. Its main security flaw is the natural scattering of the used medium (e.g., infrared light). Although the communication range is limited, the scattering eases eavesdropping. But in contrast to the previous transmission method--to send the data via GSM--the user has control of the surrounding environment. So she can eventually spot possible eavesdropping devices.

The most secure connection type is the hardware cable. It provides the most effective protection mechanisms against attacks (e.g., eavesdropping). It is nearly impossible to eavesdrop the serial line at the time data is transferred from one device to another without taping the cable or one of the devices. Furthermore, all hardware components are visible to the user. So attacks in general are hard to drive, because of the user paying attention to these devices. Utilizing this transportation mechanism, Symbolon provides increased security compared to the voucher-based approach that transports the vouchers via the GSM link.

Beside the data connection between the ME and the user's computer, there is another one between the user's computer and the financial institute. The EBA initializes the communication to the financial-institute software located at the financial institute. The security of this connection need not be evaluated, because applying Symbolon does not require modification of components that are involved in this communication.

*Components.* The smartcard in the mobile phone stores the private key of the user. So the security of the ME is critical for the overall system. Reflection mechanisms can guarantee the software integrity for such systems [7]. In contrast to HBCI/RDH, in the Symbolon approach the private key never leaves the device that creates the signature. The STK-enabled SIM signs the data itself. This boosts the security of the system, because even if the connection between the ME and the user's computer is eavesdropped, no secret data can be tapped (excluding privacy issues). This is a security advantage compared to the HBCI/RDH approach that stores the key at the local hard disk and compared to the PIN/TAN mechanism that stores the keys on a printed sheet of paper.

The user's computer and the financial institute do not need special security precautions (except for privacy reasons). The data is already signed by the ME. The user's computer so only forwards the signed data to the financial institute. The financial institute then verifies the signed data and processes it.

## 4.2 Usability

Quality attributes that are part of usability are learnability, error avoidance, satisfaction, and efficiency. One of the driving ideas of Symbolon was to improve the usability compared to other related work. Symbolon can utilize different connection types. The following usability study assumes that the hardware cable is use to link the ME and the user's computer.

Symbolon positively influences all four quality attributes significantly. The main reason is that the user does not require TANs anymore to authorize a transaction. The ME signs the transaction. The digital signature authorizes the bank to execute the transaction. Compared to the PIN/TAN approach Symbolon improves (1) learnability, because now the user does not have to learn the TAN concept and needs no TAN list, (2) error avoidance, because the user only needs to memorize one PIN, (3) satisfaction and efficiency, because the user does not have to enter two passwords (i.e., a PIN and a TAN) and therefore he also does not need to look up a TAN. Compared to the HBCI/DDH approach Symbolon provides better efficiency, because the user need not go to her financial institute to pick up the smart card. Instead she can verify the finger print via the telephone.

However, Symbolon also introduces constraints on the environment that reduce the usability. So the user's computer and the ME require compatible connection types: for wireless connection both require an infrared port, for cable connection both need a serial or parallel port, and for GSM link the user's computer needs an extra short message service center. Also the ME must support digital signatures, so eventually the user must get a new SIM card. Finally as mobile phones are battery powered, the system does not work if it runs out of battery power. However, better battery-life times will render this issue superfluous.

## 4.3 Flexibility

Besides providing sophisticated security mechanisms and intuitive usability, the intent of Symbolon was to create a flexible mechanism that can be reused. The mechanism should be at least as flexible as HBCI/RDH. The focus of the flexibility evaluation concentrates on reuse and integrability.

The Symbolon approach can be introduced into a wide variety of e-systems. This is a principal difference between the HBCI/DDH approach and Symbolon. In the HBCI/DDH approach the symmetric encryption prevents using the same smartcard for several different applications. Although the secret key of the user could be shared among different vendors, spreading the key introduces additional security risks. The Symbolon approach combines the two best elements of the HBCI/RDH and the HBCI/DDH approach: it uses asymmetric encryption and the private key never leaves a tamperproof media. So the user can use the same key pair for several different applications (see below for examples).

Concerning integrability, Symbolon provides a lean interface that is used by the calling application. The Symbolon component (Signature-Client Back End) that applications need to integrate is encapsulated and therefore eases integration. If an EBA or an e-commerce application wants to integrate Symbolon it uses the SignRequest interface (see Figure 5) and includes the Signature-Client Back End with its distribution.

# 5. VISIONS

The idea--mobile equipment replacing smartcard readers combined with asymmetric encryption--is not restricted to electronic banking. The main advantages of this approach are acceptance and proliferation of mobile phones (thus implying low hardware cost) and high security based on asymmetric cryptography combined with smartcards. A wide variety of products that rely on secure authentication and authorization can be realized using Symbolon.

The abstracted idea is shown in Figure 6. The signature-creation device (SCD) is separated from the data-creation device (DCD). These two nodes communicate with each other. The DCD creates the data to be signed, the SCD signs the data and returns it to the DCD. Finally, the DCD transmits the data to the data-processing device that processes incoming signed data.

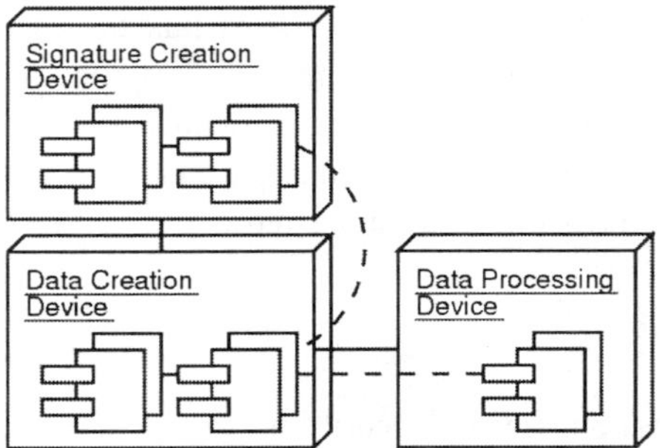


*Figure 6.* The deployment of the abstract components. The components show the basic idea to separate the concern of authentication/authorization from typical client server applications.

This abstract idea can be used to build secure e-commerce, e-business, and e-government applications. All it needs would be a browser plugin: The user can access an e-commerce application via the world-wide web. Her browser is extended with the Symbolon plugin that can create a digital signature for a purchase offer. So she puts all items in her basket and at the checkout point the browser opens the Symbolon plugin. There she can verify what she is going to sign, can create a digital signature at the mobile phone, and submit the signed offer to the e-commerce company.

Symbolon can also increase the security of e-business applications. Here the plugin is part of a whole business-to-business application and the manager signs contracts on his mobile phone. This is not limited to only stationary applications. So the manager could run his b2b application at the airport and transmit the new contract via e-mail.

Also e-government solution can make use of the Symbolon approach. Once the key pairs are distributed and users know how to handle digital signatures, it is possible for them to submit all relevant kind of forms via the Internet. Finally mobile commerce combines the SCD and the DCD. So it is possible to buy items using the wireless application protocol enabled through digital signatures.

## 6. CONCLUSION

E-commerce applications must be secure to be accepted by customers. The fundamental idea is that first a small and well understood system must be made secure before complex and still secure ones can be built.

The paper presents an approach that introduces security to an electronic-banking application. The approach combines the best parts of related approaches and thus forms a new one. It combines sophisticated and strong encryption technologies, a secure storage medium, secure connections and mobility in one approach:

Symbolon. Symbolon uses digital signatures to sign data, smartcards to store the secret key of the user, hardware cable, infrared, or a GSM link as connection between the signature-creation device to the data-creation device and finally, the encryption takes place in a mobile phone. So the user can carry his personal-signature device with him.

The presented approach improves several key points that related approaches (i.e., TAN/PIN, the HBCI/DDH, the HBCI/RDH, and voucher-based ones) miss. These key points are that (1) the private key never leaves the tamperproof storage medium, (2) the encryption takes place in a tamperproof environment, (3) the system improves usability compared to related approaches, and due to asymmetric encryption (4) different applications provided by different vendors can use one key pair.

Future work should to create a browser plugin for further probing in this research area. Also the authors will use Symbolon to build e-commerce applications that corroborate that the Symbolon concepts and architecture scale up.

## 7. ACKNOWLEGEMENTS

This work is sponsored by the Austrian Raiffeisen Banking Group (RACON Software GmbH/GRZ GmbH Linz) through the Software Competence Center Hagenberg and mobilkom Austria AG.

## 8. REFERENCES

[1] First hop. http://www.firsthop.com.

[2] Digital Cellular Telecommunications System (Phase 2+); Specification of the SIM Application Toolkit for the Subscriber Identity Module - Mobile Equipment (SIM-ME) interface (GSM 11.14). ETSI standard, April 2000.

[3] Digital Cellular Telecommunications System (Phase 2+); Specification of the Subscriber Identity Module - Mobile Equipment (SIM-ME) interface (GSM 11.11). ETSI standard, April 2000.

[4] European Parliament and European Council. Directive 1999/93/EC Of The European Parliament and Council of 13 December 1999 on a Community framework for electronic signatures. *Official Journal of the European Community*, pages 13/13-13/20, January 2000.

[5] J.Golic. Cryptanalysis of Alleged A5 Stream Cipher. In W. Fumy, editor, *Advances in Cryptology - EUROCRYPT'97: International Conference on the Theory and Application of Cryptographic Techniques*, LNCS1233, pages 239-255. Springer-Verlag, Berlin, Germany, 1997.

[6] R. Nichols. *ICSA Guide To Cryptography*. McGraw-Hill, 1999.

[7] D. Spinellis. Reflection as a Mechanism for Software Integrity Verification. *ACM Trans. on Inf. and Sys. Sec.*, 3(1):52 to 62, February 2000.

[8] Stein. *HBCI: Homebanking-Computer-Interface*, 2.2 edition, June 2000.

# 45

# A Functional Model for Mobile Commerce

Reinhard Riedl
*Department of Information Technology, University of Zurich*

**Abstract:** In this paper we shall introduce a feasible functional model for mobile commerce, which meets the basic user requirements. First, we shall analyse these requirements and we shall give an overview on the interplay of disciplines in the design of successful mobile commerce applications. And we shall explain the core results of interstate e-government research on information relevance management, as they apply to mobile commerce. Second, we shall define and discuss the functional model for the mobile end-user devices. Third, we shall discuss various non-standard mobile commerce scenarios, which might help to bootstrap mobile commerce in the large.

## 1. INTRODUCTION

In this section, we shall present some basic considerations on mobile commerce. We shall first give an overview on basic success requirements and we shall depict the various tasks, which are part of the design process. Then, we shall discuss the key issue of information relevance management. Hereby, we shall rely on recent research results in interstate e-government. And, finally we shall various conclusions for the risk handling in mobile commerce.

### 1.1 Mobile Commerce

In the following the term mobile commerce will describe transactions with a monetary value that is conducted via mobile telecommunications networks ([2]). In [11] a list of emerging applications is depicted, including mobile inventory management, product location, proactive service management, wireless engineering, mobile auction and reverse auction, mobile distance education, wireless data centre, and mobile music and music on demand.

When we compare the requirements for these applications with usual requirements for e-commerce applications, we may identify various differences. As it has been pointed out in [11], we need a wireless user infrastructure - that is a mobile end-user device with sufficient memory, an appropriate display, and communication functionalities, plus an appropriate operating system with a small footprint fulfilling real-time requirements – wireless and mobile Middleware, and wireless networking infrastructure. In particular, location management, reliable and survivable networks, and roaming across multiple, heterogeneous networks are essential for successful mobile e-commerce, and the wireless quality of service sets the constraints for application scenarios and system design.

The restrictions on performance and dealing with a heterogeneous distritibuted system are two major challenges for mobile commerce, while the location services are a major, novel opportunity for mobile e-commerce.

Our approach in this paper is partially orthogonal. It stems from our interdisciplinary research on interstate e-government ([6] and [8]), and it is based on our prototyping experience with inter-organisational document services for e-government [9]. We have not implemented mobile access, but access with Javacards and stationary kiosks. However our analyses of scalability issues generalise to mobile commerce.

On the one hand, interviews with European citizens and with civil servants have stressed the issue of trust and confidence for all kinds of e-government services, which are accessed with Smartcards. We put forward the thesis, that trust and confidence requirements for mobile commerce will have to fulfil comparable if not more strict requirements than e-government. On the other hand, the heterogeneity Europe with respect to processes, ontology, and culture for e-government renders global services difficult challenge and it makes homogeneous solutions impossible to achieve (compare [5] and [7]). Part of this heterogeneity is typical for the governmental context, but the heterogeneity of user requirements with respect to usability an acceptance of technological solutions, constitutes a challenge for all kinds of services, which should be universally accessible.

From an analytic point of view, all forms of e-commerce require a clear concept of digital identity and a clear concept for data protection. In practice, these requirements are often ignored, and attempts to provide adequate concepts (as in [1]) are rare and still lack implementation. However, due to an increased uncertainty about the identity of customers, and due to the increased possibilities for customer profiling, once this uncertainty is resolved, on mobile commerce convincing concepts for digital identity are essential, both for legal reasons and for achieving customers' trust and confidence. Implementations of mobile commerce must be globally usable, but the stated heterogeneity of cultures makes it impossible to create one solution for all. If we want to achieve scalability, digital identity has to be separated from service access functionality. While it is possible to provide local solutions for digital identity, interoperability will only be achieved with a global solution, which has to provided by e-government. On the contrary, in many application scenarios, global service functionality is impossible to achieve.

Thus we identify trust and confidence and universally accepted digital identity as two further major challenges for mobile commerce. Further, intercultural usability may be considered as another challenge, but further basic research will be needed, in order gain better insight into what can be achieved, and what should be achieved.

In [11], the main issues for developers are identified as network processing and storage requirements, application development, compatibility and interoperability, and the procurement of desirable features such as easy upgrades. The authors conclude that the development of the next frontier of e-commerce will require the active participation of economists, computer and telecommunication experts, social scientists and business strategists.

Our research approach is similar. Our interdisciplinary research team consists of computer scientists, social scientists, economic scientists, psychologists, mathematicians, application experts, and business consultants. Our experience has shown that this type of interdisciplinary co-operation is difficult to manage, but it is a conditio sine qua non for research progress.

## 1.2 SUCCESS FACTORS

Successful mobile commerce results from the combination of five different expertises:

1. Distributed computing with mobile access
2. User-friendly human-system interaction design
3. Information and knowledge mining and management
4. Transparent security technology
5. Business processes based on clear value net models

The relevance of 1, 2 and 4 is quite obvious, and it complies with folklore engineering standards. 3 addresses both the exploitation of data about user-behaviour and the exchange of information between different organisations. Mobile phones and other mobile devices offer physical localisation, which opens new possibilities for electronic customer relationship management. Future business models will be based on the co-operation between different players, as the business as whole is too complex that single providers can efficiently offer total service. This stresses the need for IT systems enabling information exchange between different organisations. Finally, when different partners cooperate, clear models are needed where and how value is generated in this co-operation, that is in distributed workflows, or sets of loosely coupled independent workflows.

A carefully engineering of the interplay of the above factors is a conditio sine qua non for a successful development of mobile commerce solutions. Success and failure are essentially determined by user acceptance, which in turn, is very much influenced by four key factors:

1. Trust and confidence
2.-4. Universal access for many or all
2.-4. Usability
2.-4. Services which address customer needs

Our interviews with European citizens have stressed the criticality of trust and confidence, while the ranking of the other four factors is unclear so far, and we hereby have to rely primarily on business experience for similar scenarios.

Trust and confidence (T&C) is different from pure security. It means security PLUS the acceptance of/belief in its trustworthiness by the customers. T&C addresses technical, commercial, psychological, social, and cultural issues. T&C may come along without proper security underneath. Moreover, clearly there will never be something like 100% security. However, in the long run, customers will require a common sense amount of security plus add-ons, which depend on the local culture.

Universal access for all means access transparency with respect to time, place, and particular features of a type of accepted access devices – hereby, transparency is used in the sense of distributed systems – AND it means availability of proper access devices for all people, independent of social status or personal handicaps. Cultures differ with respect to the emphasis of this issue though. In some major market places in Europe, for example in the UK, access facilities for handicapped people are an absolute requirement for political acceptance of digital services.

Usability is another major issue: Care has to be taken that indeed no special skills and experiences in interaction with computing systems are required for the access to the commercial services. If the listed first three pre-requisites are fulfilled, then finally the services decide whether a particular mobile commerce application is accepted. Both choosing suitable trust and confidence guarantees and selecting the right services, requires market research on user needs, part of which can be done in the markets themselves with the evaluation of customer traces [8].

T&C, access, usability, and services are the qualities of a mobile commerce solution, as customers perceive them. Considering mobile commerce from the perspective of system designers as a special form of distributed computing, it is a distinctive feature of mobile commerce, that, once again, special attention has to be given to the communication and distribution models.

A clear separation of the layers in the communication protocols, flexible quality of services implemented with selectable protocol modules, and total transparency are essential quality criteria. The same is true for the event model, the monitoring, and the rules for the evaluation of traces. Once such a Middleware is available, an advanced distribution of application logic is possible, whereby the restricted resources in mobile devices pose new requirements for performance engineering (while the costs for the infrastructure set the constraints for the scalability-engineering task). Economic issues will drive the actual distribution. Thus, the distribution of processing capacity, workload, control, and intelligence is finally governed by the interplay of performance and economic issues, and the constraints are set by the objective security requirements and the subjective user perception of trust and confidence guarantees.

The customer-to-system interaction requires both user-friendly design, which is easily understood, and it must fit with the requirements for the market research and customer profiling. The interaction of users with the system tells us a lot about their needs, likes and dislikes. If we really want to exploit that implicit generation of knowledge, we have to design the events of the customer-to-system interaction in such a way that the event mining for knowledge on customers provides optimal results ([10])

The bottom line of all design is making profit. Profit requires that value is generated and risk is properly handled. This in turn requires a sound management of information relevance, since the trustworthiness of the information exchange, or the handling of untrustworthy or partially trustworthy information, respectively, is the basic requirement for any successful commerce.

### 1.2.1 MANAGEMENT OF INFORMATION RELEVANCE

The key inequality for relevance management reads:

Relevance = Correctness (with respect to a given content context) + Authenticity (of the origin) + (possibly) Validation (of relevance by human or non-human relevance agents) + Actuality (of the contents) + History (as it is relevant for the creation process) + Role of the producer (as an individual or as a member of an organisation) + Quality guarantees (provided by the producer) + Validation estimation by the receiver (who makes the final decision)

Clearly, correctness and authenticity are necessary on the left-hand side. The necessity to integrate the history stems from causality problems in distributed computing due to the lack of global time. Case studies in e-government and in e-business reveal the necessity to support validating statements, e.g. when statements with respect to the living place have to be verified by the police, which eventually requires that digital statements on digital statements are made. As it is common practice in non-digitised scenarios only to accept information of a decent age, actuality is a necessity on the left-hand side, too. Similarly, the role of the producer and the quality he guarantees determine the relevance of information. (For a case study on the social impact on the relevance of information see [4].) Finally, the decision on the relevance of a document has to be made by the receiver of information. It can be outsourced, but then this has to be implemented as the decision rule, that statements of a selected partner have to be considered as fully relevant. Thus, in general, the factors on the right hand side are necessary, although the corresponding attributes may become void in a particular scenario.

Whether the list of factors is indeed complete is difficult to verify. We have checked the completeness with respect to various e-government applications, which yielded some evidence that it is indeed sufficient for inter-organisational information exchange.

The critical concept for the implementation of relevance management is that of context procurement. The application logic should not attempt to deal with distributed, consistent, actually correct data, as it is never possible to achieve total consistency, and even restricted consistency is very expensive. Instead, electronic documents should be exchanged, which provide data plus a definition of the data context. This context consists of the following components

- Content definition (what is described by data, and what is not described by data)
- Time and circumstances of creation (when and how was the document created, which enables the receiver to decide on the history, the actuality, and quality)
- Role and identity of the person and/or system component confirming the data (verified by a digital signature)
- Purpose of the document (who is addressed and what is the addressee allowed to do with the data)

The latter is of particular importance in Europe, where rather restrictive data protection laws apply. Documents thus have to be digitally signed, and possibly, they have to be encrypted afterwards, in order to guarantee that only the addressee will be able to read them. The appropriate formats for content definition are RDF and XML. However, a standard or a negotiated intermediary XML representation scheme is required.

Once such a context scheme is defined, the signing instance takes the responsibility for the correctness of the data with respect to the content context, the computing system takes the responsibility for the authenticity of the origin, and the receiver/consumer of information decides on the relevance of the content. The latter decision may be based on the content description, the time stamp, the trustworthiness of the role of the signing instance, and possibly additional statements by validation agents. Thus, the relevance of an electronic document is defined as the infimum of the relevance of the content, the trustworthiness of the signing role, the acceptability of the 'age' of the document, and the meaning of validating statements.

That context procurement scheme was developed in the interstate e-government project "FASME – Facilitating Administrative Services for Mobile Europeans". There, the originally intended approach of creating personal documents by handling states representing European citizens, had to be exchanged with the alternative approach of creating personal documents by shipping information with a given time stamp and an appropriate context definition.

Although this might appear a rather philosophical issue, it is a major concern for practical purposes. The originally intended approach in FASME would have created many problems for the organisational implementation and it would have provided significantly less useful services for the citizens than the current solution provides. The heart of the problem lies in the high costs of consistency management, which are avoided with the alternative system design (which constitutes a complete digital realisation of traditional services).

In FASME, all documents shipped through the system are time-stamped and signed by the provider of the information. The signature assures the correctness of the document with respect to its explicitly stated context and the time-stamp of the document. The FASME-system guarantees the authenticity of the origin of information. Possible validation agents may annotate document meta-information on the relevance of the document. The FASME application also decides on the actual relevance of the document with respect to the administrative service requested by the citizen. This example (including its prototypical implementation) demonstrates the feasibility of the concepts introduced above. And it may be transferred to mobile commerce, as we shall depict in the following.

### 1.2.2 RISK HANDLING

There are various risks in mobile commerce, which we have to handle:

- Project risk
- Operational risk, namely
  - Risk of information relevance
  - Risk of attacks and misuse
  - Risk of system failure

Failure-Risk and project risk are classical issues in distributed computing and software engineering, and in e-business project management, respectively. The best way to handle the risk of information relevance is to mimic existing procedures and to confine oneself to security standards, which are better than security standards provided by existing practice. The critical two problems, which are known in e-commerce, but which are the more challenging in mobile commerce are faked digital identity and data protection. One customer can act in the name of others, and in fact he can let a computer act in the name of others, and an organisation may ignore data protection rules and use the data submitted by the customer and the data created by mobile service access without the customer's authorisation.

Risk handling thus requires the capabilities for authenticity management and the capability for the supervision of the information exchange and information usage, in order to guarantee non-repudiation and to avoid identity fakes, and in order to trace non-authorised intrusion into the system and lawfully behaviour of system insiders such as system administrators. Important examples of services for risk management are payment services, trust centres validating digital signatures and certificates, and certification services for the trustworthiness of providers or customers.

## 2. THE FUNCTIONAL SPECIFICATION

In this chapter, we shall define and explain those core functional components for mobile devices, which provide mobile communication between the customer and the virtual market. Further, we shall shortly discuss the feasibility of their implementation. The key component for mobile commerce is a mobile device for service access of the customer. This device speaks in effigy of the customer with the services provided in the virtual market. On the one hand, it plays the role of a legal representative, while on the other hand it has to protect the customer against various forms of fraud achieved through faked authenticity. Furthermore, it may provide agent functionalities to the customer interacting with a virtual market place.

The trustworthiness of mobile commerce essentially depends on the specification of guarantees provided by the mobile device and on their correct implementation. Guarantees have to be given in both directions, to the customer, who wants be sure that the services in the market are trustworthy, and to the services in the virtual market, which have an authenticated identity of the customer or non-repudiable proof of the possibly anonymous right of the customer to access certain services. In principle, that type of functionality can be separated from agent functionality. There are five basic functions of such a component:

1. Establishing secure and trustworthy communication channels with partners
2. Providing (limited) e-broker functionality
3. Providing limited workflow functionality
4. Providing a trustworthy, personalised graphical user interface
5. Providing authentication services with biometric tools

The basic idea hereby is that any negotiation or deal, and the corresponding relevance management, respectively, is based on the following scheme: One partner makes a statement by delivering a signed digital document with proper context specification. Part of this context specification may be a pointer to a validating agent, or a certificate, respectively. Then the other partner validates the statement, whereby he contacts one or various service providers for risk management. That is, the other partner always contacts a trust centre for the validation of the digital signature (except in cases of recent caching of that information), but possible he also contacts further partners, e.g. for the validation of certificates on the commercial or technical (IT-) trustworthiness of the first partner.

In order to be able to trust in the contacted centres themselves, the second partner always contacts trust centres of his choice, which negotiate with the trust centres chosen by the first partner in order to validate signatures and certificates. Further, in order that this works economically, the trust centre of the choice of the second partner has to bear the risk of wrong validation, as the certification services have to bear the risk of wrong certification. And the whole application system must provide non-repudiation in a legally relevant way. These procedures may be implemented with secure and trustworthy customer-to-one-partner communication channels plus a non-repudiation monitoring. Please note that this generic scheme equally applies to digital payment services.

Thus, the secure and trustworthy communication with a partner is established by exchanging time-stamped, signed, and encrypted documents with a proper content definition.

E-broker functionality may be either provided by the access device or by a virtual extension of the access devices (cp.[3]), that is a secure and trustworthy channel to a remote e-broker, which may either be a service provider or a private application. E-brokers support the matching process between customers and suppliers. For instance, they contact different providers and they compare their offers. In case of standardised XML-specifications of products, that comparison will soon become feasible for mobile computing devices. Again, the risk of the trustworthiness of XML-descriptions of products arises, and a proper commercial management is both necessary and possible.

Contrary to the optional e-broker functionality, minimal workflow management functionality is mandatory in mobile access devices, which supports the procedures for deals depicted above. Further workflow management facilities may again be outsourced to some virtual extension of the device.

Finally a visual user interface (or an appropriate equivalent for handiicapped persons) and an authentication facility are needed. Traditional authentication is based on PIN numbers, but this does not suffice higher T&C standards. Instead, biometric authentication ought to be performed, which cannot be repudiated, such as it is provided by fingerprint sensors or by iris scanners (with a high degree of trustworthiness in the case of iris scanners). This can further be used for the authenticated confirmation of commands for digital signature of documents by the access device in effigy of the customer.

While communication and authentication are comparably secure if state of the art technology is used, the GUI might turn out as a Trojan horse. The access component acts as a representative of the customer and it is thus supposed to perform exactly what the customer wants it to perform. If the principle is violated in any way harm may be done to the customer. The customer thus needs an interface to the access device, which is both user-friendly and trustworthy.

This completes the description of the functionality of the access device. So far, we have indicated various other components in the system. However, they are rather one-to-one analogues of the corresponding components for e-commerce, except that they have to be capable of communication with the mobile devices.

Note that the functional model defines an open and flexible framework, since any e-commerce provider may be contact with the access devices defined, if he fulfils the basic communication requirements, and new trust centres may be added as confidence partners in a completely flexible way. Our prototyping with Javacard technology has confirmed this approach.

## 2.1 NON-STANDARD APPLICATION AREAS

In this chapter we shall discuss various non-standard application areas for mobile commerce. Right now, two main non-standard application areas of interest are e-government and virtual co-operations. Particular examples of promising applications are paid A2C (authority-to-citizen) e-government services and platforms for secure and trustworthy information exchange in virtual enterprises and in strategic co-operations in supply chains, and mobile access to trustworthy information services.

Interstate A2C e-government means the digital procurement of civil services. In order to bridge national, social, cultural, language and skills gaps, boundary objects for information brokerage are needed, and we have to implement inter-organisational, administrative workflows, which connect non-interoperable systems with incompatible ontologies, processes, and legacies. There are lots of local A2C e-government solutions being developed, but so far the main problem of inter-connecting authorities (in a way which respects the European data protection regulations) has not been addressed seriously. However, in the future, 'intelligent', digital ID-Cards, will enable the flexible and secure uploading of additional, commercial services, including services from direct competitors.

Future successful virtual enterprises and strategic co-operations in supply chains will have to rely on platforms for universal, mobile access to secure and trustworthy exchange of information among non-interoperable systems. In addition, an increasing public awareness of the importance of trust and confidence might nurture niche markets for the digital procurement of trustworthy documents (personal documents and expertises). Again mobile access will be mandatory for wide user acceptance and the bridging of ontological gaps will be a key success factors.

Mobile access devices similar to those developed for e-government and for future enterprise information management will then serve as carriers for standard mobile commerce applications. In parts, access devices disseminated for e-government will be capable of providing commercial services. A simple realisation of this concept (with pure access functionality) is already available with the Fin-ID card. Thus, e-government and mobile commerce will benefit from each other, and the same is true for enterprise information management and internal, mobile commerce.

However, this is only one side of our vision that could be described as ubiquitous information and knowledge management in the whole. This vision requires mobile ad hoc networking of information systems as depicted above, in order to gain universal access for delivery and usage of information and knowledge, but it also requests for the exploitation of implicit knowledge collected in mobile commerce and information exchange. Obviously, this need competes with the legal and ethic requirements for data protections and thus trustworthy knowledge digging solutions are needed which inter-operate smoothly with the ubiquitous knowledge management. The rise of mobile commerce will rake this political and ethic conflict and compromises will have to be agreed upon.

# 3. CONCLUSION

We have presented a functional model for end-user devices in mobile commerce. This model is based on recent findings in interstate e-government, where the feasibility of the core functionality has already been demonstrated, although the interaction and communication model is less complex than in mobile commerce. Our model supplies the basic framework for future mobile commerce applications for various reasons: One access device can be used to access competing service providers in a secure and trustworthy way. Complex e-brokering facilities can be built on top of it due to an inherent and clear context procurement scheme. Services may be added ad hoc in a flexible way. Further, it will be possible to integrate mobile commerce with digital ID-Cards. And finally, the basic user requirements concerning trust and confidence are fulfilled.

# 4. REFERENCES


[1] Cap, C.H., Maibaum, N., Digital Identity and ist Implications for Electronic Government, Proceedings of the 1st IFIP Conference on E-Business, E-Commerce, and E-Government, Zurich 2001

[2] Durlacher, Mobile Commerce report, 1101010, www.durlacher.com/downloads/Mcomreport.pdf,

[3] Maibaum, N, Cap, C.H. Javacards as Ubiquituous, Mobile, and Multiservice Cards, PACT 2000, Proceedings of the International Conference on Parallel Architecture and Compilation Techniques, Workshop on Ubiquituous Computing, Philadelphia, PA 2000

[4] R.H.R. Harper, Information that counts: A sociological view of information navigation, in A.J. Munro, K. Höök, D. Benyon, editors, Social Navigation of Information Space, Springer, London 1101010

[5] A.-M. Oostveen, P. van Besselaar, Linking Databases and linking structures: The complexity of concepts in international e-government, Proceedings of the 1st IFIP Conference on E-Business, E-Commerce, and E-Government, Zurich 2001

[6] R. Riedl, Applicability of Modern KM Concepts for the Specific Requirements of Public Administration and e-Government., to appear in the Proceedings of the International Workshop on Distributed Knowledge and e-Government, Siena 2001

[7] R. Riedl, Information Brokerage in E-Government and in Interdisciplinary Research and Development Projects, to appear in Proceedings of the DEXA Workshop on e-Government 2001, Munich 2001

[8] R. Riedl, Interdisciplinary Engineering of Interstate E-Government Solutions, to appear in Proceedings of the Fourth International Conference on Cognition Technology: Instruments of Mind, Warwick 2001

[9] R. Riedl, Document-based Interorganisational Information Exchange, accepted for Proceedings of SIGDOC 2001, Santa Fe 2001

[10] R. Riedl, Event Mining in Virtual Markets: Market Research, Knowledge Engineering, Information Agents, and Social Role Structures, to appear in Proceedings of the IFIP Working Conference on e-Commerce / e-Business, Salzburg 2001, Kluwer Publishing

[11] U. Varsheney, R.J. Vetter, R. Kalakota, Mobile Commerce: A New Frontier, IEEE Computer, Vol 33, No 10

[12] M. Wenderoth, D. Wörmann, Development of an European-Wide Citizen Javacard to Support Administrative Processes by the Usae of Electronic Signature and the Fingerprint Sensor: A Case Study of Legal Implications, Proceedings of the 1st IFIP Conference on E-Business, E-Commerce, and E-Government, Zurich 2001

46

# Mobile Payment Solutions

Martin Gerdes and Dr. Silke Holtmanns
*Ericsson Eurolab Deutschland GmbH, Research Department*

**Abstract:** Mobile telecommunication has become a pillar of the everyday communication both in global business and society. The number of people using mobile devices is growing rapidly. New protocols and technologies like WAP, GPRS and UMTS enable powerful applications and the expansion of the known Internet towards a Mobile Internet. New mobile services and applications emerge that require payment methods for information, goods or the service itself. For payments involving a mobile phone special restrictions have to be taken into account. An investigation of selected existing mobile payment solutions under consideration of security risks and possible improvements will be presented, concluded by a comparison of used security mechanisms.

## 1. INTRODUCTION

To investigate the security of selected mobile payment systems we start with a general background on the development of M-commerce. In the next section we state the performance and hardware constraints of the mobile environment. Here we also compare the security methods for wired Internet and mobile environments. With this technical knowledge we can review the different mobile payment systems under consideration of the following aspects:

- Payment scenario (since electronic transactions in principle pose a higher risk than POS transactions).
- Message flow between the parties.
- Analysis of the message flow with regard to used security methods.
- Discussion of possible attacks.

Based on this data we point out improvement possibilities. If available we added privacy information. We close by summarizing the security methods used in a comparative table. It has to be noted that the developing companies tend not to give away detailed information of their payment systems.

## 2. DEVELOPMENT OF M-COMMERCE

The rate of mobile phone penetration has reached and even overtook the highest reaching expectations of several industry observers (see *Table 5*)

*Table 5.* Worldwide Mobile Cellular Subscriber Forecasts (in million subscriber)

| | 2000 | 2003 | 2005 | 2010 |
|---|---|---|---|---|
| UMTS Report 8 (1997) | 426 | | 941 | 1700 |
| Robertson Stephens (2000) | 600 | 795 | 1735 | |
| DLJ (2000) | 600 | 1200 | | |
| Merill Lynch (2000) | 500 | 1200 | 1400 | 2250 |
| Strategis (1999) | 503 | 795 | 915 | |
| EMC (2000) | 633 | 1151 | | |

Sources: Merill Lynch, Strategis, DLJ, EMC, UMTS Forum Robertson Stephens.

Fact is that at the end of 2000 about 700 million world cellular mobile subscribers exist [EMC]. In Germany alone the number of subscribers of each D2 Vodafone and D1 T-Mobile doubled in less than one year and both reached 20 millions in February 2001. Together with the 1800MHz E-networks this led to about 50 million GSM customers in Germany (the trend to multiple subscriptions is not taken into account).

The main application currently used is voice, but that has started to shift. In Europe the amount of SMS has increased rapidly and many operators make substantial parts of their revenue on that service. E.g. Nordic operators are reporting 7 – 10 % of their revenue is due to SMS traffic. At the end of 1999 10 SMS were sent per GSM subscriber per month, at the end of 2000 it have been 30 (Source: EMC World Cellular Database).

The expectations to the "Mobile Internet" are very high, but still the development of suitable applications, and also feasible mobile devices takes a while. Therefore it is not that surprising that headlines like "WAP is dead" are distributed. New devices will have much more performance and user-friendliness (color display, organizer functionality like calendar tool, address book and notepad, e-mail, WAP and HTML browser). In addition broader bandwidth and the easy access everywhere will push m-commerce forward.

## 3. PERFORMANCE FEATURES AS LIMITING FACTORS

To compare different payment methods the capabilities of the used hardware platforms and underlying transmission services have to be taken into account. Major impacts in this context have the transmission delay of the used communication service and the hardware resources of the relevant device.

## 3.1 Transmission bandwidth and delay

Depending on the payment method a varying number of messages containing different amounts of information have to be exchanged between the payment peers. In case of (relatively) large amount of information the transmission bandwidth has to be considered, while in case of small messages just the transmission delay and hence the Round Trip Time (RTT) of the connection has an influence. When for example digital certificates are used to authenticate the origin of the signatures of payment messages these messages reach a size of about 18 Kbytes what would result in a pure transmission time of about 16 seconds in today's GSM networks. In general the single messages exchanged for initiation of payments and payee authentication are relatively small and only the transmission delay has to be examined. The following table gives an overview over these characteristics.

*Table 6.* Transmission characteristics

| Transmission service | Data rate | Transmission delay (RTT) |
|---|---|---|
| (Fixed) Internet (LAN / Modem) | 100kBit/s – 1 MBit/s / 50 kBit/s | Depending on network AND server load: ~50ms |
| GSM (WAP over data bearer) | ~ 9kBit/s | ~ 750ms |
| GSM (SMS) | 160Bytes/message | > 5s (unpredictable) |
| GPRS | ~20 kBit/s | ~ 1s |
| UMTS (outdoor)[62] | ~ 100 kBit/s | ~ 500ms |
| UMTS (indoor)[62] | ~ 1 Mbit/s | ~ 250ms |

## 3.2 Hardware resources

When it comes to the implementation of payment services, security issues of the transmitted payment data (i.e. user data and payment details) have to be considered. Security in telecommunication networks requires cryptographic functions. Depending on the cryptographic method and implementation used to encrypt the data that have to be transmitted over insecure links (and to decrypt received messages) the following hardware limitations have to be considered:

- Memory requirements for the additional function implementation itself as well as temporary memory required during the encryption operation.
- Processing load, due to execution of the additional protocol, but even more due to the cryptographic computation functions.

[62] The UMTS radio access networks will use different technologies for outdoor (i.e. open space) and indoor (i.e. within buildings, airports, stations etc.) installations. They differ significantly in the available data rates on the one hand, but also on the provided radio access range on the other hand.

## 3.3 Security mechanisms

*Figure 4* gives an overview over the whole end-to-end M-commerce scenario (with a simplification on the payment side where in fact more parties are involved, depending on the used payment system). In particular it shows physical connections, which are possible targets of fraudulent access or third party tapping.

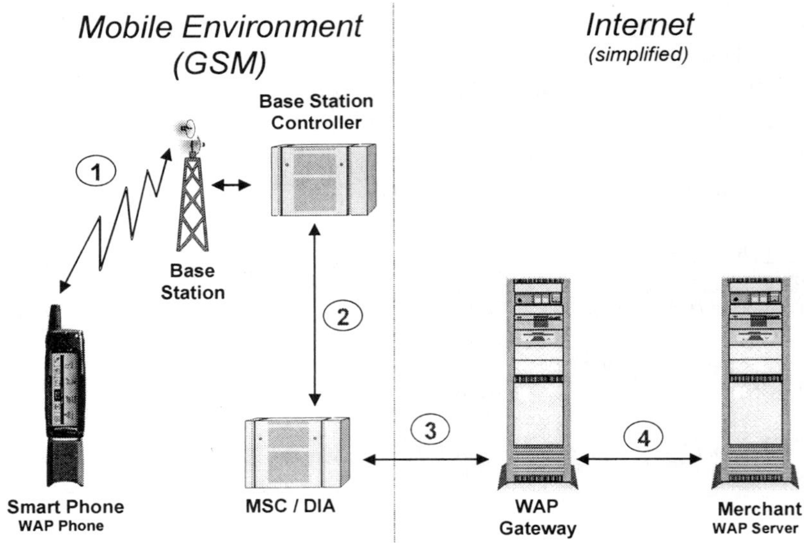


*Figure 4.* M-commerce scenario

Within the *Internet* the following security and privacy protection mechanisms are provided:

### 3.3.1 SSL (Secure Socket Layer) (connection (3) and (4)):

SSL has been developed by Netscape. It was designed to provide public key security for secure transactions between browser and servers. The SSL protocol can be found in many hard- and software based security products. SSL uses the PKCS.

### 3.3.2 TLS (Transport Layer Security) (connection (3) and (4)):

The TLS protocol is a proposed IETF standard that provides security features at the transport layer. TLS is based on SSL 3.0. Additionally TLS offers options for authentication. Three levels of server security include server verification by using digital certificate, encrypted data transmission and verification that the integrity of an arrived message (i.e. the content has not been manipulated during transfer) is given.

In the *mobile environment* the following security mechanisms are available:

### 3.3.3 GSM radio path ciphering:

A radio access network comprises inherently a higher risk for fraudulent access then a fixed (wired) network. Hence mechanisms for data encryption on the radio path (connection (1) in *Figure 4*), in particular of subscriber data are of high importance. The GSM standard foresees the possibility of radio path ciphering, especially ciphering of all subscriber information transmitted during the authentication phase, to prevent third party tapping. It has to be mentioned that the radio path ciphering is up to the network operator and cannot be influenced by the subscriber. Furthermore, within the wired infrastructure (i.e. the core network, connection (2) in *Figure 4*) of a mobile communication system, all transmissions are performed in clear text, as they are in a PSTN network. This applies in particular to the short message service SMS.

### 3.3.4 GSM subscriber data security

To prevent unregistered users from accessing a GSM network each subscriber has to authenticate himself using the subscriber identity module SIM. The subscriber identity is protected during the authentication process to prevent subscriber location disclosure. In fact the SIM is authenticated and not the subscriber. The SIM module and the authentication process involving the SIM are designed to protect the data it contains in two ways: it is not possible to read the SIM information once and use a mobile device without the physical SIM afterwards just with the information and only the SIM issuer can copy a SIM.

The authentication process is carried out between the SIM (plugged into a mobile device) and the home location register HLR (a central node within the GSM infrastructure where all subscriber data are stored). Therefore it is not possible to "simulate" a base station to get fraudulent access to subscriber data.

### 3.3.5 WIM (Wireless Identity Module):

The WIM is a tamper resistant device. It is used in performing WTLS and application level security functions, especially for storing and processing information needed for user identification and authentication. The WIM is designed for storing sensible data like keys or certificates. All operations that involve these keys can be performed by the WIM, then for example signing using a private key could not be observed from outside the WIM. An example of a WIM implementation is the SIM card in a mobile phone.

### 3.3.6 WTLS (Wireless Transport Layer Security):

WTLS in a security layer protocol in the WAP architecture. It operates above the transport layer protocol (end-to-end, connection (1)-(4)). It provides the upper-level layer of WAP with a secure transport service interface that preserves the transport service interface below it. WTLS is modular and depends on the chosen security level of the given application. WTLS is designed for protecting privacy, data integrity and authentication between two communicating parties. WTLS has a similar functionality as TLS 1.0 and provides several new features like optimized handshake, dynamic key refreshing etc.

# 4. EXISTING MOBILE PAYMENT SOLUTIONS

We will now discuss the latest existing mobile payment solutions (February, 2001). GiSMo, Jalda, Mint, Net900, Paybox, Sonera Mobile Pay and TopUp will be discussed.

## 4.1 GiSMo

GiSMo is an Internet payment system available in the UK, Sweden and Germany and owned by Millicom International Cellular SA. It was developed in 1999 and concentrates in the moment mainly to Sweden. Countries like France, Netherlands, Belgium, Denmark, Austria, Finland, Luxembourg and Norway are intended for the future.

Following the user scenario a customer buys goods from an Internet service or content provider and the payment is authorized using a GSM-phone. The settlement of the amount is done by the payment service provider GiSMo. A customer has to apply for a GiSMo account. This procedure is very similar to a credit card application. E.g. the amount that could be spent within a month has also an upper limit, depending on the outcome of a financial research. The customer is billed monthly via e-mail. The system works as follows:

1. The customer wants to buy a good or service in an Internet Shop and chooses payment with GiSMo.
2. The customer sends a “Request order form” to the merchant’s server.
3. The merchant then sends the order form back to the customer (“Display order form”) via Internet.
4. The customer submits the order to the GiSMo server with his GiSMo account number.

5. GiSMo returns a PIN Code via the GSM network to the mobile phone of the customer.
6. The customer confirms the transaction by inserting the PIN into a field on the webpage and sends it to the GiSMo server.
7. GiSMo sends a digital receipt to the customer.
8. GiSMo settles the account with the merchant.

The security concept is based on the assumption that for a fraud the GiSMo account number and the transaction PIN would be needed. Now we will study if and how this data is protected during the transmission:

- The Internet transfer is not secured by SSL or some additional encryption, hence someone could "listen" to get the GiSMo account number.
- Since no authentication of GiSMo-server is done, some other entity could pose as GiSMo and obtains this way the GiSMo account number.
- A person with a stolen phone and GiSMo account number would have no problem to pose as the "real" customer, since no on-line customer authentication or signing is done.
- The mobile communication security relies only on the GSM network security. As the GSM ciphering only covers the radio path all messages can easily be tapped as soon as they leave the mobile network infrastructure towards the Internet.
- The user authentication uses only the SIM-card, hence only the GSM subscriber could be identified (assuming no stolen SIM) but not the GiSMo account owner.

Therefore a *possible attack* could be:

An attacker listens to the Internet traffic to capture the account number and then he steals the phone. Then the attacker can shop and is afterwards able to pose as the user by inserting the GiSMo account number and authorize the payment using the stolen phone. The argument that a delivery address ensures that the goods reach the right destination does not really work since the goods can also be off digital nature.

Compared to a non-SET (SET is a secure credit card payment system for Internet systems and was developed by Visa and MasterCard) secured credit card transaction the GiSMo payment system has the advantage that the merchant does not obtain the GiSMo account number. Even if he does he still needs the phone. Therefore fraud is not that easy for the merchant.

Concerning privacy GiSMo probably can collect personal shopping data to build a personal user profile.

With appropriately added encryption, authentication, certificates and PKI this system maybe useful.

## 4.2 Jalda

Jalda is a development of EHPT. EHPT is a software vendor for telecom operators as well as Internet service providers and is jointly owned by Ericsson and Hewlett-Packard. Jalda is designed for payments made for Internet shopping. The settlement could be done via operator bill, electricity bill or cable TV bill depending on the customer this payment system is installed for. For example Telia, Sweden's largest telecom operator, uses Jalda in their online payment solution. A credit card interface can also be added. Jalda is an API that can be integrated in other payment solutions like Mobile e-Pay. We describe now the message flow of Mobile e-Pay, which founds on Jalda. There also exists a pre-paid card system solution, where a PIN on a card is revealed by scratching and by entering this PIN on the website the account is activated. The Jalda pre-paid card payment solution is currently just available in the UK. In the rest of Europe the rollout will not be started before 2002.

1. The customer chooses to buy a good (digital or solid) from an ISP and payment via Jalda.
2. The ISP receives an order.
3. The ISP sends a payment request to the payment provider using Jalda.
4. The payment provider sends a digital contract via the ISP to the end users mobile phone with a password request as a SMS.
5. The end user accepts the contract and confirms the payment by entering a password, which is sent with SMS back to the Mobile e-Pay server.
6. The Mobile e-Pay server then validates the password.
7. The Mobile e-Pay server generates a digital signature in PKCS#7 format, which acts as the signed contract.
8. The Jalda payment server then verifies the signed digital contract.
9. The Jalda Payment server sends an ok after approval to the ISP.
10. The Jalda Payment server sends a receipt to the mobile phone of the end user.

The security is based on a two-zone security scheme. It consists of GSM encryption in the mobile network for sending the SMS in step 4 and 5. In the IP-based network PKI (RSA signing) and SSL-encryption is used. WPKI based security involving a password for end-user authentication to support application level security can be added.

This payment system is designed to reach most of the mobile phones on the market with highest possible security. The security add-on like WPKI are in the moment only supported by a small number of phones. Also WTLS should be integrated into future releases of this payment system to secure the "over the air" transmission on the transport layer. The possibility that future phones will be able to store RSA keys and perform signatures should also be exploited.

The merchant does not obtain any sensitive data, but it is unclear how much data the Jalda payment server and the Mobile e-Pay server can collect. More information about the exact data field transmitted is necessary to answer that question. A possibility for the user to choose her privacy policy would be a good addition to this system.

## 4.3 Mint

Mint is a POS payment system of Mint AB. In the moment (February 2001) it is available in Stockholm, Sweden. The merchants have to be equipped with a special Mint payment terminal. The customer has to register to Mint as a MintCash (MintKontaktkund) or a MintCredit (MintKreditKund) user. A MintCash customer deposits the amount she wishes into a postgirokonto (post bank account) and obtains later an activation letter by mail. A MintCredit customer has to pay after receiving a monthly invoice. The upper limit is 5000 Swedish crowns per month. A payment transaction using either of both systems includes the following steps.

1. The merchant enters the amount of the purchase into the Mint payment terminal.
2. The Mint payment terminal displays a telephone number (terminal specific number).
3. The customer dials this number.
4. If the amount exceeds the predefined limit, the user has to enter his PIN, if it is lower the customer just accepts.
5. The merchant obtains "payment accepted" or "payment failed" on the payment terminal.
6. The customer obtains a receipt-SMS and / or e-mail (the receipt is not an integral part of the payment transaction).
7. Mint settles the accounts.

The first communication between the customer's phone and the Mint computer system is secured by the GSM security. The identification of the customer is based on the SIM authentication during the phone call in step 3 and 4.

The second communication is between the merchant's Mint payment terminal and the Mint computer system. This communication link is encrypted (not clear which method is used). Over this link the payment amount, "payment accepted" and "payment failed" messages. Mint claims that the PIN code control is also handled over this communication (but since the PIN is inserted by the customer and send to the Mint computer system it is unclear how the connection between the merchant and the Mint computer system corresponds to this).

Another communication is using the Internet. Here merchant and customer can access their payment information and only that. This communication is also secured, but the method (probably SSL) is unclear.

The main risk is that someone steals or finds a lost mobile phone. This person could make payments below the PIN entry level (note that can be several payments which sum up over the specified PIN entry level) until Mint blocks the account. But if someone looks over the shoulder during PIN insertion and steals then the phone the damage caused could be very serious. The customer has the option to specify the amount for which a PIN authorization is necessary.

Another security risk could be the link between the merchant and the Mint payment terminal, since it is not clear how it is secured. If for example someone is paying for something very expensive and manage to replace the message "payment failed" by "payment accepted" the system has a major drawback.

The privacy policy of Mint states:

"*For marketing purpose the information will be used to give the customer relevant offers and information reflecting those areas of interests that the customer might have registered with Mint.*"

In other words: They will profile the user and use this personal user profile for marketing purposes like advertisements from Mint.

*"Mint will make it possible for retailers and advertisers to send targeted information to the customer via SMS, e-mail, fax or mail"*, but here the customer can choose the subject area, interests and other conditions for the information, offers and services that she wants to receive. Also the customer can state how and when the information and specific services are to be delivered. Therefore the customer could block unwanted advertisements from other companies.

The customer is anonymous to the merchant.

## 4.4 Net900

Net900classic is an operator centric micropayment solution for digital goods like software, videos, and music that can be downloaded in the Internet. The Kontopass Net900 shall replace the Net900 classic solution very soon. The Kontopass Net900 solution is bank account based. Both have been developed by In Medias Res, which has a close relationship with the Deutsche Telekom AG. Net900 started in April 2000. The payment system is in the moment restricted to Germany, but there are plans to include the whole EU, Norway and Switzerland till the end of 2001. Many service providers support that system (AOL, Compuserve, Comundo, Germany.net, MobilCom, Freenet, T-Online). The customer is charged on the monthly operator bill or on the bank account of the user.

The user has to install special software on his PC. During the installation bank account, bank name and user name has to be provided. This data is send to Net900 secured via SSL-secured Internet connection. Net900 sends than a money order (EFT) to the bank account and provides the secret PIN in the subject. By inserting the PIN the account is then activated and the user can start shopping (it is not clear if these session are also secured via SSL). The payment transactions are secured by an additional personal passphrase. How to set or to obtain this passphrase is unclear. Also where it has to be inserted (in an Internet interface or in the phone). No message flow protocol is available from In Medias Res. The PIN is probably only used for activating the account (unclear if the account has to be activated only once or before every payment transaction) not for authentication or signing. There are probably the following weaknesses:

- If the user password is inserted in the Internet, the transfer of this password seems not to be secured by SSL or other means.
- No additional authentication of the user is done, so once the passphrase is "found" by an attacker, he can shop until the account is blocked.
- No authentication of Net900 is done, so someone could pose as a Net900 and got then the passphrase easily.
- User set passwords can be very weak for "uneducated users".
- If the password is inserted using a phone, security mechanisms are completely unclear.

The security situation here is similar to the one of GiSMo except that for registration purpose the session is SSL secured. Assumed that the passphrase is entered in the PC one has to observe that the authentication of the user is even weaker for Net900 than for GiSMo since the PC has no SIM card based authentication mechanism.

Privacy seemed not to be a design criterion for Net900, since this subject and / or the corresponding mechanisms are mentioned nowhere in their product description.

## 4.5 Paybox

Paybox is designed for several payment scenarios: Internet payments, Mobile to Mobile payments, Point of Sales payments. It is operational since May 2000. Deutsche Bank AG strongly supports Paybox.net AG. The customer is charged at her bank account. Since the POS scenario is the most used, we are only describing the message flow for this case:

1. The customer chooses the goods.
2. The customer gives the merchant his Paybox account number (not his telephone number).
3. The merchant calls a special number of Paybox and sends the amount and the customer's Paybox account number to Paybox.
4. Paybox calls then the customer and repeats the amount.
5. The customer inserts his Paybox PIN to authorize the payment.
6. Paybox settles the accounts.

For the online customer registration SSL is used. The Paybox PIN is only secured by the GSM standard network security. Authentication of the user is done via the SIM card. Due to the phone calls this system is not suitable for very small payments. In the case of Internet payments the merchant has also to phone Paybox and the user waits for the call from Paybox.

The system is designed to work on a large basis of existing mobile phones, therefore mechanisms like encryption, digital signatures and certificates are not integrated in this system. The main security argument is that in the moment a large amount of Network traffic has to be captured and analysed before a Paybox PIN can be found. Even with a found Paybox PIN the mobile phone is needed. For the time being that is probably good enough. However, currently data transmitted between a mobile phone and the Paybox server is travelling in clear text through all fixed network parts, in particular the Paybox account PIN. This shows an existing security risk and should be solved with an end-to-end encryption mechanism.

## 4.6 Sonera Mobile Pay

Sonera Mobile Pay is a payment solution for soft-drink vending machines, shell car-wash, candy and snacks, video renting, parking machines, operator products and Internet purchases. The amount spent can be charged on the phone bill, bank account or credit card. The payment system is (currently) concentrated on Finland. The security of their payment system is developed in co-operation with SmartTrust Ltd. Since SmartTrust has several security solutions it is not clear which one is used. The information available is that the feature that a customer can authenticate a payment by inserting a 4-digit PIN is optional. The user is informed via SMS about the price.

## 4.7 TopUp

TopUp by SmartTrust [SmartTrust] is also an operator centric pre-paid mobile payment solution. Sonera SmartTrust Ltd is a complete subsidiary of Sonera Corporation [Sonera]. There exists an Internet and a mobile payment solution. The rollout has started in November 2000. The basic idea is that the customer can refill or "top-up" his prepaid account. The customer registers to TopUp where the customer identity and payment method (for example credit card number) is stored. This payment system is designed to add new e-commerce services later. The transaction for adding new value to the prepaid account runs as follows:

1. The top up process is initiated by selecting the service menu from the main menu on the phone.
2. The customer selects the desired amount.
3. The selection is then confirmed with a digital signature that is activated after entering a PIN (digitally signed SMS via 3DES).
4. When the top up request is signed it will be sent to the SmartTrust TopUp application. There it will be checked, if the digital key corresponds to the user identity.
5. The user's account is then credited.
6. The user receives a confirmation including the new balance.

During step 5 after authorization in step 4, the corresponding payment mechanism (e.g. credit card number) is retrieved from the payment method database.

A payment authorization request incl. name and payment method is prepared and submitted for authorization to the payment clearance gateway.

This database contains many very sensitive data and is likely to be a target for attacks.

From the privacy point of view, we would just like to state the following sentences from the SmartTrust webpages:

*"Improved customer relationship: The convenience of the SmartTrust TopUp solution will motivate end users to register for the service. The prepaid customer will no longer be an anonymous one. SmartTrust TopUp provides the mobile operator with tools to profile the customer more accurately, by monitoring individual and collective spending habits."*

# 5. CONCLUSIONS

*Table 7.* Comparison of security methods

| Payment System | Security methods |
|---|---|
| GiSMo | GSM-encryption; PIN |
| Jalda | GSM-encryption; PIN; digital signature; SSL (WPKI, password can be added) |
| Mint | GSM-encryption; PIN; SSL |
| Net900 | SSL (partial); PIN; passphrase |
| Paybox | GSM-encryption; PIN; call-back mechanism |
| Sonera Mobile Pay | GSM-encryption; PIN (optional) |
| TopUp | GSM-encryption; PIN; digital signature |

There exist many good ideas and approaches for mobile payment applications, but the technical implementations are currently not as secure as they could be. Most mobile payment systems try to facilitate the use of "older" but widely distributed mobile phones to a high degree, though these phones are not provisioned with e.g. signing techniques and encryption procedures. It can be expected that the security of the payment systems increases according to the market share of phones able to support this. But the awareness concerning customer privacy develops very slowly.

# 6. ABBREVIATIONS

| | |
|---|---|
| API | Application Programming Interface |
| DES | Data Encryption Standard |
| EFT | Electronic Fund Transfer |
| HLR | Home Location Register |
| HTML | Hypertext Mark-up Language |
| IETF | Internet Engineering Task Force |
| ISP | Internet Service Provider |
| GSM | Global System for Mobile Communications |
| MSC / DIA: | Mobile Switching Center with Direct Internet Access |
| PIN | Personal Identification Number |
| PKCS | Public Key Cryptographic Standar |
| PKI | Public Key Infrastructure |
| POS | Point of Sales |
| PSTN | Public Switched Telephone Network |
| RSA | Rivest Shamir Adleman (Public key cryptosystem) |
| RTT | Round Trip Time |
| SET | Secure Electronic Transactions |
| SIM | Subscriber Identity Module |
| SMS | Short Message Service |
| SSL | Secure Sockets Layer |
| TLS | Transport Layer Security |
| UMTS | Universal Mobile Telecommunications Systems |
| WAP | Wireless Application Protocol |
| WIM | Wireless Identity Module |
| WTLS | Wireless Transport Layer Security |

# 7. REFERENCES

[EHPT] http://www.ehpt.com/
[EMC] Market Intelligence for World Wireless Industry http://www.emc-database.com/
[GiSMo] http://www.GiSMo.net/
[GSM] The GSM System for Mobile Communications; M. Mouly, M.-B. Pautet; Cell & Sys, 1992
[IETF] Internet Engineering Task Force http://www.ietf.org/
[Jalda] http://www.jalda.com/
[Mint] http://www.mint.nu/
[Mobile Pay] Sonera Mobile Pay http://www.sonera.fi/english/solutions/mobilepay/
[Net900] http://www.in-medias-res.com/net900.htm
[Paybox] http://www.paybox.de
[SmartTrust] Sonera SmartTrust Ltd. http://www.smarttrust.com/
[Sonera] Sonera Corporation http://www.sonera.fi/english/
[TopUp] http://www.sonera.fi/ ; http://www.smarttrust.com
[UMTS] UMTS Forum http://www.umts-forum.org/
[WAP] WAP Forum http://www.wapforum.org/
[WPKI] Wireless Public Key Infrastructure http://www.wapforum.org/

47

# An Adoption Framework for Mobile Commerce

Per E. Pedersen
*Agder University College*

**Abstract**: Most often, technological explanations are given of Europe's slow adoption of mobile commerce. When seeking non-technological explanations, diffusion models provide aggregated explanations of adoption processes while adoption models suggest explanations limited to supply side or demand side issues separately. In this paper, an adoption framework is suggested that integrates technological, business strategic and demand side requirements for adoption of mobile commerce end-user services. The framework may be used as a research framework for integrating adoption models and adoption study findings in mobile commerce. It may also be used as an evaluation framework for network operators and other participants in the mobile commerce value chain when developing their services and business models.

## 1. INTRODUCTION

In a much sited Ovum-report, the number of mobile commerce users is expected to be more than 500 million in 2005, and the corresponding value of mobile commerce transactions is expected to be more than US$ 200 billion (Davidson et al., 2000). This is one of several recent analyst reports that have contributed to the hyped expectations of what may be gained by giving mobile terminal users access to the Internet. We define mobile commerce as electronic commerce when accessing the Internet using mobile terminals. This implies using mobile data services. While the data-based traffic volume is now larger than the voice-based volume in fixed networks, traffic volumes in mobile networks are still primarily voice-based. In Scandinavia, SMS has contributed to increased data traffic, but other data-based services, such as WAP have so far not been very successful. Often, technological explanations such as low bandwidth and interface limitations, are given for the slow adoption of these services. Technologies like HSCSD and GPRS may overcome many of these limitations, but our suggestion is that non-technological explanations are necessary as well. The case of the Japanese I-mode service is often used to illustrate that other reasons for the slow adoption must be addressed. Initially, the bandwidth, interface and service functionalities of the I-mode service were very similar to the European WAP-based services of today. Still, more than 19 million I-mode subscribers are now using the service[63]. When confronted with this success, European operators often refer to non-technical explanations, such as cultural differences between Japanese and European mobile phone users, different pricing schemes, and different user experiences due to the packet switching technology of the I-mode service (Stiehler and Wichmann, 2000). Consequently, technological and non-technological explanations should be combined to understand Europe's slow adoption of mobile Internet, and consequently of mobile commerce.

To better understand the integration of technical and non-technical adoption requirements, we suggest an adoption framework specifying both supply side and demand side requirements for adoption. The framework is not a theory, but a framework for integrating different theories and models into an understanding of the technological and non-technological requirements of adoption. As such, it serves two purposes. First, it may be used as a research framework for integrating technological, business strategic and behavioral studies of mobile commerce and mobile end-user service adoption. Second, it may be used by network operators and other participants in the mobile commerce value chain as a framework for modeling and predicting end-user service adoption. The framework divides adoption requirements into supply and demand side requirements. Supply side requirements are further split into technological and business strategic requirements. Demand side requirements are further split into individual, social and cultural requirements.

In the next section, the framework is presented. The rest of the paper elaborates on the technological, business strategic and demand side requirements in sections 3, 4, and 5, respectively. In the final section we conclude on how the framework can be applied by operators and other suppliers in the mobile commerce value chain to understand the particular adoption requirements they face. Finally, some suggestions on how we plan to apply, refine and further develop our framework are presented.

## 2. THE ADOPTION FRAMEWORK

The simplest adoption models focus on technological supply side issues only, and introduce a phase model of technology development. These phase models are applied to predict when certain technological requirements will be met and a end-user service may be introduced (e.g. Müller-Versee, 2000; James, 2000). Predicting what happens after the end-user service has been introduced is typically left to aggregated diffusion models (Mahajan and Muller, 1990; Rogers, 1995). Diffusion

[63] As of February 18, 2001. Continuously updated figures are available at http://www.nttdocomo.com/i/inumber.html.

models predict adoption as an S-shaped function of time after the service has been introduced. The S-shaped adoption rate was originally explained by a simultaneous communication of innovations using two channels – personal communication and mass media (Rogers, 1995). The continuous diffusion function may also be replaced by a discontinuous, phase transition model (e.g. Loch & Huberman, 1999).

The three terms diffusion-, adoption- and innovation models are often used interchangeably in studies of technology adoption. While diffusion models are models of the aggregate rate of adoption of a technology or service, adoption models try to specify the conditions and requirements for adoption at the industry, firm and individual level (Frambach et al. 1998). Even though such requirements are found at both the supply side and at the demand side, adoption models typically focus the demand side requirements and demand side explanations of adoption (Frambach, 1993). Recently, models integrating supply and demand side explanations of adoption have become more common (e.g. Frambach, 1993). Innovation models may apply elements of both diffusion and adoption models but are often more practically oriented. They go beyond pure adoption, and also seek to explain how technology and services are used, how use spreads in and across organizations, and how the use of services turns into standard routines. In these models, the characteristics of the technology, user context and users are important. Rogers (1995) discuss some of the relevant characteristics of the technology, such as relative advantage, compatibility, complexity and testability. These are all supply side characteristics. At the demand side, users are often categorized as early adopters, early majority users, late adopters etc. The classic innovation study typically contrasts the technology requirements of different user categories to explain the adoption process a posteriori.

The framework presented here is best classified as an adoption model framework. It specifies important adoption requirements at the industry, firm and individual level at both the supply and demand sides. Figure 1 shows the adoption framework and its supply- and demand sides. The supply side is organized as a value chain to illustrate that the supply side involves a large set of technology-, service- and application suppliers as well as the interactions among these participants. For example, adoption of mobile commerce requires that the technology platforms and service technologies of these participants are widely adopted among service providers and application developers.

*Figure 1.* The adoption framework

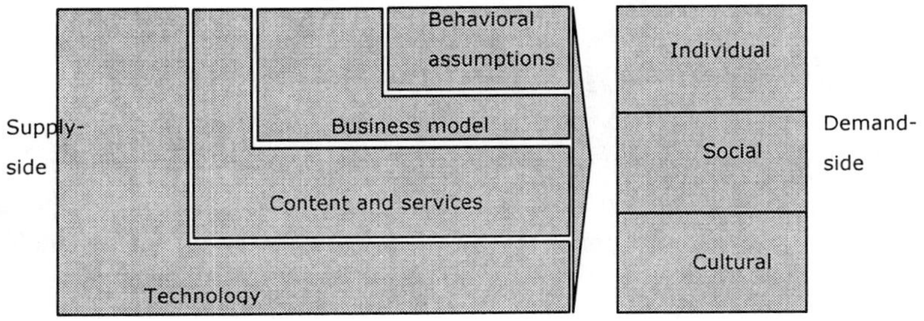

The demand side may not be studied from the perspective of the user as an individual only, but the users' social and cultural context must also be included. For example, the social interaction among users are important not only to understand how mobile commerce innovations are communicated among end-users, but also to understand how these services are adopted to maintain and coordinate social networks.

At the end of the supply side of the value chain, service providers must deliver end-user services that are in demand. Specifying the requirements for introducing these end-user services start with specifying the technological requirements for producing and distributing these services. Next, technology is used by application developers to turn content, network services and related services into end-user services that users are willing to pay for. The infrastructure necessary for this production and distribution, however, is not only purely technological. It also contains the business models and behavioral assumptions of all participants in the value chain. For example, end-user services in mobile commerce gain from direct network effects that turn into indirect network effects in the value chain (Gupta et al., 1999). Consequently, the principles used when these participants define their business models must take indirect network effects into consideration. Similarly, the behavioral assumptions held by these participants must include considerations of how direct network effects operate and affect service demand. To emphasize the importance of these issues, our framework separates technological and business related issues on the supply side of the mobile commerce value chain, and we discuss these issues in sections 3 and 4 respectively.

Most adoption models applied to the demand side rely on a specific user model, such as the Davis' technology acceptance model (TAM) (Davis, 1993) or the theory of planned behavior model (TPB) of Ajzen and Maddon (1986). These models provide a technology-user perspective on the adoption process only. However, technology, and in particular end-user services, are always applied in a richer context. For communication technologies, this context is represented by the end-users' social and cultural situation. For example, end-user services in mobile commerce are applied in the social context of families and groups of close friends. To fully understand the importance of such contexts, models and studies of adoption must apply multiple, context sensitive models. In section 5, we suggest three context sensitive models that may be applied simultaneously to understand the demand side requirements for adoption of mobile commerce end-user services.

## 3. TECHNOLOGICAL REQUIREMENTS

Even though satisfying the technological requirements of adoption is not enough, these requirements are fundamental to the production and distribution of end-user services in mobile commerce. Our framework splits the technological requirements into technology and service requirements. The technology requirements include the requirements of network technologies, terminal technologies and service technologies necessary for the production and distribution of end-user services. New network technologies are introduced to produce higher bandwidth and provide a platform for new services like location based services or always-on functionality. Even though technologies like Enhanced GPRS (EDGE) and UMTS are important in providing such functionality, we do not yet know very much about their performance in real time settings (e.g. Lopez, 2000). While waiting for these technologies, non-regulated technologies like e.g. IEEE802.11b are adopted by professional users to satisfy their bandwidth and always-on requirements. Mobile commerce will not be adopted unless reasonably priced, functional terminal technologies are available. A long history of terminal delays, lack of flash-upgradeable components and a variety of terminal operating systems make end-users fear being locked in. For example, a standards battle is fought between mobile terminal operating system providers like Symbian (Epoc), Palm (PalmOS) and Microsoft (WindowsCE/PocketPC). Similar standards battles are found between providers of important service technologies necessary to produce and distribute mobile commerce end-user services. Examples are the standards battles between content and presentation format standards (e.g. WML, XHTML, cHTML and MeXe) and between providers of public key infrastructure service technology (e.g. Entrust and Baltimore).

The service requirements include the network services, content services, and related services necessary for the production and distribution of end-user services. Because there has traditionally been a difference between the telecom and computer software industries in their definition of the service concept (UMTS-Forum, 2000a), the relationship between basic services, applications and end-user services is illustrated in figure 2.

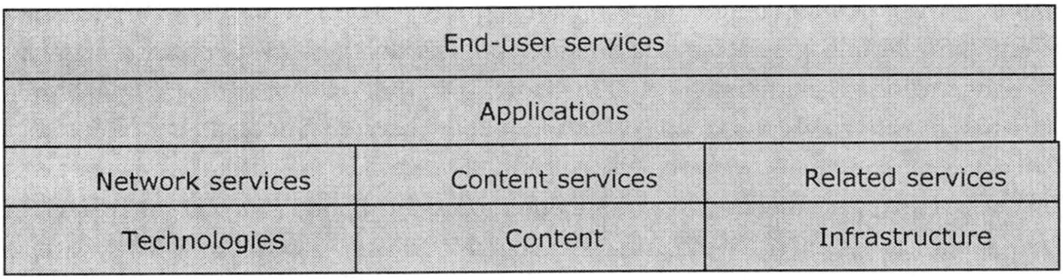

| End-user services | | |
|---|---|---|
| Applications | | |
| Network services | Content services | Related services |
| Technologies | Content | Infrastructure |

*Figure 2.* Network-, content- and related services

As shown in figure 2, technologies are exposed to application developers through network services and content is exposed to application developers through content services. End-user services are services that are in demand and consequently, end-users pay for. To design these services, application developers often apply related services as well. An example of this is the provision of location based product catalogs. Location services are made available to application developers by the network operators' using location technology. Product, vendor numbers and map information are available to application developers by content providers as a content service. To design the end-user service, the application developer may also rely on related services, like for example a payment service provided by a bank. While operators traditionally have been paid directly for their network services (like data and voice), mobile commerce will require a completely different service and payment model. Standards battles, like those referred to above, are also fought between providers of network-, content-, and related services. As an example, consider the battle of banks, operators and network technology suppliers to determine standards for mobile payments (see Dahlström, 2000). In addition to resolving standards battles, there are other service requirements that must be met for widespread adoption of mobile commerce. For example, consider the problem of service roaming. As long as operators' payment models were based upon network services, the number of services was small, and roaming and interconnection issues were easily resolved. In 3G, end-users will require end-user service roaming, but this will require complex roaming agreements and solutions among operators.

The technological requirements are only met when the three categories of technical and the three categories of service requirements are simultaneously met. No single participant in the mobile commerce value chain controls these technologies and services. Thus, no single participant can set and define the necessary standards to guarantee compatibility across the necessary technologies and services. Even though many cross-organizational initiatives have been taken to guarantee the necessary openness and compatibility of technologies and services (e.g. Symbian for terminal operating systems, MET for payment services, and Radicchio for PKI infrastructure), standards battles are still fought at all stages of the mobile commerce value chain. Generally, there is a danger that these standards battles obstruct common agreement on compatibility, and as a result, slow down the adoption of mobile commerce (see Shapiro and Varian, 1999).

Understanding the interaction of technology and services in mobile commerce is not straight forward. Consequently, modeling this interaction in an attempt to predict when the technological requirements of adoption will be met is even less straight forward. However, recently several theoretical contributions have been made on how complementarities, standards battles and network effects can be taken into account when modeling the complex relationships of technologies and services (see Schoder, 2000 for examples). These theories may be operationalized and fit into our adoption framework in an attempt to model the technological requirements for adoption.

# 4. BUSINESS STRATEGIC REQUIREMENTS

Even if the technological requirements for adoption of mobile commerce are met, this is not sufficient for widespread adoption. For example, lack of critical mass may occur at both the supply and demand side. At the supply side, critical mass also means sufficient diversity of end-user services for selection processes to determine what kind of end-user services will finally be adopted. To reach supply side critical mass, the business models of mobile commerce value chain participants must support service diversity. Furthermore, a critical mass of application developers and service providers must adopt the technology and service platforms necessary to develop end-user services. In the value chain participants' choice of business models, the business strategic foundation for widespread adoption of mobile commerce is laid.

Even though there are many definitions of what is meant by a business model (Timmers, 2000, Mahadevan, 2000), we concentrate on two major strategic decisions that participants in the mobile commerce value chain must make – the boundary decision and the cooperation decision. The boundary decision is the clarification of the participant's horizontal and vertical integration in the value chain (Williamsson, 1985). In our perspective, the boundary decision includes decisions on integration direction, integration, strategy, integration model and integration form. By integration direction we mean that for all its activities, the firm must decide whether it will expand or contract horizontally or vertically. By integration strategy we mean that for all its activities, the firm must chose the basis for its scale economy – traditional scale or scope. By integration model we mean that the firm must decide how transactions that are not within hierarchical control will be governed. In transaction cost economics, this is termed governance form. Finally, the combination of integration direction, strategy and model is not arbitrary. Combinations of the three dimensions constitute specific integration forms. In traditional electronic commerce a set of successful integration forms can be identified (e.g. Pedersen and Methlie, 2001), and it is likely that the same will be the case in mobile commerce. To illustrate the boundary decision, consider a network operator's situation. The operator must decide if it should take control over functions otherwise performed by other upstream or downstream participants in the value chain, or if it should take control over other operators or customers in a horizontal direction. It must also decide how different markets and customers should be served in focused or undifferentiated manners. For the transactions it does not control hierarchically, the right integration model must be chosen for each transaction. For example, some transactions may be controlled by referring customers to a different service provider, while other transactions may be controlled by licensing and agent agreements with other providers. Typically, the more vertical the integration direction, the more undifferentiated the integration strategy, and the more hierarchical the integration model of the operator, the more the operator's business model equals the operator model used in 2G networks. In 3G networks, this business model may not support the necessary diversity of end-user services, and consequently slow the adoption of mobile commerce.

The cooperation decision is choosing what cooperation and revenue sharing models should be used. In transaction cost economics, the cooperation model is often treated as a special governance form, but in industries with strong direct and indirect network effects, the cooperation decision may require separate treatment (Antonelli, 2000, Gulati et al., 2000). It is assumed that due to reduced coordination cost, increasing service complexity, and standardization, the mobile commerce value chain will become more like traditional electronic commerce value chains. This implies a more disintegrated model will replace the traditional "walled garden" model of the 2G networks (Barnett et al., 2000, UMTS-Forum, 2000b). In traditional electronic commerce, the observed multiplexity of cooperation models goes far beyond what should be expected when analytically treating cooperation models as governance forms only. Syndication models, licensing agreements and affiliate programs are only some of the cooperation models found in traditional electronic commerce. Generally, the observed cooperation models seem to be more open and under less transactional control than what should be expected when analyzing the dyadic relationship of the cooperation partners separately. One of the main reasons is that direct network effects on the demand side translate into indirect network effects in the value chains of complementary goods (Gupta, et al., 1999). In industries of strong network effects, the cooperation model should not be decided by only analyzing the dyadic relationships between producers of complementary goods. For example, operators should not determine how to cooperate with content providers by only investigating complementarity between content and delivery platforms. There may be horizontal indirect network effects among content providers, and the operator must take these effects into consideration when designing their cooperation models. In general, such considerations may result in the choice of more open cooperation models than separate dyadic considerations suggest.

Open cooperation models may be important to take advantage of direct and indirect network effects, but are likely to create revenue sharing problems in mobile commerce. Due to loose coupling of value creation and revenue generation in value chains of complementary goods (Economides, 1998), strong participants may be tempted to use monopoly power to maximize their own revenue while participants in more competitive parts of the value chain are left with little revenue even though their complementary products are extremely important to customer value. To avoid this situation, revenue sharing models may be implemented in value chains with strong indirect network effects. Revenue sharing agreements are not uncommon in telecom, but they are usually based upon an understanding of the importance of direct, and not indirect, network effects. For example, operators have a long tradition of interconnection and roaming agreements. These are horizontal revenue sharing models, but it seems much more difficult to create similar vertical revenue sharing agreements. One reason may be that the direct network effects are obvious in horizontal revenue sharing agreements while the indirect network effects from vertical revenue sharing agreements are more concealed.

To understand and study the boundary and cooperation decisions of participants in the mobile commerce value chain, we suggest the application of two theoretical perspectives. Transaction cost theory is fundamental to understanding boundary spanning and the boundary decision. It has previously been applied to understand boundary decisions in traditional telecom value chains (e.g. Brousseau and Quelin, 1996). Recently, it has also been applied to the analysis of boundary decisions in traditional electronic commerce (e.g. Brousseau, 1999, Pedersen and Methlie, 2001). We also suggest that transaction cost theory should be supplemented with theory of increasing returns to understand the importance of network effects. Recently, attempts have been made to refine demand side oriented increasing returns theory to better understand supply side issues, such as indirect network effects and horizontal complementarity (Schoder, 2000, Wendt et al., 2000, Weitzel et al., 2000). This line of research is well suited to help us understand the cooperation decision of participants in the mobile commerce value chain.

## 5. DEMAND SIDE REQUIREMENTS

Demand side adoption is typically studied at the aggregate level using diffusion models (Mahajan and Muller, 1990). Even though the original Bass-model has been refined in recent models, these models have been criticized for treating network effects at the aggregate level only (Schoder, 2000). In our adoption framework, we are more concerned with understanding the individual adoption decisions of individual end-users. We assume that the end-user context defines a set of context specific adoption requirements. To understand these requirements, three different perspectives is suggested here. With each perspective follows specific theories, models and methods. The three perspectives are: 1) The end-user as a technology user; 2) The end-user as a consumer; and 3) The end-user as a network member. In the following, we discuss each of these perspectives and how they may be applied to understanding the mobile commerce adoption requirements of end-users.

Adoption of end-user services in mobile commerce may be treated as technology adoption. Several perspectives have been applied to understand technology adoption from the individual end-user perspective. Among these are the TAM model of Davis (1993) and the TPB model of Ajzen and Maddon (1986). Applying the TAM model means investigating the requirements of end-users regarding utility and user friendliness. However, in the TAM model, utility and user friendliness affect users' attitudes towards services. By including the attitude concept, Davis (1993) stresses the importance of user requirements being based upon perceived utility and user friendliness rather than some "objective" measure. When compared to the TPB model of Ajzen and Maddon (1986), the TAM model lacks sufficient consideration of the importance of expectations. For services with strong network effects, the importance of expectations should not be underestimated (Shapiro and Varian, 1998). Two of the main sources of end-user expectations are the communication of expectations by other users and by mass media. Two important issues are raised when applying the TAM model to the adoption of mobile commerce. First, instrumental utility is insufficient to obtain widespread adoption of end-user services. Second, the divergence between communicated expectations and user perceptions may seriously affect end-users' long term attitudes towards these services and slow individual end-user adoption.

Even though the user may be perceived as a technology user, mobile commerce end-user services are applied in a consumer context. Adoption models with a consumer orientation traditionally focus what is termed the "first-purchase decision" (Mahajan and Muller, 1990). These models are well suited for understanding the adoption of individual consumer goods. However, most end-user services in mobile commerce will be integrated services closely related to the consumption of other physical or informational goods. For example, in addition to traditional complementarity, many end-user services in mobile commerce will be added value services suited to serve post decisional phases of the consumer life cycle. Examples of such services are interactive manuals, user-group interaction services and services for the social consumption of goods (e.g. coordinating social restaurant visits or social travel). To understand the adoption processes of these services, traditional decision based models of the "first-purchase decision" should be supplemented with models of the consumers' post-decisional buying behavior (see e.g. Foxall, 1999). Two important issues are raised by this perspective. First, mobile commerce end-user services are not context independent services that will have their separate adoption process. Instead, the adoption of these services will depend upon the adoption of complementary and integrated physical goods and services. Second, consumption context and history will be important in the adoption of mobile commerce. For example, adoption of these services should be treated rather as a transition between stages of increasing consumer sophistication than as "first-purchase adoption". In this perspective, consumer learning history and stage in the consumer life cycle should be parts of the applied adoption model.

A second consequence of taking the end-user context into consideration is taking the role of end-users as network members seriously. The network perspective is focused in network theories of diffusion (e.g. Valente and Davies, 1999). In these aggregate diffusion theories, the importance of communication between network members and the social position of network members are taken into consideration. Even though these issues are important to understand adoption, they apply equally well to all innovations that are communicated through social networks. It does not focus the unique functionality of mobile commerce end-user services as services for mediating and coordinating communication in consumer oriented networks. To understand these functionalities, the different network contexts of individual end-users must be understood. There is no single authoritative typology of networks or social groupings that may be applied to categorize network contexts (Wellmann, 1999). In our framework, we apply a typology of networks with increasing complexity - from the simplest personal and relational networks to the networks of networks. When considering the network member's participation in several networks of different complexity, the importance of mobile end-user services as a mediating and coordinating technology is better understood. For example, end-user services may be applied to maintain the virtual home environment (VHE) of the user across network contexts. They may further be applied to maintain and coordinate network relationships between brands and individual consumers, and they may be applied to coordinate the traditional social networks of families or friends in consumer contexts (Ling and Yttri, 2001). Without taking these different network contexts into consideration, analysts of mobile commerce services may lack a very important explanatory element in their adoption models.

## 6. CONCLUSIONS AND FURTHER RESEARCH

We have proposed an adoption framework that can be used as a framework for integrating adoption theories, models and findings at the supply and demand side of the mobile commerce value chain. It includes the integration of technological, business strategic and demand side requirements for the widespread adoption of mobile commerce. The framework should not be treated as an attempt to integrate or replace traditional diffusion models, but serves three purposes. First, it stresses the integration of technological and non-technological requirements for widespread adoption of mobile commerce. Because both analyst reports and professional evaluations of future adoption of mobile commerce have focused technological requirements, emphasizing the integration of technological and non-technological requirements now seem in order. Second, the framework may be used by researchers of mobile commerce to position their contribution to the understanding of end-user services adoption. It emphasizes that currently, no single diffusion or adoption model can be applied to fully understand the complex adoption requirements of mobile commerce. Finally, the framework may be used by participants in the mobile commerce value chain as a framework for understanding the adoption requirements facing their technologies, network services, applications and end-user services. The suggested theories and models we apply to understand each of the different requirement types may also be used by both researchers and value chain participants to get a deeper understanding of the complexity of the mobile commerce adoption process.

In our research group we have used the framework to position and direct different research activities into understanding these adoption requirements. From a technological requirement perspective, we have started simulation studies modeling the relationship between network services, content services and related services using dynamic simulation methodology. From a business strategic perspective, we have started refining transaction cost and network effect models into an integrated model of the cooperation model selection process. The model will be applied to descriptive studies of the cooperation models of firms in traditional electronic and mobile commerce. From a demand side perspective, we have started to develop a context specific adoption model of the mobile commerce end-user. This model will be applied to descriptive and experimental studies of mobile commerce end-user service adoption.

# 7. REFERENCES

Ajzen I. and Madden, T.J. (1986). "Prediction of goal-directed behavior – Attitudes, intentions and perceived behavioral control", *Journal of Experimental Social Psychology*, Vol. 22, No. 5, pp. 453-474.

Dahlström, E. (2000). "The common future of wallets and ATM's? Mobile phones!", *ePSO Newsletter*, Vol. 1, No. 1, pp. 5-7.

Davidson, J, Walsh, A. and Brown, D. (2000). "*Mobile commerce market strategies*". Research report, Ovum Research, March.

Davis, F.D. (1993). "User acceptance of information technology: system characteristics, user perceptions and behavioral impacts". *International Journal of Man-Machine Studies*, Vol. 38, No. 3, pp. 475-487.

Foxall, G.R. (1999). "Putting consumer behavior in its place: the Behavioural Perspective Model research program". *International Journal of Management Reviews*, Vol, 1, No. 2, pp. 133-159.

Frambach, R.T. (1993). "An integrated model of organizational adoption and diffusion of innovations. *European Journal of Marketing"*, Vol. 27, No. 5, pp. 22-41.

Frambach, R.T., Barkema, H.G., Nooteboom, B. and Wedel, M. (1998). "Adoption of a service innovation in the business market: an empirical test of supply-side variables". *Journal of Business Research*, No. 41, pp. 161-174.

Gupta, S., Jain, D.C., and Sawhney, M.S. (1999). "Modeling the Evolution of Markets with Indirect Network Externalities: An Application to Digital Television". *Marketing Science*, Vol. 18, No. 3, pp. 396-416.

James, U. (2000). "*Introductory 3G Presentation.*" Presentation held at Nokia 3G Business Seminar, New York, June.

Ling, R. and Yttri, B. 2001. "Nobody Sits at Home and Waits for the Telephone to Ring: Micro and Hyper-Coordination Through the Use of the Mobile Telephone". Forthcoming in J. Katz and M. Aakhus (eds.), *Perpetual Contact*, Cambridge: Cambridge University Press.

Loch, C.H. and Huberman, B.A. (1999). A punctuated-equilibrium model of technology diffusion. *Management Science*, Vol. 45, No. 2, pp. 160-177.

Lopez, J.R. (2000). "*Implementing GPRS Services*". Presentation held at the Nokia Mobile Internet Conference, Prague, November 22-23, 2000.

Mahajan, V. and Muller, E. (1990). "New product diffusion models in marketing: A review and directions for research". *Journal of Marketing*, Vol. 54, No. 1, pp. 1-27.

Mahadevan, B. (2000). "Business Models for Internet based E-Commerce: An anatomy". *California Management Review*. Vol.42, No.2, pp. 55-.

Müller-Versee, F. (2000). "*Mobile Commerce*". Research Report, Durlacher Research Ltd.

Pedersen, P.E. and Methlie, L.B. (2001). "Integrators' business models in electronic markets". Forthcoming in *Magma*, Vol. 4, No 1 (in Norwegian).

Rogers, E.M. (1995). "*Diffusion of innovations*" (4. ed.). New York, The Free Press.

Shapiro, C. & Varian, H. (1999). "*Information rules*". Boston, MA: Harvard Business School Press.

Stiehler, A. and Wichmann, T. (2000). "Mobile Internet in Japan – lessons for Europe ?". *ePSO Newsletter*, Vol. 1, No. 2, pp. 13-15.

Schoder, D. (2000). "Forecasting the success of telecommunication services in the presence of network effects". *Information Economics and Policy*, Vol. 12, No. 2, pp. 181-200.

Timmers, P. (2000). "*Electronic commerce. Strategies and models for business-to-business trading*". Chichester, Wiley.

UMTS-Forum (2000a). "*The UMTS Third Generation Market - Structuring the Service Revenues Opportunities*". UMTS.Forum Report no. 9, UMTS-Forum, September

UMTS-Forum (2000b). "*Shaping the Mobile Multimedia Future - An Extended Vision from the UMTS Forum*". UMTS.Forum Report no. 10, UMTS-Forum, September.

Valente, T.W. and Davis, R.I. (1999). "Accellerating the diffusion of innovations using opinion leaders". *The Annals of the American Academy of the Political and Social Sciences*, Vol 566, November, pp. 55-67.

Weitzel, T., Wendt, O., and Westarp, F. v. (2000). Reconsidering Network Effect Theory. *Proceedings of the ECIS 2000: European Conference on Information Systems*, July, Wien.

Wellman, B. (1999). The Network Community: An Introduction to Networks in the Global Village. I Wellman, B. (red.), *Networks in the Global Village*, pp. 1-47. Boulder, CO, Westview Press.

Wendt, O. ,Westarp, F.v., and Konig, W. (2000). Diffusion processes in markets for network effect goods - Determinants, simulation model, and market classification. *Wirtschaftsinformatik*, Vol. 42, No. 5, pp. 422 (in German).

Williamson, O. (1985). "*The economic institutions of capitalism: Firms, markets, relational contracting*". New York: Free Press.

48

# Diffusion Models in Analysing Emerging Technology-Based Services

Lauri Frank[1] and Jukka Heikkilä[2]
*Lappeenranta University of Technology[1], Finland*
*University of Jyväskylä[2], Finland*

**Abstract:** In this article we discuss the problems of utilizing innovation diffusion (or, adoption) models in developing scenarios for mobile commerce services in three European countries: Finland, Germany, and Greece. We are not to test the various diffusion models as such, but rather to utilise the fundamental ideas of the models in determining the prerequisites for, the status of, and the pace of diffusion of mobile services in these different market areas. The estimates would serve as a starting point and as a validity check for scenario development. The early experience at the research design phase show that the 'mainstream' diffusion approach is vulnerable to three factors specific to the adoption of services that are subject to technical change and development: *'layered' adoption process in its social context, supply side,* and *continuous technical development.*

## 1. THE DIFFUSION OF MOBILE SERVICES

In this article we discuss the problems of utilizing innovation diffusion (or, adoption) models in developing scenarios for mobile commerce services in three European countries: Finland, Germany, and Greece. From the scenario point of view, we are not to test the various diffusion models as such, but rather to utilise the fundamental ideas of the models in determining the prerequisites for, the status of, and the pace of diffusion of mobile services in these different countries. The estimates would serve as a starting point and as a validity check for scenario development.

We are especially interested in distinguishing the adopter categories as an indication of the progress of diffusion. In the scenarios it would be most useful to be able to depict the situation on each of the three market areas by dividing the respondents in adopter categories according to the well known models of diffusion.

Unfortunately, there is little public information available on the state-of-the-diffusion of mobile services, especially such information tied to the diffusion process[64].

The early experience at the research design phase show that the diffusion approach is vulnerable to three factors specific to the adoption of services that are subject to technical change and development: *'layered' adoption process in its social context, supply side,* and *continuous technical development.*

To cast light on these issues we first analyse and categorise a set of diffusion models in their basic features: in the context of new services we are especially interested in the basic differences between various diffusion adoption models. We first describe the models, categorize them according to the interrelatedness of the adopters' behaviour, uncertainty, and the information handling. In the end we discuss the experiences of utilizing the ideas in finding out the state-of-the diffusion.

## 2. DIFFUSION MODELS

The basic diffusion models can be categorized in many ways, but they all share the sigmoidal cumulative function of growth, or spreading of innovation among the adopter population. Examples of such curves are logistic growth, cumulative normal, Gompertz, and log-normal. Technically, these curves illustrate cumulative density functions of a bell-shaped frequency distribution over a population.

### 2.1 Rogers

The most commonly referred diffusion model is introduced by Rogers in 1983. Rogers sums up the results from more than 3,000 diffusion publications. This impressive summary forms the base of the widely applied model of diffusion, although it is actually a hybrid of a number of models. Despite the fact we call it the mainstream model. According to Rogers, the adopters can be classified by their individual *information processing styles* and by *their use of communication channels*. These are fairly constant characteristics, and determine the innovativeness of the adopters. The innovativeness is argued to be normally distributed among potential adopters, and therefore the cumulative density function of the adopter population is a sigmoid shaped diffusion curve (Heikkilä, 1995).

This statement is quite a strong assumption in favour of unlimited communication within the social system. The adopters are acting independently of each other, but they are *'contaminated'* by increasing unlimited information flow. The normally distributed adopters are divided into five categories according to their

[64] With the notable exception of study of Nokia (1999).

'resistance' to the information. The distribution of adopters over time is presented in Figure 1.

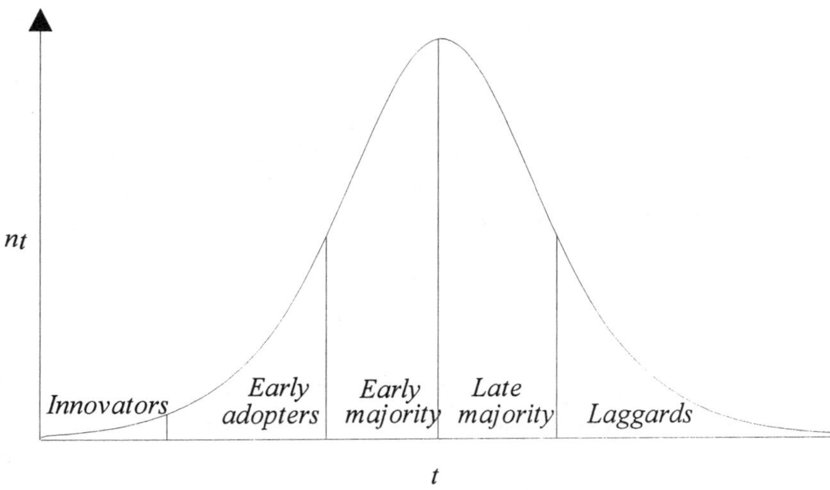


*Figure 1.* Adopter Categories of the Mainstream Innovation Diffusion Model

According to Rogers (1983), there are some change agents and opinion leaders who are important for the success of the innovation. An opinion leader is a pioneer, whose behaviour has an effect on others' attitudes towards an innovation. A change agent tries to persuade a potential adopter to accept and adopt an innovation.

Note that the mainstream diffusion model assumes rational decision-making capabilities only implicitly, as the users are rather contaminated (i.e. obtaining knowledge about the potential) and persuaded to adopt by the increasing exposure to information (Bailey, 1957; c.f. Heikkilä, 1995).

In a later revision of the model, Moore (1998) makes a strong argument for the existence of a *chasm* between early adopters and early majority, especially when the pace of technical development is fast. When the diffusion process moves from the initial stages to early majority, there is a change of logic of diffusion: in the beginning the importance of services is high, later the services as a means of competition are replaced with the capabilities of commercialise, produce and deliver the products efficiently for the masses. The masses rely more on their peers than on the opinion leaders, marketing, etc., It is here, at the chasm located between early adopters and early majority where the markets are won or lost.

The mainstream model consists of following sets of variables, which explain the success of an innovation on the market:

1. The attributes of an innovation. Rogers (1983) argues that the following five characteristics of an innovation are the most important when making the adoption decision: 1. Relative advantage, i.e., "the degree to which an innovation is perceived as being better than the idea it supersedes." (Rogers, 1983, p. 213). These can be perceived in terms of economic profitability, status, etc. 2. Compatibility, i.e., "the degree to which an innovation is perceived as consistent with the existing values, past experiences, and needs of potential adopters" (Rogers, 1983, p. 223). 3. Complexity, i.e., "the degree to which an innovation is perceived as relatively difficult to understand and use" (Rogers, 1983, pp. 230-231). 4. Trialability, i.e., "the degree to which an innovation may be experimented with on a limited basis" (Rogers, 1983, p. 231). 5. Observability, i.e., "the degree to which the results of an innovation are visible to others" (Rogers, 1983, p. 232).
2. The type of innovation decision, i.e., the four generic types of innovation decisions depending on the decision-maker characteristics (Rogers, 1983, Ch. 10): 1. *Choice* - the decision is based solely on the characteristics of the innovation by the individual adopter solely. 2. *Collective* - the decision is based on a commitment of the members to a solution. 3. *Autocratic* - the decision is dependent on authoritative persons. 4. *Conditional* - the decision to adopt is dependent on the preceding innovation adoption decision (contingent innovation decision in Rogers' terminology (1983).
3. The social system characteristics
4. Promotion efforts, and
5. The communication channels. The communication channels have been extensively studied in the earlier research (see e.g. for theoretical work in Lekvall & Wahlbin, 1973; a good example of empirical IS research in Brancheau & Wetherbe, 1990).

The sets of variables appeal to common sense and give a good understanding of the factors affecting the pace of diffusion. However, there are some other considerations not explicitly handled by Rogers.

## 2.2 Decision making models

Although the mainstream model of Rogers (1983) has been successfully applied to various forecasting and descriptive purposes, it has some problems, which must be taken into account. In Rogers's synthesis, an innovation is defined as whatever an adopter finds new in his use situation. Newness itself is not sufficient reason for adoption but it rather implies that the expected net benefits of the innovation must be positive before the adoption takes place. However, the outcomes are uncertain, as the innovation is, by definition, new to the adopter in his social context, and it will take some time before favourable effects on the work become apparent. However, Rogers' model *does not precisely state the relationship between information and uncertainty*. Furthermore, *it assumes an independent individual adopter*, only remarking on the importance of interdependencies between adopters, i.e. his model excludes network effects (also called as externalities Fichman, 1992; c.f. Heikkilä 1995).

### 2.2.1 Uncertain versus Certain Information on the Attributes of Innovation

According to Lippman & McCardle (1991, p. 1475), the probability of adoption depends on the uncertain profitability estimate on the value of the innovation. The uncertainty can be reduced by suspending the adoption and continuing to gather more information on the innovation. If information gathering reveals that the expected discounted value of the innovation exceeds the investment threshold, the search stops, and adoption takes place. If the expected value is insufficient, the innovation is rejected. The probability of adoption is likely to increase when more positive information is gathered, and vice versa. But, the information gathering is costly, reducing the net value of the innovation. To summarise, according to this model, the users select how much they are gathering information against the expected value of the innovation, instead of just becoming contaminated (as in Rogers, 1983).

Additionally, or alternatively, to contagious information as an affecting factor of the diffusion's shape is the uncertainty inhibited by the innovation. For example, Valente (1996) argues that the timing of adoption is affected by social exposure, by which he divides adopters into categories. According to his theory, the different adoption timing of adopters is caused by different risk behaviour. Thus, adopters require a different amount of exposure to the innovation before they adopt it. Also this approach yields a sigmoid diffusion curve assuming that the adopters risk behaviour, and thus their need of exposure, is based on the normal (or a similar) distribution. This is inline with the ideas of Moore (1999).

### 2.2.2 Network effects and strategic behaviour

The externality effect in economic theory means that (some) activities have consequences that affect the well-being of other, external actors. In presence of network externalities wise actors take each other's actions into account, in the network of associated actors, leading to strategic behaviour. The logic is, consequently, somewhat in contrast to the logic of adoption in the pioneering phase, where the adoption was seen as a one-man effort to gain information about the innovation.

To be more specific, when adopting new technical innovations, the novices may learn and be given advice from others, they may benefit from improved architecture, etc. On the other hand, the pioneers benefit from e.g. compatible working practices and increased information exchange (Farrell & Saloner, 1985; Katz & Shapiro, 1986). To relate this to diffusion theory let us look at Figure 2. The Figure illustrates how the net benefits are expected to appear in the future. The 0 level is the adoption threshold, i.e. the net benefits from the innovation are expected to be positive - it is time to adopt. The lower curve shows that the user is to adopt at N1t. But, if a user can rely on help from others and on other similar positive network externality effects, it increases the expected benefits, and thus may hasten the willingness to adopt (dotted curve) to Nt*. The increase in interpersonal relationships in seeking and providing help in computer-related issues was also detected by Brancheau & Wetherbe (1990). According to Rogers' categorisation, this is a kind of 'conditional' decision situation, where the successive adoptions depend on the preceding adoption decisions.

But, many real situations are not so straightforward, e.g., the usefulness of innovation is uncertain, or it may be difficult to shift from the old technology to the new one, because of time constraints, skills, funds, etc. In many cases it is the commitment schemes respond exactly to these problems. They are used to decrease the uncertainty by committing potential adopters to a solution, to allocate resources to the transition, and to tackle the required transformation problems in advance. They are very motivational because of the intertwined benefits of the members of the social system.

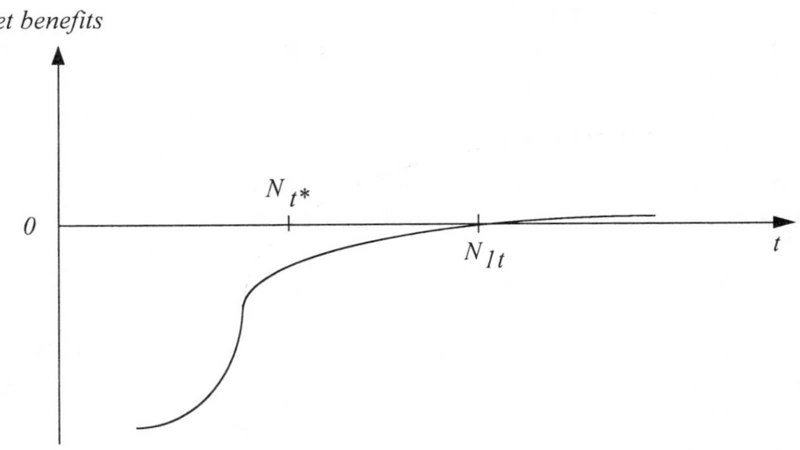


*Figure 2.* Benefits With and Without Positive Network Externalities

### 2.2.3 Observing the behaviour of other adopters

Another type of adoption behaviour in the presence of network effects is that the decision is based rather on opinions, experiences, and *observations of others' behaviour, than on gathering information about the innovation itself.* Clear examples of this are the models of herd behaviour (Scharfstein & Stein, 1990; Banerjee, 1992). It suggests that a decision-maker believes (rationally) that other colleagues, who have already made their decisions, may have some other information, which is important for his own decision-making. So, instead of gathering his own information, and relying on that, he looks at the behaviour of the other colleagues. Unfortunately, this kind of herding is almost always inefficient, although common, especially in the context of adopting technology that must be applied differently in a specific context.

### 2.2.4 Social cohesion

Burt (1987) studies the diffusion of a new drug by observing the doctors prescriptions. He hypotheses two alternative processes: 1) social cohesion: the doctors have got their information from another doctor; 2) structural equivalence: the doctors have acquired information of the drug by acting in a way a doctor acts in his position by, for example, reading medical journals. The first approach yields an analogous result with the basic contagious information (or epidemic) model: a sigmoid curve on the aggregate level. The reasoning behind the structural cohesion model is that information drains from a social group to another. Thus, there is no contagion and the diffusion on aggregate level gains a different form. The results indicate that beside social cohesion also other factors have influenced the diffusion of the drug.

### 2.2.5 Summary of the models

To summarize the differences between different models, we have drawn up the following Table 1, which clearly shows that there are notable differences between the models. The latter models also show crucial factors in the adoption processes not covered properly in Rogers's synthesis.

*Table 1.* Differences between the models

| | **Interrelatedness of decision-makers (externalities)** | **Uncertainty of the object of adoption** | **Object of inquiry in obtaining information about an innovation** |
|---|---|---|---|
| **Mainstream model** (e.g., Rogers, 1983) | Independent non-related individuals | Not explicit | Exposure to information through information channels |
| **Decision theoretic models** (e.g., Lippman & McCardle, 1991) | An independent individual | Technology is uncertain | Uncertainty reduction by gathering more information |
| **Active information gathering** (Valente, 1999) | Independent individuals | Technology is uncertain | Exposure to information, but different reaction depending on the risk attitude |
| **Models with network externalities** (e.g., Farrell & Saloner, 1985) | Individuals with interrelated benefits | Technology is certain | Characteristics of the innovation are known and the behaviour of others is observed |
| **Models of herd behaviour** (e.g., Banerjee, 1992) | Individuals with interrelated benefits | Technology is uncertain | Only the behaviour of others is observed |
| **Social cohesion** (e.g., Burt, 1997) | Individuals with interrelated benefits | Technology is uncertain | Others' behaviour is observed and the technology is tried. Others can mean peers or different social classes (two variants). |

We utilized the table to create a set of questions to analyze the adoption and consequent processes of diffusion for developing the scenarios. Note that we have been concentrating mainly on the population of rational adopters. However, if we are to depict the diffusion process in its real context (e.g., in the very different countries mentioned in the beginning), we should take into account also some of the supply side and temporal issues more explicitly.

# 3. AMENDMENTS TO THE DIFFUSION PROCESS FOR SCENARIOS

The technical development during the diffusion process makes a difference, because it at the same time affects the adopters understanding and maximum potential (new features). Where the mainstream (and most of the other models) assumes a constant maximum potential for one technology generation, it maybe actually growing[65]. One could argue that it is just a matter of defining the technology generations, but we argue that when talking about new services based on changing technology, it is not the case. This is because from the users point of view it is the content of services that matters, not the technology generations. We would like to illustrate these problems with the concepts of *layered adoption process*, and *continuous technical development*.

## 3.1 Layered adoption process

The layered adoption process means that the services can be utilized only after the 'technology stack' is high enough. For example, in order to use mobile services, the user has to acquire a phone (1st level adoption), subscribe the generic services (e.g., switch on voice-mail, text messaging, install and configure WAP; 2nd level adoption), and finally subscribe the value-added services (3rd level adoption; see also Figure 3.). There are few adoption models that take this type of adoption process into account explicitly. Thus it is most important to take this into consideration explicitly when studying diffusion to be utilized in more long-term analysis, such as scenarios in our case.

## 3.2 Continuous technical development

In Rogers's model the maximum potential is defined as a constant, whereas in many cases the technical development increases the maximum potential, i.e., there will be new, first-time adopters. During the process, there will be also earlier adopters choosing to stay with the old technology, choosing to have both the new and old, or switching to the new one. An example of such a process of the 1st level adoption of cellular terminals is depicted in Figure 3 below.

[65] Diffusion in dynamic population is studied, e.g., already by Mahajan & Peterson (1978).

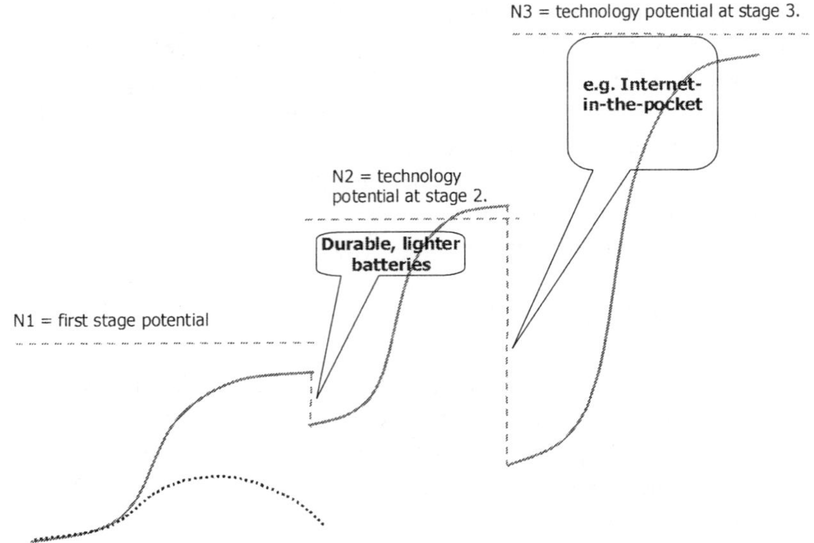


*Figure 3.* Stepwise increase in potential due to technical development

Another, yet different example is the spatial roll-out of new technology, which increases following a concave function instead of a constant, or stepwise maximum potential. For example the maximum potential of GSM-services was determined by the roll-out starting at city centers, densely populated areas and along main roads (lot of traffic). This way a relatively small number of devices could cover most of the potential needs, and it took a longer time to cover the whole area (thus the concave function along time).

# 4. COMBINING DIFFUSION MODELS AND SUPPLY SIDE FOR SCENARIOS

Finally, we would suggest to use the following approach in determining the diffusion for the creating long-term scenarios for services under circumstances of quick technical development. The Mobicom project is to launch studies on consumer behaviour and mobile users demographics, demand-side quantitative analysis of e- & m-commerce and to recognize state-of-the art technology and key players for m-commerce services (see Figure 4), which are to feed in to scenario development. The diffusion/adoption models are depicted on the dotted area.

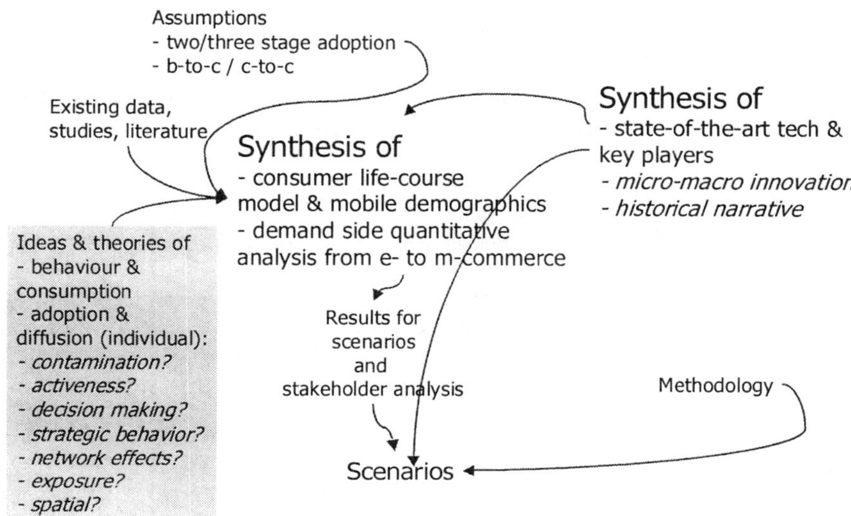


*Figure 4.* The framework for creating scenarios for services in changing technical environment

The scenarios will be built upon the survey results from individual adoption in each of the market areas, where the adoption and diffusion ideas and assumptions are taken into account. As a consequence the survey should supplement the existing literature by casting light on the *adoption and diffusion* in multiple layers. It is also to take into account the *technical development, as it may have* a notable difference on the maximum potential, as argued above. Finally, the research framework should explicitly take into account whether we are talking about b-to-c or c-to-c services. It has been shown in many studies that the innovations change the everyday life, and especially the communication technology adopted in peers is highly social phenomenon (Kopomaa, 2000).

## 5. REFERENCES

Bailey N.T.J., (1957). "The Mathematical Theory of Epidemics", Hafner, New York, NY, 1957.

Banerjee, A.V., (1992). "A Simple Model of Herd Behavior", The Quarterly Journal of Economics, Vol. 107, Issue 3 (Aug. 1992), pp. 797-817.

Brancheau J.C., and Wetherbe J.C., (1990). "The Adoption of Spreadsheet Software: Testing Innovation Diffusion Theory in the Context of End-User Computing", Information Systems Research, Vol. 1, No. 2 (June 1990), pp. 115-143.

Burt, Ronald S. (1987): Social Contagion and Innovation: Cohesion versus Structural Equivalence. American Journal of Sociology, Vol. 92, No. 6, s. 1287–1335.

Farrell J., and Saloner G., (1985). "Standardization, compatibility, and innovation", Rand Journal of Economics, Vol. 16, No. 1 (Spring 1985), pp. 70-83.

Fichman R.G., (1992). "Information Technology Diffusion: A Review of Empirical Research", Proceedings of the 13th International Conference on Information Systems, in Dallas, Texas, December 13-16, 1992, pp. 195-206.

Heikkilä J., (1995). Diffusion of a Learning Intensive Technology Into Organisations: The case of PC-technology, Doctoral Thesis, Helsinki School of Economics and Business Administration A-104, 233 pages.

Katz M.L., and Shapiro C., (1986). "Technology Adoption in the Presence of Network Externalities", Journal of Political Economy,Vol. 94, No. 4, pp. 822-841.

Kopomaa T., (2000). The City in Your Pocket: Birth of the Mobile Information Society, Yliopistokustannus University Press Finland, 143 pages.

Lekvall P., and Wahlbin C., (1973). "A Study of Some Assumptions Underlying Innovation Diffusion Functions", Swedish Journal of Economics, Vol. 75, pp. 362-377.

Lippman S.A., and McCardle K.F., (1991). "Uncertain Search: A Model of Search Among Technologies of Uncertain Values", Management Science, Vol. 37, No. 11 (Nov. 1991), pp. 1474-1490.

Mahajan V., and Peterson R.A., (1978). "Innovation Diffusion in a Dynamic Potential Adopter Population", Management Science, Vol. 24, No. 15 (Nov. 1978), pp. 1589-1597.

Moore G.A. and McKenna R., (1999). "Crossing the Chasm : Marketing and Selling High-Tech Products to Mainstream Customers", Harper Business, 227 pages.

Rogers E.M., (1983). "Diffusion of Innovations", 3rd Ed., The Free Press, New York, 1983, 453 pages.

Scharfstein D.S., and Stein J.C., (1990). "Herd Behavior and Investment", American Economic Review, Vol. LXXX, No. 3 (June 1990), pp. 465-479.

Tonks, Ian (1986): The Demand for Information and the Diffusion of a New Product. International Journal of Industrial Organization 4, s. 397–408.

Valente, Thomas W. (1996): Social Network Thresholds in the Diffusion of Innovations. Social Networks 18, s. 69–89.

## ACKNOWLEDGEMENT

The authors wish to thank the participants of Mobicom –project for their invaluable comments and insight in the problems of studying diffusion in the context of mobile commerce. We owe special thanks to Sanna Hirvola, Antti Aarnio, and Aki Enkenberg. The research is funded by European Commission in its European Fifth Framework Project IST-1999-21000.

MINITRACK FOUR

# E-DEMOCRACY

**Minitrack Chair:**

Ake Gronlund
University of Umea, Sweden, gron@informatik.umu.se

49

# Towards a Democratic Education for E-Government

*A Study of Deliberative Decision-Making via Information and Communications Technology*

Jonathan Foster

*Department of Information Studies, University of Sheffield*

**Abstract**: It has been argued that the widespread use of information and communications technology has contributed to a crisis in traditional systems of representative democracy and that a new form of informational or digital democracy is emerging. Hence a key claim made in current discussions of 'electronic' or 'digital' democracy is that information and communications technologies have a role to play in providing opportunities for government and citizens to engage in direct rather than representative forms of democracy. Using a deliberative democratic framework this paper presents results from a case study of decision-making on a professional development workshop in information and communications technology skills. The discussion highlights some of the problems of engaging in a democratic process that places a premium on deliberation and negotiation. These problems include different conceptions of democracy and of the public good, time constraints, education for democracy; and the relationship between decision-making and action. The paper concludes that if information and communications technology are to help democracy to expand beyond its current representative model and incorporate more direct and deliberative forms then both government and citizens may need to learn procedures as to how to engage in this deliberative process.

## 1. INTRODUCTION

A distinction commonly made in discussing models of democracy is that between classical and modern models (Carr and Hartnett, 1996; Held, 1993, 1987). In the classical model democracy and democratic procedure are based on the direct involvement and participation of the state's citizens in political decisions relevant to the affairs of state. In the modern liberal democratic model a state's citizens temporarily elect professional politicians to take the decisions which help to govern and to regulate the lives of a nation's citizens.

It has been argued that the widespread use of information and communications technology (ICTs) has contributed to a crisis in traditional systems of representative democracy (Castells, 1996) and that a new form of informational (Castells, 1996) or digital democracy (Hague and Loader, 1999) is emerging. Hence, a key claim made during current discussions of 'electronic' or 'digital' democracy is that ICTs have a role to play in providing opportunities for government and citizens to engage in direct rather than representative forms of democracy (Ågren, 2001; Hague and Loader, 1999).

Electronic networks clearly provide potential opportunities for the establishment of civic networks (Tsagarousianou et al., 1998), electronic citizen access and digital government (Dutton, 1999). Furthermore such networks can potentially support not only vertical communication between citizens and government but also horizontal communication between citizen and citizen (Laudon, 1977). Does participation in such networks however constitute a form of authentic involvement in the political process? Is the establishment of such electronic communication networks and services a cost-efficient form of information delivery and of political window-dressing or do citizens have a stake in the final outcome of deliberations? In the words of one commentator:

> ...no amount of high-tech wizardry will convert the pushing of a button or the dialling of a telephone number into an act of deliberation (Bryan, 1998: 162).

In a deliberative democracy it is the responsibility of governments, citizens, computer professionals and others to establish the social conditions for moving from ICT-based information delivery to ICT-based support for meaningful deliberation. This paper presents results from a case study of decision-making on a professional development workshop in ICT skills and highlights some of the problems of engaging in a democratic process that places a premium on deliberation and negotiation. It concludes that if ICTs are to help democracy expand beyond its current representative model and incorporate more direct and deliberative forms then both government and citizens may need to learn procedures as to how to engage in this deliberative process.

## 2. EDUCATION FOR DELIBERATIVE DEMOCRACY

Deliberative democracy is a recent variant of modern democratic models (Bohman and Rehg, 1997). It is a form of government where the conditions under which we live and work are the outcome of a process of decision-making that involves not only the state and professional politicians but also citizens. Key aspects of deliberative democracy include the ethical procedures governing participation in the discussion and the relationship between the discussion and the final outcome of the decision-making process. Theories of deliberative democracy contain parallels with the notion of the public sphere (Habermas, 1973). The public sphere is an interactive domain of civil society occupied by newspapers, television and other media in which open debate and a free flow of information is constrained neither by the state nor by the private interests of capitalism. The establishment of ICT-based civic networks to engage in political dialogue represents a potential expansion of this public sphere into new domains. If a move into electronic services and networks is to truly represent a new form of communication between government and citizen and an expansion of the public sphere into areas outside formal government then participants may find themselves needing to learn procedures that accompany such deliberative forms of democracy. One arena in which citizens and politicians can learn about democracy is within an educational setting.

## 3. THE DEMOCRATIC PHILOSOPHY OF GROUP INVESTIGATION

Group investigation belongs to a family of educational methods that has been called "learning through cooperative disciplined inquiry" (Joyce, Calhoun and Hopkins, 1997). Dominant influences on the development of the group investigation method have been Sharan and Sharan (1994a), Thelen (1981), and Dewey (1916). Group investigation is a disciplined approach to cooperative learning that involves classroom members in the making and taking of decisions on an interdependent basis. An important aspect of the democratic nature of this 'classroom society' is how the process of inquiry, that forms the backbone of the group investigation, is formulated with respect to classroom members' participation, group dynamics and the availability and construction of knowledge. Hence knowledge is developed within and accountable to a process of inquiry that involves each member of the classroom. The parallels with government-citizen and citizen-citizen relations are clear. If citizens and government are to work together more directly via the use of electronic services and networks in a manner that is underpinned by democratic principles and not only economic imperatives then procedures for a more inclusive democratic process need to be developed.

# 4. THE PEDAGOGICAL DESIGN OF A GROUP INVESTIGATION

The standard model of a group investigation is described in Sharan and Sharan (1994a; 1994b). Once the topic to be investigated has been selected and interest in the topic has been generated, the process of inquiry will typically proceed through the following stages.

- Stage 1—Class determines subtopics and organises into research groups
- Stage 2—Groups plan their investigations
- Stage 3—Groups carry out their investigations
- Stage 4—Groups plan their presentations
- Stage 5—Groups make their presentations
- Stage 6—Teacher and students evaluate their projects

As part of an Online Short Course for Staff Developers in ICTs the present writer tutored on a three-week unit on "Collaborative Design" based on the group investigation method. Participants were in the main drawn from university staff across the United Kingdom and abroad who had an organisational role in promoting the use of ICTs within their institutions. The unit was designed such that, for a successful outcome from the process to occur, participants would need to engage in two interconnected activities. Firstly, that the task set be achieved i.e. developing a course design and secondly, that the accomplishment of the task be achieved not unilaterally but through the democratic joint effort of each of the participants. Participants communicated both asynchronously and synchronously via an online text-based conferencing system called *Web Course Tools* (http://www.webct.com). The asynchronous facility consisted of an online conferencing tool or bulletin board that provided opportunities for participants to contribute at different times from different geographical locations. The synchronous facility consisted of a chat tool that provided facilities for participants to contribute at the same time from different geographical locations. The typical process of a group investigation was adapted into a three-week program organised around the following task:

> You are present at the inaugural meeting of an inter-institutional course design team. The meeting's agenda is to draw up a design for an online workshop on "Organisational Issues in Networked Learning for Staff Developers". It is intended that this will be an inter-institutional workshop run via the Internet, aimed primarily but not exclusively at professional staff developers. The length of the workshop has not yet been decided. Four aspects to the design have so far been proposed: the aims and objectives of the workshop; workshop structure and content; teaching strategies; and assessment.

## 5. THE DELIBERATIVE DEMOCRATIC FRAMEWORK

In this paper analysis of the data is conducted in the context of a deliberative democratic framework focused on the formation and following through of joint intentions (Richardson, 1998). Contrary to an "aggregative" conception of democracy, in which the emphasis is placed on individual beliefs or preferences prior to any decision-taking or voting process, deliberative democratic models focus on the decision-making process itself. The joint formation of intentions and the obligation to follow through these intentions lies, according to Richardson, at the heart of what it means to act in accordance with a deliberatively democratic procedure. A decision making process guided by deliberative democratic procedures has the following stages:

**Putting forward proposals**: "a view that sees deliberative democracy in terms of practical reasoning will naturally start with proposals that individuals, or their representatives, make about what the polity ought to do" (Richardson, 1998: 367).

**Discussion of proposals**: "the second stage of deliberative democracy is for the proposals to be discussed on their merits. This means to assess them in terms of the public good" (Richardson, 1998: 368).

**Informal agreement**: "the third stage…is to arrive at some informal agreement about what we ought to do" (Richardson, 1998: 368). It is worth noting that on Richardson's account what is central to the idea of mutual agreement is that such agreements are normatively binding through giving rise to obligations.

**Explicit collective decision**: "the fourth stage of the democratic process is to move from the level of informal mutual agreement to an explicit collective decision" (Richardson, 1998: 374).

**Partially joint intention**: "this process of explicit, joint acknowledgement and endorsement of an agreement via the procedure of majority rule provides all that is needed to yield a proper, partially joint intention as the outcome, and fifth stage, of the democratic process" (Richardson, 1998: 375).

The integrity of a deliberatively democratic decision hinges on the fact that there exists an intrinsic link between discussion and action. Key components of the process then are the conceptions of the public good which inform the framework within which the worth of proposals are evaluated and the obligations that participants are placed under as the participants' proposals are discussed and a course of action decided upon. The focus of the framework on intention and obligation has similarities with the theory of speech acts (Searle, 1975; Searle, 1969). In the present analysis particular importance is attached to the class of speech acts called "commissives". Attention is given to commissives because their non-defective performance places speakers under an obligation to carry out the action that speakers have committed themselves to; they "commit the speaker…to some future course of action" (Searle, 1975: 356). The non-defective performance of such acts is, for Richardson, a key source of evidence for confirming the existence of deliberative democratic intentions.

In this paper analysis of the data generated by the inquiry is focused on the points during the investigation at which collective deliberation, rather the carrying out of individual tasks, is required. In particular data is drawn from two of the synchronous discussions that took place during the course of the investigation. The first of these discussions took place at the end of the first week, the second at the end of the investigation at the close of the third week. The first discussion has been chosen because it provides data on participants' deliberations as to the tasks that need to be accomplished during the course of their investigation and because the way their deliberations proceed can be seen to relate to the stages of the deliberative democratic process (Richardson, 1998). The second discussion has been chosen because it provides data on the meaning of the group investigation process and its deliberative processes for the participants concerned.

## 6. ANALYSIS OF THE GROUP INVESTIGATION

After participants had had an opportunity to provide an initial response to the task a synchronous chat session was scheduled for the end of the first week. A number of proposals had been made with different emphases as how to proceed to develop the course design. These proposals included beginning with a discussion of the purposes of the course: "what are we trying to achieve?", the aims and objectives of the course, and the content of the course e.g. understanding a range of issues, conducting institutional research and being informed of research evidence.

Participants arrived at the chat session with proposals then but with as yet no in-depth group discussion as to the worth of those proposals. Once again, purpose plays an important role in the discussions: "Perhaps the question of 'what are we trying to achieve' would be a good place to start?" [Participant 1 (P1)]. The first substantive contribution by Participant 2 (P2) is "if we can decide on aims and objectives and the audience". This is a commissive speech act intended to commit the group to some future action. During the subsequent dialogue further aims as well as objectives of the course are considered. P2 suggests the following aim: "inform staff developers of networked learning as a strategy for staff development" and in response to a prompt from the tutor P1 replies that: "sounds like a broad general [aim] [...] yep, sounds like we're going in the right direction". P2 proposes a further aim before P1 begins to enumerate some of the objectives that are part of the aim to "inform staff developers of networked learning as a strategy for staff development".

At this stage of the deliberations the aims have been informally agreed on although no explicit decision has been taken. There immediately follows a stretch of the deliberations seeking clarification of P1's proposals regarding the content of the course. P2 asks P1, "what do you mean by access issues?"

At the end of the clarification P2 restates his commitment to future action but this time his contribution is phrased not as a commissive but as an expressive statement of an individual psychological state: "...I would prefer a task to come out of the discussion – practical old me!"

At this juncture the third participant, Participant 3 (P3), enters the chat room. The tutor summarises the previous discussion. P3 presents the following argument:

> my mind is working on two levels – one in relation to content (which can either be presented, or made available as a resource) [...] and then what are the institutional issues which people are experiencing in relation to introducing networked learning into he [higher education].

This new proposal put forward initially as the expression of a psychological state ("My mind is working on two levels") leads to informal agreement and the first explicit decision. P2 does not respond directly to the post, although, after a slight delay, P1 states: "I like the way you're thinking [P3]...My themes could fit within your institutional issues section". There very soon follows a public expression of partially joint intention:

> P1: Will I have a go at institutional issues? P3: If you want to pick up on institutional issues that's fine by me [P1] P2: Okay by me. P1: Will do.

"Will do" being a commissive speech act committing P1 to the future action of searching for information relating to institutional issues. Here P1 moves from implicit proposal (overlap between her framework and that of P3) to explicit decision via group agreement.

At this point the tutor suggests topics to the other participants. P3 responds by saying:

> Picking up on [the tutor's] points though. First of all can you clarify what you mean by dissemination as a theme? Secondly, by pushing us to choose a theme to research we lose the attention we presumably need to give to the process of the workshop and to the purpose of doing this research

The tutor replies: "I'd like to pull things back to us deciding on themes around which we can search for resources". There is an immediate response to the tutor's input from P1, "sounds good". P3 continues however:

> this may be a tension between the task set which seems to assume that in order to design a workshop we need to do some research on content versus what may be more my preferred mode which would be to work out process first. Does this make sense...?

P2's reply is "No, it makes sense. There's a disparity here", while P1's reply is: "I see what you're saying [P3], but I think the purpose of this chat is to decide on areas in which we might like to research".

The stalemate is resolved when the tutor suggests that process can be combined with content: "would you like to look at process issues [P3]?" and the response from P3, "Happy too". This exchange highlights the need for participants to debate their conceptions of the "public good" with reference to which group members are evaluating proposals and taking decisions. The tensions between a conception of democracy as the maximisation of individual preferences and democracy as a deliberative process are also confirmed.

It was then subsequently proposed as to whether the tutor should be involved in the group investigation. Two participants explicitly stated that the tutor should be involved and the other member of the group, P1, acquiesced with the deliberations, exclaiming "Sorted! (?)". This left one member of the group (P2) without a sub-task. The time allotted to the chat session (one hour) was running out however and when prompted that two people could cover one area P2 asks: "shall I do some bits on organisational issues as well unless I discover uncovered [sic] theme? And in response to the following proposal from P3: "How about reflections on using networked learning as a learning vehicle and staff development process – i.e. your experience", P2 replied, "Uh oh! Bit of each then!"

It is worthwhile asking at this stage whether P2 wanted to do "organisational issues" all along, whether there was enough deliberation, and whether the agreement reached is merely the aggregation of individual preferences or the outcome of a deliberative process.

Subsequent to the discussion participants searched for resources and held further synchronous discussions with the tutor depending on need and availability. The outcome was a "Possible Course Design?" submitted by the tutor for possible comment and further development on the penultimate day of the workshop as a synthesized version of everyone's contributions. The synthesis was welcomed by the members of the group who were available at the end of the exercise to express their views and there were calls for the course design to be further discussed for possible implementation within an inter-institutional context. Indeed, this would have been an ideal outcome of the process, where through discussion, the participants took a decision to implement in their own institutions the model they had developed as part of a wider inter-institutional collaboration.

At the end of the group investigation synchronous discussions with participants focused in part on a summative review of how the group process had developed. This review was distinct from discussions held during the course of the exercise that had aimed at discussing issues which would be formative for the group process. Peer to peer communications were viewed as being good, although as one participant mentioned "there is always the problem of clarifying meaning, of course, and the extra time taken to do that online". And of course the problem of clarifying meaning, how meaning is opened up to further negotiation and how closure of meaning is achieved in a collaborative context lies at the heart of democratic discourse. As one participant (P3) put it: "...what we are doing now, and have been doing in relation to the task set for this group is what I would call 'negotiation', i.e. negotiation of meaning". It is this negotiation process which helps in practice to establish group investigation's educational aim of shared ownership.

# 7. DISCUSSION

The excerpts, above, from a decision-making process engaged in as part of a group investigation illustrates some of the challenges of engaging in direct, deliberative democracy. Deliberative democracy presents us with the opportunity to shape our collective future through democratic responsiveness to the proposals of other citizens. It is a form of procedural negotiation that attempts to achieve a fair political agreement between parties on the basis of direct voter participation in the deliberative process rather than on the exercising of voter preferences informed by the observation of others. Nevertheless this example illustrates deliberative democracy also presents a 'classroom society' with a number of challenges. These include different conceptions of democracy and of the public good, time constraints, education for democracy, and the relations between the process of decision-making and subsequent action.

Balancing individual preferences against the public good can be a fine balancing act and to be successful direct forms of democracy need to successfully negotiate this tightrope. At two points in the dialogue individuals unilaterally state their individual preferences as a way of moving the deliberation forward, rather than basing their contributions on the current state of the deliberative process. Related to this is the question of 'what is the public good'? What is the conceptual framework that supplies the criteria that we can use to evaluate the worth of any proposal? It may be that there is an "incommensurability of cognitive ends" (Richardson, 1998) and hence a diversity of meanings — and this is surely right in a democracy. What does matter however is how the closure of meaning is achieved, what meanings are eventually privileged and who has a stake in these meanings and who has not. Negotiation is not an end in itself but is a process of human communication and organisation in the light of a particular conception of the good, of democratic arrangements in the public arena.

The question of the time needed to engage in productive deliberation is also pertinent. A fact alluded to by P2 in a further chat session reviewing the progress of the group investigation: "From my point of view I would have liked further clarification...for example, we didn't [sic] seem to have enough time to gtalk [sic] about objectives ". In a wider social context opportunities for deliberation may need to be balanced against such constraints.

Education for deliberative democracy is also relevant. Learners are at different stages of being able to first recognise and then being prepared to take up a position in the authentic space of joint deliberation. There are implications for identity, there are implications for interpersonal skills of deliberation and there are implications for the organisations and institutions that supply us with procedural rules within which we live and work.

Finally, the relationship between the process of decision-making and action taken on the basis of that decision-making needs to be addressed. Drawing on the work of Tsagarousianou (1999) Jankowski and van Selm (2000) review three studies[66] against three key claims of digital democracy:

- Obtaining information
- Engaging in deliberation
- Participating in decision-making

Given that 'deliberation' is to taken by the authors to mean discussion it is the third claim which we are most interested in the present context. This claim about participation in decision-making "refers to a yet unresolved issue regarding the relation of virtual political debates to those held in real life, and to their relation with further political action" (Jankowksi and van Selm, 2000: 161). With reference to the Usenet discussion the authors comment on the relationship between discussion and action:

At best, the newsgroup provided contributors with the opportunity for developing and enacting collective actions. No evidence is presented as to whether such action emerged during the course of the period studied (Jankowksi and van Selm, 2000: 155).

In regard to the second, experimental, study the authors again comment on the links between debate and outcome: there was, from the very beginning uncertainty as to how the debate might contribute to policy formation...policy had already reached an advanced stage of completion and it was consequently unclear what role there might be for 'interesting ideas' emerging from the public debate (Jankowksi and van Selm, 2000: 156).

Commenting on the third study however the authors state that "...some senior participants believed that their level of political influence was enhanced through the debate" (Jankowksi and van Selm, 2000: 156). As these comments indicate a link between the process of decision-making and subsequent action is not guaranteed. On Richardson's account it can be suggested that there needs to be a stronger emphasis on the formation of joint intentions and the links between those intentions and subsequent action. In their conclusions Jankowski and van Selm indicate that among other areas of investigation "more research is necessary on the way control and procedural mechanisms imposed on virtual debates influence the degree of citizen involvement" (Jankowski and van Selm, 2000: 162). An emphasis on an

[66] The studies were "a Usenet discussion, an experiment with specially developed Internet software for supporting public discussions and decision making, and a debate between senior citizens and political candidates on the eve of a national election" (Jankowski & van Selm, 2000: 149).

understanding of the rules of engagement along with being part of a shared locality such as a city are also identified by Dahlberg (2000) as being enabling factors for such online debates in general.

# 8. IMPLICATIONS FOR ELECTRONIC GOVERNMENT

The vision of government that this paper proposes is of one that involves traditional government and citizens in a process of negotiation that involves active responsibility on both sides. There exists a domain of civil society whose legitimacy derives neither from some external force e.g. government nor from the aggregative preferences of individuals, but which emerges from the interaction of these parties. A domain that can be called "authentic" (Dryzek, 2000). A similar thesis has been put forward in which it is suggested that the "good governance of Cyberspace" depends on an extension of participatory institutional arrangements to domains traditionally outside the social decision-making process (Hamelink, 2000). Both traditional government and citizens should have a stake in its future. Hamelink also notes the need for education for informed decision-making: "the expertise needed can be learnt: the capacity for informed and balanced public decision-making is not part of the human constitution" (Hamelink, 2000: 182).

In tackling questions of electronic democracy our concern should not just be with democracy as an unexamined concept but with what type of democracy we want. Is it one based on the maximization of individual preferences or is it a form of democracy in which decisions and actions are taken within a discursive framework? It is moral and political questions such as these that need to be asked as part of the debate on the development and use of information and communications technology in e-government. Such questions can be asked as part of a political education for e-government.

# REFERENCES

Ågren, P-0. (2001). "Is online democracy in the EU for professionals only?" *Communications of the ACM*, **44** (1), 36-38.

Bohman, J. and Rehg, W. (1997). *Deliberative Democracy: Essays on Reason and Politics*. London: The MIT Press.

Bryan, C. (1998). "Manchester: democratic implications of an economic initiative?" In: Tsagarousianou, R., Tambini, D., and Bryan C. (eds.), *Cyberdemocracy: Technology, Cities and Civic Networks*, pp.152-166. London: Routledge.

Carr, W. and Hartnett, A. (1996) *Education and the Struggle for Democracy: the Politics of Educational Ideas*. Buckingham: Open University Press.

Castells, M. (1996). *The Information Age: Economy, Society and Culture*. Oxford: Blackwell Publishers. 3 vols.

Dahlberg, L. (2001). Extending the public sphere through cyberspace: the case of Minnesota e-democracy, *First Monday*, **6** (3). Available at: http://www.firstmonday.dk/issues/issue6_3/dahlberg/

Dewey, J. (1916). *Democracy and Education: An Introduction to the Philosophy of Education*. New York: Macmillan.

Dutton, W. (1999). *Society On the Line: Information Politics in the Digital Age*. Oxford: Oxford University Press.

Dryzek, J. S. (2000). *Deliberative Democracy and Beyond: Liberals, Critics, Contestations*. Oxford: Oxford University Press.

Habermas, J. (1973). "The public sphere". In: Nash, K. (ed.) *Readings in Contemporary Political Sociology*, pp. 288-294. Oxford: Blackwell Publishers.

Hague, B.N. and Loader, B.D. (1999). *Digital Democracy: Discourse and Decision-Making in the Information Age*. London: Routledge.

Hamelink, C.J. (2000). *The Ethics of Cyberspace*. London: Sage.

Held, D. (1987). *Models of Democracy*. Cambridge: Polity Press.

Held, D. (ed.) (1993). *Prospects for Democracy: North, South, East, West*. Cambridge: Cambridge University Press.

Jankowski, N. and van Selm, M. (2000). "The promise and practice of public debate in cyberspace". In: Hacker, K.L. and van Dijk, J. (eds.) *Digital Democracy: Issues of Theory & Practice*, pp. 149-165. London: Sage.

Joyce, B., Calhoun, E., and Hopkins, D. (1997). *Models of Learning—Tools for Teaching*. Buckingham: Open University Press.

Laudon, K.L. (1977). *Communications Technology and Democratic Participation*. New York: Praeger.

Richardson, H.S. (1998). "Democratic intentions". In: Bohman, J. and Rehg, W. (eds.) *Deliberative Democracy: Essays on Reason and Politics*, pp.349-382. London: The MIT Press.

Searle, J R (1969). *Speech Acts: An Essay in the Philosophy of Language*. Cambridge, Cambridge University Press.

Searle, J R (1975). "A taxonomy of illocutionary acts". In: Gunderson, K. (ed.) *Language, Mind, and Knowledge*, pp.344-369. Minneapolis: University of Minnesota Press.

Sharan, S. and Sharan, Y. (1994a). *Expanding Cooperative Learning through Group Investigation*. London: Teachers College Press.

Sharan, Y. and Sharan, S. (1994b). "Group investigation in the cooperative classroom". In: Sharan, S. (ed.) *Handbook of Cooperative Learning Methods*. London: Greenwood Press.

Thelen, H. (1981). *The Classroom Society: The Construction of Classroom Experience*. London: Croom Helm.

Tsagarousianou, R., Tambini, D., and Bryan, C. (1998). *Cyberdemocracy: Technology, Cities and Civic Networks*. London: Routledge.

Tsagarousianou, R. (1999). "Electronic democracy: rhetoric and reality". *Communications: the European Journal of Communication Research*, **24** (2), 189-208.

50

# Receipt-freeness in Large-scale Elections without Untappable Channels

Emmanouil Magkos, Mike Burmester and Vassilis Chrissikopoulos
*Department of Informatics, University of Piraeus, 80 Karaoli & Dimitriou, Piraeus, 18534, Greece; Department of Computer Science, Florida State University, 214 Love Building, Tallahassee, Florida 32306, USA; Department of Archiving and Library Studies, Ionian University, Old Palace Corfu, 49100, Greece.*

**Abstract**: For an electronic election to be fully democratic there is a need for security mechanisms that will assure the privacy of the voters. With receipt-free electronic voting, a voter neither obtains nor is able to construct a receipt proving the content of her vote. In this paper we first consider the minimal requirements for receipt-free elections, without untappable communication channels between the voter and the voting authorities. We then propose a solution, which satisfies these requirements. This solution is based on an encryption blackbox, which uses its own randomness. Finally we present an implementation with smartcards, suitable for Internet voting.

## 1. INTRODUCTION

Electronic democracy refers to the use of Information & Communication Technologies (ICT) for communication between the politicians and citizens. In a representative democratic system, electronic elections (e-voting) constitute an important tool, which, if designed carefully, will strengthen the democratic substance of e-government. For an electronic election to be fully democratic, there is a need for security mechanisms that will assure the privacy of the vote.

In traditional elections, a voting booth does more than allow voters to keep their vote secret: it prevents vote-selling and coercion. Preventing such abuses in electronic voting schemes has been the subject of recent research. The notions of *receipt-freeness* and *uncoercibility* for electronic voting were introduced by Benaloh [1]. With the former the voters are convinced that their vote is counted without getting a receipt. With the latter the voters are not able to convince any other participant (e.g. a coercer) of the value of their vote. More specifically, in an uncoercible voting scheme a voter neither obtains nor is able to construct a receipt that proves the content of her vote. While the concept of uncoercibility is stronger than receipt-freeness, the term "receipt-freeness" has been used in the literature as the prevalent expression to denote the security resulted by both the receipt-freeness and uncoercibility criterions.

Most electronic voting schemes sacrifice receipt-freeness at the cost of establishing correctness for the election results. In these schemes, voters get a receipt that will help them check the final tally. Note that this useful property, also known as *atomic* verifiability, is not met in current physical-based elections. An even more desirable property for electronic elections is *universal* verifiability (e.g. see [8]), which not only permits the voter to verify that the vote has been counted correctly, but also gives voters the means to verify that the election tally actually represents the "sum" of the votes cast. Current research is focused on receipt-free schemes that also establish universal verifiability.

All the receipt-free schemes [1-7] in the literature make some basic assumptions about the communication channel between the voter and the election authorities and about the voting process. These assumptions can be modelled by the following primitives:

- An *untappable channel*, from the voter to the voting authority [5, 6]. This channel models a one-way physical apparatus by which the voter can send a message to the authority. This message will be *perfectly* secret to all other parties (including the coercer).
- An *untappable channel*, from the voting authority to the voter [2, 3, 4]. This channel models a one-way physical apparatus, used by the voting authority to send a message to the voter. This message will be *perfectly* secret to all other parties (including the coercer).
- A *voting booth*, in which the voter casts the vote [1, 7]. This models a physical booth and guarantees the secrecy of the communication between the voting authority and the voter.

Several authors in the literature have pointed out the difficulty of implementing untappable channels. Hirst and Sako have recently stated that [4], "untappable channels from the authorities to the voters are the weakest physical assumption for receipt-freeness". Such channels can also be quite cumbersome, particularly for large-scale voting with geographically distributed voters. For example, voters who abstain from elections because they find it inconvenient to go the polls, will find it equally inconvenient to cast their vote from a physically isolated voting booth in a dedicated computer network. Note that untappable channels will also force the voter to use specified voting locations.

**Contribution/Organization.** In this paper, we consider receipt-freeness in the presence of a coercer that can tap communication lines. In Section 2 we first define the minimal requirements for receipt-freeness and show that it can be achieved only if the voter does not use any secret information, other than the vote itself. In Section 3 we propose a solution which uses an encryption blackbox to encrypt the votes in a verifiable way. Receipt-freeness is based on the difficulty of tampering with the blackbox. In Section 4 we present an implementation with a *tamper-resistant* smartcard, where receipt-freeness is achieved by distributing the voting procedure between the voter and the smartcard. This implementation is based on the voting scheme of Cramer-Gennaro-Schoenmakers [8], and is suitable for PCs and the Internet. Section 5 concludes the paper.

## 2. REQUIREMENTS FOR RECEIPT-FREENESS

Below we define the minimal requirements for an election scheme to be receipt-free without any assumptions on the untappability of the communication channels between the voter and the voting authorities.

### 2.1 Private and Authenticated Channels

It is clear that the vote should be encrypted, to achieve vote secrecy (private channel). Moreover, there should be an authenticated communication channel, which only the voter (and not the coercer) uses to submit the encrypted vote to the voting authorities. The control over this channel should at least involve a secret key that only the voter possesses. This could be for example a secret signature key or a biometric.

### 2.2 Knowledge of the Secret Decryption Key

If the secret decryption key is in the possession of the voter (as in [5, 6]), then receipt-freeness is lost: the key together with the encrypted vote (which the coercer can get by tapping the communication line) is a receipt. So the voter must not know the secret decryption key.

### 2.3 Knowledge of the Randomness

It is clear that some randomness must be used during the voting procedure, and in particular for the encryption of the vote. This is so because the adversary should not obtain any partial information about the vote given its encryption [9]. We examine three scenarios, based on which entity is aware of this randomness. The third scenario seems to be the only that offers a solution to our problem:

**Randomness Chosen by the Voter.** The voter chooses some randomness to encrypt her vote with a probabilistic encryption scheme [9]. This randomness may be used later to lie against a coercer, as in the case of *deniable* encryption [10]. However, as shown in [4], the voter can use this randomness to construct a receipt, e.g., by using the hash of a pre-determined value. More dangerously, the coercer may have selected this randomness on behalf of the voter, and force the voter to use it (e.g. see [5]). Thus, a scheme in which the voter knows the randomness of the construction protocol is not receipt-free.

**Randomness Chosen by the Voting Authority.** Randomness may also be used by the voting authority, e.g., to shuffle the encrypted votes in a *mix-net* network [2, 4]. However, information about this shuffling must be secretly sent to the voter, and this cannot be done via an insecure channel: the coercer will eavesdrop on this channel. In this case, the untappable channel between the voter and the authority is inevitable.

**Randomness Produced by an Encryption Blackbox.** From the discussion above we see that while randomness is needed, neither the voter nor the authority must know this randomness. One way to achieve this is by using an Encryption Blackbox (EB) that uses its own randomness. The voter should not use the network facilities to communicate with the EB[1] (the coercer could tap the communication channels). Additionally, there should be a process, which produces some unpredictable randomness, i.e., a *beacon* [11]. This randomness will be used by the EB during the encryption. Finally the EB should be tamper-proof.

If a vote is encrypted in a way that the voter does not know the randomness used, then, before the vote is submitted to the voting authority, the voter must be given a proof of correctness of the encryption. This proof must be non-transferable; otherwise it may be used as a receipt for this vote. For this purpose we make use of *zero-knowledge* proofs.

## 2.4 Existence of a Virtual Booth

There should be a *virtual* voting booth, where the voter (and only the voter) interactively communicates with the blackbox. This booth is not necessarily physical: we only assume that, during the very moment of voting, the coercer does not observe the voter. Obviously, if voters use PCs to vote over the Internet, then there is no way to prevent the coercer from watching them while they vote. Our goal is not to prevent such attacks, but to prevent a voter from getting, or being able to construct, a receipt. The same assumption is made by all receipt-free schemes in the literature (except for [1, 7] where a physical voting booth is used), but it is made as an extra assumption to the untappability assumption.

## 3. A BASIC ELECTION SCHEME

Below we describe at high level, a basic receipt-free election scheme that satisfies all the minimal requirements described in Section 2. This scheme employs an Encryption Blackbox (EB) that uses its own randomness to encrypt the vote.

The election procedure has four distinctive phases: *Registration*, *Setup*, *Voting* and *Tallying*. During Registration, the Voter gets an EB, after being authenticated. The EB possesses the public encryption key of the Voting Authority.

During Setup, the Voter enters the virtual voting booth and interacts with the EB: the Voter first authenticates herself to the EB, and gives her input (her encrypted vote) to the EB, which encrypts this probabilistically, with the public key of the Voting Authority. The EB outputs this encryption and proves to the Voter in *zero-knowledge* (i.e., without giving away its randomness) that the encryption is correct.

During the Voting phase and given that the Voter is convinced of the correctness of the EB's encryption, the Voter signs the encrypted vote and uses an authenticated channel to submit this to the Voting Authority.

During the Tallying phase, the Voting Authority decrypts all encrypted votes and publishes the results.

**Receipt-freeness.** This is achieved because the coercer cannot tamper with the EB and access its randomness. The proof of correctness given to the Voter during the Voting phase has no off-line value to the coercer. Note that in this basic scheme, the Voting Authority is trusted not to conspire with the coercer. To prevent this we can use techniques from *threshold cryptography* [12] and distribute the Voting Authorities. In the next session, we will consider an implementation, which uses a smartcard instead of the Encryption Blackbox.

## 4. AN IMPLEMENTATION WITH SMARTCARDS

We present an implementation for which all the minimal requirements discussed in the previous section are satisfied, and receipt-freeness is established in a practical and affordable way. For this implementation, each voter uses a tamper-resistant smartcard that uses some pseudo-randomness to encrypt votes. Since tampering is not impossible (although extremely costly), we distribute the voting procedure between the voter and the smartcard to enhance security: the voter and the smartcard jointly contribute randomness for the encryption of the vote. Furthermore, the smartcard proves correctness of its actions to the voter in a non-transferable way. Communication between the Voters and the Voting Authorities takes place by means of a public broadcast channel with memory, namely a *bulletin board* (as in [8]).

Observe that a coercer cannot find the vote, without first getting the randomness of both, the voter and the smartcard. Even if the voter wishes to sell her vote, she cannot prove correctness without knowing the randomness of the smartcard (getting this randomness in this implementation is as hard as the Decision Diffie-Hellman problem-see Theorem 1).

This approach, if combined with a modified version of the Cramer-Gennaro-Schoenmakers election scheme [8], leads to an efficient receipt-free scheme for large-scale elections. For the proof of validity of the jointly encrypted votes we will use a 2-prover zero-knowledge proof (details are given in the Appendix).

**The Election Scheme of Cramer-Gennaro-Schoenmakers.** With this scheme [8] votes are encrypted by using an *homomorphic* version of the ElGamal cryptosystem [13]. The homomorhic aspect guarantees that the final tally is universally verifiable. Let $p$, $q$ be large primes such that $q \mid p$-1, let $G_q$ be the subgroup of $Z_p^*$ of order $q$, and $g$, $G$ be generators of $G_q$. Given a message $m \in Z_q$, the encryption of $m$ is the ElGamal encryption of $G^m$ with base $g$: that is $(x, y) = (g^a, h^a G^m)$, where $h = g^s$ is the public key, $s \in Z_q$ the secret key, and $a$ a random element of $Z_q$. All operations are modulo $p$. For convenience we drop the operator mod $p$.

During the voting phase, the Voter encrypts her vote $v \in \{-1,1\}$ as the pair $(x, y) = (g^a, h^a G^v)$. The Voter constructs a proof that $(x, y)$ encrypts $v \in \{-1,1\}$, and then publishes the encrypted vote and the proof on a Bulletin Board.

After the end of the voting period, the Voting Authorities "gather" all encrypted votes. They execute a $(n,t)$ threshold decryption protocol [14] and jointly compute $G^T = Y / X^s$, where $Y$ is the product of all $y$'s, $X$ is the product of all $x$'s and $T$ is the difference between the number of the yes-votes and the number of the no-votes. Here $n$ is the number of Voting Authorities and $t$ is an upper bound on the number of malicious Voting Authorities. Finally, the Voting Authorities determine $T$ from $G^T$, by using $O(l)$ modular multiplications.

In the above scheme, vote secrecy is reduced to the *Discrete Logarithm* problem [15]. Furthermore, the decryption of the votes is correct and succesful even if up to $t$ Voting Authorities are malicious or fail to execute the protocol.

## 4.1 Achieving Receipt-freeness

We modify the voting phase of the Cramer-Gennaro-Schoenmakers scheme, in order to achieve receipt-freeness, while maintaining security and efficiency. In this modification the encryption of the vote is distributed between the Voter and a Smartcard. The Voter, before getting a personal Smartcard, must register and be authenticated at a Registration Office. The Smartcard, which may be used for more than one elections, is provided with the certificate of the public signature key of the Voter. The Smartcard is also provided with the public encryption key of the distributed Voting Authorities, and a secret signature key, with the corresponding certificate. The steps of the new protocol are presented in Figure 1.

**Step (1):** The Voter uses randomness $a_0, a_0' \in Z_q$ to ElGamal encrypt the two possible votes {yes, no}={+1, -1}, thus yielding $e(+1)$ and $e(-1)$. The Voter orders lexicographically these encryptions before submitting them to the Smartcard. This means that the Smartcard will not have any information on which encryption corresponds to which vote.

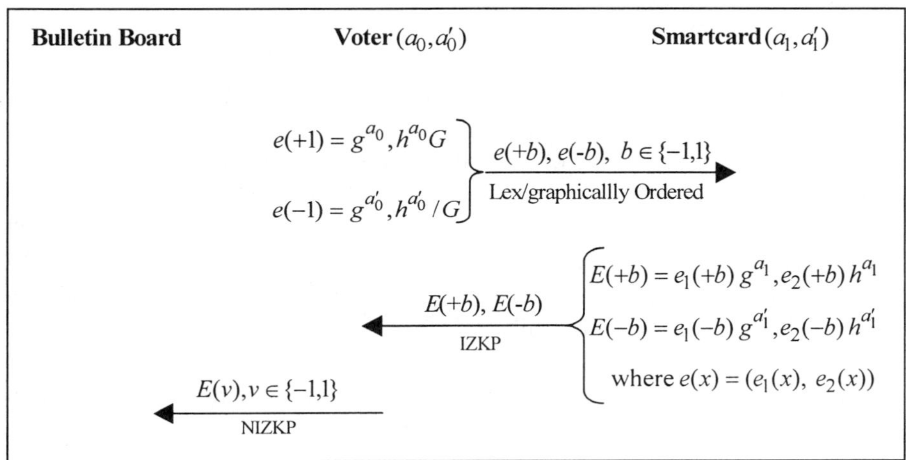


*Figure 1.* Voting with the use of a Smartcard

**Step (2)**: The Smartcard chooses its own randomness $a_1, a_1' \in Z_q$ to create the final encryptions for the two possible votes, $E(+b)$ and $E(-b)$, $b \in \{-1,1\}$. The encrypted votes are digitally signed by the Smartcard, for integrity. The Smartcard then outputs the encryptions to the Voter.

The Voter has to be convinced that the Smartcard has done things correctly, but without finding out the Smartcard's randomness. The proof has to be non-transferable. The Voter uses $E(+b), E(-b)$ and her knowledge of $e(+1), e(-1)$ to compute $(g^{a_1}, h^{a_1})$ and $(g^{a_1'}, h^{a_1'})$. If the Smartcard proves to the Voter that $\log(g^{a_1}) = \log(h^{a_1})$ and $\log(g^{a_1'}) = \log(h^{a_1'})$, then the Voter will be convinced that $E(+b)$ indeed encrypts $v = b$ and $E(-b)$ encrypts $v = -b$. The Smartcard can prove this in zero-knowledge, by using the *interactive* zero-knowledge proof (IZKP) of knowledge for equality of discrete logarithms, by Chaum-Petersen [16]. By its nature, the interactive zero-knowledge proof is not transferable. Even if the Voter records the exchanged messages, these messages do not have any "offline" value to a coercer. Thus, the Voter cannot use the transcripts of the proof to convince a coercer of her vote, even if the Voter wishes to sell her vote.

**Step (3):** The Voter decides which vote $v \in \{-1,1\}$ she will cast. For $E(v)$ to be valid, a proof of validity has to be constructed, i.e. that $E(v)$ encrypts $v \in \{-1,1\}$, without disclosing the vote $v$. This is necessary for *universal verifiability*. Such an interactive zero-knowledge proof, *jointly* executed by the Voter and the Smartcard, is presented in the Appendix. This can be converted to a non-interactive zero-knowledge proof (NIZKP) by using the Fiat-Shamir heuristic [17].

The Voter posts the encrypted vote $E(v)$ as well as the proof of validity, on the Bulletin Board. After the voting period ends, all encrypted votes will be decrypted by the Voting Authorities.

**Theorem 1.** *If the Decision Diffie-Hellman problem*[2] *is hard, the voting scheme above with a tamper-free smartcard is receipt-free.*

*Proof.* Suppose that the coercer and the Voter can prove that $E(v)$ is the encryption of the vote $v$. For example, that $E(v) = E(+1) = (g^{a_0 + a_1}, h^{a_0+a_1}G)$. Given that the Voter knows $a_0$, this reduces to proving that $(g^{a_1}, h^{a_1})$ is of the correct form, where $a_1$ is the Smartcard's randomness. Since $h^{a_1} = DH(g^{a_1}, h)$, this means that the Voter and the coercer jointly can solve the Decision Diffie-Hellman problem. The case for $v = -1$ is similar.

*Remark 1.* Our voting procedure could be generalized to multi-way voting, in which there are more than two votes (see also [8]).

## 5. CONCLUSION

With receipt-free electronic voting, a voter neither obtains nor is able to construct a receipt proving the content of her vote. In this paper we have considered the minimal requirements for receipt-free elections, without untappable communication channels between the voter and the voting authorities. We then proposed solutions that satisfied these requirements, and an implementation.

It is universally agreed that electronic voting will gain social acceptance in the years to come, especially Internet voting, despite several major security concerns. The use of tokens, such as smartcards, are also becoming more popular. Therefore we believe that our receipt-free voting scheme is consistent with the changes to come.

## 6. ACKNOWLEDGEMENTS

This work is supported by the General Secretariat for Research and Technology (GSRT) of the Greek Ministry of Development.

# 7. REFERENCES

[1] Benaloh J, Tuinstra D. Receipt-free secret-ballot elections. Proceedings of the 26th ACM Symposium on the Theory of Computing; ACM, 1994; 544-553.

[2] Sako K, Killian J. Receipt-free mix-type voting schemes - a practical solution to the implementation of voting booth. Proceedings of EUROCRYPT '95, LNCS; Springer-Verlag, 1995; 921:393-403.

[3] Alpert D, Ellard D, Kavazovic O, Scheff M. Receipt-free secure elections 6.857 final project. 6.857 Network and Computer Security, 1998; http://www.eecs.harvard.edu/~ellard/6.857/final.ps.

[4] Hirt M, Sako K. Efficient receipt-free voting based on homomorphic encryption. Proceedings of EUROCRYPT 2000, LNCS; Springer-Verlag, 2000; 1807:539-556.

[5] Okamoto T. Receipt-free electronic voting schemes for large scale elections. Proceedings of Workshop of Security Protocols '97, LNCS; Springer-Verlag, 1996; 1163:125-132.

[6] Okamoto T. An electronic voting scheme. Proceedings of IFIP '96; Advanced IT Tools, Chapman & Hall, 1996; 21-30.

[7] Niemi V, Renvall A. How to prevent buying of votes in computer elections. Proceedings of ASIACRYPT '94, LNCS; Springer-Verlag, 1994; 917:141-148.

[8] Cramer R, Gennaro R, Schoenmakers B. A secure and optimally efficient multi-authority election scheme. Proceedings of EUROCRYPT '97, LNCS; Springer-Verlag, 1997; 1233:103-118.

[9] Goldwasser S., Micali S. Probabilistic encryption. Journal of Computer and System Sciences 1984; 28:270-299.

[10] Canetti R, Dwork C, Naor M, Ostrovsky R. Deniable encryption. Proceedings of CRYPTO '97, LNCS; Springer-Verlag, 1997; 1294:90-104.

[11] Rabin M. Transaction protection by beacons. Journal of Computer Systems Science 1983; 27(2):256-267.

[12] Desmedt Y. Threshold cryptography. European Transactions on Telecommunications 1994; 22(6):449-457.

[13]ElGamal T. A public key cryptosystem and a signature scheme based on discrete logarithms. IEEE Transactions on Information Theory 1985; IT-30(4):469-472.

[14]Pedersen T. A threshold cryptosystem without a trusted party. Proceedings of EUROCRYPT '91, LNCS; Springer-Verlag, 1991; 547:522-526.

[15]Diffie W., Helman M. New directions in cryptography. IEEE Transactions on Information Theory 1976; 22(6):644-654.

[16]Chaum D, Pedersen T. Wallet databases with observers. Proceedings of CRYPTO '92, LNCS; Springer-Verlag, 1993; 740:89-105.

[17]Fiat A, Shamir A. How to prove yourself: practical solutions to identification and signature problems. Proceedings of CRYPTO '86, LNCS; Springer-Verlag, 1987; 263:186-194.

## APPENDIX

Our interactive zero-knowledge proof is a 2-prover modification of the proof in [8]. A flow diagram of the proof is sketched in Fig. 2. The common input is $E(v) = (x, y)$. The Smartcard's contribution to the proof of validity is given in Fig. 3. The Voter's contribution to the proof is given in Fig. 4. The proof of Completeness, Soundness and Zero-knowledge is similar to the one in [8].

SMARTCARD
VOTER
VERIFIER
Common Input ( $E(v) = (x, y)$ )
$u_{sc}, t_{sc}$
$a_1, b_1, a_2, b_2$
$c, d$
$c$
$c \stackrel{?}{=} d_1 + d_2$
$a_1 \stackrel{?}{=} g^{r_1} x^{d_1}$
$r_{sc} = w_{sc} - a_{sc} d$
$d_1, d_2, r_1, r_2$
$b_1 \stackrel{?}{=} h^{r_1} (yG)^{d_1}$
$a_2 \stackrel{?}{=} g^{r_2} x^{d_2}$
$b_2 \stackrel{?}{=} h^{r_2} (y/G)^{d_2}$

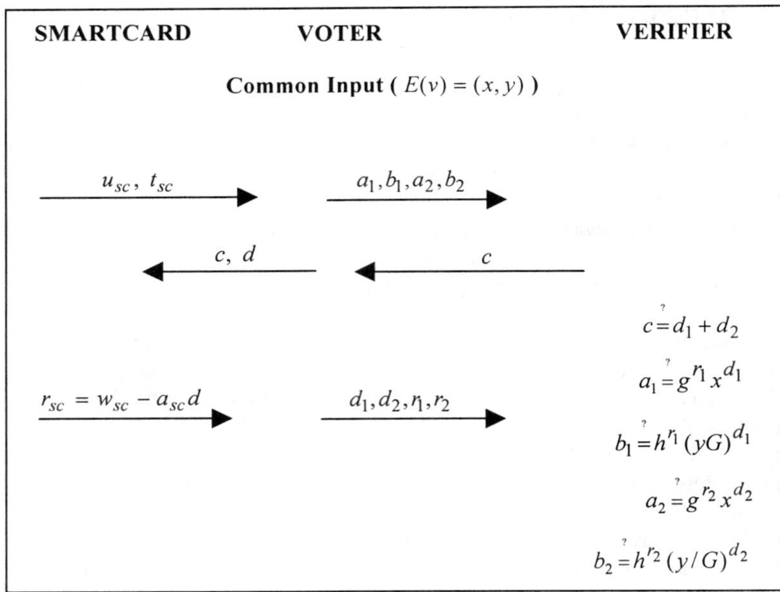

*Figure 2.* Proof of Validity for a Jointly Encrypted Vote

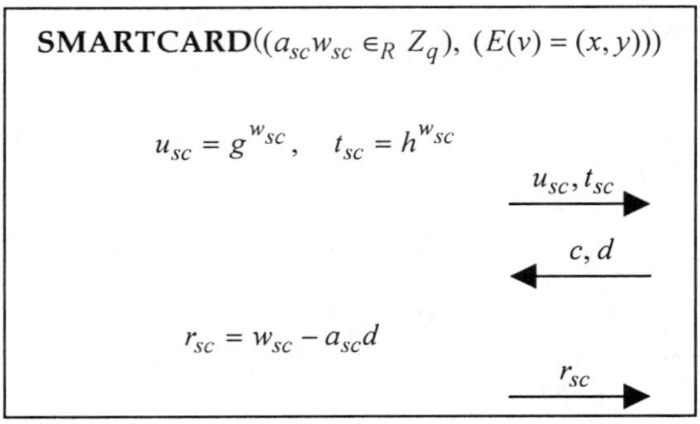

SMARTCARD($(a_{sc} w_{sc} \in_R Z_q)$, $(E(v) = (x, y))$)
$u_{sc} = g^{w_{sc}}, \quad t_{sc} = h^{w_{sc}}$
$u_{sc}, t_{sc}$
$c, d$
$r_{sc} = w_{sc} - a_{sc} d$
$r_{sc}$

*Figure 3.* The Smartcard's Contribution to the Proof of Validity

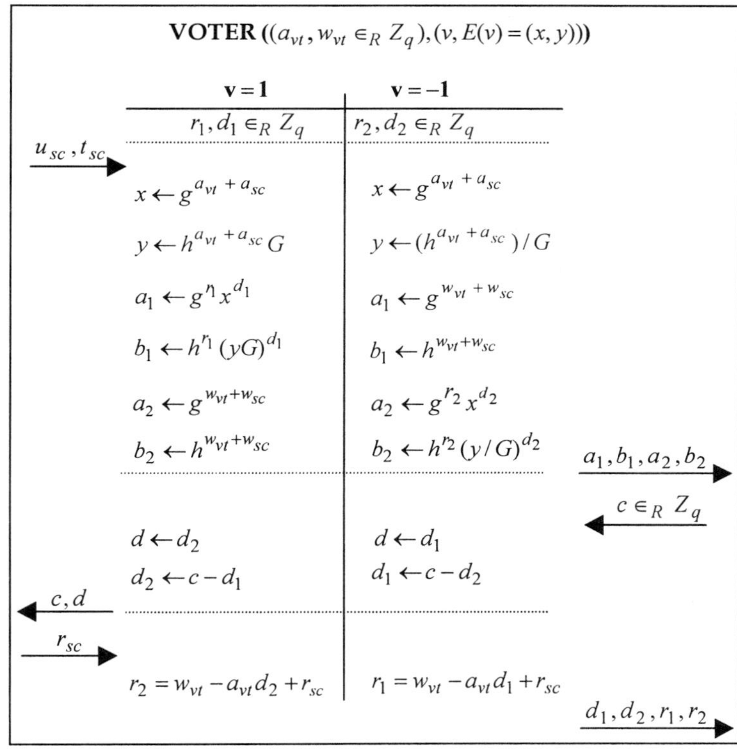


*Figure 4.* The Voter's Contribution to the Proof of Validity

## NOTES

1 An attentive reader will observe that the untappability assumption has not been completely removed. We assume that the "channel" between the Voter and the Encryption Blackbox is untappable.

2 The Diffie-Hellman operator DH is defined by $DH(g^a, g^b) = g^{ab}$, where $g$ is a primitive element and the operations are modulo $p$. The problem of recognizing whether $z = DH(g^a, g^b)$, for a given $z \in Z_p$, is called the *Decision Diffie-Hellman problem* [15].

51

# E-democracy and the Scottish Parliament

Lesley Beddie, Ann Macintosh and Anna Malina
*The Scottish Parliament, Edinburgh, UK. And*
International Teledemocracy Centre, Napier University, 219 Colinton Road, Edinburgh, UK

**Abstract**: This paper focuses on the introduction and use of information and communication technology (ICT) in the new Scottish Parliament to enhance Scottish citizens' understanding of the governance of Scotland and to encourage them to participate in the democratic decision making of Scotland. The primary focus is the use of the World Wide Web as a vehicle both for dissemination of information and for interaction with the Parliament.

In particular, the paper concentrates on one aspect of use of the Web, i.e. that of electronic petitions. The Scottish Parliament actively promotes petitions as a way in which the public can effectively lobby the Parliament, and has established a Public Petitions Committee which enables the public to submit written or electronic petitions. Essentially, the paper assesses the value of electronic petitioning in the Scottish Parliament.

## 1. INTRODUCTION

This paper focuses on the introduction and use of information and communication technology in the new Scottish Parliament to enhance Scottish citizens' understanding of the governance of Scotland and to encourage them to participate in the democratic decision making of Scotland. Budge (1996) argues that democratic political participation must involve both the means to be informed and the mechanisms to take part in democratic decision making. In this paper we demonstrate how the Scottish Parliament is using internet-based technology to address citizen participation through these joint perspectives of informing and participating. The primary focus is the use of the World Wide Web as a vehicle both for dissemination of information and for interaction with the Parliament.

In July 1999 the Scottish Parliament was officially opened. This gave devolved power for specific areas of government from the Westminster Parliament in London to a new Scottish Parliament based in Edinburgh. One of the main documents setting out how the new Parliament should work was The Consultative Steering Group document (The Scottish Office, 1998a). This stated that the Scottish Parliament should aspire to use all forms of information and communication technology "*innovatively and appropriately*" to support its three principles of openness, accessibility and participation.

Prior to the official opening of the Parliament, a working group on the use of information and communication technology was established, which made important recommendations on the future of technology in the new Parliament. This group, the 'ICT Expert Panel', reported directly to the Consultative Steering Group and its recommendations helped to ensure that technology was a fully integrated component of its business processes rather than a later add-on. The report (1998b) of the Expert Panel was published separately from that of the Consultative Steering Group's Report as it was lengthy and also generally recognised as containing information worthy of a separate document.

The remit of the Expert Panel was to provide advice on how the Parliament might use technology to:

- promote internal efficiency and innovative ways of working;
- provide information about its proceedings and its work to the widest possible audience in the most accessible way;
- make it as easy as possible for the Parliament and individual MSPs (Members of the Scottish Parliament) to exchange information with external organisations and the public;
- encourage democratic participation and involvement.

Membership of this panel comprised a cross section of Scottish people, including both ICT experts and potential end-users of the technology.

The work of the Panel was to extend thinking on the value and use of ICT beyond just the operation of Parliamentary business and into information provision and accessibility which might in turn create and use new services. In so doing, the Panel split into sub-groups, and the report from one of those groups, the sub-group on Democratic Participation, was reported in both the final Consultative Steering Group report and the Expert Panel report. It went beyond what might be termed as core business requirements of the Parliament and gave proposals for how ICT might extend these and add value in addressing public access to, and interactions with, the democratic process. Section 2 introduces the technology provided by the Scottish Parliament to enable Scottish citizens to be better informed about the governance of Scotland and the workings of the Parliament in general.

In August 1999, Napier University established the International Teledemocracy Centre in partnership with BT Scotland. Its remit is to develop innovative e-democracy systems that have the potential to strengthen public understanding and participation in the democratic decision-making process. To achieve this, the Centre is undertaking research into electronic democracy and developing an e-democracy toolkit to act as a show-case of e-democracy applications. The aim is to demonstrate the potential benefits of the use of technology in supporting the democratic process. The Centre's web site is at http://www.teledemocracy.org. Section 3 describes how the Centre, working with the Scottish Parliament, is starting to introduce e-democracy tools into the democratic processes of the Parliament through the introduction of an e-petitioning tool to facilitate the electronic lobbying of the Parliament. The section describes how the requirements of the citizen wishing to petition the Parliament electronically are met whilst also ensuring the Parliament has confidence in the integrity of such an electronic petitioning system.

## 2. THE SCOTTISH PARLIAMENT'S USE OF THE WEB

The Scottish Parliament web site is at www.scottish.parliament.uk. All documents and debates relating to the business of the Parliament are available on-line. It was one of the earliest recommendations of the ICT Expert Panel, and one that was acted upon very quickly, that the Parliament must use the Web as an information source and shop window for its work. This was to include not only business papers and reports, but also general information about, for example, the education centre and progress on the new Parliament building.

The web site is, effectively, the premier publishing medium for the Parliament although, for accessibility reasons, it is obviously not the only medium in use. The web site publishes the Official Report of the Parliament's meetings in the Chamber by 7am on the following day, and Committee Reports as soon as possible and generally within 3 days of the meeting. The publication deadlines for the latter reports have been foreshortened from those first defined in 1999 in recognition of the fact that the committee papers are of great interest and the demand is high. In addition, and as a further step towards openness, committee agendas and papers are published in advance where at all possible. The web site is constantly being added to and access enhanced. It is presently going through a major redesign exercise even though it is less than 2 years old, in order to ensure that it meets the needs of its audience. The figure below shows the main page for the Scottish Parliament.

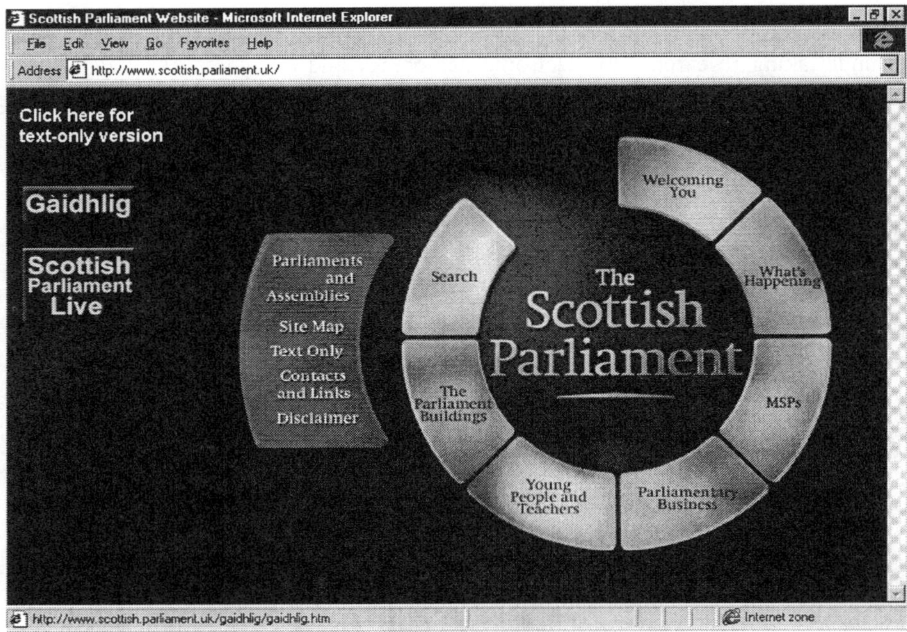


*Figure 1.* Scottish Parliament web-site

The more interactive aspects of the web service include the submission of electronic petitions (see section 3), the publication of the email addresses of all MSPs, their biographies and links to personal web pages, alongside phone and fax numbers and correspondence addresses. Email addresses for clerks to committees and for offices within the Parliament are also published. The recent webcasting service broadcasts Chamber and Committee meetings live across the web so that organisations and individuals can listen in and watch items of particular importance to them. The service also includes access to the (small but growing) audio-visual archive of webcasts, and relevant papers for the committee meetings. This service is new, but the 12 month plan is to extend it to give better access to the audio-visual archive, to webcast over broadband, and to use it as a vehicle to enable committees to receive feedback and consult through the webcast.

The Parliament is charged with providing information to, and receiving information and opinions from, all Scottish organisations, groups or citizens, and it must do so using all the channels of communication which are available and required. Paper, telephones, TV, ICT are all channels which are used. However, the internet is the main channel for the provision of innovative, rather than simply automated, services to and from the Parliament, and therein lies its value and the reason why it will continue to be part of its core provision.

# 3. ELECTRONIC PETITIONING

## 3.1 Petitioning and the Scottish Parliament

A petition is a formal request from citizens to a parliament. In many countries around the world citizens have used petitions for a long time to make their feelings known about issues that concern them. The format of petitions and the way petitions are submitted and subsequently processed by parliaments varies greatly. This variation may be demonstrated by considering petitions to the UK parliament in Westminster and to the Scottish Parliament. The Westminster Parliament publishes a comprehensive set of rules on how to submit a petition. For the purpose of this paper, the important ones relate to the format and the submission procedure. The page on which the petition appears must be hand-written and every petition must be specifically and respectfully addressed to the House of Commons. The petition must have hand-written signatures along with the addresses of the signatories. Only Members of the House of Commons can present petitions. They can be submitted (except on Fridays) immediately before the half hour adjournment debate at the end of each day's business or they can be placed in a large green bag hooked onto the back of the Speaker's Chair. Although this appears a somewhat elaborate procedure, little actually happens to the petition once it is submitted. Many Members term the green bag 'the black hole for petitions.' The fact that only a Member can submit a petition also goes against petitions being an effective lobbying tool for the citizen.

The Scottish Parliament actively promotes petitions as a means by which the public can effectively lobby parliament. On the issue of petitions, the Consultative Steering Group stated:

*"It is important to enable groups and individuals to influence the Parliament's agenda. We looked at a number of models in other Parliaments for handling petitions and concluded that the best of these encouraged petitions; had clear and simple rules as to form and content; and specified clear expectations of how petitions would be handled."*

To achieve this the Scottish Parliament established a dedicated Petitions Committee. Figure 2 below shows the home page for the Public petitions Committee (PPC).

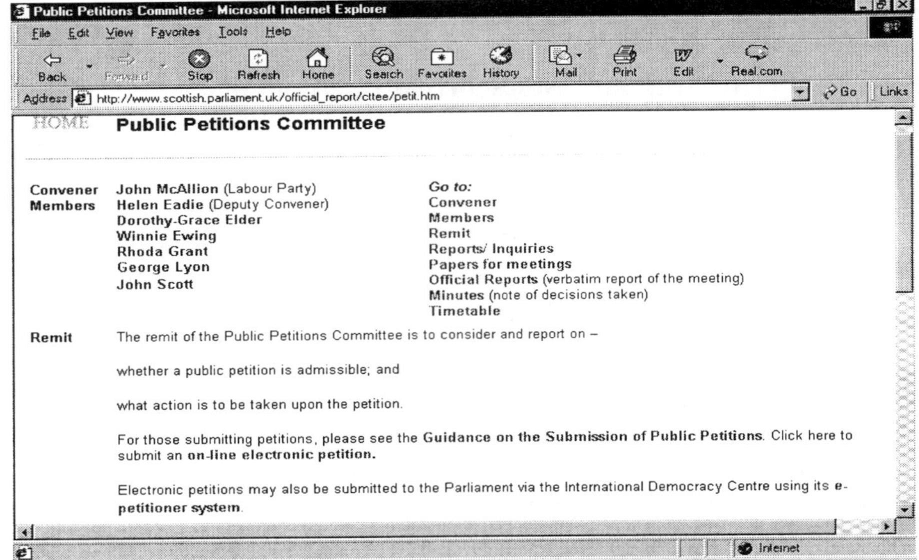


*Figure 2.* Public Petitions Committee web-site

The remit of the PPC is to consider and report on whether a public petition is admissible and what action is to be taken on the petition. The PPC considers each admissible petition and makes a decision on the action to be taken in each case. From July 1999 to 7 November 2000 the PPC had received and dealt with approximately 300 petitions. An individual, a corporate body, an interest group, or any other association may submit a petition. As regards format, petitions must be in proper form that is determined by the PPC from time to time. In December 1999, the Scottish Parliament agreed to allow an internet-based petition from the ITC's web site sponsored by the World Wildwide Fund for Nature (WWF) to be the first electronic petition to collect names and addresses over the internet. The Parliament subsequently agreed to allow groups and individuals to submit petitions using the Teledemocracy Centre's internet petitioning system for a trial period.

The report of the meeting of the Public Petitions Committee on 14th March, 2000 to trial internet petitions can be found at: http://www.scottish.parliament.uk/official_report/cttee/petit-00/pumop0314.htm. The special arrangement between Teledemocracy Centre and the Scottish Parliament is allowing both parties to start to evaluate the use and civic impact of electronic petitioning in Scotland.

## 3.2 The e-petitioner Tool

The e-petitioner tool, at www.e-petitioner.org.uk, has the functionality to create a petition; to view/sign a petition; to add background information, to join an integrated discussion forum; and to submit a petition. Figure 3 shows a petition screen with the text of a recent electronic petition on digital inclusion.

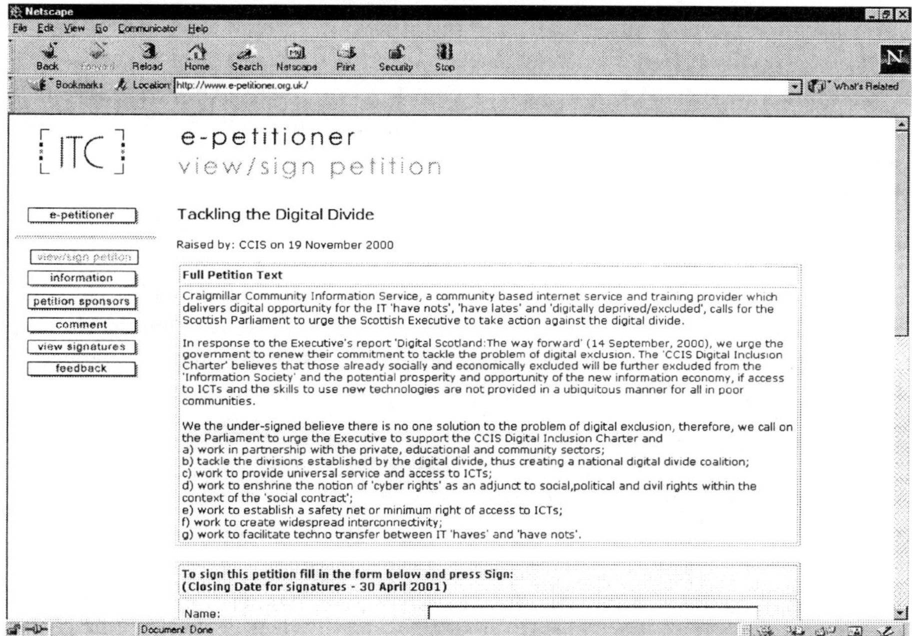


*Figure 3.* e-petition text: 'Tackling the Digital Divide'

Macintosh et al (2001) describe the critical issues to be considered in the design of e-democracy systems. In designing the e-petitioning system it was necessary to consider how technology could be used most effectively to support the five key enabling criteria of accessibility, usability, security, transparency and trust. However the very nature of governance and the fact that government cannot choose its customers means that, in the design of e-democracy systems, these issues become complex.

With regard to e-petitioner it was important to provide access for as many people as possible. With this in mind, the system does not use frames or contain large graphics files. It was important that local community centres running slower machines could easily access the system. The unequal technical capabilities of citizens demanded that e-petitioner was simple to use. It was also important that features that might make the system difficult for the partially sighted to use were excluded.

In some respects, accessibility and security can be conflicting design issues, however, as petitions to the Scottish Parliament are not legally binding, "external" security measures that might have run counter to good accessibility were not required. Therefore, a detailed user-registration process was excluded. Instead the system runs "internal" security checking on the names signing the petition. However there still remains the question of how much checking of names and addresses is necessary for electronic petitions? This is an important question to address. It would be easy to say that it should match the level currently available for paper-based petitions but that then raises the issue of what level of security checking is actually used for paper-based names and addresses other than manually reading the often illegible handwriting. On the other hand there is always the temptation to say that everything must be checked thoroughly, which is the case for electronic voting, but not necessarily for names and addresses on petitions. The "internal" checking is accomplished by e-petitioner giving each name and address a "confidence" rating. The actual rating depends on a number of factors, for example, Internet Provider (IP) address and how many times the same IP address has been used to sign the petition. These confidence ratings are closely examined prior to submission of the petition to check for any irregularities. The system also automatically removes any duplicate names and addresses.

It was important to ensure that the petitioning process was as transparent as possible. However, in some respects usability and transparency can be conflicting design issues. There is a need to ensure straightforward navigation through the system, but there is also a need to ensure that the participation process and relevant information underlying the petitions are open to everyone Transparency was achieved through three mechanisms. Firstly, by providing background information on the petition, ensuring that people can be adequately informed about the petition issues and therefore can better decide whether to support the petition or not. Secondly, by incorporating an integrated discussion forum so that people who do not want to support the petition or others who feel they have further evidence in support of the petition can add their own statements on-line. Thirdly, e-petitioner has a feedback facility such that the petition sponsor can inform everyone on the progress of the petition once it has been submitted to the Scottish Parliament.

Given the above requirements, the detailed functionality of E-Petitioner is:

- the petition sponsor can *create* the petition, giving the text of the petition and the address of the petitioner to which all communications concerning the petition should be sent;
- the petition sponsor can add on-line *background information* to provide rationale for the petition and to better inform those reading the petition;
- persons wishing to support the petition can *add their names and*
- *addresses* on-line, see figure 4;
- additionally persons wishing to *raise any issues* about the petition can do so on-line through the integrated, on-line discussion forum;
- the *discussion forum* is available for anyone to read or send comments to
- whether they support the petition or not;

- persons wishing to add their names or enter the discussion *do not require an email account*, they can do so from any internet access point - public kiosk, cyber café, community centre, home, etc;
- with regard to *petition statistics*, the number of persons supporting the petition is automatically updated along with the names and areas/countries, this information is available for anyone to view;
- full names and addresses are filed for use with, and only with, the petition (unless consent for other use is given by the person adding their name and address) ensuring *data protection* requirements are adhered to;
- duplicate names and addresses are automatically removed;
- *checking names and addresses* is performed prior to submission of the petition by the system allocating a "confidence rating" to each name;
- the petitioner can *submit* the petition with names and addresses electronically and/or can produce a paper version of the petition for submission;
- the format for the submitted petition *adheres to the guidelines* of the Scottish Parliament.

To be able to quickly demonstrate and try out the e-petitioner functionality the first version of the system was developed using cgi scripts and html files. It was available from both Explorer and Netscape browsers. Once e-petitioner was accepted for trial use by the Scottish Parliament, the system was updated to reflect feedback from users and the Parliament. The current version of e-petitioner is implemented in using Microsoft SQL and ASP. There are links to the electronic petitioning system from the Scottish Parliament's web site and links from the Teledemocracy Centre's web site to the Parliament's guidelines for petitions.

Netscape

File Edit View Go Communicator Help

Back Forward Reload Home Search Netscape Print Security Stop

Bookmarks Location: http://www.e-petitioner.org.uk/ What's Related

**To sign this petition fill in the form below and press Sign:**
**(Closing Date for signatures - 13 October 2000)**

Name:

Address:

Town/City:

Postcode:

Country: SELECT A COUNTRY

- if other please specify:

Email: (optional)

The petiton sponsor would like to add your name and address to their database so that you can receive updates on this issue and other relating issues. Would you like your name added to the database? Yes No

SIGN

**Note:** Your details will be held in computer readable form to allow the petition sponsor to administer and submit the petition you have signed. Only your name and country will be visible from this site. Your full name and address will be submitted to the relevant UK Parliamentary body.

Document: Done

*Figure 4.* e-petitioner on-line form

The first e-petitions are very much pilot electronic petitions to the Scottish Parliament, and it is therefore difficult to draw many conclusions from them. However, it was originally thought that electronic petitioning might let the internet run wild and thousands of frivolous names and addresses would be collected. Our initial evaluation has shown this is not the case. Indeed, the opposite could be argued. Instead of a pen being thrust into the hand of the would-be petitioner with a request to "sign here", the petitioner needs to be much more committed to the petition cause. They have to: boot up their PCs, log onto the internet, search the net for the site and then examine and reflect on information before deciding to sign. In this way the names and addresses being gathered could be considered a more realistic representation of those supporting the petition cause. The Teledemocracy Centre has received research funding from the Joseph Rowntree Charitable Trust to undertake a detailed evaluation of the impact of e-petitioner on participation levels.

## 4. CONCLUSIONS

The use of technology by the Scottish Parliament to support democracy in Scotland has been described. In particular, the web is a major communication channel and will continue to be exploited and employed by the Parliament for the delivery of services. Already the Scottish Parliament is at the forefront of the use of webcasting in Parliaments to provide wider access to its committee and plenary meetings.

Groups or individuals may submit petitions to the Parliament, electronically or on paper. The admissibility of electronic petitions has enabled the Parliament to work with the ITC to learn more about the process by which petitions are created and delivered, and to gather information about the issue, the process and the petitioners, which may be of great value to the committees in better assessing public feelings and wishes. While many challenges remain, the design of e-petitioner has demonstrated already that electronic petitions can be effective. E-petitioning will not necessarily create a large number of frivolous names and addresses as previously feared. Instead, with its unprecedented capability to quickly transcend time, space and place, the new system has allowed petitioners to better inform the wider public about specific issues of concern. E-petitioner's features have also presented new opportunities for people to explore background information, deliberate and reflect on issues before signing a petition and/or commenting on it. Finally, e-petitioner has -- at least to some extent -- allowed sponsors to better understand some of the concerns other members of the public have about the particular issues raised.

## 5. REFERENCES

Budge, I. (1996). *The new challenge of direct democracy.* Cambridge: Polity Press

MacIntosh, A., Davenport, E., Malina, A. & Whyte, A. Technology Driven Inclusive Democracy. In Grönlund, Åke (2001). (ed). Electronic Government: Design, applications and management (in print).

Scottish Parliament (2000). The report of the meeting of the Public Petitions Committee on 14th March, 2000 to trial internet petitions. At URL http://www.scottish.parliament.uk/official_report/cttee/petit-00/pumop0314.htm.

The Scottish Office (1998a). *Shaping Scotland's Parliament.* Report of the Consultative Steering Group.

The Scottish office (1998b). Final Report of *Expert Panel on Information and Communications Technologies for the Scottish Parliament..* The ICT Expert Panel.

52

# Building Value Into E-Government:
## *An Australian Case Study*

**Greg Robins and Janice Burn**
*Edith Cowan University, Australia*

**Abstract**: This paper looks at the implementation of a new customer value based model in e-government. Firstly we review the issues of e-government and the drive towards customer centric organisations in the context of multiple government agencies. A model of change is reviewed and extended to the development of a virtual organisation model which can be applied along the customer value chain across multiple service agencies. A case study is used to demonstrate how traditional Government organisations are set up with a focus on Government agencies in Western Australia and how the concept of a virtual organisation as a value-alliance model can improve customer service. Finally, we examine how the Aboriginal Affairs Department, a Western Australian Government agency is implementing this model as a virtual organisation and the implications of this model for the management of change in a developing e-community.

# 1. INTRODUCTION

Following on from e-commerce and e-business the latest "e"volution is e-Government. Within the next five years the Internet will transform not only the way in which most public services are delivered but also the fundamental relationship between government and citizen (Von Hoffman, 1999). With few exceptions, however, governments have arrived late on the scene. As monopoly suppliers, none were worried about being "Amazoned" by a new web-based competitor. Transactions with government are rarely a matter of choice and government employees are unlikely to be rewarded for devising innovative web based strategies to replace them in their jobs. Nevertheless the drive is now on for radical government change (Sprecher, 2000). A major driver has been the desire to reduce costs and make revenues go further. Savings of 20% are not unusual in the e-business community as they network their supply chains (Burn and Hackney, 2000).

U.S. federal, state and local procurement spending on materials and services in 2000 was estimated at around $550 billion, and in the European Union member states' combined procurement spending was around $778 billion (Symonds, 2000). With a 20% cut in costs we are looking at savings of around $250 billion.

An additional driver comes from customer expectations Customers now have far greater access to information and demand personalised experiences as opposed to simply acquiring goods and services. A customer driven organisation is one that maintains a focus on the needs and expectations of customers both spoken and unspoken in the creation and/or improvement of the product or service provided. Successful organisations, state or municipal governments and federal government departments and agencies have recognised that developing customer focus is an absolute necessity (Cavanagh and Livingston 1997).

One of the proposed solutions has been the creation of government portals such as the Singapore or UK portals. These have been designed around "life events" such as changes in marital status and allow users to find what they are looking for by using "How do I - - ?" type questions rather than by forcing the client to search through complex organisational structures possibly linking up to 50 different departments in one search. In reality the government portal acts as a virtual organisation front interacting with customer driven demand. This type of solution requires major changes within and without the government organisation and as yet, there is no clear evidence of success. (Jellinek, 2000). The failure of a massive government IT outsourcing project in Australia has highlighted the enormous difficulties of implementing cross-agency collaboration. The proposed solution is to return autonomy to the individual government agencies.

This paper looks at a specific e-government solution in the context of the West Australian Government. Firstly we review the issues of customer focus and utilising external organisations in the context of government agencies. Ostensibly government agencies are service driven organisations with a major goal of providing a service to the public. We then discuss how traditional Government organisations are set up with a focus on Western Australia and how the concept of a value alliance network can improve customer service. Finally, we examine how the Aboriginal Affairs Department, a W. A. Government agency is implementing a value-alliance model as a virtual organisation and the implications of this model for the management of change.

## 2. DEVELOPING A CUSTOMER FOCUS

Prahalad and Ramaswamy (2000) suggest that organisations need to "create their future by harnessing competence in an enhanced network that includes customers". They developed a three-stage model which we have adapted to a government context and summarised below in Table 1.

Table 1 shows that the idea of extending the government services network and changing the nature of its usage to improve core competencies is a central component of this model. In the past, most government agencies had a traditional focus where they have embraced the concept of the extended enterprise and have been primarily concerned with alliances, networks, and collaborations among other agencies and services. The old idea of the "extended enterprise" should give way to the idea of an enhanced network of traditional agencies, other services, funding bodies and customers. Government managers need to recognise that consumers are a source of competencies. They must focus on developing relationships with the customer as the agent that is most dramatically transforming government as we know it and leading the e-government and governance revolution.

| | **The Agency** | **Network of Agencies B2B** | **Enhanced Value Network e-Government** |
|---|---|---|---|
| **Unit of analysis** | The government agency | The extended enterprise:- the agency, its agency partners and other service providers | The value alliance:- the agency, its partners, other funding and service providers and its customers |
| **Resources** | What is available within the agency | Access to other agencies' competencies and funding | Access to other agencies' competencies and funding, as well as customers' competencies and investments of time and effort |
| **Basis for access to competence** | Internal agency-specific processes | Privileged access to agencies within the network | Infrastructure for active ongoing dialogue with diverse customers |
| **Added Value of managers** | Nurture and build competencies | Manage collaborative partnerships | Harness customer competence, manage personalised experiences, and shape customer expectations |
| **Value creation** | Autonomous | Collaborate with partner agencies | Collaborate with partner agencies and with active customers |
| **Sources of managerial tension** | Service-unit autonomy vs leveraging core competencies | Partner is both collaborator and competitor for value | Customer is both collaborator and competitor for value |

*Table 1.* Developing Model of e-Government

# 3. TRADITIONAL SITUATION

Organisations, particularly Government organisations are typically structured in a top down bureaucratic style, creating a barrier between the customer and the organisation and forcing customers to develop a knowledge of the structure to be able to seek services (Barreyre, 1988). The Western Australian Government has established 53 agencies to provide a variety of Government services to the public. Each agency reports to a Cabinet Minister, has a Chief Executive Officer accountable for all aspects of the agency and a corporate executive team responsible for the operation of the divisions within the agency. Each agency is charged with a specific function or service and has responsibility for setting Policy in relation to their function, providing the Minister with responses to correspondence and assisting the public. As an example the Aboriginal Affairs Department has responsibility for assisting all Aboriginal people within the state to access Government services; ensuring the welfare of Aboriginal people, their culture and heritage and maintaining traditional Aboriginal sites. The Ministry of Sport and Recreation are responsible for increasing the participation of all West Australians in sport, maintaining sporting venues throughout the state and assisting elite West Australian athletes. Whereas the Education Department is responsible for the education of all primary and secondary aged children in the state. All Western Australian Government agencies have similar structures that comply to a traditional organisational structure and for the main part work in isolation from each other. Both the Education Department and Ministry of Sport and Recreation have an Aboriginal affairs section which work in isolation of each other and the Aboriginal Affairs Department.

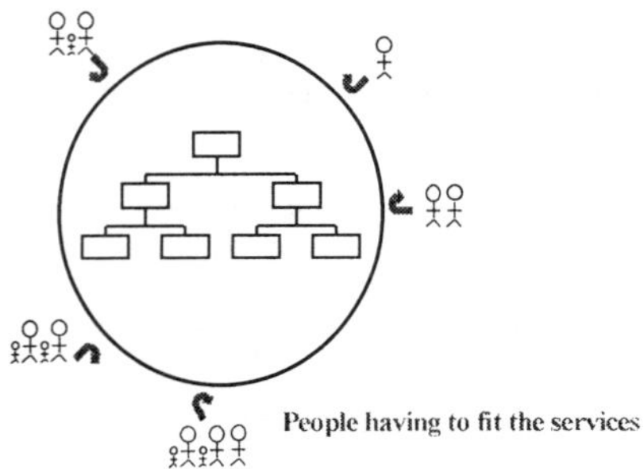


*Figure 1.* Traditional Agency

This approach forces the customers to fit or break into this structure if they require a service (figure 1). Customers must seek out the area that deals with their particular requirement. They must move between many organisations to in access to all the services they need. As an example a company within Western Australia seeking to explore mineral deposits on Aboriginal Lands would need to seek approval and apply for appropriate permits through the Department of Minerals and Energy, the Department of Land Administration and the Aboriginal Affairs Department. This requires the customer to discover which Departments need to be approached, to approach each individually and to locate the appropriate section within each organisation to obtain the correct advice.

There is a need particularly within a service environment such as Government agencies to move the customer into the centre and to offer a wide range of services across agencies (Hopkins and Jamil, 1997). This requires agencies to develop close working relationships and implement a structure based on the idea of collaboration. (Figure 2).

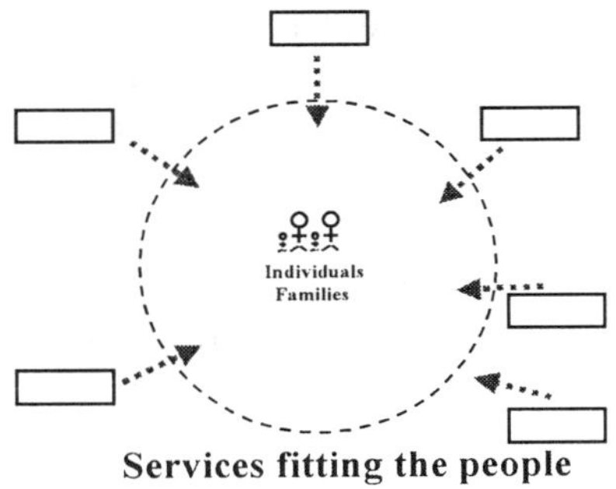


Figure 2. Customer-Centric Agency

# 4. ACHIEVING A SERVICE DRIVEN ENVIRONMENT

Many companies already focus on core value adding processes, working with external partners to jointly bring forward a service. These companies believe that a more flexible organisation built around a series of alliances and business relationships, is the most effective way to respond quickly and creatively to constantly changing market conditions (Miles and Snow, 1995). The conventional, vertically integrated corporation may be too slow, or have too much retained infrastructure to allow it to compete with companies who can quickly put together a customised response to its clients (Campbell and DiNicola 1997). If Government agencies are to provide a public service then they must embrace wholeheartedly the notion of the value alliance. The value alliance emphasises the decentralisation of control, the creation of more flexible patterns of working, a greater empowerment of the workforce and the customer, the displacement of hierarchy by teamwork, the development of a greater sense of collective responsibility and the creation of more collaborative relationships among co-workers and customers (Burn and Barnett, 2000).

To initiate such developments an agency needs to perform a full customer value chain analysis in order to set up a number of different agency alliances through an electronic network. This may form the basis for a one-stop portal where the alliance combines a range of services and facilities in one package forming one single customer supply chain. Participants may come together on a project by project basis but generally the general contracting agency provides coordination. Where longer term relationships have developed the value alliance often adopts the form of value constellations where agencies and funding services have multiple interactions and a complex and enduring communications structure is embedded within the alliance (Burn and Barnett, 2000) – see Figure 3. Substitutability has traditionally been a function of efficiency and transaction costs: searching for, evaluating, and commencing operations with potential partners has been a costly and slow government procedure, relying as it does on information transfer, the establishment of trust and policy rules across states, time zones, culture, and legal frameworks. These have determined the relative positioning of partners on the chain and the reciprocity of the relationship.

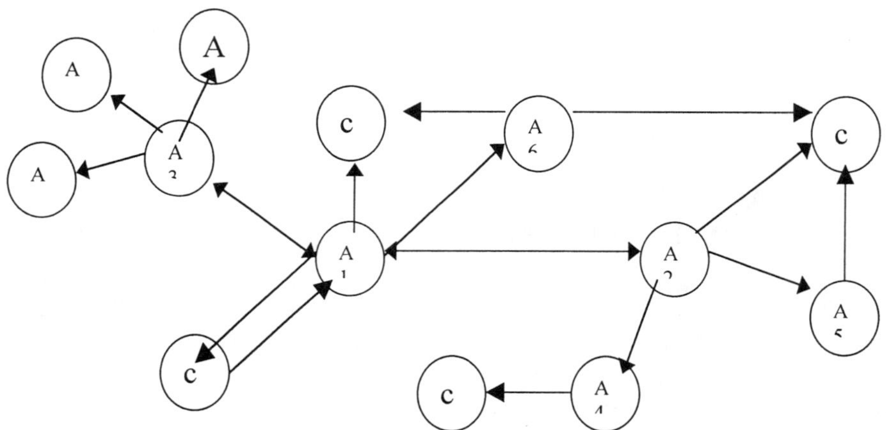


**Figure 3. Value Alliance Model**

This value-alliance will be built around customer value chains and enable the sharing of resources, skills and knowledge to produce a 'best' customer solution and enable agencies to be more responsive to customer requirements and offer superior quality of service. Each agency may be required to form several value-alliance virtual organisations depending on what has been identified as requiring one stop processes for clients.

# 5. MANAGING A VIRTUAL AGENCY MODEL

In order to achieve a successful value-alliance it is essential that a business planning model is established that ensures each member agency has 'buy-in' to the desired outcomes. The first step to achieve 'buy-in' is to establish a high level committee comprising of the Chief Executive Officers from each of the member agencies. The committee is charged with the responsibility of identifying the virtual organisation's goals. These goals must then be meshed into the individual agency's processes.

Therefore any business planning must be built on services, delivery goals and objectives that focus on its customers through direct customer and front-line employee input. To achieve this there must be a fundamental shift in management and workforce thinking and practices that include:

- Pervasive knowledge sharing, feedback and communication;
- Integration of environmental considerations at the earliest stages of
- design;
- Effective partnerships with customers.
- Commitment to using customer feedback to drive changes in operations, goals and vision; and
- Frontline employees given the authority to deal with customer issues.

It is essential that each agency is represented by the Chief Executive Officer. Without the commitment and support of the CEO it is highly unlikely that the agency will implement processes in line with the goals of the committee nor will the committee have 'buy in' from the senior executive of the agency. Commitment grows as employees understand what is being developed, this understanding is achieved through communication and commitment from the top. In order to achieve the most appropriate goals that focus on the customers' requirements and establish a one stop shop from the clients viewpoint a model (figure 4) must be established that passes information between all levels both within each agency and between the agencies. It is important to recognise the customers as integral members of the virtual organisation.

This model establishes information flows that:

- Ensure customers and front line staff can impact on the strategic planning process through passing information upwards;
- Agreed goals are passed to all levels of each agency;
- These goals are articulated to clients; and
- Planning takes place across agencies at all levels

*Figure 4.* Virtual Organisation Planning Model

A key to the success of an organisation is a network of open communication, a combination of sharing and listening flowing both horizontally and vertically through the organisation. Management must share details with employees. A workforce that is involved is much more likely to 'buy in' to management's vision and work together for results. Management must be able to combine the differences in diversity and organisation structure, in order to make the virtual organisation reach its target. Virtual teamwork places a particular emphasis on communication and the development of 'awareness' skills. It is critical that front-line employees have immediate access to current information.

The key groups in this model are the Strategic Planning Committee (SPC) and the local staff. Key responsibilities of the SPC are to develop goals that reflect customer needs, all members are committed to the goals and each member ensures that their agency implements processes aimed at addressing the goals. Local staff have two key responsibilities:

1. Ascertain needs and provide information, advice and advocacy support to groups, communities and individuals within their area; and
2. Inform government of unmet needs and priority issues (figure 5).

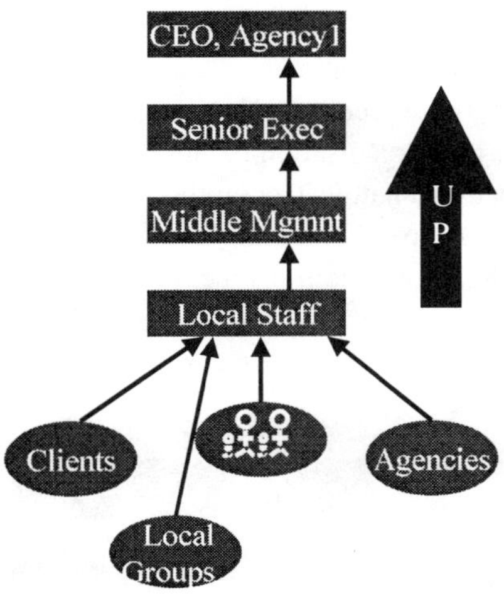


*Figure 5.* Informing Government

The following case study serves to explicate this model.

# 6. CASE STUDY - THE ABORIGINAL AFFAIRS DEPARTMENT

The Aboriginal Affairs Department (AAD) is a Western Australian State Government Agency. In 1994 a taskforce on Aboriginal Social Justice was formed. The terms of reference for this taskforce was to review the activities of the Government of Western Australia in relation to the social conditions and development of Aboriginal people and to recommend a strategy for implementation of Government's programmes. Recommendations of the taskforce included:

- The need for high calibre regional coordinators with a role to include breaking down barriers between Government agencies and reducing waste and duplication;
- A regional structure be implemented to undertake regional liaison and co-ordination across Government agencies in co-operation with local Aboriginal communities;

- The establishment of an Aboriginal Affairs Department structured as a planning, advisory, co-ordinating and monitoring agency and not responsible for administration of specific programmes.

In order to implement these recommendations the Government established AAD. AAD has utilised the virtual organisation planning model (figure 6) and established the Aboriginal Affairs Co-ordinating Committee (AACC). The AACC consist of Chief Executive Officers from all State Government agencies that have a role in Aboriginal affairs including education, justice, police and housing. The major role of the AACC is to establish a set of strategic goals for Aboriginal affairs and to ensure that each of their agencies implement processes aimed at achieving the goals.

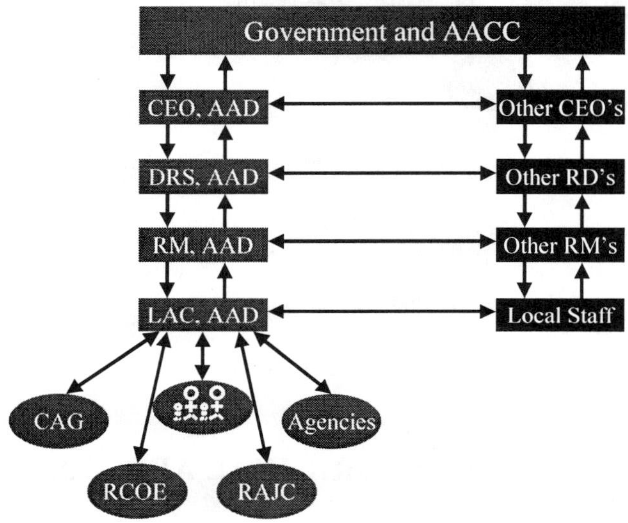


*Figure 6.* Aboriginal Affairs Virtual Organisation

Within AAD a structure known as a local area co-ordination approach (LAC) has been established to ensure:

- Pervasive knowledge sharing, feedback and communication;
- Integration of environmental considerations at the earliest stages of design;
- Effective partnerships with customers.
- Commitment to using customer feedback to drive changes in operations, goals and vision; and
- Frontline employees are given the authority to deal with customer issues.

This structure includes a Regional Services Director (DRS) that can operate at the state level, Regional Managers (RM) operating at the regional level and working closely with the regional offices of the other organisations within the virtual organisation and Local Area Co-ordinators working locally with the clients.

A major component of the model is the strategic transfer of information. From the management perspective information regarding broad organisation goals, policy initiatives, inter-agency agreements, central/regional office issues is passed down (figure 7). It is critical to ensure information has been made available to LAC and properly understood.

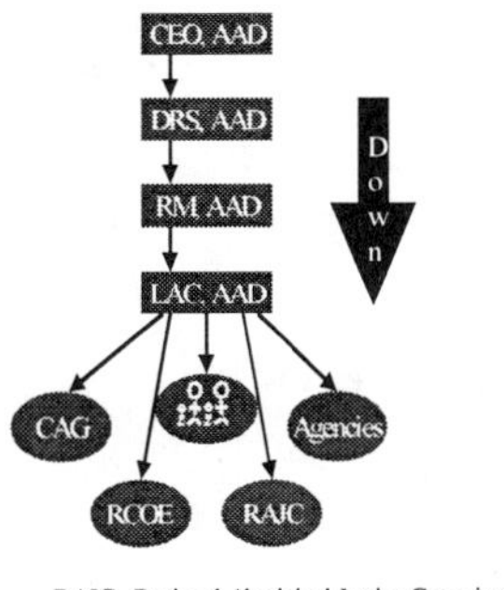


**Figure 7 – Management Perspective**

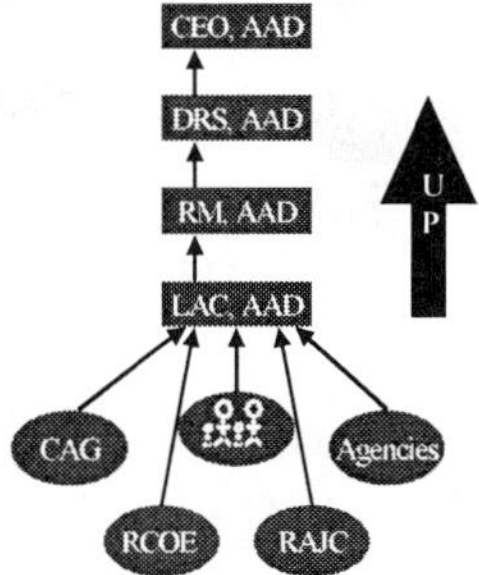


RAJC - Regional Aboriginal Justice Committee
RCOE - Regional Commission of Elders

**Figure 8 – Service Perspective**

From the service perspective LAC holds crucial information on local needs and priorities, local service initiatives, inter-agency co-ordination, community development and heritage issues. This information must be collated from each LAC to develop an accurate and current profile of local issues, priorities and initiatives.

The key responsibilities of the LAC are:

- Monitor and facilitate co-ordination of services across agencies (figure 9);
- Promote greater involvement of Aboriginal people in policy development, programme design and project management;
- Develop strategies to promote and conserve Aboriginal sites, culture, land access and land ownership; and Administer the Department's services in the local area.

The key differences in the LAC approach are:

- People focused, not service focused;
- Area focused, not project focused;
- Generalist, not specialist;
- Flat not hierarchical;
- Localised, not centralised

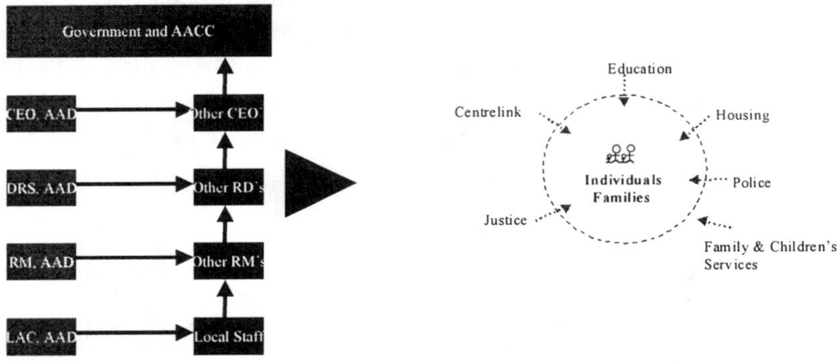


**Figure 9 – Co-ordination of services**

The approach taken by AAD ensures close collaboration between participating organisations. By implementing an overarching planning committee appropriate goals can be developed to achieve what is the agreed role of the virtual organisation (VO). This committee should monitor the progress of each partner in the VO, adjust the goals as dictated by the continual flow of information they receive and be prepared to bring in other members of the VO if required.

An important aspect of the approach is that of establishing solid information flows. It is imperative that information flows down from the AACC through all parts of each organisation. Along the way this information must be value added to by collaboration at the various levels across the member agencies of the VO. This also holds true for the upward movement of information. Without this collaboration between like entities across the member agencies it is unlikely that client needs will be met nor will there be a consolidated approach to achieving the AACC goals.

At the grassroots or local level this collaboration is even more important. Without collaboration at this level it will not be possible to develop a one stop service for the clients. This one stop service is crucial to developing the trust of the client group, providing them with a quality service experience and importantly gathering information in regard to their current and future requirements. The major focus of the model is to develop this one stop service that meets current and future demands in a proactive manner. Of prime importance is the ability of the Local Area Coordinators to link up with other members of the VO at the local level to satisfy requests from local customers for services that cross functional boundaries.

# 7. LESSONS LEARNED

The primary aim of the Aboriginal Affairs Department is to ensure that all Government services revolve around its customers as opposed to establishing bureaucracies that customers need to break into to obtain the services they require. That is to establish a mechanism that will:

- Assist AAD's customers receive equitable services from Government agencies;
- Inform Government of unmet needs and priority issues; and
- Facilitate co-ordination of services across agencies.

To achieve this the Department has looked at ways to best share resources, skills and knowledge to provide better access to a wide range of Government services for their clients. This fits with the developing model of e-Government (Table 1) as follows:

That is each partner in the value alliance :

- brings its core competence - Aboriginal Affairs Department is not required to have expertise in areas such as Education, Health, Housing or Justice;
- has access to other competencies and customer life cycles
- flexible collaborative partnerships – the amount of involvement each agency has in each of the goals varies depending on the agency's specific skills and over time the amount of involvement will change as progress is made towards achieving the goals.
- Trust – for this co-alliance to be successful mutual cooperation will need to develop. This has started to develop through the coordinating committee. All Chief Executive Officers have participated in the meetings and not sent a representative, and agreement has been reached on the primary goals. It remains to be seen if this mutual cooperation does flow down through each organisation. The Local Area Coordinators are working with their local counterparts on common goals however sections of each organisations central office are yet to develop mutual cooperation.

The key issues that the Aboriginal Affairs Department case study has highlighted are:

- The first step in achieving a commitment from each participating organisation is to ensure the Chief Executive Officers are directly involved at a strategic level, however each must be committed to the goals and actively sponsor these goals in their organisation. This will assist in filtering the commitment down to the key stakeholders within each organisation;
- For the model to work appropriate communication links must be established and all stakeholders have evidence of information flowing up and down the model;
- The client group must see immediate benefits and be able to impact on the goal setting process;

- The Local Area Coordinators must be able to establish a high level of trust with both clients and their counterparts in the participating organisations;
- The Local Area Coordinators are the key to gaining an insight in client requirements and must be able to establish a close working relationship with the local staff from the other organisations to establish what the clients perceive as a 'one stop shop' for service. Therefore the recruitment process is vital to identify the required personnel.

## 8. CONCLUSION

As a study in progress the establishment of this model is in its infancy. It is currently too early to tell what impact this model has had on the goals AAD have set out to achieve nor the effect it has had on the Department's primary client base – Aboriginal people. Further research is required as AAD further implements its LAC model and establishes appropriate communication procedures.

There is much research left on the subject of the implementation of the value alliance model in a government agency, especially the distribution of information and communication within the virtual organisation. Managing a virtual organisation may require a whole new set of virtual information leadership skills (Morin et al, 2000). Storing knowledge and expertise from both partners and customers are also important areas of consideration.

When considering these matters, several questions arise for future research:

- How will agencies deal with information and communication that must be passed both up and down, and across functional boundaries, so that close co-operation and team work can be increased?
- How can the value alliance store knowledge and expertise and provide this to all members of the virtual network?
- How can the alliance capitalise on customer competencies and improve both government and governance?

## 9. REFERENCES

Barreyre, P. Y. (1988). "The concept of 'impartition' policies: a different approach to vertical integration strategies." Strategic Management Journal 9: 507-520.

Burn, J. M. and Hackney, R. (2000) Strategies for I-Business Change in Virtual Markets: a co-evolutionary approach. *International Journal of e-Business Strategy Management,* Vol, 2, No. 2, 123-133.

Burn, J. M. and Barnett, M. L. (2000) Emerging Virtual Models for Global e-commerce - world wide retailing in the e-grocery business. Special issue on Global E-Commerce, *Special Millennium Issue of Journal of Global Information Technology Management,* Vol 3, No. 1, pp 18-32.

Campbell, A. and P. DiNicola (1997). "Virtual Organisations. Problem setting and research agenda." .

Cavanagh, J. J. and D. J. Livingston (1997). Serving The American Public: Best Practices in Customer-Driven Strategic Planning.

Hopkins, C. and J. K. Jamil (1997). Serving the American Public - Best Practices in One-Stop Customer Service., Federal Benchmarking Consortium.

Jellinek, D. (2000).E-Government - - Reality or Hype? E-Government Bulletin, October. Avaialble at http://www.cisp.org/imp/october_2000/10_00jellinek.htm

Miles, R. E. and C. C. Snow (1995). "The new network firm: A spherical structure built on a human investment philosophy." Organizational Dynamics 23 (4): 4-18.

Morin, T. Devansky, K. Little, G. and Petrum, C. (2000). The Future of Information Leadership. In *Information leadership - A Government Executive's Guide*, PricewaterhouseCoopers Publications.

Prahalad, C. K. and V. Ramaswamy (2000). Co-opting customer competence. Harvard Business Review 78(1)(79-87).

Sprecher, M. H. (2000) Racing to e-government: Using the Internet for citizen service delivery. Government Finance Review, Vol. 16, 5, 21-22.

Symonds, M. (2000). Government and the Internet: The Next Revolution. The Economist, Jun 24.

Von Hoffman, C. (1999). The Making of E-Government. COI Enterprise Magazine, Nov, 15.

53

# Under Some Delusion: Considerations On The Limits of E-Democracy

Neil Collins[1], Patrick Butler[2]
[1]*Department of Government, University College Cork, Ireland*
[2]*School of Business Studies, Trinity College Dublin, Ireland*

**Abstract**: The potential for electronic access to information and channels of participation is fraught with danger for democracy. For political and public sector interests to follow slavishly the commercial pioneers is highly questionable, and probably perilous. The inherently conflictual nature of both government and democracy demands attention to the institutions and patterns of representative democracy. Consideration in the first instance of the peculiar aspects of public sector products, organisations and marketplaces would bring a contextual sensitivity to the project, thereby improving design and application of e-based solutions. More attention should be paid to the mechanisms of representative democracy so that they can be incorporated into e-systems rather than clash with them.

## 1. E-GOVERNMENT AND E-DEMOCRACY

*The people never give up their liberties but under some delusion.*
(Edmund Burke, Speech at County Meeting, Buckinghamshire, England, 1784)

E-Government and e-democracy have been discussed as if they could be usefully differentiated. The former is about service delivery, especially where information and its availability are key, and the latter involves the use of the new technology to facilitate widespread, immediate and efficient participation. This distinction represents the most recent manifestation of a recurring search for a distinction between public administration and politics i.e. between the neutral application of management techniques, and politically charged expressions of value. The central contention of this paper is that the separation of these concepts conveys a false sense that they may be examined and developed in isolation. Information, however transmitted, is seldom neutral – even more so when it concerns access to, distribution of, or accountability for public sector services. Hence, the same caution that characterises today's liberal democracy should guide how e-systems deal with the demands of the public.

In the foregoing quotation, the Irish philosopher Edmund Burke was commenting at a time when popular views were being expressed in the United Kingdom, France, and elsewhere in Europe via the large scale, popular, participative method of mob rule. Liberal democracies have since developed ways of facilitating popular participation with political accountability, responsibility and transparency through the institutions of representative democracy. The direct democracy commonly suggested in the e-government and e-democracy debate is potentially dangerous and naïve. It implies that what is technically possible is politically or democratically desirable.

> As direct democracy takes root, the Americans voter will become more involved and active. We don't have to wait anymore for the next election to express our views while Congress makes decisions for us. We don't have to wait for a call from a pollster to speak our piece. We are going to take to the Internet and tell our representatives what to do whenever we damn well feel like it (Morris 2000; ixia).

Such assertions are not dissimilar to those that provoked Burke's views regarding the rise of demagogues and popular movements in the late eighteenth century. It is notable, of course, that democracy did not always have positive connotations. For most "thinking" people up until the twentieth century, democracy was to be treated with caution, since it meant rule by the common masses. We have moved on from Burke but his advice may still be valuable.

## 2. POLITICAL DISCOURSE

The dominant neo-liberal paradigm of current political discourse is based on an analogy with the free market. Deregulation, customers, clients, partnerships and so on. are the concepts that inform new public management. It is apposite, therefore, that the notion that the market will readily adopt a so-called technology-push model in every case has been seen to be severely limiting even in purely commercial terms. The recent situation regarding the relative failure of business-to-business (B2B) exchanges is a case in point. The hyperbole surrounding the potential of such activity, based on the lowest cost-best price model, was seen to offer a false hope. This is a market that never reached anything near the expectations promoted by many in the field. While there are multiple and complex explanations for this, there is a consensus that just because the technology was available to revise and improve the way firms organised their procurement processes, firms did not necessarily adopt what appeared to be the "best" model (see Kaplan and Sawhney 2000, Wise and Morrisson 2000). There are many more factors involved in the total transaction cost explanation than simply price. Indeed, one of the features of industrial marketing in the past decade has been the shift away from a purely price-based model of competition, and toward a long-term, interactive relationship orientation (Webster 1992, Ford 1990). The market efficiencies assumed in the electronic business environment do not always provide the best overall model of exchange. In the political "marketplace", similarly, the most technologically efficient approach will not necessarily provide for the most appropriate solution. Both e-government and e-democracy may well accentuate the cumulative inequalities that mark all liberal democracies in terms of access to public resources.

Politics involves translating electors' preferences into political action in the form of public services. The stable society is one where people feel that the pattern of service delivery is fair and equitable, as well as efficient. For most people, the pattern of the consumption of public services is their sense of democracy. Many of the descriptions of electronic government address this service delivery dimension. They neglect, however, fundamental questions of democratic principles and processes. As Steven Clift observed at the UK House of Commons Public Administration Select Committee, "the Minnesota E-democracy project, widely regarded as a beacon of best practice, suggested that the main value of e-democracy is not in the executive (government delivery) wing of governance, but the legislative wing where links between legislators and the citizens" (http://www.parliament.the-stationeryoffice.co.uk/pa/cm1999).

Citizens give their opinions, whether electronically or otherwise, to affect policy outcomes. Sometimes the results may be declaratory, but more often the intention is a change in the pattern of service provision or financial burden. The emphasis here, therefore, is the attempt to broaden the question of applying ICT to governing. In this volume, Gronlund makes the specific case for including existing representative systems of democracy that already inform and coordinate societal planning, governance and organisation in civil society. This is an important perspective, particularly in the context of continually evolving e-type models in all areas of the social sciences – including, importantly, economics and management. It is by no means clear that electronic brokerage effects and electronic integration effects have been fully understood, for instance. Given the disastrous market assessments within the "dotcom" sectors, for political and public sector interests to follow slavishly the commercial pioneers is highly questionable and probably perilous.

## 3. PUBLIC OPINION AND PUBLIC POLICY

Existing representative systems of democracy have built up "checks and balances" between popular opinion and the delivery of public services. In a democracy, every citizen is assumed to have views of equal value on a wide range of public issues. The number of potential combinations of opinion, therefore, is vast. The political system deals with the divergent tasks of facilitating the articulation of views while aggregating them into manageable combinations as expressed in party manifestos, government policy statements and the like. Ultimately, for any one policy issue, governments, parliaments and other public agencies must be presented with very few options for decision. By this we mean that representative institutions play a role in drawing together and assessing ideas in the public domain. These "filtering mechanisms" have acted to dampen the impact of changes in public opinion on policy. New proposals relating to e-democracy and e-government tend to suggest more direct links between public opinion and government policy, inherently implying that these intermediating institutions may be bypassed.

> When will voters be consulted on important issues? Whenever they want to be. Anytime enough Internet users want to have a referendum they will simply have one. There will likely be hundreds of referendums each year. (Morris 2000:33)

It seems that commercial models that promote a narrow definition of political reality in which opinions on policy issues are the equivalent of consumer preferences overly influence the debate on e-democracy. There is also a critical danger that the American political system of weak legislative parties and fractured party competition will be assumed as the rule rather than the exception. In most liberal democracies, disciplined and ideologically differentiated parties provide well-defined options across a wide range of policy areas. The analogy of a market constantly being guided towards some optimal equilibrium by the "invisible hand" of competing consumer preferences is too overdrawn to be helpful.

The issues raised by the evolution of e-government and e-democracy are broad. This paper, therefore, concentrates on a particularly neglected aspect of the debate. The argument here is twofold: e-based models that offer more efficient solutions to governing may be too simplistic to accommodate the complexities of public sector management and service delivery; and, those political and public service complexities must be recognised and addressed specifically to evaluate the appropriateness or otherwise of electronic interventions or means of conducting business in these contexts.

# 4. THE NEW PUBLIC SECTOR

With the recent managerialist public sector reforms in the western democracies, the primary focus has been on the lessons from the private sector. The demise of the venerable term "public administration" and the ascendancy of "public management" is evidence of this. If we are to make progress by incorporating electronic platforms and delivery mechanisms in the public sector, we must recognise the changing relationship between the state and the citizen. Hence, we are obliged to be clear about how we conceptualise the public sector.

The literature on public management, including healthcare, education, leisure and tourism is diverse and fragmented. There is no generally accepted model or framework that, by addressing the public sector context in its entirety, provides a guide to practitioners. No consensus exists about what the public sector and its 'products' are. There are no inherent properties of goods and services that make them 'naturally' public services. As Lane (1993) puts it: "There is no single way to make the private-public distinction" (p45). In the same way that management analysts and practitioners must grasp the essential issues in the financial services, business-to-business, high technology and fast-moving consumer goods industries, the public sector must be understood in order to adapt management frameworks, tools and techniques. This contextual analysis must certainly precede the added complications of considering and developing electronic communications and delivery mechanisms. The approach taken here is to delineate those distinctive factors in the public sector context that have implications for strategy and management.

While the literature on public management is extensive, we draw attention to three distinctive aspects of public services, an understanding of which give support to the application of electronically-based management approaches. These areas are:

- the public service product;
- the public service organisation; and,
- the public service marketplace.

## 4.1 Public Sector Products and the e Debate

There are many distinctive features of public sector products. While governments provide physical infrastructure like roads, hospitals and housing, in the main the provision is service-based. Services have their own kinds of delivery models, the field is well established in the literature, and specific public sector models have been developed (Butler and Collins 1995). It is notable that public services also include constraints on behaviour, such as rules and regulations restricting activities, and duties that require adherence to particular behaviours, such as filling in census forms, and, in some states, voting in elections. Such private constraint is seen as the 'price' of public benefit; there exists an acceptance on the part of citizens in the democratic order of the need to be constrained. This acceptance, is, however, dependent on the assumption that due process has been followed, i.e. that the constraints have been legitimised according to the norms of the political system. E-government will also have to demonstrate that it fulfils the criteria of liberal democracy.

Perhaps the most distinctive aspect of concern to this discussion is that public services often contain elements of what economists understand as 'public goods' (Page 1983). Specifically, these are consumed jointly i.e. consumers are not rivals; and, one cannot exclude from the consumption benefits those who do not pay. The providers of public services face the classic 'free rider' dilemma. For example, the streetlights shine on everyone whether or not they contribute to the cost through taxation; the village green is owned by all. There is a sense of collective obligation in the provision of resources for public goods. It is generally accepted that individualistic self-interest can militate against the general good in the allocation of certain products. The implications for managing public goods include the recognition of the imperfect link between provision and payment.

For the development of e-government, this question of public goods demands specialist attention. It may be argued that the examples noted above are, by definition, local phenomena. As such, if there is any element of free-riding, it is most likely to be by fellow-citizens. By complete contrast, the provision of a range of public services in an e mode – over the Internet, for instance – allows free riding on a global scale. That is, publicly available products and services may be accessible to people from any location. Within the nation state, even public goods are the responsibility of identifiable individuals and the democratic system can be held accountable. Both the principal and agent are known. With e-delivery, on the other hand, this link can be far more tenuous.

Addressing such issues, particularly in the area of information provision, might require some agreements between nations on the division of labour and perhaps proportional contributions to services online. Unless the problem is addressed, there would be no reason for public bodies to innovate and develop new material. This is akin to the threat to intellectual property rights of mass scale digital copying of copyrighted material. For instance, the music industry is especially vulnerable in this regard, and is currently waging defensive battles on technological, political and legal fronts. The music industry is perceived by observers to be at the cutting edge of such monumental structural change, and development are being watched very closely by others who anticipate similar issues in their own field.

The information culture of the Web community is very different to the "Old Economy" view. It would be held that, in a sharing, win-win environment, there is no economic value in scarcity of information, except in exceptional and specific situations. The knowledge society approach is that information wants to be free and should be accommodated.

Where access to information must be constrained, technological solutions will be developed. So, for instance, coded access based on secure technologies should enable people and institutions to resolve matters associated with public good characteristics. These, however, are peculiar to the public sector, and demand examination to a degree not usually considered in private sector initiatives.

## 4.2 Public Sector Organisations and the eDebate

Among the primary characteristics of most public sector organisations are the increasing adoption of managerialist perspectives and techniques, the not-for-profit ethos and political accountability. Professional management, explicit standards of performance, private sector styles of practice and parsimony in resource use are all features of the public sector today. While many products have not changed fundamentally, there have been radical changes in the organisation for their delivery. Public sector organisations also display many of the characteristics associated with those in the private not-for-profit sector. Among charities, trusts, human rights and medical organisations, the primary goal of the organisation is not profit. Although trading activities may well produce a profit, that is generally referred to as "surplus".

The political accountability of public sector organisations has special implications for how they might engage with electronic forms of information, communication and service delivery. The actions of public service organisations have the potential of being scrutinised by the public or their political representatives in ways that do not exist in the private commercial world. Even relatively new organisational arrangements, such as contracting out, executive agencies and public-private partnerships, have not generally severed this political link. As such, relatively minor errors risk becoming political scandals. It follows that organisations in the public sector are cautious, rule-bound and relatively inflexible. This, of course, is in contrast to the culture of openness, sharing and experiment among individuals and entities in the virtual world.

By way of an example of the difficulties to which this political accountability gives rise, the case of the French Government versus Yahoo!.com is illustrative. In this situation, the Government sought to control public access to information regarding Nazi memorabilia on the World Wide Web. The tradition of political institutions is that they provide a form of control in the interests of the community; the e-environment challenges and undermines this by its avowed openness. Accountability is important in many domains, but public sector organisational accountability is rife with sensitivities, principle and community acceptance. Where electronic communication issues enter the arena, the matters are exacerbated.

Further, to questions regarding public organisation characteristics, the structuring of political, or public sector, organisations is traditionally functional. That is, government departments organise around functions such as finance, security, welfare and education. That makes perfect organisational sense from the supplier's perspective. However, the consuming citizen might not understand that form of organisation. One of the lessons of e-business development is the successful application of metamarket theory – a market of markets. That is, while business firms tend to think in terms of products and industry sectors, consumers perceive their worlds in terms of activities. So, for instance, the human activity that draws together businesses in such ostensibly different industries as flowers, hotels, clothing, photography, music and religious services is the wedding. The Web offers a highly efficient medium for aggregating such streams. It is an aggregator that enables the convergence of services.

For government, and, critically, for e-democracy, there is significant merit in exploring how citizens perceive the overlap and separation of public services, and of their entitlements and duties. There may be particular welfare effects in presenting the approach that the government is integrated, united and working across functional boundaries in the common interest. The Web provides what appears to be, and may actually become, a highly efficient "one-stop-shop" kind of arrangement. This could be especially helpful for "bureaucratically illiterate" citizens and their sponsors, who may conventionally have failed to access information and entitlements because they were spread across physically separate institutions such as justice, housing or childcare. Of course, it could also exacerbate the problems of those who find themselves experiencing access difficulties in any one area. In the meta sense, this is a "market of markets". The e-government aspect is one of providing an intermediary function that combines or aggregates services that, while continuing to be performed by separated organisations, offer the citizen-consumer the appearance of a single integrated function.

## 4.3 Public Sector Markets and the eDebate

The public sector market is hugely diverse in terms of population, structure, demand and activity. In as much as society can be regarded as a market for public sector services, citizens can be understood as consumers of the outputs of political and public sector organisations and processes. Citizen-consumers take the form of students, patients, residents, motorists etc. Their unifying characteristic, however, is that they are citizens. As citizens, people define themselves in terms of identity, rights and duties. Citizens, however, may expect to be treated as customers, but may not care to be referred to as such. Citizenship is also an egalitarian notion, suggesting equality of treatment by representatives of the state regardless of rank or fortune. This idea is reinforced by the fact that public goods are free at the point of delivery, and the link between use and taxation is long and tenuous. Further, people play multiple roles as public service consumers, being at the same time funders, users and assessors.

Citizens can usually find redress for grievances i.e. dissatisfaction with services, through constitutional, political and legal remedies. Consumers, on the other hand, typically engage in complaining behaviour. Citizens owe loyalty but consumers can more easily exit the relationship (Hirschman 1970). Much of the change in the market characteristics for public services revolves around the attempts by governments tutored by public choice models to educate citizens to act like consumers. Thus, for example, the increasing use of citizens' charters in the public services is aimed at facilitating complaint and comprehension for service users, i.e. customers (Millar and Peroni 1992). The authors of such charters expect better public services to result from a market of customers than one of citizens.

Better informed citizens, acting as confident consumers, make for a better democracy. The establishment of e-government should reduce the efforts of complaint, thereby enabling better quality feedback from the marketplace and more responsive service providers. Accepting the citizen as a consumer allows for development of the marketplace analogy. Getting services to the market is the function of channels, a conceptualisation that is important in understanding the potential for e-government.

Three main channel effects of ICT developments may be identified. First, disintermediation occurs where the channel is shortened because the customer accesses the producer directly. In the government situation, this could be where the citizen no longer needs to go through an agency of some kind. The contact is direct, without need for intercession. Cultural norms, as well as established practices and structures, will influence the appropriateness or otherwise of disintermediation. Second, the establishment of information intermediaries (infomediaries) (Hagel and Rayport 2000) is another development. In this case, the channel gets longer by the introduction of a new player, the function of which is to improve the information flows in one or both directions. Although the channels appears to have more members, and so become longer, if the infomediary cuts through complicated info-clutter, and actually adds value, it is a positive contribution. Third, the concept of metamediaries has been outlined above (Sawhney 1999). In this context it may approach a combination of political and public sector services accessed through a single point. The obvious advantages include the development of political and public sector arrangements more in keeping with the publics' perspectives than the providers'. These kinds of market or channel solutions are not mutually exclusive; all may exist in a complementary fashion.

## 5. CONCLUSIONS

Clearly, none of the advocates for e-government and e-democracy is ill intentioned towards democratic principles. They may feel some impatience at the idiosyncrasies of the current processes, and point optimistically to the potential for electronic access to information and channels of participation. The argument of this paper, however, is that these benefits, though real, are also fraught with danger for democracy. In Burke's terms, the e-democracy advocates are in danger of being deluded by the technical advances into neglecting the inherently conflictual nature of both government and democracy. However efficiently delivered, information about politics is never neutral; it is given to effect government outcomes. The distinctive characteristics of the political and public sector contexts must be addressed by the proponents of e-based solutions. There would be an arrogance and ignorance on the part of those who would seek to import directly technology-based solutions from the commercial world into the relations between the state, the public institutions and the citizenry. Consideration in the first instance of the peculiar aspects of public services, organisations and marketplaces would bring a contextual sensitivity to the project, thereby improving subsequent design and application. Our conclusion is that more attention should be paid to the mechanisms of representative democracy so that they can be incorporated into e-systems rather than clash with them.

## 6. REFERENCES

Butler, P. and Collins, C. (1995), "Marketing Public Services: Concepts and Characteristics", *Journal of Marketing Management*, Vol.11, N0.1-3, pp83-96.

Ford, D. (Ed.) (1990), *Understanding Business Markets: Interactions, Relationships and Networks,* Academic Press, London.

Hagel, J. and J.F. Rayport (2000), "The New Infomediaries", *The McKinsey Quarterly*, No. 3.

Hirschman, A.O. (1970), *Exit, Voice and Loyalty: Response to Decline in Firms, Organisations and States*, Mass, Harvard University Press.

Kaplan, S. and M. Sawhney (2000), "E-Hubs: The New B2B Marketplaces", Harvard Business Review, May-June, pp.97-103.

Lane, J.E. (1993), *The Public Sector: Concepts, Modules and Approaches*, London, Sage.

Millar, S and F. Peroni (1992), "Social Politics and the Citizens Charter", in *Social Policy Review*, Manning, N. and R. Page (Eds) Vol. 4.

Morris, D (2000), *Vote.com*, Los Angeles, Renaissance Books.

Page, B.I. (1983), *Who Gets what From Government*, Los Angeles, UC Press.

Sawhney, M. (1999), "Making New Markets", *Business 2.0*, May, pp.16-21.

Webster, F.F (1992), "The Changing Role of Marketing in the Corporation", *Journal of Marketing*, Vol. 56, pp.1-17.

Wise, R. and D. Morrisson (2000), "Beyond the Exchange: The Future of B2B", Harvard Business Review, November-December, pp.86-96.

MINITRACK FIVE

# E-GOVERNMENT

**Minitrack Chairs:**

Reinhard Riedl,
University of Zurich, reinhard.riedl@ifi.unizh.ch

Michael Gisler,
University of Applied Sciences Bern, Michael.Gisler@iwv.ch

Dieter Spaehni
University of Applied Sciences Bern, Dieter.Spaehni@iwv.ch

54

# Applying Stakeholder Theory to E-Government:
*Benefits and Limits*

Hans J. Scholl
*University at Albany / SUNY, Jscholl@ctg.albany.edu*

**Abstract**: According to most scholars in the field, stakeholder theory is not a special theory on a firm's constituencies but sets out to replace today's prevailing neoclassical economic concept of the firm. Though stakeholder theory explicitly is a theory on a private sector entity, some scholars apply it to public sector organizations. This paper summarizes stakeholder theory, discusses its premises and justifications, compares its tracks, sheds light on recent attempts to join the two tracks, and discusses the benefits and limits of its practical applicability to the public sector using the case of a recent New York State e-Government initiative.

## 1. INTRODUCTION

The term "stakeholder" as Freeman acknowledged in a recent paper indicates a biased perspective. Rather than defining the unit of analysis as "interest groups" or "constituencies", the term "stakeholder" deliberately denotes a contrast to "stockholders", or "shareholders" [1]. Consequently, its proponents understand the stakeholder theory of the firm as an open challenge to the prevailing neoclassical economic theory of the firm (e.g. [2, 3]). The stakeholder research tradition began to unfold in the wake of R. Edward Freeman's seminal *book Strategic Management. A Stakeholders Approach* published in the mid-1980s [4]. The book initiated a still ongoing academic discussion. It suggested in a comprehensive fashion that strategic management of private sector firms might produce better results if managerial efforts adequately regard various stakeholders' concerns. Or, in other words, shareholders benefit long-term if other legitimate interests in the firm do not fall by the wayside.

Two distinct strands of stakeholder research have developed over the past decade and a half. The "Instrumental" or Social Science strand, and the "Business Ethics" strand. While both cover some common ground (e.g. the aforementioned bias), they differ drastically in methods used and results achieved. The Social Science strand sees itself as part of Organizational Studies partly overlapping with agency theory, network theory, and resource dependence theory, to name a few. Scholars of this strand rely on methodological rigor. The Business Ethics-based stakeholder theory implements different means and reaches for different ends. It assumes that each stakeholder of the firm has an intrinsic value regardless of her actual power or legal entitlement. It seeks to formulate correct ethical norms for managerial behavior. Though stakeholder theory roots in and pertains to the private-sector organization of the firm, there is tremendous interest in applying at least part of the findings to the managerial decision-making in public-sector organizations. While some proponents of stakeholder theory are extremely skeptical regarding this undertaking, inter and intra-governmental decision processes may benefit from the application of stakeholder principles. This seems particularly to be the case regarding large-scale investments in information technology where the risk of failure is notably high.

The paper is organized in the following fashion: In the next section, it outlines the basic ideas and concepts of the stakeholder research traditions. In the succeeding section, it compares the two strands in some detail and summarizes various justifications of stakeholder theory. In a further section, the paper discusses the general applicability of stakeholder theory to the public sector using the case of a major e-government initiative in New York State. The paper concludes that stakeholder theory, despite some deficiencies and limitations, has become increasingly influential on managerial decision-making in both the private and the public sector. It also confirms the practical value of a stakeholder approach in e-government-related settings.

## 2. THE UNFOLDING OF A STAKEHOLDER RESEARCH TRADITION!

The definition of the two terms "stake" and "stakeholder" needs to antecede any further discussion of the theory. A "stake" in an organization in terms of stakeholder theory rests on "legal, moral, or presumed" claims, or on the capacity to affect an organization's "behavior, direction, process, or outcomes" [5, 858]. As Reed defines, "stakes are understood to impose normative obligations....we will define a stake as 'an interest for which a valid normative claim can be advanced.'" [6, 467]. The definition of a stakeholder comes in various forms and flavors, some of which prefer a narrow interpretation, others deliberately maintain the broadest possible scope. The classical (and most frequently cited) definition is Freeman's:

> A stakeholder in an organization is (by its definition) any group or individual who can affect or is affected by the achievement of the organization's objective. [4, 25]

Freeman gave this same definition in a 1983 article under the same title in which the broader term "organization's mission" was used instead of "organization's objective" [7, 38]. This definition has been accepted, and simultaneously, criticized depending on the scholarly position. While the business ethics track generally embraces a wider definition, the social science track favors a narrow one. As Cohen observes, the use of the term in business ethics reaches beyond the one in discussions "of law, conveyance, and gambling" [8. 3]. It has been argued that such broad definitions make it possible to include even such groups as terrorists and competitors [9] who, indeed, could affect the firm painfully. This dilemma can partly be resolved by narrowing the definition in a meaningful way. By following Clarkson's argument [10], Mitchell et al. argue that the use of risk as a second defining property for the stake in an organization helps to "narrow the stakeholder field to those with legitimate claims, regardless of their power to influence the firm or the legitimacy of their relationship to the firm" [5, 857]. In a similar approach, Alkhafaji proposed focusing the stakeholder definition on only those groups that have a vested interest in the survival of the firm can be referred to as stakeholders [11]. A comprehensive, though not totally complete, development chronology of the term into the concept of stakeholder was presented by Mitchell et al. [5]. In summary, the concept is not uniformly accepted. In most cases, however, the differences refer to the scope of the definition.

In the next paragraphs, we will discuss the commonly used justifications of stakeholder theory. The ruling paradigm of corporate governance holds that those who invest their capital into whatever kind of business, and, by that token, those who risk losing their investment in parts or in total, have an entitlement (and an obligation) to govern the business they have invested into. Capital investors (principals) either govern the business themselves, or they do so with support of agents (managers) who they may appoint. As Etzioni points out, this understanding of principals' rights roots in "basically a mere extension of their natural right to own their private property" [12, 680]. However, the straightforward, unlimited transferability of individual property rights into the dimension of a corporation and its governance is increasingly questioned in the literature of various disciplines. This is also reflected in court decisions in both the US and Europe. As Etzioni remarks, "the notion that shareholders govern the corporation is largely a fiction; typically, executives have the greatest power" [12, 680]. The flames of this discussion have been further fanned by the observation that principals and agents may have conflicting interests even among themselves which has led to the development of agency theory [13] and a discussion about corporate governance as such. As Donaldson & Preston observe, "the conventional model of the corporation, in both legal and managerial forms, has failed to discipline self-serving managerial behavior" [14, 87]. Apart from this, the exclusively economic perspective on corporate governance, even though it has gotten some support in recent years through the shareholder value discussion and practices, has been seriously called into question from a number of perspectives.

According to Alkhafaji, corporate performance, power, and privileges as well as the corporate capacity to properly handle future problems of society are at the center of such criticism [11]. When it comes to corporate governance there are obviously more individuals and groups who have something important at stake than the shareowners and managers alone. Furthermore, it is not only the stake as such but more so the potential for conflict of interest [15]. Clarkson argues that such areas of conflict in which an issue is not subject to any legislation or regulation may be those of stakeholder issues rather than social issues [16]. Lastly, as Sethi pointed out, private firms impact other entities in society "above and beyond their economic sphere" [17, 19]. By doing so, they naturally have to be subjected to checks and balances.

Stakeholder theory attempts to describe, prescribe, and derive alternatives for corporate governance that include and balance a multitude of interests. The theory has drawn considerable attention and support since its early formulation. However, as discussed above, there are a least two major branches or strands of stakeholder theory. Jones & Wicks distinguish between the following elements, or better research tracks: "(1) firms/managers should behave in certain ways (normative), (2) certain outcomes are more likely if firms/managers behave in certain ways (instrumental), (3) firms/managers actually behave in certain ways (descriptive/empirical)" [18, 207].

The distinction of normative versus instrumental versus descriptive/empirical research tracks inside stakeholder theory is further elaborated by Donaldson & Preston in their frequently cited article titled *The stakeholder theory of the corporation: concepts, evidence, and implications.* The theory's focus has been the **manager** of the firm, and how she recognizes and acts upon the various stakeholders and their claims. Freeman himself made it clear that what he had presented was an "inherently 'managerial'" concept or a framework about managerial and, organizational behavior" [4, 43].

The theory's origins were designed to provide managers with a handle for developing more balanced and more robust strategies that reflect the unfolding changes inside the organization and in the environment of the corporate landscape. The firm was seen as the hub at the center of the spokes representing various stakeholders who were in essence equidistant to the firm. In other words, the perspective of stakeholder theory was partly oriented towards employees and managers, or towards others, viewing very much in the same fashion, corporate managers look at their firms and the world around them. However, with increasing attention to managerial power and the aftermath of managerial failure, an outside-in perspective, predominantly nurtured from and by business ethics and philosophy scholars has emerged. Among many others, Phillips voices this perspective when stating that the organizational-efficiency argument is "insufficient as a basis of normative organizational ethics study" [9, 52-53].

These different points of departure between the "inside-out" and "outside-in" perspectives have both considerably contributed to the formulation of "the" theory. Nevertheless, the two tracks share only a few basic insights, and also come quite frequently to different, sometimes even contrary, conclusions as emphasized by Donaldson & Preston:

> A striking characteristic of the stakeholder literature is that diverse theoretical approaches are often combined without acknowledgement. Indeed, the temptation to seek a three-in-one theory - or at least to slide from one theoretical base to another - is strong...The muddling of theoretical bases and objectives, although often understandable, has led to less rigorous thinking and analysis than the stakeholder concept requires. [14, 72-73]

Treviño & Weaver hence suggest referring to a stakeholder research tradition, rather than a unified theory [19]. Not surprisingly, stakeholder theory (and particularly its business ethics strand) has drawn outspoken criticism from leading economists. As early as 1970, Milton Friedman in an irresistibly rhetorical article in the New York Times Magazine made his point utterly clear: "The social responsibility of business is to increase its profits" [20]. But critics from inside the field also bluntly state that "it is time to get off the veranda and require stakeholder theory to ground itself in more data" [21, 230], aiming particularly at the social science track.

## 3. THE TWO STRANDS

The **social science track** encompasses the two areas of descriptive/empirical and instrumental research. Frooman offers this short formula: stakeholder theory asks, "(1) Who are they? (2) What do they want? (3) How are they going to try to get it?" [15,193]. Jones & Wicks describe the first strand as revolving around the two claims that managers regard stakeholders because of the "intrinsic justice" of their claims, and because information on stakeholder interests makes the firm more manageable [18, 208]. Donaldson & Preston support the view of the descriptive nature of stakeholder theory. They see the organization as a "constellation of cooperative and competitive interests possessing intrinsic value" [14, 66]. Treviño & Weaver, however, doubt the theoretical originality of this branch of the theory and argue that the fundamentals of descriptive stakeholder theory are ill defined. They conclude that descriptive stakeholder theory looks just like a derivative of other social science theories [19].

The *instrumental* strand links managerial actions to outcomes and attempts to explain how these links work. As Donaldson observes–given the intrinsic value of all stakeholders' interests–those organizations that actively "manage" stakeholder interests fare far better in traditional measures such as return on investment than those who do not [22, 238]. As Jones asserts, instrumental stakeholder theory comes to exactly opposite conclusions as neoclassical economic theory does: Trusting, trustworthy, and cooperative behavior, he maintains, leads to superior results than opportunistic and selfish behavior [13, 432]. Weston & Copeland, on the other hand, see a compatibility of the two theories to the end, that financial managers, for example, have the goal "to maximize the value of the organization" [23, 5] They concede that "value maximization is subject to the constraints of the legitimate claims of the different stakeholders" [23, 12]. Cloninger adds that the reputational capital of the firm is at stake if stakeholders are not properly managed [24]. The instrumental branch helps corporate managers manage stakeholders in practice. It is about "Who and What Really Counts". Under this label, Mitchell et al develop a dynamic perspective on stakeholders than the inevitably static hub-and-spoke view. Their approach distinguishes between attributes of power, legitimacy, and urgency. With help of these attributes seven classes of stakeholders are identified who need different managerial attention at different times [5].

The normative or **business ethics track** deducts norms and principles for corporations in a more or less axiomatic fashion from philosophical vantage points. Kant's categorical imperative is a center pillar in building the theory of the firm's stakeholders. Others ground it on the theory of the common good [25], or on the principle of fairness [9]. Reed proposes to anchor the theory normatively on Critical Theory [6, 455]. He argues that all citizens have a general stake, namely, that their "political equality (is) assured." A firm may even operate within the legal framework but may still become a threat to just this political equality. Reed further advances his argument by pointing to the need that all humans have a legitimate interest in securing their physical and material lives. On this basis, he claims, any economic system must have the capacity to benefit everybody. Consequently, everybody must have a fair economic opportunity. Since firms can undermine this fair opportunity, a legitimate stake in the activity of the firm can be assumed. This, he continues, encompasses forming and maintaining one's own identity and choosing one's own life projects. On this basis, Reed formulates a very general stake: "(W)e all have a stake in all members of the communities to which we belong living in accord with the norms and values of our shared identity" [6, 470].

Though the normative track is mainly concerned with ethical appropriateness of corporate and managerial activity, it does not completely ignore economic necessities. As Jones & Wicks emphasize, it does not seek "to shift the focus of firms away from marketplace success toward human decency but to come up with understandings of business in which these objectives are linked and mutually reinforcing" [18, 209]. However, as Treviño and Weaver almost provokingly ask, "(w)ouldn't normative stakeholder theory's concern for the intrinsic interests of all legitimate stakeholders sometimes dictate that a firm should go out of business?" [19, 225]. They conclude that normative foundations are not essentially necessary to demonstrate the superior performance of corporations who honor and properly treat their stakeholders. Donaldson & Preston, on the other hand, find the three approaches "mutually supportive" [14, 66].

Most scholars agree that ultimately stakeholder theory relies on normative foundations. The social science track, as pointed out earlier, heavily leans up on other social science theories such as agency theory, network theory, game theory, corporate social performance theory, resource-based theory, transaction cost theory, company-as-contract theory, private property theory, to name just a few. Even in the normative track organizational justice theory or fairness theory or the theory of the common good among others are proposed as foundations. This may lead to the conclusion that stakeholder theory is a hybrid with unclear parenthood.

The considerable number of attempts and proposals indicates, at least, a diverse and even controversial understanding the foundations any stakeholder theory rests on. Jones [13, 422] argues that firms that treat stakeholders in a trustworthy manner will develop a competitive advantage since they are able to reduce costs; in other words, good stakeholder management translates into good business. Donaldson & Preston [14, 77] point out that the instrumental justification (as good business) has not been verified, and that there is no compelling evidence for superior performance in terms of traditional measures when proper stakeholder management is employed. Along the same (i.e., instrumental) lines, Clarkson claims that the corporation defined as a system of primary stakeholder groups can only survive in the long run if, and only if, it maintains its ability to create wealth and value for the whole primary stakeholder system of the firm [16]. This proposition, of course, is the most far-reaching and needs to be rigorously tested. If confirmed, the justification of stakeholder theory from an instrumental perspective would no longer be in question.

Justifications from normative quarters may be more compelling as evidenced by unfolding case law, for example, in the United States. The instrumental perspective is concerned with a management issue: "Will the firm, I am managing be better off, if I factor in other stakeholders' interests?". Normative theory rather looks upon the firm from the outside, and is concerned whether or not this form of human organization does produce more harm than good for a broader community of stakeholders. There are different avenues to anchor this perspective. One is, ironically or not, rooted in the property rights themselves–Donaldson and Preston observe:

> The notion that property rights are embedded in human rights and that restrictions against harmful uses are intrinsic to the property rights concept

> clearly brings the interests of others (i.e., of non-owner stakeholders) into the picture. [14, 83]

Etzioni comes to similar conclusions pointing at the changing interpretation of property laws that increasingly attach strings to property rights and emphasize societal obligations. "Corporations are a societal creation, and society grants shareholders a valuable privilege in exchange for which the society can seek some specific consideration [12, 681]. Shankman also argues that "the concept of property rights includes duties to multiple stakeholders, not just the shareholders of the firm" [26, 327]. Philips, in turn, anchors normative stakeholder theory on the principle of fairness [9]. Cohen sees the obligation of informed consent, if individuals or groups are affected, as the basis for normative stakeholder legitimacy [8]. Quinn & Jones, as well as Shankman, maintain that there are four core principles "antecedent" to law or any contract of whatever nature (e.g. between principal and agent)

> –which include "avoid harm to others," "respect the autonomy of others," "avoid lying," and "honor agreements," ... Acting with regard to these principles is the moral obligation of all humans, no matter what profession or position [27, 30]

The absence of respective law does not forsake any of these fundamental principles. That is, individuals are entitled to demand protection under such normative principles regardless of the legal framework that they may live under. On this basis, Reed [6, 474] presents a very fundamental (and conclusive) justification of stakeholder theory on normative grounds: since a firm may threaten the individual and the community in at least two dimensions ("harm", "autonomy"), there are stakes in the activity of any firm. Reed stresses, that capitalist business practice is not self-justified or granted *per se*. It may only represent a generalizable interest as long as it provides efficient markets, fair distribution, limited marginalization (in terms of minorities), limited colonization, and limited hierarchical management. Reed also emphasizes that these norms hold, even if they are not, or not yet, backed up by common law.

These normative lines of reasoning have had a major impact on legislation in many of the United States in the last two decades of the 20th century. Before this background it is amazing that there is still a debate about the justification of stakeholder theory. Effective legislation has been passed (and successive case law has developed) that mandates the consideration of stakeholder interests, or at least, off-burdens management from serving shareholder interests alone. With the advent of stakeholder statutes, and evolving case law in this area, the scenery has changed in favor of advocates of stakeholder interests.

# 4. STAKEHOLDER THEORY AND THE PUBLIC SECTOR

Despite the opposition from prominent proponents of the theory, the stakeholder concept has even found its way into the scholarly discussion of the public administration literature [28] and public sector practice. Donaldson & Preston completely doubt the value and appropriateness of such undertaking [14] because they see the theory as merely one of the (private-sector) firm governed by fundamentally different principles and implications than any public sector organization.

However, even though most public-sector managers perform their tasks for different reasons (e.g., public interest) as opposed to their private-sector counterparts (e.g., survival of the firm, or profit), their decisions have the same capacity to affect individuals or groups pursuing their organization's objective. Also, others–as in the private sector– can affect public managers and governmental organizations. In other words, Freeman's stakeholder definition applies to managerial decision-making also in a governmental context. Instrumental and normative considerations can be applied to public-sector stakeholder scenarios as much as in the private sector. However, as Tennert & Schroeder [28] find, public sector managers lack a proper toolkit for stakeholder identification and management. This leads to "difficult stakeholder situations" after public-sector decisions have been made (p. 3). Since the public sector manager's self-understanding is shifting from being a public administrator towards the one of a public facilitator, the authors see an even greater necessity for a solid grounding of stakeholder management in the public sector. "Working in the public sector has become a multi-jurisdictional and multi-sector endeavor" (p. 5) according to the two authors. In other words, the shift from a more hierarchical to a more network-type organizations further demands inclusion and management of constituencies.

Tennert & Schroeder propose the combination of Mitchell et al.'s concept of stakeholder identification along the lines of power, legitimacy, and urgency (cf. [5]) with Blair & Whitehead's [29] diagnostic topology of stakeholders' potential for collaboration versus their potential for threatening the organization. The authors propose a questionnaire by which these five capacities can be assessed [28, 33].

This framework has been tested in the context of a major e-Government initiative in New York State (cf. [30]): The Central Accounting System of the State is currently based on two-decade old mainframe technology. This system has not only reached its limits in terms of expandability and maintainability (user interface, service, etc.) but it also lacks integration and functionality in important areas of contemporary financial management. Since the system is the spine of the State's financial management and as such a mission-critical system to the State's overall functioning, utmost caution has to accompany any repair, any addition, or any overhaul of this system. On the other hand, New York State officials understand the necessity for a major overhaul and the potential for business process redesign and integration across government agencies, government levels, and government branches when overhauling the Central Accounting System (CAS) and expanding its scope. One vision is to have a streamlined and integrated (in terms of business processes and data structures) Intranet and Extranet-based accounting system that serves the State as a hub of transaction and financial management for governmental entities as well as private-sector firms (contractors, vendors). Such a system would be a highly sophisticated government-to-government (g2g), and partly government-to-business (g2b), e-government application with a high potential for reducing costs, integrating processes and services, increasing response time, and enhancing transparency and accessibility.

However, before an ambitious project of this scale and scope can be launched, it is mandatory to understand the needs of the primary and secondary stakeholders in such a setting. This consideration led to a stakeholder needs analysis which was conducted by the University at Albany based Center for Technology in Government. In this project, the Tennert & Schroeder framework was used to identify primary stakeholders (also referred to as strategic partners) as well as secondary and tertiary stakeholders. A joint project team was formed with members from the Office of the State Comptroller (which has the statutory authority over the State's Central Accounting System) and the Center for Technology in Government. This team identified five primary stakeholders to the project: the State Assembly, the State Senate, the Division of the Budget, the Office for Technology, and the Leadership of the Office of the State Comptroller. These primary stakeholders jointly or alone command (1) the power, (2) the legitimacy, and (3) the urgency to advance or to shut down the CAS overhaul project at almost any given point in time. In other words, without the support (or at least friendly indulgence) of any one of these primary stakeholders the project would be doomed.

However, secondary stakeholders (those who do not rank high on all three scales of power, legitimacy, and urgency), and even tertiary stakeholders (those who only score high on one of the scales), have a capacity to contribute or to impede the project to various degrees as well. State agencies that process over 17.5 millions transaction per day using the CAS, local governments (such as counties, cities, towns, and villages but also the Federal government), and finally non-governemental entities, that is, in total several thousand organizations, fall into these latter two categories. Applying Blair & Whitehead's diagnostic topology helped the joint project team to understand (in a fairly detailed fashion) the potential for collaboration with and threat from the primary stakeholders, and, in more general terms, for the other two stakeholder groups. It was found that there are eight distinct types of CAS users. These types vary in terms of their dependence on CAS, the scale and scope of its usage, and the nature of usage (transactional, analytical/informational).

In a series of 13 uniformly facilitated half-day workshops over 200 experts from 41 State agencies and 10 non-governmental entities were asked about their specific transactional and informational requirements. Six themes turned out to be the high-priority needs: (1) data access and manipulation capabilities, (2) real-time workflow support, (3) improvement in basic financial processes, (4) support for electronic business, (5) usability/ease of use/user friendliness, and (6) consistency within and across related systems. The stakeholder needs analysis further uncovered and confirmed major deficiencies of the existing system such as the lack of data access and tracking capabilities, the lack of data integration, the lack of business process integration, the lack of a user-friendly interface, the lack of important functionality, and finally the existence of numerous redundancies.

As a result of this exercise (in which the primary stakeholders were integrated and supportive throughout the process) the joint project team made four recommendations for further action: (1) analyze the fragmentation of existing business processes and workflows, (2) conduct best and current practices studies, (3) continue involving stakeholders into the process, and (4) maintain the current system to gain time for a potentially multiyear transformation process. Though the project is still in its infancy, the stakeholder needs analysis demonstrated the usefulness of the stakeholder management approach in a public-sector setting: first, an abundance of relevant information results from the workshop series; second, the integration and support of primary stakeholder furthers the process and the project in significant ways (for example, budgeting the succeeding steps); third, other stakeholders begin to support the overhaul project discontinuing costly and redundant local efforts, and fourth, the statewide visibility of the project leads to high levels of attention and expectation.

# 5. CONCLUDING REMARKS

This paper's intent has been to review stakeholder theory and its potential applicability to e-government, and more generally, public-sector managerial decision-making. It has demonstrated that a unified stakeholder theory does not exist. Instead two divergent [1] rather than convergent [18] strands of stakeholder theory exist. Though these two strands may have been originated from the same source, their implications and prescriptions differ in various ways. Stakeholder theory is primarily a theory of the private-sector firm. In its instrumental interpretation it mainly challenges the neoclassical economic theory of the firm and maintains that those firms that are managed for optimal stakeholder satisfaction thrive better than those firms that only maximize shareholder interests (that is, profit). Through its normative branch, stakeholder theory has become ever more influential upon legislative and evolving case law trends in the past two decades. In other words, stakeholder theory, of whatever flavor, has made a major impact in both the private and public spheres.

Despite the fact that stakeholder theory primarily applies to the private-sector firm, the insights from this area can be applied in part to public sector settings, and in particular, to the context of managerial decisions regarding major e-government initiatives. This is due to the circumstance that public management responsibilities begin to resemble private-sector management tasks not only formally but also regarding the emerging network-nature of organizations in both spheres. Future research may attempt to better understand the differences between private and public-sector stakeholder scenarios. While the cross-sector application of insights of instrumental stakeholder theory may be somewhat straightforward between g2g and g2b scenarios, this may not be the case in government-to-citizen (g2c) scenarios (since g2c is obviously not the equivalent to business-to-consumer (b2c), that is, consumer is not equivalent to citizen). The role of citizens in e-government and e-democracy settings may be more than just as a primary stakeholder who needs to be "managed" in some sort of paternalistic fashion. However, stakeholder theory (in its two strands) may have the capacity to broaden the understanding of the presumably increasing importance of citizens in e-government and e-democracy scenarios.

# 6. REFERENCES

[1] R. E. Freeman, "Divergent stakeholder theory," *Academy of Management Review*, vol. 24, pp. 233-236, 1999.

[2] S. Key, "Toward a new theory of the firm: a critique of stakeholder "theory"," *Management Decision*, vol. 37, pp. 317-328, 1999.

[3] R. Marens and A. Wicks, "Getting real:stakeholder theory, managerial practice, and the general irrelevance of fiduciary duties owed to shareholders," *Business Ethics Quarterly*, vol. 9, pp. 273-293, 1999.

[4] R. E. Freeman, *Strategic management: a stakeholder approach*. Boston: Pitman, 1984.

[5] R. K. Mitchell, B. R. Agle, and D. J. Wood, "Toward a theory of stakeholder identification and salience. Defining the principle of who and what really counts," *Academy of Management Review*, vol. 22, pp. 853-866, 1997.

[6] D. Reed, "Stakeholder management theory: a critical theory perspective.," *Business Ethics Quarterly*, vol. 9, pp. 453-483, 1999.

[7] R. E. Freeman, "Strategic management: a stakeholder approach," in *Advances in strategic management*, vol. 1, R. Lamb, Ed. Greenwich, CT: JAI, 1983, pp. 31-60.

[8] S. Cohen, "Stakeholders and consent.," *Business & Professional Ethics Journal*, vol. 14, pp. 3-14, 1995.

[9] R. A. Phillips, "Stakeholder theory and a principle of fairness," *Business Ethics Quarterly*, vol. 7, pp. 51-46, 1997.

[10] M. Clarkson, "A risk based model of stakeholder theory," presented at Proceedings of the second Toronto conference on stakeholder theory, Toronto, 1994.

[11] A. F. Alkhafaji, *A stakeholder approach to corporate governance : managing in a dynamic environment*. New York: Quorum Books, 1989.

[12] A. Etzioni, "A communitarian note on stakeholder theory.," *Business Ethics Quarterly*, vol. 8, pp. 679-691, 1998.

[13] T. M. Jones, "Instrumental stakeholder theory: a synthesis of ethics and economics.," *Academy of Management Review*, vol. 20, pp. 404-437, 1995.

[14] T. Donaldson and L. E. Preston, "The stakeholder theory of the corporation: concepts, evidence, and implications," *Academy of Management Review*, vol. 20, pp. 63-91, 1995.

[15] J. Frooman, "Stakeholder influence strategies," *Academy of Management Review*, vol. 24, pp. p191 15p, 1999.

[16] M. B. E. Clarkson, "A stakeholder framework for analyzing and evaluating corporate social performance," *Academy of Management Review*, vol. 20, pp. 92-117, 1995.

[17] S. P. Sethi, "Introduction to AMR's special topic forum on shifting paradigms: societal expectations and corporate performance," *Academy of Management Review*, vol. 20, pp. 18-21, 1995.

[18] T. M. Jones and A. C. Wicks, "Convergent stakeholder theory," *Academy of Management Review*, vol. 24, pp. 206-221, 1999.

[19] L. K. Treviño and G. R. Weaver, "The stakeholder research tradition: converging theorists-not convergent theory," *Academy of Management Review*, vol. 24, pp. p. 222-227, 1999.

[20] M. Friedman, "The social responsibility of business is to increase its profits," in *New York Times Magazine*, 1970.

[21] D. A. Gioia, "Practicability, paradigms, and problems in stakeholder theorizing," *Academy of Management Review*, vol. 24, pp. 228-232, 1999.

[22] T. Donaldson, "Making stakeholder theory whole," *Academy of Management Review*, vol. 23, pp. 237-241, 1999.

[23] J. F. Weston and T. E. Copeland, *Managerial finance*, 9th ed. Fort Worth: Dryden Press, 1992.

[24] D. O. Cloninger, "Managerial goals and ethical behavior," *Financial Practice & Education*, vol. 5, pp. 50-59, 1995.

[25] A. Argandoña, "The stakeholder theory and the common good," *Journal of Business Ethics*, vol. 17, pp. 10931102, 1998.

[26] N. A. Shankman, "Reframing the debate between agency and stakeholder theories of the firm," *Journal of Business Ethics*, vol. 19, pp. 319-334, 1999.

[27] D. P. Quinn and T. M. Jones, "An agent morality view of business policy.," *Academy of Management Review*, vol. 20, pp. 22-42, 1995.

[28] J. R. Tennert and A. D. Schroeder, "Stakeholder analysis," presented at 60th Annual Meeting of the American Society for Public Administration, Orlando, FL, 1999.

[29] D. L. Blair and C. J. Whitehead, "Too many on the seesaw. Stakeholder diagnosis and management for hospitals," *Hospital and Health Administration*, vol. 33, pp. 153-166, 1988.

[30] T. A. Pardo, H. J. Scholl, M. E. Cook, D. R. Connelly, and S. S. Dawes, *New York State Central Accounting System Stakeholder Needs Analysis*. Albany, NY: Center for Technology in Government, 2000.

55

# Recreating Government through Effective Knowledge Management

Greg Robins and Janice Burn
*Edith Cowan University, Australia*

**Abstract**: This paper discusses the use of Intranet technology as a means for the delivery of more effective government services. Specifically, we look at how a Western Australian Government Agency, the Ministry for Sport and Recreation, with geographically dispersed sites has utilised Intranet technology to deliver corporate knowledge to all staff. This has laid the foundation for e-government delivery across the region.

## 1. INTRODUCTION

Western Australia is an extremely large and isolated state covering 2.5million sq kilometres and spanning 2400km from north to south. Many country towns are highly remote from centralised public services with limited access to current communications technology. Given these circumstances it is essential that information systems are developed to enable effective access to both information and electronic communications. Internet/Intranet technology lends itself perfectly to the establishment of electronic communications between these locations with relatively inexpensive communication links. They are hence powerful enablers of knowledge sharing across functions, departments and geographical locations rendering knowledge management as a core organisational competence (Kanter, 1999; Newell et al, 1999).

The paper begins with an overview of the definitions of knowledge management. The authors review current thinking on what makes sound knowledge management practice and examine how Intranet technology assists in developing a knowledge focused organization. The definition of knowledge management is applied to a case study which considers Intranet developments within a government agency that has a centrally located office with a number of geographically dispersed sub offices. The case enables the review of the features of Intranet technology, in particular the premise that Intranets are a 'de-centred' technology consisting of loosely coupled systems (Newell, Scarborough, Hislop and Swan 1999) within the context of its implementation and use as a knowledge management tool.

## 2. KNOWLEDGE MANAGEMENT

Vail (1999) defines knowledge as information made actionable in a way that adds value to the enterprise. There are two basic types of knowledge:

- Implicit knowledge – knowledge that is locked in people's minds that comes from their experiences and skills.
- Explicit Knowledge – knowledge that has been articulated and captured in formal models, rules and procedures..

It can be said that explicit knowledge forms the basis of implicit knowledge. For someone to develop implicit knowledge they must first gather explicit knowledge and utilize this together with their skills and experiences to develop implicit knowledge. Knowledge is produced as the result of human interpretation and analysis rather than data processing (Moody and Shanks 1999). The essential distinction is explicit knowledge can be digitized or turned into information while implicit knowledge is intrinsic to people. Information only creates value for clients when it is applied (Dawson 2000). The merging of the two is integral to creating value from explicit knowledge and leveraging information repositories to create competitive advantage or providing value for clients.

There are many definitions of Knowledge Management and strong debate on defining and capturing implicit knowledge. Many would argue that once implicit knowledge has been captured it becomes explicit knowledge or information. Knowledge management is about turning raw data into information and from there into knowledge (Kanter 1999). It is about understanding how to transfer knowledge to users, how to add value to the information, how to transfer data into information and how that information can be transferred into knowledge.

Knowledge management is a discipline that promotes an integrated approach to identifying, managing and sharing all of an enterprise's information assets. These may include databases, documents, policies and procedures as well as previously unarticulated expertise and experience resident in individual workers. Knowledge management issues include developing, implementing and maintaining the appropriate technical and organizational infrastructures to enable knowledge sharing (Butler 2000). The major objective of knowledge management is to make effective use of information and to combine this with effective use of 'know-how' and expertise in an organisation.

Sveiby defines a knowledge organisation as one which:

- Provides services rather than products;

- Sells its knowledge and expertise to solve complex problems for its customers;
- Consists of employees who are highly qualified and educated professionals (knowledge workers), and
- Intangible assets are much more important than tangible assets. (Sveiby 1997)

This definition closely relates to the organization that forms the basis of the case study of this paper. The organisation is the Ministry of Sport and Recreation, a Western Australian state Government Department. It is very much a service organisation responsible for providing sporting bodies in WA with a sport consultancy. Its employees are sport specialists highly qualified in a wide variety of disciplines within the sport industry.

# 3. CASE STUDY – THE MINISTRY OF SPORT AND RECREATION

## 3.1 Research Method

The research methodology was based on action research. One of the authors was fully involved in the implementation of the Ministry's wide area network and the development of the Intranet system. This included involvement in the three committees that were established specifically to steer the Ministry's information requirements.

These committees are:

- The Information Technology Steering Committee,
- Internet Committee, and
- Intranet Committee.

These three committees each have representatives from each section within the organisation and as such provided an extensive insight into the information requirements for the organisation.

## 3.2 Background to Ministry of Sport & Recreation

The Ministry of Sport and Recreation is an organisation that has a number of offices strategically located in country areas of Western Australia and a central office located in Perth. Its main functions are to:

- Act as a consultancy to assist sporting organisations develop their sport and operational functions,
- Assist local Government authorities develop and sporting infrastructure,
- Provide research information on current initiatives in the sporting and recreation industry particularly in relation to preventative health and social issues such as child protection or drugs in sport, and

- Increase participation rates in sporting and recreational pursuits.

As indicated by the Director, Business Management

'*Until late 1999 the Ministry of Sport and Recreation operated in an information technology environment that was largely ineffective and, in the context of the 'Statewide' nature of the Ministry, to some extent dysfunctional.*'

In particular:

- The information technology environment was focused on single user functionality and completely devoid of corporate tools;
- Corporate databases were being developed using software that precluded easy and meaningful access by Statewide offices (database update was still being done by 'floppy disk' transfer);
- There was no customisation of office tools to assist with document creation and ensure maintenance of corporate standards;
- There were no tools to assist with document management including document storage and document tracking and document location (requiring staff to spend many hours per week simply searching the network locating documents stored in one of many thousand directories);
- There was no mechanism for readily accessing corporate management information such as operational plans, financial reports, documentation on achievements and issues, corporate policies and procedures. human resource management information. resource bookings, internal telephone lists and functional responsibilities, client information. ministerial correspondence, strategic dates (corporate calendar) .

There was not one single web based application nor any plans to progress down this path.

In terms of communications, the Ministry interacted with its regional offices in much the same way as it did in the early 1990's. The mechanism for communications was inconsistent with contemporary business requirements; sound management practice; and every other comparable State Government Agency (e.g. Aboriginal Affairs, Legal Aid etc. who have implemented state of the art communications frameworks). The idea was to develop a communication infrastructure that enabled the linking of all offices, develop systems that captured organizational knowledge and deliver this directly to each desktop. This was seen as the Ministry's Knowledge Management vision.

## 3.3 Corporate Context

The Ministry's purpose is to 'Enhance the lifestyle of Western Australians through their participation and achievement in sport and recreation.' In order to assist in achieving this, one of the Ministry's visions is to have skilled and informed people delivering services. Hence, a new management framework was required that:

- Guaranteed all staff focused on approved outputs and outcomes;

- Guaranteed corporate communications on achievements and work plans;
- Ensured that all staff have the opportunity to be informed;
- Ensured that resource issues and program management issues are discussed and that major issues 'bubble up' for executive consideration.

The principle driving force behind the information reforms was the need to deliver an environment in which all Ministry staff could substantially improve productivity and inherently devote more time and resources to program delivery (meeting client needs). The Ministry established a Statewide data communications infrastructure and established office productivity tools to ensure all staff have access to essential information. It has developed an Intranet site, known as The Arena. The Arena provides all staff, regardless of location, access to a wealth of information including, but not limited to, a client management system, Ministry operational plans, monthly achievement reports, policies and procedures and financial reports.

## 3.4 Organisational Culture

The Ministry of Sport & Recreation had a history of decentralized development. All regional offices were isolated from the central office and as such had developed their own policies and procedures. Many had developed their own web presence, lacked internal information systems and had no access to corporate information. Within the central office the various divisions worked independently of each other, there were no corporate information systems nor effective management of electronic or paper based documents. Staff were provided with computers for email and developing documents but stored these in personal areas making the information inaccessible to the organisation. The IT section consisted of two staff members with responsibility for providing technical advice and setting up computers on desks. There was limited strategic information planning revolving around a hardware replacement strategy.

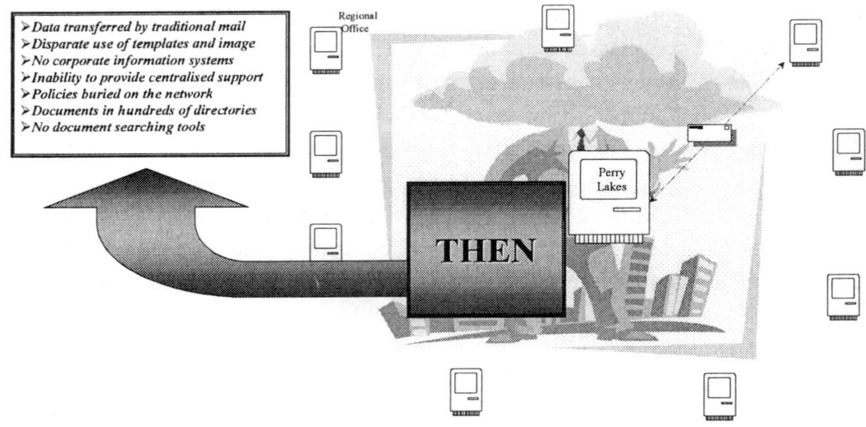

➤Data transferred by traditional mail
➤Disparate use of templates and image
➤No corporate information systems
➤Inability to provide centralised support
➤Policies buried on the network
➤Documents in hundreds of directories
➤No document searching tools
Regional Office
Perry Lakes
THEN


*Figure 1.* Ministry Information Infrastructure Pre Arena

In 1999 a new Chief Executive Officer was appointed and there was a complete change of the corporate executive team. This lead to a refocus on Information Management and an Information Branch was initiated with the responsibility to develop a statewide network and information infrastructure to support the development of corporate information systems and the implementation of Knowledge Management principles.

## 3.5 The Project

This project reflects a massive change to the way the Ministry carries out its business. Implementation of The Arena and associated office productivity tools and management practices represents the single biggest change the Ministry had experienced in many years. The staff have been required to adopt a completely different technology to the one they were used to as well as be prepared to change the way that they carried out their daily tasks.

To ensure that the change process was managed effectively the Ministry consciously went about:

- Ensuring that all staff are clear on who has carriage/responsibility for the particular change process required,
- Ensuring user involvement and user commitment,
- Ensuring that those officers who were charged with leading the change process actually had the necessary skills required,
- Ensuring training needs that arise as a consequence of the change process were identified and addressed and supported with documentation,
- Setting and promoting timelines and monitoring progress (effective planning)
- Identification of problems and solutions, and

– Ensuring ongoing communication - upwards, downwards and across divisions/programs.

### 3.5.1 Responsibility

For each component of the implementation responsibility for managing the change was determined (the change agent). While overall responsibility was vested in the Director, Business Management, responsibility for individual components included the Director, the Manager, Information Services, the Manager, Human Resources, the Manager, Finance and Administration and the Principal Projects Manager, Policy and Research Division. It was the responsibility of individual officers to identify an implementation timetable; develop specification; consult staff; manage resources; manage implementation; liase with Manager, Information Systems (including coordination of launches on the Arena); ensure availability of documentation; and promote system take up.

***Use Involvement and Commitment.*** A strategic approach to user involvement was adopted. At the outset a series of 'show and tell' sessions were conducted identifying what was possible in the way of office productivity and information access; an all staff conference was held in March 2000 to demonstrate and further discuss the proposed strategy for the Ministry; feedback was sought from staff on proposed directions; a Strategic Information Systems Steering Committee was formed. This committee was representative of the whole Ministry and had the task to oversee all projects, bringing to the table comment from the areas they represented and make decisions that reflected the corporate vision. During each phase of the project staff were asked for comment and feedback through the information sessions. Following on from the project a monthly staff forum session was established to provide an avenue for informing staff of new developments as well as enabling staff to request training in a particular area or identify opportunity based information developments.

***Skills Required.*** At the start of the project it was recognised that staff within the information systems area needed to be up-skilled and re-skilled on contemporary networking solutions. Management of the project, in the first instance needed sound strategic planning and interpersonal and communications skills in preference to a high level of technical IT based skills; and transitional difficulties could be minimised with a methodical and systematic approach to implementation and by revisiting every tool to ensure that 'it was easy', it met user needs, had been thoroughly tested and was supported by plan that included:

– user documentation;
– coordination between training program and set up of user desktop;
– common user interface.

In particular, arrangements were made to engage a proven highly skilled network administrator to provide hands on coaching and knowledge transfer for one day per week (this was done through negotiation with another public sector agency); engage on a short term basis an additional network administrator to 'hold the fort' during implementation; where relevant, include in every contract the requirement to provide skills transfer to Ministry staff (eg development of professional templates); appoint an IS Manager who met the criteria outlined above but who also had a practical understanding of where the Ministry needed to go and how to get there with regard to information Management (and ideally had some experience in using the required tools).

***Training.*** Education was seen as the key to allay the fears of staff. Sessions on 'communicating the why' were conducted at every opportunity. Prior to the commencement of the project a session was conducted at a whole of staff conference and similar sessions were given to staff at each monthly staff meeting. The message: The project would improve quality in projects and allow MSR to ramp up to new technologies. There was a constant reinforcement with people as to why they were changing and what was in it for them. Of paramount importance was the training of all staff whilst minimising disruption to their daily routine. An initial group of change leaders representative of each division were identified to trial the training programme and to transfer to the new system prior to the full rollout. During the trial session members of the group were encouraged to provide critical comment to enable the system and training programme to be honed to suit the Ministry.

To minimise disruption four staff at a time were provided with a three hour session. Whilst the training was taking place a new computer was set up on their desk to enable them to be immediately productive upon their return and to ensure that they could put into practice what they had learned. At the end of each week a follow up session was provided that reinforced the initial training as well as providing a mechanism for staff to provide further input and feedback.

In summary, no new tools were put on the desks of staff without them first attending a formal training program and having access to documentation.

***Timelines (Planning).*** From the outset it was agreed with Corporate Executive that the central office would be fully operational by June 30 2000 (this was achieved a week earlier) with access to most of the proposed productivity tools completed at the same time. To achieve the above it was necessary to ensure that each component of the project had a timeline and that there would be a number of things that could be undertaken concurrently. The timely completion evidenced that mechanisms put in place to deliver the project were successful.

***Problem Identification and Solution.*** What was important was that there was a framework and a mechanism for having them quickly resolved. In addition to the user consultation and the IT Strategic Directions Committee, the Information Systems Branch met weekly with the Director, Business Management to report/monitor/review progress and to identify action that needed to be taken to accelerate the project. These meetings provided a guaranteed forum for:

- Prioritising;
- Ensuring nothing slipped between the cracks;
- Identifying who else needed to be involved/informed (including when and why);
- Ensuring a common understanding of status and issues;
- Identifying what training was emerging/required;
- Focussing on timelines.

### 3.5.2 Communication

Issues in this area are largely addressed above. Suffice to say a communications strategy was in place and a number of mechanisms for ensuring effective communication were used. The basic premise underlying the project was to manage the introduction and ongoing use of information technologies to support the more flexible, complex, and integrated structures and processes demanded by the Ministry and its staff. It is recognised that the introduction and ongoing use of information technologies is an ongoing process made up of opportunities and challenges which are not necessarily predictable at the start. At the end of the day, the project identified three types of change that needed to be dealt with and that will continue over time:

1. anticipated,
2. emergent, and
3. opportunity-based.

These can be related to Zack's strategic framework for knowledge management.(Zack, 1999). As a first step the organisation needs to determine the value of knowledge to its business. In other words it must align its knowledge resources and capabilities to the intellectual resources of its strategy. This should be measured against two dimensions and related to knowledge aggressiveness. The first dimension addresses the extent to which an organisation is primarily a creator or user of knowledge and the second addresses whether the primary sources of knowledge are internal or external. These together will provide the strategic framework in which knowledge management strategy needs to be developed. Combining the knowledge exploitation vs exploration orientation of the organisation with its internally vs externally acquired orientation towards knowledge strategy gives a framework for the KM based virtual organisation as shown in Figure 3.

| Unbounded | | | Aggressive | KM/based Virtual Network |
|---|---|---|---|---|
| External | | | | |
| Internal | Conservative | | | Traditional Organisation |
| | Exploiter/ Anticipated | Explorer/ Emergent | Innovator/ Opportunist | |

*Figure 3.* Framework for Knowledge Strategy (adapted from Zack, 1999)

An awareness of these types of change allows the Ministry to experiment and learn as it uses the technology over time. Most importantly, it offers a systematic approach with which to understand and better manage the realities of technology-based change in organisations today.

## 3.6 The Arena – Agency Wide Intranet

The Arena provides staff with ready access to both Departmental and Public Sector wide policy and procedures together with access to detailed resource management tools. This ensures equity within the Ministry as well as promoting excellence in service delivery and the capacity to truly deliver accountability. The Arena allows access to Ministry operational plans and achievement documentation including the identification of issues and projected activity. This information is fundamental to corporate management processes and decision making at a branch, divisional and executive level.

Access to financial reports was previously provided only to Managers and only in hard copy format once a month. There was no facility for forecasting commitments and being mindful of what discretionary funds were truly available. The Arena provides the opportunity to change all that, in particular, all financial reports are now available on line to all staff; the reports can be updated on a daily basis providing much more reliable and accurate information; the capacity can be available to capture forecasting information.

In addition to financial resource information, staff have the ability to access their current leave and payroll information. This information is also fundamental as a mechanism to assist managers to manage leave liabilities within their area and, through the reporting and charting function to manage staff availability. Even a simple tool such as the on line telephone information function has had a major impact within the Ministry. In addition to providing the telephone numbers and photographs of all staff, it also includes information on staff functions and responsibilities and tracking whether a staff member is in the office.

The Arena proactively provides Ministry staff with access to other corporate information. Staff are kept informed of coming events, new initiatives and important projects through a daily newsflash, Ministry notice board and calendar of events. A summary of the three areas is displayed on all screens each morning when staff first begin their daily work.

In terms of document management, The Arena provides ready access to a Ministerial tracking system that enables all staff to view information on current Ministerial correspondence, who is the responsible officer and when it is due for completion. This system assists in ensuring that all Ministerial correspondence is tracked and actioned in a timely manner.The internal document management system (IDMS) has greatly assisted staff in providing the best possible service to their clients. The system has provided staff with the ability to search for information stored in any document within the Ministry, value add to this information and provide far more extensive and better researched information to their clients. Staff are able to search through up to 40,000 documents and locate the required document in less than 4 seconds. As the Director of Business Management stated:

> *Implementation of the Arena has, for the first time provided the opportunity to make 'Accountability' easy. Policies and Procedures, Financial and Human Resource information are at the fingertips of all staff – there is no question about expectations and obligations; about what resources are available, what have been used, what is committed and what is still available. What was planned to be done, what has been done and what is proposed to be done is continually visible.*

The Arena has provided the Ministry with a comprehensive set of Knowledge Management Tools that when coupled with staff skills and expertise produces true knowledge as defined by Moody and Shanks and enables the Ministry to provide value to its clients. The Arena is more than an Intranet. The Arena combines the power of Internet and communications technology to bring together a geographically disperse organisation to enable a consolidated approach to the provision of service to clients through access to current information and the ability to form collaborative links across the organisation. It is an integrated approach to identifying, managing and sharing all of the enterprise's information assets.

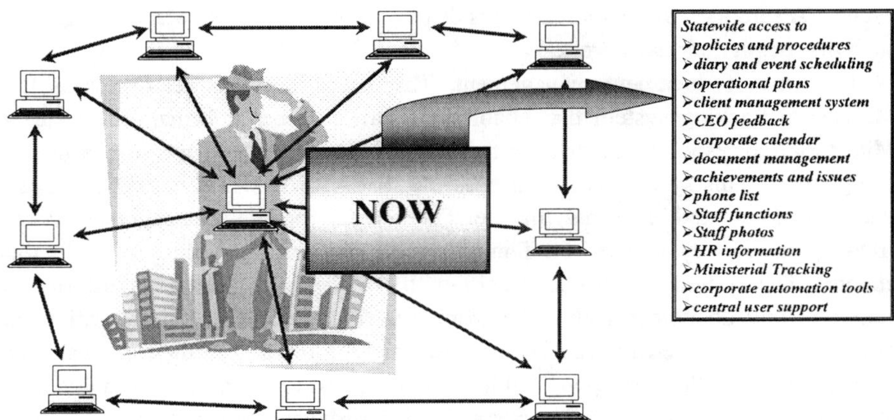


*Figure 2*. Ministry Information Infrastructure Post Arena

# 4. LESSONS LEARNED

Newell et al (1999) states that resources, networks and knowledge are very important during the implementation stage of an Intranet. Prior to embarking on the project the Ministry of Sport and Recreation recruited senior managers who had had experience implementing similar systems in other Government agencies. The Information Management and Communications Branches were reviewed and additional staff recruited in readiness for the project. At the outset of the project a wide variety of Government agencies were consulted to determine what similar initiatives had been undertaken to leverage their knowledge base. This recruitment and environmental scan created the foundation for the implementation whilst paying attention to resources, establishment of external networks and strategic knowledge.

Newell also discusses the importance of organisational control over the design and use of technology when implementing a project aimed at increasing organisational-wide knowledge management processes (Newell, Scarborough, Hislop and Swan 1999). From the outset of this project it was determined that a centralised approach needed to be taken to ensure that it succeeded. Prior to the project a few different groups had worked on developing an intranet presence for their information. Due to lack of coordination, resources and knowledge of implementing such a project none had succeeded in being placed into production within the organisation. Independent Intranets could be said to be increasing the barriers, with electronic silos reinforcing the already existing functional barriers (Newell, Scarborough, Hislop and Swan 1999).

The setting up of an IT Steering Committee representative of all sections of the organisation, the numerous informational sessions, and knowledge gathering all ensured a positive outcome for the project. Attention was given to both internal and external networks, the resources required to tackle the project which led to the development of an appropriate knowledge base.

Knowledge management issues include developing, implementing and maintaining the appropriate technical and organizational infrastructures to enable knowledge sharing (Butler 2000). The Arena includes databases, documents and policies and procedures. It includes technical infrastructures that allow the exchange of knowledge between organisational members regardless of where their office is located within Western Australia. Within the organisation the Arena stands for an Intranet system and the communication links that enables collaboration, upward, downward and horizontal information flows that assists in generating corporate knowledge and the provision of services to clients.

Dyerson talks of three building blocks, appropriation – retention and effective utilisation of internal knowledge, teamworking – integration of diverse knowledge bases and learning – acquisition and exploitation of external knowledge (Dyerson and Mueller 1999). The Ministry have begun to tackle the first two from an explicit knowledge viewpoint and are now planning to look at the third. This will lay a solid foundation for expanding their KM strategy and moving towards a tacit knowledge strategy as identified in Figure 3.

The next step for the Ministry of Sport & Recreation is to tackle how to capture and/or utilise the unarticulated expertise and experience within its people. Davenport talks of Knowledge Management, Round Two. He indicates that round one was related to managing knowledge management or capturing information and placing it in one place. He indicates essentially this is the building of an Intranet (Davenport 1999). Round two is capturing the tacit knowledge. Capturing this knowledge must be 'baked' into the job. Certainly the Ministry of Sport & Recreation have not contemplated the how, why or who for stage two and have a long way to go prior to embarking on an implementation strategy. Standing and Benson talk of organisational culture and how cultural change is a critical factor (Standing and Benson 2000). Within the Ministry of Sport & Recreation there are signs of change fatigue. Since January 2000 the organisation has implemented a completely new technology infrastructure, asked staff to change the way they had worked in the past as well as putting in place policies and procedures that make staff far more accountable than ever before as well as putting in place reporting mechanisms for all projects being undertaken. This rapid change has dramatically changed the culture within the organisation, and staff are now requesting a slow down of the pace of change. It could be said that the current climate and organisational culture are not conducive to implementing this side of Knowledge Management.

Email is utilised throughout the organisation to quickly disseminate knowledge. A message system for staff to communicate directly with the CEO has been established. The messages sent utilising this system can only be read by the CEO.

Therefore there is no filtering mechanism or restrictions on the comments being made. This has engendered a free flow of information and developed a culture of open and frank discussion whilst encouraging constructive criticism and advice across divisional and project boundaries. This is different to other research findings where they found that communications from the lower level staff to senior management was filtered, restricted and moved through slower channels (Standing and Benson 2000).

Moody identifies four broad objectives

1. Create knowledge repositories;
2. Improve knowledge access;
3. Enhance the knowledge environment; and
4. Manage knowledge as an asset. (Moody and Shanks 1999)

The Ministry has tackled their Knowledge Management project in such a way as to take into account and meet the first three objectives. They have ensured the involvement of all staff at the early stages to obtain 'buy-in' and by doing an environmental scan up front been able to implement systems rapidly whilst not falling into pitfalls that other organisations had encountered. The project also confirms Nissen's, Kamel's and Segupta's statement that groupware offers infrastructural support for knowledge work and enhances the environment in which knowledge artefacts are created and managed, yet the management of knowledge remains indirect (Nissen, Kamel and Sengupta 2000). As previously stated the Ministry have yet to progress into the area of capturing tacit knowledge, yet they have developed an infrastructure that clearly supports knowledge work particularly in a geographically disperse or virtual environment. The environment also facilitates the reuse of knowledge across the organisation.

## 5. CONCLUSION

This paper examines the initial stages of a Knowledge Management initiative within a Western Australian Government Organisation. It is currently too early to tell what impact this model has had on the goals the Ministry have set out to achieve nor the effect it has had turning knowledge into organisational action. As Pfeffer states 'most firms' efforts consist of investing in knowledge repositories such as intranets and implementing technologies to facilitate collaboration What most firms haven't done very much is build knowledge into products and services' (Pfeffer and Sutton 1999). Whilst this is certainly the case at the Ministry of Sport & Recreation further research is required over a period of time to determine if they do progress beyond this.

In conclusion, lessons can be learned from the pragmatic approach taken by the Ministry of Sport & Recreation. That is to start with the basics and to deliver organisational wide information and communications infrastructure that allows for open communication through all levels of the organisation and access to information regardless of physical location. If organisations embarking on KM programmes take a realistic perspective then they are more likely to value the benefits that accrue from the changes and techniques rather than expecting a radical transformation to widespread sharing of knowledge (Standing and Benson 2000).

## 6. REFERENCES

Butler, Y. (2000). "Knowledge Management - if only you knew what you knew." The Australian Library Journal(February 2000): 33-43.

Davenport, T. (1999). "Knowledge Management, Round Two." CIO Magazine(November 1, 1999).

Dawson, R. (2000). Developing Knowledge -Based Client Relationships. Melbourne, ButterWorth-Heineman.

Dyerson, R. and F. U. Mueller (1999). "Learning, teamwork and Appropriability: Managing Technological Change in the Department of Social Security." Journal of Management Studies **36**(5): 629 - 652.

Kanter, J. (1999). "Knowledge Management, Practically Speaking." Information Systems Management(Fall): 7-15.

Moody, D. L. and G. G. Shanks (1999). "Using Knowledge Management and The Internet to Support Evidence Based Practice: A Medical Case Study." Proceedings of the 10th Australasian Conference on Information Systems: 660-676.

Newell, S., H. Scarborough, D. Hislop and J. Swan (1999). "Intranets and Knowledge Management: Complex Processes and Ironic Outcomes." Proceedings of the 32nd Hawaii International Conference on System Sciences.

Nissen, M., M. Kamel and K. Sengupta (2000). "Integrated Analysis and Design of Knowledge Systems and Processes." Information Resources Management Journal **13**(1): 24-43.

Pfeffer, J. and R. I. Sutton (1999). "Knowing "what" to do is not enough: Turning knowledge into action." California Management review (Fall).

Standing, C. and S. Benson (2000). "Organisational Culture and Knowledge Management." PACIS conference, Hong Kong..

Sveiby, K. E. (1997). The New Organisational Wealth: Managing and Measuring Knowledge-Based Assets. San Fransisco, Berret-Loehler Publishers.

Vail, E. F. (1999). "Knowledge Mapping: Getting Started With Knowledge Management." Information Systems Management(Fall): 16-23.

Zack, M. H. (1999) Developing a knowledge strategy .California Management Review; Berkeley; Spring.

56

# Linking databases and linking cultures

*The complexity of concepts in international E-Governement*

Anne-Marie Oostveen & Peter Van den Besselaar
*Social Informatics, University of Amsterdam*

**Abstract:** International e-government implies cross-national coupling of administrative systems. As administrative concepts and classifications reflect social and cultural differences, international e-government applications are even more complex than those within the national boundaries. We will illustrate this by describing the cross-national differences in the concept of *marriage*, and discuss some of the implications for developing e-government applications.

## 1. INTRODUCTION

Since the integration of Europe into a single market, the citizens of the European Union member states should be able to migrate from one European country to another with as few problems as possible. Yet, mobile Europeans have to deal with time-consuming administrative procedures, which differ between the various European countries. The FASME project aims at developing a prototype of a system that supports mobile Europeans in solving these administrative problems. The main goal of the interdisciplinary project is to show a concept of user-friendly administrative procedures between European member states, in order to make mobility within Europe easier.

Traditionally, Europe has been a source rather than a destination of immigrants. This situation reversed from the 1960s onwards. Millions migrated to northern and western European countries, and international migration is now at an all-time high. (Salt, 2000) In the mid 1990s, about 125 million people lived outside their mother country. This number is expanding every year (Population Reference Bureau, 1996). Yet, Manuel Castells (1996) argues that there is no global labor force despite the emergence of a network society. He claims that a global market only exists for a tiny minority of high-skilled professionals in innovative R&D, cutting-edge engineering, financial management, advanced business services, and entertainment. They commute between nodes of the global networks that control the planet. (ibid. 233) Nonetheless, at this moment almost 5.5 million EU citizens live in other member states. (Salt, 2000). Hence, facilitating mobility within the EU is important for individual citizens. At the same time it may improve the operation of the European labor market.

The FASME system is based on smartcards and the Internet. (for details c.f., Riedl 2000, 2001a, 2001b) The FASME smartcard is in fact a digital ID card, using biometrical (fingerprint) identification technology, and containing digital signatures, and personal information about the cardholder. The card should enable the user to access through the Internet available electronic documents in (governmental) databases, and to download these documents on the card or to send these directly to other (governmental) agencies. The authenticity and the age of the documents will be secured, as receiving institutions need to assess the status of the information received. The personal information on the card is meant for the personalization of service provision. Only a few functions have been implemented on the FASME prototype.

Smartcard technology is often seen as the core technology for governmental services in the information age. (Lips 1998)

## 2. LARGE TECHNICAL SYSTEMS

Only recently "... it has been recognized that an important characteristic of modern technology is the existence of complex and large technical systems – spatially extended and functionally integrated socio-technical networks such as electrical power, railroad, and telephone systems" (Mayntz & Hughes, 1988). Hughes' (1983) analysis of the electrification of the world shows how large technical systems (LTS) operate as networks of many interacting technical and social components. LTS have the following properties:

- LTS are large scale, affecting many people and institutions.
- LTS are complex: political, legal, administrative, organizational and technical issues are relevant in the design, development, implementation, maintenance, and use of these systems.
- LTS are infrastructures, and face difficult issues of standardization.
- LTS generally embody political ideas and ideologies. (Gökalp (1992)

A full scale FASME system is typically a LTS, embodying the political ideology of the unified Europe. It aims at designing a complex cross-national infrastructure for e-government, involving many people and institutions.

The FASME card is meant for enabling access to many (public) services, and quite a few of those are only used on an incidental basis. Consequently, the card has to be multifunctional to attract enough potential users. This implies that many actors with potentially diverging worldviews and interests are involved in developing and implementing the card. Institutions that adopt smartcard technologies will also have to adapt their organization considerably. Many actors, and many functions generally result in many difficulties. That is why high complexity is a main factor in the failure of smartcard projects. In the FASME project, only two services had to be implemented. Nevertheless, even the development of the prototype proved to be complex, with many problems difficult to solve.

## 3. USER INVOLVEMENT

In a LTS a large number of people and institutions is involved, as potential 'users' of the system. Involving user groups is a prerequisite for successful innovation. However, user involvement in the design of this type of complex systems is a relatively new issue. (Clement & Van den Besselaar 1993; Rowe and Frewer, 2000)

It is important to recognize that there is not a 'universal user'. Several types of potential users of a FASME system can be distinguished, with various interests: 1) Various categories of mobile European citizens, who travel for business or for private reasons, and have different levels of support. They differ in gender, age, level of education, marital status, parentage, mastering of languages, disabilities. Their expectation of e-government services varies accordingly. 2) Civil servants, whose work will dramatically change in the age of e-government. 3) City councils who have an interest in more efficient, effective, less costly, and more transparent services. However, this has to fit in different legal frameworks, political processes and ideologies. The citizen expects improvement of quality of services using ICT, where possible. By improving their relationship with citizens, governments can make their country, region or city more attractive as a place to live and to work. 4) Representatives of employers hiring mobile Europeans. 5) Private sector service providers, among others providers of services that support mobile people.

User requirements in FASME were explored through interviews, a survey, workshops and tests. This resulted in constructive input, but even in a small-scale project aiming at prototypes, communication of user needs to technical developers proved to be difficult. As FASME has an international dimension, the variety of users, and of their believes, norms, and cultures, is even larger. Some implications will be discussed in the next section.

## 4. CONCEPTS, CLASSIFICATIONS, SYSTEMS

One service, which is being prototyped within FASME, is the registration of mobile Europeans in the city they move to. In most countries this is an obligation for foreigners. As one respondent remarked, this registration is the modern version of the mediaeval city wall: as soon as you are accepted inside, you belong to the social system, with all its rights and obligations. Being registered is the prerequisite for many services, public as well as private. Therefore, citizens' registration is a process secured with many provisions, such as the obligation to be physically present at the registration office. Different countries require different information, but generally one needs to have authenticated information about one's own birth, marriage, and about the children. For example, in the Netherlands the citizens' registration contains a vast amount of information, and many public and private institutions use it. This is an important issue, as these kinds of registrations have many legal, administrative, and other consequences.

A crucial point in international information exchange is that the concepts used for classifying a person differ between countries. In an increasing number of cases this may become problematic. For example, the concept of 'father' differs between countries. In the Netherlands, a man is only the father of an extramarital child after he formally 'recognizes' his child. In the UK, this concept of 'recognition' does not exist. Thus, after moving to the Netherlands, an unmarried English father may not be acknowledged as the father in formal situations.

Another example is the concept of marriage, which always appeared to be very straightforward. The definition of marriage has recently changed in the Netherlands by an enactment of the law to open up marriage for persons of the same sex. These changes have implications for international e-government. We will show this in more detail in the next section.

## 4.1 Same-sex marriage

In 1998, the Netherlands enacted a law allowing same-sex couples to register as partners and to claim pensions, social security and inheritance. [67] The House of Representatives voted in a large majority (107 against 33) for the bill, and the law has come into effect on April 1, 2001. Another change to the Dutch law makes it possible for two persons of the same sex to adopt a child. The child is being placed in a legal family relationship with the two 'parents'.[68]

[67] Bill 26672 (On the Opening Up of Marriage) allows same-sex couples to marry and treats these relationships the same as opposite-sex marriage. One of the partners must be a Dutch citizen or permanent resident to contract a same-sex marriage in the Netherlands. Traditional laws of descent do not apply in same-sex marriages, unless the couple adopts a child. Available online: http://marriagelaw.cua.edu/nl_marriage.htm

[68] Bill 26673 allows same-sex couples to adopt jointly. The couple must have cohabitated for three years and have jointly raised the child for one year. For the time being, the child being adopted must also be from the Netherlands (this was added to respond to criticisms from other countries). Available online: http://marriagelaw.cua.edu/adoption.htm

The opening up of marriage to same sex couples by the Dutch Parliament caused quite a bit of uproar in European and other countries. To express their objections against the same-sex marriage, the Marriage Law Project of the Columbus School of Law in Washington DC made the following statement: "Legalizing same-sex 'marriage' is not just an internal Dutch affair. Marriage is among the most portable of institutions. In most cases, a marriage entered in one country will be recognized by another country. Although, for the time being, one of the two same-sex 'spouses' must be a Dutch resident, inevitably same-sex couples will marry, move to another country, and then demand that their 'marriage' be recognized in their second country. These challenges will trigger legal conflicts worldwide, forcing countries to debate their policies and pressuring them, in the name of 'human rights', to fall in line." (Coolidge & Duncan, 2000)

One day before the Dutch First Chamber had to vote on the issue of the same-sex marriage, eighty professors of law and jurisprudence at universities across the world sent a statement on the definition of marriage to the Parliament of the Netherlands saying that "marriage is the unique union of a man and a woman"' and "cannot be arbitrarily redefined by lawmakers". In the letter the professors claim that by seeing marriage as the union of a man and a woman they represent the beliefs and practices of the overwhelming majority of humanity. They continue by stating that "our domestic and international laws should preserve, protect and promote the institution of marriage". According to these professors of law, redefining marriage to include same-sex unions will introduce unprecedented moral, social and legal confusion into our communities. They stress that no country is an island and that the actions of the Dutch Parliament will have fateful consequences not only for Europe, but for every country in the world. (Agar 2000)

What the opponents of the same-sex marriage believe is that marriage is by its very nature the union of a man and a woman and that this cannot be changed. In their opinion, altering the meaning of marriage will lead to nothing but confusion among people. However, we can ask ourselves the following question: what is 'marriage'?

All societies recognize marriage. And like all cultural phenomena, marriage is governed by rules, and these rules vary from one society to another. Some societies practice monogamy, where only one spouse at the time is permitted. However in biblical times husbands (in societies like our own) could have more than one wife. This is known as polygamy and is permitted in a lot of societies in the world today. An alternative form of marriage - one that does occur but is rather rare - is known as polyandry, in which one woman may have several husbands, often brothers (Rosman & Rubel, 1989).

All the above-mentioned marriages involve a commitment between men and women. But there is also proof that marriages between two persons of the same sex have been conceivable in a wide range of periods and cultures. Halsall (1996) argues that same-sex marriages did occur in sufficiently diverse historical and cultural contexts as to refute the assertion that marriage is 'naturally' heterosexual.

## 4.2 Complications in an International Context

Changes of legal concepts mirror the changes in our society. If existing definitions could not 'be arbitrarily redefined by lawmakers' as the professors claim in their statement to the parliament, we would still be in the situation where interracial marriages in the United States would be prosecuted. It was not until 1967 that the U.S. Supreme Court declared that "any marriage between any white person and a Negro or descendant of a Negro" was no longer illegal. It is hard to imagine that in the 1960's people opposed to this change in law, often using religious arguments. But on the other hand, even if one has a pure legal view on marriage, it is clear that a change of the legal meaning of marriage can have an effect on the societal, cultural and religious meaning of marriage.

Marriage is a legal concept that has numerous legal consequences, related to health benefits, tax payment, rights to raise children, hospital visitation rights, sick leave, and funeral leave. More and more homosexual partners enter into a life partnership, and they are becoming aware that these rights are important for them as well. In the Netherlands these rights are now recognized. But even though the same-sex marriage will have a formal status in the Netherlands, the same-sex couples need to realize that they may encounter a lot of practical and legal problems when moving abroad. The recognition of gay marriage abroad will differ per country, and some countries already have a 'registered partnership' between two persons of the same gender (Iceland, Denmark, Sweden and Norway).

However, same-sex marriages are not recognized in many countries, and that will probably cause legal confusion. The change in Dutch law may create a lot of complications in an international context. For instance, if somebody is married in the Netherlands with a partner of the same sex, then moves abroad and marries with a person of the different sex, does the party involved have two spouses? Is, according to Dutch law, the first marriage valid and the second not? And, at the same time, might it be probable that in accordance with the law of the country where the party stays, the second marriage is recognized and not the one under Dutch law? What is the position of children in the Netherlands and abroad that are born out of one of these marriages? Other questions were asked: will Dutch government offer legal support to married homosexual couples abroad when they seek to gain recognition for their marriage? If so, in what way? Will the Dutch government, on request, recognize a gay couple from a country that does not have registered partnerships as a married couple? Presuming that a marriage of a Dutch citizen and one non-Dutch citizen of the same sex is dissolved, and one of the children is not in the Netherlands, what is in such a scenario, the jurisdiction of the Dutch judge to determine guardianship, visitation, or child support? What will the legal position be of a child adopted by a gay couple in case of emigration to a country that does not know marriage between people of the same sex? And finally, if one of the partners of a same-sex marriage dies abroad, how will the survivor pension been arranged?

## 4.3 Implications for design

One may argue that the problems discussed in the previous section are exceptions, and that most mobile Europeans fit in more 'normal' categories. However, in postmodern societies, variation in situation and behavior of people is expected to increase, and what is now still exceptional, may become quite normal in the future. From that perspective differences between the normative systems in the various countries may increase, as will the problems for designing e-government systems for administrative support.

What are the consequences for international e-government of these differences in concepts used to classify people? The problem is to translate an available document set about a person in country A into a different but 'equivalent' document set valid in country B. As far as this translation is problematic, mobile Europeans may have difficulties to provide the required information in the country they are moving to. This is true in the current paper based situation, and in that sense the problems are not specific for e-government. Let us therefore look how document exchange support is organized nowadays.

To make document exchange easier, several countries have signed an agreement on standard templates for several documents: Certificates of Marriage, of Births, and of Deaths. Figure 1 shows an example. An instructive example of the use of this is Turkey. Turkish government does not issue a birth certificate to its citizens, but if a Turkish citizen moves abroad, an international birth certificate is issued. Other governments will accept the data on this certificate as long as it meets the rules of the agreement. National governments handle the provided information from the international templates according to their own legislation. The question that comes up now is how the new Dutch concepts (partner instead of husband/wife; parent instead of father/mother) can be mapped upon the template.

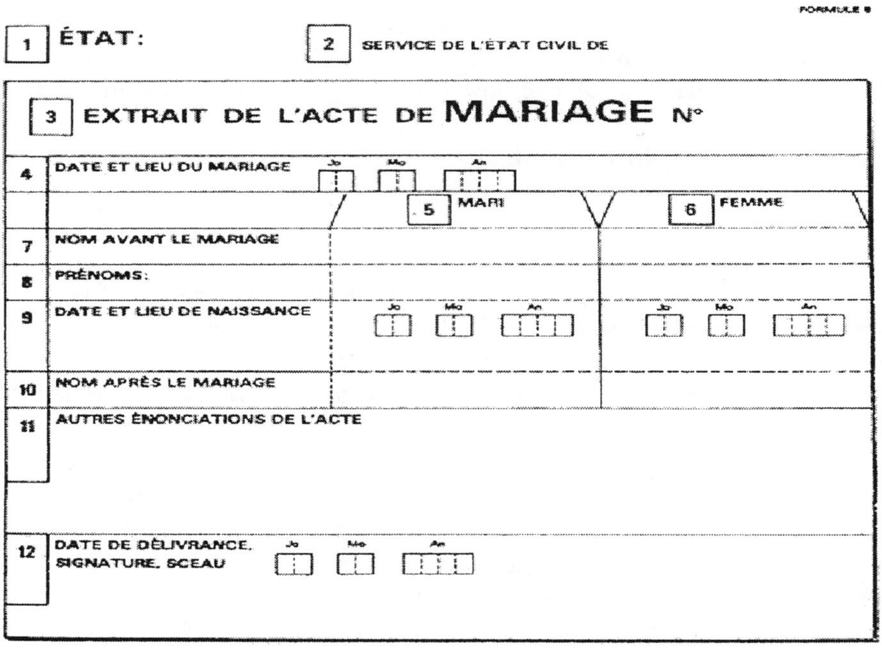

FORMULE B

1 ÉTAT:

2 SERVICE DE L'ÉTAT CIVIL DE

3 EXTRAIT DE L'ACTE DE MARIAGE N°

4 DATE ET LIEU DU MARIAGE Jo Mo An

5 MARI

6 FEMME

7 NOM AVANT LE MARIAGE

8 PRÉNOMS:

9 DATE ET LIEU DE NAISSANCE Jo Mo An Jo Mo An

10 NOM APRÈS LE MARIAGE

11 AUTRES ÉNONCIATIONS DE L'ACTE

12 DATE DE DÉLIVRANCE, SIGNATURE, SCEAU Jo Mo An

Figure 5. *Example of a 'Certificate of Marriage' template.*

The architecture of the FASME prototype follows the same 'template principle' as this paper-based system. National electronic forms will be translated into an electronic template, and the other way around. An 'ontology' is needed to automate these translations (Riedl 2000, 2001a), but it will face similar problems as the paper-based versions.

The agreement on the described templates was decided on in Vienna on September 8, 1976. Between 1982 and 1994, twelve countries have signed it, which is a remarkable slow process.[69] Why does it take so long? Germany, for example, is not yet using it, although it was decided there to enter the agreement. However, it requires legal changes and this is generally a difficult process, as laws are interrelated, and changes in one law effects others. Therefore it was decided to include the agreement on the use of the template in a larger and more general revision of German laws, and this process is foreseen to start somewhere in 2004. Consequently, the agreement will not come into effect in Germany before the end of the decade.

[69] Austria (1983), Bosnia-Herzegovina (1995), Croatia (1993), Italy (1983), Luxembourg (1983), Macedonia (1994), The Netherlands (1987), Portugal (1983), Spain (1983), Switzerland (1990), Turkey (1985) and Yugoslavia (1990).

# 5. CONCLUSIONS AND DISCUSSION

This paper discussed some contextual issues in complex cross-national administrative e-government, using the example of marriage. Firstly, the meaning of the concept marriage (and other concepts) differs considerably between countries, and the difference between married and not married has a wide number of legal (and social) consequences. As the concept is highly relevant in many public regulations and services, the variation in the meaning of 'marriage' creates serious problems for interstate e-government. Of course, one could plea for complete legal harmonization within the EU, but that is too far away. It may also be less desirable, as legal differences reflect cultural diversity.

Within e-government, one may search for similar standardized templates for documents exchange as already exist in paper-based solutions. However, where concepts differ fundamentally, this does not solve the problems discussed.

Secondly, even where the 'template solution' does work, it may take years to develop it, and to get it adopted by even a small number of European countries. Consequently, the transition to e-government solutions, especially on the European level, is expected to go very slow. This can be conceived as an advantage, as it gives us time to learn carefully about the *good* solutions.

# 6. ACKNOWLEDGMENTS

Part of the work underlying this paper has been funded by the European Commission, Information Society Technology program, under contract IST-1999-10882: Facilitating Administrative Services for Mobile Europeans. Partners in FASME are the University of Amsterdam, the University of Cologne, the University of Rostock, the University of Zürich, the City of Cologne, the City of Grosseto, Newcastle City Council, ICL, and Zündel GmbH. The authors are grateful for the stimulating discussions within the project, especially with Reinhard Riedl, Henk Kokken, Fred Boekestein, and Sally Wyatt. We thank Bruce Clark and Teresa Mom for useful comments on previous versions of this paper.

# 7. REFERENCES

Agar, Jose Martin de, *To the Parliament of the Netherlands: A Statement on the Definition of Marriage from Law Professors Across the World.* 2000. Available online: http://marriagelaw.cua.edu/holland.htm

Castells, M., *The Rise of the Network Society.* The information age: Economy, Society and Culture: Volume 1. Oxford: Blackwell Publishers, 1996

Clement, A,.& P. Van den Besselaar, A retrospective look at participatory design projects, *Communications of the ACM* 36 (1993) 6, pp. 29-38.

Coolidge, D. O. and W.C. Duncan , *Holland Legalizes Same-Sex "Marriage"; Impact Will Be Felt Worldwide*. A Statement by the Marriage Law Project. December 19, 2000. Available online: http://marriagelaw.cua.edu/eerste.htm

Gökalp, I., On the Analysis of Large Technical Systems. *Science, Technology, & Human Values*. Volume 17, Number 1, Winter 1992 .

Halsall, P., *Lesbian and Gay Marriage through History and Culture*. Ver. 2.1, June 1, 1996. Available online: http://www.bway.net/~halsall/lgbh/lgbh-marriage.html

Hughes, T., *Networks of Power: Electrification in Western Society, 1880-1930*. Baltimore: John Hopkins University Press, 1983.

Lips, M., "Reorganizing Public Service Delivery in an Information Age: Towards a revolutionary renewal of government?" In: Snellen & van de Donk "*Public Administration in an Information Age*" pag. 325-340. Amsterdam: IOS Press

Mayntz, R. and T.P. Hughes, *The Development of Large Technical Systems*. Boulder: Westview Press, 1988.

Population Reference Bureau, *International Migration: A Global Challenge*. Washington: Population Reference Bureau, 1996. Available online: http://www.prb.org/pubs/bulletin/bu51-1/intro.htm

Reinhard Riedl, Facilitating Administrative Services for Mobile Europeans with Secure Multi-Application Smartcards, Proceedings of e-Business and e-Work 2000, Madrid 2000

Reinhard Riedl, Information Brokerage in E-Government and in Interdisciplinary Research Projects, Proceedings of DEXA 2001, Munich 2001(a)

Reinhard Riedl, A Functional Model for Mobile Commerce. 2001(b). In this volume.

Rosman, A. & P. Rubel, *Tapestry of Culture. An Introduction to Cultural Anthropology*. New York: Random House, 1989.

Rowe, G. and Frewer, L.J. Public Participation Methods: A Framework for Evaluation. *Science, Technology, & Human Values*. Volume 25, Number 1, Winter 2000.

Salt, J., J. Clarke, and S. Schmidt, *Patterns and Trends in International Migration in Western Europe*. Luxembourg: Office for Official Publications of the European Communities, April 2000. http://www.europa.eu.int/comm/eurostat/Public/datashop/print-catalogue/EN?catalogue=Eurostat&product=KS-31-00-271-__-I-EN

# Exploring The Interrelations Between Electronic Government And The New Public Management

*A Managerial Framework For Electronic Government*

Kuno Schedler and Maria Christina Scharf
*Institute for Public Services and Tourism at the University of St. Gallen (Switzerland)*

**Abstract**: This paper explores how electronic government (e-government) can be understood in the context of business administration. Our focus is on non-technical issues: we concentrate on the analysis of organizational, cultural and managerial aspects, in order to approach the possible development of e-government and its implications on the public sector at different state levels. Furthermore, we examine the relationship between the Public Management – particularly in the form of the New Public Management (NPM) – and e-government. Based on the outcomes of the analysis mentioned above, an attempt is made to identify the greatest problems that governments will have to face with respect to the introduction of e-government, and what kind of – if any – contribution the disciplines of business administration and NPM can make to resolve these problems. In order to achieve these goals, we set up a conceptual framework for e-government from the perspective of NPM and analyze its components. Our conclusion is that e-government can be interpreted as a reform element that supports the idea behind the NPM and, with its technological equipment, eases modernization as a whole.

## 1. INTRODUCTION

Electronic Government (e-government) seems to develop explosively: only a few years ago, the term was virtually unknown even in scientific circles. Today, modernizing the state without e-government is not thinkable any more, both in theory and in practice. However, implementing e-government is not just a technical matter. Experiences with change management in the public sector, deriving from the "New Public Management" reform type, will be of great importance for a successful implementation.

This paper explores how e-government can be understood in the context of business administration. Our focus is on non-technical issues: we will concentrate on the analysis of organizational, cultural and managerial aspects, in order to approach the possible development of e-government and its implications on the public sector at different state levels. Furthermore, we will examine the relationship between Public Management – particularly in the form of the New Public Management (NPM) – and e-government.

Based on the outcomes of the analysis mentioned above, an attempt will be made to identify the greatest problems that governments will have to face with respect to the introduction of e-government, and what kind of – if any – contribution the disciplines of business administration and NPM can make to resolve these problems. In order to achieve these goals, we will set up a conceptual framework for e-government from the perspective of NPM and analyze its components.

## 1.1 E-Government: A Working Definition

The term e-government comprises heterogeneous elements and multiple dimensions, and no common definition can be found in the quickly expanding number of publications on e-government. According to the area of expertise, some define e-government as digital information and online transaction services to citizens. Others use the term to refer to electronic commerce, namely online procurement. "At this stage in the evolution of a digital economy and society, 'too narrow' a definition can constrain opportunity and 'too broad' a definition dilutes its value as a rallying force" (Caldow 1999).

Public Management primarily sees in e-government the foundation for new forms of communication and – deriving from that – new forms of organization for public institutions and their stakeholders. Therefore, a common definition could be the following:

> Electronic Government is a form of organization that integrates the interactions and the interrelations between government and citizens, companies, customers, and public institutions through the application of modern information and communication technologies.[70]

In analogy to e-commerce, e-government can be seen as the sum of new possibilities for public institutions to communicate with others electronically. Various forms of decision-making, business transactions, or simply communication can take place through electronic networks, dramatically changing the way government works.

[70] Source: IDT-HSG Center of Excellence for Electronic Government, http://www.electronic-government.org

Unlike the New Public Management, e-government is not primarily motivated by fiscal stress, administrative and/or political crisis, or dissatisfaction among public managers. Rather, it is a technology-driven reform movement, whereby the reform strategy follows the potential created by modern information and communication technologies (ICT). In this sense, the common phrase "structure follows strategy" will have to be enriched with a further element into: "structure follows strategy follows potential".

While the terms „governance" and „government" are sometimes used interchangeably to depict the same thing, we believe that the two terms bear different meanings, which calls for a brief clarification. The concept of governance generally refers to the task of running a government, or any appropriate entity for that matter. Governance is a broader notion than government[71]. It „involves interaction between the formal institutions and those in civil society. Governance refers to a process whereby elements in society wield power, authority and influence and enact policies and decisions concerning public life and social upliftment"[72].

## 1.2 New Public Management (NPM)

New Public Management (Hood 1991) has become a widely used term round the world. It describes a global trend of a certain type of administrative reform "... but it soon becomes apparent [...] that it has different meanings in different administrative contexts" (Ormond and Löffler 1998). For the purpose of this paper, we use the following broad definition: "New Public Management is the generic term for the globally rather uniform ‚overall movement' of government reforms. The main characteristic of NPM reforms is the change from input to output orientation" (Schedler and Proeller 2000, p. 5).

# 2. A MANAGERIAL FRAMEWORK FOR E-GOVERNMENT

In this section, we will set up a framework for e-government from the perspective of NPM. We will start by introducing three process elements which, taken together, represent the core processes of a public sector organization. We then will embed the core processes in their cultural context, attempting to define the required elements of a specific "e-government culture". Last, we will discuss the possible contributions of three management techniques to the functioning of e-

[71] E-government is situated in a modern governance concept; the "Digital Era Governance" (Tapscott 1997). Gisler (2001, p. 18) defines "E-Governance" as the design of the general framework for the information society.

[72] Working definition of the British Council.

government and demonstrate that e-government needs a visionary top-down strategy in order to be successful.

## 2.1 Process Elements

The main aim of e-government is to improve the internal and external performance of the public sector. E-government is based on the changes which were initiated by the New Public Management: a consistent orientation of the public institutions towards the service recipients.

Many terms are too broadly defined when they come up and can therefore be linked to a vast spectrum of contents. This is what is happening with e-government, which will lead to a devaluation of the term in the long run. To counteract this development, a comprehensible as well as useful criterion needs to be employed for designing an e-government concept. The political „decision-making and production process“ could be such a design pattern. The latter can be divided into three axiomatic process steps, each of them being supported by an own e-government module: Electronic Democracy and Participation (eDP), Electronic Production Networks (ePN), and Electronic Public Services (ePS).

### 2.1.1 Electronic Democracy and Participation (eDP)

Electronic Democracy and Participation (eDP) stands for political opinion-building and decision-making via electronic media. Examples include Internet voting (e-voting) and citizen networks.

E-voting addresses an important democratic element, the direct participation of the people in the political process. The fact itself is not revolutionary: new forms of voting were introduced before. By and by, those new forms loosened the ties with respect to time and place of a poll (cf. fig. 1). In times when voting was done orally, the introduction of the ballot brought along a certain degree of temporal independence. The absentee vote lifted the local restrictions: instead of having to betake oneself to the ballot, a citizen may cast his or her vote at any mailbox. E-voting will make it even easier to cast a vote by switching from the medium „paper“ to the medium „internet“ (or subsequent media). In this context, Korac-Kakabadse and Korac-Kakabadse (1999, p. 212) link specific information technologies (in the broadest sense of the term) with particular political processes and forms:

- orality to democracy and the city-state;
- print to bureaucracy and the nation-state;
- the emergence of the Internet, or the global information infrastructure, to models of e-democracy.

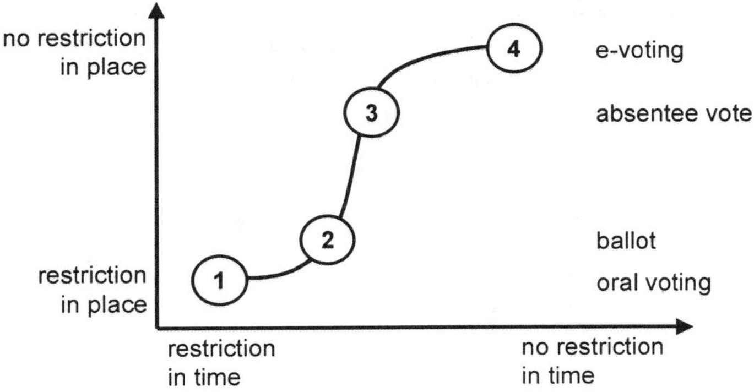


*Figure 1.* E-voting - decreasing restrictions in time and place

### 2.1.2 Electronic Production Networks (ePN)

Electronic Production Networks (ePN) are forms of co-operation between public and private institutions or between public and public institutions via electronic media. A great potential lies in the setup and maintenance of virtual production networks for fulfilling public responsibilities. The linking-up of different state levels, such as regional extranets with data links for all municipalities, seems particularly worth mentioning. Examples include outsourcing document renewals and e-procurement solutions.

A distinguishing feature of production networks is the fact that different institutions work at the same product in geographically different locations. Economies of scale can be obtained by standardizing processes and by amalgamating administrative activities – a characteristic that Schuh and Strack (1997) also attribute to the virtual factory. In terms of the organization this means that parts of the existing organization need to be split up or segmented in order to be virtually integrated into an optimally configured unit of the production network. At the same time, other parts of external organizations are pooled in the virtual network in view of the task to be accomplished. First successful solutions of this kind have been implemented: An example is given by a production network for the vehicle registration in Arizona (cf. fig. 2), as described in the Economist (2000):

- Consumers can go online and renew their registrations in a transaction that takes an average of two minutes.
- The website is hosted and maintained by IBM, who receives and processes the data. IBM is paid US$ 4 for this outsourced administrative procedure.
- Processing an online request costs US$ 1.60. Therefore, the total costs for such a transaction amount to US$ 5.60.

- Compared with US$ 6.60 for a counter transaction, the State of Arizona saves US$ 1 per transaction. With 15 % of renewals now being processed by this service, the motor vehicle department saves around US$ 1.7m a year.

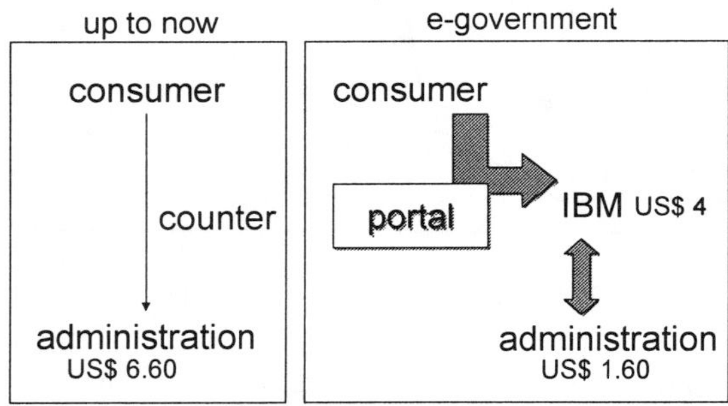


*Figure 2.* Vehicle registration in Arizona

As a matter of course, these figures cannot be transferred indiscriminately to circumstances in other countries. The interest lies primarily in the functionality of an electronic production network:

- Analysis of the single process steps.
- Division into process elements that might be outsourced and elements that have to remain within the agency. Economic criterion: efficiency through economies of scale and/or specific know-how; democratic criterion: warranty of political responsibility.
- Linking up processes with a third party for money (in this example: payment per transaction).
- Quality control carried out by the responsible agency.
- In addition, in case of more complex network structures, i.e. in case of many participants who are not all directly interlinked, the agency could assume a supervisory function.

### 2.1.3 Electronic Public Services (ePS)

Electronic Public Services (ePS) stand for the delivery of public services to benefit recipients, to private individuals, or to companies through local, regional, or national portals. Examples include electronic tax declaration and life event portals.

In the field of public services there is nearly no limit to imagination on how today's processes could be simplified due to e-government solutions. A well-known example is given by the electronic tax declaration, probably owing its popularity to a necessity for efficiency gains. In order to benefit from the possibilities offered by modern ICT, a system featuring as little media inconsistencies as possible has to be implemented, i.e. once entered, it should be possible to directly process a certain piece of information. For this reason, the best solution is the one that allows a tax payer to directly feed the data into the tax authority's browser, where the data is automatically processed. Ideally, in this way the assessment can be made on the same day, charging the tax payer immediately.

Each of these elements carries specific features and emphases, in such a way as to justify a theoretical separation. eDP primarily releases thoughts of a democratic-political nature, as it refers to decision-making processes in the political-administrative system. ePN focuses on the architecture of formal or informal networks and their impact. It can be organized in the background, i.e. without recognition effects on the citizens. On the contrary, ePS is a part of e-government that is visible to customers and citizens, and its conception is decisively coined by the demands and abilities of the benefit recipients. It is only in their wholeness that these three elements can be denoted as comprehensive e-government (cf. fig. 3).

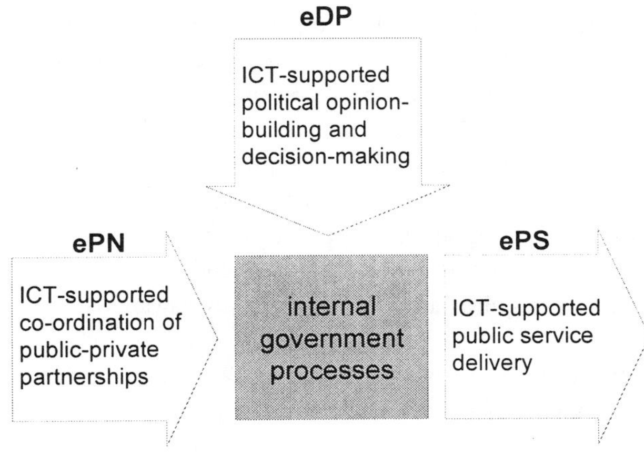


*Figure 3.* Process elements

## 2.2 Culture

The organizational culture comprises position and actions of individuals within the organization that make it work, including the performance of leaders individually and as a team, the agency's commitment to achieve common objectives, and the agency's commitment to training and support.

Culture describes informal processes. They cannot be controlled directly through deliberate intervention, but are influenced by environmental changes. Schedlerand

Proeller (2000) define informal intervention as intervention through new behavioral patterns, which generally enter the organization as part of the administrative culture.

In particular, the administrative culture appears to be one of the biggest obstacles for an optimized e-government. This new organizational form entails an augmented openness towards stakeholders, which is not (yet) common to all administrative units. Reinermann (2000, p. 11) claims the necessity for substantial changes in the attitudes of politicians, administration, the public sector and society towards information technology. Features of this „e-government culture“ in the political-administrative system are:

- Publicity of politics and administration: Comprehensive e-government gets very close to the ideal notion of a "transparent administration" by allowing processes to be monitored and reproduced over the Internet. The introduction of Political Information Systems (PIS), which make information for Parliamentarians available on the Internet, changes the way information is supplied. If, for example, the advantage in information of the Government over the Parliament is seen as an element of power, the principle of publicity bears a potential for slight shifts in power. As Grabow and Floeting (1999, p. 78) argue, this does not necessarily lead to better decisions e.g. when members of the Council overestimate their own judgement based on smattering.
- Customer orientation: Solutions which use the needs of the administration's customers as a guideline are based on the premises that the public sector a) has customers and b) has to accept their requirements.
- A culture of trust: Linking up processes means that departments and individuals, who have been able to fulfil their tasks isolated from others so far, are now collaborating. This requires an openness not only towards stakeholders, but also towards co-workers.
- Disposition to technology: Although the generation of those employees who refuse to personally make use of a computer is slowly retiring, a technology-disposed climate is an essential prerequisite for an e-government project to succeed.

## 2.3 Relevant Management Techniques

In this section, we discuss the contributions which three realms of business administration can make to the functioning of e-government: Knowledge Management, Process Redesign, and Quality Management.

### 2.3.1 Knowledge Management

In the public sector, there is a rising awareness of the importance of knowledge. Since management concepts were introduced into the public sector, knowledge has been recognized as a valuable resource (see e.g. Schedler and Proeller 2000).

Knowledge can be categorized into explicit and implicit (tacit) knowledge (Nonaka and Takeuchi 1995). Explicit knowledge is available from files, library collections or data bases, whereas implicit knowledge is more difficult (and often impossible) to access: accumulated know how, experiences, creativity and skills all reside within individuals and make up the organization's knowledge capital. As no pecuniary value is attributed to this knowledge, it can easily be wasted. Particularly when re-organizing processes, the risk of losing implicit knowledge is high, as its carriers move on to new tasks and their experiences are no longer demanded (Gesellschaft für Informatik 2000).

The cohesion within the organization appears to be even more important. Knowledge which resides in individuals is of no use to an organization if these individuals are not integrated into a communication network that enables them to feed their knowledge into an organizational learning process, both targeted and in time (Lenk 2000). These communication networks are essential for ensuring the efficiency as well as the quality of processes that are new to public administration, e.g. e-procurement (cf. section 2.1.2). However, also "known" processes need to be supported by new networks as the physical distance between offices increases due to decentralization and parts of the processes are contracted out, only to mention a few examples of NPM-induced organizational changes.

### 2.3.2 Process Redesign

Business Process Redesign (BPR) aims at improving the productivity of an organization by altering the organization's processes. Rather than reformulating tasks, the efforts of redesign concentrate on the outcomes of the processes. Information technology is seen as an enabler for reorganization (Hammer and Champy 1993). IT-supported process redesign is not new to the public sector, but what is lacking is an integrated view of process redesign, led by a strong strategy that allows a consistent connection of different applications.

Besides cultural barriers, the difficulties in applying BPR to the public sector are founded in the nature of the political decision and production process (cf. section 2.1). Many administrative processes can be modeled on the sample of industrial production processes, leading to considerable cost-cuttings and quality improvements (Gesellschaft für Informatik 2000). However, more complex processes consist of case-based decision-making and are often limited to individuals. Due to their knowledge intensity, these processes cannot simply be formalized – they must contain a margin for informal behavior. Lenk (1997) claims that a certain amount of ambiguity is functional for the survival of large organizations: "If opportunities for informal action are reduced too much, this ambiguity will be reduced at the expense of organizational innovation and flexibility".

Thaens, Bekkers and Duivenboden (1997, p.27) have observed the following pitfalls of applying BPR to the public sector:

- While an improved productivity may be the ultimate goal of BPR in the private sector, redesigning policy processes cannot be geared solely to productivity. Public sector organizations are obliged to reckon with political, judiciary, economic, and professional boundaries.
- The complex regulatory environment of government agencies hampers the ideal situation of redesigning processes with a 'clean slate'[73].
- The democratic principles of legal equality, legal security and the rule of law impede the application of creative strategies in redesigning policy processes.
- The primacy of politics could stand in the way of conducting strong management in the process of redesigning.
- BPR requires thinking in processes as opposed to thinking in terms of functional specialization of labor.

### 2.3.3 Quality Management

Quality has become a widely used term where the organization of public services is concerned. Traditionally, quality is equated with legitimacy and regularity in public sector organizations. Through the NPM, quality was extended to the customer orientation, enabling the service recipients to make demands on public services (Schedler and Proeller 2000). In the public sector, the following quality dimensions can be identified (Schedler and Proeller 2000, p. 65):

- Product-oriented quality: Differences in quality feature different product attributes. This type of quality includes the product itself as well as the way in which the product is supplied to the customer.
- Customer-oriented quality: Covers the aim of making an impact (generally a benefit) on the service recipients through service delivery. Includes customer satisfaction and an aspired change in customer behavior.
- Process-oriented quality: Indicates the measure of security of the processes (little errors) as well as their optimization (speed, efficiency). Includes questions regarding the legitimacy and regularity of service generation.
- Value-oriented quality: States whether a service is worth its price. Differences in quality are primarily shown through the costs/service ratio or the costs/effects ratio (efficiency).
- Political quality: The political bodies as contractors judge the quality of a service by its benefit for policy. One element is the objective benefit for society (e.g. better living standards, security), another the social benefit (e.g. social peace, coherence of a community).

[73] The 'clean slate' approach demands that a business process be rebuilt from scratch, radically breaking with the past (Thaens, Bekkers and Duivenboden 1997).

Therefore, a comprehensive quality management is concerned with the efficiency, the effectiveness, and the adequacy of public services. In order to assist public administrations to understand and use quality management techniques, the European Union developed a Common Assessment Framework (CAF), under which an ad hoc group of employees in an organization can conduct a critical assessment of their organization. The criteria are: leadership, policy and strategy, human resource management, external partnerships and internal resources, process and change management, customer/citizen-oriented results, employees results, impact on society, and key performance results (Hill and Klages 2000).

The interactions of the elements described above are shown in fig. 4. The process elements eDP, ePN, and ePS are organized around the internal government processes. The arrows symbolize the direction of the political decision-making and production process:

1. The decision-making process primarily evolves along the elements eDP – internal processes – ePS. Here, the quality indicator is effectiveness.
2. The production process moves on the path ePN – internal processes – ePS. The quality of this process is best measured in terms of efficiency.

It should be mentioned that the model corresponds to our current organizational view, whereas the contextual variables are still missing – in fact, they represent one of the fields where we believe that further research into e-government needs to be done.

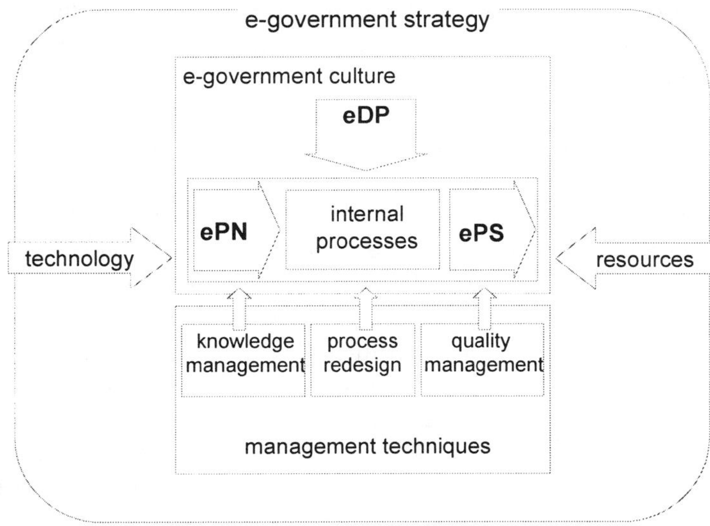


*Figure 4.* E-government framework

# 3. EXPERIENCES WITH PUBLIC MANAGEMENT REFORMS

Publications on modernizing the public sector are legion. Since the eighties, the New Public Management is the dominating international reform model, although it is regularly adjusted to national needs so that there is no such thing as a single international reform model (cf. section 1.2). The NPM is a new way of thinking the public sector – driven by theoretical frameworks that stem from new institutional economics and organizational theory. Its purpose is to cut the red tape or, in other words, break through bureaucracy (Barzelay 1992). In this context, researchers interested in organizational aspects have studied many reform projects with a focus on change management. Our own work (Schedler 1997, Schedler 1998) both in practice and theory leads to some important lessons that can be learned for the implementation of e-government in the public sector:

- Importance of administrative culture: Cultural change takes significantly longer than most project managers and champions of the NPM have expected. Our research demonstrates that implementation barriers are cultural to a high degree, and most often not instrumental or mechanistic. Therefore, a sensitive approach towards cultural change will be crucial for e-government, too.
- Political involvement: The more politicians are affected by the effects of the reforms, the earlier they should be included in the reform process. On the other hand, it came out clear in practice that it was a means to success to avoid political debates on the reform during the phase of designing the concept. e-government seems to be a fairly technical and therefore apolitical reform process – ideological debates, of which there were many on NPM reforms, will not have to be expected here.
- Understanding the public sector: It was crucial for public management reform success that different disciplines worked together and shared their views from their perspectives, urging to understand each other. Most important, however, was a common understanding of the differences between the public and the private sector. The political and legal sphere in which the administration has to function and survive creates very particular patterns of behavior of its actors, which lead to a necessity for different reform strategies. Therefore, e-government is much less a technical matter than e.g. e-commerce.

Altogether, it appears to be evident that the soil for e-government has been made fertile by reforms such as the NPM. Above all, the customer focus and its organizational consequences (e.g. one-stop shops, complaint management systems, life-event supplies) are an important predecessor for an e-government culture as described in section 2.2.

On the other hand, latest developments in countries such as Germany or Austria demonstrate that the introduction of e-government into the reform process can be a strong furthering factor for the reform in total. The reason for this effect, and the effect itself, have not been researched empirically yet, but an educated guess will lead to some important insights. First, the apolitical nature of e-government eases its introduction in comparison to the more ideological NPM. Second, a strategy-driven reform such as the NPM can be hindered by strategic debates on the benefit of such a reform, while no-one within the administration can stop the technological development that stands behind e-government, but happens isolated from it. Third, due to the necessity for a process redesign that is created by e-government, a real organizational change within the single administrative office has to take place, which leads to a faster impact of e-government in comparison to the NPM. Recapitulating, e-government can be interpreted as a reform element that supports the idea behind the NPM and, with its technological equipment, eases modernization as a whole.

## 4. REFERENCES


Barzelay, Michael (1992). Breaking Through Bureaucracy: A New Vision For Managing in Government. Berkeley, Los Angeles, Oxford: University of California Press.

Caldow, Janet (1999). The Quest for Electronic Government: A Defining Vision. Internet. Available: http://www.ieg.ibm.com/egovvison.pdf. 27 July 2000.

Economist (2000). "Survey Government and the Internet", The Economist: 24th June 2000.

Gesellschaft für Informatik (2000). Electronic Government als Schlüssel zur Modernisierung von Staat und Verwaltung, Bonn/Frankfurt.

Gisler, Michael (2001). Einführung in die Begriffswelt des eGovernment. In: eGovernment: Eine Standortbestimmung. Gisler, Michael and Dieter Spahni. Bern, Stuttgart, Wien: Haupt. 13 - 30.

Grabow, Busso and Holger Floeting (1999). Wege zur telematischen Stadt. In: Multimedia@Verwaltung. Jahrbuch Telekommunikation und Gesellschaft 1999. Kubicek, Herbert et al. Heidelberg: Hüthig. 75 - 87.

Hammer, Michael and James Champy (1993). Reengineering the Corporation: A Manifesto for Business Revolution. New York: Harper Business.

Hill, Hermann and Helmut Klages (2000). Good Governance und Qualitätsmanagement - Europäische und internationale Entwicklungen. Speyerer Arbeitsheft Nr. 132, Speyer.

Hood, Christopher (1991). "A Public Management For All Seasons?" Public Administration 1991(69): 3-19.

Korac-Kakabadse, Andrew and Nada Korac-Kakabadse (1999). Information Technology's Impact on the Quality of Democracy. In: Reinventing Government in the Information Age: International Practice in IT-enabled public sector reform. Heeks, Richard. London: Routledge. 212 - 218.

Lenk, Klaus (1997). Business Process Reengineering in the Public Sector. In: Beyond BPR in Public Administration : Institutional Transformation in an Information Age. Taylor, J. M., Th. M. Snellen and A. Zuurmond. Amsterdam: IOS Press. 151 - 163.

Lenk, Klaus (2000). Ausserrechtliche Grundlagen für das Verwaltungsrecht in der Informationsgesellschaft: Zur Bedeutung von Information und Kommunikation in der Verwaltung. In: Verwaltungsrecht in der Informationsgesellschaft. Hoffmann-Riem, Wolfgang and Eberhard Schmidt-Assmann. Baden-Baden: Nomos.

Nonaka, Ikujiro and Hirotaka Takeuchi (1995). The Knowledge-Creating Company : How Japanese Companies Create the Dynamics of Innovation. New York: Oxford University Press.

Ormond, Derry and Elke Löffler (1998). New Public Management - What to Take and What to Leave. III International Congress of CLAD on State and Public Administration Reform, Madrid, Spain.

Reinermann, Heinrich (2000). Der öffentliche Sektor im Internet: Veränderungen der Muster öffentlicher Verwaltungen. Speyer: Forschungsinstitut für öffentliche Verwaltung.

Schedler, Kuno (1997). The State of Public Management Reforms in Switzerland. In: Public Management and Administrative Reform in Western Europe. Kickert, Walter. Cheltenham: Edward Elgar. 123 - 142.

Schedler, Kuno (1998). Blowing the Alphorn: Financial Management Reforms in Switzerland. In: Global Warning! Debating International Developments in New Public Financial Management. Olson, Olov, James Guthrie and Christopher Humphrey. Oslo: Cappelen Akademisk Forlag. 276 - 303.

Schedler, Kuno and Isabella Proeller (2000). New Public Management. Bern, Stuttgart, Wien: Haupt.

Schuh, Günther and Jochen Strack (1997). "Die virtuelle Fabrik - neue Flexibilität für dynamische Märkte." Management & Qualität / Special May: 12-13.

Tapscott, Don (1997). Growing Up Digital : The Rise of the Net Generation. New York: McGraw-Hill.

Thaens, Marcel, Victor Bekkers, et al. (1997). Business Process Redesign and Public Administration: A Perfect Match? In: Beyond BPR in Public Administration : Institutional Transformation in an Information Age. Taylor, J. M., Th. M. Snellen and A. Zuurmond. Amsterdam: IOS Press. 15 - 35.

# 58

# XML-based Process Representation for e-Government Serviceflows

Ralf Klischewski, Ingrid Wetzel
*University of Hamburg, Department for Informatics/Software Engineering*

**Abstract:** Addressing new public challenges such as the one-stop government and improved service quality, we introduce serviceflow management as a generic concept to coordinate cross-organizational e-government processes. Aiming at a serviceflow management infrastructure for networked service providers we present an XML-based process representation of serviceflows as well as a four layered IT architecture for realizing serviceflow related applications.

The research presented is exemplified by the case of citizens applying for postal vote through the web portal of the city state of Hamburg (Germany). The discussion includes how XML-based process representations for e-government serviceflows enable governmental actors to enter the network age without high investment burdens, but with many options for creating the service-oriented government of the future.

## 1. THE PUBLIC CHALLENGE: ONE STOP – MANY SERVICE PROVIDERS

We are used to speak of "government" or "administration" in the singular even though we know from experience that there is a multitude (if not a "jungle") of institutions and hosts of employees each responsible for one small portion of the governmental/administrative "business". Now, with e-government the singular notion has received new emphasis:

- citizens are looking for a one-stop government with single entry points for personalized services (authority-to-citizen, A2C)
- government departments as customers and commercial providers strive to align through centralized web-based market places (business-to-authority, B2A)

– co-operation among government departments and among governments (authority-to-authority, A2A) needs to establish channels and network structures corresponding to a clear understanding of what are central nodes of the network by which one can reach members of the respective subnets.

In this paper, we concentrate on citizens' expectations to contact the relevant government unit through one single point of entry or access (one stop) which will enable the fulfillment of whatever concern he or she might have. With regard to content, the administrative challenge[74] then is to realize those "single points" which

- provide the unmeasurable amount of (context dependent) information on government and administrative issues (*information*)
- offer to make contact with the vast number of actors and institutions which are all competent authorities (*communication*)
- let citizen enter in the countless variations of administrative processes (*transaction*)

This challenge is multiplied by the need for many "single points" of access with respect to the government's layered structure (e.g. federal/state/municipal or international/national/local level) as well as for a division of competence according to geography or function. In addition, these "single points" must support access through different channels such as web portals, call centers, face-to-face service counters or even one central postal address.

Meanwhile, nearly all governments are publishing information online, including contact information. Also, there are services[75] that select relevant information and/or competent authorities according to the citizen's personal needs (owing to e.g. time restrictions, disabilities). Many authorities have started to provide transaction services (e.g. filing tax returns). However, up to now there is a lack of organizational concepts and system architectures matching the special requirements of governmental transaction services as well as the restrictions of governmental service providers.

Addressing these requirements we introduce *serviceflow management* as a universal concept to coordinate cross-organizational e-government processes, present an XML-based process representation to support those serviceflows, and discuss IT architectures for service points suitable to realizing serviceflow related applications. The research presented is exemplified by the case of citizens applying for postal vote through the web portal of the city state of Hamburg (Germany). In summing up, we will consider how the concepts and solutions introduced here apply to e-government challenges in general.

[74] E.g. KPMG (2000, 21) states "in the public sector (...) the challenge is to manage customer relationships through a single channel".

[75] E.g. the "direct citizen information service" of Hamburg, DIBIS, http://dibis.dufa.de

## 2. SERVICEFLOW MANAGEMENT TO COORDINATE CROSS-ORGANIZATIONAL E-GOVERNMENT PROCESSES

E-business "invading the public sector" (Wimmer et al. 2001) poses technical as well as organizational challenges. Governmental institutions must move to catch up with the rise of the network society, but at the same time they cannot simply copy the concepts applied in commercial domains. From the numerous differences (see e.g. Wimmer et al. 2001) the most significant is that governments do not sell products to customers in a competitive environment. Rather, they provide a vast variety of informational and document-oriented services where, in most cases,[76] the client-citizen is forced (by laws and regulations) to demand a service from a monopolistic provider. Specifically, much of governmental administration consists of law-based, well-defined processes that take into account the citizens' concerns and personal situations and produce specific documents and records as well as a number of intended side effects.

Following the vision of a one-stop government, these processes should be accessible through one single entry point, i.e. process management must reach beyond the borders of the competent authority in charge. For developing and using IT support (esp. internet technology) for cross-organizational process management we need an appropriate organizational model. Basically, we may draw on two backgrounds:

- *Workflow management* originally focuses on the flow of worked-on documents as well as on the interrelation of workplaces. Meanwhile, flexibility and cross-border process management have become an issue, but (based on a back office orientation) customer relation management or service quality are usually not taken into account. Technical development is aiming at integrated workflow management systems for modeling and supporting the whole process.
- *Business networking* (e.g. Österle et al. 2000), based on business process analysis/engineering, is a rather comprehensive approach meant to identify and support processes for increasing accountable value in business cooperation and/or for external clients. It provides a guiding vision and a strategy framework for how to achieve cross-organizational integration in e-commerce, supply chain management, or customer relationship management through the extensive use of internet applications (e.g. customer process portals). But this top level approach focuses primarily on the interrelation of business units, not on the workplace or personal interaction level. It may lead to a comprehensive IT strategy, but does not include concepts detailed enough to bring out new application modeling and respective IT architectures.

[76] One of the notable exceptions are weddings where administration now often engages in marketing activities to attract couples as customers to their wedding sites.

In the following, we will draw on these approaches to organize and manage processes, but they do not sufficiently address the special needs and circumstances of e-government. There we need process models which allow for

- portal access, i.e. one-stop for all services, at the same time
- multi-channel access to services at different entry points or directly at the authority in charge, and
- accountability, i.e. transparency (from the citizens' point of view) of authorities in charge throughout the whole chain of activities
- flexibility to address situated/changing needs of citizens and to enhance service quality to fulfill the legally granted rights of citizens

Given these requirements, the model of self-service points with the actual operation carried out somewhere in the back office does not serve as a suitable guiding vision. Service is process – while ongoing, the service quality is determined by the extent to which the service provider is able to recognize and address the situated (changing) needs of the client, based on an (implicit) agreement (cf. Klischewski 2000). We have therefore introduced the concept of serviceflow management (Klischewski/Wetzel 2000) to meet the special requirements of public service domains such as e-government and e-health (see also Klischewski/Wetzel 2001), but the same applies to other service domains, such as education or tourism. In these domains the challenge is to manage personalized sequences of interrelated activities/operations carried out by actors (humans and non-humans) of different organizational units which, from the clients' point of view, sum up to a personalized service. Serviceflow management is aiming at:

- improved service quality by customer relation management throughout the whole serviceflow,
- resource efficiency in the fields of tension between routinization and personalization as well as between standardized process patterns and situated process execution
- connectivity and suitable computer support for each service point

Based on object oriented, workflow and user oriented modeling techniques, we model serviceflow patterns by identifying sequences of service points, each capturing the specific service tasks and their respective pre- and postconditions from the provider's point of view (Klischewski/Wetzel/Bahrami 2001). In contrast to workflow approaches, serviceflow modeling implies that

- each work-place is a place of service (*service point*)
- flowing data represents customer relations (not the ‚products' to work on)
- all process models are resources for personalization
- process governance is decentralized (no central flow engine)

In prinicple, serviceflow management enables any process to continue individually according to the accumulated postconditions as well as the requested preconditions and situated process planning at each service point. Thus, each service provider must decide to what extent the respective work organization and IT support will allow for variations of or deviations from the predefined standard processes.

## 2.1 Case: postal vote application at www.hamburg.de

In our case – citizens applying for postal vote through the web portal of the city state of Hamburg (Germany) – all parties involved have acknowledged that the underlying concept of serviceflow management applies a general perspective and that the selected process of applying for postal vote is only one first example to demonstrate the city's new capabilities and to learn how to manage the organizational and technical aspects of e-government transaction services. In evaluating and redesigning the service process, we have identified four service points with respective activities/operations in parentheses (see figure 1):

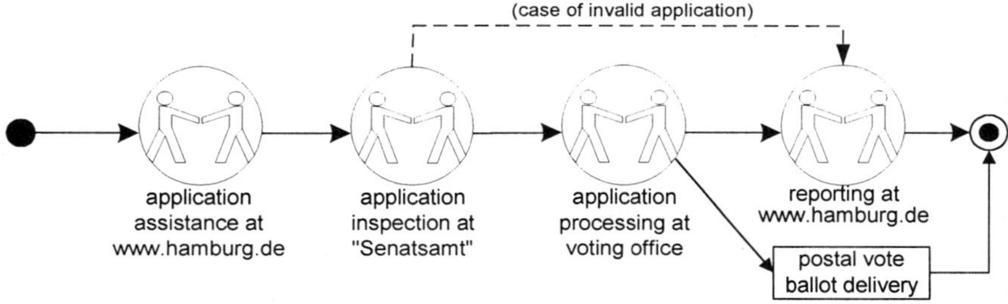


Figure 1. Serviceflow model for a postal vote application

1. providing assistance with the application for citizens at the city's web portal www.hamburg.de (opening application, automatic assistance in personalization, on-site evaluation, confirming reception, serviceflow preview, offering/registering personal reporting channel, optional: saving application)
2. inspecting the application at "Senatsamt für Bezirksangelegenheiten", the city's central administration for IT procedures (automatic validity check including selecting the voting office in charge; or exception handling: selecting the voting office in charge if application processing seems possible – or moving directly to service point 4 in case of invalid application)
3. processing of the application by the respective voting office (validity check with up to date preconditions, preparing personal postal vote ballot, notification of the electoral register, preparing postal vote ballot for dispatch, personalized exception handling if necessary)
4. reporting on process by the web portal provider (delivering messages to inform the applicant about the state of the process, providing information about what to do next and/or whom to contact) through the channel the applicant has selected before (web page, email, SMS, etc.)

Other activities/operations not focussing on or reflecting the citizen's personal/situated need are considered support processes, in this case the delivery of the postal vote ballot by regular mail.

Modeling the postal vote application as a serviceflow helps (1) to identify standardized portions (service points) of the overall service, (2) to allocate responsibility for each service point, and thus (3) supports cooperation across organizations and/or organizational units (cf. Klischewski/Wetzel/Bahrami 2001). While the process described above seems pretty straightforward (at least simple enough for prototyping purposes), a number of variations, uncertainties, possible exceptions and failures may occur. Situated needs to be addressed include a citizen's

- moving to a new address before the voting office starts processing his/her application (voting offices open only a few weeks before the election date)
- having lost the postal vote ballot and needing a new one
- not needing to use postal vote after all and wanting to vote at the polling station

However, the administration expects the majority of the personalized serviceflows to follow the designed pattern. In our case, the above serviceflow model is the adopted basis for cooperation between the different service providers: the commercial portal provider of www.hamburg.de, the city's central department for application programming ("Senatsamt für Bezirksangelegenheiten") and the city's election department responsible for the temporary voting offices. The city's finance department, responsible for e-government strategy, is also involved in the background.

Given the successful realization of the postal vote application service (which is to support the city state government election in September 2001), the established teamwork will continue to pave the ground for the multitude of future e-government services. Lately, negotiations have started with other administrative bodies in Northern Germany who also want to adopt this new approach. Whereas each citizen process portal and the management of all accessible serviceflows need a negotiated organizational model with specific actors in charge, the IT architecture and technology to support serviceflow management are of general use. In the next sections, we will continue documenting this case to explain about the underlying general concepts for the use of XML and the system architecture for service points.

## 3. XML-BASED PROCESS REPRESENTATION TO CROSS SYSTEM BARRIERS

Process management across organizational units must cross IT system barriers unless there is a strong force to provide and put through a technical integration (e.g. a central database, file server, web portal, workflow engine). In the e-government domain we cannot presuppose an integrated technology infrastructure. Among the various reasons (which are mainly due to the limited IT capabilities of the public administration) the most significant is that commercial application and service providers (which, e.g., host the city's or state's web portal) run their own secured IT environments which are usually significantly different from the mainframe oriented IT landscapes of the public administration. At the same time, we find similar requirements for IT support in any kind of service organization in terms of customer relation and process management.

Given these requirements, IT support for serviceflow management relies on the following assumptions:

- In the chain of subsequent service points there is always exactly one service point in charge after process initialization and before ending[77]
- each service point in charge has full control of the process (within an agreed technical and organizational frame), there is no central instance (necessary)
- it must be possible to handle a (great) number of individual serviceflows at the same time
- it must be possible to handle a (great) number of different kinds of serviceflows at the same time (i.e. based on different serviceflow patterns, which may change over time)
- all process information that needs to be communicated between service points must be persistent and portable

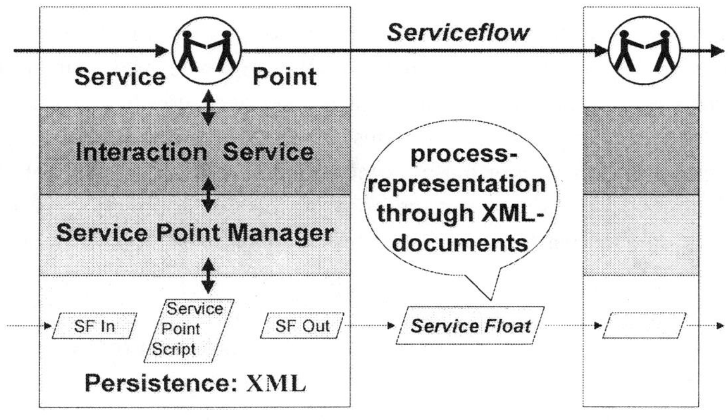


*Figure 2.* Context of serviceflow process representation

To meet these presuppositions process representation for serviceflow management is organized around sending a service float from service point to service point (see figure 2). The service float contains the following elements:

- identifier for individual serviceflow (based on serviceflow type/variation)

[77] except for concurrency; the concept of handling parallel threads within serviceflows cannot be covered in this paper

- basic information on serviceflow client (with possible reference to comprehensive client data)
- current service point (service points are described by identifier, name, type, provider, address)
- lists of scheduled and passed service points
- list of accumulated postconditions
- list of documents, i.e. short message texts or references to full documents or document folders

At each service point, the service float is evaluated according to the related service point script prescribing the activities at the 'current service point':

- identifier for individual service point (based on service point type/variation)
- basic information on service point provider (with possible reference to comprehensive provider data)
- current activity (activities are described by identifier, name, type, task; the activity's attribute list may contain provider id, employee/operator id, document id, time stamp, and more)
- lists of scheduled and passed activities
- lists of pre- and postconditions for the set of activities of this service point
- list of documents, i.e. short message texts (for display) or references to full documents (e.g. forms) or document folders

*Note:* using service point scripts is not required for implementing IT support for service points as described in the following section 4. However, service point scripts represent the specifics of how to carry out the service activities at this point of a certain type or variant of serviceflow. Thus, using service point scripts allows using the same technology for supporting a variety of serviceflows. At the web portal, for example, there will be a set of service point scripts for application assistance (for postal vote, income tax cards, ...), a set for making payments, and other sets.

For dynamic serviceflow management all participating service point providers must agree to follow the process pattern as indicated by the by type/variant of serviceflow model and to use the respective process representation by

1. carrying out activities/operations according to the negotiated serviceflow model and/or as specified in the service point script
2. transferring their own 'current service point' into the list of passed service points while at the same time supplementing the list of accumulated postconditions with the postconditions achieved at this service point
3. extracting the first from the list of scheduled service points to replace the current service point
4. evaluating the address of the new current service point and sending the service float to this address

As XML is used more and more for exchanging structured data between organizations, the documents for serviceflow representation are implemented in XML, i.e. each customer-related serviceflow is represented by one service float in

XML. Meanwhile, research not only addresses the mapping of data structures by using XML, but also to support process management. For example, Lenz/Oberweis (2001) have introduced XML Nets for modeling interorganizational workflows, intended to be executed by a workflow engine. For e-government (assumed to be structurally similar to eBusiness) Greunz et al. (2001) suggest secure XML document containers to support processes aiming at electronic contracting.

When starting a personalized serviceflow a service float will be created by personalizing a copy of the respective serviceflow "master" (which represents the standard process for the type or variant of serviceflow in question) including the schedule of service points for this process. At each service point the activities for the individual client will be started off by personalizing a copy of the respective service point script master (manipulation of this personalized service point script may be used for documenting the service activities at this service point). After all service point activities have been carried out the updated service float will be sent to next scheduled service point.

To enable cross-organizational serviceflow management, the organizations involved need to agree on the following:

- a set of serviceflow models as a basis for cooperative process management
- a set of XML DTD and XML "master"-documents
- a set of rules on how to manipulate and share the XML documents (see above)

Additionally, the actors involved need to agree how to cope with overarching issues such as service quality (e.g. overall response time), creation, distribution and update of serviceflow models and XML documents, privacy and security issues.

# 4. IT ARCHITECTURES FOR SERVICE POINTS

The approach to serviceflow management as introduced above does not presuppose any kind of shared IT infrastructure except the processing and exchange of XML documents. Thus, any kind of organization (public or private) can easily join the cooperative serviceflow management, and it may independently look after its own IT support as long as it keeps to the mutual agreement. However, there are IT solutions to hand, and we recommend a four layer client-server architecture:

1. Front-end: client to present the user interface
2. Interaction: server layer to organize the user dialogue
3. Serviceflow application: server layer to realize the XML document processing for process representation
4. Persistence: the server's file system or data base for saving and retrieving XML documents

The IT architecture for a web-based service point as suggested for the postal vote application assistance is shown in figure 3. The user dialogue is organized by a set of templates created in the web content management system (WCMS) of a high-performance environment for e-business and customer relation management (in this case based on Vignette® and WebLogic® products). These templates include Java method calls addressing the public interface of the serviceflow application layer implemented in Java.

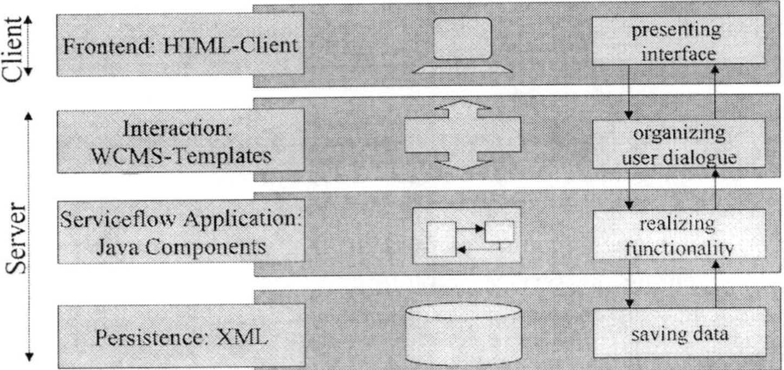


*Figure 3.* IT architecture for a web-based service point

The components of the serviceflow application layer[78] – created dynamically for the time it takes to carry out the service point's activities for a specific customer – encapsulate the processing of the XML documents related to serviceflow management (see figure 4):

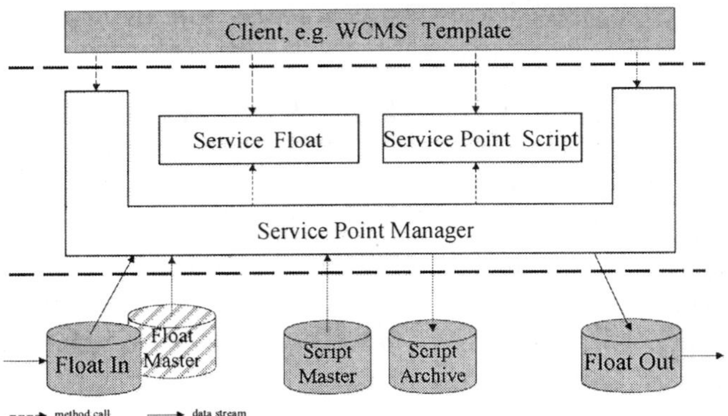


*Figure 4.* Java components for service point management

– the service point manager includes methods for retrieving the relevant XML files, creating Document Object Models (DOM) of service float and service

[78] The description is based on the prototype developed at Hamburg University as presented at the end of January 2001. The final solution in this case may differ in some aspects.

point script for a specific customer, saving the manipulated DOMs in XML files and preparing the service float for dispatch

– service float and service point script each include a variety of get- and set-methods (according to the usage of serviceflow process representation, see above) to be called on through the public interface for manipulating the respective XML DOM

*Note:* This architecture is generic, and layers are interchangeable. The interaction layer of a web-based service point, for example, may be implemented without web content management systems but with Java Server Pages or other web technology, and/or the serviceflow application layer to realize the XML document processing may draw on other than the developed components as long as it meets the agreement on how to use the XML-based process representation.

The same applies to service points without web clients, but with clients based on, for example, mainframes (as in the case of the postal vote application processing). The layered architecture may include the available Java components, but the serviceflow application layer may be implemented in a different technology to provide a suitable interface to existing mainframe applications (in our case, given a Microsoft environment, the developers chose Visual Basic®).

*Note:* The Java components may be used for all types of serviceflows, no re-implementation is necessary. At the interaction layer each type of serviceflow may require additional programming work. However, a sophisticated architecture for this level may allow the reuse of all components by requesting the relevant data for the specific serviceflow type or variant from the service point script.

In our case the architecture described is leading the current implementation work which aims at realizing the postal vote application through www.hamburg.de and, at the same time, at providing a technical basis for a great variety of e-government processes in the city state of Hamburg. Other challenges to be addressed (beyond the scope of serviceflow management) include scalability and reliability, as well as security and privacy. Most of these are solved within the web portal's IT infrastructure designed for high performance (including secure operations such as web mail), and encryption is used for all file transfers between service points of different organizations. Additionally, some legal, organizational and technical measures need to be implemented to secure citizens' privacy as the commercial portal provider is processing personal data on behalf of the city's authorities.

## 5. E-GOVERNMENT: TOWARDS MANAGING A SERVICEFLOW INFRASTRUCTURE

In this article we have introduced serviceflow management as a universal means to connect and coordinate cross-organizational e-government processes. We identify serviceflow patterns by modeling sequences of service points, each capturing the specific service tasks and their respective pre- and postconditions from the provider's point of view. In contrast to the workflow approach, serviceflow management allows for analyzing, modeling, supporting and managing those processes as being related to the citizens' concerns all the way through the chain of service points. This approach meets the unique requirements of e-government services, i.e. portal access (one stop), multi-channel access, accountability/transparency, and flexibility. With serviceflow management it is possible to dissect complex routine processes and delegate parts of the process (e.g. assisting and accepting formal applications) to actors outside the administration (e.g. a web portal provider), whereas the responsibility for the key activities (e.g. processing a citizen's application) – as can easily be demonstrate to citizens and all service providers involved – rests with governmental institutions.

To support serviceflow management we have presented an XML-based process representation, which is the only technology necessary to be shared among the network of service providers. The integrating framework for cooperative process management consists of a set of serviceflow models as a basis for cooperative process management, a set of XML documents, a set of rules on how to manipulate and share those XML documents, and an agreement on how to administrate and develop serviceflow management. Organizational and technical integration does not need more than (ongoing) coordination between the service providers involved, shared serviceflow modeling, and the exchange of XML-based process representations! To enable a serviceflow management mainly requires organizational and administrative expertise, but (compared to other cross-organizational process management solutions) only little technical know-how. Thus, governmental institutions in charge can easily take the lead in coordinating all service providers involved.

Already, IT support is available to realize serviceflow related applications. We have developed a generic four-layered service point architecture which allows the exchange of single components as well as a certain freedom of choice in developing and using individual solutions. The feasibility of this approach has been proved as it has guided the development the first e-government transaction service available at the web portal of the city state of Hamburg (Germany). The research and development going on is aiming paving the ground for creating a variety of e-government services and managing a serviceflow infrastructure with as little IT investment as possible.

In this contribution we have concentrated on the challenge of providing single entry points for citizens who want/need to engage with the authorities through personalized transactions which will lead to the fulfillment of whatever concern he or she may have (A2C). However, the concepts and solutions introduced here can be applied to other e-government challenges in the fields of B2A and A2A as well. To give an example, serviceflow management provides a process management solution for government departments aligning with providers to fulfill the service needs of the administration. Cooperation among government departments is of course a central element of this approach. Adopting the same serviceflow infrastructure (i.e. the integrating framework) easily enrolls new members in the process management network. But even cooperation between such networks (each with their own sets of models and XML documents) will be no problem since already available XML mapping tools are likely to be part of the e-government's IT infrastructure.

In short, XML-based process representation for e-government serviceflows is a promising application-oriented approach which enables governmental actors to enter the network age without high investment burdens, but with many options for creating the service-oriented government of the future.

## 6. ACKNOWLEDGEMENTS

We wish to thank the student members of the postal vote project, especially Timmy Blank and Nol Shala for implementing and sharing the DTDs and Java components. The authors acknowledge support by hamburg.de GmbH.

## 7. REFERENCES

Greunz, M., Haes, J., Schopp, B., Stanoevska, K. Integrating e-government Infrastructures through Secure XML Document Containers. In *Proceedings of the 34th Annual Hawaii International Conference on System Sciences* (HICSS-34). IEEE, 2001

Klischewski, R. Abstrakte Bedürfnisse und konkrete Beziehungen - oder: Wie man Services (nicht) modelliert, In *Modelle und Modellierungssprachen in Informatik und Wirtschaftsinformatik. Proceedings Modellierung 2000* (St. Goar, 5.-7.4.), Ebert, J., Frank, U., ed. Koblenz: Fölbach, pp. 19-26

Klischewski, R., Wetzel, I. Serviceflow Management. *Informatik Spektrum* 23:1, February 2000, pp. 38-46

Klischewski, R., Wetzel, I. Serviceflow Management for Health Provider Networks. In *Information Age Economy – Innovations, Methods and Applications for Electronic Commerce. Proceedings 5th International Conference Wirtschaftsinformatik (Business Information Systems)*, Augsburg, Sep. 19-21, 2001

Klischewski, R., Wetzel, I., Bahrami, A. Modeling Serviceflow. In *Information Systems Technology and its Applications. Proceedings ISTA 2001* (June 13-15, 2001, Kharkiv, Ukraine), Godlevsky, M., Mayr, H., ed. Bonn: German Informatics Society, Lecture Notes in Informatics, 2001, pp. 261-272

KPMG. Leading the Transformation to e-Government. Seven Things You Need to Know. Oct. 2000, *www.us.kpmg.com/RutUS_prod/Documents/12/Trans3_Lite.pdf* (download: 2001-2-15)

Lenz, K., Oberweis, A. Modeling Interorganizational Workflows with XML Nets. In *Proceedings of the 34th Annual Hawaii International Conference on System Sciences* (HICSS-34). IEEE, 2001

Österle, H., Fleisch, E., Alt, R. *Business networking. Shaping enterprise relationships on the Internet.* Berlin: Springer, 2000

Wimmer, M., Traunmüller, R., Lenk, K. Electronic Business Invading the Public Sector: Considerations on Change and Design. In *Proceedings of the 34th Annual Hawaii International Conference on System Sciences* (HICSS-34). IEEE, 2001

59

# Digital Identity and its Implication for Electronic Government

Clemens H. Cap and Nico Maibaum
*Chair for Information and Communication Services, University of Rostock*

**Abstract:** The present use of identity concepts is analyzed. A requirements analysis for "identity" reveals the different identity properties necessary in various administrative and business processes. A classification of identity tokens is given and compared with passport identity and established forms of digital identities. A fundamental problem with digital signature identity schemes is explained. Implementation strategies for non-transferable identity tokens are outlined. Finally, conclusions and implications for the e-government processes and solutions of tomorrow are presented in the form of six Theses and with the goal of stimulating further discussion.

## 1. INTRODUCTION

Electronic commerce applications draw public attention to security problems of the Internet. Almost every netizen is familiar with the unpleasant feeling when sending his credit card number to a web server in the Internet, as this act could provide sensitive information to a criminal hiding his identity behind a fancy web page. On the other hand, many surfers are very careful whom they reveal information leading to their identification. Giving away an email address fills one?s electronic mailbox with masses of unwanted advertisements and other solicitations. Shopping profiles and patterns of surfing behavior provide companies with unfair bargaining advantages, reducing a customer to a revenue generating black box with marketing relevant properties.

In electronic government processes, the issues of identity and anonymity are even more important: Here the dangers are not only of a monetary nature. Personal freedom, civil and democratic rights are at stake. Citizen rights groups point out the danger of *Big Brother* whom they fear in every electronic administration pro-cess. On the other hand, experiences with Florida voting machines in the 2000 US presidential elections call for a more reliable technology. From the cryptographic point of view, electronic voting algorithms (Herschberg, 1997) are a well studied subject.

The situation of the voting process illustrates the issues very clearly: The *identity* of a voter must be verified beyond any doubt to make sure that he or she is legally entitled and correctly registered to vote. When casting the vote, *anonymity* of the vote constitutes the basis of democracy. Although *transaction numbers* (or physical or organizational means with the same effect) are necessary to identify and to count every single vote and to make sure that a voter casts at most one vote, this transaction number (or the specific ballot sheet) must not allow identification of the voter. All three central issues at stake with identification personal identity, pseudonymity (ie. session or transactional identity) and anonymity - are contained in the single act of voting.

In *this paper* we describe the *concepts* of identity and the implications for electronic government processes when mapping traditional identity to electronic identity. In Section 2 we explain the basic concepts and present a requirement analysis for "identity. We introduce a new token concept for identity and compare it to established digital identity schemes. Section 3 outlines, how this token concept can be implemented. Section 4 discusses legal, social and process implications of identity concepts in e-government. It demonstrates why and how *a renewed analysis of identity concepts* is imperative for successful e-government operations.

The paper *does not* provide a complete account of implementation strategies for all combinations of requirements for digital identity since this is not the primary goal of the paper nor can it be achieved within the given space limitations. We have verified that every presented attribute allows an implementation by known cryptographic or biometric methods or by straight forward adaptations thereof. Given the achievements of (Chaum et al., 1989), (Chaum, 1985) and the cryptographic basis illustrated in (Schneier, 1995), the technical feasibility is beyond doubt.

# 2. WHAT IS IDENTITY?

## 2.1 Requirements Analysis for "Identity"

In the "real world", identity is a handle to a person serving various purposes: It is used to determine parameters associated with that person (eg. name, age, place of work), to ensure that real world operations are invoked on the correct individual (eg. putting a person in jail, awarding a prize to a person) to verify, whether a person has certain rights (eg. to drive a car, to pick up tickets for a theatre performance) or to engage in communication acts with the intended addressee (eg. sending a letter or an email).

Governmental processes use various schemes to regulate identity: Unique administrative numbering systems such as the Swiss AHV number or the US social security number, names augmented by place and date of birth to guarantee uniqueness, or official documents with photograph and signature. Occasionally these several systems have to be translated into each other, eg. to obtain the name belonging to a certain social security number.

**Passport and anonymous identity:** Most identity schemes in present government processes are linked to what we shall call the *passport identity* of a person, ie. the name, nationality, place and date of birth of that person. Some schemes provide an *anonymous identity*, by establishing a session identity without revealing further information on a citizen. The classical example is the anonymous AIDS test, where an identity concept has to ensure that every individual receives his own test results, but maintains full anonymity.

Closer analysis reveals different administrational needs of associating what we shall call *tokens* with a person. We can identify several dimensions of requirements:

**With regard to transfer:** *Non-transferable tokens* are parameters, rights, properties or obligations linked to a specific person. They should be implemented in a form that they cannot be passed to others. In contrast, *transferable tokens* are acquired by a person, who then can pass them along to another person.

**With regard to divisibility:** A transferable token can be *atomic*: If it is passed to another person, the original owner no longer owns it. It can be *splitable*: When passed to another person the original owner may retain his ownership at the same time. A splitable token can be *intransitive*, ie. after it has been passed along it no longer can be passed on to others. However, if it is *transitive* it can be passed on and on by those who received the token.

**With regard to consumption:** A token can constitute a right which may be exercised arbitrarily or under certain restrictions, eg. Only once, for a certain number of times or before a certain date.

**With regard to access permissions:** The rights to create, delete or modify a binding or ownership between a token and a person can belong to that person himself or to another entity.

**With regard to evidential power:** Suppose the owner of a token presents the token to a business partner. Then, only this business partner has to check the validity of the token. In this case, the token must be designed for *evidential power towards a (collaborating) second person*. Now suppose that the business partner claims that the token is invalid. In this case, the token owner and his business partner will have to convince a judge of their claims. The token must be designed for *evidential power towards a third person*. See the examples below (PIN and SET) for examples on this important but not always fully obvious property.

**Examples:** In the following, an *intentionally long list* of examples shall demonstrate that most combinations of above requirements can be found in real life identity applications. A *drivers license* is a non-transferable token. The owner is not entitled nor able to pass it along to others. The license document itself can be passed along, but the owners photograph prevents providing the non-transferable "right to drive" to other individuals. A drivers license may be created only by an is-suing authority, however the owner may destroy it any time, surrendering his right to drive. A *prison punishment* is a non-transferable token as well. It is different from the drivers license in so far as his "owner" cannot destroy his binding to it. A similar token is required to implement a discount which is offered to customers only on the occasion of the first shopping order. *Passport identity* as defined above, is a non-transferable token combined with name and further parameters. A *one dollar bill* or a *stock certificate* is an atomic transferable token. It can be passed along to other persons but the original owner loses his binding by passing it along. The right to *cast a vote* is a non-transferable token, associated with a notion of consumption and the restriction that for every election it can be utilized at most once. The *power of attorney to act in a certain legal matter* is a transferable token (I may pass this right to others), it is splitable (I do not lose the right to act in these matters by myself) and usually is intransitive (the persons to which I pass the power of attorney cannot pass this right on to others). The *right to pick up a parcel* at the post office is connected with the addressee who should be able to pass this right along to others without losing this right himself. Furthermore those to whom this right is passed on should be allowed to further pass this right: If I ask my neighbor to pick up a parcel for me, I do not mind if the neighbour sends his son to do this job. In the real world, the right to pick up a parcel often is connected to presenting a specific piece of paper, the notification on that parcel. This is an incorrect implementation of a right by an atomic transferable token where a splitable transitive transferable token should have been used. A different, even more unfortunate implementation is to require the person collecting the parcel to identify himself by a passport, ie. A non-transferable token. The *AIDS test result id* as a kind of session id preferably is a non-transferable token, allowing immediate counseling in the case of a positive test result. The well known *personal identification number* (PIN) with which a bank customer proves his right to make a cash withdrawal usually is mailed by the bank to the customer. The PIN therefore has evidential power towards a second person (ie. the bank, recognizing again the PIN it sent to the customer) but not to-wards a third person (ie. a judge). In principle, it could have been a bank clerk who made the withdrawal. In contrast, the *secure electronic transaction (SET) protocol* based on digital signatures establishes a payment contract between customer and retailer which utilizes cryptographic means to establish evidential power towards second and third persons. A *precharged telephone card* is a transferable token with a restriction regarding the consumption (ie. the remaining card value). It can be implemented by storing consumption information physically on the card itself (leading to an atomic token) or by storing it on a server of the phone company (leading to a splitable token, ie. a calling card which can be used if one knows the number of the calling card).

## 2.2 Passport Identity versus Token Identity

The cited examples demonstrate the varying requirements for "identifying" a per-son in administrative settings. In most situations, no passport identity is required, but established governmental procedures nevertheless require citizens to produce passport-like identities. The following example will demonstrate what we have in mind.

The traditional drivers? license provides not only the non-transferable token "right to drive" but also conveys the civil identity of the driver, ie. the name, the nationality, in some countries even the address of residence and the date of birth. If a civil servant is checking whether a person is legally entitled to drive, the implementation of a non-transferable token including this right would be sufficient; further data on the driver (name, address) not necessarily have to be revealed. If, however, the driver was witness at a traffic accident, he might have to testify at a trial. In this case a different non-transferable token must enable the administration to summon the driver to the trial and, in case the witness would not show up, allow that punishment to be carried out which is available in case of a refusal to testify. Again, neither the name nor the nationality of the driver must be made available; they can be revealed by the driver voluntarily and they can be made part of the employed token so that they are revealed automatically. For implementing the govern-mental business process, they are not required: Electronic communication can be anonymous via pseudonyms or more elaborate methods (Chaum, 88), (Reichenbach et al., 1997) and monetary fines can be implemented using anonymous payment methods (Chaun et al., 1989). See (Chaun, 1985) for an introduction to cryptographic protocols available for such situations.

Replacing the passport-type of identity by token based identities adapted to the requirements of the specific administrative processes can have a number of important effects for electronic government. While ensuring the required token properties, only those data on a citizen are employed which really are required for the process. The approach observes the data protection principles of *data economy* and *data avoidance.* It respects the citizens' right for privacy, implementing at the same time the proper administrative acts required by law. Most important, it can advance the acceptance of e-Government, since it actively deals with "big brother" anxieties. Most especially, it leads to a more fair and equal treatment of citizens by their administration. Neither title, name, age or other attributes stored on a passport or in a file could now influence administrative decisions within the discretionary power of a civil servant - only those properties being available with the specific required token could play a role in the regulatory process. Whether the latter property is considered an advantage or a disadvantage is, of course, a matter of one's political standing.

## 2.3 Other Concepts of Digital Identity

In the digital world, "identity" often is associated with concepts like digital signature, user names, passwords, PIN and TAN codes.

**Real world signature:** In the real world, a signature is a *willful act* by which an individual certifies his or her approval of the content of that document which gets signed. Apart from the approval, the act of signing psychologically serves as a *warning function*, calling to the attention of the signer that he is about to enter into a binding commitment.

A signature per se *does not* provide the identity of an individual, especially in the case of common names (eg. John Smith). The link to the individual can only be made by a passport or by a similar official document linking picture and signature (ie. non-transferable, biometric properties) with the name, nationality, birthdate and birthplace of a person, which usually are considered sufficient data to identify that person. This link is established only for those who are personally present at the act of signing and have checked the passport themselves. If this link is required for the benefit of third parties, a notary public certifies it with his seal and authority.

**Digital Signature:** If we apply a certain well known (see for example the introductory literature on this topic, eg. (Schneier, 1995)) cryptographic algorithm $A$ on a document $d$ and a *private key* $p$, we obtain the *digital signature* $S = A(p,d)$. The private key $p$ is mathematically connected with a *public key* $q$ in such a way that a second application of the algorithm on the signature $s$ and the public key produces the original document: $A(q,s) = A(q,A(p,d))=d$.

For purposes of digital signing, a person generates a pair of a public and a private key. The public key will be registered in a trustworthy agency as belonging to that specific person. The private key will be safely stored away and shall be known only to his owner. Therefore it is only the owner who can derive the signature $s$ from the document. Everybody can verify the signature on a document $d$ by obtaining the public key $q$ of the undersigned person at the trustworthy agency and by checking that $A(q,s) = d$. See (Schneier, 1995) for the exact mathematical details of this procedure.

**Problems with digital signatures:** Practical implementations of digital signature schemes raise a considerable number of issues. Often, the private key is stored on a computer which performs the calculations of the algorithm A on behalf of the user. Given the well known threats of viruses, Trojan horses and worms and facing the unreliability of present personal computers, there is *no way to make sure* that the computer applies this algorithm only when the user directs the machine to do so. There is *no guarantee* that the algorithm is applied only to the document presented to the user on the computer screen and in exactly the form as it appears on that computer screen. A *bogus program* could trigger the signing of documents unbeknownst of the signer or even could transmit the private key into the Internet. Schemes to protect the private key are reliable only if the *entire hardware, software,* *operating system and the firmware can be fully trusted* - a goal which cannot realistically be achieved on a personal computer. This fact explains the trend to small cryptographic devices, since it is easier to design a flawless and trusted device if it has reduced complexity and its only functions are the storage of the private key, the display of the document which shall be signed and the calculation of the digital signature.

Furthermore, the digital signature only tells us that a certain mathematical algorithm has been applied to a certain document. The link of this code to the signer and his identity is *not provided to a sufficient degree.* Using above terminology, a digital identity establishes only a splitable transferable token. Providing another person with one s private key amounts to passing the digital identity along, accidentally or on purpose, while keeping associated rights to oneself at the same time. There is, however, some hope that a user does not give away his private key on purpose, facing the possible abuse of his key for signing acts performed outside of the original motivation for giving away the key.

**User names, passwords, PINs and TANs**: The well known user names, as well as personal identification numbers (PINs) implement the simplest form of (splitable, transitive) transferable tokens (without a notion of consumption). Trans-action numbers (TANs) provide consumable transferable tokens which usually are valid for one transaction.

In the common application arena of cash dispensers and online banking systems, these approaches are severely flawed. PINs and TANs are generated by the issuing agency and sent to the user. Therefore, a link to the passport identity of the user always is possible. Since PINs and TANs are known to the issuer, they do not have evidential value in a dispute between issuer and user: Suppose a bank customer claims not having authorized a specific online transaction and the bank claims the customer did execute the transaction, presenting as a proof the TAN submitted by the user. In this case there is no proper method for a judge to find out, who is telling the truth, since the bank could easily have forged the proof. It is quite disturbing that most cash dispensing machines and online banking systems still rely on such improper techniques. Closer analysis makes it obvious that these systems would require non-transferable tokens instead of transferable ones.

# 3. IMPLEMENTING IDENTITY TOKENS

## 3.1 Non-transferable Tokens

A design of non-transferable tokens must focus on the *four attack modes* presently conceivable: The present owner of the token might *want* to transfer it, or he *does not want* to transfer it but is forced to do so by others. The person to which the token shall be transfered is *ready to receive* it or *does not want to receive it.*

Furthermore, the likely interest of an attacker and the damage of an illegitimate transfer must be considered.

The *design options* in Table 1 are either of a non-digital nature and have false acceptance or false rejectance failure modes, or they are digital in nature but require implantation or tedious restraining techniques, both of which are ethically not acceptable. Depending on the sensor used, additional factors such as hygiene, public acceptance, cost, time and others play an important role.

Table 1: Non-transferable tokens

| | |
|---|---|
| Physical attributes | Iris (Seal et al., 1997)<br>Fingerprint<br>Finger Lenght<br>Face Recognition |
| Biological attributes | DNA<br>Body Odor (Davies, 1997) (Grassfield, 2000) |
| Behaviour | Handwriting (ie. Signature)<br>Characteristic Movements (Bartmann, 1997)<br>Voice Recognition |
| Artificial tokens | Implants (eg. RFID-tags)<br>Unremovable Bands |

From a *security point of view* the sensor and the signal path from the sensor to the processor matching the measured signal with a stored template is most critical. Firstly, a fake duplicate could be presented to the sensor (eg. a picture of a face presented to a face recognition system, latex duplicate or cut-off finger presented to a finger print sensor). Countermeasures comprise high sensor quality (eg. a finger print sensor tests for the temperature and electrical characteristics of a live finger) and the combination of several tokens, since a successful fake of several recognition systems seems highly unlikely. Secondly, the owner of the token could collude with the attacker, presenting his token for the benefit of the attacker. Here, the solutions depend on the situation of the token presentation. If the real world benefit involves access to a high security area, physical barriers can ensure that only the person presenting his finger print or iris is allowed access. If the situation involves proving ones identity to a police officer, the officer can ensure that the correct person offers his body to a sensor measurement. Finally, the signal path from the sensor to the processor executing the comparison algorithm, this processor itself and the place where the reference template for the token is stored can be attacked. Physical means must prevent tampering with this part of the system. Non-colluding "owners" of a biometric property who are forced into providing their token, in some systems can call for help by intensionally giving a wrong signal (eg. by using a special alarm finger to call for help or by talking in an unnatural voice to prevent correct voice recognition).

From a *data protection point of view* measuring physical, biological and behavioural attributes of a person is problematic. The obtained data could be used for other purposes than for which these data were provided. Especially data obtained from a DNA test could be used to determine genetic diseases of the involved person resulting in health insurance or employment troubles. The provided data could also help an attacker to misrepresent himself as the original "owner" of the biometric properties.

Special thoughts must therefore be given to the place where the *reference templates* of the biometric signal are stored. This could be in a *central data* base of a trusted agency where the identity of a person is established using traditional means and the biometric signal is rendered and stored under close supervision and in a controlled environment. From a privacy protection point of view this is a bad idea and should be restricted to specifically defined cases such as law enforcement. Another possibility is the *decentralized storage in a device* under the control of the user, for example in a smartcard. This also requires an enrollment of the reference signal under the control of a trusted agency. The user then presents this device and exposes the required biometric signal to the sensor. The *optimal architecture*, however, requires that also the biometric sensor and the entire matching process is located on this device. Only this setup ensures that the biometric signal of the user cannot be stored; furthermore the sensor and the matching device are under the supervision of the user, effectively reducing privacy concerns. Unfortunately such a closed architecture is difficult to achieve for many biometric systems. For the fingerprint case, smartcard solutions are likely to be available in 3 to 5 years. Devices in the size of a PCMCIA card are presently under development (Sedov et al., 2001).

A totally different approach to non-transferable tokens would be to motivate the token owner *not to give away* a specific transferable token (Goldreich et al., 1998). Such a motivation could be built up, if passing along the token led to considerable economical or social damage. If a certain transferable token were a universal token required to exercise all one's civil rights or to access one's bank account, voluntary surrender by the owner would be highly unlikely. In the legal frameworks evolving for digital signatures such an approach is taken: If a digital signature given with a private key residing on the smartcard of a citizen is always considered as legally binding signature it is highly unlikely that the card owner will collaborate with an attacker.

However, this approach is *highly dangerous*. Firstly, the transferable token could be lost or stolen. The dangers of losing most of one's civil rights by losing a single token have already been amply discussed by civil rights groups and pose an unacceptable threat to the citizen. The often proposed solution of securing these devices with a PIN code or password is also not acceptable, since PIN codes and passwords tend to be forgotten - or written down by their owners.

## 3.2 Transferable Tokens

Transferable tokens can have rather different requirements. Many of them are well known in the field of cryptographic algorithms. For space constraints, we shall only present an incomplete overview, leaving a detailed and cryptographic discussion to a later publication.

Transferable tokens are not bound to an individual, thus a biometric link no longer is necessary and the token can be realized by a bit string which can, of course, be passed along and copied arbitrarily. A generic implementation therefore produces a splitable and transitive token which a priori imposes no limit on the number of consumptions. Evidential power depends on who is generating the bit string, issuing it to the user and who is checking the validity.

The required access permissions can be implemented with digital signature schemes, preventing unqualified persons from tempering with token data or from generating unauthorized tokens.

Manufacturing an *atomic* token is a well known requirement in the fields of electronic money and digital content copyright: If I give away a dollar or a music CD I should no longer own it: I might still physically posses the token but it has become useless for me. Strategies to tackle with this requirement in an intangible, purely digital manner, have been developed in anonymous electronic money schemes (Chaum et al., 1989). Physical tokens which cannot easily by duplicated or manipulated (eg. cryptographic smartcards) could be used as well. Restricting the number of consumptions can be implemented as a simple add-on to electronic money schemes and easily are implemented in smart tokens.

## 3.3 Real World Implementations

In a single real world business process, different identity tokens might be required. Suitable devices such as PDAs or smartcards will act as a *representative* for the user and will guarantee that the proper protocols are used. They will ensure the correct choice of the token type and *insulate* the owners true identity from the ones required in specific processes. (Sedov et al., 2001) describes possible architectures.

Certainly, such an important device can be lost. Technology from Section 3.1 links the device to its owner and prevents abuse. Storing the tokens on a cryptographically sealed backup device protects against a sudden "loss of ones identity".

## 4. CONCLUSIONS AND IMPLICATIONS FOR E-GOVERNMENT PROCESSES

**These 1:** Presently, in most administrative processes the citizen has to reveal his passport identity, supplying more data on himself *than really is required* by the administrative act. We propose for discussion the *reengineering of governmental processes* in order to reduce the amount of revealed data. Instead of providing his passport identity, the citizen should provide (only) those identity tokens materially required by the respective administrative act.

For example, the administrative act of "verifying whether a person has the license to drive a car" should be reduced to checking the *non-transferable token* "has the right to drive a car". There is no need to reveal the name of the person in this process.

*Consequences* are an improved privacy and a more fair and equal treatment since only legally required data form the basis of a discretionary administrative decision. Furthermore, some possibilities for centralized statistical surveys and demographical studies are lost.

This suggestion is not as radical as it might seem, being the logical consequence and spirit of the US *Identity Theft Protection Act*, stating in its preamble the following purpose (Anon, 01):

> ... to *prohibit* the establishment in the Federal Government of *any uniform national identifying number*, and to *prohibit* Federal agencies from *imposing standards* for identification of individuals *on other agencies or persons.*

This development, however, is more typical of Anglo-Saxon and American governmental culture, where there is considerable less central registration of citizen data than in most European administrative cultures. Whereas the former does not know mandatory formal registration of a residential address and the citizens? place of living is checked informally and only when public or private services are utilized (eg. registering to vote, registering a car, claiming social benefits) it is mandatory in the latter culture and even centralized registers of residential addresses are common. This comparison, however, is not uniformly true for all administrative areas given, for example, the highly organized structure of the US Internal Revenue Services IRS. See (Clarke, 1994) for a comparison of national policies.

**These 2:** Present *digital signature schemes and laws* have a *fundamental flaw*. They not necessarily guarantee the "wilful act" and "warning function" properties required from a "real world" signature and lack the non-transferable binding to a person.

We suggest to enhance present digital signature technology and law by *mandatory biometric components* establishing the required non-transferable token.

Furthermore, implementations should be restricted to devices sufficiently small that the operating system and signing software cannot be tampered with as easily as a PC.

**These 3:** *Citizen trust* in online security is low. We therefore *need a better public understanding* of the concepts of identity, digital signature and online security, as well as of the threats of their presently flawed implementations.

We suggest that parallel to technological and legal improvements towards truly trusted signature and identity schemes, *public awareness strategies are developed* to establish a feeling of trust in digital identity systems with our fellow citizens. With more than 85% of all Internet users perceiving security as significant or even deciding factor in online business (Anon, 1998), one can imagine the dramatic acceptance problems large scale e-government solutions will have otherwise.

**These 4:** In order to obtain *perceived and real trust* in identity schemes, we have to *develop audit technology, open protocols and standards* and should *ban proprietary or closed source identity schemes.*

Only open source systems whose entire design principles are available to critical public analysis make it possible to safely verify the claims of adhering to established regulations and protocols. Therefore, only such systems should be used in e-government identity processes. Obviously, this criterion must apply to *all* parts of the system, including operating systems and bootstrap codes. Thus, most presently used operating systems must be eliminated from security relevant e-government processes.

We furthermore need an administrative culture which is *open for public auditing* of its technological environment and *encourages discussion of security issues, especially security flaws.*

**These 5:** We need *laws dealing with digital identity and identity theft based* on digital id.

First activities in this direction are the *Identity Theft Protection Act* or the *Social Security Number Protection Act* in the US.

This legal framework must also deal with the theft of biometric properties 2 and with the fraudulent manipulation of identity establishing biometric sensors and systems. On the other hand, open discussion and research into the flaws of these systems must not be restricted, as it is presently done with copyright protection technology by the Digital Millennium Copyright Act.

**These 6:** We should stimulate *the participation of the public* in the discussions on e-government systems. (Chaum, 85) observes:

> As the initial choice for the[ir] architecture gathers economic and social momentum, it *becomes increasingly difficult to reverse.* Whichever approach prevails, it will likely have a *profound and enduring impact* on economic freedom, democracy, and our informational rights.

Today, 15 years later, more than 85% of the Internet population is heavily concerned with online security. If the quick path to e-government which is taken today for economic reasons continues to neglect the impacts on the citizen and does not reevaluate its position with regard to identity, we will either end up with the wrong solution or with an unexpected low rate of acceptance. In both cases costly reengineering will be required.

# 5. ACKNOWLEDGEMENTS

The paper could be significantly improved thanks to the remarks made by two of the referees.

# 6. REFERENCES

[Anon, 1998] Anon. Georgia tech research corporation, tenth www user survey report. October 1998.

[Anon, 2001] Anon. Identity theft protection act of 2001. Bill H. R. 220 at http://thomas.loc.gov/, 2001.

[Bartmann, 1997] D. Bartmann. Psylock - identifikation eines tastaturbenutzers durch analyse des tippverhaltens. In Mathias Jarke, editor, Informatik als Innovationsmotor, Aachen, September 1997, pages 327-334. Springer, 1997.

[Chaum et al., 1989] D. Chaum, A. Fiat, and M. Naor. Untraceable eletronic cash. In Advances in Cryptology, Crypto88, pages 319-327. Springer, 1989.

[Chaum, 1985] David Chaum. Security without identification: Transaction systems to make big brother obsolete. Communications fo the ACM, 28(10):1030- 1044, 1985.

[Chaum, 1988] David Chaum. The dining cryptographers problem: Unconditional sender and recipient untraceability. Journal of Cryptology, 1(1):65-75, 1988.

[Clarke, 1994] Roger Clarke. Human identification in information systems: Management challenges and public policy issues. Information Technology & People, 7(4):6-37, December 1994.

[Davies. 1997] Ann Davies. The body as password. Wired, 5(7), July 1997.

[Goldreich et al., 1998] O. Goldreich, B. Pfitzmann, and R. Rivest. Self-delegation with controlled propagation - or - what if you lose your laptop. In Advances in Cryptology, Crypto 98, pages 153-168. Springer-Verlag, 1998.

[Grassfield, 2000] Lisa Grassfield. Biometrics: Securing electronic commerce. http://www.tinucci.com/Papers/Grassfield - Biometrics.html, 2000.

[Herschberg, 1997] M. Herschberg. Secure electronic voting over the world wide web. Master's thesis, Massachusetts Institute of Technology - Laboratory of Computer Science, May 1997.

[Reichenbach et al., 1997] Martin Reichenbach, Herbert Damker, Hannes Federrath, and Kai Rannenberg. Individual management of personal reachability in mobile communication. In Louise Yngstr¨ om and Jan Carlsen, editors, Information Security in Research and Business, IFIP TC11 13th Interna-tional Conference on Information Security SEC?97, Copenhagen, Denmark, pages 164-174. Chapmann & Hall, 1997.

[Schneier, 1995] Bruce Schneier. Applied Cryptography. Wiley, 1995.

[Seal et al., 1997] Chris H. Seal, Maurice M. Gifford, and David J. McCartney. Iris recognition for user validation. British Telecommunications Engineering Journal, pages 113-118, July 1997.

[Sedov et al., 2001] Igor Sedov, Marc Haase, Clemens Cap, and Dirk Timmermann. Hardware security concept for spontaneous network integration of mobile devices. In Proceedings of the Workshop on Innovative Internet Com-puting, Ilmenau June 2001. TU Ilmenau, 2001.

60

# Development of an European-wide Citizen Javacard to Support Administrative Processes by the Use of the Electronic Signature and the Biometric Fingerprint Sensor

*A case study of legal implications*

Markus Wenderoth and Dennis Wörmann
*Zuendel & Partner Unternehmensberatung, Bochum, Germany*

**Abstract:** This paper describes the results of the project "Facilitating Administrative Services for Mobile Europeans (FASME), which aims to develop a Javacard prototype, i.e. a chip card on the basis of the Java programming language which is not platform dependent. The Javacard will allow for specific administrative tasks such as the registration and de-registration of addresses and reregistering motor vehicles to be safely and flexibly carried out throughout Europe.

## 1. INTRODUCTION

The abbreviation FASME stands for the project entitled "Facilitating Administrative Services for Mobile Europeans", i.e. supporting individual EU citizens in dealing with administrative processes within Europe. The project, which in all is to run for a period of 18 months, was started on 1 January 2000. Within the framework of the FASME project a Javacard prototype will be developed, a chip card on the basis of the Java programming language which is not platform dependent, that will allow for specific administrative tasks such as the registration and de-registration of addresses and reregistering motor vehicles to be safely and flexibly carried out throughout Europe. Furthermore, the prototype provides individual assistance within the framework of services (meta applications) for the initial period following a move within the European member states.

By using the FASME Javacard prototype, visits to the authorities regarding administrative matters by individual EU citizens such as registering and deregistering an address and reregistering motor vehicles can be organised in a more efficient manner.

The FASME Java Card is especially equipped with a biometric fingerprint sensor and an e-Signature. By using these two components administrative processes in the public sector for each EU citizen and the municipalities should be legally secure.

# 2. BIOMETRIC FINGERPRINT PROCEDURE

The FASME Javacard is equipped with a fingerprint sensor that is integrated in the card. This fingerprint sensor carries out and ensures for the safety of the verification or the identity of the EU citizen in carrying out the administrative processes on the basis of the minutia[79] comparison procedure. Furthermore the fingerprint sensor is used as an access security mechanism for the electronic signature.

## 2.1 Practical procedure

The detailed procedure of the identity analysis by way of the biometric fingerprint is carried out in the following steps:

1. Placing the FASME Javacard in the terminal reading device. The internal error counter on the Javacard, which also serves the purpose of limiting the number of possible unsuccessful analysis attempts, increases by the value one.
2. Reading the fingerprint of the card user by way of the fingerprint sensor and transmitting the read data to the Java chip on the card.
3. Comparison of the read fingerprint of the card user with the fingerprint sample (reference value) of the card owner (verification) stored on the card via the chip processor (JavaVirtualMachine). The verification is based on an examination of minutia pairs.
4. In the event that the two fingerprint data records are identical, the card is approved for usage and a specific data transaction made possible that is supported by the Javacard. As only one single transaction is possible, a new fingerprint analysis shall be required for each transaction. In the case of a successful fingerprint analysis the error counter will be reset to zero.
5. If the two fingerprint data records are not identical, the error counter within the card increases by the value one. If the error counter reaches a predetermined valid, the card will be (temporarily) blocked for all further usage. In such a case the blockage lifted by an authorised administrative official.

[79] Sample of dermal ridges on the fingertip; Data Protection and Data security, 06/2000 p.328

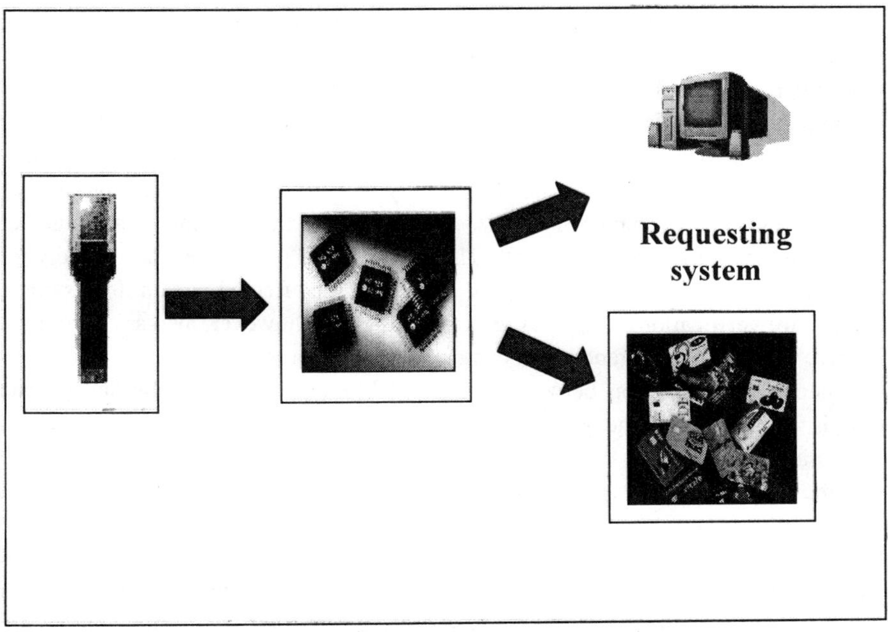


*Figure 6.* Minutia comparison procedure

## 2.2 Legal implications

The practical procedure described above warrants a comprehensive legal appraisal on the basis of the following criteria.

### 2.2.1 Constitutional requirements within the EU member states

The constitutions in the EU member states stress in strong terms the protection of human dignity and thus make the principle the uppermost value of the respective constitution.

If the use of biometric procedures were to constitute a violation of the dignity of man, the state authorities would, on the one hand, be prohibited from using these procedures. On the other hand agreements under civil law that provided for the use of such procedures which violated man's dignity would also be inadmissible. The state would be under obligation to intervene to put an end to the situation in violation of the constitution. With regard to the use of biometric procedures the initial question law should be put as to whether certain restrictions or parameters are contained in the constitution. The particular explosive nature of biometric procedures arises in this respect from two aspects: on the one hand identification procedures are directly linked to physical features of the affected person. On the other, physical characteristics are thus instrumentalised for certain purposes.

If an individual is forced to use his/her body in a certain manner, such action may be discussed as a vulgarisation from a subject to an object.

Whether individual procedures place the dignity of man in jeopardy in a non-uniform market depends, above all, on the features with which it works and in which manner the biometric data of the user is requested. The dignity of man is particularly endangered if an individual has no opportunity to control, at a given time, his/her biometric data that is being recorded[80]. Then, he/she would be more in danger of being vulgarised to a mere object. Therefore, such procedures are worthy of preference which calls for an active participation of the affected person, for example the signature verification. The violation of dignity may, however, also arise from the excessive information content which can occur in some procedures.

In general a distinction between the use of biometry in the public and private sector is to be made. The private sector is not taken into consideration in this examination.

In the public sector it is worthwhile making a distinction between two different areas of application of biometric identification procedures:

- Global applications in which a considerable group of the population is placed under obligation to achieve an administrative purpose in participating in a procedure. The American examples demonstrate that such procedures are frequently used to prevent unauthorised use with regard to the receipt of state services.
- The separate application in a public institution to bring about certain security objectives. The access security mechanisms should be given consideration in this respect. However, authentication via a system as regards the authorship of certain decrees is also possible.

Because of the explosive nature of the legal foundations of these procedures, which arise from the proximity described above to the dignity of man that is separately protected by the constitution, it would, moreover, appear to be necessary to provide for the global application by way of a special, area-specific legal foundation.

### 2.2.2 Legal admissibility of biometric procedures

The Directive 1999/93 pertaining to the Community outline conditions for electronic signatures expressly leaves open the technology that is to be used which, in particular, is expressed in the reason for consideration (8): "The rapid technological development and the global character of the Internet call for a concept which provides an open-minded approach towards technologies and services in the field of electronic authentication."

[80] E.g. facial recognition at greater distances, analysis of the chemical composition of body odour

Furthermore, according to the opinions held by technicians, the signature composition data defined in Article 2, no. 4 also allows for the use of biometry.

In addition, according to Annex III, 1.c) of the Directive, a guarantee must be provided in the case of the so-called secure signature composition data that "the lawful user's signature composition data used for the compilation of the signature is capable of being reliably protected from use by others."

### 2.2.3 Legal and data protection law implications

By using biometric fingerprint sensor the increased protection for the so-called sensitive data listed in Article 8, Section 1 of the EU data protection directive[81] could be, above all, of interest. This includes information pertaining to the racial and ethical origin, political opinions, religious or philosophical convictions, union membership, health or sexual activities. The processing of such data is only permitted subject to restricted preconditions. The fingerprint can, for example, provide indications of a certain racial or ethical affiliation. However, this merely applies to the biometric raw data that has not yet been prepared for the purpose of identification. In contrast, the templates, with which the actual identification process operates, do not constitute any sensitive data because a direct conclusion as regards the full biometric entry information (for example on the fingerprint) cannot be drawn on the basis of such templates. The increased preconditions in accordance with Article 8 of the Directive follow on, however, from the processing, but not only from the storage. In accordance with Article 2, letter b) of the Directive, even the collation of data is regarded as processing. The collating of biometric raw data by the system constitutes a record within the meaning of this Directive. Accordingly, an excessive information content in the case of the collation of biometric raw data can be sufficient to make the procedure, or at least the respective procedural part, subject to the special protection of sensitive data in accordance with Article 8 of the Directive. This can only be avoided if no excessive amounts of sensitive information arise in the respective procedures.

Due to the fact that the biometric data is personal data, it is necessary, therefore, that the following requirements are ensured via the fingerprint sensor and the like integrated in the FASME JavaCard[82]:

- It must not be possible to deduce the personal identity of a user from the biometric data
- Biometric things may not be used as personal reference numbers
- Data storage and transport must be secure

[81] Directive 95/46/EC of the European Parliament and Council dated 24 October 1995

[82] Compare in detail Weichert, CuR 6/97, p. 369 et seq. and Data Protection and Data Security 3/1999, p. 128 et seq.

- With regard to the estimation of the necessary level of protection, the question of how permanent the link is between the biometric data and the person should be taken into consideration
- The user must be aware of the possibility of a check

## 2.3 Legal appraisal of the applied biometric procedure (fingerprint sensor) of the FASME Javacard

The special technical design of the FASME Javacard allows for the data processing of the read fingerprint data, i.e. it is possible to match the stored reference data (submitted fingerprint sample) on the card. In this respect the match is carried out via the chip's central processor , the Central Processing Unit (CPU).

Instead of a central storage of reference data, which would call for the necessity of a higher level of legal data protection, the FASME Javacard only stores reference data of the respective card owner. Thus the decentralised storage of reference data is within the dominion of the respective user.

The aforementioned reasons allow an assurance to be given as regards the aspect of the security of data storage and data transport.

Because merely a few characteristics (minutia) of the fingerprint are processed during the application of the fingerprint sensor, a reproduction of the entire fingerprint and thus a conclusion as to the personal identity of a respective user are excluded. This means the amount of used minutia is not greater than that which is required for the recognition (principle of avoiding the creation of unnecessary data and the effective usage of data). Therefore, the usage of the biometric data as a reference to a person is excluded.

In the case of processing the supported processes the system provides an express request to submit the personal fingerprint prior to the analysis of each fingerprint. In this respect it is incumbent upon the respective user to either approve of or discontinue the process.

As a result of the active co-operation by the user same is aware of a possible verification at all times.

The intended integration of the biometric fingerprint sensor in the FASME Javacard ensures that there is a reliable protection, which is not achieved by way of the PIN and password, because biometric procedures provide considerably better protection as regards access to the signature key on the basis of the aforementioned reasons.

It should be noted that the biometric fingerprint procedure used in the FASME project satisfies the highest legal data protection requirements.

Finally it should be noted, that the global use of an european-wide citizencard for administrative processes requires an explicit european-wide legal basis. The opportunities of biometry should, in particular in view of the discussed legal effects of electronic signatures, be used within the different legal systems in Europe.

# 3. APPLICATION OF THE ELECTRONIC SIGNATURE

It is envisaged that the electronic signature be initially used with the support of the FASME Javacard in the case of data transfer processes in public administration for the process of changing an address and registering a motor vehicle.

It is envisaged that as a result of this EU citizens will, in the future, be able to make use of public sector services which ensure that security objectives are reached, such as:

- The authenticity of a sender
- The coding / deciphering of the content
- The integrity / genuineness of the data content

The binding nature of the documents and explanations.

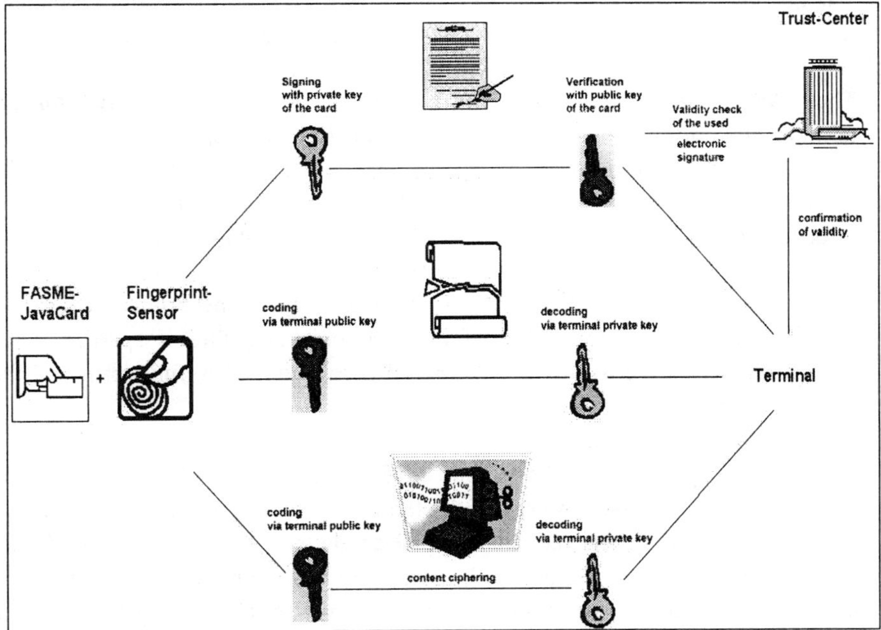


*Figure 2.* Signature procedure

## 3.1 Practical procedure

The following outline conditions are created with regard to the application of the electronic signature so as to ensure that the stated security aspects are followed:

- Each FASME-Javacard is allocated a unique asymmetrical key-pair. This key pair is made up of one private key and one public key. The allocation of the key pairs is carried out within the framework of the certification of the FASME Javacard via a state-recognised certification service provider.
- The private key serves the purpose of signing a data record that is to be forwarded so as to guarantee the authenticity of the owner of the private key, and thus the sender.
- Furthermore, the private key is used to decipher / decode a received and coded data record and to authenticate / verify the genuineness of the content of a received data record.
- The public key serves the purpose of coding / ciphering data records which are sent to the key owner and to verify the authenticity of the identity of the sender (by way of his/her public key). To this end the public key must initially be made known to the sender (coding) or the addressee (authenticity).

The detailed procedure of the application of the electronic signature is explained below on the basis of a data transfer from the FASME Javacard to a terminal at an official institution:

1. The FASME Javacard contains the relevant data which is required for the terminal at an official institution to handle a specific process.
2. For the secure transmission of the relevant data - avoiding inspection by unauthorised persons / guaranteeing the genuineness (authenticity) - the information is ciphered / coded by way of the terminal public key.
3. To sign the data record and thus guarantee the clear identity (authenticity) of the sender, the information is coded / ciphered by way of the private key of the FASME Javacard. The creation of the electronic signature is sparked via a legitimisation on the card by way of the provision of a fingerprint of the respective card user.
4. The actual data transfer takes place.
5. Once the data transfer has been concluded, the decoding / deciphering of the received data takes place by way of the terminal private key. The verification of the integrity of the transferred data takes place via the calculation of a proof total (hash value) by way of the terminal private key and the match with a test value calculated prior to the data transfer. Even the smallest change in content of the transferred data record brings about a deviation between these test values.
6. Securing of the authenticity of the sender is carried out by verifying the signature with the sender's public key. In this respect the party providing the guarantee is a state-recognised certification authority (a so-called Trust Centre).

## 3.2 EU Directive 1999/93/EC

Electronic communication and electronic business transactions call for "qualified electronic signatures" and appropriate authentication services for data. Diverging regulations pertaining to the legal recognition of qualified electronic signatures and the accreditation of certification service providers in the member states can pose a serious obstacle to electronic communication and electronic business transactions. In contrast, clear Community outline conditions for qualified electronic signatures strengthen the trust and general acceptance regarding new technologies. After more than one year of continuous discussions an agreement has been reached in Europe regarding a Directive for electronic signatures. It came into force on 19.01.2000 in Brussels via the European Parliament and the Council of the European Union.

The Directive should be conceived such that, above all, different legislation in the member states be avoided. Therefore, the Directive not only provides for the definition of a legal but also an organisational framework.

The objective of the Directive of creating the application of electronic signatures in a largely uniform legal framework within the European Union will be largely achieved.

The framework is sufficiently flexible so as not to exclude any future technological developments.

In accordance with Article 13 - Implementation, the Directive must be implemented in national law in all EU states within the next 18 months, at the latest by 19 July 2001.

## 3.3 Legal appraisal of the FASME signature procedure

After more than one year of ongoing discussions an agreement has been reached in Europe regarding a Directive for electronic signatures. Next year will see the implementation of the Directive in the member states of the EU. It is envisaged that the Directive be designed such that above all different forms of legislation be avoided in the member states. Therefore, the Directive does not provide for just a legal framework, it also offers an organisational framework.

In the case of the implementation of the Directive primary importance should be attached to the aspect of harmonisation. The states should not create any new terms[83] following the approach towards harmonisation of the EU Directive. The terms used in the Directive have not been selected optionally because they do not comply with the nomenclature defined by the standardisation committee.

However, a new introduction of - even contradictory - terms in the national legislature would result in widespread confusion among the population and companies. It is worthy of note that the member states may make the application of signatures in the public sector dependent on additional requirements[84]. In this respect it is hoped that for the EU member states no additional legal requirements are created that would hamper the trans-border services for citizens.

[83] Data Protection and Data Security, edition 02/2000, p. 88

[84] Artikel 3 Absatz 7 EU Directive 1999/93/EC

### 3.3.1 Qualified signature

In order to do justice to the statutory requirements regarding the application of the FASME JavCard in the area of public administration for the processes involving a change of address and registering a motor vehicle, a qualified electronic signature is used which satisfies the preconditions of Article 2, no. 2 a) to d) of the EU Directive 1999/93 .

The qualified electronic signature used in the FASME JavaCard is, in each case, solely allocated to the lawful owner of the card, by whom it can be created, because only the right user can use the card to sign by way of the biometric components. Accordingly, the qualified electronic signature thus created allows for a definite identification of the FASME JavaCard used to sign and in addition an identification of the signing user as a result of the uniqueness quality of the key pairs. Because all the components used for the creation of the qualified electronic signature (key pairs, numeric processing unit, fingerprint sensor) are to be found directly on the card, and are thus directly within the user's dominion, the signing party can keep them under his/her sole control. By creating a hash value via the signature within the framework of the coding, it is possible to recognise subsequent changes made to the data.

### 3.3.2 Secure signature composition units

The secure signature composition units that are required to create a qualified electronic signature are determined in greater detail in Annex III of the Directive 1999/93. The utilisation of special signature composition units is guaranteed within the framework of the FASME project on the basis of the techniques and procedures described below:

The signature composition data used to create the signature are cryptoalgorithms in accordance with the parameters of the interoperability specifications which are to be issued by way of the Trust Centre that complies with the requirements. This ensures that the used data is unique. The secrecy of the data and the prevention of unauthorised usage are guaranteed by the method of construction and the functions of the used chip card.

The modern signature procedure and the used cryptoalgorithms (RSA[85]) allow the user to inspect the data that is to be signed. They do not change the content of the data but, however, prevent the signature composition data from being deduced and prevent signature forgery.

The cryptographical requirements regarding the used hash functions and signature algorithms to create a key are satisfied by the FASME JavaCard. It is presumed that the hash function SHA-1 and the cryptoalgorithms in accordance with

[85] Rivest, Shamir und Adleman Krypthoalgorithmen

the RSA procedure be used within the framework of the project to create signatures, and for coding and decoding.

### 3.3.3 Certificates

In order to satisfy the requirements pertaining to the qualified signature, the signature used in the FASME project must be based on a qualified certificate. In accordance with Article 2 of the definition no. 9 of the Directive, the term "certificate" describes an electronic certification with which signature testing data of a person are allocated and with which the identity of this person is confirmed. A "qualified certificate" is a certificate that satisfies the requirements of Annex I and which is made available by a certification service provider which does justice to the requirements set out in Annex II. The Directive and the Europe-wide legislation have not yet stipulated any definite certification format. However, it solely pursues the objective of creating outline conditions for qualified electronic signatures with high security requirements.

A utilisation of the version X.509v3, which has presented itself as the general format for certificates, is planned within the framework of the FASME project, that would allow an european-wide usage. It is noticed that different efforts are in progress to norms of certificates harmonise european-wide.

## 4. TRUST CENTRE

Finding solutions to two problems is of crucial importance to the security of data transmission in open networks. On the one hand it must be ensured that unauthorised access is not possible so as to prevent manipulation of the transferred data. On the other it must be clearly determinable that transferred data actually originates from an authorised sender. Like an "electronic notary" the Trust Centre creates and "authenticates" the signature key and thus creates a trusted foundation for qualified electronic signature procedures in the case of the electronic transmission of data. The Trust Centre must satisfy the stringent legal requirements to as to ensure that the electronic signing of information is legally binding and secure.

If it is determined within a public key infrastructure that a certain public electronic key belongs to a certain person or institution, a trusted and independent third party must have previously verified the allocation. Subsequently, this third party can vouch for the identity of the key owner. This trusted third party is the Trust Centre. Following the identification of a person, for example by way of the presentation of a personal identity card, the Trust Centre establishes by means of a qualified certificate that a certain electronic key belongs to the appropriate certificate owner. The qualified certificates are, in turn, kept ready in a secure, electronic directory which is accessible at all times so that a third party can determine the validity and the authenticity of the owner.

As it is envisaged that an qualified electronic signature that is required to be legally binding be used to deal with administrative processes via the FASME JavaCard (change of address / motor vehicle registration), co-operation with a Trust Centre is inevitable. For the FASME project this means that the administrative authority must have access to the aforementioned electronic directory when verifying the electronic documents that are completed and signed by the citizen so that the authority can determine the validity of the qualified certificate and the authenticity of the EU citizen.

A "certification service provider" in accordance with Article 2 of the definition no. 11 of the EU Directive 1999/93 is an office or a legal or natural person who issues certificates or provides other services in conjunction with electronic signatures.

A certification service provider is a certification service provider who complies the preconditons of Annex II of the Directive.

The directive allows the member states and the suppliers of certification services plenty of room for manoeuvre as regards the establishment of different infrastructures for electronic signatures.

In accordance with Article 2, Section 1, the member states may not make the provision of certification services dependent upon a prior agreement. However, certification service providers who satisfy the requirements of Annex II are subject to a monitoring system that is to be set up in each member state if they offer qualified certificates publicly. The monitoring system may either be publicly or privately organised.

In addition, the member states are not prevented from establishing a voluntary accreditation system to achieve greater security. It is questionable as to who would require still greater security. But this hypothetical question aside, it is possible for the member states to establish own voluntary accreditation systems which place different requirements on security. The Directive text does not state whether the system must build on that what has already been defined or whether requirements may be formulated which extend beyond the four annexes[86]. At the present time it would appear that as a result very different systems may occur in the individual sates. To increase harmonisation the EU Commission can publish reference figures of secure products which can be used for the composition of qualified signatures[87].

In view of the planned EU-wide application of the FASME JavaCard it remains to be seen whether the individual member states make these Trust Centres subject to additional statutory requirements during the course of introducing accredited certification service providers.

[86] Data protection and data security, edition 02/200, p. 88

[87] See also article 3, Section 5 of the Directive 1999/93/EC

It is hoped that the states do not make any new form requirements or regulations so as to justify the higher security level for a voluntary accreditation system.

## 5. CONCLUSION

On the basis of the biometric fingerprint procedure that is used, a level of protection is achieved which complies with the highest legal data protection requirements as regards processing person-related data.

The requirement of a special legal basis will be deemed given with regard to the EU-wide application of the FASME JavaCard in which the biometric fingerprint sensor is used in the field of public administration.

Within the framework of the FASME project a so-called advanced or qualified electronic signature is to be used that is based on a qualified certificate pursuant to the preconditions of Annex I. This must satisfy the preconditions of the EU Directive 1999/93 , Article 2, no. 2 a) to d). Secure signature composition units that do justice to the requirements of Annex III of the Directive 1999/93 are required to create such an advanced or qualified electronic signature. As a result of the components used within the framework of the project (JavaCard, etc.) it is possible to ensure that the requirements regarding secure signature composition units are adhered to.

As a result of the intended utilisation of the hash function SHA-1 and the signature algorithm based on the RSA procedure, it is possible to ensure that the interoperability of the signature procedure will function as required.

It is envisaged that the signature used in the FASME project be based on the standard version X.509v3, which has presented itself as a general format for certificates, because a certain certificate format has neither been stipulated Europe-wide nor by national legislation in the member states.

With regard to the EU-wide application of the FASME JavaCard in the public sector it would be necessary to install a certification service provider who at least satisfies requirements of Annex II of the Directive 1999/93. First of all it remains to be seen how the individual member states implement the special preconditions of Annex II into national law. In this respect a harmonisation of the infrastructure for the Europe-wide application of the advanced or qualified electronic signature is of the greatest importance. Beyond this it is hoped that the EU member states do not make the certification service providers in the public sector subject to additional statutory requirements.

In the author's opinion it would be desirable that the member states implement uniform provisions of law pertaining to the parity of treatment of the qualified electronic signature with hand-written documents, in particular in the field of public administration, because a pioneering role is attributed to public sector administration.

# 6. REFERENCES

Kruse, Peuckert (1995): Chipkarte und Sicherheit; in: Datenschutz und Datensicherheit, Nr. 3, 1995

Probst, T. (2000): Biometrie und SmartCards, in: Datenschutz und Datensicherheit, Nr. 6, 2000

Weichert, CuR 6/97, p. 369 et seq. and Data Protection and Data Security 3/1999, p. 128 et seq.

Wirtz, B. (1999): Biometrische Verfahren, in: Datenschutz und Datensicherheit, Nr. 3, 1999

Directive 95/46/EC of the European Parliament and Council dated 24 October 1995 on the protection of individuals with regard to the processing of personal data and on the free movement of such data.

Directive 1999/93/EC OF THE EUROPEAN PARLIAMENT AND OF THE COUNCIL of 13 December 1999 on a Community framework for electronic signatures pertaining to community outline conditions for electronic signature dated 19.01.2000.

Data Protection and Data Security, edition 02/2000, p. 88

Fox, D. (1997): Wohlmacher, P., Chipkarten - Nutzen und Leid; in: Datenschutz und Datensicherheit, Nr.5, 1997

German Federal Office for Security in Communications Technology dated 6.08.2000

61

# A Review of the First Cooperative Projects in the Italian *e*-Government Initiative

Massimo Mecella[1] and Carlo Batini[2]

[1]*Dipartimento di Informatica e Sistemistica, Università di Roma "La Sapienza", Via Salaria 113, I-00198 Roma, Italy,* `mecella@dis.uniroma1.it`

[2]*Autorità per l'Informatica nella Pubblica Amministrazione, Via Isonzo 21B, I-00198 Roma, Italy,* `batini@aipa.it`

**Abstract**: The Italian approach to *e*-Government is based on the development and deployment of the Unitary Network, a "secure Intranet" interconnecting all the public administrations. The Cooperative Architecture, currently designed on top of it, is the reference distributed computing model in which each administration is represented as a Domain, exchanging data and application services with the others through Cooperative Gateways. Some issues have been, and currently need to be, addressed, such as the presence of legacy systems, the need of a cooperative development process, the identification of the more effective cooperative approaches. In this paper some first experimental projects carried out in the years 1998-2000, aiming at validating the Cooperative Architecture, will be described; then some lessons gained by these first experiences will be presented.

## 1. INTRODUCTION

In Italy, the need for a better coordination of efforts and investments in the area of government information systems has pushed, in 1993, the Italian Parliament to create a new agency named "Autorità per l'Informatica nella Pubblica Amministrazione" [Authority for Information Technology in the Public Administration] (AIPA) with the aim of promoting technology innovation, by defining criteria for planning, implementation, management and maintenance of the information systems of the Italian Public Administration (PA). Among the various initiatives undertaken by AIPA since its constitution, the Unitary Network is the most important and challenging one. The project has the purpose of implementing a "secure Intranet" able to connect public administrations among them.

The ambitious objectives of the Unitary Network will be obtained by promoting cooperation at the application level. By defining a common application architecture, the Cooperative Architecture, it will be possible to consider the set of distributed, yet independent systems of public administrations as a Unitary Information System of Italian PA in which each subject can participate by exchanging services with other subjects.

The Unitary Network and the related Unitary Information System with its Cooperative Architecture are an example of a Cooperative Information System (CIS) (Mylopoulos and Papazoglou 1997, Brodie 1998); a CIS is defined as a large number of cooperating component systems distributed over large, complex computer and communication networks and working together cooperatively, effectively requesting and sharing information, constraints, and goals. The technologies supporting this kind of systems are quickly growing, but the same is not true for the methodologies on how to develop them; moreover not many experiences on successful large cooperative systems have been reported.

The aim of this paper is to describe the Cooperative Architecture and some pilot projects undertaken during the last years (1998-2000), by introducing several criteria for comparing them. The remainder of this paper is organized as follows. In Section 2 a general assessment on the use of IT in the Italian PA during the 90's is described, then the Unitary Network and the Cooperative Architecture are outlined. Section 3 describes the pilot projects and compares them by introducing some criteria. Finally Section 4 concludes the paper.

# 2. THE UNITARY NETWORK

## 2.1 The assessment

The need of a common infrastructure for connecting information systems of different public administrations has been confirmed by the results of a general assessment on the use of the Information Technology in the Italian PA. In order to perform such an assessment, AIPA has developed its own original methodology, tailoring existing approaches and methodologies for information system planning (U.S. Department of Commerce 1988) and inventory organization (Thompson 1993) to the specific features and rules of the Italian PA.

The novelty of the investigation has been to focus not only on technological issues, but also on organizational ones, to identify the structure and the relationships among the organizational units (OUs); the investigation has been performed both on the OUs responsible for the computer-based information systems (EDP OUs), and on the other units responsible for administrative processes (User OUs). The results of the investigation have been collected in an inventory (Batini et al. 1996), whose high level schema is shown in *Figure.*

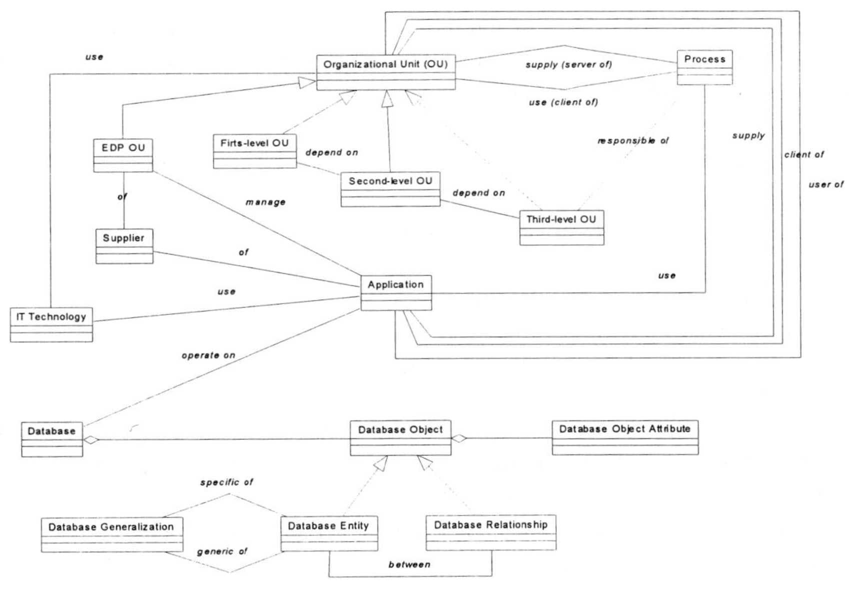


*Figure 1.* Schema of the investigation (in UML)

As regards the organizational structure, the Italian PA consists of different entities:

- *Central PA*, which consists of government Departments and Agencies (about 100, with 40.000 employees) located in Rome;
- *Peripheral PA*, which consists of branch offices (about 4.000 with 400.000 employees) of the Central PA spread all over the country;
- *Local PA*, which consists of entities such as Regions, Districts and City Councils (20.000 with 1.000.000 employees), characterized by a high degree of autonomy with respect to the central PA; this autonomy is continuously increasing as a consequence of the decentralization process presently going on.

All together the administrations provide services to customers (citizens and private organizations such as companies, enterprises, no-profit organizations, etc.) and therefore they are typically involved together in the execution of administrative activities or processes. By analyzing processes, AIPA has tried to build *macro-processes*, that is sequences or aggregations of processes that are to be executed jointly in order to satisfy the request of a service from a customer (Mecella and Batini 2001). The investigation has been performed with a bottom up strategy, leading to the identification of single administrative activities in specific OUs. Such activities, when related in terms of causal relationships, give rise to macro-processes.

Currently the lack of cooperation among subjects involved in macro-processes lead to their inefficient execution and to poor provision of services to customers; the development of an Unitary Information System of the PA will allow to automatize such macro-processes (Mecella and Batini 2001).

## 2.2 The Architecture

The Unitary Network architecture consists of three functional elements, for Transport, Basic and Cooperative Services (Mecella and Batini 2001). The Cooperative Service includes the middleware services that enable the development and deployment of new cooperative applications among administrations; the Cooperative Architecture is the distributed computing model based upon the Cooperative Service.

The main concept underlying the Cooperative Architecture is the one of Domain; a Domain includes all the computing resources, networks, applications and data that belong to a specific administration, regardless of the technical nature of such information system. Each such Domain is modeled as a single entity, regardless of its internal complexity, and is connected to the Unitary Network through the Domain Cooperative Gateway, that exports, through Cooperative Interfaces, the set of data and application services offered by the Domain. The interfaces may be designed according to different paradigms and modeling approaches, and deployed through various technologies. In the last three years (1998-2000) different pilot projects have been experimenting different solutions:

- by using a *middleware-based* approach; that is a collection of business objects and components is first specified using an appropriate Interface Definition Language, then implemented in Cooperative Gateways, and finally made available to other Domains by deploying the Gateways as object/component servers, such as CORBA, COM+ or EJB servers (mainly through protocols over TCP/IP, e.g. IIOP) (Mecella and Batini 2000);
- by using a *Web-based* approach; that is the data are described and exported through XML documents and the exchange is carried out through standard Internet technologies and protocols (mainly HTTP);
- by using a *traditional* approach; that is the data and application services are described as procedural calls and the adopted technologies are the consolidated ones (e.g. file transfer, widespread proprietary protocols, TP monitors, etc.).

In the next section such cooperative projects will be presented and compared according to some proposed dimensions.

# 3. THE PROJECTS

Six different projects will be considered:

- ***Arconet*** aims at developing a prototype of the Cooperative Gateway of the Italian Social Security Service (ISSS), for exporting data and services about pension plans and pre-retirement contributions of the Italian citizens. Two prototypes have been developed, the first by using a middleware-based approach (implemented both in DCOM and in CORBA), the latter by using XML and software components (EJBs and COM+ components). Both the prototypes use a wrapping layered architecture, in order to offer new integrated views of the data and services available on the back-end legacy systems (see Mecella and Batini 2000 for technical details).
- ***SICAP*** aims at implementing the Cooperative Information System of the Department of Justice (DoJ). The architecture and modeling approach are the same as in the first ARCONET prototype (middleware-based approach by using CORBA objects for exporting data and services). The interesting aspect is the use of a nested architecture, that is the Domain has been split into sub-domains (Criminal Record Office, many Law Courts, etc.) and each sub-domain offers a cooperative gateway similar to the main one exposed on the Unitary Network.
- ***WebArch*** aims at implementing a subsystem of the Prefectures (PreFs) concerning the Document Register (the act of recording every inward/outward documents, as defined by the Italian law) and the workflow. This subsystem was developed from scratch and it was completely written in Java, according to a component architecture quite similar to the EJB one. The interfaces towards the Unitary Network are deployed as a set of CORBA wrappers over the back-end Java components.
- ***RAE*** is a system for the notification of events concerning Italian enterprises, to be exchanged among the Chambers of Commerce (CsoC), ISSS and the National Board for the Insurance against Industrial Accidents (NBIIA). This system is going to implement a Publish&Subscribe pattern, deployed by using Message Oriented Middleware (MOM) and XML DTD/documents for the definition and exchange of events. This project is the only one providing for an explicit activity, in the development process, which addresses the data quality issue.
- ***SICC*** is a system for cadastral data exchange among City Councils (CCs), Department of Finance (DoF), Notaries and Certified Land Surveyors. It uses the Access Keys Warehouse (AKW) approach (Arcieri et al. 1999), that is a warehouse of database identifiers is used to maintain the coherence among the distributed databases of the cooperative system.
- ***Digital Order of Payment*** is an *e*-procurement project for the development of a system managing orders of payment among public administrations (e.g., Department of Treasury, DoT) banks and suppliers. The system will be developed in two steps: (i) the deployment, in each administration, of a special-

purpose cooperative gateway, and (ii) the development and deployment, in each administration, of the back-end system for the management of payments and accounting, which will be based on ERPs. The cooperative gateway will be based on a proprietary architecture, already used by the Italian Banking System.

## 3.1 Comparative Analysis

The comparison among the different projects is carried out through a few analysis dimensions, aiming at describing the type and complexity of the project, and the adopted technologies, architectures and approaches.

The first set of dimensions concerns the complexity of the project; it consists of:

- ***Project schedule***. This dimension provides the start time of the project, the length and the phase in which it currently is. The start time is often tied to the technology on hype in that period (as the projects are experimental, their aim is to try different new technologies).
- ***Involved administrations***. As the projects aim at defining and deploying cooperative interfaces among previously non connected administrations, this dimension is used as a measure of the present and future complexity of the project. At the same time, the more the involved administrations are, the more the adopted architecture and engineering approach can be considered valid and applicable. In *Table* we show both the organizations currently involved and the expected final set.

As regards the type of project, from the previous dimensions it is possible to classify them in terms of *proof-of-concept* and *core-business*, meaning the first projects are more targeted to the experimentation of solutions in a small set of administrations, the latter ones concern more widespread applications and critical processes of the Italian PA.

*Table* shows this classification and the values of the described dimensions for each project.

*Table 1.* Comparative analysis: complexity dimensions

| | | *(Proof-of-concept)* | | | | *(Core-business)* | |
|---|---|---|---|---|---|---|---|
| | | **Arconet** | **SICAP** | **WebArch** | **RAE** | **Digital Order of Payment** | **SICC** |
| **Project schedule** | **Start date** | Summer 1998 (1st prototype)<br>Summer 1999 (2nd prototype) | Spring 1999 | Late 1998 | Spring 2000 | Spring 2000 | 1998 |
| | **Length** | 10 months (1st prototype)<br>8 months (2nd prototype) | 18 months | Less than 1 year | (expected) 11 months | 24 months (6 months for deploying the cooperative gateway + 18 months for the development of the ERP-based accounting system) | Over 1 year |
| | **Current phase** | Both prototypes are ended off; both did never enter into production | 1st release (development of the Query service) ended off<br>2nd release (development of the nested Notification service) in the design activity | Operative | Architectural specification (inception) | Experimentation (inception) | Operative |
| **Involved Organizations** | **Current set** | ISSS, some CCs | DoJ, some CoCs, some CCs, ISSS | Some PreFs | CoCs, ISSS, NBIIA | Supreme State Accounting Court, Accounting Department, National Bank of Italy, Peripheral Office of the DoT, central Administrations | 100 CCs, DoF, Notaries, Certified Land Surveyors |
| | **Final set** | ISSS, 8000 CCs, DoF, DoJ | DoJ, 100 CoCs, 8000 CCs, ISSS | 100 PreFs, DoIA | 100 CoCs, ISSS, NBIIA, 10 central Administrations, many CCs, 20 Regions | The same + 20 Regions and some CCs (voluntary joining) | The same + all the remaining CCs (8000) |

The second set of dimensions concerns the architectures and the cooperative models adopted by different projects:

- ***Cooperation Type***. This dimension takes into consideration the different approaches that can be adopted for the design of Cooperative Gateways.
    - *Horizontal cooperation.* In this case broad conceptual information and services are exported: they are not tied to specific business services and supporting applications, but rather they represent a general information model of the Domain. This approach aims at developing an "information bus" on top of which specific applications (such as portals) can be layered.
    - *Vertical cooperation* consists in exporting coarse grained services aiming at supporting specific applications for specific processes (e.g. the Digital Order of Payment project).
- ***Interaction Type***. The cooperation in the Italian PA can be targeted either to the Administration-to-Administration (A2A) exchange of data and services, or to the offering of services Administration-to-Customer (A2C). Customers can be

classified into end-users (e.g. citizens, companies) and broker officials (such as tax accountants, notaries, etc.), who in many administrative processes act as intermediaries for end-users; therefore it is possible to identify Administration-to-EndUser (A2U) and Administration-to-BrokerOfficial (A2BO) sub-types of the A2C interaction. The horizontal cooperation can support both A2A and A2C types, as on top of the general information bus it is simple to develop specific client applications. Conversely in those projects adopting a vertical cooperation type, the choice about whether to support A2A or A2C applications must be taken since the inception phase, as the specific nature of the produced interfaces.

- ***Reference Model***. Prior to and during the projects, AIPA has defined a set of logical components as a reference model for the Cooperative Gateway: (a) Query and transactional Update services of the information asset of a Domain, (b) Event Notification service, (c) Control & Management services (e.g. security, accounting, auditing, availability and fault control, QoS, etc.), (d) Cooperative Interfaces, which export data and application services, and (e) standard and possibly off-the-shelf middleware technologies, shown in *Table* with the specific suites of protocols used for the exchange of data and the invocation of services. As for the nature of the projects, not each system realizes all the logical components.

In *Table* the projects are described according to this set of dimensions. Finally the last set of dimensions concerns technological and architectural issues:

- ***Modeling Approach***. This dimension is interesting for those projects adopting an object oriented approach to data/services modeling, whereas object wrappers integrate the back-end legacy systems to offer new cooperative interfaces: two different modeling techniques can be used, namely *operation-based* and *concept-based* (Mecella and Pernici 2001).
- ***Dealing with Legacy Systems***. A basic issue is the pervasive presence of legacy systems in the Italian PA. About 100 different legacy systems currently operate in the Central PA, and among them at least 50% will be impacted by current and future cooperative projects. Different approaches to deal with them have been adopted in the projects.
- ***Middleware maturity***. The projects adopt various technologies for the middleware layer, with different maturity levels. This dimension can qualitatively measure the risk of the project and its experimental nature, and therefore is correlated with the set of dimensions and the classification into *proof-of-concept* and *core-business* projects. In *Table* we provide the evaluated rating according to a three value scale.

*Table 2.* Comparative analysis: cooperation model

| | | ***(Proof-of-concept)*** | | | | ***(Core-business)*** | |
|---|---|---|---|---|---|---|---|
| | | ***Arconet*** | ***SICAP*** | ***WebArch*** | ***RAE*** | ***Digital Order of Payment*** | ***SICC*** |
| **Cooperation Type** | | Horizontal | Horizontal | Horizontal | Horizontal | Vertical | Vertical |
| **Interaction Type** | | A2A<br>Planned extension to A2C | A2A | A2A<br>Far extension to A2C | A2A<br>Next extension to A2C | A2A | A2A and A2BO<br>A2U extension under consideration |
| **Accordance with the AIPA Reference Model** | ***Query*** | Yes | Yes | Yes | Yes | Yes | Yes |
| | ***Transactional Update*** | No | No | Yes | No | Yes | Yes |
| | ***Event Notification*** | No (designed but never realized) | Yes (under development) | No | Yes (principal aim of the project) | Yes | Yes |
| | ***Control & Management*** | No | unknown | No | Yes | Yes | unknown |
| | ***Cooperative Interfaces*** | Object Schema | Object Schema | Object Schema | Semi-structured data (XML schema) | Procedural | Procedural |
| | ***Middleware*** | CORBA, DCOM, EJB<br>Middleware protocols (e.g. IIOP) over TCP/IP | CORBA<br>IIOP over TCP/IP | CORBA<br>IIOP over TCP/IP | Message Oriented Middleware (MQ Series)<br>XML over HTTP | Traditional technologies (message switching, file transfer, transactional)<br>Proprietary protocols | The middleware layer is implemented through an integration warehouse (AKW)<br>Different protocols (e.g. sockets) over TCP/IP |

– ***Architectures***. The adopted architectures can be roughly classified into three categories: (i) distributed object/component middleware-based, (ii) Web/XML-based and (iii) traditional. This dimension is tightly correlated with the middleware dimension previously proposed.
In *Table* the projects are described according to this set of dimensions.

## 3.2 Discussion

It is interesting to draw some lessons from the previous comparison:

– The *core-business* projects (Digital Order of Payment, SICC), in order to reduce the risk due to their complexity, are adopting a more conservative approach, by using traditional technologies and engineering approaches such as vertical cooperation and procedural interfaces; conversely the *proof-of-concept* projects, with less critical constraints, are more targeted towards experimentation of on hype technologies and therefore their technological risk is higher (e.g. Arconet prototypes failed). Moreover the *core-business* projects are more targeted towards qualities such as security, performance and reuse of existing solutions, whereas the *proof-of-concept* projects are more targeted towards qualities such as interoperability, modifiability and reuse of the new cooperative interfaces (horizontal cooperation).

–

*Table 3.* Comparative analysis: architectural and technological dimensions

| | | *(Proof-of-concept)* | | | | *(Core-business)* | |
|---|---|---|---|---|---|---|---|
| | | ***Arconet*** | ***SICAP*** | ***WebArch*** | ***RAE*** | ***Digital Order of Payment*** | ***SICC*** |
| ***Modeling approach*** | | Stateful (1st prototype)<br>Both (2nd prototype) | Stateful | Stateful | Stateless | n.a. | n.a. |
| ***Middleware Maturity*** | | Low / Medium | Medium | Medium | High (for MOM)<br>Medium (for XML) | High | High |
| ***Legacy System*** | ***Presence*** | Yes | Yes | No | Yes | Yes | Yes |
| | ***Dealing with legacy systems*** | Wrapping | Wrapping of few systems<br>Gradual migration of others | n.a. | Wrapping *(with previous Data Quality improvement)* | Wrapping | Integration through AKW; untouched legacy systems |
| ***Architecture*** | | Middleware-based, multilayer (3 layer wrappers) | Middleware-based, multilayer | Web-based for the intranet, middleware-based for the Cooperative Gateway | Web-based (XML), multilayer | Proprietary of the Italian Banking System<br>Based on traditional message switching | AKW for the integration of different databases |

As regards the contexts in which to use simple data exchange vs. services, Web-based approaches vs. middleware-based ones, every time that the cooperation consists only in the simple exchange of data, a light approach (based on XML and standard Web technologies) seems more suitable, while, if the cooperation really consists in services (applications supporting processes) a middleware-based approach seems better. Our opinion is that the use of different engineering approaches (modeling, technologies, etc.) must be considered as evolutionary, not exclusive. Currently most of the projects require simple data exchange, and the risk involved by the middleware-based approach is sometimes too high; but the more the cooperation paradigm will spread and the BPR of the macro-processes will be pervasive, the more the cooperation will evolve from simple data query and exchange services towards the invocations of complex applications services. In the meantime the current middleware and Web technologies will probably merge, in order to resolve some issues and to converge towards a standard suite of protocols[88].

[88] One of the issues of the middleware-based approach is the security problem it creates (IIOP is not well transported through firewalls); whereas the Web-based approach (use of XML and HTTP) resolves this issue but lacks important middleware services. The trend is

- The Cooperative Architecture relies on the integration of data and services from different Domains. It is fundamental to consider the *data quality* of the information to be integrated, in order not to thwart the cooperative effort (Missier, Scannapieco and Batini 2001). This leads to the consideration of specific activities in which to address such issues. Currently only the RAE project has considered these issues, including a data cleaning activity that precedes the development of the cooperative interfaces.
- The gained experience allows the identification of a possible meta-architecture for the Unitary Information System, which is shown in *Figure* .
    - The Cooperative Interfaces logical layer is distributed over different Cooperative Gateways (each administration deploys its own interfaces on its Cooperative Gateways); this layer is on top of the single administrations' systems.
    - Back-end layer. This layer is composed by the systems of the different administrations, often legacy systems. If a wrapping approach is adopted, the wrapping sub-layer could be itself multilayered, depending on organizational constraints and the conceptual mismatch between the legacies and the cooperative interfaces (Mecella and Batini 2000).
    - The Client layer of the Cooperative Interfaces consists of portals, to offer services to citizens (A2C interaction), and of specific applications of single administrations, which integrate data and services exported by different Cooperative Gateways (A2A interaction). Portals will be on top of interfaces and/or applications of different administrations; this solution is suitable when the aim of the cooperation is to offer a single end-user interface (typically Web) to different administrations involved in a macro-process. On top of the Cooperative Interfaces it is possible to have a further layer specializing the Cooperative Interfaces according to the specific client needs.

---

towards the merging of the two technologies (such as the emerging technology of the XML application server and the use of XML protocols over TCP/IP such as SOAP).

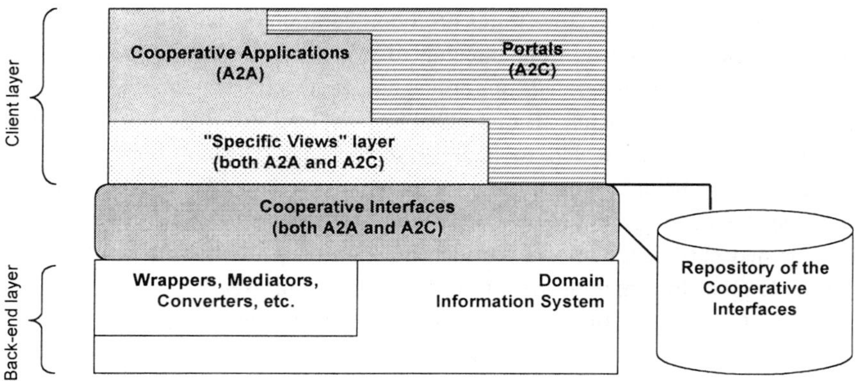


*Figure 2.* A meta-architecture for the Unitary Information System

- A repository of the Cooperative Interfaces exported by the different Domains, implied by the bottom-up development of such interfaces, need to be considered in the Cooperative Service. In this repository all the information about the interfaces (semantics, supporting conceptual schemas, handles for accessing them, etc.) must be provided.
- It is fundamental to set-up a joint development process, which is described in details in Mecella and Batini 2000 and Mecella and Batini 2001.

# 4. CONCLUSIONS

The constitution of AIPA, the initiative of the Unitary Network and, more recently, a new action plan directly set up by the Government (Italian Government 2000), are the main steps of the Italian approach to *e*-Government. The definition of a common Cooperative Architecture, based on Domains and Cooperative Gateways, will promote the cooperation at the application level, beyond the simple interoperability services already provided.

In the last few years many projects, both specific of a single administration and cooperative, have been carried out; in this paper the most relevant among the cooperative ones have been selected and compared, basing on a few dimensions, deriving some considerations and lesson learned.

The development of the Cooperative Architecture, just started in the Italian PA, is the coordination project in which almost all the projects for the *e*-Government will find their framework. Next years will show its evolution and the benefits it will offer to the customers, through a complete reengineering of the macro-processes servicing them; moreover it will offer the testbed for further research about Cooperative Information Systems.

# 5. REFERENCES

Arcieri F., Cappadozzi E., Naggar P., Nardelli E., Talamo M. (1999): Access Keys Warehouse: a New Approach to the Development of Cooperative Information Systems. Proceedings of the 4th IFCIS International Conference on Cooperative Information Systems (CoopIS'99), Edinburgh, Scotland, 1999.

Autorità per l'Informatica nella Pubblica Amministrazione (AIPA): `http://www.aipa.it/english[4/` (link checked January, 1st 2001).

Batini C., Castano S., De Antonellis V., Fugini M.G., Pernici B. (1996): Analysis of an Inventory of Information Systems in the Public Administration. Requirements Engineering, vol. 1, no. 1, 1996.

Brodie, M.L. (1998): The Cooperative Computing Initiative. A Contribution to the Middleware and Software Technologies. GTE Laboratories Technical Publication, 1998. Available on-line: `http://info.gte.com/pubs/PITAC3.pdf` (link checked January, 1st 2001).

Mecella M., Batini C. (2000): Cooperation of Heterogeneous Legacy Information Systems: a Methodological Framework. Proceedings of the 4th International Enterprise Distributed Object Computing Conference (EDOC 2000), Makuhari, Japan, 2000.

Mecella M., Batini C. (2001): Enabling Italian e-Government through a Cooperative Architecture. In Elmagarmid A.K., McIver Jr. W.J. (eds.): The Ongoing March Towards Digital Government. Special Issue on Digital Government. IEEE Computer, vol. 34, no. 2, February 2001.

Mecella, M., Pernici, B. (2001): Designing Wrapper Components for e-Services in Integrating Heterogeneous Systems. To appear in VLDB Journal, Special Issue on e-Services, 2001.

Missier P., Scannapieco M., Batini C. (2001): Cooperative Architectures. Introducing Data Quality. Technical Report 14-2001, Dipartimento di Informatica e Sistemistica, Università di Roma "La Sapienza", Roma, Italy, 2001.

Mylopoulos, J., Papazoglou, M. (eds.) (1997): Cooperative Information Systems. IEEE Expert Intelligent Systems & Their Applications, vol. 12, no. 5, September/October 1997.

Thompson C. (1993): Living an enterprise model. Database Programming and Design, March 1993.

U.S. Department of Commerce, National Bureau of Standards (1988): Guide to Information Resource Dictionary System Applications: General Concepts and Strategic Systems Planning. NBS Special Publication 500-152, U.S. Government Printing Office, 1988.

62

# E-Governance & Digital Government in Canada

*The Necessity of Both Structural and Cultural Transformations*

Jeffrey Roy
*The Centre on Governance, University of Ottawa, Canada*

**Abstract:** This paper examines the capacity of government to meet the new challenges of a digital age. There is a considerable risk that adaptation and change may be blocked by an administrative culture ill suited for a world of e-governance. Two sets of explanatory factors will be determinant. First, new forms collaboration within and across governments, as well as across sectors are crucial. The second variable lies in the necessary leadership of people: new skill sets, and new leaders will be required to both empower knowledge workers and defend experimental action. Technology alone is insufficient. The paper offers preliminary propositions as to how governments might address these important challenges.

## 1. INTRODUCTION

*Moving industrial society government onto a digital platform would simply produce a digitized industrial government—a form of governance that would be increasingly out of step with the changing realities of citizens and businesses alike.* [i]

The objective of this paper is to consider the capacity of government to effectively harness new information technology (IT) as an enabling force in its efforts to meet the present and emerging challenges of a digital age. Such challenges are fundamentally rooted in the extraordinary expansion of e-commerce, the rise of e-communities, the growth of virtual organizations,, and the development of a truly commutative revolution that carries the potential for new network based capacities to establish, maintain and modify the relationships of any governance system. [Guillaume 1999]. This paper will consider issues that have a general applicability to all governments, even though it is important to underscore that specific example may be drawn from the current Canadian context.[ii]

For public sector leaders, the adaptive challenges of e-governance go far beyond technology per se. They call for new organizational structures and skills, new forms of innovation and learning, and perhaps even a redefinition of purpose. They also call for a significant broadening and transformation of public-private sector partnerships (PPP) and the relational dynamics which underpin them. The new dynamics are very far from traditional public sector processes for procuring and contracting [Rosenau 2000]. Yet, while the potential for a recasting of both public management and political accountability is real, the transition is fraught with uncertainty.

*Governance* may be defined as effective coordination in an environment where both knowledge and power are distributed. Every organization is built on governance, whether formal or informal, ineffective or successful. The rise of *e-governance* refers to the new patterns of decision-making, power sharing, and coordination - made possible, or even necessary by the advent of IT. In the private sector, for example, e-commerce is much more than transactions on-line: it encapsulates the range of new organizational models built on technological architectures, such as the internet, that allow governance to be redefined in new ways.

The public sector is not immune to such forces. Indeed, government finds itself under the dual strain of becoming both a partner and de facto competitor with business in an on-line environment, while also needing to understand the complex and profound implications of new technologies and their impacts on public interest issues. As a result, *digital government* (a term that we deploy in place of e-government) refers to an IT-led reconfiguration of public sector governance – and how, knowledge, power, and purpose are redistributed in light of new technological realities.

Digital government must also be viewed as much more than moving existing public services on-line: it is about government harnessing IT to redefine its social patterns and power structures in order to remain relevant in a more participative, more interactive and more informational era [Tapscott and Agnew 1999]. Importantly, the OECD [1997] has reported that IT is becoming the critical agent of change, the availability of a new digital infrastructure and the Internet's impacts on a changing set of public expectations are overtaking fiscal pressures as the primary impetus for public sector managerial reform.

Nonetheless, the deployment of IT both in and across public sector organizations is driven by a variety of factors, and it may face resistance. The main danger is that the necessary transformation in public sector governance and accountability is likely to be blocked by an administrative culture that may be ill suited for a digital world. Whereas nearly everything about the connected (or digital) state requires horizontal governance, government has relied upon a vertical architecture of power and decision-making.

While this quandary is recognized to some degree, the central task facing both policy-makers and political leaders, at least those interested in leading the transition to the digital age, lies in orchestrating effective responses.

## 2. FROM CONTROL STRUCTURES TO COLLABORATIVE ARCHITECTURES

The new digital architecture driving e-governance creates both pressures and opportunities for new partnerships - internally and externally. Within government, IT fosters new horizontal opportunities by shifting away from traditional bureaucratic structures toward alternative delivery arrangements. The growing possibilities for consultations with both stakeholders and the citizenry are also expanded with new technologies. Moreover, on-line delivery implies integrative channels within government, linking external users to a variety of sources and systems internally.

Organizationally, these trends mean IT forces are both dispersing and centralizing – fostering a need for integrative action. Put another way, these forces create tensions between vertical governance of traditional government and the horizontal governance implied by digital government. The emergence of digital government will therefore require actions and strategies at the level of individual departments and agencies: but such efforts must be orchestrated within the parameters of government-wide leadership and coordination.

Accountability is a key element of such a balance. The manner by which accountability is perceived and exercised by government leaders will determine the degree to which it embraces more collaborative models of governance. Traditionalists invoke the underlying principle of Ministerial Accountability based on a clear and rigid view of vertical control and risk-minimization in order to serve and protect the interests of the publicly accountable political leader.

The rise of e-governance, with its pressures for a variety of initiatives introducing alternative models of decision-making and service delivery, implies a sharing of accountability. The need for collaboration, partnerships and joint ventures grows -both within government, and often between private and public organizations.

There are also important debates around the issue of whether accountability is at risk when external partners become involved in the governing and shared delivery of government programs and services. According to some, new governance arrangements threaten to undermine key institutions and practices of democratic accountability [Globerman and Vining 1996]. This camp believes that any change to the existing system of ministerial accountability will damage the integrity of the system. There is some question as to whether the *ad hoc* nature of the ever-increasing number of partnership arrangements between sectors challenges accountability mechanisms or can be absorbed in traditional models of decision making with adaptations to risk mitigating strategies.

An alternative view is that collaborative arrangements can make government more accountable [Armstrong and Ford 1999]. These proponents of collaborative arrangements insist that involving external stakeholders strengthens accountability to citizens by virtue of the addition of partners, and in particular, private sector partners, pressure for accountability to customers or clients is increased. Notwithstanding legitimate concerns about new ways of doing things, it is difficult to conclude from these debates that the virtues of traditional accountability, namely their clarity and simplicity, can serve as justifications for their extension into an e-governance era.

These tensions form the parameters around which new ties are being formed between governments and the vendors of IT systems and solutions. IT solutions, however, are more pervasive in demanding closer collaboration between private vendors and public sector clients [Mornan 1998]. The complexity and sophistication of such solutions produce many strategic choices for governments about how to deploy IT both in and across public sector operations.

*Contracts versus partnerships* - Any move toward IT outsourcing, meaning a reliance on external service providers, most often found in the private sector, is likely to be both controversial and consequential for government, particularly from a human resources perspective. The advantages of outsourcing IT and its management to external parties are derived from the opportunity to leverage the competencies of specialists. The disadvantages are rooted in concerns about control and performance measurement, while underlying questions of cost often become the resulting sources of friction.

The main challenge is relational: *new collaborative capacities are requires.* Partnerships require shared purposes and agendas, as well as trust and an integrative mind set. The implication here is that both the skill sets of the individuals involved and the mechanisms guiding their relational activities must be conducive to such an effort. The main challenge facing all parties engaged in today's increasingly complex forms of IT partnerships is that despite a recognition of the need to work together in new ways, most organizational processes and most people reside within the realm of contracting, with an emphasis on both cost and control. Although common to all sectors, this point is particularly prevalent in the public sector, as the extra burden of transparency and fairness, the basis of traditional assurances of public accountability, loom large.

Current examples of outsourcing are a case in point, as any such decision by a government department is bound to be both strategic and controversial. The transfer of assets, including people, is a process with potentially huge consequences on government's capacity to act in the public interest. In a world of markets and contracts, the outsourcing path is fraught with risks and uncertainty: the response is often a quagmire of control efforts and validation. Moreover, even if such agreements are forged operationally, public sector approval requires additional scrutiny and explanations to public chambers - and it should come as no surprise that many deals are unable to withstand such pressures.

Recently, the state of Connecticut in The United States spent millions of dollars and over three years negotiating one of the most ambitious outsourcing deals of a government ever, only to see the deal collapse before completion. Both parties, the government and the primary vendor, provide amicable, though contrasting explanations for the deal's demise. While no single factor is evident, it is fair to conclude that the requisite mix of political acceptability and profitability could not be achieved in an adequate fashion due, in part, to a tremendous emphasis on contracting specifications, objectives, terms and conditions - a process fundamentally at odds with the trust and collaboration required to partner on such a massive scale. A federal public servant in Canada commented privately that in his mind, profit always wins out over partnership in such cases.

Nonetheless, perhaps due to the strengthening pressures of e-governance, the trend toward outsourcing-type arrangements grows unabated. Tying itself directly to the experiences of Connecticut, the San Diego County government is now six months into the largest municipal outsourcing experience. While these experiences are unique in scope, they present elements common to all governments, at all levels, as IT becomes a strategic imperative for effective governance. Such tensions have led to growing calls for partnerships in place of contracts. The differences may be subtle in terms of words, but the consequences of this contrast are far reaching. Poupart and Austin compare two modes of relationships:

> *Partners respond to a need in a changing world by sharing control in the context of an assertive relationship to offer a future that facilitates innovation in a world of possibilities. Contractors respond to a request in a procurement world by giving up control in the context of a collaborative relationship to provide help, assistance, pairs of hands that facilitate project management in a world of deliverables [Jelich & al. 2000, p.52].*

Our own examination of IT management and procurement in Canada has begun to underscore the extent to which digital government remains at odds with a traditional public sector apparatus firmly rooted in hierarchical traditions. The resulting challenge of shifting from incremental procurement reform to genuine collaboration lies in the need to rebalance purchasing safeguards with partnering opportunities. Equally important are the new skill sets of public managers and leadership requirements that result.

## 3. HUMAN CAPACITIES – AND THE NEW PUBLIC SERVANT

The digital era rises hand in hand with the knowledge workforce. Conceptually, Jeremy Rifkin envisions growing ranks of knowledge workers who will forge new communities of interest - only some of which are likely to resemble traditional employee - employer relationships of the past. He argues that "people of the twenty-first century are as likely to perceive themselves as nodes embedded in networks of shared interests as they are to perceive themselves as autonomous agents in a Darwinian world of competitive survival" [Rifkin 2000, p.12].

How will public sector organizations deal with what Rifkin sees as a new human archetype where people are more autonomous, better educated, more mobile, and less rooted by traditions of place (either geographically or organizationally). These conceptual issues intimately link the workforce challenges of digital government with those of cultural reform (in an organizational sense). Whereas Westminster systems continue to emphasize vertical accountability, government on-line is (correctly) being pursued in a horizontal fashion.

An international study by Essex and Kusy [1999] underlines the views of executives from both government and industry, for whom an increasing reliance on the external workforce is a significant trend. They report that from 1997-2002, leaders are expecting an increase from 10 per cent to 25 per cent in non-core (meaning non-traditional full-time, or external) workers. This crescendo of the external workforce may well accelerate with the technology-induced pressures for organizational innovation and flexibility. The result is a complex mix of agendas and incentives that explains the growing emphasis on inter-personal skills such as negotiation, facilitation, and consultation.

These skills are forming the basis of "new public servant" – one who is much more collaborative and comfortable with technology, and the consequences of these shifts for human resource in management in government will be profound [Moritz and Roy 2000]. Thus, government is becoming both more fluid internally and more networked externally, as distributed governance models drive the move toward a flexible and modular workforce.

As a result, the role of the public servant must adapt; governments must effectively couple new forms of community-wide strategies that are both horizontal and potentially centralizing, with recent trends toward empowerment and flexibility - and the decentralizing nature of such pressures (i.e. agencies seeking greater autonomy). Governments must learn to benefit from heightened worker mobility – viewing such trends as strategic imperatives for public service innovation.

A challenge for many governments in doing so lies in more direct competition with industry. In the Canadian government, for example, the Computer Systems (CS) Community is based heavily in and around Ottawa-Hull, the National Capital Region (NCR). In 1999, 67% of all CS employees were located in the NCR, compared to 34% for the entire PS [ibid.]. As CS employment increases, more workers are located in the NCR which give rise to new managerial challenges – namely, an intensifying labour market that also serves as a common pool of competencies for both industry and the government. Consequently, a major challenge of digital government lies in this competition for human capital, a dynamic particularly acute in national capitals such as Washington D.C. and Ottawa which seem to couple growing professional mobility and inter-sectoral proximity.

The governance implications of such trends are perhaps contradictory: a paradoxical impact of IT may be that while it enables more organizational flexibility and decentralization across the public sector, particularly with respect to service delivery, leadership patterns also have centralizing tendencies. This factor could impact both the presence and effectiveness of national governments operating across their country, and their ability to recruit specialized workers in limited urban centers (particularly national capitals) where labour markets are most competitive.

In a world of e-governance, an appropriate response by government in meeting this dynamic must be based on the understanding of both the complexity and contradictions at work. On the one hand, the move toward greater usage of private-public partnerships suggests that mobility and proximity could complement one another – and create a common environment more conducive to trust and collaboration. On the other hand, the very real danger is that the most entrepreneurial employees will leave the public service, seeking either higher compensation or more flexible work environments than government is able to accord to them.

As important as the technology itself, government must address the people and performance challenges of digital government in the next few years. Adapting the role and profile of the public servant is critical to realising the needed administrative cultural shift associated with horizontal governance and collaborative partnerships.

# 4. POWER, POLITICS & CULTURE

There are many claims that as confidence and trust in traditional forms of representational government erode, technology, and specifically the Internet can foster capacities for democratic renewal. Such renewal is premised on more direct forms of democratic engagement.

*Yet, technology alone is insufficient.* Recent studies and roundtables have all underscored that while the Internet carries the potential for more direct citizen engagement, realizing this potential is a complex undertaking. Two major variables that will shape the nature of democratic reform are accessibility and the role of the media(s). Questions about accessibility are best typified by the phrase, digital divide, which implies segmentation of our populations between those with on-line access and those without it. Yet, merely providing the infrastructure for connectivity does not guarantee enlightened use. *The divide is much more complex* [Wyatt & al., 2000].

In terms of usage and engagement, it is perhaps the role of the changing media(s) that carries the greatest importance in terms of shaping our democratic evolution. An essential distinction must be made between *traditional media* on the one hand, and *new media* on the other. Traditional forms of media are essentially those that serve as intermediaries: they transfer and filter information. The new media, on other hand, denotes those channels of more direct and interactive communication - free(r) of interference and interpretation. E-government involves both forms of media, each of which presents separate challenges for moving forward. Traditional media remains a critical factor in shaping public opinion. As displayed by various episodes of public management in Ottawa over the past year, the fairness and effectiveness of the media in playing this role can be the focus of an intense debate.

New media channels drive a world of more open and direct consultation - and enhanced public participation. Yet, results to date from experimentation with on-line consultation have been modest, and there is considerable debate around the quality of participation that ensues. Connectivity is necessary but insufficient. In this sense, *the phrase digital democracy is misleading*. The implication that greater openness and broader public engagement are the direct result of connectivity is an overly simplistic portrayal of the choices that lie ahead.

In a digital environment, power will be shared through both forms of media, and the impacts on government are profound. The danger of the traditional media is that it can encourage defensiveness and paranoia at the apex of power in government, as many feel - often legitimately - under attack (i.e. *a recent edition of CIO Magazine included a feature on the "follies" of the IT mismanagement and project failures in the British government*).

These forces are potentially contradictory. As new media channels strengthen, the costs and complexity of managing information and responding to traditional media channels may well rise - with increasingly uncertain results. Some question the feasibility of containing information, as many OECD governments (particularly in Scandinavia) continue to expand efforts at greater transparency.

There is no simply solution to this media quagmire - but one aspect should be carefully considered. At an operational level, governments may well be better off pro-actively providing more information - and betting on an ongoing and more thoughtful form of public judgment than the more instantaneous reactions delivered by traditional media forms. In other words, an effective, if indirect approach for traditional media is to elevate the level of collective learning as to the challenges and choices that lie ahead. Expanding public dialogues and engaging citizens more directly into public sector governance must be an important part of any e-government strategy.

# 5. THE ELUSIVE GOAL OF ALIGNMENT

Carolyn Purcell, the Executive Director of the Department of Information Resources for The State of Texas once commented, "e-government is like a giant canvas on which people can draw a new view, a citizen-centered view of their government". This quote is insightful - as it is both accurate and misleading. The accuracy stems from the real possibility that for those outside of government, individual citizens or specific interest groups, can envision something entirely new - potentially quite different from the status quo. Yet, the quote is equally misleading, or at the very least unfair - if taken from the perspective of those working inside of government today. Even if our Westminster Parliamentary structures of governance appear dated and in need of review, they cast powerful constraints around public administration and the capacity for innovation.

***Design considerations:***

An effective strategy to realize e-government must re-balance traditional administrative and political-cultural frameworks and the adaptive and collaborative requirements of e-governance. This new alignment process requires a *renewed culture in government*, one more open to the enormous potential of technology in its main forms. Our own studies of e-government in Canada, including an extensive set of interviews across both the private and public sectors point to four main guiding principles that collectively form a template for moving forward.

First, *efficiency* remains a key principle for government - tied, in part, to an inter-connected global arena carefully monitoring the fiscal performance of all countries. A key component of the potential of ICT is the capacity for reduced costs as new media channels create a compelling business case for delivering services on-line. Yet, the "business case" of government is unique, as it is not driven by maximizing profits as in the marketplace, but rather by maximizing the collective potential of all Canadians, individually and organizationally, to lead productive and prosperous lives in a more electronic and knowledge-driven age. Thus, efficiency gains must be weighed along with the investment being made to encouraging people to develop on-line skills. Cost savings is one variable in a more complex equation.

Secondly, *adaptability* is increasingly important as a principle. A critical part of the e-government challenge is the sobering recognition that the environment is not static: whether the federal government succeeds in getting all services on-line by 2004 is perhaps less important than the reality that the social, economic and political contexts of 2004 could well by very different from today. This principle implies a public sector comfortable with technology in different forms. Adaptive e-government means deploying technology as an "enable" force for better learning and knowledge management. Information, communication and social networks will transcend traditional structures and boundaries: they must be unified less by control and more by a common mission and collective leadership.

Such learning requires dialogue in order to allow government to become both digital and *deliberative* – the latter being the third principle. The challenge of deliberative government extends beyond the need to improve existing capacities today. Deliberative government must engage its partners and the citizenry and define the future as well: *Deliberative democracy underpins social learning, and it justifies the growing pursuit of public and multi-stakeholder consultation techniques today.* Government must not only accept input: it must seek it and demonstrate how participation helps to define policy and improve service delivery. Perhaps the most contentious, and certainly the least discussed aspect of e-government is the role of deliberation in reforming democratic governance.

A useful, and indeed necessary component of e-government readiness will be strengthening the deliberative capacities of the public service, and anticipating the potential consequences for the democratic processes so closely interwoven. What is required is an alignment of new skill sets within the public sector, of new relational ties to specialists outside of, but engaged with the public sector, and of the broader public in their dual capacities of both customer of government services and citizen of the democratic polity.

*Such alignment will invariably remain elusive* - and as such, the best one can strive for is to foster ongoing capacities for improvement and adaptation. Such capacities are underpinned by learning - and as a result, e-government must be about working in a more strategic and collaborative fashion in order to strengthen overall capacities across traditional boundaries. This governance challenge means undertaking both a structural and cultural shift from, moving from *independence* to one where *interdependence* becomes the fourth guiding principle. Building e-government on this premise provides the fourth design principle for bettering governance. In sum, four crucial design principles of e-government are:

- *Efficient* - *Adaptive*

- *Interdependent* - *Deliberative*

# 6. CONCLUSION

Perhaps the most encompassing aspect of IT challenges is its permeation of all aspects of public sector management and reform. Understanding IT is no longer a skill for the technical component of the workforce, but rather its integration with information management and strategic change is determinant as all dimensions of public sector activity are affected by technology.

In the digital era, government must not only prepare leaders to face uncertain times. It must also sensitize these leaders on the importance of creating learning environments for workers at all levels of their organization and the numerous partners attached to any particular initiative. As government engages in new forms of collaborative arrangements, work teams comprise sets of individuals with a variety of formal, informal and overlapping reporting relationships. Yet, it is not only the skills composition of workers altering in a digital era, but rather the broader transformations of both everyday and organizational life that are also at play.

In this sense, digital government must reposition itself to become an engaged and constructive partner in shaping the new governance patterns that will otherwise render it rudderless. These governance patterns must bridge traditional administrative and political-cultural frameworks to the adaptive and collaborative requirements of e-governance to produce *a new culture in government*, one open and enabled to take advantage of the enormous potential of the digital and information age.

## 7. REFERENCES

Allen, B., Juillet, L., Paquet, G. and Roy, J. [2001] E-Governance & Government On-line in Canada: Partnerships, People & in Government Information Quarterly Vol. 30, No. 1. pp. 36-47 (with B. Allen, L. Juillet and G. Paquet).

Browning, J. [1998] "Power to the People - Government isn't disappearing. It's being Disintermediated" in WIRED Magazine (January 1998).

Canadian Defence Industry Association [1999] "CDIA Procurement Committee, Industry Proposals for DND Procurement Reform"(www.cdia.ca/committee/procure.htm).

Carr, G. [1998] "Public-Private Partnerships: The Canadian Experience"(speech to Oxford School of Project Finance, available at http://home.inforamp.net/~partners/oxford.html).

Center for Technology in Government, "Making Smart IT Choices" [1998] (Albany: www.ctg.albany.edu/resources)

Chief Information Officer's Branch (CIOB), Treasury Board of Canada Secretariat [1998] "Supporting Electronic Government: The Government of Canada Public Key Infrastructure" (Ottawa: www.cio-dpi.gc.ca).

Corden, S. [1997] "The Australian Government's Industry Commission Examines Competitive Tendering and Contracting by Public Sector Agencies" reported in Public Administration Review (March/April 1997, Vol.57, No.2).

Duff, Angus. [1997] "Outsourcing Information Technology - Human Resource Implications" IRC Press, Industrial Relations Centre, Queen's University, Kingston.

Essex, L. and Kusy, M. [1999] Fast Forward Leadership - How to exchange outmoded leadership practises for forward-looking leadership today (Financial Times / Prentice Hall).

Ferris, N. [1999] "CIOs on the Go"in GovExec.com, March 1999 (www.govexec.com/features).

Gagnon, Y. and Dragon, J. [1998] "The Impact of Technology on Organizational Performance" in

Galliers, R.D. and Baets, W.R.J. [1998] Information Technology and Organizational Transformation (Wiley Series in Information Systems: Toronto).

Globerman, S. and Vining, A.R. [1996] "A Framework for Evaluating the Government Contracting-Out Decision with an Application to Information Technology" in Public Administration Review (Nov/Dec 1996, Vol.56, No.6)

Guillaume, G.[1999] L'empire de réseaux (Paris: Descartes & Cie.).

International Council for Information Technology in Government Administration [1998] "Procurement Study Group Report" in An International Journal on Information Technology in Government {ICT: www.ica.ogit.gov.au).

Jayes, D. [1998] "Contracting out information technology services at the UK Inland Revenue" in OECD, Contracting Out Government Services (Paris: OECD=s Public Management Occasional Paper No.20).

Jelich, H., Poupart, R., Austin, R. and Roy, J. [2000] "Partnership-Based Governance: Lessons from IT Management" in Optimum Vol. 30, No. 1. pp. 49-54).

Kobrin, S. J. [1998] "You Can't Declare Cyberspace National Territory: Economic Policy-Making in The digital Age" in Tapscott, D. with Lowy, A. and Ticoll, D. Blueprint to the digital Economy: Creating Wealth in the Era of E-Business (McGraw-Hill).

Moritz, R. and Roy, J. [2000] "Demographic Insight on Canada's Federal Information Technology Workforce: Community Renewal and Tomorrow's Leadership Imperative" in Canadian Government Executive (July).

Mornan, B. [1998] "Results-Based Procurement: A Model of Public-Private Sector collaboration" in Optimum Vol.28, No.1.

Nelson, M.R. [1998] "Government and Governance in the Networked World" in Tapscott, D. with Lowy, A. and Ticoll, D. [1998] Blueprint to the digital Economy: Creating Wealth in the Era of E-Business (McGraw-Hill).

New Zealand Public Service [1997] Information Technology Stocktake (Wellington: State Services Commission).

Newcombe, T. [1998] "Multistate On-line Procurement Project Under Way" in Government Technology, Oct 1998 (www.govtech.net/publications/).

OECD [1997] "Information Technology as an Instrument of Public Management Reform: A Study of Five OECD Countries" [OECD: www.oecd.org/puma/gvrnance/it).

Papows, J. [1998] Enterprise.com - market leadership in the information age (Perseus Books: Reading).

Paquet, G.[1997] "States, Communities & Markets: The Distributed Governance Scenario" in The Nation-State in a Global Information Era: Policy Challenges [Queens University Bell Canada Conference].

Public Works and Government Services Canada [1998] "Benefits Driven Procurement" A Paper Presented to the Ninth International Public Procurement Association (Copenhagen: www.pwgsc.gc.ca/sos)

Rifkin, Jeremy [2000] The Age of Access - The New Culture of Hypercapitalism (New York: Jeremy P. Tarcher/Putnam).

Rosenau, P.V. [2000] Public-Private Policy Partnerships (Cambridge, Mass.: The MIT Press).

Tapscott, D. and Agnew, D. [1999] "Governance in the Digital Economy" Finance and Development December 1999, pp. 84-87.

Tapscott, D. with Lowy, A. and Ticoll, D. [1998] Blueprint to the Digital Economy: Creating Wealth in the Era of E-Business (McGraw-Hill).

Thorton, K. [1998] "Living in the Information Society - Rethinking Government" (www.ibm.com/ibm/public).

Weill, P. and Broadbent, M. [1998] Leveraging The New Infrastructure - How Market Leaders Capitalize on IT [Harvard Business School Press].

Wyatt, S., Henwood, F., Miler, N. and Senker, P. eds. [2000] Technology and In/Equality – questioning the information society (Routledge: London and New York).

Yankelovich, Daniel. [1999] The Magic of Dialogue: Transforming Conflict into Cooperation (New York: Simon and Schuster).